1912

The Globe Edition

POETICAL WORKS

OF

ALFRED LORD TENNYSON

MACMILLAN AND CO., Limited
LONDON · BOMBAY · CALCUTTA
MELBOURNE

THE MACMILLAN COMPANY
NEW YORK · BOSTON · CHICAGO
ATLANTA · SAN FRANCISCO

THE MACMILLAN CO. OF CANADA, Ltd.
TORONTO

POETICAL WORKS OF

ALFRED

LORD TENNYSON

POET LAUREATE

MACMILLAN AND CO., LIMITED
ST. MARTIN'S STREET, LONDON

1908

First Edition 1899.   *Reprinted* 1904, 1907, 1908

CONTENTS.

TO THE QUEEN.

Revered, beloved—O you that hold
  A nobler office upon earth
  Than arms, or power of brain, or birth
Could give the warrior kings of old,

Victoria,—since your Royal grace
  To one of less desert allows
  This laurel greener from the brows
Of him that utter'd nothing base ;

And should your greatness, and the care
  That yokes with empire, yield you time
  To make demand of modern rhyme
If aught of ancient worth be there ;

Then—while a sweeter music wakes,
  And thro' wild March the throstle calls,
  Where all about your palace-walls
The sun-lit almond-blossom shakes—

Take, Madam, this poor book of song ;
  For tho' the faults were thick as dust
  In vacant chambers, I could trust
Your kindness.   May you rule us long,

And leave us rulers of your blood
  As noble till the latest day !
  May children of our children say,
' She wrought her people lasting good ;

' Her court was pure ; her life serene ;
  God gave her peace ; her land reposed ;
  A thousand claims to reverence closed
In her as Mother, Wife, and Queen ;

' And statesmen at her council met
  Who knew the seasons when to take
  Occasion by the hand, and make
The bounds of freedom wider yet

' By shaping some august decree,
  Which kept her throne unshaken still,
  Broad-based upon her people's will,
And compass'd by the inviolate sea.'

March 1851.

T   B

JUVENILIA.

CLARIBEL.

A MELODY.

I.

WHERE Claribel low-lieth
  The breezes pause and die,
    Letting the rose-leaves fall:
But the solemn oak-tree sigheth,
  Thick-leaved, ambrosial,
  With an ancient melody
  Of an inward agony,
Where Claribel low-lieth.

II.

At eve the beetle boometh
  Athwart the thicket lone:
At noon the wild bee hummeth
  About the moss'd headstone:
At midnight the moon cometh,
  And looketh down alone.
Her song the lintwhite swelleth,
The clear-voiced mavis dwelleth,
  The callow throstle lispeth,
The slumbrous wave outwelleth,
  The babbling runnel crispeth,
The hollow grot replieth
  Where Claribel low-lieth.

NOTHING WILL DIE.

WHEN will the stream be aweary of
    flowing
      Under my eye?
When will the wind be aweary of blowing
    Over the sky?
When will the clouds be aweary of
    fleeting?
When will the heart be aweary of
    beating?
      And nature die?
Never, oh! never, nothing will die;
      The stream flows,
      The wind blows,
      The cloud fleets,
      The heart beats,
        Nothing will die.

Nothing will die;
All things will change
Thro' eternity.
'Tis the world's winter;
Autumn and summer
Are gone long ago;
Earth is dry to the centre,
But spring, a new comer,
A spring rich and strange,
Shall make the winds blow
Round and round,
Thro' and thro',
      Here and there,
      Till the air
And the ground
Shall be fill'd with life anew.

The world was never made;
It will change, but it will not fade
So let the wind range;
For even and morn
      Ever will be
      Thro' eternity.
Nothing was born;
Nothing will die;
All things will change.

ALL THINGS WILL DIE.

CLEARLY the blue river chimes in its
    flowing
        Under my eye ;
Warmly and broadly the south winds are
    blowing
        Over the sky.
One after another the white clouds are
    fleeting ;
Every heart this May morning in joyance
    is beating
        Full merrily ;
    Yet all things must die.
The stream will cease to flow ;
The wind will cease to blow ;
The clouds will cease to fleet ;
The heart will cease to beat ;
    For all things must die.
    All things must die.
Spring will come never more.
    Oh ! vanity !
Death waits at the door.
See ! our friends are all forsaking
The wine and the merrymaking.
We are call'd—we must go.
Laid low, very low,
In the dark we must lie.
The merry glees are still ;
The voice of the bird
Shall no more be heard,
Nor the wind on the hill.
    Oh ! misery !
Hark ! death is calling
While I speak to ye,
The jaw is falling,
The red cheek paling,
The strong limbs failing ;
Ice with the warm blood mixing ;
The eyeballs fixing.
Nine times goes the passing bell :
Ye merry souls, farewell.
    The old earth
    Had a birth,
    As all men know,
    Long ago.
And the old earth must die.
So let the warm winds range,
And the blue wave beat the shore ;

For even and morn
Ye will never see
Thro' eternity.
All things were born.
Ye will come never more,
For all things must die.

LEONINE ELEGIACS.

LOW-FLOWING breezes are roaming the
    broad valley dimm'd in the gloaming :
Thoro' the black-stemm'd pines only
    the far river shines.
Creeping thro' blossomy rushes and bowers
    of rose-blowing bushes,
Down by the poplar tall rivulets babble
    and fall.
Barketh the shepherd-dog cheerly ; the
    grasshopper carolleth clearly ;
Deeply the wood-dove coos ; shrilly the
    owlet halloos ;
Winds creep ; dews fall chilly : in her
    first sleep earth breathes stilly :
Over the pools in the burn water-gnats
    murmur and mourn.
Sadly the far kine loweth : the glimmer-
    ing water outfloweth :
Twin peaks shadow'd with pine slope to
    the dark hyaline.
Low-throned Hesper is stayed between
    the two peaks ; but the Naiad
Throbbing in mild unrest holds him
    beneath in her breast.
The ancient poetess singeth, that Hes-
    perus all things bringeth,
Smoothing the wearied mind : bring me
    my love, Rosalind.
Thou comest morning or even ; she
    cometh not morning or even.
False-eyed Hesper, unkind, where is my
    sweet Rosalind ?

SUPPOSED CONFESSIONS

OF A SECOND-RATE SENSITIVE MIND.

O GOD ! my God ! have mercy now.
I faint, I fall. Men say that Thou

Didst die for me, for such as *me*,
Patient of ill, and death, and scorn,
And that my sin was as a thorn
Among the thorns that girt Thy brow,
Wounding Thy soul.—That even now,
In this extremest misery
Of ignorance, I should require
A sign ! and if a bolt of fire
Would rive the slumbrous summer noon
While I do pray to Thee alone,
Think my belief would stronger grow !
Is not my human pride brought low ?
The boastings of my spirit still ?
The joy I had in my freewill
All cold, and dead, and corpse-like grown?
And what is left to me, but Thou,
And faith in Thee ?   Men pass me by ;
Christians with happy countenances—
And children all seem full of Thee !
And women smile with saint-like glances
Like Thine own mother's when she bow'd
Above Thee, on that happy morn
When angels spake to men aloud,
And Thou and peace to earth were born.
Goodwill to me as well as all—
I one of them : my brothers they :
Brothers in Christ—a world of peace
And confidence, day after day ;
And trust and hope till things should cease,
And then one Heaven receive us all.

How sweet to have a common faith !
To hold a common scorn of death !
And at a burial to hear
The creaking cords which wound and eat
Into my human heart, whene'er
Earth goes to earth, with grief, not fear,
With hopeful grief, were passing sweet !

Thrice happy state again to be
The trustful infant on the knee !
Who lets his rosy fingers play
About his mother's neck, and knows
Nothing beyond his mother's eyes.
They comfort him by night and day ;
They light his little life alway ;
He hath no thought of coming woes ;
He hath no care of life or death ;
Scarce outward signs of joy arise,
Because the Spirit of happiness

And perfect rest so inward is ;
And loveth so his innocent heart,
Her temple and her place of birth,
Where she would ever wish to dwell,
Life of the fountain there, beneath
Its salient springs, and far apart,
Hating to wander out on earth,
Or breathe into the hollow air,
Whose chillness would make visible
Her subtil, warm, and golden breath,
Which mixing with the infant's blood,
Fulfils him with beatitude.
Oh ! sure it is a special care
Of God, to fortify from doubt,
To arm in proof, and guard about
With triple-mailèd trust, and clear
Delight, the infant's dawning year.

Would that my gloomed fancy were
As thine, my mother, when with brows
Propt on thy knees, my hands upheld
In thine, I listen'd to thy vows,
For me outpour'd in holiest prayer—
For me unworthy !—and beheld
Thy mild deep eyes upraised, that knew
The beauty and repose of faith,
And the clear spirit shining thro'.
Oh ! wherefore do we grow awry
From roots which strike so deep ? why
          dare
Paths in the desert ?   Could not I
Bow myself down, where thou hast knelt,
To the earth—until the ice would melt
Here, and I feel as thou hast felt ?
What Devil had the heart to scathe
Flowers thou hadst rear'd—to brush the
          dew
From thine own lily, when thy grave
Was deep, my mother, in the clay ?
Myself ? Is it thus ? Myself ? Had I
So little love for thee ?   But why
Prevail'd not thy pure prayers ?   Why
          pray
To one who heeds not, who can save
But will not ?   Great in faith, and strong
Against the grief of circumstance
Wert thou, and yet unheard.   What if
Thou pleadest still, and seest me drive
Thro' utter dark a full-sail'd skiff,
Unpiloted i' the echoing dance

Of reboant whirlwinds, stooping low
Unto the death, not sunk ! I know
At matins and at evensong,
That thou, if thou wert yet alive,
In deep and daily prayers would'st strive
To reconcile me with thy God.
Albeit, my hope is gray, and cold
At heart, thou wouldest murmur still—
'Bring this lamb back into Thy fold,
My Lord, if so it be Thy will.'
Would'st tell me I must brook the rod
And chastisement of human pride ;
That pride, the sin of devils, stood
Betwixt me and the light of God !
That hitherto I had defied
And had rejected God—that grace
Would drop from his o'er-brimming love,
As manna on my wilderness,
If I would pray—that God would move
And strike the hard, hard rock, and thence,
Sweet in their utmost bitterness,
Would issue tears of penitence
Which would keep green hope's life.
    Alas !
I think that pride hath now no place
Nor sojourn in me. I am void,
Dark, formless, utterly destroyed.

Why not believe then ? Why not yet
Anchor thy frailty there, where man
Hath moor'd and rested ? Ask the sea
At midnight, when the crisp slope waves
After a tempest, rib and fret
The broad-imbased beach, why he
Slumbers not like a mountain tarn ?
Wherefore his ridges are not curls
And ripples of an inland mere ?
Wherefore he moaneth thus, nor can
Draw down into his vexed pools
All that blue heaven which hues and paves
The other ? I am too forlorn,
Too shaken : my own weakness fools
My judgment, and my spirit whirls,
Moved from beneath with doubt and fear.

'Yet,' said I, in my morn of youth,
The unsunn'd freshness of my strength,
When I went forth in quest of truth,
'It is man's privilege to doubt,

If so be that from doubt at length,
Truth may stand forth unmoved of change,
An image with profulgent brows,
And perfect limbs, as from the storm
Of running fires and fluid range
Of lawless airs, at last stood out
This excellence and solid form
Of constant beauty. For the Ox
Feeds in the herb, and sleeps, or fills
The horned valleys all about,
And hollows of the fringed hills
In summer heats, with placid lows
Unfearing, till his own blood flows
About his hoof. And in the flocks
The lamb rejoiceth in the year,
And raceth freely with his fere,
And answers to his mother's calls
From the flower'd furrow. In a time,
Of which he wots not, run short pains
Thro' his warm heart ; and then, from
    whence
He knows not, on his light there falls
A shadow ; and his native slope,
Where he was wont to leap and climb,
Floats from his sick and filmed eyes,
And something in the darkness draws
His forehead earthward, and he dies.
Shall man live thus, in joy and hope
As a young lamb, who cannot dream,
Living, but that he shall live on ?
Shall we not look into the laws
Of life and death, and things that seem,
And things that be, and analyse
Our double nature, and compare
All creeds till we have found the one,
If one there be ?' Ay me ! I fear
All may not doubt, but everywhere
Some must clasp Idols. Yet, my God,
Whom call I Idol ? Let Thy dove
Shadow me over, and my sins
Be unremember'd, and Thy love
Enlighten me. Oh teach me yet
Somewhat before the heavy clod
Weighs on me, and the busy fret
Of that sharp-headed worm begins
In the gross blackness underneath.

O weary life ! O weary death !
O spirit and heart made desolate !
O damned vacillating state !

THE KRAKEN.

BELOW the thunders of the upper deep ;
Far, far beneath in the abysmal sea,
His ancient, dreamless, uninvaded sleep
The Kraken sleepeth : faintest sunlights
    flee
About his shadowy sides : above him swell
Huge sponges of millennial growth and
    height ;
And far away into the sickly light,
From many a wondrous grot and secret
    cell
Unnumber'd and enormous polypi
Winnow with giant arms the slumbering
    green.
There hath he lain for ages and will lie
Battening upon huge seaworms in his
    sleep,
Until the latter fire shall heat the deep ;
Then once by man and angels to be seen,
In roaring he shall rise and on the sur-
    face die.

SONG.

THE winds, as at their hour of birth,
  Leaning upon the ridged sea,
Breathed low around the rolling earth
    With mellow preludes, ' We are free.'

The streams through many a lilied row
  Down-carolling to the crisped sea,
Low-tinkled with a bell-like flow
    Atween the blossoms, ' We are free.'

LILIAN.

I.

AIRY, fairy Lilian,
  Flitting, fairy Lilian,
When I ask her if she love me,
Claps her tiny hands above me,
    Laughing all she can ;
She'll not tell me if she love me,
  Cruel little Lilian.

II.

When my passion seeks
  Pleasance in love-sighs,
She, looking thro' and thro' me
  Thoroughly to undo me,
    Smiling, never speaks :
So innocent-arch, so cunning-simple,
From beneath her gathered wimple
  Glancing with black-beaded eyes,
Till the lightning laughters dimple
    The baby-roses in her cheeks ;
    Then away she flies.

III.

Prythee weep, May Lilian !
  Gaiety without eclipse
Wearieth me, May Lilian :
Thro' my very heart it thrilleth
  When from crimson-threaded lips
Silver-treble laughter trilleth :
  Prythee weep, May Lilian.

IV.

Praying all I•can,
If prayers will not hush thee,
  Airy Lilian,
Like a rose-leaf I will crush thee,
  Fairy Lilian.

ISABEL.

I.

EYES not down-dropt nor over - bright,
  but fed
  With the clear-pointed flame of chastity,
  Clear, without heat, undying, tended by
    Pure vestal thoughts in the trans-
    lucent fane
Of her still spirit ; locks not wide-dispread,
    Madonna - wise on either side her
    head ;
    Sweet lips whereon perpetually did
    reign
  The summer calm of golden charity,
Were fixed shadows of thy fixed mood,
  Revered Isabel, the crown and head,
The stately flower of female fortitude,
    Of perfect wifehood and pure lowli-
    head.

II.

The intuitive decision of a bright
  And thorough-edged intellect to part
    Error from crime ; a prudence to
      withhold ;
    The laws of marriage character'd in
      gold
  Upon the blanched tablets of her heart ;
A love still burning upward, giving light
To read those laws ; an accent very low
In blandishment, but a most silver flow
  Of subtle-paced counsel in distress,
Right to the heart and brain, tho' unde-
    scried,
    Winning its way with extreme gentle-
      ness
Thro' all the outworks of suspicious pride ;
A courage to endure and to obey ;
A hate of gossip parlance, and of sway,
Crown'd Isabel, thro' all her placid life,
The queen of marriage, a most perfect
  wife.

III.

The mellow'd reflex of a winter moon ;
A clear stream flowing with a muddy one,
  Till in its onward current it absorbs
    With swifter movement and in purer
      light
    The vexed eddies of its wayward
      brother :
    A leaning and upbearing parasite,
    Clothing the stem, which else had
      fallen quite
  With cluster'd flower - bells and am-
    brosial orbs
    Of rich fruit-bunches leaning on each
      other—
    Shadow forth thee :—the world hath
      not another
(Tho' all her fairest forms are types of
  thee,
And thou of God in thy great charity)
Of such a finish'd chasten'd purity.

MARIANA.

'Mariana in the moated grange.'
Measure for Measure.

WITH blackest moss the flower-plots
  Were thickly crusted, one and all :
The rusted nails fell from the knots
  That held the pear to the gable-wall.
The broken sheds look'd sad and strange :
  Unlifted was the clinking latch ;
  Weeded and worn the ancient thatch
Upon the lonely moated grange.
    She only said, ' My life is dreary,
      He cometh not,' she said ;
    She said, ' I am aweary, aweary,
      I would that I were dead !'

Her tears fell with the dews at even ;
  Her tears fell ere the dews were dried ;
She could not look on the sweet heaven,
  Either at morn or eventide.
After the flitting of the bats,
  When thickest dark did trance the sky,
  She drew her casement-curtain by,
And glanced athwart the glooming flats.
    She only said, ' The night is dreary,
      He cometh not,' she said ;
    She said, ' I am aweary, aweary,
      I would that I were dead !'

Upon the middle of the night,
  Waking she heard the night-fowl crow :
The cock sung out an hour ere light :
  From the dark fen the oxen's low
Came to her : without hope of change,
  In sleep she seem'd to walk forlorn,
  Till cold winds woke the gray-eyed
    morn
About the lonely moated grange.
    She only said, ' The day is dreary,
      He cometh not,' she said ;
    She said, ' I am aweary, aweary,
      I would that I were dead !'

About a stone-cast from the wall
  A sluice with blacken'd waters slept,
And o'er it many, round and small,
  The cluster'd marish-mosses crept.

Hard by a poplar shook alway,
　All silver-green with gnarled bark :
For leagues no other tree did mark
The level waste, the rounding gray.
　　She only said, ' My life is dreary,
　　　He cometh not,' she said ;
　　She said, ' I am aweary, aweary,
　　　I would that I were dead !'

And ever when the moon was low,
　And the shrill winds were up and away,
In the white curtain, to and fro,
　She saw the gusty shadow sway.
But when the moon was very low,
　And wild winds bound within their cell,
　The shadow of the poplar fell
Upon her bed, across her brow.
　　She only said, 'The night is dreary,
　　　He cometh not,' she said ;
　　She said, ' I am aweary, aweary,
　　　I would that I were dead !'

All day within the dreamy house,
　The doors upon their hinges creak'd ;
The blue fly sung in the pane ; the mouse
　Behind the mouldering wainscot
　　shriek'd,
Or from the crevice peer'd about.
　Old faces glimmer'd thro' the doors,
　Old footsteps trod the upper floors,
Old voices called her from without.
　　She only said, ' My life is dreary,
　　　He cometh not,' she said ;　·
　　She said, ' I am aweary, aweary,
　　　I would that I were dead !'

The sparrow's chirrup on the roof,
　The slow clock ticking, and the sound
Which to the wooing wind aloof
　The poplar made, did all confound
Her sense ; but most she loathed the hour
　When the thick-moted sunbeam lay
　Athwart the chambers, and the day
Was sloping toward his western bower.
　　Then, said she, ' I am very dreary,
　　　He will not come,' she said ;
　　She wept, ' I am aweary, aweary,
　　　Oh God, that I were dead !'

TO ——.

I.

CLEAR-HEADED friend, whose joyful scorn,
　Edged with sharp laughter, cuts atwain
　　The knots that tangle human creeds,
　　The wounding cords that bind and strain
　　　The heart until it bleeds,
Ray-fringed eyelids of the morn
　Roof not a glance so keen as thine :
　If aught of prophecy be mine,
Thou wilt not live in vain.

II.

Low-cowering shall the Sophist sit ;
　Falsehood shall bare her plaited brow :
　Fair-fronted Truth shall droop not now
With shrilling shafts of subtle wit.
Nor martyr-flames, nor trenchant swords
　Can do away that ancient lie ;
A gentler death shall Falsehood die,
Shot thro' and thro' with cunning words.

III.

Weak Truth a-leaning on her crutch,
　Wan, wasted Truth in her utmost need.
　Thy kingly intellect shall feed,
　　Until she be an athlete bold,
And weary with a finger's touch
　Those writhed limbs of lightning speed ;
Like that strange angel which of old,
　Until the breaking of the light,
Wrestled with wandering Israel,
　Past Yabbok brook the livelong night,
And heaven's mazed signs stood still
In the dim tract of Penuel.

MADELINE.

I.

THOU art not steep'd in golden languors,
　No tranced summer calm is thine,
　Ever varying Madeline.
Thro' light and shadow thou dost range,
　Sudden glances, sweet and strange,
Delicious spites and darling angers,
　And airy forms of flitting change.

II.

Smiling, frowning, evermore,
Thou art perfect in love-lore.
Revealings deep and clear are thine
Of wealthy smiles : but who may know
Whether smile or frown be fleeter?
Whether smile or frown be sweeter,
    Who may know?
Frowns perfect-sweet along the brow
Light-glooming over eyes divine,
Like little clouds sun-fringed, are thine,
    Ever varying Madeline.
Thy smile and frown are not aloof
    From one another,
    Each to each is dearest brother ;
Hues of the silken sheeny woof
Momently shot into each other.
    All the mystery is thine ;
Smiling, frowning, evermore,
Thou art perfect in love-lore,
    Ever varying Madeline.

III.

A subtle, sudden flame,
  By veering passion fann'd,
    About thee breaks and dances :
  When I would kiss thy hand,
The flush of anger'd shame
  O'erflows thy calmer glances,
And o'er black brows drops down
A sudden-curved frown :
But when I turn away,
Thou, willing me to stay,
  Wooest not, nor vainly wranglest ;
    But, looking fixedly the while,
  All my bounding heart entanglest
    In a golden-netted smile ;
Then in madness and in bliss,
If my lips should dare to kiss
Thy taper fingers amorously,
Again thou blushest angerly ;
And o'er black brows drops down
A sudden-curved frown.

SONG—THE OWL.

I.

WHEN cats run home and light is come,
  And dew is cold upon the ground,

And the far-off stream is dumb,
  And the whirring sail goes round,
  And the whirring sail goes round ;
    Alone and warming his five wits,
    The white owl in the belfry sits.

II.

When merry milkmaids click the latch,
  And rarely smells the new-mown hay,
And the cock hath sung beneath the
    thatch
  Twice or thrice his roundelay,
  Twice or thrice his roundelay ;
    Alone and warming his five wits,
    The white owl in the belfry sits,

SECOND SONG.

TO THE SAME.

I.

THY tuwhits are lull'd, I wot,
  Thy tuwhoos of yesternight,
Which upon the dark afloat,
  So took echo with delight,
  So took echo with delight,
    That her voice untuneful grown,
    Wears all day a fainter tone.

II.

I would mock thy chaunt anew ;
  But I cannot mimick it ;
Not a whit of thy tuwhoo,
  Thee to woo to thy tuwhit,
  Thee to woo to thy tuwhit,
    With a lengthen'd loud halloo,
    Tuwhoo, tuwhit, tuwhit, tuwhoo-o-o.

RECOLLECTIONS OF THE
ARABIAN NIGHTS.

WHEN the breeze of a joyful dawn blew
    free
In the silken sail of infancy,
The tide of time flow'd back with me,
  The forward-flowing tide of time ;
And many a sheeny summer-morn,
Adown the Tigris I was borne,

By Bagdat's shrines of fretted gold,
High-walled gardens green and old ;
True Mussulman was I and sworn,
    For it was in the golden prime
      Of good Haroun Alraschid.

Anight my shallop, rustling thro'
The low and bloomed foliage, drove
The fragrant, glistening deeps, and clove
The citron-shadows in the blue :
By garden porches on the brim,
The costly doors flung open wide,
Gold glittering thro' lamplight dim,
And broider'd sofas on each side :
    In sooth it was a goodly time,
    For it was in the golden prime
      Of good Haroun Alraschid.

Often, where clear-stemm'd platans guard
The outlet, did I turn away
The boat-head down a broad canal
From the main river sluiced, where all
The sloping of the moon-lit sward
Was damask-work, and deep inlay
Of braided blooms unmown, which crept
Adown to where the water slept.
    A goodly place, a goodly time,
    For it was in the golden prime
      Of good Haroun Alraschid.

A motion from the river won
Ridged the smooth level, bearing on
My shallop thro' the star-strown calm,
Until another night in night
I enter'd, from the clearer light,
Imbower'd vaults of pillar'd palm,
Imprisoning sweets, which, as they clomb
Heavenward, were stay'd beneath the
    dome
    Of hollow boughs.—A goodly time,
    For it was in the golden prime
      Of good Haroun Alraschid.

Still onward ; and the clear canal
Is rounded to as clear a lake.
From the green rivage many a fall
Of diamond rillets musical,
Thro' little crystal arches low
Down from the central fountain's flow
Fall'n silver-chiming, seemed to shake
The sparkling flints beneath the prow.

    A goodly place, a goodly time,
    For it was in the golden prime
      Of good Haroun Alraschid.

Above thro' many a bowery turn
A walk with vary-colour'd shells
Wander'd engrain'd.   On either side
All round about the fragrant marge
From fluted vase, and brazen urn
In order, eastern flowers large,
Some dropping low their crimson bells
Half-closed, and others studded wide
    With disks and tiars, fed the time
    With odour in the golden prime
      Of good Haroun Alraschid.

Far off, and where the lemon grove
In closest coverture upsprung,
The living airs of middle night
Died round the bulbul as he sung ;
Not he : but something which possess'd
The darkness of the world, delight,
Life, anguish, death, immortal love,
Ceasing not, mingled, unrepress'd,
    Apart from place, withholding time,
    But flattering the golden prime
      Of good Haroun Alraschid.

Black the garden-bowers and grots
Slumber'd : the solemn palms were ranged
Above, unwoo'd of summer wind :
A sudden splendour from behind
Flush'd all the leaves with rich gold-green,
And, flowing rapidly between
Their interspaces, counterchanged
The level lake with diamond-plots
    Of dark and bright.   A lovely time,
    For it was in the golden prime
      Of good Haroun Alraschid.

Dark-blue the deep sphere overhead,
Distinct with vivid stars inlaid,
Grew darker from that under-flame :
So, leaping lightly from the boat,
With silver anchor left afloat,
In marvel whence that glory came
Upon me, as in sleep I sank
In cool soft turf upon the bank,
    Entranced with that place and time,
    So worthy of the golden prime
      Of good Haroun Alraschid.

Thence thro' the garden I was drawn—
A realm of pleasance, many a mound,
And many a shadow-chequer'd lawn
Full of the city's stilly sound,
And deep myrrh-thickets blowing round
The stately cedar, tamarisks,
Thick rosaries of scented thorn,
Tall orient shrubs, and obelisks
     Graven with emblems of the time,
       In honour of the golden prime
         Of good Haroun Alraschid.

With dazed vision unawares
From the long alley's latticed shade
Emerged, I came upon the great
Pavilion of the Caliphat.
Right to the carven cedarn doors,
Flung inward over spangled floors,
Broad-based flights of marble stairs
Ran up with golden balustrade,
     After the fashion of the time,
       And humour of the golden prime
         Of good Haroun Alraschid.

The fourscore windows all alight
As with the quintessence of flame,
A million tapers flaring bright
From twisted silvers look'd to shame
The hollow-vaulted dark, and stream'd
Upon the mooned domes aloof
In inmost Bagdat, till there seem'd
Hundreds of crescents on the roof
     Of night new-risen, that marvellous time
       To celebrate the golden prime
         Of good Haroun Alraschid.

Then stole I up, and trancedly
Gazed on the Persian girl alone,
Serene with argent-lidded eyes
Amorous, and lashes like to rays
Of darkness, and a brow of pearl
Tressed with redolent ebony,
In many a dark delicious curl,
Flowing beneath her rose-hued zone ;
     The sweetest lady of the time,
       Well worthy of the golden prime
         Of good Haroun Alraschid.

Six columns, three on either side,
Pure silver, underpropt a rich
Throne of the massive ore, from which

Down-droop'd, in many a floating fold,
Engarlanded and diaper'd
With inwrought flowers, a cloth of gold.
Thereon, his deep eye laughter-stirr'd
With merriment of kingly pride,
     Sole star of all that place and time,
       I saw him—in his golden prime,
         THE GOOD HAROUN ALRASCHID.

ODE TO MEMORY.

ADDRESSED TO ————.

I.

THOU who stealest fire,
     From the fountains of the past,
     To glorify the present ; oh, haste,
         Visit my low desire !
Strengthen me, enlighten me !
I faint in this obscurity,
Thou dewy dawn of memory.

II.

Come not as thou camest of late,
     Flinging the gloom of yesternight
On the white day ; but robed in soften'd
     light
         Of orient state.
Whilome thou camest with the morning
     mist,
     Even as a maid, whose stately brow
The dew-impearled winds of dawn have
     kiss'd,
         When, she, as thou,
Stays on her floating locks the lovely freight
Of overflowing blooms, and earliest shoots
Of orient green, giving safe pledge of fruits,
Which in wintertide shall star
The black earth with brilliance rare.

III.

Whilome thou camest with the morning
     mist,
         And with the evening cloud,
Showering thy gleaned wealth into my
     open breast
(Those peerless flowers which in the
     rudest wind
         Never grow sere,

When rooted in the garden of the mind,
  Because they are the earliest of the year).
    Nor was the night thy shroud.
In sweet dreams softer than unbroken rest
Thou leddest by the hand thine infant
    Hope.
The eddying of her garments caught from
    thee
The light of thy great presence ; and the
    cope
  Of the half-attain'd futurity,
  Tho' deep not fathomless,
Was cloven with the million stars which
    tremble
O'er the deep mind of dauntless infancy.
Small thought was there of life's distress ;
For sure she deem'd no mist of earth
    could dull
Those spirit-thrilling eyes so keen and
    beautiful :
Sure she was nigher to heaven's spheres,
Listening the lordly music flowing from
    The illimitable years.
  O strengthen me, enlighten me !
  I faint in this obscurity,
  Thou dewy dawn of memory.

IV.

Come forth, I charge thee, arise,
Thou of the many tongues, the myriad
    eyes !
Thou comest not with shows of flaunting
    vines
    Unto mine inner eye,
    Divinest Memory !
  Thou wert not nursed by the waterfall
Which ever sounds and shines
  A pillar of white light upon the wall
Of purple cliffs, aloof descried :
Come from the woods that belt the gray
    hill-side,
The seven elms, the poplars four
That stand beside my father's door,
And chiefly from the brook that loves
To purl o'er matted cress and ribbed sand,
Or dimple in the dark of rushy coves,
Drawing into his narrow earthen urn,
    In every elbow and turn,
The filter'd tribute of the rough woodland,
    O ! hither lead thy feet !

Pour round mine ears the livelong bleat
Of the thick-fleeced sheep from wattled
    folds,
    Upon the ridged wolds,
When the first matin-song hath waken'd
    loud
Over the dark dewy earth forlorn,
What time the amber morn
Forth gushes from beneath a low-hung
    cloud.

V.

Large dowries doth the raptured eye
  To the young spirit present
    When first she is wed ;
    And like a bride of old
  In triumph led,
    With music and sweet showers
    Of festal flowers,
Unto the dwelling she must sway.
Well hast thou done, great artist Memory,
  In setting round thy first experiment
    With royal frame-work of wrought
    gold ;
Needs must thou dearly love thy first
    essay,
And foremost in thy various gallery
  Place it, where sweetest sunlight falls
  Upon the storied walls ;
    For the discovery
And newness of thine art so pleased thee,
That all which thou hast drawn of fairest
  Or boldest since, but lightly weighs
With thee unto the love thou bearest
The first-born of thy genius.   Artist-like,
Ever retiring thou dost gaze
On the prime labour of thine early days :
No matter what the sketch might be ;
Whether the high field on the bushless
    Pike,
Or even a sand-built ridge
Of heaped hills that mound the sea,
Overblown with murmurs harsh,
Or even a lowly cottage whence we see
Stretch'd wide and wild the waste enor-
    mous marsh,
Where from the frequent bridge,
Like emblems of infinity,
The trenched waters run from sky to sky ;
Or a garden bower'd close

With plaited alleys of the trailing rose,
Long alleys falling down to twilight grots,
Or opening upon level plots
Of crowned lilies, standing near
Purple-spiked lavender :
Whither in after life retired
From brawling storms,
From weary wind,
With youthful fancy re-inspired,
    We may hold converse with all forms
Of the many-sided mind,
And those whom passion hath not blinded,
Subtle-thoughted, myriad-minded.

My friend, with you to live alone,
Were how much better than to own
A crown, a sceptre, and a throne !

O strengthen me, enlighten me !
I faint in this obscurity,
Thou dewy dawn of memory.

[An Autumn] SONG.

I.

A SPIRIT haunts the year's last hours
Dwelling amid these yellowing bowers :
    To himself he talks ;
For at eventide, listening earnestly,
At his work you may hear him sob and sigh
    In the walks ;
    Earthward he boweth the heavy stalks
Of the mouldering flowers :
    Heavily hangs the broad sunflower
        Over its grave i' the earth so chilly ;
    Heavily hangs the hollyhock,
        Heavily hangs the tiger-lily.
            (see end)

II.

The air is damp, and hush'd, and close,
As a sick man's room when he taketh repose
    An hour before death ;
My very heart faints and my whole soul grieves
At the moist rich smell of the rotting leaves,

And the breath
    Of the fading edges of box beneath,
And the year's last rose.
    Heavily hangs the broad sunflower
        Over its grave i' the earth so chilly ;
    Heavily hangs the hollyhock,
        Heavily hangs the tiger-lily.

A CHARACTER.

garden lily w flowers of dull orange spotted w black or purple

WITH a half-glance upon the sky
At night he said, ' The wanderings
Of this most intricate Universe
Teach me the nothingness of things.
Yet could not all creation pierce
Beyond the bottom of his eye.

He spake of beauty : that the dull
Saw no divinity in grass,
Life in dead stones, or spirit in air ;
Then looking as 'twere in a glass,
He smooth'd his chin and sleek'd his hair,
And said the earth was beautiful.

He spake of virtue : not the gods
More purely, when they wish to charm
Pallas and Juno sitting by :
And with a sweeping of the arm,
And a lack-lustre dead-blue eye,
Devolved his rounded periods.

Most delicately hour by hour
He canvass'd human mysteries,
And trod on silk, as if the winds
Blew his own praises in his eyes,
And stood aloof from other minds
In impotence of fancied power.

With lips depress'd as he were meek,
Himself unto himself he sold :
Upon himself himself did feed :
Quiet, dispassionate, and cold,
And other than his form of creed,
With chisell'd features clear and sleek.

THE POET.

THE poet in a golden clime was born,
    With golden stars above ;
Dower'd with the hate of hate, the scorn
        of scorn,
    The love of love.

He saw thro' life and death, thro' good
    and ill,
    He saw thro' his own soul.
The marvel of the everlasting will,
    An open scroll,

Before him lay: with echoing feet he
    threaded
    The secretest walks of fame:
The viewless arrows of his thoughts were
    headed
    And wing'd with flame,

Like Indian reeds blown from his silver
    tongue,
    And of so fierce a flight,
From Calpe unto Caucasus they sung,
    Filling with light

And vagrant melodies the winds which
    bore
    Them earthward till they lit;
Then, like the arrow-seeds of the field
    flower,
    The fruitful wit

Cleaving, took root, and springing forth
    anew
    Where'er they fell, behold,
Like to the mother plant in semblance,
    grew
    A flower all gold,

And bravely furnish'd all abroad to fling
    The winged shafts of truth,
To throng with stately blooms the breath-
    ing spring
    Of Hope and Youth.

So many minds did gird their orbs with
    beams,
    Tho' one did fling the fire.
Heaven flow'd upon the soul in many
    dreams
    Of high desire.

Thus truth was multiplied on truth, the
    world
    Like one great garden show'd,
And thro' the wreaths of floating dark
    upcurl'd,
    Rare sunrise flow'd.

And Freedom rear'd in that august sunrise
    Her beautiful bold brow,
When rites and forms before his burning
    eyes
    Melted like snow.

There was no blood upon her maiden robes
    Sunn'd by those orient skies;
But round about the circles of the globes
    Of her keen eyes

And in her raiment's hem was traced in
    flame
    WISDOM, a name to shake
All evil dreams of power—a sacred name.
    And when she spake,

Her words did gather thunder as they ran,
    And as the lightning to the thunder
Which follows it, riving the spirit of man,
    Making earth wonder,

So was their meaning to her words. No
    sword
    Of wrath her right arm whirl'd,
But one poor poet's scroll, and with *his*
    word
    She shook the world.

THE POET'S MIND.

I.

VEX not thou the poet's mind
    With thy shallow wit:
Vex not thou the poet's mind;
    For thou canst not fathom it.
Clear and bright it should be ever,
Flowing like a crystal river;
Bright as light, and clear as wind.

II.

Dark-brow'd sophist, come not anear;
    All the place is holy ground;
    Hollow smile and frozen sneer
        Come not here.
    Holy water will I pour
    Into every spicy flower
Of the laurel-shrubs that hedge it around.
The flowers would faint at your cruel
    cheer.

In your eye there is death,
There is frost in your breath
Which would blight the plants.
  Where you stand you cannot hear
    From the groves within
    The wild-bird's din.
In the heart of the garden the merry bird
  chants,
It would fall to the ground if you came
  in.
  In the middle leaps a fountain
    Like sheet lightning,
    Ever brightening
  With a low melodious thunder ;
All day and all night it is ever drawn
  From the brain of the purple mountain
  Which stands in the distance yonder :
It springs on a level of bowery lawn,
And the mountain draws it from Heaven
  above,
And it sings a song of undying love ;
And yet, tho' its voice be so clear and
  full,
You never would hear it ; your ears are
  so dull ;
So keep where you are : you are foul with
  sin ;
It would shrink to the earth if you came
  in.

THE SEA-FAIRIES.

Slow sail'd the weary mariners and saw,
Betwixt the green brink and the running
  foam,
Sweet faces, rounded arms, and bosoms
  prest
To little harps of gold ; and while they
  mused
Whispering to each other half in fear,
Shrill music reach'd them on the middle
  sea.

Whither away, whither away, whither
  away ? fly no more.
Whither away from the high green field,
  and the happy blossoming shore ?
Day and night to the billow the fountain
  calls :

Down shower the gambolling waterfalls
From wandering over the lea :
Out of the live-green heart of the dells
They freshen the silvery-crimson shells,
And thick with white bells the clover-hill
  swells
High over the full-toned sea :
O hither, come hither and furl your sails,
Come hither to me and to me :
Hither, come hither and frolic and play ;
Here it is only the mew that wails ;
We will sing to you all the day :
Mariner, mariner, furl your sails,
For here are the blissful downs and dales,
And merrily, merrily carol the gales,
And the spangle dances in bight and bay,
And the rainbow forms and flies on the
  land
Over the islands free ;
And the rainbow lives in the curve of the
  sand ;
Hither, come hither and see ;
And the rainbow hangs on the poising
  wave,
And sweet is the colour of cove and cave,
And sweet shall your welcome be :
O hither, come hither, and be our lords,
For merry brides are we :
We will kiss sweet kisses, and speak
  sweet words :
O listen, listen, your eyes shall glisten
With pleasure and love and jubilee :
O listen, listen, your eyes shall glisten
When the sharp clear twang of the golden
  chords
Runs up the ridged sea.
Who can light on as happy a shore
All the world o'er, all the world o'er ?
Whither away ? listen and stay : mariner,
  mariner, fly no more.

THE DESERTED HOUSE.

I.

Life and Thought have gone away
  Side by side,
  Leaving door and windows wide :
Careless tenants they !

II.

All within is dark as night :
In the windows is no light ;
And no murmur at the door,
So frequent on its hinge before.

III.

Close the door, the shutters close,
  Or thro' the windows we shall see
  The nakedness and vacancy
Of the dark deserted house.

IV.

Come away : no more of mirth
  Is here or merry-making sound.
The house was builded of the earth,
  And shall fall again to ground.

V.

Come away : for Life and Thought
  Here no longer dwell ;
  But in a city glorious—
A great and distant city—have bought
  A mansion incorruptible.
Would they could have stayed with us !

THE DYING SWAN.

I.

THE plain was grassy, wild and bare,
Wide, wild, and open to the air,
Which had built up everywhere
  An under-roof of doleful gray.
With an inner voice the river ran,
Adown it floated a dying swan,
  And loudly did lament.
It was the middle of the day.
Ever the weary wind went on,
  And took the reed-tops as it went.

II.

Some blue peaks in the distance rose,
And white against the cold-white sky,
Shone out their crowning snows.
  One willow over the river wept,
And shook the wave as the wind did sigh;
Above in the wind was the swallow,

Chasing itself at its own wild will,
And far thro' the marish green and
  still
The tangled water-courses slept,
Shot over with purple, and green, and
  yellow.

III.

The wild swan's death-hymn took the soul
Of that waste place with joy
Hidden in sorrow : at first to the ear
The warble was low, and full and clear ;
And floating about the under-sky,
Prevailing in weakness, the coronach
  stole
Sometimes afar, and sometimes anear ;
But anon her awful jubilant voice,
With a music strange and manifold,
Flow'd forth on a carol free and bold ;
As when a mighty people rejoice
With shawms, and with cymbals, and
  harps of gold,
And the tumult of their acclaim is roll'd
Thro' the open gates of the city afar,
To the shepherd who watcheth the even-
  ing star.
And the creeping mosses and clambering
  weeds,
And the willow-branches hoar and dank,
And the wavy swell of the soughing
  reeds,
And the wave-worn horns of the echoing
  bank,
And the silvery marish-flowers that
  throng
The desolate creeks and pools among,
Were flooded over with eddying song.

A DIRGE.

I.

Now is done thy long day's work ;
Fold thy palms across thy breast,
Fold thine arms, turn to thy rest.
  Let them rave.
Shadows of the silver birk
Sweep the green that folds thy grave.
  Let them rave.

II.

Thee nor carketh care nor slander ;
Nothing but the small cold worm
Fretteth thine enshrouded form.
     Let them rave.
Light and shadow ever wander
O'er the green that folds thy grave.
     Let them rave.

III.

Thou wilt not turn upon thy bed ;
Chaunteth not the brooding bee
Sweeter tones than calumny ?
     Let them rave.
Thou wilt never raise thine head
From the green that folds thy grave.
     Let them rave.

IV.

Crocodiles wept tears for thee ;
The woodbine and eglatere
Drip sweeter dews than traitor's tear.
     Let them rave.
Rain makes music in the tree
O'er the green that folds thy grave.
     Let them rave.

V.

Round thee blow, self-pleached deep,
Bramble roses, faint and pale,
And long purples of the dale.
     Let them rave.
These in every shower creep
Thro' the green that folds thy grave.
     Let them rave.

VI.

The gold-eyed kingcups fine ;
The frail bluebell peereth over
Rare broidry of the purple clover.
     Let them rave.
Kings have no such couch as thine,
As the green that folds thy grave.
     Let them rave.

VII.

Wild words wander here and there :
God's great gift of speech abused
Makes thy memory confused :
     But let them rave.

τ

The balm-cricket carols clear
In the green that folds thy grave.
     Let them rave.

LOVE AND DEATH.

WHAT time the mighty moon was gathering light
Love paced the thymy plots of Paradise,
And all about him roll'd his lustrous eyes ;
When, turning round a cassia, full in view,
Death, walking all alone beneath a yew,
And talking to himself, first met his
          sight :
'You must begone,' said Death, 'these
          walks are mine.'
Love wept and spread his sheeny vans
          for flight ;
Yet ere he parted said, 'This hour is
          thine :
Thou art the shadow of life, and as the
          tree
Stands in the sun and shadows all beneath,
So in the light of great eternity
Life eminent creates the shade of death ;
The shadow passeth when the tree shall
          fall,
But I shall reign for ever over all.'

THE BALLAD OF ORIANA.

MY heart is wasted with my woe,
          Oriana.
There is no rest for me below,
          Oriana.
When the long dun wolds are ribb'd with
          snow,
And loud the Norland whirlwinds blow,
          Oriana,
Alone I wander to and fro,
          Oriana.

Ere the light on dark was growing,
          Oriana,
At midnight the cock was crowing,
          Oriana :

c

Winds were blowing, waters flowing,
We heard the steeds to battle going,
    Oriana ;
Aloud the hollow bugle blowing,
    Oriana.

In the yew-wood black as night,
    Oriana,
Ere I rode into the fight,
    Oriana,
While blissful tears blinded my sight
By star-shine and by moonlight,
    Oriana,
I to thee my troth did plight,
    Oriana.

She stood upon the castle wall,
    Oriana :
She watch'd my crest among them all,
    Oriana :
She saw me fight, she heard me call,
When forth there stept a foeman tall,
    Oriana,
Atween me and the castle wall,
    Oriana.

The bitter arrow went aside,
    Oriana :
The false, false arrow went aside,
    Oriana :
The damned arrow glanced aside,
And pierced thy heart, my love, my bride,
    Oriana !
Thy heart, my life, my love, my bride,
    Oriana !

Oh ! narrow, narrow was the space,
    Oriana.
Loud, loud rung out the bugle's brays,
    Oriana.
Oh ! deathful stabs were dealt apace,
The battle deepen'd in its place,
    Oriana ;
But I was down upon my face,
    Oriana.

They should have stabb'd me where I lay,
    Oriana !
How could I rise and come away,
    Oriana ?

How could I look upon the day ?
They should have stabb'd me where I lay,
    Oriana—
They should have trod me into clay,
    Oriana.

O breaking heart that will not break,
    Oriana !
O pale, pale face so sweet and meek,
    Oriana !
Thou smilest, but thou dost not speak,
And then the tears run down my cheek,
    Oriana :
What wantest thou ? whom dost thou seek,
    Oriana ?

I cry aloud : none hear my cries,
    Oriana.
Thou comest atween me and the skies,
    Oriana.
I feel the tears of blood arise
Up from my heart unto my eyes,
    Oriana.
Within thy heart my arrow lies,
    Oriana.

O cursed hand ! O cursed blow !
    Oriana !
O happy thou that liest low,
    Oriana !
All night the silence seems to flow
Beside me in my utter woe,
    Oriana.
A weary, weary way I go,
    Oriana.

When Norland winds pipe down the sea,
    Oriana,
I walk, I dare not think of thee,
    Oriana.
Thou liest beneath the greenwood tree,
I dare not die and come to thee,
    Oriana.
I hear the roaring of the sea,
    Oriana.

CIRCUMSTANCE.

Two children in two neighbour villages
Playing mad pranks along the heathy leas ;

Two strangers meeting at a festival ;
Two lovers whispering by an orchard
 wall ;
Two lives bound fast in one with golden
 ease ;
Two graves grass-green beside a gray
 church-tower,
Wash'd with still rains and daisy blos-
 somed ;
Two children in one hamlet born and
 bred ;
So runs the round of life from hour to
 hour.

THE MERMAN.

I.

Who would be
A merman bold,
Sitting alone,
Singing alone
Under the sea,
With a crown of gold,
On a throne ?

II.

I would be a merman bold,
I would sit and sing the whole of the day ;
I would fill the sea-halls with a voice of
 power ;
But at night I would roam abroad and
 play
With the mermaids in and out of the rocks,
Dressing their hair with the white sea-
 flower ;
And holding them back by their flowing
 locks
I would kiss them often under the sea,
And kiss them again till they kiss'd me
 Laughingly, laughingly ;
And then we would wander away, away
To the pale-green sea-groves straight and
 high,
 Chasing each other merrily.

III.

There would be neither moon nor star ;
But the wave would make music above
 us afar—

Low thunder and light in the magic
 night—
 Neither moon nor star.
We would call aloud in the dreamy dells,
Call to each other and whoop and cry
 All night, merrily, merrily ;
They would pelt me with starry spangles
 and shells,
Laughing and clapping their hands be-
 tween,
 All night, merrily, merrily :
But I would throw to them back in mine
Turkis and agate and almondine :
Then leaping out upon them unseen
I would kiss them often under the sea,
And kiss them again till they kiss'd me
 Laughingly, laughingly.
Oh ! what a happy life were mine
Under the hollow-hung ocean green !
Soft are the moss-beds under the sea ;
We would live merrily, merrily.

THE MERMAID.

I.

Who would be
A mermaid fair,
Singing alone,
Combing her hair
Under the sea,
In a golden curl
With a comb of pearl,
On a throne ?

II.

I would be a mermaid fair ;
I would sing to myself the whole of the
 day ;
With a comb of pearl I would comb my
 hair ;
And still as I comb'd I would sing and
 say,
'Who is it loves me? who loves not me?'
I would comb my hair till my ringlets
 would fall
 Low adown, low adown,
From under my starry sea-bud crown
 Low adown and around,
And I should look like a fountain of gold

Springing alone
With a shrill inner sound,
Over the throne
In the midst of the hall ;
Till that great sea-snake under the sea
From his coiled sleeps in the central deeps
Would slowly trail himself sevenfold
Round the hall where I sate, and look
in at the gate
With his large calm eyes for the love of
me.
And all the mermen under the sea
Would feel their immortality
Die in their hearts for the love of me.

III.

But at night I would wander away, away,
I would fling on each side my low-
flowing locks,
And lightly vault from the throne and play
With the mermen in and out of the
rocks ;
We would run to and fro, and hide and
seek,
On the broad sea-wolds in the crimson
shells,
Whose silvery spikes are nighest the sea.
But if any came near I would call, and
shriek,
And adown the steep like a wave I would
leap
From the diamond-ledges that jut from
the dells ;
For I would not be kiss'd by all who
would list,
Of the bold merry mermen under the
sea ;
They would sue me, and woo me, and
flatter me,
In the purple twilights under the sea ;
But the king of them all would carry me,
Woo me, and win me, and marry me,
In the branching jaspers under the sea ;
Then all the dry pied things that be
In the hueless mosses under the sea
Would curl round my silver feet silently,
All looking up for the love of me.
And if I should carol aloud, from aloft
All things that are forked, and horned,
and soft

Would lean out from the hollow sphere
of the sea,
All looking down for the love of me.

ADELINE.

I.

MYSTERY of mysteries,
Faintly smiling Adeline,
Scarce of earth nor all divine,
Nor unhappy, nor at rest,
But beyond expression fair
With thy floating flaxen hair ;
Thy rose-lips and full blue eyes
Take the heart from out my breast.
Wherefore those dim looks of thine,
Shadowy, dreaming Adeline ?

II.

Whence that aery bloom of thine,
Like a lily which the sun
Looks thro' in his sad decline,
And a rose-bush leans upon,
Thou that faintly smilest still,
As a Naiad in a well,
Looking at the set of day,
Or a phantom two hours old
Of a maiden past away,
Ere the placid lips be cold ?
Wherefore those faint smiles of thine,
Spiritual Adeline ?

III.

What hope or fear or joy is thine ?
Who talketh with thee, Adeline ?
For sure thou art not all alone.
Do beating hearts of salient springs
Keep measure with thine own ?
Hast thou heard the butterflies
What they say betwixt their wings ?
Or in stillest evenings
With what voice the violet woos
To his heart the silver dews ?
Or when little airs arise,
How the merry bluebell rings
To the mosses underneath ?
Hast thou look'd upon the breath
Of the lilies at sunrise ?

Wherefore that faint smile of thine,
Shadowy, dreaming Adeline?

IV.

Some honey-converse feeds thy mind,
  Some spirit of a crimson rose
  In love with thee forgets to close
His curtains, wasting odorous sighs
All night long on darkness blind.
What aileth thee? whom waitest thou
With thy soften'd, shadow'd brow,
    And those dew-lit eyes of thine,
    Thou faint smiler, Adeline?

V.

Lovest thou the doleful wind
    When thou gazest at the skies?
  Doth the low-tongued Orient
    Wander from the side of the morn,
      Dripping with Sabæan spice
  On thy pillow, lowly bent
    With melodious airs lovelorn,
Breathing Light against thy face,
While his locks a-drooping twined
  Round thy neck in subtle ring
Make a carcanet of rays,
    And ye talk together still,
  In the language wherewith Spring
    Letters cowslips on the hill? ·
Hence that look and smile of thine,
    Spiritual Adeline.

MARGARET.

I.

O sweet pale Margaret,
O rare pale Margaret,
What lit your eyes with tearful power,
Like moonlight on a falling shower?
Who lent you, love, your mortal dower
    Of pensive thought and aspect pale,
    Your melancholy sweet and frail
As perfume of the cuckoo-flower?
From the westward-winding flood,
From the evening-lighted wood,
    From all things outward you have
        won
A tearful grace, as tho' you stood
    Between the rainbow and the sun.

The very smile before you speak,
  That dimples your transparent cheek,
  Encircles all the heart, and feedeth
The senses with a still delight
    Of dainty sorrow without sound,
    Like the tender amber round,
  Which the moon about her spreadeth,
Moving thro' a fleecy night.

II.

You love, remaining peacefully,
    To hear the murmur of the strife,
    But enter not the toil of life.
Your spirit is the calmed sea,
    Laid by the tumult of the fight.
You are the evening star, alway
    Remaining betwixt dark and bright :
Lull'd echoes of laborious day
    Come to you, gleams of mellow light
    Float by you on the verge of night.

III.

What can it matter, Margaret,
    What songs below the waning stars
The lion-heart, Plantagenet,
    Sang locking thro' his prison bars?
        Exquisite Margaret, who can tell
The last wild thought of Chatelet,
    Just ere the falling axe did part
    The burning brain from the true heart,
        Even in her sight he loved so well?

IV.

A fairy shield your Genius made
    And gave you on your natal day.
Your sorrow, only sorrow's shade,
    Keeps real sorrow far away.
You move not in such solitudes,
    You are not less divine,
But more human in your moods,
    Than your twin-sister, Adeline.
Your hair is darker, and your eyes
    Touch'd with a somewhat darker hue,
    And less aërially blue, ·
    But ever trembling thro' the dew
Of dainty-woeful sympathies.

V.

O sweet pale Margaret,
O rare pale Margaret,

Come down, come down, and hear me
          speak :
Tie up the ringlets on your cheek :
          The sun is just about to set,
The arching limes are tall and shady,
          And faint, rainy lights are seen,
                    Moving in the leavy beech.
Rise from the feast of sorrow, lady,
          Where all day long you sit between
          Joy and woe, and whisper each.
Or only look across the lawn,
          Look out below your bower-eaves,
Look down, and let your blue eyes dawn
          Upon me thro' the jasmine-leaves.

ROSALIND.

I.

My Rosalind, my Rosalind,
My frolic falcon, with bright eyes,
Whose free delight, from any height of
          rapid flight,
Stoops at all game that wing the skies,
My Rosalind, my Rosalind,
My bright-eyed, wild-eyed falcon, whither,
Careless both of wind and weather,
Whither fly ye, what game spy ye,
Up or down the streaming wind ?

II.

The quick lark's closest-caroll'd strains,
The shadow rushing up the sea,
The lightning flash atween the rains,
The sunlight driving down the lea,
The leaping stream, the very wind,
That will not stay, upon his way,
To stoop the cowslip to the plains,
Is not so clear and bold and free
As you, my falcon Rosalind.
You care not for another's pains,
Because you are the soul of joy,
Bright metal all without alloy.
Life shoots and glances thro' your veins,
And flashes off a thousand ways,
Thro' lips and eyes in subtle rays.
Your hawk-eyes are keen and bright,
Keen with triumph, watching still
To pierce me thro' with pointed light ;
But oftentimes they flash and glitter

Like sunshine on a dancing rill,
And your words are seeming-bitter,
Sharp and few, but seeming-bitter
From excess of swift delight.

III.

Come down, come home, my Rosalind,
My gay young hawk, my Rosalind :
Too long you keep the upper skies ;
Too long you roam and wheel at will ;
But we must hood your random eyes,
That care not whom they kill,
And your cheek, whose brilliant hue
Is so sparkling-fresh to view,
Some red heath-flower in the dew,
Touch'd with sunrise.   We must bind
And keep you fast, my Rosalind,
Fast, fast, my wild-eyed Rosalind,
And clip your wings, and make you love :
When we have lured you from above,
And that delight of frolic flight, by day
          or night,
From North to South,
We'll bind you fast in silken cords,
And kiss away the bitter words
From off your rosy mouth.

ELEÄNORE.

I.

Thy dark eyes open'd not,
     Nor first reveal'd themselves to English
          air,
          For there is nothing here,
Which, from the outward to the inward
          brought,
Moulded thy baby thought.
Far off from human neighbourhood,
          Thou wert born, on a summer morn,
A mile beneath the cedar-wood.
Thy bounteous forehead was not fann'd
          With breezes from our oaken glades,
But thou wert nursed in some delicious
          land
          Of lavish lights, and floating shades :
And flattering thy childish thought
          The oriental fairy brought,
          At the moment of thy birth,

From old well-heads of haunted rills,
And the hearts of purple hills,
 And shadow'd coves on a sunny
  shore,
  The choicest wealth of all the
   earth,
 Jewel or shell, or starry ore,
 To deck thy cradle, Eleänore.

II.

Or the yellow-banded bees,
Thro' half-open lattices
Coming in the scented breeze,
 Fed thee, a child, lying alone,
  With whitest honey in fairy gar-
   dens cull'd—
 A glorious child, dreaming alone,
 In silk-soft folds, upon yielding down,
With the hum of swarming bees
  Into dreamful slumber lull'd.

III.

Who may minister to thee?
Summer herself should minister
  To thee, with fruitage golden-rinded
  On golden salvers, or it may be,
Youngest Autumn, in a bower
Grape - thicken'd from the light, and
  blinded
  With many a deep-hued bell-like
   flower
Of fragrant trailers, when the air
  Sleepeth over all the heaven,
  And the crag that fronts the Even,
  All along the shadowing shore,
Crimsons over an inland mere,
  Eleänore!

IV.

How may full-sail'd verse express,
 How may measured words adore
  The full-flowing harmony
Of thy swan-like stateliness,
  Eleänore?
 The luxuriant symmetry
Of thy floating gracefulness,
  Eleänore?
  Every turn and glance of thine,
  Every lineament divine,
  Eleänore,

And the steady sunset glow,
That stays upon thee? For in thee
 Is nothing sudden, nothing single;
Like two streams of incense free
 From one censer in one shrine,
 Thought and motion mingle,
Mingle ever. Motions flow
To one another, even as tho'
They were modulated so
 To an unheard melody,
Which lives about thee, and a sweep
 Of richest pauses, evermore
Drawn from each other mellow-deep;
 Who may express thee, Eleänore?

V.

I stand before thee, Eleänore;
 I see thy beauty gradually unfold,
Daily and hourly, more and more.
I muse, as in a trance, the while
 Slowly, as from a cloud of gold,
Comes out thy deep ambrosial smile.
I muse, as in a trance, whene'er
 The languors of thy love-deep eyes
Float on to me. I would I were
 So tranced, so rapt in ecstasies,
To stand apart, and to adore,
Gazing on thee for evermore,
Serene, imperial Eleänore!

VI.

Sometimes, with most intensity
Gazing, I seem to see
Thought folded over thought, smiling
  asleep,
Slowly awaken'd, grow so full and deep
In thy large eyes, that, overpower'd quite,
I cannot veil, or droop my sight,
But am as nothing in its light:
As tho' a star, in inmost heaven set,
Ev'n while we gaze on it,
Should slowly round his orb, and slowly
  grow
To a full face, there like a sun remain
Fix'd—then as slowly fade again,
 And draw itself to what it was
  before;
  So full, so deep, so slow,
  Thought seems to come and go
 In thy large eyes, imperial Eleänore.

VII.

As thunder-clouds that, hung on high,
  Roof'd the world with doubt and
    fear,
Floating thro' an evening atmosphere,
Grow golden all about the sky ;
In thee all passion becomes passionless,
Touch'd by thy spirit's mellowness,
Losing his fire and active might
    In a silent meditation,
Falling into a still delight,
    And luxury of contemplation :
As waves that up a quiet cove
    Rolling slide, and lying still
      Shadow forth the banks at will :
Or sometimes they swell and move,
  Pressing up against the land,
  With motions of the outer sea :
    And the self-same influence
    Controlleth all the soul and sense
Of Passion gazing upon thee.
His bow-string slacken'd, languid Love,
  Leaning his cheek upon his hand,
  Droops both his wings, regarding thee,
    And so would languish evermore,
    Serene, imperial Eleänore.

VIII.

But when I see thee roam, with tresses
    unconfined,
While the amorous, odorous wind
  Breathes low between the sunset and
    the moon ;
    Or, in a shadowy saloon,
On silken cushions half reclined ;
  I watch thy grace ; and in its place
  My heart a charmed slumber keeps,
    While I muse upon thy face ;
    And a languid fire creeps
      Thro' my veins to all my frame,
Dissolvingly and slowly : soon
    From thy rose-red lips MY name
Floweth ; and then, as in a swoon,
  With dinning sound my ears are rife,
  My tremulous tongue faltereth,
  I lose my colour, I lose my breath,
  I drink the cup of a costly death,
Brimm'd with delirious draughts of warm-
    est life.

I die with my delight, before
    I hear what I would hear from
      thee ;
    Yet tell my name again to me,
I _would_ be dying evermore,
  So dying ever, Eleänore.

KATE.

I KNOW her by her angry air,
Her bright black eyes, her bright black
    hair,
  Her rapid laughters wild and shrill,
As laughters of the woodpecker
  From the bosom of a hill.
  'Tis Kate—she sayeth what she will :
For Kate hath an unbridled tongue,
  Clear as the twanging of a harp.
  Her heart is like a throbbing star.
Kate hath a spirit ever strung
  Like a new bow, and bright and sharp
  As edges of the scymetar.
Whence shall she take a fitting mate ?
  For Kate no common love will feel ;
My woman-soldier, gallant Kate,
  As pure and true as blades of steel.

Kate saith ' the world is void of might.'
  Kate saith ' the men are gilded flies.'
  Kate snaps her fingers at my vows ;
Kate will not hear of lovers' sighs.
I would I were an arméd knight,
  Far-famed for well-won enterprise,
    And wearing on my swarthy brows
    The garland of new-wreathed emprise :
For in a moment I would pierce
The blackest files of clanging fight,
And strongly strike to left and right,
  In dreaming of my lady's eyes.
    Oh ! Kate loves well the bold and
      fierce ;
    But none are bold enough for Kate
    She cannot find a fitting mate.

I.

MY life is full of weary days,
  But good things have not kept aloof,
  Nor wander'd into other ways :
  I have not lack'd thy mild reproof,
Nor golden largess of thy praise.

And now shake hands across the brink
　Of that deep grave to which I go :
Shake hands once more : I cannot sink
　So far—far down, but I shall know
　Thy voice, and answer from below.

II.

When in the darkness over me
　The four-handed mole shall scrape,
Plant thou no dusky cypress-tree,
　Nor wreathe thy cap with doleful crape,
　But pledge me in the flowing grape.

And when the sappy field and wood
　Grow green beneath the showery gray,
And rugged barks begin to bud,
　And thro' damp holts new-flush'd with
　　may,
　Ring sudden scritches of the jay,

Then let wise Nature work her will,
　And on my clay her darnel grow ;
Come only, when the days are still,
　And at my headstone whisper low,
　And tell me if the woodbines blow.

EARLY SONNETS.

I.

TO ——.

As when with downcast eyes we muse and
　　brood,
And ebb into a former life, or seem
To lapse far back in some confused dream
To states of mystical similitude ;
If one but speaks or hems or stirs his chair,
Ever the wonder waxeth more and more,
So that we say, 'All this hath been before,
All this hath been, I know not when or
　　where.'
So, friend, when first I look'd upon your
　　face,
Our thought gave answer each to each, so
　　true—
Opposed mirrors each reflecting each—
That tho' I knew not in what time or place,
Methought that I had often met with you,
And either lived in either's heart and
　　speech.

II.

TO J. M. K.

My hope and heart is with thee—thou
　　wilt be
A latter Luther, and a soldier-priest
To scare church-harpies from the master's
　　feast ;
Our dusted velvets have much need of
　　thee :
Thou art no sabbath-drawler of old saws,
Distill'd from some worm-canker'd
　　homily ;
But spurr'd at heart with fieriest energy
To embattail and to wall about thy cause
With iron-worded proof, hating to hark
The humming of the drowsy pulpit-drone
Half God's good sabbath, while the worn-
　　out clerk
Brow-beats his desk below. Thou from
　　a throne
Mounted in heaven wilt shoot into the
　　dark
Arrows of lightnings. I will stand and
　　mark.

III.

Mine be the strength of spirit, full and
　　free,
Like some broad river rushing down
　　alone,
With the selfsame impulse wherewith he
　　was thrown
From his loud fount upon the echoing
　　lea :—
Which with increasing might doth forward
　　flee
By town, and tower, and hill, and cape,
　　and isle,
And in the middle of the green salt sea
Keeps his blue waters fresh for many a mile.
Mine be the power which ever to its sway
Will win the wise at once, and by degrees
May into uncongenial spirits flow ;
Ev'n as the warm gulf-stream of Florida
Floats far away into the Northern seas
The lavish growths of southern Mexico.

IV.

ALEXANDER.

WARRIOR of God, whose strong right
    arm debased
The throne of Persia, when her Satrap
    bled
At Issus by the Syrian gates, or fled
Beyond the Memmian naphtha-pits, dis-
    graced
For ever—thee (thy pathway sand-erased)
Gliding with equal crowns two serpents
    led
Joyful to that palm-planted fountain-fed
Ammonian Oasis in the waste.
There in a silent shade of laurel brown
Apart the Chamian Oracle divine
Shelter'd his unapproached mysteries :
High things were spoken there, unhanded
    down ;
Only they saw thee from the secret shrine
Returning with hot cheek and kindled
    eyes.

V.

BUONAPARTE.

HE thought to quell the stubborn hearts
    of oak,
Madman !—to chain with chains, and bind
    with bands
That island queen who sways the floods
    and lands
From Ind to Ind, but in fair daylight woke,
When from her wooden walls,—lit by
    sure hands,—
With thunders, and with lightnings, and
    with smoke,—
Peal after peal, the British battle broke,
Lulling the brine against the Coptic sands.
We taught him lowlier moods, when El-
    sinore
Heard the war moan along the distant sea,
Rocking with shatter'd spars, with sudden
    fires
Flamed over : at Trafalgar yet once more
We taught him : late he learned humility
Perforce, like those whom Gideon school'd
    with briers.

VI.

POLAND.

How long, O God, shall men be ridden
    down,
And trampled under by the last and least
Of men ? The heart of Poland hath not
    ceased
To quiver, tho' her sacred blood doth
    drown
The fields, and out of every smouldering
    town
Cries to Thee, lest brute Power be in-
    creased,
Till that o'ergrown Barbarian in the East
Transgress his ample bound to some new
    crown :—
Cries to Thee, 'Lord, how long shall
    these things be ?
How long this icy-hearted Muscovite
Oppress the region ?' Us, O Just and
    Good,
Forgive, who smiled when she was torn
    in three ;
Us, who stand now, when we should aid
    the right—
A matter to be wept with tears of blood !

VII.

CARESS'D or chidden by the slender hand,
And singing airy trifles this or that,
Light Hope at Beauty's call would perch
    and stand,
And run thro' every change of sharp and
    flat ;
And Fancy came and at her pillow sat,
When Sleep had bound her in his rosy
    band,
And chased away the still-recurring gnat,
And woke her with a lay from fairy land.
But now they live with Beauty less and
    less,
For Hope is other Hope and wanders far,
Nor cares to lisp in love's delicious creeds ;
And Fancy watches in the wilderness,
Poor Fancy sadder than a single star,
That sets at twilight in a land of reeds.

VIII.

THE form, the form alone is eloquent !
A nobler yearning never broke her rest
Than but to dance and sing, be gaily
    drest,
And win all eyes with all accomplish-
    ment :
Yet in the whirling dances as we went,
My fancy made me for a moment blest
To find my heart so near the beauteous
    breast
That once had power to rob it of content.
A moment came the tenderness of tears,
The phantom of a wish that once could
    move,
A ghost of passion that no smiles re-
    store—
For ah ! the slight coquette, she cannot
    love,
And if you kiss'd her feet a thousand
    years,
She still would take the praise, and care
    no more.

IX.

WAN Sculptor, weepest thou to take the
    cast
Of those dead lineaments that near thee
    lie ?
O sorrowest thou, pale Painter, for the
    past,
In painting some dead friend from memory?
Weep on : beyond his object Love can
    last :
His object lives : more cause to weep
    have I :
My tears, no tears of love, are flowing fast,
No tears of love, but tears that Love can
    die.
I pledge her not in any cheerful cup,
Nor care to sit beside her where she sits—
Ah pity—hint it not in human tones,
But breathe it into earth and close it up
With secret death for ever, in the pits
Which some green Christmas crams with
    weary bones.

X.

IF I were loved, as I desire to be,
What is there in the great sphere of the
    earth,
And range of evil between death and birth,
That I should fear,—if I were loved by
    thee ?
All the inner, all the outer world of pain
Clear Love would pierce and cleave, if
    thou wert mine,
As I have heard that, somewhere in the
    main,
Fresh-water springs come up through
    bitter brine.
'Twere joy, not fear, claspt hand-in-hand
    with thee,
To wait for death—mute—careless of all
    ills,
Apart upon a mountain, tho' the surge
Of some new deluge from a thousand hills
Flung leagues of roaring foam into the
    gorge
Below us, as far on as eye could see.

XI.

THE BRIDESMAID.

O BRIDESMAID, ere the happy knot was
    tied,
Thine eyes so wept that they could hardly
    see ;
Thy sister smiled and said, ' No tears for
    me !
A happy bridesmaid makes a happy bride.'
And then, the couple standing side by
    side,
Love lighted down between them full of
    glee,
And over his left shoulder laugh'd at
    thee,
' O happy bridesmaid, make a happy
    bride.'
And all at once a pleasant truth I learn'd,
For while the tender service made thee
    weep,
I loved thee for the tear thou couldst not
    hide,
And prest thy hand, and knew the press
    return'd,
And thought, ' My life is sick of single
    sleep :
O happy bridesmaid, make a happy
    bride !'

THE LADY OF SHALOTT

AND OTHER POEMS.

THE LADY OF SHALOTT.

pub 1833
[Dec. 1832] in 'Poems by Alfred Tennyson'

PART I.

(lande)
plaine

On either side the river lie
Long fields of barley and of rye,
That clothe the wold and meet the sky;
And thro' the field the road runs by
　　To many-tower'd Camelot;
And up and down the people go,
Gazing where the lilies blow
Round an island there below,
　　The island of Shalott.

only sense
in n.z.p(con-
cise)'com-
Bruimer'

Willows whiten, aspens quiver, *terrisset*
Little breezes dusk and shiver
Thro' the wave that runs for ever
By the island in the river
　　Flowing down to Camelot.
Four gray walls, and four gray towers,
Overlook a space of flowers,
And the silent isle imbowers
　　The Lady of Shalott.

chaloupe
sloop

By the margin, willow-veil'd, *'haler'*
Slide the heavy barges trail'd
By slow horses; and unhail'd = *?hailed = haunted*
The shallop flitteth silken-sail'd
　　Skimming down to Camelot:
But who hath seen her wave her hand?
Or at the casement seen her stand?
Or is she known in all the land,
　　The Lady of Shalott?

Only reapers, reaping early
In among the bearded barley,
Hear a song that echoes cheerly
From the river winding clearly,
　　Down to tower'd Camelot:
And by the moon the reaper weary,
Piling sheaves in uplands airy,
Listening, whispers ''Tis the fairy
　　Lady of Shalott.'

PART II.

There she weaves by night and day
A magic web with colours gay.

She has heard a whisper say,
A curse is on her if she stay
　　To look down to Camelot.
She knows not what the curse may be,
And so she weaveth steadily,
And little other care hath she,
　　The Lady of Shalott.

And moving thro' a mirror clear
That hangs before her all the year,
Shadows of the world appear.
There she sees the highway near
　　Winding down to Camelot:
There the river eddy whirls,
And there the surly village-churls,
And the red cloaks of market girls,
　　Pass onward from Shalott.

cheval
de selle

Sometimes a troop of damsels glad,
An abbot on an ambling pad, *(path) pale-*
Sometimes a curly shepherd-lad, *froi-*
Or long-hair'd page in crimson clad, *haque-*
　　Goes by to tower'd Camelot; *née*
And sometimes thro' the mirror blue
The knights come riding two and two:
She hath no loyal knight and true,
　　The Lady of Shalott.

But in her web she still delights
To weave the mirror's magic sights,
For often thro' the silent nights
A funeral, with plumes and lights
　　And music, went to Camelot:
Or when the moon was overhead,
Came two young lovers lately wed;
'I am half sick of shadows,' said
　　The Lady of Shalott.

PART III.

à une portée d'arc　　　　*sing) bord*

A bow-shot from her bower-eaves,
He rode between the barley-sheaves,
The sun came dazzling thro' the leaves,
And flamed upon the brazen greaves
　　Of bold Sir Lancelot.
A red-cross knight for ever kneel'd
To a lady in his shield,

That sparkled on the yellow field,
　　Beside remote Shalott.

The gemmy bridle glitter'd free,
Like to some branch of stars we see
Hung in the golden Galaxy.
The bridle bells rang merrily
　　As he rode down to Camelot :
And from his blazon'd baldric slung
A mighty silver bugle hung,
And as he rode his armour rung,
　　Beside remote Shalott.

All in the blue unclouded weather
Thick-jewell'd shone the saddle-leather,
The helmet and the helmet-feather
Burn'd like one burning flame together,
　　As he rode down to Camelot.
As often thro' the purple night,
Below the starry clusters bright,
Some bearded meteor, trailing light,
　　Moves over still Shalott.

His broad clear brow in sunlight glow'd ;
On burnish'd hooves his war-horse trode ;
From underneath his helmet flow'd
His coal-black curls as on he rode,
　　As he rode down to Camelot.
From the bank and from the river
He flash'd into the crystal mirror,
'Tirra lirra,' by the river
　　Sang Sir Lancelot.

She left the web, she left the loom,
She made three paces thro' the room,
She saw the water-lily bloom,
She saw the helmet and the plume,
　　She look'd down to Camelot.
Out flew the web and floated wide ;
The mirror crack'd from side to side ;
'The curse is come upon me,' cried
　　The Lady of Shalott.

PART IV.

IN the stormy east-wind straining,
The pale yellow woods were waning,
The broad stream in his banks complain-
　　ing,
Heavily the low sky raining
　　Over tower'd Camelot ;
Down she came and found a boat

Beneath a willow left afloat,
And round about the prow she wrote
　　The Lady of Shalott.

And down the river's dim expanse
Like some bold seër in a trance,
Seeing all his own mischance—
With a glassy countenance
　　Did she look to Camelot.
And at the closing of the day
She loosed the chain, and down she lay ;
The broad stream bore her far away,
　　The Lady of Shalott.

Lying, robed in snowy white
That loosely flew to left and right—
The leaves upon her falling light—
Thro' the noises of the night
　　She floated down to Camelot :
And as the boat-head wound along
The willowy hills and fields among,
They heard her singing her last song,
　　The Lady of Shalott.

Heard a carol, mournful, holy,
Chanted loudly, chanted lowly,
Till her blood was frozen slowly,
And her eyes were darken'd wholly,
　　Turn'd to tower'd Camelot.
For ere she reach'd upon the tide
The first house by the water-side,
Singing in her song she died,
　　The Lady of Shalott.

Under tower and balcony,
By garden-wall and gallery,
A gleaming shape she floated by,
Dead-pale between the houses high,
　　Silent into Camelot.
Out upon the wharfs they came,
Knight and burgher, lord and dame,
And round the prow they read her name,
　　The Lady of Shalott.

Who is this ? and what is here ?
And in the lighted palace near
Died the sound of royal cheer ;
And they cross'd themselves for fear,
　　All the knights at Camelot :
But Lancelot mused a little space ;
He said, ' She has a lovely face ;
God in his mercy lend her grace,
　　The Lady of Shalott.'

MARIANA IN THE SOUTH.

WITH one black shadow at its feet,
  The house thro' all the level shines,
Close-latticed to the brooding heat,
  And silent in its dusty vines :
A faint-blue ridge upon the right,
  An empty river-bed before,
  And shallows on a distant shore,
In glaring sand and inlets bright.
      But 'Ave Mary,' made she moan,
        And 'Ave Mary,' night and morn,
      And 'Ah,' she sang, 'to be all alone,
        To live forgotten, and love forlorn.'

She, as her carol sadder grew,
  From brow and bosom slowly down
Thro' rosy taper fingers drew
  Her streaming curls of deepest brown
To left and right, and made appear
  Still-lighted in a secret shrine,
  Her melancholy eyes divine,
The home of woe without a tear.
      And 'Ave Mary,' was her moan,
        'Madonna, sad is night and morn,'
      And 'Ah,' she sang, 'to be all alone,
        To live forgotten, and love forlorn.'

Till all the crimson changed, and past
  Into deep orange o'er the sea,
Low on her knees herself she cast,
  Before Our Lady murmur'd she ;
Complaining, ' Mother, give me grace
  To help me of my weary load.'
And on the liquid mirror glow'd
The clear perfection of her face.
      ' Is this the form,' she made her
        moan,
        ' That won his praises night and
          morn ? '
      And 'Ah,' she said, 'but I wake
        alone,
        I sleep forgotten, I wake forlorn.'

Nor bird would sing, nor lamb would bleat,
  Nor any cloud would cross the vault,
But day increased from heat to heat,
  On stony drought and steaming salt ;
Till now at noon she slept again,
  And seem'd knee-deep in mountain
    grass,
  And heard her native breezes pass,

And runlets babbling down the glen.
      She breathed in sleep a lower moan,
        And murmuring, as at night and
          morn,
      She thought, ' My spirit is here alone,
        Walks forgotten, and is forlorn.'

Dreaming, she knew it was a dream :
  She felt he was and was not there.
She woke : the babble of the stream
  Fell, and, without, the steady glare
Shrank one sick willow sere and small.
  The river-bed was dusty-white ;
  And all the furnace of the light
Struck up against the blinding wall.
      She whisper'd, with a stifled moan
        More inward than at night or morn,
      'Sweet Mother, let me not here alone
        Live forgotten and die forlorn.'

And, rising, from her bosom drew
  Old letters, breathing of her worth,
For ' Love,' they said, ' must needs be
    true,
  To what is loveliest upon earth.'
An image seem'd to pass the door,
  To look at her with slight, and say
  ' But now thy beauty flows away,
So be alone for evermore.'
      ' O cruel heart,' she changed her tone,
        'And cruel love, whose end is scorn,
      Is this the end to be left alone,
        To live forgotten, and die forlorn?'

But sometimes in the falling day
  An image seem'd to pass the door,
To look into her eyes and say,
  ' But thou shalt be alone no more.'
And flaming downward over all
  From heat to heat the day decreased,
  And slowly rounded to the east
The one black shadow from the wall.
      ' The day to night,' she made her
        moan,
        ' The day to night, the night to
          morn,
      And day and night I am left alone
        To live forgotten, and love forlorn.'

At eve a dry cicala sung,
  There came a sound as of the sea ;

Backward the lattice-blind she flung,
    And lean'd upon the balcony.
There all in spaces rosy-bright
    Large Hesper glitter'd on her tears,
And deepening thro' the silent spheres
Heaven over Heaven rose the night.
And weeping then she made her moan,
    'The night comes on that knows not
        morn,
When I shall cease to be all alone,
    To live forgotten, and love forlorn.'

THE TWO VOICES.

A STILL small voice spake unto me,
'Thou art so full of misery,
Were it not better not to be?'

Then to the still small voice I said;
'Let me not cast in endless shade
What is so wonderfully made.'

To which the voice did urge reply;
'To-day I saw the dragon-fly
Come from the wells where he did lie.

'An inner impulse rent the veil
Of his old husk : from head to tail
Came out clear plates of sapphire mail.

'He dried his wings : like gauze they grew;
Thro' crofts and pastures wet with dew
A living flash of light he flew.'

I said, 'When first the world began,
Young Nature thro' five cycles ran,
And in the sixth she moulded man.

'She gave him mind, the lordliest
Proportion, and, above the rest,
Dominion in the head and breast.'

Thereto the silent voice replied;
'Self-blinded are you by your pride :
Look up thro' night : the world is wide.

'This truth within thy mind rehearse,
That in a boundless universe
Is boundless better, boundless worse.

'Think you this mould of hopes and fears
Could find no statelier than his peers
In yonder hundred million spheres?'

It spake, moreover, in my mind :
'Tho' thou wert scatter'd to the wind,
Yet is there plenty of the kind.'

Then did my response clearer fall :
'No compound of this earthly ball
Is like another, all in all.'

To which he answer'd scoffingly;
'Good soul ! suppose I grant it thee,
Who'll weep for thy deficiency?

'Or will one beam be less intense,
When thy peculiar difference
Is cancell'd in the world of sense?'

I would have said, 'Thou canst not know,'
But my full heart, that work'd below,
Rain'd thro' my sight its overflow.

Again the voice spake unto me :
'Thou art so steep'd in misery,
Surely 'twere better not to be.

'Thine anguish will not let thee sleep,
Nor any train of reason keep :
Thou canst not think, but thou wilt weep.

I said, 'The years with change advance :
If I make dark my countenance,
I shut my life from happier chance.

'Some turn this sickness yet might take,
Ev'n yet.' But he : 'What drug can make
A wither'd palsy cease to shake?'

I wept, 'Tho' I should die, I know
That all about the thorn will blow
In tufts of rosy-tinted snow;

'And men, thro' novel spheres of thought
Still moving after truth long sought,
Will learn new things when I am not.'

'Yet,' said the secret voice, 'some time,
Sooner or later, will gray prime
Make thy grass hoar with early rime.

'Not less swift souls that yearn for light,
Rapt after heaven's starry flight,
Would sweep the tracts of day and night.

'Not less the bee would range her cells,
The furzy prickle fire the dells,
The foxglove cluster dappled bells.'

I said that 'all the years invent ;
Each month is various to present
The world with some development.

'Were this not well, to bide mine hour,
Tho' watching from a ruin'd tower
How grows the day of human power ? '

'The highest-mounted mind,' he said,
'Still sees the sacred morning spread
The silent summit overhead.

'Will thirty seasons render plain
Those lonely lights that still remain,
Just breaking over land and main ?

'Or make that morn, from his cold crown
And crystal silence creeping down,
Flood with full daylight glebe and town ?

'Forerun thy peers, thy time, and let
Thy feet, millenniums hence, be set
In midst of knowledge, dream'd not yet.

'Thou hast not gain'd a real height,
Nor art thou nearer to the light,
Because the scale is infinite.

''Twere better not to breathe or speak,
Than cry for strength, remaining weak,
And seem to find, but still to seek.

'Moreover, but to seem to find
Asks what thou lackest, thought resign'd,
A healthy frame, a quiet mind.'

I said, 'When I am gone away,
"He dared not tarry," men will say,
Doing dishonour to my clay.'

'This is more vile,' he made reply,
'To breathe and loathe, to live and sigh,
Than once from dread of pain to die.

'Sick art thou—a divided will
Still heaping on the fear of ill
The fear of men, a coward still.

'Do men love thee ?   Art thou so bound
To men, that how thy name may sound
Will vex thee lying underground ?

'The memory of the wither'd leaf
In endless time is scarce more brief
Than of the garner'd Autumn-sheaf.

'Go, vexed Spirit, sleep in trust ;
The right ear, that is fill'd with dust,
Hears little of the false or just.'

'Hard task, to pluck resolve,' I cried,
'From emptiness and the waste wide
Of that abyss, or scornful pride !

'Nay—rather yet that I could raise
One hope that warm'd me in the days
While still I yearn'd for human praise.

'When, wide in soul and bold of tongue,
Among the tents I paused and sung,
The distant battle flash'd and rung.

'I sung the joyful Pæan clear,
And, sitting, burnish'd without fear
The brand, the buckler, and the spear—

'Waiting to strive a happy strife,
To war with falsehood to the knife,
And not to lose the good of life—

'Some hidden principle to move,
To put together, part and prove,
And mete the bounds of hate and love—

'As far as might be, to carve out
Free space for every human doubt,
That the whole mind might orb about—

'To search thro' all I felt or saw,
The springs of life, the depths of awe,
And reach the law within the law :

'At least, not rotting like a weed,
But, having sown some generous seed,
Fruitful of further thought and deed,

'To pass, when Life her light withdraws,
Not void of righteous self-applause,
Nor in a merely selfish cause—

'In some good cause, not in mine own,
To perish, wept for, honour'd, known,
And like a warrior overthrown ;

'Whose eyes are dim with glorious tears,
When, soil'd with noble dust, he hears
His country's war-song thrill his ears :

'Then dying of a mortal stroke,
What time the foeman's line is broke,
And all the war is roll'd in smoke.'

'Yea!' said the voice, 'thy dream was good,
While thou abodest in the bud.
It was the stirring of the blood.

'If Nature put not forth her power
About the opening of the flower,
Who is it that could live an hour?

'Then comes the check, the change, the
    fall,
Pain rises up, old pleasures pall.
There is one remedy for all.

'Yet hadst thou, thro' enduring pain,
Link'd month to month with such a chain
Of knitted purport, all were vain.

'Thou hadst not between death and birth
Dissolved the riddle of the earth.
So were thy labour little-worth.

'That men with knowledge merely play'd,
I told thee—hardly nigher made,
Tho' scaling slow from grade to grade;

'Much less this dreamer, deaf and blind,
Named man, may hope some truth to find,
That bears relation to the mind.

'For every worm beneath the moon
Draws different threads, and late and soon
Spins, toiling out his own cocoon.

'Cry, faint not: either Truth is born
Beyond the polar gleam forlorn,
Or in the gateways of the morn.

'Cry, faint not, climb: the summits slope
Beyond the furthest flights of hope,
Wrapt in dense cloud from base to cope.

'Sometimes a little corner shines,
As over rainy mist inclines
A gleaming crag with belts of pines.

'I will go forward, sayest thou,
I shall not fail to find her now.
Look up, the fold is on her brow.

'If straight thy track, or if oblique,
Thou know'st not. Shadows thou dost
    strike,
Embracing cloud, Ixion-like;

'And owning but a little more
Than beasts, abidest lame and poor,
Calling thyself a little lower

'Than angels. Cease to wail and brawl!
Why inch by inch to darkness crawl?
There is one remedy for all.'

'O dull, one-sided voice,' said I,
'Wilt thou make everything a lie,
To flatter me that I may die?

'I know that age to age succeeds,
Blowing a noise of tongues and deeds,
A dust of systems and of creeds.

'I cannot hide that some have striven,
Achieving calm, to whom was given
The joy that mixes man with Heaven:

'Who, rowing hard against the stream,
Saw distant gates of Eden gleam,
And did not dream it was a dream;

'But heard, by secret transport led,
Ev'n in the charnels of the dead,
The murmur of the fountain-head—

'Which did accomplish their desire,
Bore and forebore, and did not tire,
Like Stephen, an unquenched fire.

'He heeded not reviling tones,
Nor sold his heart to idle moans,
Tho' cursed and scorn'd, and bruised
    with stones:

'But looking upward, full of grace,
He pray'd, and from a happy place
God's glory smote him on the face.'

The sullen answer slid betwixt:
'Not that the grounds of hope were
    fix'd,
The elements were kindlier mix'd.'

I said, 'I toil beneath the curse,
But, knowing not the universe,
I fear to slide from bad to worse.

'And that, in seeking to undo
One riddle, and to find the true,
I knit a hundred others new:

'Or that this anguish fleeting hence,
Unmanacled from bonds of sense,
Be fix'd and froz'n to permanence:

'For I go, weak from suffering here:
Naked I go, and void of cheer:
What is it that I may not fear?'

T

'Consider well,' the voice replied,
'His face, that two hours since hath died;
Wilt thou find passion, pain or pride?

'Will he obey when one commands?
Or answer should one press his hands?
He answers not, nor understands.

'His palms are folded on his breast:
There is no other thing express'd
But long disquiet merged in rest.

'His lips are very mild and meek:
Tho' one should smite him on the cheek,
And on the mouth, he will not speak.

'His little daughter, whose sweet face
He kiss'd, taking his last embrace,
Becomes dishonour to her race—

'His sons grow up that bear his name,
Some grow to honour, some to shame,—
But he is chill to praise or blame.

'He will not hear the north-wind rave,
Nor, moaning, household shelter crave
From winter rains that beat his grave.

'High up the vapours fold and swim:
About him broods the twilight dim:
The place he knew forgetteth him.'

'If all be dark, vague voice,' I said,
'These things are wrapt in doubt and
    dread,
Nor canst thou show the dead are dead.

'The sap dries up: the plant declines.
A deeper tale my heart divines.
Know I not Death? the outward signs?

'I found him when my years were few;
A shadow on the graves I knew,
And darkness in the village yew.

'From grave to grave the shadow crept:
In her still place the morning wept:
Touch'd by his feet the daisy slept.

'The simple senses crown'd his head:
"Omega! thou art Lord," they said,
"We find no motion in the dead."

'Why, if man rot in dreamless ease,
Should that plain fact, as taught by these,
Not make him sure that he shall cease?

'Who forged that other influence,
That heat of inward evidence,
By which he doubts against the sense?

'He owns the fatal gift of eyes,
That read his spirit blindly wise,
Not simple as a thing that dies.

'Here sits he shaping wings to fly:
His heart forebodes a mystery:
He names the name Eternity.

'That type of Perfect in his mind
In Nature can he nowhere find.
He sows himself on every wind.

'He seems to hear a Heavenly Friend,
And thro' thick veils to apprehend
A labour working to an end.

'The end and the beginning vex
His reason: many things perplex,
With motions, checks, and counterchecks.

'He knows a baseness in his blood
At such strange war with something
       good,
He may not do the thing he would.

'Heaven opens inward, chasms yawn,
Vast images in glimmering dawn,
Half shown, are broken and withdrawn.

'Ah! sure within him and without,
Could his dark wisdom find it out,
There must be answer to his doubt,

'But thou canst answer not again.
With thine own weapon art thou slain,
Or thou wilt answer but in vain.

'The doubt would rest, I dare not solve.
In the same circle we revolve.
Assurance only breeds resolve.'

As when a billow, blown against,
Falls back, the voice with which I fenced
A little ceased, but recommenced.

'Where wert thou when thy father play'd
In his free field, and pastime made,
A merry boy in sun and shade?

'A merry boy they call'd him then,
He sat upon the knees of men
In days that never come again.

'Before the little ducts began
To feed thy bones with lime, and ran
Their course, till thou wert also man :

'Who took a wife, who rear'd his race,
Whose wrinkles gather'd on his face,
Whose troubles number with his days :

'A life of nothings, nothing-worth,
From that first nothing ere his birth
To that last nothing under earth !'

'These words,' I said, 'are like the rest ;
No certain clearness, but at best
A vague suspicion of the breast :

'But if I grant, thou mightst defend
The thesis which thy words intend—
That to begin implies to end ;

'Yet how should I for certain hold,
Because my memory is so cold,
That I first was in human mould ?

'I cannot make this matter plain,
But I would shoot, howe'er in vain,
A random arrow from the brain.

'It may be that no life is found,
Which only to one engine bound
Falls off, but cycles always round.

'As old mythologies relate,
Some draught of Lethe might await
The slipping thro' from state to state.

'As here we find in trances, men
Forget the dream that happens then,
Until they fall in trance again.

'So might we, if our state were such
As one before, remember much,
For those two likes might meet and touch.

'But, if I lapsed from nobler place,
Some legend of a fallen race
Alone might hint of my disgrace ;

'Some vague emotion of delight
In gazing up an Alpine height,
Some yearning toward the lamps of
          night ;

'Or if thro' lower lives I came—
Tho' all experience past became
Consolidate in mind and frame—

'I might forget my weaker lot ;
For is not our first year forgot ?
The haunts of memory echo not.

'And men, whose reason long was blind,
From cells of madness unconfined,
Oft lose whole years of darker mind.

'Much more, if first I floated free,
As naked essence, must I be
Incompetent of memory :

'For memory dealing but with time,
And he with matter, could she climb
Beyond her own material prime ?

'Moreover, something is or seems,
That touches me with mystic gleams,
Like glimpses of forgotten dreams—

'Of something felt, like something here ;
Of something done, I know not where ;
Such as no language may declare.'

The still voice laugh'd.   'I talk,' said he,
'Not with thy dreams.   Suffice it thee
Thy pain is a reality.'

'But thou,' said I, 'hast missed thy
          mark,
Who sought'st to wreck my mortal ark,
By making all the horizon dark.

'Why not set forth, if I should do
This rashness, that which might ensue
With this old soul in organs new ?

'Whatever crazy sorrow saith,
No life that breathes with human breath
Has ever truly long'd for death.

''Tis life, whereof our nerves are scant,
Oh life, not death, for which we pant ;
More life, and fuller, that I want.'

I ceased, and sat as one forlorn.
Then said the voice, in quiet scorn,
'Behold, it is the Sabbath morn.'

And I arose, and I released
The casement, and the light increased
With freshness in the dawning east.

Like soften'd airs that blowing steal,
When meres begin to uncongeal,
The sweet church bells began to peal.

On to God's house the people prest :
Passing the place where each must rest,
Each enter'd like a welcome guest.

One walk'd between his wife and child,
With measured footfall firm and mild,
And now and then he gravely smiled.

The prudent partner of his blood
Lean'd on him, faithful, gentle, good,
Wearing the rose of womanhood.

And in their double love secure,
The little maiden walk'd demure,
Pacing with downward eyelids pure.

These three made unity so sweet,
My frozen heart began to beat,
Remembering its ancient heat.

I blest them, and they wander'd on :
I spoke, but answer came there none :
The dull and bitter voice was gone.

A second voice was at mine ear,
A little whisper silver-clear,
A murmur, ' Be of better cheer.'

As from some blissful neighbourhood,
A notice faintly understood,
' I see the end, and know the good.'

A little hint to solace woe,
A hint, a whisper breathing low,
' I may not speak of what I know.'

Like an Æolian harp that wakes
No certain air, but overtakes
Far thought with music that it makes :

Such seem'd the whisper at my side :
' What is it thou knowest, sweet voice ?'
　　I cried.
' A hidden hope,' the voice replied :

So heavenly-toned, that in that hour
From out my sullen heart a power
Broke, like the rainbow from the shower,

To feel, altho' no tongue can prove,
That every cloud, that spreads above
And veileth love, itself is love.

And forth into the fields I went,
And Nature's living motion lent
The pulse of hope to discontent.

I wonder'd at the bounteous hours,
The slow result of winter showers :
You scarce could see the grass for flowers.

I wonder'd, while I paced along :
The woods were fill'd so full with song,
There seem'd no room for sense of wrong;

And all so variously wrought,
I marvell'd how the mind was brought
To anchor by one gloomy thought ;

And wherefore rather I made choice
To commune with that barren voice,
Than him that said, ' Rejoice ! Rejoice !'

THE MILLER'S DAUGHTER.

I SEE the wealthy miller yet,
　　His double chin, his portly size,
And who that knew him could forget
　　The busy wrinkles round his eyes ?
The slow wise smile that, round about
　　His dusty forehead drily curl'd,
Seem'd half-within and half-without,
　　And full of dealings with the world ?

In yonder chair I see him sit,
　　Three fingers round the old silver cup—
I see his gray eyes twinkle yet
　　At his own jest—gray eyes lit up
With summer lightnings of a soul
　　So full of summer warmth, so glad,
So healthy, sound, and clear and whole,
　　His memory scarce can make me sad.

Yet fill my glass : give me one kiss :
　　My own sweet Alice, we must die.
There's somewhat in this world amiss
　　Shall be unriddled by and by.

There's somewhat flows to us in life,
    But more is taken quite away.
Pray, Alice, pray, my darling wife,
    That we may die the self-same day.

Have I not found a happy earth?
    I least should breathe a thought of
        pain.
Would God renew me from my birth
    I'd almost live my life again.
So sweet it seems with thee to walk,
    And once again to woo thee mine—
It seems in after-dinner talk
    Across the walnuts and the wine—

To be the long and listless boy
    Late-left an orphan of the squire,
Where this old mansion mounted high
    Looks down upon the village spire:
For even here, where I and you
    Have lived and loved alone so long,
Each morn my sleep was broken thro'
    By some wild skylark's matin song.

And oft I heard the tender dove
    In firry woodlands making moan;
But ere I saw your eyes, my love,
    I had no motion of my own.
For scarce my life with fancy play'd
    Before I dream'd that pleasant dream—
Still hither thither idly sway'd
    Like those long mosses in the stream.

Or from the bridge I lean'd to hear
    The milldam rushing down with noise,
And see the minnows everywhere
    In crystal eddies glance and poise,
The tall flag-flowers when they sprung
    Below the range of stepping-stones,
Or those three chestnuts near, that hung
    In masses thick with milky cones.

But, Alice, what an hour was that,
    When after roving in the woods
('Twas April then), I came and sat
    Below the chestnuts, when their buds
Were glistening to the breezy blue;
    And on the slope, an absent fool,
I cast me down, nor thought of you,
    But angled in the higher pool.

A love-song I had somewhere read,
    An echo from a measured strain,
Beat time to nothing in my head
    From some odd corner of the brain.
It haunted me, the morning long,
    With weary sameness in the rhymes,
The phantom of a silent song,
    That went and came a thousand times.

Then leapt a trout.   In lazy mood
    I watch'd the little circles die;
They past into the level flood,
    And there a vision caught my eye;
The reflex of a beauteous form,
    A glowing arm, a gleaming neck,
As when a sunbeam wavers warm
    Within the dark and dimpled beck.

For you remember, you had set,
    That morning, on the casement-edge
A long green box of mignonette,
    And you were leaning from the ledge
And when I raised my eyes, above
    They met with two so full and bright—
Such eyes! I swear to you, my love,
    That these have never lost their light.

I loved, and love dispell'd the fear
    That I should die an early death:
For love possess'd the atmosphere,
    And fill'd the breast with purer breath.
My mother thought, What ails the boy?
    For I was alter'd, and began
To move about the house with joy,
    And with the certain step of man.

I loved the brimming wave that swam
    Thro' quiet meadows round the mill,
The sleepy pool above the dam,
    The pool beneath it never still,
The meal-sacks on the whiten'd floor,
    The dark round of the dripping
        wheel,
The very air about the door
    Made misty with the floating meal.

And oft in ramblings on the wold,
    When April nights began to blow,
And April's crescent glimmer'd cold,
    I saw the village lights below;

I knew your taper far away,
  And full at heart of trembling hope,
From off the wold I came, and lay
  Upon the freshly-flower'd slope.

The deep brook groan'd beneath the mill ;
  And 'by that lamp,' I thought, 'she sits!'
The white chalk-quarry from the hill
  Gleam'd to the flying moon by fits.
'O that I were beside her now !
  O will she answer if I call ?
O would she give me vow for vow,
  Sweet Alice, if I told her all ?'

Sometimes I saw you sit and spin ;
  And, in the pauses of the wind,
Sometimes I heard you sing within ;
  Sometimes your shadow cross'd the
    blind.
At last you rose and moved the light,
  And the long shadow of the chair
Flitted across into the night,
  And all the casement darken'd there.

But when at last I dared to speak,
  The lanes, you know, were white with
    may,
Your ripe lips moved not, but your cheek
  Flush'd like the coming of the day ;
And so it was—half-sly, half-shy,
  You would, and would not, little one !
Although I pleaded tenderly,
  And you and I were all alone.

And slowly was my mother brought
  To yield consent to my desire :
She wish'd me happy, but she thought
  I might have look'd a little higher ;
And I was young—too young to wed :
  'Yet must I love her for your sake ;
Go fetch your Alice here,' she said :
  Her eyelid quiver'd as she spake.

And down I went to fetch my bride :
  But, Alice, you were ill at ease ;
This dress and that by turns you tried,
  Too fearful that you should not please.
I loved you better for your fears,
  I knew you could not look but well ;
And dews, that would have fall'n in tears,
  I kiss'd away before they fell.

I watch'd the little flutterings,
  The doubt my mother would not see ;
She spoke at large of many things,
  And at the last she spoke of me ;
And turning look'd upon your face,
  As near this door you sat apart,
And rose, and, with a silent grace
  Approaching, press'd you heart to heart.

Ah, well—but sing the foolish song
  I gave you, Alice, on the day
When, arm in arm, we went along,
  A pensive pair, and you were gay
With bridal flowers—that I may seem,
  As in the nights of old, to lie
Beside the mill-wheel in the stream,
  While those full chestnuts whisper by.

  It is the miller's daughter,
    And she is grown so dear, so dear,
  That I would be the jewel
    That trembles in her ear :
  For hid in ringlets day and night,
  I'd touch her neck so warm and white.

  And I would be the girdle
    About her dainty dainty waist,
  And her heart would beat against me,
    In sorrow and in rest :
  And I should know if it beat right,
  I'd clasp it round so close and tight.

  And I would be the necklace,
    And all day long to fall and rise
  Upon her balmy bosom,
    With her laughter or her sighs,
  And I would lie so light, so light,
  I scarce should be unclasp'd at night.

A trifle, sweet ! which true love spells—
  True love interprets—right alone.
His light upon the letter dwells,
  For all the spirit is his own.
So, if I waste words now, in truth
  You must blame Love.   His early rage
Had force to make me rhyme in youth,
  And makes me talk too much in age.

And now those vivid hours are gone,
  Like mine own life to me thou art,
Where Past and Present, wound in one,
  Do make a garland for the heart :

So sing that other song I made,
　Half-anger'd with my happy lot,
The day, when in the chestnut shade
　I found the blue Forget-me-not.

　　　Love that hath us in the net,
　　　Can he pass, and we forget?
　　　Many suns arise and set.
　　　Many a chance the years beget.
　　　Love the gift is Love the debt.
　　　　　Even so.
　　　Love is hurt with jar and fret.
　　　Love is made a vague regret.
　　　Eyes with idle tears are wet.
　　　Idle habit links us yet.
　　　What is love? for we forget :
　　　　　Ah, no ! no !

Look thro' mine eyes with thine.　True
　　wife,
　Round my true heart thine arms entwine
My other dearer life in life,
　Look thro' my very soul with thine !
Untouch'd with any shade of years,
　May those kind eyes for ever dwell !
They have not shed a many tears,
　Dear eyes, since first I knew them
　　well.

Yet tears they shed : they had their part
　Of sorrow : for when time was ripe,
The still affection of the heart
　Became an outward breathing type,
That into stillness past again,
　And left a want unknown before ;
Although the loss had brought us pain,
　That loss but made us love the more,

With farther lookings on.　The kiss,
　The woven arms, seem but to be
Weak symbols of the settled bliss,
　The comfort, I have found in thee :
But that God bless thee, dear — who
　　wrought
Two spirits to one equal mind—
With blessings beyond hope or thought,
　With blessings which no words can find.

Arise, and let us wander forth,
　To yon old mill across the wolds ;
For look, the sunset, south and north,
　Winds all the vale in rosy folds,

And fires your narrow casement glass,
　Touching the sullen pool below :
On the chalk-hill the bearded grass
　Is dry and dewless.　Let us go.

FATIMA.

O Love, Love, Love ! O withering might !
O sun, that from thy noonday height
Shudderest when I strain my sight,
Throbbing thro' all thy heat and light,
　Lo, falling from my constant mind,
　Lo, parch'd and wither'd, deaf and blind,
　I whirl like leaves in roaring wind.

Last night I wasted hateful hours
Below the city's eastern towers :
I thirsted for the brooks, the showers :
I roll'd among the tender flowers :
　I crush'd them on my breast, my mouth ;
　I look'd athwart the burning drouth
　Of that long desert to the south.

Last night, when some one spoke his
　　name,
From my swift blood that went and came
A thousand little shafts of flame
Were shiver'd in my narrow frame.
　O Love, O fire ! once he drew
　With one long kiss my whole soul thro'
　My lips, as sunlight drinketh dew.

Before he mounts the hill, I know
He cometh quickly : from below
Sweet gales, as from deep gardens, blow
Before him, striking on my brow.
　In my dry brain my spirit soon,
　Down-deepening from swoon to swoon,
　Faints like a dazzled morning moon.

The wind sounds like a silver wire,
And from beyond the noon a fire
Is pour'd upon the hills, and nigher
The skies stoop down in their desire ;
　And, isled in sudden seas of light,
　My heart, pierced thro' with fierce
　　delight,
　Bursts into blossom in his sight.

My whole soul waiting silently,
All naked in a sultry sky,

Droops blinded with his shining eye :
I *will* possess him or will die.
    I will grow round him in his place,
    Grow, live, die looking on his face,
    Die, dying clasp'd in his embrace.

cf. The Death of Œnone p 613
— Worcuá 85

ŒNONE.

THERE lies a vale in Ida, lovelier
Than all the valleys of Ionian hills.
The swimming vapour slopes athwart the
    glen,
Puts forth an arm, and creeps from pine
    to pine,
And loiters, slowly drawn.   On either
    hand
The lawns and meadow-ledges midway
    down
Hang rich in flowers, and far below them
    roars
The long brook falling thro' the clov'n
    ravine
In cataract after cataract to the sea.
Behind the valley topmost Gargarus
Stands up and takes the morning : but in
    front
The gorges, opening wide apart, reveal
Troas and Ilion's column'd citadel,
The crown of Troas.
                    Hither came at noon
Mournful Œnone, wandering forlorn
Of Paris, once her playmate on the hills.
Her cheek had lost the rose, and round
    her neck
Floated her hair or seem'd to float in rest.
She, leaning on a fragment twined with
    vine,
Sang to the stillness, till the mountain-
    shade
Sloped downward to her seat from the
    upper cliff.

    'O mother Ida, many-fountain'd Ida,
Dear mother Ida, harken ere I die.
For now the noonday quiet holds the hill :
The grasshopper is silent in the grass :
The lizard, with his shadow on the stone,
Rests like a shadow, and the winds are
    dead.
The purple flower droops : the golden bee

Is lily-cradled : I alone awake.
My eyes are full of tears, my heart of love,
My heart is breaking, and my eyes are
    dim,
And I am all aweary of my life.

    'O mother Ida, many-fountain'd Ida,
Dear mother Ida, harken ere I die.
Hear me, O Earth, hear me, O Hills, O
    Caves
That house the cold crown'd snake !   O
    mountain brooks,
I am the daughter of a River-God,
Hear me, for I will speak, and build up all
My sorrow with my song, as yonder walls
Rose slowly to a music slowly breathed,
A cloud that gather'd shape : for it may be
That, while I speak of it, a little while
My heart may wander from its deeper woe.

    'O mother Ida, many-fountain'd Ida,
Dear mother Ida, harken ere I die.
I waited underneath the dawning hills,
Aloft the mountain lawn was dewy-dark,
And dewy dark aloft the mountain pine :
Beautiful Paris, evil-hearted Paris,   ·
Leading a jet-black goat white-horn'd,
    white-hooved,
Came up from reedy Simois all alone.

    'O mother Ida, harken ere I die.
Far-off the torrent call'd me from the cleft :
Far up the solitary morning smote
The streaks of virgin snow.   With down-
    dropt eyes
I sat alone : white-breasted like a star
Fronting the dawn he moved ; a leopard
    skin
Droop'd from his shoulder, but his sunny
    hair
Cluster'd about his temples like a God's :
And his cheek brighten'd as the foam-bow
    brightens
When the wind blows the foam, and all
    my heart
Went forth to embrace him coming ere
    he came.

    'Dear mother Ida, harken ere I die.
He smiled, and opening out his milk-
    white palm

Disclosed a fruit of pure Hesperian gold,
That smelt ambrosially, and while I look'd
And listen'd, the full-flowing river of
    speech
Came down upon my heart.
                    ' " My own Œnone,
Beautiful-brow'd Œnone, my own soul,
Behold this fruit, whose gleaming rind
    ingrav'n
' For the most fair,' would seem to award
    it thine,
As lovelier than whatever Oread haunt
The knolls of Ida, loveliest in all grace
Of movement, and the charm of married
    brows."

   ' Dear mother Ida, harken ere I die.
He prest the blossom of his lips to mine,
And added " This was cast upon the
    board,
When all the full-faced presence of the
    Gods
Ranged in the halls of Peleus; whereupon
Rose feud, with question unto whom
    'twere due :
But light-foot Iris brought it yester-eve,
Delivering, that to me, by common voice
Elected umpire, Herè comes to-day,
Pallas and Aphroditè, claiming each
This meed of fairest. Thou, within the
    cave
Behind yon whispering tuft of oldest pine,
Mayst well behold them unbeheld, unheard
Hear all, and see thy Paris judge of
    Gods."

   ' Dear mother Ida, harken ere I die.
It was the deep midnoon : one silvery
    cloud
Had lost his way between the piney sides
Of this long glen. Then to the bower
    they came,
Naked they came to that smooth-swarded
    bower,
And at their feet the crocus brake like
    fire,
Violet, amaracus, and asphodel,
Lotos and lilies : and a wind arose,
And overhead the wandering ivy and
    vine,

This way and that, in many a wild festoon
Ran riot, garlanding the gnarled boughs
With bunch and berry and flower thro'
    and thro'.

   ' O mother Ida, harken ere I die.
On the tree-tops a crested peacock lit,
And o'er him flow'd a golden cloud, and
    lean'd
Upon him, slowly dropping fragrant dew.
Then first I heard the voice of her, to
    whom
Coming thro' Heaven, like a light that
    grows
Larger and clearer, with one mind the Gods
Rise up for reverence. She to Paris made
Proffer of royal power, ample rule
Unquestion'd, overflowing revenue
Wherewith to embellish state, " from
    many a vale
And river-sunder'd champaign clothed
    with corn,
Or labour'd mine undrainable of ore.
Honour," she said, " and homage, tax
    and toll,
From many an inland town and haven
    large,
Mast-throng'd beneath her shadowing
    citadel
In glassy bays among her tallest towers."

   ' O mother Ida, harken ere I die.
Still she spake on and still she spake of
    power,
" Which in all action is the end of all ;
Power fitted to the season ; wisdom-bred
And throned of wisdom—from all neigh-
    bour crowns
Alliance and allegiance, till thy hand
Fail from the sceptre-staff. Such boon
    from me,
From me, Heaven's Queen, Paris, to thee
    king-born,
A shepherd all thy life but yet king-born,
Should come most welcome, seeing men,
    in power
Only, are likest gods, who have attain'd
Rest in a happy place and quiet seats
Above the thunder, with undying bliss
In knowledge of their own supremacy."

'Dear mother Ida, harken ere I die.
She ceased, and Paris held the costly fruit
Out at arm's-length, so much the thought
of power
Flatter'd his spirit ; but Pallas where she
stood
Somewhat apart, her clear and bared
limbs
O'erthwarted with the brazen-headed
spear
Upon her pearly shoulder leaning cold,
The while, above, her full and earnest
eye
Over her snow-cold breast and angry
cheek
Kept watch, waiting decision, made
reply.

' " Self-reverence, self-knowledge, self-
control,
These three alone lead life to sovereign
power.
Yet not for power (power of herself
Would come uncall'd for) but to live by
law,
Acting the law we live by without fear ;
And, because right is right, to follow right
Were wisdom in the scorn of consequence."

'Dear mother Ida, harken ere I die.
Again she said : " I woo thee not with
gifts.
Sequel of guerdon could not alter me
To fairer.   Judge thou me by what I am,
So shalt thou find me fairest.
                              Yet, indeed,
If gazing on divinity disrobed
Thy mortal eyes are frail to judge of fair,
Unbias'd by self-profit, oh ! rest thee sure
That I shall love thee well and cleave to
thee,
So that my vigour, wedded to thy blood,
Shall strike within thy pulses, like a
God's,
To push thee forward thro' a life of shocks,
Dangers, and deeds, until endurance grow
Sinew'd with action, and the full-grown
will,
Circled thro' all experiences, pure law,
Commeasure perfect freedom."

'Here she ceas'd,
And Paris ponder'd, and I cried, "O
Paris,   •
Give it to Pallas !" but he heard me not,
Or hearing would not hear me, woe is me !

'O mother Ida, many-fountain'd Ida,
Dear mother Ida, harken ere I die.
Idalian Aphroditè beautiful,
Fresh as the foam, new-bathed in Paphian
wells,
With rosy slender fingers backward drew
From her warm brows and bosom her
deep hair
Ambrosial, golden round her lucid throat
And shoulder : from the violets her light
foot
Shone rosy-white, and o'er her rounded
form
Between the shadows of the vine-bunches
Floated the glowing sunlights, as she
moved.

'Dear mother Ida, harken ere I die.
She with a subtle smile in her mild eyes,
The herald of her triumph, drawing nigh
Half-whisper'd in his ear, " I promise
thee
The fairest and most loving wife in
Greece,"
She spoke and laugh'd : I shut my sight
for fear :
But when I look'd, Paris had raised his
arm,
And I beheld great Herè's angry eyes,
As she withdrew into the golden cloud,
And I was left alone within the bower ;
And from that time to this I am alone,
And I shall be alone until I die.

'Yet, mother Ida, harken ere I die.
Fairest—why fairest wife ? am I not fair?
My love hath told me so a thousand
times.
Methinks I must be fair, for yesterday,
When I past by, a wild and wanton pard,
Eyed like the evening star, with playful
tail
Crouch'd fawning in the weed.   Most
loving is she ?

Ah me, my mountain shepherd, that my
    arms
Were wound about thee, and my hot lips
    prest
Close, close to thine in that quick-falling
    dew
Of fruitful kisses, thick as Autumn rains
Flash in the pools of whirling Simois.

  'O mother, hear me yet before I die.
They came, they cut away my tallest
    pines,
My tall dark pines, that plumed the
    craggy ledge
High over the blue gorge, and all between
The snowy peak and snow-white cataract
Foster'd the callow eaglet—from beneath
Whose thick mysterious boughs in the
    dark morn
The panther's roar came muffled, while
    I sat
Low in the valley. Never, never more
Shall lone Œnone see the morning mist
Sweep thro' them ; never see them over-
    laid
With narrow moon-lit slips of silver cloud,
Between the loud stream and the trem-
    bling stars.

  'O mother, hear me yet before I die.
I wish that somewhere in the ruin'd folds,
Among the fragments tumbled from the
    glens,
Or the dry thickets, I could meet with
    her
The Abominable, that uninvited came
Into the fair Peleïan banquet-hall,
And cast the golden fruit upon the board,
And bred this change ; that I might speak
    my mind,
And tell her to her face how much I hate
Her presence, hated both of Gods and
    men.

  'O mother, hear me yet before I die.
Hath he not sworn his love a thousand
    times,
In this green valley, under this green hill,
Ev'n on this hand, and sitting on this
    stone ?

Seal'd it with kisses ? water'd it with
    tears ?
O happy tears, and how unlike to these !
O happy Heaven, how canst thou see my
    face ?
O happy earth, how canst thou bear my
    weight ?
O death, death, death, thou ever-floating
    cloud,
There are enough unhappy on this earth,
Pass by the happy souls, that love to live :
I pray thee, pass before my light of life,
And shadow all my soul, that I may die.
Thou weighest heavy on the heart within,
Weigh heavy on my eyelids : let me die.

  'O mother, hear me yet before I die.
I will not die alone, for fiery thoughts
Do shape themselves within me, more and
    more,
Whereof I catch the issue, as I hear
Dead sounds at night come from the in-
    most hills,
Like footsteps upon wool. I dimly see
My far-off doubtful purpose, as a mother
Conjectures of the features of her child
Ere it is born : her child !—a shudder comes
Across me : never child be born of me,
Unblest, to vex me with his father's eyes !

  'O mother, hear me yet before I die.
Hear me, O earth. I will not die alone,
Lest their shrill happy laughter come to
    me
Walking the cold and starless road of
    Death
Uncomforted, leaving my ancient love
With the Greek woman. I will rise and
    go
Down into Troy, and ere the stars come
    forth
Talk with the wild Cassandra, for she says
A fire dances before her, and a sound
Rings ever in her ears of armed men.
What this may be I know not, but I
    know
That, wheresoe'er I am by night and
    day,
All earth and air seem only burning
    fire.'

THE SISTERS.

WE were two daughters of one race :
She was the fairest in the face :
   The wind is blowing in turret and tree.
They were together, and she fell ;
Therefore revenge became me well.
   O the Earl was fair to see !

She died : she went to burning flame :
She mix'd her ancient blood with shame.
   The wind is howling in turret and tree.
Whole weeks and months, and early and
    late,
To win his love I lay in wait :
   O the Earl was fair to see !

I made a feast ; I bad him come ;
I won his love, I brought him home.
   The wind is roaring in turret and tree.
And after supper, on a bed,
Upon my lap he laid his head :
   O the Earl was fair to see !

I kiss'd his eyelids into rest :
His ruddy cheek upon my breast.
   The wind is raging in turret and tree.
I hated him with the hate of hell,
But I loved his beauty passing well.
   O the Earl was fair to see !

I rose up in the silent night :
I made my dagger sharp and bright.
   The wind is raving in turret and tree.
As half-asleep his breath he drew,
Three times I stabb'd him thro' and thro'.
   O the Earl was fair to see !

I curl'd and comb'd his comely head,
He look'd so grand when he was dead.
   The wind is blowing in turret and tree.
I wrapt his body in the sheet,
And laid him at his mother's feet.
   O the Earl was fair to see !

TO ——.

WITH THE FOLLOWING POEM.

I SEND you here a sort of allegory,
(For you will understand it) of a soul,
A sinful soul possess'd of many gifts,
A spacious garden full of flowering weeds,
A glorious Devil, large in heart and brain,
That did love Beauty only, (Beauty seen
   In all varieties of mould and mind)
And Knowledge for its beauty ; or if
   Good,
Good only for its beauty, seeing not
That Beauty, Good, and Knowledge, are
   three sisters
That doat upon each other, friends to
   man,
Living together under the same roof,
And never can be sunder'd without tears.
And he that shuts Love out, in turn shall
   be
Shut out from Love, and on her threshold
   lie
Howling in outer darkness.   Not for this
Was common clay ta'en from the common
   earth
Moulded by God, and temper'd with the
   tears
Of angels to the perfect shape of man.

THE PALACE OF ART.

I BUILT my soul a lordly pleasure-house,
   Wherein at ease for aye to dwell.
I said, 'O Soul, make merry and carouse,
   Dear soul, for all is well.'

A huge crag-platform, smooth as burnish'd
    brass
   I chose.   The ranged ramparts bright
From level meadow-bases of deep grass
   Suddenly scaled the light.

Thereon I built it firm.   Of ledge or
   shelf
   The rock rose clear, or winding stair.
My soul would live alone unto herself
   In her high palace there.

And 'while the world runs round and
    round,' I said,
   'Reign thou apart, a quiet king,
Still as, while Saturn whirls, his stedfast
    shade
   Sleeps on his luminous ring.'

To which my soul made answer readily :
  'Trust me, in bliss I shall abide
In this great mansion, that is built for me,
  So royal-rich and wide.'

   *   *   *   *
   *   *   *   *

Four courts I made, East, West and
    South and North,
  In each a squared lawn, wherefrom
The golden gorge of dragons spouted forth
  A flood of fountain-foam.

And round the cool green courts there
    ran a row
  Of cloisters, branch'd like mighty woods,
Echoing all night to that sonorous flow
  Of spouted fountain-floods.

And round the roofs a gilded gallery
  That lent broad verge to distant lands,
Far as the wild swan wings, to where the
    sky
  Dipt down to sea and sands.

From those four jets four currents in one
    swell
  Across the mountain stream'd below
In misty folds, that floating as they fell
  Lit up a torrent-bow.

And high on every peak a statue seem'd
  To hang on tiptoe, tossing up   .
A cloud of incense of all odour steam'd
  From out a golden cup.

So that she thought, 'And who shall
    gaze upon
  My palace with unblinded eyes,
While this great bow will waver in the sun,
  And that sweet incense rise ?'

For that sweet incense rose and never
    fail'd,
  And, while day sank or mounted higher,
The light aërial gallery, golden-rail'd,
  Burnt like a fringe of fire.

Likewise the deep-set windows, stain'd
    and traced,
  Would seem slow-flaming crimson fires
From shadow'd grots of arches interlaced,
  And tipt with frost-like spires.

   *   *   *   *
   *   *   *   *

Full of long-sounding corridors it was,
  That over-vaulted grateful gloom,
Thro' which the livelong day my soul
    did pass,
  Well-pleased, from room to room.

Full of great rooms and small the palace
    stood,
  All various, each a perfect whole
From living Nature, fit for every mood
  And change of my still soul.

For some were hung with arras green
    and blue,
  Showing a gaudy summer-morn,
Where with puff'd cheek the belted hunter
    blew
  His wreathed bugle-horn.

One seem'd all dark and red—a tract of
    sand,
  And some one pacing there alone,
Who paced for ever in a glimmering land,
  Lit with a low large moon.

One show'd an iron coast and angry
    waves.
  You seem'd to hear them climb and fall
And roar rock-thwarted under bellowing
    caves,
  Beneath the windy wall.

And one, a full-fed river winding slow
  By herds upon an endless plain,
The ragged rims of thunder brooding
    low,
  With shadow-streaks of rain.

And one, the reapers at their sultry toil.
  In front they bound the sheaves. Behind
Were realms of upland, prodigal in oil,
  And hoary to the wind.

And one a foreground black with stones
    and slags,
  Beyond, a line of heights, and higher
All barr'd with long white cloud the
    scornful crags,
  And highest, snow and fire.

And one, an English home—gray twi-
    light pour'd
  On dewy pastures, dewy trees,
Softer than sleep — all things in order
    stored,
    A haunt of ancient Peace.

Nor these alone, but every landscape fair,
  · As fit for every mood of mind,
Or gay, or grave, or sweet, or stern, was
    there
    Not less than truth design'd.

        *   *   *   *
        *   *   *   *

Or the maid-mother by a crucifix,
  In tracts of pasture sunny-warm,
Beneath branch-work of costly sardonyx
    Sat smiling, babe in arm.

Or in a clear-wall'd city on the sea,
  Near gilded organ-pipes, her hair
Wound with white roses, slept St. Cecily;
    An angel look'd at her.

Or thronging all one porch of Paradise
  A group of Houris bow'd to see
The dying Islamite, with hands and eyes
    That said, We wait for thee.

Or mythic Uther's deeply-wounded son
  In some fair space of sloping greens
Lay, dozing in the vale of Avalon,
    And watch'd by weeping queens.

Or hollowing one hand against his ear,
  To list a foot-fall, ere he saw
The wood-nymph, stay'd the Ausonian
    king to hear
    Of wisdom and of law.

Or over hills with peaky tops engrail'd,
  And many a tract of palm and rice,
The throne of Indian Cama slowly sail'd
    A summer fann'd with spice.

Or sweet Europa's mantle blew unclasp'd,
  From off her shoulder backward borne:
From one hand droop'd a crocus : one
    hand grasp'd
    The mild bull's golden horn.

Or else flush'd Ganymede, his rosy thigh
  Half-buried in the Eagle's down,
Sole as a flying star shot thro' the sky
    Above the pillar'd town.

Nor these alone : but every legend fair
  Which the supreme Caucasian mind
Carved out of Nature for itself, was there,
    Not less than life, design'd.

        *   *   *   *
        *   *   *   *

Then in the towers I placed great bells
    that swung,
  Moved of themselves, with silver sound;
And with choice paintings of wise men I
    hung
    The royal dais round.

For there was Milton like a seraph strong,
  Beside him Shakespeare bland and
    mild ;
And there the world-worn Dante grasp'd
    his song,
    And somewhat grimly smiled.

And there the Ionian father of the rest ;
  A million wrinkles carved his skin ;
A hundred winters snow'd upon his breast,
    From cheek and throat and chin.

Above, the fair hall-ceiling stately-set
  Many an arch high up did lift,
And angels rising and descending met
    With interchange of gift.

Below was all mosaic choicely plann'd
  With cycles of the human tale
Of this wide world, the times of every land
    So wrought, they will not fail.

The people here, a beast of burden slow,
  Toil'd onward, prick'd with goads and
    stings ;
Here play'd, a tiger, rolling to and fro
    The heads and crowns of kings ;

Here rose, an athlete, strong to break or
    bind
  All force in bonds that might endure,
And here once more like some sick man
    declined,
    And trusted any cure.

But over these she trod : and those great
bells
    Began to chime. She took her throne :
She sat betwixt the shining Oriels,
    To sing her songs alone.

And thro' the topmost Oriels' coloured
flame
    Two godlike faces gazed below ;
Plato the wise, and large-brow'd Verulam,
    The first of those who know.

And all those names, that in their motion
were
    Full-welling fountain-heads of change,
Betwixt the slender shafts were blazon'd
fair
    In diverse raiment strange :

Thro' which the lights, rose, amber,
emerald, blue,
    Flush'd in her temples and her eyes,
And from her lips, as morn from Memnon,
drew
    Rivers of melodies.

No nightingale delighteth to prolong
    Her low preamble all alone,
More than my soul to hear her echo'd
song
    Throb thro' the ribbed stone ;

Singing and murmuring in her feastful
mirth,
    Joying to feel herself alive,
Lord over Nature, Lord of the visible
earth,
    Lord of the senses five ;

Communing with herself : 'All these are
mine,
    And let the world have peace or wars,
'Tis one to me.' She—when young night
divine
    Crown'd dying day with stars,

Making sweet close of his delicious toils—
    Lit light in wreaths and anadems,
And pure quintessences of precious oils
    In hollow'd moons of gems,

To mimic heaven ; and clapt her hands
and cried,
    'I marvel if my still delight
In this great house so royal-rich, and wide,
    Be flatter'd to the height.

'O all things fair to sate my various eyes !
    O shapes and hues that please me well !
O silent faces of the Great and Wise,
    My Gods, with whom I dwell !

'O God-like isolation which art mine,
    I can but count thee perfect gain,
What time I watch the darkening droves
of swine
    That range on yonder plain.

'In filthy sloughs they roll a prurient skin,
    They graze and wallow, breed and
sleep ;
And oft some brainless devil enters in,
    And drives them to the deep.'

Then of the moral instinct would she prate
    And of the rising from the dead,
As hers by right of full-accomplish'd Fate;
    And at the last she said :

'I take possession of man's mind and deed.
    I care not what the sects may brawl.
I sit as God holding no form of creed,
    But contemplating all.'

    *   *   *   *

    *   *   *   *

Full oft the riddle of the painful earth
    Flash'd thro' her as she sat alone,
Yet not the less held she her solemn
mirth,
    And intellectual throne.

And so she throve and prosper'd : so
three years
    She prosper'd : on the fourth she fell,
Like Herod, when the shout was in his
ears,
    Struck thro' with pangs of hell.

Lest she should fail and perish utterly,
    God, before whom ever lie bare
The abysmal deeps of Personality,
    Plagued her with sore despair.

When she would think, where'er she
        turn'd her sight
    The airy hand confusion wrought,
Wrote, ' Mene, mene,' and divided quite
    The kingdom of her thought.

Deep dread and loathing of her solitude
    Fell on her, from which mood was
        born
Scorn of herself; again, from out that
        mood
    Laughter at her self-scorn.

' What ! is not this my place of strength,'
        she said,
    ' My spacious mansion built for me,
Whereof the strong foundation-stones
        were laid
    Since my first memory?'

But in dark corners of her palace stood
    Uncertain shapes ; and unawares
On white-eyed phantasms weeping tears
        of blood,
    And horrible nightmares,

And hollow shades enclosing hearts of
        flame,
    And, with dim fretted foreheads all,
On corpses three-months-old at noon she
        came,
    That stood against the wall.

A spot of dull stagnation, without light
    Or power of movement, seem'd my
        soul,
'Mid onward-sloping motions infinite
    Making for one sure goal.

A still salt pool, lock'd in with bars of
        sand,
    Left on the shore ; that hears all night
The plunging seas draw backward from
        the land
    Their moon-led waters white.

A star that with the choral starry dance
    Join'd not, but stood, and standing saw
The hollow orb of moving Circumstance
    Roll'd round by one fix'd law.

Back on herself her serpent pride had
        curl'd.
    ' No voice,' she shriek'd in that lone
        hall,
' No voice breaks thro' the stillness of
        this world :
    One deep, deep silence all !'

She, mouldering with the dull earth's
        mouldering sod,
    Inwrapt tenfold in slothful shame,
Lay there exiled from eternal God,
    Lost to her place and name ;

And death and life she hated equally,
    And nothing saw, for her despair,
But dreadful time, dreadful eternity,
    No comfort anywhere ;

Remaining utterly confused with fears,
    And ever worse with growing time,
And ever unrelieved by dismal tears,
    And all alone in crime :

Shut up as in a crumbling tomb, girt round
    With blackness as a solid wall,
Far off she seem'd to hear the dully sound
    Of human footsteps fall.

As in strange lands a traveller walking
        slow,
    In doubt and great perplexity,
A little before moon-rise hears the low
    Moan of an unknown sea ;

And knows not if it be thunder, or a sound *
    Of rocks thrown down, or one deep
        cry
Of great wild beasts ; then thinketh, ' I
        have found
    A new land, but I die.'

She howl'd aloud, ' I am on fire within.
    There comes no murmur of reply.
What is it that will take away my sin,
    And save me lest I die?'

So when four years were wholly finished,
    She threw her royal robes away.
' Make me a cottage in the vale,' she said,
    ' Where I may mourn and pray.

* Wisdom of Solomon xvii 18, 19
(Morley Roberts; The Private Life of
Henry Maitland [i.e. George Gissing] 1958, p 176

'Yet pull not down my palace towers,
          that are
So lightly, beautifully built :
Perchance I may return with others there
     When I have purged my guilt.'

LADY CLARA VERE DE VERE.

Lady Clara Vere de Vere,
     Of me you shall not win renown :
You thought to break a country heart
     For pastime, ere you went to town.
At me you smiled, but unbeguiled
     I saw the snare, and I retired :
The daughter of a hundred Earls,
     You are not one to be desired.

Lady Clara Vere de Vere,
     I know you proud to bear your name,
Your pride is yet no mate for mine,
     Too proud to care from whence I came.
Nor would I break for your sweet sake
     A heart that doats on truer charms.
A simple maiden in her flower
     Is worth a hundred coats-of-arms.

Lady Clara Vere de Vere,
     Some meeker pupil you must find,
For were you queen of all that is,
     I could not stoop to such a mind.
You sought to prove how I could love,
     And my disdain is my reply.
The lion on your old stone gates
     Is not more cold to you than I.

Lady Clara Vere de Vere,
     You put strange memories in my head.
Not thrice your branching limes have
          blown
Since I beheld young Laurence dead.
Oh your sweet eyes, your low replies :
     A great enchantress you may be ;
But there was that across his throat
     Which you had hardly cared to see.

Lady Clara Vere de Vere,
     When thus he met his mother's view,
She had the passions of her kind,
     She spake some certain truths of you.
Indeed I heard one bitter word
     That scarce is fit for you to hear ;
Her manners had not that repose
     Which stamps the caste of Vere de Vere.

Lady Clara Vere de Vere,
     There stands a spectre in your hall :
The guilt of blood is at your door :
     You changed a wholesome heart to gall.
You held your course without remorse,
     To make him trust his modest worth,
And, last, you fix'd a vacant stare,
     And slew him with your noble birth.

Trust me, Clara Vere de Vere,
     From yon blue heavens above us bent
The gardener Adam and his wife
     Smile at the claims of long descent.
Howe'er it be, it seems to me,
     'Tis only noble to be good.
Kind hearts are more than coronets,
     And simple faith than Norman blood.

I know you, Clara Vere de Vere,
     You pine among your halls and towers :
The languid light of your proud eyes
     Is wearied of the rolling hours.
In glowing health, with boundless wealth,
     But sickening of a vague disease,
You know so ill to deal with time,
     You needs must play such pranks as
          these.

Clara, Clara Vere de Vere,
     If time be heavy on your hands,
Are there no beggars at your gate,
     Nor any poor about your lands ?
Oh ! teach the orphan-boy to read,
     Or teach the orphan-girl to sew,
Pray Heaven for a human heart,
     And let the foolish yeoman go.

THE MAY QUEEN.

YOU must wake and call me early, call me early, mother dear ;
To-morrow 'ill be the happiest time of all the glad New-year ;
Of all the glad New-year, mother, the maddest merriest day ;
For I'm to be Queen o' the May, mother, I'm to be Queen o' the May.

There's many a black black eye, they say, but none so bright as mine ;
There's Margaret and Mary, there's Kate and Caroline :
But none so fair as little Alice in all the land they say,
So I'm to be Queen o' the May, mother, I'm to be Queen o' the May.

I sleep so sound all night, mother, that I shall never wake,
If you do not call me loud when the day begins to break :
But I must gather knots of flowers, and buds and garlands gay,
For I'm to be Queen o' the May, mother, I'm to be Queen o' the May.

As I came up the valley whom think ye should I see,
But Robin leaning on the bridge beneath the hazel-tree ?
He thought of that sharp look, mother, I gave him yesterday,
But I'm to be Queen o' the May, mother, I'm to be Queen o' the May.

He thought I was a ghost, mother, for I was all in white,
And I ran by him without speaking, like a flash of light.
They call me cruel-hearted, but I care not what they say,
For I'm to be Queen o' the May, mother, I'm to be Queen o' the May.

They say he's dying all for love, but that can never be :
They say his heart is breaking, mother—what is that to me ?
There's many a bolder lad 'ill woo me any summer day,
And I'm to be Queen o' the May, mother, I'm to be Queen o' the May.

Little Effie shall go with me to-morrow to the green,
And you'll be there, too, mother, to see me made the Queen ;
For the shepherd lads on every side 'ill come from far away,
And I'm to be Queen o' the May, mother, I'm to be Queen o' the May.

The honeysuckle round the porch has wov'n its wavy bowers,
And by the meadow-trenches blow the faint sweet cuckoo-flowers ;
And the wild marsh-marigold shines like fire in swamps and hollows gray,
And I'm to be Queen o' the May, mother, I'm to be Queen o' the May.

The night-winds come and go, mother, upon the meadow-grass,
And the happy stars above them seem to brighten as they pass ;
There will not be a drop of rain the whole of the livelong day,
And I'm to be Queen o' the May, mother, I'm to be Queen o' the May.

All the valley, mother, 'ill be fresh and green and still,
And the cowslip and the crowfoot are over all the hill,
And the rivulet in the flowery dale 'ill merrily glance and play,
For I'm to be Queen o' the May, mother, I'm to be Queen o' the May.

So you must wake and call me early, call me early, mother dear,
To-morrow 'ill be the happiest time of all the glad New-year :
To-morrow 'ill be of all the year the maddest merriest day,
For I'm to be Queen o' the May, mother, I'm to be Queen o' the May.

NEW-YEAR'S EVE.

If you're waking call me early, call me early, mother dear,
For I would see the sun rise upon the glad New-year.
It is the last New-year that I shall ever see,
Then you may lay me low i' the mould and think no more of me.   *'humus'*

To-night I saw the sun set : he set and left behind
The good old year, the dear old time, and all my peace of mind ;
And the New-year's coming up, mother, but I shall never see
The blossom on the blackthorn, the leaf upon the tree.

Last May we made a crown of flowers : we had a merry day ;
Beneath the hawthorn on the green they made me Queen of May;
And we danced about the may-pole and in the hazel copse,
Till Charles's Wain came out above the tall white chimney-tops.

There's not a flower on all the hills : the frost is on the pane :
I only wish to live till the snowdrops come again :
I wish the snow would melt and the sun come out on high :
I long to see a flower so before the day I die.

The building rook 'll caw from the windy tall elm-tree,
And the tufted plover pipe along the fallow lea,
And the swallow 'ill come back again with summer o'er the wave,
But I shall lie alone, mother, within the mouldering grave.

Upon the chancel-casement, and upon that grave of mine,
In the early early morning the summer sun 'ill shine,
Before the red cock crows from the farm upon the hill,
When you are warm-asleep, mother, and all the world is still.

When the flowers come again, mother, beneath the waning light
You'll never see me more in the long gray fields at night ;
When from the dry dark wold the summer airs blow cool
On the oat-grass and the sword-grass, and the bulrush in the pool.

You'll bury me, my mother, just beneath the hawthorn shade,
And you'll come sometimes and see me where I am lowly laid.
I shall not forget you, mother, I shall hear you when you pass,
With your feet above my head in the long and pleasant grass.

I have been wild and wayward, but you'll forgive me now ;
You'll kiss me, my own mother, and forgive me ere I go ;

insensée
désordonnée

Nay, nay, you must not weep, nor let your grief be wild,
You should not fret for me, mother, you have another child.   *(Effie)*

If I can I'll come again, mother, from out my resting-place ;
Tho' you'll not see me, mother, I shall look upon your face ;
Tho' I cannot speak a word, I shall harken what you say,
And be often, often with you when you think I'm far away.

Goodnight, goodnight, when I have said goodnight for evermore,
And you see me carried out from the threshold of the door ;
Don't let Effie come to see me till my grave be growing green :
She'll be a better child to you than ever I have been.

She'll find my garden-tools upon the granary floor :
Let her take 'em : they are hers : I shall never garden more :
But tell her, when I'm gone, to train the rosebush that I set   *caisse*
About the parlour-window and the box of mignonette.

Goodnight, sweet mother : call me before the day is born.
All night I lie awake, but I fall asleep at morn ;
But I would see the sun rise upon the glad New-year,
So, if you're waking, call me, call me early, mother dear.

CONCLUSION.

I THOUGHT to pass away before, and yet alive I am ;
And in the fields all round I hear the bleating of the lamb.
How sadly, I remember, rose the morning of the year !
To die before the snowdrop came, and now the violet's here.

O sweet is the new violet, that comes beneath the skies,
And sweeter is the young lamb's voice to me that cannot rise,
And sweet is all the land about, and all the flowers that blow,
And sweeter far is death than life to me that long to go.

It seem'd so hard at first, mother, to leave the blessed sun,
And now it seems as hard to stay, and yet His will be done !
But still I think it can't be long before I find release ;
And that good man, the clergyman, has told me words of peace.

O blessings on his kindly voice and on his silver hair !
And blessings on his whole life long, until he meet me there !
O blessings on his kindly heart and on his silver head !
A thousand times I blest him, as he knelt beside my bed.

He taught me all the mercy, for he show'd me all the sin.
Now, tho' my lamp was lighted late, there's One will let me in :
Nor would I now be well, mother, again if that could be,
For my desire is but to pass to Him that died for me.

I did not hear the dog howl, mother, or the death-watch beat,
There came a sweeter token when the night and morning meet :
But sit beside my bed, mother, and put your hand in mine,
And Effie on the other side, and I will tell the sign.

Kinds of insects whose ticking portends death 'perce-bois' horloge de la mort'

All in the wild March-morning I heard the angels call ;
It was when the moon was setting, and the dark was over all ;
The trees began to whisper, and the wind began to roll,
And in the wild March-morning I heard them call my soul.

For lying broad awake I thought of you and Effie dear ;
I saw you sitting in the house, and I no longer here ;
With all my strength I pray'd for both, and so I felt resign'd,
And up the valley came a swell of music on the wind.

I thought that it was fancy, and I listen'd in my bed,
And then did something speak to me—I know not what was said ;
For great delight and shuddèring took hold of all my mind,
And up the valley came again the music on the wind.

But you were sleeping ; and I said, ' It's not for them : it's mine.'
And if it come three times, I thought, I take it for a sign.
And once again it came, and close beside the window-bars,
Then seem'd to go right up to Heaven and die among the stars.

So now I think my time is near.   I trust it is.   I know
The blessed music went that way my soul will have to go.
And for myself, indeed, I care not if I go to-day.
But, Effie, you must comfort *her* when I am past away.

And say to Robin a kind word, and tell him not to fret ;
There's many a worthier than I, would make him happy yet.
If I had lived—I cannot tell—I might have been his wife ;
But all these things have ceased to be, with my desire of life.

O look ! the sun begins to rise, the heavens are in a glow ;
He shines upon a hundred fields, and all of them I know.
And there I move no longer now, and there his light may shine—
Wild flowers in the valley for other hands than mine.

O sweet and strange it seems to me, that ere this day is done
The voice, that now is speaking, may be beyond the sun—
For ever and for ever with those just souls and true—
And what is life, that we should moan ? why make we such ado ?

For ever and for ever, all in a blessed home—
And there to wait a little while till you and Effie come—
To lie within the light of God, as I lie upon your breast—
And the wicked cease from troubling, and the weary are at rest.

Job (iii 17) se lamente :
11 why died I not from the womb ?... been,
16 oh as an hidden untimely birth I had not
as infants which never saw light.
17 there th wicked cease from troubling ;
and there the weary be at rest.

pub 1833 [Dec. 1832] in 'Poems by Alfred Tennyson'

THE LOTOS-EATERS.

'COURAGE!' he said, and pointed toward
　　the land,
'This mounting wave will roll us shore-
　　ward soon.'
In the afternoon they came unto a land
In which it seemed always afternoon.
All round the coast the languid air did
　　swoon,
Breathing like one that hath a weary
　　dream.
Full-faced above the valley stood the
　　moon;
And like a downward smoke, the slender
　　stream
Along the cliff to fall and pause and fall
　　did seem.

A land of streams! some, like a down-
　　ward smoke,
Slow-dropping veils of thinnest lawn, did
　　go;
And some thro' wavering lights and
　　shadows broke,
Rolling a slumbrous sheet of foam below.
They saw the gleaming river seaward
　　flow
From the inner land: far off, three
　　mountain-tops,
Three silent pinnacles of aged snow,
Stood sunset-flush'd: and, dew'd with
　　showery drops,
Up-clomb the shadowy pine above the
　　woven copse.

The charmed sunset linger'd low adown
In the red West: thro' mountain clefts
　　the dale
Was seen far inland, and the yellow down
Border'd with palm, and many a winding
　　vale
And meadow, set with slender galingale;
A land where all things always seem'd
　　the same!
And round about the keel with faces
　　pale,
Dark faces pale against that rosy flame,
The mild-eyed melancholy Lotos-eaters
　　came.

Branches they bore of that enchanted
　　stem,
Laden with flower and fruit, whereof they
　　gave
To each, but whoso did receive of them,
And taste, to him the gushing of the wave
Far far away did seem to mourn and rave
On alien shores; and if his fellow spake,
His voice was thin, as voices from the
　　grave;
And deep-asleep he seem'd, yet all awake,
And music in his ears his beating heart
　　did make.

They sat them down upon the yellow
　　sand,
Between the sun and moon upon the
　　shore;
And sweet it was to dream of Fatherland,
Of child, and wife, and slave; but ever-
　　more
Most weary seem'd the sea, weary the
　　oar,
Weary the wandering fields of barren
　　foam.
Then some one said, 'We will return no
　　more;'
And all at once they sang, 'Our island
　　home
Is far beyond the wave; we will no longer
　　roam.'

CHORIC SONG.

I.

THERE is sweet music here that softer falls
Than petals from blown roses on the grass,
Or night-dews on still waters between
　　walls
Of shadowy granite, in a gleaming pass;
Music that gentlier on the spirit lies,
Than tir'd eyelids upon tir'd eyes;
Music that brings sweet sleep down from
　　the blissful skies.
Here are cool mosses deep,
And thro' the moss the ivies creep,
And in the stream the long-leaved flowers
　　weep,
And from the craggy ledge the poppy
　　hangs in sleep.

II.

Why are we weigh'd upon with heaviness,
And utterly consumed with sharp distress,
While all things else have rest from
    weariness?
All things have rest: why should we toil
    alone,
We only toil, who are the first of things,
And make perpetual moan,
Still from one sorrow to another thrown:
Nor ever fold our wings,
And cease from wanderings,
Nor steep our brows in slumber's holy
    balm;
Nor harken what the inner spirit sings,
'There is no joy but calm!'
Why should we only toil, the roof and
    crown of things?

III.

Lo! in the middle of the wood,
The folded leaf is woo'd from out the bud
With winds upon the branch, and there
Grows green and broad, and takes no care,
Sun-steep'd at noon, and in the moon
Nightly dew-fed; and turning yellow
Falls, and floats adown the air.
Lo! sweeten'd with the summer light,
The full-juiced apple, waxing over-mellow,
Drops in a silent autumn night.
All its allotted length of days,
The flower ripens in its place,
Ripens and fades, and falls, and hath no
    toil,
Fast-rooted in the fruitful soil.

IV.

Hateful is the dark-blue sky,
Vaulted o'er the dark-blue sea.
Death is the end of life; ah, why
Should life all labour be?
Let us alone. Time driveth onward fast,
And in a little while our lips are dumb.
Let us alone. What is it that will last?
All things are taken from us, and become
Portions and parcels of the dreadful Past.
Let us alone. What pleasure can we
    have
To war with evil? Is there any peace

In ever climbing up the climbing wave?
All things have rest, and ripen toward
    the grave
In silence; ripen, fall and cease:
Give us long rest or death, dark death,
    or dreamful ease.

V.

How sweet it were, hearing the down-
    ward stream,
With half-shut eyes ever to seem
Falling asleep in a half-dream!
To dream and dream, like yonder amber
    light,
Which will not leave the myrrh-bush on
    the height;
To hear each other's whisper'd speech;
Eating the Lotos day by day,
To watch the crisping ripples on the
    beach,
And tender curving lines of creamy spray;
To lend our hearts and spirits wholly
To the influence of mild-minded melan-
    choly;
To muse and brood and live again in
    memory,
With those old faces of our infancy
Heap'd over with a mound of grass,
Two handfuls of white dust, shut in an
    urn of brass!

VI.

Dear is the memory of our wedded lives,
And dear the last embraces of our wives
And their warm tears: but all hath
    suffer'd change:
For surely now our household hearths are
    cold:
Our sons inherit us: our looks are
    strange:
And we should come like ghosts to trouble
    joy.
Or else the island princes over-bold
Have eat our substance, and the minstrel
    sings
Before them of the ten years' war in Troy,
And our great deeds, as half-forgotten
    things.
Is there confusion in the little isle?
Let what is broken so remain.

The Gods are hard to reconcile :
'Tis hard to settle order once again.
There *is* confusion worse than death,
Trouble on trouble, pain on pain,
Long labour unto aged breath,
Sore task to hearts worn out by many wars
And eyes grown dim with gazing on the
　　pilot-stars.

VII.

But, propt on beds of amaranth and moly,
How sweet (while warm airs lull us,
　　blowing lowly)
With half-dropt eyelid still,
Beneath a heaven dark and holy,
To watch the long bright river drawing
　　slowly
His waters from the purple hill—
To hear the dewy echoes calling
From cave to cave thro' the thick-twined
　　vine—
To watch the emerald-colour'd water
　　falling
Thro' many a wov'n acanthus-wreath
　　divine !
Only to hear and see the far-off sparkling
　　brine,
Only to hear were sweet, stretch'd out
　　beneath the pine.

VIII.

The Lotos blooms below the barren peak :
The Lotos blows by every winding creek :
All day the wind breathes low with
　　mellower tone :
Thro' every hollow cave and alley lone
Round and round the spicy downs the
　　yellow Lotos-dust is blown.
We have had enough of action, and of
　　motion we,
Roll'd to starboard, roll'd to larboard,
　　when the surge was seething free,
Where the wallowing monster spouted
　　his foam-fountains in the sea.
Let us swear an oath, and keep it with
　　an equal mind,
In the hollow Lotos-land to live and lie
　　reclined
On the hills like Gods together, careless
　　of mankind.

For they lie beside their nectar, and the
　　bolts are hurl'd
Far below them in the valleys, and the
　　clouds are lightly curl'd
Round their golden houses, girdled with
　　the gleaming world :
Where they smile in secret, looking over
　　wasted lands,
Blight and famine, plague and earthquake,
　　roaring deeps and fiery sands,
Clanging fights, and flaming towns, and
　　sinking ships, and praying hands.
But they smile, they find a music centred
　　in a doleful song
Steaming up, a lamentation and an ancient
　　tale of wrong,
Like a tale of little meaning tho' the
　　words are strong ;
Chanted from an ill-used race of men
　　that cleave the soil,
Sow the seed, and reap the harvest with
　　enduring toil,
Storing yearly little dues of wheat, and
　　wine and oil ;
Till they perish and they suffer—some,
　　'tis whisper'd—down in hell
Suffer endless anguish, others in Elysian
　　valleys dwell,
Resting weary limbs at last on beds of
　　asphodel.
Surely, surely, slumber is more sweet
　　than toil, the shore
Than labour in the deep mid-ocean, wind
　　and wave and oar ;
Oh rest ye, brother mariners, we will
　　not wander more.

A DREAM OF FAIR WOMEN.

I READ, before my eyelids dropt their shade,
　' *The Legend of Good Women*,' long ago
Sung by the morning star of song, who
　　made
　　His music heard below ;

Dan Chaucer, the first warbler, whose
　　sweet breath
Preluded those melodious bursts that fill
The spacious times of great Elizabeth
　　With sounds that echo still.

And, for a while, the knowledge of his
    art
  Held me above the subject, as strong
    gales
Hold swollen clouds from raining, tho'
  my heart,
  Brimful of those wild tales,

Charged both mine eyes with tears. In
    every land
  I saw, wherever light illumineth,
Beauty and anguish walking hand in hand
  The downward slope to death.

Those far-renowned brides of ancient
    song
  Peopled the hollow dark, like burning
    stars,
And I heard sounds of insult, shame, and
    wrong,
  And trumpets blown for wars ;

And clattering flints batter'd with clanging
    hoofs ;
  And I saw crowds in column'd sanctu-
    aries ;
And forms that pass'd at windows and on
    roofs
  Of marble palaces ;

Corpses across the threshold ; heroes tall
  Dislodging pinnacle and parapet
Upon the tortoise creeping to the wall ;
  Lances in ambush set ;

And high shrine-doors burst thro' with
  heated blasts
  That run before the fluttering tongues
    of fire ;
White surf wind-scatter'd over sails and
  masts,
  And ever climbing higher ;

Squadrons and squares of men in brazen
  plates,
  Scaffolds, still sheets of water, divers
    woes,
Ranges of glimmering vaults with iron
  grates,
  And hush'd seraglios.

So shape chased shape as swift as, when
    to land
  Bluster the winds and tides the self-same
    way,
Crisp foam-flakes scud along the level
    sand,
  Torn from the fringe of spray.

I started once, or seem'd to start in pain,
  Resolved on noble things, and strove
    to speak,
As when a great thought strikes along
    the brain,
  And flushes all the cheek.

And once my arm was lifted to hew down
  A cavalier from off his saddle-bow,
That bore a lady from a leaguer'd town ;
  And then, I know not how,

All those sharp fancies, by down-lapsing
    thought
  Stream'd onward, lost their edges, and
    did creep
Roll'd on each other, rounded, smooth'd,
  and brought
  Into the gulfs of sleep.

At last methought that I had wander'd far
  In an old wood : fresh-wash'd in coolest
    dew
The maiden splendours of the morning star
  Shook in the stedfast blue.

Enormous elm-tree-boles did stoop and
    lean
  Upon the dusky brushwood underneath
Their broad curved branches, fledged with
  clearest green,
  New from its silken sheath.

The dim red morn had died, her journey
    done,
  And with dead lips smiled at the twi-
    light plain,
Half-fall'n across the threshold of the sun,
  Never to rise again.

There was no motion in the dumb dead air,
  Not any song of bird or sound of rill ;
Gross darkness of the inner sepulchre
  Is not so deadly still

As that wide forest.   Growths of jasmine
   turn'd
    Their humid arms festooning tree to
     tree,
And at the root thro' lush green grasses
   burn'd
    The red anemone.

I knew the flowers, I knew the leaves, I
   knew
    The tearful glimmer of the languid dawn
On those long, rank, dark wood-walks
   drench'd in dew,
    Leading from lawn to lawn.

The smell of violets, hidden in the green,
    Pour'd back into my empty soul and
     frame
The times when I remember to have been
    Joyful and free from blame.

And from within me a clear under-tone
    Thrill'd thro' mine ears in that unbliss-
     ful clime,
' Pass freely thro' : the wood is all thine
   own,
    Until the end of time.'

At length I saw a lady within call,
    Stiller than chisell'd marble, standing
     there ;
A daughter of the gods, divinely tall,
    And most divinely fair.

Her loveliness with shame and with surprise
    Froze my swift speech : she turning on
     my face
The star-like sorrows of immortal eyes,
    Spoke slowly in her place.

' I had great beauty : ask thou not my
   name :
No one can be more wise than destiny.
Many drew swords and died.   Where'er
   I came
    I brought calamity.'

' No marvel, sovereign lady : in fair field
    Myself for such a face had boldly died,'
I answer'd free ; and turning I appeal'd
    To one that stood beside.

But she, with sick and scornful looks averse,
    To her full height her stately stature
     draws ;
' My youth,' she said, ' was blasted with
   a curse :
    This woman was the cause.

' I was cut off from hope in that sad place,
    Which men call'd Aulis in those iron
     years :
My father held his hand upon his face ;
    I, blinded with my tears,

' Still strove to speak : my voice was
   thick with sighs
    As in a dream.   Dimly I could descry
The stern black-bearded kings with wolf-
   ish eyes,
    Waiting to see me die.

' The high masts flicker'd as they lay afloat ;
    The crowds, the temples, waver'd, and
     the shore ;
The bright death quiver'd at the victim's
   throat ;
    Touch'd ; and I knew no more.'

Whereto the other with a downward brow :
    ' I would the white cold heavy-plung-
     ing foam,
Whirl'd by the wind, had roll'd me deep
    below,
    Then when I left my home.'

Her slow full words sank thro' the silence
   drear,
    As thunder-drops fall on a sleeping sea :
Sudden I heard a voice that cried, ' Come
   here,
    That I may look on thee.'

I turning saw, throned on a flowery rise,
    One sitting on a crimson scarf unroll'd ;
A queen, with swarthy cheeks and bold
   black eyes,
    Brow-bound with burning gold.

She, flashing forth a haughty smile, began :
    ' I govern'd men by change, and so I
     sway'd
All moods.   'Tis long since I have seen
   a man.
    Once, like the moon, I made

'The ever-shifting currents of the blood
  According to my humour ebb and flow.
I have no men to govern in this wood:
  That makes my only woe.

'Nay—yet it chafes me that I could not
    bend
  One will; nor tame and tutor with
    mine eye
That dull cold-blooded Cæsar. Prythee,
    friend,
  Where is Mark Antony?

'The man, my lover, with whom I rode
    sublime
  On Fortune's neck: we sat as God by
    God:
The Nilus would have risen before his time
  And flooded at our nod.

'We drank the Libyan Sun to sleep,
    and lit
  Lamps which out-burn'd Canopus. O
    my life
In Egypt! O the dalliance and the wit,
  The flattery and the strife,

'And the wild kiss, when fresh from war's
    alarms,
  My Hercules, my Roman Antony,
My mailed Bacchus leapt into my arms,
  Contented there to die!

'And there he died: and when I heard
    my name
  Sigh'd forth with life I would not brook
    my fear
Of the other: with a worm I balk'd his
    fame.
  What else was left? look here!'

(With that she tore her robe apart, and half
  The polish'd argent of her breast to
    sight
Laid bare. Thereto she pointed with a
    laugh,
  Showing the aspick's bite.)

'I died a Queen. The Roman soldier
    found
  Me lying dead, my crown about my
    brows,

A name for ever!—lying robed and
    crown'd,
  Worthy a Roman spouse.'

Her warbling voice, a lyre of widest range
  Struck by all passion, did fall down
    and glance
From tone to tone, and glided thro' all
    change
  Of liveliest utterance.

When she made pause I knew not for
    delight;
  Because with sudden motion from the
    ground
She raised her piercing orbs, and fill'd with
    light
  The interval of sound.

Still with their fires Love tipt his keenest
    darts;
  As once they drew into two burning rings
All beams of Love, melting the mighty
    hearts
  Of captains and of kings.

Slowly my sense undazzled. Then I heard
  A noise of some one coming thro' the
    lawn,
And singing clearer than the crested bird
  That claps his wings at dawn.

'The torrent brooks of hallow'd Israel
  From craggy hollows pouring, late and
    soon,
Sound all night long, in falling thro' the
    dell,
  Far-heard beneath the moon.

'The balmy moon of blessed Israel
  Floods all the deep-blue gloom with
    beams divine:
All night the splinter'd crags that wall
    the dell
  With spires of silver shine.'

As one that museth where broad sunshine
    laves
  The lawn by some cathedral, thro' the
    door
Hearing the holy organ rolling waves
  Of sound on roof and floor

Within, and anthem sung, is charm'd and
  tied
    To where he stands,—so stood I, when
    that flow
Of music left the lips of her that died
  To save her father's vow ;

The daughter of the warrior Gileadite,
  A maiden pure ; as when she went
  along
From Mizpeh's tower'd gate with welcome
  light,
  With timbrel and with song.

My words leapt forth : 'Heaven heads
  the count of crimes
    With that wild oath.' She render'd
    answer high :
' Not so, nor once alone ; a thousand times
  I would be born and die.

'Single I grew, like some green plant,
  whose root
    Creeps to the garden water-pipes be-
    neath,
Feeding the flower ; but ere my flower
  to fruit
    Changed, I was ripe for death.

' My God, my land, my father—these did
  move
    Me from my bliss of life, that Nature
    gave,
Lower'd softly with a threefold cord of
  love
    Down to a silent grave.

' And I went mourning, "No fair Hebrew
  boy
    Shall smile away my maiden blame
    among
The Hebrew mothers"—emptied of all
  joy,
    Leaving the dance and song,

' Leaving the olive-gardens far below,
  Leaving the promise of my bridal
  bower,
The valleys of grape-loaded vines that
  glow
    Beneath the battled tower.

' The light white cloud swam over us.
  Anon
    We heard the lion roaring from his den ;
We saw the large white stars rise one by
  one,
    Or, from the darken'd glen,

' Saw God divide the night with flying
  flame,
    And thunder on the everlasting hills.
I heard Him, for He spake, and grief
  became
    A solemn scorn of ills.

' When the next moon was roll'd into
  the sky,
    Strength came to me that equall'd my
    desire.
How beautiful a thing it was to die
  For God and for my sire !

' It comforts me in this one thought to
  dwell,
    That I subdued me to my father's will ;
Because the kiss he gave me, ere I fell,
    Sweetens the spirit still.

' Moreover it is written that my race
  Hew'd Ammon, hip and thigh, from
  Aroer
On Arnon unto Minneth.' Here her face
  Glow'd, as I look'd at her.

She lock'd her lips : she left me where I
  stood :
    ' Glory to God,' she sang, and past
    afar,
Thridding the sombre boskage of the wood,
  Toward the morning-star.

Losing her carol I stood pensively,
  As one that from a casement leans his
  head,
When midnight bells cease ringing suddenly,
    And the old year is dead.

' Alas ! alas !' a low voice, full of care,
  Murmur'd beside me : ' Turn and look
  on me :
I am that Rosamond, whom men call fair,
    If what I was I be.

'Would I had been some maiden coarse
  and poor !
  O me, that I should ever see the light !
Those dragon eyes of anger'd Eleanor
  Do hunt me, day and night.'

She ceased in tears, fallen from hope and
  trust :
  To whom the Egyptian : ' O, you
  tamely died !
You should have clung to Fulvia's waist,
  and thrust
  The dagger thro' her side.'

With that sharp sound the white dawn's
  creeping beams,
  Stol'n to my brain, dissolved the mystery
Of folded sleep. The captain of my
  dreams
  Ruled in the eastern sky.

Morn broaden'd on the borders of the
  dark,
  Ere I saw her, who clasp'd in her last
  trance
Her murder'd father's head, or Joan of
  Arc,
  A light of ancient France ;

Or her who knew that Love can vanquish
  Death,
  Who kneeling, with one arm about
  her king,
Drew forth the poison with her balmy
  breath,
  Sweet as new buds in Spring.

No memory labours longer from the deep
  Gold-mines of thought to lift the
  hidden ore
That glimpses, moving up, than I from
  sleep
  To gather and tell o'er

Each little sound and sight. With what
  dull pain
  Compass'd, how eagerly I sought to
  strike
Into that wondrous track of dreams
  again !
  But no two dreams are like.

As when a soul laments, which hath been
  blest,
  Desiring what is mingled with past
  years,
In yearnings that can never be exprest
  By signs or groans or tears ;

Because all words, tho' cull'd with choicest
  art,
  Failing to give the bitter of the sweet,
Wither beneath the palate, and the heart
  Faints, faded by its heat.

THE BLACKBIRD.

O BLACKBIRD ! sing me something well :
  While all the neighbours shoot thee
  round,
  I keep smooth plats of fruitful ground,
Where thou may'st warble, eat and dwell.

The espaliers and the standards all
  Are thine ; the range of lawn and
  park :
  The unnetted black-hearts ripen dark,
All thine, against the garden wall.

Yet, tho' I spared thee all the spring,
  Thy sole delight is, sitting still,
  With that gold dagger of thy bill
To fret the summer jenneting.

A golden bill ! the silver tongue,
  Cold February loved, is dry :
  Plenty corrupts the melody
That made thee famous once, when
  young :

And in the sultry garden-squares,
  Now thy flute-notes are changed to
  coarse,
  I hear thee not at all, or hoarse
As when a hawker hawks his wares.

Take warning ! he that will not sing
  While yon sun prospers in the blue,
  Shall sing for want, ere leaves are
  new,
Caught in the frozen palms of Spring.

THE DEATH OF THE OLD YEAR.

FULL knee-deep lies the winter snow,
  And the winter winds are wearily sigh-
    ing :
Toll ye the church-bell sad and slow,
And tread softly and speak low,
For the old year lies a-dying.
      Old year, you must not die ;
      You came to us so readily,
      You lived with us so steadily,
      Old year, you shall not die.

He lieth still : he doth not move :
He will not see the dawn of day.
He hath no other life above.
He gave me a friend, and a true true-love,
And the New-year will take 'em away.
      Old year, you must not go ;
      So long as you have been with us,
      Such joy as you have seen with us,
      Old year, you shall not go.

He froth'd his bumpers to the brim ;
A jollier year we shall not see.
But tho' his eyes are waxing dim,
And tho' his foes speak ill of him,
He was a friend to me.
      Old year, you shall not die ;
      We did so laugh and cry with you,
      I've half a mind to die with you,
      Old year, if you must die.

He was full of joke and jest,
But all his merry quips are o'er.
To see him die, across the waste
His son and heir doth ride post-haste,
But he'll be dead before.
      Every one for his own.
      The night is starry and cold, my
        friend,
      And the New-year blithe and bold,
        my friend,
      Comes up to take his own.

How hard he breathes ! over the snow
I heard just now the crowing cock.
The shadows flicker to and fro :
The cricket chirps : the light burns low :
'Tis nearly twelve o'clock.

Shake hands, before you die.
Old year, we'll dearly rue for you :
What is it we can do for you ?
Speak out before you die.

His face is growing sharp and thin.
Alack ! our friend is gone.
Close up his eyes : tie up his chin :
Step from the corpse, and let him in
That standeth there alone,
      And waiteth at the door.
      There's a new foot on the floor, my
        friend,
      And a new face at the door, my
        friend,
      A new face at the door.

TO J. S.

THE wind, that beats the mountain, blows
  More softly round the open wold,
And gently comes the world to those
  That are cast in gentle mould.

And me this knowledge bolder made,
  Or else I had not dared to flow
In these words toward you, and invade
  Even with a verse your holy woe.

'Tis strange that those we lean on most,
  Those in whose laps our limbs are
    nursed,
Fall into shadow, soonest lost :
  Those we love first are taken first.

God gives us love.   Something to love
  He lends us ; but, when love is grown
To ripeness, that on which it throve
  Falls off, and love is left alone.

This is the curse of time.   Alas !
  In grief I am not all unlearn'd ;
Once thro' mine own doors Death did
    pass ;
  One went, who never hath return'd.

He will not smile—not speak to me
  Once more.   Two years his chair is
    seen
Empty before us.   That was he
  Without whose life I had not been.

Your loss is rarer; for this star
　　Rose with you thro' a little arc
Of heaven, nor having wander'd far
　　Shot on the sudden into dark.

I knew your brother: his mute dust
　　I honour and his living worth:
A man more pure and bold and just
　　Was never born into the earth.

I have not look'd upon you nigh,
　　Since that dear soul hath fall'n asleep.
Great Nature is more wise than I:
　　I will not tell you not to weep.

And tho' mine own eyes fill with dew,
　　Drawn from the spirit thro' the brain,
I will not even preach to you,
　　'Weep, weeping dulls the inward
　　　　pain.'

Let Grief be her own mistress still.
　　She loveth her own anguish deep
More than much pleasure.　Let her will
　　Be done—to weep or not to weep.

I will not say, 'God's ordinance
　　Of Death is blown in every wind;'
For that is not a common chance
　　That takes away a noble mind.

His memory long will live alone
　　In all our hearts, as mournful light
That broods above the fallen sun,
　　And dwells in heaven half the night.

Vain solace! Memory standing near
　　Cast down her eyes, and in her
　　　　throat
Her voice seem'd distant, and a tear
　　Dropt on the letters as I wrote.

I wrote I know not what.　In truth,
　　How *should* I soothe you anyway,
Who miss the brother of your youth?
　　Yet something I did wish to say:

For he too was a friend to me:
　　Both are my friends, and my true
　　　　breast
Bleedeth for both; yet it may be
　　That only silence suiteth best.

Words weaker than your grief would
　　make
　　Grief more.　'Twere better I should
　　　　cease
Although myself could almost take
　　The place of him that sleeps in
　　　　peace.

Sleep sweetly, tender heart, in peace:
　　Sleep, holy spirit, blessed soul,
While the stars burn, the moons increase,
　　And the great ages onward roll.

Sleep till the end, true soul and sweet.
　　Nothing comes to thee new or strange.
Sleep full of rest from head to feet;
　　Lie still, dry dust, secure of change.

ON A MOURNER.

I.

NATURE, so far as in her lies,
　　Imitates God, and turns her face
To every land beneath the skies,
　　Counts nothing that she meets with
　　　　base,
　　But lives and loves in every place;

II.

Fills out the homely quickset-screens,
　　And makes the purple lilac ripe,
Steps from her airy hill, and greens
　　The swamp, where humm'd the drop-
　　　　ping snipe,
　　With moss and braided marish-pipe;

III.

And on thy heart a finger lays,
　　Saying, 'Beat quicker, for the time '
Is pleasant, and the woods and ways
　　Are pleasant, and the beech and lime
　　Put forth and feel a gladder clime.'

IV.

And murmurs of a deeper voice,
　　Going before to some far shrine,
Teach that sick heart the stronger choice,
　　Till all thy life one way incline
　　With one wide Will that closes thine.

V.

And when the zoning eve has died
　Where yon dark valleys wind forlorn,
Come Hope and Memory, spouse and
　　bride,
　From out the borders of the morn,
　With that fair child betwixt them born.

VI.

And when no mortal motion jars
　The blackness round the tombing sod,
Thro' silence and the trembling stars
　Comes Faith from tracts no feet have
　　trod,
　And Virtue, like a household god

VII.

Promising empire ; such as those
　Once heard at dead of night to greet
Troy's wandering prince, so that he rose
　With sacrifice, while all the fleet
　Had rest by stony hills of Crete.

———

You ask me, why, tho' ill at ease,
　Within this region I subsist,
　Whose spirits falter in the mist,
And languish for the purple seas.

It is the land that freemen till,
　That sober-suited Freedom chose,
　The land, where girt with friends or
　　foes
A man may speak the thing he will ;

A land of settled government,
　A land of just and old renown,
　Where Freedom slowly broadens
　　down
From precedent to precedent :

Where faction seldom gathers head,
　But by degrees to fullness wrought,
　The strength of some diffusive thought
Hath time and space to work and spread.

Should banded unions persecute
　Opinion, and induce a time
　When single thought is civil crime,
And individual freedom mute ;

Tho' Power should make from land to
　　land
　The name of Britain trebly great—
　Tho' every channel of the State
Should fill and choke with golden sand—

Yet waft me from the harbour-mouth,
　Wild wind ! I seek a warmer sky,
　And I will see before I die
The palms and temples of the South.

———

Of old sat Freedom on the heights,
　The thunders breaking at her feet :
Above her shook the starry lights :
　She heard the torrents meet.

There in her place she did rejoice,
　Self-gather'd in her prophet-mind,
But fragments of her mighty voice
　Came rolling on the wind.

Then stept she down thro' town and field
　To mingle with the human race,
And part by part to men reveal'd
　The fullness of her face—

Grave mother of majestic works,
　From her isle-altar gazing down,
Who, God-like, grasps the triple forks,
　And, King-like, wears the crown :

Her open eyes desire the truth.
　The wisdom of a thousand years
Is in them. May perpetual youth
　Keep dry their light from tears ;

That her fair form may stand and shine,
　Make bright our days and light our
　　dreams,
Turning to scorn with lips divine
　The falsehood of extremes !

———

Love thou thy land, with love far-brought
　From out the storied Past, and used
　Within the Present, but transfused
Thro' future time by power of thought.

True love turn'd round on fixed poles,
  Love, that endures not sordid ends,
  For English natures, freemen, friends,
Thy brothers and immortal souls.

But pamper not a hasty time,
  Nor feed with crude imaginings
  The herd, wild hearts and feeble wings
That every sophister can lime.

Deliver not the tasks of might
  To weakness, neither hide the ray
  From those, not blind, who wait for
      day,
Tho' sitting girt with doubtful light.

Make knowledge circle with the winds ;
  But let her herald, Reverence, fly
  Before her to whatever sky
Bear seed of men and growth of minds.

Watch what main-currents draw the years :
  Cut Prejudice against the grain :
  But gentle words are always gain :
Regard the weakness of thy peers :

Nor toil for title, place, or touch
  Of pension, neither count on praise :
  It grows to guerdon after-days :
Nor deal in watch-words overmuch :

Not clinging to some ancient saw ;
  Not master'd by some modern term ;
  Not swift nor slow to change, but firm :
And in its season bring the law ;

That from Discussion's lip may fall
  With Life, that, working strongly,
      binds—
  Set in all lights by many minds,
To close the interests of all.

For Nature also, cold and warm,
  And moist and dry, devising long,
  Thro' many agents making strong,
Matures the individual form.

Meet is it changes should control
  Our being, lest we rust in ease.
  We all are changed by still degrees,
All but the basis of the soul.

So let the change which comes be free
  To ingroove itself with that which flies,
  And work, a joint of state, that plies
Its office, moved with sympathy.

A saying, hard to shape in act ;
  For all the past of Time reveals
  A bridal dawn of thunder-peals,
Wherever Thought hath wedded Fact.

Ev'n now we hear with inward strife
  A motion toiling in the gloom—
  The Spirit of the years to come
Yearning to mix himself with Life.

A slow-develop'd strength awaits
  Completion in a painful school ;
  Phantoms of other forms of rule,
New Majesties of mighty States—

The warders of the growing hour,
  But vague in vapour, hard to mark ;
  And round them sea and air are dark
With great contrivances of Power.

Of many changes, aptly join'd,
  Is bodied forth the second whole.
  Regard gradation, lest the soul
Of Discord race the rising wind ;

A wind to puff your idol-fires,
  And heap their ashes on the head ;
  To shame the boast so often made,
That we are wiser than our sires.

Oh yet, if Nature's evil star
  Drive men in manhood, as in youth,
  To follow flying steps of Truth
Across the brazen bridge of war—

If New and Old, disastrous feud,
  Must ever shock, like armed foes,
  And this be true, till Time shall close,
That Principles are rain'd in blood ;

Not yet the wise of heart would cease
  To hold his hope thro' shame and guilt,
  But with his hand against the hilt,
Would pace the troubled land, like
      Peace ;

Not less, tho' dogs of Faction bay,
    Would serve his kind in deed and word,
    Certain, if knowledge bring the sword,
That knowledge takes the sword away—

Would love the gleams of good that broke
    From either side, nor veil his eyes :
    And if some dreadful need should rise
Would strike, and firmly, and one stroke :

To-morrow yet would reap to-day,
    As we bear blossom of the dead ;
    Earn well the thrifty months, nor wed
Raw Haste, half-sister to Delay.

ENGLAND AND AMERICA
IN 1782.

O THOU, that sendest out the man
    To rule by land and sea,
Strong mother of a Lion-line,
Be proud of those strong sons of thine
    Who wrench'd their rights from thee !

What wonder, if in noble heat
    Those men thine arms withstood,
Retaught the lesson thou hadst taught,
And in thy spirit with thee fought—
    Who sprang from English blood !

But Thou rejoice with liberal joy,
    Lift up thy rocky face,
And shatter, when the storms are black,
In many a streaming torrent back,
    The seas that shock thy base !

Whatever harmonies of law
    The growing world assume,
Thy work is thine—The single note
From that deep chord which Hampden
        smote
    Will vibrate to the doom.

THE GOOSE.

I KNEW an old wife lean and poor,
    Her rags scarce held together ;
There strode a stranger to the door,
    And it was windy weather.

He held a goose upon his arm,
    He utter'd rhyme and reason,
'Here, take the goose, and keep you
        warm,
    It is a stormy season.'

She caught the white goose by the leg,
    A goose—'twas no great matter.
The goose let fall a golden egg
    With cackle and with clatter.

She dropt the goose, and caught the
        pelf,
    And ran to tell her neighbours ;
And bless'd herself, and cursed herself,
    And rested from her labours.

And feeding high, and living soft,
    Grew plump and able-bodied ;
Until the grave churchwarden doff'd,
    The parson smirk'd and nodded.

So sitting, served by man and maid,
    She felt her heart grow prouder :
But ah ! the more the white goose laid
    It clack'd and cackled louder.

It clutter'd here, it chuckled there ;
    It stirr'd the old wife's mettle :
She shifted in her elbow-chair,
    And hurl'd the pan and kettle.

'A quinsy choke thy cursed note !'
    Then wax'd her anger stronger.
'Go, take the goose, and wring her throat,
    I will not bear it longer.'

Then yelp'd the cur, and yawl'd the cat ;
    Ran Gaffer, stumbled Gammer.
The goose flew this way and flew that,
    And fill'd the house with clamour.

As head and heels upon the floor
    They flounder'd all together,
There strode a stranger to the door,
    And it was windy weather :

He took the goose upon his arm,
    He utter'd words of scorning ;
'So keep you cold, or keep you warm,
    It is a stormy morning.'

The wild wind rang from park and plain,
   And round the attics rumbled,
Till all the tables danced again,
   And half the chimneys tumbled.

The glass blew in, the fire blew out,
   The blast was hard and harder.

Her cap blew off, her gown blew up,
   And a whirlwind clear'd the larder:

And while on all sides breaking loose
   Her household fled the danger,
Quoth she, 'The Devil take the goose,
   And God forget the stranger!'

ENGLISH IDYLS

AND OTHER POEMS.

THE EPIC.

AT Francis Allen's on the Christmas-
   eve,—
The game of forfeits done—the girls all
   kiss'd
Beneath the sacred bush and past away—
The parson Holmes, the poet Everard
   Hall,
The host, and I sat round the wassail-
   bowl,
Then half-way ebb'd : and there we held
   a talk,
How all the old honour had from Christmas
   gone,
Or gone, or dwindled down to some odd
   games
In some odd nooks like this ; till I, tired
   out
With cutting eights that day upon the
   pond,
Where, three times slipping from the
   outer edge,
I bump'd the ice into three several stars,
Fell in a doze ; and half-awake I heard
The parson taking wide and wider
   sweeps,
Now harping on the church - commis-
   sioners,
Now hawking at Geology and schism ;
Until I woke, and found him settled down
Upon the general decay of faith
Right thro' the world, 'at home was little
   left,

And none abroad : there was no anchor,
   none,
To hold by.' Francis, laughing, clapt
   his hand
On Everard's shoulder, with ' I hold by
   him.'
' And I,' quoth Everard, ' by the wassail-
   bowl.'
' Why yes,' I said, 'we knew your gift
   that way
At college : but another which you had,
I mean of verse (for so we held it then),
What came of that ?' ' You know,' said
   Frank, ' he burnt
His epic, his King Arthur, some twelve
   books '—
And then to me demanding why ? ' Oh,
   sir,
He thought that nothing new was said,
   or else
Something so said 'twas nothing—that a
   truth
Looks freshest in the fashion of the day :
God knows : he has a mint of reasons : ask.
It pleased *me* well enough.' ' Nay, nay,'
   said Hall,
'Why take the style of those heroic times?
For nature brings not back the Mastodon,
Nor we those times ; and why should any
   man
Remodel models ? these twelve books of
   mine
Were faint Homeric echoes, nothing-
   worth,

Mere chaff and draff, much better burnt.'
'But I,'
Said Francis, 'pick'd the eleventh from
this hearth
And have it : keep a thing, its use will
come.
I hoard it as a sugar-plum for Holmes.'
He laugh'd, and I, tho' sleepy, like a
horse
That hears the corn-bin open, prick'd my
ears ;
For I remember'd Everard's college fame
When we were Freshmen : then at my
request
He brought it ; and the poet little urged,
But with some prelude of disparagement,
Read, mouthing out his hollow oes and
aes,
Deep-chested music, and to this result.

✻ MORTE D'ARTHUR.

So all day long the noise of battle roll'd
Among the mountains by the winter sea ;
Until King Arthur's table, man by man,
Had fallen in Lyonnesse about their Lord,
King Arthur : then, because his wound
was deep,
The bold Sir Bedivere uplifted him,
Sir Bedivere, the last of all his knights,
And bore him to a chapel nigh the field,
A broken chancel with a broken cross,
That stood on a dark strait of barren land.
On one side lay the Ocean, and on one
Lay a great water, and the moon was
full.
    Then spake King Arthur to Sir
    Bedivere :
'The sequel of to-day unsolders all
The goodliest fellowship of famous knights
Whereof this world holds record.   Such
a sleep
They sleep—the men I loved. I think
that we
Shall never more, at any future time,
Delight our souls with talk of knightly
deeds,
Walking about the gardens and the halls
Of Camelot, as in the days that were.
I perish by this people which I made,—

Tho' Merlin sware that I should come
again
To rule once more——but let what will be,
be,
I am so deeply smitten thro' the helm
That without help I cannot last till morn.
Thou therefore take my brand Excalibur,
Which was my pride : for thou remem-
berest how
In those old days, one summer noon, an
arm
Rose up from out the bosom of the lake,
Clothed in white samite, mystic, won-
derful,
Holding the sword—and how I row'd
across
And took it, and have worn it, like a
king :
And, wheresoever I am sung or told
In aftertime, this also shall be known :
But now delay not : take Excalibur,
And fling him far into the middle mere :
Watch what thou seëst, and lightly bring
me word.'

    To him replied the bold Sir Bedivere :
'It is not meet, Sir King, to leave thee
thus,
Aidless, alone, and smitten thro' the helm.
A little thing may harm a wounded man.
Yet I thy hest will all perform at full,
Watch what I see, and lightly bring thee
word.'

    So saying, from the ruin'd shrine he
    stept
And in the moon athwart the place of
tombs,
Where lay the mighty bones of ancient
men,
Old knights, and over them the sea-wind
sang
Shrill, chill, with flakes of foam.   He,
stepping down
By zig-zag paths, and juts of pointed rock,
Came on the shining levels of the lake.
    There drew he forth the brand
    Excalibur,
And o'er him, drawing it, the winter
moon,
Brightening the skirts of a long cloud, ran
forth

And sparkled keen with frost against the
    hilt :
For all the haft twinkled with diamond
    sparks,
Myriads of topaz-lights, and jacinth-work
Of subtlest jewellery. He gazed so long
That both his eyes were dazzled, as he
    stood,
This way and that dividing the swift
    mind,
In act to throw : but at the last it seem'd
Better to leave Excalibur conceal'd
There in the many-knotted waterflags,
That whistled stiff and dry about the
    marge.
So strode he back slow to the wounded
    King.
    Then spake King Arthur to Sir Bedi-
      vere :
'Hast thou perform'd my mission which
    I gave ?
What is it thou hast seen ? or what hast
    heard ?'
    And answer made the bold Sir Bedivere :
'I heard the ripple washing in the reeds,
And the wild water lapping on the crag.'
    To whom replied King Arthur, faint
      and pale :
'Thou hast betray'd thy nature and thy
    name,
Not rendering true answer, as beseem'd
Thy fëalty, nor like a noble knight :
For surer sign had follow'd, either hand,
Or voice, or else a motion of the mere.
This is a shameful thing for men to lie.
Yet now, I charge thee, quickly go again
As thou art lief and dear, and do the thing
I bad thee, watch, and lightly bring me
    word.'
    Then went Sir Bedivere the second time
Across the ridge, and paced beside the
    mere,
Counting the dewy pebbles, fix'd in
    thought ;
But when he saw the wonder of the hilt,
How curiously and strangely chased, he
    smote
His palms together, and he cried aloud,
    'And if indeed I cast the brand away,
Surely a precious thing, one worthy note,

Should thus be lost for ever from the earth,
Which might have pleased the eyes of
    many men.
What good should follow this, if this were
    done ?
What harm, undone ? deep harm to dis-
    obey,
Seeing obedience is the bond of rule.
Were it well to obey then, if a king demand
An act unprofitable, against himself ?
The King is sick, and knows not what he
    does.
What record, or what relic of my lord
Should be to aftertime, but empty breath
And rumours of a doubt ? but were this
    kept,
Stored in some treasure-house of mighty
    kings,
Some one might show it at a joust of arms,
Saying, "King Arthur's sword, Excalibur,
Wrought by the lonely maiden of the Lake.
Nine years she wrought it, sitting in the
    deeps
Upon the hidden bases of the hills."
So might some old man speak in the
    aftertime
To all the people, winning reverence.
But now much honour and much fame
    were lost.'
    So spake he, clouded with his own
      conceit,
And hid Excalibur the second time,
And so strode back slow to the wounded
    King.
    Then spoke King Arthur, breathing
      heavily :
'What is it thou hast seen? or what hast
    heard ?'
    And answer made the bold Sir Bedivere :
'I heard the water lapping on the crag,
And the long ripple washing in the reeds.'
    To whom replied King Arthur, much
      in wrath :
'Ah, miserable and unkind, untrue,
Unknightly, traitor-hearted ! Woe is me !
Authority forgets a dying king,
Laid widow'd of the power in his eye
That bow'd the will. I see thee what
    thou art,
For thou, the latest-left of all my knights

In whom should meet the offices of all,
Thou wouldst betray me for the precious
    hilt ;
Either from lust of gold, or like a girl
Valuing the giddy pleasure of the eyes.
Yet, for a man may fail in duty twice,
And the third time may prosper, get thee
    hence :
But, if thou spare to fling Excalibur,
I will arise and slay thee with my hands.'
    Then quickly rose Sir Bedivere, and
        ran,
And, leaping down the ridges lightly,
    plunged
Among the bulrush-beds, and clutch'd the
    sword,
And strongly wheel'd and threw it.   The
    great brand
Made lightnings in the splendour of the
    moon,
And flashing round and round, and whirl'd
    in an arch,
Shot like a streamer of the northern morn,
Seen where the moving isles of winter
    shock
By night, with noises of the northern sea.
So flash'd and fell the brand Excalibur :
But ere he dipt the surface, rose an arm
Clothed in white samite, mystic, won-
    derful,
And caught him by the hilt, and bran-
    dish'd him
Three times, and drew him under in the
    mere.
And lightly went the other to the King.
    Then spoke King Arthur, drawing
        thicker breath :
' Now see I by thine eyes that this is
    done.
Speak out : what is it thou hast heard, or
    seen ?'
    And answer made the bold Sir Bedivere :
' Sir King, I closed mine eyelids, lest the
    gems
Should blind my purpose, for I never saw,
Nor shall see, here or elsewhere, till I die,
Not tho' I live three lives of mortal men,
So great a miracle as yonder hilt.
Then with both hands I flung him, wheel-
    ing him ;

But when I look'd again, behold an arm,
Clothed in white samite, mystic, won-
    derful,
That caught him by the hilt, and bran-
    dish'd him
Three times, and drew him under in the
    mere.'
    And answer made King Arthur, breath-
        ing hard :
' My end draws nigh ; 'tis time that I
    were gone.
Make broad thy shoulders to receive my
    weight,
And bear me to the margin ; yet I fear
My wound hath taken cold, and I shall
    die.'
    So saying, from the pavement he half
        rose,
Slowly, with pain, reclining on his arm,
And looking wistfully with wide blue eyes
As in a picture.   Him Sir Bedivere
Remorsefully regarded thro' his tears,
And would have spoken, but he found
    not words,
Then took with care, and kneeling on
    one knee,
O'er both his shoulders drew the languid
    hands,
And rising bore him thro' the place of
    tombs.
    But, as he walk'd, King Arthur panted
        hard,
Like one that feels a nightmare on his bed
When all the house is mute.   So sigh'd
    the King,
Muttering and murmuring at his ear,
        ' Quick, quick !
I fear it is too late, and I shall die.'
But the other swiftly strode from ridge to
    ridge,
Clothed with his breath, and looking, as
    he walk'd,
Larger than human on the frozen hills.
He heard the deep behind him, and a
    cry
Before.   His own thought drove him, like
    a goad.
Dry clash'd his harness in the icy caves
And barren chasms, and all to left and
    right

The bare black cliff clang'd round him,
    as he based
His feet on juts of slippery crag that rang
Sharp-smitten with the dint of armed
    heels—
And on a sudden, lo ! the level lake,
And the long glories of the winter moon.
    Then saw they how there hove a dusky
    barge,
Dark as a funeral scarf from stem to stern,
Beneath them ; and descending they were
    ware
That all the decks were dense with stately
    forms
Black-stoled, black-hooded, like a dream
    —by these
Three Queens with crowns of gold—and
    from them rose
A cry that shiver'd to the tingling stars,
And, as it were one voice an agony
Of lamentation, like a wind, that shrills
All night in a waste land, where no one
    comes,
Or hath come, since the making of the
    world.
    Then murmur'd Arthur, ' Place me in
    the barge,'
And to the barge they came. There those
    three Queens
Put forth their hands, and took the King,
    and wept. ·
But she, that rose the tallest of them all
And fairest, laid his head upon her lap,
And loosed the shatter'd casque, and
    chafed his hands,
And call'd him by his name, complaining
    loud,
And dropping bitter tears against his brow
Striped with dark blood : for all his face
    was white
And colourless, and like the wither'd
    moon
Smote by the fresh beam of the springing
    east ;
And all his greaves and cuisses dash'd
    with drops
Of onset ; and the light and lustrous curls—
That made his forehead like a rising sun
High from the daïs-throne—were parch'd
    with dust ;

Or, clotted into points and hanging loose,
Mix'd with the knightly growth that
    fringed his lips.
So like a shatter'd column lay the King ;
Not like that Arthur who, with lance in
    rest,
From spur to plume a star of tournament,
Shot thro' the lists at Camelot, and charged
Before the eyes of ladies and of kings.
    Then loudly cried the bold Sir Bedivere,
' Ah ! my Lord Arthur, whither shall I
    go ?
Where shall I hide my forehead and my
    eyes ?
For now I see the true old times are dead,
When every morning brought a noble
    chance,
And every chance brought out a noble
    knight.
Such times have been not since the light
    that led
The holy Elders with the gift of myrrh.
But now the whole ROUND TABLE is
    dissolved
Which was an image of the mighty world ;
And I, the last, go forth companionless,
And the days darken round me, and the
    years,
Among new men, strange faces, other
    minds.'
    And slowly answered Arthur from the
    barge :
' The old order changeth, yielding place
    to new,
And God fulfils Himself in many ways,
Lest one good custom should corrupt the
    world.
Comfort thyself : what comfort is in me ?
I have lived my life, and that which I
    have done
May He within Himself make pure ! but
    thou,
If thou shouldst never see my face again,
Pray for my soul. More things are
    wrought by prayer
Than this world dreams of. Wherefore,
    let thy voice
Rise like a fountain for me night and day.
For what are men better than sheep or
    goats

That nourish a blind life within the brain,
If, knowing God, they lift not hands of
    prayer
Both for themselves and those who call
    them friend ?
For so the whole round earth is every way
Bound by gold chains about the feet of
    God.
But now farewell.   I am going a long way
With these thou seëst—if indeed I go—
(For all my mind is clouded with a doubt)
To the island-valley of Avilion ;
Where falls not hail, or rain, or any snow,
Nor ever wind blows loudly ; but it lies
Deep-meadow'd, happy, fair with orchard-
    lawns
And bowery hollows crown'd with summer
    sea,
Where I will heal me of my grievous
    wound.'
    So said he, and the barge with oar and
    sail
Moved from the brink, like some full-
    breasted swan
That, fluting a wild carol ere her death,
Ruffles her pure cold plume, and takes
    the flood
With swarthy webs.   Long stood Sir
    Bedivere
Revolving many memories, till the hull
Look'd one black dot against the verge
    of dawn,
And on the mere the wailing died away.

HERE ended Hall, and our last light,
    that long
Had wink'd and threaten'd darkness,
    flared and fell :
At which the Parson, sent to sleep with
    sound,
And waked with silence, grunted 'Good !'
    but we
Sat rapt : it was the tone with which he
    read—
Perhaps some modern touches here and
    there
Redeem'd it from the charge of nothing-
    ness—
Or else we loved the man, and prized his
    work ;

I know not : but we sitting, as I said,
The cock crew loud ; as at that time
    of year
The lusty bird takes every hour for dawn :
Then Francis, muttering, like a man
    ill-used,
'There now—that's nothing !' drew a
    little back,
And drove his heel into the smoulder'd
    log,
That sent a blast of sparkles up the flue :
And so to bed ; where yet in sleep I seem'd
To sail with Arthur under looming shores,
Point after point ; till on to dawn, when
    dreams
Begin to feel the truth and stir of day,
To me, methought, who waited with a
    crowd,
There came a bark that, blowing forward,
    bore
King Arthur, like a modern gentleman
Of stateliest port ; and all the people
    cried,
' Arthur is come again : he cannot die.'
Then those that stood upon the hills
    behind
Repeated—' Come again, and thrice as
    fair ;'
And, further inland, voices echo'd —
    ' Come
With all good things, and war shall be
    no more.'
At this a hundred bells began to peal,
That with the sound I woke, and heard
    indeed
The clear church-bells ring in the
    Christmas-morn.

THE GARDENER'S
DAUGHTER ;

OR, THE PICTURES.

THIS morning is the morning of the day
When I and Eustace from the city went
To see the Gardener's Daughter ; I and he,
Brothers in Art ; a friendship so complete
Portion'd in halves between us, that we
    grew
The fable of the city where we dwelt.

My Eustace might have sat for Hercules ;
So muscular he spread, so broad of breast.
He, by some law that holds in love, and
        draws
The greater to the lesser, long desired
A certain miracle of symmetry,
A miniature of loveliness, all grace
Summ'd up and closed in little ;—Juliet,
        she
So light of foot, so light of spirit—oh, she
To me myself, for some three careless
        moons,
The summer pilot of an empty heart
Unto the shores of nothing ! Know you not
Such touches are but embassies of love,
To tamper with the feelings, ere he found
Empire for life ? but Eustace painted her,
And said to me, she sitting with us then,
'When will *you* paint like this ?' and I
        replied,
My words were half in earnest, half in
        jest,)
'Tis not your work, but Love's.   Love,
        unperceived,
A more ideal Artist he than all,
Came, drew your pencil from you, made
        those eyes
Darker than darkest pansies, and that hair
More black than ashbuds in the front of
        March.'
And Juliet answer'd laughing, 'Go and see
The Gardener's daughter : trust me, after
        that,
You scarce can fail to match his master-
        piece.'
And up we rose, and on the spur we went.
   Not wholly in the busy world, nor quite
Beyond it, blooms the garden that I love.
News from the humming city comes to it
In sound of funeral or of marriage bells ;
And, sitting muffled in dark leaves, you
        hear
The windy clanging of the minster clock ;
Although between it and the garden lies
A league of grass, wash'd by a slow broad
        stream,
That, stirr'd with languid pulses of the oar,
Waves all its lazy lilies, and creeps on,
Barge-laden, to three arches of a bridge
Crown'd with the minster-towers.

The fields between
Are dewy-fresh, browsed by deep-udder'd
        kine,
And all about the large lime feathers low,
The lime a summer home of murmurous
        wings.
   In that still place she, hoarded in herself,
Grew, seldom seen ; not less among us
        lived
Her fame from lip to lip.   Who had not
        heard
Of Rose, the Gardener's daughter ? Where
        was he,
So blunt in memory, so old at heart,
At such a distance from his youth in grief,
That, having seen, forgot ?   The common
        mouth,
So gross to express delight, in praise of
        her
Grew oratory.   Such a lord is Love,
And Beauty such a mistress of the world.
   And if I said that Fancy, led by Love,
Would play with flying forms and images,
Yet this is also true, that, long before
I look'd upon her, when I heard her name
My heart was like a prophet to my heart,
And told me I should love.   A crowd of
        hopes,
That sought to sow themselves like
        winged seeds,
Born out of everything I heard and saw,
Flutter'd about my senses and my soul ;
And vague desires, like fitful blasts of
        balm
To one that travels quickly, made the air
Of Life delicious, and all kinds of thought,
That verged upon them, sweeter than the
        dream
Dream'd by a happy man, when the dark
        East,
Unseen, is brightening to his bridal morn.
   And sure this orbit of the memory folds
For ever in itself the day we went
To see her.   All the land in flowery
        squares,
Beneath a broad and equal-blowing wind,
Smelt of the coming summer, as one large
        cloud
Drew downward : but all else of heaven
        was pure

Up to the Sun, and May from verge to
verge,
And May with me from head to heel.
And now,
As tho' 'twere yesterday, as tho' it were
The hour just flown, that morn with all
its sound,
(For those old Mays had thrice the life
of these,)
Rings in mine ears. The steer forgot to
graze,
And, where the hedge-row cuts the
pathway, stood,
Leaning his horns into the neighbour field,
And lowing to his fellows. From the
woods
Came voices of the well-contented doves.
The lark could scarce get out his notes
for joy,
But shook his song together as he near'd
His happy home, the ground. To left
and right,
The cuckoo told his name to all the hills;
The mellow ouzel fluted in the elm;
The redcap whistled; and the nightingale
Sang loud, as tho' he were the bird of day.
    And Eustace turn'd, and smiling said
    to me,
'Hear how the bushes echo! by my life,
These birds have joyful thoughts. Think
you they sing
Like poets, from the vanity of song?
Or have they any sense of why they sing?
And would they praise the heavens for
what they have?'
And I made answer, 'Were there nothing
else
For which to praise the heavens but only
love,
That only love were cause enough for
praise.'
    Lightly he laugh'd, as one that read
    my thought,
And on we went; but ere an hour had
pass'd,
We reach'd a meadow slanting to the
North;
Down which a well-worn pathway courted
us
To one green wicket in a privet hedge;

This, yielding, gave into a grassy walk
Thro' crowded lilac-ambush trimly pruned;
And one warm gust, full-fed with perfume,
blew
Beyond us, as we enter'd in the cool.
The garden stretches southward. In the
midst
A cedar spread his dark-green layers of
shade.
The garden-glasses glanced, and mom-
ently
The twinkling laurel scatter'd silver lights.
    'Eustace,' I said, 'this wonder keeps
    the house.'
He nodded, but a moment afterwards
He cried, 'Look! look!' Before he ceased
I turn'd,
And, ere a star can wink, beheld her there.
    For up the porch there grew an Eastern
    rose,
That, flowering high, the last night's gale
had caught,
And blown across the walk. One arm
aloft—
Gown'd in pure white, that fitted to the
shape—
Holding the bush, to fix it back, she stood,
A single stream of all her soft brown hair
Pour'd on one side: the shadow of the
flowers
Stole all the golden gloss, and, wavering
Lovingly lower, trembled on her waist—
Ah, happy shade—and still went waver-
ing down,
But, ere it touch'd a foot, that might have
danced
The greensward into greener circles, dipt,
And mix'd with shadows of the common
ground!
But the full day dwelt on her brows, and
sunn'd
Her violet eyes, and all her Hebe bloom,
And doubled his own warmth against her
lips,
And on the bounteous wave of such a
breast
As never pencil drew. Half light, half
shade,
She stood, a sight to make an old man
young.

So rapt, we near'd the house ; but she,
a Rose
In roses, mingled with her fragrant toil,
Nor heard us come, nor from her tendance
turn'd
Into the world without ; till close at hand,
And almost ere I knew mine own intent,
This murmur broke the stillness of that
air
Which brooded round about her :
     ' Ah, one rose,
One rose, but one, by those fair fingers
cull'd,
Were worth a hundred kisses press'd on
lips
Less exquisite than thine.'
     She look'd : but all
Suffused with blushes—neither self-pos-
sess'd
Nor startled, but betwixt this mood and
that,
Divided in a graceful quiet—paused,
And dropt the branch she held, and turn-
ing, wound
Her looser hair in braid, and stirr'd her
lips
For some sweet answer, tho' no answer
came,
Nor yet refused the rose, but granted it,
And moved away, and left me, statue-like,
In act to render thanks.
     I, that whole day,
Saw her no more, altho' I linger'd there
Till every daisy slept, and Love's white
star
Beam'd thro' the thicken'd cedar in the
dusk.
 So home we went, and all the livelong
way
With solemn gibe did Eustace banter me.
' Now,' said he, ' will you climb the top
of Art.
You cannot fail but work in hues to dim
The Titianic Flora. Will you match
My Juliet ? you, not you,—the Master,
Love,
A more ideal Artist he than all.'
 So home I went, but could not sleep
for joy,
Reading her perfect features in the gloom,

Kissing the rose she gave me o'er and o'er,
And shaping faithful record of the glance
That graced the giving—such a noise of
life
Swarm'd in the golden present, such a
voice
Call'd to me from the years to come, and
such
A length of bright horizon rimm'd the
dark.
And all that night I heard the watchman
peal
The sliding season : all that night I heard
The heavy clocks knolling the drowsy
hours.
The drowsy hours, dispensers of all good,
O'er the mute city stole with folded wings,
Distilling odours on me as they went
To greet their fairer sisters of the East.
 Love at first sight, first-born, and heir
to all,
Made this night thus. Henceforward
squall nor storm
Could keep me from that Eden where she
dwelt.
Light pretexts drew me ; sometimes a
Dutch love
For tulips ; then for roses, moss or musk,
To grace my city rooms ; or fruits and
cream
Served in the weeping elm ; and more and
more
A word could bring the colour to my
cheek ;
A thought would fill my eyes with happy
dew ;
Love trebled life within me, and with
each
The year increased.
     The daughters of the year,
One after one, thro' that still garden
pass'd ;
Each garlanded with her peculiar flower
Danced into light, and died into the
shade ;
And each in passing touch'd with some
new grace
Or seem'd to touch her, so that day by
day,
Like one that never can be wholly known,

Her beauty grew ; till Autumn brought
    an hour
For Eustace, when I heard his deep ' I
    will,'
Breathed, like the covenant of a God, to
    hold
From thence thro' all the worlds : but I
    rose up
Full of his bliss, and following her dark
    eyes
Felt earth as air beneath me, till I reach'd
The wicket-gate, and found her standing
    there.
    There sat we down upon a garden
        mound,
Two mutually enfolded ; Love, the third,
Between us, in the circle of his arms
Enwound us both ; and over many a range
Of waning lime the gray cathedral towers,
Across a hazy glimmer of the west,
Reveal'd their shining windows : from
    them clash'd
The bells ; we listen'd ; with the time
    we play'd,
We spoke of other things ; we coursed
    about
The subject most at heart, more near and
    near,
Like doves about a dovecote, wheeling
    round
The central wish, until we settled there.
    Then, in that time and place, I spoke
        to her,
Requiring, tho' I knew it was mine own,
Yet for the pleasure that I took to hear,
Requiring at her hand the greatest gift,
A woman's heart, the heart of her I loved ;
And in that time and place she answer'd
    me,
And in the compass of three little words,
More musical than ever came in one,
The silver fragments of a broken voice,
Made me most happy, faltering, ' I am
    thine.'
    Shall I cease here ? Is this enough to
        say
That my desire, like all strongest hopes,
By its own energy fulfill'd itself,
Merged in completion ? Would you learn
    at full

How passion rose thro' circumstantial
    grades
Beyond all grades develop'd ? and indeed
I had not staid so long to tell you all,
But while I mused came Memory with
    sad eyes,
Holding the folded annals of my youth ;
And while I mused, Love with knit brows
    went by,
And with a flying finger swept my lips,
And spake, ' Be wise : not easily forgiven
Are those, who setting wide the doors that
    bar
The secret bridal chambers of the heart,
Let in the day.' Here, then, my words
    have end.
    Yet might I tell of meetings, of fare-
        wells —
Of that which came between, more sweet
    than each,
In whispers, like the whispers of the
    leaves
That tremble round a nightingale — in
    sighs
Which perfect Joy, perplex'd for utter-
    ance,
Stole from her sister Sorrow. Might I
    not tell
Of difference, reconcilement, pledges
    given,
And vows, where there was never need
    of vows,
And kisses, where the heart on one wild
    leap
Hung tranced from all pulsation, as above
The heavens between their fairy fleeces
    pale
Sow'd all their mystic gulfs with fleeting
    stars ;
Or while the balmy glooming, crescent-lit,
Spread the light haze along the river-
    shores,
And in the hollows ; or as once we met
Unheedful, tho' beneath a whispering
    rain
Night slid down one long stream of sigh-
    ing wind,
And in her bosom bore the baby, Sleep.
    But this whole hour your eyes have
        been intent

On that veil'd picture—veil'd, for what it
holds
May not be dwelt on by the common day.
This prelude has prepared thee.   Raise
thy soul ;
Make thine heart ready with thine eyes :
the time
Is come to raise the veil.
                    Behold her there,
As I beheld her ere she knew my heart,
My first, last love ; the idol of my youth,
The darling of my manhood, and, alas !
Now the most blessed memory of mine
age.

DORA.

WITH farmer Allan at the farm abode
William and Dora.   William was his son,
And she his niece.   He often look'd at
them,
And often thought, ' I'll make them man
and wife.'
Now Dora felt her uncle's will in all,
And yearn'd toward William ; but the
youth, because
He had been always with her in the house,
Thought not of Dora.
                    Then there came a day
When Allan call'd his son, and said,
' My son :
I married late, but I would wish to see
My grandchild on my knees before I die :
And I have set my heart upon a match.
Now therefore look to Dora ; she is well
To look to ; thrifty too beyond her age.
She is my brother's daughter : he and I
Had once hard words, and parted, and
he died
In foreign lands ; but for his sake I bred
His daughter Dora : take her for your
wife ;
For I have wish'd this marriage, night
and day,
For many years.'   But William answer'd
short ;
' I cannot marry Dora ; by my life,
I will not marry Dora.'   Then the old man
Was wroth, and doubled up his hands,
and said :

' You will not, boy ! you dare to answer
thus !
But in my time a father's word was law,
And so it shall be now for me.   Look to
it ;
Consider, William : take a month to
think,
And let me have an answer to my wish ;
Or, by the Lord that made me, you shall
pack,
And never more darken my doors again.'
But William answer'd madly ; bit his
lips,
And broke away.   The more he look'd
at her
The less he liked her ; and his ways were
harsh ;
But Dora bore them meekly.   Then
before
The month was out he left his father's
house,
And hired himself to work within the
fields ;
And half in love, half spite, he woo'd and
wed
A labourer's daughter, Mary Morrison.
    Then, when the bells were ringing,
Allan call'd
His niece and said : ' My girl, I love you
well ;
But if you speak with him that was my
son,
Or change a word with her he calls his
wife,
My home is none of yours.   My will is
law.'
And Dora promised, being meek.   She
thought,
' It cannot be : my uncle's mind will
change !'
    And days went on, and there was born
a boy
To William ; then distresses came on
him ;
And day by day he pass'd his father's
gate,
Heart-broken, and his father help'd him
not.
But Dora stored what little she could
save,

And sent it them by stealth, nor did they
 know
Who sent it ; till at last a fever seized
On William, and in harvest time he died.
 Then Dora went to Mary. Mary sat
And look'd with tears upon her boy, and
 thought
Hard things of Dora. Dora came and
 said :
'I have obey'd my uncle until now,
And I have sinn'd, for it was all thro' me
This evil came on William at the first.
But, Mary, for the sake of him that's
 gone,
And for your sake, the woman that he
 chose,
And for this orphan, I am come to you :
You know there has not been for these
 five years
So full a harvest : let me take the boy,
And I will set him in my uncle's eye
Among the wheat ; that when his heart
 is glad
Of the full harvest, he may see the boy,
And bless him for the sake of him that's
 gone.'
 And Dora took the child, and went
 her way
Across the wheat, and sat upon a mound
That was unsown, where many poppies
 grew.
Far off the farmer came into the field
And spied her not ; for none of all his
 men
Dare tell him Dora waited with the child ;
And Dora would have risen and gone to
 him,
But her heart fail'd her ; and the reapers
 reap'd,
And the sun fell, and all the land was
 dark.
 But when the morrow came, she rose
 and took
The child once more, and sat upon the
 mound ;
And made a little wreath of all the flowers
That grew about, and tied it round his hat
To make him pleasing in her uncle's eye.
Then when the farmer pass'd into the field
He spied her, and he left his men at work,

And came and said : 'Where were you
 yesterday ?
Whose child is that ? What are you doing
 here ?'
So Dora cast her eyes upon the ground,
And answer'd softly, 'This is William's
 child !'
'And did I not,' said Allan, 'did I not
Forbid you, Dora ?' Dora said again :
'Do with me as you will, but take the
 child,
And bless him for the sake of him that's
 gone !'
And Allan said, 'I see it is a trick
Got up betwixt you and the woman there.
I must be taught my duty, and by you !
You knew my word was law, and yet you
 dared
To slight it. Well—for I will take the
 boy ;
But go you hence, and never see me more.'
 So saying, he took the boy that cried
 aloud
And struggled hard. The wreath of
 flowers fell
At Dora's feet. She bow'd upon her
 hands,
And the boy's cry came to her from the
 field,
More and more distant. She bow'd
 down her head,
Remembering the day when first she came,
And all the things that had been. She
 bow'd down
And wept in secret ; and the reapers
 reap'd,
And the sun fell, and all the land was
 dark.
 Then Dora went to Mary's house, and
 stood
Upon the threshold. Mary saw the boy
Was not with Dora. She broke out in
 praise
To God, that help'd her in her widowhood.
And Dora said, ' My uncle took the boy ;
But, Mary, let me live and work with you :
He says that he will never see me more.'
Then answer'd Mary, 'This shall never be,
That thou shouldst take my trouble on
 thyself :

And, now I think, he shall not have the
    boy,
For he will teach him hardness, and to
    slight
His mother ; therefore thou and I will go,
And I will have my boy, and bring him
    home ;
And I will beg of him to take thee back :
But if he will not take thee back again,
Then thou and I will live within one
    house,
And work for William's child, until he
    grows
Of age to help us.'
             So the women kiss'd
Each other, and set out, and reach'd the
    farm.
The door was off the latch : they peep'd,
    and saw
The boy set up betwixt his grandsire's
    knees,
Who thrust him in the hollows of his arm,
And clapt him on the hands and on the
    cheeks,
Like one that loved him : and the lad
    stretch'd out
And babbled for the golden seal, that
    hung
From Allan's watch, and sparkled by the
    fire.
Then they came in : but when the boy
    beheld
His mother, he cried out to come to her :
And Allan set him down, and Mary said :
    ' O Father !—if you let me call you
    so—
I never came a-begging for myself,
Or William, or this child ; but now I
    come
For Dora : take her back ; she loves you
    well.
O Sir, when William died, he died at
    peace
With all men ; for I ask'd him, and he
    said,
He could not ever rue his marrying me—
I had been a patient wife : but, Sir, he
    said
That he was wrong to cross his father
    thus :

"God bless him !" he said, "and may
    he never know
The troubles I have gone thro' !" Then
    he turn'd
His face and pass'd—unhappy that I am !
But now, Sir, let me have my boy, for
    you
Will make him hard, and he will learn
    to slight
His father's memory ; and take Dora
    back,
And let all this be as it was before.'
    So Mary said, and Dora hid her face
By Mary. There was silence in the room ;
And all at once the old man burst in
    sobs :—
    ' I have been to blame—to blame. I
    have kill'd my son.
I have kill'd him—but I loved him—my
    dear son.
May God forgive me !—I have been to
    blame.
Kiss me, my children.'
             Then they clung about
The old man's neck, and kiss'd him many
    times.
And all the man was broken with re-
    morse ;
And all his love came back a hundred-
    fold ;
And for three hours he sobb'd o'er Wil-
    liam's child
Thinking of William.
             So those four abode
Within one house together ; and as years
Went forward, Mary took another mate ;
But Dora lived unmarried till her death.

AUDLEY COURT.

' THE Bull, the Fleece are cramm'd, and
    not a room
For love or money. Let us picnic there
At Audley Court.'
             I spoke, while Audley feast
Humm'd like a hive all round the narrow
    quay,
To Francis, with a basket on his arm,
To Francis just alighted from the boat,

And breathing of the sea.　‘With all my
　　heart,’
Said Francis.　Then we shoulder’d thro’
　　the swarm,
And rounded by the stillness of the beach
To where the bay runs up its latest horn.
　We left the dying ebb that faintly lipp’d
The flat red granite ; so by many a sweep
Of meadow smooth from aftermath we
　　reach’d
The griffin-guarded gates, and pass’d thro’
　　all
The pillar’d dusk of sounding sycamores,
And cross’d the garden to the gardener’s
　　lodge,
With all its casements bedded, and its
　　walls
And chimneys muffled in the leafy vine.
　There, on a slope of orchard, Francis
　　laid
A damask napkin wrought with horse and
　　hound,
Brought out a dusky loaf that smelt of
　　home,
And, half-cut-down, a pasty costly-made,
Where quail and pigeon, lark and leveret
　　lay,
Like fossils of the rock, with golden yolks
Imbedded and injellied ; last, with these,
A flask of cider from his father’s vats,
Prime, which I knew ; and so we sat and
　　eat
And talk’d old matters over ; who was
　　dead,
Who married, who was like to be, and
　　how
The races went, and who would rent the
　　hall :
Then touch’d upon the game, how scarce
　　it was
This season ; glancing thence, discuss’d
　　the farm,
The four-field system, and the price of
　　grain ;
And struck upon the corn-laws, where we
　　split,
And came again together on the king
With heated faces ; till he laugh’d aloud ;
And, while the blackbird on the pippin
　　hung

To hear him, clapt his hand in mine and
　　sang—
　‘Oh ! who would fight and march and
　　countermarch,
Be shot for sixpence in a battle-field,
And shovell’d up into some bloody trench
Where no one knows ? but let me live my
　　life.
　‘Oh ! who would cast and balance at
　　a desk,
Perch’d like a crow upon a three-legg’d
　　stool,
Till all his juice is dried, and all his joints
Are full of chalk ? but let me live my life.
　‘Who’d serve the state ? for if I carved
　　my name
Upon the cliffs that guard my native land,
I might as well have traced it in the sands ;
The sea wastes all : but let me live my life.
　‘Oh ! who would love ? I woo’d a
　　woman once,
But she was sharper than an eastern wind,
And all my heart turn’d from her, as a
　　thorn
Turns from the sea ; but let me live my
　　life.’
　He sang his song, and I replied with
　　mine :
I found it in a volume, all of songs,
Knock’d down to me, when old Sir
　　Robert’s pride,
His books—the more the pity, so I said—
Came to the hammer here in March—
　　and this—
I set the words, and added names I knew.
　‘Sleep, Ellen Aubrey, sleep, and dream
　　of me :
Sleep, Ellen, folded in thy sister’s arm,
And sleeping, haply dream her arm is
　　mine.
　‘Sleep, Ellen, folded in Emilia’s arm ;
Emilia, fairer than all else but thou,
For thou art fairer than all else that is.
　‘Sleep, breathing health and peace
　　upon her breast :
Sleep, breathing love and trust against
　　her lip :
I go to-night : I come to-morrow morn.
　‘I go, but I return : I would I were
The pilot of the darkness and the dream.

Sleep, Ellen Aubrey, love, and dream of
  me.'
  So sang we each to either, Francis
    Hale,
The farmer's son, who lived across the
  bay,
My friend; and I, that having where-
  withal,
And in the fallow leisure of my life
A rolling stone of here and everywhere,
Did what I would; but ere the night we
  rose
And saunter'd home beneath a moon,
  that, just
In crescent, dimly rain'd about the leaf
Twilights of airy silver, till we reach'd
The limit of the hills; and as we sank
From rock to rock upon the glooming
  quay,
The town was hush'd beneath us: lower
  down
The bay was oily calm; the harbour-
  buoy,
Sole star of phosphorescence in the calm,
With one green sparkle ever and anon
Dipt by itself, and we were glad at heart.

WALKING TO THE MAIL.

John. I'm glad I walk'd. How fresh
  the meadows look
Above the river, and, but a month ago,
The whole hill-side was redder than a fox.
Is yon plantation where this byway joins
The turnpike?
James.   Yes.
John. And when does this come by?
James. The mail? At one o'clock.
John.   What is it now?
James. A quarter to.
John.   Whose house is that I see?
No, not the County Member's with the
  vane:
Up higher with the yew-tree by it, and
  half
A score of gables.
James. That? Sir Edward Head's:
But he's abroad: the place is to be sold.
John. Oh, his. He was not broken.

James.   No, sir, he,
Vex'd with a morbid devil in his blood
That veil'd the world with jaundice, hid
  his face
From all men, and commercing with
  himself,
He lost the sense that handles daily life—
That keeps us all in order more or less—
And sick of home went overseas for
  change.
John. And whither?
James. Nay, who knows? he's here
  and there.
But let him go; his devil goes with him,
As well as with his tenant, Jocky Dawes.
John. What's that?
James. You saw the man—on Mon-
  day, was it?—
There by the humpback'd willow; half
  stands up
And bristles; half has fall'n and made a
  bridge;
And there he caught the younker tickling
  trout—
Caught *in flagrante*—what's the Latin
  word?—
Delicto: but his house, for so they say,
Was haunted with a jolly ghost, that
  shook
The curtains, whined in lobbies, tapt at
  doors,
And rummaged like a rat: no servant
  stay'd:
The farmer vext packs up his beds and
  chairs,
And all his household stuff; and with his
  boy
Betwixt his knees, his wife upon the tilt,
Sets out, and meets a friend who hails
  him, 'What!
You're flitting!' 'Yes, we're flitting,'
  says the ghost
(For they had pack'd the thing among
  the beds,)
'Oh well,' says he, 'you flitting with us
  too—
Jack, turn the horses' heads and home
  again.'
John. He left *his* wife behind; for so
  I heard.

T

James. He left her, yes.   I met my
     lady once :
A woman like a butt, and harsh as crabs.
     John.   Oh yet but I remember, ten
     years back—
'Tis now at least ten years—and then she
     was—
You could not light upon a sweeter thing :
A body slight and round, and like a pear
In growing, modest eyes, a hand, a foot
Lessening in perfect cadence, and a skin
As clean and white as privet when it
     flowers.
     James. Ay, ay, the blossom fades, and
     they that loved
At first like dove and dove were cat and
     dog.
She was the daughter of a cottager,
Out of her sphere.   What betwixt shame
     and pride,
New things and old, himself and her, she
     sour'd
To what she is : a nature never kind !
Like men, like manners : like breeds like,
     they say :
Kind nature is the best : those manners
     next
That fit us like a nature second-hand ;
Which are indeed the manners of the great.
     John. But I had heard it was this bill
     that past,
And fear of change at home, that drove
     him hence.
     James. That was the last drop in the
     cup of gall.
I once was near him, when his bailiff
     brought
A Chartist pike.   You should have seen
     him wince
As from a venomous thing : he thought
     himself
A mark for all, and shudder'd, lest a cry
Should break his sleep by night, and his
     nice eyes
Should see the raw mechanic's bloody
     thumbs
Sweat on his blazon'd chairs ; but, sir,
     you know
That these two parties still divide the
     world—

Of those that want, and those that have :
     and still
The same old sore breaks out from age
     to age
With much the same result.   Now I
     myself,
A Tory to the quick, was as a boy
Destructive, when I had not what I would.
I was at school—a college in the South :
There lived a flayflint near ; we stole his
     fruit,
His hens, his eggs ; but there was law
     for *us ;*
We paid in person.   He had a sow, sir.
     She,
With meditative grunts of much content,
Lay great with pig, wallowing in sun and
     mud.
By night we dragg'd her to the college
     tower
From her warm bed, and up the cork-
     screw stair
With hand and rope we haled the groan-
     ing sow,
And on the leads we kept her till she
     pigg'd.
Large range of prospect had the mother
     sow,
And but for daily loss of one she loved
As one by one we took them—but for
     this—
As never sow was higher in this world—
Might have been happy : but what lot is
     pure ?
We took them all, till she was left alone
Upon her tower, the Niobe of swine,
And so return'd unfarrow'd to her sty.
     John. They found you out ?
     James.   Not they.
     John.   Well—after all—
What know we of the secret of a man ?
His nerves were wrong.   What ails us,
     who are sound,
That we should mimic this raw fool the
     world,
Which charts us all in its coarse blacks
     or whites,
As ruthless as a baby with a worm,
As cruel as a schoolboy ere he grows
To Pity—more from ignorance than will

But put your best foot forward, or I
  fear
That we shall miss the mail : and here it
  comes
With five at top : as quaint a four-in-hand
As you shall see—three pyebalds and a
  roan.

EDWIN MORRIS ;

OR, THE LAKE.

O ME, my pleasant rambles by the lake,
My sweet, wild, fresh three quarters of a
  year,
My one Oasis in the dust and drouth
Of city life !   I was a sketcher then :
See here, my doing : curves of mountain,
  bridge,
Boat, island, ruins of a castle, built
When men knew how to build, upon a
  rock
With turrets lichen-gilded like a rock :
And here, new-comers in an ancient hold,
New-comers from the Mersey, million-
  aires,
Here lived the Hills—a Tudor-chimnied
  bulk
Of mellow brickwork on an isle of bowers.
  O me, my pleasant rambles by the lake
With Edwin Morris and with Edward
  Bull
The curate ; he was fatter than his cure.

  But Edwin Morris, he that knew the
  names,
Long learned names of agaric, moss and
  fern,
Who forged a thousand theories of the
  rocks,
Who taught me how to skate, to row, to
  swim,
Who read me rhymes elaborately good,
His own—I call'd him Crichton, for he
  seem'd
All-perfect, finish'd to the finger nail.

  And once I ask'd him of his early life,
And his first passion ; and he answer'd
  me ;

And well his words became him : was he
  not
A full-cell'd honeycomb of eloquence
Stored from all flowers ?   Poet-like he
  spoke.

  ' My love for Nature is as old as I ;
But thirty moons, one honeymoon to that,
And three rich sennights more, my love
  for her.
My love for Nature and my love for her,
Of different ages, like twin-sisters grew,
Twin-sisters differently beautiful.
To some full music rose and sank the sun,
And some full music seem'd to move and
  change
With all the varied changes of the dark,
And either twilight and the day between ;
For daily hope fulfill'd, to rise again
Revolving toward fulfilment, made it
  sweet
To walk, to sit, to sleep, to wake, to
  breathe.'

  Or this or something like to this he
  spoke.
Then said the fat-faced curate Edward
  Bull,
  ' I take it, God made the woman for
  the man,
And for the good and increase of the
  world.
A pretty face is well, and this is well,
To have a dame indoors, that trims us up,
And keeps us tight ; but these unreal
  ways
Seem but the theme of writers, and in-
  deed
Worn threadbare.   Man is made of solid
  stuff.
I say, God made the woman for the man,
And for the good and increase of the
  world.'

  ' Parson,' said I, ' you pitch the pipe
  too low :
But I have sudden touches, and can run
My faith beyond my practice into his :
Tho' if, in dancing after Letty Hill,
I do not hear the bells upon my cap,
I scarce have other music : yet say on.

What should one give to light on such a
    dream?'
I ask'd him half-sardonically.
                        'Give?
Give all thou art,' he answer'd, and a
    light
Of laughter dimpled in his swarthy cheek;
'I would have hid her needle in my
    heart,
To save her little finger from a scratch
No deeper than the skin: my ears could
    hear
Her lightest breath; her least remark
    was worth
The experience of the wise. I went and
    came;
Her voice fled always thro' the summer
    land;
I spoke her name alone. Thrice-happy
    days!
The flower of each, those moments when
    we met,
The crown of all, we met to part no
    more.'

  Were not his words delicious, I a beast
To take them as I did? but something
    jarr'd;
Whether he spoke too largely; that there
    seem'd
A touch of something false, some self-
    conceit,
Or over-smoothness: howsoe'er it was,
He scarcely hit my humour, and I said:

  'Friend Edwin, do not think yourself
    alone
Of all men happy. Shall not Love to
    me,
As in the Latin song I learnt at school,
Sneeze out a full God-bless-you right and
    left?
But you can talk: yours is a kindly vein:
I have, I think, — Heaven knows — as
    much within;
Have, or should have, but for a thought
    or two,
That like a purple beech among the greens
Looks out of place: 'tis from no want in
    her:

It is my shyness, or my self-distrust,
Or something of a wayward modern mind
Dissecting passion. Time will set me
    right.'

  So spoke I knowing not the things
    that were.
Then said the fat-faced curate, Edward
    Bull:
'God made the woman for the use of
    man,
And for the good and increase of the
    world.'
And I and Edwin laughed; and now we
    paused
About the windings of the marge to hear
The soft wind blowing over meadowy
    holms
And alders, garden-isles; and now we left
The clerk behind us, I and he, and ran
By ripply shallows of the lisping lake,
Delighted with the freshness and the
    sound.

  But, when the bracken rusted on their
    crags,
My suit had wither'd, nipt to death by
    him
That was a God, and is a lawyer's clerk,
The rentroll Cupid of our rainy isles.
'Tis true, we met: one hour I had, no
    more:
She sent a note, the seal an *Elle vous suit*,
The close, 'Your Letty, only yours;' and
    this
Thrice underscored. The friendly mist
    of morn
Clung to the lake. I boated over, ran
My craft aground, and heard with beat-
    ing heart
The Sweet-Gale rustle round the shelving
    keel;
And out I stept, and up I crept: she
    moved,
Like Proserpine in Enna, gathering
    flowers:
Then low and sweet I whistled thrice;
    and she,
She turn'd, we closed, we kiss'd, swore
    faith, I breathed

In some new planet: a silent cousin stole
Upon us and departed: 'Leave,' she
    cried,
'O leave me!' 'Never, dearest, never:
    here
I brave the worst:' and while we stood
    like fools
Embracing, all at once a score of pugs
And poodles yell'd within, and out they
    came
Trustees and Aunts and Uncles. 'What,
    with him!
Go' (shrill'd the cotton-spinning chorus);
    'him!'
I choked. Again they shriek'd the
    burthen—'Him!'
Again with hands of wild rejection 'Go!—
Girl, get you in!' She went—and in one
    month
They wedded her to sixty thousand pounds,
To lands in Kent and messuages in York,
And slight Sir Robert with his watery
    smile
And educated whisker. But for me,
They set an ancient creditor to work:
It seems I broke a close with force and
    arms:
There came a mystic token from the king
To greet the sheriff, needless courtesy!
I read, and fled by night, and flying
    turn'd:
Her taper glimmer'd in the lake below:
I turn'd once more, close-button'd to the
    storm;
So left the place, left Edwin, nor have seen
Him since, nor heard of her, nor cared to
    hear.

Nor cared to hear? perhaps: yet long
    ago
I have pardon'd little Letty; not indeed,
It may be, for her own dear sake but this,
She seems a part of those fresh days to me;
For in the dust and drouth of London life
She moves among my visions of the lake,
While the prime swallow dips his wing,
    or then
While the gold-lily blows, and overhead
The light cloud smoulders on the summer
    crag.

ST. SIMEON STYLITES.

ALTHO' I be the basest of mankind,
From scalp to sole one slough and crust
    of sin,
Unfit for earth, unfit for heaven, scarce
    meet
For troops of devils, mad with blasphemy,
I will not cease to grasp the hope I hold
Of saintdom, and to clamour, mourn and
    sob,
Battering the gates of heaven with storms
    of prayer,
Have mercy, Lord, and take away my sin.
    Let this avail, just, dreadful, mighty
    God,
This not be all in vain, that thrice ten
    years,
Thrice multiplied by superhuman pangs,
In hungers and in thirsts, fevers and cold,
In coughs, aches, stitches, ulcerous throes
    and cramps,
A sign betwixt the meadow and the cloud,
Patient on this tall pillar I have borne
Rain, wind, frost, heat, hail, damp, and
    sleet, and snow;
And I had hoped that ere this period closed
Thou wouldst have caught me up into thy
    rest,
Denying not these weather-beaten limbs
The meed of saints, the white robe and
    the palm.
    O take the meaning, Lord: I do not
    breathe,
Not whisper, any murmur of complaint.
Pain heap'd ten-hundred-fold to this, were
    still
Less burthen, by ten-hundred-fold, to bear,
Than were those lead-like tons of sin,
    that crush'd
My spirit flat before thee.
                        O Lord, Lord,
Thou knowest I bore this better at the
    first,
For I was strong and hale of body then;
And tho' my teeth, which now are dropt
    away,
Would chatter with the cold, and all my
    beard

Was tagg'd with icy fringes in the moon,
I drown'd the whoopings of the owl with
    sound
Of pious hymns and psalms, and some-
    times saw
An angel stand and watch me, as I sang.
Now am I feeble grown ; my end draws
    nigh ;
I hope my end draws nigh : half deaf I am,
So that I scarce can hear the people hum
About the column's base, and almost blind,
And scarce can recognise the fields I
    know ;
And both my thighs are rotted with the
    dew ;
Yet cease I not to clamour and to cry,
While my stiff spine can hold my weary
    head,
Till all my limbs drop piecemeal from the
    stone,
Have mercy, mercy : take away my sin.
    O Jesus, if thou wilt not save my soul,
Who may be saved ? who is it may be
    saved ?
Who may be made a saint, if I fail here ?
Show me the man hath suffer'd more
    than I.
For did not all thy martyrs die one death ?
For either they were stoned, or crucified,
Or burn'd in fire, or boil'd in oil, or sawn
In twain beneath the ribs ; but I die here
To-day, and whole years long, a life of
    death.
Bear witness, if I could have found a way
(And heedfully I sifted all my thought)
More slowly-painful to subdue this home
Of sin, my flesh, which I despise and hate,
I had not stinted practice, O my God.
    For not alone this pillar-punishment,
Not this alone I bore : but while I lived
In the white convent down the valley there,
For many weeks about my loins I wore
The rope that haled the buckets from the
    well,
Twisted as tight as I could knot the noose ;
And spake not of it to a single soul,
Until the ulcer, eating thro' my skin,
Betray'd my secret penance, so that all
My brethren marvell'd greatly. More
    than this

I bore, whereof, O God, thou knowest all.
    Three winters, that my soul might
    grow to thee,
I lived up there on yonder mountain
    side.
My right leg chain'd into the crag, I lay
Pent in a roofless close of ragged stones ;
Inswathed sometimes in wandering mist,
    and twice
Black'd with thy branding thunder, and
    sometimes
Sucking the damps for drink, and eating
    not,
Except the spare chance-gift of those
    that came
To touch my body and be heal'd, and live :
And they say then that I work'd miracles,
Whereof my fame is loud amongst man-
    kind,
Cured lameness, palsies, cancers. Thou,
    O God,
Knowest alone whether this was or no.
Have mercy, mercy ! cover all my sin.
    Then, that I might be more alone
    with thee,
Three years I lived upon a pillar, high
Six cubits, and three years on one of
    twelve ;
And twice three years I crouch'd on one
    that rose
Twenty by measure ; last of all, I grew
Twice ten long weary weary years to this,
That numbers forty cubits from the soil.
    I think that I have borne as much as
    this—
Or else I dream—and for so long a time,
If I may measure time by yon slow light,
And this high dial, which my sorrow
    crowns—
So much—even so.
            And yet I know not well,
For that the evil ones come here, and say,
' Fall down, O Simeon : thou hast suffer'd
    long
For ages and for ages !' then they prate
Of penances I cannot have gone thro',
Perplexing me with lies ; and oft I fall,
Maybe for months, in such blind lethargies
That Heaven, and Earth, and Time are
    choked.

But yet
Bethink thee, Lord, while thou and all
 the saints
Enjoy themselves in heaven, and men on
 earth
House in the shade of comfortable roofs,
Sit with their wives by fires, eat whole-
 some food,
And wear warm clothes, and even beasts
 have stalls,
I, 'tween the spring and downfall of the
 light,
Bow down one thousand and two hundred
 times,
To Christ, the Virgin Mother, and the
 saints ;
Or in the night, after a little sleep,
I wake : the chill stars sparkle ; I am
 wet
With drenching dews, or stiff with crack-
 ling frost.
 wear an undress'd goatskin on my
 back ;
A grazing iron collar grinds my neck ;
And in my weak, lean arms I lift the
 cross,
And strive and wrestle with thee till I
 die :
O mercy, mercy ! wash away my sin.
 O Lord, thou knowest what a man I
 am ;
A sinful man, conceived and born in sin :
'Tis their own doing ; this is none of
 mine ;
Lay it not to me. Am I to blame for
 this,
That here come those that worship me ?
 Ha ! ha !
They think that I am somewhat. What
 am I ?
The silly people take me for a saint,
And bring me offerings of fruit and
 flowers :
And I, in truth (thou wilt bear witness
 here)
Have all in all endured as much, and
 more
Than many just and holy men, whose
 names
Are register'd and calendar'd for saints.

Good people, you do ill to kneel to me.
What is it I can have done to merit this ?
I am a sinner viler than you all.
It may be I have wrought some miracles,
And cured some halt and maim'd ; but
 what of that ?
It may be, no one, even among the saints,
May match his pains with mine ; but
 what of that ?
Yet do not rise ; for you may look on me,
And in your looking you may kneel to
 God.
Speak ! is there any of you halt or maim'd?
I think you know I have some power
 with Heaven
From my long penance : let him speak
 his wish.
 Yes, I can heal him. Power goes
 forth from me.
They say that they are heal'd. Ah,
 hark ! they shout
'St. Simeon Stylites.' Why, if so,
God reaps a harvest in me. O my soul,
God reaps a harvest in thee. If this be,
Can I work miracles and not be saved ?
This is not told of any. They were saints.
It cannot be but that I shall be saved ;
Yea, crown'd a saint. They shout,
 'Behold a saint !'
And lower voices saint me from above.
Courage, St. Simeon ! This dull chrysalis
Cracks into shining wings, and hope ere
 death
Spreads more and more and more, that
 God hath now
Sponged and made blank of crimeful
 record all
My mortal archives.
    O my sons, my sons,
I, Simeon of the pillar, by surname
Stylites, among men ; I, Simeon,
The watcher on the column till the end ;
I, Simeon, whose brain the sunshine
 bakes ;
I, whose bald brows in silent hours
 become
Unnaturally hoar with rime, do now
From my high nest of penance here pro-
 claim
That Pontius and Iscariot by my side

Show'd like fair seraphs. On the coals
    I lay,
A vessel full of sin : all hell beneath
Made me boil over. Devils pluck'd my
    sleeve,
Abaddon and Asmodeus caught at me.
I smote them with the cross; they
    swarm'd again.
In bed like monstrous apes they crush'd
    my chest :
They flapp'd my light out as I read : I
    saw
Their faces grow between me and my
    book ;
With colt-like whinny and with hoggish
    whine
They burst my prayer. Yet this way
    was left,
And by this way I 'scaped them. Mortify
Your flesh, like me, with scourges and
    with thorns ;
Smite, shrink not, spare not. If it may
    be, fast
Whole Lents, and pray. I hardly, with
    slow steps,
With slow, faint steps, and much exceed-
    ing pain,
Have scrambled past those pits of fire,
    that still
Sing in mine ears. But yield not me the
    praise :
God only thro' his bounty hath thought
    fit,
Among the powers and princes of this
    world,
To make me an example to mankind,
Which few can reach to. Yet I do not
    say
But that a time may come — yea, even
    now,
Now, now, his footsteps smite the thresh-
    old stairs
Of life—I say, that time is at the doors
When you may worship me without re-
    proach ;
For I will leave my relics in your land,
And you may carve a shrine about my
    dust,
And burn a fragrant lamp before my
    bones,

When I am gather'd to the glorious
    saints.
  While I spake then, a sting of shrewd-
    est pain
Ran shrivelling thro' me, and a cloudlike
    change,
In passing, with a grosser film made thick
These heavy, horny eyes. The end ! the
    end !
Surely the end ! What's here ? a shape,
    a shade,
A flash of light. Is that the angel there
That holds a crown ? Come, blessed
    brother, come.
I know thy glittering face. I waited
    long ;
My brows are ready. What ! deny it
    now ?
Nay, draw, draw, draw nigh. So I
    clutch it. Christ !
'Tis gone : 'tis here again ; the crown !
    the crown !
So now 'tis fitted on and grows to me,
And from it melt the dews of Paradise,
Sweet ! sweet ! spikenard, and balm, and
    frankincense.
Ah ! let me not be fool'd, sweet saints :
    I trust
That I am whole, and clean, and meet
    for Heaven.
  Speak, if there be a priest, a man of
    God,
Among you there, and let him presently
Approach, and lean a ladder on the shaft,
And climbing up into my airy home,
Deliver me the blessed sacrament ;
For by the warning of the Holy Ghost,
I prophesy that I shall die to-night,
A quarter before twelve.
            But thou, O Lord,
Aid all this foolish people ; let them take
Example, pattern : lead them to thy light.

THE TALKING OAK.

ONCE more the gate behind me falls ;
  Once more before my face
I see the moulder'd Abbey-walls,
  That stand within the chace.

Beyond the lodge the city lies,
  Beneath its drift of smoke ;
And ah ! with what delighted eyes
  I turn to yonder oak.

For when my passion first began,
  Ere that, which in me burn'd,
The love, that makes me thrice a man,
  Could hope itself return'd ;

To yonder oak within the field
  I spoke without restraint,
And with a larger faith appeal'd
  Than Papist unto Saint.

For oft I talk'd with him apart,
  And told him of my choice,
Until he plagiarised a heart,
  And answer'd with a voice.

Tho' what he whisper'd under Heaven
  None else could understand ;
I found him garrulously given,
  A babbler in the land.

But since I heard him make reply
  Is many a weary hour ;
'Twere well to question him, and try
  If yet he keeps the power.

Hail, hidden to the knees in fern,
  Broad Oak of Sumner-chace,
Whose topmost branches can discern
  The roofs of Sumner-place !

Say thou, whereon I carved her name,
  If ever maid or spouse,
As fair as my Olivia, came
  To rest beneath thy boughs. —

'O Walter, I have shelter'd here
  Whatever maiden grace
The good old Summers, year by year
  Made ripe in Sumner-chace :

'Old Summers, when the monk was fat,
  And, issuing shorn and sleek,
Would twist his girdle tight, and pat
  The girls upon the cheek,

'Ere yet, in scorn of Peter's-pence,
  And number'd bead, and shrift,
Bluff Harry broke into the spence
  And turn'd the cowls adrift :

'And I have seen some score of those
  Fresh faces, that would thrive
When his man-minded offset rose
  To chase the deer at five ;

'And all that from the town would stroll,
  Till that wild wind made work
In which the gloomy brewer's soul
  Went by me, like a stork :

'The slight she-slips of loyal blood,
  And others, passing praise,
Strait-laced, but all-too-full in bud
  For puritanic stays :

'And I have shadow'd many a group
  Of beauties, that were born
In teacup-times of hood and hoop,
  Or while the patch was worn ;

'And, leg and arm with love-knots gay,
  About me leap'd and laugh'd
The modish Cupid of the day,
  And shrill'd his tinsel shaft.

'I swear (and else may insects prick
  Each leaf into a gall)
This girl, for whom your heart is sick,
  Is three times worth them all ;

'For those and theirs, by Nature's law,
  Have faded long ago ;
But in these latter springs I saw
  Your own Olivia blow,

'From when she gamboll'd on the greens
  A baby-germ, to when
The maiden blossoms of her teens
  Could number five from ten.

'I swear, by leaf, and wind, and rain,
  (And hear me with thine ears,)
That, tho' I circle in the grain
  Five hundred rings of years—

'Yet, since I first could cast a shade,
  Did never creature pass
So slightly, musically made,
  So light upon the grass :

'For as to fairies, that will flit
  To make the greensward fresh,
I hold them exquisitely knit,
  But far too spare of flesh.'

Oh, hide thy knotted knees in fern,
  And overlook the chace ;
And from thy topmost branch discern
  The roofs of Sumner-place.

But thou, whereon I carved her name,
  That oft hast heard my vows,
Declare when last Olivia came
  To sport beneath thy boughs.

'O yesterday, you know, the fair
  Was holden at the town ;
Her father left his good arm-chair,
  And rode his hunter down.

'And with him Albert came on his.
  I look'd at him with joy :
As cowslip unto oxlip is,
  So seems she to the boy.

'An hour had past—and, sitting straight
  Within the low-wheel'd chaise,
Her mother trundled to the gate
  Behind the dappled grays.

'But as for her, she stay'd at home,
  And on the roof she went,
And down the way you use to come,
  She look'd with discontent.

'She left the novel half-uncut
  Upon the rosewood shelf ;
She left the new piano shut :
  She could not please herself.

'Then ran she, gamesome as the colt,
  And livelier than a lark
She sent her voice thro' all the holt
  Before her, and the park.

'A light wind chased her on the wing,
  And in the chase grew wild,
As close as might be would he cling
  About the darling child :

'But light as any wind that blows
  So fleetly did she stir,
The flower, she touch'd on, dipt and rose,
  And turn'd to look at her.

'And here she came, and round me play'd,
  And sang to me the whole
Of those three stanzas that you made
  About my " giant bole ;"

'And in a fit of frolic mirth
  She strove to span my waist :
Alas, I was so broad of girth,
  I could not be embraced.

'I wish'd myself the fair young beech
  That here beside me stands,
That round me, clasping each in each,
  She might have lock'd her hands.

'Yet seem'd the pressure thrice as sweet
  As woodbine's fragile hold,
Or when I feel about my feet
  The berried briony fold.'

O muffle round thy knees with fern,
  And shadow Sumner-chace !
Long may thy topmost branch discern
  The roofs of Sumner-place !

But tell me, did she read the name
  I carved with many vows
When last with throbbing heart I came
  To rest beneath thy boughs ?

'O yes, she wander'd round and round
  These knotted knees of mine,
And found, and kiss'd the name she found,
  And sweetly murmur'd thine.

'A teardrop trembled from its source,
  And down my surface crept.
My sense of touch is something coarse,
  But I believe she wept.

'Then flush'd her cheek with rosy light,
    She glanced across the plain ;
But not a creature was in sight :
    She kiss'd me once again.

'Her kisses were so close and kind,
    That, trust me on my word,
Hard wood I am, and wrinkled rind,
    But yet my sap was stirr'd :

'And even into my inmost ring
    A pleasure I discern'd,
Like those blind motions of the Spring,
    That show the year is turn'd.

'Thrice-happy he that may caress
    The ringlet's waving balm—
The cushions of whose touch may press
    The maiden's tender palm.

'I, rooted here among the groves
    But languidly adjust
My vapid vegetable loves
    With anthers and with dust :

'For ah ! my friend, the days were brief
    Whereof the poets talk,
When that, which breathes within the leaf,
    Could slip its bark and walk.

'But could I, as in times foregone,
    From spray, and branch, and stem,
Have suck'd and gather'd into one
    The life that spreads in them,

'She had not found me so remiss ;
    But lightly issuing thro',
I would have paid her kiss for kiss,
    With usury thereto.'

O flourish high, with leafy towers,
    And overlook the lea,
Pursue thy loves among the bowers
    But leave thou mine to me.

O flourish, hidden deep in fern,
    Old oak, I love thee well ;
A thousand thanks for what I learn
    And what remains to tell.

''Tis little more : the day was warm ;
    At last, tired out with play,
She sank her head upon her arm
    And at my feet she lay.

'Her eyelids dropp'd their silken eaves.
    I breathed upon her eyes
Thro' all the summer of my leaves
    A welcome mix'd with sighs.

'I took the swarming sound of life—
    The music from the town—
The murmurs of the drum and fife
    And lull'd them in my own.

'Sometimes I let a sunbeam slip,
    To light her shaded eye ;
A second flutter'd round her lip
    Like a golden butterfly ;

'A third would glimmer on her neck
    To make the necklace shine ;
Another slid, a sunny fleck,
    From head to ancle fine,

'Then close and dark my arms I spread.
    And shadow'd all her rest—
Dropt dews upon her golden head,
    An acorn in her breast.

'But in a pet she started up,
    And pluck'd it out, and drew
My little oakling from the cup,
    And flung him in the dew.

'And yet it was a graceful gift—
    I felt a pang within
As when I see the woodman lift
    His axe to slay my kin.

'I shook him down because he was
    The finest on the tree.
He lies beside thee on the grass.
    O kiss him once for me.

'O kiss him twice and thrice for me,
    That have no lips to kiss,
For never yet was oak on lea
    Shall grow so fair as this.'

Step deeper yet in herb and fern,
    Look further thro' the chace,
Spread upward till thy boughs discern
    The front of Sumner-place.

This fruit of thine by Love is blest,
    That but a moment lay
Where fairer fruit of Love may rest
    Some happy future day.

I kiss it twice, I kiss it thrice,
    The warmth it thence shall win
To riper life may magnetise
    The baby-oak within.

But thou, while kingdoms overset,
    Or lapse from hand to hand,
Thy leaf shall never fail, nor yet
    Thine acorn in the land.

May never saw dismember thee,
    Nor wielded axe disjoint,
That art the fairest-spoken tree
    From here to Lizard-point.

O rock upon thy towery-top
    All throats that gurgle sweet !
All starry culmination drop
    Balm-dews to bathe thy feet !

All grass of silky feather grow—
    And while he sinks or swells
The full south-breeze around thee blow
    The sound of minster bells.

The fat earth feed thy branchy root,
    That under deeply strikes !
The northern morning o'er thee shoot,
    High up, in silver spikes !

Nor ever lightning char thy grain,
    But, rolling as in sleep,
Low thunders bring the mellow rain,
    That makes thee broad and deep !

And hear me swear a solemn oath,
    That only by thy side
Will I to Olive plight my troth,
    And gain her for my bride.

And when my marriage morn may fall,
    She, Dryad-like, shall wear
Alternate leaf and acorn-ball
    In wreath about her hair.

And I will work in prose and rhyme,
    And praise thee more in both
Than bard has honour'd beech or lime,
    Or that Thessalian growth,

In which the swarthy ringdove sat,
    And mystic sentence spoke ;
And more than England honours that,
    Thy famous brother-oak,

Wherein the younger Charles abode
    Till all the paths were dim,
And far below the Roundhead rode,
    And humm'd a surly hymn.

LOVE AND DUTY.

OF love that never found his earthly close,
What sequel ? Streaming eyes and break-
    ing hearts ?
Or all the same as if he had not been ?
    Not so. Shall Error in the round of
    time
Still father Truth ? O shall the braggart
    shout
For some blind glimpse of freedom work
    itself
Thro' madness, hated by the wise, to law
System and empire ? Sin itself be found
The cloudy porch oft opening on the Sun ?
And only he, this wonder, dead, become
Mere highway dust ? or year by year alone
Sit brooding in the ruins of a life,
Nightmare of youth, the spectre of him-
    self?
    If this were thus, if this, indeed, were
    all,
Better the narrow brain, the stony heart,
The staring eye glazed o'er with sapless
    days,
The long mechanic pacings to and fro,
The set gray life, and apathetic end.
But am I not the nobler thro' thy love ?
O three times less unworthy ! likewise
    thou

Art more thro' Love, and greater than
    thy years,
The Sun will run his orbit, and the Moon
Her circle. Wait, and Love himself will
    bring
The drooping flower of knowledge changed
    to fruit
Of wisdom. Wait: my faith is large in
    Time,
And that which shapes it to some perfect
    end.
    Will some one say, Then why not ill
      for good?
Why took ye not your pastime? To that
    man
My work shall answer, since I knew the
    right
And did it ; for a man is not as God,
But then most Godlike being most a man.
—So let me think 'tis well for thee and
    me—
Ill-fated that I am, what lot is mine
Whose foresight preaches peace, my heart
    so slow
To feel it ! For how hard it seem'd to me,
When eyes, love-languid thro' half tears
    would dwell
One earnest, earnest moment upon mine,
Then not to dare to see ! when thy low
    voice,
Faltering, would break its syllables, to
    keep
My own full-tuned,—hold passion in a
    leash,
And not leap forth and fall about thy
    neck,
And on thy bosom (deep desired relief !)
Rain out the heavy mist of tears, that
    weigh'd
Upon my brain, my senses and my soul !
    For Love himself took part against
      himself
To warn us off, and Duty loved of Love—
O this world's curse,—beloved but hated
    —came
Like Death betwixt thy dear embrace and
    mine,
And crying, 'Who is this? behold thy
    bride,'
She push'd me from thee.

                If the sense is hard
To alien ears, I did not speak to these—
No, not to thee, but to thyself in me :
Hard is my doom and thine : thou
    knowest it all.
    Could Love part thus ? was it not well
    to speak,
To have spoken once ? It could not but
    be well.
The slow sweet hours that bring us all
    things good,
The slow sad hours that bring us all
    things ill,
And all good things from evil, brought
    the night
In which we sat together and alone,
And to the want, that hollow'd all the
    heart,
Gave utterance by the yearning of an eye,
That burn'd upon its object thro' such
    tears
As flow but once a life.
                The trance gave way
To those caresses, when a hundred times
In that last kiss, which never was the last,
Farewell, like endless welcome, lived and
    died.
Then follow'd counsel, comfort, and the
    words
That make a man feel strong in speaking
    truth ;
Till now the dark was worn, and overhead
The lights of sunset and of sunrise mix'd
In that brief night ; the summer night,
    that paused
Among her stars to hear us ; stars that
    hung
Love-charm'd to listen : all the wheels of
    Time
Spun round in station, but the end had
    come.
    O then like those, who clench their
      nerves to rush
Upon their dissolution, we two rose,
There—closing like an individual life—
In one blind cry of passion and of pain,
Like bitter accusation ev'n to death,
Caught up the whole of love and utter'd
    it,
And bade adieu for ever.

Live—yet live—
Shall sharpest pathos blight us, knowing
　all
Life needs for life is possible to will—
Live happy; tend thy flowers; be tended
　by
My blessing! Should my Shadow cross
　thy thoughts
Too sadly for their peace, remand it thou
For calmer hours to Memory's darkest
　hold,
If not to be forgotten—not at once—
Not all forgotten. Should it cross thy
　dreams,
O might it come like one that looks con-
　tent,
With quiet eyes unfaithful to the truth,
And point thee forward to a distant light,
Or seem to lift a burthen from thy heart
And leave thee freër, till thou wake
　refresh'd
Then when the first low matin-chirp hath
　grown
Full quire, and morning driv'n her plow
　of pearl
Far furrowing into light the mounded
　rack,
Beyond the fair green field and eastern
　sea.

THE GOLDEN YEAR.

WELL, you shall have that song which
　Leonard wrote:
It was last summer on a tour in Wales:
Old James was with me: we that day
　had been
Up Snowdon; and I wish'd for Leonard
　there,
And found him in Llanberis: then we
　crost
Between the lakes, and clamber'd half
　way up
The counter side; and that same song of
　his
He told me; for I banter'd him, and
　swore
They said he lived shut up within himself,
A tongue-tied Poet in the feverous days,

That, setting the *how much* before the
　how,
Cry, like the daughters of the horseleech,
　'Give,
Cram us with all,' but count not me the
　herd!
　To which 'They call me what they
　　will,' he said:
'But I was born too late: the fair new
　forms,
That float about the threshold of an age,
Like truths of Science waiting to be
　caught—
Catch me who can, and make the catcher
　crown'd—
Are taken by the forelock. Let it be.
But if you care indeed to listen, hear
These measured words, my work of
　yestermorn.
　'We sleep and wake and sleep, but all
　　things move;
The Sun flies forward to his brother Sun;
The dark Earth follows wheel'd in her
　ellipse;
And human things returning on them-
　selves
Move onward, leading up the golden year.
　'Ah, tho' the times, when some new
　　thought can bud,
Are but as poets' seasons when they
　flower,
Yet oceans daily gaining on the land,
Have ebb and flow conditioning their
　march,
And slow and sure comes up the golden
　year.
　'When wealth no more shall rest in
　　mounded heaps,
But smit with freër light shall slowly
　melt
In many streams to fatten lower lands,
And light shall spread, and man be liker
　man
Thro' all the season of the golden year.
　'Shall eagles not be eagles? wrens be
　　wrens?
If all the world were falcons, what of
　that?
The wonder of the eagle were the less,
But he not less the eagle. Happy days

Roll onward, leading up the golden year.
  'Fly, happy happy sails, and bear the
      Press ;
Fly happy with the mission of the Cross ;
Knit land to land, and blowing haven-
      ward
With silks, and fruits, and spices, clear
      of toll,
Enrich the markets of the golden year.
  'But we grow old. Ah ! when shall
      all men's good
Be each man's rule, and universal Peace
Lie like a shaft of light across the land,
And like a lane of beams athwart the
      sea,
Thro' all the circle of the golden year ? '
  Thus far he flow'd, and ended ; where-
      upon
'Ah, folly !' in mimic cadence answer'd
      James—
'Ah, folly ! for it lies so far away,
Not in our time, nor in our children's
      time,
'Tis like the second world to us that live ;
'Twere all as one to fix our hopes on
      Heaven
As on this vision of the golden year.'
  With that he struck his staff against
      the rocks
And broke it,—James,—you know him,
      —old, but full
Of force and choler, and firm upon his
      feet,
And like an oaken stock in winter woods,
O'erflourish'd with the hoary clematis :
Then added, all in heat :
          'What stuff is this !
Old writers push'd the happy season
      back,—
The more fools they,—we forward :
      dreamers both :
You most, that in an age, when every
      hour
Must sweat her sixty minutes to the
      death,
Live on, God love us, as if the seedsman,
      rapt
Upon the teeming harvest, should not
      plunge
His hand into the bag : but well I know

That unto him who works, and feels he
      works,
This same grand year is ever at the
      doors.'
  He spoke ; and, high above, I heard
      them blast
The steep slate-quarry, and the great
      echo flap
And buffet round the hills, from bluff to
      bluff.

✳ ULYSSES.

It little profits that an idle king,
By this still hearth, among these barren
      crags,
Match'd with an aged wife, I mete and
      dole
Unequal laws unto a savage race,
That hoard, and sleep, and feed, and
      know not me.
I cannot rest from travel : I will drink
Life to the lees : all times I have enjoy'd
Greatly, have suffer'd greatly, both with
      those
That loved me, and alone ; on shore, and
      when
Thro' scudding drifts the rainy Hyades
Vext the dim sea : I am become a name ;
For always roaming with a hungry heart
Much have I seen and known ; cities of
      men
And manners, climates, councils, govern-
      ments,
Myself not least, but honour'd of them
      all ;
And drunk delight of battle with my
      peers,
Far on the ringing plains of windy
      Troy.
I am a part of all that I have met ;
Yet all experience is an arch wherethro'
Gleams that untravell'd world, whose
      margin fades
For ever and for ever when I move.
How dull it is to pause, to make an end,
To rust unburnish'd, not to shine in use !
As tho' to breathe were life.   Life piled
      on life
Were all too little, and of one to me

Little remains : but every hour is saved
From that eternal silence, something
    more,
A bringer of new things ; and vile it
    were
For some three suns to store and hoard
    myself,
And this gray spirit yearning in desire
To follow knowledge like a sinking star,
Beyond the utmost bound of human
    thought.

    This is my son, mine own Telemachus,
To whom I leave the sceptre and the isle—
Well-loved of me, discerning to fulfil
This labour, by slow prudence to make
    mild
A rugged people, and thro' soft degrees
Subdue them to the useful and the good.
Most blameless is he, centred in the
    sphere
Of common duties, decent not to fail
In offices of tenderness, and pay
Meet adoration to my household gods,
When I am gone. He works his work,
    I mine.

    There lies the port ; the vessel puffs
    her sail :
There gloom the dark broad seas. My
    mariners,
Souls that have toil'd, and wrought, and
    thought with me—
That ever with a frolic welcome took
The thunder and the sunshine, and
    opposed
Free hearts, free foreheads—you and I
    are old ;
Old age hath yet his honour and his toil ;
Death closes all : but something ere the
    end,
Some work of noble note, may yet be
    done,
Not unbecoming men that strove with
    Gods.
The lights begin to twinkle from the
    rocks :
The long day wanes : the slow moon
    climbs : the deep
Moans round with many voices. Come,
    my friends,
'Tis not too late to seek a newer world.

Push off, and sitting well in order smite
The sounding furrows ; for my purpose
    holds
To sail beyond the sunset, and the baths
Of all the western stars, until I die.
It may be that the gulfs will wash us
    down :
It may be we shall touch the Happy Isles,
And see the great Achilles, whom we
    knew.
Tho' much is taken, much abides ; and
    tho'
We are not now that strength which in
    old days
Moved earth and heaven ; that which we
    are, we are ;
One equal temper of heroic hearts,
Made weak by time and fate, but strong
    in will
To strive, to seek, to find, and not to yield.

TITHŌNUS.

THE woods decay, the woods decay and
    fall,
The vapours weep their burthen to the
    ground,
Man comes and tills the field and lies
    beneath,
And after many a summer dies the swan.
Me only cruel immortality
Consumes : I wither slowly in thine arms,
Here at the quiet limit of the world,
A white-hair'd shadow roaming like a
    dream
The ever-silent spaces of the East,
Far-folded mists, and gleaming halls of
    morn.

    Alas ! for this gray shadow, once a
    man—
So glorious in his beauty and thy choice,
Who madest him thy chosen, that he
    seem'd
To his great heart none other than a God !
I ask'd thee, ' Give me immortality.'
Then didst thou grant mine asking with
    a smile,
Like wealthy men who care not how they
    give.

But thy strong Hours indignant work'd
    their wills,
And beat me down and marr'd and wasted
    me,
And tho' they could not end me, left me
    maim'd
To dwell in presence of immortal youth,
Immortal age beside immortal youth,
And all I was, in ashes. Can thy love,
Thy beauty, make amends, tho' even now,
Close over us, the silver star, thy guide,
Shines in those tremulous eyes that fill
    with tears
To hear me? Let me go : take back thy
    gift :
Why should a man desire in any way
To vary from the kindly race of men,
Or pass beyond the goal of ordinance
Where all should pause, as is most meet
    for all ?

A soft air fans the cloud apart ; there
    comes
A glimpse of that dark world where I
    was born.
Once more the old mysterious glimmer
    steals
From thy pure brows, and from thy
    shoulders pure,
And bosom beating with a heart renew'd.
Thy cheek begins to redden thro' the
    gloom,
Thy sweet eyes brighten slowly close to
    mine,
Ere yet they blind the stars, and the wild
    team
Which love thee, yearning for thy yoke,
    arise,
And shake the darkness from their
    loosen'd manes,
And beat the twilight into flakes of fire.

Lo ! ever thus thou growest beautiful
In silence, then before thine answer
    given
Departest, and thy tears are on my
    cheek.

Why wilt thou ever scare me with thy
    tears,
And make me tremble lest a saying learnt,

In days far-off, on that dark earth, be
    true ?
' The Gods themselves cannot recall their
    gifts.'

Ay me ! ay me ! with what another
    heart
In days far-off, and with what other eyes
I used to watch—if I be he that watch'd—
The lucid outline forming round thee ;
    saw
The dim curls kindle into sunny rings ;
Changed with thy mystic change, and
    felt my blood
Glow with the glow that slowly crimson'd
    all
Thy presence and thy portals, while I
    lay,
Mouth, forehead, eyelids, growing dewy-
    warm
With kisses balmier than half-opening
    buds
Of April, and could hear the lips that
    kiss'd
Whispering I knew not what of wild and
    sweet,
Like that strange song I heard Apollo
    sing,
While Ilion like a mist rose into towers.

Yet hold me not for ever in thine East :
How can my nature longer mix with
    thine ?
Coldly thy rosy shadows bathe me, cold
Are all thy lights, and cold my wrinkled
    feet
Upon thy glimmering thresholds, when
    the steam
Floats up from those dim fields about the
    homes
Of happy men that have the power to
    die,
And grassy barrows of the happier dead.
Release me, and restore me to the ground ;
Thou seëst all things, thou wilt see my
    grave :
Thou wilt renew thy beauty morn by
    morn ;
I earth in earth forget these empty courts,
And thee returning on thy silver wheels.

T
H

LOCKSLEY HALL.

COMRADES, leave me here a little, while as yet 'tis early morn :
Leave me here, and when you want me, sound upon the bugle-horn.

'Tis the place, and all around it, as of old, the curlews call,
Dreary gleams about the moorland flying over Locksley Hall ;

Locksley Hall, that in the distance overlooks the sandy tracts,
And the hollow ocean-ridges roaring into cataracts.

Many a night from yonder ivied casement, ere I went to rest,
Did I look on great Orion sloping slowly to the West.

Many a night I saw the Pleiads, rising thro' the mellow shade,
Glitter like a swarm of fire-flies tangled in a silver braid.

Here about the beach I wander'd, nourishing a youth sublime
With the fairy tales of science, and the long result of Time ;

When the centuries behind me like a fruitful land reposed ;
When I clung to all the present for the promise that it closed :

When I dipt into the future far as human eye could see ;
Saw the Vision of the world, and all the wonder that would be.——

In the Spring a fuller crimson comes upon the robin's breast ;
In the Spring the wanton lapwing gets himself another crest ;

In the Spring a livelier iris changes on the burnish'd dove ;
In the Spring a young man's fancy lightly turns to thoughts of love.

Then her cheek was pale and thinner than should be for one so young,
And her eyes on all my motions with a mute observance hung.

And I said, ' My cousin Amy, speak, and speak the truth to me,
Trust me, cousin, all the current of my being sets to thee.'

On her pallid cheek and forehead came a colour and a light,
As I have seen the rosy red flushing in the northern night.

And she turn'd—her bosom shaken with a sudden storm of sighs—
All the spirit deeply dawning in the dark of hazel eyes—

Saying, ' I have hid my feelings, fearing they should do me wrong ; '
Saying, ' Dost thou love me, cousin ?' weeping, ' I have loved thee long.'

Love took up the glass of Time, and turn'd it in his glowing hands ;
Every moment, lightly shaken, ran itself in golden sands.

Love took up the harp of Life, and smote on all the chords with might ;
Smote the chord of Self, that, trembling, pass'd in music out of sight.

Many a morning on the moorland did we hear the copses ring,
And her whisper throng'd my pulses with the fulness of the Spring.

Many an evening by the waters did we watch the stately ships,
And our spirits rush'd together at the touching of the lips.

O my cousin, shallow-hearted ! O my Amy, mine no more !
O the dreary, dreary moorland ! O the barren, barren shore !

Falser than all fancy fathoms, falser than all songs have sung,
Puppet to a father's threat, and servile to a shrewish tongue !

Is it well to wish thee happy ?—having known me—to decline
On a range of lower feelings and a narrower heart than mine !

Yet it shall be : thou shalt lower to his level day by day,
What is fine within thee growing coarse to sympathise with clay.

As the husband is, the wife is : thou art mated with a clown,
And the grossness of his nature will have weight to drag thee down.

He will hold thee, when his passion shall have spent its novel force,
Something better than his dog, a little dearer than his horse.

What is this ? his eyes are heavy : think not they are glazed with wine.
Go to him : it is thy duty : kiss him : take his hand in thine.

It may be my lord is weary, that his brain is overwrought :
Soothe him with thy finer fancies, touch him with thy lighter thought.

He will answer to the purpose, easy things to understand—
Better thou wert dead before me, tho' I slew thee with my hand !

Better thou and I were lying, hidden from the heart's disgrace,
Roll'd in one another's arms, and silent in a last embrace.

Cursed be the social wants that sin against the strength of youth !
Cursed be the social lies that warp us from the living truth !

Cursed be the sickly forms that err from honest Nature's rule !
Cursed be the gold that gilds the straiten'd forehead of the fool !

Well—'tis well that I should bluster !—Hadst thou less unworthy proved—
Would to God—for I had loved thee more than ever wife was loved.

Am I mad, that I should cherish that which bears but bitter fruit ?
I will pluck it from my bosom, tho' my heart be at the root.

Never, tho' my mortal summers to such length of years should come
As the many-winter'd crow that leads the clanging rookery home.

Where is comfort ? in division of the records of the mind ?
Can I part her from herself, and love her, as I knew her, kind ?

I remember one that perish'd : sweetly did she speak and move :
Such a one do I remember, whom to look at was to love.

Can I think of her as dead, and love her for the love she bore ?
No—she never loved me truly : love is love for evermore.

Comfort ? comfort scorn'd of devils ! this is truth the poet sings,
That a sorrow's crown of sorrow is remembering happier things.

Drug thy memories, lest thou learn it, lest thy heart be put to proof,
In the dead unhappy night, and when the rain is on the roof.

Like a dog, he hunts in dreams, and thou art staring at the wall,
Where the dying night-lamp flickers, and the shadows rise and fall.

Then a hand shall pass before thee, pointing to his drunken sleep,
To thy widow'd marriage-pillows, to the tears that thou wilt weep.

Thou shalt hear the 'Never, never,' whisper'd by the phantom years,
And a song from out the distance in the ringing of thine ears ;

And an eye shall vex thee, looking ancient kindness on thy pain.
Turn thee, turn thee on thy pillow : get thee to thy rest again.

Nay, but Nature brings thee solace ; for a tender voice will cry.
'Tis a purer life than thine ; a lip to drain thy trouble dry.

Baby lips will laugh me down : my latest rival brings thee rest.
Baby fingers, waxen touches, press me from the mother's breast.

O, the child too clothes the father with a dearness not his due.
Half is thine and half is his : it will be worthy of the two.

O, I see thee old and formal, fitted to thy petty part,
With a little hoard of maxims preaching down a daughter's heart.

' They were dangerous guides the feelings—she herself was not exempt—
Truly, she herself had suffer'd '—Perish in thy self-contempt !

Overlive it—lower yet—be happy ! wherefore should I care ?
I myself must mix with action, lest I wither by despair.

What is that which I should turn to, lighting upon days like these ?
Every door is barr'd with gold, and opens but to golden keys.

Every gate is throng'd with suitors, all the markets overflow.
I have but an angry fancy : what is that which I should do ?

I had been content to perish, falling on the foeman's ground,
When the ranks are roll'd in vapour, and the winds are laid with sound.

But the jingling of the guinea helps the hurt that Honour feels,
And the nations do but murmur, snarling at each other's heels.

Can I but relive in sadness? I will turn that earlier page.
Hide me from my deep emotion, O thou wondrous Mother-Age!

Make me feel the wild pulsation that I felt before the strife,
When I heard my days before me, and the tumult of my life;

Yearning for the large excitement that the coming years would yield,
Eager-hearted as a boy when first he leaves his father's field,

And at night along the dusky highway near and nearer drawn,
Sees in heaven the light of London flaring like a dreary dawn;

And his spirit leaps within him to be gone before him then,
Underneath the light he looks at, in among the throngs of men:

Men, my brothers, men the workers, ever reaping something new:
That which they have done but earnest of the things that they shall do:

For I dipt into the future, far as human eye could see,
Saw the Vision of the world, and all the wonder that would be;

Saw the heavens fill with commerce, argosies of magic sails,
Pilots of the purple twilight, dropping down with costly bales;

Heard the heavens fill with shouting, and there rain'd a ghastly dew
From the nations' airy navies grappling in the central blue;

Far along the world-wide whisper of the south-wind rushing warm,
With the standards of the peoples plunging thro' the thunder-storm;

Till the war-drum throbb'd no longer, and the battle-flags were furl'd
In the Parliament of man, the Federation of the world.

There the common sense of most shall hold a fretful realm in awe,
And the kindly earth shall slumber, lapt in universal law.

So I triumph'd ere my passion sweeping thro' me left me dry,
Left me with the palsied heart, and left me with the jaundiced eye;

Eye, to which all order festers, all things here are out of joint:
Science moves, but slowly slowly, creeping on from point to point:

Slowly comes a hungry people, as a lion creeping nigher,
Glares at one that nods and winks behind a slowly-dying fire.

Yet I doubt not thro' the ages one increasing purpose runs,
And the thoughts of men are widen'd with the process of the suns.

What is that to him that reaps not harvest of his youthful joys,
Tho' the deep heart of existence beat for ever like a boy's?

Knowledge comes, but wisdom lingers, and I linger on the shore,
And the individual withers, and the world is more and more.

Knowledge comes, but wisdom lingers, and he bears a laden breast,
Full of sad experience, moving toward the stillness of his rest.

Hark, my merry comrades call me, sounding on the bugle-horn,
They to whom my foolish passion were a target for their scorn :

Shall it not be scorn to me to harp on such a moulder'd string ?
I am shamed thro' all my nature to have loved so slight a thing.

Weakness to be wroth with weakness ! woman's pleasure, woman's pain—
Nature made them blinder motions bounded in a shallower brain :

Woman is the lesser man, and all thy passions, match'd with mine,
Are as moonlight unto sunlight, and as water unto wine—

Here at least, where nature sickens, nothing.   Ah, for some retreat
Deep in yonder shining Orient, where my life began to beat ;

Where in wild Mahratta-battle fell my father evil-starr'd ;—
I was left a trampled orphan, and a selfish uncle's ward.

Or to burst all links of habit—there to wander far away,
On from island unto island at the gateways of the day.

Larger constellations burning, mellow moons and happy skies,
Breadths of tropic shade and palms in cluster, knots of Paradise.

Never comes the trader, never floats an European flag,
Slides the bird o'er lustrous woodland, swings the trailer from the crag ;

Droops the heavy-blossom'd bower, hangs the heavy-fruited tree—
Summer isles of Eden lying in dark-purple spheres of sea.

There methinks would be enjoyment more than in this march of mind,
In the steamship, in the railway, in the thoughts that shake mankind.

There the passions cramp'd no longer shall have scope and breathing space
I will take some savage woman, she shall rear my dusky race.

Iron jointed, supple-sinew'd, they shall dive, and they shall run,
Catch the wild goat by the hair, and hurl their lances in the sun ;

Whistle back the parrot's call, and leap the rainbows of the brooks,
Not with blinded eyesight poring over miserable books—

Fool, again the dream, the fancy ! but I *know* my words are wild,
But I count the gray barbarian lower than the Christian child.

I, to herd with narrow foreheads, vacant of our glorious gains,
Like a beast with lower pleasures, like a beast with lower pains !

Mated with a squalid savage—what to me were sun or clime ?
I the heir of all the ages, in the foremost files of time—

I that rather held it better men should perish one by one,
Than that earth should stand at gaze like Joshua's moon in Ajalon!

Not in vain the distance beacons. Forward, forward let us range,
Let the great world spin for ever down the ringing grooves of change.

Thro' the shadow of the globe we sweep into the younger day :
Better fifty years of Europe than a cycle of Cathay.

Mother-Age (for mine I knew not) help me as when life begun :
Rift the hills, and roll the waters, flash the lightnings, weigh the Sun.

O, I see the crescent promise of my spirit hath not set.
Ancient founts of inspiration well thro' all my fancy yet.

Howsoever these things be, a long farewell to Locksley Hall !
Now for me the woods may wither, now for me the roof-tree fall.

Comes a vapour from the margin, blackening over heath and holt,
Cramming all the blast before it, in its breast a thunderbolt.

Let it fall on Locksley Hall, with rain or hail, or fire or snow ;
For the mighty wind arises, roaring seaward, and I go.

GODIVA.

I waited for the train at Coventry ;
I hung with grooms and porters on the
bridge,
To watch the three tall spires ; and there
I shaped
The city's ancient legend into this :—
Not only we, the latest seed of Time,
New men, that in the flying of a wheel
Cry down the past, not only we, that prate
Of rights and wrongs, have loved the
people well,
And loathed to see them overtax'd ; but
she
Did more, and underwent, and overcame,
The woman of a thousand summers back,
Godiva, wife to that grim Earl, who ruled
In Coventry : for when he laid a tax
Upon his town, and all the mothers
brought
Their children, clamouring, 'If we pay,
we starve !'
She sought her lord, and found him, where
he strode
About the hall, among his dogs, alone,
His beard a foot before him, and his hair

A yard behind. She told him of their
tears,
And pray'd him, 'If they pay this tax,
they starve.'
Whereat he stared, replying, half-amazed,
'You would not let your little finger ache
For such as *these ?*'—'But I would die,'
said she.
He laugh'd, and swore by Peter and by
Paul :
Then fillip'd at the diamond in her ear ;
'Oh ay, ay, ay, you talk !'—'Alas !' she
said,
'But prove me what it is I would not do.'
And from a heart as rough as Esau's hand,
He answer'd, 'Ride you naked thro' the
town,
And I repeal it ;' and nodding, as in scorn,
He parted, with great strides among his
dogs.
So left alone, the passions of her mind.
As winds from all the compass shift and
blow,
Made war upon each other for an hour,
Till pity won. She sent a herald forth,
And bade him cry, with sound of trumpet,
all

The hard condition ; but that she would
    loose
The people : therefore, as they loved her
    well,
From then till noon no foot should pace
    the street,
No eye look down, she passing ; but that all
Should keep within, door shut, and
    window barr'd.
    Then fled she to her inmost bower,
        and there
Unclasp'd the wedded eagles of her belt,
The grim Earl's gift ; but ever at a breath
She linger'd, looking like a summer moon
Half-dipt in cloud : anon she shook her
    head,
And shower'd the rippled ringlets to her
    knee ;
Unclad herself in haste ; adown the stair
Stole on ; and, like a creeping sunbeam,
    slid
From pillar unto pillar, until she reach'd
The gateway ; there she found her palfrey
    trapt
In purple blazon'd with armorial gold.
    Then she rode forth, clothed on with
        chastity :
The deep air listen'd round her as she rode,
And all the low wind hardly breathed for
    fear.
The little wide-mouth'd heads upon the
    spout
Had cunning eyes to see : the barking cur
Made her cheek flame : her palfrey's foot-
    fall shot
Light horrors thro' her pulses : the blind
    walls
Were full of chinks and holes ; and
    overhead
Fantastic gables, crowding, stared: but she
Not less thro' all bore up, till, last, she saw
The white-flower'd elder-thicket from the
    field
Gleam thro' the Gothic archway in the
    wall.
    Then she rode back, clothed on with
        chastity :
And one low churl, compact of thankless
    earth,
The fatal byword of all years to come,

Boring a little auger-hole in fear,
Peep'd—but his eyes, before they had
    their will,
Were shrivell'd into darkness in his head,
And dropt before him. So the Powers,
    who wait
On noble deeds, cancell'd a sense misused :
And she, that knew not, pass'd : and all
    at once,
With twelve great shocks of sound, the
    shameless noon
Was clash'd and hammer'd from a hundred
    towers,
One after one : but even then she gain'd
Her bower ; whence reissuing, robed and
    crown'd,
To meet her lord, she took the tax away
And built herself an everlasting name.

THE DAY-DREAM.

PROLOGUE.

O LADY FLORA, let me speak :
    A pleasant hour has passed away
While, dreaming on your damask cheek,
    The dewy sister-eyelids lay.
As by the lattice you reclined,
    I went thro' many wayward moods
To see you dreaming—and, behind,
    A summer crisp with shining woods.
And I too dream'd, until at last
    Across my fancy, brooding warm,
The reflex of a legend past,
    And loosely settled into form.
And would you have the thought I had,
    And see the vision that I saw,
Then take the broidery-frame, and add
    A crimson to the quaint Macaw,
And I will tell it. Turn your face,
    Nor look with that too-earnest eye—
The rhymes are dazzled from their place
    And order'd words asunder fly.

THE SLEEPING PALACE.

I.

THE varying year with blade and sheaf
    Clothes and reclothes the happy plains,

I.

Here rests the sap within the leaf,
   Here stays the blood along the veins.
Faint shadows, vapours lightly curl'd,
   Faint murmurs from the meadows
      come,
Like hints and echoes of the world
   To spirits folded in the womb.

II.

Soft lustre bathes the range of urns
   On every slanting terrace-lawn.
The fountain to his place returns
   Deep in the garden lake withdrawn.
Here droops the banner on the tower,
   On the hall-hearths the festal fires,
The peacock in his laurel bower,
   The parrot in his gilded wires.

III.

Roof-haunting martins warm their eggs :
   In these, in those the life is stay'd.
The mantles from the golden pegs
   Droop sleepily : no sound is made,
Not even of a gnat that sings.
   More like a picture seemeth all
Than those old portraits of old kings,
   That watch the sleepers from the wall.

IV.

Here sits the Butler with a flask
   Between his knees, half-drain'd ; and
      there
The wrinkled steward at his task,
   The maid-of-honour blooming fair ;
The page has caught her hand in his :
   Her lips are sever'd as to speak :
His own are pouted to a kiss :
   The blush is fix'd upon her cheek.

V.

Till all the hundred summers pass,
   The beams, that thro' the Oriel shine,
Make prisms in every carven glass,
   And beaker brimm'd with noble wine.
Each baron at the banquet sleeps,
   Grave faces gather'd in a ring.
His state the king reposing keeps.
   He must have been a jovial king.

VI.

All round a hedge upshoots, and shows
   At distance like a little wood ;
Thorns, ivies, woodbine, mistletoes,
   And grapes with bunches red as blood ;
All creeping plants, a wall of green
   Close-matted, bur and brake and briar,
And glimpsing over these, just seen,
   High up, the topmost palace spire.

VII.

When will the hundred summers die,
   And thought and time be born again,
And newer knowledge, drawing nigh,
   Bring truth that sways the soul of men ?
Here all things in their place remain,
   As all were order'd, ages since.
Come, Care and Pleasure, Hope and Pain,
   And bring the fated fairy Prince.

THE SLEEPING BEAUTY.

I.

YEAR after year unto her feet,
   She lying on her couch alone,
Across the purple coverlet,
   The maiden's jet-black hair has grown,
On either side her tranced form
   Forth streaming from a braid of pearl :
The slumbrous light is rich and warm,
   And moves not on the rounded curl.

II.

The silk star-broider'd coverlid
   Unto her limbs itself doth mould
Languidly ever ; and, amid
   Her full black ringlets downward
      roll'd,
Glows forth each softly-shadow'd arm
   With bracelets of the diamond bright :
Her constant beauty doth inform
   Stillness with love, and day with light.

III.

She sleeps : her breathings are not heard
   In palace chambers far apart.
The fragrant tresses are not stirr'd
   That lie upon her charmed heart.

She sleeps : on either hand upswells
  The gold - fringed pillow lightly
    prest :
She sleeps, nor dreams, but ever dwells
  A perfect form in perfect rest.

THE ARRIVAL.

I.

ALL precious things, discover'd late,
  To those that seek them issue forth ;
For love in sequel works with fate,
    And draws the veil from hidden
      worth.
He travels far from other skies—
  His mantle glitters on the rocks—
A fairy Prince, with joyful eyes,
  And lighter-footed than the fox.

II.

The bodies and the bones of those
  That strove in other days to pass,
Are wither'd in the thorny close,
  Or scatter'd blanching on the grass.
He gazes on the silent dead :
  ' They perish'd in their daring deeds.'
This proverb flashes thro' his head,
  ' The many fail : the one succeeds.'

III.

He comes, scarce knowing what he
    seeks :
  He breaks the hedge : he enters
    there :
The colour flies into his cheeks :
  He trusts to light on something fair ;
For all his life the charm did talk
  About his path, and hover near
With words of promise in his walk,
  And whisper'd voices at his ear.

IV.

More close and close his footsteps
    wind :
  The Magic Music in his heart
Beats quick and quicker, till he find
  The quiet chamber far apart.

His spirit flutters like a lark,
  He stoops—to kiss her—on his knee.
' Love, if thy tresses be so dark,
  How dark those hidden eyes must be !'

THE REVIVAL.

I.

A TOUCH, a kiss ! the charm was snapt.
  There rose a noise of striking clocks,
And feet that ran, and doors that clapt,
  And barking dogs, and crowing cocks ;
A fuller light illumined all,
  A breeze thro' all the garden swept,
A sudden hubbub shook the hall,
  And sixty feet the fountain leapt.

II.

The hedge broke in, the banner blew,
  The butler drank, the steward scrawl'd,
The fire shot up, the martin flew,
    The parrot scream'd, the peacock
      squall'd,
The maid and page renew'd their strife,
    The palace bang'd, and buzz'd and
      clackt,
And all the long-pent stream of life
  Dash'd downward in a cataract.

III.

And last with these the king awoke,
  And in his chair himself uprear'd,
And yawn'd, and rubb'd his face, and
    spoke,
  ' By holy rood, a royal beard !
How say you ? we have slept, my lords.
  My beard has grown into my lap.'
The barons swore, with many words,
  'Twas but an after-dinner's nap.

IV.

' Pardy,' return'd the king, ' but still
  My joints are somewhat stiff or so.
My lord, and shall we pass the bill
  I mention'd half an hour ago ?'
The chancellor, sedate and vain,
  In courteous words return'd reply :
But dallied with his golden chain,
  And, smiling, put the question by.

THE DEPARTURE.

I.

AND on her lover's arm she leant,
  And round her waist she felt it fold,
And far across the hills they went
  In that new world which is the old :
Across the hills, and far away
  Beyond their utmost purple rim,
And deep into the dying day
  The happy princess follow'd him.

II.

' I'd sleep another hundred years,
  O love, for such another kiss ;'
' O wake for ever, love,' she hears,
  ' O love, 'twas such as this and this.'
And o'er them many a sliding star,
  And many a merry wind was borne,
And, stream'd thro' many a golden bar,
  The twilight melted into morn.

III.

' O eyes long laid in happy sleep !'
  ' O happy sleep, that lightly fled !'
' O happy kiss, that woke thy sleep !'
  ' O love, thy kiss would wake the dead !
And o'er them many a flowing range
  Of vapour buoy'd the crescent-bark,
And, rapt thro' many a rosy change,
  The twilight died into the dark.

IV.

' A hundred summers ! can it be ?
  And whither goest thou, tell me where?'
' O seek my father's court with me,
  For there are greater wonders there.'
And o'er the hills, and far away
  Beyond their utmost purple rim,
Beyond the night, across the day,
  Thro' all the world she follow'd him.

MORAL.

I.

So, Lady Flora, take my lay,
  And if you find no moral there,
Go, look in any glass and say,
  What moral is in being fair.

Oh, to what uses shall we put
  The wildweed-flower that simply blows?
And is there any moral shut
  Within the bosom of the rose ?

II.

But any man that walks the mead,
  In bud or blade, or bloom, may find,
According as his humours lead,
  A meaning suited to his mind.
And liberal applications lie
  In Art like Nature, dearest friend ;
So 'twere to cramp its use, if I
  Should hook it to some useful end.

L'ENVOI.

I.

YOU shake your head.   A random string
  Your finer female sense offends.
Well—were it not a pleasant thing
  To fall asleep with all one's friends ;
To pass with all our social ties
  To silence from the paths of men ;
And every hundred years to rise
  And learn the world, and sleep again ;
To sleep thro' terms of mighty wars,
  And wake on science grown to more,
On secrets of the brain, the stars,
  As wild as aught of fairy lore ;
And all that else the years will show,
  The Poet-forms of stronger hours,
The vast Republics that may grow,
  The Federations and the Powers ;
Titanic forces taking birth
  In divers seasons, divers climes ;
For we are Ancients of the earth,
  And in the morning of the times.

II.

So sleeping, so aroused from sleep
  Thro' sunny decads new and strange,
Or gay quinquenniads would we reap
  The flower and quintessence of change.

III.

Ah, yet would I—and would I might !
  So much your eyes my fancy take—
Be still the first to leap to light
  That I might kiss those eyes awake !

For, am I right, or am I wrong,
    To choose your own you did not care ;
You'd have *my* moral from the song,
    And I will take my pleasure there :
And, am I right or am I wrong,
    My fancy, ranging thro' and thro',
To search a meaning for the song,
    Perforce will still revert to you ;
Nor finds a closer truth than this
    All-graceful head, so richly curl'd,
And evermore a costly kiss
    The prelude to some brighter world.

IV.

For since the time when Adam first
    Embraced his Eve in happy hour,
And every bird of Eden burst
    In carol, every bud to flower,
What eyes, like thine, have waken'd
        hopes,
    What lips, like thine, so sweetly
        join'd ?
Where on the double rosebud droops
    The fulness of the pensive mind ;
Which all too dearly self-involved,
    Yet sleeps a dreamless sleep to me ;
A sleep by kisses undissolved,
    That lets thee neither hear nor see :
But break it.   In the name of wife,
    And in the rights that name may
        give,
Are clasp'd the moral of thy life,
    And that for which I care to live.

EPILOGUE.

So, Lady Flora, take my lay,
    And, if you find a meaning there,
O whisper to your glass, and say,
    ' What wonder, if he thinks me fair ? '
What wonder I was all unwise,
    To shape the song for your delight
Like long-tail'd birds of Paradise
    That float thro' Heaven, and cannot
        light ?
Or old-world trains, upheld at court
    By Cupid-boys of blooming hue—
But take it—earnest wed with sport,
    And either sacred unto you.

AMPHION.

My father left a park to me,
    But it is wild and barren,
A garden too with scarce a tree,
    And waster than a warren :
Yet say the neighbours when they call,
    It is not bad but good land,
And in it is the germ of all
    That grows within the woodland.

O had I lived when song was great
    In days of old Amphion,
And ta'en my fiddle to the gate,
    Nor cared for seed or scion !
And had I lived when song was great,
    And legs of trees were limber,
And ta'en my fiddle to the gate,
    And fiddled in the timber !

'Tis said he had a tuneful tongue,
    Such happy intonation,
Wherever he sat down and sung
    He left a small plantation ;
Wherever in a lonely grove
    He set up his forlorn pipes,
The gouty oak began to move,
    And flounder into hornpipes.

The mountain stirr'd its bushy crown,
    And, as tradition teaches,
Young ashes pirouetted down
    Coquetting with young beeches ;
And briony-vine and ivy-wreath
    Ran forward to his rhyming,
And from the valleys underneath
    Came little copses climbing.

The linden broke her ranks and rent
    The woodbine wreaths that bind her,
And down the middle, buzz ! she went
    With all her bees behind her :
The poplars, in long order due,
    With cypress promenaded,
The shock-head willows two and two
    By rivers gallopaded.

Came wet-shod alder from the wave,
    Came yews, a dismal coterie ;
Each pluck'd his one foot from the grave
    Poussetting with a sloe-tree :

Old elms came breaking from the vine,
  The vine stream'd out to follow,
And, sweating rosin, plump'd the pine
  From many a cloudy hollow.

And wasn't it a sight to see,
  When, ere his song was ended,
Like some great landslip, tree by tree,
  The country-side descended;
And shepherds from the mountain-eaves
  Look'd down, half-pleased, half-fright-
    en'd,
As dash'd about the drunken leaves
  The random sunshine lighten'd!

Oh, nature first was fresh to men,
  And wanton without measure;
So youthful and so flexile then,
  You moved her at your pleasure.
Twang out, my fiddle! shake the
    twigs!
  And make her dance attendance;
Blow, flute, and stir the stiff-set sprigs,
  And scirrhous roots and tendons.

'Tis vain! in such a brassy age
  I could not move a thistle;
The very sparrows in the hedge
  Scarce answer to my whistle;
Or at the most, when three-parts-sick
  With strumming and with scraping,
A jackass heehaws from the rick,
  The passive oxen gaping.

But what is that I hear? a sound
  Like sleepy counsel pleading;
O Lord!—'tis in my neighbour's ground,
  The modern Muses reading.
They read Botanic Treatises,
  And Works on Gardening thro' there,
And Methods of transplanting trees
  To look as if they grew there.

The wither'd Misses! how they prose
  O'er books of travell'd seamen,
And show you slips of all that grows
  From England to Van Diemen.
They read in arbours clipt and cut,
  And alleys, faded places,
By squares of tropic summer shut
  And warm'd in crystal cases.

But these, tho' fed with careful dirt,
  Are neither green nor sappy;
Half-conscious of the garden-squirt,
  The spindlings look unhappy.
Better to me the meanest weed
  That blows upon its mountain,
The vilest herb that runs to seed
  Beside its native fountain.

And I must work thro' months of toil,
  And years of cultivation,
Upon my proper patch of soil
  To grow my own plantation.
I'll take the showers as they fall,
  I will not vex my bosom:
Enough if at the end of all
  A little garden blossom.

ST. AGNES' EVE.

DEEP on the convent-roof the snows
  Are sparkling to the moon:
My breath to heaven like vapour goes:
  May my soul follow soon!
The shadows of the convent-towers
  Slant down the snowy sward,
Still creeping with the creeping hours
  That lead me to my Lord:
Make Thou my spirit pure and clear
  As are the frosty skies,
Or this first snowdrop of the year
  That in my bosom lies.

As these white robes are soil'd and dark,
  To yonder shining ground;
As this pale taper's earthly spark,
  To yonder argent round;
So shows my soul before the Lamb,
  My spirit before Thee;
So in mine earthly house I am,
  To that I hope to be.
Break up the heavens, O Lord! and far,
  Thro' all yon starlight keen,
Draw me, thy bride, a glittering star,
  In raiment white and clean.

He lifts me to the golden doors;
  The flashes come and go;
All heaven bursts her starry floors,
  And strows her lights below,

And deepens on and up ! the gates
   Roll back, and far within
For me the Heavenly Bridegroom waits,
   To make me pure of sin.
The sabbaths of Eternity,
   One sabbath deep and wide—
A light upon the shining sea—
   The Bridegroom with his bride !

SIR GALAHAD.

My good blade carves the casques of men,
   My tough lance thrusteth sure,
My strength is as the strength of ten,
   Because my heart is pure.
The shattering trumpet shrilleth high,
   The hard brands shiver on the steel,
The splinter'd spear-shafts crack and fly,
   The horse and rider reel :
They reel, they roll in clanging lists,
   And when the tide of combat stands,
Perfume and flowers fall in showers,
   That lightly rain from ladies' hands.

How sweet are looks that ladies bend
   On whom their favours fall !
For them I battle till the end,
   To save from shame and thrall :
But all my heart is drawn above,
   My knees are bow'd in crypt and
      shrine :
I never felt the kiss of love,
   Nor maiden's hand in mine.
More bounteous aspects on me beam,
   Me mightier transports move and thrill ;
So keep I fair thro' faith and prayer
   A virgin heart in work and will.

When down the stormy crescent goes,
   A light before me swims,
Between dark stems the forest glows,
   I hear a noise of hymns :
Then by some secret shrine I ride ;
   I hear a voice but none are there ;
The stalls are void, the doors are wide,
   The tapers burning fair.
Fair gleams the snowy altar-cloth,
   The silver vessels sparkle clean,
The shrill bell rings, the censer swings,
   And solemn chaunts resound between.

Sometimes on lonely mountain-meres
   I find a magic bark ;
I leap on board : no helmsman steers :
   I float till all is dark.
A gentle sound, an awful light !
   Three angels bear the holy Grail :
With folded feet, in stoles of white,
   On sleeping wings they sail.
Ah, blessed vision ! blood of God !
   My spirit beats her mortal bars,
As down dark tides the glory slides,
   And star-like mingles with the stars.

When on my goodly charger borne
   Thro' dreaming towns I go,
The cock crows ere the Christmas
      morn,
   The streets are dumb with snow.
The tempest crackles on the leads,
   And, ringing, springs from brand and
      mail ;
But o'er the dark a glory spreads,
   And gilds the driving hail.
I leave the plain, I climb the height ;
   No branchy thicket shelter yields ;
But blessed forms in whistling storms
   Fly o'er waste fens and windy fields.

A maiden knight—to me is given
   Such hope, I know not fear ;
I yearn to breathe the airs of heaven
   That often meet me here.
I muse on joy that will not cease,
   Pure spaces clothed in living beams,
Pure lilies of eternal peace,
   Whose odours haunt my dreams ;
And, stricken by an angel's hand,
   This mortal armour that I wear,
This weight and size, this heart and
      eyes,
   Are touch'd, are turn'd to finest air.

The clouds are broken in the sky,
   And thro' the mountain-walls
A rolling organ-harmony
   Swells up, and shakes and falls.
Then move the trees, the copses nod,
   Wings flutter, voices hover clear :
' O just and faithful knight of God !
   Ride on ! the prize is near.'

So pass I hostel, hall, and grange ;
　By bridge and ford, by park and pale,
All-arm'd I ride, whate'er betide,
　Until I find the holy Grail.

EDWARD GRAY.

SWEET Emma Moreland of yonder town
　Met me walking on yonder way,
' And have you lost your heart ?' she said ;
　' And are you married yet, Edward
　　Gray ?'

Sweet Emma Moreland spoke to me :
　Bitterly weeping I turn'd away :
' Sweet Emma Moreland, love no more
　Can touch the heart of Edward Gray.

' Ellen Adair she loved me well,
　Against her father's and mother's will :
To-day I sat for an hour and wept,
　By Ellen's grave, on the windy hill.

' Shy she was, and I thought her cold ;
　Thought her proud, and fled over the sea ;
Fill'd I was with folly and spite,
　When Ellen Adair was dying for me.

' Cruel, cruel the words I said !
　Cruelly came they back to-day :
" You're too slight and fickle," I said,
　" To trouble the heart of Edward Gray."

' There I put my face in the grass—
　Whisper'd, " Listen to my despair :
I repent me of all I did :
　Speak a little, Ellen Adair !"

' Then I took a pencil, and wrote
　On the mossy stone, as I lay,
" Here lies the body of Ellen Adair ;
　And here the heart of Edward Gray !"

' Love may come, and love may go,
　And fly, like a bird, from tree to tree ;
But I will love no more, no more,
　Till Ellen Adair come back to me.

' Bitterly wept I over the stone :
　Bitterly weeping I turn'd away :
There lies the body of Ellen Adair !
　And there the heart of Edward Gray !'

WILL WATERPROOF'S LYRICAL MONOLOGUE.

MADE AT THE COCK.

O PLUMP head-waiter at The Cock,
　To which I most resort,
How goes the time ? 'Tis five o'clock.
　Go fetch a pint of port :
But let it not be such as that
　You set before chance-comers,
But such whose father-grape grew fat
　On Lusitanian summers.

No vain libation to the Muse,
　But may she still be kind,
And whisper lovely words, and use
　Her influence on the mind,
To make me write my random rhymes,
　Ere they be half-forgotten ;
Nor add and alter, many times,
　Till all be ripe and rotten.

I pledge her, and she comes and dips
　Her laurel in the wine,
And lays it thrice upon my lips,
　These favour'd lips of mine ;
Until the charm have power to make
　New lifeblood warm the bosom,
And barren commonplaces break
　In full and kindly blossom.

I pledge her silent at the board ;
　Her gradual fingers steal
And touch upon the master-chord
　Of all I felt and feel.
Old wishes, ghosts of broken plans,
　And phantom hopes assemble ;
And that child's heart within the man's
　Begins to move and tremble.

Thro' many an hour of summer suns,
　By many pleasant ways,
Against its fountain upward runs
　The current of my days :
I kiss the lips I once have kiss'd ;
　The gas-light wavers dimmer ;
And softly, thro' a vinous mist,
　My college friendships glimmer.

I grow in worth, and wit, and sense,
　　Unboding critic-pen,
Or that eternal want of pence,
　　Which vexes public men,
Who hold their hands to all, and cry
　　For that which all deny them—
Who sweep the crossings, wet or dry,
　　And all the world go by them.

Ah yet, tho' all the world forsake,
　　Tho' fortune clip my wings,
I will not cramp my heart, nor take
　　Half-views of men and things.
Let Whig and Tory stir their blood ;
　　There must be stormy weather ;
But for some true result of good
　　All parties work together.

Let there be thistles, there are grapes ;
　　If old things, there are new ;
Ten thousand broken lights and shapes,
　　Yet glimpses of the true.
Let raffs be rife in prose and rhyme,
　　We lack not rhymes and reasons,
As on this whirligig of Time
　　We circle with the seasons.

This earth is rich in man and maid ;
　　With fair horizons bound :
This whole wide earth of light and shade
　　Comes out a perfect round.
High over roaring Temple-bar,
　　And set in Heaven's third story,
I look at all things as they are,
　　But thro' a kind of glory.

———

Head-waiter, honour'd by the guest
　　Half-mused, or reeling ripe,
The pint, you brought me, was the best
　　That ever came from pipe.
But tho' the port surpasses praise,
　　My nerves have dealt with stiffer.
Is there some magic in the place ?
　　Or do my peptics differ ?

For since I came to live and learn,
　　No pint of white or red
Had ever half the power to turn
　　This wheel within my head,

Which bears a season'd brain about,
　　Unsubject to confusion,
Tho' soak'd and saturate, out and out,
　　Thro' every convolution.

For I am of a numerous house,
　　With many kinsmen gay,
Where long and largely we carouse
　　As who shall say me nay :
Each month, a birth-day coming on,
　　We drink defying trouble,
Or sometimes two would meet in one,
　　And then we drank it double ;

Whether the vintage, yet unkept,
　　Had relish fiery-new,
Or elbow-deep in sawdust, slept,
　　As old as Waterloo ;
Or stow'd, when classic Canning died,
　　In musty bins and chambers,
Had cast upon its crusty side
　　The gloom of ten Decembers.

The Muse, the jolly Muse, it is !
　　She answer'd to my call,
She changes with that mood or this,
　　Is all-in-all to all :
She lit the spark within my throat,
　　To make my blood run quicker,
Used all her fiery will, and smote
　　Her life into the liquor.

And hence this halo lives about
　　The waiter's hands, that reach
To each his perfect pint of stout,
　　His proper chop to each.
He looks not like the common breed
　　That with the napkin dally ;
I think he came like Ganymede,
　　From some delightful valley.

The Cock was of a larger egg
　　Than modern poultry drop,
Stept forward on a firmer leg,
　　And cramm'd a plumper crop ;
Upon an ampler dunghill trod,
　　Crow'd lustier late and early,
Sipt wine from silver, praising God,
　　And raked in golden barley.

A private life was all his joy,
   Till in a court he saw
A something-pottle-bodied boy
   That knuckled at the taw :
He stoop'd and clutch'd him, fair and
      good,
   Flew over roof and casement :
His brothers of the weather stood
   Stock-still for sheer amazement.

But he, by farmstead, thorpe and spire,
   And follow'd with acclaims,
A sign to many a staring shire
   Came crowing over Thames.
Right down by smoky Paul's they bore,
   Till, where the street grows straiter,
One fix'd for ever at the door,
   And one became head-waiter.

———

But whither would my fancy go ?
   How out of place she makes
The violet of a legend blow
   Among the chops and steaks !
'Tis but a steward of the can,
   One shade more plump than common ;
As just and mere a serving-man
   As any born of woman.

I ranged too high : what draws me down
   Into the common day ?
Is it the weight of that half-crown,
   Which I shall have to pay ?
For, something duller than at first,
   Nor wholly comfortable,
I sit, my empty glass reversed,
   And thrumming on the table :

Half fearful that, with self at strife,
   I take myself to task ;
Lest of the fulness of my life
   I leave an empty flask :
For I had hope, by something rare
   To prove myself a poet :
But, while I plan and plan, my hair
   Is gray before I know it.

So fares it since the years began,
   Till they be gather'd up ;
The truth, that flies the flowing can,
   Will haunt the vacant cup :

And others' follies teach us not,
   Nor much their wisdom teaches ;
And most, of sterling worth, is what
   Our own experience preaches.

Ah, let the rusty theme alone !
   We know not what we know.
But for my pleasant hour, 'tis gone ;
   'Tis gone, and let it go.
'Tis gone : a thousand such have slipt
   Away from my embraces,
And fall'n into the dusty crypt
   Of darken'd forms and faces.

Go, therefore, thou ! thy betters went
   Long since, and came no more ;
With peals of genial clamour sent
   From many a tavern-door,
With twisted quirks and happy hits,
   From misty men of letters ;
The tavern-hours of mighty wits—
   Thine elders and thy betters.

Hours, when the Poet's words and looks
   Had yet their native glow :
Nor yet the fear of little books
   Had made him talk for show ;
But, all his vast heart sherris-warm'd,
   He flash'd his random speeches,
Ere days, that deal in ana, swarm'd
   His literary leeches.

So mix for ever with the past,
   Like all good things on earth !
For should I prize thee, couldst thou
      last,
   At half thy real worth ?
I hold it good, good things should pass:
   With time I will not quarrel :
It is but yonder empty glass
   That makes me maudlin-moral.

———

Head-waiter of the chop-house here,
   To which I most resort,
I too must part : I hold thee dear
   For this good pint of port.
For this, thou shalt from all things suck
   Marrow of mirth and laughter ;
And wheresoe'er thou move, good luck
   Shall fling her old shoe after.

But thou wilt never move from hence,
    The sphere thy fate allots :
Thy latter days increased with pence
    Go down among the pots :
Thou battenest by the greasy gleam
    In haunts of hungry sinners,
Old boxes, larded with the steam
    Of thirty thousand dinners.

We fret, we fume, would shift our skins,
    Would quarrel with our lot ;
Thy care is, under polish'd tins,
    To serve the hot-and-hot ;
To come and go, and come again,
    Returning like the pewit,
And watch'd by silent gentlemen,
    That trifle with the cruet.

Live long, ere from thy topmost head
    The thick-set hazel dies ;
Long, ere the hateful crow shall tread
    The corners of thine eyes :
Live long, nor feel in head or chest
    Our changeful equinoxes,
Till mellow Death, like some late guest,
    Shall call thee from the boxes.

But when he calls, and thou shalt cease
    To pace the gritted floor,
And, laying down an unctuous lease
    Of life, shalt earn no more ;
No carved cross-bones, the types of Death,
    Shall show thee past to Heaven :
But carved cross-pipes, and, underneath,
    A pint-pot neatly graven.

LADY CLARE.

IT was the time when lilies blow,
    And clouds are highest up in air,
Lord Ronald brought a lily-white doe
    To give his cousin, Lady Clare.

I trow they did not part in scorn :
    Lovers long-betroth'd were they :
They two will wed the morrow morn :
    God's blessing on the day !

'He does not love me for my birth,
    Nor for my lands so broad and fair ;
He loves me for my own true worth,
    And that is well,' said Lady Clare.

In there came old Alice the nurse,
    Said, 'Who was this that went from
        thee ?'
'It was my cousin,' said Lady Clare,
    'To-morrow he weds with me.'

'O God be thank'd !' said Alice the
        nurse,
    'That all comes round so just and fair :
Lord Ronald is heir of all your lands,
    And you are *not* the Lady Clare.'

'Are ye out of your mind, my nurse,
        my nurse ?'
    Said Lady Clare, 'that ye speak so
        wild ?'
'As God's above,' said Alice the nurse,
    'I speak the truth : you are my child.

'The old Earl's daughter died at my
        breast ;
    I speak the truth, as I live by bread !
I buried her like my own sweet child,
    And put my child in her stead.'

'Falsely, falsely have ye done,
    O mother,' she said, 'if this be true,
To keep the best man under the sun
    So many years from his due.'

'Nay now, my child,' said Alice the
        nurse,
    'But keep the secret for your life,
And all you have will be Lord Ronald's,
    When you are man and wife.'

'If I'm a beggar born,' she said,
    'I will speak out, for I dare not lie.
Pull off, pull off, the brooch of gold,
    And fling the diamond necklace by.'

'Nay now, my child,' said Alice the
        nurse,
    'But keep the secret all ye can.'
She said, 'Not so : but I will know
    If there be any faith in man.'

'Nay now, what faith ?' said Alice the
        nurse,
    'The man will cleave unto his right.'
'And he shall have it,' the lady replied,
    'Tho' I should die to-night.'

'Yet give one kiss to your mother dear!
　Alas, my child, I sinn'd for thee.'
'O mother, mother, mother,' she said,
　'So strange it seems to me.

'Yet here's a kiss for my mother dear,
　My mother dear, if this be so,
And lay your hand upon my head,
　And bless me, mother, ere I go.'

She clad herself in a russet gown,
　She was no longer Lady Clare:
She went by dale, and she went by down,
　With a single rose in her hair.

The lily-white doe Lord Ronald had
　　brought
　Leapt up from where she lay,
Dropt her head in the maiden's hand,
　And follow'd her all the way.

Down stept Lord Ronald from his tower:
　'O Lady Clare, you shame your worth!
Why come you drest like a village maid,
　That are the flower of the earth?'

'If I come drest like a village maid,
　I am but as my fortunes are:
I am a beggar born,' she said,
　'And not the Lady Clare.'

'Play me no tricks,' said Lord Ronald,
　'For I am yours in word and in deed.
Play me no tricks,' said Lord Ronald,
　'Your riddle is hard to read.'

O and proudly stood she up!
　Her heart within her did not fail:
She look'd into Lord Ronald's eyes,
　And told him all her nurse's tale.

He laugh'd a laugh of merry scorn:
　He turn'd and kiss'd her where she
　　stood:
'If you are not the heiress born,
　And I,' said he, 'the next in blood—

'If you are not the heiress born,
　And I,' said he, 'the lawful heir,
We two will wed to-morrow morn,
　And you shall still be Lady Clare.'

THE CAPTAIN.

A LEGEND OF THE NAVY.

HE that only rules by terror
　Doeth grievous wrong.
Deep as Hell I count his error.
　Let him hear my song.
Brave the Captain was: the seamen
　Made a gallant crew,
Gallant sons of English freemen,
　Sailors bold and true.
But they hated his oppression,
　Stern he was and rash;
So for every light transgression
　Doom'd them to the lash.
Day by day more harsh and cruel
　Seem'd the Captain's mood.
Secret wrath like smother'd fuel
　Burnt in each man's blood.
Yet he hoped to purchase glory,
　Hoped to make the name
Of his vessel great in story,
　Wheresoe'er he came.
So they past by capes and islands,
　Many a harbour-mouth,
Sailing under palmy highlands
　Far within the South.
On a day when they were going
　O'er the lone expanse,
In the north, her canvas flowing,
　Rose a ship of France.
Then the Captain's colour heighten'd,
　Joyful came his speech:
But a cloudy gladness lighten'd
　In the eyes of each.
'Chase,' he said: the ship flew for-
　　ward,
　And the wind did blow;
Stately, lightly, went she Norward,
　Till she near'd the foe.
Then they look'd at him they hated,
　Had what they desired:
Mute with folded arms they waited—
　Not a gun was fired.
But they heard the foeman's thunder
　Roaring out their doom;
All the air was torn in sunder,
　Crashing went the boom,

Spars were splinter'd, decks were shatter'd,
　　Bullets fell like rain ;
Over mast and deck were scatter'd
　　Blood and brains of men.
Spars were splinter'd ; decks were broken :
　　Every mother's son—
Down they dropt—no word was spoken—
　　Each beside his gun.
On the decks as they were lying,
　　Were their faces grim.
In their blood, as they lay dying,
　　Did they smile on him.
Those, in whom he had reliance
　　For his noble name,
With one smile of still defiance
　　Sold him unto shame.
Shame and wrath his heart confounded,
　　Pale he turn'd and red,
Till himself was deadly wounded
　　Falling on the dead.
Dismal error ! fearful slaughter !
　　Years have wander'd by,
Side by side beneath the water
　　Crew and Captain lie ;
There the sunlit ocean tosses
　　O'er them mouldering,
And the lonely seabird crosses
　　With one waft of the wing.

THE LORD OF BURLEIGH.

In her ear he whispers gaily,
　　' If my heart by signs can tell,
Maiden, I have watch'd thee daily,
　　And I think thou lov'st me well.'
She replies, in accents fainter,
　　' There is none I love like thee.'
He is but a landscape-painter,
　　And a village maiden she.
He to lips, that fondly falter, *q. défaillent*
　　Presses his without reproof :
Leads her to the village altar,
　　And they leave her father's roof.
' I can make no marriage present :
　　Little can I give my wife.
Love will make our cottage pleasant,
　　And I love thee more than life.'
They by parks and lodges going
　　See the lordly castles stand :

Summer woods, about them blowing,
　　Made a murmur in the land.
From deep thought himself he rouses,
　　Says to her that loves him well,
' Let us see these handsome houses
　　Where the wealthy nobles dwell.'
So she goes by him attended,
　　Hears him lovingly converse,
Sees whatever fair and splendid
　　Lay betwixt his home and hers ;
Parks with oak and chestnut shady,
　　Parks and order'd gardens great,
Ancient homes of lord and lady,
　　Built for pleasure and for state.
All he shows her makes him dearer :
　　Evermore she seems to gaze
On that cottage growing nearer,
　　Where they twain will spend their days
O but she will love him truly !
　　He shall have a cheerful home ;
She will order all things duly,
　　When beneath his roof they come.
Thus her heart rejoices greatly,
　　Till a gateway she discerns
With armorial bearings stately,
　　And beneath the gate she turns ;
Sees a mansion more majestic
　　Than all those she saw before :
Many a gallant gay domestic
　　Bows before him at the door.
And they speak in gentle murmur,
　　When they answer to his call,
While he treads with footstep firmer,
　　Leading on from hall to hall.
And, while now she wonders blindly,
　　Nor the meaning can divine,
Proudly turns he round and kindly,
　　' All of this is mine and thine.'
Here he lives in state and bounty,
　　Lord of Burleigh, fair and free,
Not a lord in all the county
　　Is so great a lord as he.
All at once the colour flushes
　　Her sweet face from brow to chin :
As it were with shame she blushes,
　　And her spirit changed within.
Then her countenance all over
　　Pale again as death did prove :
But he clasp'd her like a lover,
　　And he cheer'd her soul with love.

So she strove against her weakness,
  Tho' at times her spirit sank :
Shaped her heart with woman's meekness
  To all duties of her rank :
And a gentle consort made he,
  And her gentle mind was such
That she grew a noble lady,
  And the people loved her much.
But a trouble weigh'd upon her,
  And perplex'd her, night and morn,
With the burthen of an honour
  Unto which she was not born.
Faint she grew, and ever fainter,
  And she murmur'd, ' Oh, that he
Were once more that landscape-painter,
  Which did win my heart from me !'
So she droop'd and droop'd before him,
  Fading slowly from his side :
Three fair children first she bore him,
  Then before her time she died.
Weeping, weeping late and early,
  Walking up and pacing down,
Deeply mourn'd the Lord of Burleigh,
  Burleigh-house by Stamford-town.
And he came to look upon her,
  And he look'd at her and said,
'Bring the dress and put it on her,
  That she wore when she was wed.'
Then her people, softly treading,
  Bore to earth her body, drest
In the dress that she was wed in,
  That her spirit might have rest.

THE VOYAGE.

I.

WE left behind the painted buoy
  That tosses at the harbour-mouth ;
And madly danced our hearts with joy,
  As fast we fleeted to the South :
How fresh was every sight and sound
  On open main or winding shore !
We knew the merry world was round,
  And we might sail for evermore.

II.

Warm broke the breeze against the
    brow,
  Dry sang the tackle, sang the sail :

The Lady's-head upon the prow
  Caught the shrill salt, and sheer'd the
    gale.
The broad seas swell'd to meet the keel,
  And swept behind ; so quick the run,
We felt the good ship shake and reel,
  We seem'd to sail into the Sun !

III.

How oft we saw the Sun retire,
  And burn the threshold of the night,
Fall from his Ocean-lane of fire,
  And sleep beneath his pillar'd light !
How oft the purple-skirted robe
  Of twilight slowly downward drawn,
As thro' the slumber of the globe
  Again we dash'd into the dawn !

IV.

New stars all night above the brim
  Of waters lighten'd into view ;
They climb'd as quickly, for the rim
  Changed every moment as we flew.
Far ran the naked moon across
  The houseless ocean's heaving field,
Or flying shone, the silver boss
  Of her own halo's dusky shield ;

V.

The peaky islet shifted shapes,
  High towns on hills were dimly seen,
We past long lines of Northern capes
  And dewy Northern meadows green.
We came to warmer waves, and deep
  Across the boundless east we drove,
Where those long swells of breaker sweep
  The nutmeg rocks and isles of clove.

VI.

By peaks that flamed, or, all in shade,
  Gloom'd the low coast and quivering
    brine
With ashy rains, that spreading made
  Fantastic plume or sable pine ;
By sands and steaming flats, and floods
  Of mighty mouth, we scudded fast,
And hills and scarlet-mingled woods
  Glow'd for a moment as we past.

VII.

O hundred shores of happy climes,
    How swiftly stream'd ye by the bark !
At times the whole sea burn'd, at times
    With wakes of fire we tore the dark ;
At times a carven craft would shoot
    From havens hid in fairy bowers,
With naked limbs and flowers and fruit,
    But we nor paused for fruit nor flowers.

VIII.

For one fair Vision ever fled
    Down the waste waters day and night,
And still we follow'd where she led,
    In hope to gain upon her flight.
Her face was evermore unseen,
    And fixt upon the far sea-line ;
But each man murmur'd, 'O my Queen,
    I follow till I make thee mine.'

IX.

And now we lost her, now she gleam'd
    Like Fancy made of golden air,
Now nearer to the prow she seem'd
    Like Virtue firm, like Knowledge fair,
Now high on waves that idly burst
    Like Heavenly Hope she crown'd the
        sea,
And now, the bloodless point reversed,
    She bore the blade of Liberty.

X.

And only one among us—him
    We   pleased   not — he   was   seldom
        pleased :
He saw not far : his eyes were dim :
    But ours he swore were all diseased.
'A ship of fools,' he shriek'd in spite,
    'A ship of fools,' he sneer'd and
        wept.
And overboard one stormy night
    He cast his body, and on we swept.

XI.

And never sail of ours was furl'd,
    Nor anchor dropt at eve or morn ;
We lov'd the glories of the world,
    But laws of nature were our scorn.

For blasts would rise and rave and cease,
    But whence were those that drove the
        sail
Across the whirlwind's heart of peace,
    And to and thro' the counter gale ?

XII.

Again to colder climes we came,
    For still we follow'd where she led :
Now mate is blind and captain lame,
    And half the crew are sick or dead,
But, blind or lame or sick or sound,
    We follow that which flies before :
We know the merry world is round,
    And we may sail for evermore.

SIR LAUNCELOT AND
QUEEN GUINEVERE.

A FRAGMENT.

LIKE souls that balance joy and pain,
With tears and smiles from heaven again
The maiden Spring upon the plain
Came in a sun-lit fall of rain.
    In crystal vapour everywhere
Blue isles of heaven laugh'd between,
And far, in forest-deeps unseen,
The topmost elm-tree gather'd green
    From draughts of balmy air.

Sometimes the linnet piped his song :
Sometimes the throstle whistled strong :
Sometimes the sparhawk, wheel'd along,
Hush'd all the groves from fear of wrong :
    By grassy capes with fuller sound
In curves the yellowing river ran,
And drooping chestnut-buds began
To spread into the perfect fan,
    Above the teeming ground.

Then, in the boyhood of the year,
Sir Launcelot and Queen Guinevere
Rode thro' the coverts of the deer,
With blissful treble ringing clear.
    She seem'd a part of joyous Spring :
A gown of grass-green silk she wore,
Buckled with golden clasps before ;
A light-green tuft of plumes she bore
    Closed in a golden ring.

Now on some twisted ivy-net,
Now by some tinkling rivulet,
In mosses mixt with violet
Her cream-white mule his pastern set :
 And fleeter now she skimm'd the
  plains
Than she whose elfin prancer springs
By night to eery warblings,
When all the glimmering moorland rings
 With jingling bridle-reins.

As fast she fled thro' sun and shade,
The happy winds upon her play'd,
Blowing the ringlet from the braid :
She look'd so lovely, as she sway'd
 The rein with dainty finger-tips,
A man had given all other bliss,
And all his worldly worth for this,
To waste his whole heart in one kiss
 Upon her perfect lips.

A FAREWELL.

FLOW down, cold rivulet, to the sea,
 Thy tribute wave deliver :
No more by thee my steps shall be,
 For ever and for ever.

Flow, softly flow, by lawn and lea,
 A rivulet then a river :
No where by thee my steps shall be,
 For ever and for ever.

But here will sigh thine alder tree,
 And here thine aspen shiver ;
And here by thee will hum the bee,
 For ever and for ever.

A thousand suns will stream on thee,
 A thousand moons will quiver ;
But not by thee my steps shall be,
 For ever and for ever.

THE BEGGAR MAID.

HER arms across her breast she laid ;
 She was more fair than words can say :
Bare-footed came the beggar maid
 Before the king Cophetua.

In robe and crown the king stept down,
 To meet and greet her on her way ;
' It is no wonder,' said the lords,
 ' She is more beautiful than day.'

As shines the moon in clouded skies,
 She in her poor attire was seen :
One praised her ancles, one her eyes,
 One her dark hair and lovesome mien.
So sweet a face, such angel grace,
 In all that land had never been :
Cophetua sware a royal oath :
 ' This beggar maid shall be my queen !'

THE EAGLE.

FRAGMENT.

HE clasps the crag with crooked hands ;
Close to the sun in lonely lands,
Ring'd with the azure world, he stands.

The wrinkled sea beneath him crawls ;
He watches from his mountain walls,
And like a thunderbolt he falls.

———

MOVE eastward, happy earth, and leave
 Yon orange sunset waning slow :
From fringes of the faded eve,
 O, happy planet, eastward go ;
Till over thy dark shoulder glow
 Thy silver sister-world, and rise
 To glass herself in dewy eyes
That watch me from the glen below.

Ah, bear me with thee, smoothly borne,
 Dip forward under starry light,
And move me to my marriage-morn,
 And round again to happy night.

———

COME not, when I am dead,
 To drop thy foolish tears upon my
  grave,
To trample round my fallen head,
 And vex the unhappy dust thou wouldst
  not save.
There let the wind sweep and the plover
 cry ;
  But thou, go by.

m an old Engl ballad in Percy's 'Rel'
») ± 189
nak
p223

Child, if it were thine error or thy crime
    I care no longer, being all unblest :
Wed whom thou wilt, but I am sick of
    Time,
    And I desire to rest.
Pass on, weak heart, and leave me where
    I lie :
      Go by, go by.

THE LETTERS.

I.

STILL on the tower stood the vane,
    A black yew gloom'd the stagnant air,
I peer'd athwart the chancel pane
    And saw the altar cold and bare.
A clog of lead was round my feet,
    A band of pain across my brow ;
' Cold altar, Heaven and earth shall meet
    Before you hear my marriage vow.'

II.

I turn'd and humm'd a bitter song
    That mock'd the wholesome human
      heart,
And then we met in wrath and wrong,
    We met, but only meant to part.
Full cold my greeting was and dry ;
    She faintly smiled, she hardly moved ;
I saw with half-unconscious eye
    She wore the colours I approved.

III.

She took the little ivory chest,
    With half a sigh she turn'd the key,
Then raised her head with lips comprest,
    And gave my letters back to me.
And gave the trinkets and the rings,
    My gifts, when gifts of mine could
      please ;
As looks a father on the things
    Of his dead son, I look'd on these.

IV.

She told me all her friends had said ;
    I raged against the public liar ;
She talk'd as if her love were dead,
    But in my words were seeds of fire.

' No more of love ; your sex is known :
    I never will be twice deceived.
Henceforth I trust the man alone,
    The woman cannot be believed.

V.

' Thro' slander, meanest spawn of Hell—
    And women's slander is the worst,
And you, whom once I lov'd so well,
    Thro' you, my life will be accurst.'
I spoke with heart, and heat and force,
    I shook her breast with vague alarms—
Like torrents from a mountain source
    We rush'd into each other's arms.

VI.

We parted : sweetly gleam'd the stars,
    And sweet the vapour-braided blue,
Low breezes fann'd the belfry bars,
    As homeward by the church I drew.
The very graves appear'd to smile,
    So fresh they rose in shadow'd swells ;
' Dark porch,' I said, ' and silent aisle,
    There comes a sound of marriage bells.

THE VISION OF SIN.

I.

I HAD a vision when the night was late :
A youth came riding toward a palace-gate.
He rode a horse with wings, that would
    have flown,
But that his heavy rider kept him down.
And from the palace came a child of sin,
And took him by the curls, and led him in,
Where sat a company with heated eyes,
Expecting when a fountain should arise :
A sleepy light upon their brows and lips—
As when the sun, a crescent of eclipse,
Dreams over lake and lawn, and isles and
    capes—
Suffused them, sitting, lying, languid
    shapes,
By heaps of gourds, and skins of wine,
    and piles of grapes.

II.

Then methought I heard a mellow sound,
Gathering up from all the lower ground ;

Narrowing in to where they sat assembled
Low voluptuous music winding trembled,
Wov'n in circles: they that heard it sigh'd,
Panted hand-in-hand with faces pale,
Swung themselves, and in low tones re-
   plied ;
Till the fountain spouted, showering wide
Sleet of diamond-drift and pearly hail ;
Then the music touch'd the gates and died ;
Rose again from where it seem'd to fail,
Storm'd in orbs of song, a growing gale ;
Till thronging in and in, to where they
   waited,
As 'twere a hundred-throated nightingale,
The strong tempestuous treble throbb'd
   and palpitated ;
Ran into its giddiest whirl of sound,
Caught the sparkles, and in circles,
Purple gauzes, golden hazes, liquid mazes,
Flung the torrent rainbow round :
Then they started from their places,
Moved with violence, changed in hue,
Caught each other with wild grimaces,
Half-invisible to the view,
Wheeling with precipitate paces
To the melody, till they flew,
Hair, and eyes, and limbs, and faces,
Twisted hard in fierce embraces,
Like to Furies, like to Graces,
Dash'd together in blinding dew :
Till, kill'd with some luxurious agony,
The nerve-dissolving melody
Flutter'd headlong from the sky.

III.

And then I look'd up toward a mountain-
   tract,
That girt the region with high cliff and
   lawn :
I saw that every morning, far withdrawn
Beyond the darkness and the cataract,
God made Himself an awful rose of dawn,
Unheeded : and detaching, fold by fold,
From those still heights, and, slowly
   drawing near,
A vapour heavy, hueless, formless, cold,
Came floating on for many a month and
   year,
Unheeded : and I thought I would have
   spoken,

And warn'd that madman ere it grew too
   late :
But, as in dreams, I could not.   Mine
   was broken,
When that cold vapour touch'd the palace
   gate,
And link'd again.   I saw within my head
A gray and gap-tooth'd man as lean as
   death,
Who slowly rode across a wither'd heath,
And lighted at a ruin'd inn, and said :

IV.

' Wrinkled ostler, grim and thin !
   Here is custom come your way ;
Take my brute, and lead him in,
   Stuff his ribs with mouldy hay.

' Bitter barmaid, waning fast !
   See that sheets are on my bed ;
What ! the flower of life is past :
   It is long before you wed.

' Slip-shod waiter, lank and sour,
   At the Dragon on the heath !
Let us have a quiet hour,
   Let us hob-and-nob with Death.

' I am old, but let me drink ;
   Bring me spices, bring me wine ;
I remember, when I think,
   That my youth was half divine.

Wine is good for shrivell'd lips,
   When a blanket wraps the day,
When the rotten woodland drips,
   And the leaf is stamp'd in clay.

' Sit thee down, and have no shame,
   Cheek by jowl, and knee by knee :
What care I for any name ?
   What for order or degree ?

' Let me screw thee up a peg :
   Let me loose thy tongue with wine :
Callest thou that thing a leg ?
   Which is thinnest ? thine or mine ?

' Thou shalt not be saved by works :
   Thou hast been a sinner too :
Ruin'd trunks on wither'd forks,
   Empty scarecrows, I and you !

'Fill the cup, and fill the can :
  Have a rouse before the morn :
Every moment dies a man,
  Every moment one is born.

'We are men of ruin'd blood ;
  Therefore comes it we are wise.
Fish are we that love the mud,
  Rising to no fancy-flies.

'Name and fame ! to fly sublime
  Thro' the courts, the camps, the
    schools,
Is to be the ball of Time,
  Bandied by the hands of fools.

'Friendship !—to be two in one—
  Let the canting liar pack !
Well I know, when I am gone,
  How she mouths behind my back.

'Virtue !—to be good and just—
  Every heart, when sifted well,
Is a clot of warmer dust,
  Mix'd with cunning sparks of hell.

'O ! we two as well can look
  Whited thought and cleanly life
As the priest, above his book
  Leering at his neighbour's wife.

'Fill the cup, and fill the can :
  Have a rouse before the morn :
Every moment dies a man,
  Every moment one is born.

'Drink, and let the parties rave :
  They are fill'd with idle spleen ;
Rising, falling, like a wave,
  For they know not what they mean.

'He that roars for liberty
  Faster binds a tyrant's power ;
And the tyrant's cruel glee
  Forces on the freer hour.

'Fill the can, and fill the cup :
  All the windy ways of men
Are but dust that rises up,
  And is lightly laid again.

'Greet her with applausive breath,
  Freedom, gaily doth she tread ;
In her right a civic wreath,
  In her left a human head.

'No, I love not what is new ;
  She is of an ancient house :
And I think we know the hue
  Of that cap upon her brows.

'Let her go ! her thirst she slakes
  Where the bloody conduit runs,
Then her sweetest meal she makes
  On the first-born of her sons.

'Drink to lofty hopes that cool—
  Visions of a perfect State :
Drink we, last, the public fool,
  Frantic love and frantic hate.

'Chant me now some wicked stave,
  Till thy drooping courage rise,
And the glow-worm of the grave
  Glimmer in thy rheumy eyes.

'Fear not thou to loose thy tongue ;
  Set thy hoary fancies free ;
What is loathsome to the young
  Savours well to thee and me.

'Change, reverting to the years,
  When thy nerves could understand
What there is in loving tears,
  And the warmth of hand in hand.

'Tell me tales of thy first love—
  April hopes, the fools of chance ;
Till the graves begin to move,
  And the dead begin to dance.

'Fill the can, and fill the cup :
  All the windy ways of men
Are but dust that rises up,
  And is lightly laid again.

'Trooping from their mouldy dens
  The chap-fallen circle spreads :
Welcome, fellow-citizens,
  Hollow hearts and empty heads !

'You are bones, and what of that?
  Every face, however full,
Padded round with flesh and fat,
  Is but modell'd on a skull.

'Death is king, and Vivat Rex!
  Tread a measure on the stones,
Madam—if I know your sex,
  From the fashion of your bones.

'No, I cannot praise the fire
  In your eye—nor yet your lip:
All the more do I admire
  Joints of cunning workmanship.

'Lo! God's likeness—the ground-plan—
  Neither modell'd, glazed, nor framed:
Buss me, thou rough sketch of man,
  Far too naked to be shamed!

'Drink to Fortune, drink to Chance,
  While we keep a little breath!
Drink to heavy Ignorance!
  Hob-and-nob with brother Death!

'Thou art mazed, the night is long,
  And the longer night is near:
What! I am not all as wrong
  As a bitter jest is dear.

'Youthful hopes, by scores, to all,
  When the locks are crisp and curl'd;
Unto me my maudlin gall
  And my mockeries of the world.

'Fill the cup, and fill the can:
  Mingle madness, mingle scorn!
Dregs of life, and lees of man:
  Yet we will not die forlorn.'

v.

The voice grew faint: there came a
  further change:
Once more uprose the mystic mountain-
  range:
Below were men and horses pierced with
  worms,
And slowly quickening into lower forms;
By shards and scurf of salt, and scum of
  dross,
Old plash of rains, and refuse patch'd
  with moss.

Then some one spake: 'Behold! it was
  a crime
Of sense avenged by sense that wore with
  time.'
Another said: 'The crime of sense
  became
The crime of malice, and is equal blame.'
And one: 'He had not wholly quench'd
  his power;
A little grain of conscience made him
  sour.'
At last I heard a voice upon the slope
Cry to the summit, 'Is there any hope?'
To which an answer peal'd from that high
  land,
But in a tongue no man could understand;
And on the glimmering limit far with-
  drawn
God made Himself an awful rose of dawn.

TO ——,

AFTER READING A LIFE AND LETTERS.

'Cursed be he that moves my bones.'
     Shakespeare's Epitaph.

You might have won the Poet's name,
  If such be worth the winning now,
  And gain'd a laurel for your brow
Of sounder leaf than I can claim;

But you have made the wiser choice,
  A life that moves to gracious ends
  Thro' troops of unrecording friends,
A deedful life, a silent voice:

And you have miss'd the irreverent doom
  Of those that wear the Poet's crown:
  Hereafter, neither knave nor clown
Shall hold their orgies at your tomb.

For now the Poet cannot die,
  Nor leave his music as of old,
  But round him ere he scarce be cold
Begins the scandal and the cry:

'Proclaim the faults he would not show:
  Break lock and seal: betray the trust:
  Keep nothing sacred: 'tis but just
The many-headed beast should know.'

Ah shameless ! for he did but sing
  A song that pleased us from its worth;
  No public life was his on earth,
No blazon'd statesman he, nor king.

He gave the people of his best :
  His worst he kept, his best he gave.
  My Shakespeare's curse on clown and
      knave
Who will not let his ashes rest !

Who make it seem more sweet to be
  The little life of bank and brier,
  The bird that pipes his lone desire
And dies unheard within his tree,

Than he that warbles long and loud
  And drops at Glory's temple-gates,
  For whom the carrion vulture waits
To tear his heart before the crowd !

TO E. L., ON HIS TRAVELS
IN GREECE.

ILLYRIAN woodlands, echoing falls
  Of water, sheets of summer glass,
  The long divine Peneïan pass,
The vast Akrokeraunian walls,

Tomohrit, Athos, all things fair,
  With such a pencil, such a pen,
  You shadow forth to distant men,
I read and felt that I was there :

And trust me while I turn'd the page,
  And track'd you still on classic ground,
  I grew in gladness till I found
My spirits in the golden age.

For me the torrent ever pour'd
  And glisten'd—here and there alone
  The broad-limb'd Gods at random
      thrown
By fountain-urns ;—and Naiads oar'd

A glimmering shoulder under gloom
  Of cavern pillars ; on the swell
  The silver lily heaved and fell ;
And many a slope was rich in bloom

From him that on the mountain lea
  By dancing rivulets fed his flocks
  To him who sat upon the rocks,
And fluted to the morning sea.

BREAK, break, break,
  On thy cold gray stones, O Sea !
And I would that my tongue could utter
  The thoughts that arise in me.

O well for the fisherman's boy,
  That he shouts with his sister at play !
O well for the sailor lad,
  That he sings in his boat on the bay !

And the stately ships go on
  To their haven under the hill ;
But O for the touch of a vanish'd hand,
  And the sound of a voice that is still !

Break, break, break,
  At the foot of thy crags, O Sea !
But the tender grace of a day that is dead
  Will never come back to me.

THE POET'S SONG.

THE rain had fallen, the Poet arose,
  He pass'd by the town and out of the
     street,
A light wind blew from the gates of the
     sun,
  And waves of shadow went over the
     wheat,
And he sat him down in a lonely place,
  And chanted a melody loud and sweet,
That made the wild-swan pause in her
     cloud,
  And the lark drop down at his feet.

The swallow stopt as he hunted the fly,
  The snake slipt under a spray,
The wild hawk stood with the down on
     his beak,
  And stared, with his foot on the prey,
And the nightingale thought, 'I have
     sung many songs,
  But never a one so gay,
For he sings of what the world will be
  When the years have died away.'

From **THE TIMES** of 1859

MONDAY, JANUARY 24, 1859. Price 4d.

[16 pages.]

[*HENRY HALLAM.*]

The constellation of writers shed a brilliance on the early part of the present century is fast vanishing away. Not the least remarkable of these, the historian of the Middle Ages, of the Revival of Letters, and of the English Constitution, Henry Hallam, died on Saturday last at the great age of 81. He has left but few of his companions behind him, and, more than this, it was his bitter fate to outlive those who should have come after him, to see two sons of rare promise, who should have preserved his name, the pride of his life snatched from his eyes, the delight of his old age laid low in the dust of death. One of these was that Arthur Henry Hallam, who died in 1833, and to whom Tennyson dedicated the remarkable series of poems which have been published under the title of *In Memoriam*. . . . The poor bereaved father buried [his second son Henry Fitzmaurice Hallam, who died in 1850] in Cleveland Church, in Somersetshire, by the side of his brother, and his sister, and his mother. He selected this place, as he says in his memoir of the elder son, " not only from the connexion of kindred, but on account of its still and sequestered situation on a lone hill that overhangs the Bristol Channel." It is to this hill, and to this Channel, and to this grave to which now the remains of the old, heartbroken father are to be added, that Tennyson refers in the most pathetic of his poems,—

" And the stately ships go on
" To their haven under the hill !
" But, O for the touch of a vanished hand
" And the sound of a voice that is still !
" Break, break, break.
" At the foot of thy crags, O sea !
" But the tender grace of a day that is dead
" Will never come back to me ! "

Break, break, break
Works p 124

10 Praise the country (6).

12 Works a lift manually (6).

13 " Clerk —— and ~~may~~ Margaret Walk'd owre yon garden green " (Anon.) (8).

15 Is it what makes our Florence so " refeened " ? (12).

18 Bill herewith and fur returned to us (7, 5).

23 Not waxy playfellows ; on the contrary they seem pliant to teasing (3, 5).

24 Light blue river (6).

26 Poet's home of " shy traffickers " (6).

27 Not where you hang the unpaid accounts (8).

28 The General Post Office reconstruction is by her (6).

29 Let a Japanese admiral disembark (8).

DOWN

1 Material for a partial black - out ? (6).

2 Champagne ? That's great ! (6).

3 Her end was not so much down and out as out and down (7).

Jezabel

4 A backward rusti (4).

6 Real net lasts fo ever (7).

7 He's super, a rea star ! (8).

8 It rolls along i the rolling Englis way (8).

11 Does he call fo support ! He ma need it (7).

14 It was twenty mile from Cranford (7).

16 It's warming ? Not it (8).

17 A lot of basic fertilizer ? (4, 4).

19 I doze, being about fifty-one (7).

20 Painter out wandering around a stream (7).

may may

DRUMBL

gproher

over]

Ed" Beljame

ENOCH ARDEN

AND OTHER POEMS.

ENOCH ARDEN.

LONG lines of cliff breaking have left a chasm ;
And in the chasm are foam and yellow sands ;
Beyond, red roofs about a narrow wharf
In cluster ; then a moulder'd church ; and higher
A long street climbs to one tall-tower'd mill ;
And high in heaven behind it a gray down
With Danish barrows ; and a hazelwood,
By autumn nutters haunted, flourishes
Green in a cuplike hollow of the down.

Here on this beach a hundred years ago,
Three children of three houses, Annie Lee,
The prettiest little damsel in the port,
And Philip Ray the miller's only son,
And Enoch Arden, a rough sailor's lad
Made orphan by a winter shipwreck, play'd
Among the waste and lumber of the shore,
Hard coils of cordage, swarthy fishing-nets,
Anchors of rusty fluke, and boats up-drawn ;
And built their castles of dissolving sand
To watch them overflow'd, or following up
And flying the white breaker, daily left
The little footprint daily wash'd away.

A narrow cave ran in beneath the cliff :
In this the children play'd at keeping house.
Enoch was host one day, Philip the next,
While Annie still was mistress ; but at times
Enoch would hold possession for a week :
'This is my house and this my little wife.'
'Mine too' said Philip 'turn and turn about :'
When, if they quarrell'd, Enoch stronger-made

Was master : then would Philip, his blue eyes
All flooded with the helpless wrath of tears,
Shriek out 'I hate you, Enoch,' and at this
The little wife would weep for company,
And pray them not to quarrel for her sake,
And say she would be little wife to both.

But when the dawn of rosy childhood past,
And the new warmth of life's ascending sun
Was felt by either, either fixt his heart
On that one girl ; and Enoch spoke his love,
But Philip loved in silence ; and the girl
Seem'd kinder unto Philip than to him ;
But she loved Enoch ; tho' she knew it not,
And would if ask'd deny it.   Enoch set
A purpose evermore before his eyes,
To hoard all savings to the uttermost,
To purchase his own boat, and make a home
For Annie : and so prosper'd that at last
A luckier or a bolder fisherman,
A carefuller in peril, did not breathe
For leagues along that breaker-beaten coast
Than Enoch.   Likewise had he served a year
On board a merchantman, and made himself
Full sailor ; and he thrice had pluck'd a life
From the dread sweep of the down-streaming seas :
And all men look'd upon him favourably :
And ere he touch'd his one-and-twentieth May

He purchased his own boat, and made a
home
For Annie, neat and nestlike, halfway up
60 The narrow street that clamber'd toward
the mill.

Then, on a golden autumn eventide,
The younger people making holiday,
With bag and sack and basket, great and
small,
Went nutting to the hazels.   Philip stay'd
(His father lying sick and needing him)
An hour behind ; but as he climb'd the hill,
Just where the prone edge of the wood
began
To feather toward the hollow, saw the
pair,
Enoch and Annie, sitting hand-in-hand,
His large gray eyes and weather-beaten
face
All-kindled by a still and sacred fire,
That burn'd as on an altar.   Philip look'd,
And in their eyes and faces read his doom ;
Then, as their faces drew together,
groan'd,
And slipt aside, and like a wounded life
Crept down into the hollows of the wood ;
There, while the rest were loud in merry-
making,
Had his dark hour unseen, and rose and
past
Bearing a lifelong hunger in his heart.

So these were wed, and merrily rang
the bells,
And merrily ran the years, seven happy
years,
Seven happy years of health and com-
petence,
And mutual love and honourable toil ;
With children ; first a daughter.   In him
woke,
With his first babe's first cry, the noble
wish
To save all earnings to the uttermost,
And give his child a better bringing-up
Than his had been, or hers ; a wish re-
new'd,
When two years after came a boy to be
The rosy idol of her solitudes,

While Enoch was abroad on wrathful seas,
Or often journeying landward ; for in truth
Enoch's white horse, and Enoch's ocean-
spoil
In ocean-smelling osier, and his face,
Rough-redden'd with a thousand winter
gales,
Not only to the market-cross were known,
But in the leafy lanes behind the down,
Far as the portal-warding lion-whelp,
And peacock-yewtree of the lonely Hall,
Whose Friday fare was Enoch's minister-
ing.

Then came a change, as all things
human change.
Ten miles to northward of the narrow port
Open'd a larger haven : thither used
Enoch at times to go by land or sea ;
And once when there, and clambering on
a mast
In harbour, by mischance he slipt and
fell :
A limb was broken when they lifted
him ;
And while he lay recovering there, his
wife
Bore him another son, a sickly one :
Another hand crept too across his trade
Taking her bread and theirs : and on him
fell,
Altho' a grave and staid God-fearing
man,
Yet lying thus inactive, doubt and gloom.
He seem'd, as in a nightmare of the night,
To see his children leading evermore
Low miserable lives of hand-to-mouth,
And her, he loved, a beggar : then he
pray'd
' Save them from this, whatever comes to
me.'
And while he pray'd, the master of that
ship
Enoch had served in, hearing his mis-
chance,
Came, for he knew the man and valued
him,
Reporting of his vessel China-bound,
And wanting yet a boatswain.   Would
he go ?

There yet were many weeks before she
sail'd,
Sail'd from this port.   Would Enoch
have the place?
And Enoch all at once assented to it,
Rejoicing at that answer to his prayer.

So now that shadow of mischance
appear'd
No graver than as when some little cloud
Cuts off the fiery highway of the sun,
And isles a light in the offing: yet the
wife—
When he was gone—the children—what
to do?
Then Enoch lay long-pondering on his
plans;
To sell the boat—and yet he loved her
well—
How many a rough sea had he weather'd
in her!
He knew her, as a horseman knows his
horse—
And yet to sell her—then with what she
brought
Buy goods and stores—set Annie forth
in trade
With all that seamen needed or their
wives—
So might she keep the house while he
was gone.
Should he not trade himself out yonder?
go
This voyage more than once? yea twice
or thrice—
As oft as needed—last, returning rich,
Become the master of a larger craft,
With fuller profits lead an easier life,
Have all his pretty young ones educated,
And pass his days in peace among his
own.

Thus Enoch in his heart determined all:
Then moving homeward came on Annie
pale,
Nursing the sickly babe, her latest-born.
Forward she started with a happy cry,
And laid the feeble infant in his arms;
Whom Enoch took, and handled all his
limbs,

Appraised his weight and fondled father-
like,
But had no heart to break his purposes
To Annie, till the morrow, when he spoke.

Then first since Enoch's golden ring
had girt
Her finger, Annie fought against his will:
Yet not with brawling opposition she,
But manifold entreaties, many a tear,
Many a sad kiss by day by night renew'd
(Sure that all evil would come out of it)
Besought him, supplicating, if he cared
For her or his dear children, not to go.
He not for his own self caring but her,
Her and her children, let her plead in vain;
So grieving held his will, and bore it thro'.

For Enoch parted with his old sea-
friend,
Bought Annie goods and stores, and set
his hand
To fit their little streetward sitting-room
With shelf and corner for the goods and
stores.
So all day long till Enoch's last at home,
Shaking their pretty cabin, hammer and
axe,
Auger and saw, while Annie seem'd to
hear
Her own death-scaffold raising, shrill'd
and rang,
Till this was ended, and his careful
hand,—
The space was narrow,—having order'd
all
Almost as neat and close as Nature packs
Her blossom or her seedling, paused;
and he,
Who needs would work for Annie to the
last,
Ascending tired, heavily slept till morn.

And Enoch faced this morning of fare-
well
Brightly and boldly. All his Annie's fears,
Save, as his Annie's, were a laughter to
him.
Yet Enoch as a brave God-fearing man
Bow'd himself down, and in that mystery

Where God-in-man is one with man-in-
God,
Pray'd for a blessing on his wife and babes
Whatever came to him : and then he said
'Annie, this voyage by the grace of God
Will bring fair weather yet to all of us.
Keep a clean hearth and a clear fire for me,
For I'll be back, my girl, before you
know it.'
Then lightly rocking baby's cradle 'and
he,
This pretty, puny, weakly little one,—
Nay—for I love him all the better for it—
God bless him, he shall sit upon my knees
And I will tell him tales of foreign parts,
And make him merry, when I come home
again.
Come, Annie, come, cheer up before I go.'

Him running on thus hopefully she
heard,
And almost hoped herself; but when he
turn'd
The current of his talk to graver things
In sailor fashion roughly sermonizing
On providence and trust in Heaven, she
heard,
Heard and not heard him ; as the village
girl,
Who sets her pitcher underneath the
spring,
Musing on him that used to fill it for her,
Hears and not hears, and lets it overflow.

At length she spoke 'O Enoch, you
are wise ;
And yet for all your wisdom well know I
That I shall look upon your face no more.'

'Well then,' said Enoch, 'I shall look
on yours.
Annie, the ship I sail in passes here
(He named the day) get you a seaman's
glass,
Spy out my face, and laugh at all your
fears.'

But when the last of those last moments
came,
'Annie, my girl, cheer up, be comforted,
Look to the babes, and till I come again

Keep everything shipshape, for I must go.
And fear no more for me ; or if you fear
Cast all your cares on God ; that anchor
holds.
Is He not yonder in those uttermost
Parts of the morning ? if I flee to these
Can I go from Him ? and the sea is His,
The sea is His : He made it.'

Enoch rose,
Cast his strong arms about his drooping
wife,
And kiss'd his wonder-stricken little ones;
But for the third, the sickly one, who slept
After a night of feverous wakefulness,
When Annie would have raised him
Enoch said
'Wake him not ; let him sleep ; how
should the child
Remember this ?' and kiss'd him in his
cot.
But Annie from her baby's forehead clipt
A tiny curl, and gave it : this he kept
Thro' all his future ; but now hastily
caught
His bundle, waved his hand, and went
his way.

She when the day, that Enoch
mention'd, came,
Borrow'd a glass, but all in vain : perhaps
She could not fix the glass to suit her eye;
Perhaps her eye was dim, hand tremulous;
She saw him not : and while he stood on
deck
Waving, the moment and the vessel past.

Ev'n to the last dip of the vanishing sail
She watch'd it, and departed weeping for
him ;
Then, tho' she mourn'd his absence as his
grave,
Set her sad will no less to chime with his,
But throve not in her trade, not being bred
To barter, nor compensating the want
By shrewdness, neither capable of lies,
Nor asking overmuch and taking less,
And still foreboding 'what would Enoch
say ?'
For more than once, in days of difficulty

And pressure, had she sold her wares for
    less
Than what she gave in buying what she
    sold :
She fail'd and sadden'd knowing it ; and
    thus,
Expectant of that news which never came,
Gain'd for her own a scanty sustenance,
And lived a life of silent melancholy.

Now the third child was sickly-born
    and grew
Yet sicklier, tho' the mother cared for it
With all a mother's care : nevertheless,
Whether her business often call'd her from
    it,
Or thro' the want of what it needed most,
Or means to pay the voice who best could
    tell
What most it needed—howsoe'er it was,
After a lingering,—ere she was aware,—
Like the caged bird escaping suddenly,
The little innocent soul flitted away.

In that same week when Annie buried
    it,
Philip's true heart, which hunger'd for her
    peace
(Since Enoch left he had not look'd upon
    her),
Smote him, as having kept aloof so long.
'Surely,' said Philip, 'I may see her now,
May be some little comfort ;' therefore
    went,
Past thro' the solitary room in front,
Paused for a moment at an inner door,
Then struck it thrice, and, no one opening,
Enter'd ; but Annie, seated with her grief,
Fresh from the burial of her little one,
Cared not to look on any human face,
But turn'd her own toward the wall and
    wept.
Then Philip standing up said falteringly
'Annie, I came to ask a favour of you.'

He spoke ; the passion in her moan'd
    reply
'Favour from one so sad and so forlorn
As I am !' half abash'd him ; yet unask'd,
His bashfulness and tenderness at war,
He set himself beside her, saying to her :

'I came to speak to you of what he
    wish'd,
Enoch, your husband : I have ever said
You chose the best among us—a strong
    man :
For where he fixt his heart he set his hand
To do the thing he will'd, and bore it thro'.
And wherefore did he go this weary way,
And leave you lonely ? not to see the
    world—
For pleasure ?—nay, but for the where-
    withal
To give his babes a better bringing-up
Than his had been, or yours : that was
    his wish.
And if he come again, vext will he be
To find the precious morning hours were
    lost.
And it would vex him even in his grave,
If he could know his babes were running
    wild
Like colts about the waste. So, Annie,
    now—
Have we not known each other all our
    lives ?
I do beseech you by the love you bear
Him and his children not to say me nay—
For, if you will, when Enoch comes again
Why then he shall repay me—if you will,
Annie—for I am rich and well-to-do.
Now let me put the boy and girl to school :
This is the favour that I came to ask.'

Then Annie with her brows against the
    wall
Answer'd 'I cannot look you in the face
I seem so foolish and so broken down.
When you came in my sorrow broke me
    down ;
And now I think your kindness breaks
    me down ;
But Enoch lives ; that is borne in on me.
He will repay you : money can be repaid ;
Not kindness such as yours.'

                 And Philip ask'd
'Then you will let me, Annie ?'

                 There she turn'd,
She rose, and fixt her swimming eyes upon
    him,

T   K

And dwelt a moment on his kindly face,
Then calling down a blessing on his head
Caught at his hand, and wrung it passion-
ately,
And past into the little garth beyond.
So lifted up in spirit he moved away.

Then Philip put the boy and girl to
school,
And bought them needful books, and
everyway,
Like one who does his duty by his own,
Made himself theirs ; and tho' for Annie's
sake,
Fearing the lazy gossip of the port,
He oft denied his heart his dearest wish,
And seldom crost her threshold, yet he
sent
Gifts by the children, garden-herbs and
fruit,
The late and early roses from his wall,
Or conies from the down, and now and
then,
With some pretext of fineness in the meal
To save the offence of charitable, flour
From his tall mill that whistled on the
waste.

But Philip did not fathom Annie's
mind:
Scarce could the woman when he came
upon her,
Out of full heart and boundless gratitude
Light on a broken word to thank him
with.
But Philip was her children's all-in-all ;
From distant corners of the street they
ran
To greet his hearty welcome heartily ;
Lords of his house and of his mill were
they ;
Worried his passive ear with petty wrongs
Or pleasures, hung upon him, play'd with
him
And call'd him Father Philip. Philip
gain'd
As Enoch lost ; for Enoch seem'd to them
Uncertain as a vision or a dream,
Faint as a figure seen in early dawn
Down at the far end of an avenue,

Going we know not where : and so ten
years,
Since Enoch left his hearth and native
land,
Fled forward, and no news of Enoch
came.

It chanced one evening Annie's children
long'd
To go with others, nutting to the wood,
And Annie would go with them ; then
they begg'd
For Father Philip (as they call'd him) too :
Him, like the working bee in blossom-
dust,
Blanch'd with his mill, they found ; and
saying to him
'Come with us Father Philip' he denied;
But when the children pluck'd at him to
go,
He laugh'd, and yielded readily to their
wish,
For was not Annie with them ? and they
went.

But after scaling half the weary down,
Just where the prone edge of the wood
began
To feather toward the hollow, all her force
Fail'd her ; and sighing, 'Let me rest' she
said :
So Philip rested with her well-content ;
While all the younger ones with jubilant
cries
Broke from their elders, and tumultuously
Down thro' the whitening hazels made a
plunge
To the bottom, and dispersed, and bent
or broke
The lithe reluctant boughs to tear away
Their tawny clusters, crying to each other
And calling, here and there, about the
wood.

But Philip sitting at her side forgot
Her presence, and remember'd one dark
hour
Here in this wood, when like a wounded
life
He crept into the shadow: at last he said,

Lifting his honest forehead, 'Listen, Annie,
How merry they are down yonder in the wood.
Tired, Annie?' for she did not speak a word.
'Tired?' but her face had fall'n upon her hands;
At which, as with a kind of anger in him,
'The ship was lost,' he said, 'the ship was lost!
No more of that! why should you kill yourself
And make them orphans quite?' And Annie said
'I thought not of it: but—I know not why—
Their voices make me feel so solitary.'

Then Philip coming somewhat closer spoke.
'Annie, there is a thing upon my mind,
And it has been upon my mind so long,
That tho' I know not when it first came there,
I know that it will out at last. O Annie,
It is beyond all hope, against all chance,
That he who left you ten long years ago
Should still be living; well then—let me speak:
I grieve to see you poor and wanting help:
I cannot help you as I wish to do
Unless—they say that women are so quick—
Perhaps you know what I would have you know—
I wish you for my wife. I fain would prove
A father to your children: I do think
They love me as a father: I am sure
That I love them as if they were mine own;
And I believe, if you were fast my wife,
That after all these sad uncertain years,
We might be still as happy as God grants
To any of his creatures. Think upon it:
For I am well-to-do—no kin, no care,
No burthen, save my care for you and yours:

And we have known each other all our lives,
And I have loved you longer than you know.'

Then answer'd Annie; tenderly she spoke:
'You have been as God's good angel in our house.
God bless you for it, God reward you for it,
Philip, with something happier than myself.
Can one love twice? can you be ever loved
As Enoch was? what is it that you ask?'
'I am content' he answer'd 'to be loved
A little after Enoch.' 'O' she cried,
Scared as it were, 'dear Philip, wait a while:
If Enoch comes—but Enoch will not come—
Yet wait a year, a year is not so long:
Surely I shall be wiser in a year:
O wait a little!' Philip sadly said
'Annie, as I have waited all my life
I well may wait a little.' 'Nay' she cried
'I am bound: you have my promise—in a year:
Will you not bide your year as I bide mine?'
And Philip answer'd 'I will bide my year.'

Here both were mute, till Philip glancing up
Beheld the dead flame of the fallen day
Pass from the Danish barrow overhead;
Then fearing night and chill for Annie, rose
And sent his voice beneath him thro' the wood.
Up came the children laden with their spoil;
Then all descended to the port, and there
At Annie's door he paused and gave his hand,
Saying gently 'Annie, when I spoke to you,

That was your hour of weakness. I was
wrong,
I am always bound to you, but you are
free.'
Then Annie weeping answer'd 'I am
bound.'

She spoke; and in one moment as it
were,
While yet she went about her household
ways,
Ev'n as she dwelt upon his latest words,
That he had loved her longer than she
knew,
That autumn into autumn flash'd again,
And there he stood once more before her
face,
Claiming her promise. 'Is it a year?'
she ask'd.
'Yes, if the nuts' he said 'be ripe again:
Come out and see.' But she—she put
him off—
So much to look to—such a change—a
month—
Give her a month—she knew that she was
bound—
A month—no more. Then Philip with
his eyes
Full of that lifelong hunger, and his voice
Shaking a little like a drunkard's hand,
'Take your own time, Annie, take your
own time.'
And Annie could have wept for pity of
him;
And yet she held him on delayingly
With many a scarce-believable excuse,
Trying his truth and his long-sufferance,
Till half-another year had slipt away.

By this the lazy gossips of the port,
Abhorrent of a calculation crost,
Began to chafe as at a personal wrong.
Some thought that Philip did but trifle
with her;
Some that she but held off to draw him on;
And others laugh'd at her and Philip too,
As simple folk that knew not their own
minds,
And one, in whom all evil fancies clung
Like serpent eggs together, laughingly

Would hint at worse in either. Her own
son
Was silent, tho' he often look'd his wish;
But evermore the daughter prest upon her
To wed the man so dear to all of them
And lift the household out of poverty;
And Philip's rosy face contracting grew
Careworn and wan; and all these things
fell on her
Sharp as reproach.

At last one night it chanced
That Annie could not sleep, but earnestly
Pray'd for a sign 'my Enoch is he gone?'
Then compass'd round by the blind wall
of night
Brook'd not the expectant terror of her
heart,
Started from bed, and struck herself a
light,
Then desperately seized the holy Book,
Suddenly set it wide to find a sign,
Suddenly put her finger on the text,
'Under the palm-tree.' That was nothing
to her:
No meaning there: she closed the Book
and slept:
When lo! her Enoch sitting on a height,
Under a palm-tree, over him the Sun:
'He is gone,' she thought, 'he is happy,
he is singing
Hosanna in the highest: yonder shines
The Sun of Righteousness, and these be
palms
Whereof the happy people strowing cried
"Hosanna in the highest!"' Here she
woke,
Resolved, sent for him and said wildly to
him
'There is no reason why we should not
wed.'
'Then for God's sake,' he answer'd, 'both
our sakes,
So you will wed me, let it be at once.'

So these were wed and merrily rang the
bells,
Merrily rang the bells and they were wed
But never merrily beat Annie's heart.
A footstep seem'd to fall beside her path,

She knew not whence ; a whisper on her
    ear,
She knew not what ; nor loved she to be left
Alone at home, nor ventured out alone.
What ail'd her then, that ere she enter'd,
    often
Her hand dwelt lingeringly on the latch,
Fearing to enter : Philip thought he knew :
Such doubts and fears were common to
    her state,
Being with child : but when her child was
    born,
Then her new child was as herself renew'd,
Then the new mother came about her
    heart,
Then her good Philip was her all-in-all,
And that mysterious instinct wholly died.

    And where was Enoch ? prosperously
    sail'd
The ship ' Good Fortune,' tho' at setting
    forth
The Biscay, roughly ridging eastward,
    shook
And almost overwhelm'd her, yet unvext
She slipt across the summer of the world,
Then after a long tumble about the Cape
And frequent interchange of foul and fair,
She passing thro' the summer world again,
The breath of heaven came continually
And sent her sweetly by the golden isles,
Till silent in her oriental haven.

    There Enoch traded for himself, and
    bought
Quaint monsters for the market of those
    times,
A gilded dragon, also, for the babes.

    Less lucky her home-voyage : at first
    indeed
Thro' many a fair sea-circle, day by day,
Scarce-rocking, her full-busted figure-head
Stared o'er the ripple feathering from her
    bows :
Then follow'd calms, and then winds
    variable,
Then baffling, a long course of them ; and
    last
Storm, such as drove her under moonless
    heavens

Till hard upon the cry of ' breakers ' came
The crash of ruin, and the loss of all
But Enoch and two others.   Half the
    night,
Buoy'd upon floating tackle and broken
    spars,
These drifted, stranding on an isle at morn
Rich, but the loneliest in a lonely sea.

    No want was there of human sustenance,
Soft fruitage, mighty nuts, and nourishing
    roots ;
Nor save for pity was it hard to take
The helpless life so wild that it was tame.
There in a seaward-gazing mountain-gorge
They built, and thatch'd with leaves of
    palm, a hut,
Half hut, half native cavern.   So the
    three,
Set in this Eden of all plenteousness,
Dwelt with eternal summer, ill-content.

    For one, the youngest, hardly more than
    boy,
Hurt in that night of sudden ruin and
    wreck,
Lay lingering out a five-years' death-in-
    life.
They could not leave him.   After he was
    gone,
The two remaining found a fallen stem ;
And Enoch's comrade, careless of himself,
Fire-hollowing this in Indian fashion, fell
Sun-stricken, and that other lived alone.
In those two deaths he read God's warn-
    ing ' wait.'

    The mountain wooded to the peak, the
    lawns
And winding glades high up like ways to
    Heaven,
The slender coco's drooping crown of
    plumes,
The lightning flash of insect and of bird,
The lustre of the long convolvuluses
That coil'd around the stately stems, and
    ran
Ev'n to the limit of the land, the glows
And glories of the broad belt of the world,
All these he saw ; but what he fain had
    seen

He could not see, the kindly human face,
Nor ever hear a kindly voice, but heard
The myriad shriek of wheeling ocean-fowl,
The league-long roller thundering on the
    reef,
The moving whisper of huge trees that
    branch'd
And blossom'd in the zenith, or the sweep
Of some precipitous rivulet to the wave,
As down the shore he ranged, or all day
    long
Sat often in the seaward-gazing gorge,
A shipwreck'd sailor, waiting for a sail :
No sail from day to day, but every day
The sunrise broken into scarlet shafts
Among the palms and ferns and precipices ;
The blaze upon the waters to the east ;
The blaze upon his island overhead ;
The blaze upon the waters to the west ;
Then the great stars that globed them-
    selves in Heaven,
The hollower-bellowing ocean, and again
The scarlet shafts of sunrise—but no sail.

    There often as he watch'd or seem'd to
        watch,
So still, the golden lizard on him paused,
A phantom made of many phantoms
    moved
Before him haunting him, or he himself
Moved haunting people, things and places,
    known
Far in a darker isle beyond the line ;
The babes, their babble, Annie, the small
    house,
The climbing street, the mill, the leafy
    lanes,
The peacock-yewtree and the lonely Hall,
The horse he drove, the boat he sold, the
    chill
November dawns and dewy-glooming
    downs,
The gentle shower, the smell of dying
    leaves,
And the low moan of leaden-colour'd seas.

    Once likewise, in the ringing of his
        ears,
Tho' faintly, merrily—far and far away—
He heard the pealing of his parish bells ;

Then, tho' he knew not wherefore, started
    up
Shuddering, and when the beauteous
    hateful isle
Return'd upon him, had not his poor heart
Spoken with That, which being every-
    where
Lets none, who speaks with Him, seem
    all alone,
Surely the man had died of solitude.

    Thus over Enoch's early-silvering head
The sunny and rainy seasons came and
    went
Year after year.   His hopes to see his own,
And pace the sacred old familiar fields,
Not yet had perish'd, when his lonely
    doom
Came suddenly to an end.   Another ship
(She wanted water) blown by baffling
    winds,
Like the Good Fortune, from her destined
    course,
Stay'd by this isle, not knowing where
    she lay :
For since the mate had seen at early dawn
Across a break on the mist-wreathen isle
The silent water slipping from the hills,
They sent a crew that landing burst away
In search of stream or fount, and fill'd the
    shores
With clamour.   Downward from his
    mountain gorge
Stept the long-hair'd long-bearded solitary,
Brown, looking hardly human, strangely
    clad,
Muttering and mumbling, idiotlike it
    seem'd,
With inarticulate rage, and making signs
They knew not what : and yet he led the
    way
To where the rivulets of sweet water ran ;
And ever as he mingled with the crew,
And heard them talking, his long-bounden
    tongue
Was loosen'd, till he made them under-
    stand ;
Whom, when their casks were fill'd they
    took aboard :
And there the tale he utter'd brokenly,

Scarce-credited at first but more and more,
Amazed and melted all who listen'd to it:
And clothes they gave him and free pass-
    age home ;
But oft he work'd among the rest and
    shook
His isolation from him.   None of these
Came from his country, or could answer
    him,
If question'd, aught of what he cared to
    know.
And dull the voyage was with long delays,
The vessel scarce sea-worthy ; but ever-
    more
His fancy fled before the lazy wind
Returning, till beneath a clouded moon
He like a lover down thro' all his blood
Drew in the dewy meadowy morning-
    breath
Of England, blown across her ghostly wall :
And that same morning officers and men
Levied a kindly tax upon themselves,
Pitying the lonely man, and gave him it :
Then moving up the coast they landed him,
Ev'n in that harbour whence he sail'd
    before.

There Enoch spoke no word to any one,
But homeward—home—what home? had
    he a home ?
His home, he walk'd.   Bright was that
    afternoon,
Sunny but chill ; till drawn thro' either
    chasm,
Where either haven open'd on the deeps,
Roll'd a sea-haze and whelm'd the world
    in gray ;
Cut off the length of highway on before,
And left but narrow breadth to left and
    right
Of wither'd holt or tilth or pasturage.
On the nigh-naked tree the robin piped
Disconsolate, and thro' the dripping haze
The dead weight of the dead leaf bore it
    down :
Thicker the drizzle grew, deeper the
    gloom ;
Last, as it seem'd, a great mist-blotted light
Flared on him, and he came upon the
    place.

Then down the long street having slowly
    stolen,
His heart foreshadowing all calamity,
His eyes upon the stones, he reach'd the
    home
Where Annie lived and loved him, and
    his babes
In those far-off seven happy years were
    born ;
But finding neither light nor murmur there
(A bill of sale gleam'd thro' the drizzle)
    crept
Still downward thinking ' dead or dead
    to me ! '

Down to the pool and narrow wharf he
    went,
Seeking a tavern which of old he knew,
A front of timber-crost antiquity,
So propt, worm-eaten, ruinously old,
He thought it must have gone ; but he
    was gone
Who kept it ; and his widow Miriam
    Lane,
With daily-dwindling profits held the
    house ;
A haunt of brawling seamen once, but now
Stiller, with yet a bed for wandering men.
There Enoch rested silent many days.

But Miriam Lane was good and garru-
    lous,
Nor let him be, but often breaking in,
Told him, with other annals of the port,
Not knowing—Enoch was so brown, so
    bow'd,
So broken—all the story of his house.
His baby's death, her growing poverty,
How Philip put her little ones to school,
And kept them in it, his long wooing her,
Her slow consent, and marriage, and the
    birth
Of Philip's child : and o'er his counte-
    nance
No shadow past, nor motion : any one,
Regarding, well had deem'd he felt the
    tale
Less than the teller : only when she closed
' Enoch, poor man, was cast away and
    lost '

Hdt i 8 (Candaule a Gyggés:) ὦτα γάρ τυγχάνει ἀνθρώποισι ἐόντα ἀπιστό-
τερα ὀφθαλμῶν
Hor AP 180 Segnius irritant animos demissa per aurem,
Quam quae sunt oculis subiecta? fidelibus --

He, shaking his gray head pathetically,
Repeated muttering 'cast away and lost;'
Again in deeper inward whispers 'lost!'

But Enoch yearn'd to see her face
      again ;
'If I might look on her sweet face again
And know that she is happy.' So the
      thought
Haunted and harass'd him, and drove
      him forth,
At evening when the dull November day
Was growing duller twilight, to the hill.
There he sat down gazing on all below ;
There did a thousand memories roll upon
      him,
Unspeakable for sadness.   By and by
The ruddy square of comfortable light,
Far-blazing from the rear of Philip's
      house,
Allured him, as the beacon-blaze allures
The bird of passage, till he madly strikes
Against it, and beats out his weary life.

For Philip's dwelling fronted on the
      street,
The latest house to landward ; but be-
      hind,
With one small gate that open'd on the
      waste,
Flourish'd a little garden square and
      wall'd :
And in it throve an ancient evergreen,
A yewtree, and all round it ran a walk
Of shingle, and a walk divided it :
But Enoch shunn'd the middle walk and
      stole
Up by the wall, behind the yew ; and
      thence
That which he better might have shunn'd,
      if griefs
Like his have worse or better, Enoch
      saw.

For cups and silver on the burnish'd
      board
Sparkled and shone ; so genial was the
      hearth :
And on the right hand of the hearth he
      saw
Philip, the slighted suitor of old times,

Stout, rosy, with his babe across his
      knees ;
And o'er her second father stoopt a girl,
A later but a loftier Annie Lee,
Fair-hair'd and tall, and from her lifted
      hand
Dangled a length of ribbon and a ring
To tempt the babe, who rear'd his creasy
      arms,
Caught at and ever miss'd it, and they
      laugh'd ;
And on the left hand of the hearth he saw
The mother glancing often toward her
      babe,
But turning now and then to speak with
      him,
Her son, who stood beside her tall and
      strong,
And saying that which pleased him, for
      he smiled.

Now when the dead man come to life
      beheld
His wife his wife no more, and saw the
      babe
Hers, yet not his, upon the father's knee,
And all the warmth, the peace, the
      happiness,
And his own children tall and beautiful,
And him, that other, reigning in his place,
Lord of his rights and of his children's
      love,—
Then he, tho' Miriam Lane had told him
      all,
Because things seen are mightier than
      things heard,
Stagger'd and shook, holding the branch,
      and fear'd
To send abroad a shrill and terrible cry,
Which in one moment, like the blast of
      doom,
Would shatter all the happiness of the
      hearth.

He therefore turning softly like a thief,
Lest the harsh shingle should grate under-
      foot,
And feeling all along the garden-wall,
Lest he should swoon and tumble and be
      found,

Crept to the gate, and open'd it, and
closed,
As lightly as a sick man's chamber-door,
Behind him, and came out upon the
waste.

And there he would have knelt, but
that his knees
Were feeble, so that falling prone he dug
His fingers into the wet earth, and
pray'd.

'Too hard to bear! why did they take
me thence?
O God Almighty, blessed Saviour, Thou
That didst uphold me on my lonely isle,
Uphold me, Father, in my loneliness
A little longer! aid me, give me strength
Not to tell her, never to let her know.
Help me not to break in upon her peace.
My children too! must I not speak to
these?
They know me not. I should betray
myself.
Never: No father's kiss for me—the girl
So like her mother, and the boy, my
son.'

There speech and thought and nature
fail'd a little,
And he lay tranced; but when he rose
and paced
Back toward his solitary home again,
All down the long and narrow street he
went
Beating it in upon his weary brain,
As tho' it were the burthen of a song,
'Not to tell her, never to let her know.'

He was not all unhappy. His resolve
Upbore him, and firm faith, and ever-
more
Prayer from a living source within the
will,
And beating up thro' all the bitter world,
Like fountains of sweet water in the sea,
Kept him a living soul. 'This miller's
wife'
He said to Miriam 'that you spoke about,
Has she no fear that her first husband
lives?'

'Ay, ay, poor soul' said Miriam, 'fear
enow!
If you could tell her you had seen him
dead,
Why, that would be her comfort;' and
he thought
'After the Lord has call'd me she shall
know,
I wait His time,' and Enoch set himself,
Scorning an alms, to work whereby to live.
Almost to all things could he turn his
hand.
Cooper he was and carpenter, and wrought
To make the boatmen fishing-nets, or
help'd
At lading and unlading the tall barks,
That brought the stinted commerce of
those days;
Thus earn'd a scanty living for himself:
Yet since he did but labour for himself,
Work without hope, there was not life
in it
Whereby the man could live; and as the
year
Roll'd itself round again to meet the day
When Enoch had return'd, a languor
came
Upon him, gentle sickness, gradually
Weakening the man, till he could do no
more,
But kept the house, his chair, and last his
bed.
And Enoch bore his weakness cheerfully.
For sure no gladlier does the stranded
wreck
See thro' the gray skirts of a lifting squall
The boat that bears the hope of life
approach
To save the life despair'd of, than he saw
Death dawning on him, and the close of
all.

For thro' that dawning gleam'd a kind-
lier hope
On Enoch thinking 'after I am gone,
Then may she learn I lov'd her to the last.'
He call'd aloud for Miriam Lane and said
'Woman, I have a secret—only swear,
Before I tell you—swear upon the book
Not to reveal it, till you see me dead.'

'Dead,' clamour'd the good woman, 'hear
  him talk !
I warrant, man, that we shall bring you
  round.'
'Swear' added Enoch sternly ' on the
  book.'
And on the book, half-frighted, Miriam
  swore.
Then Enoch rolling his gray eyes upon her,
' Did you know Enoch Arden of this
  town ?'
' Know him ?' she said ' I knew him far
  away.
Ay, ay, I mind him coming down the
  street ;
Held his head high, and cared for no man,
  he.'
Slowly and sadly Enoch answer'd her ;
' His head is low, and no man cares for
  him.
I think I have not three days more to live ;
I am the man.'   At which the woman gave
A half-incredulous, half-hysterical cry.
' You Arden, you ! nay,—sure he was a
  foot
Higher than you be.'   Enoch said again
' My God has bow'd me down to what I
  am ;
My grief and solitude have broken me ;
Nevertheless, know you that I am he
Who married—but that name has twice
  been changed—
I married her who married Philip Ray.
Sit, listen.'   Then he told her of his
  voyage,
His wreck, his lonely life, his coming back,
His gazing in on Annie, his resolve,
And how he kept it.   As the woman
  heard,
Fast flow'd the current of her easy tears,
While in her heart she yearn'd incessantly
To rush abroad all round the little haven,
Proclaiming Enoch Arden and his woes;
But awed and promise-bounden she for-
  bore,
Saying only ' See your bairns before you go!
Eh, let me fetch 'em, Arden,' and arose
Eager to bring them down, for Enoch
  hung
A moment on her words, but then replied :

' Woman, disturb me not now at the
  last,
But let me hold my purpose till I die.
Sit down again ; mark me and understand,
While I have power to speak.   I charge
  you now,
When you shall see her, tell her that I died
Blessing her, praying for her, loving her;
Save for the bar between us, loving her
As when she laid her head beside my own.
And tell my daughter Annie, whom I saw
So like her mother, that my latest breath
Was spent in blessing her and praying for
  her.
And tell my son that I died blessing him.
And say to Philip that I blest him too ;
He never meant us any thing but good.
But if my children care to see me dead,
Who hardly knew me living, let them
  come,
I am their father; but she must not come,
For my dead face would vex her after-life.
And now there is but one of all my blood
Who will embrace me in the world-to-be
This hair is his : she cut it off and gave it,
And I have borne it with me all these
  years.
And thought to bear it with me to my
  grave ;
But now my mind is changed, for I shall
  see him,
My babe in bliss : wherefore when I am
  gone,
Take, give her this, for it may comfort
  her :
It will moreover be a token to her,
That I am he.'

He ceased ; and Miriam Lane
Made such a voluble answer promising all,
That once again he roll'd his eyes upon
  her
Repeating all he wish'd, and once again
She promised.

Then the third night after this,
While Enoch slumber'd motionless and
  pale,
And Miriam watch'd and dozed at intervals,

There came so loud a calling of the sea,
That all the houses in the haven rang.
He woke, he rose, he spread his arms
    abroad
Crying with a loud voice 'A sail! a sail!
I am saved;' and so fell back and spoke
    no more.

So past the strong heroic soul away.
And when they buried him the little port
Had seldom seen a costlier funeral.

THE BROOK.

HERE, by this brook, we parted; I to the
    East
And he for Italy—too late—too late:
One whom the strong sons of the world
    despise;
For lucky rhymes to him were scrip and
    share,
And mellow metres more than cent for
    cent;
Nor could he understand how money
    breeds,
Thought it a dead thing; yet himself
    could make
The thing that is not as the thing that
    is.
O had he lived! In our schoolbooks we
    say,
Of those that held their heads above the
    crowd,
They flourish'd then or then; but life in
    him
Could scarce be said to flourish, only
    touch'd
On such a time as goes before the leaf,
When all the wood stands in a mist of
    green,
And nothing perfect: yet the brook he
    loved,
For which, in branding summers of
    Bengal,
Or ev'n the sweet half-English Neilgherry
    air
I panted, seems, as I re-listen to it,
Prattling the primrose fancies of the boy,
To me that loved him; for 'O brook,'
    he says,

'O babbling brook,' says Edmund in his
    rhyme,
'Whence come you?' and the brook, why
    not? replies. *(foulque (oiseau plongeur)*
    (marais)

  I come from haunts of coot and hern,
    I make a sudden sally,
  And sparkle out among the fern,
    To bicker down a valley.

  By thirty hills I hurry down,
    Or slip between the ridges,
  By twenty thorps, a little town,
    And half a hundred bridges.

  Till last by Philip's farm I flow
    To join the brimming river,
  For men may come and men may go,
    But I go on for ever.

'Poor lad, he died at Florence, quite
    worn out,
Travelling to Naples. There is Darnley
    bridge,
It has more ivy; there the river; and there
Stands Philip's farm where brook and
    river meet.

  I chatter over stony ways,
    In little sharps and trebles,
  I bubble into eddying bays,
    I babble on the pebbles.

  With many a curve my banks I fret
    By many a field and fallow,
  And many a fairy foreland set
    With willow-weed and mallow. *épilobe*

  I chatter, chatter, as I flow
    To join the brimming river,
  For men may come and men may go,
    But I go on for ever.

'But Philip chatter'd more than brook
    or bird;
Old Philip; all about the fields you caught
His weary daylong chirping, like the dry
High-elbow'd grigs that leap in summer
    grass.

  I wind about, and in and out,
    With here a blossom sailing,
  And here and there a lusty trout,
    And here and there a grayling, *'ombre'*

  And here and there a foamy flake
    Upon me, as I travel
  With many a silvery waterbreak
    Above the golden gravel,

And draw them all along, and flow
  To join the brimming river,
For men may come and men may go,
  But I go on for ever.

  'O darling Katie Willows, his one
    child !
A maiden of our century, yet most meek ;
A daughter of our meadows, yet not
    coarse ;
Straight, but as lissome as a hazel wand ;
Her eyes a bashful azure, and her hair
In gloss and hue the chestnut, when the
    shell
Divides threefold to show the fruit within.

  'Sweet Katie, once I did her a good
    turn,
Her and her far-off cousin and betrothed,
James Willows, of one name and heart
    with her.
For here I came, twenty years back—the
    week
Before I parted with poor Edmund ; crost
By that old bridge which, half in ruins
    then,
Still makes a hoary eyebrow for the gleam
Beyond it, where the waters marry—crost,
Whistling a random bar of Bonny Doon,
And push'd at Philip's garden-gate. The
    gate,
Half - parted from a weak and scolding
    hinge,
Stuck ; and he clamour'd from a case-
    ment, " Run "
To Katie somewhere in the walks below,
" Run, Katie ! " Katie never ran : she
    moved
To meet me, winding under woodbine
    bowers,
A little flutter'd, with her eyelids down,
Fresh apple-blossom, blushing for a boon.

  'What was it ? less of sentiment than
    sense
Had Katie ; not illiterate ; nor of those
Who dabbling in the fount of fictive tears,
And nursed by mealy - mouth'd philan-
    thropies,
Divorce the Feeling from her mate the
    Deed.

  'She told me.   She and James had
    quarrell'd.   Why ?
What cause of quarrel ? None, she said,
    no cause ;
James had no cause : but when I prest
    the cause,
I learnt that James had flickering jea-
    lousies
Which anger'd her.   Who anger'd James ?
    I said.
But Katie snatch'd her eyes at once from
    mine,
And sketching with her slender pointed
    foot
Some figure like a wizard pentagram
On garden gravel, let my query pass
Unclaim'd, in flushing silence, till I ask'd
If James were coming.   " Coming every
    day,"
She answer'd, " ever longing to explain,
But evermore her father came across
With some long-winded tale, and broke
    him short ;
And James departed vext with him and
    her."
How could I help her ? " Would I—was
    it wrong ? "
(Claspt hands and that petitionary grace
Of sweet seventeen subdued me ere she
    spoke)
" O would I take her father for one hour,
For one half-hour, and let him talk to me ! "
And even while she spoke, I saw where
    James
Made toward us, like a wader in the surf,
Beyond the brook, waist-deep in meadow-
    sweet.

  'O Katie, what I suffer'd for your sake !
For in I went, and call'd old Philip out
To show the farm : full willingly he rose :
He led me thro' the short sweet-smelling
    lanes
Of his wheat-suburb, babbling as he went.
He praised his land, his horses, his
    machines ;
He praised his ploughs, his cows, his hogs,
    his dogs ;
He praised his hens, his geese, his guinea-
    hens ;

His pigeons, who in session on their roofs
Approved him, bowing at their own
    deserts :
Then from the plaintive mother's teat he
    took
Her blind and shuddering puppies, naming
    each,
And naming those, his friends, for whom
    they were :
Then crost the common into Darnley
    chase
To show Sir Arthur's deer.   In copse
    and fern
Twinkled the innumerable ear and tail.
Then, seated on a serpent-rooted beech,
He pointed out a pasturing colt, and
    said :
" That was the four-year-old I sold the
    Squire."
And there he told a long long-winded tale
Of how the Squire had seen the colt at
    grass,
And how it was the thing his daughter
    wish'd,
And how he sent the bailiff to the farm
To learn the price, and what the price he
    ask'd,
And how the bailiff swore that he was
    mad,
But he stood firm ; and so the matter
    hung ;
He gave them line : and five days after
    that
He met the bailiff at the Golden Fleece,
Who then and there had offer'd something
    more,
But he stood firm ; and so the matter
    hung ;
He knew the man ; the colt would fetch
    its price ;
He gave them line : and how by chance
    at last
(It might be May or April, he forgot,
The last of April or the first of May)
He found the bailiff riding by the farm,
And, talking from the point, he drew
    him in,
And there he mellow'd all his heart with
    ale,
Until they closed a bargain, hand in hand.

'Then, while I breathed in sight of
    haven, he,
Poor fellow, could he help it? recom-
    menced,
And ran thro' all the coltish chronicle,
Wild Will, Black Bess, Tantivy, Tallyho,
Reform, White Rose, Bellerophon, the
    Jilt,
Arbaces, and Phenomenon, and the rest,
Till, not to die a listener, I arose,
And with me Philip, talking still ; and so
We turn'd our foreheads from the falling
    sun,
And following our own shadows thrice
    as long
As when they follow'd us from Philip's
    door,
Arrived and found the sun of sweet con-
    tent
Re-risen in Katie's eyes, and all things
    well.

    I steal by lawns and grassy plots,
        I slide by hazel covers ;
    I move the sweet forget-me-nots
        That grow for happy lovers.

    I slip, I slide, I gloom, I glance,
        Among my skimming swallows ;
    I make the netted sunbeam dance
        Against my sandy shallows.

    I murmur under moon and stars
        In brambly wildernesses ;
    I linger by my shingly bars ;
        I loiter round my cresses ;

    And out again I curve and flow
        To join the brimming river,
    For men may come and men may go,
        But I go on for ever.

Yes, men may come and go ; and these
    are gone,
All gone.   My dearest brother, Edmund,
    sleeps,
Not by the well-known stream and rustic
    spire,
But unfamiliar Arno, and the dome
Of Brunelleschi ; sleeps in peace : and he,
Poor Philip, of all his lavish waste of
    words
Remains the lean P. W. on his tomb :

I scraped the lichen from it : Katie walks
By the long wash of Australasian seas
Far off, and holds her head to other stars,
And breathes in April‑autumns. All
    are gone.'

So Lawrence Aylmer, seated on a stile
In the long hedge, and rolling in his
    mind
Old waifs of rhyme, and bowing o'er the
    brook
A tonsured head in middle age forlorn,
Mused, and was mute. On a sudden a
    low breath
Of tender air made tremble in the
    hedge
The fragile bindweed‑bells and briony
    rings ;
And he look'd up. There stood a maiden
    near,
Waiting to pass. In much amaze he
    stared
On eyes a bashful azure, and on hair
In gloss and hue the chestnut, when the
    shell
Divides threefold to show the fruit with‑
    in :
Then, wondering, ask'd her 'Are you
    from the farm ?'
'Yes' answer'd she. 'Pray stay a little :
    pardon me ;
What do they call you ?' 'Katie.' 'That
    were strange.
What surname ?' 'Willows.' 'No !'
    'That is my name.'
'Indeed !' and here he look'd so self‑
    perplext,
That Katie laugh'd, and laughing blush'd,
    till he
Laugh'd also, but as one before he
    wakes,
Who feels a glimmering strangeness in
    his dream.
Then looking at her ; 'Too happy, fresh
    and fair,
Too fresh and fair in our sad world's best
    bloom,
To be the ghost of one who bore your
    name
About these meadows, twenty years ago.'

'Have you not heard ?' said Katie,
    'we came back.
We bought the farm we tenanted before.
Am I so like her ? so they said on board.
Sir, if you knew her in her English days,
My mother, as it seems you did, the days
That most she loves to talk of, come
    with me.
My brother James is in the harvest‑field :
But she—you will be welcome—O, come
    in !'

AYLMER'S FIELD.

1793.

Dust are our frames ; and, gilded dust,
    our pride
Looks only for a moment whole and
    sound ;
Like that long‑buried body of the king,
Found lying with his urns and ornaments,
Which at a touch of light, an air of
    heaven,
Slipt into ashes, and was found no more.

Here is a story which in rougher shape
Came from a grizzled cripple, whom I
    saw
Sunning himself in a waste field alone—
Old, and a mine of memories—who had
    served,
Long since, a bygone Rector of the place,
And been himself a part of what he told.

Sir Aylmer Aylmer, that almighty
    man,
The county God—in whose capacious
    hall,
Hung with a hundred shields, the family
    tree
Sprang from the midriff of a prostrate
    king—
Whose blazing wyvern weathercock'd the
    spire,
Stood from his walls and wing'd his entry‑
    gates
And swang besides on many a windy
    sign—
Whose eyes from under a pyramidal head

Saw from his windows nothing save his
    own—
What lovelier of his own had he than
    her,
His only child, his Edith, whom he loved
As heiress and not heir regretfully?
But 'he that marries her marries her
    name'
This fiat somewhat soothed himself and
    wife,
His wife a faded beauty of the Baths,
Insipid as the Queen upon a card ;
Her all of thought and bearing hardly
    more
Than his own shadow in a sickly sun.

A land of hops and poppy-mingled
    corn,
Little about it stirring save a brook !
A sleepy land, where under the same
    wheel
The same old rut would deepen year by
    year ;
Where almost all the village had one
    name ;
Where Aylmer followed Aylmer at the
    Hall
And Averill Averill at the Rectory
Thrice over ; so that Rectory and Hall,
Bound in an immemorial intimacy,
Were open to each other ; tho' to dream
That Love could bind them closer well
    had made
The hoar hair of the Baronet bristle up
With horror, worse than had he heard
    his priest
Preach an inverted scripture, sons of men
Daughters of God ; so sleepy was the
    land.

And might not Averill, had he will'd
    it so,
Somewhere beneath his own low range
    of roofs,
Have also set his many-shielded tree ?
There was an Aylmer-Averill marriage
    once.
When the red rose was redder than itself,
And York's white rose as red as Lancas-
    ter's.

With wounded peace which each had
    prick'd to death.
'Not proven' Averill said, or laughingly
'Some other race of Averills'—prov'n
    or no,
What cared he ? what, if other or the
    same ?
He lean'd not on his fathers but himself.
But Leolin, his brother, living oft
With Averill, and a year or two before
Call'd to the bar, but ever call'd away
By one low voice to one dear neighbour-
    hood,
Would often, in his walks with Edith,
    claim
A distant kinship to the gracious blood
That shook the heart of Edith hearing
    him.

Sanguine he was : a but less vivid hue
Than of that islet in the chestnut-bloom
Flamed in his cheek ; and eager eyes,
    that still
Took joyful note of all things joyful,
    beam'd,
Beneath a manelike mass of rolling gold,
Their best and brightest, when they dwelt
    on hers,
Edith, whose pensive beauty, perfect else,
But subject to the season or the mood,
Shone like a mystic star between the less
And greater glory varying to and fro,
We know not wherefore ; bounteously
    made,
And yet so finely, that a troublous touch
Thinn'd, or would seem to thin her in a
    day,
A joyous to dilate, as toward the light.
And these had been together from the
    first.
Leolin's first nurse was, five years after,
    hers :
So much the boy foreran ; but when his
    date
Doubled her own, for want of playmates,
    he
(Since Averill was a decad and a half
His elder, and their parents underground)
Had tost his ball and flown his kite, and
    roll'd

His hoop to pleasure Edith, with her dipt
Against the rush of the air in the prone
    swing,
Made blossom - ball or daisy - chain, ar-
    ranged
Her garden, sow'd her name and kept it
    green
In living letters, told her fairy-tales,
Show'd her the fairy footings on the
    grass,
The little dells of cowslip, fairy palms,
The petty marestail forest, fairy pines,
Or from the tiny pitted target blew
What look'd a flight of fairy arrows aim'd
All at one mark, all hitting : make-be-
    lieves
For Edith and himself : or else he forged,
But that was later, boyish histories
Of battle, bold adventure, dungeon,
    wreck,
Flights, terrors, sudden rescues, and true
    love
Crown'd after trial ; sketches rude and
    faint.
But where a passion yet unborn perhaps
Lay hidden as the music of the moon
Sleeps in the plain eggs of the nightingale.
And thus together, save for college-times
Or Temple-eaten terms, a couple, fair
As ever painter painted, poet sang,
Or Heaven in lavish bounty moulded,
    grew.
And more and more, the maiden woman-
    grown,
He wasted hours with Averill ; there,
    when first
The tented winter-field was broken up
Into that phalanx of the summer spears
That soon should wear the garland ; there
    again
When burr and bine were gather'd ;
    lastly there
At Christmas ; ever welcome at the Hall,
On whose dull sameness his full tide of
    youth
Broke with a phosphorescence charming
    even
My lady ; and the Baronet yet had laid
No bar between them : dull and self-
    involved,

Tall and erect, but bending from his
    height
With half - allowing smiles for all the
    world,
And mighty courteous in the main—his
    pride
Lay deeper than to wear it as his ring—
He, like an Aylmer in his Aylmerism,
Would care no more for Leolin's walking
    with her
Than for his old Newfoundland's, when
    they ran
To loose him at the stables, for he rose
Twofooted at the limit of his chain,
Roaring to make a third : and how should
    Love,
Whom the cross-lightnings of four chance-
    met eyes
Flash into fiery life from nothing, follow
Such dear familiarities of dawn ?
Seldom, but when he does, Master of all

So these young hearts not knowing that
    they loved,
Not she at least, nor conscious of a bar
Between them, nor by plight or broken
    ring
Bound, but an immemorial intimacy,
Wander'd at will, and oft accompanied
By Averill : his, a brother's love, that
    hung
With wings of brooding shelter o'er her
    peace,
Might have been other, save for Leolin's—
Who knows ? but so they wander'd, hour
    by hour
Gather'd the blossom that rebloom'd, and
    drank
The magic cup that fill'd itself anew.

A whisper half reveal'd her to herself.
For out beyond her lodges, where the
    brook
Vocal, with here and there a silence, ran
By sallowy rims, arose the labourers'
    homes,
A frequent haunt of Edith, on low knolls
That dimpling died into each other, huts
At random scatter'd, each a nest in
    bloom.

Her art, her hand, her counsel all had
    wrought
About them : here was one that, summer-
    blanch'd,
Was parcel-bearded with the traveller's-
    joy
In Autumn, parcel ivy-clad ; and here
The warm - blue breathings of a hidden
    hearth
Broke from a bower of vine and honey-
    suckle :
One look'd all rosetree, and another wore
A close-set robe of jasmine sown with
    stars :
This had a rosy sea of gillyflowers
About it ; this, a milky-way on earth,
Like visions in the Northern dreamer's
    heavens,
A lily-avenue climbing to the doors ;
One, almost to the martin-haunted eaves
A summer burial deep in hollyhocks ;
Each, its own charm ; and Edith's every-
    where ;
And Edith ever visitant with him,
He but less loved than Edith, of her
    poor :
For she—so lowly-lovely and so loving,
Queenly responsive when the loyal hand
Rose from the clay it work'd in as she
    past,
Not sowing hedgerow texts and passing
    by,
Nor dealing goodly counsel from a height
That makes the lowest hate it, but a voice
Of comfort and an open hand of help,
A splendid presence flattering the poor
    roofs
Revered as theirs, but kindlier than them-
    selves
To ailing wife or wailing infancy
Or old bedridden palsy,—was adored ;
He, loved for her and for himself. A
    grasp
Having the warmth and muscle of the
    heart,
A childly way with children, and a laugh
Ringing like proven golden coinage true,
Were no false passport to that easy realm,
Where once with Leolin at her side the
    girl,

T

Nursing a child, and turning to the
    warmth
The tender pink five-beaded baby-soles,
Heard the good mother softly whisper
    ' Bless,
God bless 'em : marriages are made in
    Heaven.'

A flash of semi-jealousy clear'd it to
    her.
My lady's Indian kinsman unannounced
With half a score of swarthy faces came.
His own, tho' keen and bold and soldierly
Sear'd by the close ecliptic, was not fair ;
Fairer his talk, a tongue that ruled the
    hour,
Tho' seeming boastful : so when first he
    dash'd
Into the chronicle of a deedful day,
Sir Aylmer half forgot his lazy smile
Of patron ' Good ! my lady's kinsman !
    good !'
My lady with her fingers interlock'd,
And rotatory thumbs on silken knees,
Call'd all her vital spirits into each ear
To listen : unawares they flitted off,
Busying themselves about the flowerage
That stood from out a stiff brocade in
    which,
The meteor of a splendid season, she,
Once with this kinsman, ah so long ago,
Stept thro' the stately minuet of those
    days :
But Edith's eager fancy hurried with him
Snatch'd thro' the perilous passes of his
    life :
Till Leolin ever watchful of her eye,
Hated him with a momentary hate.
Wife - hunting, as the rumour ran, was
    he :
I know not, for he spoke not, only
    shower'd
His oriental gifts on everyone
And most on Edith : like a storm he
    came,
And shook the house, and like a storm
    he went.

Among the gifts he left her (possibly
He flow'd and ebb'd uncertain, to return

L

When others had been tested) there was
    one,
A dagger, in rich sheath with jewels on it
Sprinkled about in gold that branch'd
    itself
Fine as ice-ferns on January panes
Made by a breath. I know not whence
    at first,
Nor of what race, the work; but as he told
The story, storming a hill-fort of thieves
He got it; for their captain after fight,
His comrades having fought their last
    below,
Was climbing up the valley; at whom
    he shot:
Down from the beetling crag to which he
    clung
Tumbled the tawny rascal at his feet,
This dagger with him, which when now
    admired
By Edith whom his pleasure was to please,
At once the costly Sahib yielded to her.

And Leolin, coming after he was gone,
Tost over all her presents petulantly:
And when she show'd the wealthy scab-
    bard, saying
'Look what a lovely piece of workman-
    ship!'
Slight was his answer 'Well—I care not
    for it:'
Then playing with the blade he prick'd
    his hand,
'A gracious gift to give a lady, this!'
'But would it be more gracious' ask'd
    the girl
'Were I to give this gift of his to one
That is no lady?' 'Gracious? No' said he.
'Me?—but I cared not for it. O pardon
    me,
I seem to be ungraciousness itself.'
'Take it' she added sweetly, 'tho' his
    gift;
For I am more ungracious ev'n than you,
I care not for it either;' and he said
'Why then I love it:' but Sir Aylmer
    past,
And neither loved nor liked the thing he
    heard.

The next day came a neighbour.
    Blues and reds
They talk'd of: blues were sure of it, he
    thought:
Then of the latest fox—where started—
    kill'd
In such a bottom: 'Peter had the brush,
My Peter, first:' and did Sir Aylmer know
That great pock-pitten fellow had been
    caught?
Then made his pleasure echo, hand to
    hand,
And rolling as it were the substance of it
Between his palms a moment up and
    down—
'The birds were warm, the birds were
    warm upon him;
We have him now:' and had Sir Aylmer
    heard—
Nay, but he must—the land was ringing
    of it—
This blacksmith border-marriage—one
    they knew—
Raw from the nursery—who could trust
    a child?
That cursed France with her egalities!
And did Sir Aylmer (deferentially
With nearing chair and lower'd accent)
    think—
For people talk'd—that it was wholly wise
To let that handsome fellow Averill walk
So freely with his daughter? people
    talk'd—
The boy might get a notion into him;
The girl might be entangled ere she knew.
Sir Aylmer Aylmer slowly stiffening
    spoke:
'The girl and boy, Sir, know their differ-
    ences!'
'Good,' said his friend, 'but watch!'
    and he, 'Enough,
More than enough, Sir! I can guard my
    own.'
They parted, and Sir Aylmer Aylmer
    watch'd.

Pale, for on her the thunders of the
    house
Had fallen first, was Edith that same
    night;

Pale as the Jephtha's daughter, a rough
　piece
Of early rigid colour, under which
Withdrawing by the counter door to that
Which Leolin open'd, she cast back upon
　him
A piteous glance, and vanish'd. He, as
　one
Caught in a burst of unexpected storm,
And pelted with outrageous epithets,
Turning beheld the Powers of the House
On either side the hearth, indignant;
　her,
Cooling her false cheek with a featherfan,
Him, glaring, by his own stale devil
　spurr'd,
And, like a beast hard-ridden, breathing
　hard.
'Ungenerous, dishonourable, base,
Presumptuous! trusted as he was with
　her,
The sole succeeder to their wealth, their
　lands,
The last remaining pillar of their house,
The one transmitter of their ancient name,
Their child.' 'Our child!' 'Our
　heiress!' 'Ours!' for still,
Like echoes from beyond a hollow, came
Her sicklier iteration. Last he said,
'Boy, mark me! for your fortunes are to
　make.
I swear you shall not make them out of
　mine.
Now inasmuch as you have practised on
　her,
Perplext her, made her half forget herself,
Swerve from her duty to herself and us—
Things in an Aylmer deem'd impossible,
Far as we track ourselves—I say that
　this—
Else I withdraw favour and countenance
From you and yours for ever—shall you
　do.
Sir, when you see her—but you shall not
　see her—
No, you shall write, and not to her, but
　me:
And you shall say that having spoken
　with me,
And after look'd into yourself, you find

That you meant nothing—as indeed you
　know
That you meant nothing. Such a match
　as this!
Impossible, prodigious!' These were
　words,
As meted by his measure of himself,
Arguing boundless forbearance: after
　which,
And Leolin's horror-stricken answer, 'I
So foul a traitor to myself and her,
Never oh never,' for about as long
As the wind-hover hangs in balance,
　paused
Sir Aylmer reddening from the storm
　within,
Then broke all bonds of courtesy, and
　crying
'Boy, should I find you by my doors
　again,
My men shall lash you from them like a
　dog;
Hence!' with a sudden execration drove
The footstool from before him, and arose;
So, stammering 'scoundrel' out of teeth
　that ground
As in a dreadful dream, while Leolin still
Retreated half-aghast, the fierce old man
Follow'd, and under his own lintel stood
Storming with lifted hands, a hoary face
Meet for the reverence of the hearth, but
　now,
Beneath a pale and unimpassion'd moon,
Vext with unworthy madness, and de-
　form'd.

　Slowly and conscious of the rageful eye
That watch'd him, till he heard the
　ponderous door
Close, crashing with long echoes thro' the
　land,
Went Leolin; then, his passions all in
　flood
And masters of his motion, furiously
Down thro' the bright lawns to his
　brother's ran,
And foam'd away his heart at Averill's
　ear:
Whom Averill solaced as he might,
　amazed:

The man was his, had been his father's,
　　friend :
He must have seen, himself had seen it
　　long ;
He must have known, himself had known :
　　besides,
He never yet had set his daughter forth
Here in the woman-markets of the west,
Where our Caucasians let themselves be
　　sold.
Some one, he thought, had slander'd
　　Leolin to him.
' Brother, for I have loved you more as
　　son
Than brother, let me tell you : I myself—
What is their pretty saying ? jilted, is it ?
Jilted I was : I say it for your peace.
Pain'd, and, as bearing in myself the
　　shame
The woman should have borne, humili-
　　ated,
I lived for years a stunted sunless life ;
Till after our good parents past away
Watching your growth, I seem'd again to
　　grow.
Leolin, I almost sin in envying you :
The very whitest lamb in all my fold
Loves you : I know her : the worst
　　thought she has
Is whiter even than her pretty hand :
She must prove true : for, brother, where
　　two fight
The strongest wins, and truth and love
　　are strength,
And you are happy : let her parents be.'

　　But Leolin cried out the more upon
　　them—
Insolent, brainless, heartless ! heiress,
　　wealth,
Their wealth, their heiress ! wealth
　　enough was theirs
For twenty matches. Were he lord of
　　this,
Why twenty boys and girls should marry
　　on it,
And forty blest ones bless him, and him-
　　self
Be wealthy still, ay wealthier. He be-
　　lieved

This filthy marriage-hindering Mammon
　　made
The harlot of the cities : nature crost
Was mother of the foul adulteries
That saturate soul with body. Name,
　　too ! name,
Their ancient name ! they *might* be
　　proud ; its worth
Was being Edith's. Ah how pale she
　　had look'd
Darling, to-night ! they must have rated
　　her
Beyond all tolerance. These old pheasant-
　　lords,
These partridge-breeders of a thousand
　　years,
Who had mildew'd in their thousands,
　　doing nothing
Since Egbert — why, the greater their
　　disgrace !
Fall back upon a name ! rest, rot in that !
Not *keep* it noble, make it nobler ? fools,
With such a vantage-ground for nobleness !
He had known a man, a quintessence of
　　man,
The life of all—who madly loved—and he,
Thwarted by one of these old father-fools,
Had rioted his life out, and made an end.
He would not do it ! her sweet face and
　　faith
Held him from that : but he had powers,
　　he knew it :
Back would he to his studies, make a name,
Name, fortune too : the world should ring
　　of him
To shame these mouldy Aylmers in their
　　graves :
Chancellor, or what is greatest would he
　　be—
' O brother, I am grieved to learn your
　　grief—
Give me my fling, and let me say my say.'

　　At which, like one that sees his own
　　excess,
And easily forgives it as his own,
He laugh'd ; and then was mute ; but
　　presently
Wept like a storm : and honest Averill
　　seeing

How low his brother's mood had fallen, fetch'd
His richest beeswing from a binn reserved
For banquets, praised the waning red, and told
The vintage—when *this* Aylmer came of age—
Then drank and past it; till at length the two,
Tho' Leolin flamed and fell again, agreed
That much allowance must be made for men.
After an angry dream this kindlier glow
Faded with morning, but his purpose held.

Yet once by night again the lovers met,
A perilous meeting under the tall pines
That darken'd all the northward of her Hall.
Him, to her meek and modest bosom prest
In agony, she promised that no force,
Persuasion, no, nor death could alter her:
He, passionately hopefuller, would go,
Labour for his own Edith, and return
In such a sunlight of prosperity
He should not be rejected. 'Write to me!
They loved me, and because I love their child
They hate me: there is war between us, dear,
Which breaks all bonds but ours; we must remain
Sacred to one another.' So they talk'd,
Poor children, for their comfort: the wind blew;
The rain of heaven, and their own bitter tears,
Tears, and the careless rain of heaven, mixt
Upon their faces, as they kiss'd each other
In darkness, and above them roar'd the pine.

So Leolin went; and as we task ourselves
To learn a language known but smatteringly
In phrases here and there at random, toil'd

Mastering the lawless science of our law,
That codeless myriad of precedent,
That wilderness of single instances,
Thro' which a few, by wit or fortune led,
May beat a pathway out to wealth and fame.
The jests, that flash'd about the pleader's room,
Lightning of the hour, the pun, the scurrilous tale,—
Old scandals buried now seven decads deep
In other scandals that have lived and died,
And left the living scandal that shall die—
Were dead to him already; bent as he was
To make disproof of scorn, and strong in hopes,
And prodigal of all brain-labour he,
Charier of sleep, and wine, and exercise,
Except when for a breathing-while at eve,
Some niggard fraction of an hour, he ran
Beside the river-bank: and then indeed
Harder the times were, and the hands of power
Were bloodier, and the according hearts of men
Seem'd harder too; but the soft river-breeze,
Which fann'd the gardens of that rival rose
Yet fragrant in a heart remembering
His former talks with Edith, on him breathed
Far purelier in his rushings to and fro,
After his books, to flush his blood with air,
Then to his books again. My lady's cousin,
Half-sickening of his pension'd afternoon,
Drove in upon the student once or twice,
Ran a Malayan amuck against the times,
Had golden hopes for France and all mankind,
Answer'd all queries touching those at home
With a heaved shoulder and a saucy smile,
And fain had haled him out into the world,
And air'd him there: his nearer friend would say
'Screw not the chord too sharply lest it snap.'

Then left alone he pluck'd her dagger
    forth
From where his worldless heart had kept
    it warm,
Kissing his vows upon it like a knight.
And wrinkled benchers often talk'd of
    him
Approvingly, and prophesied his rise :
For heart, I think, help'd head : her
    letters too,
Tho' far between, and coming fitfully
Like broken music, written as she found
Or made occasion, being strictly watch'd,
Charm'd him thro' every labyrinth till he
    saw
An end, a hope, a light breaking upon him.

But they that cast her spirit into flesh,
Her worldly-wise begetters, plagued them-
    selves
To sell her, those good parents, for her
    good.
Whatever eldest-born of rank or wealth
Might lie within their compass, him they
    lured
Into their net made pleasant by the baits
Of gold and beauty, wooing him to woo.
So month by month the noise about their
    doors,
And distant blaze of those dull banquets,
    made
The nightly wirer of their innocent hare
Falter before he took it.   All in vain.
Sullen, defiant, pitying, wroth, return'd
Leolin's rejected rivals from their suit
So often, that the folly taking wings
Slipt o'er those lazy limits down the wind
With rumour, and became in other fields
A mockery to the yeomen over ale,
And laughter to their lords : but those at
    home,
As hunters round a hunted creature draw
The cordon close and closer toward the
    death,
Narrow'd her goings out and comings in ;
Forbad her first the house of Averill,
Then closed her access to the wealthier
    farms,
Last from her own home-circle of the
    poor

They barr'd her : yet she bore it : yet her
    cheek
Kept colour : wondrous ! but, O mystery !
What amulet drew her down to that old
    oak,
So old, that twenty years before, a part
Falling had let appear the brand of John—
Once grovelike, each huge arm a tree,
    but now
The broken base of a black tower, a cave
Of touchwood, with a single flourishing
    spray.
There the manorial lord too curiously
Raking in that millennial touchwood-dust
Found for himself a bitter treasure-trove ;
Burst his own wyvern on the seal, and read
Writhing a letter from his child, for which
Came at the moment Leolin's emissary,
A crippled lad, and coming turn'd to fly,
But scared with threats of jail and halter
    gave
To him that fluster'd his poor parish wits
The letter which he brought, and swore
    besides
To play their go-between as heretofore
Nor let them know themselves betray'd ;
    and then,
Soul-stricken at their kindness to him,
    went
Hating his own lean heart and miserable

Thenceforward oft from out a despot
    dream
The father panting woke, and oft, as dawn
Aroused the black republic on his elms,
Sweeping the frothfly from the fescue
    brush'd
Thro' the dim meadow toward his
    treasure-trove,
Seized it, took home, and to my lady,—
    who made
A downward crescent of her minion mouth,
Listless in all despondence,—read ; and
    tore,
As if the living passion symbol'd there
Were living nerves to feel the rent ; and
    burnt,
Now chafing at his own great self defied,
Now striking on huge stumbling-blocks of
    scorn

In babyisms, and dear diminutives
Scatter'd all over the vocabulary
Of such a love as like a chidden child,
After much wailing, hush'd itself at last
Hopeless of answer: then tho' Averill wrote
And bad him with good heart sustain
 himself—
All would be well—the lover heeded not,
But passionately restless came and went,
And rustling once at night about the place,
There by a keeper shot at, slightly hurt,
Raging return'd : nor was it well for her
Kept to the garden now, and grove of pines,
Watch'd even there ; and one was set to
 watch
The watcher, and Sir Aylmer watch'd
 them all,
Yet bitterer from his readings : once
 indeed,
Warm'd with his wines, or taking pride
 in her,
She look'd so sweet, he kiss'd her tenderly
Not knowing what possess'd him : that
 one kiss
Was Leolin's one strong rival upon earth ;
Seconded, for my lady follow'd suit,
Seem'd hope's returning rose : and then
 ensued
A Martin's summer of his faded love,
Or ordeal by kindness ; after this
He seldom crost his child without a sneer ;
The mother flow'd in shallower acrimo-
 nies :
Never one kindly smile, one kindly word :
So that the gentle creature shut from all
Her charitable use, and face to face
With twenty months of silence, slowly lost
Nor greatly cared to lose, her hold on life.
Last, some low fever ranging round to spy
The weakness of a people or a house,
Like flies that haunt a wound, or deer, or
 men,
Or almost all that is, hurting the hurt—
Save Christ as we believe him—found the
 girl
And flung her down upon a couch of fire,
Where careless of the household faces near,
And crying upon the name of Leolin,
She, and with her the race of Aylmer,
 past.

Star to star vibrates light : may soul
 to soul
Strike thro' a finer element of her own ?
So,—from afar,—touch as at once ? or
 why
That night, that moment, when she named
 his name,
Did the keen shriek 'Yes love, yes, Edith,
 yes,'
Shrill, till the comrade of his chambers
 woke,
And came upon him half-arisen from sleep,
With a weird bright eye, sweating and
 trembling,
His hair as it were crackling into flames,
His body half flung forward in pursuit,
And his long arms stretch'd as to grasp a
 flyer :
Nor knew he wherefore he had made the
 cry ;
And being much befool'd and idioted
By the rough amity of the other, sank
As into sleep again. The second day,
My lady's Indian kinsman rushing in,
A breaker of the bitter news from home,
Found a dead man, a letter edged with
 death
Beside him, and the dagger which himself
Gave Edith, redden'd with no bandit's
 blood :
' From Edith' was engraven on the blade.

Then Averill went and gazed upon his
 death.
And when he came again, his flock be-
 lieved—
Beholding how the years which are not
 Time's
Had blasted him—that many thousand
 days
Were clipt by horror from his term of life.
Yet the sad mother, for the second death
Scarce touch'd her thro' that nearness of
 the first,
And being used to find her pastor texts,
Sent to the harrow'd brother, praying
 him
To speak before the people of her child,
And fixt the Sabbath. Darkly that day
 rose :

Autumn's mock sunshine of the faded
    woods
Was all the life of it ; for hard 'on these,
A breathless burthen of low-folded heavens
Stifled and chill'd at once ; but every roof
Sent out a listener : many too had known
Edith among the hamlets round, and
    since
The parents' harshness and the hapless
    loves
And double death were widely murmur'd,
    left
Their own gray tower, or plain-faced
    tabernacle,
To hear him ; all in mourning these, and
    those
With blots of it about them, ribbon, glove
Or kerchief ; while the church, — one
    night, except
For greenish glimmerings thro' the lancets,
    —made
Still paler the pale head of him, who
    tower'd
Above them, with his hopes in either
    grave.

Long o'er his bent brows linger'd
    Averill,
His face magnetic to the hand from which
Livid he pluck'd it forth, and labour'd
    thro'
His brief prayer-prelude, gave the verse
    ' Behold,
Your house is left unto you desolate !'
But lapsed into so long a pause again
As half amazed half frighted all his flock :
Then from his height and loneliness of
    grief
Bore down in flood, and dash'd his angry
    heart
Against the desolations of the world.

Never since our bad earth became one
    sea,
Which rolling o'er the palaces of the
    proud,
And all but those who knew the living
    God—
Eight that were left to make a purer
    world—

When since had flood, fire, earthquake,
    thunder, wrought
Such waste and havock as the idolatries,
Which from the low light of mortality
Shot up their shadows to the Heaven of
    Heavens,
And worshipt their own darkness in the
    Highest ?
' Gash thyself, priest, and honour thy
    brute Baäl,
And to thy worst self sacrifice thyself,
For with thy worst self hast thou clothed
    thy God.
Then came a Lord in no wise like to
    Baäl.
The babe shall lead the lion. Surely now
The wilderness shall blossom as the rose.
Crown thyself, worm, and worship thine
    own lusts !—
No coarse and blockish God of acreage
Stands at thy gate for thee to grovel to—
Thy God is far diffused in noble groves
And princely halls, and farms, and flowing
    lawns,
And heaps of living gold that daily grow,
And title-scrolls and gorgeous heraldries.
In such a shape dost thou behold thy
    God.
Thou wilt not gash thy flesh for *him* ; for
    thine
Fares richly, in fine linen, not a hair
Ruffled upon the scarfskin, even while
The deathless ruler of thy dying house
Is wounded to the death that cannot die ;
And tho' thou numberest with the followers
Of One who cried, "Leave all and follow
    me."
Thee therefore with His light about thy
    feet,
Thee with His message ringing in thine
    ears,
Thee shall thy brother man, the Lord from
    Heaven,
Born of a village girl, carpenter's son,
Wonderful, Prince of peace, the Mighty
    God,
Count the more base idolater of the two ;
Crueller : as not passing thro' the fire
Bodies, but souls—thy children's—thro'
    the smoke

The blight of low desires—darkening
 thine own
To thine own likeness ; or if one of these,
Thy better born unhappily from thee,
Should, as by miracle, grow straight and
 fair—
Friends, I was bid to speak of such a one
By those who most have cause to sorrow
 for her—
Fairer than Rachel by the palmy well,
Fairer than Ruth among the fields of corn,
Fair as the Angel that said " Hail !" she
 seem'd,
Who entering fill'd the house with sudden
 light.
For so mine own was brighten'd : where
 indeed
The roof so lowly but that beam of
 Heaven
Dawn'd sometime thro' the doorway ?
 whose the babe
Too ragged to be fondled on her lap,
Warm'd at her bosom ?   The poor child
 of shame
The common care whom no one cared
 for, leapt
To greet her, wasting his forgotten heart,
As with the mother he had never known,
In gambols ; for her fresh and innocent
 eyes
Had such a star of morning in their blue,
That all neglected places of the field
Broke into nature's music when they saw
 her.
Low was her voice, but won mysterious
 way
Thro' the seal'd ear to which a louder
 one
Was all but silence—free of alms her
 hand—
The hand that robed your cottage-walls
 with flowers
Has often toil'd to clothe your little ones ;
How often placed upon the sick man's
 brow
Cool'd it, or laid his feverous pillow
 smooth !
Had you one sorrow and she shared it
 not ?
One burthen and she would not lighten it ?

One spiritual doubt she did not soothe ?
Or when some heat of difference sparkled
 out,
How sweetly would she glide between
 your wraths,
And steal you from each other ! for she
 walk'd
Wearing the light yoke of that Lord of
 love,
Who still'd the rolling wave of Galilee !
And one—of him I was not bid to
 speak—
Was always with her, whom you also
 knew.
Him too you loved, for he was worthy
 love.
And these had been together from the
 first ;
They might have been together till the
 last.
Friends, this frail bark of ours, when
 sorely tried,
May wreck itself without the pilot's guilt,
Without the captain's knowledge : hope
 with me.
Whose shame is that, if he went hence
 with shame ?
Nor mine the fault, if losing both of these
I cry to vacant chairs and widow'd walls,
" My house is left unto me desolate." '

   While thus he spoke, his hearers wept ;
 but some,
Sons of the glebe, with other frowns than
 those
That knit themselves for summer shadow,
 scowl'd
At their great lord.   He, when it seem'd
 he saw
No pale sheet-lightnings from afar, but
 fork'd
Of the near storm, and aiming at his
 head,
Sat anger-charm'd from sorrow, soldier-
 like,
Erect : but when the preacher's cadence
 flow'd
Softening thro' all the gentle attributes
Of his lost child, the wife, who watch'd
 his face,

Paled at a sudden twitch of his iron
mouth;
And 'O pray God that he hold up' she
thought
'Or surely I shall shame myself and him.'

'Nor yours the blame—for who beside
your hearths
Can take her place—if echoing me you
cry
"Our house is left unto us desolate"?
But thou, O thou that killest, hadst thou
known,
O thou that stonest, hadst thou under-
stood
The things belonging to thy peace and
ours!
Is there no prophet but the voice that
calls
Doom upon kings, or in the waste "Re-
pent"?
Is not our own child on the narrow way,
Who down to those that saunter in the
broad
Cries "Come up hither," as a prophet to
us?
Is there no stoning save with flint and
rock?
Yes, as the dead we weep for testify—
No desolation but by sword and fire?
Yes, as your moanings witness, and my-
self
Am lonelier, darker, earthlier for my loss.
Give me your prayers, for he is past your
prayers,
Not past the living fount of pity in
Heaven.
But I that thought myself long-suffering,
meek,
Exceeding "poor in spirit"—how the
words
Have twisted back upon themselves, and
mean
Vileness, we are grown so proud—I
wish'd my voice
A rushing tempest of the wrath of God
To blow these sacrifices thro' the world—
Sent like the twelve-divided concubine
To inflame the tribes: but there—out
yonder—earth

Lightens from her own central Hell—O
there
The red fruit of an old idolatry—
The heads of chiefs and princes fall so
fast,
They cling together in the ghastly sack—
The land all shambles—naked marriages
Flash from the bridge, and ever-murder'd
France,
By shores that darken with the gathering
wolf,
Runs in a river of blood to the sick sea.
Is this a time to madden madness then?
Was this a time for these to flaunt their
pride?
May Pharaoh's darkness, folds as dense
as those
Which hid the Holiest from the people's
eyes
Ere the great death, shroud this great sin
from all!
Doubtless our narrow world must canvass
it:
O rather pray for those and pity them,
Who, thro' their own desire accomplish'd,
bring
Their own gray hairs with sorrow to the
grave—
Who broke the bond which they desired
to break,
Which else had link'd their race with
times to come—
Who wove coarse webs to snare her
purity,
Grossly contriving their dear daughter's
good—
Poor souls, and knew not what they did,
but sat
Ignorant, devising their own daughter's
death!
May not that earthly chastisement suffice?
Have not our love and reverence left
them bare?
Will not another take their heritage?
Will there be children's laughter in their
hall
For ever and for ever, or one stone
Left on another, or is it a light thing
That I, their guest, their host, their
ancient friend,

I made by these the last of all my race,
Must cry to these the last of theirs, as
    cried
Christ ere His agony to those that swore
Not by the temple but the gold, and made
Their own traditions God, and slew the
    Lord,
And left their memories a world's curse—
    " Behold,
Your house is left unto you desolate "?'

Ended he had not, but she brook'd no
    more :
Long since her heart had beat remorse-
    lessly,
Her crampt-up sorrow pain'd her, and a
    sense
Of meanness in her unresisting life.
Then their eyes vext her ; for on entering
He had cast the curtains of their seat
    aside—
Black velvet of the costliest—she herself
Had seen to that : fain had she closed
    them now,
Yet dared not stir to do it, only near'd
Her husband inch by inch, but when she
    laid,
Wifelike, her hand in one of his, he veil'd
His face with the other, and at once, as
    falls
A creeper when the prop is broken, fell
The woman shrieking at his feet, and
    swoon'd.
Then her own people bore along the nave
Her pendent hands, and narrow meagre
    face
Seam'd with the shallow cares of fifty
    years :
And her the Lord of all the landscape
    round
Ev'n to its last horizon, and of all
Who peer'd at him so keenly, follow'd
    out
Tall and erect, but in the middle aisle
Reel'd, as a footsore ox in crowded
    ways
Stumbling across the market to his death,
Unpitied ; for he groped as blind, and
    seem'd
Always about to fall, grasping the pews

And oaken finials till he touch'd the
    door ;
Yet to the lychgate, where his chariot
    stood,
Strode from the porch, tall and erect
    again.

But nevermore did either pass the gate
Save under pall with bearers.   In one
    month,
Thro' weary and yet ever wearier hours,
The childless mother went to seek her
    child ;
And when he felt the silence of his house
About him, and the change and not the
    change,
And those fixt eyes of painted ancestors
Staring for ever from their gilded walls
On him their last descendant, his own
    head
Began to droop, to fall ; the man became
Imbecile ; his one word was ' desolate ;'
Dead for two years before his death was
    he ;
But when the second Christmas came,
    escaped
His keepers, and the silence which he felt,
To find a deeper in the narrow gloom
By wife and child ; nor wanted at his
    end
The dark retinue reverencing death
At golden thresholds ; nor from tender
    hearts,
And those who sorrow'd o'er a vanish'd
    race,
Pity, the violet on the tyrant's grave.
Then the great Hall was wholly broken
    down,
And the broad woodland parcell'd into
    farms ;
And where the two contrived their
    daughter's good,
Lies the hawk's cast, the mole has made
    his run,
The hedgehog underneath the plantain
    bores,
The rabbit fondles his own harmless face,
The slow-worm creeps, and the thin
    weasel there
Follows the mouse, and all is open field.

SEA DREAMS.

A CITY clerk, but gently born and bred ;
His wife, an unknown artist's orphan
    child—
One babe was theirs, a Margaret, three
    years old :
They, thinking that her clear germander
    eye
Droopt in the giant-factoried city-gloom,
Came, with a month's leave given them,
    to the sea :
For which his gains were dock'd, however
    small :
Small were his gains, and hard his work ;
    besides,
Their slender household fortunes (for the
    man
Had risk'd his little) like the little thrift,
Trembled in perilous places o'er a deep :
And oft, when sitting all alone, his face
Would darken, as he cursed his credulous-
    ness,
And that one unctuous mouth which lured
    him, rogue,
To buy strange shares in some Peruvian
    mine.
Now seaward-bound for health they gain'd
    a coast,
All sand and cliff and deep-inrunning cave,
At close of day ; slept, woke, and went
    the next,
The Sabbath, pious variers from the
    church,
To chapel ; where a heated pulpiteer,
Not preaching simple Christ to simple men,
Announced the coming doom, and ful-
    minated
Against the scarlet woman and her creed ;
For sideways up he swung his arms, and
    shriek'd
'Thus, thus with violence,' ev'n as if he
    held
The Apocalyptic millstone, and himself
Were that great Angel ; 'Thus with
    violence
Shall Babylon be cast into the sea ;
Then comes the close.' The gentle-
    hearted wife

Sat shuddering at the ruin of a world ;
He at his own : but when the wordy storm
Had ended, forth they came and paced
    the shore,
Ran in and out the long sea-framing caves,
Drank the large air, and saw, but scarce
    believed
(The sootflake of so many a summer still
Clung to their fancies) that they saw, the sea.
So now on sand they walk'd, and now on
    cliff,
Lingering about the thymy promontories,
Till all the sails were darken'd in the west,
And rosed in the east : then homeward and
    to bed :
Where she, who kept a tender Christian
    hope,
Haunting a holy text, and still to that
Returning, as the bird returns, at night,
'Let not the sun go down upon your
    wrath,'
Said, 'Love, forgive him : ' but he did not
    speak ;
And silenced by that silence lay the wife,
Remembering her dear Lord who died for
    all,
And musing on the little lives of men,
And how they mar this little by their feuds.

But while the two were sleeping, a full
    tide
Rose with ground-swell, which, on the
    foremost rocks
Touching, upjetted in spirts of wild sea-
    smoke,
And scaled in sheets of wasteful foam, and
    fell
In vast sea-cataracts—ever and anon
Dead claps of thunder from within the cliffs
Heard thro' the living roar.   At this the
    babe,
Their Margaret cradled near them, wail'd
    and woke
The mother, and the father suddenly cried,
'A wreck, a wreck !' then turn'd, and
    groaning said,

'Forgive !   How many will say, "for-
    give," and find
A sort of absolution in the sound

To hate a little longer ! No ; the sin
That neither God nor man can well for-
    give,
Hypocrisy, I saw it in him at once.
Is it so true that second thoughts are best?
Not first, and third, which are a riper first?
Too ripe, too late ! they come too late
    for use.
Ah love, there surely lives in man and
    beast
Something divine to warn them of their
    foes :
And such a sense, when first I fronted him,
Said, " Trust him not ;" but after, when
    I came
To know him more, I lost it, knew him
    less ;
Fought with what seem'd my own un-
    charity ;
Sat at his table ; drank his costly wines ;
Made more and more allowance for his
    talk ;
Went further, fool ! and trusted him with
    all,
All my poor scrapings from a dozen years
Of dust and deskwork : there is no such
    mine,
None ; but a gulf of ruin, swallowing gold,
Not making.   Ruin'd ! ruin'd ! the sea
    roars
Ruin : a fearful night !'

        ' Not fearful ; fair,'
Said the good wife, ' if every star in
    heaven
Can make it fair : you do but hear the tide.
Had you ill dreams ?'

    ' O yes,' he said, ' I dream'd
Of such a tide swelling toward the land,
And I from out the boundless outer deep
Swept with it to the shore, and enter'd one
Of those dark caves that run beneath the
    cliffs.
I thought the motion of the boundless deep
Bore thro' the cave, and I was heaved
    upon it
In darkness : then I saw one lovely star
Larger and larger.   " What a world," I
    thought,

" To live in !" but in moving on I found
Only the landward exit of the cave,
Bright with the sun upon the stream
    beyond :
And near the light a giant woman sat,
All over earthy, like a piece of·earth,
A pickaxe in her hand : then out I slipt
Into a land all sun and blossom, trees
As high as heaven, and every bird that
    sings :
And here the night-light flickering in my
    eyes
Awoke me.'

    ' That was then your dream,' she said,
' Not sad, but sweet.'

            ' So sweet, I lay,' said he,
' And mused upon it, drifting up the
    stream
In fancy, till I slept again, and pieced
The broken vision ; for I dream'd that still
The motion of the great deep bore me on,
And that the woman walk'd upon the
    brink :
I wonder'd at her strength, and ask'd her
    of it :
" It came," she said, " by working in the
    mines : "
O then to ask her of my shares, I thought ;
And ask'd ; but not a word ; she shook
    her head.
And then the motion of the current ceased,
And there was rolling thunder ; and we
    reach'd
A mountain, like a wall of burs and
    thorns ;
But she with her strong feet up the steep
    hill
Trod out a path : I follow'd ; and at top
She pointed seaward : there a fleet of
    glass,
That seem'd a fleet of jewels under me,
Sailing along before a gloomy cloud
That not one moment ceased to thunder,
    past
In sunshine : right across its track there lay,
Down in the water, a long reef of gold,
Or what seem'd gold : and I was glad at
    first

To think that in our often-ransack'd world
Still so much gold was left ; and then I
    fear'd
Lest the gay navy there should splinter
    on it,
And fearing waved my arm to warn them
    off ;
An idle signal, for the brittle fleet
(I thought I could have died to save it)
    near'd,
Touch'd, clink'd, and clash'd, and
    vanish'd, and I woke,
I heard the clash so clearly. Now I see
My dream was Life ; the woman honest
    Work ;
And my poor venture but a fleet of glass
Wreck'd on a reef of visionary gold.'

    ' Nay,' said the kindly wife to comfort
        him,
' You raised your arm, you tumbled down
    and broke
The glass with little Margaret's medicine
    in it ;
And, breaking that, you made and broke
    your dream :
A trifle makes a dream, a trifle breaks.'

    ' No trifle,' groan'd the husband ;
        ' yesterday
I met him suddenly in the street, and ask'd
That which I ask'd the woman in my
    dream.
Like her, he shook his head. "Show me
    the books !"
He dodged me with a long and loose
    account.
"The books, the books !" but he, he could
    not wait,
Bound on a matter he of life and death :
When the great Books (see Daniel seven
    and ten)
Were open'd, I should find he meant me
    well ;
And then began to bloat himself, and ooze
All over with the fat affectionate smile
That makes the widow lean. "My dearest
    friend,
Have faith, have faith ! We live by faith,"
    said he ;

"And all things work together for the good
Of those "—it makes me sick to quote him
    —last
Gript my hand hard, and with God-bless-
    you went.
I stood like one that had received a blow :
I found a hard friend in his loose accounts,
A loose one in the hard grip of his hand,
A curse in his God-bless-you : then my
    eyes
Pursued him down the street, and far
    away,
Among the honest shoulders of the crowd,
Read rascal in the motions of his back,
And scoundrel in the supple-sliding knee.'

    ' Was he so bound, poor soul ?' said
        the good wife ;
' So are we all : but do not call him, love,
Before you prove him, rogue, and proved,
    forgive.
His gain is loss ; for he that wrongs his
    friend
Wrongs himself more, and ever bears
    about
A silent court of justice in his breast,
Himself the judge and jury, and himself
The prisoner at the bar, ever condemn'd :
And that drags down his life : then comes
    what comes
Hereafter : and he meant, he said he
    meant,
Perhaps he meant, or partly meant, you
    well.'

    ' "With all his conscience and one eye
        askew "—
Love, let me quote these lines, that you
    may learn
A man is likewise counsel for himself,
Too often, in that silent court of yours—
" With all his conscience and one eye
    askew,
So false, he partly took himself for true ;
Whose pious talk, when most his heart
    was dry,
Made wet the crafty crowsfoot round his
    eye ;
Who, never naming God except for gain,
So never took that useful name in vain,

Made Him his catspaw and the Cross his
   tool,
And Christ the bait to trap his dupe and
   fool ;
Nor deeds of gift, but gifts of grace he
   forged,
And snake-like slimed his victim ere he
   gorged ;
And oft at Bible meetings, o'er the rest
Arising, did his holy oily best,
Dropping the too rough H in Hell and
   Heaven,
To spread the Word by which himself
   had thriven."
How like you this old satire ?'

                     ' Nay,' she said,
' I loathe it : he had never kindly heart,
Nor ever cared to better his own kind,
Who first wrote satire, with no pity in it.
But will you hear *my* dream, for I had one
That altogether went to music ?   Still
It awed me.'

     Then she told it, having dream'd
Of that same coast.

       —But round the North, a light,
A belt, it seem'd, of luminous vapour, lay,
And ever in it a low musical note
Swell'd up and died ; and, as it swell'd,
   a ridge
Of breaker issued from the belt, and still
Grew with the growing note, and when
   the note
Had reach'd a thunderous fulness, on
   those cliffs
Broke, mixt with awful light (the same as
   that
Living within the belt) whereby she saw
That all those lines of cliffs were cliffs no
   more,
But huge cathedral fronts of every age,
Grave, florid, stern, as far as eye could see,
One after one : and then the great ridge
   drew,
Lessening to the lessening music, back,
And past into the belt and swell'd again
Slowly to music : ever when it broke
The statues, king or saint, or founder fell ;

Then from the gaps and chasms of ruin
   left
Came men and women in dark clusters
   round,
Some crying, ' Set them up ! they shall
   not fall !'
And others, ' Let them lie, for they have
   fall'n.'
And still they strove and wrangled : and
   she grieved
In her strange dream, she knew not why,
   to find
Their wildest wailings never out of tune
With that sweet note ; and ever as their
   shrieks
Ran highest up the gamut, that great wave
Returning, while none mark'd it, on the
   crowd
Broke, mixt with awful light, and show'd
   their eyes
Glaring, and passionate looks, and swept
   away
The men of flesh and blood, and men of
   stone,
To the waste deeps together.

                    ' Then I fixt
My wistful eyes on two fair images,
Both crown'd with stars and high among
   the stars,—
The Virgin Mother standing with her
   child
High up on one of those dark minster-
   fronts—
Till she began to totter, and the child
Clung to the mother, and sent out a cry
Which mixt with little Margaret's, and I
   woke,
And my dream awed me :—well—but
   what are dreams ?
Yours came but from the breaking of a
   glass,
And mine but from the crying of a
   child.'

   'Child? No !' said he, 'but this tide's
   roar, and his,
Our Boanerges with his threats of doom,
And loud-lung'd Antibabylonianisms
(Altho' I grant but little music there)

Went both to make your dream : but if
    there were
A music harmonizing our wild cries,
Sphere-music such as that you dream'd
    about,
Why, that would make our passions far
    too like
The discords dear to the musician.   No—
One shriek of hate would jar all the hymns
    of heaven :
True Devils with no ear, they howl in tune
With nothing but the Devil !'

            ' " True " indeed !
One of our town, but later by an hour
Here than ourselves, spoke with me on
    the shore ;
While you were running down the sands,
    and made
The dimpled flounce of the sea-furbelow
    flap,
Good man, to please the child.   She
    brought strange news.
Why were you silent when I spoke to-
    night ?
I had set my heart on your forgiving him
Before you knew.   We *must* forgive the
    dead.'

    ' Dead ! who is dead ?'

            ' The man your eye pursued.
A little after you had parted with him,
He suddenly dropt dead of heart-disease.'

'Dead? he? of heart-disease? what heart
    had he
To die of? dead !'

            ' Ah, dearest, if there be
A devil in man, there is an angel too,
And if he did that wrong you charge him
    with,
His angel broke his heart.   But your
    rough voice
(You spoke so loud) has roused the child
    again.
Sleep, little birdie, sleep ! will she not
    sleep
Without her " little birdie " ? well then,
    sleep,
And I will sing you " birdie." '

            Saying this,
The woman half turn'd round from him
    she loved,
Left him one hand, and reaching thro'
    the night
Her other, found (for it was close be-
    side)
And half-embraced the basket cradle-
    head
With one soft arm, which, like the pliant
    bough
That moving moves the nest and nestling,
    sway'd
The cradle, while she sang this baby song.

    What does little birdie say
    In her nest at peep of day ?
    Let me fly, says little birdie,
    Mother, let me fly away.
    Birdie, rest a little longer,
    Till the little wings are stronger.
    So she rests a little longer,
    Then she flies away.

    What does little baby say,
    In her bed at peep of day ?
    Baby says, like little birdie,
    Let me rise and fly away.
    Baby, sleep a little longer,
    Till the little limbs are stronger.
    If she sleeps a little longer,
    Baby too shall fly away.

  ' She sleeps : let us too, let all evil,
    sleep.
He also sleeps—another sleep than
    ours.
He can do no more wrong : forgive him,
    dear,
And I shall sleep the sounder !'

            Then the man,
' His deeds yet live, the worst is yet to
    come.
Yet let your sleep for this one night be
    sound :
I do forgive him !'

            ' Thanks, my love,' she said,
' Your own will be the sweeter,' and they
    slept.

(Hieron., additions to the Eusebeian Chronicle; letter of Valerius
Rufinus in Epistolas S. Hier. (Lyon 1518) iii, p. 131 v°. – D'ap. T.L.S.
–.7.17.)

LUCRETIUS.

cf. 'A. Π. δ' 56

LUCILIA, wedded to Lucretius, found
Her master cold ; for when the morning
    flush
Of passion and the first embrace had died
Between them, tho' he lov'd her none the
    less,
Yet often when the woman heard his foot
Return from pacings in the field, and ran
To greet him with a kiss, the master took
Small notice, or austerely, for—his mind
Half buried in some weightier argument,
Or fancy-borne perhaps upon the rise
And long roll of the Hexameter—he past
To turn and ponder those three hundred
    scrolls
Left by the Teacher, whom he held divine.
She brook'd it not ; but wrathful, petulant,
Dreaming some rival, sought and found
    a witch
Who brew'd the philtre which had power,
    they said,
To lead an errant passion home again.
And this, at times, she mingled with his
    drink,
And this destroy'd him ; for the wicked
    broth
Confused the chemic labour of the blood,
And tickling the brute brain within the
    man's
Made havock among those tender cells,
    and check'd
His power to shape : he loathed himself ;
    and once
After a tempest woke upon a morn
That mock'd him with returning calm,
    and cried :

   ' Storm in the night ! for thrice I heard
      the rain
Rushing ; and once the flash of a
    thunderbolt—
Methought I never saw so fierce a fork—
Struck out the streaming mountain-side,
    and show'd
A riotous confluence of watercourses
Blanching and billowing in a hollow of it,
Where all but yester-eve was dusty-dry.

' Storm, and what dreams, ye holy
    Gods, what dreams !
For thrice I waken'd after dreams. Per-
    chance
We do but recollect the dreams that come
Just ere the waking : terrible ! for it seem'd
A void was made in Nature ; all her bonds
Crack'd ; and I saw the flaring atom-
    streams
And torrents of her myriad universe,
Ruining along the illimitable inane,
Fly on to clash together again, and make
Another and another frame of things
For ever : that was mine, my dream, I
    knew it—
Of and belonging to me, as the dog
With inward yelp and restless forefoot
    plies
His function of the woodland : but the
    next !
I thought that all the blood by Sylla shed
Came driving rainlike down again on
    earth,
And where it dash'd the reddening mea-
    dow, sprang
No dragon warriors from Cadmean teeth,
For these I thought my dream would
    show to me,
But girls, Hetairai, curious in their art,
Hired animalisms, vile as those that made
The mulberry-faced Dictator's orgies
    worse
Than aught they fable of the quiet Gods.
And hands they mixt, and yell'd and
    round me drove
In narrowing circles till I yell'd again
Half-suffocated, and sprang up, and saw—
Was it the first beam of my latest day ?

   ' Then, then, from utter gloom stood
      out the breasts,
The breasts of Helen, and hoveringly a
    sword
Now over and now under, now direct,
Pointed itself to pierce, but sank down
    shamed
At all that beauty ; and as I stared, a fire,
The fire that left a roofless Ilion,
Shot out of them, and scorch'd me that
    I woke.

T

M

'Is this thy vengeance, holy Venus, thine,
Because I would not one of thine own doves,
Not ev'n a rose, were offer'd to thee? thine,
Forgetful how my rich procemion makes
Thy glory fly along the Italian field,
In lays that will outlast thy Deity?

'Deity? nay, thy worshippers. My tongue
Trips, or I speak profanely. Which of these
Angers thee most, or angers thee at all?
Not if thou be'st of those who, far aloof
From envy, hate and pity, and spite and scorn,
Live the great life which all our greatest fain
Would follow, center'd in eternal calm.

'Nay, if thou canst, O Goddess, like ourselves
Touch, and be touch'd, then would I cry to thee
To kiss thy Mavors, roll thy tender arms
Round him, and keep him from the lust of blood
That makes a steaming slaughter-house of Rome.

'Ay, but I meant not thee; I meant not her,
Whom all the pines of Ida shook to see
Slide from that quiet heaven of hers, and tempt
The Trojan, while his neat-herds were abroad;
Nor her that o'er her wounded hunter wept
Her Deity false in human-amorous tears;
Nor whom her beardless apple-arbiter
Decided fairest. Rather, O ye Gods,
Poet-like, as the great Sicilian called
Calliope to grace his golden verse—
Ay, and this Kypris also—did I take
That popular name of thine to shadow forth
The all-generating powers and genial heat

Of Nature, when she strikes thro' the thick blood
Of cattle, and light is large, and lambs are glad
Nosing the mother's udder, and the bird
Makes his heart voice amid the blaze of flowers:
Which things appear the work of mighty Gods.

'The Gods! and if I go *my* work is left
Unfinish'd—*if* I go. The Gods, who haunt
The lucid interspace of world and world,
Where never creeps a cloud, or moves a wind,
Nor ever falls the least white star of snow,
Nor ever lowest roll of thunder moans,
Nor sound of human sorrow mounts to mar
Their sacred everlasting calm! and such,
Not all so fine, nor so divine a calm,
Not such, nor all unlike it, man may gain
Letting his own life go. The Gods, the Gods!
If all be atoms, how then should the Gods
Being atomic not be dissoluble,
Not follow the great law? My master held
That Gods there are, for all men so believe.
I prest my footsteps into his, and meant
Surely to lead my Memmius in a train
Of flowery clauses onward to the proof
That Gods there are, and deathless. Meant? I meant?
I have forgotten what I meant: my mind
Stumbles, and all my faculties are lamed.

'Look where another of our Gods, the Sun,
Apollo, Delius, or of older use
All-seeing Hyperion—what you will—
Has mounted yonder; since he never sware,
Except his wrath were wreak'd on wretched man,

That he would only shine among the dead
Hereafter ; tales ! for never yet on earth
Could dead flesh creep, or bits of roast-
   ing ox
Moan round the spit—nor knows he
   what he sees ;
King of the East altho' he seem, and girt
With song and flame and fragrance, slowly
   lifts
His golden feet on those empurpled stairs
That climb into the windy halls of
   heaven :
And here he glances on an eye new-born,
And gets for greeting but a wail of pain ;
And here he stays upon a freezing orb
That fain would gaze upon him to the
   last ;
And here upon a yellow eyelid fall'n
And closed by those who mourn a friend
   in vain,
Not thankful that his troubles are no
   more.
And me, altho' his fire is on my face
Blinding, he sees not, nor at all can tell
Whether I mean this day to end myself,
Or lend an ear to Plato where he says,
That men like soldiers may not quit the
   post
Allotted by the Gods : but he that holds
The Gods are careless, wherefore need he
   care
Greatly for them, nor rather plunge at
   once,
Being troubled, wholly out of sight, and
   sink
Past earthquake—ay, and gout and stone,
   that break
Body toward death, and palsy, death-in-
   life,
And wretched age—and worst disease of
   all,
These prodigies of myriad nakednesses,
And twisted shapes of lust, unspeakable,
Abominable, strangers at my hearth
Not welcome, harpies miring every dish,
The phantom husks of something foully
   done,
And fleeting thro' the boundless universe,
And blasting the long quiet of my breast
With animal heat and dire insanity ?

'How should the mind, except it loved
   them, clasp
These idols to herself ? or do they fly
Now thinner, and now thicker, like the
   flakes
In a fall of snow, and so press in, perforce
Of multitude, as crowds that in an hour
Of civic tumult jam the doors, and bear
The keepers down, and throng, their rags
   and they
The basest, far into that council-hall
Where sit the best and stateliest of the
   land ?

'Can I not fling this horror off me
   again,
Seeing with how great ease Nature can
   smile,
Balmier and nobler from her bath of
   storm,
At random ravage ? and how easily
The mountain there has cast his cloudy
   slough,
Now towering o'er him in serenest air,
A mountain o'er a mountain,—ay, and
   within
All hollow as the hopes and fears of
   men ?

'But who was he, that in the garden
   snared
Picus and Faunus, rustic Gods ? a tale
To laugh at—more to laugh at in myself—
For look ! what is it ? there ? yon arbutus
Totters ; a noiseless riot underneath
Strikes through the wood, sets all the
   tops quivering—
The mountain quickens into Nymph and
   Faun ;
And here an Oread—how the sun delights
To glance and shift about her slippery
   sides,
And rosy knees and supple roundedness,
And budded bosom-peaks—who this way
   runs
Before the rest—A satyr, a satyr, see,
Follows ; but him I proved impossible ;
Twy-natured is no nature : yet he draws
Nearer and nearer, and I scan him now
Beastlier than any phantom of his kind

That ever butted his rough brother-brute
For lust or lusty blood or provender :
I hate, abhor, spit, sicken at him ; and she
Loathes him as well ; such a precipitate heel,
Fledged as it were with Mercury's ankle-wing,
Whirls her to me : but will she fling herself,
Shameless upon me ? Catch her, goat-foot : nay,
Hide, hide them, million-myrtled wilderness,
And cavern-shadowing laurels, hide ! do I wish—
What ?—that the bush were leafless ? or to whelm
All of them in one massacre ? O ye Gods,
I know you careless, yet, behold, to you
From childly wont and ancient use I call—
I thought I lived securely as yourselves—
No lewdness, narrowing envy, monkey-spite,
No madness of ambition, avarice, none :
No larger feast than under plane or pine
With neighbours laid along the grass, to take
Only such cups as left us friendly-warm,
Affirming each his own philosophy—
Nothing to mar the sober majesties
Of settled, sweet, Epicurean life.
But now it seems some unseen monster lays
His vast and filthy hands upon my will,
Wrenching it backward into his ; and spoils
My bliss in being ; and it was not great ;
For save when shutting reasons up in rhythm,
Or Heliconian honey in living words,
To make a truth less harsh, I often grew
Tired of so much within our little life,
Or of so little in our little life—
Poor little life that toddles half an hour
Crown'd with a flower or two, and there an end—
And since the nobler pleasure seems to fade.

Why should I, beastlike as I find myself,
Not manlike end myself?—our privilege—
What beast has heart to do it ? And what man,
What Roman would be dragg'd in triumph thus ?
Not I ; not he, who bears one name with her
Whose death-blow struck the dateless doom of kings,
When, brooking not the Tarquin in her veins,
She made her blood in sight of Collatine
And all his peers, flushing the guiltless air,
Spout from the maiden fountain in her heart.
And from it sprang the Commonwealth, which breaks
As I am breaking now !

     'And therefore now
Let her, that is the womb and tomb of all,
Great Nature, take, and forcing far apart
Those blind beginnings that have made me man,
Dash them anew together at her will
Thro' all her cycles—into man once more,
Or beast or bird or fish, or opulent flower:
But till this cosmic order everywhere
Shatter'd into one earthquake in one day
Cracks all to pieces,—and that hour perhaps
Is not so far when momentary man
Shall seem no more a something to himself,
But he, his hopes and hates, his homes and fanes,
And even his bones long laid within the grave,
The very sides of the grave itself shall pass,
Vanishing, atom and void, atom and void,
Into the unseen for ever,—till that hour,
My golden work in which I told a truth
That stays the rolling Ixionian wheel,
And numbs the Fury's ringlet-snake, and plucks
The mortal soul from out immortal hell,
Shall stand : ay, surely : then it fails at last

And perishes as I must ; for O Thou,
Passionless bride, divine Tranquillity,
Yearn'd after by the wisest of the wise,
Who fail to find thee, being as thou art
Without one pleasure and without one
   pain,
Howbeit I know thou surely must be mine
Or soon or late, yet out of season, thus
I woo thee roughly, for thou carest not
How roughly men may woo thee so they
   win—
Thus—thus: the soul flies out and dies
   in the air.'

With that he drove the knife into his
   side :
She heard him raging, heard him fall ;
   ran in,
Beat breast, tore hair, cried out upon
   herself
As having fail'd in duty to him, shriek'd
That she but meant to win him back, fell
   on him,
Clasp'd, kiss'd him, wail'd : he answer'd,
   ' Care not thou !
Thy duty ? What is duty ? Fare thee
   well !'

THE PRINCESS; *pub 1847*

A MEDLEY.

PROLOGUE.

SIR Walter Vivian all a summer's day
Gave his broad lawns until the set of sun
Up to the people : thither flock'd at noon
His tenants, wife and child, and thither
   half
The neighbouring borough with their
   Institute
Of which he was the patron. I was
   there
From college, visiting the son,—the son
A Walter too,—with others of our set,
Five others : we were seven at Vivian-
   place.

And me that morning Walter show'd
   the house,
Greek, set with busts : from vases in the
   hall
Flowers of all heavens, and lovelier than
   their names,
Grew side by side ; and on the pavement
   lay
Carved stones of the Abbey-ruin in the
   park,
Huge Ammonites, and the first bones of
   Time ;
And on the tables every clime and age

Jumbled together ; celts and calumets,
Claymore and snowshoe, toys in lava,
   fans
Of sandal, amber, ancient rosaries,
Laborious orient ivory sphere in sphere,
The cursed Malayan crease, and battle
   clubs
From the isles of palm : and higher on
   the walls,
Betwixt the monstrous horns of elk and
   deer,
His own forefathers' arms and armour
   hung.

And ' this ' he said ' was Hugh's at
   Agincourt ;
And that was old Sir Ralph's at As-
   calon :
A good knight he ! we keep a chronicle
With all about him '—which he brought,
   and I
Dived in a hoard of tales that dealt with
   knights,
Half-legend, half-historic, counts and
   kings
Who laid about them at their wills and
   died ;
And mixt with these, a lady, one that
   arm'd

Her own fair head, and sallying thro' the gate,
Had beat her foes with slaughter from her walls.

'O miracle of women,' said the book,
'O noble heart who, being strait-besieged
By this wild king to force her to his wish,
Nor bent, nor broke, nor shunn'd a soldier's death,
But now when all was lost or seem'd as lost—
Her stature more than mortal in the burst
Of sunrise, her arm lifted, eyes on fire—
Brake with a blast of trumpets from the gate,
And, falling on them like a thunderbolt,
She trampled some beneath her horses' heels,
And some were whelm'd with missiles of the wall,
And some were push'd with lances from the rock,
And part were drown'd within the whirling brook:
O miracle of noble womanhood!'

So sang the gallant glorious chronicle;
And, I all rapt in this, 'Come out,' he said,
'To the Abbey: there is Aunt Elizabeth
And sister Lilia with the rest.' We went
(I kept the book and had my finger in it)
Down thro' the park: strange was the sight to me;
For all the sloping pasture murmur'd, sown
With happy faces and with holiday.
There moved the multitude, a thousand heads:
The patient leaders of their Institute
Taught them with facts. One rear'd a font of stone
And drew, from butts of water on the slope,
The fountain of the moment, playing, now
A twisted snake, and now a rain of pearls,
Or steep-up spout whereon the gilded ball

Danced like a wisp: and somewhat lower down
A man with knobs and wires and vials fired
A cannon: Echo answer'd in her sleep
From hollow fields: and here were telescopes
For azure views; and there a group of girls
In circle waited, whom the electric shock
Dislink'd with shrieks and laughter: round the lake
A little clock-work steamer paddling plied
And shook the lilies: perch'd about the knolls
A dozen angry models jetted steam:
A petty railway ran: a fire-balloon
Rose gem-like up before the dusky groves
And dropt a fairy parachute and past:
And there thro' twenty posts of telegraph
They flash'd a saucy message to and fro
Between the mimic stations; so that sport
Went hand in hand with Science; otherwhere
Pure sport: a herd of boys with clamour bowl'd
And stump'd the wicket; babies roll'd about
Like tumbled fruit in grass; and men and maids
Arranged a country dance, and flew thro' light
And shadow, while the twangling violin
Struck up with Soldier-laddie, and overhead
The broad ambrosial aisles of lofty lime
Made noise with bees and breeze from end to end.

Strange was the sight and smacking of the time;
And long we gazed, but satiated at length
Came to the ruins. High-arch'd and ivy-claspt,
Of finest Gothic lighter than a fire,
Thro' one wide chasm of time and frost they gave
The park, the crowd, the house; but all within
The sward was trim as any garden lawn:

And here we lit on Aunt Elizabeth,
And Lilia with the rest, and lady friends
From neighbour seats: and there was
Ralph himself,
A broken statue propt against the wall,
As gay as any. Lilia, wild with sport,
Half child half woman as she was, had
wound
A scarf of orange round the stony helm,
And robed the shoulders in a rosy silk,
That made the old warrior from his ivied
nook
Glow like a sunbeam: near his tomb a
feast
Shone, silver-set; about it lay the guests,
And there we join'd them: then the
maiden Aunt
Took this fair day for text, and from it
preach'd
An universal culture for the crowd,
And all things great; but we, unworthier,
told
Of college: he had climb'd across the
spikes,
And he had squeezed himself betwixt the
bars,
And he had breathed the Proctor's dogs;
and one
Discuss'd his tutor, rough to common
men,
But honeying at the whisper of a lord;
And one the Master, as a rogue in grain
Veneer'd with sanctimonious theory.

But while they talk'd, above their heads
I saw
The feudal warrior lady-clad; which
brought
My book to mind: and opening this I
read
Of old Sir Ralph a page or two that rang
With tilt and tourney; then the tale of
her
That drove her foes with slaughter from
her walls,
And much I praised her nobleness, and
'Where,'
Ask'd Walter, patting Lilia's head (she lay
Beside him) 'lives there such a woman
now?'

Quick answer'd Lilia 'There are thou-
sands now
Such women, but convention beats them
down:
It is but bringing up; no more than that:
You men have done it: how I hate you
all!
Ah, were I something great! I wish I
were
Some mighty poetess, I would shame you
then,
That love to keep us children! O I wish
That I were some great princess, I would
build
Far off from men a college like a man's,
And I would teach them all that men are
taught;
We are twice as quick!' And here she
shook aside
The hand that play'd the patron with her
curls.

And one said smiling 'Pretty were the
sight
If our old halls could change their sex,
and flaunt
With prudes for proctors, dowagers for
deans,
And sweet girl-graduates in their golden
hair.
I think they should not wear our rusty
gowns,
But move as rich as Emperor-moths, or
Ralph
Who shines so in the corner; yet I fear,
If there were many Lilias in the brood,
However deep you might embower the
nest,
Some boy would spy it.'
                        At this upon the sward
She tapt her tiny silken-sandal'd foot:
'That's your light way; but I would
make it death
For any male thing but to peep at us.'

Petulant she spoke, and at herself she
laugh'd;
A rosebud set with little wilful thorns,
And sweet as English air could make her,
she:

But Walter hail'd a score of names upon
    her,
And 'petty Ogress,' and 'ungrateful
    Puss,'
And swore he long'd at college, only
    long'd,
All else was well, for she-society.
They boated and they cricketed ; they
    talk'd
At wine, in clubs, of art, of politics ;
They lost their weeks ; they vext the
    souls of deans ;
They rode ; they betted ; made a hundred
    friends,
And caught the blossom of the flying
    terms,
But miss'd the mignonette of Vivian-place,
The little hearth-flower Lilia.   Thus he
    spoke,
Part banter, part affection.
                'True,' she said,
'We doubt not that.   O yes, you miss'd
    us much.
I'll stake my ruby ring upon it you
    did.'

    She held it out ; and as a parrot turns
Up thro' gilt wires a crafty loving eye,
And takes a lady's finger with all care,
And bites it for true heart and not for
    harm,
So he with Lilia's.   Daintily she shriek'd
And wrung it.   'Doubt my word again !'
    he said.
'Come, listen ! here is proof that you
    were miss'd :
We seven stay'd at Christmas up to read ;
And there we took one tutor as to read :
The hard-grain'd Muses of the cube and
    square
Were out of season : never man, I think,
So moulder'd in a sinecure as he :
For while our cloisters echo'd frosty feet,
And our long walks were stript as bare
    as brooms,
We did but talk you over, pledge you all
In wassail ; often, like as many girls—
Sick for the hollies and the yews of home—
As many little trifling Lilias—play'd
Charades and riddles as at Christmas here,

And *what's my thought* and *when* and
    where and *how*,
And often told a tale from mouth to mouth
As here at Christmas.'
                She remember'd that :
A pleasant game, she thought : she liked
    it more
Than magic music, forfeits, all the rest.
But these—what kind of tales did men
    tell men,
She wonder'd, by themselves ?
                A half-disdain
Perch'd on the pouted blossom of her lips :
And Walter nodded at me ; '*He* began,
The rest would follow, each in turn ; and so
We forged a sevenfold story.   Kind ?
    what kind ?
Chimeras, crotchets, Christmas solecisms,
Seven-headed monsters only made to kill
Time by the fire in winter.'
                'Kill him now,
The tyrant ! kill him in the summer too,'
Said Lilia ; 'Why not now ?' the maiden
    Aunt.
'Why not a summer's as a winter's tale ?
A tale for summer as befits the time,
And something it should be to suit the
    place,
Heroic, for a hero lies beneath,
Grave, solemn !'
              Walter warp'd his mouth at this
To something so mock-solemn, that I
    laugh'd
And Lilia woke with sudden-shrilling
    mirth
An echo like a ghostly woodpecker,
Hid in the ruins ; till the maiden Aunt
(A little sense of wrong had touch'd her
    face
With colour) turn'd to me with 'As you
    will ;
Heroic if you will, or what you will,
Or be yourself your hero if you will.'

    'Take Lilia, then, for heroine,' clam-
    our'd he,
'And make her some great Princess, six
    feet high,
Grand, epic, homicidal ; and be you
The Prince to win her !'

'Then follow me, the Prince,'
I answer'd, 'each be hero in his turn !
Seven and yet one, like shadows in a
  dream.—
Heroic seems our Princess as required—
But something made to suit with Time
  and place,
A Gothic ruin and a Grecian house,
A talk of college and of ladies' rights,
A feudal knight in silken masquerade,
And, yonder, shrieks and strange experi-
  ments
For which the good Sir Ralph had burnt
  them all—
This *were* a medley ! we should have him
  back
Who told the "Winter's tale " to do it
  for us.
No matter : we will say whatever comes.
And let the ladies sing us, if they will,
From time to time, some ballad or a song
To give us breathing-space.'
                              So I began,
And the rest follow'd : and the women
  sang
Between the rougher voices of the men,
Like linnets in the pauses of the wind :
And here I give the story and the songs.

I.

A prince I was, blue-eyed, and fair in
  face,
Of temper amorous, as the first of May,
With lengths of yellow ringlet, like a girl,
For on my cradle shone the Northern
  star.

There lived an ancient legend in our
  house.
Some sorcerer, whom a far-off grandsire
  burnt
Because he cast no shadow, had foretold,
Dying, that none of all our blood should
  know
The shadow from the substance, and that
  one
Should come to fight with shadows and
  to fall.
For so, my mother said, the story ran.

And, truly, waking dreams were, more or
  less,
An old and strange affection of the house.
Myself too had weird seizures, Heaven
  knows what :
On a sudden in the midst of men and day,
And while I walk'd and talk'd as hereto-
  fore,
I seem'd to move among a world of ghosts,
And feel myself the shadow of a dream.
Our great court-Galen poised his gilt-head
  cane,
And paw'd his beard, and mutter'd
  'catalepsy.'
My mother pitying made a thousand
  prayers ;
My mother was as mild as any saint,
Half-canonized by all that look'd on her,
So gracious was her tact and tenderness :
But my good father thought a king a king ;
He cared not for the affection of the house ;
He held his sceptre like a pedant's wand
To lash offence, and with long arms and
  hands
Reach'd out, and pick'd offenders from
  the mass
For judgment.
            Now it chanced that I had been,
While life was yet in bud and blade,
  betroth'd
To one, a neighbouring Princess : she to me
Was proxy-wedded with a bootless calf
At eight years old ; and still from time
  to time
Came murmurs of her beauty from the
  South,
And of her brethren, youths of puissance ;
And still I wore her picture by my heart,
And one dark tress ; and all around them
  both
Sweet thoughts would swarm as bees about
  their queen.

But when the days drew nigh that I
  should wed,
My father sent ambassadors with furs
And jewels, gifts, to fetch her : these
  brought back
A present, a great labour of the loom ;
And therewithal an answer vague as wind :

Besides, they saw the king; he took the gifts;
He said there was a compact; that was true:
But then she had a will; was he to blame?
And maiden fancies; loved to live alone
Among her women; certain, would not wed.

That morning in the presence room I stood
With Cyril and with Florian, my two friends:
The first, a gentleman of broken means
(His father's fault) but given to starts and bursts
Of revel; and the last, my other heart,
And almost my half-self, for still we moved
Together, twinn'd as horse's ear and eye.

Now, while they spake, I saw my father's face
Grow long and troubled like a rising moon,
Inflamed with wrath: he started on his feet,
Tore the king's letter, snow'd it down, and rent
The wonder of the loom thro' warp and woof
From skirt to skirt; and at the last he sware
That he would send a hundred thousand men,
And bring her in a whirlwind: then he chew'd
The thrice-turn'd cud of wrath, and cook'd his spleen,
Communing with his captains of the war.

At last I spoke. 'My father, let me go.
It cannot be but some gross error lies
In this report, this answer of a king,
Whom all men rate as kind and hospitable:
Or, maybe, I myself, my bride once seen,
Whate'er my grief to find her less than fame,
May rue the bargain made.' And Florian said:
'I have a sister at the foreign court,
Who moves about the Princess; she, you know,
Who wedded with a nobleman from thence:
He, dying lately, left her, as I hear,
The lady of three castles in that land:
Thro' her this matter might be sifted clean.'
And Cyril whisper'd: 'Take me with you too.'

Then laughing 'what, if these weird seizures come
Upon you in those lands, and no one near
To point you out the shadow from the truth!
Take me: I'll serve you better in a strait;
I grate on rusty hinges here:' but 'No!'
Roar'd the rough king, 'you shall not; we ourself
Will crush her pretty maiden fancies dead
In iron gauntlets: break the council up.'

But when the council broke, I rose and past
Thro' the wild woods that hung about the town;
Found a still place, and pluck'd her likeness out;
Laid it on flowers, and watch'd it lying bathed
In the green gleam of dewy-tassell'd trees:
What were those fancies? wherefore break her troth?
Proud look'd the lips: but while I meditated
A wind arose and rush'd upon the South,
And shook the songs, the whispers, and the shrieks
Of the wild woods together; and a Voice
Went with it, 'Follow, follow, thou shalt win.'

Then, ere the silver sickle of that month
Became her golden shield, I stole from court
With Cyril and with Florian, unperceived,
Cat-footed thro' the town and half in dread
To hear my father's clamour at our backs
With Ho! from some bay-window shake the night;
But all was quiet: from the bastion'd walls

Like threaded spiders, one by one, we
    dropt,
And flying reach'd the frontier : then we
    crost
To a livelier land ; and so by tilth and
    grange,
And vines, and blowing bosks of wilder-
    ness,
We gain'd the mother-city thick with
    towers,
And in the imperial palace found the king.

His name was Gama ; crack'd and
    small his voice,
But bland the smile that like a wrinkling
    wind
On glassy water drove his cheek in lines ;
A little dry old man, without a star,
Not like a king : three days he feasted us,
And on the fourth I spake of why we
    came,
And my betroth'd. 'You do us, Prince,'
    he said,
Airing a snowy hand and signet gem,
'All honour. We remember love our-
    selves
In our sweet youth : there did a compact
    pass
Long summers back, a kind of ceremony—
I think the year in which our olives
    fail'd.
I would you had her, Prince, with all my
    heart,
With my full heart : but there were
    widows here,
Two widows, Lady Psyche, Lady Blanche ;
They fed her theories, in and out of place
Maintaining that with equal husbandry
The woman were an equal to the man.
They harp'd on this ; with this our ban-
    quets rang ;
Our dances broke and buzz'd in knots of
    talk ;
Nothing but this ; my very ears were hot
To hear them ; knowledge, so my daughter
    held,
Was all in all : they had but been, she
    thought,
As children ; they must lose the child,
    assume

The woman : then, Sir, awful odes she
    wrote,
Too awful, sure, for what they treated of,
But all she is and does is awful ; odes
About this losing of the child ; and rhymes
And dismal lyrics, prophesying change
Beyond all reason : these the women sang ;
And they that know such things—I sought
    but peace ;
No critic I—would call them master-
    pieces :
They master'd *me*. At last she begg'd a
    boon,
A certain summer-palace which I have
Hard by your father's frontier : I said no,
Yet being an easy man, gave it : and
    there,
All wild to found an University
For maidens, on the spur she fled ; and
    more
We know not,—only this : they see no
    men,
Not ev'n her brother Arac, nor the twins
Her brethren, tho' they love her, look
    upon her
As on a kind of paragon ; and I
(Pardon me saying it) were much loth to
    breed
Dispute betwixt myself and mine : but
    since
(And I confess with right) you think me
    bound
In some sort, I can give you letters to her ;
And yet, to speak the truth, I rate your
    chance
Almost at naked nothing.'
               Thus the king ;
And I, tho' nettled that he seem'd to slur
With garrulous ease and oily courtesies
Our formal compact, yet, not less (all frets
But chafing me on fire to find my bride)
Went forth again with both my friends.
    We rode
Many a long league back to the North.
    At last
From hills, that look'd across a land of
    hope,
We dropt with evening on a rustic town
Set in a gleaming river's crescent-curve,
Close at the boundary of the liberties ;

There, enter'd an old hostel, call'd mine host
To council, plied him with his richest wines,
And show'd the late-writ letters of the king.

He with a long low sibilation, stared
As blank as death in marble; then ex-claim'd
Averring it was clear against all rules
For any man to go: but as his brain
Began to mellow, 'If the king,' he said,
'Had given us letters, was he bound to speak?
The king would bear him out;' and at the last—
The summer of the vine in all his veins—
'No doubt that we might make it worth his while.
She once had past that way; he heard her speak;
She scared him; life! he never saw the like;
She look'd as grand as doomsday and as grave:
And he, he reverenced his liege-lady there;
He always made a point to post with mares;
His daughter and his housemaid were the boys:
The land, he understood, for miles about
Was till'd by women; all the swine were sows,
And all the dogs'—
            But while he jested thus,
A thought flash'd thro' me which I clothed in act,
Remembering how we three presented Maid
Or Nymph, or Goddess, at high tide of feast,
In masque or pageant at my father's court.
We sent mine host to purchase female gear;
He brought it, and himself a sight to shake
The midriff of despair with laughter, holp
To lace us up, till, each, in maiden plumes

We rustled: him we gave a costly bribe
To guerdon silence, mounted our good steeds,
And boldly ventured on the liberties.

We follow'd up the river as we rode,
And rode till midnight when the college lights
Began to glitter firefly-like in copse
And linden alley: then we past an arch,
Whereon a woman-statue rose with wings
From four wing'd horses dark against the stars;
And some inscription ran along the front,
But deep in shadow: further on we gain'd
A little street half garden and half house;
But scarce could hear each other speak for noise
Of clocks and chimes, like silver hammers falling
On silver anvils, and the splash and stir
Of fountains spouted up and showering down
In meshes of the jasmine and the rose:
And all about us peal'd the nightingale,
Rapt in her song, and careless of the snare.

There stood a bust of Pallas for a sign,
By two sphere lamps blazon'd like Heaven and Earth
With constellation and with continent,
Above an entry: riding in, we call'd;
A plump-arm'd Ostleress and a stable wench
Came running at the call, and help'd us down.
Then stept a buxom hostess forth, and sail'd,
Full-blown, before us into rooms which gave
Upon a pillar'd porch, the bases lost
In laurel: her we ask'd of that and this,
And who were tutors. 'Lady Blanche' she said,
'And Lady Psyche.'   'Which was prettiest,
Best-natured?' 'Lady Psyche.' 'Hers are we,'

One voice, we cried ; and I sat down and
    wrote,
In such a hand as when a field of corn
Bows all its ears before the roaring East ;

'Three ladies of the Northern empire
    pray
Your Highness would enroll them with
    your own,
As Lady Psyche's pupils.'
                    This I seal'd :
The seal was Cupid bent above a scroll,
And o'er his head Uranian Venus hung,
And raised the blinding bandage from his
    eyes :
I gave the letter to be sent with dawn ;
And then to bed, where half in doze I
    seem'd
To float about a glimmering night, and
    watch
A full sea glazed with muffled moonlight,
    swell
On some dark shore just seen that it was
    rich.

II.

As thro' the land at eve we went,
    And pluck'd the ripen'd ears,
We fell out, my wife and I,
O we fell out I know not why,
    And kiss'd again with tears.
And blessings on the falling out
    That all the more endears,
When we fall out with those we love
    And kiss again with tears !
For when we came where lies the child
    We lost in other years,
There above the little grave,
O there above the little grave,
    We kiss'd again with tears.

At break of day the College Portress
    came :
She brought us Academic silks, in hue
The lilac, with a silken hood to each,
And zoned with gold ; and now when
    these were on,
And we as rich as moths from dusk
    cocoons,
She, curtseying her obeisance, let us know
The Princess Ida waited : out we paced,

I first, and following thro' the porch that
    sang
All round with laurel, issued in a court
Compact of lucid marbles, boss'd with
    lengths
Of classic frieze, with ample awnings gay
Betwixt the pillars, and with great urns
    of flowers.
The Muses and the Graces, group'd in
    threes,
Enring'd a billowing fountain in the midst ;
And here and there on lattice edges lay
Or book or lute ; but hastily we past,
And up a flight of stairs into the hall.

There at a board by tome and paper
    sat,
With two tame leopards couch'd beside
    her throne,
All beauty compass'd in a female form,
The Princess ; liker to the inhabitant
Of some clear planet close upon the Sun,
Than our man's earth ; such eyes were in
    her head,
And so much grace and power, breathing
    down
From over her arch'd brows, with every
    turn
Lived thro' her to the tips of her long
    hands,
And to her feet. She rose her height,
    and said :

'We give you welcome : not without
    redound
Of use and glory to yourselves ye come,
The first-fruits of the stranger : aftertime,
And that full voice which circles round
    the grave,
Will rank you nobly, mingled up with me.
What ! are the ladies of your land so
    tall ?'
'We of the court' said Cyril. 'From
    the court'
She answer'd, 'then ye know the Prince?'
    and he :
'The climax of his age ! as tho' there were
One rose in all the world, your Highness
    that,
He worships your ideal :' she replied :

'We scarcely thought in our own hall to
  hear
This barren verbiage, current among men,
Light coin, the tinsel clink of compliment.
Your flight from out your bookless wilds
  would seem
As arguing love of knowledge and of
  power ;
Your language proves you still the child.
  Indeed,
We dream not of him : when we set our
  hand
To this great work, we purposed with
  ourself
Never to wed. You likewise will do well,
Ladies, in entering here, to cast and fling
The tricks, which make us toys of men,
  that so,
Some future time, if so indeed you will,
You may with those self-styled our lords
  ally
Your fortunes, justlier balanced, scale with
  scale.'

  At those high words, we conscious of
    ourselves,
Perused the matting ; then an officer
Rose up, and read the statutes, such as
  these :
Not for three years to correspond with
  home ;
Not for three years to cross the liberties ;
Not for three years to speak with any
  men ;
And many more, which hastily subscribed,
We enter'd on the boards : and 'Now,'
  she cried,
'Ye are green wood, see ye warp not.
  Look, our hall !
Our statues ! — not of those that men
  desire,
Sleek Odalisques, or oracles of mode,
Nor stunted squaws of West or East ; but
  she
That taught the Sabine how to rule, and
  she
The foundress of the Babylonian wall,
The Carian Artemisia strong in war,
The Rhodope, that built the pyramid,
Clelia, Cornelia, with the Palmyrene

That fought Aurelian, and the Roman
  brows
Of Agrippina. Dwell with these, and
  lose
Convention, since to look on noble forms
Makes noble thro' the sensuous organism
That which is higher. O lift your natures
  up :
Embrace our aims : work out your free-
  dom. Girls,
Knowledge is now no more a fountain
  seal'd :
Drink deep, until the habits of the slave,
The sins of emptiness, gossip and spite
And slander, die. Better not be at all
Than not be noble. Leave us : you may
  go :
To-day the Lady Psyche will harangue
The fresh arrivals of the week before ;
For they press in from all the provinces,
And fill the hive.'

            She spoke, and bowing waved
Dismissal : back again we crost the court
To Lady Psyche's : as we enter'd in,
There sat along the forms, like morning
  doves
That sun their milky bosoms on the
  thatch,
A patient range of pupils ; she herself
Erect behind a desk of satin-wood,
A quick brunette, well-moulded, falcon-
  eyed,
And on the hither side, or so she look'd,
Of twenty summers. At her left, a child,
In shining draperies, headed like a star,
Her maiden babe, a double April old,
Aglaïa slept. We sat : the Lady glanced :
Then Florian, but no livelier than the
  dame
That whisper'd 'Asses' ears,' among the
  sedge,
'My sister.' 'Comely, too, by all that's
  fair,'
Said Cyril. 'O hush, hush !' and she
  began.

  'This world was once a fluid haze of
    light,
Till toward the centre set the starry tides,
And eddied into suns, that wheeling cast

The planets : then the monster, then the
  man ;
Tattoo'd or woaded, winter-clad in skins,
Raw from the prime, and crushing down
  his mate ;
As yet we find in barbarous isles, and
  here
Among the lowest.'
              Thereupon she took
A bird's-eye-view of all the ungracious
  past ;
Glanced at the legendary Amazon
As emblematic of a nobler age ;
Appraised the Lycian custom, spoke of
  those
That lay at wine with Lar and Lucumo ;
Ran down the Persian, Grecian, Roman
  lines
Of empire, and the woman's state in each,
How far from just ; till warming with her
  theme
She fulmined out her scorn of laws Salique
And little-footed China, touch'd on
  Mahomet
With much contempt, and came to
  chivalry :
When some respect, however slight, was
  paid
To woman, superstition all awry :
However then commenced the dawn : a
  beam
Had slanted forward, falling in a land
Of promise ; fruit would follow. Deep,
  indeed,
Their debt of thanks to her who first had
  dared
To leap the rotten pales of prejudice,
Disyoke their necks from custom, and
  assert
None lordlier than themselves but that
  which made
Woman and man. She had founded ;
  they must build.
Here might they learn whatever men were
  taught :
Let them not fear : some said their heads
  were less :
Some men's were small ; not they the
  least of men ;
For often fineness compensated size :

Besides the brain was like the hand, and
  grew
With using ; thence the man's, if more
  was more ;
He took advantage of his strength to be
First in the field : some ages had been lost ;
But woman ripen'd earlier, and her life
Was longer ; and albeit their glorious
  names
Were fewer, scatter'd stars, yet since in
  truth
The highest is the measure of the man,
And not the Kaffir, Hottentot, Malay,
Nor those horn-handed breakers of the
  glebe,
But Homer, Plato, Verulam ; even so
With woman : and in arts of government
Elizabeth and others ; arts of war
The peasant Joan and others ; arts of grace
Sappho and others vied with any man :
And, last not least, she who had left her
  place,
And bow'd her state to them, that they
  might grow
To use and power on this Oasis, lapt
In the arms of leisure, sacred from the
  blight
Of ancient influence and scorn.
                          At last
She rose upon a wind of prophecy
Dilating on the future ; 'everywhere
Two heads in council, two beside the
  hearth,
Two in the tangled business of the world,
Two in the liberal offices of life,
Two plummets dropt for one to sound
  the abyss
Of science, and the secrets of the mind :
Musician, painter, sculptor, critic, more :
And everywhere the broad and bounteous
  Earth
Should bear a double growth of those
  rare souls,
Poets, whose thoughts enrich the blood
  of the world.'

She ended here, and beckon'd us : the
  rest
Parted ; and, glowing full-faced welcome,
  she

Began to address us, and was moving on
In gratulation, till as when a boat
Tacks, and the slacken'd sail flaps, all
    her voice
Faltering and fluttering in her throat, she
    cried
'My brother!' 'Well, my sister.' 'O,'
    she said,
'What do you here? and in this dress?
    and these?
Why who are these? a wolf within the
    fold!
A pack of wolves! the Lord be gracious
    to me!
A plot, a plot, a plot, to ruin all!'
'No plot, no plot,' he answer'd.
    'Wretched boy,
How saw you not the inscription on the
    gate,
LET NO MAN ENTER IN ON PAIN OF
    DEATH?'
'And if I had,' he answer'd, 'who could
    think
The softer Adams of your Academe,
O sister, Sirens tho' they be, were such
As chanted on the blanching bones of
    men?'
'But you will find it otherwise' she said.
'You jest: ill jesting with edge-tools!
    my vow
Binds me to speak, and O that iron will,
That axelike edge unturnable, our Head,
The Princess.' 'Well then, Psyche, take
    my life,
And nail me like a weasel on a grange
For warning: bury me beside the gate,
And cut this epitaph above my bones;
*Here lies a brother by a sister slain,
All for the common good of womankind.*'
'Let me die too,' said Cyril, 'having
    seen
And heard the Lady Psyche.'
                    I struck in:
'Albeit so mask'd, Madam, I love the
    truth;
Receive it; and in me behold the Prince
Your countryman, affianced years ago
To the Lady Ida: here, for here she was,
And thus (what other way was left) I
    came.'

'O Sir, O Prince, I have no country
    none;
If any, this; but none. Whate'er I was
Disrooted, what I am is grafted here.
Affianced, Sir? love-whispers may not
    breathe
Within this vestal limit, and how should
    I,
Who am not mine, say, live: the thunder-
    bolt
Hangs silent; but prepare: I speak; it
    falls.'
'Yet pause,' I said: 'for that inscription
    there,
I think no more of deadly lurks therein,
Than in a clapper clapping in a garth,
To scare the fowl from fruit: if more
    there be,
If more and acted on, what follows? war;
Your own work marr'd: for this your
    Academe,
Whichever side be Victor, in the halloo
Will topple to the trumpet down, and
    pass
With all fair theories only made to gild
A stormless summer.' 'Let the Princess
    judge
Of that' she said: 'farewell, Sir—and
    to you.
I shudder at the sequel, but I go.'

'Are you that Lady Psyche,' I re-
    join'd,
'The fifth in line from that old Florian,
Yet hangs his portrait in my father's hall
(The gaunt old Baron with his beetle brow
Sun-shaded in the heat of dusty fights)
As he bestrode my Grandsire, when he
    fell,
And all else fled? we point to it, and
    we say,
The loyal warmth of Florian is not cold,
But branches current yet in kindred
    veins.'
'Are you that Psyche,' Florian added;
    'she
With whom I sang about the morning
    hills,
Flung ball, flew kite, and raced the
    purple fly,

And snared the squirrel of the glen? are
    you
That Psyche, wont to bind my throbbing
    brow,
To smoothe my pillow, mix the foaming
    draught
Of fever, tell me pleasant tales, and read
My sickness down to happy dreams? are
    you
That brother-sister Psyche, both in one?
You were that Psyche, but what are you
    now?'
'You are that Psyche,' Cyril said, 'for
    whom
I would be that for ever which I seem,
Woman, if I might sit beside your feet,
And glean your scatter'd sapience.'
              Then once more,
'Are you that Lady Psyche,' I began,
'That on her bridal morn before she past
From all her old companions, when the
    king
Kiss'd her pale cheek, declared that
    ancient ties
Would still be dear beyond the southern
    hills;
That were there any of our people there
In want or peril, there was one to hear
And help them? look! for such are these
    and I.'
'Are you that Psyche,' Florian ask'd,
    'to whom,
In gentler days, your arrow-wounded fawn
Came flying while you sat beside the well?
The creature laid his muzzle on your lap,
And sobb'd, and you sobb'd with it, and
    the blood
Was sprinkled on your kirtle, and you
    wept.
That was fawn's blood, not brother's, yet
    you wept.
O by the bright head of my little niece,
You were that Psyche, and what are
    you now?'
'You are that Psyche,' Cyril said again,
'The mother of the sweetest little maid,
That ever crow'd for kisses.'
              'Out upon it!'
She answer'd, 'peace! and why should
    I not play

The Spartan Mother with emotion, be
The Lucius Junius Brutus of my kind?
Him you call great: he for the common
    weal,
The fading politics of mortal Rome,
As I might slay this child, if good need
    were,
Slew both his sons: and I, shall I, on
    whom
The secular emancipation turns
Of half this world, be swerved from right
    to save
A prince, a brother? a little will I yield.
Best so, perchance, for us, and well for
    you.
O hard, when love and duty clash! I fear
My conscience will not count me fleck-
    less; yet—
Hear my conditions: promise (otherwise
You perish) as you came, to slip away
To-day, to-morrow, soon: it shall be
    said,
These women were too barbarous, would
    not learn;
They fled, who might have shamed us:
    promise, all.'

    What could we else, we promised each;
       and she,
Like some wild creature newly-caged,
    commenced
A to-and-fro, so pacing till she paused
By Florian; holding out her lily arms
Took both his hands, and smiling faintly
    said:
'I knew you at the first: tho' you have
    grown
You scarce have alter'd: I am sad and
    glad
To see you, Florian. *I* give thee to death
My brother! it was duty spoke, not I.
My needful seeming harshness, pardon it.
Our mother, is she well?'
            With that she kiss'd
His forehead, then, a moment after, clung
About him, and betwixt them blossom'd
    up
From out a common vein of memory
Sweet household talk, and phrases of the
    hearth,

T

N

And far allusion, till the gracious dews
Began to glisten and to fall : and while
They stood, so rapt, we gazing, came a
   voice,
'I brought a message here from Lady
   Blanche.'
Back started she, and turning round we
   saw
The Lady Blanche's daughter where she
   stood,
Melissa, with her hand upon the lock,
A rosy blonde, and in a college gown,
That clad her like an April daffodilly
(Her mother's colour) with her lips apart,
And all her thoughts as fair within her
   eyes,
As bottom agates seen to wave and float
In crystal currents of clear morning seas.

   So stood that same fair creature at the
   ￬door.
Then Lady Psyche, 'Ah—Melissa—you !
You heard us ?' and Melissa, 'O pardon
   me
I heard, I could not help it, did not
   wish :
But, dearest Lady, pray you fear me not,
Nor think I bear that heart within my
   breast,
To give three gallant gentlemen to death.'
'I trust you,' said the other, 'for we two
Were always friends, none closer, elm
   and vine :
But yet your mother's jealous tempera-
   ment—
Let not your prudence, dearest, drowse,
   or prove
The Danaïd of a leaky vase, for fear
This whole foundation ruin, and I lose
My honour, these their lives.'   'Ah, fear
   me not '
Replied Melissa ; 'no—I would not tell,
No, not for all Aspasia's cleverness,
No, not to answer, Madam, all those
   hard things
That Sheba came to ask of Solomon.'
'Be it so' the other, 'that we still may
   lead
The new light up, and culminate in peace,
For Solomon may come to Sheba yet.'

Said Cyril, ' Madam, he the wisest man
Feasted the woman wisest then, in halls
Of Lebanonian cedar : nor should you
(Tho', Madam, *you* should answer, we
   would ask)
Less welcome find among us, if you came
Among us, debtors for our lives to you,
Myself for something more.'   He said
   not what,
But 'Thanks,' she answer'd 'Go : we have
   been too long
Together : keep your hoods about the
   face ;
They do so that affect abstraction here.
Speak little ; mix not with the rest ; and
   hold
Your promise : all, I trust, may yet be
   well.'

   We turn'd to go, but Cyril took the
   child,
And held her round the knees against his
   waist,
And blew the swoll'n cheek of a trumpeter,
While Psyche watch'd them, smiling, and
   the child
Push'd her flat hand against his face and
   laugh'd ;
And thus our conference closed.
                 And then we stroll'd
For half the day thro' stately theatres
Bench'd crescent-wise.   In each we sat,
   we heard
The grave Professor.   On the lecture
   slate
The circle rounded under female hands
With flawless demonstration : follow'd
   then
A classic lecture, rich in sentiment,
With scraps of thundrous Epic lilted out
By violet-hooded Doctors, elegies
And quoted odes, and jewels five-words
   long
That on the stretch'd forefinger of all
   Time
Sparkle for ever : then we dipt in all
That treats of whatsoever is, the state,
The total chronicles of man, the mind,
The morals, something of the frame, the
   rock,

The star, the bird, the fish, the shell, the flower,
Electric, chemic laws, and all the rest,
And whatsoever can be taught and known;
Till like three horses that have broken fence,
And glutted all night long breast-deep in corn,
We issued gorged with knowledge, and I spoke:
'Why, Sirs, they do all this as well as we.'
'They hunt old trails' said Cyril 'very well;
But when did woman ever yet invent?'
'Ungracious!' answer'd Florian; 'have you learnt
No more from Psyche's lecture, you that talk'd
The trash that made me sick, and almost sad?'
'O trash' he said, 'but with a kernel in it.
Should I not call her wise, who made me wise?
And learnt? I learnt more from her in a flash,
Than if my brainpan were an empty hull,
And every Muse tumbled a science in.
A thousand hearts lie fallow in these halls,
And round these halls a thousand baby loves
Fly twanging headless arrows at the hearts,
Whence follows many a vacant pang; but O
With me, Sir, enter'd in the bigger boy,
The Head of all the golden-shafted firm,
The long-limb'd lad that had a Psyche too;
He cleft me thro' the stomacher; and now
What think you of it, Florian? do I chase
The substance or the shadow? will it hold?
I have no sorcerer's malison on me,
No ghostly hauntings like his Highness. I
Flatter myself that always everywhere
I know the substance when I see it. Well,

Are castles shadows? Three of them? Is she
The sweet proprietress a shadow? If not,
Shall those three castles patch my tatter'd coat?
For dear are those three castles to my wants,
And dear is sister Psyche to my heart,
And two dear things are one of double worth,
And much I might have said, but that my zone
Unmann'd me: then the Doctors! O to hear
The Doctors! O to watch the thirsty plants
Imbibing! once or twice I thought to roar,
To break my chain, to shake my mane: but thou,
Modulate me, Soul of mincing mimicry!
Make liquid treble of that bassoon, my throat;
Abase those eyes that ever loved to meet
Star-sisters answering under crescent brows;
Abate the stride, which speaks of man, and loose
A flying charm of blushes o'er this cheek,
Where they like swallows coming out of time
Will wonder why they came: but hark the bell
For dinner, let us go!'
                           And in we stream'd
Among the columns, pacing staid and still
By twos and threes, till all from end to end
With beauties every shade of brown and fair
In colours gayer than the morning mist,
The long hall glitter'd like a bed of flowers.
How might a man not wander from his wits
Pierced thro' with eyes, but that I kept mine own
Intent on her, who rapt in glorious dreams,
The second-sight of some Astræan age,
Sat compass'd with professors: they, the while,

Discuss'd a doubt and tost it to and fro:
A clamour thicken'd, mixt with inmost
    terms
Of art and science: Lady Blanche alone
Of faded form and haughtiest lineaments,
With all her autumn tresses falsely brown,
Shot sidelong daggers at us, a tiger-cat
In act to spring.
                    At last a solemn grace
Concluded, and we sought the gardens:
    there
One walk'd reciting by herself, and one
In this hand held a volume as to read,
And smoothed a petted peacock down
    with that:
Some to a low song oar'd a shallop by,
Or under arches of the marble bridge
Hung, shadow'd from the heat: some
    hid and sought
In the orange thickets: others tost a ball
Above the fountain-jets, and back again
With laughter: others lay about the
    lawns,
Of the older sort, and murmur'd that their
    May
Was passing: what was learning unto
    them?
They wish'd to marry; they could rule a
    house;
Men hated learned women: but we three
Sat muffled like the Fates; and often
    came
Melissa hitting all we saw with shafts
Of gentle satire, kin to charity,
That harm'd not: then day droopt; the
    chapel bells
Call'd us: we left the walks; we mixt
    with those
Six hundred maidens clad in purest white,
Before two streams of light from wall to
    wall,
While the great organ almost burst his
    pipes,
Groaning for power, and rolling thro' the
    court
A long melodious thunder to the sound
Of solemn psalms, and silver litanies,
The work of Ida, to call down from
    Heaven
A blessing on her labours for the world.

[a mother's song]

III.

Sweet and low, sweet and low,
    Wind of the western sea,
Low, low, breathe and blow,
    Wind of the western sea!
Over the rolling waters go,
Come from the dying moon, and blow,
    Blow him again to me;
While my little one, while my pretty one, sleeps.

Sleep and rest, sleep and rest,
    Father will come to thee soon;
Rest, rest, on mother's breast,
    Father will come to thee soon;
Father will come to his babe in the nest,
Silver sails all out of the west
    Under the silver moon:
Sleep, my little one, sleep, my pretty one, sleep.

Morn in the white wake of the morning
    star
Came furrowing all the orient into gold.
We rose, and each by other drest with
    care
Descended to the court that lay three parts
In shadow, but the Muses' heads were
    touch'd
Above the darkness from their native East.

    There while we stood beside the fount,
        and watch'd
Or seem'd to watch the dancing bubble,
    approach'd
Melissa, tinged with wan from lack of
    sleep,
Or grief, and glowing round her dewy
    eyes
The circled Iris of a night of tears;
'And fly,' she cried, 'O fly, while yet
    you may!
My mother knows:' and when I ask'd
    her 'how,'
'My fault' she wept 'my fault! and yet
    not mine;
Yet mine in part.   O hear me, pardon
    me.
My mother, 'tis her wont from night to
    night
To rail at Lady Psyche and her side.
She says the Princess should have been
    the Head,
Herself and Lady Psyche the two arms;

And so it was agreed when first they
      came ;
But Lady Psyche was the right hand now,
And she the left, or not, or seldom used ;
Hers more than half the students, all the
      love.
And so last night she fell to canvass you :
Her countrywomen ! she did not envy
      her.
" Who ever saw such wild barbarians ?
Girls ?—more like men !" and at these
      words the snake,
My secret, seem'd to stir within my breast ;
And oh, Sirs, could I help it, but my
      cheek
Began to burn and burn, and her lynx
      eye
To fix and make me hotter, till she
      laugh'd :
" O marvellously modest maiden, you !
Men ! girls, like men ! why, if they had
      been men
You need not set your thoughts in rubric
      thus
For wholesale comment." Pardon, I am
      shamed
That I must needs repeat for my excuse
What looks so little graceful : " men "
      (for still
My mother went revolving on the word)
" And so they are,—very like men in-
      deed—
And with that woman closeted for hours !"
Then came these dreadful words out one
      by one,
" Why—these—*are*—men :" I shudder'd :
      " and you know it."
" O ask me nothing," I said : " And she
      knows too,
And she conceals it." So my mother
      clutch'd
The truth at once, but with no word from
      me ;
And now thus early risen she goes to
      inform
The Princess : Lady Psyche will be
      crush'd ;
But you may yet be saved, and therefore
      fly :
But heal me with your pardon ere you go.'

' What pardon, sweet Melissa, for a
      blush ?'
Said Cyril : ' Pale one, blush again : than
      wear
Those lilies, better blush our lives away.
Yet let us breathe for one hour more in
      Heaven '
He added, ' lest some classic Angel speak
In scorn of us, " They mounted, Gany-
      medes,
To tumble, Vulcans, on the second morn."
But I will melt this marble into wax
To yield us farther furlough : ' and he went.

Melissa shook her doubtful curls, and
      thought
He scarce would prosper. ' Tell us,'
      Florian ask'd,
' How grew this feud betwixt the right
      and left.'
' O long ago,' she said, ' betwixt these
      two
Division smoulders hidden ; 'tis my
      mother,
Too jealous, often fretful as the wind
Pent in a crevice : much I bear with her :
I never knew my father, but she says
(God help her) she was wedded to a fool ;
And still she rail'd against the state of
      things.
She had the care of Lady Ida's youth,
And from the Queen's decease she brought
      her up.
But when your sister came she won the
      heart
Of Ida : they were still together, grew
(For so they said themselves) inosculated ;
Consonant chords that shiver to one note ;
One mind in all things : yet my mother
      still
Affirms your Psyche thieved her theories,
And angled with them for her pupil's love :
She calls her plagiarist ; I know not what :
But I must go : I dare not tarry,' and
      light,
As flies the shadow of a bird, she fled.

Then murmur'd Florian gazing after
      her,
' An open-hearted maiden, true and pure.

If I could love, why this were she : how
　　pretty
Her blushing was, and how she blush'd
　　again,
As if to close with Cyril's random wish :
Not like your Princess cramm'd with
　　erring pride,
Nor like poor Psyche whom she drags in
　　tow.'

　'The crane,' I said, 'may chatter of
　　the crane,
The dove may murmur of the dove, but I
An eagle clang an eagle to the sphere.
My princess, O my princess ! true she errs,
But in her own grand way: being herself
Three times more noble than three score
　　of men,
She sees herself in every woman else,
And so she wears her error like a crown
To blind the truth and me : for her, and
　　her,
Hebes are they to hand ambrosia, mix
The nectar ; but—ah she—whene'er she
　　moves
The Samian Herè rises and she speaks
A Memnon smitten with the morning
　　Sun.'

　　So saying from the court we paced,
　　and gain'd
The terrace ranged along the Northern
　　front,
And leaning there on those balusters, high
Above the empurpled champaign, drank
　　the gale
That blown about the foliage underneath,
And sated with the innumerable rose,
Beat balm upon our eyelids.　Hither came
Cyril, and yawning ' O hard task,' he
　　cried ;
' No fighting shadows here !　I forced a
　　way
Thro' solid opposition crabb'd and gnarl'd.
Better to clear prime forests, heave and
　　thump
A league of street in summer solstice
　　down,
Than hammer at this reverend gentle-
　　woman.

I knock'd and, bidden, enter'd ; found
　　her there
At point to move, and settled in her eyes
The green malignant light of coming
　　storm.
Sir, I was courteous, every phrase well-
　　oil'd,
As man's could be ; yet maiden-meek I
　　pray'd
Concealment : she demanded who we
　　were,
And why we came ? I fabled nothing fair,
But, your example pilot, told her all.
Up went the hush'd amaze of hand and
　　eye.
But when I dwelt upon your old affiance,
She answer'd sharply that I talk'd astray.
I urged the fierce inscription on the gate,
And our three lives.　True—we had
　　limed ourselves
With open eyes, and we must take the
　　chance.
But such extremes, I told her, well might
　　harm
The woman's cause.　" Not more than
　　now," she said,
" So puddled as it is with favouritism."
I tried the mother's heart.　Shame might
　　befall
Melissa, knowing, saying not she knew :
Her answer was " Leave me to deal with
　　that."
I spoke of war to come and many deaths,
And she replied, her duty was to speak,
And duty duty, clear of consequences.
I grew discouraged, Sir ; but since I knew
No rock so hard but that a little wave
May beat admission in a thousand years,
I recommenced ; " Decide not ere you
　　pause. 　*
I find you here but in the second place,
Some say the third—the authentic found-
　　ress you.
I offer boldly : we will seat you highest :
Wink at our advent : help my prince to
　　gain
His rightful bride, and here I promise
　　you
Some palace in our land, where you shall
　　reign

The head and heart of all our fair she-
world,
And your great name flow on with broad-
ening time
For ever." Well, she balanced this a
little,
And told me she would answer us to-day,
Meantime be mute : thus much, nor more
I gain'd.'

He ceasing, came a message from the
Head.
'That afternoon the Princess rode to take
The dip of certain strata to the North.
Would we go with her? we should find
the land
Worth seeing ; and the river made a fall
Out yonder:' then she pointed on to
where
A double hill ran up his furrowy forks
Beyond the thick-leaved platans of the
vale.

Agreed to, this, the day fled on thro'
all
Its range of duties to the appointed hour.
Then summon'd to the porch we went.
She stood
Among her maidens, higher by the head,
Her back against a pillar, her foot on
one
Of those tame leopards. Kittenlike he
roll'd
And paw'd about her sandal. I drew
near ;
I gazed. On a sudden my strange seizure
came
Upon me, the weird vision of our house :
The Princess Ida seem'd a hollow show,
Her gay-furr'd cats a painted fantasy,
Her college and her maidens, empty
masks,
And I myself the shadow of a dream,
For all things were and were not. Yet
I felt
My heart beat thick with passion and
with awe ;
Then from my breast the involuntary sigh
Brake, as she smote me with the light of
eyes

That lent my knee desire to kneel, and
shook
My pulses, till to horse we got, and so
Went forth in long retinue following up
The river as it narrow'd to the hills.

I rode beside her and to me she said :
'O friend, we trust that you esteem'd us
not
Too harsh to your companion yestermorn ;
Unwillingly we spake.' 'No—not to her,'
I answer'd, 'but to one of whom we spake
Your Highness might have seem'd the
thing you say.'
'Again?' she cried, 'are you ambassa-
dresses
From him to me? we give you, being
strange,
A license : speak, and let the topic die.'

I stammer'd that I knew him—could
have wish'd—
'Our king expects—was there no pre-
contract?
There is no truer-hearted—ah, you seem
All he prefigured, and he could not see
The bird of passage flying south but
long'd
To follow : surely, if your Highness keep
Your purport, you will shock him ev'n to
death,
Or baser courses, children of despair.'

'Poor boy,' she said, 'can he not read
—no books?
Quoit, tennis, ball—no games? nor deals
in that
Which men delight in, martial exercise?
To nurse a blind ideal like a girl,
Methinks he seems no better than a girl;
As girls were once, as we ourself have
been :
We had our dreams ; perhaps he mixt
with them :
We touch on our dead self, nor shun to
do it,
Being other—since we learnt our meaning
here,
To lift the woman's fall'n divinity
Upon an even pedestal with man.'

She paused, and added with a haughtier
    smile
'And as to precontracts, we move, my
    friend,
At no man's beck, but know ourself and
    thee,
O Vashti, noble Vashti ! Summon'd out
She kept her state, and left the drunken
    king
To brawl at Shushan underneath the
    palms.'

'Alas your Highness breathes full
    East,' I said,
'On that which leans to you. I know
    the Prince,
I prize his truth : and then how vast a
    work
To assail this gray preëminence of man !
You grant me license ; might I use it ?
    think ;
Ere half be done perchance your life may
    fail ;
Then comes the feebler heiress of your
    plan,
And takes and ruins all ; and thus your
    pains
May only make that footprint upon sand
Which old-recurring waves of prejudice
Resmooth to nothing : might I dread
    that you,
With only Fame for spouse and your
    great deeds
For issue, yet may live in vain, and miss,
Meanwhile, what every woman counts
    her due,
Love, children, happiness ?'
                And she exclaim'd,
'Peace, you young savage of the Northern
    wild !
What ! tho' your Prince's love were like
    a God's,
Have we not made ourself the sacrifice ?
You are bold indeed : we are not talk'd
    to thus :
Yet will we say for children, would they
    grew
Like field-flowers everywhere ! we like
    them well :
But children die ; and let me tell you, girl,

Howe'er you babble, great deeds cannot
    die ;
They with the sun and moon renew their
    light
For ever, blessing those that look on
    them.
Children—that men may pluck them from
    our hearts,
Kill us with pity, break us with ourselves—
O—children—there is nothing upon earth
More miserable than she that has a son
And sees him err : nor would we work
    for fame ;
Tho' she perhaps might reap the applause
    of Great,
Who learns the one POU STO whence after-
    hands
May move the world, tho' she herself effect
But little : wherefore up and act, nor
    shrink
For fear our solid aim be dissipated
By frail successors. Would, indeed, we
    had been,
In lieu of many mortal flies, a race
Of giants living, each, a thousand years,
That we might see our own work out,
    and watch
The sandy footprint harden into stone.'

I answer'd nothing, doubtful in myself
If that strange Poet-princess with her
    grand
Imaginations might at all be won.
And she broke out interpreting my
    thoughts :

'No doubt we seem a kind of monster
    to you ;
We are used to that : for women, up till
    this
Cramp'd under worse than South-sea-isle
    taboo,
Dwarfs of the gynæceum, fail so far
In high desire, they know not, cannot
    guess
How much their welfare is a passion to
    us.
If we could give them surer, quicker
    proof—
Oh if our end were less achievable

By slow approaches, than by single act
Of immolation, any phase of death,
We were as prompt to spring against the
    pikes,
Or down the fiery gulf as talk of it,
To compass our dear sisters' liberties.'

  She bow'd as if to veil a noble tear;
And up we came to where the river sloped
To plunge in cataract, shattering on black
    blocks
A breadth of thunder.   O'er it shook the
    woods,
And danced the colour, and, below, stuck
    out
The bones of some vast bulk that lived
    and roar'd
Before man was.   She gazed awhile and
    said,
As these rude bones to us, are we to
    her
That will be.'   'Dare we dream of that,'
    I ask'd,
Which wrought us, as the workman and
    his work,
That practice betters?'   'How,' she cried,
    'you love
The metaphysics!   read and earn our prize,
A golden brooch: beneath an emerald
    plane
Sits Diotima, teaching him that died
Of hemlock;   our device;   wrought to the
    life;
She rapt upon her subject, he on her:
For there are schools for all.'   'And yet'
    I said
Methinks I have not found among them
    all
One anatomic.'   'Nay, we thought of
    that,'
She answer'd, 'but it pleased us not: in
    truth
We shudder but to dream our maids
    should ape
Those monstrous males that carve the
    living hound,
And cram him with the fragments of the
    grave,
Or in the dark dissolving human heart,
And holy secrets of this microcosm.

Dabbling a shameless hand with shameful
    jest,
Encarnalize their spirits: yet we know
Knowledge is knowledge, and this matter
    hangs:
Howbeit ourself, foreseeing casualty,
Nor willing men should come among us,
    learnt,
For many weary moons before we came,
This craft of healing.   Were you sick,
    ourself
Would tend upon you.   To your question
    now,
Which touches on the workman and his
    work.
Let there be light and there was light:
    'tis so:
For was, and is, and will be, are but is;
And all creation is one act at once,
The birth of light: but we that are not all,
As parts, can see but parts, now this,
    now that,
And live, perforce, from thought to
    thought, and make
One act a phantom of succession: thus
Our   weakness   somehow   shapes   the
    shadow, Time;
But in the shadow will we work, and
    mould
The woman to the fuller day.'
                            She spake
With kindled eyes: we rode a league
    beyond,
And, o'er a bridge of pinewood crossing,
    came
On flowery levels underneath the crag,
Full of all beauty.   'O how sweet' I said
(For I was half-oblivious of my mask)
'To linger here with one that loved us.'
    'Yea,'
She answer'd, 'or with fair philosophies
That lift the fancy; for indeed these fields
Are lovely, lovelier not the Elysian lawns,
Where paced the Demigods of old, and
    saw
The soft white vapour streak the crowned
    towers
Built to the Sun:' then, turning to her
    maids,
'Pitch our pavilion here upon the sward;

Lay out the viands.' At the word, they raised
A tent of satin, elaborately wrought
With fair Corinna's triumph; here she stood,
Engirt with many a florid maiden-cheek,
The woman-conqueror; woman-conquer'd there
The bearded Victor of ten-thousand hymns,
And all the men mourn'd at his side: but we
Set forth to climb; then, climbing, Cyril kept
With Psyche, with Melissa Florian, I
With mine affianced. Many a little hand
Glanced like a touch of sunshine on the rocks,
Many a light foot shone like a jewel set
In the dark crag: and then we turn'd, we wound
About the cliffs, the copses, out and in,
Hammering and clinking, chattering stony names
Of shale and hornblende, rag and trap and tuff,
Amygdaloid and trachyte, till the Sun
Grew broader toward his death and fell, and all
The rosy heights came out above the lawns.

IV.

The splendour falls on castle walls
  And snowy summits old in story:
The long light shakes across the lakes,
  And the wild cataract leaps in glory.
Blow, bugle, blow, set the wild echoes flying,
Blow, bugle; answer, echoes, dying, dying, dying.

O hark, O hear! how thin and clear,
  And thinner, clearer, farther going!
O sweet and far from cliff and scar
  The horns of Elfland faintly blowing!
Blow, let us hear the purple glens replying:
Blow, bugle; answer, echoes, dying, dying, dying.

O love, they die in yon rich sky,
  They faint on hill or field or river:
Our echoes roll from soul to soul,
  And grow for ever and for ever.
Blow, bugle, blow, set the wild echoes flying,
And answer, echoes, answer, dying, dying, dying.

'There sinks the nebulous star we cal the Sun,
If that hypothesis of theirs be sound'
Said Ida; 'let us down and rest;' an we
Down from the lean and wrinkled preci pices,
By every coppice-feather'd chasm an cleft,
Dropt thro' the ambrosial gloom to wher below
No bigger than a glow-worm shone th tent
Lamp-lit from the inner. Once she lean' on me,
Descending; once or twice she lent he hand,
And blissful palpitations in the blood,
Stirring a sudden transport rose and fell

But when we planted level feet, an dipt
Beneath the satin dome and enter'd in,
There leaning deep in broider'd down w sank
Our elbows: on a tripod in the midst
A fragrant flame rose, and before us glow'
Fruit, blossom, viand, amber wine, an gold.

Then she, 'Let some one sing to us lightlier move
The minutes fledged with music:' and maid,
Of those beside her, smote her harp, an sang.

'Tears, idle tears, I know not what they mean
Tears from the depth of some divine despair
Rise in the heart, and gather to the eyes,
In looking on the happy Autumn-fields,
And thinking of the days that are no more.

'Fresh as the first beam glittering on a sail,
That brings our friends up from the underworld
Sad as the last which reddens over one
That sinks with all we love below the verge;
So sad, so fresh, the days that are no more.

'Ah, sad and strange as in dark summer dawn
The earliest pipe of half-awaken'd birds
To dying ears, when unto dying eyes
The casement slowly grows a glimmering square
So sad, so strange, the days that are no more.

'Dear as remember'd kisses after death,
And sweet as those by hopeless fancy feign'd
On lips that are for others; deep as love,
Deep as first love, and wild with all regret;
O Death in Life, the days that are no more.'

She ended with such passion that the tear,
She sang of, shook and fell, an erring pearl
Lost in her bosom: but with some disdain
Answer'd the Princess, 'If indeed there haunt
About the moulder'd lodges of the Past
So sweet a voice and vague, fatal to men,
Well needs it we should cram our ears with wool
And so pace by: but thine are fancies hatch'd
In silken-folded idleness; nor is it
Wiser to weep a true occasion lost,
But trim our sails, and let old bygones be,
While down the streams that float us each and all
To the issue, goes, like glittering bergs of ice,
Throne after throne, and molten on the waste
Becomes a cloud: for all things serve their time
Toward that great year of equal mights and rights,
Nor would I fight with iron laws, in the end
Found golden: let the past be past; let be
Their cancell'd Babels: tho' the rough kex break
The starr'd mosaic, and the beard-blown goat
Hang on the shaft, and the wild figtree split
Their monstrous idols, care not while we hear
A trumpet in the distance pealing news
Of better, and Hope, a poising eagle, burns
Above the unrisen morrow:' then to me;
'Know you no song of your own land,' she said,

'Not such as moans about the retrospect,
But deals with the other distance and the hues
Of promise; not a death's-head at the wine.'

Then I remember'd one myself had made,
What time I watch'd the swallow winging south
From mine own land, part made long since, and part
Now while I sang, and maidenlike as far
As I could ape their treble, did I sing.

'O Swallow, Swallow, flying, flying South,
Fly to her, and fall upon her gilded eaves,
And tell her, tell her, what I tell to thee.

'O tell her, Swallow, thou that knowest each,
That bright and fierce and fickle is the South,
And dark and true and tender is the North.

'O Swallow, Swallow, if I could follow, and light
Upon her lattice, I would pipe and trill,
And cheep and twitter twenty million loves.

'O were I thou that she might take me in,
And lay me on her bosom, and her heart
Would rock the snowy cradle till I died.

'Why lingereth she to clothe her heart with love,
Delaying as the tender ash delays
To clothe herself, when all the woods are green?

'O tell her, Swallow, that thy brood is flown:
Say to her, I do but wanton in the South,
But in the North long since my nest is made.

'O tell her, brief is life but love is long,
And brief the sun of summer in the North,
And brief the moon of beauty in the South.

'O Swallow, flying from the golden woods,
Fly to her, and pipe and woo her, and make her mine,
And tell her, tell her, that I follow thee.'

I ceased, and all the ladies, each at each,
Like the Ithacensian suitors in old time,
Stared with great eyes, and laugh'd with alien lips,
And knew not what they meant; for still my voice
Rang false: but smiling 'Not for thee,' she said,

'O Bulbul, any rose of Gulistan
Shall burst her veil: marsh-divers, rather,
    maid,
Shall croak thee sister, or the meadow-
    crake
Grate her harsh kindred in the grass : and
    this
A mere love-poem! O for such, my friend,
We hold them slight: they mind us of
    the time
When we made bricks in Egypt. Knaves
    are men,
That lute and flute fantastic tenderness,
And dress the victim to the offering up.
And paint the gates of Hell with Paradise,
And play the slave to gain the tyranny.
Poor soul! I had a maid of honour once;
She wept her true eyes blind for such a
    one,
A rogue of canzonets and serenades.
I loved her. Peace be with her. She
    is dead.
So they blaspheme the muse! But great
    is song
Used to great ends: ourself have often
    tried
Valkyrian hymns, or into rhythm have
    dash'd
The passion of the prophetess; for song
Is duer unto freedom, force and growth
Of spirit than to junketing and love.
Love is it? Would this same mock-love,
    and this
Mock - Hymen were laid up like winter
    bats,
Till all men grew to rate us at our worth,
Not vassals to be beat, nor pretty babes
To be dandled, no, but living wills, and
    sphered
Whole in ourselves and owed to none.
    Enough!
But now to leaven play with profit, you,
Know you no song, the true growth of
    your soil,
That gives the manners of your country-
    women?'

She spoke and turn'd her sumptuous
    head with eyes
Of shining expectation fixt on mine.

Then while I dragg'd my brains for such
    a song,
Cyril, with whom the bell-mouth'd glass
    had wrought,
Or master'd by the sense of sport, began
To troll a careless, careless tavern-catch
Of Moll and Meg, and strange experiences
Unmeet for ladies. Florian nodded at
    him,
I frowning; Psyche flush'd and wann'd
    and shook;
The lilylike Melissa droop'd her brows;
'Forbear,' the Princess cried; 'Forbear,
    Sir' I;
And heated thro' and thro' with wrath
    and love,
I smote him on the breast; he started
    up;
There rose a shriek as of a city sack'd;
Melissa clamour'd 'Flee the death;' 'To
    horse'
Said Ida; 'home! to horse!' and fled,
    as flies
A troop of snowy doves athwart the dusk,
When some one batters at the dovecote-
    doors,
Disorderly the women. Alone I stood
With Florian, cursing Cyril, vext at heart,
In the pavilion : there like parting hopes
I heard them passing from me : hoof by
    hoof,
And every hoof a knell to my desires,
Clang'd on the bridge; and then another
    shriek,
'The Head, the Head, the Princess, O
    the Head!'
For blind with rage she miss'd the plank,
    and roll'd
In the river. Out I sprang from glow to
    gloom :
There whirl'd her white robe like a
    blossom'd branch
Rapt to the horrible fall : a glance I gave,
No more; but woman-vested as I was
Plunged; and the flood drew; yet I
    caught her; then
Oaring one arm, and bearing in my left
The weight of all the hopes of half the
    world,
Strove to buffet to land in vain. A tree

Was half-disrooted from his place and
    stoop'd
To drench his dark locks in the gurgling
    wave
Mid - channel. Right on this we drove
    and caught,
And grasping down the boughs I gain'd
    the shore.

There stood her maidens glimmeringly
    group'd
In the hollow bank. One reaching
    forward drew
My burthen from mine arms ; they cried
    'she lives :'
They bore her back into the tent : but I,
So much a kind of shame within me
    wrought,
Not yet endured to meet her opening eyes,
Nor found my friends ; but push'd alone
    on foot
(For since her horse was lost I left her mine)
Across the woods, and less from Indian
    craft
Than beelike instinct hiveward, found at
    length
The garden portals. Two great statues,
    Art
And Science, Caryatids, lifted up
A weight of emblem, and betwixt were
    valves
Of open-work in which the hunter rued
His rash intrusion, manlike, but his brows
Had sprouted, and the branches thereupon
Spread out at top, and grimly spiked the
    gates.

A little space was left between the
    horns,
Thro' which I clamber'd o'er at top with
    pain,
Dropt on the sward, and up the linden
    walks,
And, tost on thoughts that changed from
    hue to hue,
Now poring on the glowworm, now the
    star,
I paced the terrace, till the Bear had
    wheel'd
Thro' a great arc his seven slow suns.

                  A step
Of lightest echo, then a loftier form
Than female, moving thro' the uncertain
    gloom,
Disturb'd me with the doubt 'if this
    were she,'
But it was Florian. 'Hist O Hist,' he
    said,
'They seek us : out so late is out of
    rules.
Moreover 'seize the strangers' is the cry.
How came you here ?' I told him : 'I'
    said he,
'Last of the train, a moral leper, I,
To whom none spake, half-sick at heart,
    return'd.
Arriving all confused among the rest
With hooded brows I crept into the hall,
And, couch'd behind a Judith, underneath
The head of Holofernes peep'd and saw.
Girl after girl was call'd to trial : each
Disclaim'd all knowledge of us : last of
    all,
Melissa : trust me, Sir, I pitied her.
She, question'd if she knew us men, at
    first
Was silent ; closer prest, denied it not :
And then, demanded if her mother knew,
Or Psyche, she affirm'd not, or denied :
From whence the Royal mind, familiar
    with her,
Easily gather'd either guilt. She sent
For Psyche, but she was not there ; she
    call'd
For Psyche's child to cast it from the doors ;
She sent for Blanche to accuse her face to
    face ;
And I slipt out : but whither will you now?
And where are Psyche, Cyril ? both are
    fled :
What, if together ? that were not so well.
Would rather we had never come ! I dread
His wildness, and the chances of the dark.'

'And yet,' I said, 'you wrong him more
    than I
That struck him : this is proper to the
    clown,
Tho' smock'd, or furr'd and purpled, still
    the clown,

To harm the thing that trusts him, and to
    shame
That which he says he loves : for Cyril,
    howe'er
He deal in frolic, as to-night—the song
Might have been worse and sinn'd in
    grosser lips
Beyond all pardon—as it is, I hold
These flashes on the surface are not he.
He has a solid base of temperament :
But as the waterlily starts and slides
Upon the level in little puffs of wind,
Tho' anchor'd to the bottom, such is he.'

Scarce had I ceased when from a tamarisk
    near
Two Proctors leapt upon us, crying,
    'Names :'
He, standing still, was clutch'd ; but I
    began
To thrid the musky-circled mazes, wind
And double in and out the boles, and race
By all the fountains : fleet I was of foot :
Before me shower'd the rose in flakes ;
    behind
I heard the puff'd pursuer ; at mine ear
Bubbled the nightingale and heeded not,
And secret laughter tickled all my soul.
At last I hook'd my ankle in a vine,
That claspt the feet of a Mnemosyne,
And falling on my face was caught and
    known.

They haled us to the Princess where
    she sat
High in the hall : above her droop'd a
    lamp,
And made the single jewel on her brow
Burn like the mystic fire on a mast-
    head,
Prophet of storm : a handmaid on each
    side
Bow'd toward her, combing out her long
    black hair
Damp from the river ; and close behind
    her stood
Eight daughters of the plough, stronger
    than men,
Huge women blowzed with health, and
    wind, and rain,

And labour.   Each was like a Druid rock ;
Or like a spire of land that stands apart
Cleft from the main, and wail'd about
    with mews.

Then, as we came, the crowd dividing
    clove
An advent to the throne : and therebeside,
Half-naked as if caught at once from bed
And tumbled on the purple footcloth, lay
The lily-shining child ; and on the left,
Bow'd on her palms and folded up from
    wrong,
Her round white shoulder shaken with her
    sobs,
Melissa knelt ; but Lady Blanche erect
Stood up and spake, an affluent orator.

'It was not thus, O Princess, in old
    days :
You prized my counsel, lived upon my
    lips :
I led you then to all the Castalies ;
I fed you with the milk of every Muse ;
I loved you like this kneeler, and you me
Your second mother : those were gracious
    times.
Then came your new friend : you began
    to change—
I saw it and grieved—to slacken and to
    cool ;
Till taken with her seeming openness
You turn'd your warmer currents all to
    her,
To me you froze : this was my meed for all.
Yet I bore up in part from ancient love,
And partly that I hoped to win you back,
And partly conscious of my own deserts,
And partly that you were my civil head,
And chiefly you were born for something
    great,
In which I might your fellow-worker be,
When time should serve ; and thus a noble
    scheme
Grew up from seed we two long since had
    sown ;
In us true growth, in her a Jonah's gourd,
Up in one night and due to sudden sun :
We took this palace ; but even from the
    first

You stood in your own light and darken'd
    mine.
What student came but that you planed
    her path
To Lady Psyche, younger, not so wise,
A foreigner, and I your countrywoman,
I your old friend and tried, she new in all?
But still her lists were swell'd and mine
    were lean;
Yet I bore up in hope she would be known:
Then came these wolves: *they* knew her:
    they endured,
Long-closeted with her the yestermorn,
To tell her what they were, and she to
    hear:
And me none told: not less to an eye like
    mine
A lidless watcher of the public weal,
Last night, their mask was patent, and my
    foot
Was to you: but I thought again: I fear'd
To meet a cold " We thank you, we shall
    hear of it
From Lady Psyche:" you had gone to
    her,
She told, perforce; and winning easy grace,
No doubt, for slight delay, remain'd
    among us
In our young nursery still unknown, the
    stem
Less grain than touchwood, while my
    honest heat
Were all miscounted as malignant haste
To push my rival out of place and power.
But public use required she should be
    known;
And since my oath was ta'en for public
    use,
I broke the letter of it to keep the sense.
I spoke not then at first, but watch'd them
    well,
Saw that they kept apart, no mischief
    done;
And yet this day (tho' you should hate
    me for it)
I came to tell you; found that you had
    gone,
Ridd'n to the hills, she likewise: now, I
    thought,
That surely she will speak; if not, then I:

Did she? These monsters blazon'd what
    they were,
According to the coarseness of their kind,
For thus I hear; and known at last (my
    work)
And full of cowardice and guilty shame,
I grant in her some sense of shame, she
    flies;
And I remain on whom to wreak your
    rage,
I, that have lent my life to build up yours,
I that have wasted here health, wealth,
    and time,
And talent, I—you know it—I will not
    boast:
Dismiss me, and I prophesy your plan,
Divorced from my experience, will be chaff
For every gust of chance, and men will say
We did not know the real light, but chased
The wisp that flickers where no foot can
    tread.'

She ceased: the Princess answer'd
    coldly, ' Good:
Your oath is broken: we dismiss you: go.
For this lost lamb (she pointed to the
    child)
Our mind is changed: we take it to our-
    self.'

Thereat the Lady stretch'd a vulture
    throat,
And shot from crooked lips a haggard
    smile.
' The plan was mine. I built the nest'
    she said
' To hatch the cuckoo. Rise!' and stoop'd
    to updrag
Melissa: she, half on her mother propt,
Half-drooping from her, turn'd her face,
    and cast
A liquid look on Ida, full of prayer,
Which melted Florian's fancy as she hung,
A Niobëan daughter, one arm out,
Appealing to the bolts of Heaven; and
    while
We gazed upon her came a little stir
About the doors, and on a sudden rush'd
Among us, out of breath, as one pursued,
A woman-post in flying raiment. Fear

Stared in her eyes, and chalk'd her face,
    and wing'd
Her transit to the throne, whereby she fell
Delivering seal'd dispatches which the
    Head
Took half-amazed, and in her lion's mood
Tore open, silent we with blind surmise
Regarding, while she read, till over brow
And cheek and bosom brake the wrath-
    ful bloom
As of some fire against a stormy cloud,
When the wild peasant rights himself, the
    rick
Flames, and his anger reddens in the
    heavens ;
For anger most it seem'd, while now her
    breast,
Beaten with some great passion at her
    heart,
Palpitated, her hand shook, and we heard
In the dead hush the papers that she held
Rustle : at once the lost lamb at her feet
Sent out a bitter bleating for its dam ;
The plaintive cry jarr'd on her ire ; she
    crush'd
The scrolls together, made a sudden turn
As if to speak, but, utterance failing her,
She whirl'd them on to me, as who should
    say
'Read,' and I read—two letters—one her
    sire's.

'Fair daughter, when we sent the
    Prince your way
We knew not your ungracious laws, which
    learnt,
We, conscious of what temper you are
    built,
Came all in haste to hinder wrong, but fell
Into his father's hands, who has this night,
You lying close upon his territory,
Slipt round and in the dark invested you,
And here he keeps me hostage for his son.'

The second was my father's running
    thus :
'You have our son : touch not a hair of
    his head :
Render him up unscathed : give me your
    hand :

Cleave to your contract : tho' indeed we
    hear
You hold the woman is the better man ;
A rampant heresy, such as if it spread
Would make all women kick against their
    Lords
Thro' all the world, and which might well
    deserve
That we this night should pluck your
    palace down ;
And we will do it, unless you send us back
Our son, on the instant, whole.'
                        So far I read ;
And then stood up and spoke impetuously.

'O not to pry and peer on your reserve,
But led by golden wishes, and a hope
The child of regal compact, did I break
Your precinct ; not a scorner of your sex
But venerator, zealous it should be
All that it might be : hear me, for I bear,
Tho' man, yet human, whatsoe'er your
    wrongs,
From the flaxen curl to the gray lock a
    life
Less mine than yours : my nurse would
    tell me of you ;
I babbled for you, as babies for the moon,
Vague brightness ; when a boy, you stoop'd
    to me
From all high places, lived in all fair lights,
Came in long breezes rapt from inmost
    south
And blown to inmost north ; at eve and
    dawn
With Ida, Ida, Ida, rang the woods ;
The leader wildswan in among the stars
Would clang it, and lapt in wreaths of
    glowworm light
The mellow breaker murmur'd Ida. Now,
Because I would have reach'd you, had
    you been
Sphered up with Cassiopëia, or the en-
    throned
Persephonè in Hades, now at length,
Those winters of abeyance all worn out,
A man I came to see you : but, indeed,
Not in this frequence can I lend full
    tongue,
O noble Ida, to those thoughts that wait

On you, their centre : let me say but this,
That many a famous man and woman, town
And landskip, have I heard of, after seen
The dwarfs of presage : tho' when known, there grew
Another kind of beauty in detail
Made them worth knowing ; but in you I found
My boyish dream involved and dazzled down
And master'd, while that after-beauty makes
Such head from act to act, from hour to hour,
Within me, that except you slay me here,
According to your bitter statute-book,
I cannot cease to follow you, as they say
The seal does music ; who desire you more
Than growing boys their manhood ; dying lips,
With many thousand matters left to do,
The breath of life ; O more than poor men wealth,
Than sick men health—yours, yours, not mine—but half
Without you ; with you, whole ; and of those halves
You worthiest ; and howe'er you block and bar
Your heart with system out from mine, I hold
That it becomes no man to nurse despair,
But in the teeth of clench'd antagonisms
To follow up the worthiest till he die :
Yet that I came not all unauthorized
Behold your father's letter.'
                        On one knee
Kneeling, I gave it, which she caught, and dash'd
Unopen'd at her feet : a tide of fierce
Invective seem'd to wait behind her lips,
As waits a river level with the dam
Ready to burst and flood the world with foam :
And so she would have spoken, but there rose
A hubbub in the court of half the maids
Gather'd together: from the illumined hall

Long lanes of splendour slanted o'er a press
Of snowy shoulders, thick as herded ewes,
And rainbow robes, and gems and gem-like eyes,
And gold and golden heads ; they to and fro
Fluctuated, as flowers in storm, some red, some pale,
All open-mouth'd, all gazing to the light,
Some crying there was an army in the land,
And some that men were in the very walls,
And some they cared not ; till a clamour grew
As of a new-world Babel, woman-built,
And worse-confounded : high above them stood
The placid marble Muses, looking peace.

  Not peace she look'd, the Head : but rising up
Robed in the long night of her deep hair, so
To the open window moved, remaining there
Fixt like a beacon-tower above the waves
Of tempest, when the crimson-rolling eye
Glares ruin, and the wild birds on the light
Dash themselves dead. She stretch'd her arms and call'd
Across the tumult and the tumult fell.

  'What fear ye, brawlers ? am not I your Head ?
On me, me, me, the storm first breaks :
    I dare
All these male thunderbolts : what is it ye fear ?
Peace ! there are those to avenge us and they come :
If not,—myself were like enough, O girls,
To unfurl the maiden banner of our rights,
And clad in iron burst the ranks of war,
Or, falling, protomartyr of our cause,
Die : yet I blame you not so much for fear ;

T   O

Six thousand years of fear have made you
    that
From which I would redeem you: but
    for those
That stir this hubbub—you and you—I
    know
Your faces there in the crowd—to-morrow
    morn
We hold a great convention: then shall
    they
That love their voices more than duty,
    learn
With whom they deal, dismiss'd in shame
    to live
No wiser than their mothers, household
    stuff,
Live chattels, mincers of each other's
    fame,
Full of weak poison, turnspits for the clown,
The drunkard's football, laughing-stocks
    of Time,
Whose brains are in their hands and in
    their heels,
But fit to flaunt, to dress, to dance, to
    thrum,
To tramp, to scream, to burnish, and to
    scour,
For ever slaves at home and fools abroad.'

    She, ending, waved her hands: thereat
        the crowd
Muttering, dissolved: then with a smile,
    that look'd
A stroke of cruel sunshine on the cliff,
When all the glens are drown'd in azure
    gloom
Of thunder-shower, she floated to us and
    said: .

    'You have done well and like a
        gentleman,
And like a prince: you have our thanks
    for all:
And you look well too in your woman's
    dress:
Well have you done and like a gentleman.
You saved our life: we owe you bitter
    thanks:
Better have died and spilt our bones in
    the flood—

Then men had said—but now — What
    hinders me
To take such bloody vengeance on you
    both?—
Yet since our father—Wasps in our good
    hive,
You would-be quenchers of the light to
    be,
Barbarians, grosser than your native
    bears—
O would I had his sceptre for one hour!
You that have dared to break our bound,
    and gull'd
Our servants, wrong'd and lied and
    thwarted us—
I wed with thee! *I* bound by precontract
Your bride, your bondslave! not tho' all
    the gold
That veins the world were pack'd to
    make your crown,
And every spoken tongue should lord
    you.   Sir,
Your falsehood and yourself are hateful
    to us:
I trample on your offers and on you:
Begone: we will not look upon you more.
Here, push them out at gates.'
                            In wrath she spake.
Then those eight mighty daughters of the
    plough
Bent their broad faces toward us and
    address'd
Their motion: twice I sought to plead
    my cause,
But on my shoulder hung their heavy
    hands,
The weight of destiny: so from her face
They push'd us, down the steps, and
    thro' the court,
And with grim laughter thrust us out at
    gates.

    We cross'd the street and gain'd a petty
        mound
Beyond it, whence we saw the lights and
    heard
The voices murmuring.   While I listen'd,
    came
On a sudden the weird seizure and the
    doubt:

seem'd to move among a world of
  ghosts ;
The Princess with her monstrous woman-
  guard,
The jest and earnest working side by side,
The cataract and the tumult and the kings
Were shadows ; and the long fantastic
  night
With all its doings had and had not been,
And all things were and were not.

This went by
As strangely as it came, and on my spirits
Settled a gentle cloud of melancholy ;
Not long ; I shook it off ; for spite of
  doubts
And sudden ghostly shadowings I was one
To whom the touch of all mischance but
  came
As night to him that sitting on a hill
Sees the midsummer, midnight, Norway
  sun
Set into sunrise ; then we moved away.

  Thy voice is heard thro' rolling drums,
    That beat to battle where he stands ;
  Thy face across his fancy comes,
    And gives the battle to his hands :
  A moment, while the trumpets blow,
    He sees his brood about thy knee ;
  The next, like fire he meets the foe,
    And strikes him dead for thine and thee.

  Lilia sang : we thought her half-
  possess'd,
She struck such warbling fury thro' the
  words ;
And, after, feigning pique at what she
  call'd
The raillery, or grotesque, or false sub-
  lime—
Like one that wishes at a dance to change
The music— clapt her hands and cried
  for war,
Or some grand fight to kill and make an
  end :
And he that next inherited the tale
Half turning to the broken statue, said,
'Sir Ralph has got your colours : if I
  prove
Your knight, and fight your battle, what
  for me ?'

It chanced, her empty glove upon the
  tomb
Lay by her like a model of her hand.
She took it and she flung it. ' Fight '
  she said,
' And make us all we would be, great
  and good.'
He knightlike in his cap instead of casque,
A cap of Tyrol borrow'd frcm the hall,
Arranged the favour, and assumed the
  Prince.

v.

Now, scarce three paces measured from
  the mound,
We stumbled on a stationary voice,
And ' Stand, who goes ?' ' Two from the
  palace ' I.
' The second two : they wait,' he said,
  ' pass on ;
His Highness wakes :' and one, that
  clash'd in arms,
By glimmering lanes and walls of canvas
  led
Threading the soldier-city, till we heard
The drowsy folds of our great ensign
  shake
From blazon'd lions o'er the imperial tent
Whispers of war.

Entering, the sudden light
Dazed me half-blind : I stood and seem'd
  to hear,
As in a poplar grove when a light wind
  wakes
A lisping of the innumerous leaf and dies,
Each hissing in his neighbour's ear ; and
  then
A strangled titter, out of which there
  brake
On all sides, clamouring etiquette to
  death,
Unmeasured mirth ; while now the two
  old kings
Began to wag their baldness up and down,
The fresh young captains flash'd their
  glittering teeth,
The huge bush-bearded Barons heaved
  and blew,
And slain with laughter roll'd the gilded
  Squire.

At length my Sire, his rough cheek
    wet with tears,
Panted from weary sides ' King, you are
    free !
We did but keep you surety for our son,
If this be he, — or a draggled mawkin,
    thou,
That tends her bristled grunters in the
    sludge :'
For I was drench'd with ooze, and torn
    with briers,
More crumpled than a poppy from the
    sheath,
And all one rag, disprinced from head to
    heel.
Then some one sent beneath his vaulted
    palm
A whisper'd jest to some one near him,
    ' Look,
He has been among his shadows.' ' Satan
    take
The old women and their shadows! (thus
    the King
Roar'd) make yourself a man to fight with
    men.
Go : Cyril told us all.'
              As boys that slink
From ferule and the trespass-chiding eye,
Away we stole, and transient in a trice
From what was left of faded woman-
    slough
To sheathing splendours and the golden
    scale
Of harness, issued in the sun, that now
Leapt from the dewy shoulders of the
    Earth,
And hit the Northern hills.   Here Cyril
    met us.
A little shy at first, but by and by
We twain, with mutual pardon ask'd and
    given
For stroke and song, resolder'd peace,
    whereon
Follow'd his tale.   Amazed he fled away
Thro' the dark land, and later in the night
Had come on Psyche weeping : ' then we
    fell
Into your father's hand, and there she
    lies,
But will not speak, nor stir.'

                 He show'd a ten
A stone-shot off : we enter'd in, and ther
Among piled arms and rough accoutre
    ments,
Pitiful sight, wrapp'd in a soldier's cloak
Like some sweet sculpture draped fror
    head to foot,
And push'd by rude hands from i
    pedestal,
All her fair length upon the ground sh
    lay :
And at her head a follower of the camp
A charr'd and wrinkled piece of womar
    hood,
Sat watching like a watcher by the dea

    Then Florian knelt, and ' Come ' l
        whisper'd to her,
' Lift up your head, sweet sister : lie n
    thus.
What have you done but right? you coul
    not slay
Me, nor your prince : look up : be con
    forted :
Sweet is it to have done the thing one ough
When fall'n in darker ways.'   And lik
    wise I :
' Be comforted : have I not lost her to
In whose least act abides the namele
    charm
That none has else for me ?'   She hear
    she moved,
She moan'd, a folded voice ; and up sh
    sat,
And raised the cloak from brows as pa
    and smooth
As those that mourn half-shrouded ov
    death
In deathless marble.   ' Her,' she sai
    ' my friend—
Parted from her—betray'd her cause a
    mine—
Where shall I breathe? why kept ye n
    your faith?
O base and bad ! what comfort? no
    for me !'
To whom remorseful Cyril, ' Yet I pra
Take comfort : live, dear lady, for yo
    child !'
At which she lifted up her voice and crie

' Ah me, my babe, my blossom, ah, my
            child,
My one sweet child, whom I shall see no
            more !
For now will cruel Ida keep her back ;
And either she will die from want of care,
Or sicken with ill-usage, when they say
The child is hers—for every little fault,
The child is hers ; and they will beat my
            girl
Remembering her mother: O my flower !
Or they will take her, they will make her
            hard,
And she will pass me by in after-life
With some cold reverence worse than
            were she dead.
Ill mother that I was to leave her there,
To lag behind, scared by the cry they
            made,
The horror of the shame among them all :
But I will go and sit beside the doors,
And make a wild petition night and day,
Until they hate to hear me like a wind
Wailing for ever, till they open to me,
And lay my little blossom at my feet,
My babe, my sweet Aglaïa, my one child :
And I will take her up and go my way,
And satisfy my soul with kissing her :
Ah ! what might that man not deserve of
            me
Who gave me back my child ?'   ' Be
            comforted,'
Said Cyril, 'you shall have it :' but again
She veil'd her brows, and prone she sank,
            and so
Like tender things that being caught feign
            death,
Spoke not, nor stirr'd.
                        By this a murmur ran
Thro' all the camp and inward raced the
            scouts
With rumour of Prince Arac hard at hand.
We left her by the woman, and without
Found the gray kings at parle: and 'Look
            you ' cried
My father ' that our compact be fulfill'd :
You have spoilt this child ; she laughs at
            you and man :
She wrongs herself, her sex, and me, and
            him :

But red-faced war has rods of steel and
            fire ;
She yields, or war.'
                        Then Gama turn'd to me :
' We fear, indeed, you spent a stormy
            time
With our strange girl : and yet they say
            that still
You love her.   Give us, then, your mind
            at large :
How say you, war or not ?'
                        ' Not war, if possible,
O king,' I said, ' lest from the abuse of
            war,
The desecrated shrine, the trampled year,
The smouldering homestead, and the
            household flower
Torn from the lintel—all the common
            wrong—
A smoke go up thro' which I loom to her
Three times a monster : now she lightens
            scorn
At him that mars her plan, but then
            would hate
(And every voice she talk'd with ratify it,
And every face she look'd on justify it)
The general foe.   More soluble is this
            knot,
By gentleness than war.   I want her love.
What were I nigher this altho' we dash'd
Your cities into shards with catapults,
She would not love ;— or brought her
            chain'd, a slave,
The lifting of whose eyelash is my lord,
Not ever would she love ; but brooding
            turn
The book of scorn, till all my flitting
            chance
Were caught within the record of her
            wrongs,
And crush'd to death : and rather, Sire,
            than this
I would the old God of war himself were
            dead,
Forgotten, rusting on his iron hills,
Rotting on some wild shore with ribs of
            wreck,
Or like an old-world mammoth bulk'd in
            ice,
Not to be molten out.'

And roughly spake
My father, 'Tut, you know them not, the
    girls.
Boy, when I hear you prate I almost think
That idiot legend credible. Look you,
    Sir !
Man is the hunter ; woman is his game :
The sleek and shining creatures of the
    chase,
We hunt them for the beauty of their
    skins ;
They love us for it, and we ride them
    down.
Wheedling and siding with them ! Out !
    for shame !
Boy, there's no rose that's half so dear to
    them
As he that does the thing they dare not do,
Breathing and sounding beauteous battle,
    comes
With the air of the trumpet round him,
    and leaps in
Among the women, snares them by the
    score
Flatter'd and fluster'd, wins, tho' dash'd
    with death
He reddens what he kisses : thus I won
Your mother, a good mother, a good wife,
Worth winning ; but this firebrand—
    gentleness
To such as her ! if Cyril spake her true,
To catch a dragon in a cherry net,
To trip a tigress with a gossamer,
Were wisdom to it.'
                'Yea but Sire,' I cried,
'Wild natures need wise curbs. The
    soldier ? No :
What dares not Ida do that she should
    prize
The soldier ? I beheld her, when she rose
The yesternight, and storming in extremes,
Stood for her cause, and flung defiance
    down
Gagelike to man, and had not shunn'd the
    death,
No, not the soldier's : yet I hold her, king,
True woman : but you clash them all in
    one,
That have as many differences as we.
The violet varies from the lily as far

As oak from elm : one loves the soldie[r]
    one
The silken priest of peace, one this, or
    that,
And some unworthily ; their sinless fait[h]
A maiden moon that sparkles on a sty,
Glorifying clown and satyr ; whence the
    need
More breadth of culture : is not Ida righ[t]
They worth it ? truer to the law within
Severer in the logic of a life ?
Twice as magnetic to sweet influences
Of earth and heaven ? and she of who[m]
    you speak,
My mother, looks as whole as some serer[e]
Creation minted in the golden moods
Of sovereign artists ; not a thought, [a]
    touch,
But pure as lines of green that streak th[e]
    white
Of the first snowdrop's inner leaves ; I sa[y]
Not like the piebald miscellany, man,
Bursts of great heart and slips in sensu[al]
    mire,
But whole and one : and take them al[l]
    in-all,
Were we ourselves but half as good, as kin[d]
As truthful, much that Ida claims as rig[ht]
Had ne'er been mooted, but as frank [as]
    theirs
As dues of Nature. To our point : n[o]
    war :
Lest I lose all.'
            'Nay, nay, you spake but sens[e]
Said Gama. 'We remember love ourse[lf]
In our sweet youth ; we did not rate hi[m]
    then
This red-hot iron to be shaped with blow[s]
You talk almost like Ida : *she* can talk
And there is something in it as you say
But you talk kindlier : we esteem you f[or]
    it.—
He seems a gracious and a gallant Princ[e]
I would he had our daughter : for the res[t]
Our own detention, why, the caus[e]
    weigh'd,
Fatherly fears—you used us courteously—
We would do much to gratify your Prince—
We pardon it ; and for your ingress her[e]
Upon the skirt and fringe of our fair lan[d]

You did but come as goblins in the night,
Nor in the furrow broke the ploughman's head,
Nor burnt the grange, nor buss'd the milking-maid,
Nor robb'd the farmer of his bowl of cream:
But let your Prince (our royal word upon it,
He comes back safe) ride with us to our lines,
And speak with Arac: Arac's word is thrice
As ours with Ida: something may be done—
I know not what—and ours shall see us friends.
You, likewise, our late guests, if so you will,
Follow us: who knows? we four may build some plan
Foursquare to opposition.'
     Here he reach'd
White hands of farewell to my sire, who growl'd
An answer which, half-muffled in his beard,
Let so much out as gave us leave to go.

Then rode we with the old king across the lawns
Beneath huge trees, a thousand rings of Spring
In every bole, a song on every spray
Of birds that piped their Valentines, and woke
Desire in me to infuse my tale of love
In the old king's ears, who promised help, and oozed
All o'er with honey'd answer as we rode
And blossom-fragrant slipt the heavy dews
Gather'd by night and peace, with each light air
On our mail'd heads: but other thoughts than Peace
Burnt in us, when we saw the embattled squares,
And squadrons of the Prince, trampling the flowers
With clamour: for among them rose a cry
As if to greet the king; they made a halt;

The horses yell'd; they clash'd their arms; the drum
Beat; merrily-blowing shrill'd the martial fife;
And in the blast and bray of the long horn
And serpent-throated bugle, undulated
The banner: anon to meet us lightly pranced
Three captains out; nor ever had I seen
Such thews of men: the midmost and the highest
Was Arac: all about his motion clung
The shadow of his sister, as the beam
Of the East, that play'd upon them, made them glance
Like those three stars of the airy Giant's zone,
That glitter burnish'd by the frosty dark;
And as the fiery Sirius alters hue,
And bickers into red and emerald, shone
Their morions, wash'd with morning, as they came.

And I that prated peace, when first I heard
War-music, felt the blind wildbeast of force,
Whose home is in the sinews of a man,
Stir in me as to strike: then took the king
His three broad sons; with now a wandering hand
And now a pointed finger, told them all:
A common light of smiles at our disguise
Broke from their lips, and, ere the windy jest
Had labour'd down within his ample lungs,
The genial giant, Arac, roll'd himself
Thrice in the saddle, then burst out in words.

'Our land invaded, 'sdeath! and he himself
Your captive, yet my father wills not war:
And, 'sdeath! myself, what care I, war or no?
But then this question of your troth remains:
And there's a downright honest meaning in her;

She flies too high, she flies too high! and
    yet
She ask'd but space and fairplay for her
    scheme ;
She prest and prest it on me—I myself,
What know I of these things? but, life
    and soul!
I thought her half-right talking of her
    wrongs ;
I say she flies too high, 'sdeath! what of
    that?
I take her for the flower of womankind,
And so I often told her, right or wrong,
And, Prince, she can be sweet to those
    she loves,
And, right or wrong, I care not : this is
    all,
I stand upon her side : she made me
    swear it—
'Sdeath—and with solemn rites by candle-
    light—
Swear by St. something—I forget her
    name—
Her that talk'd down the fifty wisest men ;
She was a princess too ; and so I swore.
Come, this is all ; she will not : waive
    your claim :
If not, the foughten field, what else, at
    once
Decides it, 'sdeath! against my father's
    will.'

I lagg'd in answer loth to render up
My precontract, and loth by brainless war
To cleave the rift of difference deeper
    yet ;
Till one of those two brothers, half aside
And fingering at the hair about his lip,
To prick us on to combat ' Like to like !
The woman's garment hid the woman's
    heart.'
A taunt that clench'd his purpose like a
    blow !
For fiery-short was Cyril's counter-scoff,
And sharp I answer'd, touch'd upon the
    point
Where idle boys are cowards to their
    shame,
' Decide it here : why not? we are three
    to three.'

Then spake the third ' But three to
    three? no more?
No more, and in our noble sister's cause?
More, more, for honour : every captain
    waits
Hungry for honour, angry for his king.
More, more, some fifty on a side, that each
May breathe himself, and quick! by over-
    throw
Of these or those, the question settled die.'

' Yea,' answer'd I, ' for this wild wreath
    of air,
This flake of rainbow flying on the highest
Foam of men's deeds—this honour, if ye
    will.
It needs must be for honour if at all :
Since, what decision? if we fail, we fail,
And if we win, we fail : she would not
    keep
Her compact.' ' 'Sdeath ! but we will
    send to her,'
Said Arac, 'worthy reasons why she should
Bide by this issue : let our missive thro',
And you shall have her answer by the
    word.'

' Boys !' shriek'd the old king, but
    vainlier than a hen
To her false daughters in the pool ; for
    none
Regarded ; neither seem'd there more to
    say :
Back rode we to my father's camp, and
    found
He thrice had sent a herald to the gates,
To learn if Ida yet would cede our claim,
Or by denial flush her babbling wells
With her own people's life : three times
    he went :
The first, he blew and blew, but none
    appear'd :
He batter'd at the doors ; none came :
    the next,
An awful voice within had warn'd him
    thence :
The third, and those eight daughters of
    the plough
Came sallying thro' the gates, and caught
    his hair,

And so belabour'd him on rib and cheek
They made him wild : not less one glance
    he caught
Thro' open doors of Ida station'd there
Unshaken, clinging to her purpose, firm
Tho' compass'd by two armies and the
    noise
Of arms ; and standing like a stately Pine
Set in a cataract on an island-crag,
When storm is on the heights, and right
    and left
Suck'd from the dark heart of the long
    hills roll
The torrents, dash'd to the vale : and yet
    her will
Bred will in me to overcome it or fall.

But when I told the king that I was
    pledged
To fight in tourney for my bride, he
    clash'd
His iron palms together with a cry ;
Himself would tilt it out among the lads :
But overborne by all his bearded lords
With reasons drawn from age and state,
    perforce
He yielded, wroth and red, with fierce
    demur :
And many a bold knight started up in heat,
And sware to combat for my claim till
    death.

All on this side the palace ran the field
Flat to the garden-wall : and likewise
    here,
Above the garden's glowing blossom-belts,
A column'd entry shone and marble stairs,
And great bronze valves, emboss'd with
    Tomyris
And what she did to Cyrus after fight,
But now fast barr'd : so here upon the flat
All that long morn the lists were hammer'd
    up,
And all that morn the heralds to and fro,
With message and defiance, went and
    came ;
Last, Ida's answer, in a royal hand,
But shaken here and there, and rolling
    words
Oration-like.   I kiss'd it and I read.

' O brother, you have known the pangs
    we felt,
What heats of indignation when we heard
Of those that iron-cramp'd their women's
    feet ;
Of lands in which at the altar the poor
    bride
Gives her harsh groom for bridal-gift a
    scourge ;
Of living hearts that crack within the fire
Where smoulder their dead despots ; and
    of those,—
Mothers,—that, all prophetic pity, fling
Their pretty maids in the running flood,
    and swoops
The vulture, beak and talon, at the heart
Made for all noble motion : and I saw
That equal baseness lived in sleeker times
With smoother men : the old leaven
    leaven'd all :
Millions of throats would bawl for civil
    rights,
No woman named : therefore I set my
    face
Against all men, and lived but for mine
    own.
Far off from men I built a fold for them :
I stored it full of rich memorial :
I fenced it round with gallant institutes,
And biting laws to scare the beasts of prey
And prosper'd ; till a rout of saucy boys
Brake on us at our books, and marr'd
    our peace,
Mask'd like our maids, blustering I know
    not what
Of insolence and love, some pretext held
Of baby troth, invalid, since my will
Seal'd not the bond—the striplings !—for
    their sport !—
I tamed my leopards : shall I not tame
    these ?
Or you ? or I ? for since you think me
    touch'd
In honour—what, I would not aught of
    false—
Is not our cause pure ? and whereas I
    know
Your prowess, Arac, and what mother's
    blood
You draw from, fight ; you failing, I abide

What end soever: fail you will not. Still
Take not his life: he risk'd it for my own;
His mother lives: yet whatsoe'er you do,
Fight and fight well; strike and strike
　　　home. O dear
Brothers, the woman's Angel guards you,
　　　you
The sole men to be mingled with our
　　　cause,
The sole men we shall prize in the after-
　　　time,
Your very armour hallow'd, and your
　　　statues
Rear'd, sung to, when, this gad-fly brush'd
　　　aside,
We plant a solid foot into the Time,
And mould a generation strong to move
With claim on claim from right to right,
　　　till she
Whose name is yoked with children's,
　　　know herself;
And Knowledge in our own land make
　　　her free,
And, ever following those two crowned
　　　twins,
Commerce and conquest, shower the fiery
　　　grain
Of freedom broadcast over all that orbs
Between the Northern and the Southern
　　　morn.'

Then came a postscript dash'd across
　　　the rest.
'See that there be no traitors in your
　　　camp:
We seem a nest of traitors—none to trust
Since our arms fail'd—this Egypt-plague
　　　of men!
Almost our maids were better at their
　　　homes,
Than thus man-girdled here: indeed I
　　　think
Our chiefest comfort is the little child
Of one unworthy mother; which she left:
She shall not have it back: the child
　　　shall grow
To prize the authentic mother of her mind.
I took it for an hour in mine own bed
This morning: there the tender orphan
　　　hands

Felt at my heart, and seem'd to charm
　　　from thence
The wrath I nursed against the world:
　　　farewell.'

I ceased; he said, 'Stubborn, but she
　　　may sit
Upon a king's right hand in thunder-
　　　storms,
And breed up warriors! See now, tho'
　　　yourself
Be dazzled by the wildfire Love to sloughs
That swallow common sense, the spind-
　　　ling king,
This Gama swamp'd in lazy tolerance.
When the man wants weight, the woman
　　　takes it up,
And topples down the scales; but this is
　　　fixt
As are the roots of earth and base of all;
Man for the field and woman for the
　　　hearth:
Man for the sword and for the needle she:
Man with the head and woman with the
　　　heart:
Man to command and woman to obey;
All else confusion. Look you! the gray
　　　mare
Is ill to live with, when her whinny shrills
From tile to scullery, and her small good-
　　　man
Shrinks in his arm-chair while the fires
　　　of Hell
Mix with his hearth: but you—she's yet
　　　a colt—
Take, break her: strongly groom'd and
　　　straitly curb'd
She might not rank with those detestable
That let the bantling scald at home, and
　　　brawl
Their rights or wrongs like potherbs in
　　　the street.
They say she's comely; there's the fairer
　　　chance:
I like her none the less for rating at her!
Besides, the woman wed is not as we,
But suffers change of frame. A lusty brace
•Of twins may weed her of her folly. Boy,
The bearing and the training of a child
Is woman's wisdom.'

Thus the hard old king:
I took my leave, for it was nearly noon:
I pored upon her letter which I held,
And on the little clause 'take not his life:'
I mused on that wild morning in the
woods,
And on the 'Follow, follow, thou shalt
win:'
I thought on all the wrathful king had
said,
And how the strange betrothment was to
end:
Then I remember'd that burnt sorcerer's
curse
That one should fight with shadows and
should fall;
And like a flash the weird affection came:
King, camp and college turn'd to hollow
shows;
I seem'd to move in old memorial tilts,
And doing battle with forgotten ghosts,
To dream myself the shadow of a dream:
And ere I woke it was the point of noon,
The lists were ready. Empanoplied and
plumed
We enter'd in, and waited, fifty there
Opposed to fifty, till the trumpet blared
At the barrier like a wild horn in a land
Of echoes, and a moment, and once more
The trumpet, and again: at which the
storm
Of galloping hoofs bare on the ridge of
spears
And riders front to front, until they closed
In conflict with the crash of shivering
points,
And thunder. Yet it seem'd a dream, I
dream'd
Of fighting. On his haunches rose the
steed,
And into fiery splinters leapt the lance,
And out of stricken helmets sprang the fire.
Part sat like rocks: part reel'd but kept
their seats:
Part roll'd on the earth and rose again
and drew:
Part stumbled mixt with floundering
horses. Down
From those two bulks at Arac's side, and
down

From Arac's arm, as from a giant's flail,
The large blows rain'd, as here and every-
where
He rode the mellay, lord of the ringing
lists,
And all the plain,—brand, mace, and
shaft, and shield—
Shock'd, like an iron-clanging anvil
bang'd
With hammers; till I thought, can this
be he
From Gama's dwarfish loins? if this be so,
The mother makes us most—and in my
dream
I glanced aside, and saw the palace-front
Alive with fluttering scarfs and ladies'
eyes,
And highest, among the statues, statue-
like,
Between a cymbal'd Miriam and a Jael,
With Psyche's babe, was Ida watching us,
A single band of gold about her hair,
Like a Saint's glory up in heaven: but
she
No saint—inexorable—no tenderness—
Too hard, too cruel: yet she sees me
fight,
Yea, let her see me fall! with that I drave
Among the thickest and bore down a
Prince,
And Cyril, one. Yea, let me make my
dream
All that I would. But that large-moulded
man,
His visage all agrin as at a wake,
Made at me thro' the press, and, stagger-
ing back
With stroke on stroke the horse and
horseman, came
As comes a pillar of electric cloud,
Flaying the roofs and sucking up the
drains,
And shadowing down the champaign till
it strikes
On a wood, and takes, and breaks, and
cracks, and splits,
And twists the grain with such a roar
that Earth
Reels, and the herdsmen cry; for every-
thing

Gave way before him : only Florian, he
That loved me closer than his own right
    eye,
Thrust in between ; but Arac rode him
    down :
And Cyril seeing it, push'd against the
    Prince,
With Psyche's colour round his helmet,
    tough,
Strong, supple, sinew - corded, apt at
    arms ;
But tougher, heavier, stronger, he that
    smote
And threw him : last I spurr'd ; I felt
    my veins
Stretch with fierce heat ; a moment hand
    to hand,
And sword to sword, and horse to horse
    we hung,
Till I struck out and shouted ; the blade
    glanced,
I did but shear a feather, and dream and
    truth
Flow'd from me ; darkness closed me ;
    and I fell.

VI.

Home they brought her warrior dead :
    She nor swoon'd, nor utter'd cry :
All her maidens, watching, said,
    ' She must weep or she will die.'

Then they praised him, soft and low,
    Call'd him worthy to be loved,
Truest friend and noblest foe ;
    Yet she neither spoke nor moved.

Stole a maiden from her place,
    Lightly to the warrior stept,
Took the face-cloth from the face ;
    Yet she neither moved nor wept.

Rose a nurse of ninety years,
    Set his child upon her knee—
Like summer tempest came her tears—
    ' Sweet my child, I live for thee.'

My dream had never died or lived
    again.
As in some mystic middle state I lay ;
Seeing I saw not, hearing not I heard :
Tho', if I saw not, yet they told me all
So often that I speak as having seen.

For so it seem'd, or so they said to me,
That all things grew more tragic and
    more strange ;
That when our side was vanquish'd and
    my cause
For ever lost, there went up a great cry,
The Prince is slain. My father heard
    and ran
In on the lists, and there unlaced my
    casque
And grovell'd on my body, and after him
Came Psyche, sorrowing for Aglaïa.

But high upon the palace Ida stood
With Psyche's babe in arm : there on the
    roofs
Like that great dame of Lapidoth she
    sang.

' Our enemies have fall'n, have fall'n : the seed,
The little seed they laugh'd at in the dark,
Has risen and cleft the soil, and grown a bulk
Of spanless girth, that lays on every side
A thousand arms and rushes to the Sun.

' Our enemies have fall'n, have fall'n : they
    came ;
The leaves were wet with women's tears : they
    heard
A noise of songs they would not understand :
They mark'd it with the red cross to the fall,
And would have strown it, and are fall'n them-
    selves.

' Our enemies have fall'n, have fall'n : they
    came,
The woodmen with their axes : lo the tree !
But we will make it faggots for the hearth,
And shape it plank and beam for roof and floor,
And boats and bridges for the use of men.

' Our enemies have fall'n, have fall'n : they
    struck ;
With their own blows they hurt themselves, nor
    knew
There dwelt an iron nature in the grain :
The glittering axe was broken in their arms,
Their arms were shatter'd to the shoulder blade.

' Our enemies have fall'n, but this shall grow
A night of Summer from the heat, a breadth
Of Autumn, dropping fruits of power : and roll'd
With music in the growing breeze of Time,
The tops shall strike from star to star, the fangs
Shall move the stony bases of the world.

'And now, O maids, behold our
      sanctuary
Is violate, our laws broken : fear we not
To break them more in their behoof,
      whose arms
Champion'd our cause and won it with a
      day
Blanch'd in our annals, and perpetual feast,
When dames and heroines of the golden
      year
Shall strip a hundred hollows bare of
      Spring,
To rain an April of ovation round
Their statues, borne aloft, the three : but
      come,
We will be liberal, since our rights are
      won.
Let them not lie in the tents with coarse
      mankind,
Ill nurses ; but descend, and proffer these
The brethren of our blood and cause, that
      there
Lie bruised and maim'd, the tender
      ministries
Of female hands and hospitality.'

      She spoke, and with the babe yet in
      her arms,
Descending, burst the great bronze valves,
      and led
A hundred maids in train across the Park.
Some cowl'd, and some bare-headed, on
      they came,
Their feet in flowers, her loveliest : by
      them went
The enamour'd air sighing, and on their
      curls
From the high tree the blossom wavering
      fell,
And over them the tremulous isles of light
Slided, they moving under shade : but
      Blanche
At distance follow'd : so they came : anon
Thro' open field into the lists they wound
Timorously ; and as the leader of the
      herd
That holds a stately fretwork to the Sun,
And follow'd up by a hundred airy does,
Steps with a tender foot, light as on air,
The lovely, lordly creature floated on

To where her wounded brethren lay ;
      there stay'd ;
Knelt on one knee,—the child on one,—
      and prest
Their hands, and call'd them dear de-
      liverers,
And happy warriors, and immortal names,
And said 'You shall not lie in the tents
      but here,
And nursed by those for whom you fought,
      and served
With female hands and hospitality.'

      Then, whether moved by this, or was
      it chance,
She past my way.   Up started from my
      side
The old lion, glaring with his whelpless
      eye,
Silent ; but when she saw me lying stark,
Dishelm'd and mute, and motionlessly
      pale,
Cold ev'n to her, she sigh'd ; and when
      she saw
The haggard father's face and reverend
      beard
Of grisly twine, all dabbled with the blood
Of his own son, shudder'd, a twitch of pain
Tortured her mouth, and o'er her forehead
      past
A shadow, and her hue changed, and she
      said :
'He saved my life : my brother slew him
      for it.'
No more : at which the king in bitter
      scorn
Drew from my neck the painting and the
      tress,
And held them up : she saw them, and a
      day
Rose from the distance on her memory,
When the good Queen, her mother, shore
      the tress
With kisses, ere the days of Lady Blanche :
And then once more she look'd at my pale
      face :
Till understanding all the foolish work
Of Fancy, and the bitter close of all,
Her iron will was broken in her mind ;
Her noble heart was molten in her breast ;

She bow'd, she set the child on the earth;
she laid
A feeling finger on my brows, and
presently
'O Sire,' she said, 'he lives: he is not
dead:
O let me have him with my brethren here
In our own palace: we will tend on him
Like one of these; if so, by any means,
To lighten this great clog of thanks, that
make
Our progress falter to the woman's goal.'

She said: but at the happy word 'he
lives'
My father stoop'd, re-father'd o'er my
wounds.
So those two foes above my fallen life,
With brow to brow like night and evening
mixt
Their dark and gray, while Psyche ever
stole
A little nearer, till the babe that by us,
Half-lapt in glowing gauze and golden
brede,
Lay like a new-fall'n meteor on the grass,
Uncared for, spied its mother and began
A blind and babbling laughter, and to
dance
Its body, and reach its fatling innocent
arms
And lazy lingering fingers. She the appeal
Brook'd not, but clamouring out 'Mine—
mine—not yours,
It is not yours, but mine: give me the
child'
Ceased all on tremble: piteous was the
cry:
So stood the unhappy mother open-
mouth'd,
And turn'd each face her way: wan was
her cheek
With hollow watch, her blooming mantle
torn,
Red grief and mother's hunger in her eye,
And down dead-heavy sank her curls, and
half
The sacred mother's bosom, panting, burst
The laces toward her babe; but she nor
cared

Nor knew it, clamouring on, till Ida heard,
Look'd up, and rising slowly from me,
stood
Erect and silent, striking with her glance
The mother, me, the child; but he that
lay
Beside us, Cyril, batter'd as he was,
Trail'd himself up on one knee: then he
drew
Her robe to meet his lips, and down she
look'd
At the arm'd man sideways, pitying as it
seem'd,
Or self-involved; but when she learnt his
face,
Remembering his ill-omen'd song, arose
Once more thro' all her height, and o'er
him grew
Tall as a figure lengthen'd on the sand
When the tide ebbs in sunshine, and he
said:

'O fair and strong and terrible!
Lioness
That with your long locks play the Lion's
mane!
But Love and Nature, these are two more
terrible
And stronger. See, your foot is on our
necks,
We vanquish'd, you the Victor of your
will.
What would you more? give her the
child! remain
Orb'd in your isolation: he is dead,
Or all as dead: henceforth we let you be:
Win you the hearts of women; and
beware
Lest, where you seek the common love
of these,
The common hate with the revolving
wheel
Should drag you down, and some great
Nemesis
Break from a darken'd future, crown'd
with fire,
And tread you out for ever: but how-
soe'er
Fix'd in yourself, never in your own arms
To hold your own, deny not hers to her

Give her the child ! O if, I say, you keep
One pulse that beats true woman, if you
    loved
The breast that fed or arm that dandled
    you,
Or own one port of sense not flint to
    prayer,
Give her the child ! or if you scorn to
    lay it,
Yourself, in hands so lately claspt with
    yours,
Or speak to her, your dearest, her one
    fault
The tenderness, not yours, that could not
    kill,
Give *me* it : *I* will give it her.'
                    He said :
At first her eye with slow dilation roll'd
Dry flame, she listening ; after sank and
    sank
And, into mournful twilight mellowing,
    dwelt
Full on the child ; she took it : ' Pretty
    bud !
Lily of the vale ! half open'd bell of the
    woods !
Sole comfort of my dark hour, when a
    world
Of traitorous friend and broken system
    made
No purple in the distance, mystery,
Pledge of a love not to be mine, farewell ;
These men are hard upon us as of old,
We two must part : and yet how fain
    was I
To dream thy cause embraced in mine,
    to think
I might be something to thee, when I felt
Thy helpless warmth about my barren
    breast
In the dead prime : but may thy mother
    prove
As true to thee as false, false, false to me !
And, if thou needs must bear the yoke,
    I wish it
Gentle as freedom '—here she kiss'd it :
    then—
' All good go with thee ! take it Sir,'
    and so
Laid the soft babe in his hard-mailed hands.

Who turn'd half-round to Psyche as she
    sprang
To meet it, with an eye that swum in
    thanks ;
Then felt it sound and whole from head
    to foot,
And hugg'd and never hugg'd it close
    enough,
And in her hunger mouth'd and mumbled
    it,
And hid her bosom with it ; after that
Put on more calm and added suppliantly :

' We two were friends : I go to mine
    own land
For ever : find some other : as for me
I scarce am fit for your great plans : yet
    speak to me,
Say one soft word and let me part for-
    given.'

But Ida spoke not, rapt upon the child.
Then Arac. ' Ida— 'sdeath ! you blame
    the man ;
You wrong yourselves—the woman is so
    hard
Upon the woman. Come, a grace to me !
I am your warrior : I and mine have fought
Your battle : kiss her ; take her hand,
    she weeps :
'Sdeath ! I would sooner fight thrice o'er
    than see it.'

But Ida spoke not, gazing on the ground,
And reddening in the furrows of his chin,
And moved beyond his custom, Gama
    said :

' I've heard that there is iron in the
    blood,
And I believe it. Not one word ? not one ?
Whence drew you this steel temper ? not
    from me,
Not from your mother, now a saint with
    saints.
She said you had a heart—I heard her
    say it—
" Our Ida has a heart "—just ere she died—
" But see that some one with authority
Be near her still " and I—I sought for
    one—

All people said she had authority—
The Lady Blanche: much profit! Not
　　one word;
No! tho' your father sues: see how you
　　stand
Stiff as Lot's wife, and all the good
　　knights maim'd,
I trust that there is no one hurt to death,
For your wild whim: and was it then
　　for this,
Was it for this we gave our palace up,
Where we withdrew from summer heats
　　and state,
And had our wine and chess beneath the
　　planes,
And many a pleasant hour with her that's
　　gone,
Ere you were born to vex us? Is it kind?
Speak to her I say: is this not she of
　　whom,
When first she came, all flush'd you said
　　to me
Now had you got a friend of your own
　　age,
Now could you share your thought; now
　　should men see
Two women faster welded in one love
Than pairs of wedlock; she you walk'd
　　with, she
You talk'd with, whole nights long, up
　　in the tower,
Of sine and arc, spheroïd and azimuth,
And right ascension, Heaven knows what;
　　and now
A word, but one, one little kindly word,
Not one to spare her: out upon you,
　　flint!
You love nor her, nor me, nor any; nay,
You shame your mother's judgment too.
　　Not one?
You will not? well—no heart have you,
　　or such
As fancies like the vermin in a nut
Have fretted all to dust and bitterness.'
So said the small king moved beyond his
　　wont.

But Ida stood nor spoke, drain'd of her
　　force
By many a varying influence and so long.

Down thro' her limbs a drooping languor
　　wept:
Her head a little bent; and on her mouth
A doubtful smile dwelt like a clouded
　　moon
In a still water: then brake out my sire,
Lifting his grim head from my wounds.
　　'O you,
Woman, whom we thought woman even
　　now,
And were half fool'd to let you tend our son,
Because he might have wish'd it—but we
　　see
The accomplice of your madness unfor-
　　given,
And think that you might mix his draught
　　with death,
When your skies change again: the
　　rougher hand
Is safer: on to the tents: take up the
　　Prince.'

He rose, and while each ear was prick'd
　　to attend
A tempest, thro' the cloud that dimm'd
　　her broke
A genial warmth and light once more,
　　and shone
Thro' glittering drops on her sad friend.
　　　　　　　　　'Come hither.
O Psyche,' she cried out, 'embrace me,
　　come,
Quick while I melt; make reconcilement
　　sure
With one that cannot keep her mind an
　　hour:
Come to the hollow heart they slander so!
Kiss and be friends, like children being
　　chid!
I seem no more: *I* want forgiveness too:
I should have had to do with none but
　　maids,
That have no links with men. Ah false
　　but dear,
Dear traitor, too much loved, why?—
　　why?—Yet see,
Before these kings we embrace you yet
　　once more
With all forgiveness, all oblivion,
And trust, not love, you less.

                                        And now, O sire,
Grant me your son, to nurse, to wait upon
    him,
Like mine own brother.   For my debt to
    him,
This nightmare weight of gratitude, I
    know it ;
Taunt me no more : yourself and yours
    shall have
Free adit ; we will scatter all our maids
Till happier times each to her proper
    hearth :
What use to keep them here—now ?
    grant my prayer.
Help, father, brother, help ; speak to the
    king :
Thaw this male nature to some touch of
    that
Which kills me with myself, and drags
    me down
From my fixt height to mob me up with all
The soft and milky rabble of womankind,
Poor weakling ev'n as they are.'
                            Passionate tears
Follow'd : the king replied not: Cyril
    said :
'Your brother, Lady,—Florian,—ask for
    him
Of your great head—for he is wounded
    too—
That you may tend upon him with the
    prince.'
'Ay so,' said Ida with a bitter smile,
'Our laws are broken : let him enter
    too.'
Then Violet, she that sang the mournful
    song,
And had a cousin tumbled on the plain,
Petition'd too for him.   'Ay so,' she said,
'I stagger in the stream : I cannot keep
My heart an eddy from the brawling
    hour :
We break our laws with ease, but let it
    be.'
'Ay so ?' said Blanche : 'Amazed am I
    to hear
Your Highness : but your Highness
    breaks with ease
The law your Highness did not make :
    'twas I.

T

I had been wedded wife, I knew mankind,
And block'd them out ; but these men
    came to woo
Your Highness—verily I think to win.'

    So she, and turn'd askance a wintry eye:
But Ida with a voice, that like a bell
Toll'd by an earthquake in a trembling
    tower,
Rang ruin, answer'd full of grief and scorn.

'Fling our doors wide ! all, all, not
    one, but all,
Not only he, but by my mother's soul,
Whatever man lies wounded, friend or
    foe,
Shall enter, if he will.   Let our girls flit,
Till the storm die ! but had you stood by
    us,
The roar that breaks the Pharos from his
    base
Had left us rock.   She fain would sting
    us too,
But shall not.   Pass, and mingle with
    your likes.
We brook no further insult but are gone.'

    She turn'd ; the very nape of her white
    neck
Was rosed with indignation : but the
    Prince
Her brother came ; the king her father
    charm'd
Her wounded soul with words : nor did
    mine own
Refuse her proffer, lastly gave his hand.

    Then us they lifted up, dead weights,
    and bare
Straight to the doors : to them the doors
    gave way
Groaning, and in the Vestal entry shriek'd
The virgin marble under iron heels :
And on they moved and gain'd the hall,
    and there
Rested : but great the crush was, and
    each base,
To left and right, of those tall columns
    drown'd
In silken fluctuation and the swarm
Of female whisperers : at the further end

P

Was Ida by the throne, the two great cats
Close by her, like supporters on a shield,
Bow-back'd with fear : but in the centre
　　stood
The common men with rolling eyes ;
　　amazed
They glared upon the women, and aghast
The women stared at these, all silent,
　　save
When armour clash'd or jingled, while
　　the day,
Descending, struck athwart the hall, and
　　shot
A flying splendour out of brass and steel,
That o'er the statues leapt from head to
　　head,
Now fired an angry Pallas on the helm,
Now set a wrathful Dian's moon on flame,
And now and then an echo started up,
And shuddering fled from room to room,
　　and died
Of fright in far apartments.
　　　　　　　　　Then the voice
Of Ida sounded, issuing ordinance :
And me they bore up the broad stairs,
　　and thro'
The long-laid galleries past a hundred
　　doors
To one deep chamber shut from sound,
　　and due
To languid limbs and sickness ; left me
　　in it ;
And others otherwhere they laid ; and all
That afternoon a sound arose of hoof
And chariot, many a maiden passing home
Till happier times ; but some were left of
　　those
Held sagest, and the great lords out and in,
From those two hosts that lay beside the
　　walls,
Walk'd at their will, and everything was
　　changed.

VII.

Ask me no more : the moon may draw the sea ;
　　The cloud may stoop from heaven and take the
　　shape
　　With fold to fold, of mountain or of cape ;
But O too fond, when have I answer'd thee ?
　　　　　　Ask me no more.

Ask me no more : what answer should I give ?
　I love not hollow cheek or faded eye :
　　Yet, O my friend, I will not have thee die !
Ask me no more, lest I should bid thee live ;
　　　　　　Ask me no more.

Ask me no more : thy fate and mine are seal'd :
　I strove against the stream and all in vain :
　　Let the great river take me to the main :
No more, dear love, for at a touch I yield ;
　　　　　　Ask me no more.

So was their sanctuary violated,
So their fair college turn'd to hospital ;
At first with all confusion : by and by
Sweet order lived again with other laws :
A kindlier influence reign'd ; and every-
　　where
Low voices with the ministering hand
Hung round the sick : the maidens came,
　　they talk'd,
They sang, they read : till she not fair
　　began
To gather light, and she that was, became
Her former beauty treble ; and to and fro
With books, with flowers, with Angel
　　offices,
Like creatures native unto gracious act,
And in their own clear element, they
　　moved.

But sadness on the soul of Ida fell,
And hatred of her weakness, blent with
　　shame.
Old studies fail'd ; seldom she spoke :
　　but oft
Clomb to the roofs, and gazed alone for
　　hours
On that disastrous leaguer, swarms of men
Darkening her female field : void was her
　　use,
And she as one that climbs a peak to gaze
O'er land and main, and sees a great
　　black cloud
Drag inward from the deeps, a wall of
　　night,
Blot out the slope of sea from verge to
　　shore,
And suck the blinding splendour from the
　　sand,
And quenching lake by lake and tarn by
　　tarn

Expunge the world : so fared she gazing
   there ;
To blacken'd all her world in secret,
   blank
And waste it seem'd and vain ; till down
   she came,
And found fair peace once more among
   the sick.

And twilight dawn'd ; and morn by
   morn the lark
Shot up and shrill'd in flickering gyres,
   but I
Lay silent in the muffled cage of life :
And twilight gloom'd ; and broader-grown
   the bowers
Drew the great night into themselves,
   and Heaven,
Star after star, arose and fell ; but I,
Deeper than those weird doubts could
   reach me, lay
Quite sunder'd from the moving Universe,
Nor knew what eye was on me, nor the
   hand
That nursed me, more than infants in
   their sleep.

But Psyche tended Florian : with her
   oft,
Melissa came ; for Blanche had gone, but
   left
Her child among us, willing she should
   keep
Court-favour : here and there the small
   bright head,
A light of healing, glanced about the
   couch,
Or thro' the parted silks the tender face
Peep'd, shining in upon the wounded man
With blush and smile, a medicine in
   themselves
To wile the length from languorous hours,
   and draw
The sting from pain ; nor seem'd it strange
   that soon
He rose up whole, and those fair charities
Join'd at her side ; nor stranger seem'd
   that hearts
So gentle, so employ'd, should close in
   love,

Than when two dewdrops on the petal
   shake
To the same sweet air, and tremble deeper
   down,
And slip at once all-fragrant into one.

Less prosperously the second suit ob-
   tain'd
At first with Psyche.   Not tho' Blanche
   had sworn
That after that dark night among the fields
She needs must wed him for her own good
   name ;
Not tho' he built upon the babe restored ;
Nor tho' she liked him, yielded she, but
   fear'd
To incense the Head once more ; till on
   a day
When Cyril pleaded, Ida came behind
Seen but of Psyche : on her foot she hung
A moment, and she heard, at which her
   face
A little flush'd, and she past on ; but each
Assumed from thence a half-consent in-
   volved
In stillness, plighted troth, and were at
   peace.

Nor only these: Love in the sacred halls
Held carnival at will, and flying struck
With showers of random sweet on maid
   and man.
Nor did her father cease to press my claim,
Nor did mine own, now reconciled ; nor yet
Did those twin brothers, risen again and
   whole ;
Nor Arac, satiate with his victory.

But I lay still, and with me oft she sat:
Then came a change ; for sometimes I
   would catch
Her hand in wild delirium, gripe it hard,
And fling it like a viper off, and shriek
' You are not Ida ;' clasp it once again,
And call her Ida, tho' I knew her not,
And call her sweet, as if in irony,
And call her hard and cold which seem'd
   a truth :
And still she fear'd that I should lose my
   mind,

And often she believed that I should die:
Till out of long frustration of her care,
And pensive tendance in the all-weary
　　noons,
And watches in the dead, the dark, when
　　clocks
Throbb'd thunder thro' the palace floors,
　　or call'd
On flying Time from all their silver
　　tongues—
And out of memories of her kindlier days,
And sidelong glances at my father's grief,
And at the happy lovers heart in heart—
And out of hauntings of my spoken love,
And lonely listenings to my mutter'd
　　dream,
And often feeling of the helpless hands,
And wordless broodings on the wasted
　　cheek—
From all a closer interest flourish'd up,
Tenderness touch by touch, and last, to
　　these,
Love, like an Alpine harebell hung with
　　tears
By some cold morning glacier; frail at first
And feeble, all unconscious of itself,
But such as gather'd colour day by day.

Last I woke sane, but well-nigh close
　　to death
For weakness: it was evening: silent light
Slept on the painted walls, wherein were
　　wrought
Two grand designs; for on one side arose
The women up in wild revolt, and storm'd
At the Oppian law. Titanic shapes, they
　　cramm'd
The forum, and half-crush'd among the
　　rest
A dwarf-like Cato cower'd. On the other
　　side
Hortensia spoke against the tax; behind,
A train of dames: by axe and eagle sat,
With all their foreheads drawn in Roman
　　scowls,
And half the wolf's-milk curdled in their
　　veins,
The fierce triumvirs; and before them
　　paused
Hortensia pleading: angry was her face.

I saw the forms: I knew not where
　　was:
They did but look like hollow show
　　nor more
Sweet Ida: palm to palm she sat: the de
Dwelt in her eyes, and softer all her sha
And rounder seem'd: I moved: I sigh'
　　a touch
Came round my wrist, and tears upon m
　　hand
Then all for languor and self-pity ran
Mine down my face, and with what life
　　had,
And like a flower that cannot all unfold
So drench'd it is with tempest, to the su
Yet, as it may, turns toward him, I on h
Fixt my faint eyes, and utter'd whispe
　　ingly:

'If you be, what I think you, som
　　sweet dream,
I would but ask you to fulfil yourself:
But if you be that Ida whom I knew,
I ask you nothing: only, if a dream,
Sweet dream, be perfect. I shall d
　　to-night.
Stoop down and seem to kiss me ere
　　die.'

I could no more, but lay like one
　　trance,
That hears his burial talk'd of by h
　　friends,
And cannot speak, nor move, nor mal
　　one sign,
But lies and dreads his doom. She turn'
　　she paused;
She stoop'd; and out of languor leapt
　　cry;
Leapt fiery Passion from the brinks
　　death;
And I believed that in the living world
My spirit closed with Ida's at the lips;
Till back I fell, and from mine arms sl
　　rose
Glowing all over noble shame; and all
Her falser self slipt from her like a rob
And left her woman, lovelier in her moo
Than in her mould that other, when sl
　　came

From barren deeps to conquer all with
 love ;
And down the streaming crystal dropt ;
 and she
Far-fleeted by the purple island-sides,
Naked, a double light in air and wave,
To meet her Graces, where they deck'd
 her out
For worship without end ; nor end of mine,
Stateliest, for thee ! but mute she glided
 forth,
Nor glanced behind her, and I sank and
 slept,
Fill'd thro' and thro' with Love, a happy
 sleep.

Deep in the night I woke : she, near
 me, held
A volume of the Poets of her land :
There to herself, all in low tones, she
 read.

'Now sleeps the crimson petal, now the white ;
Nor waves the cypress in the palace walk ;
Nor winks the gold fin in the porphyry font :
The fire-fly wakens : waken thou with me.

Now droops the milkwhite peacock like a ghost,
And like a ghost she glimmers on to me.

Now lies the Earth all Danaë to the stars,
And all thy heart lies open unto me.

Now slides the silent meteor on, and leaves
A shining furrow, as thy thoughts in me.

Now folds the lily all her sweetness up,
And slips into the bosom of the lake :
So fold thyself, my dearest, thou, and slip
Into my bosom and be lost in me.'

I heard her turn the page ; she found
 a small
Sweet Idyl, and once more, as low, she
 read :

'Come down, O maid, from yonder mountain
 height :
What pleasure lives in height (the shepherd sang)
In height and cold, the splendour of the hills ?
But cease to move so near the Heavens, and cease
To glide a sunbeam by the blasted Pine,
To sit a star upon the sparkling spire ;
And come, for Love is of the valley, come,
For Love is of the valley, come thou down

And find him ; by the happy threshold, he,
Or hand in hand with Plenty in the maize,
Or red with spirted purple of the vats,
Or foxlike in the vine ; nor cares to walk
With Death and Morning on the silver horns,
Nor wilt thou snare him in the white ravine,
Nor find him dropt upon the firths of ice,
That huddling slant in furrow-cloven falls
To roll the torrent out of dusky doors :
But follow ; let the torrent dance thee down
To find him in the valley ; let the wild
Lean-headed Eagles yelp alone, and leave
The monstrous ledges there to slope, and spill
Their thousand wreaths of dangling water-smoke,
That like a broken purpose waste in air :
So waste not thou ; but come ; for all the vales
Await thee ; azure pillars of the hearth
Arise to thee ; the children call, and I
Thy shepherd pipe, and sweet is every sound,
Sweeter thy voice, but every sound is sweet ;
Myriads of rivulets hurrying thro' the lawn,
The moan of doves in immemorial elms,
And murmuring of innumerable bees.'

So she low-toned ; while with shut
 eyes I lay
Listening ; then look'd. Pale was the
 perfect face ;
The bosom with long sighs labour'd ; and
 meek
Seem'd the full lips, and mild the lumi-
 nous eyes,
And the voice trembled and the hand.
 She said
Brokenly, that she knew it, she had fail'd
In sweet humility ; had fail'd in all ;
That all her labour was but as a block
Left in the quarry ; but she still were loth,
She still were loth to yield herself to one
That wholly scorn'd to help their equal
 rights
Against the sons of men, and barbarous
 laws.
She pray'd me not to judge their cause
 from her
That wrong'd it, sought far less for truth
 than power
In knowledge : something wild within
 her breast,
A greater than all knowledge, beat her
 down.
And she had nursed me there from week
 to week :

Much had she learnt in little time.   In
part
It was ill counsel had misled the girl
To vex true hearts: yet was she but a girl—
'Ah fool, and made myself a Queen of
farce !
When comes another such? never, I think,
Till the Sun drop, dead, from the signs.'
                                Her voice
Choked, and her forehead sank upon her
hands,
And her great heart thro' all the faultful
Past
Went sorrowing in a pause I dared not
break ;
Till notice of a change in the dark world
Was lispt about the acacias, and a bird,
That early woke to feed her little ones,
Sent from a dewy breast a cry for light :
She moved, and at her feet the volume
fell.

'Blame not thyself too much,' I said,
    'nor blame
Too much the sons of men and barbarous
laws ;
These were the rough ways of the world
till now.
Henceforth thou hast a helper, me, that
know
The woman's cause is man's : they rise
or sink
Together, dwarf'd or godlike, bond or
free :
For she that out of Lethe scales with man
The shining steps of Nature, shares with
man
His nights, his days, moves with him to
one goal,
Stays all the fair young planet in her
hands—
If she be small, slight-natured, miserable,
How shall men grow? but work no more
alone !
Our place is much : as far as in us lies
We two will serve them both in aiding
her—
Will clear away the parasitic forms
That seem to keep her up but drag her
down—

Will leave her space to burgeon out of all
Within her—let her make herself her own
To give or keep, to live and learn and be
All that not harms distinctive womanhood.
For woman is not undevelopt man,
But diverse : could we make her as the
man,
Sweet Love were slain : his dearest bond
is this,
Not like to like, but like in difference.
Yet in the long years liker must they grow ;
The man be more of woman, she of man ;
He gain in sweetness and in moral height,
Nor lose the wrestling thews that throw
the world ;
She mental breadth, nor fail in childward
care,
Nor lose the childlike in the larger mind ;
Till at the last she set herself to man,
Like perfect music unto noble words ;
And so these twain, upon the skirts of
Time,
Sit side by side, full-summ'd in all their
powers,
Dispensing harvest, sowing the To-be,
Self-reverent each and reverencing each,
Distinct in individualities,
But like each other ev'n as those who love.
Then comes the statelier Eden back to
men :
Then reign the world's great bridals,
chaste and calm :
Then springs the crowning race of human-
kind.
May these things be !'
                        Sighing she spoke 'I fear
They will not.'
                    'Dear, but let us type them now
In our own lives, and this proud watch-
word rest
Of equal ; seeing either sex alone
Is half itself, and in true marriage lies
Nor equal, nor unequal : each fulfils
Defect in each, and always thought in
thought,
Purpose in purpose, will in will, they grow,
The single pure and perfect animal,
The two-cell'd heart beating, with one
full stroke,
Life.'

And again sighing she spoke : ' A
   dream
That once was mine ! what woman taught
   you this ?'

  ' Alone,' I said, ' from earlier than I
   know,
Immersed in rich foreshadowings of the
   world,
I loved the woman : he, that doth not,
   lives
A drowning life, besotted in sweet self,
Or pines in sad experience worse than
   death,
Or keeps his wing'd affections clipt with
   crime :
Yet was there one thro' whom I loved
   her, one
Not learned, save in gracious household
   ways,
Not perfect, nay, but full of tender wants,
No Angel, but a dearer being, all dipt
In Angel instincts, breathing Paradise,
Interpreter between the Gods and men,
Who look'd all native to her place, and
   yet
On tiptoe seem'd to touch upon a sphere
Too gross to tread, and all male minds
   perforce
Sway'd to her from their orbits as they
   moved,
And girdled her with music. Happy he
With such a mother ! faith in woman-
   kind
Beats with his blood, and trust in all
   things high
Comes easy to him, and tho' he trip and
   fall
He shall not blind his soul with clay.'
                    ' But I,'
Said Ida, tremulously, ' so all unlike—
It seems you love to cheat yourself with
   words :
This mother is your model. I have
   heard
Of your strange doubts : they well might
   be : I seem
A mockery to my own self. Never,
   Prince ;
You cannot love me.'

                 ' Nay but thee ' I said
' From yearlong poring on thy pictured
   eyes,
Ere seen I loved, and loved thee seen,
   and saw
Thee woman thro' the crust of iron moods
That mask'd thee from men's reverence
   up, and forced
Sweet love on pranks of saucy boyhood :
   now,
Giv'n back to life, to life indeed, thro'
   thee,
Indeed I love : the new day comes, the
   light
Dearer for night, as dearer thou for faults
Lived over : lift thine eyes ; my doubts
   are dead,
My haunting sense of hollow shows : the
   change,
This truthful change in thee has kill'd it.
   Dear,
Look up, and let thy nature strike on
   mine,
Like yonder morning on the blind half-
   world ;
Approach and fear not ; breathe upon
   my brows ;
In that fine air I tremble, all the past
Melts mist-like into this bright hour, and
   this
Is morn to more, and all the rich to-come
Reels, as the golden Autumn woodland
   reels
Athwart the smoke of burning weeds.
   Forgive me,
I waste my heart in signs : let be. My
   bride,
My wife, my life. O we will walk this
   world,
Yoked in all exercise of noble end,
And so thro' those dark gates across the
   wild
That no man knows. Indeed I love
   thee : come,
Yield thyself up : my hopes and thine are
   one :
Accomplish thou my manhood and thy-
   self ;
Lay thy sweet hands in mine and trust
   to me.'

CONCLUSION.

So closed our tale, of which I give you all
The random scheme as wildly as it rose :
The words are mostly mine ; for when we ceased
There came a minute's pause, and Walter said,
'I wish she had not yielded !' then to me,
'What, if you drest it up poetically !'
So pray'd the men, the women : I gave assent :
Yet how to bind the scatter'd scheme of seven
Together in one sheaf?   What style could suit ?
The men required that I should give throughout
The sort of mock-heroic gigantesque,
With which we banter'd little Lilia first :
The women—and perhaps they felt their power,
For something in the ballads which they sang,
Or in their silent influence as they sat,
Had ever seem'd to wrestle with burlesque,
And drove us, last, to quite a solemn close—
They hated banter, wish'd for something real,
A gallant fight, a noble princess—why
Not make her true-heroic—true-sublime ?
Or all, they said, as earnest as the close ?
Which yet with such a framework scarce could be.
Then rose a little feud betwixt the two,
Betwixt the mockers and the realists :
And I, betwixt them both, to please them both,
And yet to give the story as it rose,
I moved as in a strange diagonal,
And maybe neither pleased myself nor them.

But Lilia pleased me, for she took no part
In our dispute : the sequel of the tale
Had touch'd her ; and she sat, she pluck'd the grass,

She flung it from her, thinking : last, she fixt
A showery glance upon her aunt, and said,
'You—tell us what we are' who might have told,
For she was cramm'd with theories out of books,
But that there rose a shout : the gates were closed
At sunset, and the crowd were swarming now,
To take their leave, about the garden rails.

So I and some went out to these : we climb'd
The slope to Vivian-place, and turning saw
The happy valleys, half in light, and half
Far-shadowing from the west, a land of peace ;
Gray halls alone among their massive groves ;
Trim hamlets ; here and there a rustic tower
Half-lost in belts of hop and breadths of wheat ;
The shimmering glimpses of a stream ; the seas ;
A red sail, or a white ; and far beyond,
Imagined more than seen, the skirts of France.

'Look there, a garden !' said my college friend,
The Tory member's elder son, 'and there !
God bless the narrow sea which keeps her off,
And keeps our Britain, whole within herself,
A nation yet, the rulers and the ruled—
Some sense of duty, something of a faith,
Some reverence for the laws ourselves have made,
Some patient force to change them when we will,
Some civic manhood firm against the crowd—
But yonder, whiff ! there comes a sudden heat,

The gravest citizen seems to lose his head,
The king is scared, the soldier will not
    fight,
The little boys begin to shoot and stab,
A kingdom topples over with a shriek
Like an old woman, and down rolls the
    world
In mock heroics stranger than our own ;
Revolts, republics, revolutions, most
No graver than a schoolboys' barring
    out ;
Too comic for the solemn things they
    are,
Too solemn for the comic touches in
    them,
Like our wild Princess with as wise a
    dream
As some of theirs—God bless the narrow
    seas !
I wish they were a whole Atlantic broad.'

    'Have patience,' I replied, 'ourselves
    are full
Of social wrong ; and maybe wildest
    dreams
Are but the needful preludes of the truth :
For me, the genial day, the happy crowd,
The sport half-science, fill me with a
    faith,
This fine old world of ours is but a child
Yet in the go-cart. Patience ! Give it
    time
To learn its limbs : there is a hand that
    guides.'

    In such discourse we gain'd the garden
    rails,
And there we saw Sir Walter where he
    stood,
Before a tower of crimson holly-hoaks,
Among six boys, head under head, and
    look'd
No little lily-handed Baronet he,
A great broad-shoulder'd genial English-
    man,
A lord of fat prize-oxen and of sheep,
A raiser of huge melons and of pine,
A patron of some thirty charities,
A pamphleteer on guano and on grain,
A quarter-sessions chairman, abler none ;

Fair-hair'd and redder than a windy
    morn ;
Now shaking hands with him, now him,
    of those
That stood the nearest—now address'd
    to speech—
Who spoke few words and pithy, such as
    closed
Welcome, farewell, and welcome for the
    year
To follow : a shout rose again, and made
The long line of the approaching rookery
    swerve
From the elms, and shook the branches
    of the deer
From slope to slope thro' distant ferns,
    and rang
Beyond the bourn of sunset ; O, a shout
More joyful than the city-roar that hails
Premier or king ! Why should not these
    great Sirs
Give up their parks some dozen times a
    year
To let the people breathe ? So thrice
    they cried,
I likewise, and in groups they stream'd
    away.

    But we went back to the Abbey, and
    sat on,
So much the gathering darkness charm'd :
    we sat
But spoke not, rapt in nameless reverie,
Perchance upon the future man : the
    walls
Blacken'd about us, bats wheel'd, and
    owls whoop'd,
And gradually the powers of the night,
That range above the region of the wind,
Deepening the courts of twilight broke
    them up
Thro' all the silent spaces of the worlds,
Beyond all thought into the Heaven of
    Heavens.

    Last little Lilia, rising quietly,
Disrobed the glimmering statue of Sir
    Ralph
From those rich silks, and home well
    pleased we went.

ODE ON THE DEATH OF THE DUKE OF WELLINGTON.

PUBLISHED IN 1852.

I.

Bury the Great Duke
  With an empire's lamentation,
Let us bury the Great Duke
  To the noise of the mourning of a
      mighty nation,
Mourning when their leaders fall,
Warriors carry the warrior's pall,
And sorrow darkens hamlet and hall.

II.

Whére shall we lay the man whom we
    deplore?
Here, in streaming London's central roar.
Let the sound of those he wrought for,
And the feet of those he fought for,
Echo round his bones for evermore.

III.

Lead out the pageant : sad and slow,
As fits an universal woe,
Let the long long procession go,
And let the sorrowing crowd about it
    grow,
And let the mournful martial music blow;
The last great Englishman is low.

IV.

Mourn, for to us he seems the last,
Remembering all his greatness in the
    Past.
No more in soldier fashion will he greet
With lifted hand the gazer in the street.
O friends, our chief state-oracle is mute :
Mourn for the man of long-enduring blood,
The statesman - warrior, moderate, reso-
    lute,
Whole in himself, a common good.
Mourn for the man of amplest influence,
Yet clearest of ambitious crime,
Our greatest yet with least pretence,
Great in council and great in war,
Foremost captain of his time,
Rich in saving common-sense,

And, as the greatest only are,
In his simplicity sublime.
O good gray head which all men knew,
O voice from which their omens all men
    drew,
O iron nerve to true occasion true,
O fall'n at length that tower of strength
Which stood four-square to all the winds
    that blew !
Such was he whom we deplore.
The long self-sacrifice of life is o'er.
The great World-victor's victor will be
    seen no more.

V.

All is over and done :
Render thanks to the Giver,
England, for thy son.
Let the bell be toll'd.
Render thanks to the Giver,
And render him to the mould.
Under the cross of gold
That shines over city and river,
There he shall rest for ever
Among the wise and the bold.
Let the bell be toll'd :
And a reverent people behold
The towering car, the sable steeds :
Bright let it be with its blazon'd deeds,
Dark in its funeral fold.
Let the bell be toll'd :
And a deeper knell in the heart be
    knoll'd ;
And the sound of the sorrowing anthem
    roll'd
Thro' the dome of the golden cross ;
And the volleying cannon thunder his
    loss ;
He knew their voices of old.
For many a time in many a clime
His captain's-ear has heard them boom
Bellowing victory, bellowing doom :
When he with those deep voices wrought,
Guarding realms and kings from shame
With those deep voices our dead captain
    taught
The tyrant, and asserts his claim
In that dread sound to the great name,
Which he has worn so pure of blame,
In praise and in dispraise the same,

A man of well-attemper'd frame.
O civic muse, to such a name,
To such a name for ages long,
To such a name,
Preserve a broad approach of fame,
And ever-echoing avenues of song.

VI.

Who is he that cometh, like an honour'd
    guest,
With banner and with music, with soldier
    and with priest,
With a nation weeping, and breaking on
    my rest?
Mighty Seaman, this is he
Was great by land as thou by sea.
Thine island loves thee well, thou famous
    man,
The greatest sailor since our world began.
Now, to the roll of muffled drums,
To thee the greatest soldier comes;
For this is he
Was great by land as thou by sea;
His foes were thine; he kept us free;
O give him welcome, this is he
Worthy of our gorgeous rites,
And worthy to be laid by thee;
For this is England's greatest son,
He that gain'd a hundred fights,
Nor ever lost an English gun;
This is he that far away
Against the myriads of Assaye
Clash'd with his fiery few and won;
And underneath another sun,
Warring on a later day,
Round affrighted Lisbon drew
The treble works, the vast designs
Of his labour'd rampart-lines,
Where he greatly stood at bay,
Whence he issued forth anew,
And ever great and greater grew,
Beating from the wasted vines
Back to France her banded swarms,
Back to France with countless blows,
Till o'er the hills her eagles flew
Beyond the Pyrenean pines,
Follow'd up in valley and glen
With blare of bugle, clamour of men,
Roll of cannon and clash of arms,
And England pouring on her foes.

Such a war had such a close.
Again their ravening eagle rose
In anger, wheel'd on Europe-shadowing
    wings,
And barking for the thrones of kings;
Till one that sought but Duty's iron crown
On that loud sabbath shook the spoiler
    down;
A day of onsets of despair!
Dash'd on every rocky square
Their surging charges foam'd themselves
    away;
Last, the Prussian trumpet blew;
Thro' the long-tormented air
Heaven flash'd a sudden jubilant ray,
And down we swept and charged and
    overthrew.
So great a soldier taught us there,
What long-enduring hearts could do
In that world-earthquake, Waterloo!
Mighty Seaman, tender and true,
And pure as he from taint of craven guile,
O saviour of the silver-coasted isle,
O shaker of the Baltic and the Nile,
If aught of things that here befall
Touch a spirit among things divine,
If love of country move thee there at all,
Be glad, because his bones are laid by
    thine!
And thro' the centuries let a people's voice
In full acclaim,
A people's voice,
The proof and echo of all human fame,
A people's voice, when they rejoice
At civic revel and pomp and game,
Attest their great commander's claim
With honour, honour, honour, honour to
    him,
Eternal honour to his name.

VII.

A people's voice! we are a people yet.
Tho' all men else their nobler dreams
    forget,
Confused by brainless mobs and lawless
    Powers;
Thank Him who isled us here, and roughly
    set
His Briton in blown seas and storming
    showers,

We have a voice, with which to pay the debt
Of boundless love and reverence and regret
To those great men who fought, and kept it ours.
And keep it ours, O God, from brute control ;
O Statesmen, guard us, guard the eye, the soul
Of Europe, keep our noble England whole,
And save the one true seed of freedom sown
Betwixt a people and their ancient throne,
That sober freedom out of which there springs
Our loyal passion for our temperate kings ;
For, saving that, ye help to save mankind
Till public wrong be crumbled into dust,
And drill the raw world for the march of mind,
Till crowds at length be sane and crowns be just.
But wink no more in slothful overtrust.
Remember him who led your hosts ;
He bad you guard the sacred coasts.
Your cannons moulder on the seaward wall ;
His voice is silent in your council-hall
For ever ; and whatever tempests lour
For ever silent ; even if they broke
In thunder, silent ; yet remember all
He spoke among you, and the Man who spoke ;
Who never sold the truth to serve the hour,
Nor palter'd with Eternal God for power ;
Who let the turbid streams of rumour flow
Thro' either babbling world of high and low ;
Whose life was work, whose language rife
With rugged maxims hewn from life ;
Who never spoke against a foe ;
Whose eighty winters freeze with one rebuke
All great self-seekers trampling on the right :
Truth-teller was our England's Alfred named ;

Truth-lover was our English Duke ;
Whatever record leap to light
He never shall be shamed.

VIII.

Lo, the leader in these glorious wars
Now to glorious burial slowly borne,
Follow'd by the brave of other lands,
He, on whom from both her open hands
Lavish Honour shower'd all her stars,
And affluent Fortune emptied all her horn.
Yea, let all good things await
Him who cares not to be great,
But as he saves or serves the state.
Not once or twice in our rough island story,
The path of duty was the way to glory :
He that walks it, only thirsting
For the right, and learns to deaden
Love of self, before his journey closes,
He shall find the stubborn thistle bursting
Into glossy purples, which outredden
All voluptuous garden-roses.
Not once or twice in our fair island-story,
The path of duty was the way to glory :
He, that ever following her commands,
On with toil of heart and knees and hands,
Thro' the long gorge to the far light has won
His path upward, and prevail'd,
Shall find the toppling crags of Duty scaled
Are close upon the shining table-lands
To which our God Himself is moon and sun.
Such was he : his work is done.
But while the races of mankind endure,
Let his great example stand
Colossal, seen of every land,
And keep the soldier firm, the statesman pure :
Till in all lands and thro' all human story
The path of duty be the way to glory :
And let the land whose hearths he saved from shame
For many and many an age proclaim
At civic revel and pomp and game,
And when the long-illumined cities flame,
Their ever-loyal iron leader's fame,

With honour, honour, honour, honour to
    him,
Eternal honour to his name.

IX.

Peace, his triumph will be sung
By some yet unmoulded tongue
Far on in summers that we shall not see :
Peace, it is a day of pain
For one about whose patriarchal knee
Late the little children clung :
O peace, it is a day of pain
For one, upon whose hand and heart and
    brain
Once the weight and fate of Europe hung.
Ours the pain, be his the gain !
More than is of man's degree
Must be with us, watching here
At this, our great solemnity.
Whom we see not we revere ;
We revere, and we refrain
From talk of battles loud and vain,
And brawling memories all too free
For such a wise humility
As befits a solemn fane :
We revere, and while we hear
The tides of Music's golden sea
Setting toward eternity,
Uplifted high in heart and hope are we,
Until we doubt not that for one so true
There must be other nobler work to do
Than when he fought at Waterloo,
And Victor he must ever be.
For tho' the Giant Ages heave the hill
And break the shore, and evermore
Make and break, and work their will ;
Tho' world on world in myriad myriads
    roll
Round us, each with different powers,
And other forms of life than ours,
What know we greater than the soul ?
On God and Godlike men we build our
    trust.
Hush, the Dead March wails in the
    people's ears :
The dark crowd moves, and there are sobs
    and tears :
The black earth yawns : the mortal
    disappears ;
Ashes to ashes, dust to dust ;

He is gone who seem'd so great.—
Gone ; but nothing can bereave him
Of the force he made his own
Being here, and we believe him
Something far advanced in State,
And that he wears a truer crown
Than any wreath that man can weave him.
Speak no more of his renown,
Lay your earthly fancies down,
And in the vast cathedral leave him,
God accept him, Christ receive him.

    1852.

THE THIRD OF FEBRUARY,
1852.

My Lords, we heard you speak : you told
    us all
    That England's honest censure went
        too far ;
That our free press should cease to brawl,
    Not sting the fiery Frenchman into
        war.
It was our ancient privilege, my Lords,
To fling whate'er we felt, not fearing, into
    words.

We love not this French God, the child
    of Hell,
    Wild War, who breaks the converse of
        the wise ;
But though we love kind Peace so well,
    We dare not ev'n by silence sanction
        lies.
It might be safe our censures to withdraw ;
And yet, my Lords, not well : there is a
    higher law.

As long as we remain, we must speak free,
    Tho' all the storm of Europe on us
        break ;
No little German state are we,
    But the one voice in Europe : we *must*
        speak ;
That if to-night our greatness were struck
    dead,
There might be left some record of the
    things we said.

| see p 568

4 If you be fearful, then must we be bold.
    Our Britain cannot salve a tyrant o'er.
Better the waste Atlantic roll'd
    On her and us and ours for evermore.
What ! have we fought for Freedom from
      our prime,
At last to dodge and palter with a public
      crime ?

5 Shall we fear *him ?* our own we never
      fear'd.
    From our first Charles by force we
      wrung our claims.
Prick'd by the Papal spur, we rear'd,
    We flung the burthen of the second
      James.
I say, we *never* feared ! and as for these,
We broke them on the land, we drove
      them on the seas.

6 And you, my Lords, you make the people
      muse
    In doubt if you be of our Barons' breed—
Were those your sires who fought at
      Lewes ?
Is this the manly strain of Runnymede ?
O fall'n nobility, that, overawed,
Would lisp in honey'd whispers of this
      monstrous fraud !

7 *We* feel, at least, that silence here were sin,
    Not ours the fault if we have feeble
      hosts—
If easy patrons of their kin
    Have left the last free race with naked
      coasts !
They knew the precious things they had
      to guard :
For us, we will not spare the tyrant one
      hard word.

8 Tho' niggard throats of Manchester may
      bawl,
    What England was, shall her true sons
      forget ?
We are not cotton-spinners all,
    But some love England and her honour
      yet.
And these in our Thermopylæ shall stand,
And hold against the world this honour
      of the land.

THE CHARGE OF THE LIGHT BRIGADE. (25 æ 1854

I.

HALF a league, half a league,
    Half a league onward,
All in the valley of Death
    Rode the six hundred.
'Forward, the Light Brigade !
Charge for the guns !' he said :
Into the valley of Death
    Rode the six hundred.

II.

'Forward, the Light Brigade !'
Was there a man dismay'd ?
Not tho' the soldier knew
    Some one had blunder'd :
Their's not to make reply,
Their's not to reason why,
Their's but to do and die :
Into the valley of Death
    Rode the six hundred.

III.

Cannon to right of them,
Cannon to left of them,
Cannon in front of them
    Volley'd and thunder'd ;
Storm'd at with shot and shell
Boldly they rode and well,
Into the jaws of Death,
Into the mouth of Hell
    Rode the six hundred.

IV.

Flash'd all their sabres bare,
Flash'd as they turn'd in air
Sabring the gunners there,
Charging an army, while
    All the world wonder'd :
Plunged in the battery-smoke
Right thro' the line they broke ;
Cossack and Russian
Reel'd from the sabre-stroke
    Shatter'd and sunder'd.
Then they rode back, but not
    Not the six hundred.

v.

Cannon to right of them,
Cannon to left of them,
Cannon behind them
  Volley'd and thunder'd ;
Storm'd at with shot and shell,
While horse and hero fell,
They that had fought so well
Came thro' the jaws of Death,
Back from the mouth of Hell,
All that was left of them,
  Left of six hundred.

vi.

When can their glory fade ?
O the wild charge they made !
  All the world wonder'd.
Honour the charge they made !
Honour the Light Brigade,
  Noble six hundred !

ODE SUNG AT THE OPENING OF THE INTERNATIONAL EXHIBITION.

i.

UPLIFT a thousand voices full and sweet,
  In this wide hall with earth's invention
    stored,
  And praise the invisible universal Lord,
Who lets once more in peace the nations
    meet,
  Where Science, Art, and Labour have
    outpour'd
Their myriad horns of plenty at our feet.

ii.

O silent father of our Kings to be
Mourn'd in this golden hour of jubilee,
For this, for all, we weep our thanks to
    thee !

iii.

The world-compelling plan was thine,—
And, lo ! the long laborious miles
Of Palace ; lo ! the giant aisles,
Rich in model and design ;
Harvest-tool and husbandry,
Loom and wheel and enginery,

Secrets of the sullen mine,
Steel and gold, and corn and wine,
Fabric rough, or fairy-fine,
Sunny tokens of the Line,
Polar marvels, and a feast
Of wonder, out of West and East,
And shapes and hues of Art divine !
All of beauty, all of use,
That one fair planet can produce,
  Brought from under every star,
Blown from over every main,
And mixt, as life is mixt with pain,
  The works of peace with works of war.

iv.

Is the goal so far away ?
Far, how far no tongue can say,
Let us dream our dream to-day.

v.

O ye, the wise who think, the wise who
    reign,
From growing commerce loose her latest
    chain,
And let the fair white-wing'd peacemaker
    fly
To happy havens under all the sky,
And mix the seasons and the golden
    hours ;
Till each man find his own in all men's
    good,
And all men work in noble brotherhood,
Breaking their mailed fleets and armed
    towers,
And ruling by obeying Nature's powers,
And gathering all the fruits of earth and
    crown'd with all her flowers.

A WELCOME TO ALEXANDRA.

MARCH 7, 1863.

SEA-KINGS' daughter from over the sea,
                    Alexandra !
Saxon and Norman and Dane are we,
But all of us Danes in our welcome of
    thee,   Alexandra !
Welcome her, thunders of fort and of fleet !
Welcome her, thundering cheer of the
    street !

Welcome her, all things youthful and
   sweet,
Scatter the blossom under her feet !
Break, happy land, into earlier flowers !
Make music, O bird, in the new-budded
   bowers !
Blazon your mottoes of blessing and
   prayer´!
Welcome her, welcome her, all that is ours!
Warble, O bugle, and trumpet, blare !
Flags, flutter out upon turrets and towers !
Flames, on the windy headland flare !
Utter your jubilee, steeple and spire !
Clash, ye bells, in the merry March air !
Flash, ye cities, in rivers of fire !
Rush to the roof, sudden rocket, and
   higher
Melt into stars for the land's desire !
Roll and rejoice, jubilant voice,
Roll as a ground-swell dash'd on the
   strand,
Roar as the sea when he welcomes the
   land,
And welcome her, welcome the land's
   desire,
The sea-kings' daughter as happy as fair,
Blissful bride of a blissful heir,
Bride of the heir of the kings of the sea—
O joy to the people and joy to the
   throne,
Come to us, love us and make us your
   own :
For Saxon or Dane or Norman we,
Teuton or Celt, or whatever we be,
We are each all Dane in our welcome of
   thee,   Alexandra !

A WELCOME TO HER ROYAL HIGHNESS MARIE ALEXANDROVNA, DUCHESS OF EDINBURGH.

MARCH 7, 1874.

I.

THE Son of him with whom we strove
   for power—
   Whose will is lord thro' all his world-
     domain—

Who made the serf a man, and burst
   his chain—
Has given our Prince his own imperial
   Flower,
         Alexandrovna.
And welcome Russian flower, a people's
   pride,
   To Britain, when her flowers begin to
    blow !
   From love to love, from home to home
    you go,
From mother unto mother, stately bride,
       Marie Alexandrovna !

II.

The golden news along the steppes is
   blown,
   And at thy name the Tartar tents are
    stirr'd ;
   Elburz and all the Caucasus have
    heard ;
And all the sultry palms of India known,
       Alexandrovna.
The voices of our universal sea
   On capes of Afric as on cliffs of Kent,
   The Maoris and that Isle of Continent,
And loyal pines of Canada murmur
   thee,
       Marie Alexandrovna

III.

Fair empires branching, both, in lusty
   life !—
   Yet Harold's England fell to Norman
    swords ;
   Yet thine own land has bow'd to
    Tartar hordes
Since English Harold gave its throne a
   wife,
       Alexandrovna !
For thrones and peoples are as waifs that
   swing,
   And float or fall, in endless ebb and
    flow ;
   But who love best have best the grace
    to know
That Love by right divine is deathless
   king,
       Marie Alexandrovna !

IV.

And Love has led thee to the stranger
    land,
  Where men are bold and strongly say
    their say ;—
  See, empire upon empire smiles to-
    day,
As thou with thy young lover hand in
    hand
            Alexandrovna !
So now thy fuller life is in the west,
  Whose hand at home was gracious to
    thy poor :
  Thy name was blest within the narrow
    door ;
Here also, Marie, shall thy name be blest,
            Marie Alexandrovna !

V.

Shall fears and jealous hatreds flame again?
    Or at thy coming, Princess, every-
      where,
    The blue heaven break, and some
      diviner air
Breathe thro' the world and change the
      hearts of men,
            Alexandrovna ?
But hearts that change not, love that
      cannot cease,
  And peace be yours, the peace of soul
    in soul !
  And howsoever this wild world may roll,
Between your peoples truth and manful
    peace,
            Alfred—Alexandrovna !

THE GRANDMOTHER.

I.

And Willy, my eldest-born, is gone, you say, little Anne ?
Ruddy and white, and strong on his legs, he looks like a man.
And Willy's wife has written : she never was over-wise,
Never the wife for Willy : he wouldn't take my advice.

II.

For, Annie, you see, her father was not the man to save,
Hadn't a head to manage, and drank himself into his grave.
Pretty enough, very pretty ! but I was against it for one.
Eh !—but he wouldn't hear me—and Willy, you say, is gone.

III.

Willy, my beauty, my eldest-born, the flower of the flock ;
Never a man could fling him : for Willy stood like a rock.
' Here's a leg for a babe of a week !' says doctor ; and he would be bound,
There was not his like that year in twenty parishes round.

IV.

Strong of his hands, and strong on his legs, but still of his tongue !
I ought to have gone before him : I wonder he went so young.
I cannot cry for him, Annie : I have not long to stay ;
Perhaps I shall see him the sooner, for he lived far away.

V.

Why do you look at me, Annie ? you think I am hard and cold ;
But all my children have gone before me, I am so old :
I cannot weep for Willy, nor can I weep for the rest ;
Only at your age, Annie, I could have wept with the best.

VI.

For I remember a quarrel I had with your father, my dear,
All for a slanderous story, that cost me many a tear.
I mean your grandfather, Annie : it cost me a world of woe,
Seventy years ago, my darling, seventy years ago.

VII.

For Jenny, my cousin, had come to the place, and I knew right well
That Jenny had tript in her time : I knew, but I would not tell.
And she to be coming and slandering me, the base little liar !
But the tongue is a fire as you know, my dear, the tongue is a fire.

VIII.

And the parson made it his text that week, and he said likewise,
That a lie which is half a truth is ever the blackest of lies,
That a lie which is all a lie may be met and fought with outright,
But a lie which is part a truth is a harder matter to fight.

IX.

And Willy had not been down to the farm for a week and a day ;
And all things look'd half-dead, tho' it was the middle of May.
Jenny, to slander me, who knew what Jenny had been !
But soiling another, Annie, will never make oneself clean.

X.

And I cried myself well-nigh blind, and all of an evening late
I climb'd to the top of the garth, and stood by the road at the gate.
The moon like a rick on fire was rising over the dale,
And whit, whit, whit, in the bush beside me chirrupt the nightingale.

XI.

All of a sudden he stopt : there past by the gate of the farm,
Willy,—he didn't see me,—and Jenny hung on his arm.
Out into the road I started, and spoke I scarce knew how ;
Ah, there's no fool like the old one—it makes me angry now.

XII.

Willy stood up like a man, and look'd the thing that he meant ;
Jenny, the viper, made me a mocking curtsey and went.
And I said, ' Let us part : in a hundred years it'll all be the same,
You cannot love me at all, if you love not my good name.'

XIII.

And he turn'd, and I saw his eyes all wet, in the sweet moonshine :
' Sweetheart, I love you so well that your good name is mine.
And what do I care for Jane, let her speak of you well or ill ;
But marry me out of hand : we two shall be happy still.'

XIV.

'Marry you, Willy!' said I, 'but I needs must speak my mind,
And I fear you'll listen to tales, be jealous and hard and unkind.'
But he turn'd and claspt me in his arms, and answer'd, 'No, love, no ;'
Seventy years ago, my darling, seventy years ago.

XV.

So Willy and I were wedded : I wore a lilac gown ;
And the ringers rang with a will, and he gave the ringers a crown.
But the first that ever I bare was dead before he was born,
Shadow and shine is life, little Annie, flower and thorn.

XVI.

That was the first time, too, that ever I thought of death.
There lay the sweet little body that never had drawn a breath.
I had not wept, little Anne, not since I had been a wife ;
But I wept like a child that day, for the babe had fought for his life.

XVII.

His dear little face was troubled, as if with anger or pain :
I look'd at the still little body—his trouble had all been in vain.
For Willy I cannot weep, I shall see him another morn :
But I wept like a child for the child that was dead before he was born.

XVIII.

But he cheer'd me, my good man, for he seldom said me nay :
Kind, like a man, was he ; like a man, too, would have his way :
Never jealous—not he : we had many a happy year ;
And he died, and I could not weep—my own time seem'd so near.

XIX.

But I wish'd it had been God's will that I, too, then could have died :
I began to be tired a little, and fain had slept at his side.
And that was ten years back, or more, if I don't forget :
But as to the children, Annie, they're all about me yet.

XX.

Pattering over the boards, my Annie who left me at two,
Patter she goes, my own little Annie, an Annie like you :
Pattering over the boards, she comes and goes at her will,
While Harry is in the five-acre and Charlie ploughing the hill.

XXI.

And Harry and Charlie, I hear them too—they sing to their team :
Often they come to the door in a pleasant kind of a dream.
They come and sit by my chair, they hover about my bed—
I am not always certain if they be alive or dead.

XXII.

And yet I know for a truth, there's none of them left alive ;
For Harry went at sixty, your father at sixty-five :
And Willy, my eldest-born, at nigh threescore and ten ;
I knew them all as babies, and now they're elderly men.

XXIII.

For mine is a time of peace, it is not often I grieve ;
I am oftener sitting at home in my father's farm at eve :
And the neighbours come and laugh and gossip, and so do I ;
I find myself often laughing at things that have long gone by.

XXIV.

To be sure the preacher says, our sins should make us sad :
But mine is a time of peace, and there is Grace to be had ;
And God, not man, is the Judge of us all when life shall cease ;
And in this Book, little Annie, the message is one of Peace.

XXV.

And age is a time of peace, so it be free from pain,
And happy has been my life ; but I would not live it again.
I seem to be tired a little, that's all, and long for rest ;
Only at your age, Annie, I could have wept with the best.

XXVI.

So Willy has gone, my beauty, my eldest-born, my flower ;
But how can I weep for Willy, he has but gone for an hour,—
Gone for a minute, my son, from this room into the next ;
I, too, shall go in a minute.   What time have I to be vext ?

XXVII.

And Willy's wife has written, she never was over-wise.
Get me my glasses, Annie : thank God that I keep my eyes.
There is but a trifle left you, when I shall have past away.
But stay with the old woman now : you cannot have long to stay.

NORTHERN FARMER.

OLD STYLE.

I.

Wheer 'asta beän saw long and meä liggin' 'ere aloän ?
Noorse ? thourt nowt o' a noorse : whoy, Doctor's abeän an' agoän :
Says that I moänt 'a naw moor aäle : but I beänt a fool :
Git ma my aäle, fur I beänt a-gawin' to breäk my rule.

II.

Doctors, they knaws nowt, fur a says what's nawways true :
Naw soort o' koind o' use to saäy the things that a do.
I've 'ed my point o' aäle ivry noight sin' I beän 'ere.
An' I've 'ed my quart ivry market-noight for foorty year.

III.

Parson's a beän loikewoise, an' a sittin' 'ere o' my bed.
' The amoighty's a taäkin o' you [1] to 'issén, my friend,' a said,
An' a towd ma my sins, an's toithe were due, an' I gied it in hond ;
I done moy duty boy 'um, as I 'a done boy the lond.

IV.

Larn'd a ma' beä.   I reckons I 'annot sa mooch to larn.
But a cast oop, thot a did, 'bout Bessy Marris's barne.
Thaw a knaws I hallus voäted wi' Squoire an' choorch an' staäte,
An' i' the woost o' toimes I wur niver agin the raäte.

V.

An' I hallus coom'd to 's chooch afoor moy Sally wur deäd,
An' 'eärd 'um a bummin' awaäy loike a buzzard-clock [2] ower my 'eäd,
An' I niver knaw'd whot a meän'd but I thowt a 'ad summut to saäy,
An' I thowt a said whot a owt to 'a said an' I coom'd awaäy.

VI.

Bessy Marris's barne ! tha knaws she laäid it to meä.
Mowt a beän, mayhap, for she wur a bad un, sheä.
'Siver, I kep 'um, I kep 'um, my lass, tha mun understond ;
I done moy duty boy 'um as I 'a done boy the lond.

VII.

But Parson a cooms an' a goäs, an' a says it eäsy an' freeä
' The amoighty's a taäkin o' you to 'issén, my friend,' says 'eä.
I weänt saäy men be loiars, thaw summun said it in 'aäste :
But 'e reäds wonn sarmin a weeäk, an' I 'a stubb'd Thurnaby waäste.

VIII.

D'ya moind the waäste, my lass ? naw, naw, tha was not born then ;
Theer wur a boggle in it, I often 'eärd 'um mysen ;
Moäst loike a butter-bump, [3] fur I 'eärd 'um about an' about,
But I stubb'd 'um oop wi' the lot, an' raäved an' rembled 'um out.

IX.

Keäper's it wur ; fo' they fun 'um theer a-laäid of 'is faäce
Down i' the woild 'enemies [4] afoor I coom'd to the plaäce.
Noäks or Thimbleby—toäner [5] 'ed shot 'um as deäd as a naäil.
Noäks wur 'ang'd for it oop at 'soize—but git ma my aäle.

[1] ou as in hour.   [2] Cockchafer.   [3] Bittern.   [4] Anemones.   [5] One or other.

X.

Dubbut looök at the waäste : theer warn't not feeäd for a cow;
Nowt at all but bracken an' fuzz, an' looök at it now—
Warnt worth nowt a haäcre, an' now theer's lots o' feeäd,
Fourscoor [1] yows upon it an' some on it down i' seeäd. [2]

XI.

Nobbut a bit on it's left, an' I meän'd to 'a stubb'd it at fall,
Done it ta-year I meän'd, an' runn'd plow thruff it an' all,
If godamoighty an' parson 'ud nobbut let ma aloän,
Meä, wi' haäte hoonderd haäcre o' Squoire's, an' lond o' my oän.

XII.

Do godamoighty knaw what a's doing a-taäkin' o' meä?
I beänt wonn as saws 'ere a beän an' yonder a peä;
An' Squoire 'ull be sa mad an' all—a' dear a' dear !
And I 'a managed for Squoire coom Michaelmas thutty year.

XIII.

A mowt 'a taäen owd Joänes, as 'ant not a 'aäpoth o' sense,
Or a mowt 'a taäen young Robins—a niver mended a fence :
But godamoighty a moost taäke meä an' taäke ma now
Wi' aäf the cows to cauve an' Thurnaby hoälms to plow !

XIV.

Loook 'ow quoloty smoiles when they seeäs ma a passin' boy,
Says to thessén naw doubt 'what a man a beä sewer-loy !'
Fur they knaws what I beän to Squoire sin fust a coom'd to the 'All ;
I done moy duty by Squoire an' I done moy duty boy hall.

XV.

Squoire's i' Lunnon, an' summun I reckons 'ull 'a to wroite,
For whoä's to howd the lond ater meä thot muddles ma quoit ;
Sartin-sewer I beä, thot a weänt niver give it to Joänes,
Naw, nor a moänt to Robins—a niver rembles the stoäns.

XVI.

But summun 'ull come ater meä mayhap wi' 'is kittle o' steäm
Huzzin' an' maäzin' the blessed feälds wi' the Divil's oän teäm.
Sin' I mun doy I mun doy, thaw loife they says is sweet,
But sin' I mun doy I mun doy, for I couldn abeär to see it.

XVII.

What atta stannin' theer fur, an' doesn bring ma the aäle ?
Doctor's a 'toättler, lass, an a's hallus i' the owd taäle ;
I weänt breäk rules fur Doctor, a knaws naw moor nor a floy ;
Git ma my aäle I tell tha, an' if I mun doy I mun doy.

[1] ou as in hour.   [2] Clover.

NORTHERN FARMER.

NEW STYLE.

I.

Dosn't thou 'ear my 'erse's legs, as they canters awaäy?
Proputty, proputty, proputty—that's what I 'ears 'em saäy.
Proputty, proputty, proputty—Sam, thou's an ass for thy paaïns :
Theer's moor sense i' one o' 'is legs nor in all thy braaïns.

II.

Woä—theer's a craw to pluck wi' tha, Sam : yon's parson's 'ouse—
Dosn't thou knaw that a man mun be eäther a man or a mouse?
Time to think on it then ; for thou'll be twenty to weeäk.[1]
Proputty, proputty—woä then woä—let ma 'ear mysén speäk.

III.

Me an' thy muther, Sammy, 'as beän a-talkin' o' thee ;
Thou's beän talkin' to muther, an' she beän a tellin' it me.
Thou'll not marry for munny—thou's sweet upo' parson's lass—
Noä—thou'll marry for luvv—an' we boäth on us thinks tha an ass.

IV.

Seeä'd her todaäy goä by—Saäint's-daäy—they was ringing the bells.
She's a beauty thou thinks—an' soä is scoors o' gells,
Them as 'as munny an' all—wot's a beauty?—the flower as blaws.
But proputty, proputty sticks, an' proputty, proputty graws.

V.

Do'ant be stunt :[2] taäke time : I knaws what maäkes tha sa mad.
Warn't I craäzed fur the lasses mysén when I wur a lad?
But I knaw'd a Quaäker feller as often 'as towd ma this :
' Doänt thou marry for munny, but goä wheer munny is !'

VI.

An' I went wheer munny war : an' thy muther coom to 'and,
Wi' lots o' munny laaïd by, an' a nicetish bit o' land.
Maäybe she warn't a beauty :—I niver giv it a thowt—
But warn't she as good to cuddle an' kiss as a lass as 'ant nowt?

VII.

Parson's lass 'ant nowt, an' she weänt 'a nowt when 'e's deäd,
Mun be a guvness, lad, or summut, and addle[3] her breäd :
Why? fur 'e's nobbut a curate, an' weänt niver git hissen clear,
An' 'e maäde the bed as 'e ligs on afoor 'e coom'd to the shere.

---

[1] This week.   [2] Obstinate.   [3] Earn.

VIII.

An' thin 'e coom'd to the parish wi' lots o' Varsity debt,
Stook to his taaïl they did, an' 'e 'ant got shut on 'em yet.
An' 'e ligs on 'is back i' the grip, wi' noän to lend 'im a shuvv,
Woorse nor a far-welter'd [1] yowe : fur, Sammy, 'e married fur luvv.

IX.

Luvv ? what's luvv ? thou can luvv thy lass an' 'er munny too,
Maakin' 'em goä togither as they've good right to do.
Could'n I luvv thy muther by cause o' 'er munny laaïd by ?
Naäy—fur I luvv'd 'er a vast sight moor fur it : reäson why.

X.

Ay an' thy muther says thou wants to marry the lass,
Cooms of a gentleman burn : an' we boäth on us thinks tha an **ass**
Woä then, proputty, wiltha ?—an ass as near as mays nowt [2]—
Woä then, wiltha ? dangtha !—the bees is as fell as owt. [3]

XI.

Breäk me a bit o' the esh for his 'eäd, lad, out o' the fence !
Gentleman burn ! what's gentleman burn ? is it shillins an' pence ?
Proputty, proputty's ivrything 'ere, an', Sammy, I'm blest
If it isn't the saäme oop yonder, fur them as 'as it's the best.

XII.

Tis'n them as 'as munny as breäks into 'ouses an' steäls,
Them as 'as coäts to their backs an' taäkes their regular meäls.
Noä, but it's them as niver knaws wheer a meäl's to be 'ad.
Taäke my word for it, Sammy, the poor in a loomp is bad.

XIII.

Them or thir feythers, tha sees, mun 'a beän a laäzy lot,
Fur work mun 'a gone to the gittin' whiniver munny was got.
Feyther 'ad ammost nowt ; leästways 'is munny was 'id.
But 'e tued an' moil'd 'issén deäd, an 'e died a good un, 'e did.

XIV.

Loook thou theer wheer Wrigglesby beck cooms out by the 'ill !
Feyther run oop to the farm, an' I runs oop to the mill ;
An' I'll run oop to the brig, an' that thou'll live to see ;
And if thou marries a good un I'll leäve the land to thee.

XV.

Thim's my noätions, Sammy, wheerby I means to stick ;
But if thou marries a bad un, I'll leäve the land to Dick.—
Coom oop, proputty, proputty—that's what I 'ears 'im saäy—
Proputty, proputty, proputty—canter an' canter awaäy.

---

[1] Or fow-welter'd,—said of a sheep lying on its back.
[2] Makes nothing.   [3] The flies are as fierce as anything.

THE DAISY.

WRITTEN AT EDINBURGH.

O LOVE, what hours were thine and mine,
In lands of palm and southern pine;
  In lands of palm, of orange-blossom,
Of olive, aloe, and maize and vine.

What Roman strength Turbia show'd
In ruin, by the mountain road;
  How like a gem, beneath, the city
Of little Monaco, basking, glow'd.

How richly down the rocky dell
The torrent vineyard streaming fell
  To meet the sun and sunny waters,
That only heaved with a summer swell.

What slender campanili grew
By bays, the peacock's neck in hue;
  Where, here and there, on sandy
    beaches
A milky-bell'd amaryllis blew.

How young Columbus seem'd to rove,
Yet present in his natal grove,
  Now watching high on mountain cor-
    nice,
And steering, now, from a purple cove,

Now pacing mute by ocean's rim;
Till, in a narrow street and dim,
  I stay'd the wheels at Cogoletto,
And drank, and loyally drank to him.

Nor knew we well what pleased us most,
Not the clipt palm of which they boast;
  But distant colour, happy hamlet,
A moulder'd citadel on the coast,

Or tower, or high hill-convent, seen
A light amid its olives green;
  Or olive-hoary cape in ocean;
Or rosy blossom in hot ravine,

Where oleanders flush'd the bed
Of silent torrents, gravel-spread;
  And, crossing, oft we saw the glisten
Of ice, far up on a mountain head.

We loved that hall, tho' white and cold,
Those niched shapes of noble mould,
  A princely people's awful princes,
The grave, severe Genovese of old.

At Florence too what golden hours,
In those long galleries, were ours;
  What drives about the fresh Cascinè,
Or walks in Boboli's ducal bowers.

In bright vignettes, and each complete,
Of tower or duomo, sunny-sweet,
  Or palace, how the city glitter'd,
Thro' cypress avenues, at our feet.

But when we crost the Lombard plain
Remember what a plague of rain;
  Of rain at Reggio, rain at Parma;
At Lodi, rain, Piacenza, rain.

And stern and sad (so rare the smiles
Of sunlight) look'd the Lombard piles;
  Porch-pillars on the lion resting,
And sombre, old, colonnaded aisles.

O Milan, O the chanting quires,
The giant windows' blazon'd fires,
  The height, the space, the gloom, the
    glory!
A mount of marble, a hundred spires!

I climb'd the roofs at break of day;
Sun-smitten Alps before me lay.
  I stood among the silent statues,
And statued pinnacles, mute as they.

How faintly-flush'd, how phantom-fair,
Was Monte Rosa, hanging there
  A thousand shadowy-pencill'd valleys
And snowy dells in a golden air.

Remember how we came at last
To Como; shower and storm and blast
  Had blown the lake beyond his limit,
And all was flooded; and how we past

From Como, when the light was gray,
And in my head, for half the day,
  The rich Virgilian rustic measure
Of Lari Maxume, all the way,

Like ballad-burthen music, kept,
As on The Lariano crept,
  To that fair port below the castle
Of Queen Theodolind, where we slept ;

Or hardly slept, but watch'd awake
A cypress in the moonlight shake,
  The moonlight touching o'er a terrace
One tall Agavè above the lake.

What more ? we took our last adieu,
And up the snowy Splugen drew,
  But ere we reach'd the highest summit
I pluck'd a daisy, I gave it you.

It told of England then to me,
And now it tells of Italy.
  O love, we two shall go no longer
To lands of summer across the sea ;

So dear a life your arms enfold
Whose crying is a cry for gold :
  Yet here to-night in this dark city,
When ill and weary, alone and cold,

I found, tho' crush'd to hard and dry,
This nurseling of another sky
  Still in the little book you lent me,
And where you tenderly laid it by :

And I forgot the clouded Forth,
The gloom that saddens Heaven and
    Earth,
  The bitter east, the misty summer
And gray metropolis of the North.

Perchance, to lull the throbs of pain,
Perchance, to charm a vacant brain,
  Perchance, to dream you still beside me,
My fancy fled to the South again.

TO THE REV. F. D. MAURICE.

Come, when no graver cares employ,
Godfather, come and see your boy :
  Your presence will be sun in winter,
Making the little one leap for joy.

For, being of that honest few,
Who give the Fiend himself his due,
  Should eighty-thousand college-councils
Thunder 'Anathema,' friend, at you ;

Should all our churchmen foam in spite
At you, so careful of the right, .
  Yet one lay-hearth would give you wel-
    come
(Take it and come) to the Isle of Wight ;

Where, far from noise and smoke of town,
I watch the twilight falling brown
  All round a careless-order'd garden
Close to the ridge of a noble down.

You'll have no scandal while you dine,
But honest talk and wholesome wine,
  And only hear the magpie gossip
Garrulous under a roof of pine :

For groves or pine on either hand,
To break the blast of winter, stand ;
  And further on, the hoary Channel
Tumbles a billow on chalk and sand ;

Where, if below the milky steep
Some ship of battle slowly creep,
  And on thro' zones of light and shadow
Glimmer away to the lonely deep,

We might discuss the Northern sin
Which made a selfish war begin ;
  Dispute the claims, arrange the chances ;
Emperor, Ottoman, which shall win :

Or whether war's avenging rod
Shall lash all Europe into blood ;
  Till you should turn to dearer matters,
Dear to the man that is dear to God ;

How best to help the slender store,
How mend the dwellings, of the poor ;
  How gain in life, as life advances,
Valour and charity more and more.

Come, Maurice, come : the lawn as yet
Is hoar with rime, or spongy-wet ;
  But when the wreath of March has
    blossom'd,
Crocus, anemone, violet,

Or later, pay one visit here,
For those are few we hold as dear ;
  Nor pay but one, but come for many,
Many and many a happy year.

January, 1854.

WILL.

I.

O WELL for him whose will is strong!
He suffers, but he will not suffer long;
He suffers, but he cannot suffer wrong:
For him nor moves the loud world's
  random mock,
Nor all Calamity's hugest waves confound,
Who seems a promontory of rock,
That, compass'd round with turbulent
  sound,
In middle ocean meets the surging shock,
Tempest-buffeted, citadel-crown'd.

II.

But ill for him who, bettering not with time,
Corrupts the strength of heaven-descended
  Will,
And ever weaker grows thro' acted crime,
Or seeming-genial venial fault,
Recurring and suggesting still!
He seems as one whose footsteps halt,
Toiling in immeasurable sand,
And o'er a weary sultry land,
Far beneath a blazing vault,
Sown in a wrinkle of the monstrous hill,
The city sparkles like a grain of salt.

IN THE VALLEY OF CAUTERETZ.

ALL along the valley, stream that flashest
  white,
Deepening thy voice with the deepening
  of the night,
All along the valley, where thy waters flow,
I walk'd with one I loved two and thirty
  years ago.
All along the valley, while I walk'd to-day,
The two and thirty years were a mist that
  rolls away;
For all along the valley, down thy rocky bed,
Thy living voice to me was as the voice
  of the dead,
And all along the valley, by rock and
  cave and tree,
The voice of the dead was a living voice
  to me.

IN THE GARDEN AT SWAINSTON.

NIGHTINGALES warbled without,
  Within was weeping for thee:
Shadows of three dead men
  Walk'd in the walks with me,
  Shadows of three dead men and thou
    wast one of the three.

Nightingales sang in his woods:
  The Master was far away:
Nightingales warbled and sang
  Of a passion that lasts but a day;
  Still in the house in his coffin the Prince
    of courtesy lay.

Two dead men have I known
  In courtesy like to thee:
Two dead men have I loved
  With a love that ever will be:
  Three dead men have I loved and thou
    art last of the three.

THE FLOWER.

ONCE in a golden hour
  I cast to earth a seed.
Up there came a flower,
  The people said, a weed.

To and fro they went
  Thro' my garden-bower,
And muttering discontent
  Cursed me and my flower.

Then it grew so tall
  It wore a crown of light,
But thieves from o'er the wall
  Stole the seed by night.

Sow'd it far and wide
  By every town and tower,
Till all the people cried,
  'Splendid is the flower.'

Read my little fable:
  He that runs may read.
Most can raise the flowers now,
  For all have got the seed.

And some are pretty enough,
  And some are poor indeed ;
And now again the people
  Call it but a weed.

REQUIESCAT.

FAIR is her cottage in its place,
  Where yon broad water sweetly slowly
    glides.
It sees itself from thatch to base
  Dream in the sliding tides.

And fairer she, but ah how soon to die !
  Her quiet dream of life this hour may
    cease.
Her peaceful being slowly passes by
  To some more perfect peace.

THE SAILOR BOY.

HE rose at dawn and, fired with hope,
  Shot o'er the seething harbour-bar,
And reach'd the ship and caught the rope,
  And whistled to the morning star.

And while he whistled long and loud
  He heard a fierce mermaiden cry,
'O boy, tho' thou art young and proud,
  I see the place where thou wilt lie.

'The sands and yeasty surges mix
  In caves about the dreary bay,
And on thy ribs the limpet sticks,
  And in thy heart the scrawl shall play.'

'Fool,' he answer'd, 'death is sure
  To those that stay and those that roam,
But I will nevermore endure
  To sit with empty hands at home.

'My mother clings about my neck,
  My sisters crying, " Stay for shame ; "
My father raves of death and wreck,
  They are all to blame, they are all to
    blame.

'God help me ! save I take my part
  Of danger on the roaring sea,
A devil rises in my heart,
  Far worse than any death to me.'

THE ISLET.

' WHITHER, O whither, love, shall we go,
For a score of sweet little summers or so ?'
The sweet little wife of the singer said,
On the day that follow'd the day she was
    wed,
' Whither, O whither, love, shall we go ?'
And the singer shaking his curly head
Turn'd as he sat, and struck the keys
There at his right with a sudden crash,
Singing, ' And shall it be over the seas
With a crew that is neither rude nor rash,
But a bevy of Eroses apple-cheek'd,
In a shallop of crystal ivory-beak'd,
With a satin sail of a ruby glow,
To a sweet little Eden on earth that I
    know,
A mountain islet pointed and peak'd ;
Waves on a diamond shingle dash,
Cataract brooks to the ocean run,
Fairily-delicate palaces shine
Mixt with myrtle and clad with vine,
And overstream'd and silvery-streak'd
With many a rivulet high against the
    Sun
The facets of the glorious mountain flash
Above the valleys of palm and pine.'

' Thither, O thither, love, let us go.'

' No, no, no !
For in all that exquisite isle, my dear,
There is but one bird with a musical
    throat,
And his compass is but of a single note,
That it makes one weary to hear.'

' Mock me not ! mock me not ! love, let
    us go.'

' No, love, no.
For the bud ever breaks into bloom on
    the tree,
And a storm never wakes on the lonely
    sea,
And a worm is there in the lonely wood,
That pierces the liver and blackens the
    blood ;
And makes it a sorrow to be.'

CHILD-SONGS.

I.

THE CITY CHILD.

DAINTY little maiden, whither would you
    wander?
  Whither from this pretty home, the
    home where mother dwells?
' Far and far away,' said the dainty little
    maiden,
' All among the gardens, auriculas,
    anemones,
  Roses and lilies and Canterbury-bells.'

Dainty little maiden, whither would you
    wander?
  Whither from this pretty house, this
    city-house of ours?
' Far and far away,' said the dainty little
    maiden,
' All among the meadows, the clover and
    the clematis,
  Daisies and kingcups and honeysuckle-
    flowers.'

II.

MINNIE AND WINNIE.

MINNIE and Winnie
  Slept in a shell.
Sleep, little ladies!
  And they slept well.

Pink was the shell within,
  Silver without;
Sounds of the great sea
  Wander'd about.

Sleep, little ladies!
  Wake not soon!
Echo on echo
  Dies to the moon.

Two bright stars
  Peep'd into the shell.
' What are they dreaming of?
  Who can tell?'

Started a green linnet
  Out of the croft;
Wake, little ladies,
  The sun is aloft!

THE SPITEFUL LETTER.

HERE, it is here, the close of the year,
  And with it a spiteful letter.
My name in song has done him much
    wrong,
  For himself has done much better.

O little bard, is your lot so hard,
  If men neglect your pages?
I think not much of yours or of mine,
  I hear the roll of the ages.

Rhymes and rhymes in the range of the
    times!
  Are mine for the moment stronger?
Yet hate me not, but abide your lot,
  I last but a moment longer.

This faded leaf, our names are as brief;
  What room is left for a hater?
Yet the yellow leaf hates the greener leaf,
  For it hangs one moment later.

Greater than I—is that your cry?
  And men will live to see it.
Well—if it be so—so it is, you know;
  And if it be so, so be it.

Brief, brief is a summer leaf,
  But this is the time of hollies.
O hollies and ivies and evergreens,
  How I hate the spites and the follies!

LITERARY SQUABBLES.

AH God! the petty fools of rhyme
  That shriek and sweat in pigmy wars
Before the stony face of Time,
  And look'd at by the silent stars:

Who hate each other for a song,
  And do their little best to bite
And pinch their brethren in the throng,
  And scratch the very dead for spite:

And strain to make an inch of room
  For their sweet selves, and cannot hear
The sullen Lethe rolling doom
  On them and theirs and all things
    here:

When one small touch of Charity
  Could lift them nearer God-like state
Than if the crowded Orb should cry
  Like those who cried Diana great :

And I too, talk, and lose the touch
  I talk of.   Surely, after all,
The noblest answer unto such
  Is perfect stillness when they brawl.

THE VICTIM.

I.

A PLAGUE upon the people fell,
  A famine after laid them low,
Then thorpe and byre arose in fire,
  For on them brake the sudden foe ;
So thick they died the people cried,
  'The Gods are moved against the land,'
The Priest in horror about his altar
  To Thor and Odin lifted a hand :
      ' Help us from famine
      And plague and strife !
      What would you have of us ?
      Human life ?
      Were it our nearest,
      Were it our dearest,
      (Answer, O answer)
      We give you his life.'

II.

But still the foeman spoil'd and burn'd,
  And cattle died, and deer in wood,
And bird in air, and fishes turn'd
  And whiten'd all the rolling flood ;
And dead men lay all over the way,
  Or down in a furrow scathed with flame :
And ever and aye the Priesthood moan'd,
  Till at last it seem'd that an answer
      came.
      ' The King is happy
      In child and wife ;
      Take you his dearest,
      Give us a life.'

III.

The Priest went out by heath and hill ;
  The King was hunting in the wild ;
They found the mother sitting still ;
  She cast her arms about the child.

The child was only eight summers old,
  His beauty still with his years increased,
His face was ruddy, his hair was gold,
  He seem'd a victim due to the priest.
      The Priest beheld him,
      And cried with joy,
      ' The Gods have answer'd :
      We give them the boy.'

IV.

The King return'd from out the wild,
  He bore but little game in hand ;
The mother said, ' They have taken the
      child
  To spill his blood and heal the land :
The land is sick, the people diseased,
  And blight and famine on all the lea :
The holy Gods, they must be appeased,
  So I pray you tell the truth to me.
      They have taken our son,
      They will have his life.
      Is *he* your dearest ?
      Or I, the wife ?'

V.

The King bent low, with hand on brow,
  He stay'd his arms upon his knee :
' O wife, what use to answer now ?
  For now the Priest has judged for me.'
The King was shaken with holy fear ;
  . ' The Gods,' he said, ' would have
      chosen well ;
Yet both are near, and both are dear,
  And which the dearest I cannot tell !'
      But the Priest was happy,
      His victim won :
      ' We have his dearest,
      His only son !'

VI.

The rites prepared, the victim bared,
  The knife uprising toward the blow
To the altar-stone she sprang alone,
  'Me, not my darling, no !'
He caught her away with a sudden cry ;
  Suddenly from him brake his wife,
And shrieking ' *I* am his dearest, I—
  I am his dearest !' rush'd on the
      knife.

And the Priest was happy,
'O, Father Odin,
We give you a life.

Which was his nearest ?
Who was his dearest ?
The Gods have answer'd ;
We give them the wife !'

WAGES.

GLORY of warrior, glory of orator, glory of song,
　Paid with a voice flying by to be lost on an endless sea—
Glory of Virtue, to fight, to struggle, to right the wrong—
　Nay, but she aim'd not at glory, no lover of glory she :
Give her the glory of going on, and still to be.

The wages of sin is death : if the wages of Virtue be dust,
　Would she have heart to endure for the life of the worm and the fly ?
She desires no isles of the blest, no quiet seats of the just,
　To rest in a golden grove, or to bask in a summer sky :
Give her the wages of going on, and not to die.

THE HIGHER PANTHEISM.

THE sun, the moon, the stars, the seas, the hills and the plains—
Are not these, O Soul, the Vision of Him who reigns ?

Is not the Vision He ? tho' He be not that which He seems ?
Dreams are true while they last, and do we not live in dreams ?

Earth, these solid stars, this weight of body and limb,
Are they not sign and symbol of thy division from Him ?

Dark is the world to thee : thyself art the reason why ;
For is He not all but that which has power to feel 'I am I' ?

Glory about thee, without thee ; and thou fulfillest thy doom
Making Him broken gleams, and a stifled splendour and gloom.

Speak to Him thou for He hears, and Spirit with Spirit can meet—
Closer is He than breathing, and nearer than hands and feet.

God is law, say the wise ; O Soul, and let us rejoice,
For if He thunder by law the thunder is yet His voice.

Law is God, say some : no God at all, says the fool ;
For all we have power to see is a straight staff bent in a pool ;

And the ear of man cannot hear, and the eye of man cannot see ;
But if we could see and hear, this Vision—were it not He ?

THE VOICE AND THE PEAK.

I.

THE voice and the Peak
    Far over summit and lawn,
The lone glow and long roar
    Green-rushing from the rosy thrones of
        dawn !

II.

All night have I heard the voice
    Rave over the rocky bar,
But thou wert silent in heaven,
    Above thee glided the star.

III.

Hast thou no voice, O Peak,
    That standest high above all ?
' I am the voice of the Peak,
    I roar and rave for I fall.

IV.

' A thousand voices go
    To North, South, East, and West ;
They leave the heights and are troubled,
    And moan and sink to their rest.

V.

' The fields are fair beside them,
    The chestnut towers in his bloom ;
But they—they feel the desire of the deep—
    Fall, and follow their doom.

VI.

' The deep has power on the height,
    And the height has power on the deep ;
They are raised for ever and ever,
    And sink again into sleep.'

VII.

Not raised for ever and ever,
    But when their cycle is o'er,
The valley, the voice, the peak, the star
    Pass, and are found no more.

VIII.

The Peak is high and flush'd
    At his highest with sunrise fire ;
The Peak is high, and the stars are high,
    And the thought of a man is higher.

IX.

A deep below the deep,
    And a height beyond the height !
Our hearing is not hearing,
    And our seeing is not sight.

X.

The voice and the Peak
    Far into heaven withdrawn,
The lone glow and long roar
    Green-rushing from the rosy thrones
        of dawn !

FLOWER in the crannied wall,
I pluck you out of the crannies,
I hold you here, root and all, in my hand,
Little flower—but *if* I could understand
What you are, root and all, and all in
    all,
I should know what God and man is.

A DEDICATION.

DEAR, near and true — no truer Time
    himself
Can prove you, tho' he make you ever-
    more
Dearer and nearer, as the rapid of life
Shoots to the fall—take this and pray
    that he
Who wrote it, honouring your sweet faith
    in him,
May trust himself ; and after praise and
    scorn,
As one who feels the immeasurable
    world,
Attain the wise indifference of the wise ;
And after Autumn past—if left to pass
His autumn into seeming-leafless days—
Draw toward the long frost and longest
    night,
Wearing his wisdom lightly, like the
    fruit
Which in our winter woodland looks a
    flower.[1]

[1] The fruit of the Spindle-tree (*Euonymus
Europæus*).

EXPERIMENTS.

BOÄDICEA.

WHILE about the shore of Mona those Neronian legionaries
Burnt and broke the grove and altar of the Druid and Druidess,
Far in the East Boädicéa, standing loftily charioted,
Mad and maddening all that heard her in her fierce volubility,
Girt by half the tribes of Britain, near the colony Cámulodúne,
Yell'd and shriek'd between her daughters o'er a wild confederacy.

'They that scorn the tribes and call us Britain's barbarous populaces,
Did they hear me, would they listen, did they pity me supplicating?
Shall I heed them in their anguish? shall I brook to be supplicated?
Hear Icenian, Catieuchlanian, hear Coritanian, Trinobant!
Must their ever-ravening eagle's beak and talon annihilate us?
Tear the noble heart of Britain, leave it gorily quivering?
Bark an answer, Britain's raven! bark and blacken innumerable,
Blacken round the Roman carrion, make the carcase a skeleton,
Kite and kestrel, wolf and wolfkin, from the wilderness, wallow in it,
Till the face of Bel be brighten'd, Taranis be propitiated.
Lo their colony half-defended! lo their colony, Cámulodúne!
There the horde of Roman robbers mock at a barbarous adversary.
There the hive of Roman liars worship an emperor-idiot.
Such is Rome, and this her deity: hear it, Spirit of Cássivëlaún!

'Hear it, Gods! the Gods have heard it, O Icenian, O Coritanian!
Doubt not ye the Gods have answer'd, Catieuchlanian, Trinobant.
These have told us all their anger in miraculous utterances,
Thunder, a flying fire in heaven, a murmur heard aërially,
Phantom sound of blows descending, moan of an enemy massacred,
Phantom wail of women and children, multitudinous agonies.
Bloodily flow'd the Tamesa rolling phantom bodies of horses and men;
Then a phantom colony smoulder'd on the refluent estuary;
Lastly yonder yester-even, suddenly giddily tottering—
There was one who watch'd and told me—down their statue of Victory fell.
Lo their precious Roman bantling, lo the colony Cámulodúne,
Shall we teach it a Roman lesson? shall we care to be pitiful?
Shall we deal with it as an infant? shall we dandle it amorously?

'Hear Icenian, Catieuchlanian, hear Coritanian, Trinobant!
While I roved about the forest, long and bitterly meditating,
There I heard them in the darkness, at the mystical ceremony,
Loosely robed in flying raiment, sang the terrible prophetesses,
"Fear not, isle of blowing woodland, isle of silvery parapets!
Tho' the Roman eagle shadow thee, tho' the gathering enemy narrow thee,
Thou shalt wax and he shall dwindle, thou shalt be the mighty one yet!
Thine the liberty, thine the glory, thine the deeds to be celebrated,

T   R

Thine the myriad-rolling ocean, light and shadow illimitable,
Thine the lands of lasting summer, many-blossoming Paradises,
Thine the North and thine the South and thine the battle-thunder of God,"
So they chanted : how shall Britain light upon auguries happier ?
So they chanted in the darkness, and there cometh a victory now.

   'Hear Icenian, Catieuchlanian, hear Coritanian, Trinobant !
Me the wife of rich Prasútagus, me the lover of liberty,
Me they seized and me they tortured, me they lash'd and humiliated,
Me the sport of ribald Veterans, mine of ruffian violators !
See they sit, they hide their faces, miserable in ignominy !
Wherefore in me burns an anger, not by blood to be satiated.
Lo the palaces and the temple, lo the colony Cámulodúne !
There they ruled, and thence they wasted all the flourishing territory,
Thither at their will they haled the yellow-ringleted Britoness—
Bloodily, bloodily fall the battle-axe, unexhausted, inexorable.
Shout Icenian, Catieuchlanian, shout Coritanian, Trinobant,
Till the victim hear within and yearn to hurry precipitously
Like the leaf in a roaring whirlwind, like the smoke in a hurricane whirl'd.
Lo the colony, there they rioted in the city of Cúnobelíne !
There they drank in cups of emerald, there at tables of ebony lay,
Rolling on their purple couches in their tender effeminacy.
There they dwelt and there they rioted ; there—there—they dwell no more.
Burst the gates, and burn the palaces, break the works of the statuary,
Take the hoary Roman head and shatter it, hold it abominable,
Cut the Roman boy to pieces in his lust and voluptuousness,
Lash the maiden into swooning, me they lash'd and humiliated,
Chop the breasts from off the mother, dash the brains of the little one out,
Up my Britons, on my chariot, on my chargers, trample them under us.'

   So the Queen Boädicéa, standing loftily charioted,
Brandishing in her hand a dart and rolling glances lioness-like,
Yell'd and shriek'd between her daughters in her fierce volubility.
Till her people all around the royal chariot agitated,
Madly dash'd the darts together, writhing barbarous lineäments,
Made the noise of frosty woodlands, when they shiver in January,
Roar'd as when the roaring breakers boom and blanch on the precipices,
Yell'd as when the winds of winter tear an oak on a promontory.
So the silent colony hearing her tumultuous adversaries
Clash the darts and on the buckler beat with rapid unanimous hand,
Thought on all her evil tyrannies, all her pitiless avarice,
Till she felt the heart within her fall and flutter tremulously,
Then her pulses at the clamouring of her enemy fainted away.
Out of evil evil flourishes, out of tyranny tyranny buds.
Ran the land with Roman slaughter, multitudinous agonies.
Perish'd many a maid and matron, many a valorous legionary,
Fell the colony, city, and citadel, London, Verulam, Cámulodúne.

IN QUANTITY.

ON TRANSLATIONS OF HOMER.

Hexameters and Pentameters.

THESE lame hexameters the strong-wing'd music of Homer!
  No—but a most burlesque barbarous experiment.
When was a harsher sound ever heard, ye Muses, in England?
  When did a frog coarser croak upon our Helicon?
Hexameters no worse than daring Germany gave us,
  Barbarous experiment, barbarous hexameters.

MILTON.

Alcaics.

MIGHTY-MOUTH'D inventor of harmonies,
  skill'd to sing of Time or Eternity,
    God-gifted organ-voice of England,
      Milton, a name to resound for ages;
hose Titan angels, Gabriel, Abdiel,
  arr'd from Jehovah's gorgeous armouries,
    Tower, as the deep-domed empyrëan
      Rings to the roar of an angel onset—
 e rather all that bowery loneliness,
  e brooks of Eden mazily murmuring,
    And bloom profuse and cedar arches
      Charm, as a wanderer out in ocean,
here some refulgent sunset of India
  reams o'er a rich ambrosial ocean isle,
    And crimson-hued the stately palm-woods
      Whisper in odorous heights of even.

Hendecasyllabics.

YOU chorus of indolent reviewers,
 esponsible, indolent reviewers,
 ok, I come to the test, a tiny poem
  composed in a metre of Catullus,
  in quantity, careful of my motion,
 e the skater on ice that hardly bears him,
 st I fall unawares before the people,
 aking laughter in indolent reviewers.
 ould I flounder awhile without a tumble
 ro' this metrification of Catullus,
 ey should speak to me not without a welcome,

All that chorus of indolent reviewers.
Hard, hard, hard is it, only not to tumble,
So fantastical is the dainty metre.
Wherefore slight me not wholly, nor believe me
Too presumptuous, indolent reviewers.
O blatant Magazines, regard me rather—
Since I blush to belaud myself a moment—
As some rare little rose, a piece of inmost
Horticultural art, or half coquette-like
Maiden, not to be greeted unbenignly.

SPECIMEN OF A TRANSLATION OF THE ILIAD IN BLANK VERSE. *viii* 542-561

SO Hector spake; the Trojans roar'd applause;
Then loosed their sweating horses from the yoke,
And each beside his chariot bound his own;
And oxen from the city, and goodly sheep
In haste they drove, and honey-hearted wine
And bread from out the houses brought, and heap'd
Their firewood, and the winds from off the plain
Roll'd the rich vapour far into the heaven.
And these all night upon the bridge[1] of war
Sat glorying; many a fire before them blazed:

---

[1] Or, ridge.

*Le ciel
étoilé et
la campagne
muette*

As when in heaven the stars about the moon
Look beautiful, when all the winds are laid,
And every height comes out, and jutting peak
And valley, and the immeasurable heavens
Break open to their highest, and all the stars
Shine, and the Shepherd gladdens in his heart :

So many a fire between the ships and stream
Of Xanthus blazed before the towers of Troy,
A thousand on the plain ; and close by each
Sat fifty in the blaze of burning fire ;
And eating hoary grain and pulse the steeds,
Fixt by their cars, waited the golden dawn. *Iliad* VIII. 542-5

THE WINDOW;

OR, THE SONG OF THE WRENS.

FOUR years ago Mr. Sullivan requested me to write a little song-cycle, German fashion, for him to exercise his art upon. He had been very successful in setting such old songs as ' Orpheus with his lute,' and I drest up for him, partly in the old style, a puppet, whose almost only merit is, perhaps that it can dance to Mr. Sullivan's instrument. I am sorry that my four-year-old puppet should have to dance at all in the dark shadow of these days ; but the music is now completed, and I am bound by my promise.

December, 1870.   A. TENNYSON.

THE WINDOW.

ON THE HILL.

THE lights and shadows fly !
Yonder it brightens and darkens down on the plain.
  A jewel, a jewel dear to a lover's eye !
Oh is it the brook, or a pool, or her window pane,
    When the winds are up in the morning ?

Clouds that are racing above,
And winds and lights and shadows that cannot be still,
  All running on one way to the home of my love,
You are all running on, and I stand on the slope of the hill,
    And the winds are up in the morning !

Follow, follow the chase !
And my thoughts are as quick and as quick, ever on, on, on.
  O lights, are you flying over her sweet little face ?

And my heart is there before you come, and gone,
    When the winds are up in morning !

Follow them down the slope !
And I follow them down to the window pane of my dear,
  And it brightens and darkens and brightens like my hope,
And it darkens and brightens and darkens like my fear,
    And the winds are up in morning.

AT THE WINDOW.

Vine, vine and eglantine,
Clasp her window, trail and twine !
Rose, rose and clematis,
Trail and twine and clasp and kiss,
Kiss, kiss ; and make her a bower
  All of flowers, and drop me a flower,
  Drop me a flower.

Vine, vine and eglantine,
Cannot a flower, a flower, be mine?
Rose, rose and clematis,
Drop me a flower, a flower, to kiss,
Kiss, kiss—and out of her bower
    All of flowers, a flower, a flower,
        Dropt, a flower.

GONE.

one!
one, till the end of the year,
one, and the light gone with her, and
    left me in shadow here!
        Gone—flitted away,
aken the stars from the night and the
    sun from the day!
one, and a cloud in my heart, and a
    storm in the air!
lown to the east or the west, flitted I
    know not where!
own in the south is a flash and a groan:
    she is there! she is there!

WINTER.

he frost is here,
nd fuel is dear,
nd woods are sear,
nd fires burn clear,
nd frost is here
nd has bitten the heel of the going year.

ite, frost, bite!
ou roll up away from the light
he blue wood-louse, and the plump
    dormouse,
nd the bees are still'd, and the flies are
    kill'd,
nd you bite far into the heart of the
    house,
ut not into mine.

ite, frost, bite!
he woods are all the searer,
he fuel is all the dearer,
he fires are all the clearer,
y spring is all the nearer,
ou have bitten into the heart of the
    earth,
ut not into mine.

SPRING.

Birds' love and birds' song
    Flying here and there,
Birds' song and birds' love,
    And you with gold for hair!
Birds' song and birds' love,
    Passing with the weather,
Men's song and men's love,
    To love once and for ever.

Men's love and birds' love,
    And women's love and men's!
And you my wren with a crown of gold,
    You my queen of the wrens!
You the queen of the wrens—
    We'll be birds of a feather,
I'll be King of the Queen of the wrens,
    And all in a nest together.

THE LETTER.

Where is another sweet as my sweet,
    Fine of the fine, and shy of the shy?
Fine little hands, fine little feet—
    Dewy blue eye.
Shall I write to her? shall I go?
    Ask her to marry me by and by?
Somebody said that she'd say no;
    Somebody knows that she'll say ay!

Ay or no, if ask'd to her face?
    Ay or no, from shy of the shy?
Go, little letter, apace, apace,
        Fly;
Fly to the light in the valley below—
    Tell my wish to her dewy blue eye:
Somebody said that she'd say no;
    Somebody knows that she'll say ay!

NO ANSWER.

The mist and the rain, the mist and the
    rain!
    Is it ay or no? is it ay or no?
And never a glimpse of her window pane!
    And I may die but the grass will grow,
And the grass will grow when I am gone,
And the wet west wind and the world
    will go on.
Ay is the song of the wedded spheres.
    No is trouble and cloud and storm,

Ay is life for a hundred years,
    No will push me down to the worm,
And when I am there and dead and gone,
The wet west wind and the world will
        go on.

The wind and the wet, the wind and the
        wet !
    Wet west wind how you blow, you
        blow !
And never a line from my lady yet !
    Is it ay or no ? is it ay or no ?
Blow then, blow, and when I am gone,
The wet west wind and the world may
        go on.

NO ANSWER.

Winds are loud and you are dumb,
Take my love, for love will come,
    Love will come but once a life.
Winds are loud and winds will pass !
Spring is here with leaf and grass :
    Take my love and be my wife.
After-loves of maids and men
Are but dainties drest again :
Love me now, you'll love me then :
    Love can love but once a life.

THE ANSWER.

Two little hands that meet,
Claspt on her seal, my sweet !
Must I take you and break you,
Two little hands that meet ?
I must take you, and break you,
And loving hands must part—
Take, take—break, break—
Break—you may break my heart.
        Faint heart never won—
        Break, break, and all's done.

AY.

Be merry, all birds, to-day,
    Be merry on earth as you never were
        merry before,
Be merry in heaven, O larks, and far away,
    And merry for ever and ever, and one
        day more.
            Why ?
    For it's easy to find a rhyme.

Look, look, how he flits,
    The fire-crown'd king of the wren
        from out of the pine !
Look how they tumble the blossom, th
        mad little tits !
    'Cuck-oo ! Cuck-oo !' was ever a Ma
        so fine ?
            Why ?
    For it's easy to find a rhyme.
O merry the linnet and dove,
    And swallow and sparrow and throstl
        and have your desire !
O merry my heart, you have gotten th
        wings of love,
    And flit like the king of the wrens wit
        a crown of fire.
            Why ?
    For it's ay ay, ay ay.

WHEN.

Sun comes, moon comes,
    Time slips away.
Sun sets, moon sets,
    Love, fix a day.

' A year hence, a year hence.'
    ' We shall both be gray.'
' A month hence, a month hence.
    ' Far, far away.'

' A week hence, a week hence.'
    ' Ah, the long delay.'
' Wait a little, wait a little,
    You shall fix a day.'

' To-morrow, love, to-morrow,
    And that's an age away.'
Blaze upon her window, sun,
    And honour all the day.

MARRIAGE MORNING.

Light, so low upon earth,
    You send a flash to the sun.
Here is the golden close of love,
    All my wooing is done.
Oh, the woods and the meadows,
    Woods where we hid from the we
Stiles where we stay'd to be kind,
    Meadows in which we met !

Light, so low in the vale
   You flash and lighten afar,
For this is the golden morning of love,
   And you are his morning star.
Flash, I am coming, I come,
   By meadow and stile and wood,
Oh, lighten into my eyes and my heart,
   Into my heart and my blood !

Heart, are you great enough
   For a love that never tires ?
O heart, are you great enough for love ?
   I have heard of thorns and briers.
Over the thorns and briers,
   Over the meadows and stiles,
Over the world to the end of it
   Flash for a million miles.

IN MEMORIAM A. H. H.

OBIIT MDCCCXXXIII.

STRONG Son of God, immortal Love,
   Whom we, that have not seen thy
      face,
   By faith, and faith alone, embrace,
Believing where we cannot prove ;

Thine are these orbs of light and shade ;
   Thou madest Life in man and brute ;
   Thou madest Death ; and lo, thy foot
Is on the skull which thou hast made.

Thou wilt not leave us in the dust :
   Thou madest man, he knows not
      why,
   He thinks he was not made to die ;
And thou hast made him : thou art just.

Thou seemest human and divine,
   The highest, holiest manhood, thou :
   Our wills are ours, we know not
      how ;
Our wills are ours, to make them thine.

Our little systems have their day ;
   They have their day and cease to be :
   They are but broken lights of thee,
And thou, O Lord, art more than they.

We have but faith : we cannot know ;
   For knowledge is of things we see ;
   And yet we trust it comes from thee,
A beam in darkness : let it grow.

Let knowledge grow from more to more,
   But more of reverence in us dwell ;
   That mind and soul, according well,
May make one music as before.

But vaster. We are fools and slight ;
   We mock thee when we do not fear :
   But help thy foolish ones to bear ;
Help thy vain worlds to bear thy light.

Forgive what seem'd my sin in me ;
   What seem'd my worth since I
      began ;
   For merit lives from man to man,
And not from man, O Lord, to thee.

Forgive my grief for one removed,
   Thy creature, whom I found so fair.
   I trust he lives in thee, and there
I find him worthier to be loved.

Forgive these wild and wandering cries,
   Confusions of a wasted youth ;
   Forgive them where they fail in truth,
And in thy wisdom make me wise.

                1849.

I.

I HELD it truth, with him who sings
   To one clear harp in divers tones,
   That men may rise on stepping-stones
Of their dead selves to higher things.

But who shall so forecast the years
   And find in loss a gain to match ?
   Or reach a hand thro' time to catch
The far-off interest of tears ?

Let Love clasp Grief lest both be drown'd,
   Let darkness keep her raven gloss :
   Ah, sweeter to be drunk with loss,
To dance with death, to beat the ground.

Than that the victor Hours should scorn
　　The long result of love, and boast,
　　'Behold the man that loved and lost,
But all he was is overworn.'

II.

Old Yew, which graspest at the stones
　　That name the under-lying dead,
　　Thy fibres net the dreamless head,
Thy roots are wrapt about the bones.

The seasons bring the flower again,
　　And bring the firstling to the flock;
　　And in the dusk of thee, the clock
Beats out the little lives of men.

O not for thee the glow, the bloom,
　　Who changest not in any gale,
　　Nor branding summer suns avail
To touch thy thousand years of gloom:

And gazing on thee, sullen tree,
　　Sick for thy stubborn hardihood,
　　I seem to fail from out my blood
And grow incorporate into thee.

III.

O Sorrow, cruel fellowship,
　　O Priestess in the vaults of Death,
　　O sweet and bitter in a breath,
What whispers from thy lying lip?

'The stars,' she whispers, 'blindly run;
　　A web is wov'n across the sky;
　　From out waste places comes a cry,
And murmurs from the dying sun:

'And all the phantom, Nature, stands—
　　With all the music in her tone,
　　A hollow echo of my own,—
A hollow form with empty hands.'

And shall I take a thing so blind,
　　Embrace her as my natural good;
　　Or crush her, like a vice of blood,
Upon the threshold of the mind?

IV.

To Sleep I give my powers away;
　　My will is bondsman to the dark;
　　I sit within a helmless bark,
And with my heart I muse and say:

O heart, how fares it with thee now,
　　That thou should'st fail from thy
　　　　desire,
　　Who scarcely darest to inquire,
'What is it makes me beat so low?'

Something it is which thou hast lost,
　　Some pleasure from thine early years.
　　Break, thou deep vase of chilling
　　　　tears,
That grief hath shaken into frost!

Such clouds of nameless trouble cross
　　All night below the darken'd eyes;
　　With morning wakes the will, and
　　　　cries,
'Thou shalt not be the fool of loss.'

V.

I sometimes hold it half a sin
　　To put in words the grief I feel;
　　For words, like Nature, half reveal
And half conceal the Soul within.

But, for the unquiet heart and brain,
　　A use in measured language lies;
　　The sad mechanic exercise,
Like dull narcotics, numbing pain.

In words, like weeds, I'll wrap me o'er,
　　Like coarsest clothes against the
　　　　cold:
　　But that large grief which these
　　　　enfold
Is given in outline and no more.

VI.

One writes, that 'Other friends remain,'
　　That 'Loss is common to the race'—
　　And common is the commonplace,
And vacant chaff well meant for grain.

That loss is common would not make
　　My own less bitter, rather more:
　　Too common! Never morning wore
To evening, but some heart did break.

O father, wheresoe'er thou be,
　　Who pledgest now thy gallant son;
　　A shot, ere half thy draught be done,
Hath still'd the life that beat from thee.

O mother, praying God will save
    Thy sailor, — while thy head is
        bow'd,
    His heavy-shotted hammock-shroud
Drops in his vast and wandering grave.

Ye know no more than I who wrought
    At that last hour to please him well ;
    Who mused on all I had to tell,
And something written, something
        thought ;

Expecting still his advent home ;
    And ever met him on his way
    With wishes, thinking, ' here to-day,'
Or ' here to-morrow will he come.'

O somewhere, meek, unconscious dove,
    That sittest ranging golden hair ;
    And glad to find thyself so fair,
Poor child, that waitest for thy love !

For now her father's chimney glows
    In expectation of a guest ;
    And thinking ' this will please him
        best,'
She takes a riband or a rose ;

For he will see them on to-night ;
    And with the thought her colour
        burns ;
    And, having left the glass, she turns
Once more to set a ringlet right ;

And, even when she turn'd, the curse
    Had fallen, and her future Lord
    Was drown'd in passing thro' the
        ford,
Or kill'd in falling from his horse.

O what to her shall be the end ?
    And what to me remains of good ?
    To her, perpetual maidenhood,
And unto me no second friend.

VII.

Dark house, by which once more I stand
    Here in the long unlovely street,
    Doors, where my heart was used to
        beat
So quickly, waiting for a hand,

A hand that can be clasp'd no more—
    Behold me, for I cannot sleep,
    And like a guilty thing I creep
At earliest morning to the door.

He is not here ; but far away
    The noise of life begins again,
    And ghastly thro' the drizzling rain
On the bald street breaks the blank day.

VIII.

A happy lover who has come
    To look on her that loves him well,
    Who 'lights and rings the gateway
        bell,
And learns her gone and far from home ;

He saddens, all the magic light
    Dies off at once from bower and hall,
    And all the place is dark, and all
The chambers emptied of delight :

So find I every pleasant spot
    In which we two were wont to meet,
    The field, the chamber and the street,
For all is dark where thou art not.

Yet as that other, wandering there
    In those deserted walks, may find
    A flower beat with rain and wind,
Which once she foster'd up with care ;

So seems it in my deep regret,
    O my forsaken heart, with thee
    And this poor flower of poesy
Which little cared for fades not yet.

But since it pleased a vanish'd eye,
    I go to plant it on his tomb,
    That if it can it there may bloom,
Or dying, there at least may die.

IX.

Fair ship, that from the Italian shore
    Sailest the placid ocean-plains
    With my lost Arthur's loved remains,
Spread thy full wings, and waft him o'er.

So draw him home to those that mourn
    In vain ; a favourable speed
    Ruffle thy mirror'd mast, and lead
Thro' prosperous floods his holy urn.

All night no ruder air perplex
    Thy sliding keel, till Phosphor, bright
    As our pure love, thro' early light
Shall glimmer on the dewy decks.

Sphere all your lights around, above ;
    Sleep, gentle heavens, before the
        prow ;
    Sleep, gentle winds, as he sleeps now,
My friend, the brother of my love ;

My Arthur, whom I shall not see
    Till all my widow'd race be run ;
    Dear as the mother to the son,
More than my brothers are to me.

X.

I hear the noise about thy keel ;
    I hear the bell struck in the night :
    I see the cabin-window bright ;
I see the sailor at the wheel.

Thou bring'st the sailor to his wife,
    And travell'd men from foreign lands ;
    And letters unto trembling hands ;
And, thy dark freight, a vanish'd life.

So bring him : we have idle dreams :
    This look of quiet flatters thus
    Our home-bred fancies : O to us,
The fools of habit, sweeter seems

To rest beneath the clover sod,
    That takes the sunshine and the rains,
    Or where the kneeling hamlet drains
The chalice of the grapes of God ;

Than if with thee the roaring wells
    Should gulf him fathom-deep in brine;
    And hands so often clasp'd in mine,
Should toss with tangle and with shells.

XI.

Calm is the morn without a sound,
    Calm as to suit a calmer grief,
    And only thro' the faded leaf
The chestnut pattering to the ground :

Calm and deep peace on this high wold,
    And on these dews that drench the
        furze,
    And all the silvery gossamers
That twinkle into green and gold :

Calm and still light on yon great plain
    That sweeps with all its autumn
        bowers,
    And crowded farms and lessening
        towers,
To mingle with the bounding main :

Calm and deep peace in this wide air,
    These leaves that redden to the fall ;
    And in my heart, if calm at all,
If any calm, a calm despair :

Calm on the seas, and silver sleep,
    And waves that sway themselves in
        rest,
    And dead calm in that noble breast
Which heaves but with the heaving deep.

XII.

Lo, as a dove when up she springs
    To bear thro' Heaven a tale of woe,
    Some dolorous message knit below
The wild pulsation of her wings ;

Like her I go ; I cannot stay ;
    I leave this mortal ark behind,
    A weight of nerves without a mind,
And leave the cliffs, and haste away

O'er ocean-mirrors rounded large,
    And reach the glow of southern skies,
    And see the sails at distance rise,
And linger weeping on the marge,

And saying ; ' Comes he thus, my friend?
    Is this the end of all my care ?'
    And circle moaning in the air :
' Is this the end ?   Is this the end ?'

And forward dart again, and play
    About the prow, and back return
    To where the body sits, and learn
That I have been an hour away.

XIII.

Tears of the widower, when he sees
    A late-lost form that sleep reveals,
    And moves his doubtful arms, and
        feels
Her place is empty, fall like these ;

Which weep a loss for ever new,
    A void where heart on heart reposed ;
    And, where warm hands have prest
        and closed,
Silence, till I be silent too.

Which weep the comrade of my choice,
    An awful thought, a life removed,
    The human-hearted man I loved,
A Spirit, not a breathing voice.

Come Time, and teach me, many years,
    I do not suffer in a dream ;
    For now so strange do these things
        seem,
Mine eyes have leisure for their tears ;

My fancies time to rise on wing,
    And glance about the approaching
        sails,
    As tho' they brought but merchants'
        bales,
And not the burthen that they bring.

XIV.

If one should bring me this report,
    That thou hadst touch'd the land
        to-day,
    And I went down unto the quay,
And found thee lying in the port ;

And standing, muffled round with woe,
    Should see thy passengers in rank
    Come stepping lightly down the
        plank,
And beckoning unto those they know ;

And if along with these should come
    The man I held as half-divine ;
    Should strike a sudden hand in mine,
And ask a thousand things of home ;

And I should tell him all my pain,
    And how my life had droop'd of late,
    And he should sorrow o'er my state
And marvel what possess'd my brain ;

And I perceived no touch of change,
    No hint of death in all his frame,
    But found him all in all the same,
I should not feel it to be strange.

XV.

To-night the winds begin to rise
    And roar from yonder dropping day :
    The last red leaf is whirl'd away,
The rooks are blown about the skies ;

The forest crack'd, the waters curl'd,
    The cattle huddled on the lea ;
    And wildly dash'd on tower and tree
The sunbeam strikes along the world :

And but for fancies, which aver
    That all thy motions gently pass
    Athwart a plane of molten glass,
I scarce could brook the strain and stir

That makes the barren branches loud ;
    And but for fear it is not so,
    The wild unrest that lives in woe
Would dote and pore on yonder cloud

That rises upward always higher,
    And onward drags a labouring breast,
    And topples round the dreary west,
A looming bastion fringed with fire.

XVI.

What words are these have fall'n from me?
    Can calm despair and wild unrest
    Be tenants of a single breast,
Or sorrow such a changeling be ?

Or doth she only seem to take
    The touch of change in calm or storm;
    But knows no more of transient form
In her deep self, than some dead lake

That holds the shadow of a lark
    Hung in the shadow of a heaven ?
    Or has the shock, so harshly given,
Confused me like the unhappy bark

That strikes by night a craggy shelf,
    And staggers blindly ere she sink ?
    And stunn'd me from my power to
        think
And all my knowledge of myself ;

And made me that delirious man
    Whose fancy fuses old and new,
    And flashes into false and true,
And mingles all without a plan ?

XVII.

Thou comest, much wept for : such a breeze
  Compell'd thy canvas, and my prayer
  Was as the whisper of an air
To breathe thee over lonely seas.

For I in spirit saw thee move
  Thro' circles of the bounding sky,
  Week after week : the days go by :
Come quick, thou bringest all I love.

Henceforth, wherever thou may'st roam,
  My blessing, like a line of light,
  Is on the waters day and night,
And like a beacon guards thee home.

So may whatever tempest mars
  Mid-ocean, spare thee, sacred bark ;
  And balmy drops in summer dark
Slide from the bosom of the stars.

So kind an office hath been done,
  Such precious relics brought by thee ;
  The dust of him I shall not see
Till all my widow'd race be run.

XVIII.

'Tis well ; 'tis something ; we may stand
  Where he in English earth is laid,
  And from his ashes may be made
The violet of his native land.

'Tis little ; but it looks in truth
  As if the quiet bones were blest
  Among familiar names to rest
And in the places of his youth.

Come then, pure hands, and bear the head
  That sleeps or wears the mask of sleep,
  And come, whatever loves to weep,
And hear the ritual of the dead.

Ah yet, ev'n yet, if this might be,
  I, falling on his faithful heart,
  Would breathing thro' his lips impart
The life that almost dies in me ;

That dies not, but endures with pain,
  And slowly forms the firmer mind,
  Treasuring the look it cannot find,
The words that are not heard again.

XIX.

The Danube to the Severn gave
  The darken'd heart that beat no
    more ;
  They laid him by the pleasant shore,
And in the hearing of the wave.

There twice a day the Severn fills ;
  The salt sea-water passes by,
  And hushes half the babbling Wye,
And makes a silence in the hills.

The Wye is hush'd nor moved along,
  And hush'd my deepest grief of all,
  When fill'd with tears that cannot
    fall,
I brim with sorrow drowning song.

The tide flows down, the wave again
  Is vocal in its wooded walls ;
  My deeper anguish also falls,
And I can speak a little then.

XX.

The lesser griefs that may be said,
  That breathe a thousand tender
    vows,
  Are but as servants in a house
Where lies the master newly dead ;

Who speak their feeling as it is,
  And weep the fulness from the
    mind :
  ' It will be hard,' they say, ' to find
Another service such as this.'

My lighter moods are like to these,
  That out of words a comfort win ;
  But there are other griefs within,
And tears that at their fountain freeze ;

For by the hearth the children sit
  Cold in that atmosphere of Death,
  And scarce endure to draw the
    breath,
Or like to noiseless phantoms flit :

But open converse is there none,
  So much the vital spirits sink
  To see the vacant chair, and think,
' How good ! how kind ! and he is gone.'

XXI.

I sing to him that rests below,
 And, since the grasses round me wave,
 I take the grasses of the grave,
And make them pipes whereon to blow.

The traveller hears me now and then,
 And sometimes harshly will he speak:
 'This fellow would make weakness weak,
And melt the waxen hearts of men.'

Another answers, 'Let him be,
 He loves to make parade of pain,
 That with his piping he may gain
The praise that comes to constancy.'

A third is wroth: 'Is this an hour
 For private sorrow's barren song,
 When more and more the people throng
The chairs and thrones of civil power?

'A time to sicken and to swoon,
 When Science reaches forth her arms
 To feel from world to world, and charms
Her secret from the latest moon?'

Behold, ye speak an idle thing:
 Ye never knew the sacred dust:
 I do but sing because I must,
And pipe but as the linnets sing:

And one is glad; her note is gay,
 For now her little ones have ranged;
 And one is sad; her note is changed,
Because her brood is stol'n away.

XXII.

The path by which we twain did go,
 Which led by tracts that pleased us well,
 Thro' four sweet years arose and fell,
From flower to flower, from snow to snow:

And we with singing cheer'd the way,
 And, crown'd with all the season lent,
 From April on to April went,
And glad at heart from May to May:

But where the path we walk'd began
 To slant the fifth autumnal slope,
 As we descended following Hope,
There sat the Shadow fear'd of man;

Who broke our fair companionship,
 And spread his mantle dark and cold,
 And wrapt thee formless in the fold,
And dull'd the murmur on thy lip,

And bore thee where I could not see
 Nor follow, tho' I walk in haste,
 And think, that somewhere in the waste
The Shadow sits and waits for me.

XXIII.

Now, sometimes in my sorrow shut,
 Or breaking into song by fits,
 Alone, alone, to where he sits,
The Shadow cloak'd from head to foot,

Who keeps the keys of all the creeds,
 I wander, often falling lame,
 And looking back to whence I came,
Or on to where the pathway leads;

And crying, How changed from where it ran
 Thro' lands where not a leaf was dumb;
 But all the lavish hills would hum
The murmur of a happy Pan:

When each by turns was guide to each,
 And Fancy light from Fancy caught,
 And Thought leapt out to wed with Thought
Ere Thought could wed itself with Speech;

And all we met was fair and good,
 And all was good that Time could bring,
 And all the secret of the Spring
Moved in the chambers of the blood;

And many an old philosophy
 On Argive heights divinely sang,
 And round us all the thicket rang
To many a flute of Arcady.

XXIV.

And was the day of my delight
    As pure and perfect as I say?
    The very source and fount of Day
Is dash'd with wandering isles of night.

If all was good and fair we met,
    This earth had been the Paradise
    It never look'd to human eyes
Since our first Sun arose and set.

And is it that the haze of grief
    Makes former gladness loom so
        great?
    The lowness of the present state,
That sets the past in this relief?

Or that the past will always win
    A glory from its being far;
    And orb into the perfect star
We saw not, when we moved therein?

XXV.

I know that this was Life,—the track
    Whereon with equal feet we fared;
    And then, as now, the day prepared
The daily burden for the back.

But this it was that made me move
    As light as carrier-birds in air;
    I loved the weight I had to bear,
Because it needed help of Love:

Nor could I weary, heart or limb,
    When mighty Love would cleave in
        twain
    The lading of a single pain,
And part it, giving half to him.

XXVI.

Still onward winds the dreary way;
    I with it; for I long to prove
    No lapse of moons can canker Love,
Whatever fickle tongues may say.

And if that eye which watches guilt
    And goodness, and hath power to
        see
    Within the green the moulder'd tree,
And towers fall'n as soon as built—

Oh, if indeed that eye foresee
    Or see (in Him is no before)
    In more of life true life no more
And Love the indifference to be,

Then might I find, ere yet the morn
    Breaks hither over Indian seas,
    That Shadow waiting with the
        keys,
To shroud me from my proper scorn.

XXVII.

I envy not in any moods
    The captive void of noble rage,
    The linnet born within the cage,
That never knew the summer woods:

I envy not the beast that takes
    His license in the field of time,
    Unfetter'd by the sense of crime,
To whom a conscience never wakes;

Nor, what may count itself as blest,
    The heart that never plighted troth
    But stagnates in the weeds of sloth:
Nor any want-begotten rest.

I hold it true, whate'er befall;
    I feel it, when I sorrow most;
    'Tis better to have loved and lost
Than never to have loved at all.

XXVIII.

The time draws near the birth of Christ:
    The moon is hid; the night is still;
    The Christmas bells from hill to hill
Answer each other in the mist.

Four voices of four hamlets round,
    From far and near, on mead and
        moor,
    Swell out and fail, as if a door
Were shut between me and the sound:

Each voice four changes on the wind,
    That now dilate, and now decrease,
    Peace and goodwill, goodwill and
        peace,
Peace and goodwill, to all mankind.

This year I slept and woke with pain,
　　I almost wish'd no more to wake,
　　And that my hold on life would break
Before I heard those bells again :

But they my troubled spirit rule,
　　For they controll'd me when a boy ;
　　They bring me sorrow touch'd with joy,
The merry merry bells of Yule.

XXIX.

With such compelling cause to grieve
　　As daily vexes household peace,
　　And chains regret to his decease,
How dare we keep our Christmas-eve ;

Which brings no more a welcome guest
　　To enrich the threshold of the night
　　With shower'd largess of delight
In dance and song and game and jest ?

Yet go, and while the holly boughs
　　Entwine the cold baptismal font,
　　Make one wreath more for Use and Wont,
That guard the portals of the house ;

Old sisters of a day gone by,
　　Gray nurses, loving nothing new ;
　　Why should they miss their yearly due
Before their time ? They too will die.

XXX.

With trembling fingers did we weave
　　The holly round the Christmas hearth ;
　　A rainy cloud possess'd the earth,
And sadly fell our Christmas-eve.

At our old pastimes in the hall
　　We gambol'd, making vain pretence
　　Of gladness, with an awful sense
Of one mute Shadow watching all.

We paused : the winds were in the beech :
　　We heard them sweep the winter land ;
　　And in a circle hand-in-hand
Sat silent, looking each at each.

Then echo-like our voices rang ;
　　We sung, tho' every eye was dim,
　　A merry song we sang with him
Last year : impetuously we sang :

We ceased : a gentler feeling crept
　　Upon us : surely rest is meet :
　　'They rest,' we said, 'their sleep is sweet,'
And silence follow'd, and we wept.

Our voices took a higher range ;
　　Once more we sang : 'They do not die
　　Nor lose their mortal sympathy,
Nor change to us, although they change ;

'Rapt from the fickle and the frail
　　With gather'd power, yet the same,
　　Pierces the keen seraphic flame
From orb to orb, from veil to veil.'

Rise, happy morn, rise, holy morn,
　　Draw forth the cheerful day from night :
　　O Father, touch the east, and light
The light that shone when Hope was born.

XXXI.

When Lazarus left his charnel-cave,
　　And home to Mary's house return'd,
　　Was this demanded—if he yearn'd
To hear her weeping by his grave ?

'Where wert thou, brother, those four days ?'
　　There lives no record of reply,
　　Which telling what it is to die
Had surely added praise to praise.

From every house the neighbours met,
　　The streets were fill'd with joyful sound,
　　A solemn gladness even crown'd
The purple brows of Olivet.

Behold a man raised up by Christ !
　　The rest remaineth unreveal'd ;
　　He told it not ; or something seal'd
The lips of that Evangelist.

XXXII.

Her eyes are homes of silent prayer,
    Nor other thought her mind admits
    But, he was dead, and there he sits,
And he that brought him back is there.

Then one deep love doth supersede
    All other, when her ardent gaze
    Roves from the living brother's face,
And rests upon the Life indeed.

All subtle thought, all curious fears,
    Borne down by gladness so complete,
    She bows, she bathes the Saviour's
        feet
With costly spikenard and with tears.

Thrice blest whose lives are faithful
        prayers,
    Whose loves in higher love endure ;
    What souls possess themselves so
        pure,
Or is there blessedness like theirs ?

XXXIII.

O thou that after toil and storm
    Mayst seem to have reach'd a purer
        air,
    Whose faith has centre everywhere,
Nor cares to fix itself to form,

Leave thou thy sister when she prays,
    Her early Heaven, her happy views ;
    Nor thou with shadow'd hint confuse
A life that leads melodious days.

Her faith thro' form is pure as thine,
    Her hands are quicker unto good :
    Oh, sacred be the flesh and blood
To which she links a truth divine !

See thou, that countest reason ripe
    In holding by the law within,
    Thou fail not in a world of sin,
And ev'n for want of such a type.

XXXIV.

My own dim life should teach me this,
    That life shall live for evermore,
    Else earth is darkness at the core,
And dust and ashes all that is ;

This round of green, this orb of flame,
    Fantastic beauty ; such as lurks
    In some wild Poet, when he works
Without a conscience or an aim.

What then were God to such as I ?
    'Twere hardly worth my while to
       choose
    Of things all mortal, or to use
A little patience ere I die ;

'Twere best at once to sink to peace,
    Like birds the charming serpent
       draws,
    To drop head-foremost in the jaws
Of vacant darkness and to cease.

XXXV.

Yet if some voice that man could trust
    Should murmur from the narrow
       house,
    ' The cheeks drop in ; the body bows
Man dies : nor is there hope in dust :'

Might I not say ? 'Yet even here,
    But for one hour, O Love, I strive
    To keep so sweet a thing alive :'
But I should turn mine ears and hear

The moanings of the homeless sea,
    The sound of streams that swift or
       slow
    Draw down Æonian hills, and sow
The dust of continents to be ;

And Love would answer with a sigh,
    ' The sound of that forgetful shore
    Will change my sweetness more and
       more,
Half-dead to know that I shall die.'

O me, what profits it to put
    An idle case ? If Death were seen
    At first as Death, Love had not been,
Or been in narrowest working shut,

Mere fellowship of sluggish moods,
    Or in his coarsest Satyr-shape
    Had bruised the herb and crush'd
       the grape,
And bask'd and batten'd in the woods.

XXXVI.

Tho' truths in manhood darkly join,
  Deep-seated in our mystic frame,
  We yield all blessing to the name
Of Him that made them current coin ;

For Wisdom dealt with mortal powers,
  Where truth in closest words shall
    fail,
  When truth embodied in a tale
Shall enter in at lowly doors.

And so the Word had breath, and
    wrought
  With human hands the creed of
    creeds
  In loveliness of perfect deeds,
More strong than all poetic thought ;

Which he may read that binds the sheaf,
  Or builds the house, or digs the grave,
  And those wild eyes that watch the
    wave
In roarings round the coral reef.

XXXVII.

Urania speaks with darken'd brow :
  'Thou pratest here where thou art
    least ;
  This faith has many a purer priest,
And many an abler voice than thou.

'Go down beside thy native rill,
  On thy Parnassus set thy feet,
  And hear thy laurel whisper sweet
About the ledges of the hill.'

And my Melpomene replies,
  A touch of shame upon her cheek :
  'I am not worthy ev'n to speak
Of thy prevailing mysteries ;

'For I am but an earthly Muse,
  And owning but a little art
  To lull with song an aching heart,
And render human love his dues ;

'But brooding on the dear one dead,
  And all he said of things divine,
  (And dear to me as sacred wine
To dying lips is all he said),

'I murmur'd, as I came along,
  Of comfort clasp'd in truth reveal'd;
  And loiter'd in the master's field,
And darken'd sanctities with song.'

XXXVIII.

With weary steps I loiter on,
  Tho' always under alter'd skies
  The purple from the distance dies,
My prospect and horizon gone.

No joy the blowing season gives,
  The herald melodies of spring,
  But in the songs I love to sing
A doubtful gleam of solace lives.

If any care for what is here
  Survive in spirits render'd free,
  Then are these songs I sing of thee
Not all ungrateful to thine ear. ·

XXXIX.

Old warder of these buried bones,
  And answering now my random
    stroke
  With fruitful cloud and living smoke,
Dark yew, that graspest at the stones

And dippest toward the dreamless head,
  To thee too comes the golden hour
  When flower is feeling after flower ;
But Sorrow—fixt upon the dead,

And darkening the dark graves of men,—
  What whisper'd from her lying lips?
  Thy gloom is kindled at the tips,
And passes into gloom again.

XL.

Could we forget the widow'd hour
  And look on Spirits breathed away,
  As on a maiden in the day
When first she wears her orange-flower !

When crown'd with blessing she doth
    rise
  To take her latest leave of home,
  And hopes and light regrets that
    come
Make April of her tender eyes ;

And doubtful joys the father move,
  And tears are on the mother's face,
  As parting with a long embrace
She enters other realms of love ;

Her office there to rear, to teach,
  Becoming as is meet and fit
  A link among the days, to knit
The generations each with each ;

And, doubtless, unto thee is given
  A life that bears immortal fruit
  In those great offices that suit
The full-grown energies of heaven.

Ay me, the difference I discern !
  How often shall her old fireside
  Be cheer'd with tidings of the bride,
How often she herself return,

And tell them all they would have told,
  And bring her babe, and make her
    boast,
  Till even those that miss'd her most
Shall count new things as dear as old :

But thou and I have shaken hands,
  Till growing winters lay me low ;
  My paths are in the fields I know,
And thine in undiscover'd lands.

XLI.

Thy spirit ere our fatal loss
  Did ever rise from high to higher ;
  As mounts the heavenward altar-fire,
As flies the lighter thro' the gross.

But thou art turn'd to something strange,
  And I have lost the links that bound
  Thy changes ; here upon the ground,
No more partaker of thy change.

Deep folly ! yet that this could be—
  That I could wing my will with
    might
  To leap the grades of life and light,
And flash at once, my friend, to thee.

For tho' my nature rarely yields
  To that vague fear implied in death ;
  Nor shudders at the gulfs beneath,
The howlings from forgotten fields ;

Yet oft when sundown skirts the moor
  An inner trouble I behold,
  A spectral doubt which makes me
    cold,
That I shall be thy mate no more,

Tho' following with an upward mind
  The wonders that have come to
    thee,
  Thro' all the secular to-be,
But evermore a life behind.

XLII.

I vex my heart with fancies dim :
  He still outstript me in the race ;
  It was but unity of place
That made me dream I rank'd with him.

And so may Place retain us still,
  And he the much-beloved again,
  A lord of large experience, train
To riper growth the mind and will :

And what delights can equal those
  That stir the spirit's inner deeps,
  When one that loves but knows not,
    reaps
A truth from one that loves and knows ?

XLIII.

If Sleep and Death be truly one,
  And every spirit's folded bloom
  Thro' all its intervital gloom
In some long trance should slumber on ;

Unconscious of the sliding hour,
  Bare of the body, might it last,
  And silent traces of the past
Be all the colour of the flower :

So then were nothing lost to man ;
  So that still garden of the souls
  In many a figured leaf enrolls
The total world since life began ;

And love will last as pure and whole
  As when he loved me here in
    Time,
  And at the spiritual prime
Rewaken with the dawning soul.

XLIV.

How fares it with the happy dead?
 For here the man is more and more;
 But he forgets the days before
God shut the doorways of his head.

The days have vanish'd, tone and tint,
 And yet perhaps the hoarding sense
 Gives out at times (he knows not
  whence)
A little flash, a mystic hint;

And in the long harmonious years
 (If Death so taste Lethean springs),
 May some dim touch of earthly
  things
Surprise thee ranging with thy peers.

If such a dreamy touch should fall,
 O turn thee round, resolve the doubt;
 My guardian angel will speak out
In that high place, and tell thee all.

XLV.

The baby new to earth and sky,
 What time his tender palm is prest
 Against the circle of the breast,
Has never thought that 'this is I:'

But as he grows he gathers much,
 And learns the use of 'I,' and 'me,'
 And finds 'I am not what I see,
And other than the things I touch.'

So rounds he to a separate mind
 From whence clear memory may
  begin,
 As thro' the frame that binds him in
His isolation grows defined.

This use may lie in blood and breath,
 Which else were fruitless of their due,
 Had man to learn himself anew
Beyond the second birth of Death.

XLVI.

We ranging down this lower track,
 The path we came by, thorn and
  flower,
 Is shadow'd by the growing hour,
Lest life should fail in looking back.

So be it: there no shade can last
 In that deep dawn behind the tomb,
 But clear from marge to marge shall
  bloom
The eternal landscape of the past;

A lifelong tract of time reveal'd;
 The fruitful hours of still increase;
 Days order'd in a wealthy peace,
And those five years its richest field.

O Love, thy province were not large,
 A bounded field, nor stretching far;
 Look also, Love, a brooding star,
A rosy warmth from marge to marge.

XLVII.

That each, who seems a separate whole,
 Should move his rounds, and fusing
  all
 The skirts of self again, should fall
Remerging in the general Soul,

Is faith as vague as all unsweet:
 Eternal form shall still divide
 The eternal soul from all beside;
And I shall know him when we meet:

And we shall sit at endless feast,
 Enjoying each the other's good:
 What vaster dream can hit the mood
Of Love on earth? He seeks at least

Upon the last and sharpest height,
 Before the spirits fade away,
 Some landing-place, to clasp and say,
'Farewell! We lose ourselves in light.'

XLVIII.

If these brief lays, of Sorrow born,
 Were taken to be such as closed
 Grave doubts and answers here pro-
  posed,
Then these were such as men might scorn:

Her care is not to part and prove;
 She takes, when harsher moods
  remit,
 What slender shade of doubt may
  flit,
And makes it vassal unto love:

And hence, indeed, she sports with
    words,
    But better serves a wholesome law,
    And holds it sin and shame to draw
The deepest measure from the chords :

Nor dare she trust a larger lay,
    But rather loosens from the lip
    Short swallow-flights of song, that dip
Their wings in tears, and skim away.

XLIX.

From art, from nature, from the schools,
    Let random influences glance,
    Like light in many a shiver'd lance
That breaks about the dappled pools :

The lightest wave of thought shall lisp,
    The fancy's tenderest eddy wreathe,
    The slightest air of song shall breathe
To make the sullen surface crisp.

And look thy look, and go thy way,
    But blame not thou the winds that
      make
    The seeming-wanton ripple break,
The tender-pencil'd shadow play.

Beneath all fancied hopes and fears
    Ay me, the sorrow deepens down,
    Whose muffled motions blindly drown
The bases of my life in tears.

L.

Be near me when my light is low,
    When the blood creeps, and the
      nerves prick
    And tingle ; and the heart is sick,
And all the wheels of Being slow.

Be near me when the sensuous frame
    Is rack'd with pangs that conquer
      trust ;
    And Time, a maniac scattering dust,
And Life, a Fury slinging flame.

Be near me when my faith is dry,
    And men the flies of latter spring,
    That lay their eggs, and sting and
      sing
And weave their petty cells and die.

Be near me when I fade away,
    To point the term of human strife,
    And on the low dark verge of life
The twilight of eternal day.

LI.

Do we indeed desire the dead
    Should still be near us at our side ?
    Is there no baseness we would hide ?
No inner vileness that we dread ?

Shall he for whose applause I strove,
    I had such reverence for his blame,
    See with clear eye some hidden
      shame
And I be lessen'd in his love ?

I wrong the grave with fears untrue :
    Shall love be blamed for want of
      faith ?
    There must be wisdom with great
      Death :
The dead shall look me thro' and thro'.

Be near us when we climb or fall :
    Ye watch, like God, the rolling hours
    With larger other eyes than ours,
To make allowance for us all.

LII.

I cannot love thee as I ought,
    For love reflects the thing beloved ;
    My words are only words, and moved
Upon the topmost froth of thought.

' Yet blame not thou thy plaintive song,'
    The Spirit of true love replied ;
    ' Thou canst not move me from thy
      side,
Nor human frailty do me wrong.

' What keeps a spirit wholly true
    To that ideal which he bears ?
    What record ? not the sinless years
That breathed beneath the Syrian blue :

' So fret not, like an idle girl,
    That life is dash'd with flecks of sin.
    Abide : thy wealth is gather'd in,
When Time hath sunder'd shell from
      pearl.'

LIII.

How many a father have I seen,
    A sober man, among his boys,
    Whose youth was full of foolish
      noise,
Who wears his manhood hale and green:

And dare we to this fancy give,
    That had the wild oat not been
      sown,
    The soil, left barren, scarce had
      grown
The grain by which a man may live?

Or, if we held the doctrine sound
    For life outliving heats of youth,
    Yet who would preach it as a truth
To those that eddy round and round?

Hold thou the good: define it well:
    For fear divine Philosophy
    Should push beyond her mark, and
      be
Procuress to the Lords of Hell.

LIV.

Oh yet we trust that somehow good
    Will be the final goal of ill,
    To pangs of nature, sins of will,
Defects of doubt, and taints of blood;

That nothing walks with aimless feet;
    That not one life shall be destroy'd,
    Or cast as rubbish to the void,
When God hath made the pile complete;

That not a worm is cloven in vain;
    That not a moth with vain desire
    Is shrivell'd in a fruitless fire,
Or but subserves another's gain.

Behold, we know not anything;
    I can but trust that good shall fall
    At last—far off—at last, to all,
And every winter change to spring.

So runs my dream: but what am I?
    An infant crying in the night:
    An infant crying for the light:
And with no language but a cry.

LV.

The wish, that of the living whole
    No life may fail beyond the grave,
    Derives it not from what we have
The likest God within the soul?

Are God and Nature then at strife,
    That Nature lends such evil dreams?
    So careful of the type she seems,
So careless of the single life;

That I, considering everywhere
    Her secret meaning in her deeds,
    And finding that of fifty seeds
She often brings but one to bear,

I falter where I firmly trod,
    And falling with my weight of cares
    Upon the great world's altar-stairs
That slope thro' darkness up to God,

I stretch lame hands of faith, and grope,
    And gather dust and chaff, and call
    To what I feel is Lord of all,
And faintly trust the larger hope.

LVI.

'So careful of the type?' but no.
    From scarped cliff and quarried stone
    She cries, 'A thousand types are gone:
I care for nothing, all shall go.

'Thou makest thine appeal to me:
    I bring to life, I bring to death:
    The spirit does but mean the breath:
I know no more.' And he, shall he,

Man, her last work, who seem'd so fair,
    Such splendid purpose in his eyes,
    Who roll'd the psalm to wintry skies,
Who built him fanes of fruitless prayer,

Who trusted God was love indeed
    And love Creation's final law—
    Tho' Nature, red in tooth and claw
With ravine, shriek'd against his creed—

Who loved, who suffer'd countless ills,
    Who battled for the True, the Just,
    Be blown about the desert dust,
Or seal'd within the iron hills?

No more? A monster then, a dream,
    A discord. Dragons of the prime,
    That tare each other in their slime,
Were mellow music match'd with him.

O life as futile, then, as frail!
    O for thy voice to soothe and bless!
    What hope of answer, or redress?
Behind the veil, behind the veil.

LVII.

Peace; come away: the song of woe
    Is after all an earthly song:
    Peace; come away: we do him
        wrong
To sing so wildly: let us go.

Come; let us go: your cheeks are pale;
    But half my life I leave behind:
    Methinks my friend is richly shrined;
But I shall pass; my work will fail.

Yet in these ears, till hearing dies,
    One set slow bell will seem to toll
    The passing of the sweetest soul
That ever look'd with human eyes.

I hear it now, and o'er and o'er,
    Eternal greetings to the dead;
    And 'Ave, Ave, Ave,' said,
'Adieu, adieu' for evermore.

LVIII.

In those sad words I took farewell:
    Like echoes in sepulchral halls,
    As drop by drop the water falls
In vaults and catacombs, they fell;

And, falling, idly broke the peace
    Of hearts that beat from day to
        day,
    Half-conscious of their dying clay,
And those cold crypts where they shall
    cease.

The high Muse answer'd: 'Wherefore
        grieve
    Thy brethren with a fruitless tear?
    Abide a little longer here,
And thou shalt take a nobler leave.'

LIX.

O Sorrow, wilt thou live with me
    No casual mistress, but a wife,
    My bosom-friend and half of life;
As I confess it needs must be;

O Sorrow, wilt thou rule my blood,
    Be sometimes lovely like a bride,
    And put thy harsher moods aside,
If thou wilt have me wise and good.

My centred passion cannot move.
    Nor will it lessen from to-day;
    But I'll have leave at times to play
As with the creature of my love;

And set thee forth, for thou art mine,
    With so much hope for years to come
    That, howsoe'er I know thee, some
Could hardly tell what name were thine.

LX.

He past; a soul of nobler tone:
    My spirit loved and loves him yet,
    Like some poor girl whose heart is
        set
On one whose rank exceeds her own.

He mixing with his proper sphere,
    She finds the baseness of her lot,
    Half jealous of she knows not what,
And envying all that meet him there.

The little village looks forlorn;
    She sighs amid her narrow days,
    Moving about the household ways,
In that dark house where she was born.

The foolish neighbours come and go,
    And tease her till the day draws by;
    At night she weeps, 'How vain
        am I!
How should he love a thing so low?'

LXI.

If, in thy second state sublime,
    Thy ransom'd reason change replies
    With all the circle of the wise,
The perfect flower of human time;

And if thou cast thine eyes below,
    How dimly character'd and slight,
    How dwarf'd a growth of cold and
       night,
How blanch'd with darkness must I grow !

Yet turn thee to the doubtful shore,
    Where thy first form was made a man ;
    I loved thee, Spirit, and love, nor can
The soul of Shakspeare love thee more.

LXII.

Tho' if an eye that's downward cast
    Could make thee somewhat blench
      or fail,
    Then be my love an idle tale,
And fading legend of the past ;

And thou, as one that once declined,
    When he was little more than boy,
    On some unworthy heart with joy,
But lives to wed an equal mind ;

And breathes a novel world, the while
    His other passion wholly dies,
    Or in the light of deeper eyes
Is matter for a flying smile.

LXIII.

Yet pity for a horse o'er-driven,
    And love in which my hound has
      part,
    Can hang no weight upon my heart
In its assumptions up to heaven ;

And I am so much more than these,
    As thou, perchance, art more than I,
    And yet I spare them sympathy,
And I would set their pains at ease.

So mayst thou watch me where I weep,
    As, unto vaster motions bound,
    The circuits of thine orbit round
A higher height, a deeper deep.

LXIV.

Dost thou look back on what hath been,
    As some divinely gifted man,
    Whose life in low estate began
And on a simple village green ;

Who breaks his birth's invidious bar,
    And grasps the skirts of happy chance,
    And breasts the blows of circum-
      stance,
And grapples with his evil star ;

Who makes by force his merit known
    And lives to clutch the golden keys,
    To mould a mighty state's decrees,
And shape the whisper of the throne ;

And moving up from high to higher,
    Becomes on Fortune's crowning slope
    The pillar of a people's hope,
The centre of a world's desire ;

Yet feels, as in a pensive dream,
    When all his active powers are still,
    A distant dearness in the hill,
A secret sweetness in the stream,

The limit of his narrower fate,
    While yet beside its vocal springs
    He play'd at counsellors and kings,
With one that was his earliest mate ;

Who ploughs with pain his native lea
    And reaps the labour of his hands,
    Or in the furrow musing stands ;
' Does my old friend remember me ?'

LXV.

Sweet soul, do with me as thou wilt ;
    I lull a fancy trouble-tost
    With 'Love's too precious to be lost,
A little grain shall not be spilt.'

And in that solace can I sing,
    Till out of painful phases wrought
    There flutters up a happy thought,
Self-balanced on a lightsome wing :

Since we deserved the name of friends,
    And thine effect so lives in me,
    A part of mine may live in thee
And move thee on to noble ends.

LXVI.

You thought my heart too far diseased ;
    You wonder when my fancies play
    To find me gay among the gay,
Like one with any trifle pleased.

The shade by which my life was crost,
　　Which makes a desert in the mind,
　　Has made me kindly with my kind,
And like to him whose sight is lost ;

Whose feet are guided thro' the land,
　　Whose jest among his friends is
　　　　free,
　　Who takes the children on his knee,
And winds their curls about his hand :

He plays with threads, he beats his chair
　　For pastime, dreaming of the sky ;
　　His inner day can never die,
His night of loss is always there.

LXVII.

When on my bed the moonlight falls,
　　I know that in thy place of rest
　　By that broad water of the west,
There comes a glory on the walls :

Thy marble bright in dark appears,
　　As slowly steals a silver flame
　　Along the letters of thy name,
And o'er the number of thy years.

The mystic glory swims away ;
　　From off my bed the moonlight dies ;
　　And closing eaves of wearied eyes
I sleep till dusk is dipt in gray :

And then I know the mist is drawn
　　A lucid veil from coast to coast,
　　And in the dark church like a ghost
Thy tablet glimmers to the dawn.

LXVIII.

When in the down I sink my head,
　　Sleep, Death's twin-brother, times
　　　　my breath ;
　　Sleep, Death's twin-brother, knows
　　　　not Death,
Nor can I dream of thee as dead :

I walk as ere I walk'd forlorn,
　　When all our path was fresh with
　　　　dew,
　　And all the bugle breezes blew
Reveillée to the breaking morn.

But what is this ?　I turn about,
　　I find a trouble in thine eye,
　　Which makes me sad I know not why
Nor can my dream resolve the doubt :

But ere the lark hath left the lea
　　I wake, and I discern the truth ;
　　It is the trouble of my youth
That foolish sleep transfers to thee.

LXIX.

I dream'd there would be Spring no more,
　　That Nature's ancient power was
　　　　lost :
　　The streets were black with smoke
　　　　and frost,
They chatter'd trifles at the door :

I wander'd from the noisy town,
　　I found a wood with thorny boughs :
　　I took the thorns to bind my brows,
I wore them like a civic crown :

I met with scoffs, I met with scorns
　　From youth and babe and hoary
　　　　hairs :
　　They call'd me in the public squares
The fool that wears a crown of thorns :

They call'd me fool, they call'd me child :
　　I found an angel of the night ;
　　The voice was low, the look was
　　　　bright ;
He look'd upon my crown and smiled :

He reach'd the glory of a hand,
　　That seem'd to touch it into leaf :
　　The voice was not the voice of grief,
The words were hard to understand.

LXX.

I cannot see the features right,
　　When on the gloom I strive to paint
　　The face I know ; the hues are faint
And mix with hollow masks of night ;

Cloud-towers by ghostly masons wrought,
　　A gulf that ever shuts and gapes,
　　A hand that points, and palled shapes
In shadowy thoroughfares of thought ;

And crowds that stream from yawning
doors,
  And shoals of pucker'd faces drive ;
  Dark bulks that tumble half alive,
And lazy lengths on boundless shores ;

Till all at once beyond the will
  I hear a wizard music roll,
  And thro' a lattice on the soul
Looks thy fair face and makes it still.

LXXI.

Sleep, kinsman thou to death and trance
  And madness, thou hast forged at last
  A night-long Present of the Past
In which we went thro' summer France.

Hadst thou such credit with the soul ?
  Then bring an opiate trebly strong,
  Drug down the blindfold sense of
wrong
That so my pleasure may be whole ;

While now we talk as once we talk'd
  Of men and minds, the dust of change,
  The days that grow to something
strange,
In walking as of old we walk'd

Beside the river's wooded reach,
  The fortress, and the mountain ridge,
  The cataract flashing from the bridge,
The breaker breaking on the beach.

LXXII.

Risest thou thus, dim dawn, again,
  And howlest, issuing out of night,
  With blasts that blow the poplar
white,
And lash with storm the streaming pane ?

Day, when my crown'd estate begun
  To pine in that reverse of doom,
  Which sicken'd every living bloom,
And blurr'd the splendour of the sun ;

Who usherest in the dolorous hour
  With thy quick tears that make the
rose
  Pull sideways, and the daisy close
Her crimson fringes to the shower ;

Who might'st have heaved a windless flame
  Up the deep East, or, whispering,
play'd
  A chequer-work of beam and shade
Along the hills, yet look'd the same.

As wan, as chill, as wild as now ;
  Day, mark'd as with some hideous
crime,
  When the dark hand struck down
thro' time,
And cancell'd nature's best : but thou,

Lift as thou may'st thy burthen'd brows
  Thro' clouds that drench the morning
star,
  And whirl the ungarner'd sheaf afar,
And sow the sky with flying boughs,

And up thy vault with roaring sound
  Climb thy thick noon, disastrous day;
  Touch thy dull goal of joyless gray,
And hide thy shame beneath the ground.

LXXIII.

So many worlds, so much to do,
  So little done, such things to be,
  How know I what had need of thee,
For thou wert strong as thou wert true ?

The fame is quench'd that I foresaw,
  The head hath miss'd an earthly
wreath :
  I curse not nature, no, nor death ;
For nothing is that errs from law.

We pass ; the path that each man trod
  Is dim, or will be dim, with weeds :
  What fame is left for human deeds
In endless age ? It rests with God.

O hollow wraith of dying fame,
  Fade wholly, while the soul exults,
  And self-infolds the large results
Of force that would have forged a name.

LXXIV.

As sometimes in a dead man's face,
  To those that watch it more and more,
  A likeness, hardly seen before,
Comes out—to some one of his race :

So, dearest, now thy brows are cold,
　　I see thee what thou art, and know
　　Thy likeness to the wise below,
Thy kindred with the great of old.

But there is more than I can see,
　　And what I see I leave unsaid,
　　Nor speak it, knowing Death has
　　　made
His darkness beautiful with thee.

LXXV.

I leave thy praises unexpress'd
　　In verse that brings myself relief,
　　And by the measure of my grief
I leave thy greatness to be guess'd ;

What practice howsoe'er expert
　　In fitting aptest words to things,
　　Or voice the richest-toned that sings,
Hath power to give thee as thou wert ?

I care not in these fading days
　　To raise a cry that lasts not long,
　　And round thee with the breeze of
　　　song
To stir a little dust of praise.

Thy leaf has perish'd in the green,
　　And, while we breathe beneath the
　　　sun,
　　The world which credits what is done
Is cold to all that might have been.

So here shall silence guard thy fame ;
　　But somewhere, out of human view,
　　Whate'er thy hands are set to do
Is wrought with tumult of acclaim.

LXXVI.

Take wings of fancy, and ascend,
　　And in a moment set thy face
　　Where all the starry heavens of
　　　space
Are sharpen'd to a needle's end ;

Take wings of foresight ; lighten thro'
　　The secular abyss to come,
　　And lo, thy deepest lays are dumb
Before the mouldering of a yew ;

And if the matin songs, that woke
　　The darkness of our planet, last,
　　Thine own shall wither in the vast
Ere half the lifetime of an oak.

Ere these have clothed their branch
　　　bowers
　　With fifty Mays, thy songs are vai
　　And what are they when these rema
The ruin'd shells of hollow towers ?

LXXVII.

What hope is here for modern rhyme
　　To him, who turns a musing eye
　　On songs, and deeds, and lives, th
　　　lie
Foreshorten'd in the tract of time ?

These mortal lullabies of pain
　　May bind a book, may line a box
　　May serve to curl a maiden's lock
Or when a thousand moons shall wane

A man upon a stall may find,
　　And, passing, turn the page that te
　　A grief, then changed to somethi
　　　else,
Sung by a long-forgotten mind.

But what of that ?　My darken'd ways
　　Shall ring with music all the sam
　　To breathe my loss is more than fam
To utter love more sweet than praise.

LXXVIII.

Again at Christmas did we weave
　　The holly round the Christn
　　　hearth ;
　　The silent snow possess'd the ear
And calmly fell our Christmas-eve :

The yule-clog sparkled keen with fros
　　No wing of wind the region swep
　　But over all things brooding slep
The quiet sense of something lost.

As in the winters left behind,
　　Again our ancient games had pla
　　The mimic picture's breathing gra
And dance and song and hoodman-bli

Who show'd a token of distress?
      No single tear, no mark of pain:
      O sorrow, then can sorrow wane?
O grief, can grief be changed to less?

O last regret, regret can die!
      No—mixt with all this mystic frame,
      Her deep relations are the same,
But with long use her tears are dry.

LXXIX.

'More than my brothers are to me,'—
      Let this not vex thee, noble heart!
      I know thee of what force thou art
To hold the costliest love in fee.

But thou and I are one in kind,
      As moulded like in Nature's mint;
      And hill and wood and field did print
The same sweet forms in either mind.

For us the same cold streamlet curl'd
      Thro' all his eddying coves; the same
      All winds that roam the twilight came
In whispers of the beauteous world.

At one dear knee we proffer'd vows,
      One lesson from one book we learn'd,
      Ere childhood's flaxen ringlet turn'd
To black and brown on kindred brows.

And so my wealth resembles thine,
      But he was rich where I was poor,
      And he supplied my want the more
As his unlikeness fitted mine.

LXXX.

If any vague desire should rise,
      That holy Death ere Arthur died
      Had moved me kindly from his side,
And dropt the dust on tearless eyes;

Then fancy shapes, as fancy can,
      The grief my loss in him had wrought,
      A grief as deep as life or thought,
But stay'd in peace with God and man.

I make a picture in the brain;
      I hear the sentence that he speaks;
      He bears the burthen of the weeks
But turns his burthen into gain.

His credit thus shall set me free;
      And, influence-rich to soothe and
            save,
      Unused example from the grave
Reach out dead hands to comfort me.

LXXXI.

Could I have said while he was here,
      'My love shall now no further range;
      There cannot come a mellower
            change,
For now is love mature in ear.'

Love, then, had hope of richer store:
      What end is here to my complaint?
      This haunting whisper makes me
            faint,
'More years had made me love thee more.

But Death returns an answer sweet:
      'My sudden frost was sudden gain,
      And gave all ripeness to the grain,
It might have drawn from after-heat.'

LXXXII.

I wage not any feud with Death
      For changes wrought on form and
            face;
      No lower life that earth's embrace
May breed with him, can fright my faith.

Eternal process moving on,
      From state to state the spirit walks;
      And these are but the shatter'd stalks,
Or ruin'd chrysalis of one.

Nor blame I Death, because he bare
      The use of virtue out of earth:
      I know transplanted human worth
Will bloom to profit, otherwhere.

For this alone on Death I wreak
      The wrath that garners in my heart;
      He put our lives so far apart
We cannot hear each other speak.

LXXXIII.

Dip down upon the northern shore,
      O sweet new-year delaying long;
      Thou doest expectant nature wrong;
Delaying long, delay no more.

What stays thee from the clouded noons,
  Thy sweetness from its proper place?
  Can trouble live with April days,
Or sadness in the summer moons?

Bring orchis, bring the foxglove spire,
  The little speedwell's darling blue,
  Deep tulips dash'd with fiery dew,
Laburnums, dropping-wells of fire.

O thou, new-year, delaying long,
  Delayest the sorrow in my blood,
  That longs to burst a frozen bud
And flood a fresher throat with song.

LXXXIV.

When I contemplate all alone
  The life that had been thine below,
  And fix my thoughts on all the glow
To which thy crescent would have grown;

I see thee sitting crown'd with good,
  A central warmth diffusing bliss
  In glance and smile, and clasp and
    kiss,
On all the branches of thy blood;

Thy blood, my friend, and partly mine;
  For now the day was drawing on,
  When thou should'st link thy life
    with one
Of mine own house, and boys of thine

Had babbled 'Uncle' on my knee;
  But that remorseless iron hour
  Made cypress of her orange flower,
Despair of Hope, and earth of thee.

I seem to meet their least desire,
  To clap their cheeks, to call them mine.
  I see their unborn faces shine
Beside the never-lighted fire.

I see myself an honour'd guest,
  Thy partner in the flowery walk
  Of letters, genial table-talk,
Or deep dispute, and graceful jest;

While now thy prosperous labour fills
  The lips of men with honest praise,
  And sun by sun the happy days
Descend below the golden hills

With promise of a morn as fair;
  And all the train of bounteous hours
  Conduct by paths of growing powers,
To reverence and the silver hair;

Till slowly worn her earthly robe,
  Her lavish mission richly wrought,
  Leaving great legacies of thought,
Thy spirit should fail from off the globe;

What time mine own might also flee,
  As link'd with thine in love and fate,
  And, hovering o'er the dolorous strait
To the other shore, involved in thee,

Arrive at last the blessed goal,
  And He that died in Holy Land
  Would reach us out the shining hand,
And take us as a single soul.

What reed was that on which I leant?
  Ah, backward fancy, wherefore wake
  The old bitterness again, and break
The low beginnings of content.

LXXXV.

This truth came borne with bier and pall,
  I felt it, when I sorrow'd most,
  'Tis better to have loved and lost,
Than never to have loved at all——

O true in word, and tried in deed,
  Demanding, so to bring relief
  To this which is our common grief,
What kind of life is that I lead;

And whether trust in things above
  Be dimm'd of sorrow, or sustain'd;
  And whether love for him have
    drain'd
My capabilities of love;

Your words have virtue such as draws
  A faithful answer from the breast,
  Thro' light reproaches, half exprest
And loyal unto kindly laws.

My blood an even tenor kept,
  Till on mine ear this message falls,
  That in Vienna's fatal walls
God's finger touch'd him, and he slept.

The great Intelligences fair
    That range above our mortal state,
    In circle round the blessed gate,
Received and gave him welcome there ;

And led him thro' the blissful climes,
    And show'd him in the fountain fresh
    All knowledge that the sons of flesh
Shall gather in the cycled times.

But I remain'd, whose hopes were dim,
    Whose life, whose thoughts were little
        worth,
    To wander on a darken'd earth,
Where all things round me breathed of
        him.

O friendship, equal-poised control,
    O heart, with kindliest motion warm,
    O sacred essence, other form,
O solemn ghost, O crowned soul !

Yet none could better know than I,
    How much of act at human hands
    The sense of human will demands
By which we dare to live or die.

Whatever way my days decline,
    I felt and feel, tho' left alone,
    His being working in mine own,
The footsteps of his life in mine ;

A life that all the Muses deck'd
    With gifts of grace, that might ex-
        press
    All-comprehensive tenderness,
All-subtilising intellect :

And so my passion hath not swerved
    To works of weakness, but I find
    An image comforting the mind,
And in my grief a strength reserved.

Likewise the imaginative woe,
    That loved to handle spiritual strife,
    Diffused the shock thro' all my life,
But in the present broke the blow.

My pulses therefore beat again
    For other friends that once I met ;
    Nor can it suit me to forget
The mighty hopes that make us men.

I woo your love : I count it crime
    To mourn for any overmuch ;
    I, the divided half of such
A friendship as had master'd Time :

Which masters Time indeed, and is
    Eternal, separate from fears :
    The all-assuming months and years
Can take no part away from this :

But Summer on the steaming floods,
    And Spring that swells the narrow
        brooks,
    And Autumn, with a noise of rooks,
That gather in the waning woods,

And every pulse of wind and wave
    Recalls, in change of light or gloom,
    My old affection of the tomb,
And my prime passion in the grave :

My old affection of the tomb,
    A part of stillness, yearns to speak :
    'Arise, and get thee forth and seek
A friendship for the years to come.

'I watch thee from the quiet shore ;
    Thy spirit up to mine can reach ;
    But in dear words of human speech
We two communicate no more.'

And I, 'Can clouds of nature stain
    The starry clearness of the free ?
    How is it ? Canst thou feel for me
Some painless sympathy with pain ?'

And lightly does the whisper fall ;
    ' 'Tis hard for thee to fathom this ;
    I triumph in conclusive bliss,
And that serene result of all.'

So hold I commerce with the dead ;
    Or so methinks the dead would
        say ;
    Or so shall grief with symbols play
And pining life be fancy-fed.

Now looking to some settled end,
    That these things pass, and I shall
        prove
    A meeting somewhere, love with love,
I crave your pardon, O my friend ;

If not so fresh, with love as true,
    I, clasping brother-hands, aver
    I could not, if I would, transfer
The whole I felt for him to you.

For which be they that hold apart
    The promise of the golden hours?
    First love, first friendship, equal
        powers,
That marry with the virgin heart.

Still mine, that cannot but deplore,
    That beats within a lonely place,
    That yet remembers his embrace,
But at his footstep leaps no more,

My heart, tho' widow'd, may not rest
    Quite in the love of what is gone,
    But seeks to beat in time with one
That warms another living breast.

Ah, take the imperfect gift I bring,
    Knowing the primrose yet is dear,
    The primrose of the later year,
As not unlike to that of Spring.

LXXXVI.

Sweet after showers, ambrosial air,
    That rollest from the gorgeous
        gloom
    Of evening over brake and bloom
And meadow, slowly breathing bare

The round of space, and rapt below
    Thro' all the dewy-tassell'd wood,
    And shadowing down the horned
        flood
In ripples, fan my brows and blow

The fever from my cheek, and sigh
    The full new life that feeds thy
        breath
    Throughout my frame, till Doubt
        and Death,
Ill brethren, let the fancy fly

From belt to belt of crimson seas
    On leagues of odour streaming far,
    To where in yonder orient star
A hundred spirits whisper 'Peace.'

LXXXVII.

I past beside the reverend walls
    In which of old I wore the gown;
    I roved at random thro' the town,
And saw the tumult of the halls;

And heard once more in college fanes
    The storm their high-built organs
        make,
    And thunder-music, rolling, shake
The prophet blazon'd on the panes;

And caught once more the distant shout,
    The measured pulse of racing oars
    Among the willows; paced the shores
And many a bridge, and all about

The same gray flats again, and felt
    The same, but not the same; and
        last
    Up that long walk of limes I past
To see the rooms in which he dwelt.

Another name was on the door:
    I linger'd; all within was noise
    Of songs, and clapping hands, and
        boys
That crash'd the glass and beat the floor;

Where once we held debate, a band
    Of youthful friends, on mind and art,
    And labour, and the changing mart,
And all the framework of the land;

When one would aim an arrow fair,
    But send it slackly from the string;
    And one would pierce an outer ring,
And one an inner, here and there;

And last the master-bowman, he,
    Would cleave the mark. A willing
        ear
    We lent him. Who, but hung to
        hear
The rapt oration flowing free

From point to point, with power and
        grace
    And music in the bounds of law,
    To those conclusions when we saw
The God within him light his face,

And seem to lift the form, and glow
    In azure orbits heavenly-wise ;
    And over those ethereal eyes
The bar of Michael Angelo.

LXXXVIII.

Wild bird, whose warble, liquid sweet,
    Rings Eden thro' the budded quicks,
    O tell me where the senses mix,
O tell me where the passions meet,

Whence radiate : fierce extremes employ
    Thy spirits in the darkening leaf,
    And in the midmost heart of grief
Thy passion clasps a secret joy :

And I—my harp would prelude woe—
    I cannot all command the strings ;
    The glory of the sum of things
Will flash along the chords and go.

LXXXIX.

Witch-elms that counterchange the floor
    Of this flat lawn with dusk and
        bright ;
    And thou, with all thy breadth and
        height
Of foliage, towering sycamore ;

How often, hither wandering down,
    My Arthur found your shadows fair,
    And shook to all the liberal air
The dust and din and steam of town :

He brought an eye for all he saw ;
    He mixt in all our simple sports ;
    They pleased him, fresh from brawl-
        ing courts
And dusty purlieus of the law.

O joy to him in this retreat,
    Immantled in ambrosial dark,
    To drink the cooler air, and mark
The landscape winking thro' the heat :

O sound to rout the brood of cares,
    The sweep of scythe in morning
        dew,
    The gust that round the garden flew,
And tumbled half the mellowing pears !

O bliss, when all in circle drawn
    About him, heart and ear were fed
    To hear him, as he lay and read
The Tuscan poets on the lawn :

Or in the all-golden afternoon
    A guest, or happy sister, sung,
    Or here she brought the harp and
        flung
A ballad to the brightening moon :

Nor less it pleased in livelier moods,
    Beyond the bounding hill to stray,
    And break the livelong summer day
With banquet in the distant woods ;

Whereat we glanced from theme to
        theme,
    Discuss'd the books to love or hate,
    Or touch'd the changes of the state,
Or threaded some Socratic dream ;

But if I praised the busy town,
    He loved to rail against it still,
    For 'ground in yonder social mill
We rub each other's angles down,

' And merge ' he said ' in form and
        gloss
    The picturesque of man and man.'
    We talk'd : the stream beneath us
        ran,
The wine-flask lying couch'd in moss,

Or cool'd within the glooming wave ;
    And last, returning from afar,
    Before the crimson-circled star
Had fall'n into her father's grave,

And brushing ankle-deep in flowers,
    We heard behind the woodbine veil
    The milk that bubbled in the pail,
And buzzings of the honied hours.

XC.

He tasted love with half his mind,
    Nor ever drank the inviolate spring
    Where nighest heaven, who first
        could fling
This bitter seed among mankind ;

That could the dead, whose dying eyes
　　Were closed with wail, resume their
　　　life,
　　They would but find in child and wife
An iron welcome when they rise :

'Twas well, indeed, when warm with wine,
　　To pledge them with a kindly tear,
　　To talk them o'er, to wish them here,
To count their memories half divine ;

But if they came who past away,
　　Behold their brides in other hands ;
　　The hard heir strides about their
　　　lands,
And will not yield them for a day.

Yea, tho' their sons were none of these,
　　Not less the yet-loved sire would
　　　make
　　Confusion worse than death, and
　　　shake
The pillars of domestic peace.

Ah dear, but come thou back to me :
　　Whatever change the years have
　　　wrought,
　　I find not yet one lonely thought
That cries against my wish for thee.

XCI.

When rosy plumelets tuft the larch,
　　And rarely pipes the mounted thrush ;
　　Or underneath the barren bush
Flits by the sea-blue bird of March ;

Come, wear the form by which I know
　　Thy spirit in time among thy peers ;
　　The hope of unaccomplish'd years
Be large and lucid round thy brow.

When summer's hourly-mellowing change
　　May breathe, with many roses sweet,
　　Upon the thousand waves of wheat,
That ripple round the lonely grange ;

Come : not in watches of the night,
　　But where the sunbeam broodeth
　　　warm,
　　Come, beauteous in thine after form,
And like a finer light in light.

XCII.

If any vision should reveal
　　Thy likeness, I might count it vain
　　As but the canker of the brain ;
Yea, tho' it spake and made appeal

To chances where our lots were cast
　　Together in the days behind,
　　I might but say, I hear a wind
Of memory murmuring the past.

Yea, tho' it spake and bared to view
　　A fact within the coming year ;
　　And tho' the months, revolving near,
Should prove the phantom-warning true.

They might not seem thy prophecies,
　　But spiritual presentiments,
　　And such refraction of events
As often rises ere they rise.

XCIII.

I shall not see thee.　Dare I say
　　No spirit ever brake the band
　　That stays him from the native land
Where first he walk'd when claspt in clay?

No visual shade of some one lost,
　　But he, the Spirit himself, may come
　　Where all the nerve of sense is
　　　numb ;
Spirit to Spirit, Ghost to Ghost.

O, therefore from thy sightless range
　　With gods in unconjectured bliss,
　　O, from the distance of the abyss
Of tenfold-complicated change,

Descend, and touch, and enter ; hear
　　The wish too strong for words to
　　　name ;
　　That in this blindness of the frame
My Ghost may feel that thine is near.

XCIV.

How pure at heart and sound in head,
　　With what divine affections bold
　　Should be the man whose thought
　　　would hold
An hour's communion with the dead.

In vain shalt thou, or any, call
    The spirits from their golden day,
    Except, like them, thou too canst say,
My spirit is at peace with all.

They haunt the silence of the breast,
    Imaginations calm and fair,
    The memory like a cloudless air,
The conscience as a sea at rest :

But when the heart is full of din,
    And doubt beside the portal waits,
    They can but listen at the gates,
And hear the household jar within.

XCV.

By night we linger'd on the lawn,
    For underfoot the herb was dry ;
    And genial warmth ; and o'er the sky
The silvery haze of summer drawn ;

And calm that let the tapers burn
    Unwavering : not a cricket chirr'd :
    The brook alone far-off was heard,
And on the board the fluttering urn :

And bats went round in fragrant skies,
    And wheel'd or lit the filmy shapes
    That haunt the dusk, with ermine capes
And woolly breasts and beaded eyes ;

While now we sang old songs that peal'd
    From knoll to knoll, where, couch'd at ease,
    The white kine glimmer'd, and the trees
Laid their dark arms about the field.

But when those others, one by one,
    Withdrew themselves from me and night,
    And in the house light after light
Went out, and I was all alone,

A hunger seized my heart ; I read
    Of that glad year which once had been,
    In those fall'n leaves which kept their green,
The noble letters of the dead :

And strangely on the silence broke
    The silent-speaking words, and strange
    Was love's dumb cry defying change
To test his worth ; and strangely spoke

The faith, the vigour, bold to dwell
    On doubts that drive the coward back,
    And keen thro' wordy snares to track
Suggestion to her inmost cell.

So word by word, and line by line,
    The dead man touch'd me from the past,
    And all at once it seem'd at last
The living soul was flash'd on mine,

And mine in this was wound, and whirl'd
    About empyreal heights of thought,
    And came on that which is, and caught
The deep pulsations of the world,

Æonian music measuring out
    The steps of Time—the shocks of Chance—
    The blows of Death. At length my trance
Was cancell'd, stricken thro' with doubt.

Vague words ! but ah, how hard to frame
    In matter-moulded forms of speech,
    Or ev'n for intellect to reach
Thro' memory that which I became :

Till now the doubtful dusk reveal'd
    The knolls once more where, couch'd at ease,
    The white kine glimmer'd, and the trees
Laid their dark arms about the field :

And suck'd from out the distant gloom
    A breeze began to tremble o'er
    The large leaves of the sycamore,
And fluctuate all the still perfume,

And gathering freshlier overhead,
    Rock'd the full-foliaged elms, and swung
    The heavy-folded rose, and flung
The lilies to and fro, and said

T   T

'The dawn, the dawn,' and died away;
　　And East and West, without a
　　　　breath,
　　Mixt their dim lights, like life and
　　　　death,
To broaden into boundless day.

XCVI.

You say, but with no touch of scorn,
　　Sweet-hearted, you, whose light-
　　　　blue eyes
　　Are tender over drowning flies,
You tell me, doubt is Devil-born.

I know not: one indeed I knew
　　In many a subtle question versed,
　　Who touch'd a jarring lyre at first,
But ever strove to make it true:

Perplext in faith, but pure in deeds,
　　At last he beat his music out.
　　There lives more faith in honest
　　　　doubt,
Believe me, than in half the creeds.

He fought his doubts and gather'd
　　　　strength,
　　He would not make his judgment
　　　　blind,
　　He faced the spectres of the mind
And laid them: thus he came at length

To find a stronger faith his own;
　　And Power was with him in the
　　　　night,
　　Which makes the darkness and the
　　　　light,
And dwells not in the light alone,

But in the darkness and the cloud,
　　As over Sinai's peaks of old,
　　While Israel made their gods of
　　　　gold,
Altho' the trumpet blew so loud.

XCVII.

My love has talk'd with rocks and trees;
　　He finds on misty mountain-ground
　　His own vast shadow glory-crown'd;
He sees himself in all he sees.

Two partners of a married life—
　　I look'd on these and thought of thee
　　In vastness and in mystery,
And of my spirit as of a wife.

These two—they dwelt with eye on eye,
　　Their hearts of old have beat in
　　　　tune,
　　Their meetings made December June
Their every parting was to die.

Their love has never past away;
　　The days she never can forget
　　Are earnest that he loves her yet,
Whate'er the faithless people say.

Her life is lone, he sits apart,
　　He loves her yet, she will not weep,
　　Tho' rapt in matters dark and deep
He seems to slight her simple heart.

He thrids the labyrinth of the mind,
　　He reads the secret of the star,
　　He seems so near and yet so far,
He looks so cold: she thinks him kind.

She keeps the gift of years before,
　　A wither'd violet is her bliss:
　　She knows not what his greatness is,
For that, for all, she loves him more.

For him she plays, to him she sings
　　Of early faith and plighted vows;
　　She knows but matters of the house,
And he, he knows a thousand things.

Her faith is fixt and cannot move,
　　She darkly feels him great and wise,
　　She dwells on him with faithful eyes,
'I cannot understand: I love.'

XCVIII.

You leave us: you will see the Rhine,
　　And those fair hills I sail'd below,
　　When I was there with him; and go
By summer belts of wheat and vine

To where he breathed his latest breath,
　　That City. All her splendour seems
　　No livelier than the wisp that gleams
On Lethe in the eyes of Death.

Let her great Danube rolling fair
    Enwind her isles, unmark'd of me :
    I have not seen, I will not see
Vienna ; rather dream that there,

A treble darkness, Evil haunts
    The birth, the bridal ; friend from
      friend
    Is oftener parted, fathers bend
Above more graves, a thousand wants

Gnarr at the heels of men, and prey
    By each cold hearth, and sadness
      flings
    Her shadow on the blaze of kings :
And yet myself have heard him say,

That not in any mother town
    With statelier progress to and fro
    The double tides of chariots flow
By park and suburb under brown

Of lustier leaves ; nor more content,
    He told me, lives in any crowd,
    When all is gay with lamps, and
      loud
With sport and song, in booth and tent,

Imperial halls, or open plain ;
    And wheels the circled dance, and
      breaks
    The rocket molten into flakes
Of crimson or in emerald rain.

XCIX.

Risest thou thus, dim dawn, again,
    So loud with voices of the birds,
    So thick with lowings of the herds,
Day, when I lost the flower of men ;

Who tremblest thro' thy darkling red
    On yon swoll'n brook that bubbles
      fast
    By meadows breathing of the past,
And woodlands holy to the dead ;

Who murmurest in the foliaged eaves
    A song that slights the coming care,
    And Autumn laying here and there
A fiery finger on the leaves ;

Who wakenest with thy balmy breath
    To myriads on the genial earth,
    Memories of bridal, or of birth,
And unto myriads more, of death.

O wheresoever those may be,
    Betwixt the slumber of the poles,
    To-day they count as kindred souls ;
They know me not, but mourn with me.

C.

I climb the hill : from end to end
    Of all the landscape underneath,
    I find no place that does not breathe
Some gracious memory of my friend ;

No gray old grange, or lonely fold,
    Or low morass and whispering
      reed,
    Or simple stile from mead to mead,
Or sheepwalk up the windy wold ;

Nor hoary knoll of ash and haw
    That hears the latest linnet trill,
    Nor quarry trench'd along the hill
And haunted by the wrangling daw ;

Nor runlet tinkling from the rock ;
    Nor pastoral rivulet that swerves
    To left and right thro' meadowy
      curves,
That feed the mothers of the flock ;

But each has pleased a kindred eye,
    And each reflects a kindlier day ;
    And, leaving these, to pass away,
I think once more he seems to die.

CI.

Unwatch'd, the garden bough shall sway,
    The tender blossom flutter down,
    Unloved, that beech will gather
      brown,
This maple burn itself away ;

Unloved, the sun-flower, shining fair,
    Ray round with flames her disk of
      seed,
    And many a rose-carnation feed
With summer spice the humming air ;

Unloved, by many a sandy bar,
    The brook shall babble down the
        plain,
    At noon or when the lesser wain
Is twisting round the polar star ;

Uncared for, gird the windy grove,
    And flood the haunts of hern and
        crake ;
    Or into silver arrows break
The sailing moon in creek and cove ;

Till from the garden and the wild
    A fresh association blow,
    And year by year the landscape
        grow
Familiar to the stranger's child ;

As year by year the labourer tills
    His wonted glebe, or lops the glades ;
    And year by year our memory fades
From all the circle of the hills.

CII.

We leave the well-beloved place
    Where first we gazed upon the sky ;
    The roofs, that heard our earliest
        cry,
Will shelter one of stranger race.

We go, but ere we go from home,
    As down the garden-walks I move,
    Two spirits of a diverse love
Contend for loving masterdom.

One whispers, ' Here thy boyhood sung
    Long since its matin song, and
        heard
    The low love-language of the bird
In native hazels tassel-hung.'

The other answers, ' Yea, but here
    Thy feet have stray'd in after hours
    With thy lost friend among the
        bowers,
And this hath made them trebly dear.'

These two have striven half the day,
    And each prefers his separate claim,
    Poor rivals in a losing game,
That will not yield each other way.

I turn to go : my feet are set
    To leave the pleasant fields and
        farms ;
    They mix in one another's arms
To one pure image of regret.

CIII.

On that last night before we went
    From out the doors where I was bred,
    I dream'd a vision of the dead,
Which left my after-morn content.

Methought I dwelt within a hall,
    And maidens with me : distant hills
    From hidden summits fed with rills
A river sliding by the wall.

The hall with harp and carol rang.
    They sang of what is wise and good
    And graceful.   In the centre stood
A statue veil'd, to which they sang ;

And which, tho' veil'd, was known to me,
    The shape of him I loved, and love
    For ever : then flew in a dove
And brought a summons from the sea :

And when they learnt that I must go
    They wept and wail'd, but led the
        way
    To where a little shallop lay
At anchor in the flood below ;

And on by many a level mead,
    And shadowing bluff that made the
        banks,
    We glided winding under ranks
Of iris, and the golden reed ;

And still as vaster grew the shore
    And roll'd the floods in grander
        space,
    The maidens gather'd strength and
        grace
And presence, lordlier than before ;

And I myself, who sat apart
    And watch'd them, wax'd in every
        limb ;
    I felt the thews of Anakim,
The pulses of a Titan's heart ;

As one would sing the death of war,
　　And one would chant the history
　　Of that great race, which is to be,
And one the shaping of a star ;

Until the forward-creeping tides
　　Began to foam, and we to draw
　　From deep to deep, to where we saw
A great ship lift her shining sides.

The man we loved was there on deck,
　　But thrice as large as man he bent
　　To greet us.　Up the side I went,
And fell in silence on his neck :

Whereat those maidens with one mind
　　Bewail'd their lot ; I did them wrong :
　　'We served thee here,' they said,
　　　'so long,
And wilt thou leave us now behind ?'

So rapt I was, they could not win
　　An answer from my lips, but he
　　Replying, 'Enter likewise ye
And go with us :' they enter'd in.

And while the wind began to sweep
　　A music out of sheet and shroud,
　　We steer'd her toward a crimson cloud
That landlike slept along the deep.

CIV.

The time draws near the birth of Christ ;
　　The moon is hid, the night is still ;
　　A single church below the hill
Is pealing, folded in the mist.

A single peal of bells below,
　　That wakens at this hour of rest
　　A single murmur in the breast,
That these are not the bells I know.

Like strangers' voices here they sound,
　　In lands where not a memory strays,
　　Nor landmark breathes of other days,
But all is new unhallow'd ground.

CV.

To-night ungather'd let us leave
　　This laurel, let this holly stand :
　　We live within the stranger's land,
And strangely falls our Christmas-eve.

Our father's dust is left alone
　　And silent under other snows :
　　There in due time the woodbine
　　　blows,
The violet comes, but we are gone.

No more shall wayward grief abuse
　　The genial hour with mask and
　　　mime ;
　　For change of place, like growth of
　　　time,
Has broke the bond of dying use.

Let cares that petty shadows cast,
　　By which our lives are chiefly
　　　proved,
　　A little spare the night I loved,
And hold it solemn to the past.

But let no footstep beat the floor,
　　Nor bowl of wassail mantle warm ;
　　For who would keep an ancient form
Thro' which the spirit breathes no more?

Be neither song, nor game, nor feast ;
　　Nor harp be touch'd, nor flute be
　　　blown ;
　　No dance, no motion, save alone
What lightens in the lucid east

Of rising worlds by yonder wood.
　　Long sleeps the summer in the seed ;
　　Run out your measured arcs, and
　　　lead
The closing cycle rich in good.

CVI.

Ring out, wild bells, to the wild sky,
　　The flying cloud, the frosty light :
　　The year is dying in the night ;
Ring out, wild bells, and let him die.

Ring out the old, ring in the new,
　　Ring, happy bells, across the snow :
　　The year is going, let him go ;
Ring out the false, ring in the true.

Ring out the grief that saps the mind,
　　For those that here we see no more ;
　　Ring out the feud of rich and poor,
Ring in redress to all mankind.

Ring out a slowly dying cause,
　　And ancient forms of party strife ;
　　Ring in the nobler modes of life,
With sweeter manners, purer laws.

Ring out the want, the care, the sin,
　　The faithless coldness of the times ;
　　Ring out, . ring out my mournful
　　　rhymes,
But ring the fuller minstrel in.

Ring out false pride in place and blood,
　　The civic slander and the spite ;
　　Ring in the love of truth and right,
Ring in the common love of good.

Ring out old shapes of foul disease ;
　　Ring out the narrowing lust of gold ;
　　Ring out the thousand wars of old,
Ring in the thousand years of peace.

Ring in the valiant man and free,
　　The larger heart, the kindlier hand ;
　　Ring out the darkness of the land,
Ring in the Christ that is to be.

CVII.

It is the day when he was born,
　　A bitter day that early sank
　　Behind a purple-frosty bank
Of vapour, leaving night forlorn.

The time admits not flowers or leaves
　　To deck the banquet. Fiercely flies
　　The blast of North and East, and ice
Makes daggers at the sharpen'd eaves,

And bristles all the brakes and thorns
　　To yon hard crescent, as she hangs
　　Above the wood which grides and
　　　clangs
Its leafless ribs and iron horns

Together, in the drifts that pass
　　To darken on the rolling brine
　　That breaks the coast. But fetch
　　the wine,
Arrange the board and brim the glass ;

Bring in great logs and let them lie,
　　To make a solid core of heat ;
　　Be cheerful-minded, talk and treat
Of all things ev'n as he were by ;

We keep the day. With festal cheer,
　　With books and music, surely we
　　Will drink to him, whate'er he be,
And sing the songs he loved to hear.

CVIII.

I will not shut me from my kind,
　　And, lest I stiffen into stone,
　　I will not eat my heart alone,
Nor feed with sighs a passing wind :

What profit lies in barren faith,
　　And vacant yearning, tho' with might
　　To scale the heaven's highest height,
Or dive below the wells of Death ?

What find I in the highest place,
　　But mine own phantom chanting
　　　hymns ?
　　And on the depths of death there
　　　swims
The reflex of a human face.

I'll rather take what fruit may be
　　Of sorrow under human skies :
　　'Tis held that sorrow makes us
　　wise,
Whatever wisdom sleep with thee.

CIX.

Heart-affluence in discursive talk
　　From household fountains never
　　　dry ;
　　The critic clearness of an eye,
That saw thro' all the Muses' walk ,

Seraphic intellect and force
　　To seize and throw the doubts of
　　man ;
　　Impassion'd logic, which outran
The hearer in its fiery course ;

High nature amorous of the good,
　　But touch'd with no ascetic gloom ;
　　And passion pure in snowy bloom
Thro' all the years of April blood ;

A love of freedom rarely felt,
　　Of freedom in her regal seat
　　Of England ; not the schoolboy heat,
The blind hysterics of the Celt :

And manhood fused with female grace
In such a sort, the child would twine
A trustful hand, unask'd, in thine,
And find his comfort in thy face;

All these have been, and thee mine eyes
Have look'd on: if they look'd in
vain,
My shame is greater who remain,
Nor let thy wisdom make me wise.

CX.

Thy converse drew us with delight,
The men of rathe and riper years:
The feeble soul, a haunt of fears,
Forgot his weakness in thy sight.

On thee the loyal-hearted hung,
The proud was half disarm'd of
pride,
Nor cared the serpent at thy side
To flicker with his double tongue.

The stern were mild when thou wert by,
The flippant put himself to school
And heard thee, and the brazen fool
Was soften'd, and he knew not why;

While I, thy nearest, sat apart,
And felt thy triumph was as mine;
And loved them more, that they
were thine,
The graceful tact, the Christian art;

Nor mine the sweetness or the skill,
But mine the love that will not tire,
And, born of love, the vague desire
That spurs an imitative will.

CXI.

The churl in spirit, up or down
Along the scale of ranks, thro' all,
To him who grasps a golden ball,
By blood a king, at heart a clown;

The churl in spirit, howe'er he veil
His want in forms for fashion's
sake,
Will let his coltish nature break
At seasons thro' the gilded pale:

For who can always act? but he,
To whom a thousand memories call,
Not being less but more than all
The gentleness he seem'd to be,

Best seem'd the thing he was, and join'd
Each office of the social hour
To noble manners, as the flower
And native growth of noble mind;

Nor ever narrowness or spite,
Or villain fancy fleeting by,
Drew in the expression of an eye,
Where God and Nature met in light;

And thus he bore without abuse
The grand old name of gentleman,
Defamed by every charlatan,
And soil'd with all ignoble use.

CXII.

High wisdom holds my wisdom less,
That I, who gaze with temperate
eyes
On glorious insufficiencies,
Set light by narrower perfectness.

But thou, that fillest all the room
Of all my love, art reason why
I seem to cast a careless eye
On souls, the lesser lords of doom.

For what wert thou? some novel power
Sprang up for ever at a touch,
And hope could never hope too
much,
In watching thee from hour to hour,

Large elements in order brought,
And tracts of calm from tempest
made,
And world-wide fluctuation sway'd
In vassal tides that follow'd thought.

CXIII.

'Tis held that sorrow makes us wise;
Yet how much wisdom sleeps with
thee
Which not alone had guided me,
But served the seasons that may rise;

For can I doubt, who knew thee keen
　　In intellect, with force and skill
　　To strive, to fashion, to fulfil—
I doubt not what thou wouldst have been :

A life in civic action warm,
　　A soul on highest mission sent,
　　A potent voice of Parliament,
A pillar steadfast in the storm,

Should licensed boldness gather force,
　　Becoming, when the time has birth,
　　A lever to uplift the earth
And roll it in another course,

With thousand shocks that come and go,
　　With agonies, with energies,
　　With overthrowings, and with cries,
And undulations to and fro.

CXIV.

Who loves not Knowledge? Who shall
　　　　rail
　　Against her beauty? May she mix
　　With men and prosper ! Who shall
　　　　fix
Her pillars ? Let her work prevail.

But on her forehead sits a fire :
　　She sets her forward countenance
　　And leaps into the future chance,
Submitting all things to desire.

Half-grown as yet, a child, and vain—
　　She cannot fight the fear of death.
　　What is she, cut from love and faith,
But some wild Pallas from the brain

Of Demons ? fiery-hot to burst
　　All barriers in her onward race
　　For power. Let her know her place ;
She is the second, not the first.

A higher hand must make her mild,
　　If all be not in vain ; and guide
　　Her footsteps, moving side by side
With wisdom, like the younger child :

For she is earthly of the mind,
　　But Wisdom heavenly of the soul.
　　O, friend, who camest to thy goal
So early, leaving me behind,

I would the great world grew like thee,
　　Who grewest not alone in power
　　And knowledge, but by year and
　　　　hour
In reverence and in charity.

CXV.

Now fades the last long streak of snow,
　　Now burgeons every maze of quick
　　About the flowering squares, and
　　　　thick
By ashen roots the violets blow.

Now rings the woodland loud and long,
　　The distance takes a lovelier hue,
　　And drown'd in yonder living blue
The lark becomes a sightless song.

Now dance the lights on lawn and lea,
　　The flocks are whiter down the vale,
　　And milkier every milky sail
On winding stream or distant sea ;

Where now the seamew pipes, or dives
　　In yonder greening gleam, and fly
　　The happy birds, that change their
　　　　sky
To build and brood ; that live their lives

From land to land ; and in my breast
　　Spring wakens too ; and my regret
　　Becomes an April violet,
And buds and blossoms like the rest.

CXVI.

Is it, then, regret for buried time
　　That keenlier in sweet April wakes,
　　And meets the year, and gives and
　　　　takes
The colours of the crescent prime ?

Not all : the songs, the stirring air,
　　The life re-orient out of dust,
　　Cry thro' the sense to hearten trust
In that which made the world so fair.

Not all regret : the face will shine
　　Upon me, while I muse alone ;
　　And that dear voice, I once have
　　　　known,
Still speak to me of me and mine :

Yet less of sorrow lives in me
    For days of happy commune dead ;
    Less yearning for the friendship
        fled,
Than some strong bond which is to be.

CXVII.

O days and hours, your work is this
    To hold me from my proper place,
    A little while from his embrace,
For fuller gain of after bliss :

That out of distance might ensue
    Desire of nearness doubly sweet ;
    And unto meeting when we meet,
Delight a hundredfold accrue,

For every grain of sand that runs,
    And every span of shade that
        steals,
    And every kiss of toothed wheels,
And all the courses of the suns.

CXVIII.

Contemplate all this work of Time,
    The giant labouring in his youth ;
    Nor dream of human love and truth,
As dying Nature's earth and lime ;

But trust that those we call the dead
    Are breathers of an ampler day
    For ever nobler ends.   They say,
The solid earth whereon we tread

In tracts of fluent heat began,
    And grew to seeming-random forms,
    The seeming prey of cyclic storms,
Till at the last arose the man ;

Who throve and branch'd from clime to
        clime,
    The herald of a higher race,
    And of himself in higher place,
If so he type this work of time

Within himself, from more to more ;
    Or, crown'd with attributes of woe
    Like glories, move his course, and
        show
That life is not as idle ore,

But iron dug from central gloom,
    And heated hot with burning fears,
    And dipt in baths of hissing tears,
And batter'd with the shocks of doom

To shape and use.   Arise and fly
    The reeling Faun, the sensual feast ;
    Move upward, working out the beast,
And let the ape and tiger die.

CXIX.

Doors, where my heart was used to beat
    So quickly, not as one that weeps
    I come once more ; the city sleeps ;
I smell the meadow in the street ;

I hear a chirp of birds ; I see
    Betwixt the black fronts long-with-
        drawn
    A light-blue lane of early dawn,
And think of early days and thee,

And bless thee, for thy lips are bland,
    And bright the friendship of thine
        eye ;
    And in my thoughts with scarce a sigh
I take the pressure of thine hand.

CXX.

I trust I have not wasted breath :
    I think we are not wholly brain,
    Magnetic mockeries ; not in vain,
Like Paul with beasts, I fought with
        Death ;

Not only cunning casts in clay :
    Let Science prove we are, and then
    What matters Science unto men,
At least to me ? I would not stay.

Let him, the wiser man who springs
    Hereafter, up from childhood shape
    His action like the greater ape,
But I was *born* to other things.

CXXI.

Sad Hesper o'er the buried sun
    And ready, thou, to die with him,
    Thou watchest all things ever dim
And dimmer, and a glory done :

The team is loosen'd from the wain,
    The boat is drawn upon the shore ;
    Thou listenest to the closing door,
And life is darken'd in the brain.

Bright Phosphor, fresher for the night,
    By thee the world's great work is
        heard
    Beginning, and the wakeful bird ;
Behind thee comes the greater light :

The market boat is on the stream,
    And voices hail it from the brink ;
    Thou hear'st the village hammer
        clink,
And see'st the moving of the team.

Sweet Hesper-Phosphor, double name
    For what is one, the first, the last,
    Thou, like my present and my
        past,
Thy place is changed ; thou art the
        same.

CXXII.

Oh, wast thou with me, dearest, then,
    While I rose up against my doom,
    And yearn'd to burst the folded
        gloom,
To bare the eternal Heavens again,

To feel once more, in placid awe,
    The strong imagination roll
    A sphere of stars about my soul,
In all her motion one with law ;

If thou wert with me, and the grave
    Divide us not, be with me now,
    And enter in at breast and brow,
Till all my blood, a fuller wave,

Be quicken'd with a livelier breath,
    And like an inconsiderate boy,
    As in the former flash of joy,
I slip the thoughts of life and death ;

And all the breeze of Fancy blows,
    And every dew-drop paints a bow,
    The wizard lightnings deeply glow,
And every thought breaks out a rose.

CXXIII.

There rolls the deep where grew the tree.
    O earth, what changes hast thou
        seen !
    There where the long street roars,
        hath been
The stillness of the central sea.

The hills are shadows, and they flow
    From form to form, and nothing
        stands ;
    They melt like mist, the solid lands,
Like clouds they shape themselves and
        go.

But in my spirit will I dwell,
    And dream my dream, and hold it
        true ;
    For tho' my lips may breathe adieu,
I cannot think the thing farewell.

CXXIV.

That which we dare invoke to bless ;
    Our dearest faith ; our ghastliest
        doubt ;
    He, They, One, All ; within, with-
        out ;
The Power in darkness whom we guess ;

I found Him not in world or sun,
    Or eagle's wing, or insect's eye ;
    Nor thro' the questions men may
        try,
The petty cobwebs we have spun :

If e'er when faith had fall'n asleep,
    I heard a voice ' believe no more '
    And heard an ever-breaking shore
That tumbled in the Godless deep ;

A warmth within the breast would melt
    The freezing reason's colder part,
    And like a man in wrath the heart
Stood up and answer'd ' I have felt.'

No, like a child in doubt and fear :
    But that blind clamour made me
        wise ;
    Then was I as a child that cries,
But, crying, knows his father near ;

nd what I am beheld again
  What is, and no man understands ;
  And out of darkness came the hands
hat reach thro' nature, moulding men.

CXXV.

Whatever I have said or sung,
  Some bitter notes my harp would give,
  Yea, tho' there often seem'd to live
 contradiction on the tongue,

et Hope had never lost her youth ;
  She did but look through dimmer
    eyes ;
  Or Love but play'd with gracious lies,
ecause he felt so fix'd in truth :

nd if the song were full of care,
  He breathed the spirit of the song ;
  And if the words were sweet and
    strong
Ie set his royal signet there ;

biding with me till I sail
  To seek thee on the mystic deeps,
  And this electric force, that keeps
 thousand pulses dancing, fail.

CXXVI.

Love is and was my Lord and King,
  And in his presence I attend
  To hear the tidings of my friend,
Which every hour his couriers bring.

Love is and was my King and Lord,
  And will be, tho' as yet I keep
  Within his court on earth, and sleep
Incompass'd by his faithful guard,

And hear at times a sentinel
  Who moves about from place to place,
  And whispers to the worlds of space,
n the deep night, that all is well.

CXXVII.

And all is well, tho' faith and form
  Be sunder'd in the night of fear ;
  Well roars the storm to those that
    hear
A deeper voice across the storm,

Proclaiming social truth shall spread,
  And justice, ev'n tho' thrice again
  The red fool-fury of the Seine
Should pile her barricades with dead.

But ill for him that wears a crown,
  And him, the lazar, in his rags :
  They tremble, the sustaining crags ;
The spires of ice are toppled down,

And molten up, and roar in flood ;
  The fortress crashes from on high,
  The brute earth lightens to the sky,
And the great Æon sinks in blood,

And compass'd by the fires of Hell ;
  While thou, dear spirit, happy star,
  O'erlook'st the tumult from afar,
And smilest, knowing all is well.

CXXVIII.

The love that rose on stronger wings,
  Unpalsied when he met with Death,
  Is comrade of the lesser faith
That sees the course of human things.

No doubt vast eddies in the flood
  Of onward time shall yet be made,
  And throned races may degrade ;
Yet O ye mysteries of good,

Wild Hours that fly with Hope and Fear,
  If all your office had to do
  With old results that look like new ;
If this were all your mission here,

To draw, to sheathe a useless sword,
  To fool the crowd with glorious
    lies,
  To cleave a creed in sects and cries,
To change the bearing of a word,

To shift an arbitrary power,
  To cramp the student at his desk,
  To make old bareness picturesque
And tuft with grass a feudal tower ;

Why then my scorn might well descend
  On you and yours. I see in part
  That all, as in some piece of art,
Is toil cöoperant to an end.

CXXIX.

Dear friend, far off, my lost desire,
 So far, so near in woe and weal;
 O loved the most, when most I feel
There is a lower and a higher;

Known and unknown; human, divine;
 Sweet human hand and lips and eye;
 Dear heavenly friend that canst not
  die,
Mine, mine, for ever, ever mine;

Strange friend, past, present, and to be;
 Loved deeplier, darklier understood;
 Behold, I dream a dream of good,
And mingle all the world with thee.

CXXX.

Thy voice is on the rolling air;
 I hear thee where the waters run;
 Thou standest in the rising sun,
And in the setting thou art fair.

What art thou then? I cannot guess;
 But tho' I seem in star and flower
 To feel thee some diffusive power,
I do not therefore love thee less:

My love involves the love before;
 My love is vaster passion now;
 Tho' mix'd with God and Nature
  thou,
I seem to love thee more and more.

Far off thou art, but ever nigh;
 I have thee still, and I rejoice;
 I prosper, circled with thy voice;
I shall not lose thee tho' I die.

CXXXI.

O living will that shalt endure
 When all that seems shall suffer
  shock,
 Rise in the spiritual rock,
Flow thro' our deeds and make them pure,

That we may lift from out of dust
 A voice as unto him that hears,
 A cry above the conquer'd years
To one that with us works, and trust,

With faith that comes of self-control,
 The truths that never can be prove[d]
 Until we close with all we loved,
And all we flow from, soul in soul.

———

O true and tried, so well and long,
 Demand not thou a marriage lay;
 In that it is thy marriage day
Is music more than any song.

Nor have I felt so much of bliss
 Since first he told me that he love[d]
 A daughter of our house; nor prove[d]
Since that dark day a day like this;

Tho' I since then have number'd o'er
 Some thrice three years: they wen[t]
  and came,
 Remade the blood and changed th[e]
  frame,
And yet is love not less, but more;

No longer caring to embalm
 In dying songs a dead regret,
 But like a statue solid-set,
And moulded in colossal calm.

Regret is dead, but love is more
 Than in the summers that are flown
 For I myself with these have grow[n]
To something greater than before;

Which makes appear the songs I made
 As echoes out of weaker times,
 As half but idle brawling rhymes,
The sport of random sun and shade.

But where is she, the bridal flower,
 That must be made a wife ere noon
 She enters, glowing like the moon
Of Eden on its bridal bower:

On me she bends her blissful eyes
 And then on thee; they meet thy loo[k]
 And brighten like the star that shoo[k]
Betwixt the palms of paradise.

O when her life was yet in bud,
 He too foretold the perfect rose.
 For thee she grew, for thee she grow[s]
For ever, and as fair as good.

And thou art worthy; full of power;
 As gentle; liberal-minded, great,
  Consistent; wearing all that weight
Of learning lightly like a flower.

But now set out: the noon is near,
 And I must give away the bride;
  She fears not, or with thee beside
And me behind her, will not fear.

For I that danced her on my knee,
 That watch'd her on her nurse's arm,
  That shielded all her life from harm
At last must part with her to thee;

Now waiting to be made a wife,
 Her feet, my darling, on the dead;
  Their pensive tablets round her head,
And the most living words of life

Breathed in her ear. The ring is on,
 The 'wilt thou' answer'd, and again
  The 'wilt thou' ask'd, till out of
   twain
Her sweet 'I will' has made you one.

Now sign your names, which shall be
  read,
 Mute symbols of a joyful morn,
  By village eyes as yet unborn;
The names are sign'd, and overhead

Begins the clash and clang that tells
 The joy to every wandering breeze;
  The blind wall rocks, and on the trees
The dead leaf trembles to the bells.

O happy hour, and happier hours
 Await them. Many a merry face
  Salutes them—maidens of the place,
That pelt us in the porch with flowers.

O happy hour, behold the bride
 With him to whom her hand I gave.
  They leave the porch, they pass the
   grave
That has to-day its sunny side.

To-day the grave is bright for me,
 For them the light of life increased,
  Who stay to share the morning feast,
Who rest to-night beside the sea.

Let all my genial spirits advance
 To meet and greet a whiter sun;
  My drooping memory will not shun
The foaming grape of eastern France.

It circles round, and fancy plays,
 And hearts are warm'd and faces
   bloom,
  As drinking health to bride and
   groom
We wish them store of happy days.

Nor count me all to blame if I
 Conjecture of a stiller guest,
  Perchance, perchance, among the
   rest,
And, tho' in silence, wishing joy.

But they must go, the time draws on,
 And those white-favour'd horses
   wait;
  They rise, but linger; it is late;
Farewell, we kiss, and they are gone.

A shade falls on us like the dark
 From little cloudlets on the grass,
  But sweeps away as out we pass
To range the woods, to roam the park,

Discussing how their courtship grew,
 And talk of others that are wed,
  And how she look'd, and what he
   said,
And back we come at fall of dew.

Again the feast, the speech, the glee,
 The shade of passing thought, the
   wealth
  Of words and wit, the double health,
The crowning cup, the three-times-three,

And last the dance;—till I retire:
 Dumb is that tower which spake so
   loud,
  And high in heaven the streaming
   cloud,
And on the downs a rising fire:

And rise, O moon, from yonder down,
 Till over down and over dale
  All night the shining vapour sail
And pass the silent-lighted town,

The white-faced halls, the glancing rills,
    And catch at every mountain head,
    And o'er the friths that branch and
        spread
Their sleeping silver thro' the hills ;

And touch with shade the bridal doors,
    With tender gloom the roof, the
        wall ;
    And breaking let the splendour fall
To spangle all the happy shores

By which they rest, and ocean sounds,
    And, star and system rolling past,
    A soul shall draw from out the vast
And strike his being into bounds,

And, moved thro' life of lower phase,
    Result in man, be born and think,
    And act and love, a closer link
Betwixt us and the crowning race

Of those that, eye to eye, shall look
    On knowledge ; under whose com-
        mand
    Is Earth and Earth's, and in their
        hand
Is Nature like an open book ;

No longer half-akin to brute,
    For all we thought and loved and did,
    And hoped, and suffer'd, is but seed
Of what in them is flower and fruit ;

Whereof the man, that with me trod
    This planet, was a noble type
    Appearing ere the times were ripe,
That friend of mine who lives in God,

That God, which ever lives and loves,
    One God, one law, one element,
    And one far-off divine event,
To which the whole creation moves.

MAUD; A MONODRAMA.

PART I.

I.

I.

I HATE the dreadful hollow behind the little wood,
Its lips in the field above are dabbled with blood-red heath,
The red-ribb'd ledges drip with a silent horror of blood,
And Echo there, whatever is ask'd her, answers ' Death.'

II.

For there in the ghastly pit long since a body was found,
His who had given me life—O father ! O God ! was it well ?—
Mangled, and flatten'd, and crush'd, and dinted into the ground :
There yet lies the rock that fell with him when he fell.

III.

Did he fling himself down ? who knows ? for a vast speculation had fail'd,
And ever he mutter'd and madden'd, and ever wann'd with despair,
And out he walk'd when the wind like a broken worldling wail'd,
And the flying gold of the ruin'd woodlands drove thro' the air.

IV.

I remember the time, for the roots of my hair were stirr'd
By a shuffled step, by a dead weight trail'd, by a whisper'd fright,
And my pulses closed their gates with a shock on my heart as I heard
The shrill-edged shriek of a mother divide the shuddering night.

V.

Villainy somewhere! whose? One says, we are villains all.
Not he: his honest fame should at least by me be maintained :
But that old man, now lord of the broad estate and the Hall,
Dropt off gorged from a scheme that had left us flaccid and drain'd.

VI.

Why do they prate of the blessings of Peace? we have made them a curse,
Pickpockets, each hand lusting for all that is not its own ;
And lust of gain, in the spirit of Cain, is it better or worse
Than the heart of the citizen hissing in war on his own hearthstone?

VII.

But these are the days of advance, the works of the men of mind,
When who but a fool would have faith in a tradesman's ware or his word?
Is it peace or war? Civil war, as I think, and that of a kind
The viler, as underhand, not openly bearing the sword.

VIII.

Sooner or later I too may passively take the print
Of the golden age—why not? I have neither hope nor trust ;
May make my heart as a millstone, set my face as a flint,
Cheat and be cheated, and die : who knows? we are ashes and dust.

IX.

Peace sitting under her olive, and slurring the days gone by,
When the poor are hovell'd and hustled together, each sex, like swine,
When only the ledger lives, and when only not all men lie ;
Peace in her vineyard—yes !—but a company forges the wine.

X.

And the vitriol madness flushes up in the ruffian's head,
Till the filthy by-lane rings to the yell of the trampled wife,
And chalk and alum and plaster are sold to the poor for bread,
And the spirit of murder works in the very means of life,

XI.

And Sleep must lie down arm'd, for the villainous centre-bits
Grind on the wakeful ear in the hush of the moonless nights,
While another is cheating the sick of a few last gasps, as he sits
To pestle a poison'd poison behind his crimson lights.

XII.

When a Mammonite mother kills her babe for a burial fee,
And Timour-Mammon grins on a pile of children's bones,
Is it peace or war? better, war! loud war by land and by sea,
War with a thousand battles, and shaking a hundred thrones.

XIII.

For I trust if an enemy's fleet came yonder round by the hill,
And the rushing battle-bolt sang from the three-decker out of the foam,
That the smooth-faced snubnosed rogue would leap from his counter and till,
And strike, if he could, were it but with his cheating yardwand, home.——

XIV.

What ! am I raging alone as my father raged in his mood ?
Must *I* too creep to the hollow and dash myself down and die
Rather than hold by the law that I made, nevermore to brood
On a horror of shatter'd limbs and a wretched swindler's lie ?

XV.

Would there be sorrow for *me ?* there was *love* in the passionate shriek,
Love for the silent thing that had made false haste to the grave—
Wrapt in a cloak, as I saw him, and thought he would rise and speak
And rave at the lie and the liar, ah God, as he used to rave.

XVI.

I am sick of the Hall and the hill, I am sick of the moor and the main.
Why should I stay ? can a sweeter chance ever come to me here ?
O, having the nerves of motion as well as the nerves of pain,
Were it not wise if I fled from the place and the pit and the fear ?

XVII.

Workmen up at the Hall !—they are coming back from abroad ;
The dark old place will be gilt by the touch of a millionaire :
I have heard, I know not whence, of the singular beauty of Maud ;
I play'd with the girl when a child ; she promised then to be fair.

XVIII.

Maud with her venturous climbings and tumbles and childish escapes,
Maud the delight of the village, the ringing joy of the Hall,
Maud with her sweet purse-mouth when my father dangled the grapes,
Maud the beloved of my mother, the moon-faced darling of all,—

XIX.

What is she now ? My dreams are bad. She may bring me a curse.
No, there is fatter game on the moor ; she will let me alone.
Thanks, for the fiend best knows whether woman or man be the worse.
I will bury myself in myself, and the Devil may pipe to his own.

II.

Long have I sigh'd for a calm : God grant I may find it at last !
It will never be broken by Maud, she has neither savour nor salt,
But a cold and clear-cut face, as I found when her carriage past,
Perfectly beautiful : let it be granted her : where is the fault ?

All that I saw (for her eyes were downcast, not to be seen)
Faultily faultless, icily regular, splendidly null,
Dead perfection, no more ; nothing more, if it had not been
For a chance of travel, a paleness, an hour's defect of the rose,
Or an underlip, you may call it a little too ripe, too full,
Or the least little delicate aquiline curve in a sensitive nose,
From which I escaped heart-free, with the least little touch of spleen.

III.

Cold and clear-cut face, why come you so cruelly meek,
Breaking a slumber in which all spleenful folly was drown'd,
Pale with the golden beam of an eyelash dead on the cheek,
Passionless, pale, cold face, star-sweet on a gloom profound ;
Womanlike, taking revenge too deep for a transient wrong
Done but in thought to your beauty, and ever as pale as before
Growing and fading and growing upon me without a sound,
Luminous, gemlike, ghostlike, deathlike, half the night long
Growing and fading and growing, till I could bear it no more,
But arose, and all by myself in my own dark garden ground,
Listening now to the tide in its broad-flung shipwrecking roar,
Now to the scream of a madden'd beach dragg'd down by the wave,
Walk'd in a wintry wind by a ghastly glimmer, and found
The shining daffodil dead, and Orion low in his grave.

IV.

I.

A million emeralds break from the ruby-budded lime
In the little grove where I sit—ah, wherefore cannot I be
Like things of the season gay, like the bountiful season bland,
When the far-off sail is blown by the breeze of a softer clime,
Half-lost in the liquid azure bloom of a crescent of sea,
The silent sapphire-spangled marriage ring of the land ?

II.

Below me, there, is the village, and looks how quiet and small !
And yet bubbles o'er like a city, with gossip, scandal, and spite ;
And Jack on his ale-house bench has as many lies as a Czar ;
And here on the landward side, by a red rock, glimmers the Hall ;
And up in the high Hall-garden I see her pass like a light ;
But sorrow seize me if ever that light be my leading star !

III.

When have I bow'd to her father, the wrinkled head of the race ?
I met her to-day with her brother, but not to her brother I bow'd :
I bow'd to his lady-sister as she rode by on the moor ;
But the fire of a foolish pride flash'd over her beautiful face.
O child, you wrong your beauty, believe it, in being so proud ;
Your father has wealth well-gotten, and I am nameless and poor.

T   U

IV.

I keep but a man and a maid, ever ready to slander and steal ;
I know it, and smile a hard-set smile, like a stoic, or like
A wiser epicurean, and let the world have its way :
For nature is one with rapine, a harm no preacher can heal ;
The Mayfly is torn by the swallow, the sparrow spear'd by the shrike,
And the whole little wood where I sit is a world of plunder and prey.

V.

We are puppets, Man in his pride, and Beauty fair in her flower ;
Do we move ourselves, or are moved by an unseen hand at a game
That pushes us off from the board, and others ever succeed ?
Ah yet, we cannot be kind to each other here for an hour ;
We whisper, and hint, and chuckle, and grin at a brother's shame ;
However we brave it out, we men are a little breed.

VI.

A monstrous eft was of old the Lord and Master of Earth,
For him did his high sun flame, and his river billowing ran,
And he felt himself in his force to be Nature's crowning race.
As nine months go to the shaping an infant ripe for his birth,
So many a million of ages have gone to the making of man :
He now is first, but is he the last ? is he not too base ?

VII.

The man of science himself is fonder of glory, and vain,
An eye well-practised in nature, a spirit bounded and poor ;
The passionate heart of the poet is whirl'd into folly and vice.
I would not marvel at either, but keep a temperate brain ;
For not to desire or admire, if a man could learn it, were more
Than to walk all day like the sultan of old in a garden of spice.

VIII.

For the drift of the Maker is dark, an Isis hid by the veil.
Who knows the ways of the world, how God will bring them about
Our planet is one, the suns are many, the world is wide.
Shall I weep if a Poland fall ? shall I shriek if a Hungary fail ?
Or an infant civilisation be ruled with rod or with knout ?
I have not made the world, and He that made it will guide.

IX.

Be mine a philosopher's life in the quiet woodland ways,
Where if I cannot be gay let a passionless peace be my lot,
Far-off from the clamour of liars belied in the hubbub of lies ;
From the long-neck'd geese of the world that are ever hissing dispraise
Because their natures are little, and, whether he heed it or not,
Where each man walks with his head in a cloud of poisonous flies.

x.

And most of all would I flee from the cruel madness of love,
The honey of poison-flowers and all the measureless ill.
Ah Maud, you milkwhite fawn, you are all unmeet for a wife.
Your mother is mute in her grave as her image in marble above ;
Your father is ever in London, you wander about at your will ;
You have but fed on the roses and lain in the lilies of life.

V.

I.

A voice by the cedar tree
In the meadow under the Hall !
She is singing an air that is known to me,
A passionate ballad gallant and gay,
A martial song like a trumpet's call !
Singing alone in the morning of life,
In the happy morning of life and of May,
Singing of men that in battle array,
Ready in heart and ready in hand,
March with banner and bugle and fife
To the death, for their native land.

II.

Maud with her exquisite face,
And wild voice pealing up to the sunny
  sky,
And feet like sunny gems on an English
  green,
Maud in the light of her youth and her
  grace,
Singing of Death, and of Honour that
  cannot die,
Till I well could weep for a time so sordid
  and mean,
And myself so languid and base.

III.

Silence, beautiful voice !
Be still, for you only trouble the mind
With a joy in which I cannot rejoice,
A glory I shall not find.
Still ! I will hear you no more,
For your sweetness hardly leaves me a
  choice
But to move to the meadow and fall before
Her feet on the meadow grass, and adore,
Not her, who is neither courtly nor kind,
Not her, not her, but a voice.

VI.

I.

Morning arises stormy and pale,
No sun, but a wannish glare
In fold upon fold of hueless cloud,
And the budded peaks of the wood are
  bow'd
Caught and cuff'd by the gale :
I had fancied it would be fair.

II.

Whom but Maud should I meet
Last night, when the sunset burn'd
On the blossom'd gable-ends
At the head of the village street,
Whom but Maud should I meet ?
And she touch'd my hand with a smile
  so sweet,
She made me divine amends
For a courtesy not return'd.

III.

And thus a delicate spark
Of glowing and growing light
Thro' the livelong hours of the dark
Kept itself warm in the heart of my
  dreams,
Ready to burst in a colour'd flame ;
Till at last when the morning came
In a cloud, it faded, and seems
But an ashen-gray delight.

IV.

What if with her sunny hair,
And smile as sunny as cold,
She meant to weave me a snare
Of some coquettish deceit,
Cleopatra-like as of old
To entangle me when we met,
To have her lion roll in a silken net
And fawn at a victor's feet.

V.

Ah, what shall I be at fifty
Should Nature keep me alive,
If I find the world so bitter
When I am but twenty-five?
Yet, if she were not a cheat,
If Maud were all that she seem'd,
And her smile were all that I dream'd,
Then the world were not so bitter
But a smile could make it sweet.

VI

What if tho' her eye seem'd full
Of a kind intent to me,
What if that dandy-despot, he,
That jewell'd mass of millinery,
That oil'd and curl'd Assyrian Bull
Smelling of musk and of insolence,
Her brother, from whom I keep aloof,
Who wants the finer politic sense
To mask, tho' but in his own behoof,
With a glassy smile his brutal scorn—
What if he had told her yestermorn
How prettily for his own sweet sake
A face of tenderness might be feign'd,
And a moist mirage in desert eyes,
That so, when the rotten hustings shake
In another month to his brazen lies,
A wretched vote may be gain'd.

VII.

For a raven ever croaks, at my side,
Keep watch and ward, keep watch and
ward,
Or thou wilt prove their tool.
Yea, too, myself from myself I guard,
For often a man's own angry pride
Is cap and bells for a fool.

VIII.

Perhaps the smile and tender tone
Came out of her pitying womanhood,
For am I not, am I not, here alone
So many a summer since she died,
My mother, who was so gentle and
good?
Living alone in an empty house,
Here half-hid in the gleaming wood,
Where I hear the dead at midday moan,
And the shrieking rush of the wainscot
mouse,
And my own sad name in corners cried,
When the shiver of dancing leaves is
thrown
About its echoing chambers wide,
Till a morbid hate and horror have
grown
Of a world in which I have hardly mixt,
And a morbid eating lichen fixt
On a heart half-turn'd to stone.

IX.

O heart of stone, are you flesh, and caught
By that you swore to withstand?
For what was it else within me wrought
But, I fear, the new strong wine of
love,
That made my tongue so stammer and
trip
When I saw the treasured splendour, her
hand,
Come sliding out of her sacred glove,
And the sunlight broke from her lip?

X.

I have play'd with her when a child;
She remembers it now we meet.
Ah well, well, well, I *may* be beguiled
By some coquettish deceit.
Yet, if she were not a cheat,
If Maud were all that she seem'd,
And her smile had all that I dream'd,
Then the world were not so bitter
But a smile could make it sweet.

VII.

I.

Did I hear it half in a doze
    Long since, I know not where?
Did I dream it an hour ago,
    When asleep in this arm-chair?

II.

Men were drinking together,
    Drinking and talking of me;
'Well, if it prove a girl, the boy
    Will have plenty: so let it be.'

III.

Is it an echo of something
   Read with a boy's delight,
Viziers nodding together
   In some Arabian night?

IV.

Strange, that I hear two men,
   Somewhere, talking of me;
'Well, if it prove a girl, my boy
   Will have plenty: so let it be.'

VIII.

She came to the village church,
And sat by a pillar alone;
An angel watching an urn
Wept over her, carved in stone;
And once, but once, she lifted her
   eyes,
And suddenly, sweetly, strangely blush'd
To find they were met by my own;
And suddenly, sweetly, my heart beat
   stronger
And thicker, until I heard no longer
The snowy-banded, dilettante,
Delicate-handed priest intone;
And thought, is it pride, and mused and
   sigh'd
'No surely, now it cannot be pride.'

IX.

   I was walking a mile,
   More than a mile from the shore,
The sun look'd out with a smile
Betwixt the cloud and the moor
   And riding at set of day
   Over the dark moor land,
   Rapidly riding far away,
She waved to me with her hand.
There were two at her side,
Something flash'd in the sun,
Down by the hill I saw them ride,
In a moment they were gone:
   Like a sudden spark
Struck vainly in the night,
   Then returns the dark
With no more hope of light.

X.

I.

Sick, am I sick of a jealous dread?
Was not one of the two at her side
This new-made lord, whose splendour
   plucks
The slavish hat from the villager's head?
Whose old grandfather has lately died,
Gone to a blacker pit, for whom
Grimy nakedness dragging his trucks
And laying his trams in a poison'd gloom
Wrought, till he crept from a gutted
   mine
Master of half a servile shire,
And left his coal all turn'd into gold
To a grandson, first of his noble line,
Rich in the grace all women desire,
Strong in the power that all men adore,
And simper and set their voices lower,
And soften as if to a girl, and hold
Awe-stricken breaths at a work divine,
Seeing his gewgaw castle shine,
New as his title, built last year,
There amid perky larches and pine,
And over the sullen-purple moor
(Look at it) pricking a cockney ear.

II.

What, has he found my jewel out?
For one of the two that rode at her side
Bound for the Hall, I am sure was he:
Bound for the Hall, and I think for a
   bride.
Blithe would her brother's acceptance be.
Maud could be gracious too, no doubt
To a lord, a captain, a padded shape,
A bought commission, a waxen face,
A rabbit mouth that is ever agape—
Bought? what is it he cannot buy?
And therefore splenetic, personal, base,
A wounded thing with a rancorous cry,
At war with myself and a wretched race,
Sick, sick to the heart of life, am I.

III.

Last week came one to the county town,
To preach our poor little army down,
And play the game of the despot kings,

Tho' the state has done it and thrice as
 well :
This broad - brimm'd hawker of holy
 things,
Whose ear is cramm'd with his cotton,
 and rings
Even in dreams to the chink of his pence,
This huckster put down war ! can he tell
Whether war be a cause or a consequence?
Put down the passions that make earth
 Hell !
Down with ambition, avarice, pride,
Jealousy, down ! cut off from the mind
The bitter springs of anger and fear ;
Down too, down at your own fireside,
With the evil tongue and the evil ear,
For each is at war with mankind.

IV.

I wish I could hear again
The chivalrous battle-song
That she warbled alone in her joy !
I might persuade myself then
She would not do herself this great wrong,
To take a wanton dissolute boy
For a man and leader of men.

V.

Ah God, for a man with heart, head, hand,
Like some of the simple great ones gone
For ever and ever by,
One still strong man in a blatant land,
Whatever they call him, what care I,
Aristocrat, democrat, autocrat—one
Who can rule and dare not lie.

VI.

And ah for a man to arise in me,
That the man I am may cease to be !

XI.

I.

O let the solid ground
 Not fail beneath my feet
Before my life has found
 What some have found so sweet ;
Then let come what come may,
What matter if I go mad,
I shall have had my day.

II.

Let the sweet heavens endure,
 Not close and darken above me
Before I am quite quite sure
 That there is one to love me ;
Then let come what come may
To a life that has been so sad,
I shall have had my day.

XII.

I.

Birds in the high Hall-garden
 When twilight was falling,
Maud, Maud, Maud, Maud,
 They were crying and calling.

II.

Where was Maud ? in our wood ;
 And I, who else, was with her,
Gathering woodland lilies,
 Myriads blow together.

III.

Birds in our wood sang
 Ringing thro' the valleys,
Maud is here, here, here
 In among the lilies.

IV.

I kiss'd her slender hand,
 She took the kiss sedately ;
Maud is not seventeen,
 But she is tall and stately.

V.

I to cry out on pride
 Who have won her favour !
O Maud were sure of Heaven
 If lowliness could save her.

VI.

I know the way she went
 Home with her maiden posy,
For her feet have touch'd the meadow
 And left the daisies rosy.

VII.

Birds in the high Hall-garden
 Were crying and calling to her,
Where is Maud, Maud, Maud ?
 One is come to woo her.

VIII.

Look, a horse at the door,
  And little King Charley snarling,
Go back, my lord, across the moor,
  You are not her darling.

XIII.

I.

Scorn'd, to be scorn'd by one that I scorn,
Is that a matter to make me fret?
That a calamity hard to be borne?
Well, he may live to hate me yet.
Fool that I am to be vext with his pride!
I past him, I was crossing his lands;
He stood on the path a little aside;
His face, as I grant, in spite of spite,
Has a broad-blown comeliness, red and
    white,
And six feet two, as I think, he stands;
But his essences turn'd the live air sick,
And barbarous opulence jewel-thick
Sunn'd itself on his breast and his hands.

II.

Who shall call me ungentle, unfair,
I long'd so heartily then and there
To give him the grasp of fellowship;
But while I past he was humming an air,
Stopt, and then with a riding whip
Leisurely tapping a glossy boot,
And curving a contumelious lip,
Gorgonised me from head to foot
With a stony British stare.

III.

Why sits he here in his father's chair?
That old man never comes to his place:
Shall I believe him ashamed to be seen?
For only once, in the village street,
Last year, I caught a glimpse of his face,
A gray old wolf and a lean.
Scarcely, now, would I call him a cheat;
For then, perhaps, as a child of deceit,
She might by a true descent be untrue;
And Maud is as true as Maud is sweet:
Tho' I fancy her sweetness only due
To the sweeter blood by the other side;
Her mother has been a thing complete,
However she came to be so allied.

And fair without, faithful within,
Maud to him is nothing akin:
Some peculiar mystic grace
Made her only the child of her mother,
And heap'd the whole inherited sin
On that huge scapegoat of the race,
All, all upon the brother.

IV.

Peace, angry spirit, and let him be!
Has not his sister smiled on me?

XIV.

I.

Maud has a garden of roses
And lilies fair on a lawn;
There she walks in her state
And tends upon bed and bower,
And thither I climb'd at dawn
And stood by her garden-gate;
A lion ramps at the top,
He is claspt by a passion-flower.

II.

Maud's own little oak-room
(Which Maud, like a precious stone
Set in the heart of the carven gloom,
Lights with herself, when alone
She sits by her music and books
And her brother lingers late
With a roystering company) looks
Upon Maud's own garden-gate:
And I thought as I stood, if a hand, as
    white
As ocean-foam in the moon, were laid
On the hasp of the window, and my
    Delight
Had a sudden desire, like a glorious ghost,
    to glide,
Like a beam of the seventh Heaven, down
    to my side,
There were but a step to be made.

III.

The fancy flatter'd my mind,
And again seem'd overbold;
Now I thought that she cared for me,
Now I thought she was kind
Only because she was cold.

IV.

I heard no sound where I stood
But the rivulet on from the lawn
Running down to my own dark wood ;
Or the voice of the long sea-wave as it
    swell'd
Now and then in the dim-gray dawn ;
But I look'd, and round, all round the
    house I beheld
The death-white curtain drawn ;
Felt a horror over me creep,
Prickle my skin and catch my breath,
Knew that the death-white curtain meant
    but sleep,
Yet I shudder'd and thought like a fool
    of the sleep of death.

XV.

So dark a mind within me dwells,
    And I make myself such evil cheer,
That if *I* be dear to some one else,
    Then some one else may have much to
        fear ;
But if *I* be dear to some one else,
    Then I should be to myself more dear.
Shall I not take care of all that I think,
Yea ev'n of wretched meat and drink,
If I be dear,
If I be dear to some one else.

XVI.

I.

This lump of earth has left his estate
The lighter by the loss of his weight ;
And so that he find what he went to
    seek,
And fulsome Pleasure clog him, and
    drown
His heart in the gross mud-honey of town,
He may stay for a year who has gone for
    a week :
But this is the day when I must speak,
And I see my Oread coming down,
O this is the day !
O beautiful creature, what am I
That I dare to look her way ;
Think I may hold dominion sweet,
Lord of the pulse that is lord of her breast,

And dream of her beauty with tender
    dread,
From the delicate Arab arch of her feet
To the grace that, bright and light as the
    crest
Of a peacock, sits on her shining head,
And she knows it not : O, if she knew it,
To know her beauty might half undo it.
I know it the one bright thing to save
My yet young life in the wilds of Time,
Perhaps from madness, perhaps from crime,
Perhaps from a selfish grave.

II.

What, if she be fasten'd to this fool lord,
Dare I bid her abide by her word ?
Should I love her so well if she
Had given her word to a thing so low ?
Shall I love her as well if she
Can break her word were it even for me ?
I trust that it is not so.

III.

Catch not my breath, O clamorous heart,
Let not my tongue be a thrall to my eye,
For I must tell her before we part,
I must tell her, or die.

XVII.

Go not, happy day,
    From the shining fields,
Go not, happy day,
    Till the maiden yields.
Rosy is the West,
    Rosy is the South,
Roses are her cheeks,
    And a rose her mouth
When the happy Yes
    Falters from her lips,
Pass and blush the news
    Over glowing ships ;
Over blowing seas,
    Over seas at rest,
Pass the happy news,
    Blush it thro' the West;
Till the red man dance
    By his red cedar-tree,
And the red man's babe
    Leap, beyond the sea.

Blush from West to East,
    Blush from East to West,
Till the West is East,
    Blush it thro' the West.
Rosy is the West,
    Rosy is the South,
Roses are her cheeks,
    And a rose her mouth.

XVIII.

I.

I have led her home, my love, my only
        friend.
There is none like her, none.
And never yet so warmly ran my blood
And sweetly, on and on
Calming itself to the long-wish'd-for end,
Full to the banks, close on the promised
        good.

II.

None like her, none.
Just now the dry-tongued laurels' patter-
        ing talk
Seem'd her light foot along the garden
        walk,
And shook my heart to think she comes
        once more ;
But even then I heard her close the
        door,
The gates of Heaven are closed, and she
        is gone.

III.

There is none like her, none.
Nor will be when our summers have de-
        ceased.
O, art thou sighing for Lebanon
In the long breeze that streams to thy
        delicious East,
Sighing for Lebanon,
Dark cedar, tho' thy limbs have here in-
        creased,
Upon a pastoral slope as fair,
And looking to the South, and fed
With honey'd rain and delicate air,
And haunted by the starry head
Of her whose gentle will has changed my
        fate,
And made my life a perfumed altar-flame ;
And over whom thy darkness must have
        spread
With such delight as theirs of old, thy
        great
Forefathers of the thornless garden, there
Shadowing the snow-limb'd Eve from
        whom she came.

IV.

Here will I lie, while these long branches
        sway,
And you fair stars that crown a happy day
Go in and out as if at merry play,
Who am no more so all forlorn,
As when it seem'd far better to be born
To labour and the mattock-harden'd
        hand,
Than nursed at ease and brought to un-
        derstand
A sad astrology, the boundless plan
That makes you tyrants in your iron
        skies,
Innumerable, pitiless, passionless eyes,
Cold fires, yet with power to burn and
        brand
His nothingness into man.

V.

But now shine on, and what care I,
Who in this stormy gulf have found a
        pearl
The countercharm of space and hollow
        sky,
And do accept my madness, and would die
To save from some slight shame one
        simple girl.

VI.

Would die ; for sullen-seeming Death
        may give
More life to Love than is or ever was
In our low world, where yet 'tis sweet to
        live.
Let no one ask me how it came to pass ;
It seems that I am happy, that to me
A livelier emerald twinkles in the grass,
A purer sapphire melts into the sea.

VII.

Not die ; but live a life of truest breath,
And teach true life to fight with mortal
    wrongs.
O, why should Love, like men in drink-
    ing-songs,
Spice his fair banquet with the dust of
    death ?
Make answer, Maud my bliss,
Maud made my Maud by that long loving
    kiss,
Life of my life, wilt thou not answer this ?
' The dusky strand of Death inwoven
    here
With dear Love's tie, makes Love himself
    more dear.'

VIII.

Is that enchanted moan only the swell
Of the long waves that roll in yonder bay?
And hark the clock within, the silver
    knell
Of twelve sweet hours that past in bridal
    white,
And died to live, long as my pulses play;
But now by this my love has closed her
    sight
And given false death her hand, and stol'n
    away
To dreamful wastes where footless fancies
    dwell
Among the fragments of the golden day.
May nothing there her maiden grace
    affright !
Dear heart, I feel with thee the drowsy
    spell.
My bride to be, my evermore delight,
My own heart's heart, my ownest own,
    farewell ;
It is but for a little space I go :
And ye meanwhile far over moor and fell
Beat to the noiseless music of the night !
Has our whole earth gone nearer to the
    glow
Of your soft splendours that you look so
    bright ?
I have climb'd nearer out of lonely Hell.
Beat, happy stars, timing with things
    below,

Beat with my heart more blest than heart
    can tell,
Blest, but for some dark undercurrent
    woe
That seems to draw—but it shall not be
    so :
Let all be well, be well.

XIX.

I.

Her brother is coming back to-night.
Breaking up my dream of delight.

II.

My dream ? do I dream of bliss ?
I have walk'd awake with Truth.
O when did a morning shine
So rich in atonement as this
For my dark-dawning youth,
Darken'd watching a mother decline
And that dead man at her heart and
    mine :
For who was left to watch her but I ?
Yet so did I let my freshness die.

III.

I trust that I did not talk
To gentle Maud in our walk
(For often in lonely wanderings
I have cursed him even to lifeless things)
But I trust that I did not talk,
Not touch on her father's sin :
I am sure I did but speak
Of my mother's faded cheek
When it slowly grew so thin,
That I felt she was slowly dying
Vext with lawyers and harass'd with
    debt :
For how often I caught her with eyes all
    wet,
Shaking her head at her son and sighing
A world of trouble within !

IV.

And Maud too, Maud was moved
To speak of the mother she loved
As one scarce less forlorn,
Dying abroad and it seems apart

rom him who had ceased to share her
   heart,
And ever mourning over the feud,
The household Fury sprinkled with blood
By which our houses are torn :
How strange was what she said,
When only Maud and the brother
Hung over her dying bed—
That Maud's dark father and mine
Had bound us one to the other,
Betrothed us over their wine,
On the day when Maud was born ;
Seal'd her mine from her first sweet
   breath.
Mine, mine by a right, from birth till
   death.
Mine, mine—our fathers have sworn.

V.

But the true blood spilt had in it a heat
To dissolve the precious seal on a bond,
That, if left uncancell'd, had been so
   sweet :
And none of us thought of a something
   beyond,
A desire that awoke in the heart of the
   child,
As it were a duty done to the tomb,
To be friends for her sake, to be recon-
   ciled ;
And I was cursing them and my doom,
And letting a dangerous thought run
   wild
While often abroad in the fragrant gloom
Of foreign churches—I see her there,
Bright English lily, breathing a prayer
To be friends, to be reconciled !

VI.

But then what a flint is he !
Abroad, at Florence, at Rome,
I find whenever she touch'd on me
This brother had laugh'd her down,
And at last, when each came home,
He had darken'd into a frown,
Chid her, and forbid her to speak
To me, her friend of the years before ;
And this was what had redden'd her
   cheek
When I bow'd to her on the moor.

VII.

Yet Maud, altho' not blind
To the faults of his heart and mind,
I see she cannot but love him,
And says he is rough but kind,
And wishes me to approve him,
And tells me, when she lay
Sick once, with a fear of worse,
That he left his wine and horses and play,
Sat with her, read to her, night and day,
And tended her like a nurse.

VIII.

Kind ? but the deathbed desire
Spurn'd by this heir of the liar—
Rough but kind ? yet I know
He has plotted against me in this,
That he plots against me still.
Kind to Maud ? that were not amiss.
Well, rough but kind ; why let it be so :
For shall not Maud have her will?

IX.

For, Maud, so tender and true,
As long as my life endures
I feel I shall owe you a debt,
That I never can hope to pay ;
And if ever I should forget
That I owe this debt to you
And for your sweet sake to yours ;
O then, what then shall I say?—
If ever I *should* forget,
May God make me more wretched
Than ever I have been yet !

X.

So now I have sworn to bury
All this dead body of hate,
I feel so free and so clear
By the loss of that dead weight,
That I should grow light-headed, I fear,
Fantastically merry ;
But that her brother comes, like a blight
On my fresh hope, to the Hall to-night.

XX.

I.

Strange, that I felt so gay,
Strange, that *I* tried to-day

To beguile her melancholy;
The Sultan, as we name him,—
She did not wish to blame him—
But he vext her and perplext her
With his worldly talk and folly:
Was it gentle to reprove her
For stealing out of view
From a little lazy lover
Who but claims her as his due?
Or for chilling his caresses
By the coldness of her manners,
Nay, the plainness of her dresses?
Now I know her but in two,
Nor can pronounce upon it
If one should ask me whether
The habit, hat, and feather,
Or the frock and gipsy bonnet
Be the neater and completer;
For nothing can be sweeter
Than maiden Maud in either.

II.

But to-morrow, if we live,
Our ponderous squire will give
A grand political dinner
To half the squirelings near;
And Maud will wear her jewels,
And the bird of prey will hover,
And the titmouse hope to win her
With his chirrup at her ear.

III.

A grand political dinner
To the men of many acres,
A gathering of the Tory,
A dinner and then a dance
For the maids and marriage-makers,
And every eye but mine will glance
At Maud in all her glory.

IV.

For I am not invited,
But, with the Sultan's pardon,
I am all as well delighted,
For I know her own rose-garden,
And mean to linger in it
Till the dancing will be over;
And then, oh then, come out to me
For a minute, but for a minute,

Come out to your own true lover,
That your true lover may see
Your glory also, and render
All homage to his own darling,
Queen Maud in all her splendour.

XXI.

Rivulet crossing my ground,
And bringing me down from the Hall
This garden-rose that I found,
Forgetful of Maud and me,
And lost in trouble and moving round
Here at the head of a tinkling fall,
And trying to pass to the sea;
O Rivulet, born at the Hall,
My Maud has sent it by thee
(If I read her sweet will right)
On a blushing mission to me,
Saying in odour and colour, 'Ah, be
Among the roses to-night.'

XXII.

I.

Come into the garden, Maud,
    For the black bat, night, has flown,
Come into the garden, Maud,
    I am here at the gate alone;
And the woodbine spices are wafted
        abroad,
    And the musk of the rose is blown.

II.

For a breeze of morning moves,
    And the planet of Love is on high,
Beginning to faint in the light that she
        loves
    On a bed of daffodil sky,
To faint in the light of the sun she loves,
    To faint in his light, and to die.

III.

All night have the roses heard
    The flute, violin, bassoon;
All night has the casement jessamine
        stirr'd
    To the dancers dancing in tune;
Till a silence fell with the waking bird,
    And a hush with the setting moon.

IV.

I said to the lily, 'There is but one
  With whom she has heart to be gay.
When will the dancers leave her alone?
  She is weary of dance and play.'
Now half to the setting moon are gone,
  And half to the rising day;
Low on the sand and loud on the stone
  The last wheel echoes away.

V.

I said to the rose, 'The brief night goes
  In babble and revel and wine.
O young lord-lover, what sighs are those,
  For one that will never be thine?
But mine, but mine,' so I sware to the
    rose,
  'For ever and ever, mine.'

VI.

And the soul of the rose went into my
    blood,
  As the music clash'd in the hall;
And long by the garden lake I stood,
  For I heard your rivulet fall
From the lake to the meadow and on to
    the wood,
  Our wood, that is dearer than all;

VII.

From the meadow your walks have left
    so sweet
  That whenever a March-wind sighs
He sets the jewel-print of your feet
  In violets blue as your eyes,
To the woody hollows in which we meet
  And the valleys of Paradise.

VIII.

The slender acacia would not shake
  One long milk-bloom on the tree;
The white lake-blossom fell into the lake
  As the pimpernel dozed on the lea;
But the rose was awake all night for your
    sake,
  Knowing your promise to me;
The lilies and roses were all awake,
  They sigh'd for the dawn and thee.

IX.

Queen rose of the rosebud garden of girls,
  Come hither, the dances are done,
In gloss of satin and glimmer of pearls,
  Queen lily and rose in one;
Shine out, little head, sunning over with
    curls,
  To the flowers, and be their sun.

X.

There has fallen a splendid tear
  From the passion-flower at the gate.
She is coming, my dove, my dear;
  She is coming, my life, my fate;
The red rose cries, 'She is near, she is
    near;'
  And the white rose weeps, 'She is
    late;'
The larkspur listens, 'I hear, I hear;'
  And the lily whispers, 'I wait.'

XI.

She is coming, my own, my sweet;
  Were it ever so airy a tread,
My heart would hear her and beat,
  Were it earth in an earthy bed;
My dust would hear her and beat,
  Had I lain for a century dead;
Would start and tremble under her feet,
  And blossom in purple and red.

PART II.

I.

i.

'THE fault was mine, the fault was
    mine'—
Why am I sitting here so stunn'd and still,
Plucking the harmless wild-flower on the
    hill?—
It is this guilty hand!—
And there rises ever a passionate cry
From underneath in the darkening land—
What is it, that has been done?
O dawn of Eden bright over earth and sky,
The fires of Hell brake out of thy rising
    sun,
The fires of Hell and of Hate;

For she, sweet soul, had hardly spoken a
  word,
When her brother ran in his rage to the
  gate,
He came with the babe-faced lord ;
Heap'd on her terms of disgrace,
And while she wept, and I strove to be
  cool,
He fiercely gave me the lie,
Till I with as fierce an anger spoke,
And he struck me, madman, over the
  face,
Struck me before the languid fool,
Who was gaping and grinning by :
Struck for himself an evil stroke ;
Wrought for his house an irredeemable
  woe ;
For front to front in an hour we stood,
And a million horrible bellowing echoes
  broke
From the red-ribb'd hollow behind the
  wood,
And thunder'd up into Heaven the Christ-
  less code,
That must have life for a blow.
Ever and ever afresh they seem'd to grow.
Was it he lay there with a fading eye ?
'The fault was mine,' he whisper'd, 'fly !'
Then glided out of the joyous wood
The ghastly Wraith of one that I know ;
And there rang on a sudden a passionate
  cry,
A cry for a brother's blood :
It will ring in my heart and my ears, till
  I die, till I die.

II.

Is it gone ? my pulses beat—
What was it ? a lying trick of the brain ?
Yet I thought I saw her stand,
A shadow there at my feet,
High over the shadowy land.
It is gone ; and the heavens fall in a
  gentle rain,
When they should burst and drown with
  deluging storms
The feeble vassals of wine and anger and
  lust,
The little hearts that know not how to
  forgive :

Arise, my God, and strike, for we hold
  Thee just,
Strike dead the whole weak race of veno-
  mous worms,
That sting each other here in the dust ;
We are not worthy to live.

II.

I.

See what a lovely shell,
Small and pure as a pearl,
Lying close to my foot,
Frail, but a work divine,
Made so fairily well
With delicate spire and whorl,
How exquisitely minute,
A miracle of design !

II.

What is it ? a learned man
Could give it a clumsy name.
Let him name it who can,
The beauty would be the same.

III.

The tiny cell is forlorn,
Void of the little living will
That made it stir on the shore.
Did he stand at the diamond door
Of his house in a rainbow frill ?
Did he push, when he was uncurl'd,
A golden foot or a fairy horn
Thro' his dim water-world ?

IV.

Slight, to be crush'd with a tap
Of my finger-nail on the sand,
Small, but a work divine,
Frail, but of force to withstand,
Year upon year, the shock
Of cataract seas that snap
The three decker's oaken spine
Athwart the ledges of rock,
Here on the Breton strand !

V.

Breton, not Briton ; here
Like a shipwreck'd man on a coast
Of ancient fable and fear—

Plagued with a flitting to and fro,
A disease, a hard mechanic ghost
That never came from on high
Nor ever arose from below,
But only moves with the moving eye,
Flying along the land and the main—
Why should it look like Maud?
Am I to be overawed
By what I cannot but know
Is a juggle born of the brain?

VI.

Back from the Breton coast,
Sick of a nameless fear,
Back to the dark sea-line
Looking, thinking of all I have lost;
An old song vexes my ear;
But that of Lamech is mine.

VII.

For years, a measureless ill,
For years, for ever, to part—
But she, she would love me still;
And as long, O God, as she
Have a grain of love for me,
So long, no doubt, no doubt,
Shall I nurse in my dark heart,
However weary, a spark of will
Not to be trampled out.

VIII.

Strange, that the mind, when fraught
With a passion so intense
One would think that it well
Might drown all life in the eye,—
That it should, by being so overwrought,
Suddenly strike on a sharper sense
For a shell, or a flower, little things
Which else would have been past by!
And now I remember, I,
When he lay dying there,
I noticed one of his many rings
(For he had many, poor worm) and
　　thought
It is his mother's hair.

IX.

Who knows if he be dead?
Whether I need have fled?

Am I guilty of blood?
However this may be,
Comfort her, comfort her, all things
　　good,
While I am over the sea!
Let me and my passionate love go by,
But speak to her all things holy and
　　high,
Whatever happen to me!
Me and my harmful love go by;
But come to her waking, find her asleep,
Powers of the height, Powers of the
　　deep,
And comfort her tho' I die.

III.

Courage, poor heart of stone!
I will not ask thee why
Thou canst not understand
That thou art left for ever alone:
Courage, poor stupid heart of stone.—
Or if I ask thee why,
Care not thou to reply:
She is but dead, and the time is at hand
When thou shalt more than die.

IV.

I.

O that 'twere possible
After long grief and pain
To find the arms of my true love
Round me once again!

II.

When I was wont to meet her
In the silent woody places
By the home that gave me birth,
We stood tranced in long embraces
Mixt with kisses sweeter sweeter
Than anything on earth.

III.

A shadow flits before me,
Not thou, but like to thee:
Ah Christ, that it were possible
For one short hour to see
The souls we loved, that they might tell us
What and where they be.

IV.

It leads me forth at evening,
It lightly winds and steals
In a cold white robe before me,
When all my spirit reels
At the shouts, the leagues of lights,
And the roaring of the wheels.

V.

Half the night I waste in sighs,
Half in dreams I sorrow after
The delight of early skies ;
In a wakeful doze I sorrow
For the hand, the lips, the eyes,
For the meeting of the morrow,
The delight of happy laughter,
The delight of low replies.

VI.

'Tis a morning pure and sweet,
And a dewy splendour falls
On the little flower that clings
To the turrets and the walls ;
'Tis a morning pure and sweet,
And the light and shadow fleet ;
She is walking in the meadow,
And the woodland echo rings ;
In a moment we shall meet ;
She is singing in the meadow
And the rivulet at her feet
Ripples on in light and shadow
To the ballad that she sings.

VII.

Do I hear her sing as of old,
My bird with the shining head,
My own dove with the tender eye ?
But there rings on a sudden a passionate
    cry,
There is some one dying or dead,
And a sullen thunder is roll'd ;
For a tumult shakes the city,
And I wake, my dream is fled ;
In the shuddering dawn, behold,
Without knowledge, without pity,
By the curtains of my bed
That abiding phantom cold.

VIII.

Get thee hence, nor come again,
Mix not memory with doubt,
Pass, thou deathlike type of pain,
Pass and cease to move about !
'Tis the blot upon the brain
That *will* show itself without.

IX.

Then I rise, the eavedrops fall,
And the yellow vapours choke
The great city sounding wide ;
The day comes, a dull red ball
Wrapt in drifts of lurid smoke
On the misty river-tide.

X.

Thro' the hubbub of the market
I steal, a wasted frame,
It crosses here, it crosses there,
Thro' all that crowd confused and loud,
The shadow still the same ;
And on my heavy eyelids
My anguish hangs like shame.

XI.

Alas for her that met me,
That heard me softly call,
Came glimmering thro' the laurels
At the quiet evenfall,
In the garden by the turrets
Of the old manorial hall.

XII.

Would the happy spirit descend,
From the realms of light and song,
In the chamber or the street,
As she looks among the blest,
Should I fear to greet my friend
Or to say ' Forgive the wrong,'
Or to ask her, ' Take me, sweet,
To the regions of thy rest ' ?

XIII.

But the broad light glares and beats,
And the shadow flits and fleets
And will not let me be ;
And I loathe the squares and streets,
And the faces that one meets,
Hearts with no love for me :

ways I long to creep
to some still cavern deep,
here to weep, and weep, and weep
y whole soul out to thee.

V.

I.

ead, long dead,
ong dead !
nd my heart is a handful of dust,
nd the wheels go over my head,
nd my bones are shaken with pain,
or into a shallow grave they are thrust,
nly a yard beneath the street,
nd the hoofs of the horses beat, beat,
he hoofs of the horses beat,
eat into my scalp and my brain,
ith never an end to the stream of passing
      feet,
riving, hurrying, marrying, burying,
amour and rumble, and ringing and
      clatter,
nd here beneath it is all as bad,
or I thought the dead had peace, but it
      is not so ;
o have no peace in the grave, is that
      not sad ?
at up and down and to and fro,
ver about me the dead men gó ;
nd then to hear a dead man chatter
 enough to drive one mad.

II.

retchedest age, since Time began,
ey cannot even bury a man ;
nd tho' we paid our tithes in the days
      that are gone,
ot a bell was rung, not a prayer was
      read ;
is that which makes us loud in the
      world of the dead ;
here is none that does his work, not
      one ;
 touch of their office might have
      sufficed,
t the churchmen fain would kill their
      church,
 the churches have kill'd their Christ.

III.

See, there is one of us sobbing,
No limit to his distress ;
And another, a lord of all things, praying
To his own great self, as I guess ;
And another, a statesman there, betraying
His party-secret, fool, to the press ;
And yonder a vile physician, blabbing
The case of his patient—all for what ?
To tickle the maggot born in an empty
      head,
And wheedle a world that loves him not,
For it is but a world of the dead.

IV.

Nothing but idiot gabble !
For the prophecy given of old
And then not understood,
Has come to pass as foretold ;
Not let any man think for the public
      good,
But babble, merely for babble.
For I never whisper'd a private affair
Within the hearing of cat or mouse,
No, not to myself in the closet alone,
But I heard it shouted at once from the
      top of the house ;
Everything came to be known.
Who told *him* we were there ?

V.

Not that gray old wolf, for he came not
      back
From the wilderness, full of wolves, where
      he used to lie ;
He has gather'd the bones for his o'er-
      grown whelp to crack ;
Crack them now for yourself, and howl,
      and die.

VI.

Prophet, curse me the blabbing lip,
And curse me the British vermin, the rat ;
I know not whether he came in the
      Hanover ship,
But I know that he lies and listens mute
In an ancient mansion's crannies and
      holes :

T   X

Arsenic, arsenic, sure, would do it,
Except that now we poison our babes,
          poor souls !
It is all used up for that.

VII.

Tell him now : she is standing here at my
          head ;
Not beautiful now, not even kind ;
He may take her now ; for she never
          speaks her mind,
But is ever the one thing silent here.
She is not *of* us, as I divine ;
She comes from another stiller world of
          the dead,
Stiller, not fairer than mine.

VIII.

But I know where a garden grows,
Fairer than aught in the world beside,
All made up of the lily and rose
That blow by night, when the season is
          good,
To the sound of dancing music and flutes:
It is only flowers, they had no fruits,
And I almost fear they are not roses, but
          blood ;
For the keeper was one, so full of pride,
He linkt a dead man there to a spectral
          bride ;
For he, if he had not been a Sultan of
          brutes,
Would he have that hole in his side ?

IX.

But what will the old man say ?
He laid a cruel snare in a pit
To catch a friend of mine one storm
          day ;
Yet now I could even weep to thir
          of it ;
For what will the old man say
When he comes to the second corpse
          the pit ?

X.

Friend, to be struck by the public foe,
Then to strike him and lay him low,
That were a public merit, far,
Whatever the Quaker holds, from sin ;
But the red life spilt for a private blow
I swear to you, lawful and lawless war
Are scarcely even akin.

XI.

O me, why have they not buried me dee
          enough?
Is it kind to have made me a grave
          rough,
Me, that was never a quiet sleeper ?
Maybe still I am but half-dead ;
Then I cannot be wholly dumb ;
I will cry to the steps above my head
And somebody, surely, some kind hea
          will come
To bury me, bury me
Deeper, ever so little deeper.

PART III.

VI.

I.

My life has crept so long on a broken wing
Thro' cells of madness, haunts of horror and fear,
That I come to be grateful at last for a little thing :
My mood is changed, for it fell at a time of year
When the face of night is fair on the dewy downs,
And the shining daffodil dies, and the Charioteer
And starry Gemini hang like glorious crowns
Over Orion's grave low down in the west,
That like a silent lightning under the stars
She seem'd to divide in a dream from a band of the blest,

And spoke of a hope for the world in the coming wars—
' And in that hope, dear soul, let trouble have rest,
Knowing I tarry for thee,' and pointed to Mars
As he glow'd like a ruddy shield on the Lion's breast.

II.

And it was but a dream, yet it yielded a dear delight
To have look'd, tho' but in a dream, upon eyes so fair,
That had been in a weary world my one thing bright ;
And it was but a dream, yet it lighten'd my despair
When I thought that a war would arise in defence of the right,
That an iron tyranny now should bend or cease,
The glory of manhood stand on his ancient height,
Nor Britain's one sole God be the millionaire :
No more shall commerce be all in all, and Peace
Pipe on her pastoral hillock a languid note,
And watch her harvest ripen, her herd increase,
Nor the cannon-bullet rust on a slothful shore,
And the cobweb woven across the cannon's throat
Shall shake its threaded tears in the wind no more.

III.

And as months ran on and rumour of battle grew,
' It is time, it is time, O passionate heart,' said I
(For I cleaved to a cause that I felt to be pure and true),
' It is time, O passionate heart and morbid eye,
That old hysterical mock-disease should die.'
And I stood on a giant deck and mix'd my breath
With a loyal people shouting a battle cry,
Till I saw the dreary phantom arise and fly
Far into the North, and battle, and seas of death.

IV.

Let it go or stay, so I wake to the higher aims
Of a land that has lost for a little her lust of gold,
And love of a peace that was full of wrongs and shames,
Horrible, hateful, monstrous, not to be told ;
And hail once more to the banner of battle unroll'd !
Tho' many a light shall darken, and many shall weep
For those that are crush'd in the clash of jarring claims,
Yet God's just wrath shall be wreak'd on a giant liar ;
And many a darkness into the light shall leap,
And shine in the sudden making of splendid names,
And noble thought be freër under the sun,
And the heart of a people beat with one desire ;
For the peace, that I deem'd no peace, is over and done,
And now by the side of the Black and the Baltic deep,
And deathful-grinning mouths of the fortress, flames
The blood-red blossom of war with a heart of fire.

V.

Let it flame or fade, and the war roll down like a wind,
We have proved we have hearts in a cause, we are noble still,
And myself have awaked, as it seems, to the better mind ;
It is better to fight for the good than to rail at the ill ;
I have felt with my native land, I am one with my kind,
I embrace the purpose of God, and the doom assign'd.

IDYLLS OF THE KING.

IN TWELVE BOOKS.

'Flos Regum Arthurus.'—JOSEPH OF EXETER

DEDICATION.

THESE to His Memory —since he held
   them dear,
Perchance as finding there unconsciously
Some image of himself—I dedicate,
I dedicate, I consecrate with tears—
These Idylls.

      And indeed He seems to me
Scarce other than my king's ideal knight,
‘ Who reverenced his conscience as his
   king ;
Whose glory was, redressing human wrong ;
Who spake no slander, no, nor listen'd
   to it ;
Who loved one only and who clave to her—’
Her—over all whose realms to their last
   isle,
Commingled with the gloom of imminent
   war,
The shadow of His loss drew like eclipse,
Darkening the world.   We have lost
   him : he is gone :
We know him now : all narrow jealousies
Are silent ; and we see him as he moved,
How modest, kindly, all - accomplish'd,
   wise,
With what sublime repression of himself,
And in what limits, and how tenderly ;
Not swaying to this faction or to that ;
Not making his high place the lawless
   perch
Of wing'd ambitions, nor a vantage-ground
For pleasure ; but thro’ all this tract of
   years
Wearing the white flower of a blameless
   life,

Before a thousand peering littlenesses,
In that fierce light which beats upon
   throne,
And blackens every blot : for where is he
Who dares foreshadow for an only son
A lovelier life, a more unstain'd, than his
Or how should England dreaming of h
   sons
Hope more for these than some inheritanc
Of such a life, a heart, a mind as thine
Thou noble Father of her Kings to be,
Laborious for her people and her poor-
Voice in the rich dawn of an ampler day-
Far-sighted summoner of War and Was
To fruitful strifes and rivalries of peace-
Sweet nature gilded by the gracious glea
Of letters, dear to Science, dear to Art
Dear to thy land and ours, a Prince indee
Beyond all titles, and a household nam
Hereafter, thro’ all times, Albert the Goo

   Break not, O woman's-heart, but st
   endure ;
Break not, for thou art Royal, but endu
Remembering all the beauty of that sta
Which shone so close beside Thee th
   ye made
One light together, but has past and leav
The Crown a lonely splendour.

          May all lov
His love, unseen but felt, o’ershadow Th
The love of all Thy sons encompass Th
The love of all Thy daughters cherish Th
The love of all Thy people comfort Th
Till God's love set Thee at his side aga

THE COMING OF ARTHUR.

LEODOGRAN, the King of Cameliard,
Had one fair daughter, and none other
child ;
And she was fairest of all flesh on earth,
Guinevere, and in her his one delight.

For many a petty king ere Arthur came
Ruled in this isle, and ever waging war
Each upon other, wasted all the land ;
And still from time to time the heathen
host
Swarm'd overseas, and harried what was
left.
And so there grew great tracts of wilder-
ness,
Wherein the beast was ever more and
more,
But man was less and less, till Arthur
came.
For first Aurelius lived and fought and
died,
And after him King Uther fought and died,
But either fail'd to make the kingdom
one.
And after these King Arthur for a space,
And thro' the puissance of his Table
Round,
Drew all their petty princedoms under
him,
Their king and head, and made a realm,
and reign'd.

And thus the land of Cameliard was
waste,
Thick with wet woods, and many a beast
therein,
And none or few to scare or chase the
beast ;
So that wild dog, and wolf and boar and
bear
Came night and day, and rooted in the
fields,
And wallow'd in the gardens of the King.
And ever and anon the wolf would steal
The children and devour, but now and
then,
Her own brood lost or dead, lent her
fierce teat

To human sucklings ; and the children,
housed
In her foul den, there at their meat would
growl,
And mock their foster-mother on four feet,
Till, straighten'd, they grew up to wolf-
like men,
Worse than the wolves. And King
Leodogran
Groan'd for the Roman legions here again,
And Cæsar's eagle : then his brother king,
Urien, assail'd him : last a heathen horde,
Reddening the sun with smoke and earth
with blood,
And on the spike that split the mother's
heart
Spitting the child, brake on him, till,
amazed,
He knew not whither he should turn for
aid.

But—for he heard of Arthur newly
crown'd,
Tho' not without an uproar made by those
Who cried, ' He is not Uther's son '—the
King
Sent to him, saying, ' Arise, and help us
thou !
For here between the man and beast we
die.'

And Arthur yet had done no deed of
arms,
But heard the call, and came : and
Guinevere
Stood by the castle walls to watch him
pass ;
But since he neither wore on helm or
shield
The golden symbol of his kinglihood,
But rode a simple knight among his
knights,
And many of these in richer arms than he,
She saw him not, or mark'd not, if she
saw,
One among many, tho' his face was bare.
But Arthur, looking downward as he past,
Felt the light of her eyes into his life

Smite on the sudden, yet rode on, and
    pitch'd
His tents beside the forest.   Then he
    drave
The heathen; after, slew the beast, and
    fell'd
The forest, letting in the sun, and made
Broad pathways for the hunter and the
    knight
And so return'd.

             For while he linger'd there,
A doubt that ever smoulder'd in the hearts
Of those great Lords and Barons of his
    realm
Flash'd forth and into war : for most of
    these,
Colleaguing with a score of petty kings,
Made head against him, crying, 'Who
    is he
That he should rule us? who hath proven
    him
King Uther's son? for lo! we look at him,
And find nor face nor bearing, limbs nor
    voice,
Are like to those of Uther whom we knew.
This is the son of Gorloïs, not the King;
This is the son of Anton, not the King.'

    And Arthur, passing thence to battle,
    felt
Travail, and throes and agonies of the life,
Desiring to be join'd with Guinevere;
And thinking as he rode, 'Her father said
That there between the man and beast
    they die.
Shall I not lift her from this land of beasts
Up to my throne, and side by side with
    me?
What happiness to reign a lonely king,
Vext—O ye stars that shudder over me,
O earth that soundest hollow under me,
Vext with waste dreams? for saving I be
    join'd
To her that is the fairest under heaven,
I seem as nothing in the mighty world,
And cannot will my will, nor work my
    work
Wholly, nor make myself in mine own
    realm

Victor and lord.   But were I join'd with
    her,
Then might we live together as one life,
And reigning with one will in everything
Have power on this dark land to lighten
    it,
And power on this dead world to make
    it live.'

    Thereafter—as he speaks who tells the
    tale—
When Arthur reach'd a field-of-battle
    bright
With pitch'd pavilions of his foe, the
    world
Was all so clear about him, that he saw
The smallest rock far on the faintest hill,
And even in high day the morning star.
So when the King had set his banner
    broad,
At once from either side, with trumpet-
    blast,
And shouts, and clarions shrilling unto
    blood,
The long-lanced battle let their horses
    run.
And now the Barons and the kings pre-
    vail'd,
And now the King, as here and there
    that war
Went swaying; but the Powers who walk
    the world
Made lightnings and great thunders over
    him,
And dazed all eyes, till Arthur by main
    might,
And mightier of his hands with every
    blow,
And leading all his knighthood threw the
    kings
Carádos, Urien, Cradlemont of Wales,
Claudias, and Clariance of Northumber-
    land,
The King Brandagoras of Latangor,
With Anguisant of Erin, Morganore,
And Lot of Orkney.   Then, before a voice
As dreadful as the shout of one who sees
To one who sins, and deems himself alone
And all the world asleep, they swerved
    and brake

Flying, and Arthur call'd to stay the brands
That hack'd among the flyers, 'Ho ! they yield !'
So like a painted battle the war stood
Silenced, the living quiet as the dead,
And in the heart of Arthur joy was lord.
He laugh'd upon his warrior whom he loved
And honour'd most. 'Thou dost not doubt me King,
So well thine arm hath wrought for me to-day.'
'Sir and my liege,' he cried, 'the fire of God
Descends upon thee in the battle-field :
I know thee for my King !' Whereat the two,
For each had warded either in the fight,
Sware on the field of death a deathless love.
And Arthur said, 'Man's word is God in man :
Let chance what will, I trust thee to the death.'

Then quickly from the foughten field he sent
Ulfius, and Brastias, and Bedivere,
His new-made knights, to King Leodogran,
Saying, 'If I in aught have served thee well,
Give me thy daughter Guinevere to wife.'

Whom when he heard, Leodogran in heart
Debating—'How should I that am a king,
However much he holp me at my need,
Give my one daughter saving to a king,
And a king's son ?'—lifted his voice, and call'd
A hoary man, his chamberlain, to whom
He trusted all things, and of him required
His counsel : 'Knowest thou aught of Arthur's birth ?'

Then spake the hoary chamberlain and said,
'Sir King, there be but two old men that know :

And each is twice as old as I ; and one
Is Merlin, the wise man that ever served
King Uther thro' his magic art ; and one
Is Merlin's master (so they call him) Bleys,
Who taught him magic ; but the scholar ran
Before the master, and so far, that Bleys
Laid magic by, and sat him down, and wrote
All things and whatsoever Merlin did
In one great annal-book, where after-years
Will learn the secret of our Arthur's birth.'

To whom the King Leodogran replied,
'O friend, had I been holpen half as well
By this King Arthur as by thee to-day,
Then beast and man had had their share of me :
But summon here before us yet once more
Ulfius, and Brastias, and Bedivere.'

Then, when they came before him, the King said,
'I have seen the cuckoo chased by lesser fowl,
And reason in the chase : but wherefore now
Do these your lords stir up the heat of war,
Some calling Arthur born of Gorloïs,
Others of Anton ? Tell me, ye yourselves,
Hold ye this Arthur for King Uther's son ?'

And Ulfius and Brastias answer'd, 'Ay.'
Then Bedivere, the first of all his knights
Knighted by Arthur at his crowning, spake—
For bold in heart and act and word was he,
Whenever slander breathed against the King—

'Sir, there be many rumours on this head :
For there be those who hate him in their hearts,
Call him baseborn, and since his ways are sweet,
And theirs are bestial, hold him less than man :

And there be those who deem him more
  than man,
And dream he dropt from heaven : but
  my belief
In all this matter—so ye care to learn—
Sir, for ye know that in King Uther's
  time
The prince and warrior Gorloïs, he that
  held
Tintagil castle by the Cornish sea,
Was wedded with a winsome wife, Ygerne :
And daughters had she borne him,—one
  whereof,
Lot's wife, the Queen of Orkney, Belli-
  cent,
Hath ever like a loyal sister cleaved
To Arthur,—but a son she had not borne.
And Uther cast upon her eyes of love :
But she, a stainless wife to Gorloïs,
So loathed the bright dishonour of his
  love,
That Gorloïs and King Uther went to war :
And overthrown was Gorloïs and slain.
Then Uther in his wrath and heat besieged
Ygerne within Tintagil, where her men,
Seeing the mighty swarm about their
  walls,
Left her and fled, and Uther enter'd in,
And there was none to call to but himself.
So, compass'd by the power of the King,
Enforced she was to wed him in her tears,
And with a shameful swiftness : after-
  ward,
Not many moons, King Uther died him-
  self,
Moaning and wailing for an heir to rule
After him, lest the realm should go to
  wrack.
And that same night, the night of the new
  year,
By reason of the bitterness and grief
That vext his mother, all before his time
Was Arthur born, and all as soon as born
Deliver'd at a secret postern-gate
To Merlin, to be holden far apart
Until his hour should come ; because the
  lords
Of that fierce day were as the lords of this,
Wild beasts, and surely would have torn
  the child

Piecemeal among them, had they known ;
  for each
But sought to rule for his own self and
  hand,
And many hated Uther for the sake
Of Gorloïs. Wherefore Merlin took the
  child,
And gave him to Sir Anton, an old knight
And ancient friend of Uther ; and his wife
Nursed the young prince, and rear'd him
  with her own ;
And no man knew. And ever since the
  lords
Have foughten like wild beasts among
  themselves,
So that the realm has gone to wrack :
  but now,
This year, when Merlin (for his hour had
  come)
Brought Arthur forth, and set him in the
  hall,
Proclaiming, " Here is Uther's heir, your
  king,"
A hundred voices cried, "Away with him !
No king of ours ! a son of Gorloïs he,
Or else the child of Anton, and no king,
Or else baseborn." Yet Merlin thro' his
  craft,
And while the people clamour'd for a king,
Had Arthur crown'd ; but after, the great
  lords
Banded, and so brake out in open war.'

Then while the King debated with
  himself
If Arthur were the child of shamefulness,
Or born the son of Gorloïs, after death,
Or Uther's son, and born before his
  time,
Or whether there were truth in anything
Said by these three, there came to Came-
  liard,
With Gawain and young Modred, her two
  sons,
Lot's wife, the Queen of Orkney, Belli-
  cent ;
Whom as he could, not as he would, the
  King
Made feast for, saying, as they sat at
  meat,

'A doubtful throne is ice on summer
    seas.
Ye come from Arthur's court. Victor his
    men
Report him! Yea, but ye—think ye this
    king—
So many those that hate him, and so
    strong,
So few his knights, however brave they
    be—
Hath body enow to hold his foemen
    down?'

'O King,' she cried, 'and I will tell
    thee: few,
Few, but all brave, all of one mind with
    him;
For I was near him when the savage yells
Of Uther's peerage died, and Arthur sat
Crown'd on the daïs, and his warriors
    cried,
"Be thou the king, and we will work thy
    will
Who love thee." Then the King in low
    deep tones,
And simple words of great authority,
Bound them by so strait vows to his own
    self,
That when they rose, knighted from
    kneeling, some
Were pale as at the passing of a ghost,
Some flush'd, and others dazed, as one
    who wakes
Half-blinded at the coming of a light.

'But when he spake and cheer'd his
    Table Round
With large, divine, and comfortable words,
Beyond my tongue to tell thee—I beheld
From eye to eye thro' all their Order flash
A momentary likeness of the King:
And ere it left their faces, thro' the cross
And those around it and the Crucified,
Down from the casement over Arthur,
    smote
Flame-colour, vert and azure, in three
    rays,
One falling upon each of three fair queens,
Who stood in silence near his throne, the
    friends

Of Arthur, gazing on him, tall, with bright
Sweet faces, who will help him at his
    need.

'And there I saw mage Merlin, whose
    vast wit
And hundred winters are but as the hands
Of loyal vassals toiling for their liege.

'And near him stood the Lady of the
    Lake,
Who knows a subtler magic than his
    own—
Clothed in white samite, mystic, wonder-
    ful.
She gave the King his huge cross-hilted
    sword,
Whereby to drive the heathen out: a mist
Of incense curl'd about her, and her face
Wellnigh was hidden in the minster
    gloom;
But there was heard among the holy
    hymns
A voice as of the waters, for she dwells
Down in a deep; calm, whatsoever storms
May shake the world, and when the
    surface rolls,
Hath power to walk the waters like our
    Lord.

'There likewise I beheld Excalibur
Before him at his crowning borne, the
    sword
That rose from out the bosom of the lake,
And Arthur row'd across and took it—rich
With jewels, elfin Urim, on the hilt,
Bewildering heart and eye—the blade so
    bright
That men are blinded by it—on one side,
Graven in the oldest tongue of all this
    world,
"Take me," but turn the blade and ye
    shall see,
And written in the speech ye speak your-
    self,
"Cast me away!" And sad was Arthur's
    face
Taking it, but old Merlin counsell'd him,
"Take thou and strike! the time to cast
    away

Is yet far-off." So this great brand the
   king
Took, and by this will beat his foemen
   down.'

  Thereat Leodogran rejoiced, but
    thought
To sift his doubtings to the last, and ask'd,
Fixing full eyes of question on her face,
' The swallow and the swift are near akin,
But thou art closer to this noble prince,
Being his own dear sister ;' and she said,
' Daughter of Gorloïs and Ygerne am I ;'
' And therefore Arthur's sister ?' ask'd
   the King.
She answer'd, ' These be secret things,'
   and sign'd
To those two sons to pass, and let them be.
And Gawain went, and breaking into song
Sprang out, and follow'd by his flying hair
Ran like a colt, and leapt at all he saw :
But Modred laid his ear beside the doors,
And there half-heard ; the same that
   afterward
Struck for the throne, and striking found
   his doom.

  And then the Queen made answer,
    ' What know I ?
For dark my mother was in eyes and hair,
And dark in hair and eyes am I ; and dark
Was Gorloïs, yea and dark was Uther too,
Wellnigh to blackness ; but this King is
   fair
Beyond the race of Britons and of men.
Moreover, always in my mind I hear
A cry from out the dawning of my life,
A mother weeping, and I hear her say,
" O that ye had some brother, pretty one,
To guard thee on the rough ways of the
   world." '

   ' Ay,' said the King, ' and hear ye
    such a cry ?
But when did Arthur chance upon thee
   first ?'

   ' O King !' she cried, ' and I will tell
    thee true :
He found me first when yet a little maid :
Beaten I had been for a little fault

Whereof I was not guilty ; and out I ran
And flung myself down on a bank of
   heath,
And hated this fair world and all therein,
And wept, and wish'd that I were dead ;
   and he—
I know not whether of himself he came,
Or brought by Merlin, who, they say,
   can walk
Unseen at pleasure—he was at my side,
And spake sweet words, and comforted
   my heart,
And dried my tears, being a child with me.
And many a time he came, and evermore
As I grew greater grew with me ; and sad
At times he seem'd, and sad with him
   was I,
Stern too at times, and then I loved him
   not,
But sweet again, and then I loved him
   well.
And now of late I see him less and less,
But those first days had golden hours for
   me,
For then I surely thought he would be
   king.

   ' But let me tell thee now another tale :
For Bleys, our Merlin's master, as they
   say,
Died but of late, and sent his cry to me,
To hear him speak before he left his life.
Shrunk like a fairy changeling lay the
   mage ;
And when I enter'd told me that himself
And Merlin ever served about the King,
Uther, before he died ; and on the night
When Uther in Tintagil past away
Moaning and wailing for an heir, the two
Left the still King, and passing forth to
   breathe,
Then from the castle gateway by the
   chasm
Descending thro' the dismal night—a
   night
In which the bounds of heaven and earth
   were lost—
Beheld, so high upon the dreary deeps
It seem'd in heaven, a ship, the shape
   thereof

A dragon wing'd, and all from stem to
stern
Bright with a shining people on the decks,
And gone as soon as seen.   And then
the two
Dropt to the cove, and watch'd the great
sea fall,
Wave after wave, each mightier than the
last,
Till last, a ninth one, gathering half the
deep
And full of voices, slowly rose and plunged
Roaring, and all the wave was in a flame:
And down the wave and in the flame was
borne
A naked babe, and rode to Merlin's feet,
Who stoopt and caught the babe, and
cried "The King!
Here is an heir for Uther!"   And the
fringe
Of that great breaker, sweeping up the
strand,
Lash'd at the wizard as he spake the word,
And all at once all round him rose in fire,
So that the child and he were clothed in fire.
And presently thereafter follow'd calm,
Free sky and stars: "And this same
child," he said,
"Is he who reigns; nor could I part in
peace
Till this were told."   And saying this the
seer
Went thro' the strait and dreadful pass of
death,
Not ever to be question'd any more
Save on the further side; but when I met
Merlin, and ask'd him if these things were
truth—
The shining dragon and the naked child
Descending in the glory of the seas—
He laugh'd as is his wont, and answer'd me
In riddling triplets of old time, and said:

' "Rain, rain, and sun! a rainbow in
the sky!
A young man will be wiser by and by;
An old man's wit may wander ere he die.
Rain, rain, and sun! a rainbow on the
lea!
And truth is this to me, and that to thee;

And truth or clothed or naked let it be.
Rain, sun, and rain! and the free
blossom blows:
Sun, rain, and sun! and where is he
who knows?
From the great deep to the great deep he
goes." '

' So Merlin riddling anger'd me; but
thou
Fear not to give this King thine only child,
Guinevere: so great bards of him will sing
Hereafter; and dark sayings from of old
Ranging and ringing thro' the minds of
men,
And echo'd by old folk beside their fires
For comfort after their wage-work is done,
Speak of the King; and Merlin in our
time
Hath spoken also, not in jest, and sworn
Tho' men may wound him that he will
not die,
But pass, again to come; and then or now
Utterly smite the heathen underfoot,
Till these and all men hail him for their
king.'

She spake and King Leodogran rejoiced,
But musing 'Shall I answer yea or nay?'
Doubted, and drowsed, nodded and slept,
and saw,
Dreaming, a slope of land that ever grew,
Field after field, up to a height, the peak
Haze - hidden, and thereon a phantom
king,
Now looming, and now lost; and on the
slope
The sword rose, the hind fell, the herd
was driven,
Fire glimpsed; and all the land from
roof and rick,
In drifts of smoke before a rolling wind,
Stream'd to the peak, and mingled with
the haze
And made it thicker; while the phantom
king
Sent out at times a voice; and here or there
Stood one who pointed toward the voice,
the rest
Slew on and burnt, crying, 'No king of
ours,

No son of Uther, and no king of ours ; '
Till with a wink his dream was changed,
    the haze
Descended, and the solid earth became
As nothing, but the King stood out in
    heaven,
Crown'd.   And Leodogran awoke, and
    sent
Ulfius, and Brastias and Bedivere,
Back to the court of Arthur answering yea.

Then Arthur charged his warrior whom
    he loved
And honour'd most, Sir Lancelot, to ride
    forth
And bring the Queen ;—and watch'd him
    from the gates :
And Lancelot past away among the
    flowers,
(For then was latter April) and return'd
Among the flowers, in May, with Guine-
    vere.
To whom arrived, by Dubric the high
    saint,
Chief of the church in Britain, and before
The stateliest of her altar-shrines, the
    King
That morn was married, while in stainless
    white,
The fair beginners of a nobler time,
And glorying in their vows and him, his
    knights
Stood round him, and rejoicing in his joy.
Far shone the fields of May thro' open
    door,
The sacred altar blossom'd white with May,
The Sun of May descended on their King,
They gazed on all earth's beauty in their
    Queen,
Roll'd incense, and there past along the
    hymns
A voice as of the waters, while the two
Sware at the shrine of Christ a deathless
    love :
And Arthur said, 'Behold, thy doom is
    mine.
Let chance what will, I love thee to the
    death ! '
To whom the Queen replied with drooping
    eyes,

'King and my lord, I love thee to the
    death ! '
And holy Dubric spread his hands and
    spake,
'Reign ye, and live and love, and make
    the world
Other, and may thy Queen be one with
    thee,
And all this Order of thy Table Round
Fulfil the boundless purpose of their
    King ! '

So Dubric said ; but when they left the
    shrine
Great Lords from Rome before the portal
    stood,
In scornful stillness gazing as they past ;
Then while they paced a city all on fire
With sun and cloth of gold, the trumpets
    blew,
And Arthur's knighthood sang before the
    King :—

'Blow trumpet, for the world is white
    with May ;
Blow trumpet, the long night hath roll'd
    away !
Blow thro' the living world—"Let the
    King reign."

'Shall Rome or Heathen rule in
    Arthur's realm ?
Flash brand and lance, fall battleaxe upon
    helm,
Fall battleaxe, and flash brand ! Let the
    King reign.

'Strike for the King and live ! his
    knights have heard
That God hath told the King a secret
    word.
Fall battleaxe, and flash brand ! Let the
    King reign.

'Blow trumpet ! he will lift us from
    the dust.
Blow trumpet ! live the strength and die
    the lust !
Clang battleaxe, and clash brand ! Let
    the King reign.

'Strike for the King and die! and if
    thou diest,
The King is King, and ever wills the
    highest.
Clang battleaxe, and clash brand! Let
    the King reign

   'Blow, for our Sun is mighty in his
    May!
Blow, for our Sun is mightier day by day!
Clang battleaxe, and clash brand! Let
    the King reign.

   'The King will follow Christ, and we
    the King
In whom high God hath breathed a secret
    thing.
Fall battleaxe, and flash brand! Let the
    King reign.'

So sang the knighthood, moving to their
    hall.
There at the banquet those great Lords
    from Rome,
The slowly-fading mistress of the world,
Strode in, and claim'd their tribute as of
    yore.

But Arthur spake, 'Behold, for these have
    sworn
To wage my wars, and worship me their
    King;
The old order changeth, yielding place
    to new;
And we that fight for our fair father
    Christ,
Seeing that ye be grown too weak and
    old
To drive the heathen from your Roman
    wall,
No tribute will we pay:' so those great
    lords
Drew back in wrath, and Arthur strove
    with Rome.

And Arthur and his knighthood for a
    space
Were all one will, and thro' that strength
    the King
Drew in the petty princedoms under him,
Fought, and in twelve great battles over-
    came
The heathen hordes, and made a realm
    and reign'd.

THE ROUND TABLE.

GARETH AND LYNETTE.

THE last tall son of Lot and Bellicent,
And tallest, Gareth, in a showerful spring
Stared at the spate. A slender-shafted
    Pine
Lost footing, fell, and so was whirl'd away.
'How he went down,' said Gareth, 'as
    a false knight
Or evil king before my lance if lance
Were mine to use—O senseless cataract,
Bearing all down in thy precipitancy—
And yet thou art but swollen with cold
    snows
And mine is living blood: thou dost His
    will,

The Maker's, and not knowest, and I
    that know,
Have strength and wit, in my good
    mother's hall
Linger with vacillating obedience,
Prison'd, and kept and coax'd and
    whistled to—
Since the good mother holds me still a
    child!
Good mother is bad mother unto me!
A worse were better; yet no worse
    would I.
Heaven yield her for it, but in me put
    force
To weary her ears with one continuous
    prayer,

Until she let me fly discaged to sweep
In ever-highering eagle-circles up
To the great Sun of Glory, and thence
    swoop
Down upon all things base, and dash
    them dead,
A knight of Arthur, working out his will,
To cleanse the world. Why, Gawain,
    when he came
With Modred hither in the summertime,
Ask'd me to tilt with him, the proven
    knight.
Modred for want of worthier was the
    judge.
Then I so shook him in the saddle, he
    said,
" Thou hast half prevail'd against me,"
    said so—he—
Tho' Modred biting his thin lips was mute,
For he is alway sullen : what care I ?'

And Gareth went, and hovering round
    her chair
Ask'd, ' Mother, tho' ye count me still
    the child,
Sweet mother, do ye love the child ?'
    She laugh'd,
'Thou art but a wild-goose to question
    it.'
' Then, mother, an ye love the child,' he
    said,
' Being a goose and rather tame than wild,
Hear the child's story.' ' Yea, my well-
    beloved,
An 'twere but of the goose and golden
    eggs.'

And Gareth answer'd her with kindling
    eyes,
' Nay, nay, good mother, but this egg of
    mine
Was finer gold than any goose can lay ;
For this an Eagle, a royal Eagle, laid
Almost beyond eye-reach, on such a palm
As glitters gilded in thy Book of Hours.
And there was ever haunting round the
    palm
A lusty youth, but poor, who often saw
The splendour sparkling from aloft, and
    thought

" An I could climb and lay my hand upon
    it,
Then were I wealthier than a leash of
    kings."
But ever when he reach'd a hand to climb,
One, that had loved him from his child-
    hood, caught
And stay'd him, " Climb not lest thou
    break thy neck,
I charge thee by my love," and so the boy,
Sweet mother, neither clomb, nor brake
    his neck,
But brake his very heart in pining for it,
And past away.'

                    To whom the mother said,
' True love, sweet son, had risk'd himself
    and climb'd,
And handed down the golden treasure to
    him.'

And Gareth answer'd her with kindling
    eyes,
' Gold ? said I gold ?—ay then, why he,
    or she,
Or whosoe'er it was, or half the world
Had ventured—*had* the thing I spake of
    been
Mere gold—but this was all of that true
    steel,
Whereof they forged the brand Excalibur,
And lightnings play'd about it in the
    storm,
And all the little fowl were flurried at it,
And there were cries and clashings in the
    nest,
That sent him from his senses : let me go.'

Then Bellicent bemoan'd herself and
    said,
' Hast thou no pity upon my loneliness ?
Lo, where thy father Lot beside the hearth
Lies like a log, and all but smoulder'd
    out !
For ever since when traitor to the King
He fought against him in the Barons' war,
And Arthur gave him back his territory,
His age hath slowly droopt, and now lies
    there
A yet-warm corpse, and yet unburiable,

No more ; nor sees, nor hears, nor speaks,
    nor knows.
And both thy brethren are in Arthur's hall,
Albeit neither loved with that full love
I feel for thee, nor worthy such a love :
Stay therefore thou ; red berries charm
    the bird,
And thee, mine innocent, the jousts, the
    wars,
Who never knewest finger-ache, nor pang
Of wrench'd or broken limb—an often
    chance
In those brain-stunning shocks, and
    tourney-falls,
Frights to my heart ; but stay : follow
    the deer
By these tall firs and our fast-falling burns ;
So make thy manhood mightier day by
    day ;
Sweet is the chase : and I will seek thee
    out
Some comfortable bride and fair, to grace
Thy climbing life, and cherish my prone
    year,
Till falling into Lot's forgetfulness
I know not thee, myself, nor anything.
Stay, my best son ! ye are yet more boy
    than man.'

    Then Gareth, 'An ye hold me yet for
    child,
Hear yet once more the story of the child.
For, mother, there was once a King, like
    ours.
The prince his heir, when tall and
    marriageable,
Ask'd for a bride ; and thereupon the
    King
Set two before him. One was fair,
    strong, arm'd—
But to be won by force—and many men
Desired her ; one, good lack, no man
    desired.
And these were the conditions of the
    King :
That save he won the first by force, he
    needs
Must wed that other, whom no man
    desired,
A red-faced bride who knew herself so vile,

That evermore she long'd to hide herself,
Nor fronted man or woman, eye to eye—
Yea—some she cleaved to, but they died
    of her.
And one—they call'd her Fame ; and
    one,—O Mother,
How can ye keep me tether'd to you—
    Shame.
Man am I grown, a man's work must I do.
Follow the deer ? follow the Christ, the
    King,
Live pure, speak true, right wrong, follow
    the King—
Else, wherefore born ?'

        To whom the mother said,
' Sweet son, for there be many who deem
    him not,
Or will not deem him, wholly proven
    King—
Albeit in mine own heart I knew him
    King,
When I was frequent with him in my
    youth,
And heard him Kingly speak, and doubted
    him
No more than he, himself ; but felt him
    mine,
Of closest kin to me : yet—wilt thou leave
Thine easeful biding here, and risk thine
    all,
Life, limbs, for one that is not proven
    King ?
Stay, till the cloud that settles round his
    birth
Hath lifted but a little. Stay, sweet son.'

    And Gareth answer'd quickly, 'Not
    an hour,
So that ye yield me—I will walk thro'
    fire,
Mother, to gain it—your full leave to
    go.
Not proven, who swept the dust of ruin'd
    Rome
From off the threshold of the realm, and
    crush'd
The Idolaters, and made the people free ?
Who should be King save him who
    makes us free ?'

So when the Queen, who long had
    sought in vain
To break him from the intent to which
    he grew,
Found her son's will unwaveringly one,
She answer'd craftily, 'Will ye walk thro'
    fire?
Who walks thro' fire will hardly heed the
    smoke.
Ay, go then, an ye must : only one proof,
Before thou ask the King to make thee
    knight,
Of thine obedience and thy love to me,
Thy mother,—I demand.'

And Gareth cried,
' A hard one, or a hundred, so I go.
Nay—quick! the proof to prove me to
    the quick!'

But slowly spake the mother looking
    at him,
' Prince, thou shalt go disguised to
    Arthur's hall,
And hire thyself to serve for meats and
    drinks
Among the scullions and the kitchen-
    knaves,
And those that hand the dish across the
    bar.
Nor shalt thou tell thy name to anyone.
And thou shalt serve a twelvemonth and
    a day.'

For so the Queen believed that when
    her son
Beheld his only way to glory lead
Low down thro' villain kitchen-vassalage,
Her own true Gareth was too princely-
    proud
To pass thereby ; so should he rest with
    her,
Closed in her castle from the sound of
    arms.

Silent awhile was Gareth, then replied,
' The thrall in person may be free in soul,
And I shall see the jousts. Thy son am I,
And since thou art my mother, must
    obey.
I therefore yield me freely to thy will ;

For hence will I, disguised, and hire my-
    self
To serve with scullions and with kitchen-
    knaves ;
Nor tell my name to any—no, not the
    King.'

Gareth awhile linger'd. The mother's
    eye
Full of the wistful fear that he would go,
And turning toward him wheresoe'er he
    turn'd,
Perplext his outward purpose, till an hour,
When waken'd by the wind which with
    full voice
Swept bellowing thro' the darkness on to
    dawn,
He rose, and out of slumber calling two
That still had tended on him from his
    birth,
Before the wakeful mother heard him,
    went.

The three were clad like tillers of the
    soil.
Southward they set their faces. The birds
    made
Melody on branch, and melody in mid air.
The damp hill-slopes were quicken'd into
    green,
And the live green had kindled into
    flowers,
For it was past the time of Easterday.

So, when their feet were planted on
    the plain
That broaden'd toward the base of Came-
    lot,
Far off they saw the silver-misty morn
Rolling her smoke about the Royal
    mount,
That rose between the forest and the field.
At times the summit of the high city
    flash'd ;
At times the spires and turrets half-way
    down
Prick'd thro' the mist ; at times the great
    gate shone
Only, that open'd on the field below :
Anon, the whole fair city had disappear'd.

Then those who went with Gareth were
   amazed,
One crying, ' Let us go no further, lord.
Here is a city of Enchanters, built
By fairy Kings.' The second echo'd him,
' Lord, we have heard from our wise man
   at home
To Northward, that this King is not the
   King,
But only changeling out of Fairyland,
Who drave the heathen hence by sorcery
And Merlin's glamour.' Then the first
   again,
' Lord, there is no such city anywhere,
But all a vision.'

            Gareth answer'd them
With laughter, swearing he had glamour
   enow
In his own blood, his princedom, youth
   and hopes,
To plunge old Merlin in the Arabian sea;
So push'd them all unwilling toward the
   gate.
And there was no gate like it under
   heaven.
For barefoot on the keystone, which was
   lined
And rippled like an ever-fleeting wave,
The Lady of the Lake stood : all her dress
Wept from her sides as water flowing away ;
But like the cross her great and goodly
   arms
Stretch'd under all the cornice and
   upheld :
And drops of water fell from either hand ;
And down from one a sword was hung,
   from one
A censer, either worn with wind and
   storm ;
And o'er her breast floated the sacred fish ;
And in the space to left of her, and right,
Were Arthur's wars in weird devices done,
New things and old co-twisted, as if Time
Were nothing, so inveterately, that men
Were giddy gazing there ; and over all
High on the top were those three Queens,
   the friends
Of Arthur, who should help him at his
   need.

T

Then those with Gareth for so long a
   space
Stared at the figures, that at last it seem'd
The dragon-boughts and elvish emblem-
   ings
Began to move, seethe, twine and curl :
   they call'd
To Gareth, ' Lord, the gateway is alive.'

    And Gareth likewise on them fixt his
   eyes
So long, that ev'n to him they seem'd to
   move.
Out of the city a blast of music peal'd.
Back from the gate started the three, to
   whom
From out thereunder came an ancient
   man,
Long-bearded, saying, ' Who be ye, my
   sons ?'

    Then Gareth, ' We be tillers of the soil,
Who leaving share in furrow come to see
The glories of our King : but these, my
   men,
(Your city moved so weirdly in the mist)
Doubt if the King be King at all, or come
From Fairyland ; and whether this be built
By magic, and by fairy Kings and Queens ;
Or whether there be any city at all,
Or all a vision : and this music now
Hath scared them both, but tell thou
   these the truth.'

    Then that old Seer made answer play-
   ing on him
And saying, ' Son, I have seen the good
   ship sail
Keel upward, and mast downward, in
   the heavens,
And solid turrets topsy-turvy in air :
And here is truth ; but an it please thee
   not,
Take thou the truth as thou hast told it
   me.
For truly as thou sayest, a Fairy King
And Fairy Queens have built the city, son ;
They came from out a sacred mountain-
   cleft
Toward the sunrise, each with harp in
   hand,

Y

And built it to the music of their harps.
And, as thou sayest, it is enchanted, son,
For there is nothing in it as it seems
Saving the King; tho' some there be that
    hold
The King a shadow, and the city real :
Yet take thou heed of him, for, so thou
    pass
Beneath this archway, then wilt thou
    become
A thrall to his enchantments, for the King
Will bind thee by such vows, as is a shame
A man should not be bound by, yet the
    which
No man can keep ; but, so thou dread to
    swear,
Pass not beneath this gateway, but abide
Without, among the cattle of the field.
For an ye heard a music, like enow
They are building still, seeing the city is
    built
To music, therefore never built at all,
And therefore built for ever.'

                Gareth spake
Anger'd, 'Old Master, reverence thine
    own beard
That looks as white as utter truth, and
    seems
Wellnigh as long as thou art statured tall !
Why mockest thou the stranger that hath
    been
To thee fair-spoken ?'

            But the Seer replied,
'Know ye not then the Riddling of the
    Bards ?
"Confusion, and illusion, and relation,
Elusion, and occasion, and evasion"?
I mock thee not but as thou mockest me,
And all that see thee, for thou art not who
Thou seemest, but I know thee who thou
    art.
And now thou goest up to mock the King,
Who cannot brook the shadow of any lie.'

Unmockingly the mocker ending here
Turn'd to the right, and past along the
    plain ;
Whom Gareth looking after said, 'My
    men,

Our one white lie sits like a little ghost
Here on the threshold of our enterprise.
Let love be blamed for it, not she, nor I :
Well, we will make amends.'

               With all good cheer
He spake and laugh'd, then enter'd with
    his twain
Camelot, a city of shadowy palaces
And stately, rich in emblem and the work
Of ancient kings who did their days in
    stone ;
Which Merlin's hand, the Mage at
    Arthur's court,
Knowing all arts, had touch'd, and every-
    where
At Arthur's ordinance, tipt with lessening
    peak
And pinnacle, and had made it spire to
    heaven.
And ever and anon a knight would pass
Outward, or inward to the hall : his arms
Clash'd ; and the sound was good to
    Gareth's ear.
And out of bower and casement shyly
    glanced
Eyes of pure women, wholesome stars of
    love ;
And all about a healthful people stept
As in the presence of a gracious king.

Then into hall Gareth ascending heard
A voice, the voice of Arthur, and beheld
Far over heads in that long-vaulted hall
The splendour of the presence of the
    King
Throned, and delivering doom — and
    look'd no more—
But felt his young heart hammering in his
    ears,
And thought, 'For this half-shadow of a
    lie
The truthful King will doom me when I
    speak.'
Yet pressing on, tho' all in fear to find
Sir Gawain or Sir Modred, saw nor one
Nor other, but in all the listening eyes
Of those tall knights, that ranged about
    the throne,
Clear honour shining like the dewy star

Of dawn, and faith in their great King,
with pure
Affection, and the light of victory,
And glory gain'd, and evermore to gain.

Then came a widow crying to the King,
A boon, Sir King ! Thy father, Uther,
reft
From my dead lord a field with violence :
For howsoe'er at first he proffer'd gold,
Yet, for the field was pleasant in our eyes,
We yielded not ; and then he reft us of it
Perforce, and left us neither gold nor field.'

Said Arthur, ' Whether would ye ?
gold or field ?'
To whom the woman weeping, ' Nay, my
lord,
The field was pleasant in my husband's
eye.'

And Arthur, ' Have thy pleasant field
again,
And thrice the gold for Uther's use
thereof,
According to the years. No boon is here,
But justice, so thy say be proven true.
Accursed, who from the wrongs his father
did
Would shape himself a right !'

And while she past,
Came yet another widow crying to him,
A boon, Sir King ! Thine enemy, King,
am I.
With thine own hand thou slewest my
dear lord,
A knight of Uther in the Barons' war,
When Lot and many another rose and
fought
Against thee, saying thou wert basely
born.
I held with these, and loathe to ask thee
aught.
Yet lo ! my husband's brother had my
son
Thrall'd in his castle, and hath starved
him dead ;
And standeth seized of that inheritance
Which thou that slewest the sire hast left
the son.

So tho' I scarce can ask it thee for hate,
Grant me some knight to do the battle
for me,
Kill the foul thief, and wreak me for my
son.'

Then strode a good knight forward,
crying to him,
' A boon, Sir King ! I am her kinsman, I.
Give me to right her wrong, and slay the
man.'

Then came Sir Kay, the seneschal, and
cried,
' A boon, Sir King ! ev'n that thou grant
her none,
This railer, that hath mock'd thee in full
hall—
None ; or the wholesome boon of gyve
and gag.'

But Arthur, ' We sit King, to help the
wrong'd
Thro' all our realm. The woman loves
her lord.
Peace to thee, woman, with thy loves and
hates !
The kings of old had doom'd thee to the
flames,
Aurelius Emrys would have scourged thee
dead,
And Uther slit thy tongue : but get thee
hence—
Lest that rough humour of the kings of
old
Return upon me ! Thou that art her kin,
Go likewise ; lay him low and slay him
not,
But bring him here, that I may judge the
right,
According to the justice of the King :
Then, be he guilty, by that deathless King
Who lived and died for men, the man
shall die.'

Then came in hall the messenger of
Mark,
A name of evil savour in the land,
The Cornish king. In either hand he
bore
What dazzled all, and shone far-off as
shines

A field of charlock in the sudden sun
Between two showers, a cloth of palest
     gold,
Which down he laid before the throne,
     and knelt,
Delivering, that his lord, the vassal king,
Was ev'n upon his way to Camelot ;
For having heard that Arthur of his grace
Had made his goodly cousin, Tristram,
     knight,
And, for himself was of the greater state,
Being a king, he trusted his liege-lord
Would yield him this large honour all the
     more ;
So pray'd him well to accept this cloth of
     gold,
In token of true heart and feälty.

     Then Arthur cried to rend the cloth, to
          rend
In pieces, and so cast it on the hearth.
An oak-tree smoulder'd there.   'The
     goodly knight !
What ! shall the shield of Mark stand
     among these ?'
For, midway down the side of that long
     hall
A stately pile,—whereof along the front,
Some blazon'd, some but carven, and
     some blank,
There ran a treble range of stony
     shields, —
Rose, and high-arching overbrow'd the
     hearth.
And under every shield a knight was
     named :
For this was Arthur's custom in his hall ;
When some good knight had done one
     noble deed,
His arms were carven only ; but if twain
His arms were blazon'd also ; but if none,
The shield was blank and bare without a
     sign
Saving the name beneath ; and Gareth
     saw
The shield of Gawain blazon'd rich and
     bright,
And Modred's blank as death ; and
     Arthur cried
To rend the cloth and cast it on the hearth.

' More like are we to reave him of hi
     crown
Than make him knight because men ca
     him king.
The kings we found, ye know we stay'
     their hands
From war among themselves, but le
     them kings ;
Of whom were any bounteous, merciful,
Truth-speaking, brave, good livers, ther
     we enroll'd
Among us, and they sit within our hall.
But Mark hath tarnish'd the great nam
     of king,
As Mark would sully the low state of churl
And, seeing he hath sent us cloth of gold
Return, and meet, and hold him fror
     our eyes,
Lest we should lap him up in cloth of lead
Silenced for ever—craven—a man o
     plots,
Craft, poisonous counsels, wayside am
     bushings—
No fault of thine : let Kay the senescha
Look to thy wants, and send thee satis
     fied—
Accursed, who strikes nor lets the han
     be seen !'

     And many another suppliant cryin
          came
With noise of ravage wrought by beas
     and man,
And evermore a knight would ride away

     Last, Gareth leaning both hands heavil
Down on the shoulders of the twain, hi
     men,
Approach'd between them toward th
     King, and ask'd,
' A boon, Sir King (his voice was al
     ashamed),
For see ye not how weak and hungerwor
I seem—leaning on these ? grant me t
     serve
For meat and drink among thy kitchen
     knaves
A twelvemonth and a day, nor seek m
     name.
Hereafter I will fight.'

To him the King,
'A goodly youth and worth a goodlier
      boon !
But so thou wilt no goodlier, then must
      Kay,
The master of the meats and drinks, be
      thine.'

  He rose and past ; then Kay, a man
      of mien
Wan-sallow as the plant that feels itself
Root-bitten by white lichen,

              ' Lo ye now !
This fellow hath broken from some Abbey,
      where,
God wot, he had not beef and brewis enow,
However that might chance ! but an he
      work,
Like any pigeon will I cram his crop,
And sleeker shall he shine than any hog.'

  Then Lancelot standing near, ' Sir
      Seneschal,
Sleuth-hound thou knowest, and gray,
      and all the hounds ;
A horse thou knowest, a man thou dost
      not know :
Broad brows and fair, a fluent hair and fine,
High nose, a nostril large and fine, and
      hands
Large, fair and fine !—Some young lad's
      mystery—
But, or from sheepcot or king's hall, the boy
Is noble-natured.   Treat him with all
      grace,
Lest he should come to shame thy judging
      of him.'

  Then Kay, ' What murmurest thou of
      mystery ?
Think ye this fellow will poison the
      King's dish ?
Nay, for he spake too fool-like : mystery !
Tut, an the lad were noble, he had ask'd
For horse and armour : fair and fine,
      forsooth !
Sir Fine-face, Sir Fair-hands ? but see
      thou to it
That thine own fineness, Lancelot, some
      fine day
Undo thee not—and leave my man to me.'

  So Gareth all for glory underwent
The sooty yoke of kitchen-vassalage ;
Ate with young lads his portion by the
      door,
And couch'd at night with grimy kitchen-
      knaves.

And Lancelot ever spake him pleasantly,
But Kay the seneschal, who loved him not,
Would hustle and harry him, and labour
      him
Beyond his comrade of the hearth, and set
To turn the broach, draw water, or hew
      wood,
Or grosser tasks ; and Gareth bow'd
      himself
With all obedience to the King, and
      wrought
All kind of service with a noble ease
That graced the lowliest act in doing it.
And when the thralls had talk among
      themselves,
And one would praise the love that linkt
      the King
And Lancelot—how the King had saved
      his life
In battle twice, and Lancelot once the
      King's—
For Lancelot was the first in Tournament,
But Arthur mightiest on the battle-field—
Gareth was glad.   Or if some other told,
How once the wandering forester at dawn,
Far over the blue tarns and hazy seas,
On Caer-Eryri's highest found the King,
A naked babe, of whom the Prophet spake,
' He passes to the Isle Avilion,
He passes and is heal'd and cannot die '—
Gareth was glad.   But if their talk were
      foul,
Then would he whistle rapid as any lark,
Or carol some old roundelay, and so loud
That first they mock'd, but, after, rever-
      enced him.
Or Gareth telling some prodigious tale
Of knights, who sliced a red life-bubbling
      way
Thro' twenty folds of twisted dragon, held
All in a gap-mouth'd circle his good mates
Lying or sitting round him, idle hands,
Charm'd ; till Sir Kay, the seneschal,
      would come

Blustering upon them, like a sudden wind
Among dead leaves, and drive them all
    apart.
Or when the thralls had sport among
    themselves,
So there were any trial of mastery,
He, by two yards in casting bar or stone
Was counted best ; and if there chanced
    a joust,
So that Sir Kay nodded him leave to go,
Would hurry thither, and when he saw
    the knights
Clash like the coming and retiring wave,
And the spear spring, and good horse
    reel, the boy
Was half beyond himself for ecstasy.

So for a month he wrought among the
    thralls ;
But in the weeks that follow'd, the good
    Queen,
Repentant of the word she made him
    swear,
And saddening in her childless castle, sent,
Between the in-crescent and de-crescent
    moon,
Arms for her son, and loosed him from
    his vow.

This, Gareth hearing from a squire of
    Lot
With whom he used to play at tourney
    once,
When both were children, and in lonely
    haunts
Would scratch a ragged oval on the sand,
And each at either dash from either end—
Shame never made girl redder than Gareth
    joy.
He laugh'd ; he sprang.   ' Out of the
    smoke, at once
I leap from Satan's foot to Peter's knee—
These news be mine, none other's—nay,
    the King's—
Descend into the city :' whereon he sought
The King alone, and found, and told him
    all.

    ' I have stagger'd thy strong Gawain in
        a tilt
For pastime ; yea, he said it : joust can I.

Make me thy knight—in secret ! let my
    name
Be hidd'n, and give me the first quest, I
    spring
Like flame from ashes.'

                    Here the King's calm eye
Fell on, and check'd, and made him flush,
    and bow
Lowly, to kiss his hand, who answer'd
    him,
' Son, the good mother let me know thee
    here,
And sent her wish that I would yield thee
    thine.
Make thee my knight ? my knights are
    sworn to vows
Of utter hardihood, utter gentleness,
And, loving, utter faithfulness in love,
And uttermost obedience to the King.'

    Then Gareth, lightly springing from
        his knees,
' My King, for hardihood I can promise
    thee.
For uttermost obedience make demand
Of whom ye gave me to, the Seneschal,
No mellow master of the meats and
    drinks !
And as for love, God wot, I love not yet,
But love I shall, God willing.'

                    And the King—
' Make thee my knight in secret ? yea,
    but he,
Our noblest brother, and our truest man,
And one with me in all, he needs must
    know.'

    ' Let Lancelot know, my King, let
        Lancelot know,
Thy noblest and thy truest !'

                    And the King—
' But wherefore would ye men should
    wonder at you ?
Nay, rather for the sake of me, their
    King,
And the deed's sake my knighthood do
    the deed,
Than to be noised of.'

Merrily Gareth ask'd,
" Have I not earn'd my cake in baking
of it ?
Let be my name until I make my name !
My deeds will speak : it is but for a day.'
So with a kindly hand on Gareth's arm
Smiled the great King, and half-unwill-
ingly
Loving his lusty youthhood yielded to
him.
Then, after summoning Lancelot privily,
' I have given him the first quest : he is
not proven.
Look therefore when he calls for this in
hall,
Thou get to horse and follow him far away.
Cover the lions on thy shield, and see
Far as thou mayest, he be nor ta'en nor
slain.'

Then that same day there past into the
hall
A damsel of high lineage, and a brow
May - blossom, and a cheek of apple-
blossom,
Hawk-eyes ; and lightly was her slender
nose
Tip-tilted like the petal of a flower ;
She into hall past with her page and cried,

' O King, for thou hast driven the foe
without,
See to the foe within ! bridge, ford, beset
By bandits, everyone that owns a tower
The Lord for half a league.   Why sit ye
there ?
Rest would I not, Sir King, an I were
king,
Till ev'n the lonest hold were all as free
From cursed bloodshed, as thine altar-
cloth
From that best blood it is a sin to spill.'

' Comfort thyself,' said Arthur, ' I nor
mine
Rest : so my knighthood keep the vows
they swore,
The wastest moorland of our realm shall
be
Safe, damsel, as the centre of this hall.
What is thy name ? thy need ?'

' My name ?' she said—
' Lynette my name ; noble ; my need, a
knight
To combat for my sister, Lyonors,
A lady of high lineage, of great lands,
And comely, yea, and comelier than my-
self.
She lives in Castle Perilous : a river
Runs in three loops about her living-
place ;
And o'er it are three passings, and three
knights
Defend the passings, brethren, and a
fourth
And of that four the mightiest, holds her
stay'd
In her own castle, and so besieges her
To break her will, and make her wed with
him :
And but delays his purport till thou send
To do the battle with him, thy chief man
Sir Lancelot whom he trusts to overthrow,
Then wed, with glory : but she will not
wed
Save whom she loveth, or a holy life.
Now therefore have I come for Lancelot.'

Then Arthur mindful of Sir Gareth ask'd,
' Damsel, ye know this Order lives to
crush
All wrongers of the Realm.   But say, these
four,
Who be they ?   What the fashion of the
men ?'

' They be of foolish fashion, O Sir King,
The fashion of that old knight-errantry
Who ride abroad, and do but what they
will ;
Courteous or bestial from the moment,
such
As have nor law nor king ; and three of
these
Proud in their fantasy call themselves the
Day,
Morning-Star, and Noon-Sun, and Even-
ing-Star,
Being strong fools ; and never a whit more
wise
The fourth, who alway rideth arm'd in
black,

A huge man-beast of boundless savagery.
He names himself the Night and oftener
    Death,
And wears a helmet mounted with a skull,
And bears a skeleton figured on his arms,
To show that who may slay or scape the
    three,
Slain by himself, shall enter endless night.
And all these four be fools, but mighty men,
And therefore am I come for Lancelot.'

Hereat Sir Gareth call'd from where he
    rose,
A head with kindling eyes above the
    throng,
'A boon, Sir King—this quest !' then—
    for he mark'd
Kay near him groaning like a wounded
    bull—
'Yea, King, thou knowest thy kitchen-
    knave am I,
And mighty thro' thy meats and drinks
    am I,
And I can topple over a hundred such.
Thy promise, King,' and Arthur glancing
    at him,
Brought down a momentary brow.
        ' Rough, sudden,
And pardonable, worthy to be knight—
Go therefore,' and all hearers were amazed.

But on the damsel's forehead shame,
    pride, wrath
Slew the May-white : she lifted either arm,
' Fie on thee, King ! I ask'd for thy chief
    knight,
And thou hast given me but a kitchen-
    knave.'
Then ere a man in hall could stay her,
    turn'd,
Fled down the lane of access to the King,
Took horse, descended the slope street,
    and past
The weird white gate, and paused without,
    beside
The field of tourney, murmuring ' kitchen-
    knave.'

Now two great entries open'd from the
    hall,
At one end one, that gave upon a range

Of level pavement where the King would
    pace
At sunrise, gazing over plain and wood ;
And down from this a lordly stairway
    sloped
Till lost in blowing trees and tops of
    towers ;
And out by this main doorway past the
    King.
But one was counter to the hearth, and
    rose
High that the highest-crested helm could
    ride
Therethro' nor graze : and by this entry
    fled
The damsel in her wrath, and on to this
Sir Gareth strode, and saw without the
    door
King Arthur's gift, the worth of half a
    town,
A warhorse of the best, and near it stood
The two that out of north had follow'd
    him :
This bare a maiden shield, a casque ; that
    held
The horse, the spear ; whereat Sir Gareth
    loosed
A cloak that dropt from collar-bone to
    heel,
A cloth of roughest web, and cast it down,
And from it like a fuel-smother'd fire,
That lookt half-dead, brake bright, and
    flash'd as those
Dull-coated things, that making slide
    apart
Their dusk wing-cases, all beneath there
    burns
A jewell'd harness, ere they pass and fly.
So Gareth ere he parted flash'd in arms.
Then as he donn'd the helm, and took the
    shield
And mounted horse and graspt a spear, of
    grain
Storm-strengthen'd on a windy site, and
    tipt
With trenchant steel, around him slowly
    prest
The people, while from out of kitchen came
The thralls in throng, and seeing who had
    work'd

Lustier than any, and whom they could
    but love,
Mounted in arms, threw up their caps and
    cried,
' God bless the King, and all his fellow-
    ship !'
And on thro' lanes of shouting Gareth rode
Down the slope street, and past without
    the gate.

So Gareth past with joy ; but as the cur
Pluckt from the cur he fights with, ere his
    cause
Be cool'd by fighting, follows, being
    named,
His owner, but remembers all, and growls
Remembering, so Sir Kay beside the door
Mutter'd in scorn of Gareth whom he used
To harry and hustle.

            ' Bound upon a quest
With horse and arms—the King hath past
    his time—
My scullion knave ! Thralls to your work
    again,
For an your fire be low ye kindle mine !
Will there be dawn in West and eve in
    East?
Begone !—my knave !—belike and like
    enow
Some old head-blow not heeded in his
    youth
So shook his wits they wander in his
    prime—
Crazed ! How the villain lifted up his
    voice,
Nor shamed to bawl himself a kitchen-
    knave.
Tut : he was tame and meek enow with
    me,
Till peacock'd up with Lancelot's noticing.
Well—I will after my loud knave, and
    learn
Whether he know me for his master yet.
Out of the smoke he came, and so my
    lance
Hold, by God's grace, he shall into the
    mire—
Thence, if the King awaken from his craze,
Into the smoke again.'

            But Lancelot said,
' Kay, wherefore wilt thou go against the
    King,
For that did never he whereon ye rail,
But ever meekly served the King in thee?
Abide : take counsel ; for this lad is great
And lusty, and knowing both of lance and
    sword.'
' Tut, tell not me,' said Kay, ' ye are
    overfine
To mar stout knaves with foolish courte-
    sies : '
Then mounted, on thro' silent faces rode
Down the slope city, and out beyond the
    gate.

But by the field of tourney lingering yet
Mutter'd the damsel, ' Wherefore did the
    King
Scorn me ? for, were Sir Lancelot lackt,
    at least
He might have yielded to me one of those
Who tilt for lady's love and glory here,
Rather than—O sweet heaven ! O fie
    upon him—
His kitchen-knave.'

            To whom Sir Gareth drew
(And there were none but few goodlier
    than he)
Shining in arms, 'Damsel, the quest is mine.
Lead, and I follow.' She thereat, as one
That smells a foul-flesh'd agaric in the
    holt,
And deems it carrion of some woodland
    thing,
Or shrew, or weasel, nipt her slender nose
With petulant thumb and finger, shrilling,
    ' Hence !
Avoid, thou smellest all of kitchen-grease.
And look who comes behind,' for there
    was Kay.
' Knowest thou not me ? thy master ? I
    am Kay.
We lack thee by the hearth.'

            And Gareth to him,
' Master no more ! too well I know thee,
    ay—
The most ungentle knight in Arthur's
    hall.'

'Have at thee then,' said Kay: they
　　shock'd, and Kay
Fell shoulder-slipt, and Gareth cried again,
'Lead, and I follow,' and fast away she
　　fled.

But after sod and shingle ceased to fly
Behind her, and the heart of her good horse
Was nigh to burst with violence of the beat,
Perforce she stay'd, and overtaken spoke.

　'What doest thou, scullion, in my
　　fellowship?
Deem'st thou that I accept thee aught the
　　more
Or love thee better, that by some device
Full cowardly, or by mere unhappiness,
Thou hast overthrown and slain thy
　　master—thou!—
Dish-washer and broach-turner, loon!—
　　to me
Thou smellest all of kitchen as before.'

　'Damsel,' Sir Gareth answer'd gently,
　　'say
Whate'er ye will, but whatsoe'er ye say,
I leave not till I finish this fair quest,
Or die therefore.'

　　　　　　　'Ay, wilt thou finish it?
Sweet lord, how like a noble knight he
　　talks!
The listening rogue hath caught the man-
　　ner of it.
But, knave, anon thou shalt be met with,
　　knave,
And then by such a one that thou for all
The kitchen brewis that was ever supt
Shalt not once dare to look him in the
　　face.'

　'I shall assay,' said Gareth with a smile
That madden'd her, and away she flash'd
　　again
Down the long avenues of a boundless
　　wood,
And Gareth following was again beknaved.

　'Sir Kitchen-knave, I have miss'd the
　　only way
Where Arthur's men are set along the
　　wood;

The wood is nigh as full of thieves as
　　leaves:
If both be slain, I am rid of thee; but yet,
Sir Scullion, canst thou use that spit of
　　thine?
Fight, an thou canst: I have miss'd the
　　only way.'

　So till the dusk that follow'd evensong
Rode on the two, reviler and reviled;
Then after one long slope was mounted,
　　saw,
Bowl-shaped, thro' tops of many thousand
　　pines
A gloomy-gladed hollow slowly sink
To westward—in the deeps whereof a
　　mere,
Round as the red eye of an Eagle-owl,
Under the half-dead sunset glared; and
　　shouts
Ascended, and there brake a servingman
Flying from out of the black wood, and
　　crying,
'They have bound my lord to cast him in
　　the mere.'
Then Gareth, 'Bound am I to right the
　　wrong'd,
But straitlier bound am I to bide with
　　thee.'
And when the damsel spake contempt-
　　uously,
'Lead, and I follow,' Gareth cried again,
'Follow, I lead!' so down among the
　　pines
He plunged; and there, blackshadow'd
　　nigh the mere,
And mid-thigh-deep in bulrushes and
　　reed,
Saw six tall men haling a seventh along,
A stone about his neck to drown him
　　in it.
Three with good blows he quieted, but
　　three
Fled thro' the pines; and Gareth loosed
　　the stone
From off his neck, then in the mere beside
Tumbled it; oilily bubbled up the mere.
Last, Gareth loosed his bonds and on free
　　feet
Set him, a stalwart Baron, Arthur's friend.

'Well that ye came, or else these caitiff
    rogues
Had wreak'd themselves on me ; good
    cause is theirs
To hate me, for my wont hath ever been
To catch my thief, and then like vermin
    here
Drown him, and with a stone about his
    neck ;
And under this wan water many of them
Lie rotting, but at night let go the stone,
And rise, and flickering in a grimly light
Dance on the mere. Good now, ye have
    saved a life
Worth somewhat as the cleanser of this
    wood.
And fain would I reward thee worship-
    fully.
What guerdon will ye ?'

           Gareth sharply spake,
'None ! for the deed's sake have I done
    the deed,
In uttermost obedience to the King.
But wilt thou yield this damsel harbour-
    age ?'

  Whereat the Baron saying, 'I well
    believe
You be of Arthur's Table,' a light laugh
Broke from Lynette, 'Ay, truly of a truth,
And in a sort, being Arthur's kitchen-
    knave !—
But deem not I accept thee aught the
    more,
Scullion, for running sharply with thy spit
Down on a rout of craven foresters.
A thresher with his flail had scatter'd them.
Nay—for thou smellest of the kitchen
    still.
But an this lord will yield us harbourage,
    Well.'

  So she spake. A league beyond the
    wood,
All in a full-fair manor and a rich,
His towers where that day a feast had
    been
Held in high hall, and many a viand left,
And many a costly cate, received the
    three.

And there they placed a peacock in his
    pride
Before the damsel, and the Baron set
Gareth beside her, but at once she rose.

  'Meseems, that here is much dis-
    courtesy,
Setting this knave, Lord Baron, at my side.
Hear me—this morn I stood in Arthur's
    hall,
And pray'd the King would grant me
    Lancelot
To fight the brotherhood of Day and
    Night—
The last a monster unsubduable
Of any save of him for whom I call'd—
Suddenly bawls this frontless kitchen-
    knave,
"The quest is mine ; thy kitchen-knave
    am I,
And mighty thro' thy meats and drinks
    am I."
Then Arthur all at once gone mad replies,
"Go therefore," and so gives the quest
    to him—
Him—here—a villain fitter to stick swine
Than ride abroad redressing women's
    wrong,
Or sit beside a noble gentlewoman.'

  Then half-ashamed and part-amazed,
    the lord
Now look'd at one and now at other, left
The damsel by the peacock in his pride,
And, seating Gareth at another board,
Sat down beside him, ate and then began.

  'Friend, whether thou be kitchen-
    knave, or not,
Or whether it be the maiden's fantasy,
And whether she be mad, or else the
    King,
Or both or neither, or thyself be mad,
I ask not : but thou strikest a strong
    stroke,
For strong thou art and goodly there-
    withal,
And saver of my life ; and therefore now,
For here be mighty men to joust with,
    weigh

Whether thou wilt not with thy damsel back
To crave again Sir Lancelot of the King.
Thy pardon ; I but speak for thine avail,
The saver of my life.'

               And Gareth said,
' Full pardon, but I follow up the quest,
Despite of Day and Night and Death and Hell.'

So when, next morn, the lord whose life he saved
Had, some brief space, convey'd them on their way
And left them with God-speed, Sir Gareth spake,
' Lead, and I follow.'   Haughtily she replied,

  ' I fly no more : I allow thee for an hour.
Lion and stoat have isled together, knave,
In time of flood.   Nay, furthermore, methinks
Some ruth is mine for thee.   Back wilt thou, fool ?
For hard by here is one will overthrow
And slay thee : then will I to court again,
And shame the King for only yielding me
My champion from the ashes of his hearth.'

  To whom Sir Gareth answer'd courteously,
' Say thou thy say, and I will do my deed.
Allow me for mine hour, and thou wilt find
My fortunes all as fair as hers who lay
Among the ashes and wedded the King's son.'

  Then to the shore of one of those long loops
Wherethro' the serpent river coil'd, they came.
Rough-thicketed were the banks and steep ; the stream
Full, narrow ; this a bridge of single arc
Took at a leap ; and on the further side
Arose a silk pavilion, gay with gold

In streaks and rays, and all Lent-lily in hue,
Save that the dome was purple, and above,
Crimson, a slender banneret fluttering.
And therebefore the lawless warrior paced
Unarm'd, and calling, ' Damsel, is this he,
The champion thou hast brought from Arthur's hall ?
For whom we let thee pass.' ' Nay, nay,' she said,
' Sir Morning-Star. The King in utter scorn
Of thee and thy much folly hath sent thee here
His kitchen-knave : and look thou to thyself :
See that he fall not on thee suddenly,
And slay thee unarm'd : he is not knight but knave.'

  Then at his call, ' O daughters of the Dawn,
And servants of the Morning-Star, approach,
Arm me,' from out the silken curtain-folds
Bare-footed and bare-headed three fair girls
In gilt and rosy raiment came : their feet
In dewy grasses glisten'd ; and the hair
All over glanced with dewdrop or with gem
Like sparkles in the stone Avanturine.
These arm'd him in blue arms, and gave a shield
Blue also, and thereon the morning star.
And Gareth silent gazed upon the knight,
Who stood a moment, ere his horse was brought,
Glorying ; and in the stream beneath him, shone
Immingled with Heaven's azure waveringly,
The gay pavilion and the naked feet,
His arms, the rosy raiment, and the star.

  Then she that watch'd him, ' Wherefore stare ye so ?
Thou shakest in thy fear : there yet is time :

Flee down the valley before he get to
 horse.
Who will cry shame? Thou art not
 knight but knave.'

Said Gareth, 'Damsel, whether knave
 or knight,
Far liefer had I fight a score of times
Than hear thee so missay me and revile.
Fair words were best for him who fights
 for thee;
But truly foul are better, for they send
That strength of anger thro' mine arms,
 I know
That I shall overthrow him.'

                    And he that bore
The star, when mounted, cried from o'er
 the bridge,
'A kitchen-knave, and sent in scorn of me:
Such fight not I, but answer scorn with
 scorn.
For this were shame to do him further
 wrong
Than set him on his feet, and take his
 horse
And arms, and so return him to the
 King.
Come, therefore, leave thy lady lightly,
 knave.
Avoid: for it beseemeth not a knave
To ride with such a lady.'

                    'Dog, thou liest.
I spring from loftier lineage than thine
 own.'
He spake; and all at fiery speed the two
Shock'd on the central bridge, and either
 spear
Bent but not brake, and either knight at
 once,
Hurl'd as a stone from out of a catapult
Beyond his horse's crupper and the bridge,
Fell, as if dead; but quickly rose and
 drew,
And Gareth lash'd so fiercely with his
 brand
He drave his enemy backward down the
 bridge,
The damsel crying, 'Well-stricken,
 kitchen-knave!'

Till Gareth's shield was cloven; but one
 stroke
Laid him that clove it grovelling on the
 ground.

Then cried the fall'n, 'Take not my
 life: I yield.'
And Gareth, 'So this damsel ask it of me
Good—I accord it easily as a grace.'
She reddening, 'Insolent scullion: I of
 thee?
I bound to thee for any favour ask'd!'
'Then shall he die.' And Gareth there
 unlaced
His helmet as to slay him, but she shriek'd,
'Be not so hardy, scullion, as to slay
One nobler than thyself.' 'Damsel, thy
 charge
Is an abounding pleasure to me. Knight,
Thy life is thine at her command. Arise
And quickly pass to Arthur's hall, and say
His kitchen-knave hath sent thee. See
 thou crave
His pardon for thy breaking of his laws.
Myself, when I return, will plead for thee.
Thy shield is mine—farewell; and,
 damsel, thou,
Lead, and I follow.'

                    And fast away she fled.
Then when he came upon her, spake,
 'Methought,
Knave, when I watch'd thee striking on
 the bridge
The savour of thy kitchen came upon me
A little faintlier: but the wind hath
 changed:
I scent it twenty-fold.' And then she sang,
'"O morning star" (not that tall felon there
Whom thou by sorcery or unhappiness
Or some device, hast foully overthrown),
"O morning star that smilest in the blue,
O star, my morning dream hath proven
 true,
Smile sweetly, thou! my love hath smiled
 on me."

'But thou begone, take counsel, and
 away,
For hard by here is one that guards a
 ford—

The second brother in their fool's parable—
Will pay thee all thy wages, and to boot.
Care not for shame : thou art not knight
    but knave.'

    To whom Sir Gareth answer'd, laugh-
        ingly,
' Parables ? Hear a parable of the knave.
When I was kitchen-knave among the rest
Fierce was the hearth, and one of my
        co-mates
Own'd a rough dog, to whom he cast his
        coat,
"Guard it," and there was none to meddle
        with it.
And such a coat art thou, and thee the
        King
Gave me to guard, and such a dog am I,
To worry, and not to flee—and—knight
        or knave—
The knave that doth thee service as full
        knight
Is all as good, meseems, as any knight
Toward thy sister's freeing.'

                    ' Ay, Sir Knave !
Ay, knave, because thou strikest as a
        knight,
Being but knave, I hate thee all the more.'

    ' Fair damsel, you should worship me
        the more,
That, being but knave, I throw thine
        enemies.'

    ' Ay, ay,' she said, ' but thou shalt meet
        thy match.'

    So when they touch'd the second river-
        loop,
Huge on a huge red horse, and all in mail
Burnish'd to blinding, shone the Noonday
        Sun
Beyond a raging shallow. As if the flower,
That blows a globe of after arrowlets,
Ten thousand-fold had grown, flash'd the
        fierce shield,
All sun ; and Gareth's eyes had flying
        blots
Before them when he turn'd from watch-
        ing him.

He from beyond the roaring shallow
        roar'd,
' What doest thou, brother, in my marches
        here ?'
And she athwart the shallow shrill'd again,
' Here is a kitchen-knave from Arthur's
        hall
Hath overthrown thy brother, and hath
        his arms.'
' Ugh !' cried the Sun, and vizoring up a
        red
And cipher face of rounded foolishness,
Push'd horse across the foamings of the
        ford,
Whom Gareth met midstream : no room
        was there
For lance or tourney-skill : four strokes
        they struck
With sword, and these were mighty ; the
        new knight
Had fear he might be shamed ; but as the
        Sun
Heaved up a ponderous arm to strike the
        fifth,
The hoof of his horse slipt in the stream,
        the stream
Descended, and the Sun was wash'd away.

    Then Gareth laid his lance athwart the
        ford ;
So drew him home ; but he that fought
        no more,
As being all bone-batter'd on the rock,
Yielded ; and Gareth sent him to the
        King.
' Myself when I return will plead for thee.'
' Lead, and I follow.' Quietly she led.
' Hath not the good wind, damsel, changed
        again ?'
' Nay, not a point : nor art thou victor
        here.
There lies a ridge of slate across the ford ;
His horse thereon stumbled—ay, for I
        saw it.

    ' "O Sun " (not this strong fool whom
        thou, Sir Knave,
Hast overthrown thro' mere unhappiness),
"O Sun, that wakenest all to bliss or
        pain,

O moon, that layest all to sleep again,
Shine sweetly : twice my love hath smiled
on me."

'What knowest thou of lovesong or of
love?
Nay, nay, God wot, so thou wert nobly
born,
Thou hast a pleasant presence. Yea,
perchance,—

' "O dewy flowers that open to the
sun,
O dewy flowers that close when day is
done,
Blow sweetly : twice my love hath smiled
on me."

'What knowest thou of flowers, except,
belike,
To garnish meats with? hath not our
good King
Who lent me thee, the flower of kitchen-
dom,
A foolish love for flowers? what stick ye
round
The pasty? wherewithal deck the boar's
head?
Flowers? nay, the boar hath rosemaries
and bay.

' "O birds, that warble to the morning
sky,
O birds that warble as the day goes by,
Sing sweetly : twice my love hath smiled
on me."

'What knowest thou of birds, lark,
mavis, merle,
Linnet? what dream ye when they utter
forth
May-music growing with the growing
light,
Their sweet sun-worship? these be for the
snare
(So runs thy fancy) these be for the spit,
Larding and basting. See thou have not
now
Larded thy last, except thou turn and fly.
There stands the third fool of their
allegory.'

For there beyond a bridge of treble
bow,
All in a rose-red from the west, and all
Naked it seem'd, and glowing in the broad
Deep-dimpled current underneath, the
knight,
That named himself the Star of Evening,
stood.

And Gareth, 'Wherefore waits the
madman there
Naked in open dayshine?' 'Nay,' she
cried,
'Not naked, only wrapt in harden'd skins
That fit him like his own; and so ye cleave
His armour off him, these will turn the
blade.'

Then the third brother shouted o'er the
bridge,
'O brother-star, why shine ye here so low?
Thy ward is higher up : but have ye slain
The damsel's champion?' and the damsel
cried,

'No star of thine, but shot from Arthur's
heaven
With all disaster unto thine and thee!
For both thy younger brethren have gone
down
Before this youth; and so wilt thou, Sir
Star;
Art thou not old?'

'Old, damsel, old and hard,
Old, with the might and breath of twenty
boys.'
Said Gareth, 'Old, and over-bold in
brag!
But that same strength which threw the
Morning Star
Can throw the Evening.'

Then that other blew
A hard and deadly note upon the horn.
'Approach and arm me!' With slow
steps from out
An old storm-beaten, russet, many-stain'd
Pavilion, forth a grizzled damsel came,
And arm'd him in old arms, and brought
a helm

With but a drying evergreen for crest,
And gave a shield whereon the Star of
Even
Half-tarnish'd and half-bright, his em-
blem, shone.
But when it glitter'd o'er the saddle-bow,
They madly hurl'd together on the bridge;
And Gareth overthrew him, lighted, drew,
There met him drawn, and overthrew him
again,
But up like fire he started : and as oft
As Gareth brought him grovelling on his
knees,
So many a time he vaulted up again ;
Till Gareth panted hard, and his great
heart,
Foredooming all his trouble was in vain,
Labour'd within him, for he seem'd as one
That all in later, sadder age begins
To war against ill uses of a life,
But these from all his life arise, and cry,
' Thou hast made us lords, and canst not
put us down ! '
He half despairs ; so Gareth seem'd to
strike
Vainly, the damsel clamouring all the
while,
' Well done, knave-knight, well stricken,
O good knight-knave—
O knave, as noble as any of all the
knights—
Shame me not, shame me not. I have
prophesied—
Strike, thou art worthy of the Table
Round—
His arms are old, he trusts the harden'd
skin—
Strike—strike—the wind will never
change again.'
And Gareth hearing ever stronglier smote,
And hew'd great pieces of his armour off
him,
But lash'd in vain against the harden'd
skin,
And could not wholly bring him under,
more
Than loud Southwesterns, rolling ridge
on ridge,
The buoy that rides at sea, and dips and
springs

For ever; till at length Sir Gareth's brand
Clash'd his, and brake it utterly to the
hilt.
' I have thee now ;' but forth that other
sprang,
And, all unknightlike, writhed his wiry
arms
Around him, till he felt, despite his mail,
Strangled, but straining ev'n his uttermost
Cast, and so hurl'd him headlong o'er the
bridge
Down to the river, sink or swim, and
cried,
' Lead, and I follow.'

But the damsel said,
' I lead no longer ; ride thou at my side ;
Thou art the kingliest of all kitchen-
knaves.

' " O trefoil, sparkling on the rainy
plain,
O rainbow with three colours after rain,
Shine sweetly : thrice my love hath smiled
on me."

' Sir, — and, good faith, I fain had
added—Knight,
But that I heard thee call thyself a
knave,—
Shamed am I that I so rebuked, reviled,
Missaid thee ; noble I am ; and thought
the King
Scorn'd me and mine ; and now thy
pardon, friend,
For thou hast ever answer'd courteously,
And wholly bold thou art, and meek
withal
As any of Arthur's best, but, being knave,
Hast mazed my wit : I marvel what thou
art.

' Damsel,' he said, ' you be not all to
blame,
Saving that you mistrusted our good King
Would handle scorn, or yield you, asking,
one
Not fit to cope your quest. You said
your say ;
Mine answer was my deed. Good sooth !
I hold

He scarce is knight, yea but half-man,
    nor meet
To fight for gentle damsel, he, who lets
His heart be stirr'd with any foolish heat
At any gentle damsel's waywardness.
Shamed ? care not ! thy foul sayings
    fought for me :
And seeing now thy words are fair,
    methinks
There rides no knight, not Lancelot, his
    great self,
Hath force to quell me.'

           Nigh upon that hour
When the lone hern forgets his melancholy,
Lets down his other leg, and stretching,
    dreams
Of goodly supper in the distant pool,
Then turn'd the noble damsel smiling at
    him,
And told him of a cavern hard at hand,
Where bread and baken meats and good
    red wine
Of Southland, which the Lady Lyonors
Had sent her coming champion, waited
    him.

Anon they past a narrow comb wherein
Were slabs of rock with figures, knights
    on horse
Sculptured, and deckt in slowly-waning
    hues.
'Sir Knave, my knight, a hermit once
    was here,
Whose holy hand hath fashion'd on the
    rock
The war of Time against the soul of man.
And yon four fools have suck'd their alle-
    gory
From these damp walls, and taken but
    the form.
Know ye not these?' and Gareth lookt
    and read—
In letters like to those the vexillary
Hath left crag-carven o'er the streaming
    Gelt—
'PHOSPHORUS,' then 'MERIDIES'—
    'HESPERUS'—
'NOX'—'MORS,' beneath five figures,
    armed men,

T

Slab after slab, their faces forward all,
And running down the Soul, a Shape that
    fled
With broken wings, torn raiment and
    loose hair,
For help and shelter to the hermit's cave.
'Follow the faces, and we find it.   Look
Who comes behind?'

           For one—delay'd at first
Thro' helping back the dislocated Kay
To Camelot, then by what thereafter
    chanced,
The damsel's headlong error thro' the
    wood—
Sir Lancelot, having swum the river-
    loops—
His blue shield-lions cover'd—softly drew
Behind the twain, and when he saw the
    star
Gleam, on Sir Gareth's turning to him,
    cried,
'Stay, felon knight, I avenge me for my
    friend.'
And Gareth crying prick'd against the cry;
But when they closed—in a moment—at
    one touch
Of that skill'd spear, the wonder of the
    world—
Went sliding down so easily, and fell,
That when he found the grass within his
    hands
He laugh'd ; the laughter jarr'd upon
    Lynette :
Harshly she ask'd him, 'Shamed and
    overthrown,
And tumbled back into the kitchen-knave,
Why laugh ye? that ye blew your boast
    in vain?'
'Nay, noble damsel, but that I, the son
Of old King Lot and good Queen Belli-
    cent,
And victor of the bridges and the ford,
And knight of Arthur, here lie thrown by
    whom
I know not, all thro' mere unhappiness—
Device and sorcery and unhappiness—
Out, sword ; we are thrown !' And
    Lancelot answer'd, 'Prince,
O Gareth—thro' the mere unhappiness

Z

Of one who came to help thee, not to
    harm,
Lancelot, and all as glad to find thee
    whole,
As on the day when Arthur knighted him.'

    Then Gareth, 'Thou—Lancelot !—
        thine the hand
That threw me ?   An some chance to mar
    the boast
Thy brethren of thee make—which could
    not chance—
Had sent thee down before a lesser spear,
Shamed had I been, and sad—O Lancelot
    —thou !'

    Whereat the maiden, petulant, 'Lance-
        lot,
Why came ye not, when call'd ? and
    wherefore now
Come ye, not call'd ?   I gloried in my
    knave,
Who being still rebuked, would answer
    still
Courteous as any knight—but now, if
    knight,
The marvel dies, and leaves me fool'd
    and trick'd,
And only wondering wherefore play'd
    upon :
And doubtful whether I and mine be
    scorn'd.
Where should be truth if not in Arthur's
    hall,
In Arthur's presence ?   Knight, knave,
    prince and fool,
I hate thee and for ever.'

                And Lancelot said,
'Blessed be thou, Sir Gareth ! knight
    art thou
To the King's best wish.   O damsel, be
    you wise
To call him shamed, who is but over-
    thrown ?
Thrown have I been, nor once, but many
    a time.
Victor from vanquish'd issues at the last,
And overthrower from being overthrown.
With sword we have not striven ; and
    thy good horse

And thou are weary ; yet not less I felt
Thy manhood thro' that wearied lance
    of thine.
Well hast thou done ; for all the stream
    is freed,
And thou hast wreak'd his justice on his
    foes,
And when reviled, hast answer'd graci-
    ously,
And makest merry when overthrown.
    Prince, Knight,
Hail, Knight and Prince, and of our
    Table Round !'

    And then when turning to Lynette he
        told
The tale of Gareth, petulantly she said,
'Ay well—ay well—for worse than being
    fool'd
Of others, is to fool one's self.   A cave,
Sir Lancelot, is hard by, with meats and
    drinks
And forage for the horse, and flint for fire.
But all about it flies a honeysuckle.
Seek, till we find.'   And when they
    sought and found,
Sir Gareth drank and ate, and all his life
Past into sleep; on whom the maiden
    gazed.
'Sound sleep be thine ! sound cause to
    sleep hast thou.
Wake lusty ! Seem I not as tender to
    him
As any mother ?   Ay, but such a one
As all day long hath rated at her child,
And vext his day, but blesses him asleep—
Good lord, how sweetly smells the
    honeysuckle
In the hush'd night, as if the world were
    one
Of utter peace, and love, and gentleness !
O Lancelot, Lancelot'—and she clapt
    her hands—
'Full merry am I to find my goodly knave
Is knight and noble.   See now, sworn
    have I,
Else yon black felon had not let me pass,
To bring thee back to do the battle with
    him.
Thus an thou goest, he will fight thee first ;

Who doubts thee victor? so will my
    knight-knave
Miss the full flower of this accomplish-
    ment.'

Said Lancelot, 'Peradventure he, you
    name,
May know my shield. Let Gareth, an
    he will,
Change his for mine, and take my charger,
    fresh,
Not to be spurr'd, loving the battle as
    well
As he that rides him.' 'Lancelot-like,'
    she said,
'Courteous in this, Lord Lancelot, as in
    all.'

And Gareth, wakening, fiercely clutch'd
    the shield ;
'Ramp ye lance-splintering lions, on whom
    all spears
Are rotten sticks ! ye seem agape to roar !
Yea, ramp and roar at leaving of your
    lord !—
Care not, good beasts, so well I care for
    you.
O noble Lancelot, from my hold on these
Streams virtue—fire—thro' one that will
    not shame
Even the shadow of Lancelot under shield.
Hence : let us go.'

Silent the silent field
They traversed. Arthur's harp tho'
    summer-wan,
In counter motion to the clouds, allured
The glance of Gareth dreaming on his
    liege.
A star shot : 'Lo,' said Gareth, 'the foe
    falls !'
An owl whoopt : 'Hark the victor peal-
    ing there !'
Suddenly she that rode upon his left
Clung to the shield that Lancelot lent
    him, crying,
'Yield, yield him this again : 'tis he must
    fight :
I curse the tongue that all thro' yesterday
Reviled thee, and hath wrought on
    Lancelot now

To lend thee horse and shield : wonders
    ye have done ;
Miracles ye cannot : here is glory enow
In having flung the three : I see thee
    maim'd,
Mangled : I swear thou canst not fling
    the fourth.'

'And wherefore, damsel ? tell me all
    ye know.
You cannot scare me ; nor rough face, or
    voice,
Brute bulk of limb, or boundless savagery
Appal me from the quest.'

'Nay, Prince,' she cried,
'God wot, I never look'd upon the face,
Seeing he never rides abroad by day ;
But watch'd him have I like a phantom
    pass
Chilling the night : nor have I heard the
    voice.
Always he made his mouthpiece of a page
Who came and went, and still reported
    him
As closing in himself the strength of ten,
And when his anger tare him, massacring
Man, woman, lad and girl—yea, the soft
    babe !
Some hold that he hath swallow'd infant
    flesh,
Monster ! O Prince, I went for Lancelot
    first,
The quest is Lancelot's : give him back
    the shield.'

Said Gareth laughing, 'An he fight for
    this,
Belike he wins it as the better man :
Thus—and not else !'

But Lancelot on him urged
All the devisings of their chivalry
When one might meet a mightier than
    himself ;
How best to manage horse, lance, sword
    and shield,
And so fill up the gap where force might
    fail
With skill and fineness. Instant were
    his words.

Then Gareth, 'Here be rules. I know
    but one—
To dash against mine enemy and to win.
Yet have I watch'd thee victor in the
    joust,
And seen thy way.' 'Heaven help thee,'
    sigh'd Lynette.

Then for a space, and under cloud that
    grew
To thunder-gloom palling all stars, they
    rode
In converse till she made her palfrey halt,
Lifted an arm, and softly whisper'd,
    'There.'
And all the three were silent seeing,
    pitch'd
Beside the Castle Perilous on flat field,
A huge pavilion like a mountain peak
Sunder the glooming crimson on the
    marge,
Black, with black banner, and a long
    black horn
Beside it hanging; which Sir Gareth
    graspt,
And so, before the two could hinder him,
Sent all his heart and breath thro' all the
    horn.
Echo'd the walls; a light twinkled; anon
Came lights and lights, and once again
    he blew;
Whereon were hollow tramplings up and
    down
And muffled voices heard, and shadows
    past;
Till high above him, circled with her
    maids,
The Lady Lyonors at a window stood,
Beautiful among lights, and waving to him
White hands, and courtesy; but when
    the Prince
Three times had blown—after long hush
    —at last—
The huge pavilion slowly yielded up,
Thro' those black foldings, that which
    housed therein.
High on a nightblack horse, in nightblack
    arms,
With white breast-bone, and barren ribs
    of Death,

And crown'd with fleshless laughter—
    some ten steps—
In the half-light—thro' the dim dawn—
    advanced
The monster, and then paused, and spake
    no word.

But Gareth spake and all indignantly,
'Fool, for thou hast, men say, the strength
    of ten,
Canst thou not trust the limbs thy God
    hath given,
But must, to make the terror of thee more,
Trick thyself out in ghastly imageries
Of that which Life hath done with, and
    the clod,
Less dull than thou, will hide with
    mantling flowers
As if for pity?' But he spake no word;
Which set the horror higher: a maiden
    swoon'd;
The Lady Lyonors wrung her hands and
    wept,
As doom'd to be the bride of Night and
    Death;
Sir Gareth's head prickled beneath his
    helm;
And ev'n Sir Lancelot thro' his warm
    blood felt
Ice strike, and all that mark'd him were
    aghast.

At once Sir Lancelot's charger fiercely
    neigh'd,
And Death's dark war-horse bounded
    forward with him.
Then those that did not blink the terror,
    saw
That Death was cast to ground, and
    slowly rose.
But with one stroke Sir Gareth split the
    skull.
Half fell to right and half to left and lay.
Then with a stronger buffet he clove the
    helm
As throughly as the skull; and out from
    this
Issued the bright face of a blooming boy
Fresh as a flower new-born, and crying
    'Knight,

Slay me not : my three brethren bad me
  do it,
To make a horror all about the house,
And stay the world from Lady Lyonors.
They never dream'd the passes would be
  past.'
Answer'd Sir Gareth graciously to one
Not many a moon his younger, 'My fair
  child,
What madness made thee challenge the
  chief knight
Of Arthur's hall?' 'Fair Sir, they bad
  me do it.
They hate the King, and Lancelot, the
  King's friend,
They hoped to slay him somewhere on
  the stream,
They never dream'd the passes could be
  past.'

Then sprang the happier day from
  underground ;
And Lady Lyonors and her house, with
  dance
And revel and song, made merry over
  Death,
As being after all their foolish fears
And horrors only proven a blooming boy.
So large mirth lived and Gareth won the
  quest.

And he that told the tale in older times
Says that Sir Gareth wedded Lyonors,
But he, that told it later, says Lynette.

THE MARRIAGE OF GERAINT.

THE brave Geraint, a knight of Arthur's
  court,
A tributary prince of Devon, one
Of that great Order of the Table Round,
Had married Enid, Yniol's only child,
And loved her, as he loved the light of
  Heaven.
And as the light of Heaven varies, now
At sunrise, now at sunset, now by night
With moon and trembling stars, so loved
  Geraint
To make her beauty vary day by day,

In crimsons and in purples and in gems.
And Enid, but to please her husband's
  eye,
Who first had found and loved her in a
  state
Of broken fortunes, daily fronted him
In some fresh splendour ; and the Queen
  herself,
Grateful to Prince Geraint for service
  done,
Loved her, and often with her own white
  hands
Array'd and deck'd her, as the loveliest,
Next after her own self, in all the court.
And Enid loved the Queen, and with true
  heart
Adored her, as the stateliest and the best
And loveliest of all women upon earth.
And seeing them so tender and so close,
Long in their common love rejoiced
  Geraint.

But when a rumour rose about the Queen,
Touching her guilty love for Lancelot,
Tho' yet there lived no proof, nor yet
  was heard
The world's loud whisper breaking into
  storm,
Not less Geraint believed it ; and there fell
A horror on him, lest his gentle wife,
Thro' that great tenderness for Guinevere,
Had suffer'd, or should suffer any taint
In nature : wherefore going to the King,
He made this pretext, that his princedom
  lay
Close on the borders of a territory,
Wherein were bandit earls, and caitiff
  knights,
Assassins, and all flyers from the hand
Of Justice, and whatever loathes a law :
And therefore, till the King himself
  should please
To cleanse this common sewer of all his
  realm,
He craved a fair permission to depart,
And there defend his marches ; and the
  King
Mused for a little on his plea, but, last,
Allowing it, the Prince and Enid rode,
And fifty knights rode with them, to the
  shores

Of Severn, and they past to their own
land ;
Where, thinking, that if ever yet was wife
True to her lord, mine shall be so to me,
He compass'd her with sweet observances
And worship, never leaving her, and grew
Forgetful of his promise to the King,
Forgetful of the falcon and the hunt,
Forgetful of the tilt and tournament,
Forgetful of his glory and his name,
Forgetful of his princedom and its cares.
And this forgetfulness was hateful to her.
And by and by the people, when they met
In twos and threes, or fuller companies,
Began to scoff and jeer and babble of him
As of a prince whose manhood was all
gone,
And molten down in mere uxoriousness.
And this she gather'd from the people's
eyes :
This too the women who attired her head,
To please her, dwelling on his boundless
love,
Told Enid, and they sadden'd her the
more :
And day by day she thought to tell Geraint,
But could not out of bashful delicacy ;
While he that watch'd her sadden, was
the more
Suspicious that her nature had a taint.

At last, it chanced that on a summer
morn
(They sleeping each by either) the new sun
Beat thro' the blindless casement of the
room,
And heated the strong warrior in his
dreams ;
Who, moving, cast the coverlet aside,
And bared the knotted column of his
throat,
The massive square of his heroic breast,
And arms on which the standing muscle
sloped,
As slopes a wild brook o'er a little stone,
Running too vehemently to break upon it.
And Enid woke and sat beside the couch,
Admiring him, and thought within herself,
Was ever man so grandly made as he?
Then, like a shadow, past the people's talk

And accusation of uxoriousness
Across her mind, and bowing over him,
Low to her own heart piteously she said :

'O noble breast and all-puissant arms,
Am I the cause, I the poor cause that men
Reproach you, saying all your force is
gone?
I *am* the cause, because I dare not speak
And tell him what I think and what they
say.
And yet I hate that he should linger here;
I cannot love my lord and not his name.
Far liefer had I gird his harness on him,
And ride with him to battle and stand by,
And watch his mightful hand striking
great blows
At caitiffs and at wrongers of the world.
Far better were I laid in the dark earth,
Not hearing any more his noble voice,
Not to be folded more in these dear arms,
And darken'd from the high light in his
eyes,
Than that my lord thro' me should suffer
shame.
Am I so bold, and could I so stand by,
And see my dear lord wounded in the strife,
Or maybe pierced to death before mine
eyes,
And yet not dare to tell him what I think,
And how men slur him, saying all his force
Is melted into mere effeminacy?
O me, I fear that I am no true wife.'

Half inwardly, half audibly she spoke,
And the strong passion in her made her
weep
True tears upon his broad and naked
breast,
And these awoke him, and by great mis-
chance
He heard but fragments of her later words,
And that she fear'd she was not a true wife.
And then he thought, 'In spite of all my
care,
For all my pains, poor man, for all my
pains,
She is not faithful to me, and I see her
Weeping for some gay knight in Arthur's
hall.'

Then tho' he loved and reverenced her
    too much
To dream she could be guilty of foul act,
Right thro' his manful breast darted the
    pang
That makes a man, in the sweet face of her
Whom he loves most, lonely and miserable.
At this he hurl'd his huge limbs out of
    bed,
And shook his drowsy squire awake and
    cried,
'My charger and her palfrey;' then to her,
'I will ride forth into the wilderness;
For tho' it seems my spurs are yet to win,
I have not fall'n so low as some would
    wish.
And thou, put on thy worst and meanest
    dress
And ride with me.' And Enid ask'd,
    amazed,
'If Enid errs, let Enid learn her fault.'
But he, 'I charge thee, ask not, but obey.'
Then she bethought her of a faded silk,
A faded mantle and a faded veil,
And moving toward a cedarn cabinet,
Wherein she kept them folded reverently
With sprigs of summer laid between the
    folds,
She took them, and array'd herself therein,
Remembering when first he came on her
Drest in that dress, and how he loved her
    in it,
And all her foolish fears about the dress,
And all his journey to her, as himself
Had told her, and their coming to the
    court.

For Arthur on the Whitsuntide before
Held court at old Caerleon upon Usk.
There on a day, he sitting high in hall,
Before him came a forester of Dean,
Wet from the woods, with notice of a hart
Taller than all his fellows, milky-white,
First seen that day : these things he told
    the King.
Then the good King gave order to let blow
His horns for hunting on the morrow morn.
And when the Queen petition'd for his
    leave
To see the hunt, allow'd it easily.

So with the morning all the court were
    gone.
But Guinevere lay late into the morn,
Lost in sweet dreams, and dreaming of her
    love
For Lancelot, and forgetful of the hunt;
But rose at last, a single maiden with her,
Took horse, and forded Usk, and gain'd
    the wood ;
There, on a little knoll beside it, stay'd
Waiting to hear the hounds; but heard
    instead
A sudden sound of hoofs, for Prince
    Geraint,
Late also, wearing neither hunting-dress
Nor weapon, save a golden-hilted brand,
Came quickly flashing thro' the shallow
    ford
Behind them, and so gallop'd up the knoll.
A purple scarf, at either end whereof
There swung an apple of the purest gold,
Sway'd round about him, as he gallop'd up
To join them, glancing like a dragon-fly
In summer suit and silks of holiday.
Low bow'd the tributary Prince, and she,
Sweetly and statelily, and with all grace
Of womanhood and queenhood, answer'd
    him :
'Late, late, Sir Prince,' she said, 'later
    than we !'
'Yea, noble Queen,' he answer'd, 'and
    so late
That I but come like you to see the
    hunt,
Not join it.' 'Therefore wait with me,'
    she said ;
'For on this little knoll, if anywhere,
There is good chance that we shall hear
    the hounds :
Here often they break covert at our feet.'

And while they listen'd for the distant
    hunt,
And chiefly for the baying of Cavall,
King Arthur's hound of deepest mouth,
    there rode
Full slowly by a knight, lady, and dwarf;
Whereof the dwarf lagg'd latest, and the
    knight
Had vizor up, and show'd a youthful face,

Imperious, and of haughtiest lineaments.
And Guinevere, not mindful of his face
In the King's hall, desired his name, and
    sent
Her maiden to demand it of the dwarf ;
Who being vicious, old and irritable,
And doubling all his master's vice of pride,
Made answer sharply that she should not
    know.
'Then will I ask it of himself,' she said.
'Nay, by my faith, thou shalt not,' cried
    the dwarf ;
'Thou art not worthy ev'n to speak of
    him ;'
And when she put her horse toward the
    knight,
Struck at her with his whip, and she
    return'd
Indignant to the Queen ; whereat Geraint
Exclaiming, 'Surely I will learn the name,'
Made sharply to the dwarf, and ask'd it
    of him,
Who answer'd as before ; and when the
    Prince
Had put his horse in motion toward the
    knight,
Struck at him with his whip, and cut his
    cheek.
The Prince's blood spirted upon the scarf,
Dyeing it ; and his quick, instinctive hand
Caught at the hilt, as to abolish him :
But he, from his exceeding manfulness
And pure nobility of temperament,
Wroth to be wroth at such a worm,
    refrain'd
From ev'n a word, and so returning said :

'I will avenge this insult, noble Queen,
Done in your maiden's person to yourself :
And I will track this vermin to their
    earths :
For tho' I ride unarm'd, I do not doubt
To find, at some place I shall come at,
    arms
On loan, or else for pledge ; and, being
    found,
Then will I fight him, and will break his
    pride,
And on the third day will again be here,
So that I be not fall'n in fight. Farewell.'

'Farewell, fair Prince,' answer'd the
    stately Queen.
'Be prosperous in this journey, as in all ;
And may you light on all things that you
    love,
And live to wed with her whom first you
    love :
But ere you wed with any, bring your
    bride,
And I, were she the daughter of a
    king,
Yea, tho' she were a beggar from the
    hedge,
Will clothe her for her bridals like the
    sun.'

And Prince Geraint, now thinking that
    he heard
The noble hart at bay, now the far horn,
A little vext at losing of the hunt,
A little at the vile occasion, rode,
By ups and downs, thro' many a grassy
    glade
And valley, with fixt eye following the
    three.
At last they issued from the world of
    wood,
And climb'd upon a fair and even ridge,
And show'd themselves against the sky,
    and sank.
And thither came Geraint, and under-
    neath
Beheld the long street of a little town
In a long valley, on one side whereof,
White from the mason's hand, a fortress
    rose ;
And on one side a castle in decay,
Beyond a bridge that spann'd a dry
    ravine :
And out of town and valley came a noise
As of a broad brook o'er a shingly bed
Brawling, or like a clamour of the rooks
At distance, ere they settle for the night.

And onward to the fortress rode the
    three,
And enter'd, and were lost behind the
    walls.
'So,' thought Geraint, 'I have track'd
    him to his earth.'

And down the long street riding wearily,
Found every hostel full, and everywhere
Was hammer laid to hoof, and the hot hiss
And bustling whistle of the youth who scour'd
His master's armour; and of such a one
He ask'd, 'What means the tumult in the town?'
Who told him, scouring still, 'The sparrow-hawk!'
Then riding close behind an ancient churl,
Who, smitten by the dusty sloping beam,
Went sweating underneath a sack of corn,
Ask'd yet once more what meant the hubbub here?
Who answer'd gruffly, 'Ugh! the sparrow-hawk.'
Then riding further past an armourer's,
Who, with back turn'd, and bow'd above his work,
Sat riveting a helmet on his knee,
He put the self-same query, but the man
Not turning round, nor looking at him, said:
'Friend, he that labours for the sparrow-hawk
Has little time for idle questioners.'
Whereat Geraint flash'd into sudden spleen:
'A thousand pips eat up your sparrow-hawk!
Tits, wrens, and all wing'd nothings peck him dead!
Ye think the rustic cackle of your bourg
The murmur of the world! What is it to me?
O wretched set of sparrows, one and all,
Who pipe of nothing but of sparrow-hawks!
Speak, if ye be not like the rest, hawk-mad,
Where can I get me harbourage for the night?
And arms, arms, arms to fight my enemy? Speak!'
Whereat the armourer turning all amazed
And seeing one so gay in purple silks,
Came forward with the helmet yet in hand

And answer'd, 'Pardon me, O stranger knight;
We hold a tourney here to-morrow morn,
And there is scantly time for half the work.
Arms? truth! I know not: all are wanted here.
Harbourage? truth, good truth, I know not, save,
It may be, at Earl Yniol's, o'er the bridge
Yonder.' He spoke and fell to work again.

Then rode Geraint, a little spleenful yet,
Across the bridge that spann'd the dry ravine.
There musing sat the hoary-headed Earl,
(His dress a suit of fray'd magnificence,
Once fit for feasts of ceremony) and said:
'Whither, fair son?' to whom Geraint replied,
'O friend, I seek a harbourage for the night.'
Then Yniol, 'Enter therefore and partake
The slender entertainment of a house
Once rich, now poor, but ever open-door'd.'
'Thanks, venerable friend,' replied Geraint;
'So that ye do not serve me sparrow-hawks
For supper, I will enter, I will eat
With all the passion of a twelve hours' fast.'
Then sigh'd and smiled the hoary-headed Earl,
And answer'd, 'Graver cause than yours is mine
To curse this hedgerow thief, the sparrow-hawk:
But in, go in; for save yourself desire it,
We will not touch upon him ev'n in jest.'

Then rode Geraint into the castle court,
His charger trampling many a prickly star
Of sprouted thistle on the broken stones.
He look'd and saw that all was ruinous.
Here stood a shatter'd archway plumed with fern;

And here had fall'n a great part of a
    tower,
Whole, like a crag that tumbles from the
    cliff,
And like a crag was gay with wilding
    flowers :
320 And high above a piece of turret stair,
Worn by the feet that now were silent,
    wound
Bare to the sun, and monstrous ivy-stems
Claspt the gray walls with hairy-fibred
    arms,
And suck'd the joining of the stones, and
    look'd
325 A knot, beneath, of snakes, aloft, a grove.

And while he waited in the castle court,
The voice of Enid, Yniol's daughter, rang
Clear thro' the open casement of the hall,
Singing ; and as the sweet voice of a bird,
330 Heard by the lander in a lonely isle,
Moves him to think what kind of bird it is
That sings so delicately clear, and make
Conjecture of the plumage and the form ;
So the sweet voice of Enid moved Geraint ;
335 And made him like a man abroad at morn
When first the liquid note beloved of men
Comes flying over many a windy wave
To Britain, and in April suddenly
Breaks from a coppice gemm'd with green
    and red,
340 And he suspends his converse with a
    friend,
Or it may be the labour of his hands,
To think or say, 'There is the nightingale ;'
So fared it with Geraint, who thought
    and said,
'Here, by God's grace, is the one voice
    for me.'

345 It chanced the song that Enid sang
    was one
Of Fortune and her wheel, and Enid
    sang :

    'Turn, Fortune, turn thy wheel and
       lower the proud ;
Turn thy wild wheel thro' sunshine,
    storm, and cloud ;
Thy wheel and thee we neither love nor
    hate.

'Turn, Fortune, turn thy wheel with
    smile or frown ;
With that wild wheel we go not up or
    down ;
Our hoard is little, but our hearts are
    great.

'Smile and we smile, the lords of many
    lands ;
Frown and we smile, the lords of our
    own hands ;
For man is man and master of his fate.

'Turn, turn thy wheel above the staring
    crowd ;
Thy wheel and thou are shadows in the
    cloud ;
Thy wheel and thee we neither love nor
    hate.'

'Hark, by the bird's song ye may learn
    the nest,'
Said Yniol ; 'enter quickly.' Entering
    then,
Right o'er a mount of newly-fallen stones,
The dusky-rafter'd many-cobweb'd hall,
He found an ancient dame in dim bro-
    cade ;
And near her, like a blossom vermeil-
    white,
That lightly breaks a faded flower-sheath,
Moved the fair Enid, all in faded silk,
Her daughter. In a moment thought
    Geraint,
'Here by God's rood is the one maid for
    me.'
But none spake word except the hoary
    Earl :
'Enid, the good knight's horse stands in
    the court ;
Take him to stall, and give him corn, and
    then
Go to the town and buy us flesh and
    wine ;
And we will make us merry as we may.
Our hoard is little, but our hearts are
    great.'

He spake : the Prince, as Enid past
    him, fain
To follow, strode a stride, but Yniol caught

His purple scarf, and held, and said,
    'Forbear!
Rest! the good house, tho' ruin'd, O my
    son,
Endures not that her guest should serve
    himself.'
And reverencing the custom of the house
Geraint, from utter courtesy, forbore.

    So Enid took his charger to the stall;
And after went her way across the bridge,
And reach'd the town, and while the
    Prince and Earl
Yet spoke together, came again with one,
A youth, that following with a costrel bore
The means of goodly welcome, flesh and
    wine.
And Enid brought sweet cakes to make
    them cheer,
And in her veil enfolded, manchet bread.
And then, because their hall must also
    serve
For kitchen, boil'd the flesh, and spread
    the board,
And stood behind, and waited on the
    three.
And seeing her so sweet and serviceable,
Geraint had longing in him evermore
To stoop and kiss the tender little thumb,
That crost the trencher as she laid it
    down:
But after all had eaten, then Geraint,
For now the wine made summer in his
    veins,
Let his eye rove in following, or rest
On Enid at her lowly handmaid-work,
Now here, now there, about the dusky
    hall;
Then suddenly address the hoary Earl:

'Fair Host and Earl, I pray your
    courtesy;
This sparrow-hawk, what is he? tell me
    of him.
His name? but no, good faith, I will not
    have it:
For if he be the knight whom late I saw
Ride into that new fortress by your town,
White from the mason's hand, then have
    I sworn

From his own lips to have it — I am
    Geraint
Of Devon — for this morning when the
    Queen
Sent her own maiden to demand the name,
His dwarf, a vicious under-shapen thing,
Struck at her with his whip, and she re-
    turn'd
Indignant to the Queen; and then I swore
That I would track this caitiff to his hold,
And fight and break his pride, and have
    it of him.
And all unarm'd I rode, and thought to
    find
Arms in your town, where all the men
    are mad;
They take the rustic murmur of their
    bourg
For the great wave that echoes round the
    world;
They would not hear me speak: but if
    ye know
Where I can light on arms, or if yourself
Should have them, tell me, seeing I have
    sworn
That I will break his pride and learn his
    name,
Avenging this great insult done the
    Queen.'

    Then cried Earl Yniol, 'Art thou he
    indeed,
Geraint, a name far-sounded among men
For noble deeds? and truly I, when first
I saw you moving by me on the bridge,
Felt ye were somewhat, yea, and by your
    state
And presence might have guess'd you one
    of those
That eat in Arthur's hall at Camelot.
Nor speak I now from foolish flattery;
For this dear child hath often heard me
    praise
Your feats of arms, and often when I
    paused
Hath ask'd again, and ever loved to hear;
So grateful is the noise of noble deeds
To noble hearts who see but acts of wrong:
O never yet had woman such a pair
Of suitors as this maiden; first Limours.

A creature wholly given to brawls and
　　wine,
Drunk even when he woo'd ; and be he
　　dead
I know not, but he past to the wild land.
The second was your foe, the sparrow-
　　hawk,
My curse, my nephew—I will not let his
　　name
Slip from my lips if I can help it—he,
When I that knew him fierce and tur-
　　bulent
Refused her to him, then his pride awoke ;
And since the proud man often is the
　　mean,
He sow'd a slander in the common ear,
Affirming that his father left him gold,
And in my charge, which was not ren-
　　der'd to him ;
Bribed with large promises the men who
　　served
About my person, the more easily
Because my means were somewhat broken
　　into
Thro' open doors and hospitality ;
Raised my own town against me in the
　　night
Before my Enid's birthday, sack'd my
　　house ;
From mine own earldom foully ousted
　　me ;
Built that new fort to overawe my friends,
For truly there are those who love me
　　yet ;
And keeps me in this ruinous castle here,
Where doubtless he would put me soon
　　to death,
But that his pride too much despises
　　me :
And I myself sometimes despise myself ;
For I have let men be, and have their
　　way ;
Am much too gentle, have not used my
　　power :
Nor know I whether I be very base
Or very manful, whether very wise
Or very foolish ; only this I know,
That whatsoever evil happen to me,
I seem to suffer nothing heart or limb,
But can endure it all most patiently.'

' Well said, true heart,' replied Geraint,
　　' but arms,
That if the sparrow-hawk, this nephew,
　　fight
In next day's tourney I may break his
　　pride.'

　　And Yniol answer'd, ' Arms, indeed,
　　but old
And rusty, old and rusty, Prince Geraint,
Are mine, and therefore at thine asking,
　　thine.
But in this tournament can no man tilt,
Except the lady he loves best be there.
Two forks are fixt into the meadow
　　ground,
And over these is placed a silver wand,
And over that a golden sparrow-hawk,
The prize of beauty for the fairest there.
And this, what knight soever be in field
Lays claim to for the lady at his side,
And tilts with my good nephew there-
　　upon,
Who being apt at arms and big of bone
Has ever won it for the lady with him,
And toppling over all antagonism
Has earn'd himself the name of sparrow-
　　hawk.
But thou, that hast no lady, canst not
　　fight.'

　　To whom Geraint with eyes all bright
　　replied,
Leaning a little toward him, ' Thy leave !
Let *me* lay lance in rest, O noble host,
For this dear child, because I never saw,
Tho' having seen all beauties of our time,
Nor can see elsewhere, anything so fair.
And if I fall her name will yet remain
Untarnish'd as before ; but if I live,
So aid me Heaven when at mine utter-
　　most,
As I will make her truly my true wife.'

　　Then, howsoever patient, Yniol's heart
Danced in his bosom, seeing better days.
And looking round he saw not Enid there,
(Who hearing her own name had stol'n
　　away)
But that old dame, to whom full tenderly
And fondling all her hand in his he said,

'Mother, a maiden is a tender thing,
And best by her that bore her understood.
Go thou to rest, but ere thou go to rest
Tell her, and prove her heart toward the
　Prince.'

So spake the kindly-hearted Earl, and
　she
With frequent smile and nod departing
　found,
Half disarray'd as to her rest, the girl ;
Whom first she kiss'd on either cheek,
　and then
On either shining shoulder laid a hand,
And kept her off and gazed upon her face,
And told her all their converse in the hall,
Proving her heart : but never light and
　shade
Coursed one another more on open ground
Beneath a troubled heaven, than red and
　pale
Across the face of Enid hearing her ;
While slowly falling as a scale that falls,
When weight is added only grain by grain,
Sank her sweet head upon her gentle
　breast ;
Nor did she lift an eye nor speak a word,
Rapt in the fear and in the wonder of it ;
So moving without answer to her rest
She found no rest, and ever fail'd to draw
The quiet night into her blood, but lay
Contemplating her own unworthiness ;
And when the pale and bloodless east
　began
To quicken to the sun, arose, and raised
Her mother too, and hand in hand they
　moved
Down to the meadow where the jousts
　were held,
And waited there for Yniol and Geraint.

And thither came the twain, and when
　Geraint
Beheld her first in field awaiting him,
He felt, were she the prize of bodily force,
Himself beyond the rest pushing could
　move
The chair of Idris. Yniol's rusted arms
Were on his princely person, but thro'
　these

Princelike his bearing shone ; and errant
　knights
And ladies came, and by and by the town
Flow'd in, and settling circled all the lists.
And there they fixt the forks into the
　ground,
And over these they placed the silver wand,
And over that the golden sparrow-hawk.
Then Yniol's nephew, after trumpet
　blown,
Spake to the lady with him and pro-
　claim'd,
' Advance and take, as fairest of the fair,
What I these two years past have won
　for thee,
The prize of beauty.' Loudly spake the
　Prince,
' Forbear : there is a worthier,' and the
　knight
With some surprise and thrice as much
　disdain
Turn'd, and beheld the four, and all his
　face
Glow'd like the heart of a great fire at
　Yule,
So burnt he was with passion, crying out,
' Do battle for it then,' no more ; and
　thrice
They clash'd together, and thrice they
　brake their spears.
Then each, dishorsed and drawing, lash'd
　at each
So often and with such blows, that all the
　crowd
Wonder'd, and now and then from distant
　walls
There came a clapping as of phantom
　hands.
So twice they fought, and twice they
　breathed, and still
The dew of their great labour, and the
　blood
Of their strong bodies, flowing, drain'd
　their force.
But either's force was match'd till Yniol's
　cry,
' Remember that great insult done the
　Queen,'
Increased Geraint's, who heaved his blade
　aloft,

And crack'd the helmet thro', and bit the
    bone,
And fell'd him, and set foot upon his
    breast,
And said, 'Thy name?' To whom the
    fallen man
Made answer, groaning, 'Edyrn, son of
    Nudd!
Ashamed am I that I should tell it thee.
My pride is broken : men have seen my
    fall.'
'Then, Edyrn, son of Nudd,' replied
    Geraint,
'These two things shalt thou do, or else
    thou diest.
First, thou thyself, with damsel and with
    dwarf,
Shalt ride to Arthur's court, and coming
    there,
Crave pardon for that insult done the
    Queen,
And shalt abide her judgment on it ; next,
Thou shalt give back their earldom to thy
    kin.
These two things shalt thou do, or thou
    shalt die.'
And Edyrn answer'd, 'These things will
    I do,
For I have never yet been overthrown,
And thou hast overthrown me, and my
    pride
Is broken down, for Enid sees my fall!'
And rising up, he rode to Arthur's court,
And there the Queen forgave him easily.
And being young, he changed and came
    to loathe
His crime of traitor, slowly drew himself
Bright from his old dark life, and fell at
    last
In the great battle fighting for the King.

But when the third day from the
    hunting-morn
Made a low splendour in the world, and
    wings
Moved in her ivy, Enid, for she lay
With her fair head in the dim-yellow light,
Among the dancing shadows of the birds,
Woke and bethought her of her promise
    given

No later than last eve to Prince Geraint—
So bent he seem'd on going the third day,
He would not leave her, till her promise
    given—
To ride with him this morning to the
    court,
And there be made known to the stately
    Queen,
And there be wedded with all ceremony.
At this she cast her eyes upon her dress,
And thought it never yet had look'd so
    mean.
For as a leaf in mid-November is
To what it was in mid-October, seem'd
The dress that now she look'd on to the
    dress
She look'd on ere the coming of Geraint.
And still she look'd, and still the terror
    grew
Of that strange bright and dreadful thing,
    a court,
All staring at her in her faded silk :
And softly to her own sweet heart she said :

'This noble prince who won our
    earldom back,
So splendid in his acts and his attire,
Sweet heaven, how much I shall discredit
    him!
Would he could tarry with us here awhile,
But being so beholden to the Prince,
It were but little grace in any of us,
Bent as he seem'd on going this third day,
To seek a second favour at his hands.
Yet if he could but tarry a day or two,
Myself would work eye dim, and finger
    lame,
Far liefer than so much discredit him.'

And Enid fell in longing for a dress
All branch'd and flower'd with gold, a
    costly gift
Of her good mother, given her on the
    night
Before her birthday, three sad years ago,
That night of fire, when Edyrn sack'd
    their house,
And scatter'd all they had to all the winds:
For while the mother show'd it, and the
    two

Were turning and admiring it, the work
To both appear'd so costly, rose a cry
That Edyrn's men were on them, and they
    fled
With little save the jewels they had on,
Which being sold and sold had bought
    them bread :
And Edyrn's men had caught them in
    their flight,
And placed them in this ruin ; and she
    wish'd
The Prince had found her in her ancient
    home ;
Then let her fancy flit across the past,
And roam the goodly places that she
    knew ;
And last bethought her how she used to
    watch,
Near that old home, a pool of golden carp ;
And one was patch'd and blurr'd and
    lustreless
Among his burnish'd brethren of the pool ;
And half asleep she made comparison
Of that and these to her own faded self
And the gay court, and fell asleep again ;
And dreamt herself was such a faded form
Among her burnish'd sisters of the pool ;
But this was in the garden of a king ;
And tho' she lay dark in the pool, she
    knew
That all was bright ; that all about were
    birds
Of sunny plume in gilded trellis-work ;
That all the turf was rich in plots that
    look'd
Each like a garnet or a turkis in it ;
And lords and ladies of the high court
    went
In silver tissue talking things of state ;
And children of the King in cloth of
    gold
Glanced at the doors or gambol'd down
    the walks ;
And while she thought 'They will not
    see me,' came
A stately queen whose name was
    Guinevere,
And all the children in their cloth of gold
Ran to her, crying, 'If we have fish at
    all

Let them be gold ; and charge the
    gardeners now
To pick the faded creature from the pool,
And cast it on the mixen that it die.'
And therewithal one came and seized on
    her,
And Enid started waking, with her heart
All overshadow'd by the foolish dream,
And lo ! it was her mother grasping her
To get her well awake ; and in her hand
A suit of bright apparel, which she laid
Flat on the couch, and spoke exultingly :

'See here, my child, how fresh the
    colours look,
How fast they hold like colours of a shell
That keeps the wear and polish of the
    wave.
Why not ? It never yet was worn, I trow :
Look on it, child, and tell me if ye know
    it.'

And Enid look'd, but all confused at
    first,
Could scarce divide it from her foolish
    dream :
Then suddenly she knew it and rejoiced,
And answer'd, 'Yea, I know it ; your
    good gift,
So sadly lost on that unhappy night ;
Your own good gift !' 'Yea, surely,' said
    the dame,
'And gladly given again this happy morn.
For when the jousts were ended yesterday,
Went Yniol thro' the town, and every-
    where
He found the sack and plunder of our
    house
All scatter'd thro' the houses of the town ;
And gave command that all which once
    was ours
Should now be ours again : and yester-eve,
While ye were talking sweetly with your
    Prince,
Came one with this and laid it in my hand,
For love or fear, or seeking favour of us,
Because we have our earldom back again.
And yester-eve I would not tell you of it,
But kept it for a sweet surprise at morn.
Yea, truly is it not a sweet surprise ?

For I myself unwillingly have worn
My faded suit, as you, my child, have
  yours,
And howsoever patient, Yniol his.
Ah, dear, he took me from a goodly house,
With store of rich apparel, sumptuous fare,
And page, and maid, and squire, and
  seneschal,
And pastime both of hawk and hound,
  and all
That appertains to noble maintenance.
Yea, and he brought me to a goodly house;
But since our fortune swerved from sun to
  shade,
And all thro' that young traitor, cruel need
Constrain'd us, but a better time has
  come ;
So clothe yourself in this, that better fits
Our mended fortunes and a Prince's bride:
For tho' ye won the prize of fairest fair,
And tho' I heard him call you fairest fair,
Let never maiden think, however fair,
She is not fairer in new clothes than old.
And should some great court-lady say, the
  Prince
Hath pick'd a ragged-robin from the
  hedge,
And like a madman brought her to the
  court,
Then were ye shamed, and, worse, might
  shame the Prince
To whom we are beholden ; but I know,
When my dear child is set forth at her best,
That neither court nor country, tho' they
  sought
Thro' all the provinces like those of old
That lighted on Queen Esther, has her
  match.'

  Here ceased the kindly mother out of
    breath ;
And Enid listen'd brightening as she lay ;
Then, as the white and glittering star of
  morn
Parts from a bank of snow, and by and by
Slips into golden cloud, the maiden rose,
And left her maiden couch, and robed
  herself,
Help'd by the mother's careful hand and
  eye,

Without a mirror, in the gorgeous gown;
Who, after, turn'd her daughter round,
  and said,
She never yet had seen her half so fair ;
And call'd her like that maiden in the tale,
Whom Gwydion made by glamour out of
  flowers,
And sweeter than the bride of Cassivelaun,
Flur, for whose love the Roman Cæsar
  first
Invaded Britain, 'But we beat him back,
As this great Prince invaded us, and we,
Not beat him back, but welcomed him
  with joy.
And I can scarcely ride with you to court,
For old am I, and rough the ways and
  wild ;
But Yniol goes, and I full oft shall dream
I see my princess as I see her now,
Clothed with my gift, and gay among the
  gay.'

  But while the women thus rejoiced,
    Geraint
Woke where he slept in the high hall, and
  call'd
For Enid, and when Yniol made report
Of that good mother making Enid gay
In such apparel as might well beseem
His princess, or indeed the stately Queen,
He answer'd : ' Earl, entreat her by my
  love,
Albeit I give no reason but my wish,
That she ride with me in her faded silk.'
Yniol with that hard message went ; it fell
Like flaws in summer laying lusty corn :
For Enid, all abash'd she knew not why,
Dared not to glance at her good mother's
  face,
But silently, in all obedience,
Her mother silent too, nor helping her,
Laid from her limbs the costly-broider'd
  gift,
And robed them in her ancient suit again,
And so descended.   Never man rejoiced
More than Geraint to greet her thus
  attired ;
And glancing all at once as keenly at her
As careful robins eye the delver's toil,
Made her cheek burn and either eyelid fall,

But rested with her sweet face satisfied;
Then seeing cloud upon the mother's brow,
Her by both hands he caught, and sweetly
    said,

    'O my new mother, be not wroth or
        grieved
At thy new son, for my petition to her.
When late I left Caerleon, our great
        Queen,
In words whose echo lasts, they were so
        sweet,
Made promise, that whatever bride I
        brought,
Herself would clothe her like the sun in
        Heaven.
Thereafter, when I reach'd this ruin'd hall,
Beholding one so bright in dark estate,
I vow'd that could I gain her, our fair
        Queen,
No hand but hers, should make your Enid
        burst
Sunlike from cloud—and likewise thought
        perhaps,
That service done so graciously would
        bind
The two together; fain I would the two
Should love each other: how can Enid
        find
A nobler friend? Another thought was
        mine;
I came among you here so suddenly,
That tho' her gentle presence at the lists
Might well have served for proof that I
        was loved,
I doubted whether daughter's tenderness,
Or easy nature, might not let itself
Be moulded by your wishes for her weal;
Or whether some false sense in her own
        self
Of my contrasting brightness, overbore
Her fancy dwelling in this dusky hall;
And such a sense might make her long
        for court
And all its perilous glories: and I
        thought,
That could I someway prove such force
        in her
Link'd with such love for me, that at a
        word

(No reason given her) she could cast aside
A splendour dear to women, new to her,
And therefore dearer; or if not so new,
Yet therefore tenfold dearer by the power
Of intermitted usage; then I felt
That I could rest, a rock in ebbs and
        flows,
Fixt on her faith.   Now, therefore, I do
        rest,
A prophet certain of my prophecy,
That never shadow of mistrust can cross
Between us.   Grant me pardon for my
        thoughts:
And for my strange petition I will make
Amends hereafter by some gaudy-day,
When your fair child shall wear your
        costly gift
Beside your own warm hearth, with, on
        her knees,
Who knows? another gift of the high
        God,
Which, maybe, shall have learn'd to lisp
        you thanks.'

    He spoke: the mother smiled, but half
        in tears,
Then brought a mantle down and wrapt
        her in it,
And claspt and kiss'd her, and they rode
        away.

    Now thrice that morning Guinevere had
        climb'd
The giant tower, from whose high crest,
        they say,
Men saw the goodly hills of Somerset,
And white sails flying on the yellow sea;
But not to goodly hill or yellow sea
Look'd the fair Queen, but up the vale
        of Usk,
By the flat meadow, till she saw them
        come;
And then descending met them at the
        gates,
Embraced her with all welcome as a
        friend,
And did her honour as the Prince's bride,
And clothed her for her bridals like the
        sun;
And all that week was old Caerleon gay,.

T

For by the hands of Dubric, the high saint,
They twain were wedded with all ceremony.

And this was on the last year's Whitsuntide.
But Enid ever kept the faded silk,
Remembering how first he came on her,
Drest in that dress, and how he loved her in it,
And all her foolish fears about the dress,
And all his journey toward her, as himself
Had told her, and their coming to the court.

And now this morning when he said to her,
Put on your worst and meanest dress,'
she found
And took it, and array'd herself therein.

GERAINT AND ENID.

O PURBLIND race of miserable men,
How many among us at this very hour
Do forge a life-long trouble for ourselves,
By taking true for false, or false for true;
Here, thro' the feeble twilight of this world
Groping, how many, until we pass and reach
That other, where we see as we are seen !

So fared it with Geraint, who issuing forth
That morning, when they both had got to horse,
Perhaps because he loved her passionately,
And felt that tempest brooding round his heart,
Which, if he spoke at all, would break perforce
Upon a head so dear in thunder, said :
'Not at my side. I charge thee ride before,
Ever a good way on before ; and this
I charge thee, on thy duty as a wife,
Whatever happens, not to speak to me,
No, not a word !' and Enid was aghast ;
And forth they rode, but scarce three paces on,

When crying out, 'Effeminate as I am,
I will not fight my way with gilded arms,
All shall be iron ;' he loosed a mighty purse,
Hung at his belt, and hurl'd it toward the squire.
So the last sight that Enid had of home
Was all the marble threshold flashing, strown
With gold and scatter'd coinage, and the squire
Chafing his shoulder : then he cried again
' To the wilds !' and Enid leading down the tracks
Thro' which he bad her lead him on, they past
The marches, and by bandit-haunted holds,
Gray swamps and pools, waste places of the hern,
And wildernesses, perilous paths, they rode :
Round was their pace at first, but slacken'd soon :
A stranger meeting them had surely thought
They rode so slowly and they look'd so pale,
That each had suffer'd some exceeding wrong.
For he was ever saying to himself,
' O I that wasted time to tend upon her,
To compass her with sweet observances,
To dress her beautifully and keep her true '—
And there he broke the sentence in his heart
Abruptly, as a man upon his tongue
May break it, when his passion masters him.
And she was ever praying the sweet heavens
To save her dear lord whole from any wound.
And ever in her mind she cast about
For that unnoticed failing in herself,
Which made him look so cloudy and so cold ;
Till the great plover's human whistl
amazed

Her heart, and glancing round the waste
    she fear'd
In every wavering brake an ambuscade.
Then thought again, 'If there be such in
    me,
I might amend it by the grace of Heaven,
If he would only speak and tell me of it.'

But when the fourth part of the day
    was gone,
Then Enid was aware of three tall knights
On horseback, wholly arm'd, behind a
    rock
In shadow, waiting for them, caitiffs all ;
And heard one crying to his fellow,
    ' Look,
Here comes a laggard hanging down his
    head,
Who seems no bolder than a beaten
    hound ;
Come, we will slay him and will have his
    horse
And armour, and his damsel shall be
    ours.'

Then Enid ponder'd in her heart, and
    said :
' I will go back a little to my lord,
And I will tell him all their caitiff talk ;
For, be he wroth even to slaying me,
Far liefer by his dear hand had I die,
Than that my lord should suffer loss or
    shame.'

Then she went back some paces of
    return,
Met his full frown timidly firm, and said ;
' My lord, I saw three bandits by the
    rock
Waiting to fall on you, and heard them
    boast
That they would slay you, and possess
    your horse
And armour, and your damsel should' be
    theirs.'

He made a wrathful answer : ' Did I
    wish
Your warning or your silence ? one com-
    mand
I laid upon you, not to speak to me,

And thus ye keep it ! Well then, look
    —for now,
Whether ye wish me victory or defeat,
Long for my life, or hunger for my death,
Yourself shall see my vigour is not lost.'

Then Enid waited pale and sorrowful,
And down upon him bare the bandit
    three.
And at the midmost charging, Prince
    Geraint
Drave the long spear a cubit thro' his
    breast
And out beyond ; and then against his
    brace
Of comrades, each of whom had broken
    on him
A lance that splinter'd like an icicle,
Swung from his brand a windy buffet out
Once, twice, to right, to left, and stunn'd
    the twain
Or slew them, and dismounting like a man
That skins the wild beast after slaying
    him,
Stript from the three dead wolves of
    woman born
The three gay suits of armour which they
    wore,
And let the bodies lie, but bound the suits
Of armour on their horses, each on each,
And tied the bridle-reins of all the three
Together, and said to her, ' Drive them
    on
Before you ;' and she drove them thro'
    the waste.

He follow'd nearer : ruth began to
    work
Against his anger in him, while he watch'd
The being he loved best in all the world,
With difficulty in mild obedience
Driving them on : he fain had spoken to
    her,
And loosed in words of sudden fire the
    wrath
And smoulder'd wrong that burnt him all
    within ;
But evermore it seem'd an easier thing
At once without remorse to strike her
    dead,

Than to cry 'Halt,' and to her own
    bright face
Accuse her of the least immodesty :
And thus tongue-tied, it made him wroth
    the more
That she *could* speak whom his own ear
    had heard
Call herself false : and suffering thus he
    made
Minutes an age : but in scarce longer time
Than at Caerleon the full-tided Usk,
Before he turn to fall seaward again,
Pauses, did Enid, keeping watch, behold
In the first shallow shade of a deep wood,
Before a gloom of stubborn-shafted oaks,
Three other horsemen waiting, wholly
    arm'd,
Whereof one seem'd far larger than her
    lord,
And shook her pulses, crying, 'Look, a
    prize !
Three horses and three goodly suits of
    arms,
And all in charge of whom? a girl: set on.'
'Nay,' said the second, 'yonder comes a
    knight.'
The third, 'A craven ; how he hangs his
    head.'
The giant answer'd merrily, 'Yea, but one?
Wait here, and when he passes fall upon
    him.'

And Enid ponder'd in her heart and
    said,
'I will abide the coming of my lord,
And I will tell him all their villainy.
My lord is weary with the fight before,
And they will fall upon him unawares.
I needs must disobey him for his good ;
How should I dare obey him to his harm?
Needs must I speak, and tho' he kill me
    for it,
I save a life dearer to me than mine.'

And she abode his coming, and said to
    him
With timid firmness, 'Have I leave to
    speak ? '
He said, 'Ye take it, speaking,' and she
    spoke.

'There lurk three villains yonder in the
    wood,
And each of them is wholly arm'd, and one
Is larger-limb'd than you are, and they say
That they will fall upon you while ye
    pass.'

To which he flung a wrathful answer
    back :
'And if there were an hundred in the
    wood,
And every man were larger-limb'd than I,
And all at once should sally out upon me,
I swear it would not ruffle me so much
As you that not obey me.   Stand aside,
And if I fall, cleave to the better man.'

And Enid stood aside to wait the event,
Not dare to watch the combat, only
    breathe
Short fits of prayer, at every stroke a
    breath.
And he, she dreaded most, bare down
    upon him.
Aim'd at the helm, his lance err'd ; but
    Geraint's,
A little in the late encounter strain'd,
Struck thro' the bulky bandit's corselet
    home,
And then brake short, and down his
    enemy roll'd,
And there lay still ; as he that tells the
    tale
Saw once a great piece of a promontory,
That had a sapling growing on it, slide
From the long shore-cliff's windy walls
    to the beach,
And there lie still, and yet the sapling
    grew :
So lay the man transfixt.   His craven pair
Of comrades making slowlier at the
    Prince,
When now they saw their bulwark fallen
    stood ;
On whom the victor, to confound them
    more,
Spurr'd with his terrible war-cry ; for as
    one,
That listens near a torrent mountain
    brook,

All thro' the crash of the near cataract hears
The drumming thunder of the huger fall
At distance, were the soldiers wont to
hear
His voice in battle, and be kindled by it,
And foemen scared, like that false pair
who turn'd
Flying, but, overtaken, died the death
Themselves had wrought on many an
innocent.

Thereon Geraint, dismounting, pick'd
the lance
That pleased him best, and drew from
those dead wolves
Their three gay suits of armour, each from
each,
And bound them on their horses, each on
each,
And tied the bridle-reins of all the three
Together, and said to her, 'Drive them on
Before you,' and she drove them thro' the
wood.

He follow'd nearer still: the pain she
had
To keep them in the wild ways of the
wood,
Two sets of three laden with jingling
arms,
Together, served a little to disedge
The sharpness of that pain about her
heart:
And they themselves, like creatures gently
born
But into bad hands fall'n, and now so long
By bandits groom'd, prick'd their light
ears, and felt
Her low firm voice and tender government.

So thro' the green gloom of the wood
they past,
And issuing under open heavens beheld
A little town with towers, upon a rock,
And close beneath, a meadow gemlike
chased
In the brown wild, and mowers mowing
in it:
And down a rocky pathway from the place
There came a fair-hair'd youth, that in
his hand

Bare victual for the mowers: and Geraint
Had ruth again on Enid looking pale:
Then, moving downward to the meadow
ground,
He, when the fair-hair'd youth came by
him, said,
'Friend, let her eat; the damsel is so
faint.'
'Yea, willingly,' replied the youth; 'and
thou,
My lord, eat also, tho' the fare is coarse,
And only meet for mowers;' then set
down
His basket, and dismounting on the sward
They let the horses graze, and ate them-
selves.
And Enid took a little delicately,
Less having stomach for it than desire
To close with her lord's pleasure; but
Geraint
Ate all the mowers' victual unawares,
And when he found all empty, was
amazed;
And 'Boy,' said he, 'I have eaten all,
but take
A horse and arms for guerdon; choose
the best.'
He, reddening in extremity of delight,
'My lord, you overpay me fifty-fold.'
'Ye will be all the wealthier,' cried the
Prince.
'I take it as free gift, then,' said the boy,
'Not guerdon; for myself can easily,
While your good damsel rests, return,
and fetch
Fresh victual for these mowers of our
Earl;
For these are his, and all the field is his,
And I myself am his; and I will tell
him
How great a man thou art: he loves to
know
When men of mark are in his territory:
And he will have thee to his palace here,
And serve thee costlier than with mowers'
fare.'

Then said Geraint, 'I wish no better
fare:
I never ate with angrier appetite

Than when I left your mowers dinnerless.
And into no Earl's palace will I go.
I know, God knows, too much of
    palaces !
And if he want me, let him come to me.
But hire us some fair chamber for the
    night,
And stalling for the horses, and return
With victual for these men, and let us
    know.'

    ' Yea, my kind lord,' said the glad
      youth, and went,
Held his head high, and thought himself
    a knight,
And up the rocky pathway disappear'd,
Leading the horse, and they were left
    alone.

    But when the Prince had brought his
      errant eyes
Home from the rock, sideways he let
    them glance
At Enid, where she droopt : his own
    false doom,
That shadow of mistrust should never cross
Betwixt them, came upon him, and he
    sigh'd ;
Then with another humorous ruth re-
    mark'd
The lusty mowers labouring dinnerless,
And watch'd the sun blaze on the turning
    scythe,
And after nodded sleepily in the heat.
But she, remembering her old ruin'd hall,
And all the windy clamour of the daws
About her hollow turret, pluck'd the
    grass
There growing longest by the meadow's
    edge,
And into many a listless annulet,
Now over, now beneath her marriage
    ring,
Wove and unwove it, till the boy return'd
And told them of a chamber, and they
    went ;
Where, after saying to her, ' If ye will,
Cail for the woman of the house,' to which
She answer'd, ' Thanks, my lord ;' the
    two remain'd

Apart by all the chamber's width, and
    mute
As creatures voiceless thro' the fault of
    birth,
Or two wild men supporters of a shield,
Painted, who stare at open space, nor
    glance
The one at other, parted by the shield.

    On a sudden, many a voice along the
      street,
And heel against the pavement echoing,
    burst
Their drowse ; and either started while
    the door,
Push'd from without, drave backward to
    the wall,
And midmost of a rout of roisterers,
Femininely fair and dissolutely pale,
Her suitor in old years before Geraint,
Enter'd, the wild lord of the place,
    Limours.
He moving up with pliant courtliness,
Greeted Geraint full face, but stealthily,
In the mid-warmth of welcome and graspt
    hand,
Found Enid with the corner of his eye,
And knew her sitting sad and solitary.
Then cried Geraint for wine and goodly
    cheer
To feed the sudden guest, and sump-
    tuously
According to his fashion, bad the host
Call in what men soever were his friends,
And feast with these in honour of their
    Earl ;
' And care not for the cost ; the cost is
    mine.'

    And wine and food were brought, and
      Earl Limours
Drank till he jested with all ease, and told
Free tales, and took the word and play'd
    upon it,
And made it of two colours ; for his talk,
When wine and free companions kindled
    him,
Was wont to glance and sparkle like a gem
Of fifty facets ; thus he moved the Prince
To laughter and his comrades to applause.

Then, when the Prince was merry, ask'd
    Limours,
'Your leave, my lord, to cross the room,
    and speak
To your good damsel there who sits apart,
And seems so lonely?' 'My free leave,'
    he said;
'Get her to speak: she doth not speak to
    me.'
Then rose Limours, and looking at his
    feet,
Like him who tries the bridge he fears
    may fail,
Crost and came near, lifted adoring eyes,
Bow'd at her side and utter'd whisper-
    ingly:

'Enid, the pilot star of my lone life,
Enid, my early and my only love,
Enid, the loss of whom hath turn'd me
    wild—
What chance is this? how is it I see you
    here?
Ye are in my power at last, are in my
    power.
Yet fear me not: I call mine own self
    wild,
But keep a touch of sweet civility
Here in the heart of waste and wilderness.
I thought, but that your father came
    between,
In former days you saw me favourably.
And if it were so do not keep it back:
Make me a little happier: let me know it:
Owe you me nothing for a life half-lost?
Yea, yea, the whole dear debt of all you
    are.
And, Enid, you and he, I see with joy,
Ye sit apart, you do not speak to him,
You come with no attendance, page or
    maid,
To serve you—doth he love you as of old?
For, call it lovers' quarrels, yet I know
Tho' men may bicker with the things they
    love,
They would not make them laughable in
    all eyes,
Not while they loved them; and your
    wretched dress,
A wretched insult on you, dumbly speaks

Your story, that this man loves you no
    more.
Your beauty is no beauty to him now:
A common chance—right well I know it
    —pall'd—
For I know men: nor will ye win him
    back,
For the man's love once gone never
    returns.
But here is one who loves you as of old;
With more exceeding passion than of old:
Good, speak the word: my followers ring
    him round:
He sits unarm'd; I hold a finger up;
They understand: nay; I do not mean
    blood:
Nor need ye look so scared at what I say:
My malice is no deeper than a moat,
No stronger than a wall: there is the
    keep;
He shall not cross us more; speak but
    the word:
Or speak it not; but then by Him that
    made me
The one true lover whom you ever own'd,
I will make use of all the power I have.
O pardon me! the madness of that hour,
When first I parted from thee, moves me
    yet.'

At this the tender sound of his own
    voice
And sweet self-pity, or the fancy of it,
Made his eye moist; but Enid fear'd his
    eyes,
Moist as they were, wine-heated from the
    feast;
And answer'd with such craft as women
    use,
Guilty or guiltless, to stave off a chance
That breaks upon them perilously, and
    said:

'Earl, if you love me as in former
    years,
And do not practise on me, come with
    morn,
And snatch me from him as by violence;
Leave me to-night: I am weary to the
    death.'

Low at leave-taking, with his brandish'd
plume
Brushing his instep, bow'd the all-
amorous Earl,
And the stout Prince bad him a loud
good-night.
He moving homeward babbled to his men,
How Enid never loved a man but him,
Nor cared a broken egg-shell for her lord.

But Enid left alone with Prince Geraint,
Debating his command of silence given,
And that she now perforce must violate it,
Held commune with herself, and while
she held
He fell asleep, and Enid had no heart
To wake him, but hung o'er him, wholly
pleased
To find him yet unwounded after fight,
And hear him breathing low and equally.
Anon she rose, and stepping lightly,
heap'd
The pieces of his armour in one place,
All to be there against a sudden need ;
Then dozed awhile herself, but overtoil'd
By that day's grief and travel, evermore
Seem'd catching at a rootless thorn, and
then
Went slipping down horrible precipices,
And strongly striking out her limbs
awoke ;
Then thought she heard the wild Earl at
the door,
With all his rout of random followers,
Sound on a dreadful trumpet, summoning
her ;
Which was the red cock shouting to the
light,
As the gray dawn stole o'er the dewy
world,
And glimmer'd on his armour in the room.
And once again she rose to look at it,
But touch'd it unawares : jangling, the
casque
Fell, and he started up and stared at her.
Then breaking his command of silence
given,
She told him all that Earl Limours had
said,
Except the passage that he loved her not ;

Nor left untold the craft herself had used ;
But ended with apology so sweet,
Low-spoken, and of so few words, and
seem'd
So justified by that necessity,
That tho' he thought 'was it for him she
wept
In Devon ?' he but gave a wrathful groan,
Saying, 'Your sweet faces make good
fellows fools
And traitors. Call the host and bid him
bring
Charger and palfrey.' So she glided out
Among the heavy breathings of the
house,
And like a household Spirit at the walls
Beat, till she woke the sleepers, and
return'd :
Then tending her rough lord, tho' all
unask'd,
In silence, did him service as a squire ;
Till issuing arm'd he found the host and
cried,
'Thy reckoning, friend ?' and ere he
learnt it, 'Take
Five horses and their armours ;' and the
host
Suddenly honest, answer'd in amaze,
'My lord, I scarce have spent the worth
of one !'
'Ye will be all the wealthier,' said the
Prince,
And then to Enid, 'Forward ! and to-
day
I charge you, Enid, more especially,
What thing soever ye may hear, or see,
Or fancy (tho' I count it of small use
To charge you) that ye speak not but
obey.'

And Enid answer'd, 'Yea, my lord,
I know
Your wish, and would obey ; but riding
first,
I hear the violent threats you do not
hear,
I see the danger which you cannot see :
Then not to give you warning, that seems
hard ;
Almost beyond me : yet I would obey.'

'Yea so,' said he, 'do it : be not too
  wise ;
Seeing that ye are wedded to a man,
Not all mismated with a yawning clown,
But one with arms to guard his head and
  yours,
With eyes to find you out however far,
And ears to hear you even in his dreams.'

With that he turn'd and look'd as
  keenly at her
As careful robins eye the delver's toil ;
And that within her, which a wanton fool,
Or hasty judger would have call'd her
  guilt,
Made her cheek burn and either eyelid fall.
And Geraint look'd and was not satisfied.

Then forward by a way which, beaten
  broad,
Led from the territory of false Limours
To the waste earldom of another earl,
Doorm, whom his shaking vassals call'd
  the Bull,
Went Enid with her sullen follower on.
Once she look'd back, and when she saw
  him ride
More near by many a rood than yester-
  morn,
It wellnigh made her cheerful ; till
  Geraint
Waving an angry hand as who should
  say
'Ye watch me,' sadden'd all her heart
  again.
But while the sun yet beat a dewy blade,
The sound of many a heavily-galloping
  hoof
Smote on her ear, and turning round she
  saw
Dust, and the points of lances bicker in it.
Then not to disobey her lord's behest,
And yet to give him warning, for he rode
As if he heard not, moving back she held
Her finger up, and pointed to the dust.
At which the warrior in his obstinacy,
Because she kept the letter of his word,
Was in a manner pleased, and turning,
  stood.
And in the moment after, wild Limours,

Borne on a black horse, like a thunder-
  cloud
Whose skirts are loosen'd by the breaking
  storm,
Half ridden off with by the thing he rode,
And all in passion uttering a dry shriek,
Dash'd on Geraint, who closed with him,
  and bore
Down by the length of lance and arm
  beyond
The crupper, and so left him stunn'd or
  dead,
And overthrew the next that follow'd him,
And blindly rush'd on all the rout behind.
But at the flash and motion of the man
They vanish'd panic-stricken, like a shoal
Of darting fish, that on a summer morn
Adown the crystal dykes at Camelot
Come slipping o'er their shadows on the
  sand,
But if a man who stands upon the brink
But lift a shining hand against the sun,
There is not left the twinkle of a fin
Betwixt the cressy islets white in flower ;
So, scared but at the motion of the man,
Fled all the boon companions of the Earl,
And left him lying in the public way ;
So vanish friendships only made in wine.

Then like a stormy sunlight smiled
  Geraint,
Who saw the chargers of the two that fell
Start from their fallen lords, and wildly fly,
Mixt with the flyers.   'Horse and man,'
  he said,
'All of one mind and all right-honest
  friends !
Not a hoof left : and I methinks till now
Was honest—paid with horses and with
  arms ;
I cannot steal or plunder, no nor beg :
And so what say ye, shall we strip him
  there
Your lover? has your palfrey heart enough
To bear his armour ? shall we fast, or
  dine ?
No ?—then do thou, being right honest,
  pray
That we may meet the horsemen of Earl
  Doorm,

I too would still be honest.' Thus he
    said :
And sadly gazing on her bridle-reins,
And answering not one word, she led the
    way.

But as a man to whom a dreadful loss
Falls in a far land and he knows it not,
But coming back he learns it, and the loss
So pains him that he sickens nigh to
    death ;
So fared it with Geraint, who being prick'd
In combat with the follower of Limours,
Bled underneath his armour secretly,
And so rode on, nor told his gentle wife
What ail'd him, hardly knowing it himself,
Till his eye darken'd and his helmet
    wagg'd ;
And at a sudden swerving of the road,
Tho' happily down on a bank of grass,
The Prince, without a word, from his
    horse fell.

And Enid heard the clashing of his fall,
Suddenly came, and at his side all pale
Dismounting, loosed the fastenings of his
    arms,
Nor let her true hand falter, nor blue eye
Moisten, till she had lighted on his wound,
And tearing off her veil of faded silk
Had bared her forehead to the blistering
    sun,
And swathed the hurt that drain'd her
    dear lord's life.
Then after all was done that hand could do,
She rested, and her desolation came
Upon her, and she wept beside the way.

And many past, but none regarded her,
For in that realm of lawless turbulence,
A woman weeping for her murder'd mate
Was cared as much for as a summer shower:
One took him for a victim of Earl Doorm,
Nor dared to waste a perilous pity on him :
Another hurrying past, a man-at-arms,
Rode on a mission to the bandit Earl ;
Half whistling and half singing a coarse
    song,
He drove the dust against her veilless eyes :
Another, flying from the wrath of Doorm
Before an ever-fancied arrow, made

The long way smoke beneath him in his
    fear ;
At which her palfrey whinnying lifted
    heel,
And scour'd into the coppices and was lost,
While the great charger stood, grieved
    like a man.

But at the point of noon the huge Earl
    Doorm,
Broad-faced with under-fringe of russet
    beard,
Bound on a foray, rolling eyes of prey,
Came riding with a hundred lances up ;
But ere he came, like one that hails a ship,
Cried out with a big voice, ' What, is he
    dead ?'
' No, no, not dead !' she answer'd in all
    haste.
' Would some of your kind people take'
    him up,
And bear him hence out of this cruel sun ?
Most sure am I, quite sure, he is not dead.'

Then said Earl Doorm : ' Well, if he
    be not dead,
Why wail ye for him thus ? ye seem a child.
And be he dead, I count you for a fool ;
Your wailing will not quicken him : dead
    or not,
Ye mar a comely face with idiot tears.
Yet, since the face is comely—some of you,
Here, take him up, and bear him to our
    hall :
An if he live, we will have him of our
    band ;
And if he die, why earth has earth enough
To hide him.   See ye take the charger too,
A noble one.'

                    He spake, and past away,
But left two brawny spearmen, who
    advanced,
Each growling like a dog, when his good
    bone
Seems to be pluck'd at by the village boys
Who love to vex him eating, and he fears
To lose his bone, and lays his foot upon it,
Gnawing and growling : so the ruffians
    growl'd,
Fearing to lose, and all for a dead man,

Their chance of booty from the morning's
    raid,
Yet raised and laid him on a litter-bier,
Such as they brought upon their forays out
For those that might be wounded ; laid
    him on it
All in the hollow of his shield, and took
And bore him to the naked hall of Doorm,
(His gentle charger following him unled)
And cast him and the bier in which he
    lay
Down on an oaken settle in the hall,
And then departed, hot in haste to join
Their luckier mates, but growling as
    before,
And cursing their lost time, and the dead
    man,
And their own Earl, and their own souls,
    and her.
They might as well have blest her : she
    was deaf
To blessing or to cursing save from one.

So for long hours sat Enid by her lord,
There in the naked hall, propping his
    head,
And chafing his pale hands, and calling
    to him.
Till at the last he waken'd from his swoon,
And found his own dear bride propping
    his head,
And chafing his faint hands, and calling
    to him ;
And felt the warm tears falling on his face ;
And said to his own heart, ' She weeps
    for me :'
And yet lay still, and feign'd himself as
    dead,
That he might prove her to the uttermost,
And say to his own heart, ' She weeps
    for me.'

But in the falling afternoon return'd
The huge Earl Doorm with plunder to
    the hall.
His lusty spearmen follow'd him with
    noise :
Each hurling down a heap of things that
    rang
Against the pavement, cast his lance aside,

And doff'd his helm : and then there
    flutter'd in,
Half-bold, half-frighted, with dilated eyes,
A tribe of women, dress'd in many hues,
And mingled with the spearmen : and
    Earl Doorm
Struck with a knife's haft hard against
    the board,
And call'd for flesh and wine to feed his
    spears.
And men brought in whole hogs and
    quarter beeves,
And all the hall was dim with steam of
    flesh :
And none spake word, but all sat down
    at once,
And ate with tumult in the naked hall,
Feeding like horses when you hear them
    feed ;
Till Enid shrank far back into herself,
To shun the wild ways of the lawless tribe.
But when Earl Doorm had eaten all he
    would,
He roll'd his eyes about the hall, and
    found
A damsel drooping in a corner of it.
Then he remember'd her, and how she
    wept ;
And out of her there came a power upon
    him ;
And rising on the sudden he said, ' Eat !
I never yet beheld a thing so pale.
God's curse, it makes me mad to see you
    weep.
Eat ! Look yourself. Good luck had
    your good man,
For were I dead who is it would weep
    for me ?
Sweet lady, never since I first drew breath
Have I beheld a lily like yourself.
And so there lived some colour in your
    cheek,
There is not one among my gentlewomen
Were fit to wear your slipper for a glove.
But listen to me, and by me be ruled,
And I will do the thing I have not done,
For ye shall share my earldom with me,
    girl,
And we will live like two birds in one
    nest,

And I will fetch you forage from all
    fields,
For I compel all creatures to my will.'

    He spoke : the brawny spearman let
        his cheek
Bulge with the unswallow'd piece, and
    turning stared ;
While some, whose souls the old serpent
    long had drawn
Down, as the worm draws in the wither'd
    leaf
And makes it earth, hiss'd each at other's
    ear
What shall not be recorded—women they,
Women, or what had been those gracious
    things,
But now desired the humbling of their
    best,
Yea, would have help'd him to it : and
    all at once
They hated her, who took no thought of
    them,
But answer'd in low voice, her meek head
    yet
Drooping, 'I pray you of your courtesy,
He being as he is, to let me be.'

    She spake so low he hardly heard her
        speak,
But like a mighty patron, satisfied
With what himself had done so graci-
    ously,
Assumed that she had thank'd him, add-
    ing, 'Yea,
Eat and be glad, for I account you mine.'

    She answer'd meekly, 'How should I
        be glad
Henceforth in all the world at anything,
Until my lord arise and look upon me?'

    Here the huge Earl cried out upon her
        talk,
As all but empty heart and weariness
And sickly nothing ; suddenly seized on
    her,
And bare her by main violence to the
    board,
And thrust the dish before her, crying,
    'Eat.'

'No, no,' said Enid, vext, 'I will not
    eat
Till yonder man upon the bier arise,
And eat with me.'   'Drink, then,' he
    answer'd.   'Here !'
(And fill'd a horn with wine and held it
    to her,)
'Lo ! I, myself, when flush'd with fight,
    or hot,
God's curse, with anger—often I myself,
Before I well have drunken, scarce can
    eat :
Drink therefore and the wine will change
    your will.'

    'Not so,' she cried, 'by Heaven, I
        will not drink
Till my dear lord arise and bid me do it,
And drink with me ; and if he rise no
    more,
I will not look at wine until I die.'

    At this he turn'd all red and paced his
        hall,
Now gnaw'd his under, now his upper
    lip,
And coming up close to her, said at last :
'Girl, for I see ye scorn my courtesies,
Take warning : yonder man is surely
    dead ;
And I compel all creatures to my will.
Not eat nor drink ?   And wherefore wail
    for one,
Who put your beauty to this flout and
    scorn
By dressing it in rags ?   Amazed am I,
Beholding how ye butt against my wish,
That I forbear you thus : cross me no
    more.
At least put off to please me this poor
    gown,
This silken rag, this beggar-woman's
    weed :
I love that beauty should go beautifully :
For see ye not my gentlewomen here,
How gay, how suited to the house of one
Who loves that beauty should go beauti-
    fully ?
Rise therefore ; robe yourself in this ;
    obey.'

He spoke, and one among his gentle-
women
Display'd a splendid silk of foreign loom,
Where like a shoaling sea the lovely blue
Play'd into green, and thicker down the
front
With jewels than the sward with drops of
dew,
When all night long a cloud clings to the
hill,
And with the dawn ascending lets the day
Strike where it clung : so thickly shone
the gems.

But Enid answer'd, harder to be moved
Than hardest tyrants in their day of power,
With life-long injuries burning unavenged,
And now their hour has come ; and Enid
said :

'In this poor gown my dear lord found
me first,
And loved me serving in my father's hall :
In this poor gown I rode with him to
court,
And there the Queen array'd me like the
sun :
In this poor gown he bad me clothe
myself,
When now we rode upon this fatal quest
Of honour, where no honour can be
gain'd :
And this poor gown I will not cast aside
Until himself arise a living man,
And bid me cast it. I have griefs enough :
Pray you be gentle, pray you let me be :
I never loved, can never love but him :
Yea, God, I pray you of your gentleness,
He being as he is, to let me be.'

Then strode the brute Earl up and
down his hall,
And took his russet beard between his
teeth ;
Last, coming up quite close, and in his
mood
Crying, 'I count it of no more avail,
Dame, to be gentle than ungentle with
you ;
Take my salute,' unknightly with flat hand,
However lightly, smote her on the cheek.

Then Enid, in her utter helplessness,
And since she thought, 'He had not
dared to do it,
Except he surely knew my lord was dead,'
Sent forth a sudden sharp and bitter cry,
As of a wild thing taken in the trap,
Which sees the trapper coming thro' the
wood.

This heard Geraint, and grasping at
his sword,
(It lay beside him in the hollow shield),
Made but a single bound, and with a
sweep of it
Shore thro' the swarthy neck, and like a
ball
The russet-bearded head roll'd on the
floor.
So died Earl Doorm by him he counted
dead.
And all the men and women in the hall
Rose when they saw the dead man rise,
and fled
Yelling as from a spectre, and the two
Were left alone together, and he said :

'Enid, I have used you worse than
that dead man ;
Done you more wrong : we both have
undergone
That trouble which has left me thrice
your own :
Henceforward I will rather die than doubt.
And here I lay this penance on myself,
Not, tho' mine own ears heard you
yestermorn—
You thought me sleeping, but I heard
you say,
I heard you say, that you were no true
wife :
I swear I will not ask your meaning in
it :
I do believe yourself against yourself,
And will henceforward rather die than
doubt.'

And Enid could not say one tender
word,
She felt so blunt and stupid at the heart :
She only pray'd him, 'Fly, they will
return

And slay you; fly, your charger is with-
out,
My palfrey lost.' 'Then, Enid, shall you
ride
Behind me.' 'Yea,' said Enid, 'let us go.'
And moving out they found the stately
horse,
Who now no more a vassal to the thief,
But free to stretch his limbs in lawful fight,
Neigh'd with all gladness as they came,
and stoop'd
With a low whinny toward the pair: and
she
Kiss'd the white star upon his noble front,
Glad also; then Geraint upon the horse
Mounted, and reach'd a hand, and on his
foot
She set her own and climb'd; he turn'd
his face
And kiss'd her climbing, and she cast
her arms
About him, and at once they rode away.

And never yet, since high in Paradise
O'er the four rivers the first roses blew,
Came purer pleasure unto mortal kind
Than lived thro' her, who in that perilous
hour
Put hand to hand beneath her husband's
heart,
And felt him hers again: she did not
weep,
But o'er her meek eyes came a happy
mist
Like that which kept the heart of Eden
green
Before the useful trouble of the rain:
Yet not so misty were her meek blue
eyes
As not to see before them on the path,
Right in the gateway of the bandit hold,
A knight of Arthur's court, who laid his
lance
In rest, and made as if to fall upon him.
Then, fearing for his hurt and loss of
blood,
She, with her mind all full of what had
chanced,
Shriek'd to the stranger 'Slay not a dead
man!'

'The voice of Enid,' said the knight;
but she,
Beholding it was Edyrn son of Nudd,
Was moved so much the more, and
shriek'd again,
'O cousin, slay not him who gave you
life.'
And Edyrn moving frankly forward spake:
'My lord Geraint, I greet you with all
love;
I took you for a bandit knight of Doorm;
And fear not, Enid, I should fall upon
him,
Who love you, Prince, with something
of the love
Wherewith we love the Heaven that
chastens us.
For once, when I was up so high in pride
That I was halfway down the slope to
Hell,
By overthrowing me you threw me higher.
Now, made a knight of Arthur's Table
Round,
And since I knew this Earl, when I my-
self
Was half a bandit in my lawless hour,
I come the mouthpiece of our King to
Doorm
(The King is close behind me) bidding
him
Disband himself, and scatter all his powers,
Submit, and hear the judgment of the
King.'

'He hears the judgment of the King
of kings,'
Cried the wan Prince; 'and lo, the
powers of Doorm
Are scatter'd,' and he pointed to the field,
Where, huddled here and there on mound
and knoll,
Were men and women staring and aghast,
While some yet fled; and then he plainlier
told
How the huge Earl lay slain within his
hall.
But when the knight besought him,
'Follow me,
Prince, to the camp, and in the King's
own ear

Speak what has chanced ; ye surely have
    endured
Strange chances here alone ;' that other
    flush'd,
And hung his head, and halted in reply,
Fearing the mild face of the blameless
    King,
And after madness acted question ask'd :
Till Edyrn crying, ' If ye will not go
To Arthur, then will Arthur come to you,'
' Enough,' he said, ' I follow,' and they
    went.
But Enid in their going had two fears,
One from the bandit scatter'd in the field,
And one from Edyrn. Every now and
    then,
When Edyrn rein'd his charger at her side,
She shrank a little. In a hollow land,
From which old fires have broken, men
    may fear
Fresh fire and ruin. He, perceiving, said :

  ' Fair and dear cousin, you that most
    had cause
To fear me, fear no longer, I am changed.
Yourself were first the blameless cause to
    make
My nature's prideful sparkle in the blood
Break into furious flame ; being repulsed
By Yniol and yourself, I schemed and
    wrought
Until I overturn'd him ; then set up
(With one main purpose ever at my heart)
My haughty jousts, and took a paramour ;
Did her mock-honour as the fairest fair,
And, toppling over all antagonism,
So wax'd in pride, that I believed myself
Unconquerable, for I was wellnigh mad :
And, but for my main purpose in these
    jousts,
I should have slain your father, seized
    yourself.
I lived in hope that sometime you would
    come
To these my lists with him whom best
    you loved ;
And there, poor cousin, with your meek
    blue eyes,
The truest eyes that ever answer'd Heaven,
Behold me overturn and trample on him.

Then, had you cried, or knelt, or pray'd
    to me,
I should not less have kill'd him. And
    you came,—
But once you came,—and with your own
    true eyes
Beheld the man you loved (I speak as one
Speaks of a service done him) overthrow
My proud self, and my purpose three
    years old,
And set his foot upon me, and give me
    life.
There was I broken down ; there was I
    saved :
Tho' thence I rode all-shamed, hating
    the life
He gave me, meaning to be rid of it.
And all the penance the Queen laid upon
    me
Was but to rest awhile within her court ;
Where first as sullen as a beast new-caged,
And waiting to be treated like a wolf,
Because I knew my deeds were known,
    I found,
Instead of scornful pity or pure scorn,
Such fine reserve and noble reticence,
Manners so kind, yet stately, such a grace
Of tenderest courtesy, that I began
To glance behind me at my former life,
And find that it had been the wolf's in-
    deed :
And oft I talk'd with Dubric, the high
    saint,
Who, with mild heat of holy oratory,
Subdued me somewhat to that gentleness,
Which, when it weds with manhood,
    makes a man.
And you were often there about the Queen,
But saw me not, or mark'd not if you saw ;
Nor did I care or dare to speak with you,
But kept myself aloof till I was changed ;
And fear not, cousin ; I am changed
    indeed.'

  He spoke, and Enid easily believed,
Like simple noble natures, credulous
Of what they long for, good in friend or
    foe,
There most in those who most have done
    them ill.

And when they reach'd the camp the
King himself
Advanced to greet them, and beholding
her
Tho' pale, yet happy, ask'd her not a
word,
But went apart with Edyrn, whom he held
In converse for a little, and return'd,
And, gravely smiling, lifted her from
horse,
And kiss'd her with all pureness, brother-
like,
And show'd an empty tent allotted her,
And glancing for a minute, till he saw her
Pass into it, turn'd to the Prince, and
said :

' Prince, when of late ye pray'd me for
my leave
To move to your own land, and there
defend
Your marches, I was prick'd with some
reproof,
As one that let foul wrong stagnate and
be,
By having look'd too much thro' alien
eyes,
And wrought too long with delegated
hands,
Not used mine own : but now behold me
come
To cleanse this common sewer of all my
realm,
With Edyrn and with others : have ye
look'd
At Edyrn ? have ye seen how nobly
changed ?
This work of his is great and wonderful.
His very face with change of heart is
changed.
The world will not believe a man repents :
And this wise world of ours is mainly
right.
Full seldom doth a man repent, or use
Both grace and will to pick the vicious
quitch
Of blood and custom wholly out of him,
And make all clean, and plant himself
afresh.
Edyrn has done it, weeding all his heart

As I will weed this land before I go.
I, therefore, made him of our Table
Round,
Not rashly, but have proved him every-
way
One of our noblest, our most valorous,
Sanest and most obedient : and indeed
This work of Edyrn wrought upon himself
After a life of violence, seems to me
A thousand-fold more great and wonderful
Than if some knight of mine, risking his
life, .
My subject with my subjects under him,
Should make an onslaught single on a
realm
Of robbers, tho' he slew them one by one,
And were himself nigh wounded to the
death.'

So spake the King ; low bow'd the
Prince, and felt
His work was neither great nor wonderful,
And past to Enid's tent ; and thither came
The King's own leech to look into his
hurt ;
And Enid tended on him there ; and there
Her constant motion round him, and the
breath
Of her sweet tendance hovering over him,
Fill'd all the genial courses of his blood
With deeper and with ever deeper love,
As the south-west that blowing Bala lake
Fills all the sacred Dee.   So past the days.

But while Geraint lay healing of his
hurt,
The blameless King went forth and cast
his eyes
On each of all whom Uther left in charge
Long since, to guard the justice of the
King :
He look'd and found them wanting ; and
as now
Men weed the white horse on the Berk-
shire hills
To keep him bright and clean as hereto-
fore,
He rooted out the slothful officer
Or guilty, which for bribe had wink'd at
wrong,

And in their chairs set up a stronger race
With hearts and hands, and sent a thou-
    sand men
To till the wastes, and moving everywhere
Clear'd the dark places and let in the law,
And broke the bandit holds and cleansed
    the land.

Then, when Geraint was whole again,
    they past
With Arthur to Caerleon upon Usk.
There the great Queen once more em-
    braced her friend,
And clothed her in apparel like the day.
And tho' Geraint could never take again
That comfort from their converse which
    he took
Before the Queen's fair name was breathed
    upon,
He rested well content that all was well.
Thence after tarrying for a space they rode,
And fifty knights rode with them to the
    shores
Of Severn, and they past to their own
    land.
And there he kept the justice of the King
So vigorously yet mildly, that all hearts
Applauded, and the spiteful whisper died :
And being ever foremost in the chase,
And victor at the tilt and tournament,
They call'd him the great Prince and man
    of men.
But Enid, whom her ladies loved to call
Enid the Fair, a grateful people named
Enid the Good ; and in their halls arose
The cry of children, Enids and Geraints
Of times to be ; nor did he doubt her more,
But rested in her fealty, till he crown'd
A happy life with a fair death, and fell
Against the heathen of the Northern Sea
In battle, fighting for the blameless King.

BALIN AND BALAN.

PELLAM the King, who held and lost with
    Lot
In that first war, and had his realm restored
But render'd tributary, fail'd of late
To send his tribute ; wherefore Arthur
    call'd

His treasurer, one of many years, and
    spake,
' Go thou with him and him and bring it
    to us,
Lest we should set one truer on his throne.
Man's word is God in man.'

His Baron said
' We go but harken : there be two strange
    knights
Who sit near Camelot at a fountain-side,
A mile beneath the forest, challenging
And overthrowing every knight who
    comes.
Wilt thou I undertake them as we pass,
And send them to thee ? '

Arthur laugh'd upon him.
' Old friend, too old to be so young,
    depart,
Delay not thou for ought, but let them
    sit,
Until they find a lustier than themselves.'

So these departed. Early, one fair
    dawn,
The light-wing'd spirit of his youth
    return'd
On Arthur's heart ; he arm'd himself and
    went,
So coming to the fountain-side beheld
Balin and Balan sitting statuelike,
Brethren, to right and left the spring, that
    down,
From underneath a plume of lady-fern,
Sang, and the sand danced at the bottom
    of it.
And on the right of Balin Balin's horse
Was fast beside an alder, on the left
Of Balan Balan's near a poplartree.
' Fair Sirs,' said Arthur, ' wherefore sit
    ye here ? '
Balin and Balan answer'd ' For the sake
Of glory ; we be mightier men than all
In Arthur's court ; that also have we
    proved ;
For whatsoever knight against us came
Or I or he have easily overthrown.'
' I too,' said Arthur, ' am of Arthur's
    hall,

T

But rather proven in his Paynim wars
Than famous jousts ; but see, or proven
     or not,
Whether me likewise ye can overthrow.'
And Arthur lightly smote the brethren
     down,
And lightly so return'd, and no man knew.

Then Balin rose, and Balan, and beside
The carolling water set themselves again,
And spake no word until the shadow
     turn'd ;
When from the fringe of coppice round
     them burst
A spangled pursuivant, and crying 'Sirs,
Rise, follow ! ye be sent for by the
     King,'
They follow'd ; whom when Arthur seeing
     ask'd
' Tell me your names ; why sat ye by the
     well ?'
Balin the stillness of a minute broke
Saying 'An unmelodious name to thee,
Balin, "the Savage"—that addition
     thine—
My brother and my better, this man here,
Balan. I smote upon the naked skull
A thrall of thine in open hall, my hand
Was gauntleted, half slew him ; for I
     heard
He had spoken evil of me ; thy just wrath
Sent me a three-years' exile from thine
     eyes.
I have not lived my life delightsomely :
For I that did that violence to thy thrall,
Had often wrought some fury on myself,
Saving for Balan : those three kingless
     years
Have past—were wormwood-bitter to me.
     King,
Methought that if we sat beside the well,
And hurl'd to ground what knight soever
     spurr'd
Against us, thou would'st take me gladlier
     back,
And make, as ten-times worthier to be
     thine
Than twenty Balins, Balan knight. I
     have said.
Not so—not all. A man of thine to-day

Abash'd us both, and brake my boast.
     Thy will ?'
Said Arthur 'Thou hast ever spoken truth ;
Thy too fierce manhood would not let
     thee lie.
Rise, my true knight. As children learn,
     be thou
Wiser for falling ! walk with me, and
     move
To music with thine Order and the King.
Thy chair, a grief to all the brethren,
     stands
Vacant, but thou retake it, mine again !'

Thereafter, when Sir Balin enter'd hall,
The Lost one Found was greeted as in
     Heaven
With joy that blazed itself in woodland
     wealth
Of leaf, and gayest garlandage of flowers,
Along the walls and down the board ;
     they sat,
And cup clash'd cup ; they drank and
     some one sang,
Sweet-voiced, a song of welcome, where-
     upon
Their common shout in chorus, mount-
     ing, made
Those banners of twelve battles overhead
Stir, as they stirr'd of old, when Arthur's
     host
Proclaim'd him Victor, and the day was
     won.

Then Balan added to their Order lived
A wealthier life than heretofore with these
And Balin, till their embassage return'd.

' Sir King' they brought report ' we
     hardly found,
So bush'd about it is with gloom, the hall
Of him to whom ye sent us, Pellam, once
A Christless foe of thine as ever dash'd
Horse against horse ; but seeing that thy
     realm
Hath prosper'd in the name of Christ, the
     King
Took, as in rival heat, to holy things ;
And finds himself descended from the
     Saint

Arimathæan Joseph ; him who first
Brought the great faith to Britain over
    seas ;
He boasts his life as purer than thine
    own ;
Eats scarce enow to keep his pulse abeat ;
Hath push'd aside his faithful wife, nor
    lets
Or dame or damsel enter at his gates
Lest he should be polluted. This gray
    King
Show'd us a shrine wherein were wonders
    —yea—
Rich arks with priceless bones of martyr-
    dom,
Thorns of the crown and shivers of the
    cross,
And therewithal (for thus he told us)
    brought
By holy Joseph hither, that same spear
Wherewith the Roman pierced the side
    of Christ.
He much amazed us ; after, when we
    sought
The tribute, answer'd "I have quite fore-
    gone
All matters of this world : Garlon, mine
    heir,
Of him demand it," which this Garlon gave
With much ado, railing at thine and thee.

But when we left, in those deep woods
    we found
A knight of thine spear-stricken from
    behind,
Dead, whom we buried ; more than one
    of us
Cried out on Garlon, but a woodman
    there
Reported of some demon in the woods
Was once a man, who driven by evil
    tongues
From all his fellows, lived alone, and came
To learn black magic, and to hate his
    kind
With such a hate, that when he died, his
    soul
Became a Fiend, which, as the man in life
Was wounded by blind tongues he saw
    not whence,

Strikes from behind. This woodman
    show'd the cave
From which he sallies, and wherein he
    dwelt.
We saw the hoof-print of a horse, no
    more.'

Then Arthur, 'Let who goes before
    me, see
He do not fall behind me : foully slain
And villainously ! who will hunt for me
This demon of the woods?' Said Balan,
    'I'!
So claim'd the quest and rode away, but
    first,
Embracing Balin, 'Good my brother,
    hear !
Let not thy moods prevail, when I am
    gone
Who used to lay them ! hold them outer
    fiends,
Who leap at thee to tear thee ; shake
    them aside,
Dreams ruling when wit sleeps ! yea, but
    to dream
That any of these would wrong thee,
    wrongs thyself.
Witness their flowery welcome. Bound
    are they
To speak no evil. Truly save for fears,
My fears for thee, so rich a fellowship
Would make me wholly blest : thou one
    of them,
Be one indeed : consider them, and all
Their bearing in their common bond of
    love,
No more of hatred than in Heaven itself,
No more of jealousy than in Paradise.'

So Balan warn'd, and went ; Balin
    remain'd :
Who—for but three brief moons had
    glanced away
From being knighted till he smote the
    thrall,
And faded from the presence into years
Of exile—now would strictlier set himself
To learn what Arthur meant by courtesy,
Manhood, and knighthood ; wherefore
    hover'd round

Lancelot, but when he mark'd his high
        sweet smile
In passing, and a transitory word
Make knight or churl or child or damsel
        seem
From being smiled at happier in them-
        selves—
Sigh'd, as a boy lame-born beneath a
        height,
That glooms his valley, sighs to see the
        peak
Sun-flush'd, or touch at night the
        northern star ;
For one from out his village lately
        climb'd
And brought report of azure lands and
        fair,
Far seen to left and right ; and he him-
        self
Hath hardly scaled with help a hundred
        feet
Up from the base : so Balin marvelling
        oft
How far beyond him Lancelot seem'd to
        move,
Groan'd, and at times would mutter,
        'These be gifts,
Born with the blood, not learnable, divine,
Beyond *my* reach.   Well had I foughten
        —well—
In those fierce wars, struck hard—and
        had I crown'd
With my slain self the heaps of whom I
        slew—
So—better !—But this worship of the
        Queen,
That honour too wherein she holds him
        —this,
This was the sunshine that hath given the
        man
A growth, a name that branches o'er the
        rest,
And strength against all odds, and what
        the King
So prizes—overprizes—gentleness.
Her likewise would I worship an I might.
I never can be close with her, as he
That brought her hither.   Shall I pray
        the King
To let me bear some token of his Queen

Whereon to gaze, remembering her—
        forget
My heats and violences ? live afresh ?
What, if the Queen disdain'd to grant it !
        nay
Being so stately-gentle, would she make
My darkness blackness ? and with how
        sweet grace
She greeted my return !   Bold will I
        be—
Some goodly cognizance of Guinevere,
In lieu of this rough beast upon my
        shield,
Langued gules, and tooth'd with grinning
        savagery.'

    And Arthur, when Sir Balin sought
        him, said
' What wilt thou bear?'   Balin was bold,
        and ask'd
To bear her own crown-royal upon shield,
Whereat she smiled and turn'd her to the
        King,
Who answer'd ' Thou shalt put the crown
        to use.
The crown is but the shadow of the King,
And this a shadow's shadow, let him
        have it,
So this will help him of his violences !'
' No shadow ' said Sir Balin ' O my
        Queen,
But light to me ! no shadow, O my King,
But golden earnest of a gentler life !'

    So Balin bare the crown, and all the
        knights
Approved him, and the Queen, and all
        the world
Made music, and he felt his being move
In music with his Order, and the King.

    The nightingale, full-toned in middle
        May,
Hath ever and anon a note so thin
It seems another voice in other groves ;
Thus, after some quick burst of sudden
        wrath,
The music in him seem'd to change, and
        grow
Faint and far-off.

And once he saw the thrall
His passion half had gauntleted to death,
That causer of his banishment and shame,
Smile at him, as he deem'd, presump-
tuously :
His arm half rose to strike again, but
fell :
The memory of that cognizance on shield
Weighted it down, but in himself he
moan'd :

'Too high this mount of Camelot for
me :
These high-set courtesies are not for me.
Shall I not rather prove the worse for
these ?
Fierier and stormier from restraining,
break
Into some madness ev'n before the
Queen ?'

Thus, as a hearth lit in a mountain
home,
And glancing on the window, when the
gloom
Of twilight deepens round it, seems a
flame
That rages in the woodland far below,
So when his moods were darken'd, court
and King
And all the kindly warmth of Arthur's
hall
Shadow'd an angry distance : yet he
strove
To learn the graces of their Table, fought
Hard with himself, and seem'd at length
in peace.

Then chanced, one morning, that Sir
Balin sat
Close-bower'd in that garden nigh the
hall.
A walk of roses ran from door to door ;
A walk of lilies crost it to the bower :
And down that range of roses the great
Queen
Came with slow steps, the morning on
her face ;
And all in shadow from the counter door
Sir Lancelot as to meet her, then at once,

As if he saw not, glanced aside, and
paced
The long white walk of lilies toward the
bower.
Follow'd the Queen ; Sir Balin heard her
'Prince,
Art thou so little loyal to thy Queen,
As pass without good morrow to thy
Queen ?'
To whom Sir Lancelot with his eyes on
earth,
'Fain would I still be loyal to the Queen.'
'Yea so' she said 'but so to pass me
by—
So loyal scarce is loyal to thyself,
Whom all men rate the king of courtesy.
Let be : ye stand, fair lord, as in a
dream.'

Then Lancelot with his hand among
the flowers
'Yea—for a dream. Last night me-
thought I saw
That maiden Saint who stands with lily
in hand
In yonder shrine. All round her prest
the dark,
And all the light upon her silver face
Flow'd from the spiritual lily that she
held.
Lo ! these her emblems drew mine eyes
—away :
For see, how perfect-pure ! As light a
flush
As hardly tints the blossom of the quince
Would mar their charm of stainless
maidenhood.'

'Sweeter to me' she said 'this garden
rose
Deep-hued and many-folded ! sweeter
still
The wild-wood hyacinth and the bloom
of May.
Prince, we have ridd'n before among the
flowers
In those fair days—not all as cool as
these,
Tho' season-earlier. Art thou sad ? or
sick ?

Our noble King will send thee his own
　　leech—
Sick? or for any matter anger'd at me?'

　　Then Lancelot lifted his large eyes;
　　　　they dwelt
Deep-tranced on hers, and could not fall:
　　her hue
Changed at his gaze: so turning side by
　　side
They past, and Balin started from his
　　bower.

　　'Queen? subject? but I see not what
　　　　I see.
Damsel and lover? hear not what I
　　hear.
My father hath begotten me in his wrath.
I suffer from the things before me, know,
Learn nothing; am not worthy to be
　　knight;
A churl, a clown!' and in him gloom on
　　gloom
Deepen'd: he sharply caught his lance
　　and shield,
Nor stay'd to crave permission of the
　　King,
But, mad for strange adventure, dash'd
　　away.

　　He took the selfsame track as Balan,
　　　　saw
The fountain where they sat together,
　　sigh'd
'Was I not better there with him?' and
　　rode
The skyless woods, but under open blue
Came on the hoarhead woodman at a
　　bough
Wearily hewing. 'Churl, thine axe!'
　　he cried,
Descended, and disjointed it at a blow:
To whom the woodman utter'd wonder-
　　ingly
'Lord, thou couldst lay the Devil of
　　these woods
If arm of flesh could lay him.' Balin
　　cried
'Him, or the viler devil who plays his
　　part,

To lay that devil would lay the Devil in
　　me.'
'Nay' said the churl, 'our devil is a
　　truth,
I saw the flash of him but yestereven.
And some *do* say that our Sir Garlon too
Hath learn'd black magic, and to ride
　　unseen.
Look to the cave.' But Balin answer'd
　　him
'Old fabler, these be fancies of the churl,
Look to thy woodcraft,' and so leaving
　　him,
Now with slack rein and careless of him-
　　self,
Now with dug spur and raving at him-
　　self,
Now with droopt brow down the long
　　glades he rode;
So mark'd not on his right a cavern-chasm
Yawn over darkness, where, nor far
　　within,
The whole day died, but, dying, gleam'd
　　on rocks
Roof-pendent, sharp; and others from
　　the floor,
Tusklike, arising, made that mouth of
　　night
Whereout the Demon issued up from
　　Hell.
He mark'd not this, but blind and deaf
　　to all
Save that chain'd rage, which ever yelpt
　　within,
Past eastward from the falling sun. At
　　once
He felt the hollow-beaten mosses thud
And tremble, and then the shadow of a
　　spear,
Shot from behind him, ran along the
　　ground.
Sideways he started from the path, and
　　saw,
With pointed lance as if to pierce, a
　　shape,
A light of armour by him flash, and
　　pass
And vanish in the woods; and follow'd
　　this,
But all so blind in rage that unawares

He burst his lance against a forest bough,
Dishorsed himself, and rose again, and
  fled
Far, till the castle of a King, the hall
Of Pellam, lichen-bearded, grayly draped
With streaming grass, appear'd, low-built
  but strong ;
The ruinous donjon as a knoll of moss,
The battlement overtopt with ivytods,
A home of bats, in every tower an owl.

Then spake the men of Pellam crying
  ' Lord,
Why wear ye this crown-royal upon
  shield ? '
Said Balin ' For the fairest and the best
Of ladies living gave me this to bear.'
So stall'd his horse, and strode across the
  court,
But found the greetings both of knight
  and King
Faint in the low dark hall of banquet :
  leaves
Laid their green faces flat against the
  panes,
Sprays grated, and the canker'd boughs
  without
Whined in the wood ; for all was hush'd
  within,
Till when at feast Sir Garlon likewise
  ask'd
' Why wear ye that crown-royal ? ' Balin
  said
' The Queen we worship, Lancelot, I,
  and all,
As fairest, best and purest, granted me
To bear it ! ' Such a sound (for Arthur's
  knights
Were hated strangers in the hall) as
  makes
The white swan-mother, sitting, when she
  hears
A strange knee rustle thro' her secret
  reeds,
Made Garlon, hissing ; then he sourly
  smiled.
' Fairest I grant her : I have seen ; but
  best,
Best, purest ? *thou* from Arthur's hall,
  and yet

So simple ! hast thou eyes, or if, are these
So far besotted that they fail to see
This fair wife-worship cloaks a secret
  shame ?
Truly, ye men of Arthur be but babes.'

  A goblet on the board by Balin, boss'd
With holy Joseph's legend, on his right
Stood, all of massiest bronze : one side
  had sea
And ship and sail and angels blowing on
  it :
And one was rough with wattling, and
  the walls
Of that low church he built at Glaston-
  bury.
This Balin graspt, but while in act to
  hurl,
Thro' memory of that token on the
  shield
Relax'd his hold : ' I will be gentle ' he
  thought
' And passing gentle ' caught his hand
  away
Then fiercely to Sir Garlon 'Eyes have I
That saw to-day the shadow of a spear,
Shot from behind me, run along the
  ground ;
Eyes too that long have watch'd how
  Lancelot draws
From homage to the best and purest,
  might,
Name, manhood, and a grace, but scantly
  thine,
Who, sitting in thine own hall, canst
  endure
To mouth so huge a foulness—to thy
  guest,
Me, me of Arthur's Table. Felon talk !
Let be ! no more ! '

                    But not the less by night
The scorn of Garlon, poisoning all his
  rest,
Stung him in dreams. At length, and
  dim thro' leaves
Blinkt the white morn, sprays grated,
  and old boughs
Whined in the wood. He rose, descended, met

The scorner in the castle court, and fain,
For hate and loathing, would have past
   him by ;
But when Sir Garlon utter'd mocking-
   wise ;
'What, wear ye still that same crown-
   scandalous ?'
His countenance blacken'd, and his
   forehead veins
Bloated, and branch'd ; and tearing out
   of sheath
The brand, Sir Balin with a fiery ' Ha !
So thou be shadow, here I make thee
   ghost,'
Hard upon helm smote him, and the
   blade flew
Splintering in six, and clinkt upon the
   stones.
Then Garlon, reeling slowly backward,
   fell,
And Balin by the banneret of his helm
Dragg'd him, and struck, but from the
   castle a cry
Sounded across the court, and—men-at-
   arms,
A score with pointed lances, making at
   him—
He dash'd the pummel at the foremost
   face,
Beneath a low door dipt, and made his
   feet
Wings thro' a glimmering gallery, till he
   mark'd
The portal of King Pellam's chapel wide
And inward to the wall ; he stept behind ;
Thence in a moment heard them pass
   like wolves
Howling ; but while he stared about the
   shrine,
In which he scarce could spy the Christ
   for Saints,
Beheld before a golden altar lie
The longest lance his eyes had ever seen,
Point-painted red ; and seizing thereupon
Push'd, thro' an open casement down,
   lean'd on it,
Leapt in a semicircle, and lit on earth ;
Then hand at ear, and harkening from
   what side
The blindfold rummage buried in the walls

Might echo, ran the counter path, and
   found
His charger, mounted on him and away
An arrow whizz'd to the right, one to
   the left,
One overhead ; and Pellam's feeble cry
' Stay, stay him ! he defileth heavenly
   things
With earthly uses'—made him quickly
   dive
Beneath the boughs, and race thro' many
   a mile
Of dense and open, till his goodly horse
Arising wearily at a fallen oak,
Stumbled headlong, and cast him face to
   ground.

Half-wroth he had not ended, but all
   glad,
Knightlike, to find his charger yet un-
   lamed,
Sir Balin drew the shield from off his neck,
Stared at the priceless cognizance, and
   thought
' I have shamed thee so that now thou
   shamest me,
Thee will I bear no more,' high on a
   branch
Hung it, and turn'd aside into the woods,
And there in gloom cast himself all
   along,
Moaning ' My violences, my violences !'

But now the wholesome music of the
   wood
Was dumb'd by one from out the hall of
   Mark
A damsel-errant, warbling, as she rode
The woodland alleys, Vivien, with her
   Squire.

' The fire of Heaven has kill'd the barren
   cold,
And kindled all the plain and all the
   wold.
The new leaf ever pushes off the old.
The fire of Heaven is not the flame of
   Hell.

' Old priest, who mumble worship in
   your quire—

Old monk and nun, ye scorn the world's
    desire,
Yet in your frosty cells ye feel the fire !
The fire of Heaven is not the flame of
    Hell.

   ' The fire of Heaven is on the dusty
    ways.
The wayside blossoms open to the blaze.
The whole wood-world is one full peal
    of praise.
The fire of Heaven is not the flame of
    Hell.

   ' The fire of Heaven is lord of all things
    good,
And starve not thou this fire within thy
    blood,
But follow Vivien thro' the fiery flood !
The fire of Heaven is not the flame of
    Hell !'

    Then turning to her Squire ' This fire
    of Heaven,
This old sun-worship, boy, will rise again,
And beat the cross to earth, and break
    the King
And all his Table.'

        Then they reach'd a glade,
Where under one long lane of cloudless
    air
Before another wood, the royal crown
Sparkled, and swaying upon a restless elm
Drew the vague glance of Vivien, and her
    Squire ;
Amazed were these ; ' Lo there ' she
    cried—' a crown—
Borne by some high lord - prince of
    Arthur's hall,
And there a horse ! the rider ? where is
    he ?
See, yonder lies one dead within the
    wood.
Not dead ; he stirs !—but sleeping. I
    will speak.
Hail, royal knight, we break on thy sweet
    rest,
Not, doubtless, all unearn'd by noble
    deeds.

But bounden art thou, if from Arthur's
    hall,
To help the weak. Behold, I fly from
    shame,
A lustful King, who sought to win my
    love
Thro' evil ways : the knight, with whom
    I rode,
Hath suffer'd misadventure, and my
    squire
Hath in him small defence ; but thou,
    Sir Prince,
Wilt surely guide me to the warrior King,
Arthur the blameless, pure as any maid,
To get me shelter for my maidenhood.
I charge thee by that crown upon thy
    shield,
And by the great Queen's name, arise
    and hence.'

    And Balin rose, ' Thither no more !
    nor Prince
Nor knight am I, but one that hath
    defamed
The cognizance she gave me : here I
    dwell
Savage among the savage woods, here
    die—
Die : let the wolves' black maws en-
    sepulchre
Their brother beast, whose anger was his
    lord.
O me, that such a name as Guinevere's,
Which our high Lancelot hath so lifted
    up,
And been thereby uplifted, should thro'
    me,
My violence, and my villainy, come to
    shame.'

    Thereat she suddenly laugh'd and
    shrill, anon
Sigh'd all as suddenly. Said Balin to her
' Is this thy courtesy—to mock me, ha ?
Hence, for I will not with thee.' Again
    she sigh'd
' Pardon, sweet lord ! we maidens often
    laugh
When sick at heart, when rather we
    should weep.

I knew thee wrong'd.   I brake upon thy
        rest,
And now full loth am I to break thy
        dream,
But thou art man, and canst abide a truth,
Tho' bitter.   Hither, boy—and mark
        me well.
Dost thou remember at Caerleon once—
A year ago—nay, then I love thee not—
Ay, thou rememberest well—one summer
        dawn—
By the great tower—Caerleon upon
        Usk—
Nay, truly we were hidden : this fair
        lord,
The flower of all their vestal knighthood,
        knelt
In amorous homage—knelt—what else ?
        —O ay
Knelt, and drew down from out his
        night-black hair
And mumbled that white hand whose
        ring'd caress
Had wander'd from her own King's
        golden head,
And lost itself in darkness, till she
        cried—
I thought the great tower would crash
        down on both—
" Rise, my sweet King, and kiss me on
        the lips,
Thou art my King."   This lad, whose
        lightest word
Is mere white truth in simple nakedness,
Saw them embrace : he reddens, cannot
        speak,
So bashful, he ! but all the maiden Saints,
The deathless mother-maidenhood of
        Heaven,
Cry out upon her.   Up then, ride with
        me !
Talk not of shame ! thou canst not, an
        thou would'st,
Do these more shame than these have
        done themselves.'

   She lied with ease ; but horror-stricken
        he,
Remembering that dark bower at Camelot,
Breathed in a dismal whisper ' It is truth.'

Sunnily she smiled ' And even in this
        lone wood,
Sweet lord, ye do right well to whisper
        this.
Fools prate, and perish traitors.   Woods
        have tongues,
As walls have ears : but thou shalt go
        with me,
And we will speak at first exceeding
        low.
Meet is it the good King be not deceived.
See now, I set thee high on vantage
        ground,
From whence to watch the time, and
        eagle-like
Stoop at thy will on Lancelot and the
        Queen.'

   She ceased ; his evil spirit upon him
        leapt,
He ground his teeth together, sprang
        with a yell,
Tore from the branch, and cast on earth,
        the shield,
Drove his mail'd heel athwart the royal
        crown,
Stampt all into defacement, hurl'd it from
        him
Among the forest weeds, and cursed the
        tale,
The told-of, and the teller.

                                        That weird yell,
Unearthlier than all shriek of bird or
        beast,
Thrill'd thro' the woods ; and Balan
        lurking there
(His quest was unaccomplish'd) heard
        and thought
' The scream of that Wood-devil I came
        to quell ! '
Then nearing ' Lo ! he hath slain some
        brother-knight,
And tramples on the goodly shield to
        show
His loathing of our Order and the Queen.
My quest, meseems, is here.   Or devil
        or man
Guard thou thine head.'   Sir Balin spake
        not word,

But snatch'd a sudden buckler from the
  Squire,
And vaulted on his horse, and so they
  crash'd
In onset, and King Pellam's holy spear,
Reputed to be red with sinless blood,
Redden'd at once with sinful, for the
  point
Across the maiden shield of Balan prick'd
The hauberk to the flesh; and Balin's
  horse
Was wearied to the death, and, when
  they clash'd,
Rolling back upon Balin, crush'd the man
Inward, and either fell, and swoon'd
  away.

  Then to her Squire mutter'd the
    damsel 'Fools!
This fellow hath wrought some foulness
  with his Queen:
Else never had he borne her crown, nor
  raved
And thus foam'd over at a rival name:
But thou, Sir Chick, that scarce hast
  broken shell,
Art yet half-yolk, not even come to
  down—
Who never sawest Caerleon upon Usk—
And yet hast often pleaded for my love—
See what I see, be thou where I have
  been,
Or else Sir Chick—dismount and loose
  their casques
I fain would know what manner of men
  they be.'
And when the Squire had loosed them,
  'Goodly!—look!
They might have cropt the myriad flower
  of May,
And butt each other here, like brainless
  bulls,
Dead for one heifer!'

                  Then the gentle Squire
'I hold them happy, so they died for
  love:
And, Vivien, tho' ye beat me like your
  dog,
I too could die, as now I live, for thee.'

'Live on, Sir Boy,' she cried. 'I
  better prize
The living dog than the dead lion: away!
I cannot brook to gaze upon the dead.'
Then leapt her palfrey o'er the fallen oak,
And bounding forward 'Leave them to
  the wolves.'

But when their foreheads felt the cool-
  ing air,
Balin first woke, and seeing that true face,
Familiar up from cradle-time, so wan,
Crawl'd slowly with low moans to where
  he lay,
And on his dying brother cast himself
Dying; and *he* lifted faint eyes; he felt
One near him; all at once they found the
  world,
Staring wild-wide; then with a childlike
  wail,
And drawing down the dim disastrous
  brow
That o'er him hung, he kiss'd it, moan'd
  and spake;

'O Balin, Balin, I that fain had died
To save thy life, have brought thee to thy
  death.
Why had ye not the shield I knew? and
  why
Trampled ye thus on that which bare the
  Crown?'

Then Balin told him brokenly, and in
  gasps,
All that had chanced, and Balan moan'd
  again.

'Brother, I dwelt a day in Pellam's
  hall:
This Garlon mock'd me, but I heeded
  not.
And one said "Eat in peace! a liar is he,
And hates thee for the tribute!" this
  good knight
Told me, that twice a wanton damsel
  came,
And sought for Garlon at the castle-gates,
Whom Pellam drove away with holy
  heat.

I well believe this damsel, and the one
Who stood beside thee even now, the
        same.
" She dwells among the woods " he said
        " and meets
And dallies with him in the Mouth of
        Hell."
Foul are their lives ; foul are their lips ;
        they lied.
Pure as our own true Mother is our
        Queen.'

' O brother ' answer'd Balin ' woe is
        me !
My madness all thy life has been thy
        doom,
Thy curse, and darken'd all thy day ;
        and now
The night has come. I scarce can see
        thee now.
Goodnight ! for we shall never bid again
Goodmorrow—Dark my doom was here,
        and dark
It will be there. I see thee now no
        more.
I would not mine again should darken
        thine,
Goodnight, true brother.'

                    Balan answer'd low
' Goodnight, true brother here ! good-
        morrow there !
We two were born together, and we
        die
Together by one doom :' and while he
        spoke
Closed his death-drowsing eyes, and slept
        the sleep
With Balin, either lock'd in either's arm.

MERLIN AND VIVIEN.

A STORM was coming, but the winds
        were still,
And in the wild woods of Broceliande,
Before an oak, so hollow, huge and old
It look'd a tower of ivied masonwork,
At Merlin's feet the wily Vivien lay.

For he that always bare in bitter
        grudge
The slights of Arthur and his Table, Mark
The Cornish King, had heard a wandering
        voice,
A minstrel of Caerleon by strong storm
Blown into shelter at Tintagil, say
That out of naked knightlike purity
Sir Lancelot worship no unmarried girl
But the great Queen herself, fought in her
        name,
Sware by her—vows like theirs, that high
        in heaven
Love most, but neither marry, nor are
        given
In marriage, angels of our Lord's report.

He ceased, and then — for Vivien
        sweetly said
(She sat beside the banquet nearest Mark),
' And is the fair example follow'd, Sir,
In Arthur's household ?'—answer'd inno
        cently :

' Ay, by some few—ay, truly—youths
        that hold
It more beseems the perfect virgin knight
To worship woman as true wife beyond
All hopes of gaining, than as maiden girl.
They place their pride in Lancelot and
        the Queen.
So passionate for an utter purity
Beyond the limit of their bond, are these
For Arthur bound them not to singleness
Brave hearts and clean ! and yet—God
        guide them—young.'

Then Mark was half in heart to hurl
        his cup
Straight at the speaker, but forbore : he
        rose
To leave the hall, and, Vivien following
        him,
Turn'd to her : ' Here are snakes within
        the grass ;
And you methinks, O Vivien, save ye fear
The monkish manhood, and the mask of
        pure
Worn by this court, can stir them till they
        sting.'

And Vivien answer'd, smiling scorn-
fully,
'Why fear? because that foster'd at *thy*
court
I savour of thy—virtues? fear them? no.
As Love, if Love be perfect, casts out
fear,
So Hate, if Hate be perfect, casts out
fear.
My father died in battle against the King,
My mother on his corpse in open field;
She bore me there, for born from death
was I
Among the dead and sown upon the
wind—
And then on thee! and shown the truth
betimes,
That old true filth, and bottom of the well,
Where Truth is hidden.   Gracious lessons
thine
And maxims of the mud!   "This Arthur
pure!
Great Nature thro' the flesh herself hath
made
Gives him the lie!   There is no being
pure,
My cherub; saith not Holy Writ the
same?"—
If I were Arthur, I would have thy blood.
Thy blessing, stainless King!   I bring
thee back,
When I have ferreted out their burrow-
ings,
The hearts of all this Order in mine
hand—
Ay—so that fate and craft and folly close,
Perchance, one curl of Arthur's golden
beard.
To me this narrow grizzled fork of thine
Is cleaner-fashion'd—Well, I loved thee
first,
That warps the wit.'

Loud laugh'd the graceless Mark.
But Vivien, into Camelot stealing, lodged
Low in the city, and on a festal day
When Guinevere was crossing the great
hall
Cast herself down, knelt to the Queen,
and wail'd.

'Why kneel ye there?   What evil have
ye wrought?
Rise!' and the damsel bidden rise arose
And stood with folded hands and down-
ward eyes
Of glancing corner, and all meekly said,
'None wrought, but suffer'd much, an
orphan maid!
My father died in battle for thy King,
My mother on his corpse—in open field,
The sad sea-sounding wastes of Lyonesse—
Poor wretch—no friend!—and now by
Mark the King
For that small charm of feature mine,
pursued—
If any such be mine—I fly to thee.
Save, save me thou—Woman of women—
thine
The wreath of beauty, thine the crown of
power,
Be thine the balm of pity, O Heaven's
own white
Earth-angel, stainless bride of stainless
King—
Help, for he follows! take me to thyself!
O yield me shelter for mine innocency
Among thy maidens!'

Here her slow sweet eyes
Fear-tremulous, but humbly hopeful, rose
Fixt on her hearer's, while the Queen
who stood
All glittering like May sunshine on May
leaves
In green and gold, and plumed with green
replied,
'Peace, child! of overpraise and over-
blame
We choose the last.   Our noble Arthur,
him
Ye scarce can overpraise, will hear and
know.
Nay—we believe all evil of thy Mark—
Well, we shall test thee farther; but this
hour
We ride a-hawking with Sir Lancelot.
He hath given us a fair falcon which he
train'd;
We go to prove it.   Bide ye here the
while.'

She past ; and Vivien murmur'd after
'Go !
I bide the while.'   Then thro' the portal-
arch
Peering askance, and muttering broken-
wise,
As one that labours with an evil dream,
Beheld the Queen and Lancelot get to
horse.

' Is that the Lancelot? goodly—ay, but
gaunt :
Courteous—amends for gauntness—takes
her hand—
That glance of theirs, but for the street,
had been
A clinging kiss—how hand lingers in
hand !
Let go at last !—they ride away—to hawk
For waterfowl.   Royaller game is mine.
For such a supersensual sensual bond
As that gray cricket chirpt of at our
hearth—
Touch flax with flame—a glance will serve
—the liars !
Ah little rat that borest in the dyke
Thy hole by night to let the boundless
deep
Down upon far-off cities while they
dance—
Or dream—of thee they dream'd not—
nor of me
These—ay, but each of either : ride, and
dream
The mortal dream that never yet was
mine—
Ride, ride and dream until ye wake—to
me !
Then, narrow court and lubber King,
farewell !
For Lancelot will be gracious to the rat,
And our wise Queen, if knowing that I
know,
Will hate, loathe, fear—but honour me
the more.'

Yet while they rode together down the
plain,
Their talk was all of training, terms of art,
Diet and seeling, jesses, leash and lure.

' She is too noble ' he said ' to check at
pies,
Nor will she rake : there is no baseness
in her.'
Here when the Queen demanded as by
chance
' Know ye the stranger woman ?' ' Let
her be,'
Said Lancelot and unhooded casting off
The goodly falcon free ; she tower'd ;
her bells,
Tone under tone, shrill'd ; and they lifted
up
Their eager faces, wondering at the
strength,
Boldness and royal knighthood of the bird
Who pounced her quarry and slew it.
Many a time
As once—of old—among the flowers—
they rode.

But Vivien half-forgotten of the Queen
Among her damsels broidering sat, heard,
watch'd
And whisper'd : thro' the peaceful court
she crept
And whisper'd : then as Arthur in the
highest
Leaven'd the world, so Vivien in the
lowest,
Arriving at a time of golden rest,
And sowing one ill hint from ear to ear,
While all the heathen lay at Arthur's feet,
And no quest came, but all was joust and
play,
Leaven'd his hall.   They heard and let
her be.

Thereafter as an enemy that has left
Death in the living waters, and with-
drawn,
The wily Vivien stole from Arthur's court.

She hated all the knights, and heard in
thought
Their lavish comment when her name
was named.
For once, when Arthur walking all alone,
Vext at a rumour issued from herself
Of some corruption crept among his
knights,

Had met her, Vivien, being greeted fair,
Would fain have wrought upon his cloudy
    mood
With reverent eyes mock-loyal, shaken
    voice,
And flutter'd adoration, and at last
With dark sweet hints of some who
    prized him more
Than who should prize him most; at
    which the King
Had gazed upon her blankly and gone by:
But one had watch'd, and had not held
    his peace:
It made the laughter of an afternoon
That Vivien should attempt the blameless
    King.
And after that, she set herself to gain
Him, the most famous man of all those
    times,
Merlin, who knew the range of all their
    arts,
Had built the King his havens, ships,
    and halls,
Was also Bard, and knew the starry
    heavens;
The people call'd him Wizard; whom at
    first
She play'd about with slight and sprightly
    talk,
And vivid smiles, and faintly-venom'd
    points
Of slander, glancing here and grazing
    there;
And yielding to his kindlier moods, the
    Seer
Would watch her at her petulance, and
    play,
Ev'n when they seem'd unloveable, and
    laugh
As those that watch a kitten; thus he
    grew
Tolerant of what he half disdain'd, and
    she,
Perceiving that she was but half disdain'd,
Began to break her sports with graver fits,
Turn red or pale, would often when they
    met
Sigh fully, or all-silent gaze upon him
With such a fixt devotion, that the old
    man,

Tho' doubtful, felt the flattery, and at
    times
Would flatter his own wish in age for love,
And half believe her true: for thus at
    times
He waver'd; but that other clung to him,
Fixt in her will, and so the seasons went.

    Then fell on Merlin a great melancholy;
He walk'd with dreams and darkness,
    and he found
A doom that ever poised itself to fall,
An ever-moaning battle in the mist,
World-war of dying flesh against the life,
Death in all life and lying in all love,
The meanest having power upon the
    highest,
And the high purpose broken by the
    worm.

    So leaving Arthur's court he gain'd the
    beach;
There found a little boat, and stept into
    it;
And Vivien follow'd, but he mark'd her
    not.
She took the helm and he the sail; the
    boat
Drave with a sudden wind across the
    deeps,
And touching Breton sands, they dis-
    embark'd.
And then she follow'd Merlin all the way,
Ev'n to the wild woods of Broceliande.
For Merlin once had told her of a charm,
The which if any wrought on anyone
With woven paces and with waving arms,
The man so wrought on ever seem'd to lie
Closed in the four walls of a hollow tower,
From which was no escape for evermore;
And none could find that man for ever-
    more,
Nor could he see but him who wrought
    the charm
Coming and going, and he lay as dead
And lost to life and use and name and
    fame.
And Vivien ever sought to work the
    charm
Upon the great Enchanter of the Time,

As fancying that her glory would be great
According to his greatness whom she
    quench'd.

    There lay she all her length and kiss'd
        his feet,
As if in deepest reverence and in love.
A twist of gold was round her hair; a
    robe
Of samite without price, that more exprest
Than hid her, clung about her lissome
    limbs,
In colour like the satin-shining palm
On sallows in the windy gleams of March:
And while she kiss'd them, crying,
    'Trample me,
Dear feet, that I have follow'd thro' the
    world,
And I will pay you worship; tread me
    down
And I will kiss you for it;' he was mute:
So dark a forethought roll'd about his
    brain,
As on a dull day in an Ocean cave
The blind wave feeling round his long
    sea-hall
In silence: wherefore, when she lifted up
A face of sad appeal, and spake and said,
'O Merlin, do ye love me?' and again,
'O Merlin, do ye love me?' and once
    more,
'Great Master, do ye love me?' he was
    mute.
And lissome Vivien, holding by his heel,
Writhed toward him, slided up his knee
    and sat,
Behind his ankle twined her hollow feet
Together, curved an arm about his neck,
Clung like a snake; and letting her left
    hand
Droop from his mighty shoulder, as a leaf,
Made with her right a comb of pearl to
    part
The lists of such a beard as youth gone out
Had left in ashes: then he spoke and said,
Not looking at her, 'Who are wise in love
Love most, say least,' and Vivien an-
    swer'd quick,
'I saw the little elf-god eyeless once
In Arthur's arras hall at Camelot:

But neither eyes nor tongue—O stupid
    child !
Yet you are wise who say it; let me think
Silence is wisdom: I am silent then,
And ask no kiss;' then adding all at once,
'And lo, I clothe myself with wisdom,
    drew
The vast and shaggy mantle of his beard
Across her neck and bosom to her knee,
And call'd herself a gilded summer fly
Caught in a great old tyrant spider's web,
Who meant to eat her up in that wild
    wood
Without one word. So Vivien call'd
    herself,
But rather seem'd a lovely baleful star
Veil'd in gray vapour; till he sadly
    smiled:
'To what request for what strange boon,'
    he said,
'Are these your pretty tricks and fooleries,
O Vivien, the preamble? yet my thanks,
For these have broken up my melancholy.'

    And Vivien answer'd smiling saucily,
'What, O my Master, have ye found
    your voice?
I bid the stranger welcome. Thanks at
    last !
But yesterday you never open'd lip,
Except indeed to drink: no cup had we:
In mine own lady palms I cull'd the
    spring
That gather'd trickling dropwise from
    the cleft,
And made a pretty cup of both my hands
And offer'd you it kneeling: then you
    drank
And knew no more, nor gave me one
    poor word ;
O no more thanks than might a goat have
    given
With no more sign of reverence than a
    beard.
And when we halted at that other well,
And I was faint to swooning, and you lay
Foot-gilt with all the blossom-dust of
    those
Deep meadows we had traversed, did
    you know

at Vivien bathed your feet before her
own?
d yet no thanks: and all thro' this
wild wood
d all this morning when I fondled you:
on, ay, there was a boon, one not so
strange—
w had I wrong'd you? surely ye are
wise,
: such a silence is more wise than
kind.'

And Merlin lock'd his hand in hers
and said:
did ye never lie upon the shore,
d watch the curl'd white of the coming
wave
ss'd in the slippery sand before it
breaks?
n such a wave, but not so pleasurable,
rk in the glass of some presageful mood,
d I for three days seen, ready to fall.
d then I rose and fled from Arthur's
court
break the mood. You follow'd me
unask'd;
d when I look'd, and saw you following still,
mind involved yourself the nearest
thing
that mind-mist: for shall I tell you
truth?
a seem'd that wave about to break upon
me
d sweep me from my hold upon the
world,
use and name and fame. Your pardon,
child.
ir pretty sports have brighten'd all
again.
d ask your boon, for boon I owe you
thrice,
ce for wrong done you by confusion,
next
thanks it seems till now neglected,
last
these your dainty gambols: wherefore
ask;
d take this boon so strange and not so
strange.'

And Vivien answer'd smiling mourn-
fully:
'O not so strange as my long asking it,
Not yet so strange as you yourself are
strange,
Nor half so strange as that dark mood of
yours.
I ever fear'd ye were not wholly mine;
And see, yourself have own'd ye did me
wrong.
The people call you prophet: let it be:
But not of those that can expound them-
selves.
Take Vivien for expounder; she will call
That three-days-long presageful gloom of
yours
No presage, but the same mistrustful mood
That makes you seem less noble than
yourself,
Whenever I have ask'd this very boon,
Now ask'd again: for see you not, dear
love,
That such a mood as that, which lately
gloom'd
Your fancy when ye saw me following
you,
Must make me fear still more you are not
mine,
Must make me yearn still more to prove
you mine,
And make me wish still more to learn
this charm
Of woven paces and of waving hands,
As proof of trust. O Merlin, teach it me.
The charm so taught will charm us both
to rest.
For, grant me some slight power upon
your fate,
I, feeling that you felt me worthy trust,
Should rest and let you rest, knowing you
mine.
And therefore be as great as ye are named,
Not muffled round with selfish reticence.
How hard you look and how denyingly!
O, if you think this wickedness in me,
That I should prove it on you unawares,
That makes me passing wrathful; then
our bond
Had best be loosed for ever: but think
or not,

By Heaven that hears I tell you the clean
    truth,
As clean as blood of babes, as white as
    milk :
O Merlin, may this earth, if ever I,
If these unwitty wandering wits of mine,
Ev'n in the jumbled rubbish of a dream,
Have tript on such conjectural treachery—
May this hard earth cleave to the Nadir
    hell
Down, down, and close again, and nip
    me flat,
If I be such a traitress. Yield my boon,
Till which I scarce can yield you all I am ;
And grant my re-reiterated wish,
The great proof of your love : because I
    think,
However wise, ye hardly know me yet.'

And Merlin loosed his hand from hers
    and said,
'I never was less wise, however wise,
Too curious Vivien, tho' you talk of trust,
Than when I told you first of such a
    charm.
Yea, if ye talk of trust I tell you this,
Too much I trusted when I told you that,
And stirr'd this vice in you which ruin'd
    man
Thro' woman the first hour ; for howsoe'er
In children a great curiousness be well,
Who have to learn themselves and all the
    world,
In you, that are no child, for still I find
Your face is practised when I spell the
    lines,
I call it,—well, I will not call it vice :
But since you name yourself the summer
    fly,
I well could wish a cobweb for the gnat,
That settles, beaten back, and beaten back
Settles, till one could yield for weariness :
But since I will not yield to give you power
Upon my life and use and name and fame,
Why will ye never ask some other boon ?
Yea, by God's rood, I trusted you too much.'

And Vivien, like the tenderest-hearted
    maid
That ever bided tryst at village stile,

Made answer, either eyelid wet with tea[rs]
'Nay, Master, be not wrathful with y[our]
    maid ;
Caress her : let her feel herself forgive[n]
Who feels no heart to ask another boo[n]
I think ye hardly know the tender rhy[me]
Of "trust me not at all or all in all."[s]
I heard the great Sir Lancelot sing it on[ce]
And it shall answer for me. Listen to[

"In Love, if Love be Love, if L[ove]
    be ours,
Faith and unfaith can ne'er be eq[ual]
    powers :
Unfaith in aught is want of faith in all[

"It is the little rift within the lute,
That by and by will make the music mu[te]
And ever widening slowly silence all.

"The little rift within the lover's lu[te]
Or little pitted speck in garner'd fruit,
That rotting inward slowly moulders a[ll]

"It is not worth the keeping : let it g[o]
But shall it ? answer, darling, answer, [no]
And trust me not at all or all in all."

O Master, do ye love my tender rhym[e]

And Merlin look'd and half believ[ed]
    her true,
So tender was her voice, so fair her fa[ce]
So sweetly gleam'd her eyes behind [her]
    tears
Like sunlight on the plain behind [a]
    shower :
And yet he answer'd half indignantly :

'Far other was the song that onc[e I]
    heard
By this huge oak, sung nearly where we s[at]
For here we met, some ten or twelve of [us]
To chase a creature that was current th[ere]
In these wild woods, the hart with gold[en]
    horns.
It was the time when first the quest[ion]
    rose
About the founding of a Table Round[
That was to be, for love of God and m[en]
And noble deeds, the flower of all [the]
    world.

each incited each to noble deeds.
while we waited; one, the youngest
of us,
could not keep him silent, out he
flash'd,
into such a song, such fire for fame,
trumpet-blowings in it, coming down
such a stern and iron-clashing close,
t when he stopt we long'd to hurl
together,
should have done it; but the beauteous beast
red by the noise upstarted at our feet,
like a silver shadow slipt away
o' the dim land; and all day long we
rode
o' the dim land against a rushing
wind,
t glorious roundel echoing in our
ears,
chased the flashes of his golden horns
il they vanish'd by the fairy well
t laughs at iron—as our warriors did—
ere children cast their pins and nails,
and cry,
augh, little well!" but touch it with
a sword,
uzzes fiercely round the point; and
there
lost him: such a noble song was that.
, Vivien, when you sang me that sweet
rhyme,
t as tho' you knew this cursed charm,
e proving it on me, and that I lay
felt them slowly ebbing, name and
fame.'

nd Vivien answer'd smiling mourn-
fully:
mine have ebb'd away for evermore,
all thro' following you to this wild
wood,
ause I saw you sad, to comfort you.
now, what hearts have men! they
never mount
igh as woman in her selfless mood.
touching fame, howe'er ye scorn my
song,
e one verse more—the lady speaks it
—this:

' "My name, once mine, now thine, is
closelier mine,
For fame, could fame be mine, that fame
were thine,
And shame, could shame be thine, that
shame were mine.
So trust me not at all or all in all."

'Says she not well? and there is more
—this rhyme
Is like the fair pearl-necklace of the
Queen,
That burst in dancing, and the pearls
were spilt;
Some lost, some stolen, some as relics
kept.
But nevermore the same two sister pearls
Ran down the silken thread to kiss each
other
On her white neck—so is it with this
rhyme:
It lives dispersedly in many hands,
And every minstrel sings it differently;
Yet is there one true line, the pearl of
pearls:
"Man dreams of Fame while woman
wakes to love."
Yea! Love, tho' Love were of the gross-
est, carves
A portion from the solid present, eats
And uses, careless of the rest; but Fame,
The Fame that follows death is nothing
to us;
And what is Fame in life but half-disfame,
And counterchanged with darkness? ye
yourself
Know well that Envy calls you Devil's
son,
And since ye seem the Master of all Art,
They fain would make you Master of all
vice.'

And Merlin lock'd his hand in hers and
said,
'I once was looking for a magic weed,
And found a fair young squire who sat
alone,
Had carved himself a knightly shield of
wood,
And then was painting on it fancied arms,

Azure, an Eagle rising or, the Sun
In dexter chief; the scroll "I follow
    fame."
And speaking not, but leaning over him,
I took his brush and blotted out the bird,
And made a Gardener putting in a graff,
With this for motto, "Rather use than
    fame."
You should have seen him blush; but
    afterwards
He made a stalwart knight. O Vivien,
For you, methinks you think you love me
    well;
For me, I love you somewhat; rest: and
    Love
Should have some rest and pleasure in
    himself,
Not ever be too curious for a boon,
Too prurient for a proof against the grain
Of him ye say ye love: but Fame with
    men,
Being but ampler means to serve man-
    kind,
Should have small rest or pleasure in
    herself,
But work as vassal to the larger love,
That dwarfs the petty love of one to one.
Use gave me Fame at first, and Fame
    again
Increasing gave me use. Lo, there my
    boon!
What other? for men sought to prove me
    vile,
Because I fain had given them greater
    wits:
And then did Envy call me Devil's son:
The sick weak beast seeking to help her-
    self
By striking at her better, miss'd, and
    brought
Her own claw back, and wounded her
    own heart.
Sweet were the days when I was all un-
    known,
But when my name was lifted up, the
    storm
Brake on the mountain and I cared not
    for it.
Right well know I that Fame is half-
    disfame,

Yet needs must work my work. Th
    other fame,
To one at least, who hath not childre
    vague,
The cackle of the unborn about the gra
I cared not for it: a single misty star,
Which is the second in a line of stars
That seem a sword beneath a belt of thr
I never gazed upon it but I dreamt
Of some vast charm concluded in that s
To make fame nothing. Wherefore, i
    fear,
Giving you power upon me thro' t
    charm,
That you might play me falsely, havi
    power,
However well ye think ye love me no
(As sons of kings loving in pupilage
Have turn'd to tyrants when they ca
    to power)
I rather dread the loss of use than fam
If you—and not so much from wickedne
As some wild turn of anger, or a moo
Of overstrain'd affection, it may be,
To keep me all to your own self,—or e
A sudden spurt of woman's jealousy,—
Should try this charm on whom ye say
    love.'

    And Vivien answer'd smiling as
    wrath:
'Have I not sworn? I am not truste
    Good!
Well, hide it, hide it; I shall find it ot
And being found take heed of Vivien.
A woman and not trusted, doubtless I
Might feel some sudden turn of anger be
Of your misfaith; and your fine epithe
Is accurate too, for this full love of m
Without the full heart back may merit w
Your term of overstrain'd. So used as
My daily wonder is, I love at all.
And as to woman's jealousy, O why ne
O to what end, except a jealous one,
And one to make me jealous if I love,
Was this fair charm invented by yourse
I well believe that all about this worl
Ye cage a buxom captive here and the
Closed in the four walls of a hollow to
From which is no escape for evermore

Then the great Master merrily answer'd her :
all many a love in loving youth was mine ;
eeded then no charm to keep them mine
: youth and love ; and that full heart
 of yours
ereof ye prattle, may now assure you
 mine ;
 live uncharm'd. For those who
 wrought it first,
e wrist is parted from the hand that
 waved,
e feet unmortised from their ankle-
 bones
o paced it, ages back : but will ye hear
e legend as in guerdon for your rhyme?

There lived a king in the most Eastern
 East,
ss old than I, yet older, for my blood
th earnest in it of far springs to be.
awny pirate anchor'd in his port,
ose bark had plunder'd twenty nameless isles ;
d passing one, at the high peep of
 dawn,
 saw two cities in a thousand boats
 fighting for a woman on the sea.
d pushing his black craft among them
 all,
 lightly scatter'd theirs and brought
 her off,
ith loss of half his people arrow-slain ;
maid so smooth, so white, so wonderful,
ey said a light came from her when she
 moved :
d since the pirate would not yield her
 up,
e King impaled him for his piracy ;
en made her Queen : but those isle-
 nurtured eyes
aged such unwilling tho' successful war
 all the youth, they sicken'd ; councils
 thinn'd,
d armies waned, for magnet-like she
 drew
e rustiest iron of old fighters' hearts ;
d beasts themselves would worship ;
 camels knelt

Unbidden, and the brutes of mountain
 back
That carry kings in castles, bow'd black
 knees
Of homage, ringing with their serpent
 hands,
To make her smile, her golden ankle-bells.
What wonder, being jealous, that he sent
His horns of proclamation out thro' all
The hundred under-kingdoms that he
 sway'd
To find a wizard who might teach the King
Some charm, which being wrought upon
 the Queen
Might keep her all his own : to such a one
He promised more than ever king has
 given,
A league of mountain full of golden mines,
A province with a hundred miles of coast,
A palace and a princess, all for him :
But on all those who tried and fail'd, the
 King
Pronounced a dismal sentence, meaning
 by it
To keep the list low and pretenders back,
Or like a king, not to be trifled with—
Their heads should moulder on the city
 gates.
And many tried and fail'd, because the
 charm
Of nature in her overbore their own :
And many a wizard brow bleach'd on the
 walls :
And many weeks a troop of carrion crows
Hung like a cloud above the gateway
 towers.'

And Vivien breaking in upon him, said :
'I sit and gather honey ; yet, methinks,
Thy tongue has tript a little : ask thyself.
The lady never made *unwilling* war
With those fine eyes : she had her pleasure
 in it,
And made her good man jealous with good
 cause.
And lived there neither dame nor damsel
 then
Wroth at a lover's loss ? were all as tame,
I mean, as noble, as their Queen was fair?
Not one to flirt a venom at her eyes,

Or pinch a murderous dust into her drink,
Or make her paler with a poison'd rose?
Well, those were not our days: but did they find
A wizard? Tell me, was he like to thee?'

She ceased, and made her lithe arm round his neck
Tighten, and then drew back, and let her eyes
Speak for her, glowing on him, like a bride's
On her new lord, her own, the first of men.

He answer'd laughing, ' Nay, not like to me.
At last they found — his foragers for charms—
A little glassy-headed hairless man,
Who lived alone in a great wild on grass;
Read but one book, and ever reading grew
So grated down and filed away with thought,
So lean his eyes were monstrous; while the skin
Clung but to crate and basket, ribs and spine.
And since he kept his mind on one sole aim,
Nor ever touch'd fierce wine, nor tasted flesh,
Nor own'd a sensual wish, to him the wall
That sunders ghosts and shadow-casting men
Became a crystal, and he saw them thro' it,
And heard their voices talk behind the wall,
And learnt their elemental secrets, powers
And forces; often o'er the sun's bright eye
Drew the vast eyelid of an inky cloud,
And lash'd it at the base with slanting storm;
Or in the noon of mist and driving rain,
When the lake whiten'd and the pinewood roar'd,
And the cairn'd mountain was a shadow, sunn'd
The world to peace again: here was the man.

And so by force they dragg'd him to King.
And then he taught the King to cha
In such-wise, that no man could see more,
Nor saw she save the King, who wrou the charm,
Coming and going, and she lay as dea
And lost all use of life: but when the K
Made proffer of the league of golden min
The province with a hundred miles of coa
The palace and the princess, that old n
Went back to his old wild, and lived grass,
And vanish'd, and his book came do to me.'

And Vivien answer'd smiling sauci
' Ye have the book: the charm is writ in it:
Good: take my counsel: let me knov at once:
For keep it like a puzzle chest in ches
With each chest lock'd and padloc thirty-fold,
And whelm all this beneath as vas mound
As after furious battle turfs the slain
On some wild down above the windy de
I yet should strike upon a sudden me
To dig, pick, open, find and read charm:
Then, if I tried it, who should blame then?'

And smiling as a master smiles at
That is not of his school, nor any sch
But that where blind and naked Ignora
Delivers brawling judgments, unasham
On all things all day long, he answer'd h

' Thou read the book, my pretty Vivi
O ay, it is but twenty pages long,
But every page having an ample marg
And every marge enclosing in the mic
A square of text that looks a little blc
The text no larger than the limbs of fle
And every square of text an awful cha
Writ in a language that has long gone
So long, that mountains have arisen si

With cities on their flanks—thou read the
book !
And every margin scribbled, crost, and
cramm'd
With comment, densest condensation, hard
To mind and eye ; but the long sleepless
nights
Of my long life have made it easy to me.
And none can read the text, not even I ;
And none can read the comment but
myself :
And in the comment did I find the charm.
O, the results are simple ; a mere child
Might use it to the harm of anyone,
And never could undo it : ask no more :
For tho' you should not prove it upon me,
But keep that oath ye sware, ye might,
perchance,
Assay it on some one of the Table Round,
And all because ye dream they babble of
you.'

And Vivien, frowning in true anger,
said :
'What dare the full-fed liars say of me ?
They ride abroad redressing human
wrongs !
They sit with knife in meat and wine in
horn !
They bound to holy vows of chastity !
Were I not woman, I could tell a tale.
But you are man, you well can understand
The shame that cannot be explain'd for
shame.
Not one of all the drove should touch me :
swine !'

Then answer'd Merlin careless of her
words :
'You breathe but accusation vast and
vague,
Spleen-born, I think, and proofless. If
ye know,
Set up the charge ye know, to stand or
fall !'

And Vivien answer'd frowning wrath-
fully :
'O ay, what say ye to Sir Valence, him
Whose kinsman left him watcher o'er his
wife

And two fair babes, and went to distant
lands ;
Was one year gone, and on returning found
Not two but three ? there lay the reckling,
one
But one hour old ! What said the happy
sire ?
A seven-months' babe had been a truer gift.
Those twelve sweet moons confused his
fatherhood.'

Then answer'd Merlin, 'Nay, I know
the tale.
Sir Valence wedded with an outland dame :
Some cause had kept him sunder'd from
his wife :
One child they had : it lived with her :
she died :
His kinsman travelling on his own affair
Was charged by Valence to bring home
the child.
He brought, not found it therefore : take
the truth.'

'O ay,' said Vivien, 'overtrue a tale.
What say ye then to sweet Sir Sagramore,
That ardent man ? "to pluck the flower
in season,"
So says the song, "I trow it is no treason."
O Master, shall we call him overquick
To crop his own sweet rose before the
hour ?'

And Merlin answer'd, 'Overquick art
thou
To catch a loathly plume fall'n from the
wing
Of that foul bird of rapine whose whole
prey
Is man's good name : he never wrong'd
his bride.
I know the tale. An angry gust of wind
Puff'd out his torch among the myriad-
room'd
And many-corridor'd complexities
Of Arthur's palace : then he found a door,
And darkling felt the sculptured ornament
That wreathen round it made it seem his
own ;
And wearied out made for the couch and
slept,

A stainless man beside a stainless maid ;
And either slept, nor knew of other there ;
Till the high dawn piercing the royal rose
In Arthur's casement glimmer'd chastely
          down,
Blushing upon them blushing, and at once
He rose without a word and parted from
          her :
But when the thing was blazed about the
          court,
The brute world howling forced them into
          bonds,
And as it chanced they are happy, being
          pure.'

    'O ay,' said Vivien, 'that were likely
          too.
What say ye then to fair Sir Percivale
And of the horrid foulness that he wrought,
The saintly youth, the spotless lamb of
          Christ,
Or some black wether of St. Satan's fold.
What, in the precincts of the chapel-yard,
Among the knightly brasses of the graves,
And by the cold Hic Jacets of the dead !'

    And Merlin answer'd careless of her
          charge,
'A sober man is Percivale and pure ;
But once in life was fluster'd with new
          wine,
Then paced for coolness in the chapel-
          yard ;
Where one of Satan's shepherdesses caught
And meant to stamp him with her master's
          mark ;
And that he sinn'd is not believable ;
For, look upon his face !—but if he sinn'd,
The sin that practice burns into the blood,
And not the one dark hour which brings
          remorse,
Will brand us, after, of whose fold we be :
Or else were he, the holy king, whose
          hymns
Are chanted in the minster, worse than all.
But is your spleen froth'd out, or have ye
          more ?'

    And Vivien answer'd frowning yet in
          wrath :
'O ay ; what say ye to Sir Lancelot, friend

Traitor or true ? that commerce with the
          Queen,
I ask you, is it clamour'd by the child,
Or whisper'd in the corner ? do ye know
          it ?'

    To which he answer'd sadly, 'Yea, I
          know it.
Sir Lancelot went ambassador, at first,
To fetch her, and she watch'd him from
          her walls.
A rumour runs, she took him for the King,
So fixt her fancy on him : let them be.
But have ye no one word of loyal praise
For Arthur, blameless King and stainless
          man ?'

    She answer'd with a low and chuckling
          laugh :
'Man ! is he man at all, who knows and
          winks ?
Sees what his fair bride is and does, and
          winks ?
By which the good King means to blind
          himself,
And blinds himself and all the Table Round
To all the foulness that they work. Myself
Could call him (were it not for womanhood)
The pretty, popular name such manhood
          earns,
Could call him the main cause of all their
          crime ;
Yea, were he not crown'd King, coward,
          and fool.'

    Then Merlin to his own heart, loathing,
          said :
'O true and tender !   O my liege and
          King !
O selfless man and stainless gentleman,
Who wouldst against thine own eye-wit-
          ness fain
Have all men true and leal, all women
          pure ;
How, in the mouths of base interpreters
From over-fineness not intelligible
To things with every sense as false and foul
As the poach'd filth that floods the middl
          street,
Is thy white blamelessness accounted
          blame !'

But Vivien, deeming Merlin overborne
By instance, recommenced, and let her
    tongue
Rage like a fire among the noblest names,
Polluting, and imputing her whole self,
Defaming and defacing, till she left
Not even Lancelot brave, nor Galahad
    clean.

Her words had issue other than she
    will'd.
He dragg'd his eyebrow bushes down, and made
A snowy penthouse for his hollow eyes,
And mutter'd in himself, 'Tell *her* the
    charm !
So, if she had it, would she rail on me
To snare the next, and if she have it not
So will she rail. What did the wanton say?
" Not mount as high ; " we scarce can sink
    as low :
For men at most differ as Heaven and
    earth,
But women, worst and best, as Heaven
    and Hell.
I know the Table Round, my friends of
    old ;
All brave, and many generous, and some
    chaste.
She cloaks the scar of some repulse with
    lies ;
I well believe she tempted them and fail'd,
Being so bitter : for fine plots may fail,
Tho' harlots paint their talk as well as face
With colours of the heart that are not theirs.
I will not let her know : nine tithes of
    times
Face-flatterer and backbiter are the same.
And they, sweet soul, that most impute a
    crime
Are pronest to it, and impute themselves,
Wanting the mental range ; or low desire
Not to feel lowest makes them level all ;
Yea, they would pare the mountain to the
    plain,
To leave an equal baseness ; and in this
Are harlots like the crowd, that if they find
Some stain or blemish in a name of note,
Not grieving that their greatest are so
    small,

Inflate themselves with some insane
    delight,
And judge all nature from her feet of clay,
Without the will to lift their eyes, and see
Her godlike head crown'd with spiritual
    fire,
And touching other worlds.   I am weary
    of her.'

He spoke in words part heard, in
    whispers part,
Half-suffocated in the hoary fell
And many-winter'd fleece of throat and
    chin.
But Vivien, gathering somewhat of his
    mood,
And hearing 'harlot' mutter'd twice or
    thrice,
Leapt from her session on his lap, and
    stood
Stiff as a viper frozen ; loathsome sight,
How from the rosy lips of life and love,
Flash'd the bare-grinning skeleton of
    death !
White was her cheek ; sharp breaths of
    anger puff'd
Her fairy nostril out ; her hand half-
    clench'd
Went faltering sideways downward to her
    belt,
And feeling ; had she found a dagger
    there
(For in a wink the false love turns to
    hate)
She would have stabb'd him ; but she
    found it not :
His eye was calm, and suddenly she took
To bitter weeping like a beaten child,
A long, long weeping, not consolable.
Then her false voice made way, broken
    with sobs :

'O crueller than was ever told in tale,
Or sung in song ! O vainly lavish'd love !
O cruel, there was nothing wild or strange,
Or seeming shameful—for what shame in
    love,
So love be true, and not as yours is—
    nothing
Poor Vivien had not done to win his trust

Who call'd her what he call'd her—all
     her crime,
All—all—the wish to prove him wholly
     hers.'

  She mused a little, and then clapt her
     hands
Together with a wailing shriek, and said:
' Stabb'd through the heart's affections to
     the heart !
Seethed like the kid in its own mother's
     milk !
Kill'd with a word worse than a life of
     blows !
I thought that he was gentle, being great:
O God, that I had loved a smaller man !
I should have found in him a greater
     heart.
O, I, that flattering my true passion, saw
The knights, the court, the King, dark
     in your light,
Who loved to make men darker than they
     are,
Because of that high pleasure which I
     had
To seat you sole upon my pedestal
Of worship—I am answer'd, and hence-
     forth
The course of life that seem'd so flowery
     to me
With you for guide and master, only you,
Becomes the sea-cliff pathway broken
     short,
And ending in a ruin—nothing left,
But into some low cave to crawl, and
     there,
If the wolf spare me, weep my life away,
Kill'd with inutterable unkindliness.'

  She paused, she turn'd away, she hung
     her head,
The snake of gold slid from her hair, the
     braid
Slipt and uncoil'd itself, she wept afresh,
And the dark wood grew darker toward
     the storm
In silence, while his anger slowly died
Within him, till he let his wisdom go
For ease of heart, and half believed her
     true :

Call'd her to shelter in the hollow oak,
' Come from the storm,' and having no
     reply,
Gazed at the heaving shoulder, and the
     face
Hand-hidden, as for utmost grief or
     shame ;
Then thrice essay'd, by tenderest-touching
     terms,
To sleek her ruffled peace of mind, in
     vain.
At last she let herself be conquer'd by him,
And as the cageling newly flown returns,
The seeming-injured simple-hearted thing
Came to her old perch back, and settled
     there.
There while she sat, half-falling from his
     knees,
Half-nestled at his heart, and since he saw
The slow tear creep from her closed eye-
     lid yet,
About her, more in kindness than in love,
The gentle wizard cast a shielding arm.
But she dislink'd herself at once and rose,
Her arms upon her breast across, and
     stood,
A virtuous gentlewoman deeply wrong'd,
Upright and flush'd before him: then she
     said :

  ' There must be now no passages of love
Betwixt us twain henceforward evermore;
Since, if I be what I am grossly call'd,
What should be granted which your own
     gross heart
Would reckon worth the taking ? I will
     go.
In truth, but one thing now—better have
     died
Thrice than have ask'd it once—could
     make me stay—
That proof of trust—so often ask'd in
     vain !
How justly, after that vile term of yours,
I find with grief ! I might believe you
     then,
Who knows ? once more. Lo ! what was
     once to me
Mere matter of the fancy, now hath grown
The vast necessity of heart and life.

Farewell ; think gently of me, for I fear
My fate or folly, passing gayer youth
For one so old, must be to love thee still.
But ere I leave thee let me swear once
    more
That if I schemed against thy peace in
    this,
May yon just heaven, that darkens o'er
    me, send
One flash, that, missing all things else,
    may make
My scheming brain a cinder, if I lie.'

    Scarce had she ceased, when out of
      heaven a bolt
(For now the storm was close above them)
    struck,
Furrowing a giant oak, and javelining
With darted spikes and splinters of the
    wood
The dark earth round. He raised his
    eyes and saw
The tree that shone white-listed thro' the
    gloom.
But Vivien, fearing heaven had heard her
    oath,
And dazzled by the livid-flickering fork,
And deafen'd with the stammering cracks
    and claps
That follow'd, flying back and crying out,
' O Merlin, tho' you do not love me, save,
Yet save me !' clung to him and hugg'd
    him close ;
And call'd him dear protector in her
    fright,
Nor yet forgot her practice in her fright,
But wrought upon his mood and hugg'd
    him close.
The pale blood of the wizard at her touch
Took gayer colours, like an opal warm'd.
She blamed herself for telling hearsay
    tales :
She shook from fear, and for her fault
    she wept
Of petulancy ; she call'd him lord and
    liege,
Her seer, her bard, her silver star of eve,
Her God, her Merlin, the one passionate
    love
Of her whole life ; and ever overhead

Bellow'd the tempest, and the rotten
    branch
Snapt in the rushing of the river-rain
Above them ; and in change of glare and
    gloom
Her eyes and neck glittering went and
    came ;
Till now the storm, its burst of passion
    spent,
Moaning and calling out of other lands,
Had left the ravaged woodland yet once
    more
To peace; and what should not have been
    had been,
For Merlin, overtalk'd and overworn,
Had yielded, told her all the charm, and
    slept.

    Then, in one moment, she put forth
      the charm
Of woven paces and of waving hands,
And in the hollow oak he lay as dead,
And lost to life and use and name and
    fame.

    Then crying ' I have made his glory
      mine,'
And shrieking out ' O fool !' the harlot
    leapt
Adown the forest, and the thicket closed
Behind her, and the forest echo'd ' fool.'

LANCELOT AND ELAINE.

ELAINE the fair, Elaine the loveable,
Elaine, the lily maid of Astolat,
High in her chamber up a tower to the
    east
Guarded the sacred shield of Lancelot ;
Which first she placed where morning's
    earliest ray
Might strike it, and awake her with the
    gleam ;
Then fearing rust or soilure fashion'd for it
A case of silk, and braided thereupon
All the devices blazon'd on the shield
In their own tint, and added, of her wit,
A border fantasy of branch and flower,
And yellow-throated nestling in the nest.
Nor rested thus content, but day by day,

Leaving her household and good father,
    climb'd
That eastern tower, and entering barr'd
    her door,
Stript off the case, and read the naked
    shield,
Now guess'd a hidden meaning in his
    arms,
Now made a pretty history to herself
Of every dint a sword had beaten in it,
And every scratch a lance had made
    upon it,
Conjecturing when and where: this cut
    is fresh ;
That ten years back ; this dealt him at
    Caerlyle ;
That at Caerleon ; this at Camelot :
And ah God's mercy, what a stroke was
    there !
And here a thrust that might have kill'd,
    but God
Broke the strong lance, and roll'd his
    enemy down,
And saved him : so she lived in fantasy.

How came the lily maid by that good
    shield
Of Lancelot, she that knew not ev'n his
    name ?
He left it with her, when he rode to tilt
For the great diamond in the diamond
    jousts,
Which Arthur had ordain'd, and by that
    name
Had named them, since a diamond was
    the prize.

For Arthur, long before they crown'd
    him King,
Roving the trackless realms of Lyonnesse,
Had found a glen, gray boulder and black
    tarn.
A horror lived about the tarn, and clave
Like its own mists to all the mountain
    side :
For here two brothers, one a king, had
    met
And fought together ; but their names
    were lost ;
And each had slain his brother at a blow ;

And down they fell and made the glen
    abhorr'd :
And there they lay till all their bones
    were bleach'd,
And lichen'd into colour with the crags :
And he, that once was king, had on a
    crown
Of diamonds, one in front, and four aside.
And Arthur came, and labouring up the
    pass,
All in a misty moonshine, unawares
Had trodden that crown'd skeleton, and
    the skull
Brake from the nape, and from the skull
    the crown
Roll'd into light, and turning on its rims
Fled like a glittering rivulet to the tarn :
And down the shingly scaur he plunged,
    and caught,
And set it on his head, and in his heart
Heard murmurs, 'Lo, thou likewise shalt
    be King.'

Thereafter, when a King, he had the
    gems
Pluck'd from the crown, and show'd them
    to his knights,
Saying, 'These jewels, whereupon I
    chanced
Divinely, are the kingdom's, not the
    King's—
For public use: henceforward let there be,
Once every year, a joust for one of these :
For so by nine years' proof we needs
    must learn
Which is our mightiest, and ourselves
    shall grow
In use of arms and manhood, till we drive
The heathen, who, some say, shall rule
    the land
Hereafter, which God hinder.' Thus he
    spoke :
And eight years past, eight jousts had
    been, and still
Had Lancelot won the diamond of the
    year,
With purpose to present them to the
    Queen,
When all were won ; but meaning all at
    once

To snare her royal fancy with a boon
Worth half her realm, had never spoken
      word.

  Now for the central diamond and the
      last
And largest, Arthur, holding then his
      court
Hard on the river nigh the place which
      now
Is this world's hugest, let proclaim a joust
At Camelot, and when the time drew nigh
Spake (for she had been sick) to Guine-
      vere,
' Are you so sick, my Queen, you cannot
      move
To these fair jousts ?' ' Yea, lord,' she
      said, ' ye know it.'
' Then will ye miss,' he answer'd, ' the
      great deeds
Of Lancelot, and his prowess in the lists,
A sight ye love to look on.' And the
      Queen
Lifted her eyes, and they dwelt languidly
On Lancelot, where he stood beside the
      King.
He thinking that he read her meaning
      there,
' Stay with me, I am sick ; my love is
      more
Than many diamonds,' yielded ; and a
      heart
Love-loyal to the least wish of the Queen
(However much he yearn'd to make
      complete
The tale of diamonds for his destined boon)
Urged him to speak against the truth,
      and say,
' Sir King, mine ancient wound is hardly
      whole,
And lets me from the saddle ; ' and the
      King
Glanced first at him, then her, and went
      his way.
No sooner gone than suddenly she began :

    ' To blame, my lord Sir Lancelot,
      much to blame !
Why go ye not to these fair jousts ? the
      knights

Are half of them our enemies, and the
      crowd
Will murmur, " Lo the shameless ones,
      who take
Their pastime now the trustful King is
      gone ! " '
Then Lancelot vext at having lied in vain :
' Are ye so wise ? ye were not once so wise,
My Queen, that summer, when ye loved
      me first.
Then of the crowd ye took no more account
Than of the myriad cricket of the mead,
When its own voice clings to each blade
      of grass,
And every voice is nothing. As to
      knights,
Them surely can I silence with all ease.
But now my loyal worship is allow'd
Of all men : many a bard, without offence,
Has link'd our names together in his lay,
Lancelot, the flower of bravery, Guine-
      vere,
The pearl of beauty : and our knights at
      feast
Have pledged us in this union, while the
      King
Would listen smiling. How then ? is
      there more ?
Has Arthur spoken aught ? or would
      yourself,
Now weary of my service and devoir,
Henceforth be truer to your faultless lord ?

  She broke into a little scornful laugh :
' Arthur, my lord, Arthur, the faultless
      King,
That passionate perfection, my good
      lord—
But who can gaze upon the Sun in heaven ?
He never spake word of reproach to me,
He never had a glimpse of mine untruth,
He cares not for me : only here to-day
There gleam'd a vague suspicion in his
      eyes :
Some meddling rogue has tamper'd with
      him—else
Rapt in this fancy of his Table Round,
And swearing men to vows impossible,
To make them like himself : but, friend,
      to me

He is all fault who hath no fault at all :
For who loves me must have a touch of
  earth ;
The low sun makes the colour : I am yours,
Not Arthur's, as ye know, save by the
  bond.
And therefore hear my words : go to the
  jousts :
The tiny-trumpeting gnat can break our
  dream
When sweetest ; and the vermin voices here
May buzz so loud—we scorn them, but
  they sting.'

  Then answer'd Lancelot, the chief of
    knights :
'And with what face, after my pretext
  made,
Shall I appear, O Queen, at Camelot, I
Before a King who honours his own
  word,
As if it were his God's ?'

              'Yea,' said the Queen,
'A moral child without the craft to rule,
Else had he not lost me : but listen to me,
If I must find you wit : we hear it said
That men go down before your spear at
  a touch,
But knowing you are Lancelot ; your great
  name,
This conquers : hide it therefore ; go
  unknown :
Win ! by this kiss you will : and our true
  King
Will then allow your pretext, O my
  knight,
As all for glory ; for to speak him true,
Ye know right well, how meek soe'er he
  seem,
No keener hunter after glory breathes.
He loves it in his knights more than
  himself :
They prove to him his work : win and
  return.'

  Then got Sir Lancelot suddenly to horse,
Wroth at himself.   Not willing to be
  known,
He left the barren-beaten thoroughfare,

Chose the green path that show'd the
  rarer foot,
And there among the solitary downs,
Full often lost in fancy, lost his way ;
Till as he traced a faintly-shadow'd track,
That all in loops and links among the
  dales
Ran to the Castle of Astolat, he saw
Fired from the west, far on a hill, the
  towers.
Thither he made, and blew the gateway
  horn.
Then came an old, dumb, myriad-
  wrinkled man,
Who let him into lodging and disarm'd.
And Lancelot marvell'd at the wordless
  man ;
And issuing found the Lord of Astolat
With two strong sons, Sir Torre and Sir
  Lavaine,
Moving to meet him in the castle court ;
And close behind them stept the lily maid
Elaine, his daughter : mother of the house
There was not : some light jest among
  them rose
With laughter dying down as the great
  knight
Approach'd them : then the Lord of
  Astolat :
'Whence comest thou, my guest, and by
  what name
Livest between the lips ? for by thy state
And presence I might guess thee chief of
  those,
After the King, who eat in Arthur's halls.
Him have I seen : the rest, his Table
  Round,
Known as they are, to me they are un-
  known.'

  Then answer'd Lancelot, the chief of
    knights :
'Known am I, and of Arthur's hall, and
  known,
What I by mere mischance have brought,
  my shield.
But since I go to joust as one unknown
At Camelot for the diamond, ask me not
Hereafter ye shall know me — and the
  shield—

I pray you lend me one, if such you have,
Blank, or at least with some device not
   mine.'

Then said the Lord of Astolat, 'Here
   is Torre's :
Hurt in his first tilt was my son, Sir Torre.
And so, God wot, his shield is blank
   enough.
His ye can have.' Then added plain Sir
   Torre,
'Yea, since I cannot use it, ye may have
   it.'
Here laugh'd the father saying, 'Fie, Sir
   Churl,
Is that an answer for a noble knight?
Allow him ! but Lavaine, my younger
   here,
He is so full of lustihood, he will ride,
Joust for it, and win, and bring it in an
   hour,
And set it in this damsel's golden hair,
To make her thrice as wilful as before.'

'Nay, father, nay good father, shame
   me not
Before this noble knight,' said young
   Lavaine,
'For nothing. Surely I but play'd on
   Torre :
He seem'd so sullen, vext he could not go :
A jest, no more ! for, knight, the maiden
   dreamt
That some one put this diamond in her
   hand,
And that it was too slippery to be held,
And slipt and fell into some pool or stream,
The castle-well, belike ; and then I said
That *if* I went and *if* I fought and won it
(But all was jest and joke among ourselves)
Then must she keep it safelier. All was
   jest.
But, father, give me leave, an if he will,
To ride to Camelot with this noble knight :
Win shall I not, but do my best to win :
Young as I am, yet would I do my best.'

'So ye will grace me,' answer'd
   Lancelot,
Smiling a moment, 'with your fellowship

O'er these waste downs whereon I lost
   myself,
Then were I glad of you as guide and
   friend :
And you shall win this diamond,—as I
   hear
It is a fair large diamond,—if ye may,
And yield it to this maiden, if ye will.'
'A fair large diamond,' added plain Sir
   Torre,
'Such be for queens, and not for simple
   maids.'
Then she, who held her eyes upon the
   ground,
Elaine, and heard her name so tost about,
Flush'd slightly at the slight disparagement
Before the stranger knight, who, looking
   at her,
Full courtly, yet not falsely, thus return'd :
'If what is fair be but for what is fair,
And only queens are to be counted so,
Rash were my judgment then, who deem
   this maid
Might wear as fair a jewel as is on earth,
Not violating the bond of like to like.'

He spoke and ceased : the lily maid
   Elaine,
Won by the mellow voice before she look'd,
Lifted her eyes, and read his lineaments.
The great and guilty love he bare the
   Queen,
In battle with the love he bare his lord,
Had marr'd his face, and mark'd it ere
   his time.
Another sinning on such heights with one,
The flower of all the west and all the
   world,
Had been the sleeker for it : but in him
His mood was often like a fiend, and rose
And drove him into wastes and solitudes
For agony, who was yet a living soul.
Marr'd as he was, he seem'd the goodliest
   man
That ever among ladies ate in hall,
And noblest, when she lifted up her eyes.
However marr'd, of more than twice her
   years,
Seam'd with an ancient swordcut on the
   cheek,

And bruised and bronzed, she lifted up
    her eyes
And loved him, with that love which was
    her doom.

    Then the great knight, the darling of
        the court,
Loved of the loveliest, into that rude hall
Stept with all grace, and not with half
    disdain
Hid under grace, as in a smaller time,
But kindly man moving among his kind :
Whom they with meats and vintage of
    their best
And talk and minstrel melody entertain'd.
And much they ask'd of court and Table
    Round,
And ever well and readily answer'd he :
But Lancelot, when they glanced at
    Guinevere,
Suddenly speaking of the wordless man,
Heard from the Baron that, ten years
    before,
The heathen caught and reft him of his
    tongue.
' He learnt and warn'd me of their fierce
    design
Against my house, and him they caught
    and maim'd ;
But I, my sons, and little daughter fled
From bonds or death, and dwelt among
    the woods
By the great river in a boatman's hut.
Dull days were those, till our good Arthur
    broke
The Pagan yet once more on Badon hill.'

    ' O there, great lord, doubtless,' Lavaine
        said, rapt
By all the sweet and sudden passion of
    youth
Toward greatness in its elder, ' you have
    fought.
O tell us—for we live apart—you know
Of Arthur's glorious wars.'   And Lancelot
    spoke
And answer'd him at full, as having been
With Arthur in the fight which all day long
Rang by the white mouth of the violent
    Glem ;

And in the four loud battles by the shore
Of Duglas ; that on Bassa ; then the war
That thunder'd in and out the gloomy
    skirts
Of Celidon the forest ; and again
By castle Gurnion, where the glorious
    King
Had on his cuirass worn our Lady's Head,
Carved of one emerald center'd in a sun
Of silver rays, that lighten'd as he
    breathed ;
And at Caerleon had he help'd his lord,
When the strong neighings of the wild
    white Horse
Set every gilded parapet shuddering ;
And up in Agned-Cathregonion too,
And down the waste sand-shores of Trath
    Treroit,
Where many a heathen fell ; ' and on the
    mount
Of Badon I myself beheld the King
Charge at the head of all his Table Round,
And all his legions crying Christ and him,
And break them ; and I saw him, after,
    stand
High on a heap of slain, from spur to
    plume
Red as the rising sun with heathen blood,
And seeing me, with a great voice he cried,
" They are broken, they are broken !"
    for the King,
However mild he seems at home, nor cares
For triumph in our mimic wars, the
    jousts—
For if his own knight cast him down, he
    laughs
Saying, his knights are better men than
    he—
Yet in this heathen war the fire of God
Fills him : I never saw his like : there lives
No greater leader.'

                        While he utter'd this,
Low to her own heart said the lily maid,
' Save your great self, fair lord ;' and
    when he fell
From talk of war to traits of pleasantry—
Being mirthful he, but in a stately kind—
She still took note that when the living
    smile

Died from his lips, across him came a cloud
Of melancholy severe, from which again,
Whenever in her hovering to and fro
The lily maid had striven to make him
    cheer,
There brake a sudden-beaming tenderness
Of manners and of nature: and she
    thought
That all was nature, all, perchance, for her.
And all night long his face before her lived,
As when a painter, poring on a face,
Divinely thro' all hindrance finds the man
Behind it, and so paints him that his face,
The shape and colour of a mind and life,
Lives for his children, ever at its best
And fullest; so the face before her lived,
Dark-splendid, speaking in the silence,
    full
Of noble things, and held her from her
    sleep.
Till rathe she rose, half-cheated in the
    thought
She needs must bid farewell to sweet
    Lavaine.
First as in fear, step after step, she stole
Down the long tower-stairs, hesitating:
Anon, she heard Sir Lancelot cry in the
    court,
'This shield, my friend, where is it?'
    and Lavaine
Past inward, as she came from out the
    tower.
There to his proud horse Lancelot turn'd,
    and smooth'd
The glossy shoulder, humming to himself.
Half-envious of the flattering hand, she
    drew
Nearer and stood. He look'd, and more
    amazed
Than if seven men had set upon him, saw
The maiden standing in the dewy light.
He had not dream'd she was so beautiful.
Then came on him a sort of sacred fear,
For silent, tho' he greeted her, she stood
Rapt on his face as if it were a God's.
Suddenly flash'd on her a wild desire,
That he should wear her favour at the tilt.
She braved a riotous heart in asking for it.
'Fair lord, whose name I know not—
    noble it is,

I well believe, the noblest—will you wear
My favour at this tourney?' 'Nay,' said
    he,
'Fair lady, since I never yet have worn
Favour of any lady in the lists.
Such is my wont, as those, who know me,
    know.'
'Yea, so,' she answer'd; 'then in wearing
    mine
Needs must be lesser likelihood, noble
    lord,
That those who know should know you.'
    And he turn'd
Her counsel up and down within his mind,
And found it true, and answer'd, 'True,
    my child.
Well, I will wear it: fetch it out to me:
What is it?' and she told him 'A red
    sleeve
Broider'd with pearls,' and brought it:
    then he bound
Her token on his helmet, with a smile
Saying, 'I never yet have done so much
For any maiden living,' and the blood
Sprang to her face and fill'd her with
    delight;
But left her all the paler, when Lavaine
Returning brought the yet-unblazon'd
    shield,
His brother's; which he gave to Lancelot,
Who parted with his own to fair Elaine:
'Do me this grace, my child, to have my
    shield
In keeping till I come.' 'A grace to me,'
She answer'd, 'twice to-day. I am your
    squire!'
Whereat Lavaine said, laughing, 'Lily
    maid,
For fear our people call you lily maid
In earnest, let me bring your colour back;
Once, twice, and thrice: now get you
    hence to bed:'
So kiss'd her, and Sir Lancelot his own
    hand,
And thus they moved away: she stay'd
    a minute,
Then made a sudden step to the gate,
    and there—
Her bright hair blown about the serious
    face

T

Yet rosy-kindled with her brother's kiss—
Paused by the gateway, standing near
  the shield
In silence, while she watch'd their arms
  far-off
Sparkle, until they dipt below the downs.
Then to her tower she climb'd, and took
  the shield,
There kept it, and so lived in fantasy.

Meanwhile the new companions past
  away
Far o'er the long backs of the bushless
  downs,
To where Sir Lancelot knew there lived
  a knight
Not far from Camelot, now for forty years
A hermit, who had pray'd, labour'd and
  pray'd,
And ever labouring had scoop'd himself
In the white rock a chapel and a hall
On massive columns, like a shorecliff cave,
And cells and chambers: all were fair
  and dry;
The green light from the meadows under-
  neath
Struck up and lived along the milky roofs;
And in the meadows tremulous aspen-trees
And poplars made a noise of falling
  showers.
And thither wending there that night they
  bode.

But when the next day broke from
  underground,
And shot red fire and shadows thro' the
  cave,
They rose, heard mass, broke fast, and
  rode away:
Then Lancelot saying, 'Hear, but hold
  my name
Hidden, you ride with Lancelot of the
  Lake,'
Abash'd Lavaine, whose instant rever-
  ence,
Dearer to true young hearts than their
  own praise,
But left him leave to stammer, 'Is it
  indeed?'
And after muttering 'The great Lancelot,'

At last he got his breath and answer'd,
  'One,
One have I seen—that other, our liege
  lord,
The dread Pendragon, Britain's King of
  kings,
Of whom the people talk mysteriously,
He will be there—then were I stricken
  blind
That minute, I might say that I had seen.'

So spake Lavaine, and when they
  reach'd the lists
By Camelot in the meadow, let his eyes
Run thro' the peopled gallery which half
  round
Lay like a rainbow fall'n upon the grass,
Until they found the clear-faced King,
  who sat
Robed in red samite, easily to be known,
Since to his crown the golden dragon
  clung,
And down his robe the dragon writhed
  in gold,
And from the carven-work behind him
  crept
Two dragons gilded, sloping down to
  make
Arms for his chair, while all the rest of
  them
Thro' knots and loops and folds innu-
  merable
Fled ever thro' the woodwork, till they
  found
The new design wherein they lost them-
  selves,
Yet with all ease, so tender was the work:
And, in the costly canopy o'er him set,
Blazed the last diamond of the nameless
  king.

Then Lancelot answer'd young Lavaine
  and said,
'Me you call great: mine is the firmer
  seat,
The truer lance: but there is many a youth
Now crescent, who will come to all I am
And overcome it; and in me there dwells
No greatness, save it be some far-off touch
Of greatness to know well I am not great:

There is the man.' And Lavaine gaped
    upon him
As on a thing miraculous, and anon
The trumpets blew ; and then did either
    side,
They that assail'd, and they that held the
    lists,
Set lance in rest, strike spur, suddenly
    move,
Meet in the midst, and there so furiously
Shock, that a man far - off might well
    perceive,
If any man that day were left afield,
The hard earth shake, and a low thunder
    of arms.

And Lancelot bode a little, till he saw
Which were the weaker ; then he hurl'd
    into it
Against the stronger : little need to speak
Of Lancelot in his glory ! King, duke,
    earl,
Count, baron—whom he smote, he over-
    threw.

But in the field were Lancelot's kith
    and kin,
Ranged with the Table Round that held
    the lists,
Strong men, and wrathful that a stranger
    knight
Should do and almost overdo the deeds
Of Lancelot ; and one said to the other,
    ' Lo !
What is he ? I do not mean the force
    alone—
The grace and versatility of the man !
Is it not Lancelot ?' 'When has Lance-
    lot worn
Favour of any lady in the lists ?
Not such his wont, as we, that know him,
    know.'
' How then ? who then ?' a fury seized
    them all,
A fiery family passion for the name
Of Lancelot, and a glory one with theirs.
They couch'd their spears and prick'd their
    steeds, and thus,
Their plumes driv'n backward by the wind
    they made
In moving, all together down upon him

Bare, as a wild wave in the wide North-sea,
Green - glimmering toward the summit,
    bears, with all
Its stormy crests that smoke against the
    skies,
Down on a bark, and overbears the bark,
And him that helms it, so they overbore
Sir Lancelot and his charger, and a spear
Down-glancing lamed the charger, and a
    spear
Prick'd sharply his own cuirass, and the
    head
Pierced thro' his side, and there snapt,
    and remain'd.

Then Sir Lavaine did well and wor-
    shipfully ;
He bore a knight of old repute to the
    earth,
And brought his horse to Lancelot where
    he lay.
He up the side, sweating with agony, got,
But thought to do while he might yet
    endure,
And being lustily holpen by the rest,
His party,—tho' it seem'd half-miracle
To those he fought with,—drave his kith
    and kin,
And all the Table Round that held the
    lists,
Back to the barrier ; then the trumpets
    blew
Proclaiming his the prize, who wore the
    sleeve
Of scarlet, and the pearls ; and all the
    knights,
His party, cried ' Advance and take thy
    prize
The diamond ;' but he answer'd, 'Diamond
    me
No diamonds ! for God's love, a little air !
Prize me no prizes, for my prize is death !
Hence will I, and I charge you, follow
    me not.'

He spoke, and vanish'd suddenly from
    the field
With young Lavaine into the poplar grove.
There from his charger down he slid, and
    sat,

Gasping to Sir Lavaine, 'Draw the lance-
head :'
'Ah my sweet lord Sir Lancelot,' said
Lavaine,
'I dread me, if I draw it, you will die.'
But he, 'I die already with it : draw—
Draw,'—and Lavaine drew, and Sir
Lancelot gave
A marvellous great shriek and ghastly
groan,
And half his blood burst forth, and down
he sank
For the pure pain, and wholly swoon'd
away.
Then came the hermit out and bare him
in,
There stanch'd his wound ; and there, in
daily doubt
Whether to live or die, for many a week
Hid from the wide world's rumour by the
grove
Of poplars with their noise of falling
showers,
And ever-tremulous aspen-trees, he lay.

But on that day when Lancelot fled the
lists,
His party, knights of utmost North and
West,
Lords of waste marches, kings of desolate
isles,
Came round their great Pendragon, saying
to him,
'Lo, Sire, our knight, thro' whom we
won the day,
Hath gone sore wounded, and hath left
his prize
Untaken, crying that his prize is death.'
'Heaven hinder,' said the King, 'that
such an one,
So great a knight as we have seen to-day—
He seem'd to me another Lancelot—
Yea, twenty times I thought him Lance-
lot—
He must not pass uncared for. Where-
fore, rise,
O Gawain, and ride forth and find the
knight.
Wounded and wearied needs must he be
near.

I charge you that you get at once to horse.
And, knights and kings, there breathes
not one of you
Will deem this prize of ours is rashly
given :
His prowess was too wondrous. We will
do him
No customary honour : since the knight
Came not to us, of us to claim the prize,
Ourselves will send it after. Rise and take
This diamond, and deliver it, and return,
And bring us where he is, and how he
fares,
And cease not from your quest until ye
find.'

So saying, from the carven flower above,
To which it made a restless heart, he took,
And gave, the diamond : then from where
he sat
At Arthur's right, with smiling face arose,
With smiling face and frowning heart, a
Prince
In the mid might and flourish of his May,
Gawain, surnamed The Courteous, fair
and strong,
And after Lancelot, Tristram, and
Geraint
And Gareth, a good knight, but there-
withal
Sir Modred's brother, and the child of Lot,
Nor often loyal to his word, and now
Wroth that the King's command to sally
forth
In quest of whom he knew not, made him
leave
The banquet, and concourse of knights
and kings.

So all in wrath he got to horse and
went ;
While Arthur to the banquet, dark in
mood,
Past, thinking 'Is it Lancelot who hath
come
Despite the wound he spake of, all for
gain
Of glory, and hath added wound to wound,
And ridd'n away to die ?' So fear'd the
King,

And, after two days' tarriance there,
return'd.
Then when he saw the Queen, embrac-
ing ask'd,
'Love, are you yet so sick?' 'Nay,
lord,' she said.
'And where is Lancelot?' Then the
Queen amazed,
'Was he not with you? won he not your
prize?'
'Nay, but one like him.' 'Why that like
was he.'
And when the King demanded how she
knew,
Said, 'Lord, no sooner had ye parted
from us,
Than Lancelot told me of a common
talk
That men went down before his spear at
a touch,
But knowing he was Lancelot; his great
name
Conquer'd; and therefore would he hide
his name
From all men, ev'n the King, and to this
end
Had made the pretext of a hindering
wound,
That he might joust unknown of all, and
learn
If his old prowess were in aught decay'd;
And added, "Our true Arthur, when he
learns,
Will well allow my pretext, as for gain
Of purer glory."'

Then replied the King:
'Far lovelier in our Lancelot had it been,
In lieu of idly dallying with the truth,
To have trusted me as he hath trusted
thee.
Surely his King and most familiar friend
Might well have kept his secret. True,
indeed,
Albeit I know my knights fantastical,
So fine a fear in our large Lancelot
Must needs have moved my laughter:
now remains
But little cause for laughter: his own
kin—

Ill news, my Queen, for all who love him,
this !—
His kith and kin, not knowing, set upon
him ;
So that he went sore wounded from the
field :
Yet good news too : for goodly hopes are
mine
That Lancelot is no more a lonely heart.
He wore, against his wont, upon his helm
A sleeve of scarlet, broider'd with great
pearls,
Some gentle maiden's gift.'

'Yea, lord,' she said,
'Thy hopes are mine,' and saying that,
she choked,
And sharply turn'd about to hide her face,
Past to her chamber, and there flung
herself
Down on the great King's couch, and
writhed upon it,
And clench'd her fingers till they bit the
palm,
And shriek'd out 'Traitor' to the un-
hearing wall,
Then flash'd into wild tears, and rose
again,
And moved about her palace, proud and
pale.

Gawain the while thro' all the region
round
Rode with his diamond, wearied of the
quest,
Touch'd at all points, except the poplar
grove,
And came at last, tho' late, to Astolat :
Whom glittering in enamell'd arms the
maid
Glanced at, and cried, 'What news from
Camelot, lord ?
What of the knight with the red sleeve ?
'He won.'
'I knew it,' she said. 'But parted from
the jousts
Hurt in the side,' whereat she caught her
breath ;
Thro' her own side she felt the sharp
lance go ;

Thereon she smote her hand : wellnigh she swoon'd :
And, while he gazed wonderingly at her, came
The Lord of Astolat out, to whom the Prince
Reported who he was, and on what quest
Sent, that he bore the prize and could not find
The victor, but had ridd'n a random round
To seek him, and had wearied of the search.
To whom the Lord of Astolat, ' Bide with us,
And ride no more at random, noble Prince !
Here was the knight, and here he left a shield ;
This will he send or come for : furthermore
Our son is with him ; we shall hear anon,
Needs must we hear.' To this the courteous Prince
Accorded with his wonted courtesy,
Courtesy with a touch of traitor in it,
And stay'd ; and cast his eyes on fair Elaine :
Where could be found face daintier ? then her shape
From forehead down to foot, perfect—again
From foot to forehead exquisitely turn'd :
' Well—if I bide, lo ! this wild flower for me !'
And oft they met among the garden yews,
And there he set himself to play upon her
With sallying wit, free flashes from a height
Above her, graces of the court, and songs,
Sighs, and slow smiles, and golden eloquence
And amorous adulation, till the maid
Rebell'd against it, saying to him, ' Prince,
O loyal nephew of our noble King,
Why ask you not to see the shield he left,
Whence you might learn his name ? Why slight your King,
And lose the quest he sent you on, and prove

No surer than our falcon yesterday,
Who lost the hern we slipt her at, and went
To all the winds ?' ' Nay, by mine head,' said he,
' I lose it, as we lose the lark in heaven,
O damsel, in the light of your blue eyes ;
But an ye will it let me see the shield.'
And when the shield was brought, and Gawain saw
Sir Lancelot's azure lions, crown'd with gold,
Ramp in the field, he smote his thigh, and mock'd :
' Right was the King ! our Lancelot ! that true man !'
' And right was I,' she answer'd merrily, ' I,
Who dream'd my knight the greatest knight of all.'
' And if *I* dream'd,' said Gawain, ' that you love
This greatest knight, your pardon ! lo, ye know it !
Speak therefore : shall I waste myself in vain ?'
Full simple was her answer, ' What know I ?
My brethren have been all my fellowship ;
And I, when often they have talk'd of love,
Wish'd it had been my mother, for they talk'd,
Meseem'd, of what they knew not ; so myself—
I know not if I know what true love is,
But if I know, then, if I love not him,
I know there is none other I can love.'
' Yea, by God's death,' said he, ' ye love him well,
But would not, knew ye what all others know,
And whom he loves.' ' So be it,' cried Elaine,
And lifted her fair face and moved away :
But he pursued her, calling, ' Stay a little !
One golden minute's grace ! he wore your sleeve :

Would he break faith with one I may not
name?
Must our true man change like a leaf at
last?
Nay—like enow: why then, far be it
from me
To cross our mighty Lancelot in his
loves!
And, damsel, for I deem you know full
well
Where your great knight is hidden, let
me leave
My quest with you; the diamond also:
here!
For if you love, it will be sweet to give it;
And if he love, it will be sweet to have it
From your own hand; and whether he
love or not,
A diamond is a diamond. Fare you well
A thousand times!—a thousand times
farewell!
Yet, if he love, and his love hold, we
two
May meet at court hereafter: there, I
think,
So ye will learn the courtesies of the
court,
We two shall know each other.'

                    Then he gave,
And slightly kiss'd the hand to which he
gave,
The diamond, and all wearied of the
quest
Leapt on his horse, and carolling as he
went
A true-love ballad, lightly rode away.

   Thence to the court he past; there told
the King
What the King knew, 'Sir Lancelot is
the knight.'
And added, 'Sire, my liege, so much I
learnt;
But fail'd to find him, tho' I rode all
round
The region: but I lighted on the maid
Whose sleeve he wore; she loves him;
and to her,
Deeming our courtesy is the truest law,

I gave the diamond: she will render it;
For by mine head she knows his hiding-
place.'

   The seldom-frowning King frown'd,
and replied,
'Too courteous truly! ye shall go no more
On quest of mine, seeing that ye forget
Obedience is the courtesy due to kings.'

   He spake and parted. Wroth, but all
in awe,
For twenty strokes of the blood, without
a word,
Linger'd that other, staring after him;
Then shook his hair, strode off, and
buzz'd abroad
About the maid of Astolat, and her love.
All ears were prick'd at once, all tongues
were loosed:
'The maid of Astolat loves Sir Lance-
lot,
Sir Lancelot loves the maid of Astolat.'
Some read the King's face, some the
Queen's, and all
Had marvel what the maid might be, but
most
Predoom'd her as unworthy. One old
dame
Came suddenly on the Queen with the
sharp news.
She, that had heard the noise of it
before,
But sorrowing Lancelot should have
stoop'd so low,
Marr'd her friend's aim with pale tran-
quillity.
So ran the tale like fire about the court,
Fire in dry stubble a nine-days' wonder
flared:
Till ev'n the knights at banquet twice or
thrice
Forgot to drink to Lancelot and the
Queen,
And pledging Lancelot and the lily maid
Smiled at each other, while the Queen,
who sat
With lips severely placid, felt the knot
Climb in her throat, and with her feet
unseen

Crush'd the wild passion out against the
    floor
Beneath the banquet, where the meats
    became
As wormwood, and she hated all who
    pledged.

But far away the maid in Astolat,
Her guiltless rival, she that ever kept
The one-day-seen Sir Lancelot in her
    heart,
Crept to her father, while he mused alone,
Sat on his knee, stroked his gray face
    and said,
'Father, you call me wilful, and the fault
Is yours who let me have my will, and
    now,
Sweet father, will you let me lose my
    wits?'
'Nay,' said he, 'surely.' 'Wherefore,
    let me hence,'
She answer'd, 'and find out our dear
    Lavaine.'
'Ye will not lose your wits for dear
    Lavaine:
Bide,' answer'd he : 'we needs must hear
    anon
Of him, and of that other.' 'Ay,' she
    said,
'And of that other, for I needs must hence
And find that other, wheresoe'er he be,
And with mine own hand give his diamond
    to him,
Lest I be found as faithless in the quest
As yon proud Prince who left the quest
    to me.
Sweet father, I behold him in my dreams
Gaunt as it were the skeleton of himself,
Death-pale, for lack of gentle maiden's
    aid.
The gentler-born the maiden, the more
    bound,
My father, to be sweet and serviceable
To noble knights in sickness, as ye know
When these have worn their tokens : let
    me hence
I pray you.' Then her father nodding
    said,
'Ay, ay, the diamond : wit ye well, my
    child,

Right fain were I to learn this knight
    were whole,
Being our greatest : yea, and you must
    give it—
And sure I think this fruit is hung too
    high
For any mouth to gape for save a
    queen's—
Nay, I mean nothing : so then, get you
    gone,
Being so very wilful you must go.'

Lightly, her suit allow'd, she slipt away,
And while she made her ready for her
    ride,
Her father's latest word humm'd in her
    ear,
'Being so very wilful you must go,'
And changed itself and echo'd in her heart,
'Being so very wilful you must die.'
But she was happy enough and shook it
    off,
As we shake off the bee that buzzes at us ;
And in her heart she answer'd it and said,
'What matter, so I help him back to life?'
Then far away with good Sir Torre for
    guide
Rode o'er the long backs of the bushless
    downs
To Camelot, and before the city-gates
Came on her brother with a happy face
Making a roan horse caper and curvet
For pleasure all about a field of flowers :
Whom when she saw, 'Lavaine,' she
    cried, 'Lavaine,
How fares my lord Sir Lancelot?' He
    amazed,
'Torre and Elaine ! why here? Sir
    Lancelot !
How know ye my lord's name is Lance-
    lot ?'
But when the maid had told him all her
    tale,
Then turn'd Sir Torre, and being in his
    moods
Left them, and under the strange-statued
    gate,
Where Arthur's wars were render'd
    mystically,
Past up the still rich city to his kin,

His own far blood, which dwelt at
　　Camelot ;
And her, Lavaine across the poplar grove
Led to the caves : there first she saw the
　　casque
Of Lancelot on the wall : her scarlet
　　sleeve,
Tho' carved and cut, and half the pearls
　　away,
Stream'd from it still ; and in her heart
　　she laugh'd,
Because he had not loosed it from his
　　helm,
But meant once more perchance to tour-
　　ney in it.
And when they gain'd the cell wherein
　　he slept,
His battle-writhen arms and mighty hands
Lay naked on the wolfskin, and a dream
Of dragging down his enemy made them
　　move.
Then she that saw him lying unsleek,
　　unshorn,
Gaunt as it were the skeleton of himself,
Utter'd a little tender dolorous cry.
The sound not wonted in a place so still
Woke the sick knight, and while he roll'd
　　his eyes
Yet blank from sleep, she started to him,
　　saying,
'Your prize the diamond sent you by the
　　King :'
His eyes glisten'd : she fancied 'Is it for
　　me ?'
And when the maid had told him all the
　　tale
Of King and Prince, the diamond sent,
　　the quest
Assign'd to her not worthy of it, she knelt
Full lowly by the corners of his bed,
And laid the diamond in his open hand.
Her face was near, and as we kiss the
　　child
That does the task assign'd, he kiss'd her
　　face.
At once she slipt like water to the floor.
'Alas,' he said, 'your ride hath wearied
　　you.
Rest must you have.' 'No rest for me,'
　　she said ;

'Nay, for near you, fair lord, I am at rest.'
What might she mean by that ? his large
　　black eyes,
Yet larger thro' his leanness, dwelt upon
　　her,
Till all her heart's sad secret blazed itself
In the heart's colours on her simple face ;
And Lancelot look'd and was perplext in
　　mind,
And being weak in body said no more ;
But did not love the colour ; woman's
　　love,
Save one, he not regarded, and so turn'd
Sighing, and feign'd a sleep until he slept.

Then rose Elaine and glided thro' the
　　fields,
And past beneath the weirdly-sculptured
　　gates
Far up the dim rich city to her kin ;
There bode the night : but woke with
　　dawn, and past
Down thro' the dim rich city to the fields,
Thence to the cave : so day by day she
　　past
In either twilight ghost-like to and fro
Gliding, and every day she tended him,
And likewise many a night : and Lancelot
Would, tho' he call'd his wound a little
　　hurt
Whereof he should be quickly whole, at
　　times
Brain-feverous in his heat and agony,
　　seem
Uncourteous, even he : but the meek
　　maid
Sweetly forbore him ever, being to him
Meeker than any child to a rough nurse,
Milder than any mother to a sick child,
And never woman yet, since man's first
　　fall,
Did kindlier unto man, but her deep love
Upbore her ; till the hermit, skill'd in all
The simples and the science of that time,
Told him that her fine care had saved his
　　life.
And the sick man forgot her simple blush,
Would call her friend and sister, sweet
　　Elaine,
Would listen for her coming and regret

Her parting step, and held her tenderly,
And loved her with all love except the love
Of man and woman when they love their best,
Closest and sweetest, and had died the death
In any knightly fashion for her sake.
And peradventure had he seen her first
She might have made this and that other world
Another world for the sick man; but now
The shackles of an old love straiten'd him,
His honour rooted in dishonour stood,
And faith unfaithful kept him falsely true.

Yet the great knight in his mid-sickness made
Full many a holy vow and pure resolve.
These, as but born of sickness, could not live :
For when the blood ran lustier in him again,
Full often the bright image of one face,
Making a treacherous quiet in his heart,
Dispersed his resolution like a cloud.
Then if the maiden, while that ghostly grace
Beam'd on his fancy, spoke, he answer'd not,
Or short and coldly, and she knew right well
What the rough sickness meant, but what this meant
She knew not, and the sorrow dimm'd her sight,
And drave her ere her time across the fields
Far into the rich city, where alone
She murmur'd, ' Vain, in vain : it cannot be.
He will not love me : how then ? must I die ? '
Then as a little helpless innocent bird,
That has but one plain passage of few notes,
Will sing the simple passage o'er and o'er
For all an April morning, till the ear
Wearies to hear it, so the simple maid

Went half the night repeating, ' Must die ? '
And now to right she turn'd, and now t[o] left,
And found no ease in turning or in rest
And ' Him or death,' she mutter'd, ' death or him,'
Again and like a burthen, ' Him or death.[']

    But when Sir Lancelot's deadly hu[rt] was whole,
To Astolat returning rode the three.
There morn by morn, arraying her swe[et] self
In that wherein she deem'd she look'[d] her best,
She came before Sir Lancelot, for sh[e] thought
' If I be loved, these are my festal robes[,]
If not, the victim's flowers before he fall[.]
And Lancelot ever prest upon the maid
That she should ask some goodly gift o[f] him
For her own self or hers ; ' and do no[t] shun
To speak the wish most near to your tru[e] heart ;
Such service have ye done me, that I mak[e]
My will of yours, and Prince and Lor[d] am I
In mine own land, and what I will I can.[']
Then like a ghost she lifted up her face,
But like a ghost without the power t[o] speak.
And Lancelot saw that she withheld he[r] wish,
And bode among them yet a little space
Till he should learn it ; and one morn i[t] chanced
He found her in among the garden yews[,]
And said, ' Delay no longer, speak you[r] wish,
Seeing I go to-day : ' then out she brake[,]
' Going ? and we shall never see you more.[']
And I must die for want of one bold word.
' Speak : that I live to hear,' he said, ' i[s] yours.'
Then suddenly and passionately she spoke [:]
' I have gone mad. I love you : let m[e] die.'

'Ah, sister,' answer'd Lancelot, 'what is this?'
And innocently extending her white arms,
'Your love,' she said, 'your love—to be your wife.'
And Lancelot answer'd, 'Had I chosen to wed,
I had been wedded earlier, sweet Elaine:
But now there never will be wife of mine.'
'No, no,' she cried, 'I care not to be wife,
But to be with you still, to see your face,
To serve you, and to follow you thro' the world.'
And Lancelot answer'd, 'Nay, the world, the world,
All ear and eye, with such a stupid heart
To interpret ear and eye, and such a tongue
To blare its own interpretation—nay,
Full ill then should I quit your brother's love,
And your good father's kindness.' And she said,
'Not to be with you, not to see your face—
Alas for me then, my good days are done.'
'Nay, noble maid,' he answer'd, 'ten times nay!
This is not love: but love's first flash in youth,
Most common: yea, I know it of mine own self:
And you yourself will smile at your own self
Hereafter, when you yield your flower of life
To one more fitly yours, not thrice your age:
And then will I, for true you are and sweet
Beyond mine old belief in womanhood,
More specially should your good knight be poor,
Endow you with broad land and territory
Even to the half my realm beyond the seas,
So that would make you happy: furthermore,
Ev'n to the death, as tho' ye were my blood,

In all your quarrels will I be your knight.
This will I do, dear damsel, for your sake,
And more than this I cannot.'

 While he spoke
She neither blush'd nor shook, but deathly-pale
Stood grasping what was nearest, then replied:
'Of all this will I nothing;' and so fell,
And thus they bore her swooning to her tower.

Then spake, to whom thro' those black walls of yew
Their talk had pierced, her father: 'Ay, a flash,
I fear me, that will strike my blossom dead.
Too courteous are ye, fair Lord Lancelot.
I pray you, use some rough discourtesy
To blunt or break her passion.'

 Lancelot said,
'That were against me: what I can I will;'
And there that day remain'd, and toward even
Sent for his shield: full meekly rose the maid,
Stript off the case, and gave the naked shield;
Then, when she heard his horse upon the stones,
Unclasping flung the casement back, and look'd
Down on his helm, from which her sleeve had gone.
And Lancelot knew the little clinking sound;
And she by tact of love was well aware
That Lancelot knew that she was looking at him.
And yet he glanced not up, nor waved his hand,
Nor bad farewell, but sadly rode away.
This was the one discourtesy that he used.

So in her tower alone the maiden sat:
His very shield was gone; only the case,
Her own poor work, her empty labour, left.

But still she heard him, still his picture
    form'd
And grew between her and the pictured
    wall.
Then came her father, saying in low tones,
' Have comfort,' whom she greeted
    quietly.
Then came her brethren saying, ' Peace
    to thee,
Sweet sister,' whom she answer'd with all
    calm.
But when they left her to herself again,
Death, like a friend's voice from a distant
    field
Approaching thro' the darkness, call'd ;
    the owls
Wailing had power upon her, and she
    mixt
Her fancies with the sallow-rifted glooms
Of evening, and the moanings of the wind.

And in those days she made a little
    song,
And call'd her song ' The Song of Love
    and Death,'
And sang it : sweetly could she make
    and sing.

' Sweet is true love tho' given in vain,
    in vain ;
And sweet is death who puts an end to
    pain :
I know not which is sweeter, no, not I.

' Love, art thou sweet ? then bitter
    death must be :
Love, thou art bitter ; sweet is death to
    me.
O Love, if death be sweeter, let me die.

' Sweet love, that seems not made to
    fade away,
Sweet death, that seems to make us love-
    less clay,
I know not which is sweeter, no, not I.

' I fain would follow love, if that could
    be ;
I needs must follow death, who calls for
    me ;
Call and I follow, I follow ! let me die.'

High with the last line scaled her voice,
    and this,
All in a fiery dawning wild with wind
That shook her tower, the brothers heard,
    and thought
With shuddering, ' Hark the Phantom of
    the house
That ever shrieks before a death,' and
    call'd
The father, and all three in hurry and fear
Ran to her, and lo ! the blood-red light
    of dawn
Flared on her face, she shrilling, ' Let
    me die !'

As when we dwell upon a word we
    know,
Repeating, till the word we know so well
Becomes a wonder, and we know not why,
So dwelt the father on her face, and
    thought
' Is this Elaine ?' till back the maiden fell,
Then gave a languid hand to each, and
    lay,
Speaking a still good-morrow with her
    eyes.
At last she said, ' Sweet brothers, yester-
    night
I seem'd a curious little maid again,
As happy as when we dwelt among the
    woods,
And when ye used to take me with the
    flood
Up the great river in the boatman's boat.
Only ye would not pass beyond the cape
That has the poplar on it : there ye fixt
Your limit, oft returning with the tide.
And yet I cried because ye would not pass
Beyond it, and far up the shining flood
Until we found the palace of the King.
And yet ye would not ; but this night I
    dream'd
That I was all alone upon the flood,
And then I said, " Now shall I have my
    will :"
And there I woke, but still the wish
    remain'd.
So let me hence that I may pass at last
Beyond the poplar and far up the flood,
Until I find the palace of the King.

There will I enter in among them all,
And no man there will dare to mock at
    me ;
But there the fine Gawain will wonder at
    me,
And there the great Sir Lancelot muse
    at me ;
Gawain, who bad a thousand farewells to
    me,
Lancelot, who coldly went, nor bad me
    one :
And there the King will know me and
    my love,
And there the Queen herself will pity me,
And all the gentle court will welcome me,
And after my long voyage I shall rest !'

'Peace,' said her father, ' O my child,
    ye seem
Light-headed, for what force is yours to
    go
So far, being sick ? and wherefore would
    ye look
On this proud fellow again, who scorns
    us all ?'

Then the rough Torre began to heave
    and move,
And bluster into stormy sobs and say,
'I never loved him : an I meet with
    him,
I care not howsoever great he be,
Then will I strike at him and strike him
    down,
Give me good fortune, I will strike him
    dead,
For this discomfort he hath done the
    house.'

To whom the gentle sister made reply,
'Fret not yourself, dear brother, nor be
    wroth,
Seeing it is no more Sir Lancelot's fault
Not to love me, than it is mine to love
Him of all men who seems to me the
    highest.'

'Highest?' the father answer'd, echoing
    ' highest ?'
(He meant to break the passion in her)
    ' nay,

Daughter, I know not what you call the
    highest ;
But this I know, for all the people know it,
He loves the Queen, and in an open shame :
And she returns his love in open shame ;
If this be high, what is it to be low ?'

Then spake the lily maid of Astolat :
' Sweet father, all too faint and sick am I
For anger : these are slanders : never yet
Was noble man but made ignoble talk.
He makes no friend who never made a foe.
But now it is my glory to have loved
One peerless, without stain : so let me
    pass,
My father, howsoe'er I seem to you,
Not all unhappy, having loved God's best
And greatest, tho' my love had no return :
Yet, seeing you desire your child to live,
Thanks, but you work against your own
    desire ;
For if I could believe the things you say
I should but die the sooner ; wherefore
    cease,
Sweet father, and bid call the ghostly man
Hither, and let me shrive me clean, and
    die.'

So when the ghostly man had come and
    gone,
She with a face, bright as for sin forgiven,
Besought Lavaine to write as she devised
A letter, word for word ; and when he
    ask'd
' Is it for Lancelot, is it for my dear lord?
Then will I bear it gladly ;' she replied,
' For Lancelot and the Queen and all the
    world,
But I myself must bear it.' Then he wrote
The letter she devised ; which being writ
And folded, ' O sweet father, tender and
    true,
Deny me not,' she said—' ye never yet
Denied my fancies—this, however strange,
My latest : lay the letter in my hand
A little ere I die, and close the hand
Upon it ; I shall guard it even in death.
And when the heat is gone from out my
    heart,
Then take the little bed on which I died

For Lancelot's love, and deck it like the
    Queen's
For richness, and me also like the Queen
In all I have of rich, and lay me on it.
And let there be prepared a chariot-bier
To take me to the river, and a barge
Be ready on the river, clothed in black.
I go in state to court, to meet the Queen.
There surely I shall speak for mine own
    self,
And none of you can speak for me so well.
And therefore let our dumb old man alone
Go with me, he can steer and row, and he
Will guide me to that palace, to the
    doors.'

    She ceased : her father promised ;
    whereupon
She grew so cheerful that they deem'd her
    death
Was rather in the fantasy than the blood.
But ten slow mornings past, and on the
    eleventh
Her father laid the letter in her hand,
And closed the hand upon it, and she died.
So that day there was dole in Astolat.

    But when the next sun brake from
    underground,
Then, those two brethren slowly with bent
    brows
Accompanying, the sad chariot-bier
Past like a shadow thro' the field, that
    shone
Full-summer, to that stream whereon the
    barge,
Pall'd all its length in blackest samite, lay.
There sat the lifelong creature of the house,
Loyal, the dumb old servitor, on deck,
Winking his eyes, and twisted all his face.
So those two brethren from the chariot took
And on the black decks laid her in her bed,
Set in her hand a lily, o'er her hung
The silken case with braided blazonings,
And kiss'd her quiet brows, and saying to
    her
' Sister, farewell for ever,' and again
' Farewell, sweet sister,' parted all in tears.
Then rose the dumb old servitor, and the
    dead,

Oar'd by the dumb, went upward with
    the flood—
In her right hand the lily, in her left
The letter—all her bright hair streaming
    down—
And all the coverlid was cloth of gold
Drawn to her waist, and she herself in
    white
All but her face, and that clear-featured
    face
Was lovely, for she did not seem as dead,
But fast asleep, and lay as tho' she smiled.

    That day Sir Lancelot at the palace
    craved
Audience of Guinevere, to give at last
The price of half a realm, his costly gift,
Hard-won and hardly won with bruise and
    blow,
With deaths of others, and almost his
    own,
The nine-years-fought-for diamonds : for
    he saw
One of her house, and sent him to the
    Queen
Bearing his wish, whereto the Queen
    agreed
With such and so unmoved a majesty
She might have seem'd her statue, but
    that he,
Low-drooping till he wellnigh kiss'd her
    feet
For loyal awe, saw with a sidelong eye
The shadow of some piece of pointed lace,
In the Queen's shadow, vibrate on the
    walls,
And parted, laughing in his courtly heart.

    All in an oriel on the summer side,
Vine-clad, of Arthur's palace toward the
    stream,
They met, and Lancelot kneeling utter'd,
    ' Queen,
Lady, my liege, in whom I have my joy,
Take, what I had not won except for you,
These jewels, and make me happy, making
    them
An armlet for the roundest arm on earth,
Or necklace for a neck to which the
    swan's

Is tawnier than her cygnet's : these are
 words :
Your beauty is your beauty, and I sin
In speaking, yet O grant my worship of it
Words, as we grant grief tears. Such sin
 in words
Perchance, we both can pardon : but, my
 Queen,
I hear of rumours flying thro' your court.
Our bond, as not the bond of man and
 wife,
Should have in it an absoluter trust
To make up that defect : let rumours be :
When did not rumours fly ? these, as I
 trust
That you trust me in your own nobleness,
I may not well believe that you believe.'

 While thus he spoke, half turn'd away,
  the Queen
Brake from the vast oriel-embowering vine
Leaf after leaf, and tore, and cast them
 off,
Till all the place whereon she stood was
 green ;
Then, when he ceased, in one cold passive
 hand
Received at once and laid aside the gems
There on a table near her, and replied :

'It may be, I am quicker of belief
Than you believe me, Lancelot of the
 Lake.
Our bond is not the bond of man and wife.
This good is in it, whatsoe'er of ill,
It can be broken easier. I for you
This many a year have done despite and
 wrong
To one whom ever in my heart of hearts
I did acknowledge nobler. What are
 these ?
Diamonds for me ! they had been thrice
 their worth
Being your gift, had you not lost your
 own.
To loyal hearts the value of all gifts
Must vary as the giver's. Not for me !
For her ! for your new fancy. Only this
Grant me, I pray you : have your joys
 apart.

I doubt not that however changed, you
 keep
So much of what is graceful : and myself
Would shun to break those bounds of
 courtesy
In which as Arthur's Queen I move and
 rule :
So cannot speak my mind. An end to
 this !
A strange one ! yet I take it with Amen.
So pray you, add my diamonds to her
 pearls ;
Deck her with these ; tell her, she shines
 me down :
An armlet for an arm to which the
 Queen's
Is haggard, or a necklace for a neck
O as much fairer—as a faith once fair
Was richer than these diamonds—hers
 not mine—
Nay, by the mother of our Lord himself,
Or hers or mine, mine now to work my
 will—
She shall not have them.'

    Saying which she seized,
And, thro' the casement standing wide
 for heat,
Flung them, and down they flash'd, and
 smote the stream.
Then from the smitten surface flash'd, as
 it were,
Diamonds to meet them, and they past
 away.
Then while Sir Lancelot leant, in half
 disdain
At love, life, all things, on the window
 ledge,
Close underneath his eyes, and right
 across
Where these had fallen, slowly past the
 barge
Whereon the lily maid of Astolat
Lay smiling, like a star in blackest night.

 But the wild Queen, who saw not, burst
  away
To weep and wail in secret ; and the
 barge,
On to the palace-doorway sliding, paused.

There two stood arm'd, and kept the
door ; to whom,
All up the marble stair, tier over tier,
Were added mouths that gaped, and eyes
that ask'd
'What is it ?' but that oarsman's haggard
face,
As hard and still as is the face that men
Shape to their fancy's eye from broken
rocks
On some cliff-side, appall'd them, and
they said,
'He is enchanted, cannot speak—and she,
Look how she sleeps—the Fairy Queen,
so fair !
Yea, but how pale ! what are they ? flesh
and blood ?
Or come to take the King to Fairyland ?
For some do hold our Arthur cannot die,
But that he passes into Fairyland.'

While thus they babbled of the King,
the King
Came girt with knights : then turn'd the
tongueless man
From the half-face to the full eye, and
rose
And pointed to the damsel, and the doors.
So Arthur bad the meek Sir Percivale
And pure Sir Galahad to uplift the maid ;
And reverently they bore her into hall.
Then came the fine Gawain and wonder'd
at her,
And Lancelot later came and mused at
her,
And last the Queen herself, and pitied
her :
But Arthur spied the letter in her hand,
Stoopt, took, brake seal, and read it ;
this was all :

'Most noble lord, Sir Lancelot of the
Lake,
I, sometime call'd the maid of Astolat,
Come, for you left me taking no farewell,
Hither, to take my last farewell of you.
I loved you, and my love had no return,
And therefore my true love has been my
death.
And therefore to our Lady Guinevere,

And to all other ladies, I make moan :
Pray for my soul, and yield me burial.
Pray for my soul thou too, Sir Lancelot
As thou art a knight peerless.'

Thus he read
And ever in the reading, lords and dame
Wept, looking often from his face wh
read
To hers which lay so silent, and at times
So touch'd were they, half-thinking tha
her lips,
Who had devised the letter, moved again

Then freely spoke Sir Lancelot to ther
all :
'My lord liege Arthur, and all ye tha
hear,
Know that for this most gentle maiden'
death
Right heavy am I ; for good she was an
true,
But loved me with a love beyond all lov
In women, whomsoever I have known.
Yet to be loved makes not to love again
Not at my years, however it hold in youth
I swear by truth and knighthood that
gave
No cause, not willingly, for such a love
To this I call my friends in testimony,
Her brethren, and her father, who himsel
Besought me to be plain and blunt, an
use,
To break her passion, some discourtesy
Against my nature : what I could, I did
I left her and I bad her no farewell ;
Tho', had I dreamt the damsel woul
have died,
I might have put my wits to some roug
use,
And help'd her from herself.'

Then said the Quee
(Sea was her wrath, yet working afte
storm)
'Ye might at least have done her s
much grace,
Fair lord, as would have help'd her fror
her death.'
He raised his head, their eyes met an
hers fell,

He adding,
    ' Queen, she would not be content
Save that I wedded her, which could not
    be.
Then might she follow me thro' the world,
    she ask'd ;
It could not be. I told her that her love
Was but the flash of youth, would darken
    down
To rise hereafter in a stiller flame
Toward one more worthy of her—then
    would I,
More specially were he, she wedded, poor,
Estate them with large land and territory
In mine own realm beyond the narrow
    seas,
To keep them in all joyance : more than
    this
I could not ; this she would not, and she
    died.'

    He pausing, Arthur answer'd, ' O my
    knight,
It will be to thy worship, as my knight,
And mine, as head of all our Table Round,
To see that she be buried worshipfully.'

    So toward that shrine which then in
    all the realm
Was richest, Arthur leading, slowly went
The marshall'd Order of their Table
    Round,
And Lancelot sad beyond his wont, to see
The maiden buried, not as one unknown,
Nor meanly, but with gorgeous obsequies,
And mass, and rolling music, like a queen.
And when the knights had laid her comely
    head
Low in the dust of half-forgotten kings,
Then Arthur spake among them, ' Let
    her tomb
Be costly, and her image thereupon,
And let the shield of Lancelot at her feet
Be carven, and her lily in her hand.
And let the story of her dolorous voyage
For all true hearts be blazon'd on her tomb
In letters gold and azure !' which was
    wrought
Thereafter ; but when now the lords and
    dames

And people, from the high door stream-
    ing, brake
Disorderly, as homeward each, the Queen,
Who mark'd Sir Lancelot where he moved
    apart,
Drew near, and sigh'd in passing,
    ' Lancelot,
Forgive me ; mine was jealousy in love.'
He answer'd with his eyes upon the ground,
' That is love's curse ; pass on, my Queen,
    forgiven.'
But Arthur, who beheld his cloudy brows,
Approach'd him, and with full affection
    said,

    ' Lancelot, my Lancelot, thou in whom
    I have
Most joy and most affiance, for I know
What thou hast been in battle by my side,
And many a time have watch'd thee at
    the tilt
Strike down the lusty and long practised
    knight,
And let the younger and unskill'd go by
To win his honour and to make his name,
And loved thy courtesies and thee, a man
Made to be loved ; but now I would to
    God,
Seeing the homeless trouble in thine eyes,
Thou couldst have loved this maiden,
    shaped, it seems,
By God for thee alone, and from her face,
If one may judge the living by the dead,
Delicately pure and marvellously fair,
Who might have brought thee, now a
    lonely man
Wifeless and heirless, noble issue, sons
Born to the glory of thy name and fame,
My knight, the great Sir Lancelot of the
    Lake.'

    Then answer'd Lancelot, ' Fair she was,
    my King,
Pure, as you ever wish your knights to be.
To doubt her fairness were to want an eye,
To doubt her pureness were to want a
    heart—
Yea, to be loved, if what is worthy love
Could bind him, but free love will not be
    bound.'

T

' Free love, so bound, were freëst,' said
    the King.
' Let love be free ; free love is for the
    best :
And, after heaven, on our dull side of
    death,
What should be best, if not so pure a love
Clothed in so pure a loveliness ? yet thee
She fail'd to bind, tho' being, as I think,
Unbound as yet, and gentle, as I know.'

    And Lancelot answer'd nothing, but
        he went,
And at the inrunning of a little brook
Sat by the river in a cove, and watch'd
The high reed wave, and lifted up his eyes
And saw the barge that brought her
    moving down,
Far-off, a blot upon the stream, and said
Low in himself, 'Ah simple heart and
    sweet,
Ye loved me, damsel, surely with a love
Far tenderer than my Queen's. Pray for
    thy soul ?
Ay, that will I. Farewell too—now at
    last—
Farewell, fair lily. "Jealousy in love ?"
Not rather dead love's harsh heir, jealous
    pride ?
Queen, if I grant the jealousy as of love,
May not your crescent fear for name and
    fame
Speak, as it waxes, of a love that wanes?
Why did the King dwell on my name to
    me ?
Mine own name shames me, seeming a
    reproach,
Lancelot, whom the Lady of the Lake
Caught from his mother's arms—the
    wondrous one
Who passes thro' the vision of the night—
She chanted snatches of mysterious hymns
Heard on the winding waters, eve and
    morn
She kiss'd me saying, "Thou art fair,
    my child,
As a king's son," and often in her arms
She bare me, pacing on the dusky mere.
Would she had drown'd me in it, where'er
    it be !

For what am I ? what profits me my nam
Of greatest knight ? I fought for it, an
    have it :
Pleasure to have it, none ; to lose it, pain
Now grown a part of me : but what use i
    it ?
To make men worse by making my si
    known ?
Or sin seem less, the sinner seeming great
Alas for Arthur's greatest knight, a ma
Not after Arthur's heart ! I needs mu
    break
These bonds that so defame me : n
    without
She wills it : would I, if she will'd it ? na
Who knows ? but if I would not, the
    may God,
I pray him, send a sudden Angel down
To seize me by the hair and bear me fa
And fling me deep in that forgotte
    mere,
Among the tumbled fragments of th
    hills.'

    So groan'd Sir Lancelot in remorsefu
        pain,
Not knowing he should die a holy man.

THE HOLY GRAIL.

FROM noiseful arms, and acts of prowes
    done
In tournament or tilt, Sir Percivale,
Whom Arthur and his knighthood call'
    The Pure,
Had pass'd into the silent life of prayer,
Praise, fast, and alms ; and leaving fc
    the cowl
The helmet in an abbey far away
From Camelot, there, and not long afte
    died.

    And one, a fellow-monk among the rest
Ambrosius, loved him much beyond th
    rest,
And honour'd him, and wrought into hi
    heart
A way by love that waken'd love withir
To answer that which came : and as the
    sat

Beneath a world-old yew-tree, darkening
  half
The cloisters, on a gustful April morn
That puff'd the swaying branches into
  smoke
Above them, ere the summer when he
  died,
The monk Ambrosius question'd Percivale :

  ' O brother, I have seen this yew-tree
    smoke,
Spring after spring, for half a hundred
  years :
For never have I known the world with-
  out,
Nor ever stray'd beyond the pale : but
  thee,
When first thou camest—such a courtesy
Spake thro' the limbs and in the voice—
  I knew
For one of those who eat in Arthur's hall ;
For good ye are and bad, and like to coins,
Some true, some light, but every one of you
Stamp'd with the image of the King ; and
  now
Tell me, what drove thee from the Table
  Round,
My brother ? was it earthly passion crost ?'

  ' Nay,' said the knight ; ' for no such
    passion mine.
But the sweet vision of the Holy Grail
Drove me from all vainglories, rivalries,
And earthly heats that spring and sparkle
  out
Among us in the jousts, while women
  watch
Who wins, who falls ; and waste the
  spiritual strength
Within us, better offer'd up to Heaven.'

  To whom the monk : ' The Holy
    Grail !—I trust
We are green in Heaven's eyes ; but here
  too much
We moulder—as to things without I
  mean—
Yet one of your own knights, a guest of
  ours,
Told us of this in our refectory,

But spake with such a sadness and so low
We heard not half of what he said.   What
  is it ?
The phantom of a cup that comes and
  goes ?'

  ' Nay, monk ! what phantom ?' answer'd
    Percivale.
' The cup, the cup itself, from which our
  Lord
Drank at the last sad supper with his
  own.
This, from the blessed land of Aromat—
After the day of darkness, when the dead
Went wandering o'er Moriah—the good
  saint
Arimathæan Joseph, journeying brought
To Glastonbury, where the winter thorn
Blossoms at Christmas, mindful of our
  Lord.
And there awhile it bode ; and if a man
Could touch or see it, he was heal'd at
  once,
By faith, of all his ills.   But then the times
Grew to such evil that the holy cup
Was caught away to Heaven, and dis-
  appear'd.'

  To whom the monk : ' From our old
    books I know
That Joseph came of old to Glastonbury,
And there the heathen Prince, Arviragus,
Gave him an isle of marsh whereon to
  build ;
And there he built with wattles from the
  marsh
A little lonely church in days of yore,
For so they say, these books of ours, but
  seem
Mute of this miracle, far as I have read.
But who first saw the holy thing to-day ?'

  ' A woman,' answer'd Percivale, ' a
    nun,
And one no further off in blood from me
Than sister ; and if ever holy maid
With knees of adoration wore the stone,
A holy maid ; tho' never maiden glow'd,
But that was in her earlier maidenhood,
With such a fervent flame of human
  love,

Which being rudely blunted, glanced and shot
Only to holy things ; to prayer and praise
She gave herself, to fast and alms. And yet,
Nun as she was, the scandal of the Court,
Sin against Arthur and the Table Round,
And the strange sound of an adulterous race,
Across the iron grating of her cell
Beat, and she pray'd and fasted all the more.

'And he to whom she told her sins, or what
Her all but utter whiteness held for sin,
A man wellnigh a hundred winters old,
Spake often with her of the Holy Grail,
A legend handed down thro' five or six,
And each of these a hundred winters old,
From our Lord's time. And when King Arthur made
His Table Round, and all men's hearts became
Clean for a season, surely he had thought
That now the Holy Grail would come again ;
But sin broke out. Ah, Christ, that it would come,
And heal the world of all their wickedness !
"O Father !" ask'd the maiden, "might it come
To me by prayer and fasting?" "Nay," said he,
"I know not, for thy heart is pure as snow."
And so she pray'd and fasted, till the sun
Shone, and the wind blew, thro' her, and I thought
She might have risen and floated when I saw her.

'For on a day she sent to speak with me.
And when she came to speak, behold her eyes
Beyond my knowing of them, beautiful,
Beyond all knowing of them, wonderful,
Beautiful in the light of holiness.
And "O my brother Percivale," she said,

"Sweet brother, I have seen the Holy Grail :
For, waked at dead of night, I heard a sound
As of a silver horn from o'er the hills
Blown, and I thought, 'It is not Arthur's use
To hunt by moonlight ;' and the slender sound
As from a distance beyond distance grew
Coming upon me—O never harp nor horn,
Nor aught we blow with breath, or touch with hand,
Was like that music as it came ; and then
Stream'd thro' my cell a cold and silver beam,
And down the long beam stole the Holy Grail,
Rose-red with beatings in it, as if alive,
Till all the white walls of my cell were dyed
With rosy colours leaping on the wall ;
And then the music faded, and the Grail
Past, and the beam decay'd, and from the walls
The rosy quiverings died into the night.
So now the Holy Thing is here again
Among us, brother, fast thou too and pray,
And tell thy brother knights to fast and pray,
That so perchance the vision may be seen
By thee and those, and all the world be heal'd."

'Then leaving the pale nun, I spake of this
To all men ; and myself fasted and pray'd
Always, and many among us many a week
Fasted and pray'd even to the uttermost,
Expectant of the wonder that would be.

'And one there was among us, eve moved
Among us in white armour, Galahad.
"God make thee good as thou art beautiful,"
Said Arthur, when he dubb'd him knight
and none,

In so young youth, was ever made a
 knight
Till Galahad; and this Galahad, when
 he heard
My sister's vision, fill'd me with amaze;
His eyes became so like her own, they
 seem'd
Hers, and himself her brother more than I.

 'Sister or brother none had he; but
  some
Call'd him a son of Lancelot, and some
 said
Begotten by enchantment—chatterers
 they,
Like birds of passage piping up and down,
That gape for flies—we know not whence
 they come;
For when was Lancelot wanderingly
 lewd?

 'But she, the wan sweet maiden, shore
 away
Clean from her forehead all that wealth
 of hair
Which made a silken mat-work for her
 feet;
And out of this she plaited broad and long
A strong sword-belt, and wove with silver
 thread
And crimson in the belt a strange device,
A crimson grail within a silver beam;
And saw the bright boy-knight, and
 bound it on him,
Saying, "My knight, my love, my knight
 of heaven,
O thou, my love, whose love is one with
 mine,
I, maiden, round thee, maiden, bind my
 belt.
Go forth, for thou shalt see what I have
 seen,
And break thro' all, till one will crown
 thee king
Far in the spiritual city:" and as she
 spake
She sent the deathless passion in her eyes
Thro' him, and made him hers, and laid
 her mind
On him, and he believed in her belief.

 'Then came a year of miracle: O
  brother,
In our great hall there stood a vacant
 chair,
Fashion'd by Merlin ere he past away,
And carven with strange figures; and in
 and out
The figures, like a serpent, ran a scroll
Of letters in a tongue no man could read.
And Merlin call'd it "The Siege peril-
 ous,"
Perilous for good and ill; "for there,"
 he said,
"No man could sit but he should lose
 himself:"
And once by misadvertence Merlin sat
In his own chair, and so was lost; but he,
Galahad, when he heard of Merlin's doom,
Cried, "If I lose myself, I save myself!"

 'Then on a summer night it came to
 pass,
While the great banquet lay along the
 hall,
That Galahad would sit down in Merlin's
 chair.

 'And all at once, as there we sat, we
 heard
A cracking and a riving of the roofs,
And rending, and a blast, and overhead
Thunder, and in the thunder was a cry.
And in the blast there smote along the hall
A beam of light seven times more clear
 than day:
And down the long beam stole the Holy
 Grail
All over cover'd with a luminous cloud,
And none might see who bare it, and it
 past.
But every knight beheld his fellow's face
As in a glory, and all the knights arose,
And staring each at other like dumb men
Stood, till I found a voice and sware a
 vow.

 'I sware a vow before them all, that I,
Because I had not seen the Grail, would
 ride
A twelvemonth and a day in quest of it,
Until I found and saw it, as the nun

My sister saw it ; and Galahad sware the
vow,
And good Sir Bors, our Lancelot's cousin,
sware,
And Lancelot sware, and many among
the knights,
And Gawain sware, and louder than the
rest.'

Then spake the monk Ambrosius, asking him,
'What said the King?   Did Arthur take
the vow ?'

' Nay, for my lord,' said Percivale,
'the King,
Was not in hall : for early that same day,
Scaped thro' a cavern from a bandit hold,
An outraged maiden sprang into the hall
Crying on help : for all her shining hair
Was smear'd with earth, and either milky
arm
Red-rent with hooks of bramble, and all
she wore
Torn as a sail that leaves the rope is torn
In tempest : so the King arose and went
To smoke the scandalous hive of those
wild bees
That made such honey in his realm.
Howbeit
Some little of this marvel he too saw,
Returning o'er the plain that then began
To darken under Camelot ; whence the
King
Look'd up, calling aloud, " Lo, there !
the roofs
Of our great hall are roll'd in thunder-
smoke !
Pray Heaven, they be not smitten by the
bolt."
For dear to Arthur was that hall of ours,
As having there so oft with all his knights
Feasted, and as the stateliest under
heaven.

' O brother, had you known our mighty
hall,
Which Merlin built for Arthur long ago !
For all the sacred mount of Camelot,
And all the dim rich city, roof by roof,
Tower after tower, spire beyond spire,

By grove, and garden-lawn, and rushing
brook,
Climbs to the mighty hall that Merlin
built.
And four great zones of sculpture, set
betwixt
With many a mystic symbol, gird the hall :
And in the lowest beasts are slaying men,
And in the second men are slaying beasts,
And on the third are warriors, perfect men,
And on the fourth are men with growing
wings,
And over all one statue in the mould
Of Arthur, made by Merlin, with a crown,
And peak'd wings pointed to the Northern
Star.
And eastward fronts the statue, and the
crown
And both the wings are made of gold,
and flame
At sunrise till the people in far fields,
Wasted so often by the heathen hordes,
Behold it, crying, "We have still a King."

' And, brother, had you known our hall
within,
Broader and higher than any in all the
lands !
Where twelve great windows blazon
Arthur's wars,
And all the light that falls upon the board
Streams thro' the twelve great battles of
our King.
Nay, one there is, and at the eastern end,
Wealthy with wandering lines of mount
and mere,
Where Arthur finds the brand Excalibur.
And also one to the west, and counter to it,
And blank : and who shall blazon it ?
when and how ?—
O there, perchance, when all our wars are
done,
The brand Excalibur will be cast away.

' So to this hall full quickly rode the
King,
In horror lest the work by Merlin wrought,
Dreamlike, should on the sudden vanish,
wrapt
In unremorseful folds of rolling fire.

And in he rode, and up I glanced, and saw
The golden dragon sparkling over all :
And many of those who burnt the hold,
  their arms
Hack'd, and their foreheads grimed with
  smoke, and sear'd,
Follow'd, and in among bright faces, ours,
Full of the vision, prest : and then the
  King
Spake to me, being nearest, " Percivale,"
(Because the hall was all in tumult—some
Vowing, and some protesting), " what is
  this ?"

  ' O brother, when I told him what had
    chanced,
My sister's vision, and the rest, his face
Darken'd, as I have seen it more than
  once,
When some brave deed seem'd to be done
  in vain,
Darken ; and " Woe is me, my knights,"
  he cried,
" Had I been here, ye had not sworn
  the vow."
Bold was mine answer, " Had thyself
  been here,
My King, thou wouldst have sworn."
    " Yea, yea," said he,
" Art thou so bold and hast not seen the
  Grail ?"

  ' " Nay, lord, I heard the sound, I
    saw the light,
But since I did not see the Holy Thing,
I sware a vow to follow it till I saw."

  ' Then when he ask'd us, knight by
    knight, if any
Had seen it, all their answers were as
  one :
" Nay, lord, and therefore have we sworn
  our vows."

  ' " Lo now," said Arthur, " have ye
    seen a cloud ?
What go ye into the wilderness to see ?"

  ' Then Galahad on the sudden, and in
    a voice
Shrilling along the hall to Arthur, call'd,

" But I, Sir Arthur, saw the Holy Grail,
I saw the Holy Grail and heard a cry—
' O Galahad, and O Galahad, follow me.' "

  ' " Ah, Galahad, Galahad," said the
    King, " for such
As thou art is the vision, not for these.
Thy holy nun and thou have seen a sign—
Holier is none, my Percivale, than she—
A sign to maim this Order which I made.
But ye, that follow but the leader's bell'
(Brother, the King was hard upon his
    knights)
" Taliessin is our fullest throat of song,
And one hath sung and all the dumb will
    sing.
Lancelot is Lancelot, and hath overborne
Five knights at once, and every younger
    knight,
Unproven, holds himself as Lancelot,
Till overborne by one, he learns—and ye,
What are ye ? Galahads ?—no, nor Per-
    civales "
(For thus it pleased the King to range
    me close
After Sir Galahad) ; " nay," said he,
    " but men
With strength and will to right the
    wrong'd, of power
To lay the sudden heads of violence flat,
Knights that in twelve great battles
    splash'd and dyed
The strong White Horse in his own
    heathen blood—
But one hath seen, and all the blind will
    see.
Go, since your vows are sacred, being
    made :
Yet—for ye know the cries of all my
    realm
Pass thro' this hall—how often, O my
    knights,
Your places being vacant at my side,
This chance of noble deeds will come
    and go
Unchallenged, while ye follow wandering
    fires
Lost in the quagmire ! Many of you, yea
    most,
Return no more : ye think I show myself

Too dark a prophet : come now, let us
 · meet
The morrow morn once more in one full
 field
Of gracious pastime, that once more the
 King,
Before ye leave him for this Quest, may
 count
The yet-unbroken strength of all his
 knights,
Rejoicing in that Order which he made."

 ' So when the sun broke next from
  under ground,
All the great table of our Arthur closed
And clash'd in such a tourney and so full,
So many lances broken—never yet
Had Camelot seen the like, since Arthur
 came ;
And I myself and Galahad, for a strength
Was in us from the vision, overthrew
So many knights that all the people cried.
And almost burst the barriers in their
 heat,
Shouting, " Sir Galahad and Sir Perci-
 vale ! "

 ' But when the next day brake from
  under ground—
O brother, had you known our Camelot,
Built by old kings, age after age, so old
The King himself had fears that it would
 fall,
So strange, and rich, and dim ; for where
 the roofs
Totter'd toward each other in the sky,
Met foreheads all along the street of those
Who watch'd us pass ; and lower, and
 where the long
Rich galleries, lady-laden, weigh'd the
 necks
Of dragons clinging to the crazy walls,
Thicker than drops from thunder, showers
 of flowers
Fell as we past ; and men and boys astride
On wyvern, lion, dragon, griffin, swan,
At all the corners, named us each by
 name,
Calling " God speed ! " but in the ways
 below

The knights and ladies wept, and rich
 and poor
Wept, and the King himself could hardly
 speak
For grief, and all in middle street the
 Queen,
Who rode by Lancelot, wail'd and shriek'd
 aloud,
" This madness has come on us for our
 sins."
So to the Gate of the three Queens we
 came,
Where Arthur's wars are render'd mys-
 tically,
And thence departed every one his way.

 ' And I was lifted up in heart, and
  thought
Of all my late-shown prowess in the lists,
How my strong lance had beaten down
 the knights,
So many and famous names ; and never
 yet
Had heaven appear'd so blue, nor earth
 so green,
For all my blood danced in me, and I
 knew
That I should light upon the Holy Grail.

 ' Thereafter, the dark warning of our
  King,
That most of us would follow wandering
 fires,
Came like a driving gloom across my
 mind.
Then every evil word I had spoken once,
And every evil thought I had thought of
 old,
And every evil deed I ever did,
Awoke and cried, " This Quest is not for
 thee."
And lifting up mine eyes, I found myself
Alone, and in a land of sand and thorns,
And I was thirsty even unto death ;
And I, too, cried, " This Quest is not for
 thee."

 ' And on I rode, and when I thought
  my thirst
Would slay me, saw deep lawns, and then
 a brook,

With one sharp rapid, where the crisping
    white
Play'd ever back upon the sloping wave,
And took both ear and eye ; and o'er the
    brook
Were apple-trees, and apples by the brook
Fallen, and on the lawns.   "I will rest
    here,"
I said, "I am not worthy of the Quest ;"
But even while I drank the brook, and ate
The goodly apples, all these things at once
Fell into dust, and I was left alone,
And thirsting, in a land of sand and thorns.

'And then behold a woman at a door
Spinning ; and fair the house whereby she
    sat,
And kind the woman's eyes and innocent,
And all her bearing gracious ; and she rose
Opening her arms to meet me, as who
    should say,
"Rest here ;" but when I touch'd her,
    lo ! she, too,
Fell into dust and nothing, and the house
Became no better than a broken shed,
And in it a dead babe ; and also this
Fell into dust, and I was left alone.

'And on I rode, and greater was my
    thirst.
Then flash'd a yellow gleam across the
    world,
And where it smote the plowshare in the
    field,
The plowman left his plowing, and fell
    down
Before it ; where it glitter'd on her pail,
The milkmaid left her milking, and fell
    down
Before it, and I knew not why, but
    thought
"The sun is rising," tho' the sun had risen.
Then was I ware of one that on me moved
In golden armour with a crown of gold
About a casque all jewels ; and his horse
In golden armour jewell'd everywhere :
And on the splendour came, flashing me
    blind ;
And seem'd to me the Lord of all the
    world,

Being so huge.   But when I thought he
    meant
To crush me, moving on me, lo ! he, too,
Open'd his arms to embrace me as he
    came,
And up I went and touch'd him, and he,
    too,
Fell into dust, and I was left alone
And wearying in a land of sand and
    thorns.

'And I rode on and found a mighty
    hill,
And on the top, a city wall'd : the spires
Prick'd with incredible pinnacles into
    heaven.
And by the gateway stirr'd a crowd ; and
    these
Cried to me climbing, "Welcome, Perci-
    vale !
Thou mightiest and thou purest among
    men !"
And glad was I and clomb, but found at
    top
No man, nor any voice.   And thence I
    past
Far thro' a ruinous city, and I saw
That man had once dwelt there ; but
    there I found
Only one man of an exceeding age.
"Where is that goodly company," said I,
"That so cried out upon me ?" and he
    had
Scarce any voice to answer, and yet
    gasp'd,
"Whence and what art thou ?" and even
    as he spoke
Fell into dust, and disappear'd, and I
Was left alone once more, and cried in
    grief,
"Lo, if I find the Holy Grail itself
And touch it, it will crumble into dust."

'And thence I dropt into a lowly vale,
Low as the hill was high, and where the
    vale
Was lowest, found a chapel, and thereby
A holy hermit in a hermitage,
To whom I told my phantoms, and he
    said :

' "O son, thou hast not true humility,
The highest virtue, mother of them all ;
For when the Lord of all things made
    Himself
Naked of glory for His mortal change,
'Take thou my robe,' she said, 'for all
    is thine,'
And all her form shone forth with sudden
    light
So that the angels were amazed, and she
Follow'd Him down, and like a flying
    star
Led on the gray-hair'd wisdom of the east ;
But her thou hast not known : for what
    is this
Thou thoughtest of thy prowess and thy
    sins ?
Thou hast not lost thyself to save thyself
As Galahad." When the hermit made
    an end,
In silver armour suddenly Galahad shone
Before us, and against the chapel door
Laid lance, and enter'd, and we knelt in
    prayer.
And there the hermit slaked my burning
    thirst,
And at the sacring of the mass I saw
The holy elements alone ; but he,
"Saw ye no more? I, Galahad, saw
    the Grail,
The Holy Grail, descend upon the
    shrine :
I saw the fiery face as of a child
That smote itself into the bread, and went ;
And hither am I come ; and never yet
Hath what thy sister taught me first to
    see,
This Holy Thing, fail'd from my side, nor
    come
Cover'd, but moving with me night and
    day,
Fainter by day, but always in the night
Blood-red, and sliding down the blacken'd
    marsh
Blood-red, and on the naked mountain
    top
Blood-red, and in the sleeping mere below
Blood-red. And in the strength of this
    I rode,
Shattering all evil customs everywhere,

And past thro' Pagan realms, and made
    them mine,
And clash'd with Pagan hordes, and bore
    them down,
And broke thro' all, and in the strength
    of this
Come victor. But my time is hard at
    hand,
And hence I go ; and one will crown me
    king
Far in the spiritual city ; and come thou,
    too,
For thou shalt see the vision when I go.'

'While thus he spake, his eye, dwelling
    on mine,
Drew me, with power upon me, till I
    grew
One with him, to believe as he believed.
Then, when the day began to wane, we
    went.

'There rose a hill that none but man
    could climb,
Scarr'd with a hundred wintry water-
    courses—
Storm at the top, and when we gain'd it,
    storm
Round us and death ; for every moment
    glanced
His silver arms and gloom'd : so quick
    and thick
The lightnings here and there to left and
    right
Struck, till the dry old trunks about us,
    dead,
Yea, rotten with a hundred years of death,
Sprang into fire: and at the base we found
On either hand, as far as eye could see,
A great black swamp and of an evil smell,
Part black, part whiten'd with the bones
    of men,
Not to be crost, save that some ancient
    king
Had built a way, where, link'd with
    many a bridge,
A thousand piers ran into the great Sea.
And Galahad fled along them bridge by
    bridge,
And every bridge as quickly as he crost

Sprang into fire and vanish'd, tho' I
  yearn'd
To follow ; and thrice above him all the
  heavens
Open'd and blazed with thunder such as
  seem'd
Shoutings of all the sons of God : and first
At once I saw him far on the great Sea,
In silver-shining armour starry-clear ;
And o'er his head the Holy Vessel hung
Clothed in white samite or a luminous cloud.
And with exceeding swiftness ran the boat,
If boat it were—I saw not whence it came.
And when the heavens open'd and blazed
  again
Roaring, I saw him like a silver star—
And had he set the sail, or had the boat
Become a living creature clad with wings ?
And o'er his head the Holy Vessel hung
Redder than any rose, a joy to me,
For now I knew the veil had been with-
  drawn.
Then in a moment when they blazed again
Opening, I saw the least of little stars
Down on the waste, and straight beyond
  the star
I saw the spiritual city and all her spires
And gateways in a glory like one pearl—
No larger, tho' the goal of all the saints—
Strike from the sea ; and from the star
  there shot
A rose-red sparkle to the city, and there
Dwelt, and I knew it was the Holy Grail,
Which never eyes on earth again shall see.
Then fell the floods of heaven drowning
  the deep.
And how my feet recrost the deathful ridge
No memory in me lives ; but that I touch'd
The chapel-doors at dawn I know ; and
  thence
Taking my war-horse from the holy man,
Glad that no phantom vext me more,
  return'd
To whence I came, the gate of Arthur's
  wars.'

'O brother,' ask'd Ambrosius,—'for
  in sooth
These ancient books—and they would win
  thee—teem,

Only I find not there this Holy Grail,
With miracles and marvels like to these,
Not all unlike ; which oftentime I read,
Who read but on my breviary with ease,
Till my head swims ; and then go forth
  and pass
Down to the little thorpe that lies so close,
And almost plaster'd like a martin's nest
To these old walls—and mingle with our
  folk ;
And knowing every honest face of theirs
As well as ever shepherd knew his sheep,
And every homely secret in their hearts,
Delight myself with gossip and old wives,
And ills and aches, and teethings, lyings-
  in,
And mirthful sayings, children of the place,
That have no meaning half a league away :
Or lulling random squabbles when they
  rise,
Chafferings and chatterings at the market-
  cross,
Rejoice, small man, in this small world
  of mine,
Yea, even in their hens and in their eggs—
O brother, saving this Sir Galahad,
Came ye on none but phantoms in your
  quest,
No man, no woman ?'

            Then Sir Percivale :
'All men, to one so bound by such a vow,
And women were as phantoms. O, my
  brother,
Why wilt thou shame me to confess to thee
How far I falter'd from my quest and vow ?
For after I had lain so many nights,
A bedmate of the snail and eft and snake,
In grass and burdock, I was changed to
  wan
And meagre, and the vision had not
  come ;
And then I chanced upon a goodly town
With one great dwelling in the middle
  of it ;
Thither I made, and there was I disarm'd
By maidens each as fair as any flower :
But when they led me into hall, behold,
The Princess of that castle was the one,
Brother, and that one only, who had ever

Made my heart leap; for when I moved
    of old
A slender page about her father's hall,
And she a slender maiden, all my heart
Went after her with longing: yet we
    twain
Had never kiss'd a kiss, or vow'd a vow.
And now I came upon her once again,
And one had wedded her, and he was dead,
And all his land and wealth and state
    were hers.
And while I tarried, every day she set
A banquet richer than the day before
By me; for all her longing and her will
Was toward me as of old; till one fair
    morn,
I walking to and fro beside a stream
That flash'd across her orchard underneath
Her castle-walls, she stole upon my walk,
And calling me the greatest of all knights,
Embraced me, and so kiss'd me the first
    time,
And gave herself and all her wealth to me.
Then I remember'd Arthur's warning
    word,
That most of us would follow wandering
    fires,
And the Quest faded in my heart. Anon,
The heads of all her people drew to me,
With supplication both of knees and
    tongue:
"We have heard of thee: thou art our
    greatest knight,
Our Lady says it, and we well believe:
Wed thou our Lady, and rule over us,
And thou shalt be as Arthur in our land."
O me, my brother! but one night my vow
Burnt me within, so that I rose and fled,
But wail'd and wept, and hated mine own
    self,
And ev'n the Holy Quest, and all but her;
Then after I was join'd with Galahad
Cared not for her, nor anything upon
    earth.'

    Then said the monk, 'Poor men, when
    yule is cold,
Must be content to sit by little fires.
And this am I, so that ye care for me
Ever so little; yea, and blest be Heaven

That brought thee here to this poor house
    of ours
Where all the brethren are so hard, to
    warm
My cold heart with a friend: but O the
    pity
To find thine own first love once more—
    to hold,
Hold her a wealthy bride within thine
    arms,
Or all but hold, and then—cast her aside,
Foregoing all her sweetness, like a weed.
For we that want the warmth of double
    life,
We that are plagued with dreams of
    something sweet
Beyond all sweetness in a life so rich,—
Ah, blessed Lord, I speak too earthlywise,
Seeing I never stray'd beyond the cell,
But live like an old badger in his earth,
With earth about him everywhere, despite
All fast and penance. Saw ye none be-
    side,
None of your knights?'

            'Yea so,' said Percivale:
'One night my pathway swerving east, I
    saw
The pelican on the casque of our Sir Bors
All in the middle of the rising moon:
And toward him spurr'd, and hail'd him,
    and he me,
And each made joy of either; then he
    ask'd,
"Where is he? hast thou seen him—
    Lancelot?—Once,"
Said good Sir Bors, "he dash'd across me
    —mad,
And maddening what he rode: and when
    I cried,
'Ridest thou then so hotly on a quest
So holy,' Lancelot shouted, 'Stay me not!
I have been the sluggard, and I ride apace,
For now there is a lion in the way.'
So vanish'd."

          'Then Sir Bors had ridden on
Softly, and sorrowing for our Lancelot,
Because his former madness, once the talk
And scandal of our table, had return'd;

For Lancelot's kith and kin so worship him
That ill to him is ill to them ; to Bors
Beyond the rest : he well had been content
Not to have seen, so Lancelot might have seen,
The Holy Cup of healing ; and, indeed,
Being so clouded with his grief and love,
Small heart was his after the Holy Quest :
If God would send the vision, well : if not,
The Quest and he were in the hands of Heaven.

'And then, with small adventure met, Sir Bors
Rode to the lonest tract of all the realm,
And found a people there among their crags,
Our race and blood, a remnant that were left
Paynim amid their circles, and the stones
They pitch up straight to heaven : and their wise men
Were strong in that old magic which can trace
The wandering of the stars, and scoff'd at him
And this high Quest as at a simple thing :
Told him he follow'd—almost Arthur's words—
A mocking fire : "what other fire than he,
Whereby the blood beats, and the blossom blows,
And the sea rolls, and all the world is warm'd ?"
And when his answer chafed them, the rough crowd,
Hearing he had a difference with their priests,
Seized him, and bound and plunged him into a cell
Of great piled stones ; and lying bounden there
In darkness thro' innumerable hours
He heard the hollow-ringing heavens sweep
Over him till by miracle—what else ?—
Heavy as it was, a great stone slipt and fell,

Such as no wind could move : and thro' the gap
Glimmer'd the streaming scud : then came a night
Still as the day was loud ; and thro' the gap
The seven clear stars of Arthur's Table Round—
For, brother, so one night, because they roll
Thro' such a round in heaven, we named the stars,
Rejoicing in ourselves and in our King—
And these, like bright eyes of familiar friends,
In on him shone : "And then to me, to me,"
Said good Sir Bors, "beyond all hopes of mine,
Who scarce had pray'd or ask'd it for myself—
Across the seven clear stars—O grace to me—
In colour like the fingers of a hand
Before a burning taper, the sweet Grail
Glided and past, and close upon it peal'd
A sharp quick thunder." Afterwards, a maid,
Who kept our holy faith among her kin
In secret, entering, loosed and let him go.'

To whom the monk : 'And I remember now
That pelican on the casque : Sir Bors it was
Who spake so low and sadly at our board ;
And mighty reverent at our grace was he :
A square-set man and honest ; and his eyes,
An out-door sign of all the warmth within,
Smiled with his lips—a smile beneath a cloud,
But heaven had meant it for a sunny one :
Ay, ay, Sir Bors, who else ? But when ye reach'd
The city, found ye all your knights return'd,
Or was there sooth in Arthur's prophecy,
Tell me, and what said each, and what the King ?'

Then answer'd Percivale : ' And that can I,
Brother, and truly ; since the living words
Of so great men as Lancelot and our King
Pass not from door to door and out again,
But sit within the house. O, when we reach'd
The city, our horses stumbling as they trode
On heaps of ruin, hornless unicorns,
Crack'd basilisks, and splinter'd cocka-
trices,
And shatter'd talbots, which had left the stones
Raw, that they fell from, brought us to the hall.

' And there sat Arthur on the dais-
throne,
And those that had gone out upon the Quest,
Wasted and worn, and but a tithe of them,
And those that had not, stood before the King,
Who, when he saw me, rose, and bad me hail,
Saying, " A welfare in thine eye reproves
Our fear of some disastrous chance for thee
On hill, or plain, at sea, or flooding ford.
So fierce a gale made havoc here of late
Among the strange devices of our kings ;
Yea, shook this newer, stronger hall of ours,
And from the statue Merlin moulded for us
Half-wrench'd a golden wing ; but now—
the Quest,
This vision—hast thou seen the Holy Cup,
That Joseph brought of old to Glaston-
bury ?"

' So when I told him all thyself hast heard,
Ambrosius, and my fresh but fixt resolve
To pass away into the quiet life,
He answer'd not, but, sharply turning, ask'd
Of Gawain, " Gawain, was this Quest for thee ?"

' " Nay, lord," said Gawain, " not for such as I.
Therefore I communed with a saintly man,
Who made me sure the Quest was not for me ;
For I was much awearied of the Quest :
But found a silk pavilion in a field,
And merry maidens in it ; and then this gale
Tore my pavilion from the tenting-pin,
And blew my merry maidens all about
With all discomfort ; yea, and but for this,
My twelvemonth and a day were pleasant to me."

' He ceased ; and Arthur turn'd to whom at first
He saw not, for Sir Bors, on entering, push'd
Athwart the throng to Lancelot, caught his hand,
Held it, and there, half-hidden by him, stood,
Until the King espied him, saying to him,
" Hail, Bors ! if ever loyal man and true
Could see it, thou hast seen the Grail ;"
and Bors,
" Ask me not, for I may not speak of it :
I saw it ;" and the tears were in his eyes.

' Then there remain'd but Lancelot, for the rest
Spake but of sundry perils in the storm ;
Perhaps, like him of Cana in Holy Writ,
Our Arthur kept his best until the last ;
" Thou, too, my Lancelot," ask'd the King, " my friend,
Our mightiest, hath this Quest avail'd for thee ?"

' " Our mightiest !" answer'd Lancelot, with a groan ;
" O King !" — and when he paused, methought I spied
A dying fire of madness in his eyes—
" O King, my friend, if friend of thine I be,
Happier are those that welter in their sin,
Swine in the mud, that cannot see for slime,
Slime of the ditch : but in me lived a sin
So strange, of such a kind, that all of pure

Noble, and knightly in me twined and clung
Round that one sin, until the wholesome flower
And poisonous grew together, each as each,
Not to be pluck'd asunder ; and when thy knights
Sware, I sware with them only in the hope
That could I touch or see the Holy Grail
They might be pluck'd asunder.   Then I spake
To one most holy saint, who wept and said,
That save they could be pluck'd asunder, all
My quest were but in vain ; to whom I vow'd
That I would work according as he will'd.
And forth I went, and while I yearn'd and strove
To tear the twain asunder in my heart,
My madness came upon me as of old,
And whipt me into waste fields far away ;
There was I beaten down by little men,
Mean knights, to whom the moving of my sword
And shadow of my spear had been enow
To scare them from me once ; and then I came
All in my folly to the naked shore,
Wide flats, where nothing but coarse grasses grew ;
But such a blast, my King, began to blow,
So loud a blast along the shore and sea,
Ye could not hear the waters for the blast,
Tho' heapt in mounds and ridges all the sea
Drove like a cataract, and all the sand
Swept like a river, and the clouded heavens
Were shaken with the motion and the sound.
And blackening in the sea-foam sway'd a boat,
Half-swallow'd in it, anchor'd with a chain ;
And in my madness to myself I said,
'I will embark and I will lose myself,
And in the great sea wash away my sin.'

I burst the chain, I sprang into the boat.
Seven days I drove along the dreary deep,
And with me drove the moon and all the stars ;
And the wind fell, and on the seventh night
I heard the shingle grinding in the surge,
And felt the boat shock earth, and looking up,
Behold, the enchanted towers of Carbonek,
A castle like a rock upon a rock,
With chasm-like portals open to the sea,
And steps that met the breaker ! there was none
Stood near it but a lion on each side
That kept the entry, and the moon was full.
Then from the boat I leapt, and up the stairs.
There drew my sword.   With sudden-flaring manes
Those two great beasts rose upright like a man,
Each gript a shoulder, and I stood between ;
And, when I would have smitten them, heard a voice,
' Doubt not, go forward ; if thou doubt, the beasts
Will tear thee piecemeal.'   Then with violence
The sword was dash'd from out my hand, and fell.
And up into the sounding hall I past ;
But nothing in the sounding hall I saw,
No bench nor table, painting on the wall
Or shield of knight ; only the rounded moon
Thro' the tall oriel on the rolling sea.
But always in the quiet house I heard,
Clear as a lark, high o'er me as a lark,
A sweet voice singing in the topmost tower
To the eastward : up I climb'd a thousand steps
With pain : as in a dream I seem'd to climb
For ever : at the last I reach'd a door,
A light was in the crannies, and I heard,

' Glory and joy and honour to our Lord
And to the Holy Vessel of the Grail.'
Then in my madness I essay'd the door ;
It gave ; and thro' a stormy glare, a heat
As from a seventimes-heated furnace, I,
Blasted and burnt, and blinded as I was,
With such a fierceness that I swoon'd
away—
O, yet methought I saw the Holy Grail,
All pall'd in crimson samite, and around
Great angels, awful shapes, and wings
and eyes.
And but for all my madness and my sin,
And then my swooning, I had sworn I
saw
That which I saw ; but what I saw was
veil'd
And cover'd ; and this Quest was not for
me."

' So speaking, and here ceasing, Lance-
lot left
The hall long silent, till Sir Gawain—nay,
Brother, I need not tell thee foolish
words,—
A reckless and irreverent knight was he,
Now bolden'd by the silence of his
King,—
Well, I will tell thee : " O King, my
liege," he said,
" Hath Gawain fail'd in any quest of
thine ?
When have I stinted stroke in foughten
field ?
But as for thine, my good friend Percivale,
Thy holy nun and thou have driven men
mad,
Yea, made our mightiest madder than
our least.
But by mine eyes and by mine ears I
swear,
I will be deafer than the blue-eyed cat,
And thrice as blind as any noonday owl,
To holy virgins in their ecstasies,
Henceforward."

' " Deafer," said the blameless King,
" Gawain, and blinder unto holy things
Hope not to make thyself by idle vows,
Being too blind to have desire to see.

But if indeed there came a sign from
heaven,
Blessed are Bors, Lancelot and Percivale,
For these have seen according to their
sight.
For every fiery prophet in old times,
And all the sacred madness of the bard,
When God made music thro' them, could
but speak
His music by the framework and the
chord ;
And as ye saw it ye have spoken truth.

' " Nay—but thou errest, Lancelot :
never yet
Could all of true and noble in knight and
man
Twine round one sin, whatever it might
be,
With such a closeness, but apart there
grew,
Save that he were the swine thou spakest
of,
Some root of knighthood and pure nobleness ;
Whereto see thou, that it may bear its
flower.

' " And spake I not too truly, O my
knights ?
Was I too dark a prophet when I said
To those who went upon the Holy Quest,
That most of them would follow wan-
dering fires,
Lost in the quagmire ?—lost to me and
gone,
And left me gazing at a barren board,
And a lean Order—scarce return'd a
tithe—
And out of those to whom the vision came
My greatest hardly will believe he saw ;
Another hath beheld it afar off,
And leaving human wrongs to right them-
selves,
Cares but to pass into the silent life.
And one hath had the vision face to
face,
And now his chair desires him here in
vain,
However they may crown him otherwhere.

' "And some among you held, that if
the King
Had seen the sight he would have sworn
the vow :
Not easily, seeing that the King must
guard
That which he rules, and is but as the hind
To whom a space of land is given to
plow.
Who may not wander from the allotted
field
Before his work be done ; but, being done,
Let visions of the night or of the day
Come, as they will ; and many a time
they come,
Until this earth he walks on seems not
earth,
This light that strikes his eyeball is not
light,
This air that smites his forehead is not air
But vision—yea, his very hand and foot—
In moments when he feels he cannot die,
And knows himself no vision to himself,
Nor the high God a vision, nor that One
Who rose again : ye have seen what ye
have seen."

' So spake the King : I knew not all
he meant.'

PELLEAS AND ETTARRE.

KING ARTHUR made new knights to fill
the gap
Left by the Holy Quest ; and as he sat
In hall at old Caerleon, the high doors
Were softly sunder'd, and thro' these a
youth,
Pelleas, and the sweet smell of the fields
Past, and the sunshine came along with
him.

' Make me thy knight, because I know,
Sir King,
All that belongs to knighthood, and I love.'
Such was his cry : for having heard the
King
Had let proclaim a tournament—the prize
A golden circlet and a knightly sword,
Full fain had Pelleas for his lady won

The golden circlet, for himself the sword :
And there were those who knew him near
the King,
And promised for him : and Arthur made
him knight.

And this new knight, Sir Pelleas of the
isles—
But lately come to his inheritance,
And lord of many a barren isle was he—
Riding at noon, a day or twain before,
Across the forest call'd of Dean, to find
Caerleon and the King, had felt the sun
Beat like a strong knight on his helm,
and reel'd
Almost to falling from his horse ; but
saw
Near him a mound of even-sloping side,
Whereon a hundred stately beeches grew,
And here and there great hollies under
them ;
But for a mile all round was open space,
And fern and heath : and slowly Pelleas
drew
To that dim day, then binding his good
horse
To a tree, cast himself down ; and as he
lay
At random looking over the brown earth
Thro' that green-glooming twilight of the
grove,
It seem'd to Pelleas that the fern without
Burnt as a living fire of emeralds,
So that his eyes were dazzled looking at it.
Then o'er it crost the dimness of a cloud
Floating, and once the shadow of a bird
Flying, and then a fawn ; and his eyes
closed.
And since he loved all maidens, but no
maid
In special, half-awake he whisper'd,
' Where ?
O where ? I love thee, tho' I know thee
not.
For fair thou art and pure as Guinevere,
And I will make thee with my spear and
sword
As famous—O my Queen, my Guinevere,
For I will be thine Arthur when we
meet.'

T   2 F

Suddenly waken'd with a sound of talk
And laughter at the limit of the wood,
And glancing thro' the hoary boles, he saw,
Strange as to some old prophet might
　　have seem'd
A vision hovering on a sea of fire,
Damsels in divers colours like the cloud
Of sunset and sunrise, and all of them
On horses, and the horses richly trapt
Breast-high in that bright line of bracken
　　stood :
And all the damsels talk'd confusedly,
And one was pointing this way, and one
　　that,
Because the way was lost.

　　　　　　　And Pelleas rose,
And loosed his horse, and led him to the
　　light.
There she that seem'd the chief among
　　them said,
' In happy time behold our pilot-star !
Youth, we are damsels-errant, and we ride,
Arm'd as ye see, to tilt against the knights
There at Caerleon, but have lost our way :
To right ? to left ? straight forward ? back
　　again ?
Which ? tell us quickly.'

　　　　　　Pelleas gazing thought,
' Is Guinevere herself so beautiful ?'
For large her violet eyes look'd, and her
　　bloom
A rosy dawn kindled in stainless heavens,
And round her limbs, mature in woman-
　　hood ;
And slender was her hand and small her
　　shape ;
And but for those large eyes, the haunts
　　of scorn,
She might have seem'd a toy to trifle with,
And pass and care no more.　But while
　　he gazed
The beauty of her flesh abash'd the boy,
As tho' it were the beauty of her soul :
For as the base man, judging of the good,
Puts his own baseness in him by default
Of will and nature, so did Pelleas lend
All the young beauty of his own soul to
　　hers,

Believing her ; and when she spake to
　　him,
Stammer'd, and could not make her a
　　reply.
For out of the waste islands had he come,
Where saving his own sisters he had known
Scarce any but the women of his isles,
Rough wives, that laugh'd and scream'd
　　against the gulls,
Makers of nets, and living from the sea.

　　Then with a slow smile turn'd the lady
　　round
And look'd upon her people ; and as when
A stone is flung into some sleeping tarn,
The circle widens till it lip the marge,
Spread the slow smile thro' all her com-
　　pany.
Three knights were thereamong ; and they
　　too smiled,
Scorning him ; for the lady was Ettarre,
And she was a great lady in her land.

　　Again she said, ' O wild and of the
　　woods,
Knowest thou not the fashion of our
　　speech ?
Or have the Heavens but given thee a fair
　　face,
Lacking a tongue ?'

　　　　　　　　' O damsel,' answer'd he,
' I woke from dreams ; and coming out
　　of gloom
Was dazzled by the sudden light, and
　　crave
Pardon : but will ye to Caerleon ?　I
Go likewise : shall I lead you to the King ?'

　　' Lead then,' she said ; and thro' the
　　woods they went.
And while they rode, the meaning in his
　　eyes,
His tenderness of manner, and chaste awe,
His broken utterances and bashfulness,
Were all a burthen to her, and in her
　　heart
She mutter'd, ' I have lighted on a fool,
Raw, yet so stale !'　But since her mind
　　was bent
On hearing, after trumpet blown, her name

And title, ' Queen of Beauty,' in the lists
Cried—and beholding him so strong, she
    thought
That peradventure he will fight for me,
And win the circlet : therefore flatter'd
    him,
Being so gracious, that he wellnigh deem'd
His wish by hers was echo'd ; and her
    knights
And all her damsels too were gracious to
    him,
For she was a great lady.

        And when they reach'd
Caerleon, ere they past to lodging, she,
Taking his hand, ' O the strong hand,'
    she said,
' See ! look at mine ! but wilt thou fight
    for me,
And win me this fine circlet, Pelleas,
That I may love thee ?'

        Then his helpless heart
Leapt, and he cried, ' Ay ! wilt thou if I
    win ?'
'Ay, that will I,' she answer'd, and she
    laugh'd,
And straitly nipt the hand, and flung it
    from her ;
Then glanced askew at those three knights
    of hers,
Till all her ladies laugh'd along with her.

' O happy world,' thought Pelleas, 'all,
    meseems,
Are happy ; I the happiest of them all.'
Nor slept that night for pleasure in his
    blood,
And green wood-ways, and eyes among
    the leaves ;
Then being on the morrow knighted,
    sware
To love one only. And as he came away,
The men who met him rounded on their
    heels
And wonder'd after him, because his face
Shone like the countenance of a priest of
    old
Against the flame about a sacrifice
Kindled by fire from heaven : so glad
    was he.

Then Arthur made vast banquets, and
    strange knights
From the four winds came in : and each
    one sat,
Tho' served with choice from air, land,
    stream, and sea,
Oft in mid - banquet measuring with his
    eyes
His neighbour's make and might : and
    Pelleas look'd
Noble among the noble, for he dream'd
His lady loved him, and he knew himself
Loved of the King : and him his new-
    made knight
Worshipt, whose lightest whisper moved
    him more
Than all the ranged reasons of the world.

Then blush'd and brake the morning
    of the jousts,
And this was call'd 'The Tournament of
    Youth :'
For Arthur, loving his young knight,
    withheld
His older and his mightier from the lists,
That Pelleas might obtain his lady's love,
According to her promise, and remain
Lord of the tourney. And Arthur had
    the jousts
Down in the flat field by the shore of Usk
Holden : the gilded parapets were crown'd
With faces, and the great tower fill'd with
    eyes
Up to the summit, and the trumpets blew.
There all day long Sir Pelleas kept the
    field
With honour : so by that strong hand of
    his
The sword and golden circlet were
    achieved.

Then rang the shout his lady loved :
    the heat
Of pride and glory fired her face ; her eye
Sparkled ; she caught the circlet from his
    lance,
And there before the people crown'd
    herself :
So for the last time she was gracious to
    him.

Then at Caerleon for a space—her look
Bright for all others, cloudier on her
   knight—
Linger'd Ettarre : and seeing Pelleas
   droop,
Said Guinevere, 'We marvel at thee
   much,
O damsel, wearing this unsunny face
To him who won thee glory !' And she
   said,
'Had ye not held your Lancelot in your
   bower,
My Queen, he had not won.' Whereat
   the Queen,
As one whose foot is bitten by an ant,
Glanced down upon her, turn'd and went
   her way.

But after, when her damsels, and her-
   self,
And those three knights all set their
   faces home,
Sir Pelleas follow'd. She that saw him
   cried,
'Damsels—and yet I should be shamed
   to say it—
I cannot bide Sir Baby. Keep him back
Among yourselves. Would rather that
   we had
Some rough old knight who knew the
   worldly way,
Albeit grizzlier than a bear, to ride
And jest with : take him to you, keep
   him off,
And pamper him with papmeat, if ye will,
Old milky fables of the wolf and sheep,
Such as the wholesome mothers tell their
   boys.
Nay, should ye try him with a merry one
To find his mettle, good : and if he fly
   us,
Small matter ! let him.' This her
   damsels heard,
And mindful of her small and cruel hand,
They, closing round him thro' the journey
   home,
Acted her hest, and always from her side
Restrain'd him with all manner of device,
So that he could not come to speech
   with her.

And when she gain'd her castle, upsprang
   the bridge,
Down rang the grate of iron thro' the
   groove,
And he was left alone in open field.

'These be the ways of ladies,' Pelleas
   thought,
'To those who love them. trials of our
   faith.
Yea, let her prove me to the uttermost,
For loyal to the uttermost am I.'
So made his moan ; and, darkness falling,
   sought
A priory not far off, there lodged, but
   rose
With morning every day, and, moist or
   dry,
Full-arm'd upon his charger all day long
Sat by the walls, and no one open'd to
   him.

And this persistence turn'd her scorn
   to wrath.
Then calling her three knights, she
   charged them, 'Out !
And drive him from the walls.' And out
   they came,
But Pelleas overthrew them as they
   dash'd
Against him one by one ; and these
   return'd,
But still he kept his watch beneath the
   wall.

Thereon her wrath became a hate ;
   and once,
A week beyond, while walking on the
   walls
With her three knights, she pointed
   downward, 'Look,
He haunts me—I cannot breathe—be-
   sieges me ;
Down ! strike him ! put my hate into
   your strokes,
And drive him from my walls.' And
   down they went,
And Pelleas overthrew them one by one ;
And from the tower above him cried
   Ettarre,
'Bind him, and bring him in.'

He heard her voice ;
Then let the strong hand, which had
    overthrown
Her minion-knights, by those he over-
    threw
Be bounden straight, and so they brought
    him in.

Then when he came before Ettarre,
    the sight
Of her rich beauty made him at one
    glance
More bondsman in his heart than in his
    bonds.
Yet with good cheer he spake, ' Behold
    me, Lady,
A prisoner, and the vassal of thy will ;
And if thou keep me in thy donjon here,
Content am I so that I see thy face
But once a day : for I have sworn my
    vows,
And thou hast given thy promise, and I
    know
That all these pains are trials of my faith,
And that thyself, when thou hast seen me
    strain'd
And sifted to the utmost, wilt at length
Yield me thy love and know me for thy
    knight.'

Then she began to rail so bitterly,
With all her damsels, he was stricken
    mute ;
But when she mock'd his vows and the
    great King,
Lighted on words : ' For pity of thine
    own self,
Peace, Lady, peace : is he not thine and
    mine ?'
' Thou fool,' she said, ' I never heard his
    voice
But long'd to break away.   Unbind him
    now,
And thrust him out of doors ; for save
    he be
Fool to the midmost marrow of his bones,
He will return no more.'   And those, her
    three,
Laugh'd, and unbound, and thrust him
    from the gate.

And after this, a week beyond, again
She call'd them, saying, ' There he
    watches yet,
There like a dog before his master's door !
Kick'd, he returns : do ye not hate him,
    ye ?
Ye know yourselves : how can ye bide at
    peace,
Affronted with his fulsome innocence ?
Are ye but creatures of the board and bed,
No men to strike ?   Fall on him all at
    once,
And if ye slay him I reck not : if ye fail,
Give ye the slave mine order to be bound,
Bind him as heretofore, and bring him in :
It may be ye shall slay him in his bonds.'

She spake ; and at her will they couch'd
    their spears,
Three against one : and Gawain passing
    by,
Bound upon solitary adventure, saw
Low down beneath the shadow of those
    towers
A villainy, three to one : and thro' his
    heart
The fire of honour and all noble deeds
Flash'd, and he call'd, ' I strike upon thy
    side—
The caitiffs !'   ' Nay,' said Pelleas, ' but
    forbear ;
He needs no aid who doth his lady's will.'

So Gawain, looking at the villainy done,
Forbore, but in his heat and eagerness
Trembled and quiver'd, as the dog, with-
    held
A moment from the vermin that he sees
Before him, shivers, ere he springs and
    kills.

And Pelleas overthrew them, one to
    three ;
And they rose up, and bound, and brought
    him in.
Then first her anger, leaving Pelleas,
    burn'd
Full on her knights in many an evil name
Of craven, weakling, and thrice-beaten
    hound :

'Yet, take him, ye that scarce are fit to
   touch,
Far less to bind, your victor, and thrust
   him out,
And let who will release him from his
   bonds.
And if he comes again '—there she brake
   short ;
And Pelleas answer'd, ' Lady, for indeed
I loved you and I deem'd you beautiful,
I cannot brook to see your beauty marr'd
Thro' evil spite : and if ye love me not,
I cannot bear to dream you so forsworn :
I had liefer ye were worthy of my love,
Than to be loved again of you—farewell ;
And tho' ye kill my hope, not yet my love,
Vex not yourself : ye will not see me
   more.'

While thus he spake, she gazed upon
   the man
Of princely bearing, tho' in bonds, and
   thought,
'Why have I push'd him from me? this
   man loves,
If love there be : yet him I loved not.
   Why ?
I deem'd him fool? yea, so? or that in
   him
A something—was it nobler than my-
   self ?—
Seem'd my reproach ? He is not of my
   kind.
He could not love me, did he know me
   well.
Nay, let him go—and quickly.' And her
   knights
Laugh'd not, but thrust him bounden out
   of door.

Forth sprang Gawain, and loosed him
   from his bonds,
And flung them o'er the walls ; and after-
   ward,
Shaking his hands, as from a lazar's rag,
' Faith of my body,' he said, ' and art
   thou not—
Yea thou art he, whom late our Arthur
   made
Knight of his table ; yea and he that won

The circlet ? wherefore hast thou so
   defamed
Thy brotherhood in me and all the rest,
As let these caitiffs on thee work their
   will ?'

And Pelleas answer'd, ' O, their wills
   are hers
For whom I won the circlet ; and mine,
   hers,
Thus to be bounden, so to see her face,
Marr'd tho' it be with spite and mockery
   now,
Other than when I found her in the
   woods ;
And tho' she hath me bounden but in spite,
And all to flout me, when they bring me
   in,
Let me be bounden, I shall see her face ;
Else must I die thro' mine unhappiness.'

And Gawain answer'd kindly tho' in
   scorn,
' Why, let my lady bind me if she will,
And let my lady beat me if she will :
But an she send her delegate to thrall
These fighting hands of mine—Christ kill
   me then
But I will slice him handless by the wrist,
And let my lady sear the stump for him,
Howl as he may. But hold me for your
   friend :
Come, ye know nothing : here I pledge
   my troth,
Yea, by the honour of the Table Round,
I will be leal to thee and work thy work,
And tame thy jailing princess to thine
   hand.
Lend me thine horse and arms, and I will
   say
That I have slain thee. She will let me
   in
To hear the manner of thy fight and fall ;
Then, when I come within her counsels,
   then
From prime to vespers will I chant thy
   praise
As prowest knight and truest lover, more
Than any have sung thee living, till she
   long

To have thee back in lusty life again,
Not to be bound, save by white bonds
    and warm,
Dearer than freedom. Wherefore now
    thy horse
And armour : let me go : be comforted :
Give me three days to melt her fancy,
    and hope
The third night hence will bring thee
    news of gold.'

Then Pelleas lent his horse and all his
    arms,
Saving the goodly sword, his prize, and
    took
Gawain's, and said, ' Betray me not, but
    help—
Art thou not he whom men call light-of-
    love ?'

' Ay,' said Gawain, ' for women be so
    light.'
Then bounded forward to the castle walls,
And raised a bugle hanging from his neck,
And winded it, and that so musically
That all the old echoes hidden in the
    wall
Rang out like hollow woods at hunting-
    tide.

Up ran a score of damsels to the tower ;
' Avaunt,' they cried, ' our lady loves thee
    not.'
But Gawain lifting up his vizor said,
' Gawain am I, Gawain of Arthur's court,
And I have slain this Pelleas whom ye
    hate :
Behold his horse and armour. Open
    gates,
And I will make you merry.'

                And down they ran,
Her damsels, crying to their lady, ' Lo !
Pelleas is dead—he told us—he that hath
His horse and armour : will ye let him in ?
He slew him ! Gawain, Gawain of the
    court,
Sir Gawain—there he waits below the
    wall,
Blowing his bugle as who should say him
    nay.'

And so, leave given, straight on thro'
    open door
Rode Gawain, whom she greeted cour-
    teously.
' Dead, is it so ?' she ask'd. ' Ay, ay,'
    said he,
' And oft in dying cried upon your name.'
' Pity on him,' she answer'd, ' a good
    knight,
But never let me bide one hour at peace.
' Ay,' thought Gawain, ' and you be fair
    enow :
But I to your dead man have given my
    troth,
That whom ye loathe, him will I make
    you love.'

So those three days, aimless about the
    land,
Lost in a doubt, Pelleas wandering
Waited, until the third night brought a
    moon
With promise of large light on woods and
    ways.

Hot was the night and silent ; but a
    sound
Of Gawain ever coming, and this lay—
Which Pelleas had heard sung before the
    Queen,
And seen her sadden listening—vext his
    heart,
And marr'd his rest—' A worm within the
    rose.'

' A rose, but one, none other rose had I,
A rose, one rose, and this was wondrous
    fair,
One rose, a rose that gladden'd earth and
    sky,
One rose, my rose, that sweeten'd all
    mine air—
I cared not for the thorns ; the thorns
    were there.

' One rose, a rose to gather by and by,
One rose, a rose, to gather and to wear,
No rose but one—what other rose had I ?
One rose, my rose ; a rose that will not
    die,—
He dies who loves it,—if the worm be
    there.'

This tender rhyme, and evermore the
    doubt,
' Why lingers Gawain with his golden
    news ? '
So shook him that he could not rest, but
    rode
Ere midnight to her walls, and bound his
    horse
Hard by the gates. Wide open were the
    gates,
And no watch kept ; and in thro' these
    he past,
And heard but his own steps, and his
    own heart
Beating, for nothing moved but his own
    self,
And his own shadow. Then he crost
    the court,
And spied not any light in hall or bower,
But saw the postern portal also wide
Yawning ; and up a slope of garden, all
Of roses white and red, and brambles mixt
And overgrowing them, went on, and
    found,
Here too, all hush'd below the mellow
    moon,
Save that one rivulet from a tiny cave
Came lightening downward, and so spilt
    itself
Among the roses, and was lost again.

Then was he ware of three pavilions
    rear'd
Above the bushes, gilden-peakt : in one,
Red after revel, droned her lurdane knights
Slumbering, and their three squires across
    their feet :
In one, their malice on the placid lip
Froz'n by sweet sleep, four of her damsels
    lay :
And in the third, the circlet of the jousts
Bound on her brow, were Gawain and
    Ettarre.

Back, as a hand that pushes thro' the
    leaf
To find a nest and feels a snake, he drew :
Back, as a coward slinks from what he
    fears
To cope with, or a traitor proven, or hound

Beaten, did Pelleas in an utter shame
Creep with his shadow thro' the court
    again,
Fingering at his sword-handle until he
    stood
There on the castle-bridge once more, and
    thought,
' I will go back, and slay them where they
    lie.'

And so went back, and seeing them yet
    in sleep
Said, ' Ye, that so dishallow the holy
    sleep,
Your sleep is death,' and drew the sword,
    and thought,
' What ! slay a sleeping knight ? the King
    hath bound
And sworn me to this brotherhood ; '
    again,
' Alas that ever a knight should be so
    false.'
Then turn'd, and so return'd, and groan-
    ing laid
The naked sword athwart their naked
    throats,
There left it, and them sleeping ; and she
    lay,
The circlet of the tourney round her
    brows,
And the sword of the tourney across her
    throat.

And forth he past, and mounting on
    his horse
Stared at her towers that, larger than
    themselves
In their own darkness, throng'd into the
    moon.
Then crush'd the saddle with his thighs,
    and clench'd
His hands, and madden'd with himself
    and moan'd :

' Would they have risen against me in
    their blood
At the last day ? I might have answer'd
    them
Even before high God. O towers so
    strong,

Huge, solid, would that even while I gaze
The crack of earthquake shivering to your base
Split you, and Hell burst up your harlot roofs
Bellowing, and charr'd you thro' and thro' within,
Black as the harlot's heart—hollow as a skull !
Let the fierce east scream thro' your eye-let-holes,
And whirl the dust of harlots round and round
In dung and nettles ! hiss, snake—I saw him there—
Let the fox bark, let the wolf yell. Who yells
Here in the still sweet summer night, but I—
I, the poor Pelleas whom she call'd her fool ?
Fool, beast—he, she, or I ? myself most fool ;
Beast too, as lacking human wit — disgraced,
Dishonour'd all for trial of true love—
Love ?—we be all alike : only the King
Hath made us fools and liars. O noble vows !
O great and sane and simple race of brutes
That own no lust because they have no law !
For why should I have loved her to my shame ?
I loathe her, as I loved her to my shame.
I never loved her, I but lusted for her—
Away—'

He dash'd the rowel into his horse,
And bounded forth and vanish'd thro' the night.

Then she, that felt the cold touch on her throat,
Awaking knew the sword, and turn'd herself
To Gawain: 'Liar, for thou hast not slain
This Pelleas ! here he stood, and might have slain
Me and thyself.' And he that tells the tale

Says that her ever-veering fancy turn'd
To Pelleas, as the one true knight on earth,
And only lover ; and thro' her love her life
Wasted and pined, desiring him in vain.

But he by wild and way, for half the night,
And over hard and soft, striking the sod
From out the soft, the spark from off the hard,
Rode till the star above the wakening sun,
Beside that tower where Percivale was cowl'd,
Glanced from the rosy forehead of the dawn.
For so the words were flash'd into his heart
He knew not whence or wherefore : ' O sweet star,
Pure on the virgin forehead of the dawn !'
And there he would have wept, but felt his eyes
Harder and drier than a fountain bed
In summer : thither came the village girls
And linger'd talking, and they come no more
Till the sweet heavens have fill'd it from the heights
Again with living waters in the change
Of seasons : hard his eyes ; harder his heart
Seem'd ; but so weary were his limbs, that he,
Gasping, 'Of Arthur's hall am I, but here,
Here let me rest and die,' cast himself down,
And gulf'd his griefs in inmost sleep ; so lay,
Till shaken by a dream, that Gawain fired
The hall of Merlin, and the morning star
Reel'd in the smoke, brake into flame, and fell.

He woke, and being ware of some one nigh,
Sent hands upon him, as to tear him, crying,
'False! and I held thee pure as Guinevere.'

But Percivale stood near him and
    replied,
' Am I but false as Guinevere is pure ?
Or art thou mazed with dreams ? or being
    one
Of our free-spoken Table hast not heard
That Lancelot '—there he check'd him-
    self and paused.

Then fared it with Sir Pelleas as with
    one
Who gets a wound in battle, and the sword
That made it plunges thro' the wound
    again,
And pricks it deeper : and he shrank and
    wail'd,
' Is the Queen false ?' and Percivale was
    mute.
' Have any of our Round Table held their
    vows ?'
And Percivale made answer not a word.
' Is the King true ?'   ' The King !' said
    Percivale.
' Why then let men couple at once with
    wolves.
What ! art thou mad ?'

But Pelleas, leaping up,
Ran thro' the doors and vaulted on his
    horse
And fled : small pity upon his horse had
    he,
Or on himself, or any, and when he met
A cripple, one that held a hand for alms—
Hunch'd as he was, and like an old dwarf-
    elm
That turns its back on the salt blast, the
    boy
Paused not, but overrode him, shouting,
    ' False,
And false with Gawain !' and so left him
    bruised
And batter'd, and fled on, and hill and
    wood
Went ever streaming by him till the gloom,
That follows on the turning of the world,
Darken'd the common path : he twitch'd
    the reins,
And made his beast that better knew it,
    swerve

Now off it and now on ; but when he sa
High up in heaven the hall that Merl
    built,
Blackening against the dead-green strip
    of even,
' Black nest of rats,' he groan'd, ' ye bui
    too high.'

Not long thereafter from the city gat
Issued Sir Lancelot riding airily,
Warm with a gracious parting from t
    Queen,
Peace at his heart, and gazing at a star
And marvelling what it was : on who
    the boy,
Across the silent seeded meadow-grass
Borne, clash'd : and Lancelot, sayin
    ' What name hast thou
That ridest here so blindly and
    hard?'
' No name, no name,' he shouted,
    scourge am I
To lash the treasons of the Table Roun
' Yea, but thy name ?'   ' I have ma
    names,' he cried :
' I am wrath and shame and hate and e
    fame,
And like a poisonous wind I pass
    blast
And blaze the crime of Lancelot and t
    Queen.'
' First over me,' said Lancelot, ' sh
    thou pass.'
' Fight therefore,' yell'd the youth, an
    either knight
Drew back a space, and when they close
    at once
The weary steed of Pelleas flounderi
    flung
His rider, who call'd out from the da
    field,
' Thou art false as Hell : slay me : I ha
    no sword.'
Then Lancelot, ' Yea, between thy lips
    and sharp ;
But here will I disedge it by thy death
' Slay then,' he shriek'd, ' my will is to
    slain,'
And Lancelot, with his heel upon
    fall'n,

olling his eyes, a moment stood, then
spake :
Rise, weakling ; I am Lancelot ; say thy
say.'

And Lancelot slowly rode his warhorse
back
o Camelot, and Sir Pelleas in brief while
aught his unbroken limbs from the dark
field,
nd follow'd to the city. It chanced that
both
rake into hall together, worn and pale.
here with her knights and dames was
Guinevere.
ull wonderingly she gazed on Lancelot
o soon return'd, and then on Pelleas,
him
Vho had not greeted her, but cast himself
own on a bench, hard-breathing. 'Have
ye fought ?'
he ask'd of Lancelot. 'Ay, my Queen,'
he said.
And thou hast overthrown him ?' 'Ay,
my Queen.'
hen she, turning to Pelleas, 'O young
knight,
ath the great heart of knighthood in
thee fail'd
o far thou canst not bide, unfrowardly,
fall from *him* ?' Then, for he answer'd
not,
Or hast thou other griefs ? If I, the
Queen,
ay help them, loose thy tongue, and let
me know.'
ut Pelleas lifted up an eye so fierce
he quail'd ; and he, hissing 'I have no
sword,'
prang from the door into the dark.
The Queen
ook'd hard upon her lover, he on her ;
nd each foresaw the dolorous day to
be :
nd all talk died, as in a grove all song
eneath the shadow of some bird of prey ;
hen a long silence came upon the hall,
nd Modred thought, 'The time is hard
at hand.'

THE LAST TOURNAMENT.

DAGONET, the fool, whom Gawain in his
mood
Had made mock-knight of Arthur's Table
Round,
At Camelot, high above the yellowing
woods,
Danced like a wither'd leaf before the hall.
And toward him from the hall, with harp
in hand,
And from the crown thereof a carcanet
Of ruby swaying to and fro, the prize
Of Tristram in the jousts of yesterday,
Came Tristram, saying, 'Why skip ye
so, Sir Fool ?'

For Arthur and Sir Lancelot riding once
Far down beneath a winding wall of rock
Heard a child wail. A stump of oak
half-dead,
From roots like some black coil of carven
snakes,
Clutch'd at the crag, and started thro'
mid air
Bearing an eagle's nest : and thro' the tree
Rush'd ever a rainy wind, and thro' the
wind
Pierced ever a child's cry : and crag and
tree
Scaling, Sir Lancelot from the perilous
nest,
This ruby necklace thrice around her neck,
And all unscarr'd from beak or talon,
brought
A maiden babe ; which Arthur pitying
took,
Then gave it to his Queen to rear : the
Queen
But coldly acquiescing, in her white arms
Received, and after loved it tenderly,
And named it Nestling ; so forgot herself
A moment, and her cares ; till that young
life
Being smitten in mid heaven with mortal
cold
Past from her ; and in time the carcanet
Vext her with plaintive memories of the
child :

So she, delivering it to Arthur, said,
'Take thou the jewels of this dead innocence,
And make them, an thou wilt a tourney-
  prize.'

  To whom the King, 'Peace to thine
    eagle-borne
Dead nestling, and this honour after
  death,
Following thy will! but, O my Queen,
  I muse
Why ye not wear on arm, or neck, or
  zone
Those diamonds that I rescued from the
  tarn,
And Lancelot won, methought, for thee
  to wear.'

  'Would rather you had let them fall,'
    she cried,
'Plunge and be lost—ill-fated as they
  were,
A bitterness to me!—ye look amazed,
Not knowing they were lost as soon as
  given—
Slid from my hands, when I was leaning
  out
Above the river—that unhappy child
Past in her barge: but rosier luck will go
With these rich jewels, seeing that they
  came
Not from the skeleton of a brother-slayer,
But the sweet body of a maiden babe.
Perchance—who knows?—the purest of
  thy knights
May win them for the purest of my maids.'

  She ended, and the cry of a great jousts
With trumpet-blowings ran on all the
  ways
From Camelot in among the faded fields
To furthest towers; and everywhere the
  knights
Arm'd for a day of glory before the King.

  But on the hither side of that loud morn
Into the hall stagger'd, his visage ribb'd
From ear to ear with dogwhip-weals, his
  nose

Bridge-broken, one eye out, and one hand
  off,
And one with shatter'd fingers dangling
  lame,
A churl, to whom indignantly the King,

  'My churl, for whom Christ died, what
    evil beast
Hath drawn his claws athwart thy face?
  or fiend?
Man was it who marr'd heaven's image
  in thee thus?'

  Then, sputtering thro' the hedge of
    splinter'd teeth,
Yet strangers to the tongue, and with
  blunt stump
Pitch-blacken'd sawing the air, said the
  maim'd churl,

  'He took them and he drave them to
    his tower—
Some hold he was a table-knight of thine—
A hundred goodly ones—the Red Knight
  he—
Lord, I was tending swine, and the Red
  Knight
Brake in upon me and drave them to his
  tower;
And when I call'd upon thy name as one
That doest right by gentle and by churl,
Maim'd me and maul'd, and would outright have slain,
Save that he sware me to a message
  saying,
"Tell thou the King and all his liars, that I
Have founded my Round Table in the
  North,
And whatsoever his own knights have
  sworn
My knights have sworn the counter to
  it—and say
My tower is full of harlots, like his court,
But mine are worthier, seeing they profess
To be none other than themselves—and say
My knights are all adulterers like his own,
But mine are truer, seeing they profess
To be none other; and say his hour is come,
The heathen are upon him, his long lance
Broken, and his Excalibur a straw."'

Then Arthur turn'd to Kay the sene-
schal,
'Take thou my churl, and tend him
curiously
Like a king's heir, till all his hurts be
whole.
The heathen — but that ever - climbing
wave,
Hurl'd back again so often in empty foam,
Hath lain for years at rest—and renegades,
Thieves, bandits, leavings of confusion,
whom
The wholesome realm is purged of other-
where,
Friends, thro' your manhood and your
fëalty,—now
Make their last head like Satan in the
North.
My younger knights, new-made, in whom
your flower
Waits to be solid fruit of golden deeds,
Move with me toward their quelling,
which achieved,
The loneliest ways are safe from shore to
shore.
But thou, Sir Lancelot, sitting in my place
Enchair'd to-morrow, arbitrate the field ;
For wherefore shouldst thou care to mingle
with it,
Only to yield my Queen her own again ?
Speak, Lancelot, thou art silent : is it
well ?'

Thereto Sir Lancelot answer'd, ' It is
well :
Yet better if the King abide, and leave
The leading of his younger knights to me.
Else, for the King has will'd it, it is well.'

Then Arthur rose and Lancelot follow'd
him,
And while they stood without the doors,
the King
Turn'd to him saying, ' Is it then so well?
Or mine the blame that oft I seem as he
Of whom was written, " A sound is in his
ears "?
The foot that loiters, bidden go,—the
glance
That only seems half-loyal to command,—

A manner somewhat fall'n from rever-
ence—
Or have I dream'd the bearing of our
knights
Tells of a manhood ever less and lower ?
Or whence the fear lest this my realm,
uprear'd,
By noble deeds at one with noble vows,
From flat confusion and brute violences,
Reel back into the beast, and be no
more ?'

He spoke, and taking all his younger
knights,
Down the slope city rode, and sharply
turn'd
North by the gate. In her high bower
the Queen,
Working a tapestry, lifted up her head,
Watch'd her lord pass, and knew not that
she sigh'd.
Then ran across her memory the strange
rhyme
Of bygone Merlin, ' Where is he who
knows ?
From the great deep to the great deep he
goes.'

But when the morning of a tournament,
By these in earnest those in mockery call'd
The Tournament of the Dead Innocence,
Brake with a wet wind blowing, Lancelot,
Round whose sick head all night, like
birds of prey,
The words of Arthur flying shriek'd, arose,
And down a streetway hung with folds of
pure
White samite, and by fountains running
wine,
Where children sat in white with cups of
gold,
Moved to the lists, and there, with slow
sad steps
Ascending, fill'd his double - dragon'd
chair.

He glanced and saw the stately galleries,
Dame, damsel, each thro' worship of their
Queen
White-robed in honour of the stainless
child,

And some with scatter'd jewels, like a bank
Of maiden snow mingled with sparks of fire.
He look'd but once, and vail'd his eyes again.

The sudden trumpet sounded as in a dream
To ears but half-awaked, then one low roll
Of Autumn thunder, and the jousts began:
And ever the wind blew, and yellowing leaf
And gloom and gleam, and shower and shorn plume
Went down it. Sighing weariedly, as one
Who sits and gazes on a faded fire,
When all the goodlier guests are past away,
Sat their great umpire, looking o'er the lists.

He saw the laws that ruled the tournament
Broken, but spake not; once, a knight cast down
Before his throne of arbitration cursed
The dead babe and the follies of the King;
And once the laces of a helmet crack'd,
And show'd him, like a vermin in its hole,
Modred, a narrow face: anon he heard
The voice that billow'd round the barriers roar
An ocean-sounding welcome to one knight,
But newly-enter'd, taller than the rest,
And armour'd all in forest green, whereon
There tript a hundred tiny silver deer,
And wearing but a holly-spray for crest,
With ever-scattering berries, and on shield
A spear, a harp, a bugle—Tristram—late
From overseas in Brittany return'd,
And marriage with a princess of that realm,
Isolt the White—Sir Tristram of the Woods—
Whom Lancelot knew, had held sometime with pain
His own against him, and now yearn'd to shake
The burthen off his heart in one full shock
With Tristram ev'n to death: his strong hands gript
And dinted the gilt dragons right and left,
Until he groan'd for wrath—so many of those,

That ware their ladies' colours on the casque,
Drew from before Sir Tristram to the bounds,
And there with gibes and flickering mockeries
Stood, while he mutter'd, 'Craven crests! O shame!
What faith have these in whom they sware to love?
The glory of our Round Table is no more.'

So Tristram won, and Lancelot gave, the gems,
Not speaking other word than 'Hast thou won?
Art thou the purest, brother? See, the hand
Wherewith thou takest this, is red!' to whom
Tristram, half plagued by Lancelot's languorous mood,
Made answer, 'Ay, but wherefore toss me this
Like a dry bone cast to some hungry hound?
Let be thy fair Queen's fantasy. Strength of heart
And might of limb, but mainly use and skill,
Are winners in this pastime of our King.
My hand—belike the lance hath dript upon it—
No blood of mine, I trow; but O chief knight,
Right arm of Arthur in the battlefield,
Great brother, thou nor I have made the world;
Be happy in thy fair Queen as I in mine.'

And Tristram round the gallery made his horse
Caracole; then bow'd his homage, bluntly saying,
'Fair damsels, each to him who worships each
Sole Queen of Beauty and of love, behold
This day my Queen of Beauty is not here.'
And most of these were mute, some anger'd, one
Murmuring, 'All courtesy is dead,' and one,
'The glory of our Round Table is no more.'

Then fell thick rain, plume droopt and
mantle clung,
And pettish cries awoke, and the wan day
Went glooming down in wet and weari-
ness :
But under her black brows a swarthy one
Laugh'd shrilly, crying, 'Praise the patient
saints,
Our one white day of Innocence hath past,
Tho' somewhat draggled at the skirt. So
be it.
The snowdrop only, flowering thro' the
year,
Would make the world as blank as
Winter-tide.
Come—let us gladden their sad eyes, our
Queen's
And Lancelot's, at this night's solemnity
With all the kindlier colours of the field.'

So dame and damsel glitter'd at the
feast
Variously gay : for he that tells the tale
Liken'd them, saying, as when an hour of
cold
Falls on the mountain in midsummer
snows,
And all the purple slopes of mountain
flowers
Pass under white, till the warm hour
returns
With veer of wind, and all are flowers
again ;
So dame and damsel cast the simple white,
And glowing in all colours, the live grass,
Rose-campion, bluebell, kingcup, poppy,
glanced
About the revels, and with mirth so loud
Beyond all use, that, half-amazed, the
Queen,
And wroth at Tristram and the lawless
jousts,
Brake up their sports, then slowly to her
bower
Parted, and in her bosom pain was lord.

And little Dagonet on the morrow
morn,
High over all the yellowing Autumn-tide,
Danced like a wither'd leaf before the hall.

Then Tristram saying, 'Why skip ye so,
Sir Fool ?'
Wheel'd round on either heel, Dagonet
replied,
' Belike for lack of wiser company ;
Or being fool, and seeing too much wit
Makes the world rotten, why, belike I skip
To know myself the wisest knight of all.'
' Ay, fool,' said Tristram, ' but 'tis eating
dry
To dance without a catch, a roundelay
To dance to.' Then he twangled on his
harp,
And while he twangled little Dagonet stood
Quiet as any water-sodden log
Stay'd in the wandering warble of a brook ;
But when the twangling ended, skipt again ;
And being ask'd, ' Why skipt ye not, Sir
Fool ?'
Made answer, ' I had liefer twenty years
Skip to the broken music of my brains
Than any broken music thou canst make.'
Then Tristram, waiting for the quip to
come,
' Good now, what music have I broken,
fool ?'
And little Dagonet, skipping, ' Arthur,
the King's ;
For when thou playest that air with Queen
Isolt,
Thou makest broken music with thy bride,
Her daintier namesake down in Brittany—
And so thou breakest Arthur's music too.'
' Save for that broken music in thy brains,
Sir fool,' said Tristram, ' I would break
thy head.
Fool, I came late, the heathen wars were
o'er,
The life had flown, we sware but by the
shell—
I am but a fool to reason with a fool—
Come, thou art crabb'd and sour : but
lean me down,
Sir Dagonet, one of thy long asses' ears,
And harken if my music be not true.

' " Free love—free field—we love but
while we may :
The woods are hush'd, their music is no
more :

The leaf is dead, the yearning past away:
New leaf, new life—the days of frost are
    o'er :
New life, new love, to suit the newer day:
New loves are sweet as those that went
    before :
Free love—free field—we love but while
    we may."

    ' Ye might have moved slow-measure
        to my tune,
Not stood stockstill.   I made it in the
    woods,
And heard it ring as true as tested gold.'

    Bût Dagonet with one foot poised in
        his hand,
' Friend, did ye mark that fountain
    yesterday
Made to run wine?—but this had run
    itself
All out like a long life to a sour end—
And them that round it sat with golden
    cups
To hand the wine to whosoever came—
The twelve small damosels white as
    Innocence,
In honour of poor Innocence the babe,
Who left the gems which Innocence the
    Queen
Lent to the King, and Innocence the King
Gave for a prize—and one of those white
    slips
Handed her cup and piped, the pretty one,
"Drink, drink, Sir Fool," and thereupon
    I drank,
Spat — pish — the cup was gold, the
    draught was mud.'

    And Tristram, ' Was it muddier than
        thy gibes ?
Is all the laughter gone dead out of thee?—
Not marking how the knighthood mock
    thee, fool—
" Fear God : honour the King—his one
    true knight—
Sole follower of the vows "—for here be
    they
Who knew thee swine enow before I came,
Smuttier than blasted grain : but when
    the King

Had made thee fool, thy vanity so shot up
It frighted all free fool from out thy heart;
Which left thee less than fool, and less
    than swine,
A naked aught—yet swine I hold thee still,
For I have flung thee pearls and find thee
    swine.'

    And little Dagonet mincing with his feet,
' Knight, an ye fling those rubies round
    my neck
In lieu of hers, I'll hold thou hast some
    touch
Of music, since I care not for thy pearls.
Swine?   I have wallow'd, I have wash'd
    —the world
Is flesh and shadow—I have had my day.
The dirty nurse, Experience, in her kind
Hath foul'd me—an I wallow'd, then I
    wash'd—
I have had my day and my philosophies—
And thank the Lord I am King Arthur's
    fool.
Swine, say ye? swine, goats, asses, rams
    and geese
Troop'd round a Paynim harper once,
    who thrumm'd
On such a wire as musically as thou
Some such fine song—but never a king's
    fool.'

    And Tristram, ' Then were swine,
        goats, asses, geese
The wiser fools, seeing thy Paynim bard
Had such a mastery of his mystery
That he could harp his wife up out of hell.'

    Then Dagonet, turning on the ball of
        his foot,
' And whither harp'st thou thine ? down !
    and thyself
Down ! and two more : a helpful harper
    thou,
That harpest downward! Dost thou know
    the star
We call the harp of Arthur up in heaven?'

    And Tristram, ' Ay, Sir Fool, for when
        our King
Was victor wellnigh day by day, the
    knights,

Glorying in each new glory, set his name
High on all hills, and in the signs of
    heaven.'

    And Dagonet answer'd, ' Ay, and when
        the land
Was freed, and the Queen false, ye set
    yourself
To babble about him, all to show your
    wit—
And whether he were King by courtesy,
Or King by right—and so went harping
    down
The black king's highway, got so far, and
    grew
So witty that ye play'd at ducks and
    drakes
With Arthur's vows on the great lake of
    fire.
Tuwhoo! do ye see it? do ye see the
    star?'

    ' Nay, fool,' said Tristram, ' not in
        open day.'
And Dagonet, ' Nay, nor will: I see it
    and hear.
It makes a silent music up in heaven,
And I, and Arthur and the angels hear,
And then we skip.'   ' Lo, fool,' he said,
    ' ye talk
Fool's treason: is the King thy brother
    fool?'
Then little Dagonet clapt his hands and
    shrill'd,
' Ay, ay, my brother fool, the king of
    fools!
Conceits himself as God that he can make
Figs out of thistles, silk from bristles, milk
From burning spurge, honey from hornet-
    combs,
And men from beasts—Long live the king
    of fools!'

    And down the city Dagonet danced
        away;
But thro' the slowly-mellowing avenues
And solitary passes of the wood
Rode Tristram toward Lyonnesse and
    the west.
Before him fled the face of Queen Isolt
With ruby-circled neck, but evermore

Past, as a rustle or twitter in the wood
Made dull his inner, keen his outer eye
For all that walk'd, or crept, or perch'd,
    or flew.
Anon the face, as, when a gust hath
    blown,
Unruffling waters re-collect the shape
Of one that in them sees himself, return'd;
But at the slot or fewmets of a deer,
Or ev'n a fall'n feather, vanish'd again.

    So on for all that day from lawn to lawn
Thro' many a league-long bower he rode.
    At length
A lodge of intertwisted beechen-boughs
Furze-cramm'd, and bracken-rooft, the
    which himself
Built for a summer day with Queen Isolt
Against a shower, dark in the golden
    grove
Appearing, sent his fancy back to where
She lived a moon in that low lodge with
    him:
Till Mark her lord had past, the Cornish
    King,
With six or seven, when Tristram was
    away,
And snatch'd her thence; yet dreading
    worse than shame
Her warrior Tristram, spake not any
    word,
But bode his hour, devising wretchedness.

    And now that desert lodge to Tristram
        lookt
So sweet, that halting, in he past, and
    sank
Down on a drift of foliage random-blown;
But could not rest for musing how to
    smoothe
And sleek his marriage over to the Queen.
Perchance in lone Tintagil far from all
The tonguesters of the court she had not
    heard.
But then what folly had sent him overseas
After she left him lonely here? a name?
Was it the name of one in Brittany,
Isolt, the daughter of the King?   ' Isolt
Of the white hands ' they call'd her: the
    sweet name

Allured him first, and then the maid her-
    self,
Who served him well with those white
    hands of hers,
And loved him well, until himself had
    thought
He loved her also, wedded easily,
But left her all as easily, and return'd.
The black-blue Irish hair and Irish eyes
Had drawn him home — what marvel?
    then he laid
His brows upon the drifted leaf and
    dream'd.

He seem'd to pace the strand of Brittany
Between Isolt of Britain and his bride,
And show'd them both the ruby-chain,
    and both
Began to struggle for it, till his Queen
Graspt it so hard, that all her hand was red.
Then cried the Breton, 'Look, her hand
    is red !
These be no rubies, this is frozen blood,
And melts within her hand—her hand is
    hot
With ill desires, but this I gave thee, look,
Is all as cool and white as any flower.'
Follow'd a rush of eagle's wings, and then
A whimpering of the spirit of the child,
Because the twain had spoil'd her car-
    canet.

He dream'd ; but Arthur with a hun-
    dred spears
Rode far, till o'er the illimitable reed,
And many a glancing plash and sallowy
    isle,
The wide-wing'd sunset of the misty marsh
Glared on a huge machicolated tower
That stood with open doors, whereout
    was roll'd
A roar of riot, as from men secure
Amid their marshes, ruffians at their ease
Among their harlot-brides, an evil song.
'Lo there,' said one of Arthur's youth,
    for there,
High on a grim dead tree before the tower,
A goodly brother of the Table Round
Swung by the neck : and on the boughs
    a shield

Showing a shower of blood in a field noir,
And therebeside a horn, inflamed the
    knights
At that dishonour done the gilded spur,
Till each would clash the shield, and blow
    the horn.
But Arthur waved them back. Alone he
    rode.
Then at the dry harsh roar of the great
    horn,
That sent the face of all the marsh aloft
An ever upward-rushing storm and cloud
Of shriek and plume, the Red Knight
    heard, and all,
Even to tipmost lance and topmost helm,
In blood-red armour sallying, howl'd to
    the King,

'The teeth of Hell flay bare and gnash
    thee flat !—
Lo ! art thou not that eunuch-hearted
    King
Who fain had clipt free manhood from
    the world—
The woman-worshipper ? Yea, God's
    curse, and I !
Slain was the brother of my paramour
By a knight of thine, and I that heard
    her whine
And snivel, being eunuch-hearted too,
Sware by the scorpion-worm that twists
    in hell,
And stings itself to everlasting death,
To hang whatever knight of thine I fought
And tumbled. Art thou King?—Look
    to thy life !'

He ended : Arthur knew the voice ; the
    face
Wellnigh was helmet-hidden, and the
    name
Went wandering somewhere darkling in
    his mind.
And Arthur deign'd not use of word or
    sword,
But let the drunkard, as he stretch'd from
    horse
To strike him, overbalancing his bulk,
Down from the causeway heavily to the
    swamp

Fall, as the crest of some slow-arching
wave,
Heard in dead night along that table-
shore,
Drops flat, and after the great waters
break
Whitening for half a league, and thin
themselves,
Far over sands marbled with moon and
cloud,
From less and less to nothing ; thus he fell
Head-heavy ; then the knights, who
watch'd him, roar'd
And shouted and leapt down upon the
fall'n ;
There trampled out his face from being
known,
And sank his head in mire, and slimed
themselves :
Nor heard the King for their own cries,
but sprang
Thro' open doors, and swording right and
left
Men, women, on their sodden faces,
hurl'd
The tables over and the wines, and slew
Till all the rafters rang with woman-yells,
And all the pavement stream'd with
massacre :
Then, echoing yell with yell, they fired
the tower,
Which half that autumn night, like the
live North,
Red-pulsing up thro' Alioth and Alcor,
Made all above it, and a hundred meres
About it, as the water Moab saw
Come round by the East, and out beyond
them flush'd
The long low dune, and lazy-plunging sea.

So all the ways were safe from shore to
shore,
But in the heart of Arthur pain was lord.

Then, out of Tristram waking, the red
dream
Fled with a shout, and that low lodge
return'd,
Mid-forest, and the wind among the
boughs.

He whistled his good warhorse left to
graze
Among the forest greens, vaulted upon him,
And rode beneath an ever-showering leaf,
Till one lone woman, weeping near a
cross,
Stay'd him. 'Why weep ye ?' 'Lord,'
she said, 'my man
Hath left me or is dead ;' whereon he
thought—
'What, if she hate me now ? I would
not this.
What, if she love me still ? I would not
that.
I know not what I would '—but said to
her,
'Yet weep not thou, lest, if thy mate
return,
He find thy favour changed and love thee
not '—
Then pressing day by day thro' Lyonnesse
Last in a roky hollow, belling, heard
The hounds of Mark, and felt the goodly
hounds
Yelp at his heart, but turning, past and
gain'd
Tintagil, half in sea, and high on land,
A crown of towers.

Down in a casement sat,
A low sea-sunset glorying round her hair
And glossy-throated grace, Isolt the
Queen.
And when she heard the feet of Tristram
grind
The spiring stone that scaled about her
tower,
Flush'd, started, met him at the doors,
and there
Belted his body with her white embrace,
Crying aloud, 'Not Mark—not Mark,
my soul !
The footstep flutter'd me at first : not he :
Catlike thro' his own castle steals my
Mark,
But warrior-wise thou stridest thro' his
halls
Who hates thee, as I him—ev'n to the
death.
My soul, I felt my hatred for my Mark

Quicken within me, and knew that thou
　　wert nigh.'
To whom Sir Tristram smiling, 'I am
　　here.
Let be thy Mark, seeing he is not thine.'

　And drawing somewhat backward she
　　replied,
'Can he be wrong'd who is not ev'n his
　　own,
But save for dread of thee had beaten me,
Scratch'd, bitten, blinded, marr'd me
　　somehow—Mark?
What rights are his that dare not strike
　　for them?
Not lift a hand—not, tho' he found me
　　thus!
But harken! have ye met him? hence he
　　went
To-day for three days' hunting—as he
　　said—
And so returns belike within an hour.
Mark's way, my soul!—but eat not thou
　　with Mark,
Because he hates thee even more than
　　fears;
Nor drink: and when thou passest any
　　wood
Close vizor, lest an arrow from the bush
Should leave me all alone with Mark and
　　hell.
My God, the measure of my hate for
　　Mark
Is as the measure of my love for thee.'

　So, pluck'd one way by hate and one
　　by love,
Drain'd of her force, again she sat, and
　　spake
To Tristram, as he knelt before her,
　　saying,
'O hunter, and O blower of the horn,
Harper, and thou hast been a rover too,
For, ere I mated with my shambling king,
Ye twain had fallen out about the bride
Of one—his name is out of me—the prize,
If prize she were—(what marvel—she
　　could see)—
Thine, friend; and ever since my craven
　　seeks

To wreck thee villainously: but, O Sir
　　Knight,
What dame or damsel have ye kneel'd to
　　last?'

　And Tristram, 'Last to my Queen
　　Paramount,
Here now to my Queen Paramount of love
And loveliness—ay, lovelier than when
　　first
Her light feet fell on our rough Lyonnesse,
Sailing from Ireland.'

　　　　　　　Softly laugh'd Isolt;
'Flatter me not, for hath not our great
　　Queen
My dole of beauty trebled?' and he said,
'Her beauty is her beauty, and thine
　　thine,
And thine is more to me—soft, gracious,
　　kind—
Save when thy Mark is kindled on thy lips
Most gracious; but she, haughty, ev'n to
　　him,
Lancelot; for I have seen him wan enow
To make one doubt if ever the great Queen
Have yielded him her love.'

　　　　　　　To whom Isolt,
'Ah then, false hunter and false harper,
　　thou
Who brakest thro' the scruple of my
　　bond,
Calling me thy white hind, and saying
　　to me
That Guinevere had sinn'd against the
　　highest,
And I—misyoked with such a want of
　　man—
That I could hardly sin against the lowest.'

　He answer'd, 'O my soul, be com-
　　forted!
If this be sweet, to sin in leading-strings,
If here be comfort, and if ours be sin,
Crown'd warrant had we for the crowning
　　sin
That made us happy: but how ye greet
　　me—fear
And fault and doubt—no word of that
　　fond tale—

Thy deep heart-yearnings, thy sweet
        memories
Of Tristram in that year he was away.'

And, saddening on the sudden, spake
        Isolt,
'I had forgotten all in my strong joy
To see thee—yearnings?—ay! for, hour
        by hour,
Here in the never-ended afternoon,
O sweeter than all memories of thee,
Deeper than any yearnings after thee
Seem'd those far-rolling, westward-
        smiling seas,
Watch'd from this tower. Isolt of Britain
        dash'd
Before Isolt of Brittany on the strand,
Would that have chill'd her bride-kiss?
        Wedded her?
Fought in her father's battles? wounded
        there?
The King was all fulfill'd with grateful-
        ness,
And she, my namesake of the hands, that
        heal'd
Thy hurt and heart with unguent and
        caress—
Well—can I wish her any huger wrong
Than having known thee? her too hast
        thou left
To pine and waste in those sweet
        memories.
O were I not my Mark's, by whom all
        men
Are noble, I should hate thee more than
        love.'

And Tristram, fondling her light hands,
        replied,
'Grace, Queen, for being loved: she
        loved me well.
Did I love her? the name at least I loved.
Isolt?—I fought his battles, for Isolt!
The night was dark; the true star set.
        Isolt!
The name was ruler of the dark——Isolt?
Care not for her! patient, and prayerful,
        meek,
Pale-blooded, she will yield herself to
        God.'

And Isolt answer'd, 'Yea, and why
        not I?
Mine is the larger need, who am not meek,
Pale-blooded, prayerful. Let me tell
        thee now.
Here one black, mute midsummer night
        I sat,
Lonely, but musing on thee, wondering
        where,
Murmuring a light song I had heard thee
        sing,
And once or twice I spake thy name aloud.
Then flash'd a levin-brand; and near me
        stood,
In fuming sulphur blue and green, a
        fiend—
Mark's way to steal behind one in the
        dark—
For there was Mark: "He has wedded
        her," he said,
Not said, but hiss'd it: then this crown
        of towers
So shook to such a roar of all the sky,
That here in utter dark I swoon'd away,
And woke again in utter dark, and cried,
"I will flee hence and give myself to
        God"—
And thou wert lying in thy new leman's
        arms.'

Then Tristram, ever dallying with her
        hand,
'May God be with thee, sweet, when old
        and gray,
And past desire!' a saying that anger'd
        her.
'"May God be with thee, sweet, when
        thou art old,
And sweet no more to me!" I need
        Him now.
For when had Lancelot utter'd aught so
        gross
Ev'n to the swineherd's malkin in the
        mast?
The greater man, the greater courtesy.
Far other was the Tristram, Arthur's
        knight!
But thou, thro' ever harrying thy wild
        beasts—
Save that to touch a harp, tilt with a lance

Becomes thee well—art grown wild beast
    thyself.
How darest thou, if lover, push me even
In fancy from thy side, and set me far
In the gray distance, half a life away,
Her to be loved no more? Unsay it,
    unswear!
Flatter me rather, seeing me so weak,
Broken with Mark and hate and solitude,
Thy marriage and mine own, that I
    should suck
Lies like sweet wines: lie to me: I believe.
Will ye not lie? not swear, as there ye
    kneel,
And solemnly as when ye sware to him,
The man of men, our King—My God,
    the power
Was once in vows when men believed the
    King!
They lied not then, who sware, and thro'
    their vows
The King prevailing made his realm:—
    I say,
Swear to me thou wilt love me ev'n when
    old,
Gray-hair'd, and past desire, and in de-
    spair.'

    Then Tristram, pacing moodily up and
    down,
'Vows! did you keep the vow you made
    to Mark
More than I mine? Lied, say ye? Nay,
    but learnt,
The vow that binds too strictly snaps
    itself—
My knighthood taught me this—ay, being
    snapt—
We run more counter to the soul thereof
Than had we never sworn. I swear no
    more.
I swore to the great King, and am for-
    sworn.
For once—ev'n to the height—I honour'd
    him.
"Man, is he man at all?" methought,
    when first
I rode from our rough Lyonnesse, and
    beheld
That victor of the Pagan throned in hall—

His hair, a sun that ray'd from off a brow
Like hillsnow high in heaven, the steel-
    blue eyes,
The golden beard that clothed his lips
    with light—
Moreover, that weird legend of his birth,
With Merlin's mystic babble about his end
Amazed me; then, his foot was on a stool
Shaped as a dragon; he seem'd to me no
    man,
But Michaël trampling Satan; so I sware,
Being amazed: but this went by—The
    vows!
O ay—the wholesome madness of an
    hour—
They served their use, their time; for
    every knight
Believed himself a greater than himself,
And every follower eyed him as a God;
Till he, being lifted up beyond himself,
Did mightier deeds than elsewise he had
    done,
And so the realm was made; but then
    their vows—
First mainly thro' that sullying of our
    Queen—
Began to gall the knighthood, asking
    whence
Had Arthur right to bind them to himself?
Dropt down from heaven? wash'd up
    from out the deep?
They fail'd to trace him thro' the flesh
    and blood
Of our old kings: whence then a doubt-
    ful lord
To bind them by inviolable vows,
Which flesh and blood perforce would
    violate:
For feel this arm of mine—the tide within
Red with free chase and heather-scented
    air,
Pulsing full man; can Arthur make me
    pure
As any maiden child? lock up my tongue
From uttering freely what I freely hear?
Bind me to one? The wide world
    laughs at it.
And worldling of the world am I, and
    know
The ptarmigan that whitens ere his hour

Woos his own end ; we are not angels here
Nor shall be : vows—I am woodman of
   the woods,
And hear the garnet-headed yaffingale
Mock them : my soul, we love but while
   we may ;
And therefore is my love so large for thee,
Seeing it is not bounded save by love.'

   Here ending, he moved toward her,
   and she said,
' Good : an I turn'd away my love for thee
To some one thrice as courteous as thy-
   self—
For courtesy wins woman all as well
As valour may, but he that closes both
Is perfect, he is Lancelot—taller indeed,
Rosier and comelier, thou—but say I loved
This knightliest of all knights, and cast
   thee back
Thine own small saw, "We love but
   while we may,"
Well then, what answer ?'

          He that while she spake,
Mindful of what he brought to adorn her
   with,
The jewels, had let one finger lightly touch
The warm white apple of her throat,
   replied,
' Press this a little closer, sweet, until—
Come, I am hunger'd and half-anger'd—
   meat,
Wine, wine—and I will love thee to the
   death,
And out beyond into the dream to come.'

   So then, when both were brought to
   full accord,
She rose, and set before him all he will'd ;
And after these had comforted the blood
With meats and wines, and satiated their
   hearts—
Now talking of their woodland paradise,
The deer, the dews, the fern, the founts,
   the lawns ;
Now mocking at the much ungainliness,
And craven shifts, and long crane legs of
   Mark—
Then Tristram laughing caught the harp,
   and sang :

' Ay, ay, O ay—the winds that bend
   the brier !
A star in heaven, a star within the mere !
Ay, ay, O ay—a star was my desire,
And one was far apart, and one was near :
Ay, ay, O ay—the winds that bow the
   grass !
And one was water and one star was fire,
And one will ever shine and one will pass.
Ay, ay, O ay—the winds that move the
   mere.'

   Then in the light's last glimmer Tris-
   tram show'd
And swung the ruby carcanet. She cried,
' The collar of some Order, which our
   King
Hath newly founded, all for thee, my soul,
For thee, to yield thee grace beyond thy
   peers.'

   ' Not so, my Queen,' he said, ' but the
   red fruit
Grown on a magic oak-tree in mid-heaven,
And won by Tristram as a tourney-prize,
And hither brought by Tristram for his
   last
Love - offering and peace-offering unto
   thee.'

   He spoke, he turn'd, then, flinging
   round her neck,
Claspt it, and cried ' Thine Order, O my
   Queen !'
But, while he bow'd to kiss the jewell'd
   throat,
Out of the dark, just as the lips had
   touch'd,
Behind him rose a shadow and a shriek—
' Mark's way,' said Mark, and clove him
   thro' the brain.

   That night came Arthur home, and
   while he climb'd,
All in a death - dumb autumn - dripping
   gloom,
The stairway to the hall, and look'd and
   saw
The great Queen's bower was dark,—
   about his feet
A voice clung sobbing till he question'd it,

'What art thou?' and the voice about his
    feet
Sent up an answer, sobbing, 'I am thy
    fool,
And I shall never make thee smile again.'

GUINEVERE.

QUEEN GUINEVERE had fled the court,
    and sat
There in the holy house at Almesbury
Weeping, none with her save a little
    maid,
A novice: one low light betwixt them
    burn'd
Blurr'd by the creeping mist, for all
    abroad,
Beneath a moon unseen albeit at full,
The white mist, like a face-cloth to the
    face,
Clung to the dead earth, and the land
    was still.

    For hither had she fled, her cause of
    flight
Sir Modred; he that like a subtle beast
Lay couchant with his eyes upon the
    throne,
Ready to spring, waiting a chance: for
    this
He chill'd the popular praises of the King
With silent smiles of slow disparagement;
And tamper'd with the Lords of the
    White Horse,
Heathen, the brood by Hengist left; and
    sought
To make disruption in the Table Round
Of Arthur, and to splinter it into feuds
Serving his traitorous end; and all his
    aims
Were sharpen'd by strong hate for Lance-
    lot.

    For thus it chanced one morn when
    all the court,
Green-suited, but with plumes that
    mock'd the may,
Had been, their wont, a-maying and
    return'd,
That Modred still in green, all ear and eye,

Climb'd to the high top of the garden-
    wall
To spy some secret scandal if he might,
And saw the Queen who sat betwixt her
    best
Enid, and lissome Vivien, of her court
The wiliest and the worst; and more
    than this
He saw not, for Sir Lancelot passing by
Spied where he couch'd, and as the
    gardener's hand
Picks from the colewort a green cater-
    pillar,
So from the high wall and the flowering
    grove
Of grasses Lancelot pluck'd him by the
    heel,
And cast him as a worm upon the way;
But when he knew the Prince tho' marr'd
    with dust,
He, reverencing king's blood in a bad man,
Made such excuses as he might, and these
Full knightly without scorn; for in those
    days
No knight of Arthur's noblest dealt in
    scorn;
But, if a man were halt or hunch'd, in him
By those whom God had made full-limb'd
    and tall,
Scorn was allow'd as part of his defect,
And he was answer'd softly by the King
And all his Table. So Sir Lancelot holp
To raise the Prince, who rising twice or
    thrice
Full sharply smote his knees, and smiled,
    and went:
But, ever after, the small violence done
Rankled in him and ruffled all his heart,
As the sharp wind that ruffles all day long
A little bitter pool about a stone
On the bare coast.

            But when Sir Lancelot told
This matter to the Queen, at first she
    laugh'd
Lightly, to think of Modred's dusty fall,
Then shudder'd, as the village wife who
    cries
'I shudder, some one steps across my
    grave;'

Then laugh'd again, but faintlier, for in-
deed
She half-foresaw that he, the subtle beast,
Would track her guilt until he found, and
hers
Would be for evermore a name of scorn.
Henceforward rarely could she front in
hall,
Or elsewhere, Modred's narrow foxy face,
Heart-hiding smile, and gray persistent
eye:
Henceforward too, the Powers that tend
the soul,
To help it from the death that cannot die,
And save it even in extremes, began
To vex and plague her.   Many a time for
hours,
Beside the placid breathings of the King,
In the dead night, grim faces came and
went
Before her, or a vague spiritual fear—
Like to some doubtful noise of creaking
doors,
Heard by the watcher in a haunted house,
That keeps the rust of murder on the
walls—
Held her awake: or if she slept, she
dream'd
An awful dream ; for then she seem'd to
stand
On some vast plain before a setting sun,
And from the sun there swiftly made at her
A ghastly something, and its shadow flew
Before it, till it touch'd her, and she
turn'd—
When lo ! her own, that broadening from
her feet,
And blackening, swallow'd all the land,
and in it
Far cities burnt, and with a cry she woke.
And all this trouble did not pass but grew ;
Till ev'n the clear face of the guileless
King,
And trustful courtesies of household life,
Became her bane ; and at the last she
said,
' O Lancelot, get thee hence to thine own
land,
For if thou tarry we shall meet again,
And if we meet again, some evil chance

Will make the smouldering scandal break
and blaze
Before the people, and our lord the King.
And Lancelot ever promised, but re-
main'd,
And still they met and met.   Again she
said,
' O Lancelot, if thou love me get thee
hence.'
And then they were agreed upon a night
(When the good King should not be there)
to meet
And part for ever.   Vivien, lurking, heard.
She told Sir Modred.   Passion-pale they
met
And greeted.   Hands in hands, and eye
to eye.
Low on the border of her couch they sat
Stammering and staring.   It was their
last hour,
A madness of farewells.   And Modred
brought
His creatures to the basement of the tower
For testimony ; and crying with full voice
' Traitor, come out, ye are trapt at last,'
aroused
Lancelot, who rushing outward lionlike
Leapt on him, and hurl'd him headlong,
and he fell
Stunn'd, and his creatures took and bare
him off,
And all was still : then she, ' The end is
come,
And I am shamed for ever;' and he said,
' Mine be the shame; mine was the sin:
but rise,
And fly to my strong castle overseas :
There will I hide thee, till my life shall end,
There hold thee with my life against the
world.'
She answer'd, ' Lancelot, wilt thou hold
me so ?
Nay, friend, for we have taken our farewells.
Would God that thou couldst hide me
from myself !
Mine is the shame, for I was wife, and thou
Unwedded: yet rise now, and let us fly,
For I will draw me into sanctuary,
And bide my doom.'   So Lancelot got
her horse,

Set her thereon, and mounted on his own,
And then they rode to the divided way,
There kiss'd, and parted weeping: for
  he past,
Love-loyal to the least wish of the Queen,
Back to his land; but she to Almesbury
Fled all night long by glimmering waste
  and weald,
And heard the Spirits of the waste and
  weald
Moan as she fled, or thought she heard
  them moan:
And in herself she moan'd 'Too late, too
  late!'
Till in the cold wind that foreruns the
  morn,
A blot in heaven, the Raven, flying high,
Croak'd, and she thought, 'He spies a
  field of death;
For now the Heathen of the Northern Sea,
Lured by the crimes and frailties of the
  court,
Begin to slay the folk, and spoil the land.'

And when she came to Almesbury she
  spake
There to the nuns, and said, 'Mine
  enemies
Pursue me, but, O peaceful Sisterhood,
Receive, and yield me sanctuary, nor ask
Her name to whom ye yield it, till her
  time
To tell you:' and her beauty, grace and
  power,
Wrought as a charm upon them, and
  they spared
To ask it.

So the stately Queen abode
For many a week, unknown, among the
  nuns;
Nor with them mix'd, nor told her name,
  nor sought,
Wrapt in her grief, for housel or for
  shrift,
But communed only with the little maid,
Who pleased her with a babbling heed-
  lessness
Which often lured her from herself; but
  now,

This night, a rumour wildly blown about
Came, that Sir Modred had usurp'd the
  realm,
And leagued him with the heathen, while
  the King
Was waging war on Lancelot: then she
  thought,
'With what a hate the people and the
  King
Must hate me,' and bow'd down upon
  her hands
Silent, until the little maid, who brook'd
No silence, brake it, uttering 'Late! so
  late!
What hour, I wonder, now?' and when
  she drew
No answer, by and by began to hum
An air the nuns had taught her; 'Late,
  so late!'
Which when she heard, the Queen look'd
  up, and said,
'O maiden, if indeed ye list to sing,
Sing, and unbind my heart that I may
  weep.'
Whereat full willingly sang the little
  maid.

'Late, late, so late! and dark the
  night and chill!
Late, late, so late! but we can enter still.
Too late, too late! ye cannot enter now.

'No light had we: for that we do
  repent;
And learning this, the bridegroom will
  relent.
Too late, too late! ye cannot enter now.

'No light: so late! and dark and chill
  the night!
O let us in, that we may find the light!
Too late, too late: ye cannot enter now.

'Have we not heard the bridegroom is
  so sweet?
O let us in, tho' late, to kiss his feet!
No, no, too late! ye cannot enter now.'

So sang the novice, while full passionately,
Her head upon her hands, remembering

ler thought when first she came, wept
the sad Queen.
Then said the little novice prattling to her,

'O pray you, noble lady, weep no
more ;
But let my words, the words of one so
small,
Who knowing nothing knows but to obey,
And if I do not there is penance given—
Comfort your sorrows ; for they do not
flow
From evil done ; right sure am I of that,
Who see your tender grace and stateliness.
But weigh your sorrows with our lord the
King's,
And weighing find them less ; for gone is
he
To wage grim war against Sir Lancelot
there,
Round that strong castle where he holds
the Queen ;
And Modred whom he left in charge of
all,
The traitor—Ah sweet lady, the King's
grief
For his own self, and his own Queen, and
realm,
Must needs be thrice as great as any of
ours.
For me, I thank the saints, I am not
great.
For if there ever come a grief to me
I cry my cry in silence, and have done.
None knows it, and my tears have brought
me good :
But even were the griefs of little ones
As great as those of great ones, yet this
grief
Is added to the griefs the great must
bear,
That howsoever much they may desire
Silence, they cannot weep behind a
cloud :
As even here they talk at Almesbury
About the good King and his wicked
Queen,
And were I such a King with such a Queen,
Well might I wish to veil her wickedness,
But were I such a King, it could not be.'

Then to her own sad heart mutter'd the
Queen,
'Will the child kill me with her innocent
talk ?'
But openly she answer'd, 'Must not I,
If this false traitor have displaced his lord,
Grieve with the common grief of all the
realm ?'

'Yea,' said the maid, 'this is all
woman's grief,
That *she* is woman, whose disloyal life
Hath wrought confusion in the Table
Round
Which good King Arthur founded, years
ago,
With signs and miracles and wonders,
there
At Camelot, ere the coming of the Queen.'

Then thought the Queen within herself
again,
'Will the child kill me with her foolish
prate ?'
But openly she spake and said to her,
'O little maid, shut in by nunnery walls,
What canst thou know of Kings and
Tables Round,
Or what of signs and wonders, but the
signs
And simple miracles of thy nunnery ?'

To whom the little novice garrulously,
'Yea, but I know : the land was full of
signs
And wonders ere the coming of the Queen.
So said my father, and himself was knight
Of the great Table—at the founding of it ;
And rode thereto from Lyonnesse, and
he said
That as he rode, an hour or maybe twain
After the sunset, down the coast, he heard
Strange music, and he paused, and turn-
ing—there,
All down the lonely coast of Lyonnesse,
Each with a beacon-star upon his head,
And with a wild sea-light about his feet,
He saw them—headland after headland
flame
Far on into the rich heart of the west :

And in the light the white mermaiden
    swam,
And strong man-breasted things stood
    from the sea,
And sent a deep sea-voice thro' all the
    land,
To which the little elves of chasm and cleft
Made answer, sounding like a distant horn.
So said my father—yea, and furthermore,
Next morning, while he past the dim-lit
    woods,
Himself beheld three spirits mad with
    joy
Come dashing down on a tall wayside
    flower,
That shook beneath them, as the thistle
    shakes
When three gray linnets wrangle for the
    seed :
And still at evenings on before his horse
The flickering fairy-circle wheel'd and
    broke
Flying, and link'd again, and wheel'd and
    broke
Flying, for all the land was full of life.
And when at last he came to Camelot,
A wreath of airy dancers hand-in-hand
Swung round the lighted lantern of the
    hall ;
And in the hall itself was such a feast
As never man had dream'd ; for every
    knight
Had whatsoever meat he long'd for served
By hands unseen ; and even as he said
Down in the cellars merry bloated things
Shoulder'd the spigot, straddling on the
    butts
While the wine ran : so glad were spirits
    and men
Before the coming of the sinful Queen.'

Then spake the Queen and somewhat
    bitterly,
'Were they so glad? ill prophets were
    they all,
Spirits and men : could none of them
    foresee,
Not even thy wise father with his signs
And wonders, what has fall'n upon the
    realm ?'

To whom the novice garrulously again
'Yea, one, a bard ; of whom my father
    said,
Full many a noble war-song had he sung
Ev'n in the presence of an enemy's fleet
Between the steep cliff and the coming
    wave ;
And many a mystic lay of life and death
Had chanted on the smoky mountain
    tops,
When round him bent the spirits of the
    hills
With all their dewy hair blown back like
    flame :
So said my father—and that night the bard
Sang Arthur's glorious wars, and sang
    the King
As wellnigh more than man, and rail'd at
    those
Who call'd him the false son of Gorloïs :
For there was no man knew from whence
    he came ;
But after tempest, when the long wave
    broke
All down the thundering shores of Bude
    and Bos,
There came a day as still as heaven, and
    then
They found a naked child upon the sands
Of dark Tintagil by the Cornish sea ;
And that was Arthur ; and they foster'd
    him
Till he by miracle was approven King :
And that his grave should be a mystery
From all men, like his birth ; and could
    he find
A woman in her womanhood as great
As he was in his manhood, then, he sang,
The twain together well might change the
    world.
But even in the middle of his song
He falter'd, and his hand fell from the
    harp,
And pale he turn'd, and reel'd, and would
    have fall'n,
But that they stay'd him up ; nor would
    he tell
His vision ; but what doubt that he fore-
    saw
This evil work of Lancelot and the Queen ?'

Then thought the Queen, 'Lo! they
    have set her on,
Our simple-seeming Abbess and her nuns,
To play upon me,' and bow'd her head
    nor spake.
Whereat the novice crying, with clasp'd
    hands,
Shame on her own garrulity garrulously,
Said the good nuns would check her
    gadding tongue
Full often, 'and, sweet lady, if I seem
To vex an ear too sad to listen to me,
Unmannerly, with prattling and the tales
Which my good father told me, check
    me too
Nor let me shame my father's memory,
    one
Of noblest manners, tho' himself would say
Sir Lancelot had the noblest; and he
    died,
Kill'd in a tilt, come next, five summers
    back,
And left me; but of others who remain,
And of the two first-famed for courtesy—
And pray you check me if I ask amiss—
But pray you, which had noblest, while
    you moved
Among them, Lancelot or our lord the
    King?'

    Then the pale Queen look'd up and
    answer'd her,
Sir Lancelot, as became a noble knight,
Was gracious to all ladies, and the same
In open battle or the tilting-field
Forbore his own advantage, and the King
In open battle or the tilting-field
Forbore his own advantage, and these
    two
Were the most nobly-manner'd men of
    all;
For manners are not idle, but the fruit
Of loyal nature, and of noble mind.'

    'Yea,' said the maid, 'be manners such
    fair fruit?
Then Lancelot's needs must be a thou-
    sand-fold
Less noble, being, as all rumour runs,
The most disloyal friend in all the world.'

To which a mournful answer made the
    Queen:
'O closed about by narrowing nunnery-
    walls,
What knowest thou of the world, and all
    its lights
And shadows, all the wealth and all the
    woe?
If ever Lancelot, that most noble knight,
Were for one hour less noble than himself,
Pray for him that he scape the doom of
    fire,
And weep for her who drew him to his
    doom.'

    'Yea,' said the little novice, 'I pray for
    both;
But I should all as soon believe that his,
Sir Lancelot's, were as noble as the King's,
As I could think, sweet lady, yours
    would be
Such as they are, were you the sinful
    Queen.'

So she, like many another babbler, hurt
Whom she would soothe, and harm'd
    where she would heal;
For here a sudden flush of wrathful heat
Fired all the pale face of the Queen, who
    cried,
'Such as thou art be never maiden more
For ever! thou their tool, set on to plague
And play upon, and harry me, petty spy
And traitress.' When that storm of anger
    brake
From Guinevere, aghast the maiden rose,
White as her veil, and stood before the
    Queen
As tremulously as foam upon the beach
Stands in a wind, ready to break and fly,
And when the Queen had added 'Get
    thee hence,'
Fled frighted. Then that other left alone
Sigh'd, and began to gather heart again,
Saying in herself, 'The simple, fearful
    child
Meant nothing, but my own too-fearful
    guilt,
Simpler than any child, betrays itself.
But help me, heaven, for surely I repent.

For what is true repentance but in
    thought—
Not ev'n in inmost thought to think again
The sins that made the past so pleasant
    to us:
And I have sworn never to see him more,
To see him more.'

            And ev'n in saying this,
Her memory from old habit of the mind
Went slipping back upon the golden days
In which she saw him first, when Lancelot
    came,
Reputed the best knight and goodliest
    man,
Ambassador, to lead her to his lord
Arthur, and led her forth, and far ahead
Of his and her retinue moving, they,
Rapt in sweet talk or lively, all on love
And sport and tilts and pleasure, (for the
    time
Was maytime, and as yet no sin was
    dream'd,)
Rode under groves that look'd a paradise
Of blossom, over sheets of hyacinth
That seem'd the heavens upbreaking thro'
    the earth,
And on from hill to hill, and every day
Beheld at noon in some delicious dale
The silk pavilions of King Arthur raised
For brief repast or afternoon repose
By couriers gone before; and on again,
Till yet once more ere set of sun they
    saw
The Dragon of the great Pendragonship,
That crown'd the state pavilion of the
    King,
Blaze by the rushing brook or silent well.

    But when the Queen immersed in such
        a trance,
And moving thro' the past unconsciously,
Came to that point where first she saw
    the King
Ride toward her from the city, sigh'd to
    find
Her journey done, glanced at him, thought
    him cold,
High, self-contain'd, and passionless, not
    like him,

'Not like my Lancelot'—while she
    brooded thus
And grew half-guilty in her thought
    again,
There rode an armed warrior to the doors
A murmuring whisper thro' the nunnery
    ran,
Then on a sudden a cry, 'The King.'
    She sat
Stiff-stricken, listening; but when armed
    feet
Thro' the long gallery from the outer door
Rang coming, prone from off her seat she
    fell,
And grovell'd with her face against the
    floor:
There with her milkwhite arms and
    shadowy hair
She made her face a darkness from the
    King:
And in the darkness heard his armed feet
Pause by her; then came silence, then a
    voice,
Monotonous and hollow like a Ghost's
Denouncing judgment, but tho' changed
    the King's:

    'Liest thou here so low, the child
        one
I honour'd, happy, dead before thy shame
Well is it that no child is born of thee.
The children born of thee are sword and
    fire,
Red ruin, and the breaking up of laws,
The craft of kindred and the Godless host
Of heathen swarming o'er the Northern
    Sea;
Whom I, while yet Sir Lancelot, my right
    arm,
The mightiest of my knights, abode with
    me,
Have everywhere about this land of Christ
In twelve great battles ruining overthrew
And knowest thou now from whence I
    come—from him,
From waging bitter war with him: and
    he,
That did not shun to smite me in worse
    way,
Had yet that grace of courtesy in him left

He spared to lift his hand against the King
Who made him knight : but many a
  knight was slain ;
And many more, and all his kith and kin
Clave to him, and abode in his own land.
And many more when Modred raised
  revolt,
Forgetful of their troth and fealty, clave
To Modred, and a remnant stays with me.
And of this remnant will I leave a part,
True men who love me still, for whom I
  live,
To guard thee in the wild hour coming on,
Lest but a hair of this low head be harm'd.
Fear not : thou shalt be guarded till my
  death.
Howbeit I know, if ancient prophecies
Have err'd not, that I march to meet my
  doom.
Thou hast not made my life so sweet to
  me,
That I the King should greatly care to
  live ;
For thou hast spoilt the purpose of my life.
Bear with me for the last time while I
  show,
Ev'n for thy sake, the sin which thou hast
  sinn'd.
For when the Roman left us, and their law
Relax'd its hold upon us, and the ways
Were fill'd with rapine, here and there a
  deed
Of prowess done redress'd a random
  wrong.
But I was first of all the kings who drew
The knighthood-errant of this realm and
  all
The realms together under me, their
  Head,
In that fair Order of my Table Round,
A glorious company, the flower of men,
To serve as model for the mighty world,
And be the fair beginning of a time.
I made them lay their hands in mine and
  swear
To reverence the King, as if he were
Their conscience, and their conscience as
  their King,
To break the heathen and uphold the
  Christ,

To ride abroad redressing human wrongs,
To speak no slander, no, nor listen to it,
To honour his own word as if his God's,
To lead sweet lives in purest chastity,
To love one maiden only, cleave to her,
And worship her by years of noble deeds,
Until they won her ; for indeed I knew
Of no more subtle master under heaven
Than is the maiden passion for a maid,
Not only to keep down the base in man,
But teach high thought, and amiable
  words
And courtliness, and the desire of fame,
And love of truth, and all that makes a
  man.
And all this throve before I wedded thee,
Believing, "lo mine helpmate, one to feel
My purpose and rejoicing in my joy."
Then came thy shameful sin with Lance-
  lot ;
Then came the sin of Tristram and Isolt ;
Then others, following these my mightiest
  knights,
And drawing foul ensample from fair
  names,
Sinn'd also, till the loathsome opposite
Of all my heart had destined did obtain,
And all thro' thee ! so that this life of mine
I guard as God's high gift from scathe
  and wrong,
Not greatly care to lose ; but rather think
How sad it were for Arthur, should he live,
To sit once more within his lonely hall,
And miss the wonted number of my
  knights,
And miss to hear high talk of noble deeds
As in the golden days before thy sin.
For which of us, who might be left, could
  speak
Of the pure heart, nor seem to glance at
  thee ?
And in thy bowers of Camelot or of Usk
Thy shadow still would glide from room
  to room,
And I should evermore be vext with thee
In hanging robe or vacant ornament,
Or ghostly footfall echoing on the stair.
For think not, tho' thou wouldst not love
  thy lord,
Thy lord has wholly lost his love for thee.

I am not made of so slight elements.
Yet must I leave thee, woman, to thy
shame.
I hold that man the worst of public foes
Who either for his own or children's sake,
To save his blood from scandal, lets the
wife
Whom he knows false, abide and rule the
house :
For being thro' his cowardice allow'd
Her station, taken everywhere for pure,
She like a new disease, unknown to men,
Creeps, no precaution used, among the
crowd,
Makes wicked lightnings of her eyes, and
saps
The fealty of our friends, and stirs the
pulse
With devil's leaps, and poisons half the
young.
Worst of the worst were that man he that
reigns !
Better the King's waste hearth and aching
heart
Than thou reseated in thy place of light,
The mockery of my people, and their
bane.'

He paused, and in the pause she crept
an inch
Nearer, and laid her hands about his feet.
Far off a solitary trumpet blew.
Then waiting by the doors the warhorse
neigh'd
As at a friend's voice, and he spake again :

' Yet think not that I come to urge thy
crimes,
I did not come to curse thee, Guinevere,
I, whose vast pity almost makes me die
To see thee, laying there thy golden head,
My pride in happier summers, at my feet.
The wrath which forced my thoughts on
that fierce law,
The doom of treason and the flaming
death,
(When first I learnt thee hidden here) is
past.
The pang — which while I weigh'd thy
heart with one

Too wholly true to dream untruth in thee,
Made my tears burn — is also past —
part.
And all is past, the sin is sinn'd, and I,
Lo ! I forgive thee, as Eternal God
Forgives : do thou for thine own soul the
rest.
But how to take last leave of all I loved?
O golden hair, with which I used to play
Not knowing ! O imperial-moulded form,
And beauty such as never woman wore,
Until it came a kingdom's curse with
thee—
I cannot touch thy lips, they are not mine,
But Lancelot's : nay, they never were the
King's.
I cannot take thy hand ; that too is flesh,
And in the flesh thou hast sinn'd ; and
mine own flesh,
Here looking down on thine polluted, cries
" I loathe thee :" yet not less, O Guine-
vere,
For I was ever virgin save for thee,
My love thro' flesh hath wrought into my
life
So far, that my doom is, I love thee still.
Let no man dream but that I love thee still.
Perchance, and so thou purify thy soul,
And so thou lean on our fair father Christ,
Hereafter in that world where all are pure
We two may meet before high God, and
thou
Wilt spring to me, and claim me thine,
and know
I am thine husband—not a smaller soul,
Nor Lancelot, nor another. Leave me
that,
I charge thee, my last hope. Now must
I hence.
Thro' the thick night I hear the trumpet
blow :
They summon me their King to lead mine
hosts
Far down to that great battle in the west,
Where I must strike against the man they
call
My sister's son—no kin of mine, who
leagues
With Lords of the White Horse, heathen,
and knights,

Traitors—and strike him dead, and meet
    myself
Death, or I know not what mysterious
    doom.
And thou remaining here wilt learn the
    event ;
But hither shall I never come again,
Never lie by thy side ; see thee no more—
Farewell !'

And while she grovell'd at his feet,
She felt the King's breath wander o'er her
    neck,
And in the darkness o'er her fallen head,
Perceived the waving of his hands that
    blest.

Then, listening till those armed steps
    were gone,
Rose the pale Queen, and in her anguish
    found
The casement : 'peradventure,' so she
    thought,
If I might see his face, and not be seen.'
And lo, he sat on horseback at the door !
And near him the sad nuns with each a
    light
Stood, and he gave them charge about the
    Queen,
To guard and foster her for evermore.
And while he spake to these his helm was
    lower'd,
To which for crest the golden dragon
    clung
Of Britain ; so she did not see the face,
Which then was as an angel's, but she
    saw,
Yet with the mists and smitten by the
    lights,
The Dragon of the great Pendragonship
Blaze, making all the night a steam of
    fire.
And even then he turn'd ; and more and
    more
The moony vapour rolling round the King,
Who seem'd the phantom of a Giant in it,
Enwound him fold by fold, and made him
    gray
And grayer, till himself became as mist
Before her, moving ghostlike to his doom.

Then she stretch'd out her arms and
    cried aloud
'Oh Arthur !' there her voice brake
    suddenly,
Then—as a stream that spouting from a
    cliff
Fails in mid air, but gathering at the base
Re-makes itself, and flashes down the
    vale—
Went on in passionate utterance :

                'Gone—my lord !
Gone thro' my sin to slay and to be slain !
And he forgave me, and I could not speak.
Farewell ? I should have answer'd his
    farewell.
His mercy choked me. Gone, my lord
    the King,
My own true lord ! how dare I call him
    mine ?
The shadow of another cleaves to me,
And makes me one pollution : he, the
    King,
Call'd me polluted : shall I kill myself ?
What help in that ? I cannot kill my sin,
If soul be soul ; nor can I kill my shame ;
No, nor by living can I live it down.
The days will grow to weeks, the weeks
    to months,
The months will add themselves and make
    the years,
The years will roll into the centuries,
And mine will ever be a name of scorn.
I must not dwell on that defeat of fame.
Let the world be ; that is but of the world
What else ? what hope ? I think there was
    a hope,
Except he mock'd me when he spake of
    hope ;
His hope he call'd it ; but he never mocks,
For mockery is the fume of little hearts.
And blessed be the King, who hath for-
    given
My wickedness to him, and left me hope
That in mine own heart I can live down
    sin
And be his mate hereafter in the heavens
Before high God. Ah great and gentle
    lord,
Who wast, as is the conscience of a saint

2 H

Among his warring senses, to thy
    knights—
To whom my false voluptuous pride, that
    took
Full easily all impressions from below,
Would not look up, or half-despised the
    height
To which I would not or I could not
    climb—
I thought I could not breathe in that fine
    air
That pure severity of perfect light—
I yearn'd for warmth and colour which I
    found
In Lancelot—now I see thee what thou
    art,
Thou art the highest and most human
    too,
Not Lancelot, nor another. Is there
    none
Will tell the King I love him tho' so late?
Now—ere he goes to the great Battle?
    none :
Myself must tell him in that purer life,
But now it were too daring. Ah my
    God,
What might I not have made of thy fair
    world,
Had I but loved thy highest creature
    here?
It was my duty to have loved the highest :
It surely was my profit had I known :
It would have been my pleasure had I
    seen.
We needs must love the highest when we
    see it,
Not Lancelot, nor another.'

               Here her hand
Grasp'd, made her vail her eyes : she
    look'd and saw
The novice, weeping, suppliant, and said
    to her,
'Yea, little maid, for am *I* not forgiven?'
Then glancing up beheld the holy nuns
All round her, weeping ; and her heart
    was loosed
Within her, and she wept with these and
    said,

'Ye know me then, that wicked one,
    who broke
The vast design and purpose of the King.
O shut me round with narrowing nunnery-
    walls,
Meek maidens, from the voices crying
    "shame."
I must not scorn myself : he loves me still.
Let no one dream but that he loves me
    still.
So let me, if you do not shudder at me,
Nor shun to call me sister, dwell with
    you ;
Wear black and white, and be a nun like
    you,
Fast with your fasts, not feasting with
    your feasts ;
Grieve with your griefs, not grieving at
    your joys,
But not rejoicing ; mingle with your rites
Pray and be pray'd for ; lie before you
    shrines ;
Do each low office of your holy house ;
Walk your dim cloister, and distribute dole
To poor sick people, richer in His eyes
Who ransom'd us, and haler too than I
And treat their loathsome hurts and heal
    mine own ;
And so wear out in almsdeed and in prayer
The sombre close of that voluptuous day
Which wrought the ruin of my lord the
    King.'

    She said : they took her to themselves
    and she
Still hoping, fearing 'is it yet too late?'
Dwelt with them, till in time their Abbess
    died.
Then she, for her good deeds and her
    pure life,
And for the power of ministration in her
And likewise for the high rank she had
    borne,
Was chosen Abbess, there, an Abbess,
    lived
For three brief years, and there, an
    Abbess, past
To where beyond these voices there is
    peace.

End of 'The Round Table.'

THE PASSING OF ARTHUR.

ʜᴀᴛ story which the bold Sir Bedivere,
ʀst made and latest left of all the
knights,
ᴏld, when the man was no more than a
voice
the white winter of his age, to those
ith whom he dwelt, new faces, other
minds.

For on their march to westward,
Bedivere,
ʜo slowly paced among the slumbering
host,
ᴇard in his tent the moanings of the
King:

'I found Him in the shining of the stars,
mark'd Him in the flowering of His
fields,
ᴛt in His ways with men I find Him not.
ᴠaged His wars, and now I pass and die.
me! for why is all around us here
ᴔ if some lesser god had made the world,
ᴛt had not force to shape it as he would,
ll the High God behold it from beyond,
ɴd enter it, and make it beautiful?
ᴇr else as if the world were wholly fair,
ᴜt that these eyes of men are dense and
dim,
ɴd have not power to see it as it is:
ᴇrchance, because we see not to the
close;—
ᴏr I, being simple, thought to work His
will,
ɴd have but stricken with the sword in
vain;
ɴd all whereon I lean'd in wife and friend
traitor to my peace, and all my realm
ᴇels back into the beast, and is no more.
ʏ God, thou hast forgotten me in my
death:
ᴀy—God my Christ—I pass but shall
not die.'

Then, ere that last weird battle in the
west,
ʜere came on Arthur sleeping, Gawain
kill'd

In Lancelot's war, the ghost of Gawain
blown
Along a wandering wind, and past his ear
Went shrilling, 'Hollow, hollow all
delight!
Hail, King! to-morrow thou shalt pass
away.
Farewell! there is an isle of rest for thee.
And I am blown along a wandering
wind,
And hollow, hollow, hollow all delight.'
And fainter onward, like wild birds that
change
Their season in the night and wail their
way
From cloud to cloud, down the long wind
the dream
Shrill'd; but in going mingled with dim
cries
Far in the moonlit haze among the hills,
As of some lonely city sack'd by night,
When all is lost, and wife and child with
wail
Pass to new lords; and Arthur woke and
call'd,
'Who spake? A dream. O light upon
the wind,
Thine, Gawain, was the voice—are these
dim cries
Thine? or doth all that haunts the waste
and wild
Mourn, knowing it will go along with me?'

This heard the bold Sir Bedivere and
spake:
'O me, my King, let pass whatever will,
Elves, and the harmless glamour of the
field;
But in their stead thy name and glory cling
To all high places like a golden cloud
For ever: but as yet thou shalt not pass.
Light was Gawain in life, and light in
death
Is Gawain, for the ghost is as the man;
And care not thou for dreams from him,
but rise—
I hear the steps of Modred in the west,

And with him many of thy people, and
knights
Once thine, whom thou hast loved, but
grosser grown
Than heathen, spitting at their vows and
thee.
Right well in heart they know thee for
the King.
Arise, go forth and conquer as of old.'

Then spake King Arthur to Sir Bedi-
vere :
' Far other is this battle in the west
Whereto we move, than when we strove
in youth,
And brake the petty kings, and fought
with Rome,
Or thrust the heathen from the Roman
wall,
And shook him thro' the north. Ill doom
is mine
To war against my people and my knights.
The king who fights his people fights
himself.
And they my knights, who loved me once,
the stroke
That strikes them dead is as my death to
me.
Yet let us hence, and find or feel a way
Thro' this blind haze, which ever since I
saw
One lying in the dust at Almesbury,
Hath folded in the passes of the world.'

Then rose the King and moved his host
by night,
And ever push'd Sir Modred, league by
league,
Back to the sunset bound of Lyonnesse—
A land of old upheaven from the abyss
By fire, to sink into the abyss again ;
Where fragments of forgotten peoples
dwelt,
And the long mountains ended in a coast
Of ever-shifting sand, and far away
The phantom circle of a moaning sea.
There the pursuer could pursue no more,
And he that fled no further fly the King ;
And there, that day when the great light
of heaven

Burn'd at his lowest in the rolling yea[r]
On the waste sand by the waste sea th[at]
closed.
Nor ever yet had Arthur fought a figh[t]
Like this last, dim, weird battle of t[he]
west.
A deathwhite mist slept over sand a[nd]
sea :
Whereof the chill, to him who breath[ed]
it, drew
Down with his blood, till all his heart w[as]
cold
With formless fear ; and ev'n on Artl[ur]
fell
Confusion, since he saw not whom [he]
fought.
For friend and foe were shadows in t[he]
mist,
And friend slew friend not knowing wh[om]
he slew ;
And some had visions out of gold[en]
youth,
And some beheld the faces of old gho[sts]
Look in upon the battle ; and in the m[ist]
Was many a noble deed, many a base
And chance and craft and strength i[n]
single fights,
And ever and anon with host to host
Shocks, and the splintering spear, t[he]
hard mail hewn,
Shield-breakings, and the clash of bran[d]
the crash
Of battleaxes on shatter'd helms, a[nd]
shrieks
After the Christ, of those who falling do[wn]
Look'd up for heaven, and only saw t[he]
mist ;
And shouts of heathen and the trai[tor]
knights,
Oaths, insult, filth, and monstrous bl[as]
phemies,
Sweat, writhings, anguish, labouring [of]
the lungs
In that close mist, and cryings for t[he]
light,
Moans of the dying, and voices of the dea[d]

Last, as by some one deathbed aft[er]
wail
Of suffering, silence follows, or thro' dea[th]

r deathlike swoon, thus over all that
shore,
ave for some whisper of the seething seas,
dead hush fell ; but when the dolorous
day
rew drearier toward twilight falling,
came
bitter wind, clear from the North, and
blew
he mist aside, and with that wind the tide
ose, and the pale King glanced across
the field
f battle : but no man was moving there ;
or any cry of Christian heard thereon,
or yet of heathen ; only the wan wave
rake in among dead faces, to and fro
waying the helpless hands, and up and
down
umbling the hollow helmets of the
fallen,
nd shiver'd brands that once had fought
with Rome,
nd rolling far along the gloomy shores
he voice of days of old and days to be.

Then spake King Arthur to Sir Bedivere,
nd whiter than the mist that all day long
Had held the field of battle was the King:

' Hearest thou this great voice that
shakes the world,
nd wastes the narrow realm whereon we
move,
nd beats upon the faces of the dead,
Ay dead, as tho' they had not died for
me ?—
) Bedivere, for on my heart hath fall'n
Confusion, till I know not what I am,
Nor whence I am, nor whether I be King.
Behold, I seem but King among the dead.'

Then spake the bold Sir Bedivere :
' My King,
King everywhere ! and so the dead have
kings,
here also will I worship thee as King.
Yet still thy life is whole, and still I live
Who love thee ; but who hates thee, he
that brought

The heathen back among us, yonder
stands,
Modred, unharm'd, the traitor of thine
house.'

Then spake the King: 'My house hath
been my doom.
But call not thou this traitor of my house
Who hath but dwelt beneath one roof with
me.
My house are rather they who sware my
vows,
Yea, even while they brake them, own'd
me King.
And well for thee, saying in my dark hour,
When all the purport of my throne hath
fail'd,
That quick or dead thou holdest me for
King.
King am I, whatsoever be their cry ;
And one last act of kinghood shalt thou
see
Yet, ere I pass.' And uttering this the
King
Made at the man : then Modred smote
his liege
Hard on that helm which many a heathen
sword
Had beaten thin ; while Arthur at one
blow,
Striking the last stroke with Excalibur,
Slew him, and all but slain himself, he fell.

So all day long the noise of battle roll'd
Among the mountains by the winter sea ;
Until King Arthur's Table, man by man,
Had fall'n in Lyonnesse about their lord,
King Arthur. Then, because his wound
was deep,
The bold Sir Bedivere uplifted him,
And bore him to a chapel nigh the field,
A broken chancel with a broken cross,
That stood on a dark strait of barren land :
On one side lay the Ocean, and on one
Lay a great water, and the moon was full.

Then spake King Arthur to Sir Bedi-
vere :
' The sequel of to-day unsolders all
The goodliest fellowship of famous knights

Whereof this world holds record. Such
    a sleep
They sleep—the men I loved. I think
    that we
Shall never more, at any future time,
Delight our souls with talk of knightly
    deeds,
Walking about the gardens and the halls
Of Camelot, as in the days that were.
I perish by this people which I made,—
Tho' Merlin sware that I should come
    again
To rule once more ; but, let what will be,
    be,
I am so deeply smitten thro' the helm
That without help I cannot last till morn.
Thou therefore take my brand Excalibur,
Which was my pride : for thou remem-
    berest how
In those old days, one summer noon, an
    arm
Rose up from out the bosom of the lake,
Clothed in white samite, mystic, won-
    derful,
Holding the sword—and how I row'd
    across
And took it, and have worn it, like a king ;
And, wheresoever I am sung or told
In aftertime, this also shall be known :
But now delay not : take Excalibur,
And fling him far into the middle mere :
Watch what thou seëst, and lightly bring
    me word.'

To him replied the bold Sir Bedivere :
'It is not meet, Sir King, to leave thee
    thus,
Aidless, alone, and smitten thro' the
    helm—
A little thing may harm a wounded man ;
Yet I thy hest will all perform at full,
Watch what I see, and lightly bring thee
    word.'

So saying, from the ruin'd shrine he
    stept,
And in the moon athwart the place of
    tombs,
Where lay the mighty bones of ancient
    men,

Old knights, and over them the sea-win
    sang
Shrill, chill, with flakes of foam. He
    stepping down
By zigzag paths, and juts of pointed rock
Came on the shining levels of the lake.

There drew he forth the brand Excali
    bur,
And o'er him, drawing it, the winte
    moon,
Brightening the skirts of a long cloud
    ran forth
And sparkled keen with frost against th
    hilt :
For all the haft twinkled with diamon
    sparks,
Myriads of topaz-lights, and jacinth-wor
Of subtlest jewellery. He gazed so lon
That both his eyes were dazzled as h
    stood,
This way and that dividing the swift min
In act to throw : but at the last it seem'
Better to leave Excalibur conceal'd
There in the many-knotted waterflags,
That whistled stiff and dry about th
    marge.
So strode he back slow to the wounde
    King.

Then spake King Arthur to Sir Bedi
    vere :
'Hast thou perform'd my mission whic
    I gave ?
What is it thou hast seen ? or what has
    heard ?'

And answer made the bold Sir Bed
    vere :
'I heard the ripple washing in the reed
And the wild water lapping on the crag

To whom replied King Arthur, fair
    and pale :
'Thou hast betray'd thy nature and th
    name,
Not rendering true answer, as beseem'd
Thy fëalty, nor like a noble knight :
For surer sign had follow'd, either hand
Or voice, or else a motion of the mere.
This is a shameful thing for men to lie.

Yet now, I charge thee, quickly go again,
As thou art lief and dear, and do the thing
I bade thee, watch, and lightly bring me
    word.'

Then went Sir Bedivere the second time
Across the ridge, and paced beside the
    mere,
Counting the dewy pebbles, fix'd in
    thought ;
But when he saw the wonder of the hilt,
How curiously and strangely chased, he
    smote
His palms together, and he cried aloud :

'And if indeed I cast the brand away,
Surely a precious thing, one worthy note,
Should thus be lost for ever from the
    earth,
Which might have pleased the eyes of
    many men.
What good should follow this, if this were
    done ?
What harm, undone ?   Deep harm to
    disobey,
Seeing obedience is the bond of rule.
Were it well to obey then, if a king
    demand
An act unprofitable, against himself ?
The King is sick, and knows not what
    he does.
What record, or what relic of my lord
Should be to aftertime, but empty breath
And rumours of a doubt ? But were this
    kept,
Stored in some treasure-house of mighty
    kings,
Some one might show it at a joust of arms,
Saying, "King Arthur's sword, Excali-
    bur,
Wrought by the lonely maiden of the
    Lake.
Nine years she wrought it, sitting in the
    deeps
Upon the hidden bases of the hills."
So might some old man speak in the after-
    time
To all the people, winning reverence.
But now much honour and much fame
    were lost.'

So spake he, clouded with his own
    conceit,
And hid Excalibur the second time,
And so strode back slow to the wounded
    King.

Then spoke King Arthur, breathing
    heavily :
'What is it thou hast seen ? or what hast
    heard ?'

And answer made the bold Sir Bedi-
    vere :
'I heard the water lapping on the crag,
And the long ripple washing in the reeds.'

To whom replied King Arthur, much
    in wrath :
'Ah, miserable and unkind, untrue,
Unknightly, traitor-hearted ! Woe is me
Authority forgets a dying king,
Laid widow'd of the power in his eye
That bow'd the will. I see thee what
    thou art,
For thou, the latest-left of all my knights,
In whom should meet the offices of all,
Thou wouldst betray me for the precious
    hilt ;
Either from lust of gold, or like a girl
Valuing the giddy pleasure of the eyes.
Yet, for a man may fail in duty twice,
And the third time may prosper, get thee
    hence :
But, if thou spare to fling Excalibur,
I will arise and slay thee with my hands.'

Then quickly rose Sir Bedivere, and
    ran,
And, leaping down the ridges lightly,
    plunged
Among the bulrush beds, and clutch'd
    the sword,
And strongly wheel'd and threw it. The
    great brand
Made lightnings in the splendour of the
    moon,
And flashing round and round, and
    whirl'd in an arch,
Shot like a streamer of the northern morn,
Seen where the moving isles of winter
    shock

By night, with noises of the Northern Sea.
So flash'd and fell the brand Excalibur :
But ere he dipt the surface, rose an arm
Clothed in white samite, mystic, won-
　　derful,
And caught him by the hilt, and brandish'd
　　him
Three times, and drew him under in the
　　mere.
And lightly went the other to the King.

　Then spoke King Arthur, drawing
　　thicker breath :
' Now see I by thine eyes that this is done.
Speak out : what is it thou hast heard, or
　　seen ?'

　And answer made the bold Sir Bedi-
　　vere :
'Sir King, I closed mine eyelids, lest the
　　gems
Should blind my purpose, for I never
　　saw,
Nor shall see, here or elsewhere, till I die,
Not tho' I live three lives of mortal men,
So great a miracle as yonder hilt.
Then with both hands I flung him, wheel-
　　ing him ;
But when I look'd again, behold an arm,
Clothed in white samite, mystic, won-
　　derful,
That caught him by the hilt, and
　　brandish'd him
Three times, and drew him under in the
　　mere.'

　And answer made King Arthur, breath-
　　ing hard :
' My end draws nigh ; 'tis time that I
　　were gone.
Make broad thy shoulders to receive my
　　weight,
And bear me to the margin ; yet I fear
My wound hath taken cold, and I shall
　　die.'

　So saying, from the pavement he half
　　rose,
Slowly, with pain, reclining on his arm,
And looking wistfully with wide blue eyes
As in a picture.　Him Sir Bedivere

Remorsefully regarded thro' his tears,
And would have spoken, but he found
　　not words ;
Then took with care, and kneeling on
　　one knee,
O'er both his shoulders drew the languid
　　hands,
And rising bore him thro' the place of
　　tombs.

　But, as he walk'd, King Arthur panted
　　hard,
Like one that feels a nightmare on his bed
When all the house is mute.　So sigh'd
　　the King,
Muttering and murmuring at his ear,
　　' Quick, quick !
I fear it is too late, and I shall die.'
But the other swiftly strode from ridge to
　　ridge,
Clothed with his breath, and looking, as
　　he walk'd,
Larger than human on the frozen hills.
He heard the deep behind him, and a cry
Before.　His own thought drove him like
　　a goad.
Dry clash'd his harness in the icy caves
And barren chasms, and all to left and
　　right
The bare black cliff clang'd round him,
　　as he based
His feet on juts of slippery crag that rang
Sharp - smitten with the dint of armed
　　heels—
And on a sudden, lo ! the level lake,
And the long glories of the winter moon.

　Then saw they how there hove a dusky
　　barge,
Dark as a funeral scarf from stem to stern,
Beneath them ; and descending they were
　　ware
That all the decks were dense with stately
　　forms,
Black-stoled, black-hooded, like a dream
　　—by these
Three Queens with crowns of gold : and
　　from them rose
A cry that shiver'd to the tingling stars,
And, as it were one voice, an agony

Of lamentation, like a wind that shrills
All night in a waste land, where no one
     comes,
Or hath come, since the making of the
     world.

     Then murmur'd Arthur, ' Place me in
          the barge.'
So to the barge they came.   There those
     three Queens
Put forth their hands, and took the King,
     and wept.
But she, that rose the tallest of them all
And fairest, laid his head upon her lap,
And loosed the shatter'd casque, and
     chafed his hands,
And call'd him by his name, complaining
     loud,
And dropping bitter tears against a brow
Striped with dark blood : for all his face
     was white
And colourless, and like the wither'd
     moon
Smote by the fresh beam of the spring-
     ing east ;
And all his greaves and cuisses dash'd with
     drops
Of onset ; and the light and lustrous
     curls—
That made his forehead like a rising sun
High from the daïs-throne—were parch'd
     with dust ;
Or, clotted into points and hanging loose,
Mix'd with the knightly growth that
     fringed his lips.
So like a shatter'd column lay the King ;
Not like that Arthur who, with lance in
     rest,
From spur to plume a star of tournament,
Shot thro' the lists at Camelot, and
     charged
Before the eyes of ladies and of kings.

     Then loudly cried the bold Sir
          Bedivere :
'Ah ! my Lord Arthur, whither shall I go ?
Where shall I hide my forehead and my
     eyes ?
For now I see the true old times are
     dead,

When every morning brought a noble
     chance,
And every chance brought out a noble
     knight.
Such times have been not since the light
     that led
The holy Elders with the gift of myrrh.
But now the whole Round Table is dis-
     solved
Which was an image of the mighty world,
And I, the last, go forth companionless,
And the days darken round me, and the
     years,
Among new men, strange faces, other
     minds.'

     And slowly answer'd Arthur from the
          barge :
' The old order changeth, yielding place
     to new,
And God fulfils himself in many ways,
Lest one good custom should corrupt the
     world.
Comfort thyself : what comfort is in me ?
I have lived my life, and that which I
     have done
May He within himself make pure ! but
     thou,
If thou shouldst never see my face again,
Pray for my soul.   More things are
     wrought by prayer
Than this world dreams of.   Wherefore,
     let thy voice
Rise like a fountain for me night and day.
For what are men better than sheep or goats
That nourish a blind life within the brain,
If, knowing God, they lift not hands of
     prayer
Both for themselves and those who call
     them friend ?
For so the whole round earth is every way
Bound by gold chains about the feet of
     God.
But now farewell.   I am going a long way
With these thou seëst—if indeed I go
(For all my mind is clouded with a
     doubt)—
To the island-valley of <u>Avilion</u> ;
Where falls not hail, or rain, or any snow,
Nor ever wind blows loudly ; but it lies

Deep-meadow'd, happy, fair with orchard
  lawns
And bowery hollows crown'd with summer
  sea,
Where I will heal me of my grievous
  wound.'

  So said he, and the barge with oar and
    sail
Moved from the brink, like some full-
  breasted swan
That, fluting a wild carol ere her death,
Ruffles her pure cold plume, and takes
  the flood
With swarthy webs.   Long stood Sir
  Bedivere
Revolving many memories, till the hull
Look'd one black dot against the verge of
  dawn,
And on the mere the wailing died away.

  But when that moan had past for ever-
    more,
The stillness of the dead world's winter
  dawn
Amazed him, and he groan'd, ' The King
  is gone.'
And therewithal came on him the weird
  rhyme,
' From the great deep to the great deep
  he goes.'

  Whereat he slowly turn'd and slowly
    clomb
The last hard footstep of that iron
  crag ;

Thence mark'd the black hull moving yet,
  and cried,
' He passes to be King among the dead,
And after healing of his grievous wound
He comes again ; but—if he come no
  more—
O me, be yon dark Queens in yon black
  boat,
Who shriek'd and wail'd, the three
  whereat we gazed
On that high day, when, clothed with
  living light,
They stood before his throne in silence,
  friends
Of Arthur, who should help him at his
  need ?'

  Then from the dawn it seem'd there
    came, but faint
As from beyond the limit of the world,
Like the last echo born of a great cry,
Sounds, as if some fair city were one voice
Around a king returning from his wars.

  Thereat once more he moved about,
    and clomb
Ev'n to the highest he could climb, and
  saw,
Straining his eyes beneath an arch of hand,
Or thought he saw, the speck that bare
  the King,
Down that long water opening on the deep
Somewhere far off, pass on and on, and go
From less to less and vanish into light.
And the new sun rose bringing the new
  year.

TO THE QUEEN.

O LOYAL to the royal in thyself,
And loyal to thy land, as this to thee——
Bear witness, that rememberable day,
When, pale as yet, and fever-worn, the
  Prince
Who scarce had pluck'd his flickering life
  again
From halfway down the shadow of the
  grave,
Past with thee thro' thy people and their
  love,

And London roll'd one tide of joy thro'
  all
Her trebled millions, and loud leagues of
  man
And welcome ! witness, too, the silent cry,
The prayer of many a race and creed,
  and clime—
Thunderless lightnings striking under sea
From sunset and sunrise of all thy realm,
And that true North, whereof we lately
  heard

A strain to shame us 'keep you to your-
  selves ;
So loyal is too costly ! friends—your love
Is but a burthen : loose the bond, and go.'
Is this the tone of empire ? here the faith
That made us rulers ? this, indeed, her
  voice
And meaning, whom the roar of Hougou-
  mont
Left mightiest of all peoples under heaven ?
What shock has fool'd her since, that she
  should speak
So feebly ? wealthier—wealthier—hour
  by hour !
The voice of Britain, or a sinking land,
Some third-rate isle half-lost among her
  seas ?
There rang her voice, when the full city
  peal'd
Thee and thy Prince ! The loyal to their
  crown
Are loyal to their own far sons, who love
Our ocean-empire with her boundless
  homes
For ever-broadening England, and her
  throne
In our vast Orient, and one isle, one isle,
That knows not her own greatness : if
  she knows
And dreads it we are fall'n.——But thou,
  my Queen,
Not for itself, but thro' thy living love
For one to whom I made it o'er his grave
Sacred, accept this old imperfect tale,
New-old, and shadowing Sense at war
  with Soul,
Ideal manhood closed in real man,
Rather than that gray king, whose name,
  a ghost,
Streams like a cloud, man-shaped, from
  mountain peak,
And cleaves to cairn and cromlech still ;
  or him

Of Geoffrey's book, or him of Malleor's,
  one
Touch'd by the adulterous finger of a time
That hover'd between war and wanton-
  ness,
And crownings and dethronements : take
  withal
Thy poet's blessing, and his trust that
  Heaven
Will blow the tempest in the distance back
From thine and ours : for some are scared,
  who mark,
Or wisely or unwisely, signs of storm,
Waverings of every vane with every wind,
And wordy trucklings to the transient
  hour,
And fierce or careless looseners of the
  faith,
And Softness breeding scorn of simple
  life,
Or Cowardice, the child of lust for gold,
Or Labour, with a groan and not a voice,
Or Art with poisonous honey stol'n from
  France,
And that which knows, but careful for
  itself,
And that which knows not, ruling that
  which knows
To its own harm : the goal of this great
  world
Lies beyond sight : yet—it our slowly-
  grown
And crown'd Republic's crowning com-
  mon-sense,
That saved her many times, not fail——
  their fears
Are morning shadows huger than the
  shapes
That cast them, not those gloomier which
  forego
The darkness of that battle in the West,
Where all of high and holy dies away.

THE LOVER'S TALE.

THE original Preface to 'The Lover's Tale' states that it was composed in my nineteenth year. Two only of the three parts then written were printed, when, feeling the imperfection of the poem, I withdrew it from the press. One of my friends however who, boylike, admired the boy's work, distributed among our common associates of that hour some copies of these two parts, without my knowledge, without the omissions and amendments which I had in contemplation, and marred by the many misprints of the compositor. Seeing that these two parts have of late been mercilessly pirated, and that what I had deemed scarce worthy to live is not allowed to die, may I not be pardoned if I suffer the whole poem at last to come into the light—accompanied with a reprint of the sequel—a work of my mature life—'The Golden Supper'?

May 1879.

ARGUMENT.

JULIAN, whose cousin and foster-sister, Camilla, has been wedded to his friend and rival, Lionel, endeavours to narrate the story of his own love for her, and the strange sequel. He speaks (in Parts II. and III.) of having been haunted by visions and the sound of bells, tolling for a funeral, and at last ringing for a marriage; but he breaks away, overcome, as he approaches the Event, and a witness to it completes the tale.

I.

HERE far away, seen from the topmost cliff,
Filling with purple gloom the vacancies
Between the tufted hills, the sloping seas
Hung in mid-heaven, and half-way down
 rare sails,
White as white clouds, floated from sky
 to sky.
Oh! pleasant breast of waters, quiet bay,
Like to a quiet mind in the loud world,
Where the chafed breakers of the outer
 sea
Sank powerless, as anger falls aside
And withers on the breast of peaceful love;
Thou didst receive the growth of pines
 that fledged
The hills that watch'd thee, as Love
 watcheth Love,
In thine own essence, and delight thyself
To make it wholly thine on sunny days.
Keep thou thy name of 'Lover's Bay.'
 See, sirs,
Even now the Goddess of the Past, that
 takes
The heart, and sometimes touches but
 one string
That quivers, and is silent, and sometimes
Sweeps suddenly all its half-moulder'd
 chords
To some old melody, begins to play

That air which pleased her first. I feel
 thy breath;
I come, great Mistress of the ear and eye:
Thy breath is of the pinewood; and tho'
 years
Have hollow'd out a deep and stormy
 strait
Betwixt the native land of Love and me,
Breathe but a little on me, and the sail
Will draw me to the rising of the sun,
The lucid chambers of the morning star,
And East of Life.

  Permit me, friend, I prythee,
To pass my hand across my brows, and
 muse
On those dear hills, that never more will
 meet
The sight that throbs and aches beneath
 my touch,
As tho' there beat a heart in either eye;
For when the outer lights are darken'd
 thus,
The memory's vision hath a keener edge.
It grows upon me now—the semicircle
Of dark-blue waters and the narrow fringe
Of curving beach—its wreaths of dripping
 green—
Its pale pink shells—the summerhouse
 aloft
That open'd on the pines with doors of
 glass,

A mountain nest—the pleasure-boat that
   rock'd,
Light-green with its own shadow, keel to
   keel,
Upon the dappled dimplings of the wave,
That blanch'd upon its side.

                    O Love, O Hope !
They come, they crowd upon me all at
   once—
Moved from the cloud of unforgotten
   things,
That sometimes on the horizon of the
   mind
Lies folded, often sweeps athwart in
   storm—
Flash upon flash they lighten thro' me—
   days
Of dewy dawning and the amber eves
When thou and I, Camilla, thou and I
Were borne about the bay or safely
   moor'd
Beneath a low-brow'd cavern, where the
   tide
Plash'd, sapping its worn ribs ; and all
   without
The slowly-ridging rollers on the cliffs
Clash'd, calling to each other, and thro'
   the arch
Down those loud waters, like a setting
   star,
Mixt with the gorgeous west the light-
   house shone,
And silver-smiling Venus ere she fell
Would often loiter in her balmy blue,
To crown it with herself.

                    Here, too, my love
Waver'd at anchor with me, when day
   hung
From his mid-dome in Heaven's airy
   halls ;
Gleams of the water-circles as they broke,
Flicker'd like doubtful smiles about her
   lips,
Quiver'd a flying glory on her hair,
Leapt like a passing thought across her
   eyes ;
And mine with one that will not pass,
   till earth

And heaven pass too, dwelt on my heaven,
   a face
Most starry-fair, but kindled from within
As 'twere with dawn.   She was dark-
   hair'd, dark-eyed :
Oh, such dark eyes ! a single glance of
   them
Will govern a whole life from birth to
   death,
Careless of all things else, led on with light
In trances and in visions : look at them,
You lose yourself in utter ignorance ;
You cannot find their depth ; for they go
   back,
And farther back, and still withdraw
   themselves
Quite into the deep soul, that evermore
Fresh springing from her fountains in the
   brain,
Still pouring thro', floods with redundant
   life
Her narrow portals.

                    Trust me, long ago
I should have died, if it were possible
To die in gazing on that perfectness
Which I do bear within me : I had died,
But from my farthest lapse, my latest ebb,
Thine image, like a charm of light and
   strength
Upon the waters, push'd me back again
On these deserted sands of barren life.
Tho' from the deep vault where the heart
   of Hope
Fell into dust, and crumbled in the dark—
Forgetting how to render beautiful
Her countenance with quick and health-
   ful blood—
Thou didst not sway me upward ; could
   I perish
While thou, a meteor of the sepulchre,
Didst swathe thyself all round Hope's
   quiet urn
For ever ?   He, that saith it, hath o'er-
   stept
The slippery footing of his narrow wit,
And fall'n away from judgment.   Thou
   art light,
To which my spirit leaneth all her flowers,
And length of days, and immortality

Of thought, and freshness ever self-re-
new'd.
For Time and Grief abode too long with
Life,
And, like all other friends i' the world, at
last
They grew aweary of her fellowship :
So Time and Grief did beckon unto
Death,
And Death drew nigh and beat the doors
of Life ;
But thou didst sit alone in the inner house,
A wakeful portress, and didst parle with
Death, —
'This is a charmed dwelling which I
hold ;'
So Death gave back, and would no
further come.
Yet is my life nor in the present time,
Nor in the present place. To me alone,
Push'd from his chair of regal heritage,
The Present is the vassal of the Past :
So that, in that I *have* lived, do I live,
And cannot die, and am, in having been—
A portion of the pleasant yesterday,
Thrust forward on to-day and out of
place ;
A body journeying onward, sick with
toil,
The weight as if of age upon my limbs,
The grasp of hopeless grief about my
heart,
And all the senses weaken'd, save in that,
Which long ago they had glean'd and
garner'd up
Into the granaries of memory—
The clear brow, bulwark of the precious
brain,
Chink'd as you see, and seam'd—and all
the while
The light soul twines and mingles with
the growths
Of vigorous early days, attracted, won,
Married, made one with, molten into all
The beautiful in Past of act or place,
And like the all-enduring camel, driven
Far from the diamond fountain by the
palms,
Who toils across the middle moonlit
nights,

Or when the white heats of the blinding
noons
Beat from the concave sand ; yet in him
keeps
A draught of that sweet fountain that he
loves,
To stay his feet from falling, and his spirit
From bitterness of death.

　　　　　　　　Ye ask me, friends,
When I began to love. How should I
tell you ?
Or from the after-fulness of my heart,
Flow back again unto my slender spring
And first of love, tho' every turn and
depth
Between is clearer in my life than all
Its present flow. Ye know not what ye
ask.
How should the broad and open flower
tell
What sort of bud it was, when, prest
together
In its green sheath, close-lapt in silken
folds,
It seem'd to keep its sweetness to itself,
Yet was not the less sweet for that it
seem'd ?
For young Life knows not when young
Life was born,
But takes it all for granted : neither Love,
Warm in the heart, his cradle, can re-
member
Love in the womb, but resteth satisfied,
Looking on her that brought him to the
light :
Or as men know not when they fall asleep
Into delicious dreams, our other life,
So know I not when I began to love.
This is my sum of knowledge—that my
love
Grew with myself—say rather, was my
growth,
My inward sap, the hold I have on earth,
My outward circling air wherewith I
breathe,
Which yet upholds my life, and evermore
Is to me daily life and daily death :
For how should I have lived and not
have loved ?

Can ye take off the sweetness from the
  flower,
The colour and the sweetness from the
  rose,
And place them by themselves; or set
  apart
Their motions and their brightness from
  the stars,
And then point out the flower or the star?
Or build a wall betwixt my life and love,
And tell me where I am? 'Tis even
  thus:
In that I live I love; because I love
I live: whate'er is fountain to the one
Is fountain to the other; and whene'er
Our God unknits the riddle of the one,
There is no shade or fold of mystery
Swathing the other.

            Many, many years,
(For they seem many and my most of life,
And well I could have linger'd in that
  porch,
So unproportion'd to the dwelling-place,)
In the Maydews of childhood, opposite
The flush and dawn of youth, we lived
  together,
Apart, alone together on those hills.

  Before he saw my day my father died,
And he was happy that he saw it not;
But I and the first daisy on his grave
From the same clay came into light at
  once.
As Love and I do number equal years,
So she, my love, is of an age with me.
How like each other was the birth of
  each!
On the same morning, almost the same
  hour,
Under the selfsame aspect of the stars,
(Oh falsehood of all starcraft!) we were
  born.
How like each other was the birth of each!
The sister of my mother—she that bore
Camilla close beneath her beating heart,
Which to the imprison'd spirit of the child,
With its true-touched pulses in the flow
And hourly visitation of the blood,
Sent notes of preparation manifold,

And mellow'd echoes of the outer world—
My mother's sister, mother of my love,
Who had a twofold claim upon my heart,
One twofold mightier than the other was,
In giving so much beauty to the world,
And so much wealth as God had charged
  her with—
Loathing to put it from herself for ever,
Left her own life with it; and dying thus,
Crown'd with her highest act the placid
  face
And breathless body of her good deeds
  past.

  So were we born, so orphan'd. She
  was motherless
And I without a father. So from each
Of those two pillars which from earth
  uphold
Our childhood, one had fallen away, and
  all
The careful burthen of our tender years
Trembled upon the other. He that gave
Her life, to me delightedly fulfill'd
All lovingkindnesses, all offices
Of watchful care and trembling tender
  ness.
He waked for both: he pray'd for both
  he slept
Dreaming of both: nor was his love the
  less
Because it was divided, and shot forth
Boughs on each side, laden with whole-
  some shade,
Wherein we nested sleeping or awake,
And sang aloud the matin-song of life.

  She was my foster-sister: on one arm
The flaxen ringlets of our infancies
Wander'd, the while we rested: one soft
  lap
Pillow'd us both: a common light of eyes
Was on us as we lay: our baby lips,
Kissing one bosom, ever drew from thence
The stream of life, one stream, one life,
  one blood,
One sustenance, which, still as thought
  grew large,
Still larger moulding all the house of
  thought,

Made all our tastes and fancies like,
perhaps—
All—all but one; and strange to me,
and sweet,
Sweet thro' strange years to know that
whatsoe'er
Our general mother meant for me alone,
Our mutual mother dealt to both of us :
So what was earliest mine in earliest life,
I shared with her in whom myself remains.
    As was our childhood, so our infancy,
They tell me, was a very miracle
Of fellow-feeling and communion.
They tell me that we would not be alone,—
We cried when we were parted ; when I
wept,
Her smile lit up the rainbow on my tears,
Stay'd on the cloud of sorrow ; that we
loved
The sound of one-another's voices more
Than the gray cuckoo loves his name, and
learn'd
To lisp in tune together ; that we slept
In the same cradle always, face to face,
Heart beating time to heart, lip pressing
lip,
Folding each other, breathing on each
other,
Dreaming together (dreaming of each
other
They should have added), till the morning
light
Sloped thro' the pines, upon the dewy
pane
Falling, unseal'd our eyelids, and we woke
To gaze upon each other. If this be
true,
At thought of which my whole soul
languishes
And faints, and hath no pulse, no breath
—as tho'
A man in some still garden should infuse
Rich atar in the bosom of the rose,
Till, drunk with its own wine, and over-
full
Of sweetness, and in smelling of itself,
It fall on its own thorns—if this be true—
And that way my wish leads me evermore
Still to believe it—'tis so sweet a thought,
Why in the utter stillness of the soul

Doth question'd memory answer not, nor
tell
Of this our earliest, our closest-drawn,
Most loveliest, earthly-heavenliest har-
mony ?
    O blossom'd portal of the lonely house,
Green prelude, April promise, glad new-
year
Of Being, which with earliest violets
And lavish carol of clear-throated larks
Fill'd all the March of life !—I will not
speak of thee,
These have not seen thee, these can never
know thee,
They cannot understand me. Pass we
then
A term of eighteen years. Ye would but
laugh,
If I should tell you how I hoard in
thought
The faded rhymes and scraps of ancient
crones,
Gray relics of the nurseries of the world,
Which are as gems set in my memory,
Because she learnt them with me ; or
what use
To know her father left us just before
The daffodil was blown ? or how we
found
The dead man cast upon the shore ? All
this
Seems to the quiet daylight of your minds
But cloud and smoke, and in the dark of
mine
Is traced with flame. Move with me to
the event.
    There came a glorious morning, such a
one
As dawns but once a season. Mercury
On such a morning would have flung
himself
From cloud to cloud, and swum with
balanced wings
To some tall mountain : when I said to
her,
' A day for Gods to stoop,' she answered,
' Ay,
And men to soar:' for as that other
gazed,
Shading his eyes till all the fiery cloud,

The prophet and the chariot and the
    steeds,
Suck'd into oneness like a little star
Were drunk into the inmost blue, we
    stood,
When first we came from out the pines at
    noon,
With hands for eaves, uplooking and
    almost
Waiting to see some blessed shape in
    heaven,
So bathed we were in brilliance. Never
    yet
Before or after have I known the spring
Pour with such sudden deluges of light
Into the middle summer ; for that day
Love, rising, shook his wings, and charged
    the winds
With spiced May-sweets from bound to
    bound, and blew
Fresh fire into the sun, and from within
Burst thro' the heated buds, and sent his
    soul
Into the songs of birds, and touch'd far-
    off
His mountain-altars, his high hills, with
    flame
Milder and purer.

            Thro' the rocks we wound :
The great pine shook with lonely sounds
    of joy
That came on the sea-wind. As moun-
    tain streams
Our bloods ran free : the sunshine seem'd
    to brood
More warmly on the heart than on the
    brow.
We often paused, and, looking back, we
    saw
The clefts and openings in the mountains
    fill'd
With the blue valley and the glistening
    brooks,
And all the low dark groves, a land of
    love !
A land of promise, a land of memory,
A land of promise flowing with the milk
And honey of delicious memories !

And down to sea, and far as eye could
    ken,
Each way from verge to verge a Holy
    Land,
Still growing holier as you near'd the
    bay,
For there the Temple stood.

            When we had reach'd
The grassy platform on some hill, I
    stoop'd,
I gather'd the wild herbs, and for her
    brows
And mine made garlands of the selfsame
    flower,
Which she took smiling, and with my
    work thus
Crown'd her clear forehead. Once or
    twice she told me
(For I remember all things) to let grow
The flowers that run poison in their veins.
She said, ' The evil flourish in the world.'
Then playfully she gave herself the lie—
' Nothing in nature is unbeautiful ;
So, brother, pluck and spare not.' So
    I wove
Ev'n the dull-blooded poppy-stem, 'whose
    flower,
Hued with the scarlet of a fierce sunrise,
Like to the wild youth of an evil prince,
Is without sweetness, but who crowns
    himself
Above the naked poisons of his heart
In his old age.' A graceful thought of
    hers
Grav'n on my fancy ! And oh, how like
    a nymph,
A stately mountain nymph she look'd !
    how native
Unto the hills she trod on ! While I
    gazed
My coronal slowly disentwined itself
And fell between us both ; tho' while I
    gazed
My spirit leap'd as with those thrills of
    bliss
That strike across the soul in prayer, and
    show us
That we are surely heard. Methought a
    light

Burst from the garland I had wov'n, and
stood
A solid glory on her bright black hair ;
A light methought broke from her dark,
dark eyes,
And shot itself into the singing winds ;
A mystic light flash'd ev'n from her white
robe
As from a glass in the sun, and fell about
My footsteps on the mountains.

Last we came
To what our people call 'The Hill of
Woe.'
A bridge is there, that, look'd at from
beneath
Seems but a cobweb filament to link
The yawning of an earthquake-cloven
chasm.
And thence one night, when all the winds
were loud,
A woful man (for so the story went)
Had thrust his wife and child and dash'd
himself
Into the dizzy depth below. Below,
Fierce in the strength of far descent, a
stream
Flies with a shatter'd foam along the
chasm.
    The path was perilous, loosely strown
with crags :
We mounted slowly ; yet to both there
came
The joy of life in steepness overcome,
And victories of ascent, and looking down
On all that had look'd down on us ; and
joy
In breathing nearer heaven ; and joy to
me,
High over all the azure-circled earth,
To breathe with her as if in heaven itself ;
And more than joy that I to her became
Her guardian and her angel, raising her
Still higher, past all peril, until she saw
Beneath her feet the region far away,
Beyond the nearest mountain's bosky
brows,
Arise in open prospect—heath and hill,
And hollow lined and wooded to the lips,
And steep-down walls of battlemented rock

Gilded with broom, or shatter'd into
spires,
And glory of broad waters interfused,
Whence rose as it were breath and steam
of gold,
And over all the great wood rioting
And climbing, streak'd or starr'd at
intervals
With falling brook or blossom'd bush—
and last,
Framing the mighty landscape to the west,
A purple range of mountain-cones, be-
tween
Whose interspaces gush'd in blinding
bursts
The incorporate blaze of sun and sea.

At length
Descending from the point and standing
both,
There on the tremulous bridge, that from
beneath
Had seem'd a gossamer filament up in air,
We paused amid the splendour. All the
west
And ev'n unto the middle south was
ribb'd
And barr'd with bloom on bloom. The
sun below,
Held for a space 'twixt cloud and wave,
shower'd down
Rays of a mighty circle, weaving over
That various wilderness a tissue of light
Unparallel'd. On the other side, the
moon,
Half-melted into thin blue air, stood still,
And pale and fibrous as a wither'd leaf,
Nor yet endured in presence of His eyes
To indue his lustre ; most unloverlike,
Since in his absence full of light and joy,
And giving light to others. But this
most,
Next to her presence whom I loved so
well,
Spoke loudly even into my inmost heart
As to my outward hearing : the loud
stream,
Forth issuing from his portals in the crag
(A visible link unto the home of my
heart),

Ran amber toward the west, and nigh
    the sea
Parting my own loved mountains was
    received,
Shorn of its strength, into the sympathy
Of that small bay, which out to open
    main
Glow'd intermingling close beneath the
    sun.
Spirit of Love ! that little hour was bound
Shut in from Time, and dedicate to
    thee :
Thy fires from heaven had touch'd it,
    and the earth
They fell on became hallow'd evermore.

  We turn'd : our eyes met : hers were
    bright, and mine
Were dim with floating tears, that shot
    the sunset
In lightnings round me ; and my name
    was borne
Upon her breath.   Henceforth my name
    has been
A hallow'd memory like the names of old,
A center'd, glory-circled memory,
And a peculiar treasure, brooking not
Exchange or currency : and in that hour
A hope flow'd round me, like a golden
    mist
Charm'd amid eddies of melodious airs,
A moment, ere the onward whirlwind
    shatter it,
Waver'd and floated — which was less
    than Hope,
Because it lack'd the power of perfect
    Hope ;
But which was more and higher than all
    Hope,
Because all other Hope had lower aim ;
Even that this name to which her gracious
    lips
Did lend such gentle utterance, this one
    name,
In some obscure hereafter, might in-
    wreathe
(How lovelier, nobler then !) her life, her
    love,
With my life, love, soul, spirit, and heart
    and strength.

'Brother,' she said, 'let this be call'd
    henceforth
The Hill of Hope ;' and I replied, 'O
    sister,
My will is one with thine ; the Hill of
    Hope.'
Nevertheless, we did not change the name.

  I did not speak : I could not speak my
    love.
Love lieth deep : Love dwells not in lip-
    depths.
Love wraps his wings on either side the
    heart,
Constraining it with kisses close and warm,
Absorbing all the incense of sweet thoughts
So that they pass not to the shrine of
    sound.
Else had the life of that delighted hour
Drunk in the largeness of the utterance
Of Love ; but how should Earthly mea-
    sure mete
The Heavenly-unmeasured or unlimited
    Love,
Who scarce can tune his high majestic
    sense
Unto the thundersong that wheels the
    spheres,
Scarce living in the Æolian harmony,
And flowing odour of the spacious air,
Scarce housed within the circle of this
    Earth,
Be cabin'd up in words and syllables,
Which pass with that which breathes
    them ?   Sooner Earth
Might go round Heaven, and the strait
    girth of Time
Inswathe the fulness of Eternity,
Than language grasp the infinite of Love.

  O day which did enwomb that happy
    hour,
Thou art blessed in the years, divinest day !
O Genius of that hour which dost uphold
Thy coronal of glory like a God,
Amid thy melancholy mates far-seen,
Who walk before thee, ever turning round
To gaze upon thee till their eyes are dim
With dwelling on the light and depth of
    thine,

Thy name is ever worshipp'd among
    hours !
Had I died then, I had not seem'd to die,
For bliss stood round me like the light of
    Heaven,—
Had I died then, I had not known the
    death ;
Yea had the Power from whose right
    hand the light
Of Life issueth, and from whose left hand
    floweth
The Shadow of Death, perennial efflu-
    ences,
Whereof to all that draw the wholesome
    air,
Somewhile the one must overflow the
    other ;
Then had he stemm'd my day with night,
    and driven
My current to the fountain whence it
    sprang,—
Even his own abiding excellence—
On me, methinks, that shock of gloom
    had fall'n
Unfelt, and in this glory I had merged
The other, like the sun I gazed upon,
Which seeming for the moment due to
    death,
And dipping his head low beneath the
    verge,
Yet bearing round about him his own day,
In confidence of unabated strength,
Steppeth from Heaven to Heaven, from
    light to light,
And holdeth his undimmed forehead far
Into a clearer zenith, pure of cloud.

We trod the shadow of the downward
    hill ;
We past from light to dark. On the
    other side
Is scoop'd a cavern and a mountain hall,
Which none have fathom'd. If you go
    far in
(The country people rumour) you may
    hear
The moaning of the woman and the child,
Shut in the secret chambers of the rock.
I too have heard a sound—perchance of
    streams

Running far on within its inmost halls,
The home of darkness ; but the cavern-
    mouth,
Half overtrailed with a wanton weed,
Gives birth to a brawling brook, that
    passing lightly
Adown a natural stair of tangled roots,
Is presently received in a sweet grave
Of eglantines, a place of burial
Far lovelier than its cradle ; for unseen,
But taken with the sweetness of the place,
It makes a constant bubbling melody
That drowns the nearer echoes. Lower
    down
Spreads out a little lake, that, flooding,
    leaves
Low banks of yellow sand ; and from the
    woods
That belt it rise three dark, tall cy-
    presses,—
Three cypresses, symbols of mortal woe,
That men plant over graves.

                        Hither we came,
And sitting down upon the golden moss,
Held converse sweet and low—low con-
    verse sweet,
In which our voices bore least part. The
    wind
Told a lovetale beside us, how he woo'd
The waters, and the waters answering
    lisp'd
To kisses of the wind, that, sick with love,
Fainted at intervals, and grew again
To utterance of passion. Ye cannot
    shape
Fancy so fair as is this memory.
Methought all excellence that ever was
Had drawn herself from many thousand
    years,
And all the separate Edens of this earth,
To centre in this place and time. I
    listen'd,
And her words stole with most prevailing
    sweetness
Into my heart, as thronging fancies come
To boys and girls when summer days are
    new,
And soul and heart and body are all at
    ease :

What marvel my Camilla told me all?
It was so happy an hour, so sweet a place,
And I was as the brother of her blood,
And by that name I moved upon her
    breath ;
Dear name, which had too much of near-
    ness in it
And heralded the distance of this time !
At first her voice was very sweet and low,
As if she were afraid of utterance ;
But in the onward current of her speech,
(As echoes of the hollow-banked brooks
Are fashion'd by the channel which they
    keep),
Her words did of their meaning borrow
    sound,
Her cheek did catch the colour of her
    words.
I heard and trembled, yet I could but
    hear ;
My heart paused — my raised eyelids
    would not fall,
But still I kept my eyes upon the sky.
I seem'd the only part of Time stood still,
And saw the motion of all other things ;
While her words, syllable by syllable,
Like water, drop by drop, upon my ear
Fell ; and I wish'd, yet wish'd her not
    to speak ;
But she spake on, for I did name no wish,
What marvel my Camilla told me all
Her maiden dignities of Hope and Love—
' Perchance,' she said, ' return'd.' Even
    then the stars
Did tremble in their stations as I gazed ;
But she spake on, for I did name no wish,
No wish—no hope. Hope was not wholly
    dead,
But breathing hard at the approach of
    Death,—
Camilla, my Camilla, who was mine
No longer in the dearest sense of mine—
For all the secret of her inmost heart,
And all the maiden empire of her mind,
Lay like a map before me, and I saw
There, where I hoped myself to reign as
    king,
There, where that day I crown'd myself
    as king,
There in my realm and even on my throne,

Another ! then it seem'd as tho' a link
Of some tight chain within my inmost
    frame
Was riven in twain : that life I heeded not
Flow'd from me, and the darkness of the
    grave,
The darkness of the grave and utter night,
Did swallow up my vision ; at her feet,
Even the feet of her I loved, I fell,
Smit with exceeding sorrow unto Death.

Then had the earth beneath me yawn-
    ing cloven
With such a sound as when an iceberg
    splits
From cope to base—had Heaven from
    all her doors,
With all her golden thresholds clashing,
    roll'd
Her heaviest thunder—I had lain as
    dead,
Mute, blind and motionless as then I lay ;
Dead, for henceforth there was no life
    for me !
Mute, for henceforth what use were
    words to me !
Blind, for the day was as the night to
    me !
The night to me was kinder than the
    day ;
The night in pity took away my day,
Because my grief as yet was newly born
Of eyes too weak to look upon the light;
And thro' the hasty notice of the ear
Frail Life was startled from the tender
    love
Of him she brooded over. Would I had
    lain
Until the plaited ivy-tress had wound
Round my worn limbs, and the wild brier
    had driven
Its knotted thorns thro' my unpaining
    brows,
Leaning its roses on my faded eyes.
The wind had blown above me, and the
    rain
Had fall'n upon me, and the gilded snake
Had nestled in this bosom-throne of
    Love,
But I had been at rest for evermore.

Long time entrancement held me.   All
   too soon
Life (like a wanton too-officious friend,
Who will not *hear* denial, vain and rude
With proffer of unwish'd-for services)
Entering all the avenues of sense
Past thro' into his citadel, the brain,
With hated warmth of apprehensiveness.
And first the chillness of the sprinkled
   brook
Smote on my brows, and then I seem'd
   to hear
Its murmur, as the drowning seaman
   hears,
Who with his head below the surface
   dropt
Listens the muffled booming indistinct
Of the confused floods, and dimly knows
His head shall rise no more : and then
   came in
The white light of the weary moon
   above,
Diffused and molten into flaky cloud.
Was my sight drunk that it did shape to
   me
Him who should own that name ? Were
   it not well
If so be that the echo of that name
Ringing within the fancy had updrawn
A fashion and a phantasm of the form
It should attach to ?   Phantom !—had
   the ghastliest
That ever lusted for a body, sucking
The foul steam of the grave to thicken
   by it,
There in the shuddering moonlight
   brought its face
And what it has for eyes as close to
   mine
As he did—better that than his, than he
The friend, the neighbour, Lionel, the
   beloved,
The loved, the lover, the happy Lionel,
The low-voiced, tender-spirited Lionel,
All joy, to whom my agony was a joy.
O how her choice did leap forth from his
   eyes !
O how her love did clothe itself in smiles
About his lips ! and—not one moment's
   grace—

Then when the effect weigh'd seas upon
   my head
To come my way ! to twit me with the
   cause !

Was not the land as free thro' all her
   ways
To him as me ?   Was not his wont to
   walk
Between the going light and growing
   night ?
Had I not learnt my loss before he came ?
Could that be more because he came my
   way ?
Why should he not come my way if he
   would ?
And yet to-night, to-night—when all my
   wealth
Flash'd from me in a moment and I fell
Beggar'd for ever—why *should* he come
   my way
Robed in those robes of light I must not
   wear,
With that great crown of beams about his
   brows—
Come like an angel to a damned soul,
To tell him of the bliss he had with
   God—
Come like a careless and a greedy heir
That scarce can wait the reading of the
   will
Before he takes possession ?   Was mine
   a mood
To be invaded rudely, and not rather
A sacred, secret, unapproached woe,
Unspeakable ?   I was shut up with
   Grief ;
She took the body of my past delight,
Narded and swathed and balm'd it for
   herself,
And laid it in a sepulchre of rock
Never to rise again.   I was led mute
Into her temple like a sacrifice ;
I was the High Priest in her holiest
   place,
Not to be loudly broken in upon.

Oh friend, thoughts deep and heavy as
   these well-nigh
O'erbore the limits of my brain : but he

Bent o'er me, and my neck his arm up-
stay'd.
I thought it was an adder's fold, and once
I strove to disengage myself, but fail'd,
Being so feeble: she bent above me, too ;
Wan was her cheek ; for whatsoe'er of
blight
Lives in the dewy touch of pity had made
The red rose there a pale one—and her
eyes—
I saw the moonlight glitter on their
tears—
And some few drops of that distressful
rain
Fell on my face, and her long ringlets
moved,
Drooping and beaten by the breeze, and
brush'd
My fallen forehead in their to and fro,
For in the sudden anguish of her heart
Loosed from their simple thrall they had
flow'd abroad,
And floated on and parted round her neck,
Mantling her form halfway. She, when
I woke,
Something she ask'd, I know not what,
and ask'd,
Unanswer'd, since I spake not ; for the
sound
Of that dear voice so musically low,
And now first heard with any sense of
pain,
As it had taken life away before,
Choked all the syllables, that strove to
rise
From my full heart.

                    The blissful lover, too,
From his great hoard of happiness distill'd
Some drops of solace ; like a vain rich
man,
That, having always prosper'd in the
world,
Folding his hands, deals comfortable
words
To hearts wounded for ever ; yet, in
truth,
Fair speech was his and delicate of
phrase,

Falling in whispers on the sense, ad-
dress'd
More to the inward than the outward
ear,
As rain of the midsummer midnight soft,
Scarce-heard, recalling fragrance and the
green
Of the dead spring : but mine was wholly
dead,
No bud, no leaf, no flower, no fruit for
me.
Yet who had done, or who had suffer'd
wrong ?
And why was I to darken their pure love,
If, as I found, they two did love each
other,
Because my own was darken'd ? Why
was I
To cross between their happy star and
them ?
To stand a shadow by their shining doors,
And vex them with my darkness ? Did
I love her ?
Ye know that I did love her ; to this
present
My full-orb'd love has waned not. Did
I love her,
And could I look upon her tearful eyes ?
What had *she* done to weep ? Why
should *she* weep ?
O innocent of spirit—let my heart
Break rather—whom the gentlest airs of
Heaven
Should kiss with an unwonted gentleness.
Her love did murder mine ? What then ?
She deem'd
I wore a brother's mind : she call'd me
brother :
She told me all her love : she shall not
weep.

The brightness of a burning thought,
awhile
In battle with the glooms of my dark will,
Moonlike emerged, and to itself lit up
There on the depth of an unfathom'd woe
Reflex of action. Starting up at once,
As from a dismal dream of my own death,
I, for I loved her, lost my love in Love;
I, for I loved her, graspt the hand she lov'd,

And laid it in her own, and sent my cry
Thro' the blank night to Him who loving
made
The happy and the unhappy love, that He
Would hold the hand of blessing over them,
Lionel, the happy, and her, and her, his
bride !
Let them so love that men and boys may
say,
' Lo ! how they love each other !' till
their love
Shall ripen to a proverb, unto all
Known, when their faces are forgot in
the land—
One golden dream of love, from which
may death
Awake them with heaven's music in a life
More living to some happier happiness,
Swallowing its precedent in victory.
And as for me, Camilla, as for me,—
The dew of tears is an unwholesome dew,
They will but sicken the sick plant the
more.
Deem that I love thee but as brothers do,
So shalt thou love me still as sisters do ;
Or if thou dream aught farther, dream
but how
I could have loved thee, had there been
none else
To love as lovers, loved again by thee.

Or this, or somewhat like to this, I
spake,
When I beheld her weep so ruefully ;
For sure my love should ne'er indue the
front
And mask of Hate, who lives on others'
moans.
Shall Love pledge Hatred in her bitter
draughts,
And batten on her poisons? Love forbid !
Love passeth not the threshold of coid
Hate,
And Hate is strange beneath the roof of
Love.
O Love, if thou be'st Love, dry up these
tears
Shed for the love of Love ; for tho' mine
image,
The subject of thy power, be cold in her,

Yet, like cold snow, it melteth in the
source
Of these sad tears, and feeds their down-
ward flow.
So Love, arraign'd to judgment and to
death,
Received unto himself a part of blame,
Being guiltless, as an innocent prisoner,
Who, when the woful sentence hath been
past,
And all the clearness of his fame hath gone
Beneath the shadow of the curse of man,
First falls asleep in swoon, wherefrom
awaked,
And looking round upon his tearful friends,
Forthwith and in his agony conceives
A shameful sense as of a cleaving crime—
For whence without some guilt should
such grief be ?

So died that hour, and fell into the
abysm
Of forms outworn, but not to me outworn,
Who never hail'd another—was there
one ?
There might be one—one other, worth
the life
That made it sensible.   So that hour died
Like odour rapt into the winged wind
Borne into alien lands and far away.

There be some hearts so airily built,
that they,
They—when their love is wreck'd—if
Love can wreck—
On that sharp ridge of utmost doom ride
highly
Above the perilous seas of Change and
Chance ;
Nay, more, hold out the lights of cheer-
fulness ;
As the tall ship, that many a dreary year
Knit to some dismal sandbank far at sea,
All thro' the livelong hours of utter dark,
Showers slanting light upon the dolorous
wave.
For me—what light, what gleam on those
black ways
Where Love could walk with banish'd
Hope no more ?

It was ill-done to part you, Sisters fair;
Love's arms were wreath'd about the
  neck of Hope,
And Hope kiss'd Love, and Love drew
  in her breath
In that close kiss, and drank her
  whisper'd tales.
They said that Love would die when
  Hope was gone,
And Love mourn'd long, and sorrow'd
  after Hope;
At last she sought out Memory, and they
  trod
The same old paths where Love had
  walk'd with Hope,
And Memory fed the soul of Love with
  tears.

II.

FROM that time forth I would not see
  her more;
But many weary moons I lived alone—
Alone, and in the heart of the great forest.
Sometimes upon the hills beside the sea
All day I watch'd the floating isles of shade,
And sometimes on the shore, upon the
  sands
Insensibly I drew her name, until
The meaning of the letters shot into
My brain; anon the wanton billow wash'd
Them over, till they faded like my love.
The hollow caverns heard me—the black
  brooks
Of the midforest heard me—the soft
  winds,
Laden with thistledown and seeds of
  flowers,
Paused in their course to hear me, for my
  voice
Was all of thee: the merry linnet knew
  me,
The squirrel knew me, and the dragonfly
Shot by me like a flash of purple fire.
The rough brier tore my bleeding palms;
  the hemlock,
Brow-high, did strike my forehead as I
  past;
Yet trod I not the wildflower in my path,
Nor bruised the wildbird's egg.

Was this the end?
Why grew we then together in one plot?
Why fed we from one fountain? drew
  one sun?
Why were our mothers' branches of one
  stem?
Why were we one in all things, save in
  that
Where to have been one had been the
  cope and crown
Of all I hoped and fear'd?—if that same
  nearness
Were father to this distance, and that
  one
Vauntcourier to this *double?* if Affection
Living slew Love, and Sympathy hew'd
  out
The bosom-sepulchre of Sympathy?

Chiefly I sought the cavern and the hill
Where last we roam'd together, for the
  sound
Of the loud stream was pleasant, and the
  wind
Came wooingly with woodbine smells.
  Sometimes
All day I sat within the cavern-mouth,
Fixing my eyes on those three cypress-
  cones
That spired above the wood; and with
  mad hand
Tearing the bright leaves of the ivy-
  screen,
I cast them in the noisy brook beneath,
And watch'd them till they vanish'd from
  my sight
Beneath the bower of wreathed eglan-
  tines:
And all the fragments of the living rock
(Huge blocks, which some old trembling
  of the world
Had loosen'd from the mountain, till they
  fell
Half-digging their own graves) these in
  my agony
Did I make bare of all the golden moss,
Wherewith the dashing runnel in the
  spring
Had liveried them all over. In my
  brain

The spirit seem'd to flag from thought to
    thought,
As moonlight wandering thro' a mist : my
    blood
Crept like marsh drains thro' all my lan-
    guid limbs ;
The motions of my heart seem'd far
    within me,
Unfrequent, low, as tho' it told its pulses ;
And yet it shook me, that my frame
    would shudder,
As if 'twere drawn asunder by the rack.
But over the deep graves of Hope and
    Fear,
And all the broken palaces of the Past,
Brooded one master-passion evermore,
Like to a low-hung and a fiery sky
Above some fair metropolis, earth-
    shock'd, —
Hung round with ragged rims and burn-
    ing folds, —
Embathing all with wild and woful hues,
Great hills of ruins, and collapsed masses
Of thundershaken columns indistinct,
And fused together in the tyrannous
    light—
Ruins, the ruin of all my life and me !

    Sometimes I thought Camilla was no
    more,
Some one had told me she was dead,
    and ask'd
If I would see her burial : then I seem'd
To rise, and through the forest-shadow
    borne
With more than mortal swiftness, I ran
    down
The steepy sea-bank, till I came upon
The rear of a procession, curving round
The silver-sheeted bay : in front of which
Six stately virgins, all in white, upbare
A broad earth-sweeping pall of whitest
    lawn,
Wreathed round the bier with garlands :
    in the distance,
From out the yellow woods upon the
    hill
Look'd forth the summit and the pinna-
    cles
Of a gray steeple—thence at intervals

A low bell tolling.   All the pageantry,
Save those six virgins which upheld the
    bier,
Were stoled from head to foot in flowing
    black ;
One walk'd abreast with me, and veil'd
    his brow,
And he was loud in weeping and in praise
Of her, we follow'd : a strong sympathy
Shook all my soul : I flung myself upon
    him
In tears and cries : I told him all my love,
How I had loved her from the first ;
    whereat
He shrank and howl'd, and from his brow
    drew back
His hand to push me from him ; and the
    face,
The very face and form of Lionel
Flash'd thro' my eyes into my innermost
    brain,
And at his feet I seem'd to faint and fall,
To fall and die away.   I could not rise
Albeit I strove to follow.   They past on,
The lordly Phantasms ! in their floating
    folds
They past and were no more : but I had
    fallen
Prone by the dashing runnel on the grass.

    Alway the inaudible invisible thought,
Artificer and subject, lord and slave,
Shaped by the audible and visible,
Moulded the audible and visible ;
All crisped sounds of wave and leaf and
    wind,
Flatter'd the fancy of my fading brain ;
The cloud-pavilion'd element, the wood,
The mountain, the three cypresses, the
    cave,
Storm, sunset, glows and glories of the
    moon
Below black firs, when silent-creeping
    winds
Laid the long night in silver streaks and
    bars,
Were wrought into the tissue of my
    dream :
The moanings in the forest, the loud
    brook,

Cries of the partridge like a rusty key
Turn'd in a lock, owl - whoop and dor-
  hawk-whirr
Awoke me not, but were a part of sleep,
And voices in the distance calling to me
And in my vision bidding me dream on,
Like sounds without the twilight realm
  of dreams,
Which wander round the bases of the
  hills,
And murmur at the low-dropt eaves of
  sleep,
Half-entering the portals.   Oftentimes
The vision had fair prelude, in the end
Opening on darkness, stately vestibules
To caves and shows of Death : whether
  the mind,
With some revenge—even to itself un-
  known,—
Made strange division of its suffering
With her, whom to have suffering view'd
  had been
Extremest pain ; or that the clear-eyed
  Spirit,
Being blunted in the Present, grew at
  length
Prophetical and prescient of whate'er
The Future had in store : or that which
  most
Enchains belief, the sorrow of my spirit
Was of so wide a compass it took in
All I had loved, and my dull agony,
Ideally to her transferr'd, became
Anguish intolerable.

The day waned ;
Alone I sat with her : about my brow
Her warm breath floated in the utterance
Of silver-chorded tones : her lips were
  sunder'd
With smiles of tranquil bliss, which broke
  in light
Like morning from her eyes—her elo-
  quent eyes,
(As I have seen them many a hundred
  times)
Fill'd all with pure clear fire, thro' mine
  down rain'd
Their spirit-searching splendours.   As a
  vision

Unto a haggard prisoner, iron-stay'd
In damp and dismal dungeons under-
  ground,
Confined on points of faith, when strength
  is shock'd
With torment, and expectancy of worse
Upon the morrow, thro' the ragged walls,
All unawares before his half-shut eyes,
Comes in upon him in the dead of night,
And with the excess of sweetness and of
  awe,
Makes the heart tremble, and the sight
  run over
Upon his steely gyves ; so those fair eyes
Shone on my darkness, forms which ever
  stood
Within the magic cirque of memory,
Invisible but deathless, waiting still
The edict of the will to reassume
The semblance of those rare realities
Of which they were the mirrors.   Now
  the light
Which was their life, burst through the
  cloud of thought
Keen, irrepressible.

It was a room
Within the summer-house of which I spake,
Hung round with paintings of the sea,
  and one
A vessel in mid-ocean, her heaved prow
Clambering, the mast bent and the ravin
  wind
In her sail roaring.   From the outer day,
Betwixt the close-set ivies came a broad
And solid beam of isolated light,
Crowded with driving atomies, and fell
Slanting upon that picture, from prime
  youth
Well-known well - loved.   She drew it
  long ago
Forthgazing on the waste and open sea,
One morning when the upblown billow
  ran
Shoreward beneath red clouds, and I had
  pour'd
Into the shadowing pencil's naked forms
Colour and life : it was a bond and seal
Of friendship, spoken of with tearful
  smiles ;

A monument of childhood and of love ;
The poesy of childhood ; my lost love
Symbol'd in storm. We gazed on it
together
In mute and glad remembrance, and
each heart
Grew closer to the other, and the eye
Was riveted and charm-bound, gazing
like
The Indian on a still-eyed snake, low-
couch'd—
A beauty which is death ; when all at
once
That painted vessel, as with inner life,
Began to heave upon that painted sea ;
An earthquake, my loud heart-beats,
made the ground
Reel under us, and all at once, soul, life
And breath and motion, past and flow'd
away
To those unreal billows : round and
round
A whirlwind caught and bore us ; mighty
gyres
Rapid and vast, of hissing spray wind-
driven
Far thro' the dizzy dark. Aloud she
shriek'd ;
My heart was cloven with pain ; I wound
my arms
About her : we whirl'd giddily ; the wind
Sung ; but I clasp'd her without fear :
her weight
Shrank in my grasp, and over my dim
eyes,
And parted lips which drank her breath,
down-hung
The jaws of Death : I, groaning, from
me flung
Her empty phantom : all the sway and
whirl
Of the storm dropt to windless calm, and I
Down welter'd thro' the dark ever and
ever.

III.

I came one day and sat among the
stones
Strewn in the entry of the moaning
cave ;

A morning air, sweet after rain, ran
over
The rippling levels of the lake, and
blew
Coolness and moisture and all smells of
bud
And foliage from the dark and dripping
woods
Upon my fever'd brows that shook and
throbb'd
From temple unto temple. To what
height
The day had grown I know not. Then
came on me
The hollow tolling of the bell, and all
The vision of the bier. As heretofore
I walk'd behind with one who veil'd his
brow.
Methought by slow degrees the sullen
bell
Toll'd quicker, and the breakers on the
shore
Sloped into louder surf : those that went
with me,
And those that held the bier before my
face,
Moved with one spirit round about the
bay,
Trod swifter steps ; and while I walk'd
with these
In marvel at that gradual change, I
thought
Four bells instead of one began to ring,
Four merry bells, four merry marriage-
bells,
In clanging cadence jangling peal on
peal—
A long loud clash of rapid marriage-
bells.
Then those who led the van, and those
in rear,
Rush'd into dance, and like wild Bac-
chanals
Fled onward to the steeple in the
woods :
I, too, was borne along and felt the
blast
Beat on my heated eyelids : all at once
The front rank made a sudden halt ; the
bells

Lapsed into frightful stillness ; the surge fell
From thunder into whispers ; those six maids
With shrieks and ringing laughter on the sand
Threw down the bier ; the woods upon the hill
Waved with a sudden gust that sweeping down
Took the edges of the pall, and blew it far
Until it hung, a little silver cloud
Over the sounding seas : I turn'd : my heart
Shrank in me, like a snowflake in the hand,
Waiting to see the settled countenance
Of her I loved, adorn'd with fading flowers.
But she from out her death-like chrysalis,
She from her bier, as into fresher life,
My sister, and my cousin, and my love,
Leapt lightly clad in bridal white—her hair
Studded with one rich Provence rose—a light
Of smiling welcome round her lips—her eyes
And cheeks as bright as when she climb'd the hill.
One hand she reach'd to those that came behind,
And while I mused nor yet endured to take
So rich a prize, the man who stood with me
Stept gaily forward, throwing down his robes,
And claspt her hand in his : again the bells
Jangled and clang'd : again the stormy surf
Crash'd in the shingle : and the whirling rout
Led by those two rush'd into dance, and fled
Wind-footed to the steeple in the woods,

Till they were swallow'd in the leafy bowers,
And I stood sole beside the vacant bier.

There, there, my latest vision—then the event !

IV.

THE GOLDEN SUPPER.[1]

(*Another speaks.*)

HE flies the event : he leaves the event to me :
Poor Julian—how he rush'd away ; the bells,
Those marriage-bells, echoing in ear and heart—
But cast a parting glance at me, you saw,
As who should say 'Continue.' Well he had
One golden hour—of triumph shall I say ?
Solace at least—before he left his home.

Would you had seen him in that hour of his !
He moved thro' all of it majestically—
Restrain'd himself quite to the close—but now—

Whether they *were* his lady's marriage-bells,
Or prophets of them in his fantasy,
I never ask'd : but Lionel and the girl
Were wedded, and our Julian came again
Back to his mother's house among the pines.
But these, their gloom, the mountains and the Bay,
The whole land weigh'd him down as Ætna does
The Giant of Mythology : he would go,
Would leave the land for ever, and had gone
Surely, but for a whisper, 'Go not yet,'
Some warning — sent divinely — as it seem'd

[1] This poem is founded upon a story in Boccaccio. See Introduction, p. 476.

By that which follow'd — but of this I
    deem
As of the visions that he told—the event
Glanced back upon them in his after
    life,
And partly made them—tho' he knew it
    not.

And thus he stay'd and would not look
    at her—
No not for months : but, when the
    eleventh moon
After their marriage lit the lover's Bay,
Heard yet once more the tolling bell, and
    said,
Would you could toll me out of life, but
    found—
All softly as his mother broke it to him—
A crueller reason than a crazy ear,
For that low knell tolling his lady dead—
Dead—and had lain three days without
    a pulse :
All that look'd on her had pronounced
    her dead.
And so they bore her (for in Julian's land
They never nail a dumb head up in
    elm),
Bore her free-faced to the free airs of
    heaven,
And laid her in the vault of her own kin.

What did he then ? not die : he is here
    and hale—
Not plunge headforemost from the moun-
    tain there,
And leave the name of Lover's Leap :
    not he :
He knew the meaning of the whisper now,
Thought that he knew it. 'This, I stay'd
    for this ;
O love, I have not seen you for so long.
Now, now, will I go down into the grave,
I will be all alone with all I love,
And kiss her on the lips. She is his no
    more :
The dead returns to me, and I go down
To kiss the dead.'

The fancy stirr'd him so
He rose and went, and entering the dim
    vault,

And, making there a sudden light, beheld
All round about him that which all will
    be.
The light was but a flash, and went again.
Then at the far end of the vault he saw
His lady with the moonlight on her face :
Her breast as in a shadow-prison, bars
Of black and bands of silver, which the
    moon
Struck from an open grating overhead
High in the wall, and all the rest of her
Drown'd in the gloom and horror of the
    vault.

'It was my wish,' he said, 'to pass, to
    sleep,
To rest, to be with her — till the great
    day
Peal'd on us with that music which rights
    all,
And raised us hand in hand.' And
    kneeling there
Down in the dreadful dust that once was
    man,
Dust, as he said, that once was loving
    hearts,
Hearts that had beat with such a love as
    mine—
Not such as mine, no, nor for such as
    her—
He softly put his arm about her neck
And kiss'd her more than once, till help-
    less death
And silence made him bold—nay, but I
    wrong him,
He reverenced his dear lady even in
    death ;
But, placing his true hand upon her
    heart,
'O, you warm heart,' he moan'd, 'not
    even death
Can chill you all at once :' then starting,
    thought
His dreams had come again. 'Do I
    wake or sleep ?
Or am I made immortal, or my love
Mortal once more ?' It beat—the heart
    —it beat :
Faint—but it beat : at which his own
    began

To pulse with such a vehemence that it
    drown'd
The feebler motion underneath his hand.
But when at last his doubts were satisfied,
He raised her softly from the sepulchre,
And, wrapping her all over with the cloak
He came in, and now striding fast, and
    now
Sitting awhile to rest, but evermore
Holding his golden burthen in his arms,
So bore her thro' the solitary land
Back to the mother's house where she
    was born.

    There the good mother's kindly minis-
        tering,
With half a night's appliances, recall'd
Her fluttering life : she rais'd an eye that
    ask'd
'Where ?' till the things familiar to her
    youth
Had made a silent answer: then she spoke
'Here ! and how came I here ?' and
    learning it
(They told her somewhat rashly as I
    think)
At once began to wander and to wail,
'Ay, but you know that you must give
    me back :
Send ! bid him come ;' but Lionel was
    away—
Stung by his loss had vanish'd, none
    knew where.
'He casts me out,' she wept, 'and goes'
    —a wail
That seeming something, yet was nothing,
    born
Not from believing mind, but shatter'd
    nerve,
Yet haunting Julian, as her own reproof
At some precipitance in her burial.
Then, when her own true spirit had
    return'd,
'Oh yes, and you,' she said, 'and none
    but you ?
For you have given me life and love again,
And none but you yourself shall tell him
    of it,
And you shall give me back when he
    returns.'

'Stay then a little,' answer'd Julian,
    'here,
And keep yourself, none knowing, to
    yourself ;
And I will do your will.   I may not stay,
No, not an hour ; but send me notice of
    him
When he returns, and then will I return,
And I will make a solemn offering of you
To him you love.'   And faintly she
    replied,
'And I will do *your* will, and none shall
    know.'

    Not know ? with such a secret to be
    known.
But all their house was old and loved
    them both,
And all the house had known the loves
    of both ;
Had died almost to serve them any way,
And all the land was waste and solitary:
And then he rode away ; but after this,
An hour or two, Camilla's travail came
Upon her, and that day a boy was born,
Heir of his face and land, to Lionel.

    And thus our lonely lover rode away,
And pausing at a hostel in a marsh,
There fever seized upon him : myself was
    then
Travelling that land, and meant to rest
    an hour ;
And sitting down to such a base repast,
It makes me angry yet to speak of it—
I heard a groaning overhead, and climb'd
The moulder'd stairs (for everything was
    vile)
And in a loft, with none to wait on him,
Found, as it seem'd, a skeleton alone,
Raving of dead men's dust and beating
    hearts.

    A dismal hostel in a dismal land,
A flat malarian world of reed and rush !
But there from fever and my care of him
Sprang up a friendship that may help us
    yet.
For while we roam'd along the dreary
    coast,

And waited for her message, piece by piece
I learnt the drearier story of his life ;
And, tho' he loved and honour'd Lionel,
Found that the sudden wail his lady made
Dwelt in his fancy : did he know her worth,
Her beauty even ? should he not be taught,
Ev'n by the price that others set upon it,
The value of that jewel he had to guard ?

Suddenly came her notice and we past,
I with our lover to his native Bay.

This love is of the brain, the mind, the soul :
That makes the sequel pure ; tho' some of us
Beginning at the sequel know no more.
Not such am I : and yet I say the bird
That will not hear my call, however sweet,
But if my neighbour whistle answers him—
What matter ? there are others in the wood.
Yet when I saw her (and I thought him crazed,
Tho' not with such a craziness as needs
A cell and keeper), those dark eyes of hers—
Oh ! such dark eyes ! and not her eyes alone,
But all from these to where she touch'd on earth,
For such a craziness as Julian's look'd
No less than one divine apology.

So sweetly and so modestly she came
To greet us, her young hero in her arms !
'Kiss him,' she said. 'You gave me life again.
He, but for you, had never seen it once.
His other father you ! Kiss him, and then
Forgive him, if his name be Julian too.'

Talk of lost hopes and broken heart ! his own
Sent such a flame into his face, I knew
Some sudden vivid pleasure hit him there.

But he was all the more resolved to go,
And sent at once to Lionel, praying him
By that great love they both had borne the dead,
To come and revel for one hour with him
Before he left the land for evermore ;
And then to friends—they were not many —who lived
Scatteringly about that lonely land of his,
And bad them to a banquet of farewells.

And Julian made a solemn feast : I never
Sat at a costlier ; for all round his hall
From column on to column, as in a wood,
Not such as here—an equatorial one,
Great garlands swung and blossom'd ; and beneath,
Heirlooms, and ancient miracles of Art,
Chalice and salver, wines that, Heaven knows when,
Had suck'd the fire of some forgotten sun,
And kept it thro' a hundred years of gloom,
Yet glowing in a heart of ruby—cups
Where nymph and god ran ever round in gold—
Others of glass as costly— some with gems
Moveable and resettable at will,
And trebling all the rest in value—Ah heavens !
Why need I tell you all ?—suffice to say
That whatsoever such a house as his,
And his was old, has in it rare or fair
Was brought before the guest : and they the guests,
Wonder'd at some strange light in Julian's eyes
(I told you that he had his golden hour),
And such a feast, ill-suited as it seem'd
To such a time, to Lionel's loss and his
And that resolved self-exile from a land
He never would revisit, such a feast
So rich, so strange, and stranger ev'n than rich,
But rich as for the nuptials of a king.

And stranger yet, at one end of the hall
Two great funereal curtains, looping down,
Parted a little ere they met the floor,
About a picture of his lady, taken
Some years before, and falling hid the frame.
And just above the parting was a lamp :
So the sweet figure folded round with night
Seem'd stepping out of darkness with a smile.

Well then—our solemn feast—we ate and drank,
And might—the wines being of such nobleness—
Have jested also, but for Julian's eyes,
And something weird and wild about it all :
What was it ? for our lover seldom spoke,
Scarce touch'd the meats ; but ever and anon
A priceless goblet with a priceless wine
Arising, show'd he drank beyond his use ;
And when the feast was near an end, he said :

'There is a custom in the Orient, friends—
I read of it in Persia—when a man
Will honour those who feast with him, he brings
And shows them whatsoever he accounts
Of all his treasures the most beautiful,
Gold, jewels, arms, whatever it may be.
This custom——'

Pausing here a moment, all
The guests broke in upon him with meeting hands
And cries about the banquet—'Beautiful !
Who could desire more beauty at a feast ?'

The lover answer'd, 'There is more than one
Here sitting who desires it.   Laud me not
Before my time, but hear me to the close.
This custom steps yet further when the guest
Is loved and honour'd to the uttermost.

For after he hath shown him gems or gold,
He brings and sets before him in rich guise
That which is thrice as beautiful as these,
The beauty that is dearest to his heart—
" O my heart's lord, would I could show you," he says,
" Ev'n my heart too."   And I propose to-night
To show you what is dearest to my heart,
And my heart too.

'But solve me first a doubt.
I knew a man, nor many years ago ;
He had a faithful servant, one who loved
His master more than all on earth beside.
He falling sick, and seeming close on death,
His master would not wait until he died,
But bad his menials bear him from the door,
And leave him in the public way to die.
I knew another, not so long ago,
Who found the dying servant, took him home,
And fed, and cherish'd him, and saved his life.
I ask you now, should this first master claim
His service, whom does it belong to ? him
Who thrust him out, or him who saved his life ?'

This question, so flung down before the guests,
And balanced either way by each, at length
When some were doubtful how the law would hold,
Was handed over by consent of all
To one who had not spoken, Lionel.

Fair speech was his, and delicate of phrase.
And he beginning languidly—his loss
Weigh'd on him yet—but warming as he went,
Glanced at the point of law, to pass it by,
Affirming that as long as either lived,

By all the laws of love and gratefulness,
The service of the one so saved was due
All to the saver—adding, with a smile,
The first for many weeks—a semi-smile
As at a strong conclusion—'body and
        soul
And life and limbs, all his to work his will.'

Then Julian made a secret sign to me
To bring Camilla down before them all.
And crossing her own picture as she came,
And looking as much lovelier than herself
Is lovelier than all others—on her head
A diamond circlet, and from under this
A veil, that seemed no more than gilded
        air,
Flying by each fine ear, an Eastern gauze
With seeds of gold—so, with that grace
        of hers,
Slow-moving as a wave against the wind,
That flings a mist behind it in the sun—
And bearing high in arms the mighty babe,
The younger Julian, who himself was
        crown'd
With roses, none so rosy as himself—
And over all her babe and her the jewels
Of many generations of his house
Sparkled and flash'd, for he had decked
        them out
As for a solemn sacrifice of love—
So she came in :—I am long in telling it,
I never yet beheld a thing so strange,
Sad, sweet, and strange together—floated
        in—
While all the guests in mute amazement
        rose—
And slowly pacing to the middle hall,
Before the board, there paused and stood,
        her breast
Hard-heaving, and her eyes upon her feet,
Not daring yet to glance at Lionel.
But him she carried, him nor lights nor
        feast
Dazed or amazed, nor eyes of men ; who
        cared
Only to use his own, and staring wide
And hungering for the gilt and jewell'd
        world
About him, look'd, as he is like to prove,
When Julian goes, the lord of all he saw.

'My guests,' said Julian : 'you are
        honour'd now
Ev'n to the uttermost : in her behold
Of all my treasures the most beautiful,
Of all things upon earth the dearest to me.'
Then waving us a sign to seat ourselves,
Led his dear lady to a chair of state.
And I, by Lionel sitting, saw his face
Fire, and dead ashes and all fire again
Thrice in a second, felt him tremble too,
And heard him muttering, 'So like, so
        like ;
She never had a sister.   I knew none.
Some cousin of his and hers—O God, so
        like !'
And then he suddenly ask'd her if she
        were.
She shook, and cast her eyes down, and
        was dumb.
And then some other question'd if she
        came
From foreign lands, and still she did not
        speak.
Another, if the boy were hers : but she
To all their queries answer'd not a word,
Which made the amazement more, till
        one of them
Said, shuddering, 'Her spectre !'   But
        his friend
Replied, in half a whisper, 'Not at least
The spectre that will speak if spoken to.
Terrible pity, if one so beautiful
Prove, as I almost dread to find her,
        dumb !'

But Julian, sitting by her, answer'd all :
'She is but dumb, because in her you
        see
That faithful servant whom we spoke
        about,
Obedient to her second master now ;
Which will not last.   I have here to-night
        a guest
So bound to me by common love and
        loss—
What ! shall I bind him more ? in his
        behalf,
Shall I exceed the Persian, giving him
That which of all things is the dearest to
        me,

Not only showing? and he himself pronounced
That my rich gift is wholly mine to give.

'Now all be dumb, and promise all of
you
Not to break in on what I say by word
Or whisper, while I show you all my
heart.'
And then began the story of his love
As here to-day, but not so wordily—
The passionate moment would not suffer
that—
Past thro' his visions to the burial ; thence
Down to this last strange hour in his own
hall ;
And then rose up, and with him all his
guests
Once more as by enchantment ; all but he,
Lionel, who fain had risen, but fell again,
And sat as if in chains—to whom he said :

'Take my free gift, my cousin, for
your wife ;
And were it only for the giver's sake,
And tho' she seem so like the one you lost,
Yet cast her not away so suddenly,
Lest there be none left here to bring her
back :
I leave this land for ever.' Here he
ceased.

Then taking his dear lady by one hand,
And bearing on one arm the noble babe,
He slowly brought them both to Lionel.
And there the widower husband and dead
wife
Rush'd each at each with a cry, that rather
seem'd
For some new death than for a life renew'd ;
Whereat the very babe began to wail ;
At once they turn'd, and caught and
brought him in
To their charm'd circle, and, half killing
him
With kisses, round him closed and claspt
again.
But Lionel, when at last he freed himself
From wife and child, and lifted up a face
All over glowing with the sun of life,
And love, and boundless thanks—the
sight of this

So frighted our good friend, that turning
to me
And saying, 'It is over : let us go'—
There were our horses ready at the
doors—
We bad them no farewell, but mounting
these
He past for ever from his native land ;
And I with him, my Julian, back to mine.

TO ALFRED TENNYSON
MY GRANDSON.

GOLDEN-HAIR'D Ally whose name is one with
mine,
Crazy with laughter and babble and earth's new
wine,
Now that the flower of a year and a half is thine,
O little blossom, O mine, and mine of mine,
Glorious poet who never hast written a line,
Laugh, for the name at the head of my verse is
thine.
May'st thou never be wrong'd by the name that
is mine !

THE FIRST QUARREL.

(IN THE ISLE OF WIGHT.)

I.

'WAIT a little,' you say, 'you are sure
it 'll all come right,'
But the boy was born i' trouble, an' looks
so wan an' so white :
Wait ! an' once I ha' waited—I hadn't
to wait for long.
Now I wait, wait, wait for Harry.—No,
no, you are doing me wrong !
Harry and I were married : the boy can
hold up his head,
The boy was born in wedlock, but after
my man was dead ;
I ha' work'd for him fifteen years, an' I
work an' I wait to the end.
I am all alone in the world, an' you are
my only friend.

II.

Doctor, if *you* can wait, I'll tell you the
tale o' my life.
When Harry an' I were children, he call'd
me his own little wife ;

I was happy when I was with him, an'
    sorry when he was away,
An' when we play'd together, I loved him
    better than play ;
He workt me the daisy chain—he made
    me the cowslip ball,
He fought the boys that were rude, an' I
    loved him better than all.
Passionate girl tho' I was, an' often at
    home in disgrace,
I never could quarrel with Harry—I had
    but to look in his face.

III.

There was a farmer in Dorset of Harry's
    kin, that had need
Of a good stout lad at his farm ; he sent,
    an' the father agreed ;
So Harry was bound to the Dorsetshire
    farm for years an' for years ;
I walked with him down to the quay,
    poor lad, an' we parted in tears.
The boat was beginning to move, we
    heard them a-ringing the bell,
'I'll never love any but you, God bless
    you, my own little Nell.'

IV.

I was a child, an' he was a child, an' he
    came to harm ;
There was a girl, a hussy, that workt with
    him up at the farm,
One had deceived her an' left her alone
    with her sin an' her shame,
And so she was wicked with Harry ; the
    girl was the most to blame.

V.

And years went over till I that was little
    had grown so tall,
The men would say of the maids, 'Our
    Nelly's the flower of 'em all.'
I didn't take heed o' *them*, but I taught
    myself all I could
To make a good wife for Harry, when
    Harry came home for good.

VI.

Often I seem'd unhappy, and often as
    happy too,
For I heard it abroad in the fields 'I'll
    never love any but you ;'

'I'll never love any but you' the morning
    song of the lark,
'I'll never love any but you' the nightin-
    gale's hymn in the dark.

VII.

And Harry came home at last, but he
    look'd at me sidelong and shy,
Vext me a bit, till he told me that so
    many years had gone by,
I had grown so handsome and tall—that
    I might ha' forgot him somehow—
For he thought—there were other lads—
    he was fear'd to look at me now.

VIII.

Hard was the frost in the field, we were
    married o' Christmas day,
Married among the red berries, an' all as
    merry as May—
Those were the pleasant times, my house
    an' my man were my pride,
We seem'd like ships i' the Channel a-
    sailing with wind an' tide.

IX.

But work was scant in the Isle, tho' he
    tried the villages round,
So Harry went over the Solent to see if
    work could be found ;
An' he wrote 'I ha' six weeks' work,
    little wife, so far as I know ;
I'll come for an hour to-morrow, an' kiss
    you before I go.'

X.

So I set to righting the house, for wasn't
    he coming that day ?
An' I hit on an old deal-box that was
    push'd in a corner away,
It was full of old odds an' ends, an' a
    letter along wi' the rest,
I had better ha' put my naked hand in a
    hornets' nest.

XI.

'Sweetheart'—this was the letter—this
    was the letter I read—
'You promised to find me work near you,
    an' I wish I was dead—

Didn't you kiss me an' promise? you
haven't done it, my lad,
An' I almost died o' your going away,
an' I wish that I had.'

XII.

I too wish that I had—in the pleasant
times that had past,
Before I quarrell'd with Harry — *my*
quarrel—the first an' the last.

XIII.

For Harry came in, an' I flung him the
letter that drove me wild,
An' he told it me all at once, as simple as
any child,
' What can it matter, my lass, what I did
wi' my single life?
I ha' been as true to you as ever a man to
his wife;
An' *she* wasn't one o' the worst.' 'Then,'
I said, 'I'm none o' the best.'
An' he smiled at me, ' Ain't you, my love?
Come, come, little wife, let it rest!
The man isn't like the woman, no need
to make such a stir.'
But he anger'd me all the more, an' I said
' You were keeping with her,
When I was a-loving you all along an' the
same as before.'
An' he didn't speak for a while an' he
anger'd me more and more.
Then he patted my hand in his gentle
way, ' Let bygones be!'
' Bygones! you kept yours hush'd,' I said,
' when you married me!
By-gones ma' be come-agains; an' *she*—
in her shame an' her sin—
You'll have her to nurse my child, if I
die o' my lying in!
You'll make her its second mother! I
hate her—an' I hate you!'
Ah, Harry, my man, you had better ha'
beaten me black an' blue
Than ha' spoken as kind as you did,
when I were so crazy wi' spite,
' Wait a little, my lass, I am sure it 'ill
all come right.'

XIV.

An' he took three turns in the rain, an' I
watch'd him, an' when he came in

I felt that my heart was hard, he was all
wet thro' to the skin,
An' I never said ' off wi' the wet,' I never
said ' on wi' the dry,'
So I knew my heart was hard, when he
came to bid me goodbye.
' You said that you hated me, Ellen, but
that isn't true, you know;
I am going to leave you a bit—you'll kiss
me before I go?'

XV.

' Going! you're going to her—kiss her—
if you will,' I said—
I was near my time wi' the boy, I must
ha' been light i' my head—
' I had sooner be cursed than kiss'd!'—I
didn't know well what I meant,
But I turn'd my face from *him*, an' he
turn'd *his* face an' he went.

XVI.

And then he sent me a letter, ' I've gotten
my work to do;
You wouldn't kiss me, my lass, an' I
never loved any but you;
I am sorry for all the quarrel an' sorry for
what she wrote,
I ha' six weeks' work in Jersey an' go to'
night by the boat.'

XVII.

An' the wind began to rise, an' I thought
of him out at sea,
An' I felt I had been to blame; he was
always kind to me.
' Wait a little, my lass, I am sure it 'ill
all come right'—
An' the boat went down that night—the
boat went down that night.

RIZPAH.

17—.

I.

WAILING, wailing, wailing, the wind
over land and sea—
And Willy's voice in the wind, 'O mother,
come out to me.'

Why should he call me to-night, when he
　　knows that I cannot go?
For the downs are as bright as day, and
　　the full moon stares at the snow.

II.

We should be seen, my dear ; they would
　　spy us out of the town.
The loud black nights for us, and the
　　storm rushing over the down,
When I cannot see my own hand, but am
　　led by the creak of the chain,
And grovel and grope for my son till I
　　find myself drenched with the rain.

III.

Anything fallen again ? nay—what was
　　there left to fall ?
I have taken them home, I have number'd
　　the bones, I have hidden them all.
What am I saying ? and what are *you ?*
　　do you come as a spy ?
Falls ? what falls ? who knows ?　As the
　　tree falls so must it lie.

IV.

Who let her in ? how long has she been ?
　　you—what have you heard ?
Why did you sit so quiet ? you never have
　　spoken a word.
O—to pray with me—yes—a lady—none
　　of their spies—
But the night has crept into my heart,
　　and begun to darken my eyes.

V.

Ah—you, that have lived so soft, what
　　should *you* know of the night,
The blast and the burning shame and the
　　bitter frost and the fright ?
I have done it, while you were asleep—
　　you were only made for the day.
I have gather'd my baby together—and
　　now you may go your way.

VI.

Nay—for it's kind of you, Madam, to sit
　　by an old dying wife.
But say nothing hard of my boy, I have
　　only an hour of life.

I kiss'd my boy in the prison, before he
　　went out to die.
' They dared me to do it,' he said, and he
　　never has told me a lie.
I whipt him for robbing an orchard once
　　when he was but a child—
' The farmer dared me to do it,' he said ;
　　he was always so wild—
And idle—and couldn't be idle—my
　　Willy—he never could rest.
The King should have made him a soldier,
　　he would have been one of his best.

VII.

But he lived with a lot of wild mates, and
　　they never would let him be good ;
They swore that he dare not rob the mail,
　　and he swore that he would ;
And he took no life, but he took one
　　purse, and when all was done
He flung it among his fellows—I'll none
　　of it, said my son.

VIII.

I came into court to the Judge and the
　　lawyers.　I told them my tale,
God's own truth—but they kill'd him,
　　they kill'd him for robbing the mail.
They hang'd him in chains for a show—
　　we had always borne a good name—
To be hang'd for a thief—and then put
　　away—isn't that enough shame ?
Dust to dust—low down—let us hide !
　　but they set him so high
That all the ships of the world could
　　stare at him, passing by.
God 'ill pardon the hell-black raven and
　　horrible fowls of the air,
But not the black heart of the lawyer who
　　kill'd him and hang'd him there.

IX.

And the jailer forced me away.　I had
　　bid him my last goodbye ;
They had fasten'd the door of his cell.
　　' O mother !' I heard him cry.
I couldn't get back tho' I tried, he had
　　something further to say,
And now I never shall know it.　The
　　jailer forced me away.

X.

Then since I couldn't but hear that cry
    of my boy that was dead,
They seized me and shut me up: they
    fasten'd me down on my bed.
'Mother, O mother!'—he call'd in the
    dark to me year after year—
They beat me for that, they beat me—
    you know that I couldn't but hear;
And then at the last they found I had
    grown so stupid and still
They let me abroad again — but the
    creatures had worked their will.

XI.

Flesh of my flesh was gone, but bone of
    my bone was left—
I stole them all from the lawyers—and
    you, will you call it a theft?—
My baby, the bones that had suck'd me,
    the bones that had laughed and
    had cried—
Theirs? O no! they are mine—not
    theirs—they had moved in my side.

XII.

Do you think I was scared by the bones?
    I kiss'd 'em, I buried 'em all—
I can't dig deep, I am old—in the night
    by the churchyard wall.
My Willy 'ill rise up whole when the
    trumpet of judgment 'ill sound,
But I charge you never to say that I laid
    him in holy ground.

XIII.

They would scratch him up—they would
    hang him again on the cursed tree.
Sin? O yes—we are sinners, I know—
    let all that be,
And read me a Bible verse of the Lord's
    good will toward men—
' Full of compassion and mercy, the Lord '
    —let me hear it again;
' Full of compassion and mercy—long-
    suffering.' Yes, O yes!
For the lawyer is born but to murder—
    the Saviour lives but to bless.

He'll never put on the black cap except
    for the worst of the worst,
And the first may be last—I have heard it
    in church—and the last may be
    first.
Suffering—O long-suffering—yes, as the
    Lord must know,
Year after year in the mist and the wind
    and the shower and the snow.

XIV.

Heard, have you? what? they have told
    you he never repented his sin.
How do they know it? are *they* his
    mother? are *you* of his kin?
Heard! have you ever heard, when the
    storm on the downs began,
The wind that 'ill wail like a child and
    the sea that 'ill moan like a man?

XV.

Election, Election and Reprobation—it's
    all very well.
But I go to-night to my boy, and I shall
    not find him in Hell.
For I cared so much for my boy that the
    Lord has look'd into my care,
And He means me I'm sure to be happy
    with Willy, I know not where.

XVI.

And if *he* be lost—but to save *my* soul,
    that is all your desire:
Do you think that I care for *my* soul if
    my boy be gone to the fire?
I have been with God in the dark—go,
    go, you may leave me alone—
You never have borne a child—you are
    just as hard as a stone.

XVII.

Madam, I beg your pardon! I think
    that you mean to be kind,
But I cannot hear what you say for my
    Willy's voice in the wind—
The snow and the sky so bright—he used
    but to call in the dark,
And he calls to me now from the church
    and not from the gibbet—for hark!

Nay—you can hear it yourself—it is
    coming—shaking the walls—
Willy—the moon's in a cloud——Good-
    night. I am going. He calls.

THE NORTHERN COBBLER.

I.

Waäit till our Sally cooms in, fur thou
    mun a' sights[1] to tell.
Eh, but I be maäin glad to seeä tha sa
    'arty an' well.
'Cast awaäy on a disolut land wi' a
    vartical soon[2]!'
Strange fur to goä fur to think what
    saäilors a' seëan an' a' doon ;
'Summat to drink—sa' 'ot ?' I 'a nowt
    but Adam's wine :
What's the 'eät o' this little 'ill-side to
    the 'eät o' the line ?

II.

'What's i' tha bottle a-stanning theer ?'
    I'll tell tha. Gin.
But if thou wants thy grog, tha mun goä
    fur it down to the inn.
Naay—fur I be maäin-glad, but thaw tha
    was iver sa dry,
Thou gits naw gin fro' the bottle theer,
    an' I'll tell tha why.

III.

Meä an' thy sister was married, when
    wur it ? back-end o' June,
Ten year sin', and wa 'greed as well as a
    fiddle i' tune :
I could fettle and clump owd booöts and
    shoes wi' the best on 'em all,
As fer as fro' Thursby thurn hup to
    Harmsby and Hutterby Hall.

[1] The vowels *aï*, pronounced separately though
in the closest conjunction, best render the sound
of the long *i* and *y* in this dialect. But since such
words as *craïin'*, *daïin'*, *whaï*, *aï* (I), etc., look
awkward except in a page of express phonetics,
I have thought it better to leave the simple *i* and
y, and to trust that my readers will give them the
broader pronunciation.

[2] The *oo* short, as in 'wood.'

We was busy as beeäs i' the bloom an' as
    'appy as 'art could think,
An' then the babby wur burn, and then
    I taäkes to the drink.

IV.

An' I weänt gaäinsaäy it, my lad, thaw I
    be hafe shaämed on it now,
We could sĭng a good song at the Plow, we
    could sing a good song at the Plow ;
Thaw once of a frosty night I slither'd an'
    hurted my huck,[1]
An' I coom'd neck-an-crop soomtimes
    slaäpe down i' the squad an' the
    muck :
An' once I fowt wi' the Taäilor—not hafe
    ov a man, my lad——
Fur he scrawm'd an' scratted my faäce
    like a cat, an' it maäde 'er sa mad
That Sally she turn'd a tongue-banger,[2]
    an' raäted ma, ' Sottin' thy braäins
Guzzlin' an' soäkin' an' smoäkin' an'
    hawmin'[3] about i' the laänes,
Soä sow-droonk that tha doesn not touch
    thy 'at to the Squire ;'
An' I looök'd cock-eyed at my noäse an'
    I seeäd 'im a-gittin' o' fire ;
But sin' I wur hallus i' liquor an' hallus
    as droonk as a king,
Foälks' coostom flitted awaäy like a kite
    wi' a brokken string.

V.

An' Sally she wesh'd foälks' cloäths to
    keep the wolf fro' the door,
Eh but the moor she riled me, she druv
    me to drink the moor,
Fur I fun', when 'er back wur turn'd,
    wheer Sally's owd stockin' wur 'id,
An' I grabb'd the munny she maäde, and
    I weär'd it o' liquor, I did.

VI.

An' one night I cooms 'oäm like a bull
    gotten loose at a faäir,
An' she wur a-waäitin' fo'mma, an' cryin'
    and teärin' 'er 'aäir,

[1] Hip.   [2] Scold.   [3] Lounging.

An' I tummled athurt the craädle an'
    sweär'd as I'd breäk ivry stick
O' furnitur 'ere i' the 'ouse, an' I gied
    our Sally a kick,
An' I mash'd the taäbles an' chairs, an'
    she an' the babby beäl'd,[1]
Fur I knaw'd naw moor what I did nor
    a mortal beäst o' the feäld.

VII.

An' when I waäked i' the murnin' I seeäd
    that our Sally went laämed
Cos' o' the kick as I gied 'er, an' I wur
    dreädful ashaämed ;
An' Sally wur sloomy[2] an' draggle taäil'd
    in an owd turn gown,
An' the babby's faäce wurn't wesh'd an'
    the 'ole 'ouse hupside down.

VIII.

An' then I minded our Sally sa pratty
    an' neät an' sweeät,
Straät as a pole an' cleän as a flower fro'
    'eäd to feeät :
An' then I minded the fust kiss I gied
    'er by Thursby thurn ;
Theer wur a lark a-singin' 'is best of a
    Sunday at murn,
Couldn't see 'im, we 'eärd 'im a-mountin'
    oop 'igher an' 'igher,
An' then 'e turn'd to the sun, an' 'e
    shined like a sparkle o' fire.
' Doesn't tha see 'im,' she axes, ' fur I
    can see 'im ?' an' I
Seeäd nobbut the smile o' the sun as
    danced in 'er pratty blue eye ;
An' I says ' I mun gie tha a kiss,' an'
    Sally says ' Noä, thou moänt,'
But I gied 'er a kiss, an' then anoother,
    an' Sally says ' doänt !'

IX.

An' when we coom'd into Meeätin', at
    fust she wur all in a tew,
But, arter, ye sing'd the 'ymn togither
    like birds on a beugh ;

An' Muggins 'e preäch'd o' Hell-fire an'
    the loov o' God fur men,
An' then upo' coomin' awaäy Sally gied
    me a kiss ov 'ersen.

X.

Heer wur a fall fro' a kiss to a kick like
    Saätan as fell
Down out o' heaven i' Hell-fire—thaw
    theer's naw drinkin' i' Hell ;
Meä fur to kick our Sally as kep the wolf
    fro' the door,
All along o' the drink, fur I loov'd 'er
    as well as afoor.

XI.

Sa like a greät num-cumpus I blubber'd
    awaäy o' the bed—
' Weänt niver do it naw moor ;' an'
    Sally looökt up an' she said,
' I'll upowd it[1] tha weänt ; thou'rt like
    the rest o' the men,
Thou'll goä sniffin' about the tap till tha
    does it ageän.
Theer's thy hennemy, man, an' I knaws,
    as knaws tha sa well,
That, if tha seeäs 'im an' smells 'im tha'll
    foller 'im slick into Hell.'

XII.

' Naäy,' says I, ' fur I weänt goä sniffin'
    about the tap.'
' Weänt tha ?' she says, an' mysen I
    thowt i' mysen ' mayhap.'
' Noä :' an' I started awaäy like a shot,
    an' down to the Hinn,
An' I browt what tha seeäs stannin' theer,
    yon big black bottle o' gin.

XIII.

' That caps owt,'[2] says Sally, an' saw she
    begins to cry,
But I puts it inter 'er 'ands an' I says to
    'er, ' Sally,' says I,
' Stan' 'im theer i' the naäme o' the Lord
    an' the power ov 'is Graäce,
Stan' 'im theer, fur I'll looök my hennemy
    straït i' the faäce,

---

[1] Bellowed, cried out.
[2] Sluggish, out of spirits.

[1] I'll uphold it.
[2] That's beyond everything.

Stan' 'im theer i' the winder, an' let ma
    looök at 'im then,
'E seeäms naw moor nor watter, an' 'e's
    the Divil's oän sen.'

XIV.

An' I wur down i' tha mouth, couldn't do
    naw work an' all,
Nasty an' snaggy an' shaäky, an' poonch'd
    my 'and wi' the hawl,
But she wur a power o' coomfut, an'
    sattled 'ersen o' my knee,
An' coäxd an' coodled me oop till ageän
    I feel'd mysen free.

XV.

An' Sally she tell'd it about, an' foälk
    stood a-gawmin'[1] in,
As thaw it wur summat bewitch'd istead
    of a quart o' gin ;
An' some on 'em said it wur watter—an'
    I wur chousin' the wife,
Fur I couldn't 'owd 'ands off gin, wur it
    nobbut to saäve my life ;
An' blacksmith 'e strips me the thick ov
    'is airm, an' 'e shaws it to me,
'Feëal thou this ! thou can't graw this
    upo' watter !' says he.
An' Doctor 'e calls o' Sunday an' just as
    candles was lit,
'Thou moänt do it,' he says, 'tha mun
    breäk 'im off bit by bit.'
'Thou'rt but a Methody-man,' says Par-
    son, and laäys down 'is 'at,
An' 'e points to the bottle o' gin, 'but I
    respecks tha fur that ;'
An' Squire, his oän very sen, walks down
    fro' the 'All to see,
An' 'e spanks 'is 'and into mine, 'fur I
    respecks tha,' says 'e ;
An' coostom ageän draw'd in like a wind
    fro' far an' wide,
And browt me the booöts to be cobbled
    fro' hafe the coontryside.

XVI.

An' theer 'e stans an' theer 'e shall stan
    to my dying daäy ;

[1] Staring vacantly.

I 'a gotten to loov 'im ageän in anoother
    kind of a waäy,
Proud on 'im, like, my lad, an' I keeäps
    'im cleän an' bright,
Loovs 'im, an' roobs 'im, an' doosts 'im,
    an' puts 'im back i' the light.

XVII.

Wouldn't a pint a' sarved as well as a
    quart ? Naw doubt :
But I liked a bigger feller to fight wi' an'
    fowt it out.
Fine an' meller 'e mun be by this, if I
    cared to taäste,
But I moänt, my lad, and I weänt, fur
    I'd feäl mysen cleän disgraäced.

XVIII.

An' once I said to the Missis, 'My lass,
    when I cooms to die,
Smash the bottle to smithers, the Divil's
    in 'im,' said I.
But arter I chaänged my mind, an' if
    Sally be left aloän,
I'll hev 'im a-buried wi'mma an' taäke
    'im afoor the Throän.

XIX.

Coom thou 'eer—yon laädy a-steppin'
    along the streeät,
Doesn't tha knaw 'er—sa pratty, an' feät,
    an' neät, an' sweeät ?
Look at the cloäths on 'er back, thebbe
    ammost spick-span-new,
An' Tommy's faäce be as fresh as a codlin
    wesh'd i' the dew.

XX.

'Ere be our Sally an' Tommy, an' we be
    a-goin to dine,
Baäcon an' taätes, an' a beslings pud-
    din'[1] an' Adam's wine ;
But if tha wants ony grog tha mun goä
    fur it down to the Hinn,
Fur I weänt shed a drop on 'is blood,
    noä, not fur Sally's oän kin.

[1] A pudding made with the first milk of the cow
after calving.

THE REVENGE.

A BALLAD OF THE FLEET.

I.

At Flores in the Azores Sir Richard
    Grenville lay,
And a pinnace, like a flutter'd bird, came
    flying from far away :
'Spanish ships of war at sea ! we have
    sighted fifty-three !'
Then sware Lord Thomas Howard :
    ' 'Fore God I am no coward ;
But I cannot meet them here, for my
    ships are out of gear,
And the half my men are sick. I must
    fly, but follow quick.
We are six ships of the line ; can we
    fight with fifty-three ?'

II.

Then spake Sir Richard Grenville : 'I
    know you are no coward ;
You fly them for a moment to fight with
    them again.
But I've ninety men and more that are
    lying sick ashore.
I should count myself the coward if I left
    them, my Lord Howard,
To these Inquisition dogs and the devil-
    doms of Spain.'

III.

So Lord Howard past away with five
    ships of war that day,
Till he melted like a cloud in the silent
    summer heaven ;
But Sir Richard bore in hand all his sick
    men from the land
Very carefully and slow,
Men of Bideford in Devon,
And we laid them on the ballast down
    below ;
For we brought them all aboard,
And they blest him in their pain, that they
    were not left to Spain,
To the thumbscrew and the stake, for the
    glory of the Lord.

IV.

He had only a hundred seamen to work
    the ship and to fight,
And he sailed away from Flores till the
    Spaniard came in sight,
With his huge sea-castles heaving upon
    the weather bow.
'Shall we fight or shall we fly ?
Good Sir Richard, tell us now,
For to fight is but to die !
There'll be little of us left by the time
    this sun be set.'
And Sir Richard said again : ' We be all
    good English men.
Let us bang these dogs of Seville, the
    children of the devil,
For I never turn'd my back upon Don or
    devil yet.'

V.

Sir Richard spoke and he laugh'd, and
    we roar'd a hurrah, and so
The little Revenge ran on sheer into the
    heart of the foe,
With her hundred fighters on deck, and
    her ninety sick below ;
For half of their fleet to the right and
    half to the left were seen,
And the little Revenge ran on thro' the
    long sea-lane between.

VI.

Thousands of their soldiers look'd down
    from their decks and laugh'd,
Thousands of their seamen made mock at
    the mad little craft
Running on and on, till delay'd
By their mountain-like San Philip that,
    of fifteen hundred tons,
And up-shadowing high above us with
    her yawning tiers of guns,
Took the breath from our sails, and we
    stay'd.

VII.

And while now the great San Philip hung
    above us like a cloud
Whence the thunderbolt will fall
Long and loud,

Four galleons drew away
From the Spanish fleet that day,
And two upon the larboard and two upon
the starboard lay,
And the battle-thunder broke from them
all.

VIII.

But anon the great San Philip, she bethought herself and went
Having that within her womb that had
left her ill content ;
And the rest they came aboard us, and
they fought us hand to hand,
For a dozen times they came with their
pikes and musqueteers,
And a dozen times we shook 'em off as a
dog that shakes his ears
When he leaps from the water to the land.

IX.

And the sun went down, and the stars
came out far over the summer sea,
But never a moment ceased the fight of
the one and the fifty-three.
Ship after ship, the whole night long,
their high-built galleons came,
Ship after ship, the whole night long,
with her battle-thunder and flame ;
Ship after ship, the whole night long, drew
back with her dead and her shame.
For some were sunk and many were shatter'd, and so could fight us no
more—
God of battles, was ever a battle like this
in the world before ?

X.

For he said ' Fight on ! fight on !'
Tho' his vessel was all but a wreck ;
And it chanced that, when half of the
short summer night was gone,
With a grisly wound to be drest he had
left the deck,
But a bullet struck him that was dressing
it suddenly dead,
And himself he was wounded again in the
side and the head,
And he said ' Fight on ! fight on !'

XI.

And the night went down, and the sun
smiled out far over the summer sea,
And the Spanish fleet with broken sides
lay round us all in a ring ;
But they dared not touch us again, for
they fear'd that we still could sting,
So they watch'd what the end would be.
And we had not fought them in vain,
But in perilous plight were we,
Seeing forty of our poor hundred were
slain,
And half of the rest of us maim'd for life
In the crash of the cannonades and the
desperate strife ;
And the sick men down in the hold were
most of them stark and cold,
And the pikes were all broken or bent,
and the powder was all of it spent ;
And the masts and the rigging were lying
over the side ;
But Sir Richard cried in his English pride,
' We have fought such a fight for a day
and a night
As may never be fought again !
We have won great glory, my men !
And a day less or more
At sea or ashore,
We die—does it matter when ?
Sink me the ship, Master Gunner—sink
her, split her in twain !
Fall into the hands of God, not into the
hands of Spain !'

XII.

And the gunner said ' Ay, ay,' but the
seamen made reply :
' We have children, we have wives,
And the Lord hath spared our lives.
We will make the Spaniard promise, if
we yield, to let us go ;
We shall live to fight again and to strike
another blow.'
And the lion there lay dying, and they
yielded to the foe.

XIII.

And the stately Spanish men to their
flagship bore him then,

Where they laid him by the mast, old
   Sir Richard caught at last,
And they praised him to his face with
   their courtly foreign grace ;
But he rose upon their decks, and he cried :
'I have fought for Queen and Faith like
   a valiant man and true ;
I have only done my duty as a man is
   bound to do :
With a joyful spirit I Sir Richard Gren-
   ville die !'
And he fell upon their decks, and he died.

XIV.

And they stared at the dead that had
   been so valiant and true,
And had holden the power and glory of
   Spain so cheap
That he dared her with one little ship
   and his English few ;
Was he devil or man ? He was devil
   for aught they knew,
But they sank his body with honour down
   into the deep,
And they mann'd the Revenge with a
   swarthier alien crew,
And away she sail'd with her loss and
   long'd for her own ;
When a wind from the lands they had
   ruin'd awoke from sleep,
And the water began to heave and the
   weather to moan,
And or ever that evening ended a great
   gale blew,
And a wave like the wave that is raised
   by an earthquake grew,
Till it smote on their hulls and their sails
   and their masts and their flags,
And the whole sea plunged and fell on
   the shot-shatter'd navy of Spain,
And the little Revenge herself went down
   by the island crags
To be lost evermore in the main.

THE SISTERS.

THEY have left the doors ajar ; and by
   their clash,
And prelude on the keys, I know the
   song,

Their favourite—which I call 'The Tables
   Turned.'
Evelyn begins it ' O diviner Air.'

EVELYN.

O diviner Air,
Thro' the heat, the drowth, the dust, the
   glare,
Far from out the west in shadowing
   showers,
Over all the meadow baked and bare,
Making fresh and fair
All the bowers and the flowers,
Fainting flowers, faded bowers,
Over all this weary world of ours,
Breathe, diviner Air !

A sweet voice that—you scarce could
   better that.
Now follows Edith echoing Evelyn.

EDITH.

O diviner light,
Thro' the cloud that roofs our noon with
   night,
Thro' the blotting mist, the blinding
   showers,
Far from out a sky for ever bright,
Over all the woodland's flooded bowers,
Over all the meadow's drowning flowers,
Over all this ruin'd world of ours,
Break, diviner light !

Marvellously like, their voices—and them-
   selves !
Tho' one is somewhat deeper than the
   other,
As one is somewhat graver than the other—
Edith than Evelyn. Your good Uncle,
   whom
You count the father of your fortune,
   longs
For this alliance : let me ask you then,
Which voice most takes you ? for I do
   not doubt
Being a watchful parent, you are taken
With one or other : tho' sometimes I
   fear
You may be flickering, fluttering in a
   doubt '

Between the two—which must not be—
      which might
Be death to one : they both are beautiful:
Evelyn is gayer, wittier, prettier, says
The common voice, if one may trust it :
      she ?
No ! but the paler and the graver, Edith.
Woo her and gain her then : no waver-
      ing, boy !
The graver is perhaps the one for you
Who jest and laugh so easily and so well.
For love will go by contrast, as by likes.

No sisters ever prized each other more.
Not so : their mother and her sister loved
More passionately still.
                  But that my best
And oldest friend, your Uncle, wishes it,
And that I know you worthy everyway
To be my son, I might, perchance, be loath
To part them, or part from them : and
      yet one
Should marry, or all the broad lands in
      your view
From this bay window—which our house
      has held
Three hundred years—will pass collater-
      ally.

My father with a child on either knee,
A hand upon the head of either child,
Smoothing their locks, as golden as his
      own
Were silver, 'get them wedded' would
      he say.
And once my prattling Edith ask'd him
      'why?'
Ay, why? said he, 'for why should I go
      lame ?'
Then told them of his wars, and of his
      wound.
For see — this wine — the grape from
      whence it flow'd
Was blackening on the slopes of Portugal,
When that brave soldier, down the terrible
      ridge
Plunged in the last fierce charge at
      Waterloo,
And caught the laming bullet. He left
me this,

Which yet retains a memory of its youth,
As I of mine, and my first passion.
Here's to your happy union with my child !

      Yet must you change your name : no
            fault of mine !
You say that you can do it as willingly
As birds make ready for their bridal-
      time
By change of feather: for all that, my
      boy,
Some birds are sick and sullen when they
      moult.
An old and worthy name ! but mine that
      stirr'd
Among our civil wars and earlier too
Among the Roses, the more venerable.
I care not for a name—no fault of mine.
Once more—a happier marriage than my
      own !

      You see yon Lombard poplar on the
            plain.
The highway running by it leaves a breadth
Of sward to left and right, where, long
      ago,
One bright May morning in a world of
      song,
I lay at leisure, watching overhead
The aërial poplar wave, an amber spire.

      I dozed ; I woke.   An open landaulet
Whirl'd by, which, after it had past me,
      show'd
Turning my way, the loveliest face on
      earth.
The face of one there sitting opposite,
On whom I brought a strange unhappi-
      ness,
That time I did not see.

                  Love at first sight
May seem — with goodly rhyme and
      reason for it—
Possible—at first glimpse, and for a face
Gone in a moment—strange.   Yet once,
      when first
I came on lake Llanberris in the dark,
A moonless night with storm—one light-
      ning-fork

Flash'd out the lake ; and tho' I loiter'd
there
The full day after, yet in retrospect
That less than momentary thunder-sketch
Of lake and mountain conquers all the day.

The Sun himself has limn'd the face
for me.
Not quite so quickly, no, nor half as well.
For look you here—the shadows are too
deep,
And like the critic's blurring comment
make
The veriest beauties of the work appear
The darkest faults : the sweet eyes frown :
the lips
Seem but a gash.   My sole memorial
Of Edith—no, the other,—both indeed.

So that bright face was flash'd thro'
sense and soul
And by the poplar vanish'd—to be found
Long after, as it seem'd, beneath the tall
Tree-bowers, and those long-sweeping
beechen boughs
Of our New Forest.   I was there alone :
The phantom of the whirling landaulet
For .ever past me by : when one quick
peal
Of laughter drew me thro' the glimmer-
ing glades
Down to the snowlike sparkle of a cloth
On fern and foxglove.   Lo, the face again,
My Rosalind in this Arden—Edith—all
One bloom of youth, health, beauty,
happiness,
And moved to merriment at a passing jest.

There one of those about her knowing
me
Call'd me to join them ; so with these I
spent
What seem'd my crowning hour, my day
of days.

I woo'd her then, nor unsuccessfully,
The worse for her, for me ! was I content ?
Ay—no, not quite ; for now and then I
thought
Laziness, vague love-longings, the bright
May,

Had made a heated haze to magnify
The charm of Edith—that a man's ideal
Is high in Heaven, and lodged with
Plato's God,
Not findable here—content, and not con-
tent,
In some such fashion as a man may be
That having had the portrait of his friend
Drawn by an artist, looks at it, and says,
'Good ! very like ! not altogether he.'

As yet I had not bound myself by
words,
Only, believing I loved Edith, made
Edith love *me*.   Then came the day
when I,
Flattering myself that all my doubts were
fools
Born of the fool this Age that doubts of
all—
Not I that day of Edith's love or mine—
Had braced my purpose to declare my-
self :
I stood upon the stairs of Paradise.
The golden gates would open at a word.
I spoke it—told her of my passion, seen
And lost and found again, had got so far,
Had caught her hand, her eyelids fell—I
heard
Wheels, and a noise of welcome at the
doors—
On a sudden after two Italian years
Had set the blossom of her health again,
The younger sister, Evelyn, enter'd—
there,
There was the face, and altogether she.
The mother fell about the daughter's
neck,
The sisters closed in one another's arms,
Their people throng'd about them from
the hall,
And in the thick of question and reply
I fled the house, driven by one angel face,
And all the Furies.

I was bound to her ;
I could not free myself in honour—bound
Not by the sounded letter of the word,
But counterpressures of the yielded hand
That timorously and faintly echoed mine,

Quick blushes, the sweet dwelling of her
  eyes
Upon me when she thought I did not
  see—
Were these not bonds? nay, nay, but
  could I wed her
Loving the other? do her that great
  wrong?
Had I not dream'd I loved her yester-
  morn?
Had I not known where Love, at first a
  fear,
Grew after marriage to full height and
  form?
Yet after marriage, that mock-sister
  there—
Brother-in-law—the fiery nearness of it—
Unlawful and disloyal brotherhood—
What end but darkness could ensue from
  this
For all the three? So Love and Honour
  jarr'd
Tho' Love and Honour join'd to raise
  the full
High-tide of doubt that sway'd me up
  and down
Advancing nor retreating.

                    Edith wrote:
'My mother bids me ask' (I did not tell
  you—
A widow with less guile than many a child.
God help the wrinkled children that are
  Christ's
As well as the plump cheek—she wrought
  us harm,
Poor soul, not knowing) 'are you ill?'
  (so ran
The letter) 'you have not been here of
  late.
You will not find me here. At last I go
On that long-promised visit to the North.
I told your wayside story to my mother
And Evelyn. She remembers you.
  Farewell.
Pray come and see my mother. Almost
  blind
With ever-growing cataract, yet she thinks
She sees you when she hears. Again
  farewell.'

Cold words from one I had hoped to
  warm so far
That I could stamp my image on her
  heart !
'Pray come and see my mother, and
  farewell.'
Cold, but as welcome as free airs of
  heaven
After a dungeon's closeness. Selfish,
  strange !
What dwarfs are men ! my strangled
  vanity
Utter'd a stifled cry—to have vext myself
And all in vain for her—cold heart or
  none—
No bride for me. Yet so my path was
  clear
To win the sister.
                    Whom I woo'd and won.
For Evelyn knew not of my former suit,
Because the simple mother work'd upon
By Edith pray'd me not to whisper of it.
And Edith would be bridesmaid on the
  day.

But on that day, not being all at ease,
I from the altar glancing back upon her,
Before the first 'I will' was utter'd, saw
The bridesmaid pale, statuelike, passion-
  less—
'No harm, no harm' I turn'd again, and
  placed
My ring upon the finger of my bride.

So, when we parted, Edith spoke no
  word,
She wept no tear, but round my Evelyn
  clung
In utter silence for so long, I thought
'What, will she never set her sister free?'

We left her, happy each in each, and
  then,
As tho' the happiness of each in each
Were not enough, must fain have torrents,
  lakes,
Hills, the great things of Nature and the
  fair,
To lift us as it were from commonplace,
And help us to our joy. Better have
  sent

Our Edith thro' the glories of the earth,
To change with her horizon, if true Love
Were not his own imperial all-in-all.

    Far off we went. My God, I would
      not live
Save that I think this gross hard-seeming
    world
Is our misshaping vision of the Powers
Behind the world, that make our griefs
    our gains.

    For on the dark night of our marriage-
      day
The great Tragedian, that had quench'd
    herself
In that assumption of the bridesmaid—
    she
That loved me—our true Edith—her
    brain broke
With over-acting, till she rose and fled
Beneath a pitiless rush of Autumn rain
To the deaf church—to be let in—to pray
Before *that* altar—so I think ; and there
They found her beating the hard Protest-
    ant doors.
She died and she was buried ere we
    knew.

    I learnt it first. I had to speak. At
      once
The bright quick smile of Evelyn, that
    had sunn'd
The morning of our marriage, past away :
And on our home-return the daily want
Of Edith in the house, the garden, still
Haunted us like her ghost ; and by and
    by,
Either from that necessity for talk
Which lives with blindness, or plain
    innocence
Of nature, or desire that her lost child
Should earn from both the praise of
    heroism,
The mother broke her promise to the
    dead,
And told the living daughter with what
    love
Edith had welcomed my brief wooing of
    her,
And all her sweet self-sacrifice and death.

Henceforth that mystic bond betwixt
    the twins—
Did I not tell you they were twins ?—
    prevail'd
So far that no caress could win my wife
Back to that passionate answer of full
    heart
I had from her at first. Not that her love,
Tho' scarce as great as Edith's power of
    love,
Had lessen'd, but the mother's garrulous
    wail
For ever woke the unhappy Past again,
Till that dead bridesmaid, meant to be
    my bride,
Put forth cold hands between us, and I
    fear'd
The very fountains of her life were
    chill'd ;
So took her thence, and brought her
    here, and here
She bore a child, whom reverently we
    call'd
Edith ; and in the second year was born
A second—this I named from her own
    self,
Evelyn ; then two weeks—no more—she
    joined,
In and beyond the grave, that one she
    loved.
    Now in this quiet of declining life,
Thro' dreams by night and trances of the
    day,
The sisters glide about me hand in hand,
Both beautiful alike, nor can I tell
One from the other, no, nor care to tell
One from the other, only know they
    come,
They smile upon me, till, remembering
    all
The love they both have borne me, and
    the love
I bore them both—divided as I am
From either by the stillness of the grave—
I know not which of these I love the
    best.

    But *you* love Edith ; and her own true
    eyes
Are traitors to her ; our quick Evelyn—

T

2 L

The merrier, prettier, wittier, as they
talk,
And not without good reason, my good
son—
Is yet untouch'd : and I that hold them
both
Dearest of all things—well, I am not
sure—
But if there lie a preference eitherway,
And in the rich vocabulary of Love
' Most dearest ' be a true superlative—
I think *I* likewise love your Edith most.

THE VILLAGE WIFE ; OR, THE ENTAIL.[1]

I.

'Ouse-keeper sent tha my lass, fur New
Squire coom'd last night.
Butter an' heggs—yis—yis. I'll goä wi'
tha back : all right ;
Butter I warrants be prime, an' I war-
rants the heggs be as well,
Hafe a pint o' milk runs out when ya
breäks the shell.

II.

Sit thysen down fur a bit : hev a glass o'
cowslip wine !
I liked the owd Squire an' 'is gells as
thaw they was gells o' mine,
Fur then we was all es one, the Squire
an' 'is darters an' me,
Hall but Miss Annie, the heldest, I niver
not took to she :
But Nelly, the last of the cletch,[2] I liked
'er the fust on 'em all,
Fur hoffens we talkt o' my darter es died
o' the fever at fall :
An' I thowt 'twur the will o' the Lord, but
Miss Annie she said it wur draäins,
Fur she hedn't naw coomfut in 'er, an'
arn'd naw thanks fur 'er paäins,
Eh ! thebbe all wi' the Lord my childer,
I han't gotten none !
Sa new Squire's coom'd wi' 'is taäil in 'is
'and, an' owd Squire's gone.

1 See note to ' Northern Cobbler.'
2 A brood of chickens.

III.

Fur 'staäte be i' taäil, my lass : tha dosn'
knaw what that be ?
But I knaws the law, I does, for the
lawyer ha towd it me.
' When theer's naw 'eäd to a 'Ouse by
the fault o' that ere maäle—
The gells they counts fur nowt, and the
next un he taäkes the taäil.'

IV.

What be the next un like ? can tha tell
ony harm on 'im lass ?—
Naay sit down—naw 'urry—sa cowd !—
hev another glass !
Straänge an' cowd fur the time ! we may
happen a fall o' snaw—
Not es I cares fur to hear ony harm, but
I likes to knaw.
An' I 'oäps es 'e beänt boooklarn'd : but
'e dosn' not coom fro' the shere ;
We'd anew o' that wi' the Squire, an' we
haätes boooklarnin' ere.

V.

Fur Squire wur a Varsity scholard, an'
niver lookt arter the land—
Whoäts or tonups or taätes—'e 'ed hallus
a boook i' 'is 'and,
Hallus aloän wi' 'is boooks, thaw nigh
upo' seventy year.
An' boooks, what's boooks ? thou knaws
thebbe naither 'ere nor theer.

VI.

An' the gells, they hedn't naw taäils, an'
the lawyer he towd it me
That 'is taäil were soä tied up es he
couldn't cut down a tree !
' Drat the trees,' says I, to be sewer I
haätes 'em, my lass,
Fur we puts the muck o' the land an'
they sucks the muck fro' the grass.

VII.

An' Squire wur hallus a-smilin', an' gied
to the tramps goin' by—
An' all o' the wust i' the parish—wi'
hoffens a drop in 'is eye.

An' ivry darter o' Squire's hed her awn
   ridin-erse to 'ersen,
An' they rampaged about wi' their grooms,
   an' was 'untin' arter the men,
An' hallus a-dallackt [1] an' dizen'd out,
   an' a-buyin' new cloäthes,
While 'e sit like a greät glimmer-gowk [2]
   wi' 'is glasses athurt 'is noäse,
An' 'is noäse sa grufted wi' snuff es it
   couldn't be scroob'd awaäy,
Fur atween 'is reädin' an' writin' 'e snifft
   up a box in a daäy,
An' 'e niver runn'd arter the fox, nor
   arter the birds wi' 'is gun,
An' 'e niver not shot one 'are, but 'e
   leäved it to Charlie 'is son,
An' 'e niver not fish'd 'is awn ponds, but
   Charlie 'e cotch'd the pike,
For 'e warn't not burn to the land, an' 'e
   didn't take kind to it like ;
But I eärs es 'e'd gie fur a howry [3] owd
   book thutty pound an' moor,
An' 'e'd wrote an owd book, his awn sen,
   sa I knaw'd es 'e'd coom to be poor ;
An' 'e gied—I be fear'd fur to tell tha 'ow
   much—fur an owd scratted stoän,
An' 'e digg'd up a loomp i' the land an'
   'e got a brown pot an' a boän,
An' 'e bowt owd money, es wouldn't goä,
   wi' good gowd o' the Queen,
An' 'e bowt little statutes all-naäkt an'
   which was a shaame to be seen ;
But 'e niver looökt ower a bill, nor 'e
   niver not seed to owt,
An' 'e niver knawd nowt but boooks, an'
   boooks, as thou knaws, beänt nowt.

VIII.

But owd Squire's laädy es long es she
   lived she kep 'em all clear,
Thaw es long es she lived I niver hed
   none of 'er darters 'ere ;
But arter she died we was all es one, the
   childer an' me,
An' sarvints runn'd in an' out, an' offens
   we hed 'em to tea.
Lawk ! 'ow I laugh'd when the lasses 'ud
   talk o' their Missis's waäys,

[1] Overdrest in gay colours.   [2] Owl.
[3] Filthy.

An' the Missisis talk'd o' the lasses.—I'll
   tell tha some o' these daäys.
Hoänly Miss Annie were saw stuck oop,
   like 'er mother afoor—
'Er an' 'er blessed darter—they niver
   derken'd my door.

IX.

An' Squire 'e smiled an' 'e smiled till 'e'd
   gotten a fright at last,
An' 'e calls fur 'is son, fur the 'turney's
   letters they foller'd sa fast ;
But Squire wur afear'd o' 'is son, an' 'e
   says to 'im, meek as a mouse,
' Lad, thou mun cut off thy taäil, or the
   gells 'ull goä to the 'Ouse,
Fur I finds es I be that i' debt, es I 'oäps
   es thou'll 'elp me a bit,
An' if thou'll 'gree to cut off thy taäil I
   may saäve mysen yit.'

X.

But Charlie 'e sets back 'is ears, an' 'e
   sweärs, an' 'e says to 'im ' Noa.
I've gotten the 'staäte by the taäil an'
   be dang'd if I iver let goa !
Coom ! coom ! feyther,' 'e says, ' why
   shouldn't thy boooks be sowd ?
I hears es soom o' thy boooks mebbe
   worth their weight i' gowd.'

XI.

Heäps an' heäps o' boooks, I ha' see'd
   'em, belong'd to the Squire,
But the lasses 'ed teärd out leäves i' the
   middle to kindle the fire ;
Sa moäst on 'is owd big boooks fetch'd
   nigh to nowt at the saäle,
And Squire were at Charlie ageän to git
   'im to cut off 'is taäil.

XII.

Ya wouldn't find Charlie's likes—'e were
   that outdacious at 'oäm,
Not thaw ya went fur to raäke out Hell
   wi' a small-tooth coämb—
Droonk wi' the Quoloty's wine, an' droonk
   wi' the farmer's aäle,
Mad wi' the lasses an' all—an' 'e wouldn't
   cut off the taäil.

XIII.

Thou's coom'd oop by the beck ; and a
    thurn be a-grawin' theer,
I niver ha seed it sa white wi' the Maäy
    es I see'd it to-year—
Theerabouts Charlie joompt—and it gied
    me a scare tother night,
Fur I thowt it wur Charlie's ghoäst i'
    the derk, fur it looökt sa white.
'Billy,' says 'e, 'hev a joomp!'—thaw
    the banks o' the beck be sa high,
Fur he ca'd 'is 'erse Billy-rough-un, thaw
    niver a hair wur awry ;
But Billy fell bakkuds o' Charlie, an'
    Charlie 'e brok 'is neck,
Sa theer wur a hend o' the taäil, fur 'e
    lost 'is taäil i' the beck.

XIV.

Sa 'is taäil wur lost an' 'is booöks wur
    gone an' 'is boy wur deäd,
An' Squire 'e smiled an' 'e smiled, but 'e
    niver not lift oop 'is 'eäd :
Hallus a soft un Squire! an' 'e smiled,
    fur 'e hedn't naw friend,
Sa feyther an' son was buried togither,
    an' this wur the hend.

XV.

An' Parson as hesn't the call, nor the
    mooney, but hes the pride,
'E reäds of a sewer an' sartan 'oäp o' the
    tother side ;
But I beänt that sewer es the Lord, how-
    siver they praäy'd an' praäy'd,
Lets them inter 'eaven eäsy es leäves their
    debts to be paäid.
Siver the mou'ds rattled down upo' poor
    owd Squire i' the wood,
An' I cried along wi' the gells, fur they
    weänt niver coom to naw good.

XVI.

Fur Molly the long un she walkt awaäy
    wi' a hofficer lad,
An' nawbody 'eärd on 'er sin, sa o' coorse
    she be gone to the bad !
An' Lucy wur laäme o' one leg, sweet-
    'arts she niver 'ed none—

Straänge an' unheppen [1] Miss Lucy ! we
    naämed her ' Dot an' gaw one !'
An' Hetty wur weak i' the hattics, wi'out
    ony harm i' the legs,
An' the fever 'ed baäked Jinny's 'eäd as
    bald as one o' them heggs,
An' Nelly wur up fro' the craädle as big
    i' the mouth as a cow,
An' saw she mun hammergrate,[2] lass, or
    she weänt git a maäte onyhow !
An' es for Miss Annie es call'd me afoor
    my awn foälks to my faäce
' A hignorant village wife as 'ud hev to
    be larn'd her awn plaäce,'
Hes fur Miss Hannie the heldest hes now
    be a-grawin' sa howd,
I knaws that mooch o' sheä, es it beänt
    not fit to be towd !

XVII.

Sa I didn't not taäke it kindly ov owd
    Miss Annie to saäy
Es I should be talkin ageän 'em, es soon
    es they went awaäy,
Fur, lawks ! 'ow I cried when they went,
    an' our Nelly she gied me 'er 'and,
Fur I'd ha done owt for the Squire an' 'is
    gells es belong'd to the land ;
Booöks, es I said afoor, thebbe neyther
    'ere nor theer !
But I sarved 'em wi' butter an' heggs fur
    huppuds o' twenty year.

XVIII.

An' they hallus paäid what I hax'd, sa I
    hallus deal'd wi' the Hall,
An' they knaw'd what butter wur, an' they
    knaw'd what a hegg wur an' all ;
Hugger - mugger they lived, but they
    wasn't that eäsy to pleäse,
Till I gied 'em Hinjian curn, an' they
    laäid big heggs es tha seeas ;
An' I niver puts saäme [3] i' *my* butter,
    they does it at Willis's farm,
Taäste another drop o' the wine—tweänt
    do tha naw harm.

---

1 Ungainly, awkward.
2 Emigrate.   3 Lard.

XIX.

Sa new Squire's coom'd wi' 'is taäil in 'is
    'and, an' owd Squire's gone ;
I heard 'im a roomlin' by, but arter my
    nightcap wur on ;
Sa I han't clapt eyes on 'im yit, fur he
    coom'd last night sa laäte—
Pluksh ! ! ![1] the hens i' the peäs ! why
    didn't tha hesp the gaäte ?

IN THE CHILDREN'S
HOSPITAL.

EMMIE.

I.

OUR doctor had call'd in another, I never
    had seen him before,
But he sent a chill to my heart when I
    saw him come in at the door,
Fresh from the surgery-schools of France
    and of other lands—
Harsh red hair, big voice, big chest, big
    merciless hands !
Wonderful cures he had done, O yes, but
    they said too of him
He was happier using the knife than in
    trying to save the limb,
And that I can well believe, for he look'd
    so coarse and so red,
I could think he was one of those who
    would break their jests on the dead,
And mangle the living dog that had loved
    him and fawn'd at his knee—
Drench'd with the hellish oorali—that
    ever such things should be !

II.

Here was a boy—I am sure that some of
    our children would die
But for the voice of Love, and the smile,
    and the comforting eye—
Here was a boy in the ward, every bone
    seem'd out of its place—
Caught in a mill and crush'd—it was all
    but a hopeless case :

[1] A cry accompanied by a clapping of hands to
scare trespassing fowl.

And he handled him gently enough ; but
    his voice and his face were not kind,
And it was but a hopeless case, he had
    seen it and made up his mind,
And he said to me roughly 'The lad will
    need little more of your care.'
'All the more need,' I told him, 'to seek
    the Lord Jesus in prayer ;
They are all his children here, and I pray
    for them all as my own :'
But he turn'd to me, 'Ay, good woman,
    can prayer set a broken bone ?'
Then he mutter'd half to himself, but I
    know that I heard him say
'All very well—but the good Lord Jesus
    has had his day.'

III.

Had ? has it come ? It has only dawn'd.
    It will come by and by.
O how could I serve in the wards if the
    hope of the world were a lie ?
How could I bear with the sights and the
    loathsome smells of disease
But that He said 'Ye do it to me, when
    ye do it to these'?

IV.

So he went. And we past to this ward
    where the younger children are laid:
Here is the cot of our orphan, our dar-
    ling, our meek little maid ;
Empty you see just now ! We have lost
    her who loved her so much—
Patient of pain tho' as quick as a sensitive
    plant to the touch ;
Hers was the prettiest prattle, it often
    moved me to tears,
Hers was the gratefullest heart I have
    found in a child of her years—
Nay you remember our Emmie ; you used
    to send her the flowers ;
How she would smile at 'em, play with
    'em, talk to 'em hours after hours !
They that can wander at will where the
    works of the Lord are reveal'd
Little guess what joy can be got from a
    cowslip out of the field ;
Flowers to these 'spirits in prison' are all
    they can know of the spring,

They freshen and sweeten the wards like
    the waft of an Angel's wing ;
And she lay with a flower in one hand and
    her thin hands crost on her breast—
Wan, but as pretty as heart can desire,
    and we thought her at rest,
Quietly sleeping—so quiet, our doctor
    said 'Poor little dear,
Nurse, I must do it to-morrow ; she'll
    never live thro' it, I fear.'

V.

I walk'd with our kindly old doctor as
    far as the head of the stair,
Then I return'd to the ward ; the child
    didn't see I was there.

VI.

Never since I was nurse, had I been so
    grieved and so vext !
Emmie had heard him.   Softly she call'd
    from her cot to the next,
'He says I shall never live thro' it, O
    Annie, what shall I do ?'
Annie consider'd.   'If I,' said the wise
    little Annie, 'was you,
I should cry to the dear Lord Jesus to
    help me, for, Emmie, you see,
It's all in the picture there : "Little
    children should come to me."'
(Meaning the print that you gave us, I
    find that it always can please
Our children, the dear Lord Jesus with
    children about his knees.)
'Yes, and I will,' said Emmie, 'but then
    if I call to the Lord,
How should he know that it's me ? such
    a lot of beds in the ward !'
That was a puzzle for Annie.   Again she
    consider'd and said :
'Emmie, you put out your arms, and you
    leave 'em outside on the bed—
The Lord has so *much* to see to ! but,
    Emmie, you tell it him plain,
It's the little girl with her arms lying out
    on the counterpane.'

VII.

I had sat three nights by the child—I
    could not watch her for four—

My brain had begun to reel—I felt I
    could do it no more.
That was my sleeping-night, but I thought
    that it never would pass.
There was a thunderclap once, and a
    clatter of hail on the glass,
And there was a phantom cry that I heard
    as I tost about,
The motherless bleat of a lamb in the
    storm and the darkness without ;
My sleep was broken besides with dreams
    of the dreadful knife
And fears for our delicate Emmie who
    scarce would escape with her life ;
Then in the gray of the morning it seem'd
    she stood by me and smiled,
And the doctor came at his hour, and we
    went to see to the child.

VIII.

He had brought his ghastly tools : we
    believed her asleep again—
Her dear, long, lean, little arms lying out
    on the counterpane ;
Say that His day is done ! Ah why should
    we care what they say ?
The Lord of the children had heard her,
    and Emmie had past away.

DEDICATORY POEM TO THE PRINCESS ALICE.

DEAD PRINCESS, living Power, if that,
    which lived
True life, live on—and if the fatal kiss,
Born of true life and love, divorce thee
    not
From earthly love and life—if what we call
The spirit flash not all at once from out
This shadow into Substance—then perhaps
The mellow'd murmur of the people's
    praise
From thine own State, and all our
    breadth of realm,
Where Love and Longing dress thy deeds
    in light,
Ascends to thee ; and this March morn
    that sees
Thy Soldier-brother's bridal orange-bloom

Break thro' the yews and cypress of thy
    grave,
And thine Imperial mother smile again,
May send one ray to thee! and who can
    tell—
Thou—England's England-loving daugh-
    ter—thou
Dying so English thou wouldst have her
    flag
Borne on thy coffin—where is he can
    swear
But that some broken gleam from our
    poor earth
May touch thee, while remembering thee,
    I lay
At thy pale feet this ballad of the deeds
Of England, and her banner in the East?

THE DEFENCE OF
LUCKNOW.

I.

BANNER of England, not for a season, O
    banner of Britain, hast thou
Floated in conquering battle or flapt to
    the battle-cry!
Never with mightier glory than when we
    had rear'd thee on high
Flying at top of the roofs in the ghastly
    siege of Lucknow—
Shot thro' the staff or the halyard, but
    ever we raised thee anew,
And ever upon the topmost roof our
    banner of England blew.

II.

Frail were the works that defended the
    hold that we held with our lives—
Women and children among us, God help
    them, our children and wives!
Hold it we might—and for fifteen days
    or for twenty at most.
'Never surrender, I charge you, but
    every man die at his post!'
Voice of the dead whom we loved, our
    Lawrence the best of the brave:
Cold were his brows when we kiss'd
    him—we laid him that night in
    his grave.

'Every man die at his post!' and there
    hail'd on our houses and halls
Death from their rifle-bullets, and death
    from their cannon-balls,
Death in our innermost chamber, and
    death at our slight barricade,
Death while we stood with the musket, and
    death while we stoopt to the spade,
Death to the dying, and wounds to the
    wounded, for often there fell,
Striking the hospital wall, crashing thro'
    it, their shot and their shell,
Death—for their spies were among us, their
    marksmen were told of our best,
So that the brute bullet broke thro' the
    brain that could think for the rest;
Bullets would sing by our foreheads, and
    bullets would rain at our feet—
Fire from ten thousand at once of the
    rebels that girdled us round—
Death at the glimpse of a finger from
    over the breadth of a street,
Death from the heights of the mosque and
    the palace, and death in the ground!
Mine? yes, a mine! Countermine! down,
    down! and creep thro' the hole!
Keep the revolver in hand! you can hear
    him—the murderous mole!
Quiet, ah! quiet—wait till the point of
    the pickaxe be thro'!
Click with the pick, coming nearer and
    nearer again than before—
Now let it speak, and you fire, and the
    dark pioneer is no more;
And ever upon the topmost roof our
    banner of England blew!

III.

Ay, but the foe sprung his mine many
    times, and it chanced on a day
Soon as the blast of that underground
    thunderclap echo'd away,
Dark thro' the smoke and the sulphur like
    so many fiends in their hell—
Cannon-shot, musket-shot, volley on
    volley, and yell upon yell—
Fiercely on all the defences our myriad
    enemy fell.
What have they done? where is it? Out
    yonder. Guard the Redan!

Storm at the Water-gate ! storm at the
    Bailey-gate ! storm, and it ran
Surging and swaying all round us, as
    ocean on every side
Plunges and heaves at a bank that is
    daily devour'd by the tide—
So many thousands that if they be bold
    enough, who shall escape ?
Kill or be kill'd, live or die, they shall
    know we are soldiers and men !
Ready ! take aim at their leaders—their
    masses are gapp'd with our grape—
Backward they reel like the wave, like
    the wave flinging forward again,
Flying and foil'd at the last by the hand-
    ful they could not subdue ;
And ever upon the topmost roof our
    banner of England blew.

IV.

Handful of men as we were, we were
    English in heart and in limb,
Strong with the strength of the race to
    command, to obey, to endure,
Each of us fought as if hope for the garri-
    son hung but on him ;
Still—could we watch at all points ? we
    were every day fewer and fewer.
There was a whisper among us, but only
    a whisper that past :
'Children and wives—if the tigers leap
    into the fold unawares—
Every man die at his post—and the foe
    may outlive us at last—
Better to fall by the hands that they love,
    than to fall into theirs !'
Roar upon roar in a moment two mines
    by the enemy sprung
Clove into perilous chasms our walls and
    our poor palisades.
Rifleman, true is your heart, but be sure
    that your hand be as true !
Sharp is the fire of assault, better aimed
    are your flank fusillades—
Twice do we hurl them to earth from the
    ladders to which they had clung,
Twice from the ditch where they shelter
    we drive them with hand-grenades ;
And ever upon the topmost roof our
    banner of England blew.

V.

Then on another wild morning another
    wild earthquake out-tore
Clean from our lines of defence ten or
    twelve good paces or more.
Rifleman, high on the roof, hidden there
    from the light of the sun—
One has leapt up on the breach, crying
    out : ' Follow me, follow me !'—
Mark him—he falls ! then another, and
    him too, and down goes he.
Had they been bold enough then, who
    can tell but the traitors had won ?
Boardings and rafters and doors—an em-
    brasure ! make way for the gun !
Now double-charge it with grape ! It is
    charged and we fire, and they
    run.
Praise to our Indian brothers, and let the
    dark face have his due !
Thanks to the kindly dark faces who
    fought with us, faithful and few,
Fought with the bravest among us, and
    drove them, and smote them, and
    slew,
That ever upon the topmost roof our
    banner in India blew.

VI.

Men will forget what we suffer and not
    what we do. We can fight !
But to be soldier all day and be sentinel
    all thro' the night—
Ever the mine and assault, our sallies,
    their lying alarms,
Bugles and drums in the darkness, and
    shoutings and soundings to arms,
Ever the labour of fifty that had to be
    done by five,
Ever the marvel among us that one should
    be left alive,
Ever the day with its traitorous death
    from the loopholes around,
Ever the night with its coffinless corpse
    to be laid in the ground,
Heat like the mouth of a hell, or a deluge
    of cataract skies,
Stench of old offal decaying, and infinite
    torment of flies,

Thoughts of the breezes of May blowing
over an English field,
Cholera, scurvy, and fever, the wound
that *would* not be heal'd,
Lopping away of the limb by the pitiful-
pitiless knife,—
Torture and trouble in vain,—for it never
could save us a life.
Valour of delicate women who tended the
hospital bed,
Horror of women in travail among the
dying and dead,
Grief for our perishing children, and
never a moment for grief,
Toil and ineffable weariness, faltering
hopes of relief,
Havelock baffled, or beaten, or butcher'd
for all that we knew—
Then day and night, day and night, coming
down on the still-shatter'd walls
Millions of musket-bullets, and thousands
of cannon-balls—
But ever upon the topmost roof our
banner of England blew.

VII.

Hark cannonade, fusillade! is it true what
was told by the scout,
Outram and Havelock breaking their way
through the fell mutineers?
Surely the pibroch of Europe is ringing
again in our ears!
All on a sudden the garrison utter a jubi-
lant shout,
Havelock's glorious Highlanders answer
with conquering cheers,
Sick from the hospital echo them, women
and children come out,
Blessing the wholesome white faces of
Havelock's good fusileers,
Kissing the war-harden'd hand of the
Highlander wet with their tears!
Dance to the pibroch!—saved! we are
saved!—is it you? is it you?
Saved by the valour of Havelock, saved
by the blessing of Heaven!
'Hold it for fifteen days!' we have held
it for eighty-seven!
And ever aloft on the palace roof the old
banner of England blew.

SIR JOHN OLDCASTLE, LORD COBHAM.

(IN WALES.)

MY friend should meet me somewhere
hereabout
To take me to that hiding in the hills.

I have broke their cage, no gilded one,
I trow—
I read no more the prisoner's mute wail
Scribbled or carved upon the pitiless stone;
I find hard rocks, hard life, hard cheer, or
none,
For I am emptier than a friar's brains;
But God is with me in this wilderness,
These wet black passes and foam-churn-
ing chasms—
And God's free air, and hope of better
things.

I would I knew their speech; not now
to glean,
Not now—I hope to do it—some scatter'd
ears,
Some ears for Christ in this wild field of
Wales—
But, bread, merely for bread. This
tongue that wagg'd
They said with such heretical arrogance
Against the proud archbishop Arundel—
So much God's cause was fluent in it—is
here
But as a Latin Bible to the crowd;
'Bara!'—what use? The Shepherd,
when I speak,
Vailing a sudden eyelid with his hard
'Dim Saesneg' passes, wroth at things
of old—
No fault of mine. Had he God's word
in Welsh
He might be kindlier: happily come the
day!

Not least art thou, thou little Bethle-
hem
In Judah, for in thee the Lord was born;
Nor thou in Britain, little Lutterworth,
Least, for in thee the word was born again.

Heaven - sweet Evangel, ever - living
    word,
Who whilome spakest to the South in
    Greek
About the soft Mediterranean shores,
And then in Latin to the Latin crowd,
As good need was—thou hast come to
    talk our isle.
Hereafter thou, fulfilling Pentecost,
Must learn to use the tongues of all the
    world.
Yet art thou thine own witness that thou
    bringest
Not peace, a sword, a fire.
                    What did he say,
My frighted Wiclif-preacher whom I
    crost
In flying hither? that one night a crowd
Throng'd the waste field about the city
    gates:
The king was on them suddenly with a
    host.
Why there? they came to hear their
    preacher.   Then
Some cried on Cobham, on the good
    Lord Cobham;
Ay, for they love me ! but the king—nor
    voice
Nor finger raised against him—took and
    hang'd,
Took, hang'd and burnt—how many—
    thirty-nine—
Call'd it rebellion—hang'd, poor friends,
    as rebels
And burn'd alive as heretics ! for your
    Priest
Labels—to take the king along with
    him—
All heresy, treason: but to call men
    traitors
May make men traitors.
                    Rose of Lancaster,
Red in thy birth, redder with household
    war,
Now reddest with the blood of holy men,
Redder to be, red rose of Lancaster—
If somewhere in the North, as Rumour
    sang
Fluttering the hawks of this crown-lust-
    ing line—

By firth and loch thy silver sister grow,[1]
That were my rose, there my allegiance
    due.
Self-starved, they say — nay, murder'd,
    doubtless dead.
So to this king I cleaved : my friend was
    he,
Once my fast friend : I would have given
    my life
To help his own from scathe, a thousand
    lives
To save his soul.   He might have come
    to learn
Our Wiclif's learning : but the worldly
    Priests
Who fear the king's hard common-sense
    should find
What rotten piles uphold their mason-
    work,
Urge him to foreign war.   O had he
    will'd
I might have stricken a lusty stroke for
    him,
But he would not ; far liever led my
    friend
Back to the pure and universal church,
But he would not : whether that heirless
    flaw
In his throne's title make him feel so
    frail,
He leans on Antichrist ; or that his mind,
So quick, so capable in soldiership,
In matters of the faith, alas the while !
More worth than all the kingdoms of
    this world,
Runs in the rut, a coward to the Priest.

    Burnt—good Sir Roger Acton, my
        dear friend !
Burnt too, my faithful preacher, Beverley!
Lord give thou power to thy two wit-
    nesses !
Lest the false faith make merry over
    them !
Two—nay but thirty-nine have risen and
    stand,
Dark with the smoke of human sacrifice,
Before thy light, and cry continually—
Cry—against whom ?

            [1] Richard II.

Him, who should bear the sword
Of Justice—what! the kingly, kindly boy;
Who took the world so easily heretofore,
My boon companion, tavern-fellow—him
Who gibed and japed—in many a merry
    tale
That shook our sides—at Pardoners,
    Summoners,
Friars, absolution-sellers, monkeries
And nunneries, when the wild hour and
    the wine
Had set the wits aflame.
              Harry of Monmouth,
Or Amurath of the East?
                  Better to sink
Thy fleurs-de-lys in slime again, and fling
Thy royalty back into the riotous fits
Of wine and harlotry—thy shame, and
    mine,
Thy comrade—than to persecute the
    Lord,
And play the Saul that never will be Paul.

Burnt, burnt! and while this mitred
    Arundel
Dooms our unlicensed preacher to the
    flame,
The mitre-sanction'd harlot draws his
    clerks
Into the suburb—their hard celibacy,
Sworn to be veriest ice of pureness, molten
Into adulterous living, or such crimes
As holy Paul—a shame to speak of
    them—
Among the heathen—
              Sanctuary granted
To bandit, thief, assassin—yea to him
Who hacks his mother's throat—denied
    to him,
Who finds the Saviour in his mother
    tongue.
The Gospel, the Priest's pearl, flung
    down to swine—
The swine, lay-men, lay-women, who
    will come,
God willing, to outlearn the filthy friar.
Ah rather, Lord, than that thy Gospel,
    meant
To course and range thro' all the world,
    should be

Tether'd to these dead pillars of the
    Church—
Rather than so, if thou wilt have it so,
Burst vein, snap sinew, and crack heart,
    and life
Pass in the fire of Babylon! but how
    long,
O Lord, how long!
           My friend should meet me here
Here is the copse, the fountain and—a
    Cross!
To thee, dead wood, I bow not head no
    knees.
Rather to thee, green boscage, work of
    God,
Black holly, and white-flower'd wayfar-
    ing-tree!
Rather to thee, thou living water, drawn
By this good Wiclif mountain down from
    heaven,
And speaking clearly in thy native
    tongue—
No Latin—He that thirsteth, come and
    drink!

Eh! how I anger'd Arundel asking me
To worship Holy Cross! I spread mine
    arms,
God's work, I said, a cross of flesh and
    blood
And holier. That was heresy. (My good
    friend
By this time should be with me.)
    'Images?'
'Bury them as God's truer images
Are daily buried.' 'Heresy.—Penance?'
    'Fast,
Hairshirt and scourge—nay, let a man
    repent,
Do penance in his heart, God hears him.'
    'Heresy—
Not shriven, not saved?' 'What profits
    an ill Priest
Between me and my God? I would not
    spurn
Good counsel of good friends, but shrive
    myself
No, not to an Apostle.' 'Heresy.'
(My friend is long in coming.) 'Pil-
    grimages?'

'Drink, bagpipes, revelling, devil's-
    dances, vice.
The poor man's money gone to fat the
    friar.
Who reads of begging saints in Scripture?'
    —'Heresy'—
(Hath he been here—not found me—gone
    again?
Have I mislearnt our place of meeting?)
    'Bread—
Bread left after the blessing?' how they
    stared,
That was their main test-question—
    glared at me!
'He veil'd Himself in flesh, and now He
    veils
His flesh in bread, body and bread
    together.'
Then rose the howl of all the cassock'd
    wolves,
'No bread, no bread. God's body!'
    Archbishop, Bishop,
Priors, Canons, Friars, bellringers,
    Parish-clerks—
'No bread, no bread!'—'Authority of
    the Church,
Power of the keys!'—Then I, God help
    me, I
So mock'd, so spurn'd, so baited two
    whole days—
I lost myself and fell from evenness,
And rail'd at all the Popes, that ever since
Sylvester shed the venom of world-wealth
Into the church, had only prov'n them-
    selves
Poisoners, murderers. Well—God par-
    don all—
Me, them, and all the world—yea, that
    proud Priest,
That mock-meek mouth of utter Anti-
    christ,
That traitor to King Richard and the
    truth,
Who rose and doom'd me to the fire.
                                Amen!
Nay, I can burn, so that the Lord of life
Be by me in my death.
                    Those three! the fourth
Was like the Son of God! Not burnt
    were they.

On *them* the smell of burning had not
    past.
That was a miracle to convert the king.
These Pharisees, this Caiaphas-Arundel
What miracle could turn? *He* here
    again,
He thwarting their traditions of Him-
    self,
He would be found a heretic to Himself,
And doom'd to burn alive.
                        So, caught, I burn.
Burn? heathen men have borne as much
    as this,
For freedom, or the sake of those they
    loved,
Or some less cause, some cause far less
    than mine;
For every other cause is less than mine.
The moth will singe her wings, and
    singed return,
Her love of light quenching her fear of
    pain—
How now, my soul, we do not heed the
    fire?
Faint-hearted? tut!—faint-stomach'd!
    faint as I am,
God willing, I will burn for Him.
                                Who comes?
A thousand marks are set upon my
    head.
Friend?—foe perhaps—a tussle for it
    then!
Nay, but my friend. Thou art so well
    disguised,
I knew thee not. Hast thou brought
    bread with thee?
I have not broken bread for fifty hours.
None? I am damn'd already by the
    Priest
For holding there was bread where bread
    was none—
No bread. My friends await me yonder?
    Yes.
Lead on then. *Up* the mountain? Is
    it far?
Not far. Climb first and reach me down
    thy hand.
I am not like to die for lack of bread,
For I must live to testify by fire.[1]

---

[1] He was burnt on Christmas Day, 1417.

COLUMBUS.

CHAINS, my good lord : in your raised
    brows I read
Some wonder at our chamber ornaments.
We brought this iron from our isles of
    gold.

Does the king know you deign to visit
    him
Whom once he rose from off his throne
    to greet
Before his people, like his brother king ?
I saw your face that morning in the crowd.

At Barcelona—tho' you were not then
So bearded. Yes. The city deck'd
    herself
To meet me, roar'd my name ; the king,
    the queen
Bad me be seated, speak, and tell them all
The story of my voyage, and while I
    spoke
The crowd's roar fell as at the ' Peace,
    be still !'
And when I ceased to speak, the king,
    the queen,
Sank from their thrones, and melted into
    tears,
And knelt, and lifted hand and heart and
    voice
In praise to God who led me thro' the
    waste.
And then the great ' Laudamus ' rose to
    heaven.

Chains for the Admiral of the Ocean !
    chains
For him who gave a new heaven, a new
    earth,
As holy John had prophesied of me,
Gave glory and more empire to the kings
Of Spain than all their battles ! chains
    for him
Who push'd his prows into the setting sun,
And made West East, and sail'd the
    Dragon's mouth,
And came upon the Mountain of the
    World,
And saw the rivers roll from Paradise !

Chains ! we are Admirals of the Ocean,
    we,
We and our sons for ever. Ferdinand
Hath sign'd it and our Holy Catholic
    queen—
Of the Ocean—of the Indies—Admirals
    we—
Our title, which we never mean to yield,
Our guerdon not alone for what we did,
But our amends for all we might have
    done—
The vast occasion of our stronger life—
Eighteen long years of waste, seven in
    your Spain,
Lost, showing courts and kings a truth
    the babe
Will suck in with his milk hereafter—
    earth
A sphere.

Were *you* at Salamanca ? No.
We fronted there the learning of all
    Spain,
All their cosmogonies, their astronomies :
Guess - work *they* guess'd it, but the
    golden guess
Is morning-star to the full round of truth.
No guess-work ! I was certain of my goal ;
Some thought it heresy, but that would
    not hold.
King David call'd the heavens a hide, a
    tent
Spread over earth, and so this earth was
    flat :
Some cited old Lactantius : could it be
That trees grew downward, rain fell up-
    ward, men
Walk'd like the fly on ceilings ? and be-
    sides,
The great Augustine wrote that none
    could breathe
Within the zone of heat ; so might there
    be
Two Adams, two mankinds, and that
    was clean
Against God's word : thus was I beaten
    back,
And chiefly to my sorrow by the Church,
And thought to turn my face from Spain,
    appeal

Once more to France or England; but
	our Queen
Recall'd me, for at last their Highnesses
Were half-assured this earth might be a
	sphere.

All glory to the all-blessed Trinity,
All glory to the mother of our Lord,
And Holy Church, from whom I never
	swerved
Not even by one hair's-breadth of heresy,
I have accomplish'd what I came to do.

Not yet—not all—last night a dream—
	I sail'd
On my first voyage, harass'd by the frights
Of my first crew, their curses and their
	groans.
The great flame-banner borne by Tene-
	riffe,
The compass, like an old friend false at last
In our most need, appall'd them, and the
	wind
Still westward, and the weedy seas—at
	length
The landbird, and the branch with berries
	on it,
The carven staff—and last the light, the
	light
On Guanahani! but I changed the name;
San Salvador I call'd it; and the light
Grew as I gazed, and brought out a broad
	sky
Of dawning over—not those alien palms,
The marvel of that fair new nature—not
That Indian isle, but our most ancient
	East
Moriah with Jerusalem; and I saw
The glory of the Lord flash up, and beat
Thro' all the homely town from jasper,
	sapphire,
Chalcedony, emerald, sardonyx, sardius,
Chrysolite, beryl, topaz, chrysoprase,
Jacynth, and amethyst—and those twelve
	gates,
Pearl—and I woke, and thought—death
	—I shall die—
I am written in the Lamb's own Book
	of Life
To walk within the glory of the Lord

Sunless and moonless, utter light—but
	no!
The Lord had sent this bright, strange
	dream to me
To mind me of the secret vow I made
When Spain was waging war against
	the Moor—
I strove myself with Spain against the
	Moor.
There came two voices from the Sepul-
	chre,
Two friars crying that if Spain should
	oust
The Moslem from her limit, he, the fierce
Soldan of Egypt, would break down and
	raze
The blessed tomb of Christ; whereon I
	vow'd
That, if our Princes harken'd to my
	prayer,
Whatever wealth I brought from that new
	world
Should, in this old, be consecrate to lead
A new crusade against the Saracen,
And free the Holy Sepulchre from thrall.

Gold? I had brought your Princes
	gold enough
If left alone! Being but a Genovese,
I am handled worse than had I been a
	Moor,
And breach'd the belting wall of Cambalu,
And given the Great Khan's palaces to
	the Moor,
Or clutch'd the sacred crown of Prester
	John,
And cast it to the Moor: but *had* I
	brought
From Solomon's now-recover'd Ophir all
The gold that Solomon's navies carried
	home,
Would that have gilded *me*? Blue blood
	of Spain,
Tho' quartering your own royal arms of
	Spain,
I have not: blue blood and black blood
	of Spain,
The noble and the convict of Castile,
Howl'd me from Hispaniola; for you
	know

The flies at home, that ever swarm about
And cloud the highest heads, and murmur
  down
Truth in the distance—these outbuzz'd
  me so
That even our prudent king, our righteous
  queen—
I pray'd them being so calumniated
They would commission one of weight
  and worth
To judge between my slander'd self and
  me—
Fonseca my main enemy at their court,
They sent me out *his* tool, Bovadilla, one
As ignorant and impolitic as a beast—
Blockish irreverence, brainless greed—
  who sack'd
My dwelling, seized upon my papers,
  loosed
My captives, feed the rebels of the crown,
Sold the crown-farms for all but nothing,
  gave
All but free leave for all to work the
  mines,
Drove me and my good brothers home in
  chains,
And gathering ruthless gold—a single
  piece
Weigh'd nigh four thousand Castillanos
  —so
They tell me—weigh'd him down into the
  abysm—
The hurricane of the latitude on him fell,
The seas of our discovering over-roll
Him and his gold ; the frailer caravel,
With what was mine, came happily to the
  shore.
There was a glimmering of God's hand.

                    And God
Hath more than glimmer'd on me. O
  my lord,
I swear to you I heard his voice between
The thunders in the black Veragua
  nights,
'O soul of little faith, slow to believe !
Have I not been about thee from thy
  birth ?
Given thee the keys of the great Ocean-
  sea ?

Set thee in light till time shall be no
  more ?
Is it I who have deceived thee or the
  world ?
Endure ! thou hast done so well for men,
  that men
Cry out against thee : was it otherwise
With mine own Son ?'

                And more than once in days
Of doubt and cloud and storm, when
  drowning hope
Sank all but out of sight, I heard his
  voice,
'Be not cast down. I lead thee by the
  hand,
Fear not.' And I shall hear his voice
  again—
I know that he has led me all my life,
I am not yet too old to work his will—
His voice again.

                Still for all that, my lord,
I lying here bedridden and alone,
Cast off, put by, scouted by court and
  king—
The first discoverer starves—his followers,
  all
Flower into fortune—our world's way—
  and I,
Without a roof that I can call mine own,
With scarce a coin to buy a meal withal,
And seeing what a door for scoundrel
  scum
I open'd to the West, thro' which the lust,
Villany, violence, avarice, of your Spain
Pour'd in on all those happy naked isles—
Their kindly native princes slain or slaved,
Their wives and children Spanish concu-
  bines,
Their innocent hospitalities quench'd in
  blood,
Some dead of hunger, some beneath the
  scourge,
Some over-labour'd, some by their own
  hands,—
Yea, the dear mothers, crazing Nature,
  kill
Their babies at the breast for hate of
  Spain—

Ah God, the harmless people whom we
      found
In Hispaniola's island-Paradise !
Who took us for the very Gods from
      Heaven,
And we have sent them very fiends from
      Hell ;
And I myself, myself not blameless, I
Could sometimes wish I had never led
      the way.

      Only the ghost of our great Catholic
            Queen
Smiles on me, saying, 'Be thou com-
      forted !
This creedless people will be brought to
      Christ
And own the holy governance of Rome.'

      But who could dream that we, who
            bore the Cross
Thither, were excommunicated there,
For curbing crimes that scandalised the
      Cross,
By him, the Catalonian Minorite,
Rome's Vicar in our Indies ? who believe
These hard memorials of our truth to
      Spain
Clung closer to us for a longer term
Than any friend of ours at Court ? and yet
Pardon—too harsh, unjust.   I am rack'd
      with pains.

      You see that I have hung them by my
            bed,
And I will have them buried in my grave.

      Sir, in that flight of ages which are
            God's
Own voice to justify the dead—perchance
Spain once the most chivalric race on
      earth,
Spain then the mightiest, wealthiest realm
      on earth,
So made by me, may seek to unbury me,
To lay me in some shrine of this old Spain,
Or in that vaster Spain I leave to Spain.
Then some one standing by my grave
      will say,
'Behold the bones of Christopher
      Colon '—

'Ay, but the chains, what do *they* mean
      —the chains ?'—
I sorrow for that kindly child of Spain
Who then will have to answer, 'These
      same chains
Bound these same bones back thro' the
      Atlantic sea,
Which he unchain'd for all the world to
      come.'

      O Queen of Heaven who seest the souls
            in Hell
And purgatory, I suffer all as much
As they do—for the moment.   Stay, my
      son
Is here anon : my son will speak for me
Ablier than I can in these spasms that
      grind
Bone against bone.   You will not.   One
      last word.

      You move about the Court, I pray you
            tell
King Ferdinand who plays with me, that
      one,
Whose life has been no play with him
      and his
Hidalgos —shipwrecks, famines, fevers,
      fights,
Mutinies, treacheries—wink'd at, and
      condoned—
That I am loyal to him till the death,
And ready—tho' our Holy Catholic
      Queen,
Who fain had pledged her jewels on my
      first voyage,
Whose hope was mine to spread the
      Catholic faith,
Who wept with me when I return'd in
      chains,
Who sits beside the blessed Virgin now,
To whom I send my prayer by night and
      day—
She is gone—but you will tell the King,
      that I,
Rack'd as I am with gout, and wrench'd
      with pains
Gain'd in the service of His Highness,
      yet
Am ready to sail forth on one last voyage.

And readier, if the King would hear, to
lead
One last crusade against the Saracen,
And save the Holy Sepulchre from
thrall.

Going? I am old and slighted : you
have dared
Somewhat perhaps in coming? my poor
thanks !
I am but an alien and a Genovese.

THE VOYAGE OF MAELDUNE.

(FOUNDED ON AN IRISH LEGEND.
A.D. 700.)

I.

I WAS the chief of the race—he had
stricken my father dead—
But I gather'd my fellows together, I
swore I would strike off his head.
Each of them look'd like a king, and was
noble in birth as in worth,
And each of them boasted he sprang from
the oldest race upon earth.
Each was as brave in the fight as the
bravest hero of song,
And each of them liefer had died than
have done one another a wrong.
He lived on an isle in the ocean—we
sail'd on a Friday morn—
He that had slain my father the day
before I was born.

II.

And we came to the isle in the ocean,
and there on the shore was he.
But a sudden blast blew us out and away
thro' a boundless sea.

III.

And we came to the Silent Isle that we
never had touch'd at before,
Where a silent ocean always broke on a
silent shore,
And the brooks glitter'd on in the light
without sound, and the long
waterfalls

Pour'd in a thunderless plunge to the base
of the mountain walls,
And the poplar and cypress unshaken by
storm flourish'd up beyond sight,
And the pine shot aloft from the crag to
an unbelievable height,
And high in the heaven above it there
flicker'd a songless lark,
And the cock couldn't crow, and the bull
couldn't low, and the dog couldn't
bark.
And round it we went, and thro' it, but
never a murmur, a breath—
It was all of it fair as life, it was all of it
quiet as death,
And we hated the beautiful Isle, for
whenever we strove to speak
Our voices were thinner and fainter than
any flittermouse-shriek ;
And the men that were mighty of tongue
and could raise such a battle-cry
That a hundred who heard it would rush
on a thousand lances and die—
O they to be dumb'd by the charm !—so
fluster'd with anger were they
They almost fell on each other ; but after
we sail'd away.

IV.

And we came to the Isle of Shouting, we
landed, a score of wild birds
Cried from the topmost summit with
human voices and words ;
Once in an hour they cried, and whenever
their voices peal'd
The steer fell down at the plow and the
harvest died from the field,
And the men dropt dead in the valleys
and half of the cattle went lame,
And the roof sank in on the hearth, and
the dwelling broke into flame ;
And the shouting of these wild birds ran
into the hearts of my crew,
Till they shouted along with the shouting and seized one another and
slew ;
But I drew them the one from the other ;
I saw that we could not stay,
And we left the dead to the birds and we
sail'd with our wounded away.

V.

And we came to the Isle of Flowers : their breath met us out on the seas,
For the Spring and the middle Summer sat each on the lap of the breeze ;
And the red passion-flower to the cliffs, and the dark-blue clematis, clung,
And starr'd with a myriad blossom the long convolvulus hung ;
And the topmost spire of the mountain was lilies in lieu of snow,
And the lilies like glaciers winded down, running out below
Thro' the fire of the tulip and poppy, the blaze of gorse, and the blush
Of millions of roses that sprang without leaf or a thorn from the bush ;
And the whole isle-side flashing down from the peak without ever a tree
Swept like a torrent of gems from the sky to the blue of the sea ;
And we roll'd upon capes of crocus and vaunted our kith and our kin,
And we wallow'd in beds of lilies, and chanted the triumph of Finn,
Till each like a golden image was pollen'd from head to feet
And each was as dry as a cricket, with thirst in the middle-day heat.
Blossom and blossom, and promise of blossom, but never a fruit !
And we hated the Flowering Isle, as we hated the isle that was mute,
And we tore up the flowers by the million and flung them in bight and bay,
And we left but a naked rock, and in anger we sail'd away.

VI.

And we came to the Isle of Fruits : all round from the cliffs and the capes,
Purple or amber, dangled a hundred fathom of grapes,
And the warm melon lay like a little sun on the tawny sand,
And the fig ran up from the beach and rioted over the land,
And the mountain arose like a jewell'd throne thro' the fragrant air,

Glowing with all-colour'd plums and with golden masses of pear,
And the crimson and scarlet of berries that flamed upon bine and vine,
But in every berry and fruit was the poisonous pleasure of wine ;
And the peak of the mountain was apples, the hugest that ever were seen,
And they prest, as they grew, on each other, with hardly a leaflet between,
And all of them redder than rosiest health or than utterest shame,
And setting, when Even descended, the very sunset aflame ;
And we stay'd three days, and we gorged and we madden'd, till every one drew
His sword on his fellow to slay him, and ever they struck and they slew ;
And myself, I had eaten but sparely, and fought till I sunder'd the fray,
Then I bad them remember my father's death, and we sail'd away.

VII.

And we came to the Isle of Fire : we were lured by the light from afar,
For the peak sent up one league of fire to the Northern Star ;
Lured by the glare and the blare, but scarcely could stand upright,
For the whole isle shudder'd and shook like a man in a mortal affright ;
We were giddy besides with the fruits we had gorged, and so crazed that at last
There were some leap'd into the fire ; and away we sail'd, and we past
Over that undersea isle, where the water is clearer than air :
Down we look'd : what a garden ! O bliss, what a Paradise there !
Towers of a happier time, low down in a rainbow deep
Silent palaces, quiet fields of eternal sleep !
And three of the gentlest and best of my people, whate'er I could say,
Plunged head down in the sea, and the Paradise trembled away.

VIII.

And we came to the Bounteous Isle, where
    the heavens lean low on the land,
And ever at dawn from the cloud glitter'd
    o'er us a sunbright hand,
Then it open'd and dropt at the side of
    each man, as he rose from his
    rest,
Bread enough for his need till the labour-
    less day dipt under the West ;
And we wander'd about it and thro' it.
    O never was time so good !
And we sang of the triumphs of Finn, and
    the boast of our ancient blood,
And we gazed at the wandering wave as
    we sat by the gurgle of springs,
And we chanted the songs of the Bards
    and the glories of fairy kings ;
But at length we began to be weary, to
    sigh, and to stretch and yawn,
Till we hated the Bounteous Isle and the
    sunbright hand of the dawn,
For there was not an enemy near, but the
    whole green Isle was our own,
And we took to playing at ball, and we
    took to throwing the stone,
And we took to playing at battle, but
    that was a perilous play,
For the passion of battle was in us, we
    slew and we sail'd away.

IX.

And we past to the Isle of Witches and
    heard their musical cry—
'Come to us, O come, come' in the
    stormy red of a sky
Dashing the fires and the shadows of
    dawn on the beautiful shapes,
For a wild witch naked as heaven stood
    on each of the loftiest capes,
And a hundred ranged on the rock like
    white sea-birds in a row,
And a hundred gamboll'd and pranced
    on the wrecks in the sand below,
And a hundred splash'd from the ledges,
    and bosom'd the burst of the
    spray,
But I knew we should fall on each other,
    and hastily sail'd away.

X.

And we came in an evil time to the Isle
    of the Double Towers,
One was of smooth-cut stone, one carved
    all over with flowers,
But an earthquake always moved in the
    hollows under the dells,
And they shock'd on each other and butted
    each other with clashing of bells,
And the daws flew out of the Towers and
    jangled and wrangled in vain,
And the clash and boom of the bells rang
    into the heart and the brain,
Till the passion of battle was on us, and
    all took sides with the Towers,
There were some for the clean-cut stone,
    there were more for the carven
    flowers,
And the wrathful thunder of God peal'd
    over us all the day,
For the one half slew the other, and after
    we sail'd away.

XI.

And we came to the Isle of a Saint who
    had sail'd with St. Brendan of
    yore,
He had lived ever since on the Isle and
    his winters were fifteen score,
And his voice was low as from other
    worlds, and his eyes were sweet,
And his white hair sank to his heels and
    his white beard fell to his feet,
And he spake to me, 'O Maeldune, let
    be this purpose of thine !
Remember the words of the Lord when
    he told us "Vengeance is mine !"
His fathers have slain thy fathers in war
    or in single strife,
Thy fathers have slain his fathers, each
    taken a life for a life,
Thy father had slain his father, how long
    shall the murder last ?
Go back to the Isle of Finn and suffer
    the Past to be Past.'
And we kiss'd the fringe of his beard and
    we pray'd as we heard him pray,
And the Holy man he assoil'd us, and
    sadly we sail'd away.

XII.

And we came to the Isle we were blown
    from, and there on the shore was he,
The man that had slain my father. I
    saw him and let him be.
O weary was I of the travel, the trouble,
    the strife and the sin,
When I landed again, with a tithe of my
    men, on the Isle of Finn.

DE PROFUNDIS:

THE TWO GREETINGS.

To H. T. August 11, 1852.

I.

Out of the deep, my child, out of the
    deep,
Where all that was to be, in all that was,
Whirl'd for a million æons thro' the vast
Waste dawn of multitudinous · eddying
    light—
Out of the deep, my child, out of the
    deep,
Thro' all this changing world of change-
    less law,
And every phase of ever-heightening life,
And nine long months of antenatal gloom,
With this last moon, this crescent—her
    dark orb
Touch'd with earth's light—thou comest,
    darling boy ;
Our own ; a babe in lineament and limb
Perfect, and prophet of the perfect man ;
Whose face and form are hers and mine
    in one,
Indissolubly married like our love ;
Live, and be happy in thyself, and serve
This mortal race thy kin so well, that men
May bless thee as we bless thee, O young
    life
Breaking with laughter from the dark ;
    and may
The fated channel where thy motion lives
Be prosperously shaped, and sway thy
    course
Along the years of haste and random youth
Unshatter'd ; then full-current thro' full
    man :

And last in kindly curves, with gentlest fall,
By quiet fields, a slowly-dying power,
To that last deep where we and thou are
    still.

II.

I.

Out of the deep, my child, out of the
    deep,
From that great deep, before our world
    begins,
Whereon the Spirit of God moves as he
    will—
Out of the deep, my child, out of the
    deep,
From that true world within the world
    we see,
Whereof our world is but the bounding
    shore—
Out of the deep, Spirit, out of the deep,
With this ninth moon, that sends the
    hidden sun
Down yon dark sea, thou comest, darling
    boy.

II.

For in the world, which is not ours, They
    said
' Let us make man ' and that which
    should be man,
From that one light no man can look upon,
Drew to this shore lit by the suns and
    moons
And all the shadows. O dear Spirit
    half-lost
In thine own shadow and this fleshly sign
That thou art thou—who wailest being
    born
And banish'd into mystery, and the pain
Of this divisible-indivisible world
Among the numerable-innumerable
Sun, sun, and sun, thro' finite - infinite
    space
In finite-infinite Time—our mortal veil
And shatter'd phantom of that infinite
    One,
Who made thee unconceivably Thyself
Out of His whole World-self and all in
    all—

Live thou ! and of the grain and husk,
    the grape
And ivyberry, choose ; and still depart
From death to death thro' life and life,
    and find
Nearer and ever nearer Him, who
    wrought
Not Matter, nor the finite-infinite,
But this main-miracle, that thou art thou,
With power on thine own act and on the
    world.

THE HUMAN CRY.

I.

HALLOWED be Thy name—Halleluiah !—
    Infinite Ideality !
    Immeasurable Reality !
    Infinite Personality !
Hallowed be Thy name—Halleluiah !

II.

We feel we are nothing—for all is Thou
    and in Thee ;
We feel we are something—*that* also has
    come from Thee ;
We know we are nothing—but Thou wilt
    help us to be.
Hallowed be Thy name—Halleluiah !

PREFATORY SONNET

TO THE 'NINETEENTH CENTURY.'

THOSE that of late had fleeted far and fast
To touch all shores, now leaving to the
    skill
Of others their old craft seaworthy still,
Have charter'd this ; where, mindful of
    the past,
Our true co-mates regather round the
    mast ;
Of diverse tongue, but with a common
    will
Here, in this roaring moon of daffodil
And crocus, to put forth and brave the
    blast ;
For some, descending from the sacred
    peak

Of hoar high-templed Faith, have leagued
    again
Their lot with ours to rove the world
    about ;
And some are wilder comrades, sworn to
    seek
If any golden harbour be for men
In seas of Death and sunless gulfs of
    Doubt.

TO THE REV. W. H. BROOK-FIELD.

BROOKS, for they call'd you so that knew
    you best,
Old Brooks, who loved so well to mouth
    my rhymes,
How oft we two have heard St. Mary's
    chimes !
How oft the Cantab supper, host and
    guest,
Would echo helpless laughter to your
    jest !
How oft with him we paced that walk of
    limes,
Him, the lost light of those dawn-golden
    times,
Who loved you well ! Now both are gone
    to rest.
You man of humorous-melancholy mark,
Dead of some inward agony—is it so ?
Our kindlier, trustier Jaques, past away !
I cannot laud this life, it looks so dark :
Σκιᾶς ὄναρ—dream of a shadow, go—
God bless you. I shall join you in a
    day.

MONTENEGRO.

THEY rose to where their sovran eagle
    sails,
They kept their faith, their freedom, on
    the height,
Chaste, frugal, savage, arm'd by day and
    night
Against the Turk ; whose inroad nowhere
    scales
Their headlong passes, but his footstep
    fails,

And red with blood the Crescent reels
    from fight
Before their dauntless hundreds, in prone
    flight
By thousands down the crags and thro'
    the vales.
O smallest among peoples! rough rock-
    throne
Of Freedom! warriors beating back the
    swarm
Of Turkish Islam for five hundred years,
Great Tsernogora! never since thine own
Black ridges drew the cloud and brake
    the storm
Has breathed a race of mightier moun-
    taineers.

TO VICTOR HUGO.

VICTOR in Drama, Victor in Romance,
Cloud-weaver of phantasmal hopes and
    fears,

French of the French, and Lord of human
    tears;
Child-lover; Bard whose fame-lit laurels
    glance
Darkening the wreaths of all that would
    advance,
Beyond our strait, their claim to be thy
    peers;
Weird Titan by thy winter weight of
    years
As yet unbroken, Stormy voice of
    France!
Who dost not love our England—so they
    say;
I know not—England, France, all man
    to be
Will make one people ere man's race be
    run:
And I, desiring that diviner day,
Yield thee full thanks for thy full
    courtesy
To younger England in the boy my son.

TRANSLATIONS, ETC.

BATTLE OF BRUNANBURH.

Constantinus, King of the Scots, after having
sworn allegiance to Athelstan, allied himself with
the Danes of Ireland under Anlaf, and invading
England, was defeated by Athelstan and his
brother Edmund with great slaughter at Brunanburh in the year 937.

I.

[1] ATHELSTAN King,
  Lord among Earls,
  Bracelet-bestower and
  Baron of Barons,
  He with his brother,
  Edmund Atheling,
  Gaining a lifelong
  Glory in battle,
  Slew with the sword-edge
  There by Brunanburh,

[1] I have more or less availed myself of my
son's prose translation of this poem in the *Con-
temporary Review* (November 1876).

  Brake the shield-wall,
  Hew'd the lindenwood,[2]
  Hack'd the battleshield,
Sons of Edward with hammer'd brands.

II.

  Theirs was a greatness
  Got from their Grandsires—
  Theirs that so often in
  Strife with their enemies
Struck for their hoards and their hearths
  and their homes.

III.

  Bow'd the spoiler,
  Bent the Scotsman,
  Fell the shipcrews
  Doom'd to the death.
All the field with blood of the fighters
  Flow'd, from when first the great
  Sun-star of morningtide,

[2] Shields of lindenwood.

Lamp of the Lord God
Lord everlasting,
Glode over earth till the glorious creature
Sank to his setting.

IV.

There lay many a man
Marr'd by the javelin,
Men of the Northland
Shot over shield.
There was the Scotsman
Weary of war.

V.

We the West-Saxons,
Long as the daylight
Lasted, in companies
Troubled the track of the host that we
hated,
Grimly with swords that were sharp from
the grindstone,
Fiercely we hack'd at the flyers before
us.

VI.

Mighty the Mercian,
Hard was his hand-play,
Sparing not any of
Those that with Anlaf,
Warriors over the
Weltering waters
Borne in the bark's-bosom,
Drew to this island:
Doom'd to the death.

VII.

Five young kings put asleep by the sword-
stroke,
Seven strong Earls of the army of Anlaf
Fell on the war-field, numberless numbers,
Shipmen and Scotsmen.

VIII.

Then the Norse leader,
Dire was his need of it,
Few were his following,
Fled to his warship:
Fleeted his vessel to sea with the king
in it,
Saving his life on the fallow flood.

IX.

Also the crafty one,
Constantinus,
Crept to his North again,
Hoar-headed hero !

X.

Slender warrant had
He to be proud of
The welcome of war-knives—
He that was reft of his
Folk and his friends that had
Fallen in conflict,
Leaving his son too
Lost in the carnage,
Mangled to morsels,
A youngster in war !

XI.

Slender reason had
He to be glad of
The clash of the war-glaive—
Traitor and trickster
And spurner of treaties—
He nor had Anlaf
With armies so broken
A reason for bragging
That they had the better
In perils of battle
On places of slaughter—
The struggle of standards,
The rush of the javelins,
The crash of the charges,[1]
The wielding of weapons—
The play that they play'd with
The children of Edward.

XII.

Then with their nail'd prows
Parted the Norsemen, a
Blood-redden'd relic of
Javelins over
The jarring breaker, the deep-
sea billow,
Shaping their way toward Dy-
flen[2] again,
Shamed in their souls.

[1] Lit. 'the gathering of men.'   [2] Dublin.

XIII.

Also the brethren,
King and Atheling,
Each in his glory,
Went to his own in his own West-Saxon-
land,
Glad of the war.

XIV.

Many a carcase they left to be carrion,
Many a livid one, many a sallow-skin—
Left for the white-tail'd eagle to tear it,
and
Left for the horny-nibb'd raven to rend
it, and
Gave to the garbaging war-hawk to gorge
it, and
That gray beast, the wolf of the weald.

XV.

Never had huger
Slaughter of heroes
Slain by the sword-edge—
Such as old writers
Have writ of in histories—
Hapt in this isle, since
Up from the East hither
Saxon and Angle from
Over the broad billow
Broke into Britain with
Haughty war-workers who
Harried the Welshman, when
Earls that were lured by the
Hunger of glory gat
Hold of the land.

ACHILLES OVER THE TRENCH.

ILIAD, xviii. 202.

So saying, light-foot Iris pass'd away.
Then rose Achilles dear to Zeus ; and
round
The warrior's puissant shoulders Pallas
flung
Her fringed ægis, and around his head
The glorious goddess wreath'd a golden
cloud,
And from it lighted an all-shining
flame.
As when a smoke from a city goes to
heaven
Far off from out an island girt by foes,
All day the men contend in grievous
war
From their own city, but with set of
sun
Their fires flame thickly, and aloft the
glare
Flies streaming, if perchance the neigh-
bours round
May see, and sail to help them in the
war ;
So from his head the splendour went to
heaven.
From wall to dyke he stept, he stood,
nor join'd
The Achæans — honouring his wise
mother's word—
There standing, shouted, and Pallas far
away
Call'd ; and a boundless panic shook the
foe.
For like the clear voice when a trumpet
shrills,
Blown by the fierce beleaguerers of a
town,
So rang the clear voice of Æakidês ;
And when the brazen cry of Æakidês
Was heard among the Trojans, all their
hearts
Were troubled, and the full-maned horses
whirl'd
The chariots backward, knowing griefs
at hand ;
And sheer-astounded were the charioteers
To see the dread, unweariable fire
That always o'er the great Peleion's
head
Burn'd, for the bright-eyed goddess made
it burn.
Thrice from the dyke he sent his mighty
shout,
Thrice backward reel'd the Trojans and
allies ;
And there and then twelve of their noblest
died
Among their spears and chariots.

TO PRINCESS FREDERICA
ON HER MARRIAGE.

O you that were eyes and light to the
    King till he past away
From the darkness of life—
He saw not his daughter—he blest her :
    the blind King sees you to-day,
He blesses the wife.

SIR JOHN FRANKLIN.

ON THE CENOTAPH IN WESTMINSTER
ABBEY.

Not here ! the white North has thy
    bones ; and thou,
    Heroic sailor-soul,
Art passing on thine happier voyage now
    Toward no earthly pole.

TO DANTE.

(WRITTEN AT REQUEST OF THE
FLORENTINES.)

King, that hast reign'd six hundred years,
    and grown
In power, and ever growest, since thine
    own
Fair Florence honouring thy nativity,
Thy Florence now the crown of Italy,
Hath sought the tribute of a verse from
    me,
I, wearing but the garland of a day,
Cast at thy feet one flower that fades
    away.

TIRESIAS

AND OTHER POEMS.

TO MY GOOD FRIEND
ROBERT BROWNING,
WHOSE GENIUS AND GENIALITY WILL BEST APPRECIATE WHAT MAY BE BEST,
AND MAKE MOST ALLOWANCE FOR WHAT MAY BE WORST,
THIS VOLUME IS AFFECTIONATELY DEDICATED.

TO E. FITZGERALD.

Old Fitz, who from your suburb grange,
    Where once I tarried for a while,
Glance at the wheeling Orb of change,
    And greet it with a kindly smile ;
Whom yet I see as there you sit
    Beneath your sheltering garden-tree,
And while your doves about you flit,
    And plant on shoulder, hand and knee,
Or on your head their rosy feet,
    As if they knew your diet spares
Whatever moved in that full sheet
    Let down to Peter at his prayers ;
Who live on milk and meal and grass ;
    And once for ten long weeks I tried
Your table of Pythagoras,

And seem'd at first 'a thing enskied'
    (As Shakespeare has it) airy-light
    To float above the ways of men,
Then fell from that half-spiritual height
    Chill'd, till I tasted flesh again
One night when earth was winter-black,
    And all the heavens flash'd in frost ;
And on me, half-asleep, came back
    That wholesome heat the blood had lost,
And set me climbing icy capes
    And glaciers, over which there roll'd
To meet me long-arm'd vines with grapes
    Of Eshcol hugeness ; for the cold
Without, and warmth within me, wrought
    To mould the dream ; but none can say
That Lenten fare makes Lenten thought,
    Who reads your golden Eastern lay,

Than which I know no version done
   In English more divinely well ;
A planet equal to the sun
   Which cast it, that large infidel
Your Omar ; and your Omar drew
   Full-handed plaudits from our best
In modern letters, and from two,
   Old friends outvaluing all the rest,
Two voices heard on earth no more ;
   But we old friends are still alive,
And I am nearing seventy-four,
   While you have touch'd at seventy-five,
And so I send a birthday line
   Of greeting ; and my son, who dipt
In some forgotten book of mine
   With sallow scraps of manuscript,
And dating many a year ago,
   Has hit on this, which you will take
My Fitz, and welcome, as I know
   Less for its own than for the sake
Of one recalling gracious times,
   When, in our younger London days,
You found some merit in my rhymes,
   And I more pleasure in your praise.

TIRESIAS.

I WISH I were as in the years of old,
While yet the blessed daylight made itself
Ruddy thro' both the roofs of sight, and
   woke
These eyes, now dull, but then so keen
   to seek
The meanings ambush'd under all they
   saw,
The flight of birds, the flame of sacrifice,
What omens may foreshadow fate to man
And woman, and the secret of the Gods.
   My son, the Gods, despite of human
     prayer,
Are slower to forgive than human kings.
The great God, Arês, burns in anger still
Against the guiltless heirs of him from
   Tyre,
Our Cadmus, out of whom thou art,
   who found
Beside the springs of Dircê, smote, and
   still'd
Thro' all its folds the multitudinous beast,
The dragon, which our trembling fathers
   call'd

The God's own son.
        A tale, that told to me,
When but thine age, by age as winter-
   white
As mine is now, amazed, but made me
   yearn
For larger glimpses of that more than man
Which rolls the heavens, and lifts, and
   lays the deep,
Yet loves and hates with mortal hates
   and loves,
And moves unseen among the ways of
   men.
   Then, in my wanderings all the lands
     that lie
Subjected to the Heliconian ridge
Have heard this footstep fall, altho' my
   wont
Was more to scale the highest of the
   heights
With some strange hope to see the nearer
   God.
   One naked peak—the sister of the sun
Would climb from out the dark, and
   linger there
To silver all the valleys with her shafts—
There once, but long ago, five-fold thy
   term
Of years, I lay ; the winds were dead
   for heat ;
The noonday crag made the hand burn ;
   and sick
For shadow—not one bush was near—
   I rose
Following a torrent till its myriad falls
Found silence in the hollows underneath.
   There in a secret olive-glade I saw
Pallas Athene climbing from the bath
In anger ; yet one glittering foot disturb'd
The lucid well ; one snowy knee was prest
Against the margin flowers ; a dreadful
   light
Came from her golden hair, her golden
   helm
And all her golden armour on the grass,
And from her virgin breast, and virgin eyes
Remaining fixt on mine, till mine grew
   dark
For ever, and I heard a voice that said
' Henceforth be blind, for thou hast seen
   too much,

And speak the truth that no man may
    believe.'
  Son, in the hidden world of sight, that
    lives
Behind this darkness, I behold her still,
Beyond all work of those who carve the
    stone,
Beyond all dreams of Godlike woman-
    hood,
Ineffable beauty, out of whom, at a
    glance,
And as it were, perforce, upon me flash'd
The power of prophesying—but to me
No power—so chain'd and coupled with
    the curse
Of blindness and their unbelief, who
    heard
And heard not, when I spake of famine,
    plague,
Shrine-shattering earthquake, fire, flood,
    thunderbolt,
And angers of the Gods for evil done
And expiation lack'd—no power on Fate,
Theirs, or mine own! for when the
    crowd would roar
For blood, for war, whose issue was their
    doom,
To cast wise words among the multitude
Was flinging fruit to lions; nor, in
    hours
Of civil outbreak, when I knew the twain
Would each waste each, and bring on
    both the yoke
Of stronger states, was mine the voice to
    curb
The madness of our cities and their
    kings.
  Who ever turn'd upon his heel to hear
My warning that the tyranny of one
Was prelude to the tyranny of all?
My counsel that the tyranny of all
Led backward to the tyranny of one?
  This power hath work'd no good to
    aught that lives,
And these blind hands were useless in
    their wars.
O therefore that the unfulfill'd desire,
The grief for ever born from griefs to be,
The boundless yearning of the Prophet's
    heart—

Could *that* stand forth, and like a statue,
    rear'd
To some great citizen, win all praise
    from all
Who past it, saying, 'That was he!'
             In vain!
Virtue must shape itself in deed, and
    those
Whom weakness or necessity have cramp'd
Within themselves, immerging, each, his
    urn
In his own well, draw solace as he may.
  Menœceus, thou hast eyes, and I can
    hear
Too plainly what full tides of onset sap
Our seven high gates, and what a weight
    of war
Rides on those ringing axles! jingle of
    bits,
Shouts, arrows, tramp of the hornfooted
    horse
That grind the glebe to powder! Stony
    showers
Of that ear-stunning hail of Arês crash
Along the sounding walls. Above,
    below,
Shock after shock, the song-built towers
    and gates
Reel, bruised and butted with the
    shuddering
War-thunder of iron rams; and from
    within
The city comes a murmur void of joy,
Lest she be taken captive—maidens,
    wives,
And mothers with their babblers of the
    dawn,
And oldest age in shadow from the
    night,
Falling about their shrines before their
    Gods,
And wailing 'Save us.'
             And they wail to thee!
These eyeless eyes, that cannot see thine
    own,
See this, that only in thy virtue lies
The saving of our Thebes; for, yester-
    night,
To me, the great God Arês, whose one
    bliss

Is war, and human sacrifice—himself
Blood-red from battle, spear and helmet
 tipt
With stormy light as on a mast at sea,
Stood out before a darkness, crying
 'Thebes,
Thy Thebes shall fall and perish, for I
 loathe
The seed of Cadmus—yet if one of these
By his own hand—if one of these——'
                                    My son,
No sound is breathed so potent to
 coerce,
And to conciliate, as their names who
 dare
For that sweet mother land which gave
 them birth
Nobly to do, nobly to die.   Their names,
Graven on memorial columns, are a
 song
Heard in the future ; few, but more than
 wall
And rampart, their examples reach a
 hand
Far thro' all years, and everywhere they
 meet
And kindle generous purpose, and the
 strength
To mould it into action pure as theirs.
   Fairer thy fate than mine, if life's best
 end
Be to end well ! and thou refusing this,
Unvenerable will thy memory be
While men shall move the lips : but if
 thou dare—
Thou, one of these, the race of Cadmus
 —then
No stone is fitted in yon marble girth
Whose echo shall not tongue thy glorious
 doom,
Nor in this pavement but shall ring thy
 name
To every hoof that clangs it, and the
 springs
Of Dircê laving yonder battle-plain,
Heard from the roofs by night, will mur-
 mur thee
To thine own Thebes, while Thebes thro'
 thee shall stand
Firm-based with all her Gods.

                            The Dragon's cave
Half hid, they tell me, now in flowing
 vines—
Where once he dwelt and whence he
 roll'd himself
At dead of night—thou knowest, and
 that smooth rock
Before it, altar-fashion'd, where of late
The woman-breasted Sphinx, with wings
 drawn back,
Folded her lion paws, and look'd to
 Thebes.
There blanch the bones of whom she
 slew, and these
Mixt with her own, because the fierce
 beast found
A wiser than herself, and dash'd herself
Dead in her rage : but thou art wise
 enough,
Tho' young, to love thy wiser, blunt the
 curse
Of Pallas, hear, and tho' I speak the
 truth
Believe I speak it, let thine own hand
 strike
Thy youthful pulses into rest and quench
The red God's anger, fearing not to plunge
Thy torch of life in darkness, rather—
 thou
Rejoicing that the sun, the moon, the
 stars
Send no such light upon the ways of men
As one great deed.
                   Thither, my son, and there
Thou, that hast never known the embrace
 of love,
Offer thy maiden life.
                        This useless hand !
I felt one warm tear fall upon it.   Gone !
He will achieve his greatness.
                              But for me,
I would that I were gather'd to my rest,
And mingled with the famous kings of
 old,
On whom about their ocean-islets flash
The faces of the Gods—the wise man's
 word,
Here trampled by the populace underfoot,
There crown'd with worship—and these
 eyes will find

The men I knew, and watch the chariot
    whirl
About the goal again, and hunters race
The shadowy lion, and the warrior-
    kings,
In height and prowess more than human,
    strive
Again for glory, while the golden lyre
Is ever sounding in heroic ears
Heroic hymns, and every way the vales
Wind, clouded with the grateful incense-
    fume
Of those who mix all odour to the Gods
On one far height in one far-shining fire.

'One height and one far-shining fire'
    And while I fancied that my friend
For this brief idyll would require
    A less diffuse and opulent end,
And would defend his judgment well,
    If I should deem it over nice—
The tolling of his funeral bell
    Broke on my Pagan Paradise,
And mixt the dream of classic times
    And all the phantoms of the dream,
With present grief, and made the rhymes,
    That miss'd his living welcome, seem
Like would-be guests an hour too late,
    Who down the highway moving on
With easy laughter find the gate
    Is bolted, and the master gone.
Gone into darkness, that full light
    Of friendship ! past, in sleep, away
By night, into the deeper night !
    The deeper night ? A clearer day
Than our poor twilight dawn on earth—
    If night, what barren toil to be !
What life, so maim'd by night, were
    worth
    Our living out ? Not mine to me
Remembering all the golden hours
    Now silent, and so many dead,
And him the last ; and laying flowers,
    This wreath, above his honour'd head,
And praying that, when I from hence
    Shall fade with him into the unknown,
My close of earth's experience
    May prove as peaceful as his own.

THE WRECK.

I.

Hide me, Mother ! my Fathers belong'd
    to the church of old,
I am driven by storm and sin and death
    to the ancient fold,
I cling to the Catholic Cross once more,
    to the Faith that saves,
My brain is full of the crash of wrecks,
    and the roar of waves,
My life itself is a wreck, I have sullied a
    noble name,
I am flung from the rushing tide of the
    world as a waif of shame,
I am roused by the wail of a child, and
    awake to a livid light,
And a ghastlier face than ever has haunted
    a grave by night,
I would hide from the storm without, I
    would flee from the storm within,
I would make my life one prayer for a
    soul that died in his sin,
I was the tempter, Mother, and mine was
    the deeper fall :
I will sit at your feet, I will hide my face,
    I will tell you all.

II.

He that they gave me to, Mother, a
    heedless and innocent bride—
I never have wrong'd his heart, I have
    only wounded his pride—
Spain in his blood and the Jew—— dark
    visaged, stately and tall—
A princelier looking man never stept thro'
    a Prince's hall.
And who, when his anger was kindled,
    would venture to give him the nay?
And a man men fear is a man to be loved
    by the women they say.
And I could have loved him too, if the
    blossom can doat on the blight,
Or the young green leaf rejoice in the frost
    that sears it at night ;
He would open the books that I prized,
    and toss them away with a yawn,

Repell'd by the magnet of Art to the which
　　my nature was drawn,
The word of the Poet by whom the deeps
　　of the world are stirr'd,
The music that robes it in language beneath
　　and beyond the word !
My Shelley would fall from my hands when
　　he cast a contemptuous glance
From where he was poring over his
　　Tables of Trade and Finance ;
My hands, when I heard him coming
　　would drop from the chords or the
　　keys,
But ever I fail'd to please him, however
　　I strove to please—
All day long far-off in the cloud of the
　　city, and there
Lost, head and heart, in the chances of
　　dividend, consol, and share—
And at home if I sought for a kindly
　　caress, being woman and weak,
His formal kiss fell chill as a flake of snow
　　on the cheek :
And so, when I bore him a girl, when I
　　held it aloft in my joy,
He look'd at it coldly, and said to me
　　' Pity it isn't a boy.'
The one thing given me, to love and to
　　live for, glanced at in scorn !
The child that I felt I could die for—as
　　if she were basely born !
I had lived a wild-flower life, I was planted
　　now in a tomb ;
The daisy will shut to the shadow, I closed
　　my heart to the gloom ;
I threw myself all abroad—I would play
　　my part with the young
By the low foot-lights of the world—and
　　I caught the wreath that was flung.

III.

Mother, I have not—however their
　　tongues may have babbled of me—
Sinn'd thro' an animal vileness, for all
　　but a dwarf was he,
And all but a hunchback too ; and I
　　look'd at him, first, askance,
With pity—not he the knight for an
　　amorous girl's romance !

Tho' wealthy enough to have bask'd in
　　the light of a dowerless smile,
Having lands at home and abroad in a
　　rich West-Indian isle ;
But I came on him once at a ball, the
　　heart of a listening crowd—
Why, what a brow was there ! he was
　　seated—speaking aloud
To women, the flower of the time, and
　　men at the helm of state—
Flowing with easy greatness and touch-
　　ing on all things great,
Science, philosophy, song—till I felt my-
　　self ready to weep
For I knew not what, when I heard that
　　voice,—as mellow and deep
As a psalm by a mighty master and peal'd
　　from an organ,—roll
Rising and falling—for, Mother, the voice
　　was the voice of the soul ;
And the sun of the soul made day in the
　　dark of his wonderful eyes.
Here was the hand that would help me,
　　would heal me—the heart that
　　was wise !
And he, poor man, when he learnt that
　　I hated the ring I wore,
He helpt me with death, and he heal'd
　　me with sorrow for evermore.

IV.

For I broke the bond. That day my
　　nurse had brought me the child.
The small sweet face was flush'd, but it
　　coo'd to the Mother and smiled.
' Anything ailing,' I ask'd her, ' with
　　baby ?' She shook her head,
And the Motherless Mother kiss'd it, and
　　turn'd in her haste and fled.

V.

Low warm winds had gently breathed us
　　away from the land—
Ten long sweet summer days upon deck,
　　sitting hand in hand—
When he clothed a naked mind with the
　　wisdom and wealth of his own,
And I bow'd myself down as a slave to
　　his intellectual throne,

When he coin'd into English gold some
    treasure of classical song,
When he flouted a statesman's error, or
    flamed at a public wrong,
When he rose as it were on the wings of
    an eagle beyond me, and past
Over the range and the change of the
    world from the first to the last,
When he spoke of his tropical home in
    the canes by the purple tide,
And the high star-crowns of his palms on
    the deep-wooded mountain-side,
And cliffs all robed in lianas that dropt
    to the brink of his bay,
And trees like the towers of a minster,
    the sons of a winterless day.
'Paradise there!' so he said, but I seem'd
    in Paradise then
With the first great love I had felt for the
    first and greatest of men;
Ten long days of summer and sin—if it
    must be so—
But days of a larger light than I ever
    again shall know—
Days that will glimmer, I fear, thro' life
    to my latest breath;
'No frost there,' so he said, 'as in truest
    Love no Death.'

VI.

Mother, one morning a bird with a warble
    plaintively sweet
Perch'd on the shrouds, and then fell
    fluttering down at my feet;
I took it, he made it a cage, we fondled
    it, Stephen and I,
But it died, and I thought of the child
    for a moment, I scarce know why.

VII.

But if sin be sin, not inherited fate, as
    many will say,
My sin to my desolate little one found
    me at sea on a day,
When her orphan wail came borne in the
    shriek of a growing wind,
And a voice rang out in the thunders of
    Ocean and Heaven 'Thou hast
    sinn'd.'

And down in the cabin were we, for the
    towering crest of the tides
Plunged on the vessel and swept in a
    cataract off from her sides,
And ever the great storm grew with a
    howl and a hoot of the blast
In the rigging, voices of hell—then came
    the crash of the mast.
'The wages of sin is death,' and there I
    began to weep,
'I am the Jonah, the crew should cast
    me into the deep,
For ah God, what a heart was mine to
    forsake her even for you.'
'Never the heart among women,' he said,
    'more tender and true.'
'The heart! not a mother's heart, when
    I left my darling alone.'
'Comfort yourself, for the heart of the
    father will care for his own.'
'The heart of the father will spurn her,'
    I cried, 'for the sin of the wife,
The cloud of the mother's shame will
    enfold her and darken her life.'
Then his pale face twitch'd; 'O Stephen,
    I love you, I love you, and yet '—
As I lean'd away from his arms—' would
    God, we had never met!'
And he spoke not—only the storm; till
    after a little, I yearn'd
For his voice again, and he call'd to me
    'Kiss me!' and there—as I
    turn'd—
'The heart, the heart!' I kiss'd him, I
    clung to the sinking form,
And the storm went roaring above us,
    and he—was out of the storm.

VIII.

And then, then, Mother, the ship stag-
    ger'd under a thunderous shock,
That shook us asunder, as if she had
    struck and crash'd on a rock;
For a huge sea smote every soul from the
    decks of The Falcon but one;
All of them, all but the man that was
    lash'd to the helm had gone;
And I fell—and the storm and the days
    went by, but I knew no more—

Lost myself—lay like the dead by the
    dead on the cabin floor,
Dead to the death beside me, and lost to
    the loss that was mine,
With a dim dream, now and then, of a
    hand giving bread and wine,
Till I woke from the trance, and the ship
    stood still, and the skies were
    blue,
But the face I had known, O Mother,
    was not the face that I knew.

IX.

The strange misfeaturing mask that I saw
    so amazed me, that I
Stumbled on deck, half mad. I would
    fling myself over and die!
But one—he was waving a flag—the one
    man left on the wreck—
'Woman'—he graspt at my arm—'stay
    there'—I crouch'd upon deck—
'We are sinking, and yet there's hope:
    look yonder,' he cried, 'a sail'
In a tone so rough that I broke into
    passionate tears, and the wail
Of a beaten babe, till I saw that a boat
    was nearing us—then
All on a sudden I thought, I shall look
    on the child again.

X.

They lower'd me down the side, and
    there in the boat I lay
With sad eyes fixt on the lost sea-home,
    as we glided away,
And I sigh'd, as the low dark hull dipt
    under the smiling main,
'Had I stay'd with *him*, I had now—
    with *him*—been out of my pain.'

XI.

They took us aboard: the crew were
    gentle, the captain kind;
But *I* was the lonely slave of an often-
    wandering mind;
For whenever a rougher gust might
    tumble a stormier wave,
'O Stephen,' I moan'd, 'I am coming
    to thee in thine Ocean-grave.'

And again, when a balmier breeze curl'd
    over a peacefuller sea,
I found myself moaning again 'O child,
    I am coming to thee.'

XII.

The broad white brow of the Isle—that
    bay with the colour'd sand—
Rich was the rose of sunset there, as we
    drew to the land;
All so quiet the ripple would hardly
    blanch into spray
At the feet of the cliff; and I pray'd—
    'my child'—for I still could
    pray—
'May her life be as blissfully calm, be
    never gloom'd by the curse
Of a sin, not hers!'
        Was it well with the child?
        I wrote to the nurse
Who had borne my flower on her hireling
    heart; and an answer came
Not from the nurse—nor yet to the wife
    —to her maiden name!
I shook as I open'd the letter—I knew
    that hand too well—
And from it a scrap, clipt out of the
    'deaths' in a paper, fell.
'Ten long sweet summer days' of fever,
    and want of care!
And gone—that day of the storm—O
    Mother, she came to me there.

DESPAIR.

A man and his wife having lost faith in a God,
and hope of a life to come, and being utterly
miserable in this, resolve to end themselves by
drowning. The woman is drowned, but the man
rescued by a minister of the sect he had aban-
doned.

I.

Is it you, that preach'd in the chapel
    there looking over the sand?
Follow'd us too that night, and dogg'd
    us, and drew me to land?

II

What did I feel that night? You are
    curious. How should I tell?

Does it matter so much what I felt?
    You rescued me—yet—was it
    well
That you came unwish'd for, uncall'd,
    between me and the deep and my
    doom,
Three days since, three more dark days
    of the Godless gloom
Of a life without sun, without health, with-
    out hope, without any delight
In anything here upon earth? but ah
    God, that night, that night
When the rolling eyes of the lighthouse
    there on the fatal neck
Of land running out into rock—they had
    saved many hundreds from wreck—
Glared on our way toward death, I re-
    member I thought, as we past,
Does it matter how many they saved?
    we are all of us wreck'd at last—
' Do you fear?' and there came thro' the
    roar of the breaker a whisper, a
    breath,
' Fear? am I not with you? I am
    frighted at life not death.'

III.

And the suns of the limitless Universe
    sparkled and shone in the sky,
Flashing with fires as of God, but we
    knew that their light was a lie—
Bright as with deathless hope—but,
    however they sparkled and shone,
The dark little worlds running round
    them were worlds of woe like our
    own—
No soul in the heaven above, no soul on
    the earth below,
A fiery scroll written over with lamenta-
    tion and woe.

IV.

See, we were nursed in the drear night-
    fold of your fatalist creed,
And we turn'd to the growing dawn, we
    had hoped for a dawn indeed,
When the light of a Sun that was coming
    would scatter the ghosts of the
    Past,

T

And the cramping creeds that had
    madden'd the peoples would
    vanish at last,
And we broke away from the Christ, our
    human brother and friend,
For He spoke, or it seem'd that He
    spoke, of a Hell without help,
    without end.

V.

Hoped for a dawn and it came, but the
    promise had faded away;
We had past from a cheerless night to
    the glare of a drearier day;
He is only a cloud and a smoke who was
    once a pillar of fire,
The guess of a worm in the dust and the
    shadow of its desire—
Of a worm as it writhes in a world of the
    weak trodden down by the strong,
Of a dying worm in a world, all massacre,
    murder, and wrong.

VI.

O we poor orphans of nothing—alone on
    that lonely shore—
Born of the brainless Nature who knew
    not that which she bore !
Trusting no longer that earthly flower
    would be heavenly fruit—
Come from the brute, poor souls—no souls
    —and to die with the brute——

VII.

Nay, but I am not claiming your pity : I
    know you of old—
Small pity for those that have ranged from
    the narrow warmth of your fold,
Where you bawl'd the dark side of your
    faith and a God of eternal rage,
Till you flung us back on ourselves, and
    the human heart, and the Age.

VIII.

But pity—the Pagan held it a vice—was
    in her and in me,
Helpless, taking the place of the pitying
    God that should be !

Pity for all that aches in the grasp of an
    idiot power,
And pity for our own selves on an earth
    that bore not a flower;
Pity for all that suffers on land or in air
    or the deep,
And pity for our own selves till we long'd
    for eternal sleep.

IX.

'Lightly step over the sands! the waters
    —you hear them call!
Life with its anguish, and horrors, and
    errors—away with it all!'
And she laid her hand in my own—she
    was always loyal and sweet—
Till the points of the foam in the dusk
    came playing about our feet.
There was a strong sea-current would
    sweep us out to the main.
'Ah God' tho' I felt as I spoke I was
    taking the name in vain—
'Ah God' and we turn'd to each other,
    we kiss'd, we embraced, she and I,
Knowing the Love we were used to be-
    lieve everlasting would die:
We had read their know-nothing books
    and we lean'd to the darker side—
Ah God, should we find Him, perhaps,
    perhaps, if we died, if we died;
We never had found Him on earth, this
    earth is a fatherless Hell—
'Dear Love, for ever and ever, for ever
    and ever farewell,'
Never a cry so desolate, not since the
    world began,
Never a kiss so sad, no, not since the
    coming of man!

X.

But the blind wave cast me ashore, and
    you saved me, a valueless life.
Not a grain of gratitude mine! You
    have parted the man from the wife.
I am left alone on the land, she is all
    alone in the sea;
If a curse meant ought, I would curse
    you for not having let me be.

XI.

Visions of youth—for my brain was drunk
    with the water, it seems;
I had past into perfect quiet at length
    out of pleasant dreams,
And the transient trouble of drowning—
    what was it when match'd with
    the pains
Of the hellish heat of a wretched life
    rushing back thro' the veins?

XII.

Why should I live? one son had forged
    on his father and fled,
And if I believed in a God, I would
    thank him, the other is dead,
And there was a baby-girl, that had
    never look'd on the light:
Happiest she of us all, for she past from
    the night to the night.

XIII.

But the crime, if a crime, of her eldest-
    born, her glory, her boast,
Struck hard at the tender heart of the
    mother, and broke it almost;
Tho', glory and shame dying out for ever
    in endless time,
Does it matter so much whether crown'd
    for a virtue, or hang'd for a crime?

XIV.

And ruin'd by *him*, by *him*, I stood
    there, naked, amazed
In a world of arrogant opulence, fear'd
    myself turning crazed,
And I would not be mock'd in a mad-
    house! and she, the delicate wife,
With a grief that could only be cured, if
    cured, by the surgeon's knife,—

XV.

Why should we bear with an hour of
    torture, a moment of pain,
If every man die for ever, if all his griefs
    are in vain,
And the homeless planet at length will be
    wheel'd thro' the silence of space,

Tennyson "The Ancient Sage"
p 547   (1885)

---

ad p 549 b 1 "But^ᵗ the Nameless is nor Day
nor Hour...": of "The Princess":
For is was, & is, & will be, are but is...
...Our weakness somehow shapes the Shadow
Time.

---

expli: pp 551 b – 552

Born 1809, son of a parson d. 1892

cf. "Lucretius" p 161, esp. last words of
Lucr. p / 65 a and last words of poem.

Style & Verse.   Long, sweeping, rhetori-
cal sentences.   Harmonious, inner
rhymes or assonances (beginning of passage). – Images. – Didactic poetry, not
very moving.

titles it is more than ever e

This year we are please
than before. From these, we
able to choose those you woul
presents for the youngsters.

Just indicate with a ti
we will reserve them for you.

We strongly recommend y
so make sure of not disappoin
the most popular titles may b

September 1955
P/G/515C

Motherless evermore of an ever-vanishing
race,
When the worm shall have writhed its
last, and its last brother-worm
will have fled
From the dead fossil skull that is left in
the rocks of an earth that is dead?

XVI.

Have I crazed myself over their horrible
infidel writings? O yes,
For these are the new dark ages, you see,
of the popular press,
When the bat comes out of his cave, and
the owls are whooping at noon,
And Doubt is the lord of this dunghill
and crows to the sun and the
moon,
Till the Sun and the Moon of our science
are both of them turn'd into blood,
And Hope will have broken her heart,
running after a shadow of good;
For their knowing and know-nothing
books are scatter'd from hand to
hand—
We have knelt in your know-all chapel
too looking over the sand.

XVII.

What! I should call on that Infinite
Love that has served us so well?
Infinite cruelty rather that made ever-
lasting Hell,
Made us, foreknew us, foredoom'd us, and
does what he will with his own;
Better our dead brute mother who never
has heard us groan!

XVIII.

Hell? if the souls of men were immortal,
as men have been told,
The lecher would cleave to his lusts, and
the miser would yearn for his gold,
And so there were Hell for ever! but
were there a God as you say,
His Love would have power over Hell
till it utterly vanish'd away.

XIX.

Ah yet—I have had some glimmer, at
times, in my gloomiest woe,
Of a God behind all—after all—the great
God for aught that I know;
But the God of Love and of Hell to-
gether—they cannot be thought,
If there be such a God, may the Great
God curse him and bring him to
nought!

XX.

Blasphemy! whose is the fault? is it
mine? for why would you save
A madman to vex you with wretched
words, who is best in his grave?
Blasphemy! ay, why not, being damn'd
beyond hope of grace?
O would I were yonder with her, and
away from your faith and your
face!
Blasphemy! true! I have scared you
pale with my scandalous talk,
But the blasphemy to *my* mind lies all in
the way that you walk.

XXI.

Hence! she is gone! can I stay? can I
breathe divorced from the Past?
You needs must have good lynx-eyes if I
do not escape you at last.
Our orthodox coroner doubtless will find
it a felo-de-se,
And the stake and the cross-road, fool,
if you will, does it matter to me?

THE ANCIENT SAGE.

A THOUSAND summers ere the time of
Christ
From out his ancient city came a Seer
Whom one that loved, and honour'd
him, and yet
Was no disciple, richly garb'd, but worn
From wasteful living, follow'd—in his
hand
A scroll of verse—till that old man before

a dialogue between a Believer (in God) in the immortality of the Soul

[a sage like the Buddha (ca 500 BC) and a Nihilist. in the form of a comment, or gloss.

nb 1885. wr after read'g a "k on the life & maxims of Lao Tse (ca 600 to 500 BC). Lao Tse is the founder of Taoism.

A cavern whence an affluent fountain pour'd
From darkness into daylight, turn'd and spoke.

This wealth of waters might but seem to draw
From yon dark cave, but, son, the source is higher,
Yon summit half-a-league in air—and higher,
The cloud that hides it—higher still, the heavens
Whereby the cloud was moulded, and whereout
The cloud descended.   Force is from the heights.
I am wearied of our city, son, and go
To spend my one last year among the hills.
What hast thou there?   Some deathsong for the Ghouls
To make their banquet relish?   let me read.

" How far thro' all the bloom and brake
    That nightingale is heard !
What power but the bird's could make
    This music in the bird ?
How summer-bright are yonder skies,
    And earth as fair in hue !
And yet what sign of aught that lies
    Behind the green and blue ?
But man to-day is fancy's fool
    As man hath ever been.
The nameless Power, or Powers, that rule
    Were never heard or seen."

If thou would'st hear the Nameless, and wilt dive
Into the Temple-cave of thine own self,
There, brooding by the central altar, thou
May'st haply learn the Nameless hath a voice,
By which thou wilt abide, if thou be wise,
As if thou knewest, tho' thou canst not know;
For Knowledge is the swallow on the lake
That sees and stirs the surface-shadow there

But never yet hath dipt into the abysm,
The Abysm of all Abysms, beneath, within
The blue of sky and sea, the green of earth,
And in the million-millionth of a grain
Which cleft and cleft again for evermore,
And ever vanishing, never vanishes,
To me, my son, more mystic than myself,
Or even than the Nameless is to me.
    And when thou sendest thy free soul thro' heaven,
Nor understandest bound nor boundlessness,
Thou seest the Nameless of the hundred names.
    And if the Nameless should withdraw from all
Thy frailty counts most real, all thy world
Might vanish like thy shadow in the dark.

" And since—from when this earth began—
    The Nameless never came
Among us, never spake with man,
    And never named the Name "—

Thou canst not prove the Nameless, O my son,
Nor canst thou prove the world thou movest in,
Thou canst not prove that thou art body alone,
Nor canst thou prove that thou art spirit alone,
Nor canst thou prove that thou art both in one :
Thou canst not prove thou art immortal, no
Nor yet that thou art mortal—nay my son,
Thou canst not prove that I, who speak with thee,
Am not thyself in converse with thyself,
For nothing worthy proving can be proven,
Nor yet disproven : wherefore thou be wise,
Cleave ever to the sunnier side of doubt,
And cling to Faith beyond the forms of Faith !

She reels not in the storm of warring
    words,
She brightens at the clash of 'Yes' and
    'No,'
She sees the Best that glimmers thro' the
    Worst,
She feels the Sun is hid but for a night,
She spies the summer thro' the winter
    bud,
She tastes the fruit before the blossom
    falls,
She hears the lark within the songless egg,
She finds the fountain where they wail'd
    'Mirage'!

"What Power? aught akin to Mind,
    The mind in me and you?
Or power as of the Gods gone blind
    Who see not what they do?"

But some in yonder city hold, my son,
That none but Gods could build this
    house of ours,
So beautiful, vast, various, so beyond
All work of man, yet, like all work of
    man,
A beauty with defect——till That which
    knows,
And is not known, but felt thro' what we
    feel
Within ourselves is highest, shall descend
On this half-deed, and shape it at the
    last
According to the Highest in the Highest.

"What Power but the Years that make
    And break the vase of clay,
And stir the sleeping earth, and wake
    The bloom that fades away?
What rulers but the Days and Hours
    That cancel weal with woe,
And wind the front of youth with flowers,
    And cap our age with snow?"

    The days and hours are ever glancing
      by,
And seem to flicker past thro' sun and
    shade,
Or short, or long, as Pleasure leads, or
    Pain ;

But with the Nameless is nor Day nor
    Hour ;
Tho' we, thin minds, who creep from
    thought to thought,
Break into 'Thens' and 'Whens' the
    Eternal Now :
This double seeming of the single world !—
My words are like the babblings in a
    dream
Of nightmare, when the babblings break
    the dream.
But thou be wise in this dream-world of
    ours,
Nor take thy dial for thy deity,
But make the passing shadow serve thy
    will.

"The years that made the stripling wise
    Undo their work again,
And leave him, blind of heart and eyes,
    The last and least of men ;
Who clings to earth, and once would dare
    Hell-heat or Arctic cold,
And now one breath of cooler air
    Would loose him from his hold ;
His winter chills him to the root,
    He withers marrow and mind ;
The kernel of the shrivell'd fruit
    Is jutting thro' the rind ;
The tiger spasms tear his chest,
    The palsy wags his head ;
The wife, the sons, who love him best
Would fain that he were dead ;
The griefs by which he once was wrung
    Were never worth the while "—

Who knows ? or whether this earth-narrow
    life
Be yet but yolk, and forming in the shell ?

"The shaft of scorn that once had stung
    But wakes a dotard smile."

The placid gleam of sunset after storm !

"The statesman's brain that sway'd the
    past
    Is feebler than his knees ;
The passive sailor wrecks at last
    In ever-silent seas ;

The warrior hath forgot his arms,
　　The Learned all his lore ;
The changing market frets or charms
　　The merchant's hope no more ;
The prophet's beacon burn'd in vain,
　　And now is lost in cloud ;
The plowman passes, bent with pain,
　　To mix with what he plow'd ;
The poet whom his Age would quote
　　As heir of endless fame—
He knows not ev'n the book he wrote,
　　Not even his own name.
For man has overlived his day
　　And, darkening in the light,
Scarce feels the senses break away
　　To mix with ancient Night."

The shell must break before the bird can fly.

Death

" The years that when my Youth began
　　Had set the lily and rose
By all my ways where'er they ran,
　　Have ended mortal foes ;
My rose of love for ever gone,
　　My lily of truth and trust—
They made her lily and rose in one,
　　And changed her into dust.
O rosetree planted in my grief,
　　And growing, on her tomb,
Her dust is greening in your leaf,
　　Her blood is in your bloom.
O slender lily waving there,
　　And laughing back the light,
In vain you tell me ' Earth is fair '
　　When all is dark as night."

My son, the world is dark with griefs and
　　graves,
So dark that men cry out against the
　　Heavens.
Who knows but that the darkness is in
　　man ?
The doors of Night may be the gates of
　　Light ;
For wert thou born or blind or deaf, and
　　then
Suddenly heal'd, how would'st thou glory
　　in all
The splendours and the voices of the
　　world !

And we, the poor earth's dying race, and yet
No phantoms, watching from a phantom
　　shore
Await the last and largest sense to make
The phantom walls of this illusion fade,
And show us that the world is wholly fair.

Nihilism

" But vain the tears for darken'd years
　　As laughter over wine,
And vain the laughter as the tears,
　　O brother, mine or thine,

For all that laugh, and all that weep
　　And all that breathe are one
Slight ripple on the boundless deep
　　That moves, and all is gone."

But that one ripple on the boundless deep
Feels that the deep is boundless, and
　　itself　*(Pascal)*
For ever changing form, but evermore
One with the boundless motion of the
　　deep.　*roseau pensant*

" Yet wine and laughter friends ! and set
　　The lamps alight, and call
For golden music, and forget　*hedonis*
　　The darkness of the pall."

If utter darkness closed the day, my
　　son——
But earth's dark forehead flings athwart
　　the heavens
Her shadow crown'd with stars—and
　　yonder—out
To northward—some that never set, but
　　pass
From sight and night to lose themselves
　　in day.
I hate the black negation of the bier,
And wish the dead, as happier than our
　　selves
And higher, having climb'd one step
　　beyond
Our village miseries, might be borne in
　　white
To burial or to burning, hymn'd from
　　hence
With songs in praise of death, and
　　crown'd with flowers !

*Eloge de la mort ; les morts
sont plus heureux q[ue] les viva[nts]*

*[handwritten: * autobiogr. (cf. Wordsworth)]*

"O worms and maggots of to-day
  Without their hope of wings!"

[handwritten: Faith:-)]

But louder than thy rhyme the silent Word
Of that world-prophet in the heart of man.

  "Tho' some have gleams or so they say
  Of more than mortal things."

[handwritten: with:-)]

To-day? but what of yesterday? for oft
On me, when boy, there came what then
    I call'd,
Who knew no books and no philosophies,
In my boy-phrase 'The Passion of the
    Past.'
The first gray streak of earliest summer-
    dawn,
The last long stripe of waning crimson
    gloom,
As if the late and early were but one—
A height, a broken grange, a grove, a
    flower
Had murmurs 'Lost and gone and lost
    and gone!'
A breath, a whisper—some divine fare-
    well—
Desolate sweetness—far and far away—
What had he loved, what had he lost,
    the boy?
I know not and I speak of what has been.
  And more, my son! for more than
    once when I
Sat all alone, revolving in myself
The word that is the symbol of myself,
The mortal limit of the Self was loosed,
And past into the Nameless, as a cloud
Melts into Heaven. I touch'd my limbs,
    the limbs
Were strange not mine—and yet no shade
    of doubt,
But utter clearness, and thro' loss of Self
The gain of such large life as match'd
    with ours
Were Sun to spark—unshadowable in
    words,
Themselves but shadows of a shadow-
    world.

  "And idle gleams will come and go,
  But still the clouds remain;"

The clouds themselves are children of the
    Sun.

  "And Night and Shadow rule below
  When only Day should reign."

And Day and Night are children of the
    Sun,
And idle gleams to thee are light to me. *[handwritten: p 551 a]*
Some say, the Light was father of the
    Night,
And some, the Night was father of the *[handwritten: The problem of evil]*
    Light,
No night no day!—I touch thy world
    again—
No ill no good! such counter-terms, my
    son,
Are border-races, holding, each its own *[handwritten: ?]*
By endless war: but night enough is there
In yon dark city: get thee back: and *[handwritten: occasions]*
    since
The key to that weird casket, which for *[handwritten: for doing good]*
    thee
But holds a skull, is neither thine nor *[handwritten: & possibility of pro-]*
    mine,
But in the hand of what is more than man, *[handwritten: gress]*
Or in man's hand when man is more than *[handwritten: on earth]*
    man,
Let be thy wail and help thy fellow men,
And make thy gold thy vassal not thy
    king,
And fling free alms into the beggar's bowl, *[handwritten: 1]*
And send the day into the darken'd heart; *[handwritten: generosity]*
Nor list for guerdon in the voice of men,
A dying echo from a falling wall;
Nor care—for Hunger hath the Evil eye—
To vex the noon with fiery gems, or fold *[handwritten: 2]*
Thy presence in the silk of sumptuous *[handwritten: modesty]*
    looms;
Nor roll thy viands on a luscious tongue *[handwritten: 3]*
Nor drown thyself with flies in honied *[handwritten: moderate (sobriety)]*
    wine;
Nor thou be rageful, like a handled bee, *[handwritten: 4]*
And lose thy life by usage of thy sting; *[handwritten: no]*
Nor harm an adder thro' the lust for harm, *[handwritten: cruelty]*
Nor make a snail's horn shrink for wan-
    tonness;
And more—think well! Do-well will *[handwritten: 5]*
    follow thought, *[handwritten: rapelle]*
And in the fatal sequence of this world

[handwritten: 2 of the 8 parts of the Buddhist Path: 1 right opinion 4 right actions]

An evil thought may soil thy children's
    blood ;
But curb the beast would cast thee in the
    mire,
And leave the hot swamp of voluptuous-
    ness
A cloud between the Nameless and thyself,
And lay thine uphill shoulder to the
    wheel,
And climb the Mount of Blessing, whence,
    if thou
Look higher, then—perchance—thou
    mayest—beyond
A hundred ever-rising mountain lines,
And past the range of Night and Shadow
    —see
The high-heaven dawn of more than
    mortal day
Strike on the Mount of Vision !
                So, farewell.

THE FLIGHT.

I.

ARE you sleeping ? have you forgotten ?
    do not sleep, my sister dear !
How *can* you sleep ? the morning brings
    the day I hate and fear ;
The cock has crow'd already once, he
    crows before his time ;
Awake ! the creeping glimmer steals, the
    hills are white with rime.

II.

Ah, clasp me in your arms, sister, ah,
    fold me to your breast !
Ah, let me weep my fill once more, and
    cry myself to rest !
To rest ? to rest and wake no more were
    better rest for me,
Than to waken every morning to that
    face I loathe to see :

III.

I envied your sweet slumber, all night so
    calm you lay,
The night was calm, the morn is calm,
    and like another day ;

But I could wish yon moaning sea would
    rise and burst the shore,
And such a whirlwind blow these woods,
    as never blew before.

IV

For, one by one, the stars went down
    across the gleaming pane,
And project after project rose, and all of
    them were vain ;
The blackthorn-blossom fades and falls
    and leaves the bitter sloe,
The hope I catch at vanishes and youth
    is turn'd to woe.

V.

Come, speak a little comfort ! all night
    I pray'd with tears,
And yet no comfort came to me, and
    now the morn appears,
When he will tear me from your side,
    who bought me for his slave :
This father pays his debt with me, and
    weds me to my grave.

VI.

What father, this or mine, was he, who,
    on that summer day
When I had fall'n from off the crag we
    clamber'd up in play,
Found, fear'd me dead, and groan'd, and
    took and kiss'd me, and again
He kiss'd me ; and I loved him then ;
    he *was* my father then.

VII.

No father now, the tyrant vassal of a
    tyrant vice !
The Godless Jephtha vows his child . . .
    to one cast of the dice.
These ancient woods, this Hall at last
    will go—perhaps have gone,
Except his own meek daughter yield her
    life, heart, soul to one—

VIII.

To one who knows I scorn him. O the
    formal mocking bow,

The cruel smile, the courtly phrase that
    masks his malice now—
But often in the sidelong eyes a gleam of
    all things ill—
It is not Love but Hate that weds a
    bride against her will;

IX.

Hate, that would pluck from this true
    breast the locket that I wear,
The precious crystal into which I braided
    Edwin's hair!
The love that keeps this heart alive beats
    on it night and day—
One golden curl, his golden gift, before
    he past away.

X.

He left us weeping in the woods; his
    boat was on the sand;
How slowly down the rocks he went,
    how loth to quit the land!
And all my life was darken'd, as I saw
    the white sail run,
And darken, up that lane of light into
    the setting sun.

XI.

How often have we watch'd the sun fade
    from us thro' the West,
And follow Edwin to those isles, those
    islands of the Blest!
Is *he* not there? would I were there, the
    friend, the bride, the wife,
With him, where summer never dies,
    with Love, the Sun of life!

XII.

O would I were in Edwin's arms—once
    more—to feel his breath
Upon my cheek—on Edwin's ship, with
    Edwin, ev'n in death,
Tho' all about the shuddering wreck the
    death-white sea should rave,
Or if lip were laid to lip on the pillows
    of the wave.

XIII.

Shall I take *him?* I kneel with *him?* I
    swear and swear forsworn
To love him most, whom most I loathe,
    to honour whom I scorn?
The Fiend would yell, the grave would
    yawn, my mother's ghost would
    rise—
To lie, to lie—in God's own house—the
    blackest of all lies!

XIV.

Why—rather than that hand in mine,
    tho' every pulse would freeze,
I'd sooner fold an icy corpse dead of
    some foul disease:
Wed him? I will not wed him, let them
    spurn me from the doors,
And I will wander till I die about the
    barren moors.

XV.

The dear, mad bride who stabb'd her
    bridegroom on her bridal night—
If mad, then I am mad, but sane, if she
    were in the right.
My father's madness makes me mad—
    but words are only words!
I am not mad, not yet, not quite—There!
    listen how the birds

XVI.

Begin to warble yonder in the budding
    orchard trees!
The lark has past from earth to Heaven
    upon the morning breeze!
How gladly, were I one of those, how
    early would I wake!
And yet the sorrow that I bear is sorrow
    for *his* sake.

XVII.

They love their mates, to whom they
    sing; or else their songs, that meet
The morning with such music, would
    never be so sweet!
And tho' these fathers will not hear, the
    blessed Heavens are just,

And Love is fire, and burns the feet
　　would trample it to dust.

XVIII.

A door was open'd in the house—who?
　　who? my father sleeps!
A stealthy foot upon the stair! he—some
　　one—this way creeps!
If he? yes, he . . . lurks, listens, fears
　　his victim may have fled—
He! where is some sharp-pointed thing?
　　he comes, and finds me dead.

XIX.

Not he, not yet! and time to act—but
　　how my temples burn!
And idle fancies flutter me, I know not
　　where to turn;
Speak to me, sister; counsel me; this
　　marriage must not be.
You only know the love that makes the
　　world a world to me!

XX.

Our gentle mother, had *she* lived—but
　　we were left alone:
That other left us to ourselves; he cared
　　not for his own;
So all the summer long we roam'd in
　　these wild woods of ours,
My Edwin loved to call us then 'His
　　two wild woodland flowers.'

XXI.

Wild flowers blowing side by side in
　　God's free light and air,
Wild flowers of the secret woods, when
　　Edwin found us there,
Wild woods in which we roved with him,
　　and heard his passionate vow,
Wild woods in which we rove no more,
　　if we be parted now!

XXII.

You will not leave me thus in grief to
　　wander forth forlorn;
We never changed a bitter word, not
　　once since we were born;
Our dying mother join'd our hands; she
　　knew this father well;
She bad us love, like souls in Heaven,
　　and now I fly from Hell,

XXIII.

And you with me; and we shall light
　　upon some lonely shore,
Some lodge within the waste sea-dunes,
　　and hear the waters roar,
And see the ships from out the West go
　　dipping thro' the foam,
And sunshine on that sail at last which
　　brings our Edwin home.

XXIV.

But look, the morning grows apace, and
　　lights the old church-tower,
And lights the clock! the hand points
　　five—O me—it strikes the hour—
I bide no more, I meet my fate, whatever
　　ills betide!
Arise, my own true sister, come forth!
　　the world is wide.

XXV.

And yet my heart is ill at ease, my eyes
　　are dim with dew,
I seem to see a new-dug grave up yonder
　　by the yew!
If we should never more return, but
　　wander hand in hand
With breaking hearts, without a friend,
　　and in a distant land.

XXVI.

O sweet, they tell me that the world is
　　hard, and harsh of mind,
But can it be so hard, so harsh, as those
　　that should be kind?
That matters not: let come what will;
　　at last the end is sure,
And every heart that loves with truth is
　　equal to endure.

TOMORROW.

I.

HER, that yer Honour was spakin' to?
 Whin, yer Honour? last year—
Standin' here be the bridge, when last
 yer Honour was here?
An' yer Honour ye gev her the top of the
 mornin', 'Tomorra' says she.
What did they call her, yer Honour?
 They call'd her Molly Magee.
An' yer Honour's the thrue ould blood
 that always manes to be kind,
But there's rason in all things, yer
 Honour, for Molly was out of her
 mind.

II.

Shure, an' meself remimbers wan night
 comin' down be the sthrame,
An' it seems to me now like a bit of
 yisther-day in a dhrame—
Here where yer Honour seen her—there
 was but a slip of a moon,
But I hard thim—Molly Magee wid her
 batchelor, Danny O'Roon—
'You've been takin' a dhrop o' the
 crathur' an' Danny says 'Troth,
 an' I been
Dhrinkin' yer health wid Shamus O'Shea
 at Katty's shebeen; [1]
But I must be lavin' ye soon.' 'Ochone
 are ye goin' away?'
'Goin' to cut the Sassenach whate' he
 says 'over the say'—
'An' whin will ye meet me agin?' an' I
 hard him 'Molly asthore,
I'll meet you agin tomorra,' says he, 'be
 the chapel-door.'
'An' whin are ye goin' to lave me?'
 'O' Monday mornin'' says he;
'An' shure thin ye'll meet me tomorra?'
 'Tomorra, tomorra, Machree!'
Thin Molly's ould mother, yer Honour,
 that had no likin' for Dan,
Call'd from her cabin an' tould her to
 come away from the man,

[1] Grog-shop.

An' Molly Magee kem flyin' acrass me,
 as light as a lark,
An' Dan stood there for a minute, an'
 thin wint into the dark.
But wirrah! the storm that night—the
 tundher, an' rain that fell,
An' the sthrames runnin' down at the
 back o' the glin 'ud 'a dhrownded
 Hell.

III.

But airth was at pace nixt mornin', an'
 Hiven in its glory smiled,
As the Holy Mother o' Glory that smiles
 at her sleepin' child—
Ethen—she stept an the chapel-green,
 an' she turn'd herself roun'
Wid a diamond dhrop in her eye, for
 Danny was not to be foun',
An' many's the time that I watch'd her
 at mass lettin' down the tear,
For the Divil a Danny was there, yer
 Honour, for forty year.

IV.

Och, Molly Magee, wid the red o' the
 rose an' the white o' the May,
An' yer hair as black as the night, an'
 yer eyes as bright as the day!
Achora, yer laste little whishper was
 sweet as the lilt of a bird!
Acushla, ye set me heart batin' to music
 wid ivery word!
An' sorra the Queen wid her sceptre in
 sich an illigant han',
An' the fall of yer foot in the dance was
 as light as snow an the lan',
An' the sun kem out of a cloud whiniver
 ye walkt in the shtreet,
An' Shamus O'Shea was yer shadda, an'
 laid himself undher yer feet,
An' I loved ye meself wid a heart and a
 half, me darlin', and he
'Ud 'a shot his own sowl dead for a kiss
 of ye, Molly Magee.

V.

But shure we wor betther frinds whin I
 crack'd his skull for her sake,

An' he ped me back wid the best he
   could give at ould Donovan's
   wake—
For the boys wor about her agin whin
   Dan didn't come to the fore,
An' Shamus along wid the rest, but she
   put thim all to the door.
An', afther, I thried her meself av the
   bird 'ud come to me call,
But Molly, begorrah, 'ud listhen to
   naither at all, at all.

VI.

An' her nabours an frinds 'ud consowl an'
   condowl wid her, airly and late,
'Your Danny,' they says, 'niver crasst
   over say to the Sassenach whate ;
He's gone to the States, aroon, an' he's
   married another wife,
An' ye'll niver set eyes an the face of
   the thraithur agin in life !
An' to dhrame of a married man, death
   alive, is a mortial sin.'
But Molly says 'I'd his hand-promise, an'
   shure he'll meet me agin.'

VII.

An' afther her paärints had inter'd glory,
   an' both in wan day,
She began to spake to herself, the
   crathur, an' whishper, an' say
'Tomorra, Tomorra !' an' Father Mo-
   lowny he tuk her in han',
'Molly, you're manin',' he says, 'me
   dear, av I undherstan',
That ye'll meet your paärints agin an'
   yer Danny O'Roon afore God
Wid his blessed Marthyrs an' Saints ;'
   an' she gev him a frindly nod,
'Tomorra, Tomorra,' she says, an' she
   didn't intind to desave,
But her wits wor dead, an' her hair was
   as white as the snow an a grave.

VIII.

Arrah now, here last month they wor
   diggin' the bog, an' they foun'
Dhrownded in black bog-wather a corp
   lyin' undher groun'.

IX.

Yer Honour's own agint, he says to me
   wanst, at Katty's shebeen,
'The Divil take all the black lan', for a
   blessin' 'ud come wid the green !'
An' where 'ud the poor man, thin, cut
   his bit o' turf for the fire ?
But och ! bad scran to the bogs whin
   they swallies the man intire !
An' sorra the bog that's in Hiven wid all
   the light an' the glow,
An' there's hate enough, shure, widout
   thim in the Divil's kitchen below.

X.

Thim ould blind nagers in Agypt, I hard
   his Riverence say,
Could keep their haithen kings in the
   flesh for the Jidgemint day,
An', faix, be the piper o' Moses, they kep
   the cat an' the dog,
But it 'ud 'a been aisier work av they
   lived be an Irish bog.

XI.

How-an-iver they laid this body they
   foun' an the grass
Be the chapel-door, an' the people 'ud
   see it that wint in to mass—
But a frish gineration had riz, an' most
   of the ould was few,
An' I didn't know him meself, an' nōne
   of the parish knew.

XII.

But Molly kem limpin' up wid her stick,
   she was lamed iv a knee,
Thin a slip of a gossoon call'd, 'Div ye
   know him, Molly Magee ?'
An' she stood up strait as the Queen of
   the world—she lifted her head—
'He said he would meet me tomorra !'
   an' dhropt down dead an the dead.

XIII.

Och, Molly, we thought, machree, ye
   would start back agin into life,
Whin we laid yez, aich by aich, at yer
   wake like husban' an' wife.

Sorra the dhry eye thin but was wet for
    the frinds that was gone !
Sorra the silent throat but we hard it
    cryin' ' Ochone !'
An' Shamus O'Shea that has now ten
    childer, hansome an' tall,
Him an' his childer wor keenin' as if he
    had lost thim all.

XIV.

Thin his Riverence buried thim both in
    wan grave be the dead boor-tree,[1]
The young man Danny O'Roon wid his
    ould woman, Molly Magee.

XV.

May all the flowers o' Jeroosilim blossom
    an' spring from the grass,
Imbrashin' an' kissin' aich other—as ye
    did—over yer Crass !
An' the lark fly out o' the flowers wid his
    song to the Sun an' the Moon,
An' tell thim in Hiven about Molly Magee
    an' her Danny O'Roon,
Till Holy St. Pether gets up wid his kays
    an' opens the gate !
An' shure, be the Crass, that's betther
    nor cuttin' the Sassenach whate
To be there wid the Blessed Mother, an'
    Saints an' Marthyrs galore,
An' singin' yer ' Aves.' an' ' Pathers' for
    iver an' ivermore.

XVI.

An' now that I tould yer Honour what-
    iver I hard an' seen,
Yer Honour 'ill give me a thrifle to dhrink
    yer health in potheen.

THE SPINSTER'S SWEET-ARTS.

I.

Milk for my sweet-arts, Bess ! fur it mun
    be the time about now
When Molly cooms in fro' the far-end
    close wi' her paäils fro' the cow.

---

1 Elder-tree.

Eh ! tha be new to the plaäce—thou'rt
    gaäpin'—doesn't tha see
I calls 'em arter the fellers es once was
    sweet upo' me ?

II.

Naäy to be sewer it be past 'er time.
    What maäkes 'er sa laäte ?
Goä to the laäne at the back, an' looök
    thruf Maddison's gaäte !

III.

Sweet-arts ! Molly belike may 'a lighted
    to-night upo' one.
Sweet-arts ! thanks to the Lord that I
    niver not listen'd to noän !
So I sits i' my oän armchair wi' my oän
    kettle theere o' the hob,
An' Tommy the fust, an' Tommy the
    second, an' Steevie an' Rob.

IV.

Rob, coom oop 'ere o' my knee. Thou
    sees that i' spite o' the men
I 'a kep' thruf thick an' thin my two
    'oonderd a-year to mysen ;
Yis ! thaw tha call'd me es pretty es ony
    lass i' the Shere ;
An' thou be es pretty a Tabby, but Robby
    I seed thruf ya theere.

V.

Feyther 'ud saäy I wur ugly es sin, an' I
    beänt not vaäin,
But I niver wur downright hugly, thaw
    soom 'ud 'a thowt ma plaäin,
An' I wasn't sa plaäin i' pink ribbons, ye
    said I wur pretty i' pinks,
An' I liked to 'ear it I did, but I beänt
    sich a fool as ye thinks ;
Ye was stroäkin ma down wi' the 'air, as
    I be a-stroäkin o' you,
But whiniver I looöked i' the glass I wur
    sewer that it couldn't be true ;
Niver wur pretty, not I, but ye knaw'd it
    wur pleasant to 'ear,
Thaw it warn't not me es wur pretty, but
    my two 'oonderd a-year.

VI.

D'ya mind the murnin' when we was a-
 walkin' togither, an' stood
By the claäy'd-oop pond, that the foälk
 be sa scared at, i' Gigglesby wood,
Wheer the poor wench drowndid hersen,
 black Sal, es 'ed been disgraäced?
An' I feel'd thy arm es I stood wur a-
 creeäpin about my waäist;
An' me es wur allus afear'd of a man's
 gittin' ower fond,
I sidled awaäy an' awaäy till I plumpt foot
 fust i' the pond;
And, Robby, I niver 'a liked tha sá well,
 as I did that daäy,
Fur tha joompt in thysen, an' tha hoickt
 my feet wi' a flop fro' the claäy.
Ay, stick oop thy back, an' set oop thy
 taäil, tha may gie ma a kiss,
Fur I walk'd wi' tha all the way hoam
 an' wur niver sa nigh saäyin' Yis.
But wa boäth was i' sich a clat we was
 shaämed to cross Gigglesby Greeän,
Fur a cat may looök at a king thou knaws
 but the cat mun be cleän.
Sa we boäth on us kep out o' sight o' the
 winders o' Gigglesby Hinn—
Naäy, but the claws o' tha! quiet! they
 pricks cleän thruf to the skin—
An' wa boäth slinkt 'oäm by the brokken
 shed i' the laäne at the back,
Wheer the poodle runn'd at tha once, an'
 thou runn'd oop o' the thack;
An' tha squeedg'd my 'and i' the shed,
 fur theere we was forced to 'ide,
Fur I seed that Steevie wur coomin', and
 one o' the Tommies beside.

VII.

Theere now, what art'a mewin at, Steevie?
 for owt I can tell—
Robby wur fust to be sewer, or I mowt
 'a liked tha as well.

VIII.

But, Robby, I thowt o' tha all the while
 I wur chaängin' my gown,
An' I thowt shall I chaänge my staäte?
 but, O Lord, upo' coomin' down—

My bran-new carpet es fresh es a midder
 o' flowers i' Maäy—
Why 'edn't tha wiped thy shoes? it wur
 clatted all ower wi' claäy.
An' I could 'a cried ammost, fur I seed
 that it couldn't be,
An' Robby I gied tha a raätin that sattled
 thy coortin o' me.
An' Molly an' me was agreed, as we was
 a-cleänin' the floor,
That a man be a durty thing an' a trouble
 an' plague wi' indoor.
But I rued it arter a bit, fur I stuck to
 tha moor na the rest,
But I couldn't 'a lived wi' a man an' I
 knaws it be all fur the best.

IX.

Naäy—let ma stroäk tha down till I
 maäkes tha es smooth es silk,
But if I 'ed married tha, Robby, thou'd
 not 'a been worth thy milk,
Thou'd niver 'a cotch'd ony mice but 'a
 left me the work to do,
And 'a taäen to the bottle beside, so es
 all that I 'ears be true;
But I loovs tha to maäke thysen 'appy,
 an' soa purr awaäy, my dear,
Thou 'ed wellnigh purr'd ma awaäy fro'
 my oän two 'oonderd a-year.

X.

Sweärin agean, you Toms, as ye used to
 do twelve year sin'!
Ye niver 'eärd Steevie sweär 'cep' it wur
 at a dog coomin' in,
An' boäth o' ye mun be fools to be hallus
 a-shawin' your claws,
Fur I niver cared nothink for neither—
 an' one o' ye deäd ye knaws!
Coom give hoäver then, weant ye? I
 warrant ye soom fine daäy—
Theere, lig down—I shall hev to gie one
 or tother awaäy.
Can't ye taäke pattern by Steevie? ye
 shant hev a drop fro' the paäil.
Steevie be right good manners bang thruf
 to the tip o' the taäil.

XI.

Robby, git down wi'tha, wilt tha? let
    Steevie coom oop o' my knee.
Steevie, my lad, thou 'ed very nigh been
    the Steevie fur me !
Robby wur fust to be sewer, 'e wur burn
    an' bred i' the 'ouse,
But thou be es 'ansom a tabby es iver
    patted a mouse.

XII.

An' I beänt not vaäin, but I knaws I 'ed
    led tha a quieter life
Nor her wi' the hepitaph yonder ! "A
    faäithful an' loovin' wife !"
An' 'cos o' thy farm by the beck, an' thy
    windmill oop o' the croft,
Tha thowt tha would marry ma, did tha ?
    but that wur a bit ower soft,
Thaw thou was es soäber es daäy, wi' a
    niced red faäce, an' es cleän
Es a shillin' fresh fro' the mint wi' a bran-
    new 'eäd o' the Queeän,
An' thy farmin' es cleän es thysen', fur,
    Steevie, tha kep' it sa neät
That I niver not spied sa much es a
    poppy along wi' the wheät,
An' the wool of a thistle a-flyin' an'
    seeädin' tha haäted to see ;
'Twur es bad es a battle-twig[1] 'ere i' my
    oän blue chaumber to me.
Ay, roob thy whiskers ageän ma, fur I
    could 'a taäen to tha well,
But fur thy bairns, poor Steevie, a
    bouncin' boy an' a gell.

XIII.

An' thou was es fond o' thy bairns es I
    be mysen o' my cats,
But I niver not wish'd fur childer, I
    hevn't naw likin' fur brats ;
Pretty anew when ya dresses 'em oop,
    an' they goäs fur a walk,
Or sits wi' their 'ands afoor 'em, an'
    doesn't not 'inder the talk !
But their bottles o' pap, an' their mucky
    bibs, an' the clats an' the clouts,

[1] Earwig.

An' their mashin' their toys to pieäces
    an' maäkin' ma deäf wi' their
    shouts,
An' hallus a-joompin' about ma as if they
    was set upo' springs,
An' a haxin' ma hawkard questions, an'
    saäyin' ondecent things,
An' a-callin' ma 'hugly' mayhap to my
    faäce, or a teärin' my gown—
Dear ! dear ! dear ! I mun part them
    Tommies—Steevie git down.

XIV.

Ye be wuss nor the men-tommies, you.
    I tell'd ya, na moor o' that !
Tom, lig theere o' the cushion, an' tother
    Tom 'ere o' the mat.

XV.

Theere ! I ha' master'd *them !* IIed I
    married the Tommies—O Lord,
To loove an' obaäy the Tommies ! I
    couldn't 'a stuck by my word.
To be horder'd about, an' waäked, when
    Molly 'd put out the light,
By a man coomin' in wi' a hiccup at ony
    hour o' the night !
An' the taäble staäin'd wi' 'is aäle, an' the
    mud o' 'is boots o' the stairs,
An' the stink o' 'is pipe i' the 'ouse,
    an' the mark o' 'is 'eäd o' the
    chairs !
An' noän o' my four sweet-arts 'ud 'a let
    me 'a hed my oän waäy,
Sa I likes 'em best wi' taäils when they
    'evn't a word to saäy.

XVI.

An' I sits i' my oän little parlour, an'
    sarved by my oän little lass,
Wi' my oän little garden outside, an' my
    oän bed o' sparrow-grass,
An' my oän door-poorch wi' the wood-
    bine an' jessmine a-dressin' it
    greeän,
An' my oän fine Jackman i' purple a
    roäbin' the 'ouse like a Queeän.

XVII.

An' the little gells bobs to ma hoffens es
    I be abroad i' the laänes,
When I goäs fur to coomfut the poor es
    be down wi' their haäches an'
    their paäins:
An' a haäf-pot o' jam, or a mossel o' meät
    when it beänt too dear,
They maäkes ma a graäter Laädy nor 'er
    i' the mansion theer,
Hes 'es hallus to hax of a man how much
    to spare or to spend;
An' a spinster I be an' I will be, if soä
    pleäse God, to the hend.

XVIII.

Mew! mew!—Bess wi' the milk! what
    ha maäde our Molly sa laäte?
It should 'a been 'ere by seven, an' theere
    —it be strikin' height—
'Cushie wur craäzed fur 'er cauf' well—I
    'eärd 'er a maäkin' 'er moän,
An' I thowt to mysen 'thank God that I
    hevn't naw cauf o' my oän.'
Theere!
      Set it down!
          Now Robby!
    You Tommies shall waäit to-night
Till Robby an' Steevie 'es 'ed their lap
    —an' it sarves ye right.

LOCKSLEY HALL

SIXTY YEARS AFTER.

LATE, my grandson! half the morning have I paced these sandy tracts,
Watch'd again the hollow ridges roaring into cataracts,

Wander'd back to living boyhood while I heard the curlews call,
I myself so close on death, and death itself in Locksley Hall.

So—your happy suit was blasted—she the faultless, the divine;
And you liken—boyish babble—this boy-love of yours with mine.

I myself have often babbled doubtless of a foolish past;
Babble, babble; our old England may go down in babble at last.

'Curse him!' curse your fellow-victim? call him dotard in your rage
Eyes that lured a doting boyhood well might fool a dotard's age.

Jilted for a wealthier! wealthier? yet perhaps she was not wise;
I remember how you kiss'd the miniature with those sweet eyes.

In the hall there hangs a painting—Amy's arms about my neck—
Happy children in a sunbeam sitting on the ribs of wreck.

In my life there was a picture, she that clasp'd my neck had flown;
I was left within the shadow sitting on the wreck alone.

Yours has been a slighter ailment, will you sicken for her sake?
You, not you! your modern amourist is of easier, earthlier make.

Amy loved me, Amy fail'd me, Amy was a timid child;
But your Judith—but your worldling—*she* had never driven me wild.

She that holds the diamond necklace dearer than the golden ring,
She that finds a winter sunset fairer than a morn of Spring.

She that in her heart is brooding on his briefer lease of life,
While she vows 'till death shall part us,' she the would-be-widow wife.

She the worldling born of worldlings—father, mother—be content,
Ev'n the homely farm can teach us there is something in descent.

Yonder in that chapel, slowly sinking now into the ground,
Lies the warrior, my forefather, with his feet upon the hound.

Cross'd! for once he sail'd the sea to crush the Moslem in his pride;
Dead the warrior, dead his glory, dead the cause in which he died.

Yet how often I and Amy in the mouldering aisle have stood,
Gazing for one pensive moment on that founder of our blood.

There again I stood to-day, and where of old we knelt in prayer,
Close beneath the casement crimson with the shield of Locksley—there,

All in white Italian marble, looking still as if she smiled,
Lies my Amy dead in child-birth, dead the mother, dead the child.

Dead—and sixty years ago, and dead her aged husband now—
I this old white-headed dreamer stoopt and kiss'd her marble brow.

Gone the fires of youth, the follies, furies, curses, passionate tears,
Gone like fires and floods and earthquakes of the planet's dawning years.

Fires that shook me once, but now to silent ashes fall'n away.
Cold upon the dead volcano sleeps the gleam of dying day.

Gone the tyrant of my youth, and mute below the chancel stones,
All his virtues—I forgive them—black in white above his bones.

Gone the comrades of my bivouac, some in fight against the foe,
Some thro' age and slow diseases, gone as all on earth will go.

Gone with whom for forty years my life in golden sequence ran,
She with all the charm of woman, she with all the breadth of man,

Strong in will and rich in wisdom, Edith, yet so lowly-sweet,
Woman to her inmost heart, and woman to her tender feet,

Very woman of very woman, nurse of ailing body and mind,
She that link'd again the broken chain that bound me to my kind.

Here to-day was Amy with me, while I wander'd down the coast,
Near us Edith's holy shadow, smiling at the slighter ghost.

Gone our sailor son thy father, Leonard early lost at sea;
Thou alone, my boy, of Amy's kin and mine art left to me.

T   2 O

Gone thy tender-natured mother, wearying to be left alone,
Pining for the stronger heart that once had beat beside her own.

Truth, for Truth is Truth, he worshipt, being true as he was brave;
Good, for Good is Good, he follow'd, yet he look'd beyond the grave,

Wiser there than you, that crowning barren Death as lord of all,
Deem this over-tragic drama's closing curtain is the pall!

Beautiful was death in him, who saw the death, but kept the deck,
Saving women and their babes, and sinking with the sinking wreck,

Gone for ever! Ever? no—for since our dying race began,
Ever, ever, and for ever was the leading light of man.

Those that in barbarian burials kill'd the slave, and slew the wife
Felt within themselves the sacred passion of the second life.

Indian warriors dream of ampler hunting grounds beyond the night;
Ev'n the black Australian dying hopes he shall return, a white.

Truth for truth, and good for good! The Good, the True, the Pure, the Just—
Take the charm 'For ever' from them, and they crumble into dust.

Gone the cry of 'Forward, Forward,' lost within a growing gloom;
Lost, or only heard in silence from the silence of a tomb.

Half the marvels of my morning, triumphs over time and space,
Staled by frequence, shrunk by usage into commonest commonplace!

'Forward' rang the voices then, and of the many mine was one.
Let us hush this cry of 'Forward' till ten thousand years have gone.

Far among the vanish'd races, old Assyrian kings would flay
Captives whom they caught in battle—iron-hearted victors they.

Ages after, while in Asia, he that led the wild Moguls,
Timur built his ghastly tower of eighty thousand human skulls,

Then, and here in Edward's time, an age of noblest English names,
Christian conquerors took and flung the conquer'd Christian into flames.

Love your enemy, bless your haters, said the Greatest of the great;
Christian love among the Churches look'd the twin of heathen hate.

From the golden alms of Blessing man had coin'd himself a curse:
Rome of Cæsar, Rome of Peter, which was crueller? which was worse?

France had shown a light to all men, preach'd a Gospel, all men's good;
Celtic Demos rose a Demon, shriek'd and slaked the light with blood.

Hope was ever on her mountain, watching till the day begun—
Crown'd with sunlight—over darkness—from the still unrisen sun.

Have we grown at last beyond the passions of the primal clan?
'Kill your enemy, for you hate him,' still, 'your enemy' was a man.

Have we sunk below them? peasants maim the helpless horse, and drive
Innocent cattle under thatch, and burn the kindlier brutes alive.

Brutes, the brutes are not your wrongers—burnt at midnight, found at morn,
Twisted hard in mortal agony with their offspring, born-unborn,

Clinging to the silent mother! Are we devils? are we men?
Sweet St. Francis of Assisi, would that he were here again,

He that in his Catholic wholeness used to call the very flowers
Sisters, brothers—and the beasts—whose pains are hardly less than ours!

Chaos, Cosmos! Cosmos, Chaos! who can tell how all will end?
Read the wide world's annals, you, and take their wisdom for your friend.

Hope the best, but hold the Present fatal daughter of the Past,
Shape your heart to front the hour, but dream not that the hour will last.

Ay, if dynamite and revolver leave you courage to be wise:
When was age so cramm'd with menace? madness? written, spoken lies?

Envy wears the mask of Love, and, laughing sober fact to scorn,
Cries to Weakest as to Strongest, 'Ye are equals, equal-born.'

Equal-born? O yes, if yonder hill be level with the flat.
Charm us, Orator, till the Lion look no larger than the Cat,

Till the Cat thro' that mirage of overheated language loom
Larger than the Lion,—Demos end in working its own doom.

Russia bursts our Indian barrier, shall we fight her? shall we yield?
Pause! before you sound the trumpet, hear the voices from the field.

Those three hundred millions under one Imperial sceptre now,
Shall we hold them? shall we loose them? take the suffrage of the plow.

Nay, but these would feel and follow Truth if only you and you,
Rivals of realm-ruining party, when you speak were wholly true.

Plowmen, Shepherds, have I found, and more than once, and still could find,
Sons of God, and kings of men in utter nobleness of mind,

Truthful, trustful, looking upward to the practised hustings-liar;
So the Higher wields the Lower, while the Lower is the Higher.

Here and there a cotter's babe is royal-born by right divine;
Here and there my lord is lower than his oxen or his swine.

Chaos, Cosmos! Cosmos, Chaos! once again the sickening game;
Freedom, free to slay herself, and dying while they shout her name.

Step by step we gain'd a freedom known to Europe, known to all;
Step by step we rose to greatness,—thro' the tonguesters we may fall.

You that woo the Voices—tell them 'old experience is a fool,'
Teach your flatter'd kings that only those who cannot read can rule.

Pluck the mighty from their seat, but set no meek ones in their place;
Pillory Wisdom in your markets, pelt your offal at her face.

Tumble Nature heel o'er head, and, yelling with the yelling street,
Set the feet above the brain and swear the brain is in the feet.

Bring the old dark ages back without the faith, without the hope,
Break the State, the Church, the Throne, and roll their ruins down the slope.

Authors—essayist, atheist, novelist, realist, rhymester, play your part,
Paint the mortal shame of nature with the living hues of Art.

Rip your brothers' vices open, strip your own foul passions bare;
Down with Reticence, down with Reverence—forward—naked—let them stare.

Feed the budding rose of boyhood with the drainage of your sewer;
Send the drain into the fountain, lest the stream should issue pure.

Set the maiden fancies wallowing in the troughs of Zolaism,—
Forward, forward, ay and backward, downward too into the abysm.

Do your best to charm the worst, to lower the rising race of men;
Have we risen from out the beast, then back into the beast again?

Only 'dust to dust' for me that sicken at your lawless din,
Dust in wholesome old-world dust before the newer world begin.

Heated am I? you—you wonder—well, it scarce becomes mine age—
Patience! let the dying actor mouth his last upon the stage.

Cries of unprogressive dotage ere the dotard fall asleep?
Noises of a current narrowing, not the music of a deep?

Ay, for doubtless I am old, and think gray thoughts, for I am gray:
After all the stormy changes shall we find a changeless May?

After madness, after massacre, Jacobinism and Jacquerie,
Some diviner force to guide us thro' the days I shall not see?

When the schemes and all the systems, Kingdoms and Republics fall,
Something kindlier, higher, holier—all for each and each for all?

All the full-brain, half-brain races, led by Justice, Love, and Truth;
All the millions one at length with all the visions of my youth?

All diseases quench'd by Science, no man halt, or deaf or blind;
Stronger ever born of weaker, lustier body, larger mind?

Earth at last a warless world, a single race, a single tongue—
I have seen her far away—for is not Earth as yet so young?—

Every tiger madness muzzled, every serpent passion kill'd,
Every grim ravine a garden, every blazing desert till'd,

Robed in universal harvest up to either pole she smiles,
Universal ocean softly washing all her warless Isles.

Warless? when her tens are thousands, and her thousands millions, then—
All her harvest all too narrow—who can fancy warless men?

Warless? war will die out late then. Will it ever? late or soon?
Can it, till this outworn earth be dead as yon dead world the moon?

Dead the new astronomy calls her. . . . On this day and at this hour,
In this gap between the sandhills, whence you see the Locksley tower,

Here we met, our latest meeting—Amy—sixty years ago—
She and I—the moon was falling greenish thro' a rosy glow,

Just above the gateway tower, and even where you see her now—
Here we stood and claspt each other, swore the seeming-deathless vow. . . .

Dead, but how her living glory lights the hall, the dune, the grass!
Yet the moonlight is the sunlight, and the sun himself will pass.

Venus near her! smiling downward at this earthlier earth of ours,
Closer on the Sun, perhaps a world of never fading flowers.

Hesper, whom the poet call'd the Bringer home of all good things.
All good things may move in Hesper, perfect peoples, perfect kings.

Hesper—Venus—were we native to that splendour or in Mars,
We should see the Globe we groan in, fairest of their evening stars.

Could we dream of wars and carnage, craft and madness, lust and spite,
Roaring London, raving Paris, in that point of peaceful light?

Might we not in glancing heavenward on a star so silver-fair,
Yearn, and clasp the hands and murmur, 'Would to God that we were there'?

Forward, backward, backward, forward, in the immeasurable sea,
Sway'd by vaster ebbs and flows than can be known to you or me.

All the suns—are these but symbols of innumerable man,
Man or Mind that sees a shadow of the planner or the plan?

Is there evil but on earth? or pain in every peopled sphere?
Well be grateful for the sounding watchword 'Evolution' here,

Evolution ever climbing after some ideal good,
And Reversion ever dragging Evolution in the mud.

What are men that He should heed us? cried the king of sacred song;
Insects of an hour, that hourly work their brother insect wrong,

While the silent Heavens roll, and Suns along their fiery way,
All their planets whirling round them, flash a million miles a day.

Many an Æon moulded earth before her highest, man, was born,
Many an Æon too may pass when earth is manless and forlorn,

Earth so huge, and yet so bounded—pools of salt, and plots of land—
Shallow skin of green and azure—chains of mountain, grains of sand

Only That which made us, meant us to be mightier by and by,
Set the sphere of all the boundless Heavens within the human eye,

Sent the shadow of Himself, the boundless, thro' the human soul;
Boundless inward, in the atom, boundless outward, in the Whole.

*   *   *   *   *   *   *

Here is Locksley Hall, my grandson, here the lion-guarded gate.
Not to-night in Locksley Hall—to-morrow—you, you come so late.

Wreck'd—your train—or all but wreck'd? a shatter'd wheel? a vicious boy
Good, this forward, you that preach it, is it well to wish you joy?

Is it well that while we range with Science, glorying in the Time,
City children soak and blacken soul and sense in city slime?

There among the glooming alleys Progress halts on palsied feet,
Crime and hunger cast our maidens by the thousand on the street.

There the Master scrimps his haggard sempstress of her daily bread,
There a single sordid attic holds the living and the dead.

There the smouldering fire of fever creeps across the rotted floor,
And the crowded couch of incest in the warrens of the poor.

Nay, your pardon, cry your 'forward,' yours are hope and youth, but I
Eighty winters leave the dog too lame to follow with the cry,

Lame and old, and past his time, and passing now into the night;
Yet I would the rising race were half as eager for the light.

Light the fading gleam of Even? light the glimmer of the dawn?
Aged eyes may take the growing glimmer for the gleam withdrawn.

Far away beyond her myriad coming changes earth will be
Something other than the wildest modern guess of you and me.

Earth may reach her earthly-worst, or if she gain her earthly-best,
Would she find her human offspring this ideal man at rest?

Forward then, but still remember how the course of Time will swerve,
Crook and turn upon itself in many a backward streaming curve.

Not the Hall to-night, my grandson ! Death and Silence hold their own.
Leave the Master in the first dark hour of his last sleep alone.

Worthier soul was he than I am, sound and honest, rustic Squire,
Kindly landlord, boon companion—youthful jealousy is a liar.

Cast the poison from your bosom, oust the madness from your brain.
Let the trampled serpent show you that you have not lived in vain.

Youthful ! youth and age are scholars yet but in the lower school,
Nor is he the wisest man who never proved himself a fool.

Yonder lies our young sea-village—Art and Grace are less and less :
Science grows and Beauty dwindles—roofs of slated hideousness !

There is one old Hostel left us where they swing the Locksley shield,
Till the peasant cow shall butt the ' Lion passant ' from his field.

Poor old Heraldry, poor old History, poor old Poetry, passing hence,
In the common deluge drowning old political common-sense !

Poor old voice of eighty crying after voices that have fled !
All I loved are vanish'd voices, all my steps are on the dead.

All the world is ghost to me, and as the phantom disappears,
Forward far and far from here is all the hope of eighty years.

*   *   *   *   *   *   *

In this Hostel—I remember—I repent it o'er his grave—
Like a clown—by chance he met me—I refused the hand he gave.

From that casement where the trailer mantles all the mouldering bricks—
I was then in early boyhood, Edith but a child of six—

While I shelter'd in this archway from a day of driving showers—
Peept the winsome face of Edith like a flower among the flowers.

Here to-night ! the Hall to-morrow, when they toll the Chapel bell !
Shall I hear in one dark room a wailing, ' I have loved thee well.'

Then a peal that shakes the portal—one has come to claim his bride,
Her that shrank, and put me from her, shriek'd, and started from my side—

Silent echoes ! You, my Leonard, use and not abuse your day,
Move among your people, know them, follow him who led the way,

Strove for sixty widow'd years to help his homelier brother men,
Served the poor, and built the cottage, raised the school, and drain'd the fen.

Hears he now the Voice that wrong'd him ? who shall swear it cannot be ?
Earth would never touch her worst, were one in fifty such as he.

Ere she gain her Heavenly-best, a God must mingle with the game :
Nay, there may be those about us whom we neither see nor name,

Felt within us as ourselves, the Powers of Good, the Powers of Ill,
Strowing balm, or shedding poison in the fountains of the Will.

Follow you the Star that lights a desert pathway, yours or mine.
Forward, till you see the highest Human Nature is divine.

Follow Light, and do the Right—for man can half-control his doom
Till you find the deathless Angel seated in the vacant tomb.

Forward, let the stormy moment fly and mingle with the Past.
I that loathed, have come to love him.   Love will conquer at the last

Gone at eighty, mine own age, and I and you will bear the pall;
Then I leave thee Lord and Master, latest Lord of Locksley Hall.

see p 222

PROLOGUE
TO GENERAL HAMLEY.

OUR birches yellowing and from each
   The light leaf falling fast,
While squirrels from our fiery beech
   Were bearing off the mast,
You came, and look'd and loved the view
   Long-known and loved by me,
Green Sussex fading into blue
   With one gray glimpse of sea;
And, gazing from this height alone,
   We spoke of what had been
Most marvellous in the wars your own
   Crimean eyes had seen;
And now—like old-world inns that take
   Some warrior for a sign
That therewithin a guest may make
   True cheer with honest wine—
Because you heard the lines I read
   Nor utter'd word of blame,
I dare without your leave to head
   These rhymings with your name,
Who know you but as one of those
   I fain would meet again,
Yet know you, as your England knows
   That you and all your men
Were soldiers to her heart's desire,
   When, in the vanish'd year,
You saw the league-long rampart-fire
   Flare from Tel-el-Kebir
Thro' darkness, and the foe was driven,
   And Wolseley overthrew
Arâbi, and the stars in heaven
   Paled, and the glory grew.

THE CHARGE OF THE HEAVY
BRIGADE AT BALACLAVA.

OCTOBER 25, 1854.

I.

THE charge of the gallant three hundred,
   the Heavy Brigade!
Down the hill, down the hill, thousands
   of Russians,
Thousands of horsemen, drew to the
   valley—and stay'd;
For Scarlett and Scarlett's three hundred
   were riding by
When the points of the Russian lances
   arose in the sky;
And he call'd ' Left wheel into line!'
   and they wheel'd and obey'd.
Then he look'd at the host that had
   halted he knew not why,
And he turn'd half round, and he bad his
   trumpeter sound
To the charge, and he rode on ahead, as
   he waved his blade
To the gallant three hundred whose glory
   will never die—
' Follow,' and up the hill, up the hill, up
   the hill,
Follow'd the Heavy Brigade.

II.

The trumpet, the gallop, the charge,
   and the might of the fight!

Thousands of horsemen had gather'd
    there on the height,
With a wing push'd out to the left and
    a wing to the right,
And who shall escape if they close ? but
    he dash'd up alone
Thro' the great gray slope of men,
Sway'd his sabre, and held his own
Like an Englishman there and then ;
All in a moment follow'd with force
Three that were next in their fiery
    course,
Wedged themselves in between horse
    and horse,
Fought for their lives in the narrow gap
    they had made—
Four amid thousands! and up the hill,
    up the hill,
Gallopt the gallant three hundred, the
    Heavy Brigade.

III.

Fell like a cannonshot,
Burst like a thunderbolt,
Crash'd like a hurricane,
Broke thro' the mass from below,
Drove thro' the midst of the foe,
Plunged up and down, to and fro,
Rode flashing blow upon blow,
Brave Inniskillens and Greys
Whirling their sabres in circles of light !
And some of us, all in amaze,
Who were held for a while from the
    fight,
And were only standing at gaze,
When the dark-muffled Russian crowd
Folded its wings from the left and the
    right,
And roll'd them around like a cloud,—
O mad for the charge and the battle
    were we,
When our own good redcoats sank from
    sight,
Like drops of blood in a dark-gray
    sea,
And we turn'd to each other, whispering,
    all dismay'd,
'Lost are the gallant three hundred of
    Scarlett's Brigade !'

IV.

'Lost one and all' were the words
Mutter'd in our dismay ;
But they rode like Victors and Lords
Thro' the forest of lances and swords
In the heart of the Russian hordes,
They rode, or they stood at bay—
Struck with the sword-hand and slew,
Down with the bridle-hand drew
The foe from the saddle and threw
Underfoot there in the fray—
Ranged like a storm or stood like a rock
In the wave of a stormy day ;
Till suddenly shock upon shock
Stagger'd the mass from without,
Drove it in wild disarray,
For our men gallopt up with a cheer and
    a shout,
And the foeman surged, and waver'd, and
    reel'd
Up the hill, up the hill, up the hill, out
    of the field,
And over the brow and away.

V.

Glory to each and to all, and the charge
    that they made !
Glory to all the three hundred, and all
    the Brigade !

NOTE.—The 'three hundred' of the 'Heavy
Brigade' who made this famous charge were the
Scots Greys and the 2nd squadron of Inniskil-
lings ; the remainder of the 'Heavy Brigade'
subsequently dashing up to their support.

The 'three' were Scarlett's aide-de-camp,
Elliot, and the trumpeter and Shegog the orderly,
who had been close behind him.

EPILOGUE.

IRENE.

NOT this way will you set your name
    A star among the stars.

POET.

What way?

IRENE.

You praise when you should blame
The barbarism of wars.
A juster epoch has begun.

POET.

Yet tho' this cheek be gray,
And that bright hair the modern sun,
Those eyes the blue to-day,
You wrong me, passionate little friend.
I would that wars should cease,
I would the globe from end to end
Might sow and reap in peace,
And some new Spirit o'erbear the old,
Or Love with wreaths of flowers.
From war with kindly links of gold,
Or Love with wreaths of flowers.
Slav, Teuton, Kelt, I count them all
My friends and brother souls,
With all the peoples, great and small,
That wheel between the poles.
But since, our mortal shadow, Ill
To waste this earth began—
Perchance from some abuse of Will
In worlds before the man
Involving ours—he needs must fight
To make true peace his own,
He needs must combat might with might,
Or Might would rule alone ;
And who loves War for War's own sake
Is fool, or crazed, or worse ;
But let the patriot-soldier take
His meed of fame in verse ;
Nay—tho' that realm were in the wrong
For which her warriors bleed,
It still were right to crown with song
The warrior's noble deed—
A crown the Singer hopes may last,
For so the deed endures ;
But Song will vanish in the Vast ;
And that large phrase of yours
'A Star among the stars,' my dear,
Is girlish talk at best ;
For dare we dally with the sphere
As he did half in jest,
Old Horace?   'I will strike' said he
'The stars with head sublime,'
But scarce could see, as now we see,
The man in Space and Time,

So drew perchance a happier lot
Than ours, who rhyme to-day.
The fires that arch this dusky dot—
Yon myriad-worlded way—
The vast sun-clusters' gather'd blaze,
World-isles in lonely skies,
Whole heavens within themselves, amaze
Our brief humanities ;
And so does Earth ; for Homer's fame,
Tho' carved in harder stone—
The falling drop will make his name
As mortal as my own.

IRENE.

No !

POET.

Let it live then—ay, till when?
Earth passes, all is lost
In what they prophesy, our wise men,
Sun-flame or sunless frost,
And deed and song alike are swept
Away, and all in vain
As far as man can see, except
The man himself remain ;
And tho', in this lean age forlorn,
Too many a voice may cry
That man can have no after-morn,
Not yet of these am I.
The man remains, and whatsoe'er
He wrought of good or brave
Will mould him thro' the cycle-year
That dawns behind the grave.

And here the Singer for his Art
Not all in vain may plead
'The song that nerves a nation's heart,
Is in itself a deed.'

TO VIRGIL.

WRITTEN AT THE REQUEST OF THE
MANTUANS FOR THE NINETEENTH
CENTENARY OF VIRGIL'S DEATH.

I.

ROMAN VIRGIL, thou that singest
Ilion's lofty temples robed in fire,

Ilion falling, Rome arising,
        wars, and filial faith, and Dido's
                pyre;

II.

Landscape-lover, lord of language
        more than he that sang the Works
                and Days,
All the chosen coin of fancy
        flashing out from many a golden
                phrase;

III.

Thou that singest wheat and woodland,
        tilth and vineyard, hive and horse
                and herd;
All the charm of all the Muses
        often flowering in a lonely word;

IV.

Poet of the happy Tityrus
        piping underneath his beechen
                bowers;
Poet of the poet-satyr
        whom the laughing shepherd
                bound with flowers;

V.

Chanter of the Pollio, glorying
        in the blissful years again to be,
Summers of the snakeless meadow,
        unlaborious earth and oarless sea;

VI.

Thou that seëst Universal
        Nature moved by Universal
                Mind;
Thou majestic in thy sadness
        at the doubtful doom of human
                kind;

VII.

Light among the vanish'd ages;
        star that gildest yet this phantom
                shore;
Golden branch amid the shadows,
        kings and realms that pass to rise
                no more;

VIII.

Now thy Forum roars no longer,
        fallen every purple Cæsar's
                dome—
Tho' thine ocean-roll of rhythm
        sound for ever of Imperial
                Rome—

IX.

Now the Rome of slaves hath perish'd,
        and the Rome of freemen holds
                her place,
I, from out the Northern Island
        sunder'd once from all the human
                race,

X.

I salute thee, Mantovano,
        I that loved thee since my day
                began,
Wielder of the stateliest measure
        ever moulded by the lips of man.

THE DEAD PROPHET.

182-.

I.

DEAD!
        And the Muses cried with a stormy cry
'Send them no more, for evermore.
        Let the people die.'

II.

Dead!
        'Is it *he* then brought so low?'
And a careless people flock'd from the
        fields
        With a purse to pay for the show.

III.

Dead, who had served his time,
        Was one of the people's kings,
Had labour'd in lifting them out of slime,
        And showing them, souls have wings!

IV.

Dumb on the winter heath he lay.
  His friends had stript him bare,
And roll'd his nakedness everyway
  That all the crowd might stare.

V.

A storm-worn signpost not to be read,
  And a tree with a moulder'd nest
On its barkless bones, stood stark by the
    dead;
  And behind him, low in the West,

VI.

With shifting ladders of shadow and light,
  And blurr'd in colour and form,
The sun hung over the gates of Night,
  And glared at a coming storm.

VII.

Then glided a vulturous Beldam forth,
  That on dumb death had thriven;
They call'd her 'Reverence' here upon
    earth,
  And 'The Curse of the Prophet' in
    Heaven.

VIII.

She knelt—'We worship him'—all but
    wept—
  'So great so noble was he!'
She clear'd her sight, she arose, she swept
  The dust of earth from her knee.

IX.

'Great! for he spoke and the people
    heard,
  And his eloquence caught like a flame
From zone to zone of the world, till his
    Word
  Had won him a noble name.

X.

Noble! he sung, and the sweet sound ran
  Thro' palace and cottage door,
For he touch'd on the whole sad planet
    of man,
  The kings and the rich and the poor;

XI.

And he sung not alone of an old sun set,
  But a sun coming up in his youth!
Great and noble—O yes—but yet—
  For man is a lover of Truth,

XII.

And bound to follow, wherever she go
  Stark-naked, and up or down,
Thro' her high hill-passes of stainless
    snow,
  Or the foulest sewer of the town—

XIII.

Noble and great—O ay—but then,
  Tho' a prophet should have his due,
Was he noblier-fashion'd than other men?
  Shall we see to it, I and you?

XIV.

For since he would sit on a Prophet's
    seat,
  As a lord of the Human soul,
We needs must scan him from head to
    feet
  Were it but for a wart or a mole?'

XV.

His wife and his child stood by him in
    tears,
  But she—she push'd them aside.
'Tho' a name may last for a thousand
    years,
  Yet a truth is a truth,' she cried.

XVI.

And she that had haunted his pathway
    still,
  Had often truckled and cower'd
When he rose in his wrath, and had
    yielded her will
  To the master, as overpower'd,

XVII.

She tumbled his helpless corpse about.
  'Small blemish upon the skin!
But I think we know what is fair without
  Is often as foul within.'

XVIII.

She crouch'd, she tore him part from part,
  And out of his body she drew
The red 'Blood-eagle'[1] of liver and
    heart ;
  She held them up to the view ;

XIX.

She gabbled, as she groped in the dead,
  And all the people were pleased ;
' See, what a little heart,' she said,
  ' And the liver is half-diseased ! '

XX.

She tore the Prophet after death,
  And the people paid her well.
Lightnings flicker'd along the heath ;
  One shriek'd ' The fires of Hell ! '

EARLY SPRING.

I.

ONCE more the Heavenly Power
  Makes all things new,
And domes the red-plow'd hills
  With loving blue ;
The blackbirds have their wills,
  The throstles too.

II.

Opens a door in Heaven ;
  From skies of glass
A Jacob's ladder falls
  On greening grass,
And o'er the mountain-walls
  Young angels pass.

III.

Before them fleets the shower,
  And burst the buds,
And shine the level lands,
  And flash the floods ;
The stars are from their hands
  Flung thro' the woods,

[1] Old Viking term for lungs, liver, etc., when
torn by the conqueror out of the body of the
conquered.

IV.

The woods with living airs
  How softly fann'd,
Light airs from where the deep,
  All down the sand,
Is breathing in his sleep,
  Heard by the land.

V.

O follow, leaping blood,
  The season's lure !
O heart, look down and up
  Serene, secure,
Warm as the crocus cup,
  Like snowdrops, pure !

VI.

Past, Future glimpse and fade
  Thro' some slight spell,
A gleam from yonder vale,
  Some far blue fell,
And sympathies, how frail,
  In sound and smell !

VII.

Till at thy chuckled note,
  Thou twinkling bird,
The fairy fancies range,
  And, lightly stirr'd,
Ring little bells of change
  From word to word.

VIII.

For now the Heavenly Power
  Makes all things new,
And thaws the cold, and fills
  The flower with dew ;
The blackbirds have their wills,
  The poets too.

PREFATORY POEM TO MY BROTHER'S SONNETS.

Midnight, June 30, 1879.

I.

MIDNIGHT—in no midsummer tune
The breakers lash the shores :

The cuckoo of a joyless June
Is calling out of doors :

And thou hast vanish'd from thine own
To that which looks like rest,
True brother, only to be known
By those who love thee best.

II.

Midnight—and joyless June gone by,
And from the deluged park
The cuckoo of a worse July
Is calling thro' the dark :

But thou art silent underground,
And o'er thee streams the rain,
True poet, surely to be found
When Truth is found again.

III.

And, now to these unsummer'd skies
The summer bird is still,
Far off a phantom cuckoo cries
From out a phantom hill ;

And thro' this midnight breaks the sun
Of sixty years away,
The light of days when life begun,
The days that seem to-day,

When all my griefs were shared with thee,
As all my hopes were thine—
As all thou wert was one with me,
May all thou art be mine !

'FRATER AVE ATQUE VALE.'

Row us out from Desenzano, to your
    Sirmione row !
So they row'd, and there we landed—'O
    venusta Sirmio !'
There to me thro' all the groves of olive
    in the summer glow,
There beneath the Roman ruin where the
    purple flowers grow,
Came that 'Ave atque Vale' of the Poet's
    hopeless woe,
Tenderest of Roman poets nineteen-
    hundred years ago,

'Frater Ave atque Vale'—as we wander'd
    to and fro
Gazing at the Lydian laughter of the
    Garda Lake below
Sweet Catullus's all-but-island, olive-
    silvery Sirmio !

HELEN'S TOWER.[1]

HELEN'S TOWER, here I stand,
Dominant over sea and land.
Son's love built me, and I hold
Mother's love in letter'd gold.
Love is in and out of time,
I am mortal stone and lime.
Would my granite girth were strong
As either love, to last as long !
I should wear my crown entire
To and thro' the Doomsday fire,
And be found of angel eyes
In earth's recurring Paradise.

EPITAPH ON LORD STRAT-
FORD DE REDCLIFFE.

IN WESTMINSTER ABBEY.

THOU third great Canning, stand among
    our best
    And noblest, now thy long day's work
    hath ceased,
Here silent in our Minster of the West
    Who wert the voice of England in the
    East.

EPITAPH
ON GENERAL GORDON.

IN THE GORDON BOYS' NATIONAL
MEMORIAL HOME NEAR WOKING.

WARRIOR of God, man's friend, and
    tyrant's foe,
    Now somewhere dead far in the waste
    Soudan,
Thou livest in all hearts, for all men know
    This earth has never borne a nobler
    man.

1 Written at the request of my friend, Lord
    Dufferin.

EPITAPH ON CAXTON.

In St. Margaret's, Westminster.

Fiat Lux (his motto).

THY prayer was 'Light—more Light—
  while Time shall last !'
Thou sawest a glory growing on the night,
But not the shadows which that light
  would cast,
Till shadows vanish in the Light of Light.

TO THE DUKE OF ARGYLL.

O Patriot Statesman, be thou wise to
    know
The limits of resistance, and the bounds
Determining concession ; still be bold
Not only to slight praise but suffer scorn ;
And be thy heart a fortress to maintain
The day against the moment, and the
    year
Against the day ; thy voice, a music
    heard
Thro' all the yells and counter-yells of
    feud
And faction, and thy will, a power to
    make
This ever-changing world of circumstance,
In changing, chime with never-changing
    Law.

HANDS ALL ROUND.

FIRST pledge our Queen this solemn
    night,
  Then drink to England, every guest ;
That man's the best Cosmopolite
  Who loves his native country best.
May freedom's oak for ever live
  With stronger life from day to day ;
That man's the true Conservative
  Who lops the moulder'd branch away.
      Hands all round !
  God the traitor's hope confound !

To this great cause of Freedom drink,
    my friends,
  And the great name of England, round
    and round.

To all the loyal hearts who long
  To keep our English Empire whole !
To all our noble sons, the strong
  New England of the Southern Pole !
To England under Indian skies,
  To those dark millions of her realm !
To Canada whom we love and prize,
  Whatever statesman hold the helm.
      Hands all round !
  God the traitor's hope confound !
To this great name of England drink,
    my friends,
  And all her glorious empire, round and
    round.

To all our statesmen so they be
  True leaders of the land's desire !
To both our Houses, may they see
  Beyond the borough and the shire !
We sail'd wherever ship could sail,
  We founded many a mighty state ;
Pray God our greatness may not fail
  Thro' craven fears of being great.
      Hands all round !
  God the traitor's hope confound !
To this great cause of Freedom drink,
    my friends,
  And the great name of England, round
    and round.

FREEDOM.

I.

O THOU so fair in summers gone,
  While yet thy fresh and virgin soul
Inform'd the pillar'd Parthenon,
  The glittering Capitol ;

II.

So fair in southern sunshine bathed,
  But scarce of such majestic mien
As here with forehead vapour-swathed
  In meadows ever green ;

III.

For thou—when Athens reign'd and
    Rome,
  Thy glorious eyes were dimm'd with
    pain
To mark in many a freeman's home
  The slave, the scourge, the chain;

IV.

O follower of the Vision, still
  In motion to the distant gleam,
Howe'er blind force and brainless will
  May jar thy golden dream

V.

Of Knowledge fusing class with class,
  Of civic Hate no more to be,
Of Love to leaven all the mass,
  Till every Soul be free;

VI.

Who yet, like Nature, wouldst not mar
  By changes all too fierce and fast
This order of Her Human Star,
  This heritage of the past;

VII.

O scorner of the party cry
  That wanders from the public good,
Thou—when the nations rear on high
  Their idol smear'd with blood,

VIII.

And when they roll their idol down—
  Of saner worship sanely proud;
Thou loather of the lawless crown
  As of the lawless crowd;

IX.

How long thine ever-growing mind
  Hath still'd the blast and strown the
    wave,
Tho' some of late would raise a wind
  To sing thee to thy grave,

X.

Men loud against all forms of power—
  Unfurnish'd brows, tempestuous
    tongues—
Expecting all things in an hour—
  Brass mouths and iron lungs !

TO H.R.H. PRINCESS BEATRICE.

Two Suns of Love make day of human
  life,
Which else with all its pains, and griefs,
  and deaths,
Were utter darkness—one, the Sun of
  dawn
That brightens thro' the Mother's tender
  eyes,
And warms the child's awakening world
    —and one
The later-rising Sun of spousal Love,
Which from her household orbit draws
  the child
To move in other spheres. The Mother
  weeps
At that white funeral of the single life,
Her maiden daughter's marriage; and
  her tears
Are half of pleasure, half of pain—the
  child
Is happy—ev'n in leaving *her !* but Thou,
True daughter, whose all-faithful, filial
  eyes
Have seen the loneliness of earthly thrones,
Wilt neither quit the widow'd Crown
  nor let
This later light of Love have risen in vain,
But moving thro' the Mother's home,
  between
The two that love thee, lead a summer
  life,
Sway'd by each Love, and swaying to
  each Love,
Like some conjectured planet in mid
  heaven
Between two Suns, and drawing down
  from both
The light and genial warmth of double day.

THE FLEET.[1]

I.

YOU, you, *if* you shall fail to understand
  What England is, and what her all-in-
  all,
On you will come the curse of all the
land,
  Should this old England fall
    Which Nelson left so great.

[1] The speaker said that 'he should like to be
assured that other outlying portions of the
Empire, the Crown colonies, and important
coaling stations were being as promptly and as
thoroughly fortified as the various capitals of the
self-governing colonies. He was credibly in-
formed this was not so. It was impossible, also,
not to feel some degree of anxiety about the
efficacy of present provision to defend and pro-
tect, by means of swift well-armed cruisers, the
immense mercantile fleet of the Empire. A third
source of anxiety, so far as the colonies were
concerned, was the apparently insufficient provision for the rapid manufacture of armaments and
their prompt despatch when ordered to their
colonial destination. Hence the necessity for
manufacturing appliances equal to the require-
ments, not of Great Britain alone, but of the
whole Empire. But the keystone of the whole
was the necessity for an overwhelmingly powerful
fleet and efficient defence for all necessary coaling
stations. This was as essential for the colonies
as for Great Britain. It was the one condition
for the continuance of the Empire. All that
Continental Powers did with respect to armies
England should effect with her navy. It was
essentially a defensive force, and could be moved
rapidly from point to point, but it should be equal
to all that was expected from it. It was to
strengthen the fleet that colonists would first
readily tax themselves, because they realised how
essential a powerful fleet was to the safety, not
only of that extensive commerce sailing in every
sea, but ultimately to the security of the distant
portions of the Empire. Who could estimate the
loss involved in even a brief period of disaster to
the Imperial Navy? Any amount of money
timely expended in preparation would be quite
insignificant when compared with the possible
calamity he had referred to.'—*Extract from Sir
Graham Berry's Speech at the Colonial Institute, 9th November* 1886.

T

II.

His isle, the mightiest Ocean-power on
earth,
  Our own fair isle, the lord of every sea—
Her fuller franchise—what would that be
worth—
  Her ancient fame of Free—
    Were she . . . a fallen state?

III.

Her dauntless army scatter'd, and so
small,
  Her island-myriads fed from alien
  lands—
The fleet of England is her all-in-all;
  Her fleet is in your hands,
    And in her fleet her Fate.

IV.

You, you, that have the ordering of her
fleet,
  If you should only compass her disgrace,
When all men starve, the wild mob's
million feet
  Will kick you from your place,
    But then too late, too late.

OPENING OF THE INDIAN AND COLONIAL EXHIBI-TION BY THE QUEEN.

*Written at the Request of the Prince
of Wales.*

I.

WELCOME, welcome with one voice!
In your welfare we rejoice,
Sons and brothers that have sent,
From isle and cape and continent,
Produce of your field and flood,
Mount and mine, and primal wood;
Works of subtle brain and hand,
And splendours of the morning land,
Gifts from every British zone;
  Britons, hold your own!

2 P

II

May we find, as ages run,
The mother featured in the son ;
And may yours for ever be
That old strength and constancy
Which has made your fathers great
In our ancient island State,
And wherever her flag fly,
Glorying between sea and sky,
Makes the might of Britain known;
    Britons, hold your own !

III.

Britain fought her sons of yore—
Britain fail'd ; and never more,
Careless of our growing kin,
Shall we sin our fathers' sin,
Men that in a narrower day—
Unprophetic rulers they—
Drove from out the mother's nest
That young eagle of the West
To forage for herself alone ;
    Britons, hold your own !

IV.

Sharers of our glorious past,
Brothers, must we part at last ?
Shall we not thro' good and ill
Cleave to one another still ?
Britain's myriad voices call,
' Sons, be welded each and all,
Into one imperial whole,
One with Britain, heart and soul !
One life, one flag, one fleet, one Throne !'
    Britons, hold your own !

POETS AND THEIR BIBLIO-
GRAPHIES.

OLD poets foster'd under friendlier skies,
    Old Virgil who would write ten lines,
        they say,
    At dawn, and lavish all the golden
        day
To make them wealthier in his readers'
    eyes ;

And you, old popular Horace, you the
    wise
    Adviser of the nine-years-ponder'd lay,
    And you, that wear a wreath of sweeter
        bay,
Catullus, whose dead songster never dies;
If, glancing downward on the kindly
    sphere
    That once had roll'd you round and
        round the Sun,
    You see your Art still shrined in
        human shelves,
You should be jubilant that you flourish'd
    here
Before the Love of Letters, overdone,
Had swampt the sacred poets with
    themselves.

TO W. C. MACREADY.

. 1851.

FAREWELL, Macready, since to-night we
    part ;
    Full-handed thunders often have
        confessed
    Thy power, well-used to move the
        public breast.
We thank thee with our voice, and from
    the heart.
Farewell, Macready, since this night we
    part,
    Go, take thine honours home ; rank
        with the best,
    Garrick and statelier Kemble, and
        the rest
Who made a nation purer through their
    art.
Thine is it that our drama did not die,
    Nor flicker down to brainless panto-
        mime,
    And those gilt gauds men-children
        swarm to see.
Farewell, Macready ; moral, grave, sub-
    lime ;
Our Shakespeare's bland and universal
    eye
    Dwells pleased, through twice a
        hundred years, on thee.

DEMETER

AND OTHER POEMS.

TO THE MARQUIS OF DUFFERIN AND AVA.

I.

At times our Britain cannot rest,
　At times her steps are swift and rash;
　She moving, at her girdle clash
The golden keys of East and West.

II.

Not swift or rash, when late she lent
　The sceptres of her West, her East,
　To one, that ruling has increased
Her greatness and her self-content.

III.

Your rule has made the people love
　Their ruler. Your viceregal days
　Have added fulness to the phrase
Of 'Gauntlet in the velvet glove.'

IV.

But since your name will grow with Time,
　Not all, as honouring your fair fame
　Of Statesman, have I made the name
A golden portal to my rhyme:

V.

But more, that you and yours may know
　From me and mine, how dear a debt
　We owed you, and are owing yet
To you and yours, and still would owe.

VI.

For he—your India was his Fate,
　And drew him over sea to you—
　He fain had ranged her thro' and thro',
To serve her myriads and the State,—

VII.

A soul that, watch'd from earliest youth,
　And on thro' many a brightening year,

Had never swerved for craft or fear,
By one side-path, from simple truth;

VIII.

Who might have chased and claspt
　　Renown
　And caught her chaplet here—and there
　In haunts of jungle-poison'd air
The flame of life went wavering down;

IX.

But ere he left your fatal shore,
　And lay on that funereal boat,
　Dying, 'Unspeakable' he wrote
'Their kindness,' and he wrote no more;

X.

And sacred is the latest word;
　And now the Was, the Might-have-
　　been,
　And those lone rites I have not seen,
And one drear sound I have not heard,

XI.

Are dreams that scarce will let me be,
　Not there to bid my boy farewell,
　When That within the coffin fell,
Fell—and flash'd into the Red Sea,

XII.

Beneath a hard Arabian moon
　And alien stars. To question, why
　The sons before the fathers die,
Not mine! and I may meet him soon;

XIII.

But while my life's late eve endures,
　Nor settles into hueless gray,
　My memories of his briefer day
Will mix with love for you and yours.

ON THE JUBILEE OF QUEEN VICTORIA.

I.

FIFTY times the rose has flower'd and faded,
Fifty times the golden harvest fallen,
Since our Queen assumed the globe, the sceptre.

II.

She beloved for a kindliness
Rare in Fable or History,
Queen, and Empress of India,
Crown'd so long with a diadem
Never worn by a worthier,
Now with prosperous auguries
Comes at last to the bounteous
Crowning year of her Jubilee.

III.

Nothing of the lawless, of the Despot,
Nothing of the vulgar, or vainglorious,
All is gracious, gentle, great and Queenly.

IV.

You then joyfully, all of you,
Set the mountain aflame to-night,
Shoot your stars to the firmament,
Deck your houses, illuminate
All your towns for a festival,
And in each let a multitude
Loyal, each, to the heart of it,
One full voice of allegiance,
Hail the fair Ceremonial
Of this year of her Jubilee.

V.

Queen, as true to womanhood as Queen-hood,
Glorying in the glories of her people,
Sorrowing with the sorrows of the lowest !

VI.

You, that wanton in affluence,
Spare not now to be bountiful,
Call your poor to regale with you,
All the lowly, the destitute,
Make their neighbourhood health-fuller,
Give your gold to the Hospital,
Let the weary be comforted,
Let the needy be banqueted,
Let the maim'd in his heart rejoice
At this glad Ceremonial,
And this year of her Jubilee.

VII.

Henry's fifty years are all in shadow,
Gray with distance Edward's fifty sum-mers,
Ev'n her Grandsire's fifty half forgotten.

VIII.

You, the Patriot Architect,
You that shape for Eternity,
Raise a stately memorial,
Make it regally gorgeous,
Some Imperial Institute,
Rich in symbol, in ornament,
Which may speak to the centuries,
All the centuries after us,
Of this great Ceremonial,
And this year of her Jubilee.

IX.

Fifty years of ever-broadening Commerce !
Fifty years of ever-brightening Science !
Fifty years of ever-widening Empire !

X.

You, the Mighty, the Fortunate,
You, the Lord-territorial,
You, the Lord-manufacturer,
You, the hardy, laborious,
Patient children of Albion,
You, Canadian, Indian,
Australasian, African,
All your hearts be in harmony,
All your voices in unison,
Singing ' Hail to the glorious
Golden year of her Jubilee !'

XI.

Are there thunders moaning in the distance ?

Are there spectres moving in the darkness?

Trust the Hand of Light will lead her people,

Till the thunders pass, the spectres vanish,

And the Light is Victor, and the darkness

Dawns into the Jubilee of the Ages.

TO PROFESSOR JEBB,

WITH THE FOLLOWING POEM.

FAIR things are slow to fade away,
Bear witness you, that yesterday [1]
   From out the Ghost of Pindar in you
Roll'd an Olympian; and they say [2]

That here the torpid mummy wheat
Of Egypt bore a grain as sweet
   As that which gilds the glebe of England,
Sunn'd with a summer of milder heat.

So may this legend for awhile,
If greeted by your classic smile,
   Tho' dead in its Trinacrian Enna,
Blossom again on a colder isle.

DEMETER AND PERSEPHONE.

(IN ENNA.)

FAINT as a climate-changing bird that flies
All night across the darkness, and at dawn
Falls on the threshold of her native land,
And can no more, thou camest, O my child,
Led upward by the God of ghosts and dreams,
Who laid thee at Eleusis, dazed and dumb

[1] In Bologna.
[2] They say, for the fact is doubtful.

With passing thro' at once from state to state,
Until I brought thee hither, that the day,
When here thy hands let fall the gather'd flower,
Might break thro' clouded memories once again
On thy lost self. A sudden nightingale
Saw thee, and flash'd into a frolic of song
And welcome; and a gleam as of the moon,
When first she peers along the tremulous deep,
Fled wavering o'er thy face, and chased away
That shadow of a likeness to the king
Of shadows, thy dark mate. Persephone!
Queen of the dead no more—my child!
Thine eyes
Again were human-godlike, and the Sun
Burst from a swimming fleece of winter gray,
And robed thee in his day from head to feet—
'Mother!' and I was folded in thine arms.

Child, those imperial, disimpassion'd eyes
Awed even me at first, thy mother—eyes
That oft had seen the serpent-wanded power
Draw downward into Hades with his drift
Of flickering spectres, lighted from below
By the red race of fiery Phlegethon;
But when before have Gods or men beheld
The Life that had descended re-arise,
And lighted from above him by the Sun?
So mighty was the mother's childless cry,
A cry that rang thro' Hades, Earth, and Heaven!

So in this pleasant vale we stand again,
The field of Enna, now once more ablaze
With flowers that brighten as thy footstep falls,

All flowers——but for one black blur of
     earth
Left by that closing chasm, thro' which
     the car
Of dark Aïdoneus rising rapt thee
     hence.
And here, my child, tho' folded in thine
     arms,
I feel the deathless heart of motherhood
Within me shudder, lest the naked glebe
Should yawn once more into the gulf,
     and thence
The shrilly whinnyings of the team of
     Hell,
Ascending, pierce the glad and songful
     air,
And all at once their arch'd necks, mid-
     night-maned,
Jet upward thro' the mid-day blossom.
     No!
For, see, thy foot has touch'd it; all the
     space
Of blank earth-baldness clothes itself
     afresh,
And breaks into the crocus-purple hour
That saw thee vanish.

          Child, when thou wert gone,
I envied human wives, and nested birds,
Yea, the cubb'd lioness; went in search
     of thee
Thro' many a palace, many a cot, and
     gave
Thy breast to ailing infants in the night,
And set the mother waking in amaze
To find her sick one whole; and forth
     again
Among the wail of midnight winds, and
     cried,
'Where is my loved one? Wherefore
     do ye wail?'
And out from all the night an answer
     shrill'd,
'We know not, and we know not why we
     wail.'
I climb'd on all the cliffs of all the seas,
And ask'd the waves that moan about
     the world
'Where? do ye make your moaning for
     my child?'

And round from all the world the voices
     came
'We know not, and we know not why
     we moan.'
'Where'? and I stared from every eagle-
     peak,
I thridded the black heart of all the
     woods,
I peer'd thro' tomb and cave, and in the
     storms
Of Autumn swept across the city, and
     heard
The murmur of their temples chanting
     me,
Me, me, the desolate Mother! 'Where'?
     —and turn'd,
And fled by many a waste, forlorn of
     man,
And grieved for man thro' all my grief
     for thee,—
The jungle rooted in his shatter'd hearth,
The serpent coil'd about his broken shaft,
The scorpion crawling over naked
     skulls;—
I saw the tiger in the ruin'd fane
Spring from his fallen God, but trace of
     thee
I saw not; and far on, and, following out
A league of labyrinthine darkness, came
On three gray heads beneath a gleaming
     rift.
'Where'? and I heard one voice from
     all the three
'We know not, for we spin the lives of
     men,
And not of Gods, and know not why we
     spin!
There is a Fate beyond us.' Nothing
     knew.

     Last as the likeness of a dying man,
Without his knowledge, from him flits to
     warn
A far-off friendship that he comes no
     more,
So he, the God of dreams, who heard
     my cry,
Drew from thyself the likeness of thyself
Without thy knowledge, and thy shadow
     past

Before me, crying 'The Bright one in
 the highest
Is brother of the Dark one in the lowest,
And Bright and Dark have sworn that I,
 the child
Of thee, the great Earth-Mother, thee,
 the Power
That lifts her buried life from gloom to
 bloom,
Should be for ever and for evermore
The Bride of Darkness.'

   So the Shadow wail'd.
Then I, Earth-Goddess, cursed the Gods
 of Heaven.
I would not mingle with their feasts; to
 me
Their nectar smack'd of hemlock on the
 lips,
Their rich ambrosia tasted aconite.
The man, that only lives and loves an
 hour,
Seem'd nobler than their hard Eternities.
My quick tears kill'd the flower, my
 ravings hush'd
The bird, and lost in utter grief I fail'd
To send my life thro' olive-yard and vine
And golden grain, my gift to helpless
 man.
Rain-rotten died the wheat, the barley-
 spears
Were hollow-husk'd, the leaf fell, and
 the sun,
Pale at my grief, drew down before his
 time
Sickening, and Ætna kept her winter
 snow.
 Then He, the brother of this Darkness,
 He
Who still is highest, glancing from his
 height
On earth a fruitless fallow, when he
 miss'd
The wonted steam of sacrifice, the praise
And prayer of men, decreed that thou
 should'st dwell
For nine white moons of each whole year
 with me,
Three dark ones in the shadow with thy
 King.

Once more the reaper in the gleam of
 dawn
Will see me by the landmark far away,
Blessing his field, or seated in the dusk
Of even, by the lonely threshing-floor,
Rejoicing in the harvest and the grange.
 Yet I, Earth-Goddess, am but ill-
 content
With them, who still are highest. Those
 gray heads,
What meant they by their 'Fate beyond
 the Fates'
But younger kindlier Gods to bear us
 down,
As we bore down the Gods before us? Gods,
To quench, not hurl the thunderbolt, to
 stay,
Not spread the plague, the famine; Gods
 indeed,
To send the noon into the night and
 break
The sunless halls of Hades into Heaven?
Till thy dark lord accept and love the Sun,
And all the Shadow die into the Light,
When thou shalt dwell the whole bright
 year with me,
And souls of men, who grew beyond
 their race,
And made themselves as Gods against
 the fear
Of Death and Hell; and thou that hast
 from men,
As Queen of Death, that worship which
 is Fear,
Henceforth, as having risen from out the
 dead,
Shalt ever send thy life along with mine
From buried grain thro' springing blade,
 and bless
Their garner'd Autumn also, reap with me,
Earth-mother, in the harvest hymns of
 Earth
The worship which is Love, and see no
 more
The Stone, the Wheel, the dimly-
 glimmering lawns
Of that Elysium, all the hateful fires
Of torment, and the shadowy warrior glide
Along the silent field of Asphodel.

OWD ROÄ.[1]

NAÄY, noä mander[2] o' use to be callin'
　　'im Roä, Roä, Roä,
Fur the dog's stoän-deäf, an' e's blind, 'e
　　can naither stan' nor goä.

But I meäns fur to maäke 'is owd aäge
　　as 'appy as iver I can,
Fur I owäs owd Roäver moor nor I iver
　　owäd mottal man.

Thou's rode of 'is back when a babby,
　　afoor thou was gotten too owd,
Fur 'e'd fetch an' carry like owt, 'e was
　　allus as good as gowd.

Eh, but 'e'd fight wi' a will *when* 'e
　　fowt ; 'e could howd[3] 'is oan,
An' Roä was the dog as knaw'd when
　　an' wheere to bury his boane.

An' 'e kep his heäd hoop like a king, an'
　　'e'd niver not down wi' 'is taäil,
Fur 'e'd niver done nowt to be shaämed
　　on, when we was i' Howlaby
　　Daäle.

An' 'e sarved me sa well when 'e lived,
　　that, Dick, when 'e cooms to be
　　deäd,
I thinks as I'd like fur to hev soom soort
　　of a sarvice reäd.

Fur 'e's moor good sense na the Parlia-
　　ment man 'at stans fur us 'ere,
An' I'd voät fur 'im, my oän sen, if 'e
　　could but stan fur the Shere.

' Faäithful an' True '—them words be i'
　　Scriptur—an' Faäithful an' True
Ull be fun'[4] upo' four short legs ten times
　　fur one upo' two.

An' maäybe they'll walk upo' two but I
　　knaws they runs upo' four,[5]—
Bedtime, Dicky ! but waäit till tha 'eärs
　　it be strikin' the hour.

Fur I wants to tell tha o' Roä when we
　　lived i' Howlaby Daäle,
Ten year sin—Naäy—naäy ! tha mun
　　nobbut hev' one glass of aäle.

Straänge an' owd-farran'd[1] the 'ouse, an'
　　belt[2] long afoor my daäy
Wi' haäfe o' the chimleys a-twizzen'd[3]
　　an' twined like a band o' haäy.

The fellers as maäkes them picturs, 'ud
　　coom at the fall o' the year,
An' sattle their ends upo stools to pictur
　　the door-poorch theere,

An' the Heagle 'as hed two heäds stannin'
　　theere o' the brokken stick ;[4]
An' they niver 'ed seed sich ivin'[5] as
　　graw'd hall ower the brick ;

An' theere i' the 'ouse one night—but it's
　　down, an' all on it now
Goan into mangles an' tonups,[6] an'
　　raäved slick thruf by the plow—

Theere, when the 'ouse wur a house, one
　　night I wur sittin' aloän,
Wi' Roäver athurt my feeät, an' sleeäpin
　　still as a stoän,

Of a Christmas Eäve, an' as cowd as
　　this, an' the midders[7] as white,
An' the fences all on 'em bolster'd oop
　　wi' the windle[8] that night ;

An' the cat wur a-sleeäpin alongside
　　Roäver, but I wur awaäke,
An' smoäkin' an' thinkin' o' things—
　　Doänt maäke thysen sick wi' the
　　caäke.

Fur the men ater supper 'ed sung their
　　songs an' 'ed 'ed their beer,
An' 'ed goän their waäys ; ther was
　　nobbut three, an' noän on 'em
　　theere.

---

[1] 'Owd-farran'd,' old-fashioned.　　[2] Built.
[3] 'Twizzen'd,' twisted.　　[4] On a staff *ragulé.*
[5] Ivy.　　[6] Mangolds and turnips.
[7] Meadows.　　[8] Drifted snow.

---

[1] Old Rover.　　[2] Manner.　　[3] Hold.
[4] Found.　　[5] 'Ou' as in 'house.'

They was all on 'em fear'd o' the Ghoäst
  an' dussn't not sleeäp i' the 'ouse,
But Dicky, the Ghoäst moästlins[1] was
  nobbut a rat or a mouse.

An' I looökt out wonst[2] at the night,
  an' the daäle was all of a thaw,
Fur I seed the beck coomin' down like
  a long black snaäke i' the snaw,

An' I heärd greät heäps o' the snaw
  slushin' down fro' the bank to
  the beck,
An' then as I stood i' the doorwaäy, I
  feeäld it drip o' my neck.

Saw I turn'd in ageän, an' I thowt o'
  the good owd times 'at was goan,
An' the munney they maäde by the war,
  an' the times 'at was coomin' on ;

Fur I thowt if the Staäte was a gawin'
  to let in furriners' wheät,
Howiver was British farmers to stan'
  ageän o' their feeät.

Howiver was I fur to find my rent an'
  to paäy my men ?
An' all along o' the feller[3] as turn'd 'is
  back of hissen.

Thou slep i' the chaumber above us, we
  couldn't ha' 'eärd tha call,
Sa Moother 'ed tell'd ma to bring tha
  down, an' thy craädle an' all ;

Fur the gell o' the farm 'at slep wi' tha
  then 'ed gotten wer leäve,
Fur to goä that night to 'er foälk by cause
  o' the Christmas Eäve ;

But I cleän forgot tha, my lad, when
  Moother 'ed gotten to bed,
An' I slep i' my chair hup-on-end, an' the
  Freeä Traäde runn'd 'i my 'ead,

Till I dreäm'd 'at Squire walkt in, an' I
  says to him ' Squire, ya're laäte,'
Then I seed at 'is faäce wur as red as the
  Yule-block theer i' the graäte.

An' 'e says ' can ya paäy me the rent to-
  night ?' an' I says to 'im ' Noä,'
An' 'e cotch'd howd hard o' my hairm,[1]
  ' Then hout to-night tha shall goä.'

' Tha'll niver,' says I, ' be a-turnin ma
  hout upo' Christmas Eäve '?
Then I waäked an' I fun it was Roäver
  a-tuggin' an' teärin' my slieäve.

An' I thowt as 'e'd goän cleän-wud,[2] fur
  I noäwaäys knaw'd 'is intent ;
An' I says ' Git awaäy, ya beäst,' an' I
  fetcht 'im a kick an' 'e went.

Then 'e tummled up stairs, fur I 'eärd
  'im, as if 'e'd 'a brokken 'is neck,
An' I'd cleär forgot, little Dicky, thy
  chaumber door wouldn't sneck ;[3]

An' I slep' i' my chair ageän wi' my hairm
  hingin' down to the floor,
An' I thowt it was Roäver a-tuggin' an'
  teärin' me wuss nor afoor,

An' I thowt 'at I kick'd 'im ageän, but I
  kick'd thy Moother istead.
' What arta snorin' theere fur ? the house
  is afire,' she said.

Thy Moother 'ed beän a-naggin' about
  the gell o' the farm,
She offens 'ud spy summut wrong when
  there warn't not a mossel o' harm ;

An' she didn't not solidly meän I wur
  gawin' that waäy to the bad,
Fur the gell[4] was as howry a trollope
  as iver traäpes'd i' the squad.

But Moother was free of 'er tongue, as I
  offens 'ev tell'd 'er mysen,
Sa I kep i' my chair, fur I thowt she
  was nobbut a-rilin' ma then.

An' I says ' I'd be good to tha, Bess, if
  tha'd onywaäys let ma be good,'

---

[1] Arm.   [2] Mad.   [3] Latch.
[4] The girl was as dirty a slut as ever trudged
in the mud, but there is a sense of slatternliness
in 'traäpes'd' which is not expressed in 'trudged.'

---

[1] 'Moästlins,' for the most part, generally.
  [2] Once.   [3] Peel.

But she skelpt ma haäfe ower i' the chair,
an' screeäd like a Howl gone
wud [1]—

'Ya mun run fur the lether.[2] Git oop,
if ya're onywaäys good for owt.'
And I says 'If I beänt noäwaäys—not
nowadaäys—good fur nowt—

Yit I beänt sich a Nowt [3] of all Nowts
as 'ull hallus do as 'e's bid.'
'But the stairs is afire,' she said ; then I
seed 'er a-cryin', I did.

An' she beäld 'Ya mun saäve little Dick,
an' be sharp about it an' all,'
Sa I runs to the yard fur a lether, an'
sets 'im ageän the wall,

An' I claums an' I mashes the winder
hin, when I gits to the top,
But the heät druv hout i' my heyes till I
feäld mysen ready to drop.

Thy Moother was howdin' the lether, an'
tellin' me not to be skeärd,
An' I wasn't afeärd, or I thinks leäst-
waäys as I wasn't afeärd ;

But I couldn't see fur the smoäke wheere
thou was a-liggin, my lad,
An' Roäver was theere i' the chaumber
a-yowlin' an' yaupin' like mad ;

An' thou was a-beälin' likewise, an' a-
squeälin', as if tha was bit,
An' it wasn't a bite but a burn, fur the
merk's [4] o' thy shou'der yit ;

Then I call'd out Roä, Roä, Roä, thaw
I didn't haäfe think as 'e'd 'ear,
*But 'e coom'd thruf the fire wi' my bairn
i' 'is mouth to the winder theere !*

He coom'd like a Hangel o' marcy as
soon as 'e 'eärd 'is naäme,
Or like tother Hangel i' Scriptur 'at
summun seed i' the flaäme,

When summun 'ed hax'd fur a son, an'
'e promised a son to she,
An' Roä was as good as the Hangel i'
saävin' a son fur me.

Sa I browt tha down, an' I says 'I mun
gaw up ageän fur Roä.'
'Gaw up ageän fur the varmint ?' I
tell'd 'er 'Yeäs I mun goä.'

An' I claumb'd up ageän to the winder,
an' clemm'd [1] owd Roä by the 'eäd,
An' 'is 'air coom'd off i' my 'ands an' I
taäked 'im at fust fur deäd ;

Fur 'e smell'd like a herse a-singein', an'
seeäm'd as blind as a poop,
An' haäfe on 'im bare as a bublin'. [2] I
couldn't wakken 'im oop,

But I browt 'im down, an' we got to the
barn, fur the barn wouldn't burn
Wi' the wind blawin' hard tother waäy,
an' the wind wasn't like to turn.

An' *I* kep a-callin' o' Roä till 'e waggled
'is taäil fur a bit,
But the cocks kep a-crawin' an' crawin'
all night, an' I 'ears 'em yit ;

An' the dogs was a-yowlin' all round, and
thou was a-squeälin' thysen,
An' Moother was naggin' an' groänin' an'
moänin' an' naggin' ageän ;

An' I 'eärd the bricks an' the baulks [3]
rummle down when the roof gev
waäy,
Fur the fire was a-raägin' an' raävin' an'
roarin' like judgment daäy.

Warm enew theere sewer-ly, but the barn
was as cowd as owt,
An' we cuddled and huddled togither, an'
happt [4] wersens oop as we mowt.

An' I browt Roä round, but Moother 'ed
beän sa soäk'd wi' the thaw
'At she cotch'd 'er death o' cowd that
night, poor soul, i' the straw.

---

1 She half overturned me and shrieked like an
owl gone mad.   2 Ladder.
3 A thoroughly insignificant or worthless
person.   4 Mark.

1 Clutched.
2 'Bubbling,' a young unfledged bird.
3 Beams.   4 Wrapt ourselves.

Haäfe o' the parish runn'd oop when the
   rigtree [1] was tummlin' in—
Too laäte—but it's all ower now—hall
   hower—an' ten year sin ;

Too laäte, tha mun git tha to bed, but
   I'll coom an' I'll squench the light,
Fur we moänt 'ev naw moor fires—and
   soa little Dick, good-night.

[1] The beam that runs along the roof of the
house just beneath the ridge.

VASTNESS.

I.

MANY a hearth upon our dark globe
   sighs after many a vanish'd face,
Many a planet by many a sun may roll
   with the dust of a vanish'd race.

II.

Raving politics, never at rest—as this
   poor earth's pale history runs,—
What is it all but a trouble of ants in the
   gleam of a million million of suns ?

III.

Lies upon this side, lies upon that side,
   truthless violence mourn'd by the
   Wise,
Thousands of voices drowning his own in
   a popular torrent of lies upon lies ;

IV.

Stately purposes, valour in battle, glorious
   annals of army and fleet,
Death for the right cause, death for the
   wrong cause, trumpets of victory,
   groans of defeat ;

V.

Innocence seethed in her mother's milk,
   and Charity setting the martyr
   aflame ;
Thraldom who walks with the banner of
   Freedom, and recks not to ruin a
   realm in her name.

VI.

Faith at her zenith, or all but lost in the
   gloom of doubts that darken the
   schools ;
Craft with a bunch of all-heal in her
   hand, follow'd up by her vassal
   legion of fools ;

VII.

Trade flying over a thousand seas with
   her spice and her vintage, her silk
   and her corn ;
Desolate offing, sailorless harbours,
   famishing populace, wharves forlorn ;

VIII.

Star of the morning, Hope in the sunrise ;
   gloom of the evening, Life at a
   close ;
Pleasure who flaunts on her wide down-
   way with her flying robe and her
   poison'd rose ;

IX.

Pain, that has crawl'd from the corpse of
   Pleasure, a worm which writhes
   all day, and at night
Stirs up again in the heart of the sleeper,
   and stings him back to the curse
   of the light ;

X.

Wealth with his wines and his wedded
   harlots ; honest Poverty, bare to
   the bone ;
Opulent Avarice, lean as Poverty ;
   Flattery gilding the rift in a
   throne ;

XI.

Fame blowing out from her golden
   trumpet a jubilant challenge to
   Time and to Fate ;
Slander, her shadow, sowing the nettle on
   all the laurel'd graves of the Great ;

XII.

Love for the maiden, crown'd with
　　marriage, no regrets for aught
　　that has been,
Household happiness, gracious children,
　　debtless competence, golden mean;

XIII.

National hatreds of whole generations,
　　and pigmy spites of the village
　　spire;
Vows that will last to the last death-
　　ruckle, and vows that are snapt
　　in a moment of fire;

XIV.

He that has lived for the lust of the
　　minute, and died in the doing it,
　　flesh without mind;
He that has nail'd all flesh to the Cross,
　　till Self died out in the love of
　　his kind;

XV.

Spring and Summer and Autumn and
　　Winter, and all these old revolu-
　　tions of earth;
All new-old revolutions of Empire—
　　change of the tide—what is all of
　　it worth?

XVI.

What the philosophies, all the sciences,
　　poesy, varying voices of prayer?
All that is noblest, all that is basest, all
　　that is filthy with all that is fair?

XVII.

What is it all, if we all of us end but in
　　being our own corpse-coffins at
　　last,
Swallow'd in Vastness, lost in Silence,
　　drown'd in the deeps of a mean-
　　ingless Past?

XVIII.

What but a murmur of gnats in the
　　gloom, or a moment's anger of
　　bees in their hive?—

＊　　　＊　　　＊　　　＊

Peace, let it be! for I loved him, and
　　love him for ever: the dead are
　　not dead but alive.

Dedicated to the Hon. J. Russell
Lowell.

THE RING.

MIRIAM AND HER FATHER.

Miriam (singing).

MELLOW moon of heaven,
　　Bright in blue,
Moon of married hearts,
　　Hear me, you!

Twelve times in the year
　　Bring me bliss,
Globing Honey Moons
　　Bright as this.

Moon, you fade at times
　　From the night.
Young again you grow
　　Out of sight.

Silver crescent-curve,
　　Coming soon,
Globe again, and make
　　Honey Moon.

Shall not *my* love last,
　　Moon, with you,
For ten thousand years
　　Old and new?

Father.　And who was he with such
　　love-drunken eyes
They made a thousand honey moons of
　　one?
Miriam.　The prophet of his own, my
　　Hubert—his
The words, and mine the setting. 'Air
　　and Words,'
Said Hubert, when I sang the song, 'are
　　bride
And bridegroom.'　Does it please you?

Father. Mainly, child,
Because I hear your Mother's voice in
yours.
She——, why, you shiver tho' the wind
is west
With all the warmth of summer.
Miriam. Well, I felt
On a sudden I know not what, a breath
that past
With all the cold of winter.
Father (muttering to himself). Even
so.
The Ghost in Man, the Ghost that once
was Man,
But cannot wholly free itself from Man,
Are calling to each other thro' a dawn
Stranger than earth has ever seen; the
veil
Is rending, and the Voices of the day
Are heard across the Voices of the dark.
No sudden heaven, nor sudden hell, for
man,
But thro' the Will of One who knows
and rules—
And utter knowledge is but utter love—
Æonian Evolution, swift or slow,
Thro' all the Spheres—an ever opening
height,
An ever lessening earth—and she perhaps,
My Miriam, breaks her latest earthly link
With me to-day.
Miriam. You speak so low, what is it?
Your 'Miriam breaks'—is making a new
link
Breaking an old one?
Father. No, for we, my child,
Have been till now each other's all-in-all.
Miriam. And you the lifelong guard-
ian of the child.
Father. I, and one other whom you
have not known.
Miriam. And who? what other?
Father. Whither are you bound?
For Naples which we only left in May?
Miriam. No! father, Spain, but
Hubert brings me home
With April and the swallow. Wish me
joy!
Father. What need to wish when
Hubert weds in you

The heart of Love, and you the soul of
Truth
In Hubert?
Miriam. Tho' you used to call me
once
The lonely maiden-Princess of the wood,
Who meant to sleep her hundred sum-
mers out
Before a kiss should wake her.
Father. Ay, but now
Your fairy Prince has found you, take
this ring.
Miriam. ' Io t'amo '—and these dia-
monds—beautiful!
' From Walter,' and for me from you then?
Father. Well,
One way for Miriam.
Miriam. Miriam am I not?
Father. This ring bequeath'd you by
your mother, child,
Was to be given you—such her dying
wish—
Given on the morning when you came of
age
Or on the day you married. Both the
days
Now close in one. The ring is doubly
yours.
Why do you look so gravely at the tower?
Miriam. I never saw it yet so all
ablaze
With creepers crimsoning to the pinnacles,
As if perpetual sunset linger'd there,
And all ablaze too in the lake below!
And how the birds that circle round the
tower
Are cheeping to each other of their flight
To summer lands!
Father. And that has made you grave?
Fly—care not. Birds and brides must
leave the nest.
Child, I am happier in your happiness
Than in mine own.
Miriam. It is not that!
Father. What else?
Miriam. That chamber in the tower.
Father. What chamber, child?
Your nurse is here?
Miriam. My Mother's nurse and mine.
She comes to dress me in my bridal veil.

Father. What did she say?

Miriam. She said, that you and I
Had been abroad for my poor health so
long
She fear'd I had forgotten her, and I
ask'd
About my Mother, and she said, 'Thy
hair
Is golden like thy Mother's, not so fine.'

Father. What then? what more?

Miriam. She said—perhaps indeed
She wander'd, having wander'd now so
far
Beyond the common date of death—that
you,
When I was smaller than the statuette
Of my dear Mother on your bracket here—
You took me to that chamber in the tower,
The topmost—a chest there, by which
you knelt—
And there were books and dresses—left
to me,
A ring too which you kiss'd, and I, she
said,
I babbled, Mother, Mother—as I used
To prattle to her picture—stretch'd my
hands
As if I saw her; then a woman came
And caught me from my nurse. I hear
her yet—
A sound of anger like a distant storm.

Father. Garrulous old crone.

Miriam. Poor nurse!

Father. I bad her keep,
Like a seal'd book, all mention of the
ring,
For I myself would tell you all to-day.

Miriam. 'She too might speak to-
day,' she mumbled. Still,
I scarce have learnt the title of your book,
But you will turn the pages.

Father. Ay, to-day!
I brought you to that chamber on your
third
September birthday with your nurse, and
felt
An icy breath play on me, while I stoopt
To take and kiss the ring.

Miriam. This very ring
Io t'amo?

Father. Yes, for some wild hope
was mine
That, in the misery of my married life,
Miriam your Mother might appear to me.
She came to you, not me. The storm,
you hear
Far-off, is Muriel—your stepmother's
voice.

Miriam. Vext, that you thought my
Mother came to me?
Or at my crying 'Mother?' or to find
My Mother's diamonds hidden from her
there,
Like worldly beauties in the Cell, not
shown
To dazzle all that see them?

Father. Wait a while.
Your Mother and step-mother—Miriam
Erne
And Muriel Erne—the two were cousins
—lived
With Muriel's mother on the down, that
sees
A thousand squares of corn and meadow,
far
As the gray deep, a landscape which
your eyes
Have many a time ranged over when a
babe.

Miriam. I climb'd the hill with
Hubert yesterday,
And from the thousand squares, one
silent voice
Came on the wind, and seem'd to say
'Again.'
We saw far off an old forsaken house,
Then home, and past the ruin'd mill.

Father. And there
I found these cousins often by the brook,
For Miriam sketch'd and Muriel threw
the fly;
The girls of equal age, but one was fair,
And one was dark, and both were beauti-
ful.
No voice for either spoke within my heart
Then, for the surface eye, that only doats
On outward beauty, glancing from the one
To the other, knew not that which
pleased it most,
The raven ringlet or the gold; but both

Were dowerless, and myself, I used to
walk
This Terrace—morbid, melancholy ; mine
And yet not mine the hall, the farm, the
field ;
For all that ample woodland whisper'd
' debt,'
The brook that feeds this lakelet mur-
mur'd ' debt,'
And in yon arching avenue of old elms,
Tho' mine, not mine, I heard the sober
rook
And carrion crow cry ' Mortgage.'
 Miriam.   Father's fault
Visited on the children !
 Father.   Ay, but then
A kinsman, dying, summon'd me to
Rome—
He left me wealth—and while I journey'd
hence,
And saw the world fly by me like a dream,
And while I communed with my truest
self,
I woke to all of truest in myself,
Till, in the gleam of those mid-summer
dawns,
The form of Muriel faded, and the face
Of Miriam grew upon me, till I knew ;
And past and future mix'd in Heaven
and made
The rosy twilight of a perfect day.
 Miriam.   So glad ? no tear for him,
who left you wealth,
Your kinsman ?
 Father.   I had seen the man but once ;
He loved my name not me ; and then I
pass'd
Home, and thro' Venice, where a jeweller,
So far gone down, or so far up in life,
That he was nearing his own hundred,
sold
This ring to me, then laugh'd ' the ring
is weird.'
And weird and worn and wizard-like was
he.
' Why weird ?' I ask'd him ; and he said
   ' The souls
Of two repentant Lovers guard the ring ;'
Then with a ribald twinkle in his bleak
eyes—

' And if you give the ring to any maid,
They still remember what it cost them
here,
And bind the maid to love you by the
ring ;
And if the ring were stolen from the
maid,
The theft were death or madness to the
thief,
So sacred those Ghost Lovers hold the
gift.'
And then he told their legend :
       ' Long ago
Two lovers parted by a scurrilous tale
Had quarrell'd, till the man repenting
sent
This ring " Io t'amo " to his best beloved,
And sent it on her birthday. She in
wrath
Return'd it on her birthday, and that day
His death-day, when, half-frenzied by the
ring,
He wildly fought a rival suitor, him
The causer of that scandal, fought and
fell ;
And she that came to part them all too
late,
And found a corpse and silence, drew the
ring
From his dead finger, wore it till her
death,
Shrined him within the temple of her
heart,
Made every moment of her after life
A virgin victim to his memory,
And dying rose, and rear'd her arms, and
cried
" I see him, Io t'amo, Io t'amo." '
 Miriam.   Legend or true ? so tender
should be true !
Did *he* believe it ? did you ask him ?
 Father.   Ay !
But that half skeleton, like a barren
ghost
From out the fleshless world of spirits,
laugh'd :
A hollow laughter !
 Miriam.   Vile, so near the ghost
Himself, to laugh at love in death ! But
you ?

Father. Well, as the bygone lover
　thro' this ring
Had sent his cry for her forgiveness, I
Would call thro' this ' Io t'amo ' to the
　heart
Of Miriam; then I bad the man en-
　grave
' From Walter ' on the ring, and send it
　—wrote
Name, surname, all as clear as noon, but
　he—
Some younger hand must have engraven
　the ring—
His fingers were so stiffen'd by the frost
Of seven and ninety winters, that he
　scrawl'd
A ' Miriam ' that might seem a ' Muriel ';
And Muriel claim'd and open'd what I
　meant
For Miriam, took the ring, and flaunted
　it
Before that other whom I loved and love.
　A mountain stay'd me here, a minster
　there,
A galleried palace, or a battlefield,
Where stood the sheaf of Peace: but—
　coming home—
And on your Mother's birthday—all but
　yours—
A week betwixt—and when the tower as
　now
Was all ablaze with crimson to the roof,
And all ablaze too plunging in the lake
Head-foremost—who were those that
　stood between
The tower and that rich phantom of the
　tower?
Muriel and Miriam, each in white, and
　like
May-blossoms in mid autumn—was it
　they?
A light shot upward on them from the
　lake.
What sparkled there? whose hand was
　that? they stood
So close together.　I am not keen of
　sight,
But coming nearer—Muriel had the ring—
' O Miriam ! have you given your ring to
　her?

O Miriam !'　Miriam redden'd, Muriel
　clench'd
The hand that wore it, till I cried again:
' O Miriam, if you love me take the ring !'
She glanced at me, at Muriel, and was
　mute.
' Nay, if you cannot love me, let it be.'
Then—Muriel standing ever statue-like—
She turn'd, and in her soft imperial way
And saying gently: ' Muriel, by your
　leave,'
Unclosed the hand, and from it drew the
　ring,
And gave it me, who pass'd it down her
　own,
' Io t'amo, all is well then.'　Muriel fled.
　Miriam.　Poor Muriel !
　Father.　　　　　Ay, poor Muriel
　when you hear
What follows !　Miriam loved me from
　the first,
Not thro' the ring; but on her marriage-
　morn
This birthday, death-day, and betrothal
　ring,
Laid on her table overnight, was gone;
And after hours of search and doubt and
　threats,
And hubbub, Muriel enter'd with it,
　' See !—
Found in a chink of that old moulder'd
　floor !'
My Miriam nodded with a pitying smile,
As who should say ' that those who lose
　can find.'
　Then I and she were married for a
　year,
One year without a storm, or even a
　cloud ;
And you my Miriam born within the
　year ;
And she my Miriam dead within the
　year.
　I sat beside her dying, and she gaspt :
' The books, the miniature, the lace are
　hers,
My ring too when she comes of age, or
　when
She marries ; you—you loved me, kept
　your word.

You love me still "Io t'amo."—Muriel
—no—
She cannot love; she loves her own
    hard self,
Her firm will, her fix'd purpose. Pro-
    mise me,
Miriam not Muriel—she shall have the
    ring.'
And there the light of other life, which
    lives
Beyond our burial and our buried eyes,
Gleam'd for a moment in her own on
    earth.
I swore the vow, then with my latest
    kiss
Upon them, closed her eyes, which would
    not close,
But kept their watch upon the ring and
    you.
Your birthday was her death-day.
    Miriam.   O poor Mother !
And you, poor desolate Father, and
    poor me,
The little senseless, worthless, wordless
    babe,
Saved when your life was wreck'd !
    Father.   Desolate ? yes !
Desolate as that sailor, whom the storm
Had parted from his comrade in the
    boat,
And dash'd half dead on barren sands,
    was I.
Nay, you were my one solace; only—
    you
Were always ailing. Muriel's mother
    sent,
And sure am I, by Muriel, one day came
And saw you, shook her head, and patted
    yours,
And smiled, and making with a kindly
    pinch
Each poor pale cheek a momentary rose—
' *That* should be fix'd,' she said ; 'your
    pretty bud,
So blighted here, would flower into full
    health
Among our heath and bracken. Let her
    come !
And we will feed her with our mountain
    air,

T

And send her home to you rejoicing.'
    No—
We could not part. And once, when
    you my girl
Rode on my shoulder home—the tiny fist
Had graspt a daisy from your Mother's
    grave—
By the lych-gate was Muriel. 'Ay,' she
    said,
' Among the tombs in this damp vale of
    yours !
You scorn my Mother's warning, but the
    child
Is paler than before. We often walk
In open sun, and see beneath our feet
The mist of autumn gather from your
    lake,
And shroud the tower ; and once we
    only saw
Your gilded vane, a light above the
    mist '—
(Our old bright bird that still is veering
    there
Above his four gold letters) 'and the
    light,'
She said, 'was like that light '—and there
    she paused,
And long ; till I believing that the girl's
Lean fancy, groping for it, could not find
One likeness, laugh'd a little and found
    her two—
' A warrior's crest above the cloud of
    war '—
' A fiery phœnix rising from the smoke,
The pyre he burnt in.'—'Nay,' she said,
    ' the light
That glimmers on the marsh and on the
    grave.'
And spoke no more, but turn'd and
    pass'd away.
    Miriam, I am not surely one of those
Caught by the flower that closes on the
    fly,
But after ten slow weeks her fix'd intent,
In aiming at an all but hopeless mark
To strike it, struck ; I took, I left you
    there ;
I came, I went, was happier day by day ;
For Muriel nursed you with a mother's
    care ;

2 Q

Till on that clear and heather-scented
  height
The rounder cheek had brighten'd into
  bloom.
She always came to meet me carrying
  you,
And all her talk was of the babe she
  loved ;
So, following her old pastime of the brook,
She threw the fly for me ; but oftener left
That angling to the mother.   'Muriel's
  health
Had weaken'd, nursing little Miriam.
  Strange !
She used to shun the wailing babe, and
  doats
On this of yours.'   But when the matron
  saw
That hinted love was only wasted bait,
Not risen to, she was bolder.   'Ever
  since
You sent the fatal ring '—I told her 'sent
To Miriam,' 'Doubtless—ay, but ever
  since
In all the world my dear one sees but
  you—
In your sweet babe she finds but you—
  she makes
Her heart a mirror that reflects but you.'
And then the tear fell, the voice broke.
  Her heart !
I gazed into the mirror, as a man
Who sees his face in water, and a stone,
That glances from the bottom of the
  pool,
Strike upward thro' the shadow ; yet at
  last,
Gratitude—loneliness—desire to keep
So skilled a nurse about you always—
  nay !
Some half remorseful kind of pity too—
Well ! well, you know I married Muriel
  Erne.
  'I take thee Muriel for my wedded
  wife '—
I had forgotten it was your birthday,
  child—
When all at once with some electric thrill
A cold air pass'd between us, and the
  hands

Fell from each other, and were join'd
  again.
  No second cloudless honeymoon was
  mine.
For by and by she sicken'd of the farce,
She dropt the gracious mask of mother-
  hood,
She came no more to meet me, carrying
  you,
Nor ever cared to set you on her knee,
Nor ever let you gambol in her sight,
Nor ever cheer'd you with a kindly smile,
Nor ever ceased to clamour for the ring ;
Why had I sent the ring at first to her ?
Why had I made her love me thro' the
  ring,
And then had changed ? so fickle are
  men—the best !
Not she—but now my love was hers
  again,
The ring by right, she said, was hers
  again.
At times too shrilling in her angrier
  moods,
'That weak and watery nature love you ?
  No !
" *Io* t'amo, *Io* t'amo" !' flung herself
Against my heart, but often while her
  lips
Were warm upon my cheek, an icy breath,
As from the grating of a sepulchre,
Past over both.   I told her of my vow,
No pliable idiot I to break my vow ;
But still she made her outcry for the ring ;
For one monotonous fancy madden'd
  her,
Till I myself was madden'd with her cry,
And even that 'Io t'amo,' those three
  sweet
Italian words, became a weariness.
  My people too were scared with eerie
  sounds,
A footstep, a low throbbing in the walls,
A noise of falling weights that never fell,
Weird whispers, bells that rang without
  a hand,
Door-handles turn'd when none was at
  the door,
And bolted doors that open'd of them-
  selves :

And one betwixt the dark and light had
seen
Her, bending by the cradle of her babe.
   Miriam. And I remember once that
being waked
By noises in the house—and no one near—
I cried for nurse, and felt a gentle hand
Fall on my forehead, and a sudden face
Look'd in upon me like a gleam and
pass'd,
And I was quieted, and slept again.
Or is it some half memory of a dream?
   Father. Your fifth September birth-
day.
   Miriam. And the face,
The hand,—my Mother.
   Father. Miriam, on that day
Two lovers parted by no scurrilous tale—
Mere want of gold—and still for twenty
years
Bound by the golden cord of their first
love—
Had ask'd us to their marriage, and to
share
Their marriage-banquet. Muriel, paler
then
Than ever you were in your cradle,
moan'd,
 I am fitter for my bed, or for my grave,
I cannot go, go you.' And then she rose,
She clung to me with such a hard embrace,
So lingeringly long, that half-amazed
I parted from her, and I went alone.
And when the bridegroom murmur'd,
' With this ring,'
I felt for what I could not find, the key,
The guardian of her relics, of *her* ring.
I kept it as a sacred amulet
About me,—gone! and gone in that
embrace!
Then, hurrying home, I found her not
in house
Or garden—up the tower—an icy air
Fled by me.—There, the chest was open
—all
The sacred relics tost about the floor—
Among them Muriel lying on her face—
I raised her, call'd her ' Muriel, Muriel
wake !'
The fatal ring lay near her; the glazed eye

Glared at me as in horror. Dead! I
took
And chafed the freezing hand. A red
mark ran
All round one finger pointed straight,
the rest
Were crumpled inwards. Dead!—and
maybe stung
With some remorse, had stolen, worn the
ring—
Then torn it from her finger, or as if—
For never had I seen her show remorse—
As if—
   Miriam. —those two Ghost lovers—
   Father. Lovers yet—
   Miriam. Yes, yes!
   Father. —but dead so long, gone up
so far,
That now their ever-rising life has dwarf'd
Or lost the moment of their past on earth,
As we forget our wail at being born.
As if—
   Miriam. a dearer ghost had—
   Father. —wrench'd it away.
   Miriam. Had floated in with sad
reproachful eyes,
Till from her own hand she had torn the
ring
In fright, and fallen dead. And I myself
Am half afraid to wear it.
   Father. Well, no more!
No bridal music this! but fear not you!
You have the ring she guarded; that
poor link
With earth is broken, and has left her
free,
Except that, still drawn downward for
an hour,
Her spirit hovering by the church, where
she
Was married too, may linger, till she
sees
Her maiden coming like a Queen, who
leaves
Some colder province in the North to
gain
Her capital city, where the loyal bells
Clash welcome—linger, till her own, the
babe
She lean'd to from her Spiritual sphere,

Her lonely maiden - Princess, crown'd
    with flowers,
Has enter'd on the larger woman-world
Of wives and mothers.

               But the bridal veil—
Your nurse is waiting. Kiss me child
    and go.

FORLORN.

I.

' HE is fled—I wish him dead—
    He that wrought my ruin—
O the flattery and the craft
    Which were my undoing . . .
      In the night, in the night,
      When the storms are blowing.

II.

' Who was witness of the crime?
    Who shall now reveal it?
He is fled, or he is dead,
    Marriage will conceal it . . .
      In the night, in the night,
      While the gloom is growing.'

III.

Catherine, Catherine, in the night,
    What is this you're dreaming?
There is laughter down in Hell
    At your simple scheming . . .
      In the night, in the night,
      When the ghosts are fleeting.

IV.

You to place a hand in his
    Like an honest woman's,
You that lie with wasted lungs
    Waiting for your summons . . .
      In the night, O the night!
      O the deathwatch beating!

V.

There will come a witness soon
    Hard to be confuted,
All the world will hear a voice
    Scream you are polluted . . .
      In the night! O the night,
      When the owls are wailing!

VI.

Shame and marriage, Shame and
    marriage,
    Fright and foul dissembling,
Bantering bridesman, reddening priest,
    Tower and altar trembling . . .
      In the night, O the night,
      When the mind is failing!

VII.

Mother, dare you kill your child?
    How your hand is shaking!
Daughter of the seed of Cain,
    What is this you're taking? . . .
      In the night, O the night,
      While the house is sleeping.

VIII.

Dreadful! has it come to this,
    O unhappy creature?
You that would not tread on a worm
    For your gentle nature . . .
      In the night, O the night,
      O the night of weeping!

IX.

Murder would not veil your sin,
    Marriage will not hide it,
Earth and Hell will brand your name,
    Wretch you must abide it . . .
      In the night, O the night,
      Long before the dawning.

X.

Up, get up, and tell him all,
    Tell him you were lying!
Do not die with a lie in your mouth,
    You that know you're dying . . .
      In the night, O the night,
      While the grave is yawning.

XI.

No—you will not die before,
    Tho' you'll ne'er be stronger;
You will live till *that* is born,
    Then a little longer . . .
      In the night, O the night,
      While the Fiend is prowling.

XII.

Death and marriage, Death and
    marriage !
Funeral hearses rolling !
Black with bridal favours mixt !
    Bridal bells with tolling ! . . .
    In the night, O the night,
    When the wolves are howling.

XIII.

Up, get up, the time is short,
    Tell him now or never !
Tell him all before you die,
    Lest you die for ever . . .
    In the night, O the night,
    Where there's no forgetting.

XIV.

Up she got, and wrote him all,
    All her tale of sadness,
Blister'd every word with tears,
    And eased her heart of madness . . .
    In the night, and nigh the dawn,
    And while the moon was setting.

HAPPY.

THE LEPER'S BRIDE.

I.

WHY wail you, pretty plover ? and what
    is it that you fear ?
    Is he sick your mate like mine ? have
        you lost him, is he fled ?
And there—the heron rises from his
    watch beside the mere,
    And flies above the leper's hut, where
        lives the living-dead.

II.

Come back, nor let me know it ! would
    he live and die alone ?
    And has he not forgiven me yet, his
        over-jealous bride,
Who am, and was, and will be his, his
    own and only own,
    To share his living death with him,
        die with him side by side ?

III.

Is that the leper's hut on the solitary
    moor,
    Where noble Ulric dwells forlorn, and
        wears the leper's weed ?
The door is open.   He ! is he standing
    at the door,
    My soldier of the Cross ? it is he and
        he indeed !

IV.

My roses—will he take them *now*—mine,
    his—from off the tree
    We planted both together, happy in
        our marriage morn ?
O God, I could blaspheme, for he fought
    Thy fight for Thee,
    And Thou hast made him leper to
        compass him with scorn—

V.

Hast spared the flesh of thousands, the
    coward and the base,
    And set a crueller mark than Cain's
        on him, the good and brave !
He sees me, waves me from him.   I will
    front him face to face.
    You need not wave me from you.   I
        would leap into your grave.
    *   *   *   *

VI.

My warrior of the Holy Cross and of the
    conquering sword,
    The roses that you cast aside—once
        more I bring you these.
No nearer ? do you scorn me when you
    tell me, O my lord,
    You would not mar the beauty of your
        bride with your disease.

VII.

You say your body is so foul—then here
    I stand apart,
    Who yearn to lay my loving head upon
        your leprous breast.
The leper plague may scale my skin but
    never taint my heart ;
    Your body is not foul to me, and body
        is foul at best.

VIII.

I loved you first when young and fair,
but now I love you most;
 The fairest flesh at last is filth on which
the worm will feast;
This poor rib-grated dungeon of the holy
human ghost,
 This house with all its hateful needs no
cleaner than the beast,

IX.

This coarse diseaseful creature which in
Eden was divine,
 This Satan-haunted ruin, this little
city of sewers,
This wall of solid flesh that comes between
your soul and mine,
 Will vanish and give place to the
beauty that endures,

X.

The beauty that endures on the Spiritual
height,
 When we shall stand transfigured, like
Christ on Hermon hill,
And moving each to music, soul in soul
and light in light,
 Shall flash thro' one another in a
moment as we will.

XI.

Foul! foul! the word was yours not
mine, I worship that right hand
 Which fell'd the foes before you as the
woodman fells the wood,
And sway'd the sword that lighten'd back
the sun of Holy land,
 And clove the Moslem crescent moon,
and changed it into blood.

XII.

And once I worshipt all too well this
creature of decay,
 For Age will chink the face, and Death
will freeze the supplest limbs—
Yet you in your mid manhood—O the
grief when yesterday
 They bore the Cross before you to the
chant of funeral hymns.

XIII.

'Libera me, Domine!' you sang the
Psalm, and when
 The Priest pronounced you dead, and
flung the mould upon your feet,
A beauty came upon your face, not that
of living men,
 But seen upon the silent brow when
life has ceased to beat.

XIV.

'Libera *nos*, Domine'—you knew not
one was there
 Who saw you kneel beside your bier,
and weeping scarce could see;
May I come a little nearer, I that heard,
and changed the prayer
 And sang the married 'nos' for the
solitary 'me.'

XV.

My beauty marred by you? by you! so
be it. All is well
 If I lose it and myself in the higher
beauty, yours.
My beauty lured that falcon from his
eyry on the fell,
 Who never caught one gleam of the
beauty which endures—

XVI.

The Count who sought to snap the bond
that link'd us life to life,
 Who whisper'd me 'your Ulric loves'
—a little nearer still—
He hiss'd, 'Let us revenge ourselves,
your Ulric woos my wife'—
 A lie by which he thought he could
subdue me to his will.

XVII.

I knew that you were near me when I
let him kiss my brow;
 Did he touch me on the lips? I was
jealous, anger'd, vain,
And I meant to make *you* jealous. Are
you jealous of me now?
 Your pardon, O my love, if I ever gave
you pain.

XVIII.

You never once accused me, but I wept
  alone, and sigh'd
  In the winter of the Present for the
    summer of the Past;
That icy winter silence—how it froze you
    from your bride,
  Tho' I made one barren effort to break
    it at the last.

XIX.

I brought you, you remember, these roses,
  when I knew
  You were parting for the war, and you
    took them tho' you frown'd;
You frown'd and yet you kiss'd them.
    All at once the trumpet blew,
  And you spurr'd your fiery horse, and
    you hurl'd them to the ground.

XX.

You parted for the Holy War without a
  word to me,
  And clear myself unask'd—not I. My
    nature was too proud.
And him I saw but once again, and far
    away was he,
  When I was praying in a storm—the
    crash was long and loud—

XXI.

That God would ever slant His bolt from
  falling on your head—
  Then I lifted up my eyes, he was coming
    down the fell—
I clapt my hands. The sudden fire from
    Heaven had dash'd him dead,
  And sent him charr'd and blasted to
    the deathless fire of Hell.

XXII.

See, I sinn'd but for a moment. I re-
  pented and repent,
  And trust myself forgiven by the God
    to whom I kneel.
A little nearer? Yes. I shall hardly be
    content
  Till I be leper like yourself, my love,
    from head to heel.

XXIII.

O foolish dreams, that you, that I, would
  slight our marriage oath:
  I held you at that moment even dearer
    than before;
Now God has made you leper in His
    loving care for both,
  That we might cling together, never
    doubt each other more.

XXIV.

The Priest, who join'd you to the dead,
  has join'd our hands of old;
  If man and wife be but one flesh, let
    mine be leprous too,
As dead from all the human race as if
    beneath the mould;
  If you be dead, then I am dead, who
    only live for you.

XXV.

Would Earth tho' hid in cloud not be
  follow'd by the Moon?
  The leech forsake the dying bed for
    terror of his life?
The shadow leave the Substance in the
    brooding light of noon?
  Or if *I* had been the leper would you
    have left the wife?

XXVI.

Not take them? Still you wave me off
  —poor roses—must I go—
  I have worn them year by year—from
    the bush we both had set—
What? fling them to you?—well—that
    were hardly gracious. No!
  Your plague but passes by the touch.
    A little nearer yet!

XXVII.

There, there! he buried you, the Priest;
  the Priest is not to blame,
  He joins us once again, to his either
    office true:
I thank him. I am happy, happy.
    Kiss me. In the name
  Of the everlasting God, I will live and
    die with you.

[DEAN MILMAN has remarked that the protection and care afforded by the Church to this blighted race of lepers was among the most beautiful of its offices during the Middle Ages. The leprosy of the thirteenth and fourteenth centuries was supposed to be a legacy of the crusades, but was in all probability the offspring of meagre and unwholesome diet, miserable lodging and clothing, physical and moral degradation. The services of the Church in the seclusion of these unhappy sufferers were most affecting. The stern duty of looking to the public welfare is tempered with exquisite compassion for the victims of this loathsome disease. The ritual for the sequestration of the leprous differed little from the burial service. After the leper had been sprinkled with holy water, the priest conducted him into the church, the leper singing the psalm 'Libera me domine,' and the crucifix and bearer going before. In the church a black cloth was stretched over two trestles in front of the altar, and the leper leaning at its side devoutly heard mass. The priest, taking up a little earth in his cloak, threw it on one of the leper's feet, and put him out of the church, if it did not rain too heavily ; took him to his hut in the midst of the fields, and then uttered the prohibitions : 'I forbid you entering the church . . . . or entering the company of others. I forbid you quitting your home without your leper's dress.' He concluded : 'Take this dress, and wear it in token of humility; take these gloves, take this clapper, as a sign that you are forbidden to speak to any one. You are not to be indignant at being thus separated from others, and as to your little wants, good people will provide for you, and God will not desert you.' Then in this old ritual follow these sad words : 'When it shall come to pass that the leper shall pass out of this world, he shall be buried in his hut, and not in the churchyard.' At first there was a doubt whether wives should follow their husbands who had been leprous, or remain in the world and marry again. The Church decided that the marriage-tie was indissoluble, and so bestowed on these unhappy beings this immense source of consolation. With a love stronger than this living death, lepers were followed into banishment from the haunts of men by their faithful wives. Readers of Sir J. Stephen's *Essays on Ecclesiastical Biography* will recollect the description of the founder of the Franciscan order, how, controlling his involuntary disgust, St. Francis of Assisi washed the feet and dressed the sores of the lepers, once at least reverently applying his lips to their wounds.—BOUCHER-JAMES.]

This ceremony of *quasi*-burial varied considerably at different times and in different places. In some cases a grave was dug, and the leper's face was often covered during the service.

TO ULYSSES.[1]

I.

ULYSSES, much-experienced man,
　Whose eyes have known this globe of
　　ours,
　Her tribes of men, and trees, and
　　flowers,
From Corrientes to Japan,

II.

To you that bask below the Line,
　I soaking here in winter wet—
　The century's three strong eights have
　　met
To drag me down to seventy-nine

III.

In summer if I reach my day—
　To you, yet young, who breathe the
　　balm
　Of summer-winters by the palm
And orange grove of Paraguay,

IV.

I tolerant of the colder time,
　Who love the winter woods, to trace
　On paler heavens the branching grace
Of leafless elm, or naked lime,

V.

And see my cedar green, and there
　My giant ilex keeping leaf
　When frost is keen and days are brief—
Or marvel how in English air

VI.

My yucca, which no winter quells,
　Altho' the months have scarce begun,
　Has push'd toward our faintest sun
A spike of half-accomplish'd bells—

VII.

Or watch the waving pine which here
　The warrior of Caprera set,[2]

[1] 'Ulysses,' the title of a number of essays by W. G. Palgrave. He died at Monte Video before seeing my poem.

[2] Garibaldi said to me, alluding to his barren island, 'I wish I had your trees.'

A name that earth will not forget
Till earth has roll'd her latest year—

VIII.

I, once half-crazed for larger light
    On broader zones beyond the foam,
    But chaining fancy now at home
Among the quarried downs of Wight,

IX.

Not less would yield full thanks to you
    For your rich gift, your tale of lands
    I know not,[1] your Arabian sands;
Your cane, your palm, tree-fern, bamboo,

X.

The wealth of tropic bower and brake;
    Your Oriental Eden-isles,[2]
    Where man, nor only Nature smiles;
Your wonder of the boiling lake;[3]

XI.

Phra-Chai, the Shadow of the Best,[4]
    Phra-bat[5] the step; your Pontic coast;
    Crag-cloister;[6] Anatolian Ghost;[7]
Hong-Kong,[8] Karnac,[9] and all the rest.

XII.

Thro' which I follow'd line by line
    Your leading hand, and came, my friend,
    To prize your various book, and send
A gift of slenderer value, mine.

[1] The tale of Nejd.
[2] The Philippines.
[3] In Dominica.
[4] The Shadow of the Lord. Certain obscure markings on a rock in Siam, which express the image of Buddha to the Buddhist more or less distinctly according to his faith and his moral worth.
[5] The footstep of the Lord on another rock.
[6] The monastery of Sumelas.
[7] Anatolian Spectre stories.
[8] The Three Cities.
[9] Travels in Egypt.

TO MARY BOYLE.

WITH THE FOLLOWING POEM.

I.

'SPRING-FLOWERS'! While you still delay to take
    Your leave of Town,
Our elmtree's ruddy-hearted blossom-flake
    Is fluttering down.

II.

Be truer to your promise. There! I heard
    Our cuckoo call.
Be needle to the magnet of your word,
    Nor wait, till all

III.

Our vernal bloom from every vale and plain
    And garden pass,
And all the gold from each laburnum chain
    Drop to the grass.

IV.

Is memory with your Marian gone to rest,
    Dead with the dead?
For ere she left us, when we met, you prest
    My hand, and said

V.

'I come with your spring-flowers.' You came not, friend;
    My birds would sing,
You heard not. Take then this spring-flower I send,
    This song of spring,

VI.

Found yesterday—forgotten mine own rhyme
    By mine old self,
As I shall be forgotten by old Time,
    Laid on the shelf—

VII.

A rhyme that flower'd betwixt the whitening sloe
    And kingcup blaze,
And more than half a hundred years ago,
    In rick-fire days,

VIII.

When Dives loathed the times, and paced
his land'
    In fear of worse,
And sanguine Lazarus felt a vacant hand
    Fill with *his* purse.

IX.

For lowly minds were madden'd to the
height
    By tonguester tricks,
And once—I well remember that red
night
    When thirty ricks,

X.

All flaming, made an English homestead
Hell—
    These hands of mine
Have helpt to pass a bucket from the well
    Along the line,

XI.

When this bare dome had not begun to
gleam
    Thro' youthful curls,
And you were then a lover's fairy dream,
    His girl of girls ;

XII.

And you, that now are lonely, and with
Grief
    Sit face to face,
Might find a flickering glimmer of relief
    In change of place.

XIII.

What use to brood ? this life of mingled
pains
    And joys to me,
Despite of every Faith and Creed, remains
    The Mystery.

XIV.

Let golden youth bewail the friend, the
wife,
    For ever gone.
He dreams of that long walk thro' desert
life
    Without the one.

XV.

The silver year should cease to mourn
and sigh—
    Not long to wait—
So close are we, dear Mary, you and I
    To that dim gate.

XVI.

Take, read ! and be the faults your Poet
makes
    Or many or few,
He rests content, if his young music
wakes
    A wish in you

XVII.

To change our dark Queen-city, all her
realm
    Of sound and smoke,
For his clear heaven, and these few lanes
of elm
    And whispering oak.

THE PROGRESS OF SPRING.

I.

THE groundflame of the crocus breaks
the mould,
    Fair Spring slides hither o'er the
Southern sea,
Wavers on her thin stem the snowdrop
cold
    That trembles not to kisses of the bee:
Come, Spring, for now from all the
dripping eaves
The spear of ice has wept itself away,
And hour by hour unfolding woodbine
leaves
    O'er his uncertain shadow droops the
day.

She comes ! The loosen'd rivulets run ;
  The frost-bead melts upon her golden
    hair ;
Her mantle, slowly greening in the Sun,
  Now wraps her close, now arching
    leaves her bare
To breaths of balmier air ;

II.

Up leaps the lark, gone wild to welcome
    her,
  About her glance the tits, and shriek
    the jays,
Before her skims the jubilant woodpecker,
  The linnet's bosom blushes at her gaze,
While round her brows a woodland culver
    flits,
  Watching her large light eyes and
    gracious looks,
And in her open palm a halcyon sits
  Patient—the secret splendour of the
    brooks.
Come, Spring ! She comes on waste and
    wood,
  On farm and field : but enter also here,
Diffuse thyself at will thro' all my blood,
  And, tho' thy violet sicken into sere,
Lodge with me all the year !

III.

Once more a downy drift against the
    brakes,
  Self-darken'd in the sky, descending
    slow !
But gladly see I thro' the wavering flakes
Yon blanching apricot like snow in snow.
These will thine eyes not brook in forest-
    paths,
  On their perpetual pine, nor round
    the beech ;
They fuse themselves to little spicy baths,
  Solved in the tender blushes of the
    peach ;
They lose themselves and die
  On that new life that gems the haw-
    thorn line ;
Thy gay lent-lilies wave and put them by,
  And out once more in varnish'd glory
    shine
Thy stars of celandine.

IV.

She floats across the hamlet. Heaven
    lours,
  But in the tearful splendour of her
    smiles
I see the slowly-thickening chestnut
    towers
  Fill out the spaces by the barren tiles.
Now past her feet the swallow circling
    flies,
  A clamorous cuckoo stoops to meet
    her hand ;
Her light makes rainbows in my closing
    eyes,
  I hear a charm of song thro' all the
    land.
Come, Spring ! She comes, and Earth
    is glad
  To roll her North below thy deepening
    dome,
But ere thy maiden birk be wholly clad,
  And these low bushes dip their twigs
    in foam,
Make all true hearths thy home.

V.

Across my garden ! and the thicket stirs,
  The fountain pulses high in sunnier jets,
The blackcap warbles, and the turtle
    purrs,
  The starling claps his tiny castanets.
Still round her forehead wheels the
    woodland dove,
  And scatters on her throat the sparks
    of dew,
The kingcup fills her footprint, and above
  Broaden the glowing isles of vernal
    blue.
Hail ample presence of a Queen,
  Bountiful, beautiful, apparell'd gay,
Whose mantle, every shade of glancing
    green,
  Flies back in fragrant breezes to display
A tunic white as May !

VI.

She whispers, 'From the South I bring
    you balm,
  For on a tropic mountain was I born,

While some dark dweller by the coco-
palm
    Watch'd my far meadow zoned with
airy morn ;
From under rose a muffled moan of
floods ;
  I sat beneath a solitude of snow ;
There no one came, the turf was fresh,
the woods
    Plunged gulf on gulf thro' all their
vales below.
I saw beyond their silent tops
    The steaming marshes of the scarlet
cranes,
The slant seas leaning on the mangrove
copse,
    And summer basking in the sultry
plains
  About a land of canes ;

VII.

'Then from my vapour-girdle soaring
forth
    I scaled the buoyant highway of the
birds,
And drank the dews and drizzle of the
North,
    That I might mix with men, and hear
their words
On pathway'd plains; for—while my
hand exults
    Within the bloodless heart of lowly
flowers
To work old laws of Love to fresh
results,
  Thro' manifold effect of simple powers—
I too would teach the man
    Beyond the darker hour to see the
bright,
That his fresh life may close as it began,
  The still-fulfilling promise of a light
Narrowing the bounds of night.'

VIII.

So wed thee with my soul, that I may
mark
    The coming year's great good and
varied ills,
And new developments, whatever spark

Be struck from out the clash of warring
wills ;
Or whether, since our nature cannot rest,
    The smoke of war's volcano burst
again
From hoary deeps that belt the changeful
West,
    Old Empires, dwellings of the kings
of men ;
Or should those fail, that hold the helm,
    While the long day of knowledge
grows and warms,
And in the heart of this most ancient
realm
    A hateful voice be utter'd, and alarms
    Sounding 'To arms ! to arms !'

IX.

A simpler, saner lesson might he learn
    Who reads thy gradual process, Holy
Spring.
Thy leaves possess the season in their
turn,
    And in their time thy warblers rise on
wing.
How surely glidest thou from March to
May,
    And changest, breathing it, the sullen
wind,
Thy scope of operation, day by day,
    Larger and fuller, like the human
mind !
Thy warmths from bud to bud
    Accomplish that blind model in the
seed,
And men have hopes, which race the
restless blood,
    That after many changes may succeed
Life, which is Life indeed.

MERLIN AND THE GLEAM.

I.

O young Mariner,
You from the haven
Under the sea-cliff,
You that are watching
The gray Magician

With eyes of wonder,
I am Merlin,
And *I* am dying,
I am Merlin
Who follow The Gleam.

II.

Mighty the Wizard
Who found me at sunrise
Sleeping, and woke me
And learn'd me Magic !
Great the Master,
And sweet the Magic,
When over the valley,
In early summers,
Over the mountain,
On human faces,
And all around me,
Moving to melody,
Floated The Gleam.

III.

Once at the croak of a Raven
    who crost it,
A barbarous people,
Blind to the magic,
And deaf to the melody,
Snarl'd at and cursed me.
A demon vext me,
The light retreated,
The landskip darken'd,
The melody deaden'd,
The Master whisper'd
'Follow The Gleam.'

IV.

Then to the melody,
Over a wilderness
Gliding, and glancing at
Elf of the woodland,
Gnome of the cavern,
Griffin and Giant,
And dancing of Fairies
In desolate hollows,
And wraiths of the mountain,
And rolling of dragons
By warble of water,
Or cataract music
Of falling torrents,
Flitted The Gleam.

V.

Down from the mountain
And over the level,
And streaming and shining on
Silent river,
Silvery willow,
Pasture and plowland,
Innocent maidens,
Garrulous children,
Homestead and harvest,
Reaper and gleaner,
And rough-ruddy faces
Of lowly labour,
Slided The Gleam—

VI.

Then, with a melody
Stronger and statelier,
Led me at length
To the city and palace
Of Arthur the king;
Touch'd at the golden
Cross of the churches,
Flash'd on the Tournament,
Flicker'd and bicker'd
From helmet to helmet,
And last on the forehead
Of Arthur the blameless
Rested The Gleam.

VII.

Clouds and darkness
Closed upon Camelot;
Arthur had vanish'd
I knew not whither,
The king who loved me,
And cannot die;
For out of the darkness
Silent and slowly
The Gleam, that had waned to a
    wintry glimmer
On icy fallow
And faded forest,
Drew to the valley
Named of the shadow,
And slowly brightening
Out of the glimmer,
And slowly moving again to a melody
Yearningly tender,

Fell on the shadow,
No longer a shadow,
But clothed with The Gleam.

VIII.

And broader and brighter
The Gleam flying onward,
Wed to the melody,
Sang thro' the world;
And slower and fainter,
Old and weary,
But eager to follow,
I saw, whenever
In passing it glanced upon
Hamlet or city,
That under the Crosses
The dead man's garden,
The mortal hillock,
Would break into blossom;
And so to the land's
Last limit I came——
And can no longer,
But die rejoicing,
For thro' the Magic
Of Him the Mighty,
Who taught me in childhood,
There on the border
Of boundless Ocean,
And all but in Heaven
Hovers The Gleam.

IX.

Not of the sunlight,
Not of the moonlight,
Not of the starlight!
O young Mariner,
Down to the haven,
Call your companions,
Launch your vessel,
And crowd your canvas,
And, ere it vanishes
Over the margin,
After it, follow it,
Follow The Gleam.

ROMNEY'S REMORSE.

'I read Hayley's Life of Romney the other
day—Romney wanted but education and reading
to make him a very fine painter; but his ideal
was not high nor fixed. How touching is the
close of his life! He married at nineteen, and
because Sir Joshua and others had said that
"marriage spoilt an artist" almost immediately
left his wife in the North and scarce saw her till
the end of his life; when old, nearly mad and
quite desolate, he went back to her and she
received him and nursed him till he died. This
quiet act of hers is worth all Romney's pictures!
even as a matter of Art, I am sure.' (*Letters
and Literary Remains of Edward Fitzgerald*,
vol. i.)

'BEAT, little heart—I give you this and
        this'
    Who are you? What! the Lady
        Hamilton?
Good, I am never weary painting you.
To sit once more? Cassandra, Hebe,
        Joan,
Or spinning at your wheel beside the
        vine—
Bacchante, what you will; and if I
        fail
To conjure and concentrate into form
And colour all you are, the fault is less
In me than Art. What Artist ever yet
Could make pure light live on the canvas?
        Art!
Why should I so disrelish that short word?
    Where am I? snow on all the hills!
        so hot,
So fever'd! never colt would more delight
To roll himself in meadow grass than I
To wallow in that winter of the hills.
    Nurse, were you hired? or came of
        your own will
To wait on one so broken, so forlorn?
Have I not met you somewhere long ago?
I am all but sure I have—in Kendal
        church—
O yes! I hired you for a season there,
And then we parted; but you look so
        kind
That you will not deny my sultry throat
One draught of icy water. There—you
        spill
The drops upon my forehead. Your
        hand shakes.
I am ashamed. I am a trouble to you,
Could kneel for your forgiveness. Are
        they tears?

For me—they do me too much grace—
    for me?
O Mary, Mary!
        Vexing you with words !
Words only, born of fever, or the fumes
Of that dark opiate dose you gave me,
    —words,
Wild babble. I have stumbled back
    again
Into the common day, the sounder self.
God stay me there, if only for your sake,
The truest, kindliest, noblest-hearted wife
That ever wore a Christian marriage-
    ring.
    My curse upon the Master's apothegm,
That wife and children drag an Artist
    down !
This seem'd my lodestar in the Heaven
    of Art,
And lured me from the household fire on
    earth.
To you my days have been a life-long lie,
Grafted on half a truth ; and tho' you say
'Take comfort you have won the Painter's
    fame,'
The best in me that sees the worst in me,
And groans to see it, finds no comfort
    there.
    What fame? I am not Raphaël,
    Titian—no
Nor even a Sir Joshua, some will cry.
Wrong there ! The painter's fame? but
    mine, that grew
Blown into glittering by the popular
    breath,
May float awhile beneath the sun, may
    roll
The rainbow hues of heaven about it—
        There !
The colour'd bubble bursts above the
    abyss
Of Darkness, utter Lethe.

              Is it so?
Her sad eyes plead for my own fame
    with me
To make it dearer.

        Look, the sun has risen
To flame along another dreary day.

Your hand. How bright you keep your
    marriage-ring !
Raise me. I thank you.

          Has your opiate then
Bred this black mood ? or am I conscious,
    more
Than other Masters, of the chasm
    between
Work and Ideal ? Or does the gloom
    of Age
And suffering cloud the height I stand
    upon
Even from myself ? stand ? stood . . .
    no more.
               And yet
The world would lose, if such a wife as
    you
Should .vanish unrecorded. Might I
    crave
One favour ? I am bankrupt of all claim
On your obedience, and my strongest
    wish
Falls flat before your least unwillingness.
Still would you—if it please you—sit
    to me?
    ·I dream'd last night of that clear
    summer noon,
When seated on a rock, and foot to foot
With your own shadow in the placid lake,
You claspt our infant daughter, heart to
    heart.
I had been among the hills, and brought
    you down
A length of staghorn-moss, and this you
    twined
About her cap. I see the picture yet,
Mother and child. A sound from far
    away,
No louder than a bee among the flowers,
A fall of water lull'd the noon asleep.
You still'd it for the moment with a song
Which often echo'd in me, while I stood
Before the great Madonna-masterpieces
Of ancient Art in Paris, or in Rome.
    Mary, my crayons ! if I can, I will.
You should have been—I might have
    made you once,
Had I but known you as I know you
    now—

The true Alcestis of the time. Your
    song—
Sit, listen ! I remember it, a proof
That I—even I—at times remember'd
    you.

   'Beat upon mine, little heart ! beat,
    beat !
   Beat upon mine ! you are mine, my
    sweet !
   All mine from your pretty blue eyes
    to your feet,
             My sweet.'

Less profile ! turn to me—three-quarter
    face.

   'Sleep, little blossom, my honey, my
    bliss !
   For I give you this, and I give you
    this !
   And I blind your pretty blue eyes with
    a kiss !
             Sleep !'

Too early blinded by the kiss of death—

   'Father and Mother will watch you
    grow '—

You watch'd not I, she did not grow,
    she died.

   'Father and Mother will watch you
    grow,
   And gather the roses whenever they
    blow,
   And find the white heather wherever
    you go,
             My sweet.'

Ah, my white heather only blooms in
    heaven
With Milton's amaranth. There, there,
    there ! a child
Had shamed me at it—Down, you idle
    tools,
Stampt into dust—tremulous, all awry,
Blurr'd like a landskip in a ruffled pool,—
Not one stroke firm. This Art, that
    harlot-like
Seduced me from you, leaves me harlot-
    like,
Who love her still, and whimper, im-
    potent

To win her back before I die—and
    then—
Then, in the loud world's bastard judg-
    ment-day,
One truth will damn me with the mind-
    less mob,
Who feel no touch of my temptation,
    more
Than all the myriad lies, that blacken
    round
The corpse of every man that gains a
    name ;
'This model husband, this fine Artist'!
    Fool,
What matters ?   Six foot deep of burial
    mould
Will dull their comments ! Ay, but when
    the shout
Of His descending peals from Heaven,
    and throbs
Thro' earth, and all her graves, if *He*
    should ask
'Why left you wife and children ? for
    my sake,
According to my word ?' and I replied
'Nay, Lord, for *Art*,' why, that would
    sound so mean
That all the dead, who wait the doom of
    Hell
For bolder sins than mine, adulteries,
Wife-murders,—nay, the ruthless Mussul-
    man
Who flings his bowstrung Harem in the
    sea,
Would turn, and glare at me, and point
    and jeer,
And gibber at the worm, who, living,
    made
The wife of wives a widow-bride, and
    lost
Salvation for a sketch.
               I am wild again !
The coals of fire you heap upon my head
Have crazed me.   Someone knocking
    there without ?
No ! Will my Indian brother come ? to
    find
Me or my coffin ? Should I know the
    man ?
This worn-out Reason dying in her house

May leave the windows blinded, and if
so,
Bid him farewell for me, and tell him—
Hope!
I hear a death-bed Angel whisper 'Hope.'
" The miserable have no medicine
But only Hope!" He said it . . . in
the play.
His crime was of the senses; of the mind
Mine; worse, cold, calculated.

Tell my son—
O let me lean my head upon your breast.
' Beat little heart' on this fool brain of
mine.
I once had friends—and many—none
like you.
I love you more than when we married.
Hope!
O yes, I hope, or fancy that, perhaps,
Human forgiveness touches heaven, and
thence—
For you forgive me, you are sure of that—
Reflected, sends a light on the forgiven.

PARNASSUS.

Exegi monumentum . . .
Quod non . . .
Possit diruere . . .
. . . innumerabilis
Annorum series et fuga temporum.—HORACE.

I.

WHAT be those crown'd forms high over
the sacred fountain?
Bards, that the mighty Muses have raised
to the heights of the mountain,
And over the flight of the Ages! O
Goddesses, help me up thither!
Lightning may shrivel the laurel of
Cæsar, but mine would not wither.
Steep is the mountain, but you, you will
help me to overcome it,
And stand with my head in the zenith,
and roll my voice from the summit,
Sounding for ever and ever thro' Earth
and her listening nations,
And mixt with the great Sphere-music of
stars and of constellations.

T

II.

What be those two shapes high over the
sacred fountain,
Taller than all the Muses, and huger
than all the mountain?
On those two known peaks they stand
ever spreading and heightening;
Poet, that evergreen laurel is blasted by
more than lightning!
Look, in their deep double shadow the
crown'd ones all disappearing!
Sing like a bird and be happy, nor hope
for a deathless hearing!
' Sounding for ever and ever?' pass on!
the sight confuses—
These are Astronomy and Geology, terrible Muses!

III.

If the lips were touch'd with fire from off
a pure Pierian altar,
Tho' their music here be mortal need the
singer greatly care?
Other songs for other worlds! the fire
within him would not falter;
Let the golden Iliad vanish, Homer here
is Homer there.

BY AN EVOLUTIONIST.

THE Lord let the house of a brute to the
soul of a man,
And the man said ' Am I your debtor?'
And the Lord—' Not yet: but make it
as clean as you can,
And then I will let you a better.'

I.

If my body come from brutes, my soul
uncertain, or a fable,
Why not bask amid the senses while
the sun of morning shines,
I, the finer brute rejoicing in my hounds,
and in my stable,
Youth and Health, and birth and
wealth, and choice of women and
of wines?

2 R

II.

What hast thou done for me, grim Old
    Age, save breaking my bones on
    the rack?
Would I had past in the morning that
    looks so bright from afar!

OLD AGE.

Done for thee? starved the wild beast
    that was linkt with thee eighty
    years back.
Less weight now for the ladder - of -
    heaven that hangs on a star.

I.

If my body come from brutes, tho'
    somewhat finer than their own,
I am heir, and this my kingdom.
    Shall the royal voice be mute?
No, but if the rebel subject seek to drag
    me from the throne,
Hold the sceptre, Human Soul, and
    rule thy Province of the brute.

II.

I have climb'd to the snows of Age, and
    I gaze at a field in the Past,
Where I sank with the body at times
    in the sloughs of a low desire,
But I hear no yelp of the beast, and the
    Man is quiet at last
As he stands on the heights of his life
    with a glimpse of a height that is
    higher.

FAR—FAR—AWAY.

(FOR MUSIC.)

WHAT sight so lured him thro' the fields
    he knew
As where earth's green stole into heaven's
    own hue,
        Far—far—away?

What sound was dearest in his native dells?
The mellow lin-lan-lone of evening bells
        Far—far—away.

What vague world-whisper, mystic pain
    or joy,
Thro' those three words would haunt him
    when a boy,
        Far—far—away?

A whisper from his dawn of life? a
    breath
From some fair dawn beyond the doors
    of death
        Far—far—away?

Far, far, how far? from o'er the gates of
    Birth,
The faint horizons, all the bounds of earth,
        Far—far—away?

What charm in words, a charm no words
    could give?
O dying words, can Music make you live
        Far—far—away?

POLITICS.

WE move, the wheel must always move,
    Nor always on the plain,
And if we move to such a goal
    As Wisdom hopes to gain,
Then you that drive, and know your Craft,
    Will firmly hold the rein,
Nor lend an ear to random cries,
    Or you may drive in vain,
For some cry 'Quick' and some cry
    'Slow,'
    But, while the hills remain,
Up hill 'Too-slow' will need the whip,
    Down hill 'Too-quick,' the chain.

BEAUTIFUL CITY.

BEAUTIFUL city, the centre and crater
    of European confusion,
O you with your passionate shriek for
    the rights of an equal humanity,
How often your Re-volution has proven
    but E-volution
Roll'd again back on itself in the tides of
    a civic insanity!

THE ROSES ON THE TERRACE.

ROSE, on this terrace fifty years ago,
  When I was in my June, you in your
    May,
Two words, ' *My* Rose ' set all your face
    aglow,
  And now that I am white, and you are
    gray,
That blush of fifty years ago, my dear,
  Blooms in the Past, but close to me
    to-day
As this red rose, which on our terrace here
  Glows in the blue of fifty miles away.

THE PLAY.

ACT first, this Earth, a stage so gloom'd
    with woe
  You all but sicken at the shifting scenes.
And yet be patient.   Our Playwright
    may show
  In some fifth Act what this wild Drama
    means.

ON ONE WHO AFFECTED
AN EFFEMINATE MANNER.

WHILE man and woman still are incom-
    plete,
I prize that soul where man and woman
    meet,
Which types all Nature's male and female
    plan,
But, friend, man-woman is not woman-
    man.

TO ONE WHO RAN DOWN
THE ENGLISH.

YOU make our faults too gross, and thence
    maintain
Our darker future.   May your fears be
    vain !
At times the small black fly upon the pane
May seem the black ox of the distant plain.

THE SNOWDROP.

MANY, many welcomes
February fair-maid,
Ever as of old time,
Solitary firstling,
Coming in the cold time,
Prophet of the gay time,
Prophet of the May time,
Prophet of the roses,
Many, many welcomes
February fair-maid !

THE THROSTLE.

' SUMMER is coming, summer is coming.
    I know it, I know it, I know it.
Light again, leaf again, life again, love
    again,'
    Yes, my wild little Poet.

Sing the new year in under the blue.
    Last year you sang it as gladly.
' New, new, new, new '! Is it then *so*
    new
    That you should carol so madly ?

' Love again, song again, nest again, young
    again,'
    Never a prophet so crazy !
And hardly a daisy as yet, little friend,
    See, there is hardly a daisy.

' Here again, here, here, here, happy
    year ' !
    O warble unchidden, unbidden !
Summer is coming, is coming, my dear,
    And all the winters are hidden.

THE OAK.

LIVE thy Life,
  Young and old,
Like yon oak,
Bright in spring,
  Living gold ;

Summer-rich
    Then ; and then
Autumn-changed,
Soberer-hued
    Gold again.

All his leaves
    Fall'n at length,
Look, he stands,
Trunk and bough,
    Naked strength.

IN MEMORIAM.

W. G. WARD.

FAREWELL, whose living like I shall
        not find,
    Whose Faith and Work were bells of
        full accord,
My friend, the most unworldly of man-
        kind,
    Most generous of all Ultramontanes,
        Ward,
How subtle at tierce and quart of mind
        with mind,
    How loyal in the following of thy
        Lord !

THE DEATH OF ŒNONE

AND OTHER POEMS.

JUNE BRACKEN AND HEATHER.

To E. T.

THERE on the top of the down,
The wild heather round me and over me
　　June's high blue,
When I look'd at the bracken so bright
　　and the heather so brown,
I thought to myself I would offer this
　　book to you,
This, and my love together,
To you that are seventy-seven,
With a faith as clear as the heights of
　　the June-blue heaven,
And a fancy as summer-new
As the green of the bracken amid the
　　gloom of the heather.

TO THE MASTER OF BALLIOL.

I.

DEAR Master in our classic town,
You, loved by all the younger gown
　　There at Balliol,
Lay your Plato for one minute down,

II.

And read a Grecian tale re-told,
Which, cast in later Grecian mould,
　　Quintus Calaber
Somewhat lazily handled of old ;

III.

And on this white midwinter day—
For have the far-off hymns of May,
　　All her melodies,
All her harmonies echo'd away ?—

IV.

To-day, before you turn again
To thoughts that lift the soul of men,
　　Hear my cataract's
Downward thunder in hollow and glen,

V.

Till, led by dream and vague desire,
The woman, gliding toward the pyre,
　　Find her warrior
Stark and dark in his funeral fire.

THE DEATH OF ŒNONE

ŒNONE sat within the cave from out
Whose ivy-matted mouth she used to gaze
Down at the Troad ; but the goodly view
Was now one blank, and all the serpent
　　vines
Which on the touch of heavenly feet had
　　risen,
And gliding thro' the branches over-
　　bower'd
The naked Three, were wither'd long
　　ago,
And thro' the sunless winter morning-
　　mist
In silence wept upon the flowerless earth.
　And while she stared at those dead
　　cords that ran
Dark thro' the mist, and linking tree to
　　tree,
But once were gayer than a dawning sky
With many a pendent bell and fragrant
　　star,
Her Past became her Present, and she
　　saw
Him, climbing toward her with the
　　golden fruit,
Him, happy to be chosen Judge of Gods,
Her husband in the flush of youth and
　　dawn,
Paris, himself as beauteous as a God.

Anon from out the long ravine below,
She heard a wailing cry, that seem'd at
first
Thin as the batlike shrillings of the Dead
When driven to Hades, but, in coming
near,
Across the downward thunder of the
brook
Sounded ' Œnone '; and on a sudden he,
Paris, no longer beauteous as a God,
Struck by a poison'd arrow in the fight,
Lame, crooked, reeling, livid, thro' the
mist
Rose, like the wraith of his dead self,
and moan'd
' Œnone, *my* Œnone, while we dwelt
Together in this valley—happy then—
Too happy had I died within thine
arms,
Before the feud of Gods had marr'd our
peace,
And sunder'd each from each. I am
dying now
Pierced by a poison'd dart. Save me.
Thou knowest,
Taught by some God, whatever herb or
balm
May clear the blood from poison, and
thy fame
Is blown thro' all the Troad, and to thee
The shepherd brings his adder-bitten
lamb,
The wounded warrior climbs from Troy
to thee.
My life and death are in thy hand. The
Gods
Avenge on stony hearts a fruitless prayer
For pity. Let me owe my life to thee.
I wrought thee bitter wrong, but thou
forgive,
Forget it. Man is but the slave of Fate.
Œnone, by thy love which once was
mine,
Help, heal me. I am poison'd to the
heart.'
' And I to mine ' she said ' Adulterer,
Go back to thine adulteress and die ! '
He groan'd, he turn'd, and in the mist
at once
Became a shadow, sank and disappear'd,

But, ere the mountain rolls into the plain,
Fell headlong dead ; and of the shepherds
one
Their oldest, and the same who first had
found
Paris, a naked babe, among the woods
Of Ida, following lighted on him there,
And shouted, and the shepherds heard
and came.
One raised the Prince, one sleek'd the
squalid hair,
One kiss'd his hand, another closed his
eyes,
And then, remembering the gay playmate
rear'd
Among them, and forgetful of the man,
Whose crime had half unpeopled Ilion,
these
All that day long labour'd, hewing the
pines,
And built their shepherd-prince a funeral
pile ;
And, while the star of eve was drawing
light
From the dead sun, kindled the pyre,
and all
Stood round it, hush'd, or calling on his
name.
But when the white fog vanish'd like
a ghost
Before the day, and every topmost pine
Spired into bluest heaven, still in her
cave,
Amazed, and ever seeming stared upon
By ghastlier than the Gorgon head, a
face,—
His face deform'd by lurid blotch and
blain—
There, like a creature frozen to the heart
Beyond all hope of warmth, Œnone sat
Not moving, till in front of that ravine
Which drowsed in gloom, self-darken'd
from the west,
The sunset blazed along the wall of Troy.
Then her head sank, she slept, and
thro' her dream
A ghostly murmur floated, ' Come to me,
Œnone ! I can wrong thee now no
more,
Œnone, my Œnone,' and the dream

Wail'd in her, when she woke beneath
the stars.
  What star could burn so low? not
    Ilion yet.
What light was there? She rose and
  slowly down,
By the long torrent's ever-deepen'd roar,
Paced, following, as in trance, the silent
  cry.
She waked a bird of prey that scream'd
  and past;
She roused a snake that hissing writhed
  away;
A panther sprang across her path, she
  heard
The shriek of some lost life among the
  pines,
But when she gain'd the broader vale,
  and saw
The ring of faces redden'd by the flames
Enfolding that dark body which had lain
Of old in her embrace, paused—and then
  ask'd
Falteringly, 'Who lies on yonder pyre?'
But every man was mute for reverence.
Then moving quickly forward till the heat
Smote on her brow, she lifted up a voice
Of shrill command, 'Who burns upon
  the pyre?'
Whereon their oldest and their boldest
  said,
'He, whom thou wouldst not heal!' and
  all at once
The morning light of happy marriage
  broke
Thro' all the clouded years of widowhood,
And muffling up her comely head, and
  crying
'Husband!' she leapt upon the funeral
  pile,
And mixt herself with *him* and past in
  fire.

ST. TELEMACHUS.

HAD the fierce ashes of some fiery peak
Been hurl'd so high they ranged about
  the globe?
For day by day, thro' many a blood-red
  eve,

In that four-hundredth summer after
  Christ,
The wrathful sunset glared against a cross
Rear'd on the tumbled ruins of an old
  fane
No longer sacred to the Sun, and flamed
On one huge slope beyond, where in his
  cave
The man, whose pious hand had built
  the cross,
A man who never changed a word with
  men,
Fasted and pray'd, Telemachus the Saint.
  Eve after eve that haggard anchorite
Would haunt the desolated fane, and
  there
Gaze at the ruin, often mutter low
'Vicisti Galilæe'; louder again,
Spurning a shatter'd fragment of the
  God,
'Vicisti Galilæe!' but—when now
Bathed in that lurid crimson—ask'd 'Is
  earth
On fire to the West? or is the Demon-
  god
Wroth at his fall?' and heard an answer
  'Wake
Thou deedless dreamer, lazying out a life
Of self-suppression, not of selfless love.'
And once a flight of shadowy fighters
  crost
The disk, and once, he thought, a shape
  with wings
Came sweeping by him, and pointed to
  the West,
And at his ear he heard a whisper
  'Rome'
And in his heart he cried 'The call ot
  God!'
And call'd arose, and, slowly plunging
  down
Thro' that disastrous glory, set his face
By waste and field and town of alien
  tongue,
Following a hundred sunsets, and the
  sphere
Of westward-wheeling stars; and every
  dawn
Struck from him his own shadow on to
  Rome.

Foot-sore, way-worn, at length he
    touch'd his goal,
The Christian city.   All her splendour
    fail'd
To lure those eyes that only yearn'd to
    see,
Fleeting betwixt her column'd palace-
    walls,
The shape with wings.   Anon there past
    a crowd
With shameless laughter, Pagan oath,
    and jest,
Hard Romans brawling of their mon-
    strous games ;
He, all but deaf thro' age and weari-
    ness,
And muttering to himself ' The call of
    God '
And borne along by that full stream of
    men,
Like some old wreck on some indrawing
    sea,
Gain'd their huge Colosseum.   The caged
    beast
Yell'd, as he yell'd of yore for Christian
    blood.
Three slaves were trailing a dead lion
    away,
One, a dead man.   He stumbled in, and
    sat
Blinded ; but when the momentary gloom,
Made by the noonday blaze without, had
    left
His aged eyes, he raised them, and
    beheld
A blood-red awning waver overhead,
The dust send up a steam of human
    blood,
The gladiators moving toward their fight,
And eighty thousand Christian faces
    watch
Man murder man.   A sudden strength
    from heaven,
As some great shock may wake a palsied
    limb,
Turn'd him again to boy, for up he
    sprang,
And glided lightly down the stairs, and
    o'er

The barrier that divided beast from man
Slipt, and ran on, and flung himself
    between
The gladiatorial swords, and call'd ' For-
    bear
In the great name of Him who died for
    men,
Christ Jesus ! '   For one moment after-
    ward
A silence follow'd as of death, and then
A hiss as from a wilderness of snakes,
Then one deep roar as of a breaking sea,
And then a shower of stones that stoned
    him dead,
And then once more a silence as of death.
    His dream became a deed that woke
    the world,
For while the frantic rabble in half-amaze
Stared at him dead, thro' all the nobler
    hearts
In that vast Oval ran a shudder of shame.
The Baths, the Forum gabbled of his
    death,
And preachers linger'd o'er his dying
    words,
Which would not die, but echo'd on to
    reach
Honorius, till he heard them, and de-
    creed
That Rome no more should wallow in
    this old lust
Of Paganism, and make her festal hour
Dark with the blood of man who mur-
    der'd man.

[For Honorius, who succeeded to the sover-
eignty over Europe, suppress the gladiatorial
combats practised of old in Rome, on occasion
of the following event.   There was one Telemachus, embracing the ascetic mode of life, who
setting out from the East and arriving at Rome
for this very purpose, while that accursed spec-
tacle was being performed, entered himself the
circus, and descending into the arena, attempted
to hold back those who wielded deadly weapons
against each other.   The spectators of the murderous fray, possest with the drunken glee of
the demon who delights in such bloodshed, stoned
to death the preacher of peace.   The admirable
Emperor learning this put a stop to that evil ex-
hibition.—Theodoret's *Ecclesiastical History*.]

AKBAR'S DREAM.

AN INSCRIPTION BY ABUL FAZL FOR
A TEMPLE IN KASHMIR (Blochmann xxxii.).

O GOD in every temple I see people that
see thee, and in every language I hear
spoken, people praise thee.
    Polytheism and Islám feel after thee.
    Each religion says, ' Thou art one, with-
out equal.'
    If it be a mosque people murmur the
holy prayer, and if it be a Christian Church,
people ring the bell from love to Thee.
    Sometimes I frequent the Christian
cloister, and sometimes the mosque.
    But it is thou whom I search from
temple to temple.
    Thy elect have no dealings with either
heresy or orthodoxy ; for neither of them
stands behind the screen of thy truth.
    Heresy to the heretic, and religion to
the orthodox,
    But the dust of the rose-petal belongs to
the heart of the perfume seller.

AKBAR *and* ABUL FAZL *before the palace
at Futehpur-Sikri at night.*

' LIGHT of the nations ' ask'd his
        Chronicler
Of Akbar ' what has darken'd thee to-
        night ? '
Then, after one quick glance upon the
        stars,
And turning slowly toward him, Akbar
        said
' The shadow of a dream—an idle one
It may be. Still I raised my heart to
        heaven,
I pray'd against the dream. To pray,
        to do—
To pray, to do according to the prayer,
Are, both, to worship Alla, but the
        prayers,
That have no successor in deed, are faint
And pale in Alla's eyes, fair mothers
        they
Dying in childbirth of dead sons. I vow'd
Whate'er my dreams, I still would do
        the right

Thro' all the vast dominion which a sword,
That only conquers men to conquer
        peace,
Has won me. Alla be my guide !
                            But come,
My noble friend, my faithful counsellor,
Sit by my side. While thou art one
        with me,
I seem no longer like a lonely man
In the king's garden, gathering here and
        there
From each fair plant the blossom choicest-
        grown
To wreathe a crown not only for the
        king
But in due time for every Mussulmân,
Brahmin, and Buddhist, Christian, and
        Parsee,
Thro' all the warring world of Hindustan
    Well spake thy brother in his hymn to
        heaven
" Thy glory baffles wisdom. All the
        tracks
Of science making toward Thy Perfect-
        ness
Are blinding desert sand ; we scarce can
        spell
The Alif of Thine alphabet of Love."
    He knows Himself, men nor themselves
        nor Him,
For every splinter'd fraction of a sect
Will clamour " *I* am on the Perfect Way,
All else is to perdition."
                            Shall the rose
Cry to the lotus " No flower thou " ? the
        palm
Call to the cypress " I alone am fair " ?
The mango spurn the melon at his foot ?
" Mine is the one fruit Alla made for
        man."
    Look how the living pulse of Alla beats
Thro' all His world. If every single star
Should shriek its claim " I only am in
        heaven "
Why that were such sphere-music as the
        Greek
Had hardly dream'd of. There is light
        in all,
And light, with more or less of shade,
        in all

Man-modes of worship ; but our Ulama,
Who "sitting on green sofas contem-
    plate
The torment of the damn'd" already,
    these
Are like wild brutes new-caged—the
    narrower
The cage, the more their fury. Me they
    front
With sullen brows. What wonder ! I
    decreed
That even the dog was clean, that men
    may taste
Swine-flesh, drink wine ; they know too
    that whene'er
In our free Hall, where each philosophy
And mood of faith may hold its own,
    they blurt
Their furious formalisms, I but hear
The clash of tides that meet in narrow
    seas,—
Not the Great Voice not the true Deep.
                              To drive
A people from their ancient fold of Faith,
And wall them up perforce in mine—
    unwise,
Unkinglike ;—and the morning of my
    reign
Was redden'd by that cloud of shame
    when I . . .
  I hate the rancour of their castes and
    creeds,
I let men worship as they will, I reap
No revenue from the field of unbelief.
I cull from every faith and race the best
And bravest soul for counsellor and
    friend.
I loathe the very name of infidel.
I stagger at the Korân and the sword.
I shudder at the Christian and the stake;
Yet "Alla," says their sacred book, "is
    Love,"
And when the Goan Padre quoting Him,
Issa Ben Mariam, his own prophet, cried
"Love one another little ones" and
    "bless"
Whom ? even "your persecutors"! there
    methought
The cloud was rifted by a purer gleam
Than glances from the sun of our Islâm.

And thou rememberest what a fury
    shook
Those pillars of a moulder'd faith, when
    he,
That other, prophet of their fall, pro-
    claimed
His Master as "the Sun of Righteous-
    ness,"
Yea, Alla here on earth, who caught
    and held
His people by the bridle-rein of Truth.
  What art thou saying? "And was
    not Alla call'd
In old Irân the Sun of Love ? and Love
The net of truth ? "
                  A voice from old Irân !
Nay, but I know it—*his*, the hoary Sheik,
On whom the women shrieking "Atheist"
    flung
Filth from the roof, the mystic melodist
Who all but lost himself in Alla, him
Abû Saîd——
            —a sun but dimly seen
Here, till the mortal morning mists of
    earth
Fade in the noon of heaven, when creed
    and race
Shall bear false witness, each of each, no
    more,
But find their limits by that larger light,
And overstep them, moving easily
Thro' after-ages in the love of Truth,
The truth of Love.
                The sun, the sun ! they rail
At me the Zoroastrian. Let the Sun,
Who heats our earth to yield us grain
    and fruit,
And laughs upon thy field as well as
    mine,
And warms the blood of Shiah and
    Sunnee,
Symbol the Eternal ! Yea and may not
    kings
Express Him also by their warmth of
    love
For all they rule—by equal law for all ?
By deeds a light to men ?
                        But no such light
Glanced from our Presence on the face
    of one,

Who breaking in upon us yestermorn,
With all the Hells a-glare in either eye,
Yell'd "hast *thou* brought us down a
  new Korân
From heaven? art *thou* the Prophet?
  canst *thou* work
Miracles?" and the wild horse, anger,
  plunged
To fling me, and fail'd. Miracles! no,
  not I
Nor he, nor any. I can but lift the torch
Of Reason in the dusky cave of Life,
And gaze on this great miracle, the
  World,
Adoring That who made, and makes,
  and is,
And is not, what I gaze on—all else
  Form,
Ritual, varying with the tribes of men.
    Ay but, my friend, thou knowest I
  hold that forms
Are needful: only let the hand that rules,
With politic care, with utter gentleness,
Mould them for all his people.
              And what are forms?
Fair garments, plain or rich, and fitting
  close
Or flying looselier, warm'd but by the
  heart
Within them, moved but by the living
  limb,
And cast aside, when old, for newer,—
  Forms!
The Spiritual in Nature's market-place—
The silent Alphabet-of-heaven-in-man
Made vocal—banners blazoning a Power
That is not seen and rules from far away—
A silken cord let down from Paradise,
When fine Philosophies would fail, to
  draw
The crowd from wallowing in the mire
  of earth,
And all the more, when these behold
  their Lord,
Who shaped the forms, obey them, and
  himself
Here on this bank in *some* way live the
  life
Beyond the bridge, and serve that Infinite
Within us, as without, that All-in-all,

And over all, the never-changing One
And ever-changing Many, in praise of
  Whom
The Christian bell, the cry from off the
  mosque,
And vaguer voices of Polytheism
Make but one music, harmonising
  "Pray."
    There westward—under yon slow-
  falling star,
The Christians own a Spiritual Head;
And following thy true counsel, by thine
  aid,
Myself am such in our Islâm, for no
Mirage of glory, but for power to fuse
My myriads into union under one;
To hunt the tiger of oppression out
From office; and to spread the Divine
  Faith
Like calming oil on all their stormy
  creeds,
And fill the hollows between wave and
  wave;
To nurse my children on the milk of
  Truth,
And alchemise old hates into the gold
Of Love, and make it current; and beat
  back
The menacing poison of intolerant priests,
Those cobras ever setting up their hoods—
One Alla! one Kalifa!
              Still—at times
A doubt, a fear,—and yester afternoon
I dream'd,—thou knowest how deep a
  well of love
My heart is for my son, Saleem, mine
  heir,—
And yet so wild and wayward that my
  dream—
He glares askance at thee as one of those
Who mix the wines of heresy in the cup
Of counsel—so—I pray thee——
              Well, I dream'd
That stone by stone I rear'd a sacred
  fane,
A temple, neither Pagod, Mosque, nor
  Church,
But loftier, simpler, always open-door'd
To every breath from heaven, and Truth
  and Peace

And Love and Justice came and dwelt
    therein ;
But while we stood rejoicing, I and thou,
I heard a mocking laugh "the new
    Korân ! "
And on the sudden, and with a cry
    " Saleem "
Thou, thou—I saw thee fall before me,
    and then
Me too the black-wing'd Azrael over-
    came,
But Death had ears and eyes ; I watch'd
    my son,
And those that follow'd, loosen, stone
    from stone,
All my fair work ; and from the ruin
    arose
The shriek and curse of trampled millions,
    even
As in the time before ; but while I
    groan'd,
From out the sunset pour'd an alien race,
Who fitted stone to stone again, and
    Truth,
Peace, Love and Justice came and dwelt
    therein,
Nor in the field without were seen or
    heard
Fires of Súttee, nor wail of baby-wife,
Or Indian widow ; and in sleep I said
" All praise to Alla by whatever hands
My mission be accomplish'd ! " but we
    hear
Music : our palace is awake, and morn
Has lifted the dark eyelash of the Night
From off the rosy cheek of waking Day.
Our hymn to the sun. They sing it.
    Let us go.'

HYMN.

I.

Once again thou flamest heavenward,
    once again we see thee rise.
Every morning is thy birthday gladdening
    human hearts and eyes.
    Every morning here we greet it,
        bowing lowly down before thee,
Thee the Godlike, thee the changeless in
    thine ever-changing skies.

II.

Shadow-maker, shadow-slayer, arrowing
    light from clime to clime,
Hear thy myriad laureates hail thee
    monarch in their woodland rhyme.
    Warble bird, and open flower, and,
        men, below the dome of azure
Kneel adoring Him the Timeless in the
    flame that measures Time!

NOTES TO AKBAR'S DREAM.

The great Mogul Emperor Akbar was born
October 14, 1542, and died 1605. At 13 he succeeded his father Humayun ; at 18 he himself
assumed the sole charge of government. He
subdued and ruled over fifteen large provinces ;
his empire included all India north of the Vindhya
Mountains—in the south of India he was not so
successful. His tolerance of religions and his
abhorrence of religious persecution put our Tudors
to shame. He invented a new eclectic religion
by which he hoped to unite all creeds, castes and
peoples : and his legislation was remarkable for
vigour, justice and humanity.

'*Thy glory baffles wisdom.*' The Emperor
quotes from a hymn to the Deity by Faizi, brother
of Abul Fazl, Akbar's chief friend and minister,
who wrote the *Ain i Akbari* (Annals of Akbar).
His influence on his age was immense. It may
be that he and his brother Faizi led Akbar's
mind away from Islám and the Prophet—this
charge is brought against him by every Muham-
madan writer ; but Abul Fazl also led his sovereign to a true appreciation of his duties, and
from the moment that he entered Court, the
problem of successfully ruling over mixed races,
which Islám in few other countries had to solve,
was carefully considered, and the policy of toleration was the result (Blochmann xxix.).

Abul Fazl thus gives an account of himself
'The advice of my Father with difficulty kept me
back from acts of folly ; my mind had no rest and
my heart felt itself drawn to the sages of Mongolia
or to the hermits on Lebanon. I longed for
interviews with the Llamás of Tibet or with the
padres of Portugal, and I would gladly sit with
the priests of the Parsis and the learned of the
Zendavesta. I was sick of the learned of my own
land.'

He became the intimate friend and adviser of
Akbar, and helped him in his tolerant system of
government. Professor Blochmann writes 'Im-
pressed with a favourable idea of the value of his
Hindu subjects, he (Akbar) had resolved when
pensively sitting in the evenings on the solitary

stone at Futehpur-Sikri to rule with an even hand all men in his dominions; but as the extreme views of the learned and the lawyers continually urged him to persecute instead of to heal, he instituted discussions, because, believing himself to be in error, he thought it his duty as ruler to inquire.' 'These discussions took place every Thursday night in the Ibadat-khana a building at Futehpur-Sikri, erected for the purpose' (Malleson).

In these discussions Abul Fazl became a great power, and he induced the chief of the disputants to draw up a document defining the 'divine Faith' as it was called, and assigning to Akbar the rank of a Mujahid, or supreme khalifah, the vicegerent of the one true God.

Abul Fazl was finally murdered at the instigation of Akbar's son Salim, who in his Memoirs declares that it was Abul Fazl who had perverted his father's mind so that he denied the divine mission of Mahomet, and turned away his love from his son.

Faizi. When Akbar conquered the North-West Provinces of India, Faizi, then 20, began his life as a poet, and earned his living as a physician. He is reported to have been very generous and to have treated the poor for nothing. His fame reached Akbar's ears who commanded him to come to the camp at Chitor. Akbar was delighted with his varied knowledge and scholarship and made the poet teacher to his sons. Faizi at 33 was appointed Chief Poet (1588). He collected a fine library of 4300 MSS. and died at the age of 40 (1595) when Akbar incorporated his collection of rare books in the Imperial Library.

The warring world of Hindostan. Akbar's rapid conquests and the good government of his fifteen provinces with their complete military, civil and political systems make him conspicuous among the great kings of history.

The Goan Padre. Abul Fazl relates that 'one night the Ibadat-khana was brightened by the presence of Padre Rodolpho, who for intelligence and wisdom was unrivalled among Christian doctors. Several carping and bigoted men attacked him and this afforded an opportunity for the display of the calm judgment and justice of the assembly. These men brought forward the old received assertions, and did not attempt to arrive at truth by reasoning. Their statements were torn to pieces, and they were nearly put to shame, when they began to attack the contradictions of the Gospel, but they could not prove their assertions. With perfect calmness, and earnest conviction of the truth he replied to their arguments.

Abû Sa'îd. 'Love is the net of Truth, Love is the noose of God' is a quotation from the great Sufee poet Abû Sa'îd—born A.D. 968, died at the age of 83. He is a mystical poet, and some of his expressions have been compared to our George Herbert. Of Shaikh Abû Sa'îd it is recorded that he said, 'when my affairs had reacht a certain pitch I buried under the dust my books and opened a shop on my own account (*i.e.* began to teach with authority), and verily men represented me as that which I was not, until it came to this, that they went to the Qâdhî and testified against me of unbelieverhood; and women got upon the roofs and cast unclean things upon me.' (*Vide* reprint from article in *National Review*, March 1891, by C. J. Pickering.)

Aziz. I am not aware that there is any record of such intrusion upon the king's privacy, but the expressions in the text occur in a letter sent by Akbar's foster-brother Aziz, who refused to come to court when summoned and threw up his government, and 'after writing an insolent and reproachful letter to Akbar in which he asked him if he had received a book from heaven, or if he could work miracles like Mahomet that he presumed to introduce a new religion, warned him that he was on the way to eternal perdition, and concluded with a prayer to God to bring him back into the path of salvation' (Elphinstone).

'The Koran, the Old and New Testament, and the Psalms of David are called *books* by way of excellence, and their followers "People of the Book"' (Elphinstone).

Akbar according to Abdel Kadir had his son Murad instructed in the Gospel, and used to make him begin his lessons 'In the name of Christ' instead of in the usual way 'In the name of God.'

*To drive
A people from their ancient fold of Truth,* etc. Malleson says 'This must have happened because Akbar states it, but of the forced conversions I have found no record. This must have taken place whilst he was still a minor, and whilst the chief authority was wielded by Bairam.'

'*I reap no revenue from the field of unbelief.*' The Hindus are fond of pilgrimages and Akbar removed a remunerative tax raised by his predecessors on pilgrimages. He also abolished the fezza or capitation tax on those who differed from the Mahomedan faith. He discouraged all *excessive* prayers, fasts and pilgrimages.

Suttee. Akbar decreed that every widow who showed the least desire not to be burnt on her husband's funeral pyre, should be let go free and unharmed.

baby-wife.   He forbad marriage before the age of puberty.

Indian widow.   Akbar ordained that re-marriage was lawful.

Music.   'About a watch before daybreak,' says Abul Fazl, the musicians played to the king in the palace.   'His Majesty had such a know-ledge of the science of music as trained musicians do not possess.'

'*The Divine Faith*.'   The Divine Faith slowly passed away under the immediate successors of Akbar.   An idea of what the Divine Faith was may be gathered from the inscription at the head of the poem.   The document referred to, Abul Fazl says 'brought about excellent results (1) the Court became a gathering place of the sages and learned of all creeds; the good doctrines of all religious systems were recognized, and their de-fects were not allowed to obscure their good features; (2) perfect toleration or peace with all was established; and (3) the perverse and evil-minded were covered with shame on seeing the disinterested motives of His Majesty, and these stood in the pillory of disgrace.'   Dated Septem-ber 1579—Ragab 987 (Blochmann xiv.).

THE BANDIT'S DEATH.

TO SIR WALTER SCOTT.[1]

O GREAT AND GALLANT SCOTT,
TRUE GENTLEMAN, HEART, BLOOD AND BONE,
I WOULD IT HAD BEEN MY LOT
TO HAVE SEEN THEE, AND HEARD THEE, AND
      KNOWN.

SIR, do you see this dagger? nay, why
      do you start aside?
I was not going to stab you, tho' I *am*
      the Bandit's bride.

You have set a price on his head : I may
      claim it without a lie.
What have I here in the cloth?   I will
      show it you by-and-by.

[1] I have adopted Sir Walter Scott's version of the following story as given in his last journal (Death of Il Bizarro)—but I have taken the liberty of making some slight alterations.

Sir, I was once a wife.   I had one brief
      summer of bliss.
But the Bandit had woo'd me in vain,
      and he stabb'd my Piero with this.

And he dragg'd me up there to his cave
      in the mountain, and there one
      day
He had left his dagger behind him.   I
      found it.   I hid it away.

For he reek'd with the blood of Piero ;
      his kisses were red with his crime,
And I cried to the Saints to avenge me.
      They heard, they bided their time.

In a while I bore him a son, and he
      loved to dandle the child,
And that was a link between us ; but I
      —to be reconciled?—

No, by the Mother of God, tho' I think
      I hated him less,
And—well, if I sinn'd last night, I will
      find the Priest and confess.

Listen ! we three were alone in the dell
      at the close of the day.
I was lilting a song to the babe, and it
      laugh'd like a dawn in May.

Then on a sudden we saw your soldiers
      crossing the ridge,
And he caught my little one from me :
      we dipt down under the bridge

By the great dead pine—you know it—
      and heard as we crouch'd below,
The clatter of arms, and voices, and men
      passing to and fro.

Black was the night when we crept away
      —not a star in the sky—
Hush'd as the heart of the grave, till the
      little one utter'd a cry.

I whisper'd 'give it to me,' but he would
      not answer me—then
He gript it so hard by the throat that
      the boy never cried again.

We return'd to his cave—the link was broken—he sobb'd and he wept,
And cursed himself; then he yawn'd, for the wretch *could* sleep, and he slept

Ay, till dawn stole into the cave, and a ray red as blood
Glanced on the strangled face—I could make Sleep Death, if I would—

Glared on at the murder'd son, and the murderous father at rest, . . .
I drove the blade that had slain my husband thrice thro' his breast.

He was loved at least by his dog : it was chain'd, but its horrible yell
' She has kill'd him, has kill'd him, has kill'd him ' rang out all down thro' the dell,

Till I felt I could end myself too with the dagger—so deafen'd and dazed—
Take it, and save me from it ! I fled. I was all but crazed

With the grief that gnaw'd at my heart, and the weight that dragg'd at my hand ;
But thanks to the Blessed Saints that I came on none of his band ;

And the band will be scatter'd now their gallant captain is dead,
For I with this dagger of his—do you doubt me ? Here is his head !

THE CHURCH - WARDEN AND THE CURATE.

This is written in the dialect which was current in my youth at Spilsby and in the country about it.

I.

Eh ? good daäy ! good daäy ! thaw it bean't not mooch of a daäy,
Nasty, casselty [1] weather ! an' mea haäfe down wi' my haäy ! [2]

[1] 'Casselty,' casualty, chance weather.
[2] 'Haäfe down wi' my haäy,' while my grass is only half-mown.

II.

How be the farm gittin on ? noäways. Gittin on i'deeäd !
Why, tonups was haäfe on 'em fingers an' toäs,[1] an' the mare brokken-kneeäd,
An' pigs didn't sell at fall,[2] an' wa lost wer Haldeny cow,
An' it beäts ma to knaw wot she died on, but wool's looking oop ony how.

III.

An' soä they've maäde tha a parson, an' thou'll git along, niver fear,
Fur I beän chuch-warden mysen i' the parish fur fifteen year.
Well—sin ther beä chuch-wardens, ther mun be parsons an' all,
An' if t'öne stick alongside t'uther [3] the chuch weänt happen a fall.

IV.

Fur I wur a Baptis wonst, an' ageän the toithe an' the raäte,
Till I fun [4] that it warn't not the gaäinist [5] waäy to the narra Gaäte.
An' I can't abeär 'em, I can't, fur a lot on 'em coom'd ta-year [6]—
I wur down wi' the rheumatis then—to *my* pond to wesh thessens theere—
Sa I sticks like the ivin [7] as long as I lives to the owd chuch now,
Fur they wesh'd their sins i' *my* pond, an' I doubts they poison'd the cow.

V.

Ay, an' ya seed the Bishop. They says 'at he coom'd fra nowt—
Burn i' traäde. Sa I warrants 'e niver said haäfe wot 'e thowt,
But 'e creeäpt an' 'e crawl'd along, till 'e feeäld 'e could howd 'is oän,
Then 'e married a greät Yerl's darter, an' sits o' the Bishop's throän.

[1] 'Fingers and toes,' a disease in turnips.
[2] 'Fall,' autumn.
[3] 'If t'öne stick alongside t'uther,' if the one hold by the other. One is pronounced like ' own.'
[4] 'Fun,' found. [5] 'Gaäinist,' nearest.
[6] 'Ta-year,' this year. [7] 'Ivin,' ivy.

VI.

Now I'll gie tha a bit o' my mind an'
　　tha weänt be taakin' offence,
Fur thou be a big scholard now wi' a
　　hoonderd haäcre o' sense—
But sich an obstropulous [1] lad—naay,
　　naay—fur I minds tha sa well,
Tha'd niver not hopple [2] thy tongue, an'
　　the tongue's sit afire o' Hell,
As I says to my missis to-daay, when she
　　hurl'd a plaäte at the cat
An' anoother ageän my noäse.　Ya was
　　niver sa bad as that.

VII.

But I minds when i' Howlaby beck won
　　daäy ya was ticklin' o' trout,
An' keeäper 'e seed ya an roon'd, an' 'e
　　beal'd [3] to ya 'Lad coom hout'
An' ya stood oop naäkt i' the beck, an'
　　ya tell'd 'im to knaw his awn
　　plaäce
An' ya call'd 'im a clown, ya did, an' ya
　　thraw'd the fish i' 'is faäce,
An' 'e torn'd [4] as red as a stag-tuckey's [5]
　　wattles, but theer an' then
I coämb'd 'im down, fur I promised ya'd
　　niver not do it ageän.

VIII.

An' I cotch'd tha wonst i' my garden,
　　when thou was a height-year-
　　howd, [6]
An' I fun thy pockets as full o' my pip-
　　pins as iver they'd 'owd, [7]
An' thou was as peärky [8] as owt, an' tha
　　maäde me as mad as mad,
But I says to tha 'keeap 'em, an' wel-
　　come' fur thou was the Parson's
　　lad.

[1] 'Obstropulous,' obstreperous—here the Curate makes a sign of deprecation.
[2] 'Hopple' or 'hobble,' to tie the legs of a
skittish cow when she is being milked.
[3] 'Beal'd,' bellowed.
[4] In such words as 'torned' (turned), 'hurled,'
the *r* is hardly audible.
[5] 'Stag-tuckey,' turkey-cock.
[6] 'Height-year-howd,' eight-year-old.
[7] ''Owd,' hold.　　[8] 'Peärky,' pert.

IX.

An Parson 'e 'ears on it all, an' then
　　taäkes kindly to me,
An' then I wur chose Chuch-warden an'
　　coom'd to the top o' the tree,
Fur Quoloty's hall my friends, an' they
　　maäkes ma a help to the poor,
When I gits the plaäte fuller o' Soondays
　　nor ony chuch-warden afoor,
Fur if iver thy feyther 'ed riled me I kep'
　　mysen meeäk as a lamb,
An' saw by the Graäce o' the Lord, Mr.
　　Harry, I ham wot I ham.

X.

But Parson 'e *will* speäk out, saw, now
　　'e be sixty-seven,
He'll niver swap Owlby an' Scratby fur
　　owt but the Kingdom o' Heaven;
An' thou'll be 'is Curate 'ere, but, if iver
　　tha meäns to git 'igher,
Tha mun tackle the sins o' the Wo'ld, [1]
　　an' not the faults o' the Squire.
An' I reckons tha'll light of a livin' some-
　　wheers i' the Wowd [2] or the Fen,
If tha cottons down to thy betters, an'
　　keeäps thysen to thysen.
But niver not speäk plaäin out, if tha
　　wants to git forrards a bit,
But creeäp along the hedge-bottoms, an'
　　thou'll be a Bishop yit.

XI.

Naäy, but tha *mun* speäk hout to the
　　Baptises here i' the town,
Fur moäst on 'em talks ageän tithe, an'
　　I'd like tha to preäch 'em down,
Fur *they*'ve bin a-preächin' *mea* down,
　　they heve, an' I haätes 'em now,
Fur they leäved their nasty sins i' *my*
　　pond, an' it poison'd the cow.

[1] 'Wo'ld,' the world.　Short *o.*
[2] 'Wowd,' wold.

CHARITY.

I.

WHAT am I doing, you say to me,
  'wasting the sweet summer hours'?
Haven't you eyes? I am dressing the
  grave of a woman with flowers.

II.

For a woman ruin'd the world, as God's
  own scriptures tell,
And a man ruin'd mine, but a woman,
  God bless her, kept me from Hell.

III.

Love me? O yes, no doubt—how long
  —till you threw me aside !
Dresses and laces and jewels and never
  a ring for the bride.

IV.

All very well just now to be calling me
  darling and sweet,
And after a while would it matter so
  much if I came on the street?

V.

You when I met you first—when *he*
  brought you !—I turn'd away
And the hard blue eyes have it still, that
  stare of a beast of prey.

VI.

You were his friend—you—you—when
  he promised to make me his bride,
And you knew that he meant to betray
  me—you knew—you knew that
  he lied.

VII.

He married an heiress, an orphan with
  half a shire of estate,—
I sent him a desolate wail and a curse,
  when I learn'd my fate.

VIII.

For I used to play with the knife, creep
  down to the river-shore,

T

IX.

Moan to myself 'one plunge—then quiet
  for evermore.'

IX.

Would the man have a touch of remorse
  when he heard what an end was
  mine?
Or brag to his fellow rakes of his conquest
  over their wine?

X.

Money—my hire—*his* money—I sent
  him back what he gave,—
Will you move a little that way? your
  shadow falls on the grave.

XI.

Two trains clash'd : then and there he
  was crush'd in a moment and
  died,
But the new-wedded wife was unharm'd,
  tho' sitting close at his side.

XII.

She found my letter upon him, my wail
  of reproach and scorn ;
I had cursed the woman he married, and
  him, and the day I was born.

XIII.

They put him aside for ever, and after a
  week—no more—
A stranger as welcome as Satan—a widow
  came to my door :

XIV.

So I turn'd my face to the wall, I was
  mad, I was raving-wild,
I was close on that hour of dishonour,
  the birth of a baseborn child.

XV.

O you that can flatter your victims, and
  juggle, and lie and cajole,
Man, can you even guess at the love of
  a soul for a soul?

XVI.

I had cursed her as woman and wife,
 and in wife and woman I found
The tenderest Christ-like creature that
 ever stept on the ground.

XVII.

She watch'd me, she nursed me, she fed
 me, she sat day and night by my
 bed,
Till the joyless birthday came of a boy
 born happily dead.

XVIII.

And her name? what was it? I ask'd
 her. She said with a sudden glow
On her patient face 'My dear, I will
 tell you before I go.'

XIX.

And I when I learnt it at last, I shriek'd,
 I sprang from my seat,
I wept, and I kiss'd her hands, I flung
 myself down at her feet,

XX.

And we pray'd together for *him*, for *him*
 who had given her the name.
She has left me enough to live on. I
 need no wages of shame.

XXI.

She died of a fever caught when a nurse
 in a hospital ward.
She is high in the Heaven of Heavens,
 she is face to face with her Lord,

XXII.

And He sees not her like anywhere in
 this pitiless world of ours!
I have told you my tale. Get you gone.
 I am dressing her grave with
 flowers.

KAPIOLANI.

Kapiolani was a great chieftainess who lived in the Sandwich Islands at the beginning of this century. She won the cause of Christianity by openly defying the priests of the terrible goddess Peelè. In spite of their threats of vengeance she ascended the volcano Mauna-Loa, then clambered down over a bank of cinders 400 feet high to the great lake of fire (nine miles round)—Kilauëä—the home and haunt of the goddess, and flung into the boiling lava the consecrated berries which it was sacrilege for a woman to handle.

I.

When from the terrors of Nature a
 people have fashion'd and worship
 a Spirit of Evil,
Blest be the Voice of the Teacher who
 calls to them
'Set yourselves free!'

II.

Noble the Saxon who hurl'd at his Idol
 a valorous weapon in olden
 England!
Great and greater, and greatest of women,
 island heroine, Kapiolani
Clomb the mountain, and flung the berries,
 and dared the Goddess, and freed
 the people
Of Hawa-i-ee!

III.

A people believing that Peelè the Goddess
 would wallow in fiery riot and
 revel
On Kilauëä,
Dance in a fountain of flame with her
 devils, or shake with her thunders
 and shatter her island,
Rolling her anger
Thro' blasted valley and flaring forest
 in blood-red cataracts down to
 the sea!

IV.

Long as the lava-light
Glares from the lava-lake
Dazing the starlight,

Long as the silvery vapour in daylight
Over the mountain
Floats, will the glory of Kapiolani be
    mingled with either on Hawa-i-ee.

v.

What said her Priesthood?
' Woe to this island if ever a woman
    should handle or gather the berries
    of Peelè !
Accurséd were she !
And woe to this island if ever a woman
    should climb to the dwelling of
    Peelè the Goddess !
Accurséd were she !'

vi.

One from the Sunrise
Dawn'd on His people, and slowly before
    him
Vanish'd shadow-like
Gods and Goddesses,
None but the terrible Peelè remaining as
    Kapiolani ascended her mountain,
Baffled her priesthood,
Broke the Taboo,
Dipt to the crater,
Call'd on the Power adored by the
    Christian, and crying ' I dare her,
    let Peelè avenge herself' !
Into the flame-billow dash'd the berries,
    and drove the demon from Hawa-
    i-ee.

THE DAWN.

"You are but children."
    Egyptian Priest to Solon.

i.

RED of the Dawn !
Screams of a babe in the red-hot palms
    of a Moloch of Tyre,
Man with his brotherless dinner on
    man in the tropical wood,
Priests in the name of the Lord passing
    souls thro' fire to the fire,
Head-hunters and boats of Dahomey
    that float upon human blood !

ii.

Red of the Dawn !
Godless fury of peoples, and Christless
    frolic of kings,
And the bolt of war dashing down
    upon cities and blazing farms,
For Babylon was a child new-born,
    and Rome was a babe in arms,
And London and Paris and all the rest
    are as yet but in leading-strings.

iii.

Dawn not Day,
While scandal is mouthing a bloodless
    name at *her* cannibal feast,
And rake-ruin'd bodies and souls go
    down in a common wreck,
And the press of a thousand cities is
    prized for it smells of the beast,
Or easily violates virgin Truth for a
    coin or a cheque.

iv.

Dawn not Day !
Is it Shame, so few should have climb'd
    from the dens in the level below,
Men, with a heart and a soul, no
    slaves of a four-footed will ?
But if twenty million of summers are
    stored in the sunlight still,
We are far from the noon of man, there
    is time for the race to grow.

v.

Red of the Dawn !
Is it turning a fainter red ? so be it, but
    when shall we lay
The Ghost of the Brute that is walking
    and haunting us yet, and be free ?
In a hundred, a thousand winters?
    Ah, what will *our* children be,
The men of a hundred thousand, a
    million summers away ?

THE MAKING OF MAN.

WHERE is one that, born of woman,
    altogether can escape
From the lower world within him, moods
    of tiger, or of ape ?

Man as yet is being made, and ere the
    crowning Age of ages,
Shall not æon after æon pass and touch
    him into shape?

All about him shadow still, but, while
    the races flower and fade,
Prophet-eyes may catch a glory slowly
    gaining on the shade,
    Till the peoples all are one, and all
      their voices blend in choric
Hallelujah to the Maker ' It is finish'd.
    Man is made.'

THE DREAMER.

On a midnight in midwinter when all
    but the winds were dead,
' The meek shall inherit the earth ' was
    a Scripture that rang thro' his
    head,
Till he dream'd that a Voice of the Earth
    went wailingly past him and said :

    ' I am losing the light of my Youth
    And the Vision that led me of old,
    And I clash with an iron Truth,
    When I make for an Age of gold,
    And I would that my race were run,
    For teeming with liars, and madmen,
      and knaves,
    And wearied of Autocrats, Anarchs,
      and Slaves,
    And darken'd with doubts of a Faith
      that saves,
    And crimson with battles, and hollow
      with graves,
    To the wail of my winds, and the
      moan of my waves
    I whirl, and I follow the Sun.'

Was it only the wind of the Night shrill-
    ing out Desolation and wrong
Thro' a dream of the dark? Yet he
    thought that he answer'd her wail
    with a song—

    Moaning your losses, O Earth,
    Heart-weary and overdone !
    But all's well that ends well,
    Whirl, and follow the Sun !

He is racing from heaven to heaven
    And less will be lost than won,
For all's well that ends well,
    Whirl, and follow the Sun !

The Reign of the Meek upon earth,
    O weary one, has it begun ?
But all's well that ends well,
    Whirl, and follow the Sun !

For moans will have grown sphere-
    music
    Or ever your race be run !
And all's well that ends well,
    Whirl, and follow the Sun !

MECHANOPHILUS.

(In the time of the first railways.)

Now first we stand and understand,
    And sunder false from true,
And handle boldly with the hand,
    And see and shape and do.

Dash back that ocean with a pier,
    Strow yonder mountain flat,
A railway there, a tunnel here,
    Mix me this Zone with that !

Bring me my horse—my horse? my wings
    That I may soar the sky,
For Thought into the outward springs,
    I find her with the eye.

O will she, moonlike, sway the main,
    And bring or chase the storm,
Who was a shadow in the brain,
    And is a living form ?

Far as the Future vaults her skies,
    From this my vantage ground
To those still-working energies
    I spy nor term nor bound.

As we surpass our fathers' skill,
    Our sons will shame our own ;
A thousand things are hidden still
    And not a hundred known.

6—0, 5—7, 6—2).

N. Pietrangeli (Italy) beat F. Contreras (Mexico)
(6—3, 6—2, 6—3).

G. Pilet (France) beat P. Scholl (Germany) (8—6,
6—0, 2—6, 8—6).

J. Drobny (Egypt) beat M. Llamas (Mexico) (6—2,
10—8, 6—1).

N. A. Fraser (Australia) beat R. N. Howe (Australia)
(6—1, 4—6, 2, 6—3).

R. Emerson (Australia) beat I. C. Vermaak (S. Africa)
(6—1, 6—2, 7—5).

WOMEN'S SINGLES
SECOND ROUND

Miss C. C. Truman (G.B.) beat Miss L. Bassi (Italy)
(6—1, 6—3).

Miss Y. Ramirez (Mexico) beat Miss C. Ramorino
(Italy) (6—1, 7—5).

Miss L. Pericoli (Italy) beat Miss K. Fageros (U.S.)
(6—1, 6—2).

Miss J. S. Hopps (U.S.) beat Mrs. A. Bellani (Italy)
(6—4, 7—5).

Miss S. Reynolds (S. Africa) beat Mrs. N. Hopman
(Australia) (8—6, 4—6, 6—0).

Miss M. E. Bueno (Brazil) beat Mrs. N. Migliori
(Italy) (6—1, 6—3).

Mrs. M. Reitano (Australia) beat Miss R. M. Reyes
(Mexico) (6—8, 6—1, 8—6).

Miss S. Lazzarino (Italy) beat Miss R. Schuurman
(S. Africa) (6—3, 5—7, 6—3).

MIXED DOUBLES
FIRST ROUND

M. G. Davies and Miss C. C. Truman (G.B.) beat
M. Drisaldi and Miss L. Veronesi (Italy) (6—2,
(6—3).—*Reuter* and *Associated Press*.

GUILDFORD TOURNAMENT

MEN'S SINGLES.—QUARTER FINAL ROUND.—B.
Wheeler (Rhodesia) beat H. F. Walton (2—6, 6—2,
6—3); A. Palafox (Mexico) beat J. Hammill (S. Africa)
(6—1, 6—4); A. E. Bailey (Australia) beat R. Mandel-
stam (S. Africa) (6—3, 2—6, 6—3); T. Heckler (S.
Africa) beat N. Nette (Australia) (6—3, 10—8).

WOMEN'S SINGLES.—QUARTER FINAL ROUND.—
Miss J. Cross (S. Africa) beat Mrs. S. M. Bramley
(6—0, 6—4); Miss P. J. Wheeler beat Mrs. G. E.
Marshall (Kenya) (6—4, 6—4); Mrs. J. L. Deloford
beat Mrs. R. B. R. Wilson (6—4, 6—2); Miss R. M.
Morrison (New Zealand) beat Miss M. Hammill (S.
Africa) (6—1, 6—3).

RUGBY FIVES OFFICERS

Cambridge University Rugby Fives Club
have elected the following officers for
1959-60; Captain, B. W. J. G. Wilson (Sed-
bergh and Christ's); secretary, R. M.
Morgan (Sherborne and Caius).

From **THE TIMES** of 1859

MONDAY, MAY 9, 1859.   Price 4d.

[16 pages.] *Tennyson*

p 629

["The War"]

" There is a sound of thunder afar,
   Storm in the South that darkens the day,
Storm of battle and thunder of war,
   Well, if it do not roll our way.
      Storm ! storm ! Riflemen form !
      Ready, be ready to meet the storm !
      Riflemen, riflemen, riflemen form !

Be not deaf to the sound that warns !
   Be not gull'd by a despot's plea !
Are figs of thistles, or grapes of thorns ?
   How should a despot set men free ?
      Form ! form ! Riflemen form !
      Ready, be ready to meet the storm !
      Riflemen, riflemen, riflemen form !

Let your Reforms for a moment go,
   Look to your butts and take good aims.
Better a rotten borough or so,
   Than a rotten fleet or a city in flames !
      Form ! form ! Riflemen form !
      Ready, be ready to meet the storm !
      Riflemen, riflemen, riflemen form !

Form, be ready to do or die !
   Form in Freedom's name and the
                                    Queen's !
True, that we have a faithful ally,
   But only the Devil knows what he means.
      Form ! form ! Riflemen form !
      Ready, be ready to meet the storm !
      Riflemen, riflemen, riflemen form ! T."

                                        T."

** The general election, still in progress,
and largely concerned with the issue of
Disraeli's Reform Bill, seemed to the Poet
Laureate, Mr. Tennyson, to be dangerously
distracting attention from the ambiguous
pose of the despot Napoleon III as the
champion of Italian freedom.

And had some prophet spoken true
    Of all we shall achieve,
The wonders were so wildly new,
    That no man would believe.

Meanwhile, my brothers, work, and wield
    The forces of to-day,
And plow the Present like a field,
    And garner all you may !

You, what the cultured surface grows,
    Dispense with careful hands :
Deep under deep for ever goes,
    Heaven over heaven expands.

RIFLEMEN FORM !

THERE is a sound of thunder afar,
Storm in the South that darkens the day !
Storm of battle and thunder of war !
Well if it do not roll our way.
Storm, Storm, Riflemen form !
Ready, be ready against the storm !
Riflemen, Riflemen, Riflemen form !

Be not deaf to the sound that warns,
Be not gull'd by a despot's plea !
Are figs of thistles ? or grapes of thorns ?
How can a despot feel with the Free ?
Form, Form, Riflemen Form !
Ready, be ready to meet the storm !
Riflemen, Riflemen, Riflemen form !

Let your reforms for a moment go !
Look to your butts, and take good aims !
Better a rotten borough or so
Than a rotten fleet and a city in flames !
Storm, Storm, Riflemen form !
Ready, be ready against the storm !
Riflemen, Riflemen, Riflemen form !

Form, be ready to do or die !
Form in Freedom's name and the Queen's !
True we have got—*such* a faithful ally
That only the Devil can tell what he
    means.
Form, Form, Riflemen Form !
Ready, be ready to meet the storm !
Riflemen, Riflemen, Riflemen form ! [1]

[1] I have been asked to republish this old poem,
which was first published in ' The Times,' May
9, 1859, before the Volunteer movement began.

THE TOURNEY.

RALPH would fight in Edith's sight,
    For Ralph was Edith's lover,
Ralph went down like a fire to the fight
Struck to the left and struck to the right
    Roll'd them over and over.
' Gallant Sir Ralph,' said the king.

Casques were crack'd and hauberks hack'd
    Lances snapt in sunder,
Rang the stroke, and sprang the blood,
Knights were thwack'd and riven, and
    hew'd
    Like broad oaks with thunder.
' O what an arm,' said the king.

Edith bow'd her stately head,
    Saw them lie confounded,
Edith Montfort bow'd her head,
Crown'd her knight's, and flush'd as red
    As poppies when she crown'd it.
' Take her Sir Ralph,' said the king.

THE WANDERER.

THE gleam of household sunshine ends,
And here no longer can I rest ;
Farewell !— You will not speak, my
    friends,
Unfriendly of your parted guest.

O well for him that finds a friend,
Or makes a friend where'er he come,
And loves the world from end to end,
And wanders on from home to home !

O happy he, and fit to live,
On whom a happy home has power
To make him trust his life, and give
His fealty to the halcyon hour !

I count you kind, I hold you true ;
But what may follow who can tell ?
Give me a hand—and you—and you—
And deem me grateful, and farewell !

POETS AND CRITICS.

This thing, that thing is the rage,
Helter-skelter runs the age ;
Minds on this round earth of ours
Vary like the leaves and flowers,
    Fashion'd after certain laws ;
Sing thou low or loud or sweet,
All at all points thou canst not meet,
    Some will pass and some will pause.

What is true at last will tell :
Few at first will place thee well ;
Some too low would have thee shine,
Some too high—no fault of thine—
    Hold thine own, and work thy will !
Year will graze the heel of year,
But seldom comes the poet here,
    And the Critic's rarer still.

A VOICE SPAKE OUT OF THE SKIES.

A Voice spake out of the skies
To a just man and a wise—
' The world and all within it
Will only last a minute !'
And a beggar began to cry
' Food, food or I die' !
Is it worth his while to eat,
Or mine to give him meat,
If the world and all within it
Were nothing the next minute ?

DOUBT AND PRAYER.

Tho' Sin too oft, when smitten by Thy
    rod,
Rail at ' Blind Fate' with many a vain
    ' Alas !'
From sin thro' sorrow into Thee we pass
By that same path our true forefathers
    trod ;
And let not Reason fail me, nor the sod
Draw from my death Thy living flower
    and grass,
Before I learn that Love, which is, and
    was

My Father, and my Brother, and my
    God !
Steel me with patience ! soften me with
    grief !
Let blow the trumpet strongly while I
    pray,
Till this embattled wall of unbelief
My prison, not my fortress, fall away !
Then, if Thou willest, let my day be
    brief,
So Thou wilt strike Thy glory thro' the
    day.

FAITH.

I.

Doubt no longer that the Highest is the
    wisest and the best,
Let not all that saddens Nature blight
    thy hope or break thy rest,
    Quail not at the fiery mountain, at the
      shipwreck, or the rolling
Thunder, or the rending earthquake, or
    the famine, or the pest !

II.

Neither mourn if human creeds be lower
    than the heart's desire !
Thro' the gates that bar the distance
    comes a gleam of what is higher.
    Wait till Death has flung them open,
      when the man will make the Maker
Dark no more with human hatreds in the
    glare of deathless fire !

THE SILENT VOICES.

When the dumb Hour, clothed in black,
Brings the Dreams about my bed,
Call me not so often back,
Silent Voices of the dead,
Toward the lowland ways behind me,
And the sunlight that is gone !
Call me rather, silent voices,
Forward to the starry track
Glimmering up the heights beyond me,
On, and always on !

GOD AND THE UNIVERSE.

I.

WILL my tiny spark of being wholly
vanish in your deeps and heights?
Must my day be dark by reason, O ye
Heavens, of your boundless nights,
Rush of Suns, and roll of systems, and
your fiery clash of meteorites?

II.

'Spirit, nearing yon dark portal at the
limit of thy human state,
Fear not thou the hidden purpose of that
Power which alone is great,
Nor the myriad world, His shadow, nor
the silent Opener of the Gate.'

THE DEATH OF THE DUKE OF CLARENCE AND AVONDALE.

To the Mourners.

THE bridal garland falls upon the bier,
The shadow of a crown, that o'er him
hung,
Has vanish'd in the shadow cast by
Death.
So princely, tender, truthful, reverent,
pure—
Mourn! That a world-wide Empire
mourns with you,
That all the Thrones are clouded by
your loss,
Were slender solace. Yet be comforted;
For if this earth be ruled by Perfect
Love,
Then, after his brief range of blameless
days,
The toll of funeral in an Angel ear
Sounds happier than the merriest mar-
riage-bell.
The face of Death is toward the Sun
of Life,
His shadow darkens earth: his truer
name
Is 'Onward,' no discordance in the
roll
And march of that Eternal Harmony
Whereto the worlds beat time, tho' faintly
heard
Until the great Hereafter. Mourn in
hope!

SONGS FROM THE PLAYS.

FROM 'QUEEN MARY.'

SHAME upon you, Robin,
    Shame upon you now !
Kiss me would you ? with my hands
    Milking the cow ?
    Daisies grow again,
    Kingcups blow again,
And you came and kiss'd me milking the
    cow.

Robin came behind me,
    Kiss'd me well I vow ;
Cuff him could I ? with my hands
    Milking the cow ?
    Swallows fly again,
    Cuckoos cry again,
And you came and kiss'd me milking the
    cow.

Come, Robin, Robin,
    Come and kiss me now ;
Help it can I ? with my hands
    Milking the cow ?
    Ringdoves coo again,
    All things woo again.
Come behind and kiss me milking the
    cow !

HAPLESS doom of woman happy in be-
    trothing !
Beauty passes like a breath and love is
    lost in loathing :
Low, my lute ; speak low, my lute, but
    say the world is nothing—
        Low, lute, low !
Love will hover round the flowers when
    they first awaken ;
Love will fly the fallen leaf, and not be
    overtaken ;
Low, my lute ! oh low, my lute ! we
    fade and are forsaken—
        Low, dear lute, low !

FROM 'HAROLD.'

TWO young lovers in winter weather,
    None to guide them,
Walk'd at night on the misty heather ;
Night, as black as a raven's feather ;
Both were lost and found together,
    None beside them.

Lost, lost, the light of day,
    'I am beside thee.'
Lost, lost, we have lost the way.
    'Love, I will guide thee.'
Whither, O whither ? into the river,
Where we two may be lost together,
And lost for ever ? 'Oh ! never, oh !
    never,
Tho' we be lost and be found together.'

FROM 'BECKET.'

OVER ! the sweet summer closes,
    The reign of the roses is done ;
Over and gone with the roses,
    And over and gone with the sun.

Over ! the sweet summer closes,
    And never a flower at the close ;
Over and gone with the roses,
    And winter again and the snows.

DUET.

1. Is it the wind of the dawn that I hear
   in the pine overhead ?
2. No ; but the voice of the deep as it
   hollows the cliffs of the land.
1. Is there a voice coming up with the
   voice of the deep from the strand,
   One coming up with a song in the
   flush of the glimmering red ?
2. Love that is born of the deep coming
   up with the sun from the sea.
1. Love that can shape or can shatter a
   life till the life shall have fled ?
2. Nay, let us welcome him, Love that
   can lift up a life from the dead.
1. Keep him away from the lone little
   isle. Let us be, let us be.
2. Nay, let him make it his own, let him
   reign in it—he, it is he,
   Love that is born of the deep coming
   up with the sun from the sea.

BABBLE in bower
    Under the rose !
Bee mustn't buzz,
    Whoop—but he knows.

Kiss me, little one,
    Nobody near !
Grasshopper, grasshopper,
    Whoop—you can hear.

Kiss in the bower,
    Tit on the tree !
Bird mustn't tell,
    Whoop—he can see.

RAINBOW, stay,
Gleam upon gloom,
Bright as my dream,
Rainbow, stay !
But it passes away,
Gloom upon gleam,
Dark as my doom—
O rainbow stay.

FROM 'THE CUP.'

MOON on the field and the foam,
    Moon on the waste and the wold,
Moon bring him home, bring him home
    Safe from the dark and the cold,
Home, sweet moon, bring him home,
    Home with the flock to the fold—
Safe from the wolf to the fold.

ARTEMIS, Artemis, hear us, O Mother,
    hear us, and bless us !
Artemis, thou that art life to the wind, to
    the wave, to the glebe, to the fire !
Hear thy people who praise thee ! O help
    us from all that oppress us !
Hear thy priestesses hymn thy glory ! O
    yield them all their desire !

FROM 'THE FALCON.'

*Boccace V. 9
La Fontaine
Le Faucon*

' DEAD mountain flowers, dead mountain-
    meadow flowers,
Dearer than when you made your moun-
    tain gay,
Sweeter than any violet of to-day,
Richer than all the wide world-wealth of
    May,
To me, tho' all your bloom has died
    away,
You bloom again, dead mountain-meadow
    flowers.
        O mountain flowers !
            Dead flowers ! '

FROM 'THE PROMISE OF MAY.'

THE town lay still in the low sun-light,
The hen cluckt late by the white farm
    gate,
The maid to her dairy came in from the
    cow,
The stock-dove coo'd at the fall of night,
The blossom had open'd on every bough ;
    O joy for the promise of May, of May,
    O joy for the promise of May.

But a red fire woke in the heart of the
    town,
And a fox from the glen ran away with
    the hen,
And a cat to the cream, and a rat to the
    cheese ;
And the stock-dove coo'd, till a kite
    dropt down,
And a salt wind burnt the blossoming
    trees ;
    O grief for the promise of May, of May,
    O grief for the promise of May.

WHAT did ye do, and what did ye saäy,
Wi' the wild white rose, an' the wood-
    bine sa gaäy,
An' the midders all mow'd, an' the sky
    sa blue—
What did ye saäy, and what did ye do,
When ye thowt there were nawbody
    watchin' o' you,
And you an' your Sally was forkin' the
    haäy,
    At the end of the daäy,
    For the last loäd hoäm ?

What did we do, and what did we saäy,
Wi' the briar sa green, an' the willer sa
    graäy,
An' the midders all mow'd, an' the sky
    sa blue—
Do ye think I be gawin' to tell it to you,
What we mowt saäy, and what we mowt
    do,
When me an' my Sally was forkin' the
    haäy,
    At the end of the daäy,
    For the last loäd hoäm ?

But what did ye saäy, and what did ye
    do,
Wi' the butterflies out, and the swallers
    at plaäy,
An' the midders all mow'd, an' the sky
    sa blue ?
Why, coom then, owd feller, I'll tell it
    to you ;
For me an' my Sally we sweär'd to be
    true,

To be true to each other, let 'appen what
    maäy,
    Till the end of the daäy
    And the last loäd hoäm.

GEE oop ! whoä ! Gee oop ! whoä !
Scizzars an' Pumpy was good uns to goä
    Thruf slush an' squad
    When roäds was bad,
But hallus ud stop at the Vine-an'-the-
    Hop,
Fur boäth on 'em knawed as well as
    mysen
That beer be as good fur 'erses as men.
    Gee oop ! whoä ! Gee oop ! whoä !
Scizzars an' Pumpy was good uns to goä.

O MAN, forgive thy mortal foe,
Nor ever strike him blow for blow ;
For all the souls on earth that live
To be forgiven must forgive.
Forgive him seventy times and seven ;
For all the blessed souls in Heaven
Are both forgivers and forgiven.

O HAPPY lark, that warblest high
    Above thy lowly nest,
O brook, that brawlest merrily by
    Thro' fields that once were blest,
O tower spiring to the sky,
    O graves in daisies drest,
O Love and Life, how weary am I,
    And how I long for rest.

FROM 'THE FORESTERS.'

THE warrior Earl of Allendale,
    He loved the Lady Anne ;
The lady loved the master well,
    The maid she loved the man.

All in the castle garden,
    Or ever the day began,
The lady gave a rose to the Earl,
    The maid a rose to the man.

'I go to fight in Scotland
  With many a savage clan;'
The lady gave her hand to the Earl,
  The maid her hand to the man.

'Farewell, farewell, my warrior Earl!'
  And ever a tear down ran.
She gave a weeping kiss to the Earl,
  And the maid a kiss to the man.

———

LOVE flew in at the window
  As Wealth walk'd in at the door.
'You have come for you saw Wealth
    coming,' said I.
But he flutter'd his wings with a sweet
    little cry,
  I'll cleave to you rich or poor.

Wealth dropt out of the window,
  Poverty crept thro' the door.
'Well now you would fain follow Wealth,'
    said I,
But he flutter'd his wings as he gave me
    the lie,
  I cling to you all the more.

———

DRINKING SONG.

LONG live Richard,
  Robin and Richard!
Long live Richard!
  Down with John!
Drink to the Lion-heart
  Every one!
Pledge the Plantagenet,
  Him that is gone.
Who knows whither?
  God's good Angel
Help him back hither,
  And down with John!
Long live Robin,
  Robin and Richard!
Long live Robin,
  And down with John!

To sleep! to sleep! The long bright
    day is done,
And darkness rises from the fallen sun.
To sleep! to sleep!
Whate'er thy joys, they vanish with the
    day;
Whate'er thy griefs, in sleep they fade
    away.
To sleep! to sleep!
Sleep, mournful heart, and let the past
    be past!
Sleep, happy soul! all life will sleep at
    last.
To sleep! to sleep!

———

THERE is no land like England
  Where'er the light of day be;
There are no hearts like English hearts
  Such hearts of oak as they be.
There is no land like England
  Where'er the light of day be;
There are no men like Englishmen
  So tall and bold as they be.

Full Chorus.

And these will strike for England
  And man and maid be free
To foil and spoil the tyrant
  Beneath the greenwood tree.

There is no land like England
  Where'er the light of day be;
There are no wives like English wives
  So fair and chaste as they be.
There is no land like England
  Where'er the light of day be;
There are no maids like English maids
  So beautiful as they be.

Full Chorus.

And these shall wed with freemen,
  And all their sons be free,
To sing the songs of England
  Beneath the greenwood tree.

Up with you, out of the forest and over
    the hills and away,
And over this Robin Hood's bay!
Up thro' the light of the seas by the
    moon's long-silvering ray!
To a land where the fay,
Not an eye to survey,
In the night, in the day,
Can have frolic and play.
Up with you, all of you, out of it! hear
    and obey.
Man, lying here alone,
Moody creature,
Of a nature
Stronger, sadder than my own,
Were I human, were I human,
I could love you like a woman.
Man, man,
You shall wed your Marian.
She is true, and you are true,
And you love her and she loves you;
Both be happy, and adieu for ever and
    for evermore—adieu.

———

By all the deer that spring
Thro' wood and lawn and ling,
    When all the leaves are green;
By arrow and gray goosewing,
When horn and echo ring,
We care so much for a King;
    We care not much for a Queen—
        For a Queen, for a Queen o' the
            woods.

By all the leaves of spring,
And all the birds that sing
    When all the leaves are green;
By arrow and by bowstring,
We care so much for a King
    That we would die for a Queen—
        For a Queen, for a Queen o' the
            woods.

———

The bee buzz'd up in the heat.
'I am faint for your honey, my sweet.'
The flower said 'Take it, my dear,
For now is the spring of the year.
    So come, come!'
        'Hum!'
And the bee buzz'd down from the heat.

And the bee buzz'd up in the cold
When the flower was wither'd and old.
'Have you still any honey, my dear?'
She said 'It's the fall of the year,
    But come, come!'
        'Hum!'
And the bee buzz'd off in the cold.

Now the King is home again, and never-
    more to roam again,
Now the King is home again, the King
    will have his own again,
Home again, home again, and each will
    have his own again,
All the birds in merry Sherwood sing
    and sing him home again.

CROSSING THE BAR.

Sunset and evening star,
    And one clear call for me!
And may there be no moaning of the bar,
    When I put out to sea,

But such a tide as moving seems asleep,
    Too full for sound and foam,
When that which drew from out the
        boundless deep
    Turns again home.

Twilight and evening bell,
    And after that the dark!
And may there be no sadness of farewell,
    When I embark;

For tho' from out our bourne of Time
    and Place
    The flood may bear me far,
I hope to see my Pilot face to face
    When I have crost the bar.

INDEX TO POEMS.

INDEX TO THE FIRST LINES.

T

> What does little birdie say 160

INDEX TO 'IN MEMORIAM'

P. 247.

INDEX TO SONGS.

Printed by R. & R. CLARK, LIMITED, *Edinburgh.*

Macmillan's
GLOBE LIBRARY

Crown 8vo.   Cloth.   3s. 6d. each

The volumes marked with an asterisk (*) are also issued in green limp leather, with full gilt backs and gilt edges, price 5s. net each

BOSWELL

* BOSWELL'S LIFE OF JOHNSON. Edited with an Introduction by MOWBRAY MORRIS.

BURNS

* POEMS, SONGS, AND LETTERS, being the complete Works of Robert Burns, edited from the best printed and manuscript authorities, with Glossarial Index and a Biographical Memoir by ALEXANDER SMITH.

CHAUCER

* THE WORKS OF GEOFFREY CHAUCER. Edited by ALFRED W. POLLARD, W. FRANK HEATH, MARK H. LIDDELL and W. S. McCORMICK.

COWPER

* THE POETICAL WORKS OF WILLIAM COWPER. Edited with Notes and Biographical Introduction by W. BENHAM, B.D.

DEFOE

ROBINSON CRUSOE. Edited after the Original Editions, with a Biographical Introduction by HENRY KINGSLEY, F.R.G.S.

MILTON

*THE POETICAL WORKS OF JOHN MILTON. With Introductions by Professor MASSON.

PEPYS

*THE DIARY OF SAMUEL PEPYS. With Introduction and Notes by G. GREGORY SMITH.

POPE

*THE POETICAL WORKS OF ALEXANDER POPE. Edited, with Notes and Introductory Memoir, by Dr. A. W. WARD.

SCOTT

*POETICAL WORKS OF SIR WALTER SCOTT. With a Biographical and Critical Memoir by F. T. PALGRAVE.

SHAKESPEARE

*THE WORKS OF WILLIAM SHAKESPEARE. Edited by W. G. CLARK, M.A., and W. ALDIS WRIGHT, M.A.

SPENSER

*THE COMPLETE WORKS OF EDMUND SPENSER. Edited from the original editions and manuscripts by R. MORRIS. With a Memoir by J. W. HALES, M.A.

TENNYSON

*THE POETICAL WORKS OF ALFRED, LORD TENNYSON. Also in extra cloth, gilt edges. 4s. 6d.

VIRGIL

THE WORKS OF VIRGIL, rendered into English Prose. With Introductions, Running Analysis, Notes, and Index. By J. LONSDALE, M.A., and S. LEE, M.A.

The Globe Library

SOME PRESS OPINIONS OF THE SERIES

THE SATURDAY REVIEW

" The 'Globe' Editions are admirable for their scholarly editing, their typographical excellence, their compendious form and their cheapness."

THE DAILY TELEGRAPH

"The 'Globe' Editions are unmatched for their combination of editorial capability and care with excellence of production and lowness of price."

THE LITERARY WORLD

·' These ' Globe ' Editions are not only truly cheap, which many so-called cheap editions are not, but excellent in every way. The matter is of the very best, being reproductions of old standard authors, the type is remarkably clear and pleasant to the eye, and the volumes are handsomely though not showily got up. They are just the books which a young man, with only a limited sum to spend on literary purchases, must rejoice to add to his own select library."

THE BRITISH QUARTERLY

" In elegance and scholarliness the ' Globe' Editions of Messrs. Macmillan surpass any popular series of our classics hitherto given to the public. Wonderfully beautiful, distinct and compendious, as near an approach to miniature perfection as has ever been made."

THE GLASGOW HERALD

" The famous, accurate and marvellously cheap editions for which the people are indebted to Messrs. Macmillan & Co."

MACMILLAN & CO., LTD.
ST. MARTIN'S STREET
LONDON
W.C.

N.5.10.08